**CollegeBoard**

SAT

# The Official SAT Study Guide

Second Edition

**College Board, New York**

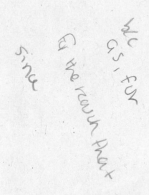

This publication was written and edited by the College Board, with archival material from Educational Testing Service. Cover Design: Beth Oliver. Assistant Director: Arthur Sprogis. Assessment Managers: James Daubs, Ed Hardin, Joel Harris. Senior Director, Mathematics: Robin O'Callaghan. Senior Assessment Specialists: Elizabeth Daniel, Beth Hart, Colleen McDermott.

Special thanks to Jim Gwyn, Senior Project Manager, and Suellen Leavy, Book Compositor/Desktop Publisher.

## About the College Board

The College Board is a mission-driven not-for-profit organization that connects students to college success and opportunity. Founded in 1900, the College Board was created to expand access to higher education. Today, the membership association is made up of over 6,000 of the world's leading educational institutions and is dedicated to promoting excellence and equity in education. Each year, the College Board helps more than seven million students prepare for a successful transition to college through programs and services in college readiness and college success — including the SAT® and the Advanced Placement Program®. The organization also serves the education community through research and advocacy on behalf of students, educators and schools.

For further information, visit www.collegeboard.org.

Copies of this book (item # 008525) are available from your bookseller or may be ordered from College Board Publications, P.O. Box 869010, Plano, TX 75074-0998 (tel. 800-323-7155). The price is $21.99 per copy. Purchase orders above $25 are accepted.

Editorial inquiries concerning this book should be addressed to the College Board, 45 Columbus Avenue, New York, NY 10023-6992.

ISBN-13: 978-0-87447-852-5

ISBN-10: 0-87447-852-9

9   15 14 13 12

Distributed by Macmillan

# CONTENTS

# Contents

# PREFACE

The best way to prepare for the SAT® is to take challenging high school classes, read extensively and write as often as possible. For more immediate help, you should review the concepts covered and practice problems similar to those you will see on the SAT. This guide from the College Board — the test maker — is the only place you'll find questions written to the SAT test specifications and actual SAT tests.

As you read through and practice with *The Official SAT Study Guide*™, you will gain confidence in your abilities and will be more prepared to succeed. This guide provides you with:

- opportunities to familiarize yourself with the format of the test

- practice on the different question types

- hundreds of practice questions

- instructional help with the concepts covered

- approaches to use for answering different types of questions

- experience taking official practice tests, helping you learn how to pace yourself

- numerous opportunities to sharpen your skills in writing effective essays

- feedback that will help you focus on areas that may need improvement

## Special Features

This book is filled with helpful suggestions. This icon appears next to the "Keep in Mind" boxes, which are located in the margins to remind you of approaches and other points that will help you prepare for the test. Plus, for every chapter that describes specific sections of the test, you'll find a "Recap" section for review.

A computer icon appears next to information you can find online at www.collegeboard.org/SATstudyguide. You can even enter your test answers online and receive personalized feedback for each of this guide's 10 full-length practice tests. This feedback makes it easy for you to focus on the areas you need to study further. As a book owner, you can review explanations to the questions in this guide's 10 official practice tests. Subscribers to *The Official SAT Online Course*™ have access to interactive instruction, additional sets of practice questions, practice essay questions and six additional official practice tests, and have responses to essays in this book and in *The Official SAT Online Course* scored automatically.

## How *The Official SAT Study Guide*™ Is Organized

The first three chapters introduce the SAT and offer helpful approaches to test taking. Chapter 3 includes a comprehensive description of the Preliminary SAT/National Merit Scholarship Qualifying Test (PSAT/NMSQT®).

Chapters 4-21 address the SAT's critical reading, writing and mathematics sections. Each chapter has in-depth descriptions of the types of questions on the test and several approaches to answering them. The solutions to sample questions will help you better understand the concepts underlying similar problems on the test.

As you work through this guide, you'll become familiar with the instructions, questions and types of answers that are on the SAT. Some questions, such as the student-produced response questions in Chapter 20, have answers that must be given in specific formats.

You'll find additional practice for each type of question in Chapter 7 (Critical Reading), Chapter 13 (Writing) and Chapter 21 (Mathematics). Chapters 15-18 detail the mathematics concepts and operations that will appear on the SAT.

Chapter 9 includes an example of an essay topic with sample scored essays. You will also learn about holistic scoring and the SAT Scoring Guide.

To help you prepare for the essay portion of the SAT, this guide includes essay questions like the ones you'll see on test day. To help you understand how the essays are scored, each essay question is accompanied by sample essays written by students. Corresponding essay samples are actual student responses to previously administered SAT Subject Tests in Writing, which are no longer given.

Part V provides 10 official practice tests to help you become familiar with the test and practice under timed conditions. You don't have to practice on *all* of them. You may wish to review questions on the practice tests that you find particularly challenging. If you'd like more practice in critical reading, for example, you could focus on that section of the test or the critical reading sample and practice questions. It's a good idea to take at least *one* official practice test, under timed conditions, to get an idea of the concentration and pacing needed to complete the test.

There are two types of practice tests in this guide. The first three practice tests are recently administered SAT tests from 2006 and 2007. As for the other official practice tests, the vast majority of questions have appeared in SAT tests before March 2005. All of the questions in this book are written by our test development experts and comply with the College Board's SAT specifications.

## We're Here to Help

The College Board hopes that you find this guide helpful and easy to use; please visit www.collegeboard.org for the most up-to-date information on the SAT. We wish you well as you work through the admissions process.

# PART I
# Getting Started

# CHAPTER 1

# Introducing the SAT®

## About the SAT®

Are you thinking about going to college? If you are, there's probably an SAT® in your future. Taking the SAT is the first step in finding the right college for you — one where you'll best succeed in discovering the tools necessary to pursue your passions.

The SAT helps colleges get to know you better by giving them insight into how you think, solve problems and communicate. The SAT measures what you've learned in the classroom — basic skills such as reading, writing and mathematics — and how well you apply that knowledge.

Your SAT score is just one of many factors that colleges look at when they consider your application. They also look at your academic record, your involvement in school activities, your application essay and your letters of recommendation.

The SAT is taken by more than two million students every year at thousands of testing centers (usually high schools) around the world. Many high school students take the SAT twice — once in the spring of their junior year and again in the fall of their senior year.

## Who Is Responsible for the SAT?

The SAT is a program of the College Board, a not-for-profit membership association to which more than 5,900 schools, colleges and universities belong. The College Board, whose mission is to connect students to college success and opportunity, was founded more than 100 years ago. Every year, the College Board serves seven million students and their parents, 23,000 high schools, and 3,800 colleges through major programs and services in college readiness, college admission, guidance, assessment, financial aid and enrollment. Among its best-known programs are the SAT®, the PSAT/NMSQT® and the Advanced Placement Program® (AP®).

## How Is the SAT Developed?

The SAT Test Development Committees, made up of college professors and high school teachers who are experts in their fields, oversee all aspects of test development to ensure that the SAT is carefully designed to be a fair test for all students.

All questions undergo a very thorough review process. In fact, each question is pretested before it is placed on the scored sections of the test. The goal is to make the questions clear, appropriately challenging and fair for all students regardless of gender or ethnicity.

How do the SAT Test Development Committees know which skills should be measured? They do their homework! The College Board meets with college faculty, high school teachers and experts in different subjects from across the country and surveys educators about their reading, writing and mathematics curricula. The College Board also reviews research on what skills are necessary for success in college. The skills measured by the SAT align with the subjects that you're learning in your high school classroom.

The SAT has evolved over time to keep up to date with current teaching practices and college and high school curricula. For example, in 1994, a new SAT mathematics section was introduced that allowed students to use calculators for the first time. Since writing is critical to succeeding in college, the College Board added a writing section to the SAT in 2005.

## How Is the Test Organized?

The SAT features eight types of questions in sections on critical reading, writing and mathematics. Table 1.1 provides an overview of each section. The table also shows the type of questions, the total number of questions in each section and the time allotted for each section. You have 3 hours and 45 minutes to complete the SAT.

The SAT also includes a variable section in critical reading, multiple-choice writing or mathematics for which 25 minutes is allotted. The variable section is used to help make sure that your scores are comparable to scores on other editions of the SAT. This variable section will not count toward your final score. Still, because you won't know which section is the variable, you need to do your best on the entire test. Remember, the official practice tests in this book do not include the variable section.

**Table 1.1** Number and Type of Questions with Time Allotted for Each Section of the SAT

| Sections of the SAT | Type of Questions | No. of Questions | Time Allotted |
|---|---|---|---|
| **Critical Reading** | Sentence completion | 19 | |
| | Passage-based reading | 48 | |
| | *Total critical reading questions* | *67* | 70 minutes (two 25-minute sections and one 20-minute section) |
| **Writing** | Identifying sentence errors | 18 | |
| | Improving sentences | 25 | |
| | Improving paragraphs | 6 | |
| | Essay writing | 1 essay | |
| | *Total writing questions* | *49 + Essay* | 60 minutes (one 25-minute essay, one 25-minute multiple-choice section and one 10-minute multiple-choice section) |
| **Mathematics** | Multiple choice | 44 | |
| | Student-produced response (grid-ins) | 10 | |
| | *Total mathematics questions* | *54* | 70 minutes (two 25-minute sections and one 20-minute section) |

# How Is the SAT Scored?

Here's how SAT scores are calculated.

1. *Multiple-choice questions*: You receive one point for each question answered correctly. For each question that you attempt but answer incorrectly, ¼ point is subtracted from the total number of correct answers. No points are added or subtracted for unanswered questions. If the final score includes a fraction, the score is rounded to the nearest whole number.

 2. *Student-produced response questions in the mathematics section*: Nothing is subtracted for wrong answers.

3. *The essay* will receive a score of 2 to 12. However, a blank essay, essays that are not written on topic, essays written in pen or essays deemed illegible after several attempts have been made to read them will receive a score of 0.

 **Essay Practice**

To practice the essay, check out *The Official SAT Online Course*™ at www.satonlinecourse.org.

A statistical process called *equating* scales your scores from 200 (lowest) to 800 (highest). Scores are equated to adjust for minor differences between test forms. Equating assures you and colleges that a score of 500 on the mathematics section of one form of the test indicates the same ability level as 500 on the mathematics section of another form of the test.

### Score Range

No test can ever measure your skills precisely, but the SAT can provide good estimates. Students who take the SAT many times within a short period of time usually find that their scores tend to vary, but not by very much. The score range is an estimate of how your scores might vary if you were tested many times.

### Percentiles

In addition to the scaled scores of 200 to 800 on each of the three sections of the test, you also will receive corresponding SAT percentile scores. The percentile score compares your scores to the scores of other students who took the test. The comparison is given as a number between 1 and 99 signifying what percentage of students earned a score lower than yours. For example, suppose your percentile is 53. That means you performed better than 53 out of every 100 test-takers in the comparison group.

Your percentile changes depending on the group with which you are being compared.

The national percentile is based on all recently graduated college-bound seniors from across the nation who took the test.

The state percentile is based on all recently graduated college-bound seniors from your state who took the test.

## Additional Services

The following services are available to you when you register for the SAT or when you receive your scores. You can learn more about these tools at sat.collegeboard.org.

### SAT® Skills Insight™

SAT Skills Insight is a free online tool that shows you the skills you have and highlights those you need to improve, including:

- Skills tested on the SAT

- Skills typical of students who score within a particular score band

- Suggestions for how to sharpen those skills

- Real SAT questions and answers

You can use your real SAT scores and your practice test scores when using SAT Skills Insight.

### My SAT Online Score Report

My SAT Online Score Report is a free online tool that gives you the meaning behind your numbers and insight into your strengths and weaknesses. It offers:

- Details of performance by question type and difficulty level

- National, state and high school percentiles

- Your essay question and scanned response

- The ability to search for career and major possibilities

### Score Choice™

Score Choice™ gives you the option to choose the SAT scores you send to colleges by test date — in accordance with a college or university's score-use practice. Designed to reduce your stress and improve the test-day experience, Score Choice gives you an opportunity to show colleges the scores you feel best represent your abilities.

Score Choice is optional, so if you don't actively choose to use it, all of your scores will be sent automatically. Since most colleges only consider your best scores, you should still feel comfortable reporting scores from all of your test dates.

Each college, university and scholarship program has different score-use practices. Our easy-to-use score-reporting process displays score-use practices for each participating institution, but you should also check with colleges to ensure that you are following their score-reporting requirements. E-mail reminders will be sent to you if you have not sent SAT scores to any colleges by the typical deadlines.

Remember:

- Scores from an entire SAT test (critical reading, writing and mathematics sections) will be sent — scores of individual sections from different test dates cannot be selected independently.

- You can send any or all scores to a college on a single report — it will not cost more to send one, multiple or all test scores.

- You receive four free score reports with your registration. We continue to recommend that you take full advantage of these reports.

### Question-and-Answer Service (QAS)

The Question-and-Answer Service (QAS) provides a report that lists the question number, the correct answer, the answer you gave, the type of question and the difficulty level of that question. You will also receive the actual questions from the edition of the SAT you took. QAS is offered for specific testing dates only (usually October, January and May). For the testing dates for which the Question-and-Answer Service is available, please visit sat.collegeboard.org. You can order QAS when you register for the SAT, or when you complete the order form sent with your score report. QAS can be ordered up to five months after the test date.

## Student Answer Service (SAS)

The Student Answer Service (SAS) provides a report that lists the question number, the difficulty of each SAT question and whether you answered it correctly, incorrectly or did not answer. Also included are the question or content types for each test section. Actual test questions are not included. SAS is available for all test dates for which QAS is not available. SAS can be ordered when you register for the SAT, or when you complete the order form sent with your score report. SAS can be ordered up to five months after the test date.

## Student Search Service®

The Student Search Service® helps colleges find prospective students. If you take the PSAT/NMSQT, the SAT or any AP Exam, you can be included in this free service.

Here's how it works: During SAT registration, indicate that you want to be part of the Student Search. Your name is put in a database along with other information such as your address, high school grade point average, date of birth, grade level, high school, e-mail address, intended college major and extracurricular activities.

Colleges and scholarship programs then use the Student Search to help them locate and recruit students with characteristics that might be a good match with their schools.

Here are some points to keep in mind about the Student Search Service:

- Being part of Student Search is voluntary. You may take the test even if you don't join Student Search.

- Colleges participating in the Search do not receive your exam scores. Colleges can ask for the names of students within certain score ranges, but your exact score is not reported.

- Being *contacted* by a college doesn't mean you have been *admitted*. You can be admitted only after you apply. The Student Search Service is simply a way for colleges to reach prospective students.

- Student Search Service will share your contact information only with approved colleges and scholarship programs that are recruiting students like you. Your name will never be sold to a private company or mailing list.

# CHAPTER 2
# How to Do Your Best on the SAT

This chapter offers suggestions for how to get ready for the SAT, how to pace yourself while taking the test, how to approach each type of question and how to feel more confident on test day.

## There's No Substitute for Studying

Preparing for the SAT is like studying for any exam. You'll feel a lot more confident if you review the test's format and become familiar with its content. You've actually been preparing for the SAT all of your academic life. The best way to get ready for the SAT is to work hard in school, take challenging courses, and read and write as much as you can.

- *Learning to read effectively* gives you the ability to figure out what the author means as well as what the author says.

- *Improving your vocabulary* gives you tools to figure out new words from the context in which they are used.

- *Developing your problem-solving abilities* helps you figure out what to do and how to do it and helps you deal with challenging problems even when you think you're stumped.

- *Strengthening your writing* helps you develop and express your ideas clearly and convincingly.

### How to Get Ready for the SAT

Practice may not make perfect, but it definitely helps. That's why taking the PSAT/NMSQT (Preliminary SAT/National Merit Scholarship Qualifying Test) is one of the best ways to get familiar with the SAT. It includes questions like those on the SAT — covering critical reading, writing and mathematics — but at a level appropriate for juniors in high school. At 2 hours and 10 minutes, the PSAT/NMSQT is shorter than the SAT, which lasts 3 hours and 45 minutes.

After taking the PSAT/NMSQT, you will receive a comprehensive score report that reviews all the questions and answers, including your answers, and provides feedback on your skills. The skills section identifies skills that need improvement and provides teacher suggestions on how to improve. You'll also receive your test back so that you can revisit test questions to help improve problem areas. If you take the test as a junior, you can qualify to enter competitions for scholarships sponsored by National Merit Scholarship Corporation and other scholarship programs. For more information about the PSAT/NMSQT, see Chapter 3.

## Online Resources

The College Board offers a wide range of free and low-cost online tools to help you get ready for test day. Available at www.satcollegeboard.org, the leading Web site for SAT and college-planning information, these resources can help you get familiar with and practice for the SAT.

### THE OFFICIAL SAT QUESTION OF THE DAY™

Practice a different question each day with the College Board's popular SAT Question of the Day. Visit our Web site or sign up to receive daily test questions via e-mail.

### THE OFFICIAL SAT PRACTICE TEST

Print or enter your answers online as you take an official SAT practice test. See how you score and get detailed answer explanations to help you better understand where you need to improve.

### THE OFFICIAL SAT ONLINE COURSE™

The most comprehensive online tool to help you get ready for the SAT, *The Official SAT Online Course™* features 18 interactive lessons, official practice questions and tests, sample essays, automated essay scoring, personalized score reports and more.

**The Official SAT Online Course™**

This book entitles you to a discount on *The Official SAT Online Course.* To learn more, visit www.satonlinecourse.org.

By using *The Official SAT Study Guide™*, and *The Official SAT Online Course* together, you'll benefit from the best of both formats — print and Internet. As a book buyer, you're entitled to a $10 discount for *The Official SAT Online Course.* To receive the discount, you will need to visit www.collegeboard.org/satonlinecourse and answer questions about your book. You may already have access to *The Official SAT Online Course* through your school. To learn whether your school subscribes, ask a teacher or a counselor.

**SAT SKILLS INSIGHT**

As mentioned previously, this free online tool can help you understand what's tested on the test and what skills you need to do well and to achieve your desired score. You'll see that the skills on the test are the same skills you've been learning in the classroom!

**MY SAT**

Online registration is easy to use and always available. Most students register for the test online. You choose your test date and test center, provide credit card information and get immediate registration confirmation. After the test, visit My SAT to receive your scores, view your score history and see where you sent your scores. You can also view a copy of your essay.

**BOOK OWNERS' AREA**

Available exclusively to owners of this book, the online book owners' area provides valuable feedback and can be used as a study tool in helping you identify where you need to focus your efforts. After you've taken an official practice test in this book, you can enter you answers online. **We'll provide a practice score report and answer explanations for each practice test.** For more information, go to www.collegeboard.org/SATstudyguide.

> **Keep in Mind**
>
> Log on to www.collegeboard.org/SATstudyguide to access practice score report and answer explanations for each practice test.

## *College Planning*

The College Board Web site (www.collegeboard.org) provides all of the tools and tips you need to prepare for your move from high school to college. You'll find complete and trusted information on College Board tests — including the SAT, SAT Subject Tests, CLEP, AP and PSAT/NMSQT — as well as valuable resources for college planning.

Get started with these popular features of the site:

> **Keep in Mind**
>
> Register early for the test so you have the best chance of getting the test center nearest to your home.

- *College Search.* Find the right colleges for you and explore colleges you're already interested in — using the Web's most popular college search engine. Get guidance to make informed choices, research the latest and trusted information about colleges, and see how you compare to students who enrolled and got in.

- *My Organizer.* Organize your college planning activities in one place, save a list of your favorite colleges, and get customized reminders to stay on track. A calendar shows upcoming dates and deadlines for your colleges.

- *Pay for College.* Get expert advice and tools to help you afford college — including college financing calculators and a scholarship search. You'll also find the CSS/Financial Aid PROFILE, which you can complete online.

- *Real Advice:* Get help on just about every topic that relates to college planning, from how to get started, to how to choose — with videos and articles packed with advice from students and experts. Checklists and how-to guides break things down into simple steps.

## Before the Test

*Know what to expect* from the test: the types of questions, the number of questions and their order on the test.

*Understand the directions* for all eight types of questions. Take time to carefully read the directions for the questions. That way, you won't have to spend extra time studying the directions on the day you take the SAT. If you understand the instructions, you'll feel more confident and be less likely to make careless errors.

**Start your mental preparation the day before the test.**

- Get a good night's sleep.

- Have everything that you need for the test ready the night before.

- Review **Test Day Checklist** to make sure you have everything you'll need the next day.

## On Test Day

*Arrive at the test center by 7:45 a.m.*, unless your admission ticket specifies a different time. Remember to take the following items:

- your photo admission ticket

- an acceptable photo ID
  - driver's license (with your photo)
  - school identification card
  - valid passport
  - student ID form that has been prepared by your school on school stationery and includes a recognizable photo and the school seal, which overlaps the photo

- several No. 2 (soft lead) pencils and soft erasers

## Test Day Checklist

| I Need | I Have |
|---|---|
| appropriate photo ID | _____ |
| <u>photo</u> admission ticket | _____ |
| several No. 2 pencils and soft erasers | _____ |
| calculator with fresh batteries | _____ |
| watch | _____ |
| snack | _____ |
| **I know the way to the test center** and have instructions for finding the entrance on Saturday or Sunday. | _____ |
| **I am leaving at _____ a.m.** This will give me plenty of time in case I run into delays. | _____ |
| **My alarm is set.** | _____ |

**\*\*Be on Time or You Can't Take the Test.\*\***

## Keep in Mind

Effective with the 2012-13 academic year, enhanced SAT security measures are in place for students participating in any of the national and international SAT administration during a given academic year. Some of the enhanced security measures include:

**Registration Enhancements**

- Students are required to submit a current, recognizable photo during registration that will be included on the Admission Ticket.
  - Students registering online are required to upload a digital photo.
  - Students registering by mail are required to enclose a photo with the paper registration form.
  - The student's appearance in the photo must match how the student will look on the day of the test.

**Test Day Enhancements**

- Students are required to present their Admission Ticket for entry to their designated test center.
  - Students who register online will be able to print the Admission Ticket by logging on to their online College Board account.
  - Students who registered by mail can choose to have the Admission Ticket mailed or emailed prior to test day.

- Students arriving at the test center without both their Admission Ticket and an acceptable form of photo ID will not be admitted to the test center.

- Test center changes are not permitted on test day.

- Test-type changes are not permitted on test day.

- Standby (walk-in) testing is not permitted.

For additional information on Test Day Tips and policies, visit www.sat.org/test-day

## During the Test

*Read and think carefully.* Consider all the choices in each question. Don't lose points on easy questions through careless mistakes.

*Use your test booklet.* Your answer sheet must be kept neat and free of stray marks, but you can mark up your test booklet. You can write whatever you want, wherever you want, in the section of the booklet you're working on. You will not receive credit for anything written in the booklet, though.

Here are some pointers for using your test booklet.

> **Time and Hassle Savers**
>
> **Mark** skipped questions in your test booklet.
>
> **Cross out** choices to eliminate as you move through the test.
>
> **When skipping questions, be sure** you leave the right circles on the answer sheet blank (to avoid marking answers to the wrong questions).

- Mark each question that you *don't* answer so that you can easily find it again.

- Draw a line through each choice as you eliminate it when you work on a question.

- Mark sections, sentences or words in reading passages.

- In mathematics, make drawings to help you figure out word problems. Mark key information on graphs. Add information to drawings and diagrams as you work on them.

*Check your answer sheet regularly to make sure you are in the right place.* Losing your place on the answer sheet will affect your test results. Check the number of the question and the number on the answer sheet every few questions. This is especially important when you skip a question.

### Pacing and Timing

Each question on the test takes a certain amount of time to read and answer. That's where pacing comes in. If you had unlimited time, or very few questions to answer, pacing might not be important. But the test ends in 3 hours and 45 minutes whether or not you finished answering every question. So you have to keep moving through the test. Remember that you are allotted a certain amount of time for each section and are not allowed to move on to the next section if you finish early.

Skilled test-takers develop a sense of timing. They spend time on the questions they are most likely to answer correctly and leave some time for review.

## Easy Does It

*Work at an even, steady pace, but keep moving.* Don't spend so much time working through hard questions that you lose time to find and answer the easier ones.

Work on less time-consuming questions before moving on to those that demand more time. Save time by marking questions as you work on them and crossing out choices you can eliminate as you move through the test.

Most questions within a section range from easy to hard. Within a group of questions, such as Identifying Sentence Errors, the easier ones come first and the questions become more difficult as you move along.

If you find that one kind of question is too difficult, quickly read through the rest of the questions in that group. There might be others you can answer. Then go on to the next group of questions in that section.

The questions in the passage-based reading and improving paragraph sets don't range from easy to hard. An easier passage-based reading question might follow a harder one. (See Chapters 4 through 6 for details on the critical reading section of the SAT.)

*Keep track of time during the test.* The SAT includes 10 sections for which you have a total of 3 hours and 45 minutes to complete. First check to see how much time you have to complete each section. Then, while practicing for and taking the test, develop a habit of occasionally checking your progress through the test. That way you know when you are one-fourth of the way through the time allotted for a section, when you are halfway through and when you have five minutes left. If you finish a section before time is called, use the remaining time to check your answers.

*Know which questions are best for you.* After practicing the different kinds of questions on the tests in this book, you will probably know which you feel most comfortable with. Some types of questions may take you longer than others. You might want to begin with that type of question rather than at the beginning of the section. But you'll have to be careful. Be sure to mark in your test booklet what you skipped so that you can return to it.

## Getting Started

*Skip questions.* All questions are worth the same number of points regardless of the type or difficulty. So if you can't answer a question without spending a long time figuring it out, go on to the next one. If you aren't sure about how to answer a question, or you don't know where to begin, stop working on that question. You may have time to come back to it. Remember to mark the question in your test booklet so that you can find it later.

*Answer the easy ones first.* Once you know where the easy and hard questions are, answer the easy questions before tackling the more time-consuming questions. All questions are worth the same number of points.

## Making an Educated Guess

When you're not sure of an answer, try making an educated guess. This may be help-ful for the multiple-choice questions and for the mathematics questions for which you come up with your own answer.

*Multiple-choice questions.* When you are not sure of an answer to a multiple-choice question, eliminate all the choices that you know are wrong and make an educated guess from the remaining ones. The more choices you can eliminate, the better your chance of choosing the right answer and earning one point. To correct for random guessing, ¼ point is subtracted for each incorrect answer. Because of this, random guessing probably won't improve your score. In fact, it could lower your score. If you can't eliminate any choice, move on. You can return to the question later if there is time.

*Student-produced response questions.* For the mathematics questions that are not multiple choice, fill in your best educated guess. You lose no points for incorrect answers to these problems. If you have no idea how to approach a problem, move on. Again, you can return to it later if there is time.

## How to Make an Educated Guess

Here are some SAT questions that show how to make an educated guess.

### EDUCATED GUESSING EXAMPLES

#### 1. Sentence Completion

He was ------- businessman, but in his personal life he was kind, thoughtful, and -------.

(A) a competent . . self-centered
(B) an avaricious . . menacing
(C) a scrupulous . . tactful
(D) a ruthless . . magnanimous
(E) an amiable . . compassionate

#### What to do

Start with the second blank in the sentence:

He was ------- businessman, but in his personal life he was kind, thoughtful, and -------.

The word must be *positive* because it is in a series with the words *kind* and *thoughtful.* The second words in (A) and (B) — *self-centered* and *menacing* — are both *negative,* so you can eliminate those two choices.

That leaves (C), (D) or (E) as possible correct answers, giving you one chance in three of getting it right. Make an educated guess.

Even though you may get this particular question wrong, it is to your advantage to make an educated guess if you can eliminate one or more of the answer choices as definitely wrong.

The correct answer is (D).

### 2. Mathematics/Multiple Choice

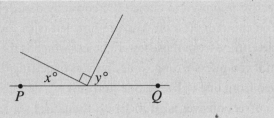

In the figure above, *PQ* is a straight line. Which of the following must be true about *x* and *y*?

(A)  $x + y = 180$
(B)  $90 + x = 180 - y$
(C)  $90 + x = y$
(D)  $2x = y$
(E)  $2y = x$

### What to do

Which of the answer choices can you eliminate by estimation?

- Clearly, the answer cannot be choice (A) because both $x°$ and $y°$ are less than 90°. Cross off choice (A).

- Choice (B) looks possible, but what about (C)?

- It's pretty obvious that (C) is not the answer because $90 + x$ is greater than *y*. Cross off choice (C).

- Choice (D) looks possible, so don't cross it off.

- But choice (E) is not possible, so cross it off.

Now you're left with only two possible answers, (B) and (D). If you were simply guessing, you are now faced with only two choices.

If you notice that $x° + y°$ must equal 90° and examine choice (B), you will see that $90 + x = 180 - y$ simplifies to $x + y = 90$.

The correct answer is choice (B).

### 3. Identifying Sentence Errors

<u>Carefully</u> designed programs of healthy diet and regular exercise <u>has provided</u> growing
  **A**                                                 **B**

teenagers <u>not only</u> healthier lungs and hearts, but also <u>improved</u> skin, teeth, and hair.
        **C**                                   **D**

No error
  **E**

### What to do

Read the sentence through entirely to see if the error is clear to you immediately. If it is not, consider the most common errors people make in writing sentences: grammar, usage, diction and idiom. Choice (A) is an adverb (ending in -ly) and it does indeed modify the adjective *designed*, so that potential error is eliminated. Likewise, the adjective *improved* in choice (D) correctly describes the nouns "skin, teeth, and hair." You can cross (D) off. You are now left with choices (B), (C) and (E), and you might determine from those fewer choices which is the actual answer for this item.

Even if you guess wrong, your chances of getting this question correct have been improved from one in five to one in three.

The correct answer is (B) because the plural subject *programs* requires a plural verb, which would be "have provided" rather than the singular "has provided."

# Get Confident

How you do on the SAT depends on how well you apply your knowledge. But your results can also reflect how you feel on the day you take the test. Your scores can be affected if you are nervous and distracted, if you are concentrating poorly or if you have negative feelings.

## Think Positively

Getting down on yourself during the test does more than make you feel bad. It can take away the confidence you need to solve problems. It can distract you. Keep up your confidence and focus on each question.

The SAT shows what you know and what you know you can do. The test has no trick questions.

If you have taken challenging course work in high school, you should be feeling good about yourself and your capabilities.

## Stay Focused

Ignore distractions. Think only of the question in front of you. If you catch yourself daydreaming, bring your focus back to the test.

## Concentrate on Your Own Progress

Suppose you get stuck on a question. Suppose you run into a batch of questions that are particularly difficult for you. You might be tempted to look around to see how everyone else is doing. Don't do it! You'll just see that others are filling in their answer sheets.

Think of this:

- Everyone works at a different pace. Your neighbors may not be working on the same question that has puzzled you.

- Thinking about what someone else is doing takes away time you could be using on the test.

- Within a testing room, the sections of the test are in different sequences. Students sitting near you may be working on different sections.

## Keep the Test in Perspective

The SAT is important, but how you do on one test won't decide whether you get into college.

- The test is only *one* factor of many in the college admissions decision.

- Nonacademic admissions criteria are important, too. These include extracurricular activities and personal recommendations. College admissions officers at individual colleges will usually be glad to discuss their schools' admissions policies with you.

- If you don't do as well as you hoped to, you can take the test again or use Score Choice to show colleges the scores that you feel best represent your abilities. Most colleges look at your highest score on each section, so even if you opt to use Score Choice you should feel comfortable sending all of your scores.

## You're in Control

Making a plan for taking the SAT will keep you in control during the test: Practice each type of question. Remember that the easier questions generally come first in each section. Learn how to pace yourself. Learn how to make an educated guess. If you're in control, you'll improve your chances of doing your best.

# Taking the Test Again

Research shows that most students do better on the SAT if they take the test a second time. Again, as mentioned in Chapter 1, approximately one out of every two high school students taking the SAT takes it more than once. Most who repeat the test take it once in the spring of their junior year and once in the fall of their senior year. There is no evidence that taking the test more than twice is beneficial to your score. But remember, all of the work you've done in school — including your reading, writing and mathematics — is what really helps you to do your best on the test and to be better prepared for college.

# PREFACE
# RECAP

## Recap

### *Before the Test*

- Learn the directions for all eight question types.

- Get a good night's sleep.

- Have everything that you need for the test ready the night before.

- Make sure you know how to get to the test center and have any special instructions for finding the entrance on Saturday or Sunday.

- Leave early enough so that you will have plenty of time in case of delays while traveling to the test center.

### *During the Test*

- First answer all the easy questions you can.

- Keep moving.

- Keep in mind that most questions are arranged from easy to hard.

- Remember which questions are best for you.

- Remember that all questions are worth the same point value.

- Eliminate choices.

- Make an educated guess.

- Watch the time you spend on any one question.

- Use your test booklet as scratch paper, and mark questions to go back to.

- Check your answer sheet regularly to make sure you're answering the right question.

- Keep your answer sheet neat.

### *Feeling Confident*

- Think positively. Negative thoughts will just distract you from doing your best.

- Stay focused. Think only about the question you are trying to answer.

- Concentrate on your own progress. Don't pay attention to what others in the room are doing or how quickly they may be working.

- Keep the test in perspective. The SAT is not the only factor in college admissions decisions, and you can always take the test again.

- Remember, you're in control. You can always choose the scores you send with Score Choice.

# CHAPTER 3

# About the PSAT/NMSQT®

If you want practice for the SAT, then the PSAT/NMSQT is for you. (PSAT/NMSQT stands for Preliminary SAT/National Merit Scholarship Qualifying Test.) This test also gives you a chance to enter scholarship competitions sponsored by the National Merit Scholarship Corporation and, through the Student Search Service, a chance to hear from colleges looking for students like you.

The PSAT/NMSQT measures the critical reading, mathematics and writing skills that you've been developing throughout your school years.

The test is given by high schools in October. Your school counselor can help you sign up for the PSAT/NMSQT. Many students take the test during their sophomore and junior years — but only test scores from their junior year are used for scholarship competitions. Ask your school counselor for a copy of the *Official Student Guide to the PSAT/NMSQT,* which includes a complete practice test.

## Why You Should Take the PSAT/NMSQT

Taking the test helps you to:

- practice for the SAT

- assess your critical reading, mathematics and writing skills. A comprehensive score report gives helpful feedback on the skills you need to work on

- compare yourself with other college-bound students from around the country

- receive projected SAT scores

- qualify for entry into scholarship competitions sponsored by the National Merit Scholarship Corporation

- participate in the Student Search Service to receive information from colleges and scholarship organizations

## Types of Questions

The PSAT/NMSQT includes critical reading, mathematics and writing skills questions. (See Table 3.1 for details.)

The PSAT/NMSQT allows 2 hours and 10 minutes and includes five sections:

- Two 25-minute critical reading sections

- Two 25-minute mathematics sections

- One 30-minute writing skills section

## Score Report

Your PSAT/NMSQT Score Report gives you feedback on your test performance and other valuable information:

- PSAT/NMSQT scores for critical reading, mathematics and writing skills

- Score ranges

- Percentiles (for juniors or sophomores)

- Selection index used by the National Merit Scholarship Corporation for initial entry into their scholarship competitions (sum of your scores in all three sections)

- Comprehensive question-by-question feedback

- Academic skills feedback

- Online access to questions and answer explanations

- Basic eligibility criteria and status for National Merit Scholarships

- Guidance information to help in college and career planning

## Preparing for the PSAT/NMSQT

As in preparing for the SAT, the best way you can prepare for the PSAT/NMSQT is to take challenging academic courses, work hard in school and read extensively. To become familiar with the questions that appear on the test:

- Review the SAT test-taking reminders and approaches on these pages.

- Read Chapter 2, "How to Do Your Best on the SAT."

- Before the test, become familiar with question types and directions by doing practice questions, which are also covered in the *Official Student Guide to the PSAT/NMSQT*.

▪ Take the complete Practice Test included with your *Official Student Guide to the PSAT/NMSQT.*

**Table 3.1** Number and Types of Questions with Time Allotted for Each Section of the PSAT/NMSQT

| Section | No. of Questions | Time Allotted |
|---|---|---|
| **Critical Reading** (multiple-choice questions) | | |
| Sentence completion | 13 | |
| Passage-based reading | 35 | |
| *Total critical reading questions* | *48* | *50 minutes (two 25-minute sections)* |
| **Mathematics** | | |
| Multiple choice | 28 | |
| Student-produced response (grid-ins) | 10 | |
| *Total mathematics questions* | *38* | *50 minutes (two 25-minute sections)* |
| **Writing Skills** (multiple-choice questions) | | |
| Identifying sentence errors | 14 | |
| Improving sentences | 20 | |
| Improving paragraphs | 5 | |
| *Total writing questions* | *39* | *30 minutes (one section)* |

## Pointers for the PSAT/NMSQT

1. Know the directions for each type of question.

2. Expect easy questions at the start of each group of questions (except in passage-based reading in the critical reading section and improving paragraphs in the writing skills section).

3. Answer as many easy questions as you can because all questions are worth the same number of points.

4. Read all the answer choices for multiple-choice questions.

5. Make sure you understand what the question is asking.

6. Do scratchwork in the test booklet.

7. Work steadily.

8. Understand the concept of educated guessing — that is, if you cannot find the correct answer, eliminate the choice or choices that you know are wrong and make an educated guess from the remaining answers.

9. Bring a calculator that you are comfortable using.

10. Practice and have a thorough understanding of how to complete math student-produced response questions.

11. Relax.

## Preparing for the Critical Reading and Mathematics Sections

The types of critical reading and mathematics questions on the PSAT/NMSQT are the same as on the SAT. Here's what you'll need to do to prepare:

- Review the critical reading and mathematics chapters in this book.

- Go through the mathematics review chapters carefully (see Chapters 15 to 18). If it is close to exam time, concentrate on the mathematics skills and concepts that you've studied but may need to review. If you have time before the test, start learning some of the unfamiliar skills and concepts.

- Practice applying the approaches and reminders on the sample tests.

## Preparing for the Writing Section

The writing skills section of the PSAT/NMSQT includes the three types of grammar and usage multiple-choice questions that appear on the SAT writing section:

- Identifying sentence errors

- Improving sentences

- Improving paragraphs

The writing section includes 39 questions on grammar and usage, and it assesses your ability to use language in a clear, consistent manner and to improve writing by revising and editing.

Test questions do not ask you to define or use grammatical terms and do not test spelling or capitalization. The PSAT/NMSQT does not include an essay portion.

Here are some ideas on how to approach the writing skills section of the test:

- If you cannot find the correct answer, eliminate the choice or choices that you know are wrong and make an educated guess from the remaining answers.

- Review the writing multiple-choice chapters in this book (Chapters 8 and 10 to 13).

- Try to answer the sample writing questions in this book and study the explanations for each sample.

## Important Review in September

When the *Official Student Guide to the PSAT/NMSQT* arrives at your school in September (ask your counselor for it), review the explanation sections and then take the full-length practice test. If any questions pose problems for you, use this book again to review those question types to improve your understanding. And, of course, work in class and with your teachers to hone your academic skills daily.

# PART II

# The Critical Reading Section

# CHAPTER 4

# About the Critical Reading Section

When you get to the critical reading section, you'll find two types of multiple-choice questions:

- *Sentence completion.* There are 19 multiple-choice questions that test your vocabulary and your ability to understand fairly complex sentences.

- *Passage-based reading.* There are 48 questions that are based on passages that range from 100 to 850 words. The content of the passages is drawn from the humanities, literary fiction, social studies, and natural sciences.

*Critical reading skills are fundamental building blocks of academic success.* The two types of critical reading questions test how well you understand the written word. Your ability to read carefully and to think about what you read is essential to your success in college. In college, you will have to learn a great deal on your own from your assigned reading, even in courses that are not language arts, such as mathematics and science. Building your vocabulary is a valuable life skill. Having a large and varied vocabulary can help you better express yourself. The best way to improve your vocabulary is by reading.

## Approaches to the Critical Reading Section

▶ *Work on sentence completion questions first.* About one-third of the critical reading questions are sentence completions. Work on these first in any section that includes both types of critical reading questions. The sentence completion questions take less time to finish than the passage-based reading questions. But remember to save enough time to read the passages.

**Keep in Mind**

Answer the sentence completion questions you're comfortable with before moving on to the passage-based reading questions.

► *Mark your test booklet.* As you work on one of the critical reading test sections, you may want to use the following three-step approach:

1. Begin with the set of sentence completions. Answer as many questions as you can. In your test booklet, mark each question you don't answer so that you can easily go back to it.

2. After moving through the sentence completions, go back and take a quick glance at the questions you marked. Answer the ones you can without spending a lot of time on any one question.

3. Then move on to the passage-based reading questions.

► *Remember that the difficulty of sentence completion questions increases as you move through a question set.* When these questions become difficult to answer, give the rest of them a quick read before you skip ahead to the passage-based reading questions. All sentence completion questions are based in part on your knowledge of vocabulary. It doesn't take long to read these questions, and you may pick up a correct answer or two. You may see a word that you know that might improve your chances of answering the question correctly.

> **Keep in Mind**
>
> **Keep track of the questions you want to go back to and read again by marking the questions in your test booklet. When skipping questions, though, be sure to keep track of your place on the answer sheet.**

► *Use the process of elimination.* If you have time to go back to some of the difficult questions that you skipped, try eliminating choices you know are wrong. (This is a good approach for the entire test.) Sometimes you can get to the correct answer that way. If not, eliminating choices will at least allow you to make educated guesses.

► *Consider related words, familiar sayings and phrases, roots, prefixes and suffixes.* If you don't know what a word means right away, stop for a moment. Have you ever heard or seen a word that may be related to it? You can get help from common sayings and phrases. If you don't know a word but are familiar with a phrase that uses it, you might be able to figure out the word. For instance, you may not immediately remember what the words *ovation* and *annul* mean. But you probably would recognize them in the phrases "a standing ovation" and "annul a marriage." If you can recall a phrase or saying in which a word is used, you may be able to figure out what it means in another context.

**CHAPTER 5**
# Sentence Completion

Having a broad vocabulary always comes in handy, especially when you're doing parts of the SAT such as the sentence completion questions. Having the ability to understand the logic of complex sentences is also helpful in this section of the SAT. In addition, several approaches can help you work through even the toughest questions.

The following box provides the directions that will appear on the test. The directions include a sample question.

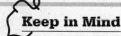

**Keep in Mind**

Be familiar with the test directions before test day.

---

Each sentence below has one or two blanks, each blank indicating that something has been omitted. Beneath the sentence are five words or sets of words labeled A through E. Choose the word or set of words that, when inserted in the sentence, best fits the meaning of the sentence as a whole.

**Example:**

Hoping to ------- the dispute, negotiators proposed a compromise that they felt would be ------- to both labor and management.

(A) enforce . . useful
(B) end . . divisive
(C) overcome . . unattractive
(D) extend . . satisfactory
(E) resolve . . acceptable          Ⓐ Ⓑ Ⓒ Ⓓ ●

---

## Types of Questions

The SAT has two different types of sentence completion questions: vocabulary in context and logic based. Following are some examples of each type of question.

### Vocabulary-in-Context Questions

To answer this type of question, you need to know how the words are used in the context of the sentence. If you know the definitions of the words involved, you have a better chance of selecting the correct answer.

There are both one-blank and two-blank vocabulary-in-context questions.

### EXAMPLE 1

Ravens appear to behave -------, actively helping one another to find food.

(A) mysteriously
(B) warily
(C) aggressively
(D) cooperatively
(E) defensively

*Answer:* The correct answer is (D).

*Explanation:* This sentence asks you to look for a word that describes how the ravens behave. The information after the comma restates and defines the meaning of the missing word. You are told that the ravens "actively help one another." Only one word among the choices accurately describes this behavior: *cooperatively*.

### EXAMPLE 2

Both ------- and -------, Wilson seldom spoke and never spent money.

(A) vociferous . . generous
(B) garrulous . . stingy
(C) effusive . . frugal
(D) taciturn . . miserly
(E) reticent . . munificent

*Answer:* The correct answer is (D).

*Explanation:* In this sentence, you are looking for two words that describe Wilson. One of the words has to mean that he "seldom spoke" and the other that he "never spent money." The correct answer is "taciturn . . miserly." *Taciturn* means "shy, unwilling to talk." *Miserly* means "like a miser, extremely stingy."

## Logic-Based Questions

The following questions require you to know the meanings of the words, know how the words are used in context and understand the logic of a rather complicated sentence.

### EXAMPLE 1

After observing several vicious territorial fights, Jane Goodall had to revise her earlier opinion that these particular primates were always ------- animals.

(A) ignorant
(B) inquisitive
(C) responsive
(D) cruel
(E) peaceful

*Answer:* The correct answer is (E).

*Explanation:* To answer this question, you have to follow the logical flow of the ideas in the sentence. A few key words reveal that logic. First, the introductory word "After" tells you that the information at the beginning of the sentence is going to affect what comes later. The word *after* also gives an order to the events in the sentence.

Second, the word *revise* tells you that something is going to change. It is going to change *after* the events described at the beginning of the sentence. So the events at the beginning really cause the change.

Finally, the end of the sentence—"her earlier opinion that these particular primates were always ------- animals"—tells you what is changing. The word filling the blank should convey a meaning you would have to revise after seeing the animals fight. *Peaceful* is the only such word among the five choices.

## EXAMPLE 2

> Although its publicity has been -------, the film itself is intelligent, well-acted, handsomely produced, and altogether --------.
>
> (A) tasteless . . respectable
> (B) extensive . . moderate
> (C) sophisticated . . amateur
> (D) risqué . . crude
> (E) perfect . . spectacular

*Answer:* The correct answer is (A).

*Explanation:* The first thing to notice about this sentence is that it has two parts or clauses. The first clause begins with "Although," the second clause begins with "the film."

The logic of the sentence is determined by the way the two clauses relate to each other. The two parts have contrasting or conflicting meanings. Why? Because one of the clauses begins with "Although." The word *although* is used to introduce an idea that conflicts with something else in the sentence: *Although* something is true, something else that you would expect to be true is not.

The answer is "tasteless . . respectable." You would not expect a film with "tasteless publicity" to be "altogether respectable." But the introductory word *although* tells you that you should expect the unexpected.

# Approaches to the Sentence Completion Questions

➤ *Start out by reading the entire sentence, saying "blank" for the blank(s).* This gives you an overall sense of the meaning of the sentence and helps you figure out how the parts of the sentence relate to each other.

➤ *Always begin by trying to determine the* standard *dictionary definitions of the words in the sentence and the answers.* To answer sentence completion questions, you usually don't have to know a nonstandard meaning of a word.

➤ *Keep in mind that* introductory *and* transitional *words are extremely important.* They can be the key to figuring out the logic of a sentence. They tell you how the parts of the sentence relate to each other. For example, look at the following common introductory and transitional words:

- but
- although
- however
- yet
- even though

These words indicate that the two parts of the sentence will contradict or be in contrast with each other. There are many other introductory and transitional words that you should watch for when working on sentence completion questions. *Always* read the sentences carefully, and don't ignore any of the details.

➤ *Be aware that some of the most difficult sentence completion questions contain negatives, which can make following the logic of the sentences challenging.* Negatives in two clauses of a sentence can be even more of a challenge, as in this example:

> According to Burgess, a novelist *should not* preach, for sermonizing *has no place* in good fiction.

A negative appears in each clause of this sentence. The transitional word *for* indicates that the second part of the sentence will explain the first.

➤ *Figure out what sort of word(s) should fill the blank(s) before looking at the choices; then look for a choice that is similar to the one(s) you thought of.* For many one-blank questions, especially the easier ones, you'll find the word you thought of among the choices. Other times, a close synonym for your word will be one of the choices.

For example, try answering the following sentence completion question without looking at the choices:

Once Murphy left home for good, he wrote no letters to his worried mother; he did not, therefore, live up to her picture of him as her ------- son.

The transitional word *therefore* indicates that the information in the *second* part of the sentence is a direct, logical result of the information in the *first* part. What words might fit in the blank?

_____     _____

_____     _____

The second part of the sentence includes a negative ("he did not . . . live up to her picture . . ."), so the blank must be a *positive* term. Words like *perfect, sweet, respectful, devoted*—all could fit in the blank. Now, look at the actual choices:

(A) misunderstood
(B) elusive
(C) destructive
(D) persuasive
(E) dutiful

Choice (E) *dutiful* is the only choice that is even close to the ones suggested. Therefore, (E) is the correct answer.

You can also try this technique with two-blank questions. You are less likely to come up with as close a word match, but it will help you get a feel for the meaning and logic of the sentence.

► *With two-blank questions, try eliminating some answers based on just one blank.* If one word in an answer doesn't make sense in the sentence, then you can reject the entire choice. For example, try approaching two-blank questions like this:

- Work with *one* of the blanks alone. Eliminate any choices in which the word doesn't make sense.

- Work on the *other* blank alone. Eliminate any choices in which that word doesn't make sense. If only one choice is left, that is the correct answer. If more than one choice remains, go to the next step.

- Work on *both* blanks together only for the remaining choices.

- Always read the complete sentence *with both words in place* to make sure your choice makes sense.

Example 2 of the logic-based questions shows how this approach works. Here it is again:

> Although its publicity has been -------, the film itself is intelligent, well-acted, handsomely produced, and altogether -------.
>
> (A) tasteless . . respectable
> (B) extensive . . moderate
> (C) sophisticated . . amateur
> (D) risqué . . crude
> (E) perfect . . spectacular

As you can see, the first blank is not tightly controlled by the words immediately around it. The first word depends on the word in the second blank. So start with the second blank.

The second blank is part of a list that includes "intelligent, well-acted, handsomely produced, and altogether _____." The word *and* indicates that the last word in the list (i.e., the blank) should be a *positive* word, in general agreement with the others. With that in mind, examine the second words in the following answer choices:

- intelligent, well-acted . . . and altogether respectable
- intelligent, well-acted . . . and altogether moderate
- intelligent, well-acted . . . and altogether amateur
- intelligent, well-acted . . . and altogether crude
- intelligent, well-acted . . . and altogether spectacular

*Amateur* and *crude* are definitely not complimentary. No matter what the rest of the sentence says, neither of these words makes sense in the second blank. So you can eliminate the answers that contain *amateur* and *crude*.

With two choices eliminated, the question becomes much easier to deal with.

▶ *Remember that the instructions for all the sentence completion questions ask you to choose the* best *answer.* One choice may seem to make sense, but it still might not be the *best* of the five choices. Unless you read all the choices, you may select only the *second best* and thus answer incorrectly.

▶ *Check your choice by reading the entire sentence with the answer you have selected in place to make sure the sentence makes sense.* This step is extremely important, especially if you have eliminated choices while working through the question. For example, choice (A) in Example 2 is correct because the words *respectable* and *tasteless* contrast with each other. Such a contrast is logically consistent because of the *although* construction of the sentence.

# Sample Questions

Each sentence below has one or two blanks, each blank indicating that something has been omitted. Beneath the sentence are five words or sets of words labeled A through E. Choose the word or set of words that, when inserted in the sentence, best fits the meaning of the sentence as a whole.

**Example:**

Hoping to ------- the dispute, negotiators proposed a compromise that they felt would be ------- to both labor and management.

(A) enforce . . useful
(B) end . . divisive
(C) overcome . . unattractive
(D) extend . . satisfactory
(E) resolve . . acceptable            Ⓐ Ⓑ Ⓒ Ⓓ ●

---

1. A judgment made before all the facts are known must be called -------.

    (A) harsh
    (B) deliberate     w. purpose
    (C) sensible
    (D) premature
    (E) fair

2. Despite their ------- proportions, the murals of Diego Rivera give his Mexican compatriots the sense that their history is ------- and human in scale, not remote and larger than life.

    (A) monumental . . accessible
    (B) focused . . prolonged
    (C) vast . . ancient
    (D) realistic . . extraneous
    (E) narrow . . overwhelming

3. The research is so ------- that it leaves no part of the issue unexamined.

    (A) comprehensive
    (B) rewarding
    (C) sporadic
    (D) economical
    (E) problematic

4. A dictatorship ------- its citizens to be docile and finds it expedient to make outcasts of those who do not -------.

    (A) forces . . rebel
    (B) expects . . disobey
    (C) requires . . conform
    (D) allows . . withdraw
    (E) forbids . . agree

5. Alice Walker's prize-winning novel exemplifies the strength of first-person narratives; the protagonist tells her own story so effectively that any additional commentary would be -------.

    (A) subjective
    (B) eloquent
    (C) superfluous
    (D) incontrovertible
    (E) impervious

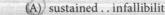

6. The Supreme Court's reversal of its previous ruling on the issue of states' rights ------- its reputation for -------.

(A) sustained . . infallibility
(B) compromised . . consistency
(C) bolstered . . doggedness
(D) aggravated . . inflexibility
(E) dispelled . . vacillation

# Answers and Explanations

1. A judgment made before all the facts are known must be called -------.

   (A) harsh
   (B) deliberate
   (C) sensible
   (D) premature
   (E) fair

*Answer:* The correct answer is (D).

*Explanation:* Getting the correct answer to this question depends almost entirely on knowing the definitions of the five words you must choose from. Which of the choices describes a judgment made before "all the facts are known"? Such a judgment, by definition, is not "deliberate," and the sentence doesn't tell us whether the judgment was "harsh" or lenient, "sensible" or silly, "fair" or unfair. *Premature* means hasty or early; therefore, it fits the blank perfectly.

This is the kind of one-blank vocabulary question for which you might be able to predict the answer based on the information given in the sentence. You might have thought of other words that could have completed the sentence satisfactorily—for instance, *rash, hasty* or *risky*—but none of them nor any synonyms for them appear among the choices. When you see the choices, you should recognize that *premature* has connotations similar to the words you thought of.

> **Keep in Mind**
>
> Know your vocabulary. Think carefully about the meanings of the words in the answer choices.

2. Despite their ------- proportions, the murals of Diego Rivera give his Mexican compatriots the sense that their history is ------- and human in scale, not remote and larger than life.

   (A) monumental . . accessible
   (B) focused . . prolonged
   (C) vast . . ancient
   (D) realistic . . extraneous
   (E) narrow . . overwhelming

*Answer:* The correct answer is (A).

*Explanation:* The keys to this sentence are the word "Despite," the words "human in scale," and the words "not remote and larger than life." The word filling the first blank has to be one that would relate closely to something that seems "larger than life," as (A) *monumental* does, but so does (C) *vast.* The word filling the second blank has to fit with "human in scale," which (A) *accessible* does. If you focus on only one of the two blanks, you will be able to eliminate several choices before you even think about the other blank, as in this case, where it is possible to eliminate answers (B), (D) and (E) almost immediately.

> **Keep in Mind**
>
> Watch for key introductory and transitional words that determine how the parts of the sentence relate. Then try answering two-blank questions one blank at a time. If you can eliminate one word in a choice, the entire choice can be ruled out.

**3.** The research is so ------- that it leaves no part of the issue unexamined.

(A) comprehensive
(B) rewarding
(C) sporadic
(D) economical
(E) problematic

### Keep in Mind

Think about the logic of the sentence without looking at the choices. Then look for the choice that has a similar meaning to the words you thought of.

*Answer:* The correct answer is (A)

*Explanation:* Try filling in the blank without reading the answer choices. What kind of words would fit? Words like *complete, thorough* or *extensive* could all fit. Now look at the answer choices. Choice (A) *comprehensive* is very similar to the words suggested, and none of the other choices fit at all.

If no possible answer occurs to you before you look at the choices, try to relate each choice to the details of the sentence. In this case you are looking for a word that would match the detail "it leaves no part of the issue unexamined."

**4.** A dictatorship ------- its citizens to be docile and finds it expedient to make outcasts of those who do not -------.

(A) forces . . rebel
(B) expects . . disobey
(C) requires . . conform
(D) allows . . withdraw
(E) forbids . . agree

### Keep in Mind

Think carefully about the standard dictionary definitions of the important words in the sentence. Small words such as *not* can make a big difference. When you choose your answer, read the entire sentence with the blank(s) filled in to be sure that it makes sense.

*Answer:* The correct answer is (C).

*Explanation:* Answering this question depends in part on your knowledge of vocabulary. You have to know what the words *dictatorship, docile* and *expedient* mean. You also have to watch out for key words such as *not.*

The first word in each of the five choices is an action a dictatorship might take, so you are more likely to find the correct answer by first examining the second word. Recognizing that the second word refers to what happens to "outcasts," and observing the crucial word *not,* you can eliminate *rebel* and *disobey.* That leaves *conform, withdraw* and *agree* as behaviors a dictatorship might want to see displayed in its people.

*Conformity* and *agreement* are certainly qualities a dictator would want in the people. The tendency to *withdraw* is less likely, because people who are out of sight might also be out of the dictator's control; also, it is illogical to make outcasts of everyone who does not *withdraw.* So choice (D) can be eliminated. If a dictator wants the people to *conform,* requiring them to be docile would help, so choice (C) looks good. In choice (E), if the dictator is going to cast out those who do not *agree,* which is a very possible political reality, the first part of the sentence is illogical: dictatorships do not forbid people to be docile (gentle). Choice (C) is clearly the most logical and meaningful of the choices.

---

**5.** Alice Walker's prize-winning novel exemplifies the strength of first-person narratives; the protagonist tells her own story so effectively that any additional commentary would be -------.

(A) subjective
(B) eloquent
(C) superfluous
(D) incontrovertible
(E) impervious

---

*Answer:* The correct answer is (C).

*Explanation:* This single-blank vocabulary question is best approached by trying to supply a satisfactory completion before you read the answer choices. You may be able to answer the question more quickly if you don't have to plug in each choice one by one to see if it makes any sense.

> **Keep in Mind**
>
> Think about the meaning of the sentence before you look at the choices. Get a sense of what you're looking for before you start looking.

Words like *prize-winning, strength* and *effectively* tell you that the writer thinks that Alice Walker's novel is well written and that the main character "tells her own story" very well. Therefore, would "additional commentary" be necessary or unnecessary? Once you've figured out that it is unnecessary, you can look for an answer with a similar meaning, which is choice (C) *superfluous.*

---

**6.** The Supreme Court's reversal of its previous ruling on the issue of states' rights ------- its reputation for -------.

(A) sustained . . infallibility
(B) compromised . . consistency
(C) bolstered . . doggedness
(D) aggravated . . inflexibility
(E) dispelled . . vacillation

---

*Answer:* The correct answer is (B).

*Explanation:* Getting the correct answer to this question depends mainly on your knowledge of the meanings of the word choices. You have to know the definitions of the words before you can try the choices one by one to arrive at the correct pair.

You also need to think about the central idea in the sentence: the Court's "reversal" does what to its "reputation" for what? The logic is complicated, and the vocabulary in the choices is difficult. You have to think for a moment about the attitude the sentence is probably trying to communicate. Most people would agree that the Supreme Court members think long and hard before they make a ruling. Reversing one of those rulings is probably an unusual and undesirable event. In each choice,

**Keep in Mind**

When you read the sentence to yourself, substitute the word *blank* for each blank. Try to figure out what the sentence is saying before you start plugging in the choices.

the second word suggests a "reputation" the Court might have. Which of those words most probably names a reputation we most usually expect of the Supreme Court?

- *Infallibility* in choice (A) and *consistency* in choice (B) — perhaps.

- *Doggedness* in choice (C) is less likely: it suggests *persistence* more than *correctness*.

- *Inflexibility* in choice (D) implies an unwillingness to keep an open mind, which is not a quality we would admire at our highest levels of justice.

- And *vacillation*, in choice (E), is something we do not want to see in the Court at all.

Look more closely at (A) and (B). If we choose (A), the sentence says that the reversal of the previous ruling *sustained* the Court's reputation for *infallibility*. That is contradictory, so it cannot be the right answer. If we choose (B), the sentence means that the reversal of its ruling *compromised* (or imperiled or jeopardized) one of its most valued qualities, its *consistency*. That sounds like a meaningful sentence, and it is in fact the correct answer.

## Recap

1. Be familiar with the directions before test day.

2. Answer as many easy questions as you can before spending time on the harder ones.

3. Read the sentence, substituting the word *blank* for each blank, to give you an overall sense of the meaning of the sentence.

4. Always begin by trying to determine the *standard* dictionary definitions of the key words in the sentence and the answer choices.

5. Know your vocabulary: think carefully about the meanings of the words in the answer choices.

6. Watch for key *introductory* and *transitional* words (e.g., *but*, *although*, *however*, *yet*, *even though*). These determine how the parts of the sentence relate. Also watch carefully for negatives.

7. Think about the logic of the sentence without looking at the choices. Try figuring out words to fill in the blank or blanks without looking at the answer choices. Then look for the choice that is similar to the ones you thought of.

8. Try answering two-blank questions one blank at a time. If you can eliminate one word in an answer, the entire choice can be eliminated.

9. Always check all the answer choices before making a final decision. A choice may seem okay, but it may still not be the best answer. Make sure that the answer you select is the *best* choice.

10. Check your answer to make sure it makes sense by reading the entire sentence with your choice in place.

11. Eliminate answers that you know are wrong, and make an educated guess from those remaining.

# Practice Questions

Each sentence below has one or two blanks, each blank indicating that something has been omitted. Beneath the sentence are five words or sets of words labeled A through E. Choose the word or set of words that, when inserted in the sentence, <u>best</u> fits the meaning of the sentence as a whole.

**Example:**

Hoping to ------- the dispute, negotiators proposed a compromise that they felt would be ------- to both labor and management.

(A)  enforce . . useful
(B)  end . . divisive
(C)  overcome . . unattractive
(D)  extend . . satisfactory
(E)  resolve . . acceptable

---

1.  In many cases, the formerly ------- origins of diseases have now been identified through modern scientific techniques.

 (A)  insightful
 (B)  mysterious
 (C)  cruel
 (D)  notable
 (E)  useful

2.  Freeing embedded fossils from rock has become less ------- for paleontologists, who now have tiny vibrating drills capable of working with great speed and delicacy.

 (A)  exploratory
 (B)  conclusive
 (C)  tedious
 (D)  respected
 (E)  demeaning

3.  Many people find Stanley Jordan's music not only entertaining but also -------; listening to it helps them to relax and to ------- the tensions they feel at the end of a trying day.

 (A)  soothing . . heighten
 (B)  therapeutic . . alleviate
 (C)  sweet . . underscore
 (D)  exhausting . . relieve
 (E)  interesting . . activate

4.  Marine biologist Sylvia Earle makes a career of expanding the limits of deep-sea mobility, making hitherto-impossible tasks ------- through the new technology designed by her company.

 (A)  famous
 (B)  feasible
 (C)  fantastic
 (D)  controversial
 (E)  captivating

5. Two anomalies regarding her character are apparent: she is unfailingly ------- yet bursting with ambition, and she is truly ------- but unable to evoke reciprocal warmth in those with whom she works.

   (A) aspiring . . generous
   (B) mercenary . . impartial
   (C) impulsive . . resolute
   (D) persistent . . reserved
   (E) humble . . compassionate

6. In many parts of East Africa at that time, wild animals were so ------- that it was almost impossible for a photographer to approach close enough to film them.

   (A) rare
   (B) large
   (C) wary
   (D) numerous
   (E) unsightly

7. The unflattering reviews that his latest recording received were ------- by his fans, who believe that everything he performs is a triumph of artistic -------.

   (A) dismissed . . creativity
   (B) hailed . . responsibility
   (C) suppressed . . self-promotion
   (D) accepted . . genius
   (E) regretted . . pretension

8. The board members, accustomed to the luxury of being chauffeured to corporate meetings in company limousines, were predictably ------- when they learned that this service had been -------.

   (A) satisfied . . annulled
   (B) stymied . . extended
   (C) displeased . . upheld
   (D) disgruntled . . suspended
   (E) concerned . . provided

9. Misrepresentative graphs and drawings ------- the real data and encourage readers to accept ------- arguments.

   (A) obscure . . legitimate
   (B) distort . . spurious
   (C) illustrate . . controversial
   (D) complement . . unresolved
   (E) replace . . esteemed

10. Conservative historians who represent a traditional account as ------- because of its age may be guilty of taking on trust what they should have ------- in a conscientious fashion.

   (A) ancient . . established
   (B) false . . reiterated
   (C) mythical . . fabricated
   (D) accurate . . examined
   (E) suspicious . . challenged

11. The art of Milet Andrejevic often presents us with an idyllic vision that is subtly
------- by more sinister elements, as if suggesting the ------- beauty of our
surroundings.

    (A) enhanced . . pristine
    (B) invaded . . flawed
    (C) altered . . unmarred
    (D) redeemed . . hallowed
    (E) devastated . . bland

12. State commissioner Ming Hsu expected that her Commission on International
Trade would not merely ------- the future effects of foreign competition on local
businesses but would also offer practical strategies for successfully resisting such
competition.

    (A) counteract
    (B) intensify
    (C) imagine
    (D) forecast
    (E) excuse

13. Since many teachers today draw on material from a variety of sources, disciplines,
and ideologies for their lessons, their approach could best be called -------.

    (A) eclectic
    (B) simplistic
    (C) invidious
    (D) impromptu
    (E) dogmatic

14. Unprecedented turmoil in the usually thriving nation has made the formerly -------
investors leery of any further involvement.

    (A) pessimistic
    (B) cautious
    (C) clandestine
    (D) reticent
    (E) sanguine

15. Despite its apparent -------, much of early Greek philosophical thought was actually
marked by a kind of unconscious dogmatism that led to ------- assertions.

    (A) liberality . . doctrinaire
    (B) independence . . autonomous
    (C) intransigence . . authoritative
    (D) fundamentalism . . arrogant
    (E) legitimacy . . ambiguous

## Answer Key

1. B
2. C
3. B
4. B
5. E
6. C
7. A
8. D
9. B
10. D
11. B
12. D
13. A
14. E
15. A

Additional practice questions can be found in *The Official SAT Online Course* at www.collegeboard.org/satonlinecourse.

# CHAPTER 6
# Passage-based Reading

When you answer passage-based reading questions, how carefully you read and how well you understand the information in a passage are more important than how much you know about the subject. Like much of the reading you'll be doing in college, the passages will present important issues, ideas or events to think about.

## Types of Passages

Here's what to expect from the passages.

- The passages range in length from about 100 to 850 words.

- Some selections are from a single source, and others consist of a pair of related passages on a shared issue or theme. For each pair, one of the passages supports, opposes or complements the other's point of view.

- The passages cover subjects in the humanities, social studies, natural sciences and literary fiction.

- The passages vary in style and tone. They include narrative, persuasive, expository and/or literary elements.

- A set of questions follows each passage or pair of related passages.

## Approaches to Reading the Passages

▶ *Mark the passages or make short notes.* Be careful that you don't mark too much. The idea of marking the passage is to help you find information quickly. Nothing will stand out if you underline or mark most of the passage.

Some students scribble a short note in the margin — a few words at most — that summarizes what a paragraph or key sentence is about. But don't spend more time marking the passage than you will save. The idea is to answer the questions, not just mark your test booklet.

▶ *Use your knowledge and experience carefully.* No matter what you know or what you believe, you cannot change what the writer has said or suggested. You must distinguish between what you think the writer *should* have said or what you would *like* the writer to believe and what the writer's words *actually* say or imply.

▶ *Read actively.* You may find that asking yourself questions about the passage will help you stay more engaged and absorb more information. Here are some questions you can ask yourself: Is the passage a factual account of an event? What is the purpose of the passage? Is the writer trying to inform you, amuse you or influence you?

▶ *If you are having a hard time with a passage, read the questions before you finish the passage.* This will give you a sense of what to look for. Looking at the questions first, though, might be a waste of time if you don't know what the passage is about. You may want to try both methods when working through practice questions.

## Types of Questions

Three types of questions may be asked about a passage: extended reasoning, vocabulary in context and literal comprehension. You will be asked questions involving single passages, paired long passages and paired paragraphs.

### Extended Reasoning Questions

Extended reasoning questions ask you to draw conclusions from or evaluate the information in the passage. The answers to these questions may not be directly stated in the passage but can be inferred from it. Extended reasoning questions also ask about the overall theme or meaning of the passage, the author's purpose or attitude, or the tone of the passage. Extended reasoning questions often include words or phrases like:

- probably

- apparently

- seems

- suggests

- it can be inferred

- the author implies

For these types of questions, you need to be an especially careful reader if you want to understand the information in a passage and figure out what the writer is saying. You should be able to *follow the logic* of the passage and to recognize points that would strengthen or weaken the writer's argument.

Extended reasoning questions require you to do some or all of the following:

- Determine the main idea of a passage or the author's primary purpose in writing the passage.

- Interpret a specific part of a passage, such as a particular word, image, phrase, example or quotation. Infer what purpose it serves rather than what it means.

- Figure out what the information presented in the passage suggests, what can be inferred about the author's views, or how the author of one passage would be likely to react to or evaluate an idea expressed in a related passage.

- Determine what the author's tone or attitude is in a specific section of the passage or in the passage as a whole.

- Understand a specific idea or relationship in a passage and identify a parallel or analogous idea.

## FACTS, ASSUMPTIONS AND INFERENCES

To answer extended reasoning questions correctly, it helps to know the difference between facts, assumptions and inferences.

*Facts:* Statements known to be true and that can be shown to be true are called *facts.* Here are some examples.

- There are 31 days in July.

- It is against the law to drive over the speed limit.

*Assumptions:* These are suppositions or propositions that writers make to reach their conclusions.

Sometimes, the assumptions that writers make may not be stated within the passage. To read critically, you must be able to recognize these unstated assumptions. These assumptions may be accurate or inaccurate — at least from your point of view. For example, think about some of the underlying assumptions in the following three statements.

1. "The principal has promised a big victory dance after the championship game next week." Two possible assumptions here are:
   - The principal hopes the team will win the championship game.
   - The principal is looking for a way to reward the whole school for the team's success.

2. "Let's have a picnic tomorrow." Two possible assumptions here are:
   - The speaker would like to spend time with the person he or she is talking to.

- Picnics are fun.

3. "Reducing the workforce will increase the profits." Two possible assumptions here are:
    - Profits are more important than people.
    - A connection exists between the number of employees and the amount of profit each employee produces.

*Inferences:* These are conclusions you reach based on what has been said in a passage.

*To infer* is to arrive at a conclusion through reasoning. In the paragraph that follows, for example, it can be *inferred* that all the examples are taken from the author's own life. Phrases such as "I've counted . . . my mailbox," "promised me prizes" and "I wrote this con artist" show that the author's opinions are based on *personal experience,* though this is not stated outright.

The problem of junk mail has grown to epidemic proportions. I've counted no fewer than 616 pieces of junk mail in my mailbox in a given month! Not only is the sheer magnitude appalling, but the antics of these "post office pirates" are equally disturbing. For example, one enterprising salesman promised me prizes ranging from a car to a transistor radio if I would drive 200 miles to look at a piece of property. I wrote this con artist and told him I'd come if he paid for the gas, but I never heard from him.

## LOGIC, STYLE AND TONE

Many extended reasoning questions will ask you about the way the author develops and presents the ideas in the passage. Some questions will ask you to consider the *tone* or *attitude* of the author. They may also ask you to think about how a reader may react.

In well-written material, the writer uses both *style* and *tone* to express what he or she has to say and to try to influence the reader. Recognizing the author's purpose — whether it is to tell an exciting story, to express enjoyment or to start a revolution — is an important part of reading.

## *Vocabulary-in-Context Questions*

Some passage-based reading questions ask about the meaning of a word as it is used in the passage. Even if you don't know the word, you can sometimes figure it out from the passage and the answer choices. The *context* — that is, the particular situation in which the word is used, including information given in neighboring sentences — helps determine its meaning.

For example, you are likely to know that the word *smart* has several meanings. It can mean "intelligent," "stylish" and "sassy." In the sentence "We knew his smart mouth would get him into a lot of trouble some day," the *context* tells us that we are not talking about intelligence or fashion sense. Chances are, neither of those will get someone into a lot of trouble. The context, or the association between the words *smart* and *trouble,* tells us that the meaning intended here is "sassy."

Usually you can work out the answer to a vocabulary-in-context question just by reading the sentence in which it is included. But sometimes you may also have to read the sentence that comes before or after it. When a word has several meanings, a vocabulary-in-context question won't necessarily use the most common meaning.

When answering vocabulary-in-context questions, keep the following in mind:

- One word can have many meanings. The answer choices will often include several different meanings of the word.

- Questions asking for the meaning of a word or phrase refer to the meaning in the context in which the word or phrase is being used in the passage.

- It helps to go back to the passage and reread the surrounding text of the word that is used. Be sure to read enough of the context to thoroughly understand the meaning of the word.

## Literal Comprehension Questions

For this type of question, you need to understand information that is directly presented in the passage. These questions measure a skill you'll be using a lot in college: reading to acquire information.

Here are some approaches to answering literal comprehension questions:

- Find the place in the passage where the detail is discussed. Reread enough of the text to find the answer. Even if you know something about the subject of the passage, remember to answer the question based on what is actually stated in the passage.

- Recognize different ways of stating the same fact or idea. Sometimes the description of the fact or idea in the *question* is different from the wording in the *passage*.

- Cross out incorrect responses as you eliminate them. Remember, you may write anywhere in your test booklet.

- Read questions carefully, looking for words such as *except, not* and *only,* and for other words that describe exactly what you are asked to do with the information.

- Be sure you can support your answer by referring to words or phrases within the passage that support it.

## Questions Involving Paired Passages and Paragraphs

At least one long and one paragraph reading selection will involve a pair of passages. The pair of passages will have a common theme or subject. One of the passages will oppose, support or in some way relate to the other.

**Table 6.1** Key Words and Phrases for Understanding the Questions

Understanding the following key words and phrases will help you understand what the questions are really asking.

| When you see this . . . | Remember that . . . |
| --- | --- |
| "according to the author" "according to the passage" | You must answer the question in terms of the statements, assumptions, or inferences that the writer is making, even if you *disagree* with what the writer has said. The question is meant to see if you understand what the writer has written. |
| "best" | This is an important word in test questions because it usually asks you to find the *most suitable* or *most acceptable* of the answer choices. This means that even though you may find a response that *seems* to fit, you still need to look at the rest of the responses in order to be sure that you have selected the *best* one. Sometimes you may think none of the answers are particularly good, but you must pick the one that is *best*. |
| "chiefly" | This means "above the rest," "mostly," "mainly but not exclusively." When you see *chiefly*, you will probably be looking for the *most central* element or *most important* explanation of something. |
| "except" | A question with *except* usually asks you to identify words or phrases that don't belong with the other choices. |
| "(the author) implies" "(it can be) inferred" "(the author) suggests" | These terms ask you to come to a conclusion that is *suggested* by the information in the passage but *not directly stated* by the author. Make sure that your inference is indeed based on the material in the passage rather than your own ideas or opinions. |
| "least" | Opposite of *most*. |
| "mainly" | Most important, or *chiefly*. |
| "most" | Frequently used as a qualifier, as in *most likely*, *most frequently*, *most reasonable*. A qualifier recognizes that there are exceptions to *most* situations and tries to allow for those exceptions. |
| "only" | *Only* means "just the one." For example, "This is the *only* . . . for me." It also can indicate a restriction, as in "You can go *only* after you wash the car." |
| "primarily" | Most important, or *chiefly*. |

When a question asks you to compare two passages, don't try to remember everything from both passages. Instead, take one choice at a time. Review the relevant parts of each passage before you select your answer.

Suppose a question asks you to identify something that is true in *both* passages. It is often easier to start by eliminating choices that are *not* true for one of the passages. Don't be fooled by a choice that is true for one passage but not for the other.

## Approaches to Passage-based Reading Questions

▶ *Keep in mind that the answers come from the passage.* Every single answer to these questions can be found in or directly inferred from the passage. Read the passages carefully.

▶ *Remember, every word counts.* Be aware of words describing people, events and things. If someone's face is described as "handsome" or "scarred," if an event is "surprising" or if a word is "whispered" or "spoken with a smile," *pay attention.* Details like these are mentioned to give you an understanding of what the author wants you to feel or think.

▶ *Read the questions and answers carefully.* Table 6.1 offers additional guidance. With most passage-based reading questions, you have to:

1. think about what the question is asking

2. look back at the passage for information that will help you with the question

3. think again about how you can use the information to answer the question correctly

▶ *Don't forget that an answer choice can be both* true *and* wrong. The correct choice is the one that *best* answers the question, not *any* choice that makes a true statement. To keep from selecting a choice that is true but wrong, *carefully* read the passage, the questions and the answer choices.

▶ *Make sure the reading passage supports your answer.* There should always be information and details in the passage that provide support for your answer. Look for specific words, phrases and sentences that help to prove your choice is correct. Even with the inference, tone and attitude questions — the ones in which you have to read between the lines — you can find evidence in the passage to support the correct choice.

▶ *Try eliminating choices.* Compare each choice to the passage and you'll find that some choices can be eliminated as definitely wrong. Then it should be easier to choose the correct answer from the remaining choices.

▶ *Double-check the other choices.* When you have made your choice, quickly read the other choices again to make sure there isn't a *better* answer.

▶ *Don't jump from passage to passage.* You will spend a lot of time reading some of the passages before you're ready to answer even one question. So take the time to answer as many questions as you can about each passage before you move on to another. Consider these suggestions:

- Move around within a set of questions to find the ones you can answer quickly.

- Stay with a passage until you are sure you have answered as many questions as you can. If you return to the passage later, you'll probably have to read it again.

- Go back to any questions you skipped. When you've gone through all the questions about a passage, review any you left out or weren't sure of. Sometimes information you picked up while thinking about one question will help you answer another.

# Sample Questions

The passages below are followed by questions based on their content; questions following a pair of related passages may also be based on the relationship between the paired passages. Answer the questions on the basis of what is <u>stated</u> or <u>implied</u> in the passages and in any introductory material that may be provided.

**Questions 1-2 are based on the following passage.**

Art forgery is a peculiar curse. Reliant on camouflage and deception, on the rhetoric of the believable lie, it is an act both audacious and self-effacing. For the imitation
*Line* to succeed in fooling us, it must resemble one or more
5 works that we have been led to believe are undoctored originals. Without something to mimic, the fake could not exist. And the forger of old masters' drawings, like the forger of twenty-dollar bills or United States' passports, must be skilled enough to fool eyes that by now
10 are practiced at uncovering deceit.

1. The primary purpose of the passage is to

    (A) describe the motivations of art forgers
    (B) indicate the artistic merit of particular forgeries
    (C) discuss the challenges facing art forgers
    (D) catalogue the skills of a successful art forger
    (E) illustrate the public's ignorance about art forgery

2. The author refers to art forgery as an act that is "self-effacing" (line 3) because it requires that the forger

    *draw attention away from yourself*

    (A) undergo an arduous apprenticeship
    (B) work in the style of another artist
    (C) forgo many opportunities for financial gain
    (D) never take his or her work too seriously
    (E) regard original artworks with reverence

**Questions 3-4 are based on the following passage.**

A cousin of the tenacious Asian longhorned beetle—
which since its initial discovery in 1996 in New York City
has caused tens of millions of dollars in damage annually
*Line* —the citrus longhorned beetle was discovered on a juniper
5 bush in August 2001 in Tukwila, Washington. Exotic pests
such as the longhorned beetle are a growing problem—an
unintended side effect of human travel and commerce
that can cause large-scale mayhem to local ecosystems.
To stop the citrus beetle, healthy trees were destroyed
10 even though there was no visible evidence of infestation,
and normal environmental regulations were suspended
so that a rapid response could be mounted.

**3.** Which best describes the function of the opening sentence ("A cousin . . . Washington")?

(A) It underscores how frequently pests are transferred from one geographical region to another.
(B) It suggests the potential harm the citrus longhorned beetle could cause in the United States.
(C) It illustrates how the Asian longhorned beetle was introduced into the United States.
(D) It describes how the citrus longhorned beetle was first discovered.
(E) It compares the destructiveness of the Asian longhorned beetle to that of the citrus beetle.

**4.** The passage suggests that the actions undertaken in lines 9-12 are best characterized as

(A) tested and reliable
(B) deliberate and effective
(C) costly and unpopular
(D) preemptive and aggressive
(E) unprecedented and unfounded

**Questions 5-8 are based on the following passages.**

**Passage 1**

Today any accessible, fast-moving story written in
unaffected prose is deemed to be "genre fiction"—at best
an excellent "read" or a "page turner" but never literature
Line  with a capital L. Everything written in self-conscious,
5  writerly prose, on the other hand, is now considered to be
"literary fiction"—not necessarily *good* literary fiction,
mind you, but always worthier of respectful attention than
even the best-written thriller or romance. It is these works
that receive full-page critiques, often one in the Sunday
10  book-review section and another in the same newspaper
during the week. It is these works, and these works only,
that make the annual short lists of award committees.

**Passage 2**

One reason why most literary novels don't appeal to
the ordinary reader looking for a "good story" is that
15  they aren't intended to. Just as nuclear physicists strive
to impress other nuclear physicists and dog breeders
value the admiration of fellow dog breeders over that of
the uninitiated masses, so people who write serious fiction
seek the high opinion of other literary novelists, of creative
20  writing teachers, and of reviewers and critics. They want
very badly to be "literary," and for many of them this
means avoiding techniques associated with commercial
and genre fiction—specifically too much emphasis on
plot. Who, after all, wants to be accused of writing "action
25  movies in book form"?

**5.** The author of Passage 1 implies that "literature with a capital L" (lines 3-4) is fiction that is

(A) considered classic by scholars of English literature
(B) written in a mannered and pretentious style
(C) unafraid to address highbrow themes and weighty issues
(D) successful both critically and financially
(E) unfairly ignored by the book-buying public

6. The author of Passage 2 suggests that authors who write "self-conscious, writerly prose" (lines 4-5, Passage 1) are

   (A) unlikely ever to produce great work
   (B) trying to improve their chances of popular success
   (C) more talented than writers of mainstream fiction
   (D) seeking the approval of like-minded writers
   (E) not capable of depicting a realistic fictional world

7. In the two passages, quotation marks are primarily used to

   (A) call attention to some common ways of categorizing fiction
   (B) suggest that some literary terms are meaningless
   (C) note labels to which writers typically object
   (D) ridicule the modes of writing most popular with the public
   (E) emphasize the importance of a shared terminology

8. Which of the following best describes the relationship between the two passages?

   (A) Passage 2 presents evidence that rebuts the argument made in Passage 1.
   (B) Passage 2 explicitly defines terms that Passage 1 assumes are well-known.
   (C) Passage 2 supplies an explanation for a state of affairs described in Passage 1.
   (D) Passage 2 focuses on an exception to a general rule established in Passage 1.
   (E) Passage 2 provides a humorous view of a situation that Passage 1 finds inexplicable.

**Questions 9-19 are based on the following passages.**

*In Passage 1, the author presents his view of the early years of the silent film industry. In Passage 2, the author draws on her experiences as a mime to generalize about her art. (A mime is a performer who, without speaking, entertains through gesture, facial expression, and movement.)*

### Passage 1

Talk to those people who first saw films when they were silent, and they will tell you the experience was magic. The silent film had extraordinary powers to draw
Line members of an audience into the story, and an equally
5 potent capacity to make their imaginations work. It required the audience to become engaged—to supply voices and sound effects. The audience was the final, creative contributor to the process of making a film.

The finest films of the silent era depended on two
10 elements that we can seldom provide today—a large and receptive audience and a well-orchestrated score. For the audience, the fusion of picture and live music added up to more than the sum of the respective parts.

The one word that sums up the attitude of the silent
15 filmmakers is *enthusiasm*, conveyed most strongly before formulas took shape and when there was more room for experimentation. This enthusiastic uncertainty often resulted in such accidental discoveries as new camera or editing techniques. Some films experimented
20 with players; the 1915 film *Regeneration*, for example, by using real gangsters and streetwalkers, provided startling local color. Other films, particularly those of Thomas Ince, provided tragic endings as often as films by other companies supplied happy ones.
25 Unfortunately, the vast majority of silent films survive today in inferior prints that no longer reflect the care that the original technicians put into them. The modern versions of silent films may appear jerky and flickery, but the vast picture palaces did not attract four to six
30 thousand people a night by giving them eyestrain. A silent film depended on its visuals; as soon as you degrade those, you lose elements that go far beyond the image on the surface. The acting in silents was often very subtle, very restrained, despite legends to the contrary.

### Passage 2

35 Mime opens up a new world to the beholder, but it does so insidiously, not by purposely injecting points of interest in the manner of a tour guide. Audiences are not unlike visitors to a foreign land who discover that the modes, manners, and thoughts of its inhabitants are not
40 meaningless oddities, but are sensible in context.

I remember once when an audience seemed perplexed at what I was doing. At first, I tried to gain a more immediate response by using slight exaggerations. I soon realized that these actions had nothing to do with the
45 audience's understanding of the character. What I had believed to be a failure of the audience to respond in the

manner I expected was, in fact, only their concentration on what I was doing; they were enjoying a gradual awakening—a slow transference of their understanding
50 from their own time and place to one that appeared so unexpectedly before their eyes. This was evidenced by their growing response to succeeding numbers.

Mime is an elusive art, as its expression is entirely dependent on the ability of the performer to imagine a
55 character and to re-create that character for each performance. As a mime, I am a physical medium, the instrument upon which the figures of my imagination play their dance of life. The individuals in my audience also have responsibilities—they must be alert
60 collaborators. They cannot sit back, mindlessly complacent, and wait to have their emotions titillated by mesmeric musical sounds or visual rhythms or acrobatic feats, or by words that tell them what to think. Mime is an art that, paradoxically, appeals both to those who respond
65 instinctively to entertainment and to those whose appreciation is more analytical and complex.

Between these extremes lie those audiences conditioned to resist any collaboration with what is played before them, and these the mime must seduce despite
70 themselves. There is only one way to attack those reluctant minds—take them unaware! They will be delighted at an unexpected pleasure.

9. Both passages are primarily concerned with the subject of

   (A) shocking special effects
   (B) varied dramatic styles
   (C) visual elements in dramatic performances
   (D) audience resistance to theatrical performances
   (E) nostalgia for earlier forms of entertainment

10. The author of Passage 1 uses the phrase "enthusiastic uncertainty" in line 17 to suggest that the filmmakers were

   (A) excited to be experimenting in a new field
   (B) delighted at the opportunity to study new technology
   (C) optimistic in spite of the obstacles that faced them
   (D) eager to challenge existing conventions
   (E) eager to please but unsure of what the public wanted

11. In lines 19-24, *Regeneration* and the films of Thomas Ince are presented as examples of

  (A) formulaic and uninspired silent films
  (B) profitable successes of a flourishing industry
  (C) suspenseful action films drawing large audiences
  (D) daring applications of an artistic philosophy
  (E) unusual products of a readiness to experiment

12. In context, the reference to "eyestrain" (line 30) conveys a sense of

  (A) irony regarding the incompetence of silent film technicians
  (B) regret that modern viewers are unable to see high quality prints of silent films
  (C) resentment that the popularity of picture palaces has waned in recent years
  (D) pleasure in remembering a grandeur that has passed
  (E) amazement at the superior quality of modern film technology

13. In line 34, "legends" most nearly means

  (A) ancient folklore
  (B) obscure symbols
  (C) history lessons
  (D) famous people
  (E) common misconceptions

14. The author of Passage 2 most likely considers the contrast of mime artist and tour guide appropriate because both

  (A) are concerned with conveying factual information
  (B) employ artistic techniques to communicate their knowledge
  (C) determine whether others enter a strange place
  (D) shape the way others perceive a new situation
  (E) explore new means of self-expression

15. The incident described in lines 41-52 shows the author of Passage 2 to be similar to the silent film-makers of Passage 1 in the way she

  (A) required very few props
  (B) used subtle technical skills to convey universal truths
  (C) learned through trial and error
  (D) combined narration with visual effects
  (E) earned a loyal audience of followers

16. In lines 41-52, the author most likely describes a specific experience in order to

  (A) dispel some misconceptions about what a mime is like
  (B) show how challenging the career of a mime can be
  (C) portray the intensity required to see the audience's point of view
  (D) explain how unpredictable mime performances can be
  (E) indicate the adjustments an audience must make in watching mime

17. In lines 60-63, the author's description of techniques used in the types of performances is

  (A) disparaging
  (B) astonished
  (C) sorrowful
  (D) indulgent
  (E) sentimental

18. What additional information would reduce the apparent similarity between these two art forms?

  (A) Silent film audiences were also accustomed to vaudeville and theatrical presentations.
  (B) Silent films could show newsworthy events as well as dramatic entertainment.
  (C) Dialogue in the form of captions was integrated into silent films.
  (D) Theaters running silent films gave many musicians steady jobs.
  (E) Individual characters created for silent films became famous in their own right.

19. Both passages mention which of the following as being important to the artistic success of the dramatic forms they describe?

  (A) Effective fusion of disparate dramatic elements
  (B) Slightly exaggerated characterization
  (C) Incorporation of realistic details
  (D) Large audiences
  (E) Audience involvement

# Answers and Explanations

**1.** The primary purpose of the passage is to

(A) describe the motivations of art forgers
(B) indicate the artistic merit of particular forgeries
(C) discuss the challenges facing art forgers
(D) catalogue the skills of a successful art forger
(E) illustrate the public's ignorance about art forgery

> **Keep in Mind**
>
> Don't be misled by an answer that looks correct but is not supported by the actual text. Choice (D) is attractive, but it's not as accurate as choice (C).

*Answer:* The correct answer is (C).

*Explanation:* The passage primarily calls attention to the difficulties inherent in art forgery. Choice (C) is correct because the passage primarily discusses several challenges inherent in art forgery. Here's why each of the other choices is incorrect:

- Choice (A) is incorrect because the passage does not discuss why people become art forgers.

- Choice (B) is incorrect because the passage does not discuss individual forgeries or their artistic merit.

- Choice (D) is incorrect. Although the passage indicates that forgers need to be skilled enough to fool people who are experienced at detecting forgeries, it does not list or discuss the particular skills that make art forgers successful.

- Choice (E) is incorrect. The passage does not discuss the public's lack of knowledge about art forgery.

**2.** The author refers to art forgery as an act that is "self-effacing" (line 3) because it requires that the forger

(A) undergo an arduous apprenticeship
(B) work in the style of another artist
(C) forgo many opportunities for financial gain
(D) never take his or her work too seriously
(E) regard original artworks with reverence

*Answer:* The correct answer is (B).

*Explanation:* The reference to "self-effacing" in line 3 suggests that a successful art forgery cannot call attention to the forger. It must appear to be a creation of the original artist. Choice (B) is correct because forgery involves employing the style of another artist rather than working in one's own style. It requires removing oneself from one's work.

Here's why each of the other choices is incorrect:

- Choice (A) is incorrect because the author does not discuss apprenticeships undertaken by art forgers. Moreover, if forgers did undertake arduous apprenticeships, the experience would not necessarily be self-effacing.

- Choices (C) and (D) are incorrect because the author does not discuss the financial rewards of forging art, nor does the author suggest that the art forgers should not take their work too seriously.

- Choice (E) is incorrect because the author does not indicate that art forgers must view original art with reverence. In fact, the author states that art forgery is an "audacious" act. A forger might not perform this audacious act if he or she viewed the original work with reverence.

> **Keep in Mind**
>
> A key word in the question may be the clue you need to arrive at the best answer. Pay attention to the words that carry the meaning of the sentence.

3. Which best describes the function of the opening sentence ("A cousin . . . Washington")?

   (A) It underscores how frequently pests are transferred from one geographical region to another.
   (B) It suggests the potential harm the citrus longhorned beetle could cause in the United States.
   (C) It illustrates how the Asian longhorned beetle was introduced into the United States.
   (D) It describes how the citrus longhorned beetle was first discovered.
   (E) It compares the destructiveness of the Asian longhorned beetle to that of the citrus beetle.

*Answer:* The correct answer is (B).

*Explanation:* The opening sentence of the passage indicates that the citrus longhorned beetle is a relative of the Asian longhorned beetle, which has wreaked havoc on the plant life in the United States. Choice (B) is correct because the opening sentence establishes that the Asian and citrus longhorned beetles are cousins and points out the devastation that the Asian beetle has caused; the implication is that the citrus beetle might be as damaging to plant life as its "tenacious" relative.

Here's why each of the other choices is not the correct answer:

- Choice (A) is incorrect because the opening sentence does not discuss how frequently pests are transferred from different geographical regions.

- Choices (C) and (D) are incorrect because the opening sentence, while mentioning both the Asian and citrus longhorned beetles, does not indicate how the Asian beetle was introduced to New York City, nor does it describe how the citrus beetle was initially discovered.

> **Keep in Mind**
>
> In some questions the syntax, or structure, of the sentence will guide you to the right answer. In this case, the structure of the sentence emphasizes the comparison between the two beetles, suggesting that the second is much like the first.

- Choice (E) is incorrect because the opening sentence makes no direct comparison between the damage caused by the Asian longhorned beetle and that caused by the citrus longhorned beetle; in fact, the passage does not provide information about the destructiveness of the citrus longhorned beetle.

4. The passage suggests that the actions undertaken in lines 9-12 are best characterized as

   (A) tested and reliable
   (B) deliberate and effective
   (C) costly and unpopular
   (D) preemptive and aggressive
   (E) unprecedented and unfounded

### Keep in Mind

Careful reading is the key to finding the correct answer. It may be tempting to apply a personal opinion, as in choice (C), but your answer must be found in the passage itself.

*Answer:* The correct answer is (D).

*Explanation:* Lines 9-12 indicate that to contain the possible spread of the citrus longhorned beetle quickly, such actions as killing healthy trees and relaxing environmental regulations and procedures were executed. Choice (D) is correct because the actions described in lines 9-12 were both preventative and bold: energetic measures undertaken to avert a potential environmental disaster.

Here's why each of the other choices is not the correct answer:

- Choice (A) is incorrect because the actions in lines 9-12 are not described as having been employed before, nor is there evidence that the actions have been repeated successfully.

- Choice (B) is incorrect because nothing in lines 9-12 suggests that the actions were careful and unhurried, nor is there any discussion of the effectiveness of these actions.

- Choice (C) is incorrect because although the actions described in lines 9-12 might be expensive and unpopular, nothing in the passage directly supports this interpretation.

- Choice (E) is incorrect because the passage provides no evidence that the actions in lines 9-12 had not been undertaken before; furthermore, the actions were not unwarranted, given the awareness of the damage that the Asian longhorned beetle had already caused.

> 5. The author of Passage 1 implies that "literature with a capital L." (lines 3-4) is fiction that is
>
> (A) considered classic by scholars of English literature
> (B) written in a mannered and pretentious style
> (C) unafraid to address highbrow themes and weighty issues
> (D) successful both critically and financially
> (E) unfairly ignored by the book-buying public

*Answer:* The correct answer is (B).

*Explanation:* The author of Passage 1 uses the phrase "literature with a capital L" to describe fiction written in a particular kind of prose. Choice (B) is correct because the passage suggests that "literature with a capital L" is written in "self-conscious, writerly prose." Prose written this way can also be described as "mannered and pretentious."

Here's why each of the other choices is not the correct answer:

- Choice (A) is incorrect because the passage does not discuss either the opinion of scholars or the issue of what is considered "classic."

- Choice (C) is incorrect because the passage doesn't focus on the types of themes and issues addressed by literary fiction.

- Choice (D) is incorrect because the passage doesn't discuss how literary fiction fares in the marketplace.

- Choice (E) is incorrect. Although the passage focuses on the amount of critical attention paid to literary fiction, it doesn't suggest that such fiction is undeservedly ignored by the book-buying public.

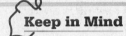

**Keep in Mind**

Rereading the relevant part of the passage should lead you to the correct answer. This question asks for an understanding of a remark in the context of its neighboring sentences.

> 6. The author of Passage 2 suggests that authors who write "self-conscious, writerly prose" (lines 4-5, Passage 1) are
>
> (A) unlikely ever to produce great work
> (B) trying to improve their chances of popular success
> (C) more talented than writers of mainstream fiction
> (D) seeking the approval of like-minded writers
> (E) not capable of depicting a realistic fictional world

*Answer:* The correct answer is (D).

*Explanation:* Passage 1 uses the phrase "self-conscious, writerly prose" to describe the style of "literary fiction." The question asks what the author of Passage 2 suggests about writers who employ this style. Choice (D) is correct because Passage 2 argues that writers of literary fiction hope to appeal to other people well versed in literary fiction: "literary novelists," "creative writing teachers," book "reviewers" and "critics." So these writers using "self-conscious, writerly prose" are "seeking the approval of like-minded writers."

**Keep in Mind**

The correct answer is found by rereading the highlighted phrase in the context of the surrounding sentences.

Here's why each of the other choices is not the correct answer:

- Choice (A) is incorrect because Passage 2 focuses on why literary novelists write as they do, not on whether they are likely to produce great novels.

- Choice (B) is incorrect because Passage 2 argues that literary novelists are interested in impressing a very specific audience; they are not seeking greater popular success.

- Choice (C) is incorrect because Passage 2 does not suggest that authors of literary fiction are either more or less talented than writers of mainstream fiction.

- Choice (E) is incorrect because Passage 2 doesn't consider the issue of realism in writing.

---

7. In the two passages, quotation marks are primarily used to

   (A) call attention to some common ways of categorizing fiction
   (B) suggest that some literary terms are meaningless
   (C) note labels to which writers typically object
   (D) ridicule the modes of writing most popular with the public
   (E) emphasize the importance of a shared terminology

---

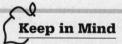

**Keep in Mind**

Consider *all* the information before making a judgment. This question asks you to make an inference from the writer's stylistic choices. By comparing the choices to the content and meaning of each passage in its entirety, you will be able to see the purpose of the quotation marks.

*Answer:* The correct answer is (A).

*Explanation:* Choice (A) is correct because the authors of both passages put quotation marks around certain words and phrases to call attention to the terms frequently used to characterize different kinds of fiction.

Here's why each of the other choices is not the correct answer:

- Choice (B) is incorrect because neither passage suggests that these literary terms are without meaning. In fact, both imply that these terms are commonly used when talking about fiction, and that they refer to specific, identifiable types of writing.

- Choice (C) is incorrect. While these words and phrases can be considered labels, neither passage suggests that writers typically object to them.

- Choice (D) is incorrect. Although Passage 1 offers a negative view of mannered "literary fiction," it does not criticize popular fiction. Passage 2 makes no judgment at all about the inherent quality of either literary or popular fiction.

- Choice (E) is incorrect. Although the quoted words and phrases are a shared terminology, neither passage emphasizes the value of sharing these terms. In fact, Passage 1 implies that the use of such terms is unfortunate because only fiction considered to be "literary" is given serious attention.

8. Which of the following best describes the relationship between the two passages?

   (A) Passage 2 presents evidence that rebuts the argument made in Passage 1.

   (B) Passage 2 explicitly defines terms that Passage 1 assumes are well known.

   (C) Passage 2 supplies an explanation for a state of affairs described in Passage 1.

   (D) Passage 2 focuses on an exception to a general rule established in Passage 1.

   (E) Passage 2 provides a humorous view of a situation that Passage 1 finds inexplicable.

*Answer:* The correct answer is (C).

*Explanation:* Passage 1 argues that literary fiction is reviewed more thoroughly than genre fiction and is the only kind of fiction recognized by award committees. Passage 2 argues that writers of literary fiction write to impress other literary novelists, reviewers and critics. This would explain why such fiction receives more serious attention from reviewers and award committees, as described in Passage 1. Therefore, choice (C) is correct.

   Here's why each of the other choices is not the correct answer:

- Choice (A) is incorrect because Passage 2 does not rebut the argument made in Passage 1. In fact, it assumes that the situation described in Passage 1 is accurate.

- Choice (B) is incorrect because, although Passage 2 uses some of the same terms as Passage 1, it does not define them any more explicitly.

- Choice (D) is incorrect because Passage 2 does not focus on an exception to the situation described in Passage 1. In fact, it does not discuss a specific case at all.

- Choice (E) is incorrect because Passage 1 does not indicate that the situation it describes is inexplicable. In addition, Passage 2 does not provide a particularly funny view of this subject.

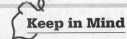

**Keep in Mind**

This is the type of question you might find easiest to answer if you eliminate answers that are wrong. Each of the incorrect answers is directly contradicted by material in the passages. You are left with the correct answer by process of elimination.

9. Both passages are primarily concerned with the subject of

   (A) shocking special effects

   (B) varied dramatic styles

   (C) visual elements in dramatic performances

   (D) audience resistance to theatrical performances

   (E) nostalgia for earlier forms of entertainment

*Answer:* The correct answer is (C).

*Explanation:* This question asks you to think about *both* passages. Notice that the question asks you to look for the main subject or focus of the pair of passages, not simply to recognize that one passage is about silent film and the other about mime.

The discussion in Passage 1 is most concerned with the effectiveness of silent films for audiences of that era. The discussion in Passage 2 is most concerned with what makes a mime performance effective for the audience. The main subject for *both* passages is how a silent, visual form of entertainment affects an audience. Choice (C) is correct because it refers to performance in a visual art form.

Here's why each of the other choices is incorrect:

**Keep in Mind**

When comparing two reading passages, review the relevant parts of each passage as you consider the choices.

- Choice (A) is incorrect because "shocking special effects" is not a main subject of either passage.

- Choice (B) is incorrect because, although "varied dramatic styles" (used by film performers and in mime) is briefly touched on in both passages, it is not the main subject of the pair of passages.

- Choice (D) is incorrect because "audience resistance to theatrical performances" is too specific: both authors are making points about the overall role of audiences in the performance. Choice (D) is also incorrect because that topic is primarily addressed only in Passage 2.

- Choice (E) is incorrect because a tone of nostalgia appears only in Passage 1.

---

**10.** The author of Passage 1 uses the phrase "enthusiastic uncertainty" in line 17 to suggest that the filmmakers were

(A) excited to be experimenting in a new field
(B) delighted at the opportunity to study new technology
(C) optimistic in spite of the obstacles that faced them
(D) eager to challenge existing conventions
(E) eager to please but unsure of what the public wanted

---

**Keep in Mind**

Read each choice carefully and compare what it says to the information in the passage.

*Answer:* The correct answer is (A).

*Explanation:* Look at the beginning of the third paragraph of Passage 1. The filmmakers were "enthusiastic" about a new kind of art form in which they could experiment. And experimentation led to "accidental discoveries" (line 18), which suggests "uncertainty," all of which is said, though in a slightly different way, in choice (A).

Here's why each of the other choices is incorrect:

- Choice (B) is incorrect because the filmmakers were delighted to use the new technology rather than to study it.

- Choice (C) can be eliminated because the passage does not talk about "obstacles" faced by the filmmakers.

- Choice (D) is specifically contradicted by line 16, which refers to these film-makers as working "before formulas took shape." The word *formulas* in this context means the same thing as "conventions."

- Choice (E) is incorrect because the "uncertainty" of the filmmakers was related to the new technology and how to use it, not to "what the public wanted."

---

**11.** In lines 19-24, *Regeneration* and the films of Thomas Ince are presented as examples of

(A) formulaic and uninspired silent films
(B) profitable successes of a flourishing industry
(C) suspenseful action films drawing large audiences
(D) daring applications of an artistic philosophy
(E) unusual products of a readiness to experiment

---

*Answer:* The correct answer is (E).

*Explanation:* The author's argument in the third paragraph is that there was lots of "room for experimentation" (line 17) in the silent film industry. Both *Regeneration* and Ince's films are specifically mentioned as examples of that "readiness to experiment," as referred to in choice (E).

Here's why each of the other choices is incorrect:

**Keep in Mind**

As you consider the choices, think of the words, phrases and sentences in the passage that relate to the question you are answering. Be aware of how the ideas in the passage are presented. What is the author's point? How does the author explain and support important points?

- Choice (A) is directly contradicted in two ways by the information in the passage. First, line 16 says that the filmmakers worked "before formulas took shape," so their work could not be "formulaic." Second, the author refers to *Regeneration* as having some "startling" effects and indicates that the endings of Ince's films were different from the endings of other films of the time. So it would not be correct to describe these films as "uninspired."

- Choices (B), (C) and (D) are incorrect because the author does not argue that these films were "profitable," "suspenseful" or "applications of an artistic philosophy." He argues that they are examples of a willingness to "experiment."

---

**12.** In context, the reference to "eyestrain" (line 30) conveys a sense of

(A) irony regarding the incompetence of silent film technicians
(B) regret that modern viewers are unable to see high-quality prints of silent films
(C) resentment that the popularity of picture palaces has waned in recent years
(D) pleasure in remembering a grandeur that has passed
(E) amazement at the superior quality of modern film technology

---

*Answer:* The correct answer is (B).

*Explanation:* The author draws a distinction between the way silent films look when viewed today — "jerky and flickery" (line 28) — and the way they looked when they were originally shown. He implies that thousands of people would not have come to the movie houses if the pictures had given them "eyestrain." The author indicates that the perception of silent films today is unfortunate. This feeling can be described as "regret," choice (B).

Here's why each of the other choices is incorrect:

- Choice (A) is incorrect because there is no indication in the passage that silent film technicians were "incompetent." The author even mentions "the care" taken by "the original technicians" (lines 26-27).

- Both choices (C) and (D) are incorrect because they do not answer this question. Remember, the question refers to the statement about "eyestrain." The remark about eyestrain concerns the technical quality of the films, not the "popularity of picture palaces" or a "grandeur that has passed."

- Choice (E) is incorrect for two reasons. First, no sense of "amazement" is conveyed in the statement about eyestrain. Second, the author does not say that modern films are "superior" to silent films, only that the "prints" of silent films are "inferior" to what they once were (lines 25-26).

---

**13.** In line 34, "legends" most nearly means

(A) ancient folklore
(B) obscure symbols
(C) history lessons
(D) famous people
(E) common misconceptions

---

*Answer:* The correct answer is (E).

*Explanation:* A *legend* is an idea or story that has come down from the past. A secondary meaning of *legend* is anything made up rather than based on fact. Throughout the final paragraph of Passage 1, the author emphasizes that people today have the wrong idea about the visual quality of silent films. In the last sentence, the author states that the acting was "often very subtle" and "very restrained," and then he adds, "despite legends to the contrary." According to the author, silent film acting is today thought of as unsubtle and unrestrained, but that is a misconception, an idea not based on fact, a "legend." Choice (E) is the best of the answer choices.

Here's why each of the other choices is incorrect:

- Choice (A) is incorrect because, although it is the most common meaning of *legend*, it doesn't make any sense here. There is no reference to or suggestion about "ancient folklore."

- Choice (B) is incorrect because it has no support at all in the passage.

- Choice (C) is incorrect because the author does not refer to "history lessons" in this sentence, but to mistaken notions about the performances in silent films.

- Choice (D) is incorrect because it simply doesn't make sense. In line 34, the word *legends* refers to acting, not to people.

---

**14.** The author of Passage 2 most likely considers the contrast of mime artist and tour guide appropriate because both

(A) are concerned with conveying factual information
(B) employ artistic techniques to communicate their knowledge
(C) determine whether others enter a strange place
(D) shape the way others perceive a new situation
(E) explore new means of self-expression

---

*Answer:* The correct answer is (D).

*Explanation:* To answer this question, you have to find a choice that describes a similarity between the performances of a mime and the work of a tour guide. The author begins Passage 2 by saying that a mime "opens up a new world to the beholder," but in a "manner" (or way) different from that of a tour guide. Thus the author assumes that contrasting the mime and the tour guide is appropriate because both of them "shape the way others perceive a new situation," choice (D).

Here's why each of the other choices is incorrect:

> **Keep in Mind**
>
> Pay close attention when authors make connections, comparisons or contrasts. These parts of passages help you identify the authors' points of view and assumptions.

- Choice (A) is incorrect because although it may correctly describe a tour guide, it doesn't fit the mime. Nowhere in the passage does the author say the mime conveys "factual information."

- Choice (B) is incorrect because although it is true for the mime, it is not true for the tour guide.

- Choice (C) is incorrect because the author of Passage 2 contrasts how mimes and tour guides introduce others to "a new world," not how they *determine* entrance to "a strange place."

- Choice (E) is incorrect because the author does not discuss "self-expression" as a tour guide's work, and because she indicates that, as a mime, she expresses a particular character, not her own personality.

**15.** The incident described in lines 41-52 shows the author of Passage 2 to be similar to the silent filmmakers of Passage 1 in the way she

(A) required very few props
(B) used subtle technical skills to convey universal truths
(C) learned through trial and error
(D) combined narration with visual effects
(E) earned a loyal audience of followers

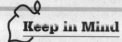

**Keep in Mind**

When a question following a pair of passages asks you to identify something that is common to *both* passages or true for *both* passages, eliminate any answer that is true for *only one* of the two passages.

*Answer:* The correct answer is (C).

*Explanation:* The question focuses on the story related in lines 41-52 and asks you to explain how that story shows that the mime is similar to silent filmmakers. So the correct answer has to express a point made about the mime in lines 41-52 that is also true for the filmmakers described in Passage 1. Lines 41-52 show the mime changing her performance when she found something that did not work. Passage 1 says that filmmakers learned through "experimentation" and "accidental discoveries." So all of these people *learned through trial and error,* choice (C).

Here's why each of the other choices is incorrect:

- Choices (A), (B), (D) and (E) are incorrect answers because they don't include traits both *described in lines 41-52 and shared with the filmmakers.*

- Choice (A) is incorrect because "props" aren't mentioned in either passage.

- Choice (B) is incorrect because "conveying universal truths" is not discussed in Passage 1.

- Choice (D) is incorrect because a mime performs without speaking or *narration.*

- Choice (E) is incorrect because Passage 1 describes loyal audiences but lines 41-52 do not.

**16.** In lines 41-52, the author most likely describes a specific experience in order to

(A) dispel some misconceptions about what a mime is like
(B) show how challenging the career of a mime can be
(C) portray the intensity required to see the audience's point of view
(D) explain how unpredictable mime performances can be
(E) indicate the adjustments an audience must make in watching mime

*Answer:* The correct answer is (E).

*Explanation:* The correct answer must explain why the author of Passage 2 described a particular experience in lines 41-52. The author's point is that she learned the audience was "enjoying a gradual awakening." Only choice (E) indicates that the story shows the "adjustments" the audience had to make to appreciate her performance.

Here's why each of the other choices is incorrect:

▪ Choice (A) is incorrect because the only "misconception" that is dispelled is the author's "misconception" about the audience.

▪ Choice (B) is incorrect because, while the story might suggest that mime is a "challenging career," that is not the author's point in describing the experience.

▪ Choice (C) is incorrect because there is no reference to "intensity" on the part of the mime.

▪ Choice (D) is incorrect because the emphasis of lines 41-52 is not on how "unpredictable" mime performance is but on what the author learned from her failure to understand the audience's initial reaction.

> **Keep in Mind**
>
> Every word counts. When you're asked about the author's intent in describing something, you have to pay close attention to how the author uses details to explain, support or challenge the point being made.

17. In lines 60-63, the author's description of techniques used in the types of performances is

    (A) disparaging
    (B) astonished
    (C) sorrowful
    (D) indulgent
    (E) sentimental

*Answer:* The correct answer is (A).

*Explanation:* The sentence beginning in line 60 says that when viewing mime, the audience "cannot sit back, mindlessly complacent." The author then says that other types of performances "titillate" audience emotions by "mesmeric musical sounds" or "acrobatic feats." The author uses these kinds of words to belittle other techniques — her tone is *disparaging*, which is the answer in choice (A).

Here's why each of the other choices is incorrect:

> **Keep in Mind**
>
> To figure out the author's attitude or tone or how the author feels about something, think about how the author uses language in the passage.

▪ Choices (B), (C) and (E) are incorrect because no "astonishment," "sorrow" or "sentimentalism" is suggested in lines 60-63.

▪ Choice (D) is incorrect because it is almost the opposite of what the author means. She is not at all "indulgent" toward these other types of performance.

18. What additional information would reduce the apparent similarity between these two art forms?

    (A) Silent film audiences were also accustomed to vaudeville and theatrical presentations.
    (B) Silent films could show newsworthy events as well as dramatic entertainment.
    (C) Dialogue in the form of captions was integrated into silent films.
    (D) Theaters running silent films gave many musicians steady jobs.
    (E) Individual characters created for silent films became famous in their own right.

**Keep in Mind**

This question asks you to think about the two reading passages *together*. Remember that you should also consider the information in the *introduction* when you compare passages.

*Answer:* The correct answer is (C).

*Explanation:* This question asks you to do two things: first, figure out a similarity between silent films and mime; second, choose an answer with information that isn't found in either passage but would make mime performance and silent films seem *less* similar.

If you think about the art forms discussed in the two passages, you should realize that neither uses *speech*. This is an important similarity. Silent films include music but not spoken words. As stated in the introduction to the two passages, a mime entertains "without speaking." Choice (C) adds the information that "dialogue" between characters was part of silent films. Characters "spoke" to each other even though audiences read captions instead of hearing spoken words. So silent film indirectly used speech and thus was different from mime, which relies on *gesture, facial expression* and *movement*.

Here's why the other choices are incorrect:

- Choices (A), (B), (D) and (E) are incorrect because they don't deal with the fundamental *similarity* between the two art forms — the absence of words. These may all be interesting things to know about silent film, but "vaudeville" performances (choice A), "newsworthy events" (choice B), "steady jobs" for musicians (choice D) and fame of "individual characters" (choice E) have nothing to do with mime. None of these things is related to an apparent similarity between mime and silent films.

19. Both passages mention which of the following as being important to the artistic success of the dramatic forms they describe?

    (A) Effective fusion of disparate dramatic elements
    (B) Slightly exaggerated characterization
    (C) Incorporation of realistic details
    (D) Large audiences
    (E) Audience involvement

*Answer:* The correct answer is (E).

*Explanation:* Passage 1 very clearly states in lines 5-8 that audience involvement was important to the success of silent films. In lines 58-60 of Passage 2, the author makes a similarly strong statement about how important it is for the *audience* to be *involved* in mime performance; thus choice (E) is correct.

Here's why each of the other choices is incorrect:

- Choices (A)-(D) are incorrect because they don't refer to ideas mentioned in *both* passages as "important to the artistic success of the dramatic forms."

- Choice (A) is incorrect because Passage 1 talks about the "fusion" of pictures and music, but Passage 2 is not concerned at all with "disparate dramatic elements."

- Choice (B) is incorrect because although it refers to something mentioned in Passage 2 (line 43), it is *not* something important to the success of a mime performance. And Passage 1 says that the "acting in silents was often very subtle, very restrained" (lines 33-34), which is the opposite of "exaggerated."

- Choice (C) is incorrect because it is mentioned only in Passage 1 (lines 20-22), and not as an element "important to the artistic success" of silent films in general.

- Choice (D) is incorrect because the author of Passage 1 says that silent films did enjoy "large audiences," but he doesn't say that "large audiences" were critical to the "artistic success" of the films. Passage 2 doesn't mention the size of the audiences at all.

## Recap

1. Be familiar with the directions before test day.

2. Keep in mind that, in this section of the test (unlike other sections of the SAT), questions do not increase in difficulty from easy to hard.

3. Don't forget that all passages have numbered lines, so when a question refers to a particular line or lines in the passage, go back and read the matching line(s) before answering the question.

4. Think of all possible meanings of a word. One word can have many meanings; the answer choices of vocabulary-in-context questions will often include several different meanings of the word.

5. Remember that the information you need to answer each question is *always* in the passage(s) — specific words, phrases and/or sentences that help to prove your choice is correct. All questions ask you to base your answer on what you read in the passages, introductions and (sometimes) footnotes. Keep in mind that there should *always* be information in the passage(s) that supports your choice.

6. Bear in mind that *every* word counts. Details that explain, support or challenge a point in a passage can help you understand how the author wants you to feel or think.

7. Try marking up the passages or making short notes in the sample test and practice questions in this book.

8. If you are having a hard time with a passage, read the questions before you finish the passage.

9. When comparing two reading passages, review the relevant parts of each passage as you consider the choices.

10. Read the *questions and answers* carefully — this is as important as reading the *passage* carefully. Read *actively* to absorb as much information as possible.

11. Remember that an answer can be *true* and still be the *wrong* answer to a particular question.

12. Don't be misled by an answer that looks correct but is not supported by the actual text.

13. Look for a key word in the question stem, which may be the clue you need to arrive at the best answer.

14. Pay attention to the syntax, or structure, of the sentence in some questions, which will guide you to the right answer.

15. Don't apply your personal opinion: instead, read carefully, because you must find your answer in the text passage itself.

16. To figure out the author's attitude or tone or how the author feels about something, think about how the author uses language in the passage.

17. Reread the relevant part of the passage to find the correct answer. Examine the context in which words are used. Also, don't try to remember *everything* from the passage(s): instead, refer back to the passage(s) as you work your way through the possible answers.

18. Pay close attention when authors make connections, comparisons or contrasts. These parts of the passages can help you identify the authors' points of view and assumptions.

19. Do not be too quick to make a judgment without considering all the information.

20. If you're not sure of the correct answer, try eliminating choices and make an educated guess. If a question following a pair of reading passages asks you to identify something that is common to *both* passages or true for *both* passages, eliminate any answer that is true for *only one* of the two passages.

21. When you have made your choice, double-check the other choices to make sure there isn't a better one.

22. Don't get bogged down on difficult questions. You might want to skim a set of questions and start by answering those you feel sure of. Then concentrate on the harder questions. *But don't skip between sets of reading questions, because when you return to a passage you'll probably have to read it again.*

23. When you have gone through all the questions associated with a passage, go back and review any you left out or weren't sure about.

# Practice Questions

The passages below are followed by questions based on their content; questions following a pair of related passages may also be based on the relationship between the paired passages. Answer the questions on the basis of what is <u>stated</u> or <u>implied</u> in the passages and in any introductory material that may be provided.

---

Questions 1-2 are based on the following passage.

The Internet is rapidly becoming another means of disseminating information traditionally made available through radio and television stations. Indeed, it is now
Line possible for journalists and the public to access new
5 releases of audio- and videotapes, satellite media tours, and on-line news conferences via their computers. The number of news sites on the Internet grows each day. As one media company executive notes, "With many of these Web sites generating new content every hour
10 and exponentially larger audiences, on-line news sites represent a dynamic and vital outlet for news."

1. In the passage, the author emphasizes which aspect of the Internet?

   (A) Its speed
   (B) Its cost
   (C) Its growth
   (D) Its design
   (E) Its accuracy

2. Which of the following best captures the attitude of the "company executive" (line 8) toward the Internet?

   (A) Anxiety
   (B) Distrust
   (C) Ambivalence
   (D) Excitement
   (E) Curiosity

**Questions 3-6 are based on the following passages.**

**Passage 1**
A recent study comparing the DNA of Native Americans and central Siberians has established that the two populations share common ancestors. Many anthropol-
Line ogists see this as proof of the Bering Strait migration
5 theory, which holds that between 11,000 and 6,000 years ago, ancestors of Native Americans migrated southward from Asia to North America across a land bridge that had joined the two continents. Apache scholar Ramon Riley sees it differently. Noting that tribal legends locate Apache
10 origins squarely in the American Southwest, he offers an alternative explanation of the newfound genetic link. "The migration was just the other way around," he says. "They spread north from here." In support of this view, Riley argues that the Athabaskan languages spoken by the northern
15 tribes—in the Pacific Northwest, Canada, and Alaska—are "much more diluted" than that spoken by the Apache.

**Passage 2**

Stanford University linguist Merritt Ruhlen has discovered striking similarities between Ket, a nearly extinct
language spoken in central Siberia, and various languages
20  of the Athabaskan group, traditionally spoken by Native
Americans living along the western edge of North America,
including the Apache in the southwestern United States.
Citing 36 separate instances of correspondences between Ket
and Athabaskan words, Ruhlen concludes that both linguistic
25  traditions ultimately derive from a single language, one
presumably spoken by a prehistoric population from which
both the Siberians and Native Americans are descended.

3. The two passages are similar in that each one

   (A) traces the origins of Ket to a Native American language
   (B) uses genetic evidence to support its position
   (C) discusses research linking Native Americans to a population in Siberia
   (D) attempts to reconcile traditional myth and historical fact
   (E) hypothesizes that a land mass once connected Asia and North America

4. The anthropologists mentioned in Passage 1, lines 3-4, would most likely claim
   that Merritt Ruhlen's conclusion (Passage 2, lines 24-27) is

   (A) inconsistent with the DNA evidence
   (B) further confirmation of the Bering Strait migration theory
   (C) a validation of some Native American legends
   (D) based on a misunderstanding of Siberian culture
   (E) evidence that Ket is no longer spoken in central Siberia

5. Ramon Riley (Passage 1, line 8) would most likely argue that the "prehistoric
   population" (Passage 2, line 26) was originally located in

   (A) central Siberia
   (B) the southwestern United States
   (C) the Pacific Northwest
   (D) Canada
   (E) Alaska

6. Passage 1 differs from Passage 2 in that only Passage 1

   (A) provides evidence of linguistic similarities between two languages
   (B) contends that different groups descended from the same population
   (C) questions the feasibility of a population migration between continents
   (D) discusses the multiple languages spoken in central Siberia
   (E) offers conflicting interpretations of a recent scientific discovery

**Questions 7-12 are based on the following passage.**

*The following passage is an excerpt from a book written by two female historians about professional women who began their careers in science in the late nineteenth and early twentieth centuries.*

The strong efforts to gain equality for women in the scientific workplace began to show results in the last quarter of the twentieth century; women have secured
Line positions as research scientists and won recognition and
5 promotion within their fields. Though the modern struggle for equality in scientific fields is the same in many ways as it was in the early part of the century, it is also different. The women who first began undertaking careers in science had little support from any part of the society in which they
10 lived. This vanguard had to struggle alone against the social conditioning they had received as women members of that society and against the male-dominated scientific community.
    Women scientific researchers made a seemingly
15 auspicious beginning. In the first quarter of the twentieth century, some women scientists who engaged in research worked at the most prestigious institutes of the period and enjoyed more career mobility than women researchers would experience again for several decades. Florence
20 Sabin, an anatomist at the Rockefeller Institute of Medical Research noted for her research on the lymphatic system, is one important example. This encouraging beginning, however, was not to be followed by other successes for many decades. To have maintained an active role in
25 research institutions, women would have had to share some of the decision-making power: they needed to be part of hiring, promotion, and funding decisions. Unfortunately, these early women scientists were excluded from the power structure of scientific research. As a result, they found it
30 almost impossible to provide opportunities for a younger set of female colleagues seeking employment in a research setting, to foster their productivity and facilitate their career mobility, and eventually to allow them access to the top ranks.
35     Even those with very high professional aspirations accepted subordinate status as assistants if doing so seemed necessary to gain access to research positions—and too often these were the only positions offered them in their chosen careers. Time and again they pulled back from
40 offering any real resistance or challenge to the organizational structure that barred their advancement. But we must remember that these women scientists were few in number, their participation in decision-making positions was virtually nil, and their political clout was minimal.
45 Thus they could easily become highly visible targets for elimination from the staff, especially if their behavior was judged in the least imprudent.
    Women's awareness that they were unequal colleagues, included in professional settings only on the
50 sufferance of male colleagues, who held the positions of power, conflicted with their belief in meritocracy. They wanted to believe that achieving persons would be welcomed for their abilities and contributions. Yet they were surrounded by evidence to the contrary. An assistant
55 professor of zoology observed that the men who were

heads of departments were insistent on having other men in the department; they told her that women ought to be satisfied teaching high school. She relates that, during her ten years in the department, men were given at least six
00 positions that she was qualified for and wanted desperately, but for which she was not even considered because she was a woman.

7. The primary purpose of the passage is to

   (A) explain a situation
   (B) refute an argument
   (C) propose a change
   (D) predict an outcome
   (E) honor an achievement

8. The passage as a whole suggests that "career mobility" (lines 18 and 32-33) means the

   (A) freedom to work on projects that one is most interested in
   (B) freedom to publish research findings no matter how controversial they are
   (C) ability to obtain funding to travel to important professional meetings
   (D) ability to find a job in any part of the country
   (E) ability to advance in one's chosen field

9. The statement that women could be eliminated from their jobs if their behavior was "the least imprudent" (line 47) suggests primarily that they

   (A) were more likely than their male colleagues to be rebellious
   (B) participated in the creation of the standards by which the performance of researchers was judged
   (C) could gain advancement if they avoided political confrontations about their rights as women
   (D) were judged by a standard different from the one used to judge their male colleagues
   (E) were as critical of their colleagues as their colleagues were of them

10. The last paragraph of the passage suggests that for the majority of women scientists, the "belief in meritocracy" (line 51) was

   (A) justified, considering the opportunities available to them
   (B) fortunate, because it provided them with attainable goals
   (C) inconsistent with the fact that they were discriminated against on the job
   (D) understandable, in that the concept had worked for the previous generation of women scientists
   (E) trend-setting, in that their views soon received universal acceptance

11. The example of the assistant professor of zoology (lines 54-62) serves primarily to indicate the

    (A) extent of male bias against women in scientific fields at a particular time
    (B) results of a woman's challenging male dominance in the early part of this century
    (C) reasons for women's right to equal treatment
    (D) inability of men and women to work together in an academic setting
    (E) early attempts of women to achieve a share of scientific awards

12. All of the following questions can be explicitly answered on the basis of the passage EXCEPT:

    (A) What conditions did women scientists find it necessary to struggle against in the first quarter of the twentieth century?
    (B) What specific steps were taken in the early part of the twentieth century to help women gain equality in the scientific workplace?
    (C) What changes in the organization of the scientific community would have enhanced the position of women scientists as the twentieth century advanced?
    (D) What were the views of some women scientific researchers on the subject of meritocracy?
    (E) What degree of success was attained by the generation of women scientists who followed those who came into prominence earlier in the twentieth century?

**Questions 13-25 are based on the following passage.**

*The following excerpt is the beginning of a memoir, published in 1989, by a woman who emigrated with her family from Poland to Canada when she was a teenager.*

It is April 1959, I'm standing at the railing of the Batory's upper deck, and I feel that my life is ending. I'm looking out at the crowd that has gath-
Line ered on the shore to see the ship's departure from
5  Gdynia—a crowd that, all of a sudden, is irrevoca-
bly on the other side—and I want to break out, run back, run toward the familiar excitement, the waving hands, the exclamations. We can't be leav-ing all this behind—but we are. I am thirteen
10 years old, and we are emigrating. It's a notion of such crushing, definitive finality that to me it might as well mean the end of the world.
    My sister, four years younger than I, is clutch-ing my hand wordlessly; she hardly understands
15 where we are, or what is happening to us. My parents are highly agitated; they had just been put through a body search by the customs police. Still, the officials weren't clever enough, or suspicious enough, to check my sister and me—lucky for us,
20 since we are both carrying some silverware we were not allowed to take out of Poland in large

pockets sewn onto our skirts especially for this purpose, and hidden under capacious sweaters.
    When the brass band on the shore strikes up the
25 jaunty mazurka rhythms of the Polish anthem, I am pierced by a youthful sorrow so powerful that I suddenly stop crying and try to hold still against the pain. I desperately want time to stop, to hold the ship still with the force of my will. I am suf-
30 fering my first, severe attack of nostalgia, or *tesknota*—a word that adds to nostalgia the tonalities of sadness and longing. It is a feeling whose shades and degrees I'm destined to know inti-mately, but at this hovering moment, it comes
35 upon me like a visitation from a whole new geog-raphy of emotions, an annunciation of how much an absence can hurt. Or a premonition of absence, because at this divide, I'm filled to the brim with what I'm about to lose—images of Cracow, which
40 I loved as one loves a person, of the sunbaked villages where we had taken summer vacations, of the hours I spent poring over passages of music with my piano teacher, of conversations and esca-pades with friends. Looking ahead, I come across
45 an enormous, cold blankness—a darkening, and erasure, of the imagination, as if a camera eye has snapped shut, or as if a heavy curtain has been pulled over the future. Of the place where we're going—Canada—I know nothing. There are vague
50 outlines of half a continent, a sense of vast spaces and little habitation. When my parents were hiding in a branch-covered forest bunker during the war, my father had a book with him called *Canada Fragrant with Resin* which, in his horrible confine-
55 ment, spoke to him of majestic wilderness, of animals roaming without being pursued, of free-dom. That is partly why we are going there, rather than to Israel, where most of our Jewish friends have gone. But to me, the word "Canada" has
60 ominous echoes of the "Sahara." No, my mind rejects the idea of being taken there, I don't want to be pried out of my childhood, my pleasures, my safety, my hopes for becoming a pianist. The Batory pulls away, the foghorn emits its lowing, shofar*
65 sound, but my being is engaged in a stubborn refusal to move. My parents put their hands on my shoulders consolingly; for a moment, they allow themselves to acknowledge that there's pain in this departure, much as they wanted it.
70   Many years later, at a stylish party in New York, I met a woman who told me that she had an enchanted childhood. Her father was a highly posi-tioned diplomat in an Asian country, and she had lived surrounded by sumptuous elegance. . . . No
75 wonder, she said, that when this part of her life came to an end, at age thirteen, she felt she had been exiled from paradise, and had been searching for it ever since.

---

* A trumpet made from a ram's horn and sounded in the synagogue on the Jewish High Holy Days.

No wonder. But the wonder is what you can
80  make a paradise out of. I told her that I grew up
in a lumpen* apartment in Cracow, squeezed into
three rudimentary rooms with four other people,
surrounded by squabbles, dark political rumblings,
memories of wartime suffering, and daily struggle
85  for existence. And yet, when it came time to
leave, I, too, felt I was being pushed out of the
happy, safe enclosures of Eden.

* Pertaining to dispossessed, often displaced, individuals
who have been cut off from the socioeconomic class with
which they would ordinarily have been identified.

13. This passage serves mainly to

(A) provide a detailed description of what the
author loved most about her life in Poland
(B) recount the author's experience of leaving
Cracow
(C) explain why the author's family chose to
emigrate
(D) convey the author's resilience during times of
great upheaval
(E) create a factual account of the author's family
history

14. In lines 2-3, "I feel that my life is ending" most
nearly reflects the author's

(A) overwhelming sense of the desperate life that
she and her family have led
(B) sad realization that she is leaving a familiar life
(C) unsettling premonition that she will not
survive the voyage to Canada
(D) severe state of depression that may lead her to
seek professional help
(E) irrational fear that she will be permanently
separated from her family

15. In lines 5-6, the author's description of the crowd
on the shore suggests that

(A) her family does not expect to find a warm
welcome in Canada
(B) her relatives will not be able to visit her in
Canada
(C) her family's friends have now turned against
them
(D) she will find it difficult to communicate with
her Polish friends
(E) the step she is taking is irreversible

16. The passage as a whole suggests that the author
differs from her parents in that she

(A) has happier memories of Poland than her
parents do
(B) is more sociable than they are
(C) feels no response to the rhythms of the Polish
anthem
(D) has no desire to wave to the crowd on the shore
(E) is not old enough to comprehend what she is
leaving behind

17. For the author, the experience of leaving Cracow
can best be described as

(A) enlightening
(B) exhilarating
(C) annoying
(D) wrenching
(E) ennobling

18. In lines 17-19, the author's description of the
customs police suggests that the author views
them with

(A) alarm
(B) skepticism
(C) disrespect
(D) caution
(E) paranoia

19. In lines 29-37, the author indicates that "nostalgia"
differs from "tesknota" in that

(A) tesknota cannot be explained in English
(B) tesknota denotes a gloomy, bittersweet
yearning
(C) tesknota is a feeling that never ends
(D) nostalgia is a more painful emotion than
tesknota
(E) nostalgia connotes a greater degree of desire
than tesknota

20. By describing her feelings as having "shades and
degrees" (line 33), the author suggests that

(A) she is allowing herself to grieve only a little at a
time
(B) she is numb to the pain of her grief
(C) she is overwhelmed by her emotions
(D) her sadness is greatest at night
(E) her emotional state is multifaceted

21. In lines 33-34, the phrase "I'm destined to know intimately" implies that the author

(A) cannot escape the path her father has chosen for the family
(B) believes that the future will bring many new emotional experiences
(C) will be deeply affected by the experience of emigrating
(D) must carefully analyze her conflicting emotional reactions
(E) has much to learn about the experience of emigrating

22. The author refers to the "camera eye" (line 46) and the "heavy curtain" (line 47) in order to suggest

(A) the difference between reality and art
(B) the importance of images to the human mind
(C) the difference between Poland and Canada
(D) her inability to overcome her fear of death
(E) her inability to imagine her future life

23. The description of the author as "engaged in a stubborn refusal to move" (lines 65-66) suggests her

(A) determination to claim her space on the crowded deck of the ship
(B) refusal to accept the change in her life
(C) wish to strike back at her parents for taking her away from Poland
(D) resolve not to become a Canadian citizen
(E) need to stay in close proximity to her family

24. In lines 66-69, the author suggests that her parents' comforting gesture indicates

(A) a recognition of feelings of distress over their departure
(B) their exhilaration and relief at the thought of personal freedom
(C) a great deal of ambivalence regarding their decision
(D) pain so great that they can feel no joy in their departure
(E) a complete loss of feeling due to the stressful events

25. The author mentions the anecdote about the person she met at a "stylish party in New York" (line 70) in order to

(A) prove that the author had become less childlike and more sophisticated
(B) demonstrate that the author's parents had become affluent in Canada
(C) describe how wealthy children are raised in Asian countries
(D) make an important point about childhood happiness
(E) show that the author had ultimately lived in the United States as well as Canada

**Questions 26-31 are based on the following passage.**

*The following passage is adapted from the writings of a Nobel Prize–winning scientist.*

Any scientist who is not a hypocrite will admit the important part that luck plays in scientific discovery. Our estimate of the importance of luck
Line is inherently biased: we know when we benefit
5 from luck, but in the nature of things cannot assess how often bad luck deprives us of the chance of making what might have been an important discovery.

A colleague and I carried out an experiment in
10 which little tissue fragments, which were very difficult to work with, were injected into mice of different strains. If we had been more experienced, we would have injected only white blood cells (which would have been easier to handle) into the
15 mice. We now know that if we had done this, we would not have discovered actively acquired tolerance* because the grafts would have in effect rejected their hosts. Obviously, we were lucky, but our scientific training enabled us to recognize the
20 significance of the accident. I think, therefore, that there was no need for the distinguished neurophysiologist Hodgkin to refer to his "feeling of guilt about suppressing the part which chance and good fortune played in what now seems to be a rather
25 logical development."

It might nevertheless seem as if luck plays a dominant role in scientific discovery. I would like to challenge this view for the following reasons: we sometimes describe as "lucky" a person who
30 wins a prize in a lottery at long odds; but if we describe such an event as luck, what word shall we use to describe the accidental discovery on a park bench of a lottery ticket that turns out to be the winning one?

35 The two cases are quite different. A person who buys a lottery ticket is putting himself or herself in the way of winning a prize. This individual has, so to speak, purchased candidacy for such a turn of events and all the rest is a matter of mathematical
40 probabilities. So it is with scientists. A scientist is anyone who, by observations and experiments conducted, by the literature read, and even by the company kept, puts himself or herself in the way of making a discovery. These individuals, by delib-
45 erate action, have enormously enlarged their awareness—their candidacy for good fortune—and will now take into account evidence of a kind that a beginner or a casual observer would probably overlook or misinterpret. I honestly do not think
50 that blind luck of the kind enjoyed by someone who finds a winning lottery ticket for which he or she has not paid plays an important part in science or that many important discoveries arise from the casual intersection of two lines.

*Evidence that transplanting living tissues between adult organisms is possible.

55     Nearly all successful scientists have emphasized
the importance of preparedness of mind, and I
want to emphasize that this preparedness of mind
is worked for and paid for by a great deal of exer-
tion and reflection. If these exertions lead to a
60 discovery, then I think it would be inappropriate
to credit such a discovery to luck.

26. The outcome of the experiment described in lines
9-12 suggests that

(A) luck worked against the scientists at first
(B) the injection of only white blood cells into the
mice allowed the two scientists to make their
discovery
(C) the mice represented the perfect animals on
which to conduct the experiment
(D) the scientists involved were able to capitalize
on luck
(E) scientific experiments occur in the concrete
world, not in the abstract world of theory

27. In lines 35-40, the author uses the example of the
lottery winner in order to

(A) suggest that blind luck occurs more frequently
than people realize
(B) suggest that luck plays a more important part
in most events than people realize
(C) suggest that luck is not the correct term to
use when referring to a significant scientific
discovery
(D) illustrate that those who rely solely on luck are
unlikely to find success
(E) illustrate that the two forms of luck are
analogous

28. In lines 44-45, "deliberate" most nearly means

(A) cunning
(B) slow
(C) compelling
(D) cautious
(E) intentional

29. The author implies that a scientist achieves
"candidacy for good fortune" (line 46) by

(A) making careful and repeated mathematical
calculations
(B) playing hunches rather than depending on
research
(C) performing enough experiments to increase
the statistical probability of success
(D) obtaining knowledge that allows him or her
to recognize important evidence
(E) understanding the difference between luck
and discovery

30. The meaning of the phrase "casual intersection
of two lines" (line 54) is most clearly conveyed by
which of the following?

(A) Informal kinds of experiments
(B) Two detailed plans
(C) Geometrically precise experiments
(D) Unanticipated coincidence
(E) Predetermined events

31. The primary purpose of the passage is to

(A) delineate a single definition of luck
(B) show that scientists discover what they
intend to find
(C) compare science to a game
(D) share the pleasure in making scientific
discoveries
(E) discuss the role of luck in science

## Answer Key

| | | | |
|---|---|---|---|
| 1. | C | 17. | D |
| 2. | D | 18. | C |
| 3. | C | 19. | B |
| 4. | B | 20. | E |
| 5. | B | 21. | C |
| 6. | E | 22. | E |
| 7. | A | 23. | B |
| 8. | E | 24. | A |
| 9. | D | 25. | D |
| 10. | C | 26. | D |
| 11. | A | 27. | C |
| 12. | B | 28. | E |
| 13. | B | 29. | D |
| 14. | B | 30. | D |
| 15. | E | 31. | E |
| 16. | A | | |

**Additional practice questions can be found in *The Official SAT Online Course* at www.collegeboard.org/satonlinecourse.**

# CHAPTER 7
# Practice for the Critical Reading Section

Here's a chance to practice the test-taking skills and concepts you've been working on. Try out different ways of approaching questions before you take the practice tests in the last section of this book. This chapter is intended to give you practice with the different types of questions, so it isn't arranged in the same way as the actual SAT.

# Practice Questions—Sentence Completion

Each sentence below has one or two blanks, each blank indicating that something has been omitted. Beneath the sentence are five words or sets of words labeled A through E. Choose the word or set of words that, when inserted in the sentence, <u>best</u> fits the meaning of the sentence as a whole.

**Example:**

Hoping to ------- the dispute, negotiators proposed a compromise that they felt would be ------- to both labor and management.

   (A) enforce . . useful
   (B) end . . divisive
   (C) overcome . . unattractive
   (D) extend . . satisfactory
   (E) resolve . . acceptable   

1. Investigation of the epidemic involved determining what was ------- about the people who were affected, what made them differ from those who remained well.

   (A) chronic
   (B) unique
   (C) fortunate
   (D) misunderstood
   (E) historical

2. Because management ------- the fact that employees find it difficult to work alertly at repetitious tasks, it sponsors numerous projects to ------- enthusiasm for the job.

   (A) recognizes . . generate
   (B) disproves . . create
   (C) respects . . quench
   (D) controls . . regulate
   (E) surmises . . suspend

3. They did their best to avoid getting embroiled in the quarrel, preferring to maintain their ------- as long as possible.

   (A) consciousness
   (B) suspense
   (C) interest
   (D) decisiveness
   (E) neutrality

4. The strong affinity of these wild sheep for mountains is not -------: mountain slopes represent ------- because they effectively limit the ability of less agile predators to pursue the sheep.

   (A) useful . . peril
   (B) accidental . . security
   (C) instinctive . . attainment
   (D) restrained . . nourishment
   (E) surprising . . inferiority

5. Even those who do not ------- Robinson's views ------- him as a candidate who has courageously refused to compromise his convictions.

   (A) shrink from . . condemn
   (B) profit from . . dismiss
   (C) concur with . . recognize
   (D) disagree with . . envision
   (E) dissent from . . remember

6. The alarm voiced by the committee investigating the accident had a ------- effect, for its dire predictions motivated people to take precautions that ------- an ecological disaster.

   (A) trivial . . prompted
   (B) salutary . . averted
   (C) conciliatory . . supported
   (D) beneficial . . exacerbated
   (E) perverse . . vanquished

7. At the age of forty-five, with a worldwide reputation and an as yet unbroken string of notable successes to her credit, Carson was at the ------- of her career.

   (A) paradigm
   (B) zenith
   (C) fiasco
   (D) periphery
   (E) inception

8. The fact that they cherished religious objects more than most of their other possessions ------- the ------- role of religion in their lives.

   (A) demonstrates . . crucial
   (B) obliterates . . vital
   (C) limits . . daily
   (D) concerns . . informal
   (E) denotes . . varying

9. Mary Cassatt, an Impressionist painter, was the epitome of the ------- American: a native of Philadelphia who lived most of her life in Paris.

   (A) conservative
   (B) provincial
   (C) benevolent
   (D) prophetic
   (E) expatriate

10. In the nineteenth century many literary critics saw themselves as stern, authoritarian figures defending society against the ------- of those ------- beings called authors.

   (A) depravities . . wayward
   (B) atrocities . . exemplary
   (C) merits . . ineffectual
   (D) kudos . . antagonistic
   (E) indictments . . secretive

# Practice Questions—Passage-based Reading

The passages below are followed by questions based on their content; questions following a pair of related passages may also be based on the relationship between the paired passages. Answer the questions on the basis of what is <u>stated</u> or <u>implied</u> in the passages and in any introductory material that may be provided.

**Questions 1-11 are based on the following passage.**

*Fear of communism swept through the United States in the years following the Russian Revolution of 1917. Several states passed espionage acts that restricted*
Line *political discussion, and radicals of all descriptions were*
5 *rounded up in so-called Red Raids conducted by the attorney general's office. Some were convicted and imprisoned; others were deported. This was the background of a trial in Chicago involving twenty men charged under Illinois's espionage statute with*
10 *advocating the violent overthrow of the government. The charge rested on the fact that all the defendants were members of the newly formed Communist Labor party.*
*The accused in the case were represented by Clarence Darrow, one of the foremost defense attorneys in the*
15 *country. Throughout his career, Darrow had defended the poor and the despised against exploitation and prejudice. He defended the rights of labor unions, for example, at a time when many sought to outlaw the strike, and he was resolute in defending constitutional*
20 *freedoms. The following are excerpts from Darrow's summation to the jury.*

Members of the Jury. . . . If you want to convict these twenty men, then do it. I ask no consideration on behalf of any one of them. They are no better than any other
25 twenty men or women; they are no better than the millions down through the ages who have been prosecuted and convicted in cases like this. And if it is necessary for my clients to show that America is like all the rest, if it is necessary that my clients shall go to prison to show it,
30 then let them go. They can afford it if you members of the jury can; make no mistake about that. . . .
The State says my clients "dare to criticize the Constitution." Yet this police officer (who the State says is a fine, right-living person) twice violated the federal Con-
35 stitution while a prosecuting attorney was standing by. They entered Mr. Owen's home without a search warrant. They overhauled his papers. They found a flag, a red one, which he had the same right to have in his house that you have to keep a green one, or a yellow one, or any
40 other color, and the officer impudently rolled it up and put another flag on the wall, nailed it there. By what right was that done? What about this kind of patriotism that

violates the Constitution? Has it come to pass in this country that officers of the law can trample on constitu-
45 tional rights and then excuse it in a court of justice? . . .
Most of what has been presented to this jury to stir up feeling in your souls has not the slightest bearing on proving conspiracy in this case. Take Mr. Lloyd's speech in Milwaukee. It had nothing to do with conspiracy.
50 Whether the speech was a joke or was serious, I will not attempt to discuss. But I will say that if it was serious it was as mild as a summer's shower compared with many of the statements of those who are responsible for working conditions in this country. We have heard from people
55 in high places that those individuals who express sympathy with labor should be stood up against a wall and shot. We have heard people of position declare that individuals who criticize the actions of those who are getting rich should be put in a cement ship with leaden sails and sent
60 out to sea. Every violent appeal that could be conceived by the brain has been used by the powerful and the strong. I repeat, Mr. Lloyd's speech was gentle in comparison. . .
My clients are condemned because they say in their platform that, while they vote, they believe the ballot is
65 secondary to education and organization. Counsel suggests that those who get something they did not vote for are sinners, but I suspect you the jury know full well that my clients are right. Most of you have an eight-hour day. Did you get it by any vote you ever cast? No. It came
70 about because workers laid down their tools and said we will no longer work until we get an eight-hour day. That is how they got the twelve-hour day, the ten-hour day, and the eight-hour day—not by voting but by laying down their tools. Then when it was over and the victory won
75 . . then the politicians, in order to get the labor vote, passed legislation creating an eight-hour day. That is how things changed; victory preceded law. . . .
You have been told that if you acquit these defendants you will be despised because you will endorse everything
80 they believe. But I am not here to defend my clients' opinions. I am here to defend their right to express their opinions. I ask you, then, to decide this case upon the facts as you have heard them, in light of the law as you understand it, in light of the history of our country, whose in-
85 stitutions you and I are bound to protect.

1. Which best captures the meaning of the word "consideration" in line 23?

   (A) Leniency
   (B) Contemplation
   (C) Due respect
   (D) Reasoned judgment
   (E) Legal rights

2. By "They can afford it if you members of the jury can" (lines 30-31), Darrow means that

(A) no harm will come to the defendants if they are convicted in this case
(B) the jurors will be severely criticized by the press if they convict the defendants
(C) the defendants are indifferent about the outcome of the trial
(D) the verdict of the jury has financial implications for all of the people involved in the trial
(E) a verdict of guilty would be a potential threat to everyone's rights

3. Lines 32-45 suggest that the case against Owen would have been dismissed if the judge had interpreted the Constitution in which of the following ways?

(A) Defendants must have their rights read to them when they are arrested.
(B) Giving false testimony in court is a crime.
(C) Evidence gained by illegal means is not admissible in court.
(D) No one can be tried twice for the same crime.
(E) Defendants cannot be forced to give incriminating evidence against themselves.

4. In line 47, the word "bearing" most nearly means

(A) connection
(B) posture
(C) endurance
(D) location
(E) resemblance

5. In lines 46-62, Darrow's defense rests mainly on convincing the jury that

(A) a double standard is being employed
(B) the prosecution's evidence is untrustworthy
(C) the defendants share mainstream American values
(D) labor unions have the right to strike
(E) the defendants should be tried by a federal rather than a state court

6. The information in lines 46-62 suggests that the prosecution treated Mr. Lloyd's speech primarily as

(A) sarcasm to be resented
(B) propaganda to be ridiculed
(C) criticism to be answered
(D) a threat to be feared
(E) a bad joke to be dismissed

7. Darrow accuses "people in high places" (lines 54-55) of

(A) conspiring to murder members of the Communist party
(B) encouraging violence against critics of wealthy business owners
(C) pressuring members of the jury to convict the defendants
(D) advocating cruel and unusual punishment for criminals
(E) insulting the public's intelligence by making foolish suggestions

8. The word "education" (line 65) is a reference to the need for

(A) establishing schools to teach the philosophy of the Communist Labor party
(B) making workers aware of their economic and political rights
(C) teaching factory owners about the needs of laborers
(D) creating opportunities for on-the-job training in business
(E) helping workers to continue their schooling

9. The statement "victory preceded law" (line 77) refers to the fact that

(A) social reform took place only after labor unions organized support for their political candidates
(B) politicians need to win the support of labor unions if they are to be elected
(C) politicians can introduce legislative reform only if they are elected to office
(D) politicians did not initiate improved working conditions but legalized them after they were in place
(E) politicians have shown that they are more interested in winning elections than in legislative reform

10. Judging from lines 78-80, the jury had apparently been told that finding the defendants innocent would be the same as

(A) denying the importance of the Constitution
(B) giving people the right to strike
(C) encouraging passive resistance
(D) inhibiting free speech
(E) supporting communist doctrine

11. In order for Darrow to win the case, it would be most crucial that the jurors possess

(A) a thorough understanding of legal procedures and terminology
(B) a thorough understanding of the principles and beliefs of the Communist Labor party
(C) sympathy for labor's rights to safe and comfortable working conditions
(D) the ability to separate the views of the defendants from the rights of the defendants
(E) the courage to act in the best interests of the nation's economy

**Questions 12-17 are based on the following passage.**

*The following is adapted from a translation of a novel first published in 1894. The author of the novel was a Puerto Rican legislator.*

The thin crescent of the new moon was greeted by torrential rains. Juan del Salto, confined by the weather, was at his desk amidst a sea of paper. He
Line reached into one of the pigeonholes and extracted
5 a bundle wrapped in a rubber band: his son's letters.

Gabriel, twenty-four years old, was in his final semester of law studies in Spain. Although Gabriel was away from Puerto Rico and already a man,
10 Juan regarded as unfinished his mission as a father. He must prepare Gabriel for the disappointments of reality, and with consummate tact, without wounding his optimism, he sent him brief accounts of the island, entrusting him with the
15 maturity to form his own convictions. Juan removed the most recent letter from the bundle and began to reread it, tenderly.

"Don't think," Gabriel wrote, "that I have come to believe our land is a paradise. I know all too
20 well that life is a struggle everywhere. But I cannot conceal from you the sorrow that your words have caused me, and a few paragraphs in your letter have struck me with the impact of cold water.

25 "In the first paragraph, Father, you wrote *just as stirring the air with a fan will never split mountains, fits of lyrical passion will not solve arduous problems.* Those words caused me to tear up an 'Ode to the Patria' which I had written. In the ode,
30 I sang the glories of my land, basing it upon its natural opulence and upon the romanticism of a great cloud of loving sentiment. I tore it up, convinced that it was like the breeze of a fan, spending its force in the void of futility.

35 "Second paragraph . . . *since Humanity owns the world, as it grows it must become worthy of the splendor of its creation. Many societies succumb to theories without ever having the good fortune to put a single one of their philosophical
40 speculations into practice. . . . Nations are like individuals: they achieve more when they plan to plant a tiny tree, and do it, than when they propose to raise an entire forest and then fall asleep in the furrows. Reality! Here you have the
45 great lever. We should concern ourselves with what already exists, in order to achieve what should be. By only singing of what we would like it to be, we accomplish nothing.* I sense a severe criticism in these words, and since I know how
50 much you love our land, that criticism is immensely important to me."

Juan enjoyed rereading it all. His son had imagination and wit. He loved everything with childlike candor, but was simultaneously a thinker begin-
55 ning the great journey along life's rugged trail. Juan

loved him infinitely, as though Gabriel were made of fragile Bohemian crystal.

Thus passed the hours of that nostalgic day.

12. The passage is primarily concerned with a

(A) father's attempt to regain his son's affection
(B) son's skill at setting his father's mind at ease
(C) father's desire for his son to include artistic sentiments in his life
(D) son's ambition to return to his homeland as a successful lawyer and poet
(E) father's efforts to guide his son's intellectual and emotional growth

13. Juan apparently considers "lyrical passion" (line 27) to be

(A) a necessary component in the creation of enduring poetry
(B) an effective technique for inspiring action in others
(C) an emotion that Gabriel needs to experience
(D) of little consequence in practical matters
(E) less compelling than other artistic feelings

14. Gabriel's stated reason for destroying his "Ode to the Patria" most strongly suggests that

(A) Gabriel's optimistic illusions had been shattered
(B) Gabriel's writing skills suddenly embarrassed him
(C) Gabriel had reversed his feelings about Puerto Rico
(D) Juan had previously ridiculed similar pieces
(E) Juan had successfully turned Gabriel's attention back to his studies

15. Which of the following best paraphrases the point made by mentioning trees and forests in lines 42-43?

(A) Detailed planning is essential in large operations.
(B) Even the strongest structure will come to ruin if it is built on a weak foundation.
(C) Following through on a small project is preferable to simply conceiving a large one.
(D) If individuals work together harmoniously, the entire community will prosper.
(E) The most invigorating work is that which is self-generated, not that assigned by others.

16. It can be inferred from the passage that Gabriel sees his father as a man who

    (A) has strong views that are well worth considering
    (B) has made great sacrifices to send him to law school
    (C) expects him to become a powerful and important leader
    (D) writes harsh observations that need to be moderated
    (E) is somewhat unsure of himself despite his confident manner

17. It can be inferred from the letters cited in the passage that which of the following exchanges has already occurred?

    (A) Juan voiced doubts about Gabriel's economic decisions.
    (B) Juan encouraged Gabriel to consider practicing law in Spain.
    (C) Gabriel sought his father's advice on affairs of the heart.
    (D) Gabriel displayed a clear reluctance to accept criticism.
    (E) Gabriel expressed some loftily idealistic thoughts.

**Questions 18-22 are based on the following passage.**

*This excerpt discusses the relationship between plants and their environments.*

Why do some desert plants grow tall and thin
like organ pipes? Why do most trees in the tropics
keep their leaves year round? Why in the Arctic
Line tundra are there no trees at all? After many years
5 without convincing general answers, we now
know much about what sets the fashion in plant
design.
   Using terminology more characteristic of a ther-
mal engineer than of a botanist, we can think of
10 plants as mechanisms that must balance their heat
budgets. A plant by day is staked out under the
Sun with no way of sheltering itself. All day long
it absorbs heat. If it did not lose as much heat as it
gained, then eventually it would die. Plants get rid
15 of their heat by warming the air around them, by
evaporating water, and by radiating heat to the
atmosphere and the cold, black reaches of space.
Each plant must balance its heat budget so that its
temperature is tolerable for the processes of life.
20    Plants in the Arctic tundra lie close to the
ground in the thin layer of still air that clings
there. A foot or two above the ground are the
winds of Arctic cold. Tundra plants absorb heat
from the Sun and tend to warm up; they probably
25 balance most of their heat budgets by radiating
heat to space, but also by warming the still air
that is trapped among them. As long as Arctic
plants are close to the ground, they can balance

their heat budgets. But if they should stretch up as
30 a tree does, they would lift their working parts,
their leaves, into the streaming Arctic winds.
Then it is likely that the plants could not absorb
enough heat from the Sun to avoid being cooled
below a critical temperature. Your heat budget
35 does not balance if you stand tall in the Arctic.
   Such thinking also helps explain other characteristics of plant design. A desert plant faces the
opposite problem from that of an Arctic plant—
the danger of overheating. It is short of water and
40 so cannot cool itself by evaporation without dehy-
drating. The familiar sticklike shape of desert
plants represents one of the solutions to this problem: the shape exposes the smallest possible
surface to incoming solar radiation and provides
45 the largest possible surface from which the plant
can radiate heat. In tropical rain forests, by way of
contrast, the scorching Sun is not a problem for
plants because there is sufficient water.
   This working model allows us to connect the
50 general characteristics of the forms of plants in
different habitats with factors such as temperature,
availability of water, and presence or absence of
seasonal differences. Our Earth is covered with a
patchwork quilt of meteorological conditions, and
55 the patterns of this patchwork are faithfully
reflected by the plants.

18. The passage primarily focuses on which of the following characteristics of plants?

    (A) Their ability to grow equally well in all environments
    (B) Their effects on the Earth's atmosphere
    (C) Their ability to store water for dry periods
    (D) Their fundamental similarity of shape
    (E) Their ability to balance heat intake and output

19. Which of the following could best be substituted for the words "sets the fashion in" (line 6) without changing the intended meaning?

    (A) improves the appearance of
    (B) accounts for the uniformity of
    (C) defines acceptable standards for
    (D) determines the general characteristics of
    (E) reduces the heat budgets of

20. According to the passage, which of the following is most responsible for preventing trees from growing tall in the Arctic?

    (A) The hard, frozen ground
    (B) The small amount of available sunshine
    (C) The cold, destructive winds
    (D) The large amount of snow that falls each year
    (E) The absence of seasonal differences in temperature

**21.** The author suggests that the "sticklike shape of desert plants" (lines 41-42) can be attributed to the

(A) inability of the plants to radiate heat to the air around them
(B) presence of irregular seasonal differences in the desert
(C) large surface area that the plants must expose to the Sun
(D) absence of winds strong enough to knock down tall, thin plants
(E) extreme heat and aridity of the habitat

**22.** The contrast mentioned in lines 46-48 specifically concerns the

(A) availability of moisture
(B) scorching heat of the Sun
(C) seasonal differences in temperature
(D) variety of plant species
(E) heat radiated by plants to the atmosphere

**Questions 23-28 are based on the following passage.**

*The following description of a small town is from a novel by an African American which was published in 1973.*

In that place, where they tore the nightshade
and blackberry patches from their roots to make
room for the Medallion City Golf Course, there
Line was once a neighborhood. It stood in the hills
5 above the valley town of Medallion and spread all
the way to the river. It is called the suburbs now,
but when Black people lived there it was called
the Bottom. One road, shaded by beeches, oaks,
maples, and chestnuts, connected it to the valley.
10 The beeches are gone now, and so are the pear
trees where children sat and yelled down through
the blossoms to passersby. Generous funds have
been allotted to level the stripped and faded buildings that clutter the road from Medallion up to the
15 golf course. They are going to raze the Time and a
Half Pool Hall, where feet in long tan shoes once
pointed down from chair rungs. A steel ball will
knock to dust Irene's Palace of Cosmetology,
where women used to lean their heads back on
20 sink trays and doze while Irene lathered Nu Nile
into their hair. Men in khaki work clothes will pry
loose the slats of Reba's Grill, where the owner
cooked in her hat because she claimed she
couldn't remember the ingredients without it.
25 There will be nothing left of the Bottom (the
footbridge that crossed the river is already gone),
but perhaps it is just as well, since it wasn't a
town anyway: just a neighborhood where on quiet
days people in valley houses could hear singing
30 sometimes, banjoes sometimes, and, if a valley
man happened to have business up in those hills—
collecting rent or insurance payments—he might

see a dark woman in a flowered dress doing a bit
of cakewalk to the lively notes of a mouth organ.
35 Her bare feet would raise the saffron dust that
floated down on the coveralls and bunion-split
shoes of the man breathing music in and out of his
harmonica. The Black people watching her would
laugh and rub their knees, and it would be easy for
40 the valley man to hear the laughter and not notice
the adult pain that rested somewhere under the
eyelids, somewhere under their head rags and soft
felt caps, somewhere in the palm of the hand,
somewhere behind the frayed lapels, somewhere in
45 the sinew's curve. He'd have to stand in the back
of Greater Saint Matthew's Church and let the
tenor's voice dress him in silk, or touch the hands
of the spoon carvers (who had not worked in eight
years) and let the fingers that danced on wood kiss
50 his skin. Otherwise the pain would escape him
even though the laughter was part of the pain.

**23.** The author's perspective on the Bottom is that of

(A) an unsympathetic outsider
(B) an adult recalling early dreams
(C) a participant defending a course of action
(D) an angry protester trying to prevent an undesirable event
(E) a sad observer of a transformation

**24.** The name "the Bottom" is incongruous because the neighborhood

(A) contains only demolished buildings
(B) has become more prosperous since it was named
(C) is a fertile piece of land
(D) has only recently been established
(E) is located in hills above a valley

**25.** "Generous" as used to describe "funds" (line 12) is intended to seem

(A) ironic, because the funds are being used to destroy something
(B) progressive, because the narrator is showing how times change
(C) objective, because the narrator knows the amount
(D) humorous, because the cleanup is not truly expensive
(E) equivocal, because the funds are inadequate

26. In the second paragraph, the author conveys a feeling of tension by juxtaposing which two of the following elements?

    (A) The assertion that the neighborhood's destruction is insignificant *versus* the carefully drawn richness of its life
    (B) The author's expression of affection for the neighborhood *versus* frustration at its reluctance to change
    (C) Nostalgia about the way the town used to be *versus* a sense of excitement about its future
    (D) Appreciation for the town's natural beauty *versus* disapproval of its ramshackle state
    (E) Sadness about the town's fate *versus* sympathy for the reasons for it

27. The author's statement that the valley man might not perceive the pain underlying the laughter of the Bottom's residents (lines 38-45) emphasizes that the Bottom's residents

    (A) had frequent contact with other residents of the valley
    (B) understood the valley man well, even though they did not see him often
    (C) were not the carefree people they might appear to be
    (D) concealed their real feelings from outsiders
    (E) were concerned about the destruction of their neighborhood

28. The author portrays the Bottom as a place

    (A) that lacked economic prosperity but had a rich emotional life
    (B) that was too filled with sadness to be able to survive
    (C) that needed to become more up-to-date in order to prosper
    (D) whose effect on its residents was difficult for them to understand
    (E) in which people paid more attention to the way things seemed to others than to the way things really were

**Questions 29-30 are based on the following passage.**

"I am a very serious woman," was Bella Savitzky Abzug's simple but powerful response to those who made light of her often boisterous activism. Abzug's
*Line* forceful manner and flamboyant appearance may
5 have drawn ridicule from some of her adversaries in the American political arena, but this very serious woman dedicated her life to the public service on behalf of the oppressed and ignored. Abzug gained fame nationally as the first Jewish woman elected to the
10 United States Congress and later internationally as a leader in the global women's movement, where her courage and indomitable spirit made a lasting impression on younger activists.

29. The tone of the quotation in line 1 is best described as

    (A) dignified
    (B) apologetic
    (C) exhilarated
    (D) hostile
    (E) cynical

30. The primary purpose of the passage is to

    (A) provide a character sketch of a political figure
    (B) promote interest in the global women's movement
    (C) emphasize the importance of public service to a society
    (D) explore both sides of a national controversy
    (E) champion the rights of those whose voices are not heard

## Answer Key

### Sentence Completion

| | | | |
|---|---|---|---|
| 1. | B | 6. | B |
| 2. | A | 7. | B |
| 3. | E | 0. | A |
| 4. | B | 9. | E |
| 5. | C | 10. | A |

### Passage-based Reading

| | | | |
|---|---|---|---|
| 1. | A | 16. | A |
| 2. | E | 17. | E |
| 3. | C | 18. | E |
| 4. | A | 19. | D |
| 5. | A | 20. | C |
| 6. | D | 21. | E |
| 7. | B | 22. | A |
| 8. | B | 23. | E |
| 9. | D | 24. | E |
| 10. | E | 25. | A |
| 11. | D | 26. | A |
| 12. | E | 27. | C |
| 13. | D | 28. | A |
| 14. | A | 29. | A |
| 15. | C | 30. | A |

 **Additional practice questions can be found in** *The Official SAT Online Course* **at www.collegeboard.org/satonlinecourse.**

# PART III
# The Writing Section

# CHAPTER 8

# About the Writing Section

Writing is a skill needed for success in both college and the workplace. The writing section gives you a chance to demonstrate the writing skills you've developed through your high school course work, particularly in English class, and through writing outside of school, such as personal journal entries and letters. The section is composed of:

- *An essay:* You will have to write a first draft of an original essay, under timed conditions.

- *Multiple choice questions:* You will have to recognize sentence errors, choose the best version of a piece of writing and improve paragraphs within a writing context.

The multiple choice sections measure your ability to
- communicate ideas clearly and effectively;
- improve a piece of writing through revision and editing;
- recognize and identify sentence-level errors;
- understand grammatical elements and structures and how they relate to one another in a sentence;
- recognize correctly formed grammatical structures;
- clearly express ideas through sentence combining and use of transitional words and phrases; and
- improve coherence of ideas within and among paragraphs.

In the essay component of the writing section, the student-written essay assesses your ability to develop and express ideas effectively. It evaluates your ability to do the kind of writing required in college — writing that develops a point of view, presents ideas logically and clearly, and uses precise language. You're not expected to be an expert in any particular field. The topic of the essay (also called a *prompt*) allows you to support your ideas by using what you've learned from your course work, your readings outside of school and your experiences in and out of school. The essay must be written in a limited time, which doesn't allow for many revisions, so it is considered and scored as a first draft.

The multiple-choice component includes 49 questions on grammar, usage, paragraph organization and multi paragraph coherence, and assesses your ability to use language in a clear, consistent manner and to improve a piece of writing through revision and editing.

The multiple choice questions don't ask you to define or use grammatical terms and don't test spelling or capitalization. In some questions, punctuation marks, such as the semicolon, may help you choose the correct answer. But questions like those mainly test the structure in which the punctuation appears.

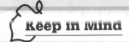

**Keep in Mind**

The multiple-choice questions include three types:
1. improving sentences (see Chapter 10)
2. identifying sentence errors (see Chapter 11)
3. improving paragraphs (see Chapter 12)

## Approaches to the Multiple-Choice Questions

▶ *Read the directions carefully,* and then follow them.

▶ *Look at the explanations for each correct answer* when you use the practice materials in this book. Even if you got the question right, you may learn something from the explanation.

▶ *Eliminate the choices you are sure are wrong when you are not sure of the answer.* Make an educated guess from those that remain.

## How the Writing Section Is Scored

You will be given two subscores for the writing section: a multiple-choice subscore that will range from 20 to 80 and an essay subscore that will range from 2 to 12. If you write an essay that is not on the assigned topic, you will receive an essay subscore of 0. The essay subscore will contribute about 30 percent toward the total writing score, and the score on the multiple-choice questions will contribute about 70 percent. The total writing score will be placed on the College Board 200- to 800-point scale.

## Developing Writing Skills

Good writing, especially in college, requires you to develop your ideas with relevant and appropriate information. This is true for any subject that you'll be studying, whether it's English, history, science, social studies, mathematics or fine arts. Though each of your instructors may have different expectations for your writing assignments, every instructor will want ideas that are well thought out and clearly expressed.

To write better, you have to write more. Practice helps improve your writing skills.

To write better, you have to read more. Reading helps improve the way you use language.

The more you read — challenging material in particular — the more you'll be exposed to interesting and provocative ideas and to varied, even unusual, ways of using language. If you read well-written books and articles, you may be inspired to use similar language in your own writing.

Table 8.1 lists characteristics of effective writing and provides examples of ineffective sentences and corrected sentences. You will need to recognize these characteristics when you work on the writing multiple-choice sections.

> **Keep in Mind**
>
> Successful college writing includes:
> - well-developed ideas, with relevant and accurate supporting information
> - clearly expressed thesis statements
> - good organization
> - appropriate, accurate and varied vocabulary
> - variety of syntax (sentence structure)

**Table 8.1** Characteristics of Effective Writing, with Examples

| Characteristics of Effective Writing | Examples of Ineffective Writing | Corrected Sentences |
|---|---|---|
| **1. Consistency** | | |
| Sequence of tenses | After he broke his arm, he is home for two weeks. | After he broke his arm, he was home for two weeks. |
| Shift of pronoun | If you are tense, one should try to relax. | If you are tense, you should try to relax. |
| Parallelism | The master carpenter showed us how to countersink the nails, how to varnish the wood, and getting a smooth surface was also demonstrated. | The master carpenter showed us how to countersink the nails, varnish the wood, and get a smooth surface. |
| Noun-number agreement | Ann and Sarah want to be a pilot. | Ann and Sarah want to be pilots. |
| Subject-verb agreement | There is eight people on shore. | There are eight people on shore. |
| **2. Logical Expression of Ideas** | | |
| Coordination and subordination | Nancy has a rash, and she is probably allergic to something. | Nancy has a rash; she is probably allergic to something. |
| Logical comparison | Harry grew more vegetables than his neighbor's garden. | Harry grew more vegetables than his neighbor. |
| Modification and word order | Barking loudly, the tree had the dog's leash wrapped around it. | Barking loudly, the dog had wrapped his leash around the tree. |

*(continued)*

**Table 8.1** (*continued*)

| Characteristics of Effective Writing | Examples of Ineffective Writing | Corrected Sentences |
|---|---|---|
| **3. Clarity and Precision** | | |
| Ambiguous and vague pronouns | *In the newspaper they say that few people voted.* | *The newspaper reported that few people voted.* |
| Diction | *He circumvented the globe on his trip.* | *He circumnavigated the globe on his trip.* |
| Wordiness | *There are many problems in the contemporary world in which we live.* | *There are many problems in our contemporary world.* |
| Missing subject | *If your car is parked here while not eating in the restaurant, it will be towed away.* | *If you park here and do not eat in the restaurant, your car will be towed away.* |
| Weak passive verbs | *When you bake a cake, the oven should be preheated.* | *When you bake a cake, you should preheat the oven.* |
| **4. Appropriate Use of Conventions** | | |
| Adjective and adverb confusion | *His friends agree that he drives reckless.* | *His friends agree that he drives recklessly.* |
| Pronoun case | *He sat between you and I at the stadium.* | *He sat between you and me at the stadium.* |
| Idiom | *Natalie had a different opinion towards her.* | *Natalie had a different opinion of her.* |
| Comparison of modifiers | *Of the sixteen executives, Meg makes more money.* | *Of the sixteen executives, Meg makes the most money.* |
| Sentence fragment | *Whether or not the answer seems correct.* | *The answer seems to be correct.* |
| Comma splice or fused sentence | *Shawna enjoys crossword puzzles, she works on one every day.* | *Shawna enjoys crossword puzzles, and she works on one every day.* |

# CHAPTER 9

# The Essay

The ability to write effectively is one of the key factors in doing well in college. Writing is an essential part of learning. Through the writing process, you develop, examine and refine your ideas. Through formal writing assignments, you demonstrate what you understand and how well you are able to communicate it to others. The SAT essay measures your ability to write effectively under timed conditions.

The SAT essay is similar to the on-demand writing done in many college classes. You will be given 25 minutes to respond to an essay topic, also called a prompt. The topic will be general enough for you to respond to without needing advanced knowledge on a specific subject. The topic will be relevant to a wide range of fields and interests — literature, the arts, sports, politics, technology, science, history and current events. The essay readers are not looking for one correct viewpoint. You may support a viewpoint that is described in the prompt or you may develop a different viewpoint. However, you must write on the topic you are given, or your essay will receive a score of 0.

There is no formula for writing an effective essay. You are free to choose your own writing style. For example, you can write an essay that is narrative, expository, persuasive or argumentative. Furthermore, there are no guidelines on how to organize your essay; use the approach that best fits your topic and point of view. Good writing is not strict adherence to a formula; rather, it is the strong development of ideas, the ability to connect to an audience, precise use of language, effective organization and appropriate choices of evidence.

> **Keep in Mind**
>
> **You must use a pencil on the essay. Essays written in pen cannot be scanned and will appear blank (and receive a score of zero).**

Your essay will show how well you can develop, support and present your point of view. You will need to support your ideas with reasoning. You can draw on any part of your knowledge base that supports your reasoning, including any or all of the following:

- what you have learned in school
- what you have read in and outside of school in literature, science or other areas
- current events
- your extracurricular and outside activities
- your observations and your own experiences

You are not expected to produce a polished piece of writing in the 25 minutes that you have to write the essay. Readers scoring the essays know that you did not have the topic ahead of time or the time to make significant revisions.

**The First Section**

The essay is the *first* part of the SAT.

How well you write is more important than how much you write, but to cover the topic adequately you will probably need to write at least one page. Your essay must be completely written on the lines provided on your answer sheet. For an example of the answer sheet, look at the practice tests in the back of the book. You will have enough space if you write on every line, avoid wide margins and keep your handwriting to a reasonable size. It's important that your handwriting be legible. As long as your handwriting is clear, you may write in print or script. But remember that the SAT reader isn't familiar with your handwriting.

## How the Essays Are Scored

Essays written for the SAT are scored using a holistic approach. In holistic scoring, an essay is considered in its entirety rather than feature by feature. The reader reads the entire essay and determines a score based on an overall impression. To score essays written on specific topics, readers are trained to use the SAT Scoring Guide shown in Exhibit 9.1 in conjunction with sample essays illustrating each score point.

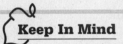
**Keep In Mind**

A perfect score for an essay is 12 (two scores of 6). The majority of papers will fall in the middle of the scoring range of 2 to 12.

The readers are on your side. They are urged to be positive and reward what is done well rather than to penalize what is done poorly. The readers know that the essays are written by high school students as first drafts under timed conditions. The readers are reminded to ignore handwriting and to avoid judging an essay by its length.

To ensure accurate and reliable scoring, two readers independently evaluate and score each essay on a scale of 1 to 6. Therefore, the combined score for readers will range from 2 to 12. If the readers' scores are different by more than one point on the six-point scale, a third reader, the scoring director, resolves the difference. On the SAT, fewer than 3 percent of the essays scored go to a third reader.

SAT readers, who are experienced high school teachers and college professors, receive extensive training and practice in holistic scoring using the Scoring Guide. The readers are required to qualify for scoring by completing a rigorous online training course that will familiarize them with holistic scoring and teach them to

**Keep In Mind**

If the readers' scores are different by more than one point on the six-point scale, a third reader, the scoring director, scores the essay.

evaluate essays. To qualify after training, a reader must score a high percentage of practice papers in exact agreement with the preassigned scores as determined by expert readers. During live scoring, the readers are monitored in real time, and scoring directors review readers' scoring of selected essays.

**Exhibit 9.1** SAT Scoring Guide

| Score of 6 | Score of 5 | Score of 4 |
|---|---|---|
| An essay in this category demonstrates *clear and consistent mastery,* although it may have a few minor errors. A typical essay | An essay in this category demonstrates *reasonably consistent mastery,* although it will have occasional errors or lapses in quality. A typical essay | An essay in this category demonstrates *adequate mastery,* although it will have lapses in quality. A typical essay |
| • effectively and insightfully develops a point of view on the issue and demonstrates outstanding critical thinking, using clearly appropriate examples, reasons and other evidence to support its position | • effectively develops a point of view on the issue and demonstrates strong critical thinking, generally using appropriate examples, reasons and other evidence to support its position | • develops a point of view on the issue and demonstrates competent critical thinking, using adequate examples, reasons and other evidence to support its position |
| • is well organized and clearly focused, demonstrating clear coherence and smooth progression of ideas | • is well organized and focused, demonstrating coherence and progression of ideas | • is generally organized and focused, demonstrating some coherence and progression of ideas |
| • exhibits skillful use of language, using a varied, accurate and apt vocabulary | • exhibits facility in the use of language, using appropriate vocabulary | • exhibits adequate but inconsistent facility in the use of language, using generally appropriate vocabulary |
| • demonstrates meaningful variety in sentence structure | • demonstrates variety in sentence structure | • demonstrates some variety in sentence structure |
| • is free of most errors in grammar, usage, and mechanics | • is generally free of most errors in grammar, usage, and mechanics | • has some errors in grammar, usage, and mechanics |

| Score of 3 | Score of 2 | Score of 1 |
|---|---|---|
| An essay in this category demonstrates *developing mastery,* and is marked by ONE OR MORE of the following weaknesses: | An essay in this category demonstrates *little mastery,* and is flawed by ONE OR MORE of the following weaknesses: | An essay in this category demonstrates *very little* or *no mastery,* and is severely flawed by ONE OR MORE of the following weaknesses: |
| • develops a point of view on the issue, demonstrating some critical thinking, but may do so inconsistently or use inadequate examples, reasons or other evidence to support its position | • develops a point of view on the issue that is vague or seriously limited, and demonstrates weak critical thinking, providing inappropriate or insufficient examples, reasons, or other evidence to support its position | • develops no viable point of view on the issue, or provides little or no evidence to support its position |
| • is limited in its organization or focus, or may demonstrate some lapses in coherence or progression of ideas | • is poorly organized and/or focused, or demonstrates serious problems with coherence or progression of ideas | • is disorganized or unfocused, resulting in a disjointed or incoherent essay |
| • displays developing facility in the use of language, but sometimes uses weak vocabulary or inappropriate word choice | • displays very little facility in the use of language, using very limited vocabulary or incorrect word choice | • displays fundamental errors in vocabulary |
| • lacks variety or demonstrates problems in sentence structure | • demonstrates frequent problems in sentence structure | • demonstrates severe flaws in sentence structure |
| • contains an accumulation of errors in grammar, usage and mechanics | • contains errors in grammar, usage and mechanics so serious that meaning is somewhat obscured | • contains pervasive errors in grammar, usage or mechanics that persistently interfere with meaning |

**Essays not written on the essay assignment will receive a score of zero.**

## Approaches to the Essay

▶ *Read the prompt carefully, and make sure you write on the topic given.* Essays not on topic will receive a zero.

▶ *Decide your viewpoint on the topic.* If you have trouble focusing on the main point, try completing this sentence: "When people finish reading my essay, I want them to understand that

_____

_____

_____

The words you use to fill in that blank might well become part of your thesis statement.

▶ *Spend a couple of minutes on planning.* Use your test booklet to create a quick sentence outline. Begin with the thesis from the above approach. Follow it with two or three single-sentence statements of examples or reasons you will use to develop your point of view. For example, suppose you are answering the essay question given as the sample later in this chapter:

> Think carefully about the issue presented in the following excerpt and the assignment below.
>
> > Some people believe that there is only one foolproof plan, perfect solution, or correct interpretation. But nothing is ever that simple. For better or worse, for every so-called final answer there is another way of seeing things. There is always a "however."
>
> **Assignment:** Is there always another explanation or another point of view? Plan and write an essay in which you develop your point of view on this issue. Support your position with reasoning and examples taken from your reading, studies, experience, or observations.

The student sample that scored a 6 may have been the result of an outline like this:

- Thesis: An attribute can be either a vice or a virtue, depending on a person's point of view.

- Point 1 — I had always believed that perfectionism was a virtue: it was a motivator to achieve high goals, which I had done.

- Point 2 — Later, I discovered that others, including a teacher, perceived my perfectionism to be a vice, resulting in fatigue, stress and illness.

- Conclusion — There is always a "however." I realized that perfectionism is neither all good nor all bad.

You have only 25 minutes to write your essay, so don't spend too much time outlining. A little planning time, however, may be essential to make sure that your essay does not stray too far from your focused thesis statement.

➤ *Vary the sentence structure in your writing.* Good writing uses a variety of sentence types to show the proper relationships between ideas. Simple sentences communicate single observations. Compound sentences show that two ideas are related and are roughly equal in weight, and complex sentences show that of two related ideas, one is more important than the other. Essays that receive high scores almost always use a variety of sentence structures. Sentence variety also makes your writing more engaging and easier to read! Remember that as you write. Here are samples of the three kinds of sentences:

- *Simple:* "My best friend lives two blocks away from me." This sentence is called *simple* because there is one subject — "my friend" — and one verb — "lives." It makes a single observation.

- *Compound:* "My best friend lives two blocks away from me, but her house is much nicer than mine." This sentence is *compound* because it comprises what could be two or more simple sentences that are connected with one of the words we call coordinating conjunctions — *and, or, but, for* or *nor.* These words indicate that there is a relationship between these two observations and that the two statements are of roughly equal importance. You may learn that the words *so* and *yet* sometimes function as coordinating conjunctions as well. Either half of the compound sentence could have been a simple sentence by itself.

- *Complex:* "Although my friend lives two blocks away from me, I don't go to her house very often." This sentence is *complex* because it contains two observations but they are *not* of equal importance. The first one — "although my friend lives two blocks away from me" — cannot be written as a simple sentence because of the connecting word "although." That word, called a *subordinating conjunction,* expresses the relationship between the two ideas and indicates that the other observation, the one that does not begin with a subordinating conjunction, is the more important one. The fact that you don't go to your friend's house very often is, in this sentence, more important than the fact that she lives only two blocks away.

All your ideas will not be related to each other in the same way, so you should *vary* the sentence structure that communicates how your ideas are related to each other.

➤ *Use clear, precise and appropriate vocabulary.* Appropriate words are accurate and specific, not necessarily long and obscure. Avoid too many abstract and indefinite words, and seek concrete, specific ones in their place. Consider the differences in these two sentences:

1. The place where we stopped to eat was full of people dressed up more than we were.

2. The restaurant where we stopped for lunch was full of men wearing jackets and ties and women wearing suits and dresses — a noticeable contrast to our jeans and T-shirts.

Although the first sentence is grammatically correct, it is general and unspecific. A reader will not easily see the contrast between the speaker and the other people in the restaurant. The second version creates a much more concrete and vivid image in the reader's mind, and it communicates more effectively the contrast between the speaker and the other customers.

The sentence is not improved by substituting unnecessarily fancy words where concrete, everyday ones do just fine: "The dining establishment where we rested for our midday repast was peopled with representatives of the paying public who wore garments more typically associated with the office and business world than our comfortable and casual attire."

Good writing uses mature and sophisticated language, but some writers think readers are impressed by fancy vocabulary and convoluted sentences. Those writers are wrong.

➤ *Leave time to review what you've written.* Although you won't have time for full-scale revision, do leave time for rereading your essay and making minor changes in the wording or even in the structure of what you have written. Occasionally a more appropriate word, or a clearer way to make a point, will occur to you. Don't be afraid to make these minor changes if they improve your essay.

## Writing Exercise: Using Action Verbs

Writing exercises and practice can help you prepare further for the essay component of the SAT. One of the best ways you can improve your writing is to minimize the use of the same verb — especially the verb *to be*.

Reliance on the verb *to be* in any of its eight parts (*be, am, are, is, was, were, being, been*) makes your writing sluggish and unclear. More than any other kind of word, the verbs you use communicate what is happening so, whenever possible, try to use a verb to convey the *action* of your sentence. For example, consider this sentence:

"The decision of the manager to bring about an end to the practice of overtime assignments and schedule the right number of workers in the first place was greeted with approval by a unanimous number of workers."

What a horrible sentence! It limps along until the passive verb "was greeted," and it mercifully ends a few words later. (A verb or sentence is *passive,* or in the passive voice, if someone or something other than the subject performs its actions. In this case, the actual subject of the sentence is "decision," but the action, the greeting, was done by the workers. A sentence in which the subject performs the action is called an *active* sentence.) The main idea of the sentence, however, has little to do with greeting. It is supposed to communicate the fact that workers *approved* something that the manager *decided* to do.

you have a few choices available. Suppose you want to indicate the *time* sequence. You could write:

> "After the manager decided to stop assigning overtime and to schedule the right number of workers in the first place, the workers unanimously approved the manager's decision."

On the other hand, if you want to indicate *cause,* you could write:

> "Because the manager decided to stop assigning overtime and to schedule the right number of workers in the first place, the workers unanimously approved the manager's decision."

Yet you are not happy about the repeated word "decided/decision." Should you change one of them? Can you do that without confusing the reader? Yes, you can, when you realize that it is the decision of the first clause that the workers approve. What you have been trying to communicate is:

> "Workers unanimously approved the manager's decision to stop assigning overtime and to schedule the right number of workers in the first place."

How much better that reads than the original version! Here's the original sentence again:

> "The decision of the manager to bring about an end to the practice of overtime assignments and schedule the right number of workers in the first place was greeted with approval by a unanimous number of workers."

To sum up, you have made the following improvements:

- You have expressed the action of the sentence as a verb.

- You have used the subject of the sentence to tell who performed that action.

- You have reduced the number of abstract nouns.

- You have reduced the number of prepositional phrases.

Following are a few more unclear sentences that need the same type of revision as in the example. You may find this process slow at first, but with practice, you will make these revisions quickly.

Work out your revisions, and then compare them to the suggested revisions that follow. Remember that there will be several good revisions available for each. Yours will be good if you follow these suggestions:

- Avoid the verb *to be* in favor of a verb that communicates action.

- Reduce the number of abstract nouns.

- Replace prepositional phrases with single-word adjectives a~~ you can.

1. *Original:* The price [of the toy] [on the shelf] [of the store] *was intended* to be a reflection [of the hard work] [of many workers] and the high cost [of materials].
   *Rewrite:* The toys [on the shelf] *cost* so much because a lot [of people] *worked* hard to make them and the materials *were* expensive.

2. *Original:* [Under the management] [of the new owners] [of the store] the store *is designed* to serve the basic needs [of the majority] [of the people] [in the neighborhood].
   *Rewrite:* The new owners *will manage* the store so that it serves most [of the neighborhood people's needs].

3. *Original:* The audience *was impressed* [by the skill] [of the actors] and the imagination [of the director] [of the film] [at the theater] [around the corner] [from my house].
   *Rewrite:* The actors' skill and the director's imagination *impressed* the audience who *attended* the theater [around the corner] [from my house].
   *Or:* The actors' skill and the director's imagination *impressed* the audience who *attended* the neighborhood theater.

4. *Original:* The most important idea [in the introduction] [of the essay] *is* [at the end] [of the paragraph] that *is found* [at the beginning] [of the paper].
   *Rewrite:* In the introduction to the essay, the most important idea *is found* at the end of the first paragraph.

# Writing Exercise: Using Abstract and Concrete Language

Another way to improve your writing is to recognize the difference between *abstract* language and *concrete* language — and to provide concrete illustrations whenever you write about something abstract.

For example, when you read a word like *success,* you know what it means, but you probably also know that the same word will mean something different to someone else. On the other hand, "a score of 520 on the SAT math section" means the same to anyone who reads it. This is true because *success* is an abstract word, whereas "a score of 520" is a concrete expression.

What would you consider to be an example of success? For some, it might be a position on the varsity tennis team. For others, it might be passing a driver's test.

All these examples can be seen as concrete illustrations of the abstract term *success.* If you are writing about success, you do not clarify your meaning by providing synonyms, such as *achievement, accomplishment* or *reaching a goal.* You achieve clarity by providing specific illustrations so that your reader knows what *you* mean by the term.

### Example Exercise: Using Concrete Language

How would you illustrate success? Write three concrete illustrations of success here:

1. _____

2. _____

3. _____

### Example Exercise: Using Abstract Language

*Beauty,* *happiness* and *courage* are three other abstract nouns. How would you illustrate them? Provide three examples of each of them, and then, if possible, compare your responses to a friend's.

*Beauty:*

1. _____

2. _____

3. _____

*Happiness:*

1. _____

2. _____

3. _____

*Courage:*

1. _____

2. _____

3. _____

If we examine the sentence for words that contain some potential for action, we'll see many: *decision, bring, end, practice, assignments, scheduling, workers, greeting* and *approval.* Unfortunately, none of these can be the *verb* of the sentence because they appear in other grammatical structures (i.e., in this sentence, they appear as abstract nouns, infinitives and gerunds, which are defined and illustrated in the section below). Each functions as the subject or the object of a preposition, but not as a verb. If you could revise the sentence so that one or more of these potential verbs becomes the action-bearing word, you will have a more dynamic and accurate sentence.

## Quick Grammar Review

Although you will not be asked to define or use grammatical terms on the SAT, familiarity with the preceding grammatical terms will make it easier to understand the principles of this writing exercise on action verbs. Here are some definitions:

- *Abstract nouns* are those nouns (i.e., naming words) that refer to ideas, thoughts or intangible things. The abstract nouns in the sample sentence are *decision, end, practice, assignments,* and *approval.* They are general rather than specific.

- *Infinitives* are verb forms that use the word *to.* In the sample sentence, the infinitive is "to bring." Other examples are "We hoped *to see* our cousin during her visit," or "What do you want *to do* with the money you've earned?"

- *Gerunds* are specialized verb forms that end in "-ing," take the place of nouns and indicate an action of some kind. In the sentence "*Running* is an excellent form of exercise," *running* is a gerund because it takes the place of a noun and names an action. Not all words ending in "-ing" are gerunds, but all gerunds end in "-ing."

- *Present participles* are also verb forms that end in "-ing." Instead of naming an action, though, the participle describes a noun. For example, the word *singing* can be either a gerund or a present participle depending on its use. In the sentence "*Singing* makes me feel happy," it is a gerund because it names an action. In the sentence "The *singing* bird woke me up at four o'clock," it is a participle because it describes the bird.

- A *preposition* is a word that shows a particular relationship, such as direction or location, between a noun and the rest of the sentence. Prepositions are usually very short words, such as *in, of, to* or *by.* Prepositions are usually followed by nouns, which are called their *objects.* In the following illustrations, the preposition is italicized and the object is underlined:
  - the rooms *in* my <u>house</u>
  - the name *of* my <u>friend</u>
  - the trip *to* <u>Chicago</u>
  - the tree *by* my <u>window</u>

- A *prepositional phrase* contains a preposition and its object and whatever describing words accompany that object.

## Revising Sentences to Use Action Verbs

If you revise your sentences so that the verb indicates the action and the subject tells who or what performed that action, you will probably see three other improvements:

1. You will change the passive voice to active.

2. You will reduce the number of abstract nouns.

3. You will eliminate strings of prepositional phrases.

If you decide that the real action of the sample sentence lies in the word *approval,* begin by making that the verb. Then decide who approved of what. You should be able to construct this much of the sentence so far:

"Workers approved when the manager decided . . ."

Now you can add the details from the original sentence that you think are necessary:

"Workers unanimously approved when the manager decided to bring about an end to the practice of overtime assignments and schedule the right number of workers in the first place."

This revision is much better, but it is not as good as it can be. There are still several abstract nouns: *end, practice, assignments.* Take a moment and determine if these nouns imply actions (they do), and who performs these actions. Do the workers end, practice and assign? Or does the manager do these things? Once you think about it, you'll realize it's the manager who ends, the manager who practices and the manager who assigns. This is a lot of activity hiding in nonaction words, and all of it is being done by someone who is not the subject of the sentence. How can you express this action with the manager as the subject?

"The manager decided to end assigning overtime and to schedule the right number of workers in the first place."

Instead of "to end assigning overtime," you would probably write:

"The manager decided to stop assigning overtime . . ."

You see that you don't need the word "practice" at all. You've eliminated one unnecessary abstract noun. Now you have two sentences:

"The manager decided to stop assigning overtime and to schedule the right number of workers in the first place."

"Workers unanimously approved the manager's decision."

You can leave this revision as two sentences if you like. These two sentences are certainly clearer than the original. But you might also realize that there is a relationship between them, and you want to combine them in a way that communicates that relationship. Because the relationship is chronological (i.e., the decision came first, then the approval after) or causative (i.e., the decision caused the approval), you have a few choices available. Suppose you want to indicate the *time* sequence. You could write:

"After the manager decided to stop assigning overtime and to schedule the right number of workers in the first place, the workers unanimously approved the manager's decision."

On the other hand, if you want to indicate *cause,* you could write:

"Because the manager decided to stop assigning overtime and to schedule the right number of workers in the first place, the workers unanimously approved the manager's decision."

Yet you are not happy about the repeated word "decided/decision." Should you change one of them? Can you do that without confusing the reader? Yes, you can, when you realize that it is the decision of the first clause that the workers approve. What you have been trying to communicate is:

"Workers unanimously approved the manager's decision to stop assigning overtime and to schedule the right number of workers in the first place."

How much better that reads than the original version! Here's the original sentence again:

"The decision of the manager to bring about an end to the practice of overtime assignments and schedule the right number of workers in the first place was greeted with approval by a unanimous number of workers."

To sum up, you have made the following improvements:

- You have expressed the action of the sentence as a verb.

- You have used the subject of the sentence to tell who performed that action.

- You have reduced the number of abstract nouns.

- You have reduced the number of prepositional phrases.

Following are a few more unclear sentences that need the same type of revision as in the example. You may find this process slow at first, but with practice, you will make these revisions quickly.

Work out your revisions, and then compare them to the suggested revisions that follow. Remember that there will be several good revisions available for each. Yours will be good if you follow these suggestions:

- Avoid the verb *to be* in favor of a verb that communicates action.

- Reduce the number of abstract nouns.

- Replace prepositional phrases with single-word adjectives and adverbs when you can.

## Example Exercise: Rewriting Sentences Using Action Verbs

1.  The price of the toy on the shelf of the store was intended to be a reflection of the hard work of many workers and the high cost of materials.

    *Rewrite:*

    _____

    _____

    _____

2.  Under the management of the new owners of the store the store is designed to serve the basic needs of the majority of the people in the neighborhood.

    *Rewrite:*

    _____

    _____

    _____

3.  The audience was impressed by the skill of the actors and the imagination of the director of the film at the theater around the corner from my house.

    *Rewrite:*

    _____

    _____

    _____

4.  The most important idea in the introduction of the essay is at the end of the paragraph that is found at the beginning of the paper.

    *Rewrite:*

    _____

    _____

    _____

### POSSIBLE REWRITES THAT IMPROVE THE ORIGINAL SENTENCES

Here are some possible responses to the exercise. Yours may or may not look like these, but successful ones will share the features mentioned above. The original sentence comes first, followed by a suggested revision. The verbs are italicized and the prepositional phrases are placed within brackets.

### *Example Exercise: Using Concrete Language*

How would you illustrate success? Write three concrete illustrations of success here:

1. _____

2. _____

3. _____

### *Example Exercise: Using Abstract Language*

*Beauty, happiness* and *courage* are three other abstract nouns. How would you illustrate them? Provide three examples of each of them, and then, if possible, compare your responses to a friend's.

*Beauty:*

1. _____

2. _____

3. _____

*Happiness:*

1. _____

2. _____

3. _____

*Courage:*

1. _____

2. _____

3. _____

1. *Original:* The price [of the toy] [on the shelf] [of the store] *was intended* to be a reflection [of the hard work] [of many workers] and the high cost [of materials].

   *Rewrite:* The toys [on the shelf] *cost* so much because a lot [of people] *worked* hard to make them and the materials *were* expensive.

2. *Original:* [Under the management] [of the new owners] [of the store] the store *is designed* to serve the basic needs [of the majority] [of the people] [in the neighborhood].

   *Rewrite:* The new owners *will manage* the store so that it serves most [of the neighborhood people's needs].

3. *Original:* The audience *was impressed* [by the skill] [of the actors] and the imagination [of the director] [of the film] [at the theater] [around the corner] [from my house].

   *Rewrite:* The actors' skill and the director's imagination *impressed* the audience who *attended* the theater [around the corner] [from my house].

   *Or:* The actors' skill and the director's imagination *impressed* the audience who *attended* the neighborhood theater.

4. *Original:* The most important idea [in the introduction] [of the essay] *is* [at the end] [of the paragraph] that *is found* [at the beginning] [of the paper].

   *Rewrite:* In the introduction to the essay, the most important idea *is found* at the end of the first paragraph.

# Writing Exercise: Using Abstract and Concrete Language

Another way to improve your writing is to recognize the difference between *abstract* language and *concrete* language — and to provide concrete illustrations whenever you write about something abstract.

For example, when you read a word like *success,* you know what it means, but you probably also know that the same word will mean something different to someone else. On the other hand, "a score of 520 on the SAT math section" means the same to anyone who reads it. This is true because *success* is an abstract word, whereas "a score of 520" is a concrete expression.

What would you consider to be an example of success? For some, it might be a position on the varsity tennis team. For others, it might be passing a driver's test.

All these examples can be seen as concrete illustrations of the abstract term *success.* If you are writing about success, you do not clarify your meaning by providing synonyms, such as *achievement, accomplishment* or *reaching a goal.* You achieve clarity by providing specific illustrations so that your reader knows what *you* mean by the term.

Most of the time, you know a word is abstract because you have a sense of its meaning. In some cases, however, the end of the word tells us it is an abstract noun. Common abstract noun endings include -age (as you saw in *courage*), -ance, -ment, -ness (as you saw in *happiness*), -ity (or just -ty, as you saw in *beauty*) and -tion. Although many abstract nouns have no such endings, so many do that it is a good idea to become familiar with them. Can you think of examples of abstract nouns with each of these suffixes?

-age                    -ance                   -ment

_____         _____         _____

_____         _____         _____

_____         _____         _____

-ness                   -ity or -ty             -tion

_____         _____         _____

_____         _____         _____

_____         _____         _____

## Example Exercise: Writing Concrete Descriptions of Abstract Concepts

To help improve the clarity of your writing, look again at several of the abstract words you provided, and think of illustrations that would make the terms more concrete for a reader:

*Abstract word:* _____

*Concrete illustrations:* _____

_____

_____

*Abstract word:* _____

*Concrete illustrations:* _____

_____

_____

Abstract word: _____

Concrete illustrations: _____

_____

_____

# The Benefit of Using Both Abstract and Concrete Language

You may have realized already that there is a strong parallel between the concepts of abstract/concrete and general/specific. Abstract words tend to be general. They concern ideas rather than things, the intangible rather than the tangible. Their value is their ability to communicate thoughts, feelings and opinions. Most of your essays (in high school, in college and on the SAT) will be about ideas rather than things. Your thesis statement is probably going to be an observation about an idea, a principle, a theory or a belief — in other words, something abstract.

Essays that discuss only concrete topics — such as a car, a piece of jewelry or a friend who moved away — and that never present any abstract ideas about those concrete things will probably not effectively connect to your audience. For example, your friend who moved away is important to you, but until you *connect* that event in the reader's mind with an *abstract idea,* such as loneliness, or loss, or loyalty, that friend's absence doesn't mean much to the reader. Similarly, a ring that you inherited from your grandmother is precious to you, but it's not precious to your reader until you write of it in terms of its sentimental value, your family's heritage, your grandmother's generosity or your love for her — all of which are abstract concepts. The best essays are about *ideas,* and you should develop them with appropriate concrete illustrations to clarify your position on those ideas.

A frequent observation among teachers of writing (and readers of examination essays) is that student writers do not provide enough concrete illustrations. They rarely feel that a student essay has too many facts. How can you, as a writer, be sure that you have enough concrete information in your essay? For example, read this opening paragraph from E. B. White's essay "Once More to the Lake," and observe his use of abstract language (underlined) and concrete illustrations (in italics):

"One summer, along about *1904,* my father rented a camp on *a lake in Maine* and took us all there for *the month of August.* We all got *ringworm from some kittens* and had to rub *Pond's Extract* on *our arms and legs night and morning,* and my *father rolled over in a canoe with all his clothes on;* but outside of that the vacation was a <u>success</u> and from then on none of us ever thought there was any place in the world like *that lake in Maine.* We returned summer after summer — always *on August 1st for one month.* I have since become a saltwater man, but sometimes in summer there are days when the <u>restlessness</u> *of the tides* and fearful <u>cold</u> *of the sea water* and *incessant wind that blows across the afternoon and into the evening* make me wish for the <u>placidity</u> of a lake in the woods. A few weeks ago this <u>feeling</u> got so strong I bought myself *a couple of bass hooks and a spinner* and returned to the lake where we used to go, for *a week's fishing* and to revisit old haunts."

White's abstract ideas, especially <u>success</u> and <u>placidity</u>, are well illustrated by the many concrete details he provides (again, in italics). Although you may not consider a month of camping by a lake in Maine to be a successful family vacation — you might prefer an amusement park or a city's museums and theaters — you still know exactly what White is talking about and his opinion on that subject. How much less satisfying this paragraph would be if he had written the following:

"My father used to take us on vacation, but we all got sick and he fell in the water. Even so, we had a good time. We always used to go to the same place around the same time of year. After I grew up I liked other things, but sometimes I miss the old family place, so I got some old fishing gear and went back."

Obviously, the ability to manage abstract and concrete language makes a tremendous difference in the success of White's writing here.

A point worth noting is that proper nouns (i.e., those that begin with capital letters) and numbers are very concrete. The presence of such concrete language, when possible, gives your writing specificity — which makes your writing more interesting.

## Example Exercise: Rewriting Sentences Using Concrete Language

For each of the abstract statements below, rewrite the sentence and make it more concrete by providing specific language.

1. What we did yesterday afternoon was lots of fun.

*Rewrite:*

_____

_____

_____

2. I have strong feelings about the attitude you are expressing on that topic.

*Rewrite:*

_____

_____

_____

3. That is my favorite performer singing that song on the radio.

*Rewrite:*

_____

_____

_____

4. That book is the most amazing thing I have ever read.

*Rewrite:*

_____

_____

_____

5. When my friend told me her news, I thought she was the luckiest girl in the world.

*Rewrite:*

_____

_____

_____

6. If you want to be healthy, you have to take care of yourself.

*Rewrite:*

_____

_____

_____

## POSSIBLE REWRITES THAT IMPROVE THE ORIGINAL SENTENCES

Following are some possible revisions of the preceding sentences. Yours will certainly be quite different, depending on what concrete details you have included. In these sample responses, the concrete details are printed in italics.

1. **Original:** What we did yesterday afternoon was lots of fun.
   **Rewrite:** *The trip to the mall and the ride on the roller coaster* were lots of fun.

2. **Original:** I have strong feelings about the attitude you are expressing on that topic.
   **Rewrite:** I feel very *worried* when I hear *how stubbornly you defend the bullies* who *tease children.*

3. *Original:* That is my favorite performer singing that song on the radio.
   *Rewrite:* That is my favorite singer, *Miley Cyrus,* singing *"See You Again"* on the radio.

4. *Original:* That book is the most amazing thing I have ever read.
   *Rewrite:* Of all the books I have ever read, *The Samurai's Garden* best showed me *how selfless love can be.*

5. *Original:* When my friend told me her news, I thought she was the luckiest girl in the world.
   *Rewrite:* When Louisa told me *that she had won a basketball scholarship,* I thought she was the luckiest girl in the world.

6. *Original:* If you want to be healthy, you have to take care of yourself.
   *Rewrite:* If you want to be healthy, you have to eat *fruits and vegetables,* get at least *a half hour of exercise every day* and *sleep seven hours a night.*

## Sample Essays

The rest of this chapter offers examples from students that illustrate every possible score. Although all of the sample essays were *handwritten* by students, they are shown *typed* here, in boxes, for ease of reading. However, we are presenting one in handwriting to remind you that it is important to write legibly and clearly. The essays have been typed *exactly* as each student wrote his or her essay, without any corrections to spelling, punctuation or paragraph breaks.

The following is a sample prompt:

 **Automated Score**

To receive an automated score for your response to this essay question, check out *The Official SAT Online Course* at www.collegeboard.org/satonlinecourse.

> Think carefully about the issue presented in the following excerpt and the assignment below.
>
> > Some people believe that there is only one foolproof plan, perfect solution, or correct interpretation. But nothing is ever that simple. For better or worse, for every so-called final answer there is another way of seeing things. There is always a "however."
>
> **Assignment:** Is there always another explanation or another point of view? Plan and write an essay in which you develop your point of view on this issue. Support your position with reasoning and examples taken from your reading, studies, experience, or observations.

*Essay #1: This essay received a score of 6.*

Part A (Writing Sample)       Begin your composition on this side. If you need more space, continue on the reverse side.

I admit, with pride, that I am a perfectionist. ~~with pride~~.
I see it as the force which motivates me to
achieve high goals. I owe my good grades,
my success as a dancer as well as my
organized room to my drive to be perfect.
However, others view my perfectionism as
a flaw. Others see me crying over the
"B+" I received on the math test and
blame my "emotional instability," as they call
it, on my perfectionism. Whether one considers it is a vice
or a virtue depends on his or her point
of view.

May is AP Test season and for me
that means severely high levels of stress.
I could be spotted walking down the halls
of the school with my Barron's AP
World History book under my right arm
and a highlighter in my pocket It
was imperative that I study hard enough
to receive a grade of "5" on the ~~test~~
~~I~~ All my stressing and constant studying
gave me ~~dark~~ dark circles under my eyes

Continue on the reverse side if necessary.

and a ~~strong~~ head cold. ~~I~~ One day, shortly before the ~~test,~~ ~~end of~~ my french teacher approached me and asked me if I was alright. I explained that I was just tired and stressed from studying for APs. She paused when I finished speaking. Then she stared me straight in the eye and said, "Everyone choses their own poison." I was dumbfounded. What did she mean? Then it dawned on me; she see's my drive for perfection in the spring that feeds my ultimate downfall. My perfectionism is my vice, according to her and yet all this time I thought it was my greatest virtue.

Now I understand that my perfectionism is not "all good"; it was after all responsible for the lack of plenty of sleep as well as being responsible for my head cold. However, I maintain that it is not "all bad" either. I ~~continued to~~ study for the AP World History test ~~and~~, although the scores are not back yet, I have a hunch I did well on it. So is perfectionism a vice or a virtue? It depends on whom you are talking to.

### WHY ESSAY #1 RECEIVED A SCORE OF 6

This response demonstrates *clear and consistent mastery* by insightfully exploring the writer's drive for perfectionism. The writer effectively develops the position that whether another person considers this perfectionism "a vice or virtue depends on his or her point of view." This response demonstrates *outstanding* critical thinking by not only describing the writer's own intense motivation and the resulting physical and emotional strain, but also by providing examples of ways that others negatively see the writer's drive. ("Others see me crying over the 'B+' I received on the math test and blame my 'emotional instability,' as they call it, on my perfectionism." "My perfectionism is my vice, according to her and yet all this time I thought it was my greatest virtue.")

By considering others' viewpoints, the writer is able to look more objectively at his or her motivation. ("Now I understand that my perfectionism is not 'all good,' it was after all responsible for the lack of plenty of sleep as well as being responsible for my head cold. However, I maintain that it is not 'all bad' either.") This well-organized essay smoothly moves from one idea to the next, demonstrating a clear coherence. Using a varied, accurate and apt vocabulary, the essay exhibits the skillful use of language and demonstrates a meaningful variety in sentence structure ("May is AP test season and for me that means severely high levels of stress. I could be spotted walking down the halls of the school with my *Barron's AP World History* book under my right arm and a highlighter in my pocket. It was imperative that I study hard enough to receive a grade of '5' on the test"). This *outstanding* response scored a 6.

*Essay #2: This essay also received a score of 6.*

There is always a "however." Each situation has its benefits and its drawbacks. In the field of market finance, we find a compelling example that supports this thesis.

The Roaring Twenties was a decade during which the American economy saw a rapid boom. In fact, America's bull markets, such as the New York Stock Exchange had become so financially inviting by 1927 that even America's middle class poured its money into America's financial forums. Unfortunately, on October 4, 1929 the Booming Twenties came to an abrupt halt when the New York Stock Exchange crashed.

The Crash had many negative consequences. Most notably, the stock market crash of 1929 launched America into the Great Depression, a time of starvation and unemployment for millions of American citizens. The widespread optimism of the 1920's quickly turned into an almost suicidal pessimism. Indeed, the Great Depression represents a crippling consequence of the stock market crash of 1929.

However, Franklin Delano Roosevelt established institutions and regulations to prevent future economic catastrophes. Cognizant of the Crash's causes, such as pool corruption, overpriced stock values, and margin buying, Roosevelt implemented the Social Security Act, the FDIC, and stricter rules monitoring credit. His aggressive policies not only ameliorated the uncomfortable climate of the Great Depression, but also laid the groundwork for a safer, more successful economy.

The American public also realized the many positive results of the stock market crash of 1929. In particular, American citizens now have an entirely different fiscal outlook from the one they had before the Crash. Speculators have proven to be more prudent and insightful, as they often research market trends before investing. Perhaps most importantly, American investors are not as easily swayed by popular optimism and eager advertisement.

 While the stock market crash of 1929 was the embryo of the Great Depression, the Crash also set the foundation for a sounder economy. If we recognize the good and the bad of the Crash, we are destined to make fewer economic mistakes.

### WHY ESSAY #2 RECEIVED A SCORE OF 6

In this *outstanding* essay, the writer develops insightfully the main idea that "Each situation has its benefits and its drawbacks" by focusing on how the tragedy of the 1929 stock market crash and the Great Depression necessitated changes that led eventually to a sounder national economy. This response demonstrates *outstanding* critical thinking by demonstrating that while the 1929 Crash "launched America into the Great Depression," it also motivated Franklin Delano Roosevelt to instigate changes that "laid the groundwork for a safer, more successful economy" and provided Americans with valuable financial lessons.

 Paragraphs two and three describe the devastation that followed the crash of the 1920s' booming economy. Paragraphs four and five explore the idea that while the Great Depression was a time of "almost suicidal pessimism," positive actions were taken to ensure that such a catastrophe would not occur again.

 This well-organized essay uses clearly focused and appropriate details to demonstrate a smooth progression of ideas. Using a varied, apt and accurate vocabulary, the writer exhibits a skillful use of language. ("The American public also realized the many positive results of the stock market crash of 1929. In particular, American citizens now have an entirely different fiscal outlook from the one they had before the Crash.") This essay demonstrates *clear and consistent mastery* and scored a 6.

*Essay #3: This essay received a score of 5.*

The statement "There is always a 'however'" is extremely accurate, for most things in life come with conditions. Most of the time it is not always as easy as saying that you want to do something and then doing it, or saying that you want something and then getting it. There is always some sort of condition or stipulation set by someone else that you must follow. This word 'however' is especially relevant to teenagers, whose parents and teachers take advantage of it to spoil whatever plans or ideas they may have had.

Take for example a typical teenage boy who has just been assigned a project to do in his history class. The teacher begins the assignment with, "You have full freedom to choose the topic of your project." And here marks the entrance of the dreadful 'however.' The teacher continues, "HOWEVER, the project must have some relevance to the current situation in the Middle East." The boy's head, which had previously been swimming with ideas, was now drained of all topics, for he had no clue what was happening in the Middle East. Then the boy finally comes up with a topic and goes to discuss it with his teacher. The teacher begins, "That is a very intelligent and well thought out idea." The boy is elated, but then that word rears its ugly head. The teacher continues, "HOWEVER, it is not relevant enough to the situation at hand." And that one word has singlehandedly ruined that boy's day.

Another example would be a teenage girl getting ready for a night out with her friends. She is just about to walk out the door when her mother begins, "Your outfit is very lovely." Automatically the girl becomes suspicious. The mother continues,

"HOWEVER, I cannot let you leave this house wearing it." The girl changes her outfit and returns when her mother begins again, "You may take my car." The girl is excited, for she was afraid she would have to walk. Then the mother continues, "HOWEVER, you must bring it back by 9:30." And the girl's evening plans are cut short and her night is ruined.

The word however is very powerful. It has the ability to ruin entire days and nights when used incorrectly. The modern teenager especially feels the harsh usage of 'however', for his or her teachers and parents always make some sort of condition or stipulation on every activity that he or she wants to participate in.

### WHY ESSAY #3 RECEIVED A SCORE OF 5

In this essay, the writer effectively develops the main idea that parents and teachers use the word *however* to destroy the plans of the modern teenager by making "some sort of condition or stipulation on every activity that he or she wants to participate in." The essay demonstrates strong critical thinking by providing four appropriate, focused examples of instances when an initial offer from an adult is ruined by a subsequent "however."

This focused response is well organized, moving easily from example to example and demonstrating a progression of ideas. The writer consistently exhibits facility in the use of language and demonstrates variety in sentence structure. ("The teacher continues, 'HOWEVER, the project must have some relevance to the current situation in the Middle East.' The boy's head, which had previously been swimming with ideas, was now drained of all topics, for he had no clue what was happening in the Middle East.")

To receive a score of 6, this response needs to demonstrate *outstanding* critical thinking by using the evidence more insightfully to develop the position instead of simply providing one example after another. Overall, this *effective* response demonstrates *reasonably consistent mastery* and scored a 5.

**Essay #4: This essay also received a score of 5.**

There is always a "however." Is it not true that every little situation in life seems to always have some sort of a catch to it? Whether it be a "but", or "however"; or even "one more thing", everything seems to come already attached to something else. There is this one episode of the TV show "Friends", where Joey challenges Phoebe to find and act on a perfectly selfless deed. Just one little example is all she had to find, but as we see through her search, finding a selfless deed is not as easy as it may sound. This also relates to the infamous Holden Caulfield of J.D. Salinger's "Catcher in the Rye" In Holden's search for "true people", he continuously ends up disappointed, finding faults with every person he meets and placing them under his "phony category" And in this crazy world of today we all strive to achieve and "get ahead", but with each thing that one person gains, it becomes unavailable for another

In Phoebe's quest to find a selfless deed, she finds it almost impossible to prove Joey wrong as with every good deed that we perform, we feel good about ourselves. Even if the deed is a total sacrifice onto yourself, you end up feeling better about you as a person, and how you helped mankind just a little. And so this "however" permeates each and every aspect of our lives, even managing to butt in to self sacrifices, good deeds, and random acts of kindness.

In Holden's case he finds the "however" in everything. Seeing lawyers not as protectors of justice and the law, but rather as greedy people who love the thrill and power of conducting themselves within the law. Holden manages to find the "phony" in everyone, and hurts himself by never seeing the good in people.

    While this "however" might exist and be found to intertwine itself in most situations of life, we as humans can't dwell on it. Because to dwell on all the "buts" and "howevers" of life, would only bring negative and depressing feelings. With everything in life, you can gain something, but in consequence, someone else will lose what you gain. It is an ongoing cycle called life. Life is a tryout, an audition, an application, and as long as you try your best and at least try to avoid the "howevers", you should be okay.

### WHY ESSAY #4 RECEIVED A SCORE OF 5

This response demonstrates *reasonably consistent mastery* by developing effectively the point of view that "every little situation in life seems to always have some sort of a catch to it." The writer demonstrates strong critical thinking by selecting two appropriate examples of how a character's search for "truth" is, for different reasons, unsuccessful because of a "however." The writer uses an episode of *Friends* to illustrate the idea that, because there is always an attachment to the gratification from helping others and performing "good deeds," perfectly selfless acts do not exist. The response also explores how Holden Caulfield's focus on the negative aspects of people prevents him from ever "seeing the good in people" or finding "true people."

The writer concludes by acknowledging the inevitability of "howevers" and "buts" in the life cycle and advocates not letting them become distractions from the positive aspects of life. There is a variety in sentence structure. ("Just one little example is all she had to find, but as we see through her search, finding a selfless deed is not as easy as it may sound. This also relates to the infamous Holden Caulfield of J. D. Salinger's 'Catcher in the Rye' In Holden's search for 'true people,' he continuously ends up disappointed, finding faults with every person he meets and placing them under his 'phony category.'")

To receive a score of 6, this essay would have to exhibit a stronger organizational structure and smoother progression of ideas by focusing on fully developing one example before moving to the next. This *effective* essay scored a 5.

**Essay #5: This essay received a score of 4.**

I most certainly agree with the thesis "There is always a 'however.'-" Both history and literature bear witness to the undeniable fact that no matter how a situation may seem, there will always be another factor to consider that may shed a new light on the circumstance

The conclusion of the Second World War can perhaps exemplify this maxim. Although the Allied powers reigned triumphant over fascism, there was a "however" that would perhaps marr their victory. This "however" was the establishing threat of Communism. Despite the colossal victory the Allies had achieved, there was still another aspect, a "however" that was inevitable

Literature as well is a testament to this thesis, as evidenced by the tragic play of Romeo and Juliet. Overcoming almost insurmountable odds, the scion and daughter of family rivalries fall in deep and true love. "However," their love is offset by the consuming hatred between their families. Although the situation as in the end of World War II seemed hopeful and bright, there are always "however" that offset the circumstances

As both history and great works of literature attest to, there can be no consummately perfect (or disasterous situation without at least one "however." This statement is indeed proven veritable.

### WHY ESSAY #5 RECEIVED A SCORE OF 4

This response demonstrates *adequate mastery* by developing the point of view that "Both history and literature bear witness to the undeniable fact that no matter how a situation may seem, there will always be another factor to consider that may shed a new light on the circumstance." The writer demonstrates competent critical thinking by selecting two adequate examples to illustrate situations that seem "hopeful and bright" but are clouded by the inevitable "however." Paragraph two discusses how the "colossal victory the Allies had achieved" at the end of World War II was marred by the "threat of Communism." Paragraph three briefly discusses Romeo and Juliet's forbidden love.

The response is generally focused and demonstrates some progression of ideas and coherence. The writer exhibits adequate facility in the use of language and displays some variety in sentence structure. ("Although the Allied powers reigned triumphant over fascism, there was a 'however' that would perhaps marr their victory. This 'however' was the establishing threat of Communism. Despite the colossal victory the Allies had achieved, there was still another aspect, a 'however' that was inevitable.") Although this response is *competent,* to achieve a higher score, the writer would need to develop the point of view more effectively by demonstrating clearer focus and providing more detailed evidence. This essay scored a 4.

**Essay #6: This essay also received a score of 4.**

Rarely in life is there a situation where only one answer is correct. In fact, even assuming there is only one right often leads to an ill thought out decision. Sometimes the best way to learn is to find the "however" and persue all possible answers to the fullest extent.

This is a lesson I learned in my English class this year  As we read in books, we would want to have discussions about their meaning and their implications in our lives. These discussions led to many heated debates on various topics througout the year. At first, my classmates and I would become angry at each other for disagreeing and at the teacher for structuring his lessons so these arguments would occur. But then my perspective changed  I came to class one day unsure of how I felt on the topic. As I sat in class I listened to each argument, trying to learn what the correct answer was  Eventually I found my own feelings on the subject, but I also found something else. There really was no "right" answer, and my opinion was strengthened by being tested by opposing views.

As the year went on many of my classmates seemed to realize this as well. English remained a debate, but not an angry one. It became a time to share your perspective while listening to the others' "howevers."

### WHY ESSAY #6 RECEIVED A SCORE OF 4

This *competent* response develops the point of view that "Sometimes the best way to learn is to find the 'however' and persue all possible answers to the fullest extent." The writer demonstrates competent critical thinking by focusing on an adequate, personal example to support the position. The response describes the change from the writer's initial anger with other points of view in class to an understanding that his or her own "opinion was strengthened by being tested by opposing views."

This essay is generally organized to chronicle the shift in the writer's position and therefore demonstrates a progression of ideas. Using generally appropriate vocabulary, the writer exhibits adequate facility in the use of language. ("These discussions led to many heated debates on various topics throughout the year. At first, my classmates and I would become angry at each other for disagreeing and at the teacher for structuring his lessons so these arguments would occur.")

However, to receive a higher score, this writer would need to develop the position more effectively by discussing in further depth the ways the example supports the point of view, in addition to retelling the anecdote. Thus, this response demonstrates *adequate mastery* and scored a 4.

**Essay #7: This essay received a score of 3.**

> The statement "There is always a however" suggests that there is always another explanation or point of view. However there is not always another explanation or point of view. In many cases there is only one solution to a problem, no matter how one looks at it. Because of this, the statement "There is always a however" is a false statement despite the fact that it may be seen as true by some people.
>
> The statement is not true in mathematical equations. If a teacher were to ask for the answer to the problem one plus one, the answer would be two. In this case there is no however. The answer is two and there is no other answer.
>
> The statement is also false in certain physical aspects of life. If someone were to pitch a baseball and the batter did not hit it, you cound say the batter did hit it because it is completely evident that he didn't. There is no however.
>
> The term "however" certainly applies to aspects of life, but not all of them and therefore not always. Because of those times where it doesn't apply the statement, "There is always a however" is false.

**WHY ESSAY #7 RECEIVED A SCORE OF 3**

This response demonstrates *developing mastery* by asserting the point of view that "in many cases there is only one solution to a problem, no matter how one looks at it." The writer demonstrates some critical thinking by attempting to prove that "the statement 'There is always a however' is false."

Although the writer attempts to support the main idea, evidence provided is too limited and repetitive to be adequate. ("If a teacher were to ask for the answer to the problem one plus one, the answer would be two. In this case there is no however. The answer is two and there is no other answer.")

To receive a higher score, this essay needs to demonstrate clearer focus and stronger critical thinking by developing the position further. Therefore, the essay remains in the *inadequate* category and scored a 3.

**Essay #8: This essay received a score of 2.**

"There is always a 'however.'" This statement is true. It means that a second explanation is always possible. Also, it tells us that the truth is not always easy to see. This is easy to see in The Great Gatsby, by F. Scott Fitzgerald.

In this novel, Jay Gatsby has devoted the last five years of his life to the woman he loves, named Daisy Fay. Due to the class status of Gatsby, he can not marry Daisy when he wants to. He then becomes determined to get wealthy and pursue his love. Later in life, when he becomes rich and meets Daisy, the two fall back in love. However, Gatsby became a mobster in order to get wealthy. Upon finding this information, Daisy realizes that Gatsby is not the man she wants to marry.

To conclude, Daisy wanted to marry Gatsby, but he was not wealthy. When he became wealthy, they could not marry, because he became a mobster.

**WHY ESSAY #8 RECEIVED A SCORE OF 2**

This *seriously limited* essay begins to develop the point of view that "the truth is not always easy to see," but it provides only one vague and insufficient example to support this position. Although the writer does demonstrate some critical thinking by selecting the appropriate example of Jay Gatsby's deception, the response lacks the focus and organization necessary to exhibit coherence and a progression of ideas.

Furthermore, the response displays little facility in the use of language, using a limited vocabulary. ("However, Gatsby became a mobster in order to get wealthy. . . . Daisy wanted to marry Gatsby, but he was not wealthy. When he became wealthy, they could not marry, because he became a mobster.") To receive a higher score, this essay would need to exhibit more facility in the use of language and demonstrate stronger critical thinking by providing more relevant evidence to support the point of view. Consequently, this response demonstrates *little mastery* and scored a 2.

*Essay #9: This essay received a score of 1.*

> There is always a "however" in any point of view. The idea can be quite complex in different situations. Knowing the possibility of a "however" in an important instance can be helpful, unpleasing or both. The importance of another possible explanation or point of view has helped many things such as medicine, advance.
>
> When researchers and doctors began the challenge to explore Parkinson's Disease, they found themselves always questioning the other explanation, or asking to find a different. When American doctors became aware of a mysterious case in California,

**WHY ESSAY #9 RECEIVED A SCORE OF 1**

This brief response is fundamentally lacking. Although the response attempts to develop a point of view ("There is always a 'however' in any point of view."), there is little evidence provided to support this position. The sparse support is incomplete and simply too limited to be organized or focused, resulting in an incoherent essay. Vocabulary is vague ("Knowing the possibility of a 'however' in an important instance can be helpful, unpleasing or both.") and fails to further the progression of ideas. To achieve a higher score, this response would have to exhibit a clearer focus and provide further evidence to support its position. Thus, this response demonstrates only *very little mastery* and scored a 1.

# CHAPTER 10

# Improving Sentences

Improving or revising written English is a pivotal part of successful writing. The questions in this chapter focus on an important skill: the ability to recognize and write clear, effective and accurate sentences. This is a skill you'll need when writing and making revisions to your writing in high school, in college and beyond.

The following box provides the directions and the example that will appear on the test.

The following sentences test correctness and effectiveness of expression. Part of each sentence or the entire sentence is underlined; beneath each sentence are five ways of phrasing the underlined material. Choice A repeats the original phrasing; the other four choices are different. If you think the original phrasing produces a better sentence than any of the alternatives, select choice A; if not, select one of the other choices.

In making your selection, follow the requirements of standard written English; that is, pay attention to grammar, choice of words, sentence construction, and punctuation. Your selection should result in the most effective sentence — clear and precise, without awkwardness or ambiguity.

**Example:**

Laura Ingalls Wilder published her first book <u>and she was sixty-five years old then</u>.

(A) and she was sixty-five years old then
(B) when she was sixty-five
(C) at age sixty-five years old
(D) upon the reaching of sixty-five years
(E) at the time when she was sixty-five

Here's another example. This one includes an explanation to help you understand the reasoning behind the correct answer.

**EXAMPLE**

Although several groups were absolutely opposed to the outside support given to the revolutionary government, other groups <u>were as equal in their adamant approval of</u> that support.

(A) were as equal in their adamant approval of
(B) held equally adamant approval of
(C) were equally adamant in approving
(D) had approved equally adamantly
(E) held approval equally adamant of

*Answer:* The correct answer is (C).

*Explanation:* Choice (C) is correct because it expresses the second part of the sentence in a way that is parallel to the first part. Two groups are being compared: groups "absolutely opposed to" and groups "equally adamant in." Both phrases now have a common structure: an adverb modifying an adjective followed by a preposition.

## Approaches to Improving Sentences

▶ *Read the entire sentence before you look at the choices.* Choice A is always the same as the original phrasing, so you may see that the right answer is to leave the sentence unchanged.

▶ *Remember that the right answer will result in the most effective sentence.* This is different from what you will be asked to do for Identifying Sentence Errors (Chapter 11).

▶ *Read each choice along with the entire sentence.* Don't read the choices on their own.

▶ *Look for common problem areas in sentences.* These include noun/verb agreement, parallelism, placement of modifiers and the use of relative clauses.

▶ *Read all five versions of the sentence aloud, if possible, while you're practicing.* You will not be able to do this during the actual test, of course. Your ear may tell you what your eye initially misses.

▶ *Read more slowly than you normally do.* Our brains sometimes make automatic corrections that we don't notice. Reading more slowly will help you pay closer attention.

▶ *Use your test booklet to help you by marking each question that you don't answer.* Then you can easily find it later.

## Writing Exercise: Using Parallelism

You can improve your writing enormously by using parallelism, which is simply using similar structures in a series. Because parallelism puts the content of a sentence into a recognizable pattern, it's easier to understand a parallel sentence. For example, note the parallelism in these sentences:

- Hawaii is *famous* <u>for its beautiful beaches</u>, and Montana is *well known* <u>for its majestic mountains</u>.

- Sharon wanted to have the party *at her house* <u>on Saturday night</u> rather than *in a restaurant* <u>on Sunday afternoon</u>.

In the first sentence, Hawaii and Montana are the two subjects. They are both described with adjectives (which are italicized — i.e., *famous* and *well known*), and what they are famous and well known for in each case follows in a prepositional phrase (which is underlined). The parallelism extends to the fact that the noun in each prepositional phrase is preceded by an adjective:

| Hawaii | is | *famous* | <u>for its beautiful beaches</u> | and |
| Montana | is | *well known* | <u>for its majestic mountains</u> | |

How would you describe the parallelism of the second sentence?

| Sharon wanted to have the party | (where?) | *at her house* |
| | (when?) | <u>on Saturday night</u> |
| rather than | (where?) | *in a restaurant* |
| | (when?) | <u>on Sunday afternoon</u>. |

In general, try to balance a word with a word, a phrase with a phrase and a clause with a clause. Within those patterns, if you want to be a careful writer, try to balance similar *types* of words — for example, adjectives with adjectives, prepositional phrases with prepositional phrases, or noun clauses with noun clauses. For example, notice the clumsiness of this sentence:

"On a hot day, I like swimming or to sit in the shade."

A better, clearer way to write this sentence would use a parallel expression:

"On a hot day, I like to *swim* or *sit* in the shade."

Often the parallelism involves items in a series:

"The telephone message was short, quiet and what I couldn't understand."

This sentence would be clearer if it had three adjectives (italicized):

"The telephone message was *short, quiet* and *hard to understand*."

## *Example Exercise: Rewriting Sentences Using Parallelism*

Rewrite these sentences, using parallelism:

1. Our vacation plans include exploring the city, visiting old friends, and to spend a few days doing nothing at all.

   *Rewrite:*

   _____

   _____

   _____

2. Sean had to choose between his brother's baseball game and going to his girl-friend's recital.

   *Rewrite:*

   _____

   _____

   _____

3. A teacher needs patience and to be fair.

   *Rewrite:*

   _____

   _____

   _____

4. I decided to buy the gift whether the store took credit cards or even making me pay cash.

   *Rewrite:*

   _____

   _____

   _____

5. The movie was not entertaining or an experience that was pleasant.

   *Rewrite:*

   _____

   _____

   _____

6. She is hoping for a career in medicine, law, or to be an engineer.

   *Rewrite:*

   _____

   _____

   _____

7. I try to be honest, hardworking, and to pay attention to my friends.

   *Rewrite:*

   _____

   _____

   _____

8. The produce in that store is fresh, well displayed, and costs too much.

   *Rewrite:*

   _____

   _____

   _____

**POSSIBLE REWRITES THAT IMPROVE THE ORIGINAL SENTENCES**

In the following rewritten sentences, the parallel items are italicized, and an explanation follows each rewrite.

1. *Original:* Our vacation plans include exploring the city, visiting old friends, and to spend a few days doing nothing at all.

   *Rewrite:* Our vacation plans include *exploring* the city, *visiting* old friends and *spending* a few days doing nothing at all.

   *Rationale:* The three parallel words are all *gerunds* — that is, verbs ending in -ing — that are doing the job of a noun: in this case, telling what the vacation plans include. Nouns often answer the question "what." Gerunds look like present participles, which are also verbs ending in -ing, but participles do the work of an adjective, which is to describe a noun. If you want an even more thorough understanding of grammar, consider this: the gerund is not only a noun but is simultaneously performing as a verb. In this case, like the transitive verbs they are, each one takes an object (underlined): exploring <u>the city</u>, visiting <u>old friends</u>, and spending <u>a few days</u>.

2. *Original:* Sean had to choose between his brother's baseball game and going to his girlfriend's recital.

   *Rewrite:* Sean had to choose between *his brother's baseball game* and *his girlfriend's recital.*

   *Rationale:* The parallel items are in similar form: his brother's *this* and his girlfriend's *that.*

3. *Original:* A teacher needs patience and to be fair.

   *Rewrite:* A teacher needs *patience* and *fairness.*

   *Or:* A teacher needs to be *patient* and *fair.*

   *Rationale:* The teacher needs two qualities. It does not matter whether they are expressed as nouns (i.e., *patience* and *fairness*) or infinitives (i.e., *to be patient* and [*to be*] *fair*). Either parallel expression is fine.

4. *Original:* I decided to buy the gift whether the store took credit cards or even making me pay cash.

  *Rewrite:* I decided to buy the gift whether the store *took* credit cards or even *made* me pay cash.

  *Rationale:* I decided to buy the gift whether the store did *this* or did *that* — *took credit cards* or (even) *made me pay.* You achieve the parallelism when you put both expressions into the same form, in this case, the past tense verb following the subject "store."

5. *Original:* The movie was not entertaining or an experience that was pleasant.

  *Rewrite:* The movie was not *entertaining* or *pleasant.*

  *Or:* The movie was neither *entertaining* nor *pleasant.*

  *Rationale:* Two words tell what the movie was not: entertaining and pleasant. Those two adjectives would make the sentence parallel in structure. Also, remember that when you use the negative word *neither,* you must use the equally negative word *nor.* That pair of connectors emphasizes the parallelism of the sentence.

6. *Original:* She is hoping for a career in medicine, law or to be an engineer.

  *Rewrite:* She is hoping for a career in *medicine, law* or *engineering.*

  *Rationale:* The series following "in" tells of three choices, so they should be expressed in parallel structure: medicine, law and engineering. Another possible parallel expression is to name the three professions: She is hoping to be a *doctor,* a *lawyer* or an *engineer.*

7. *Original:* I try to be honest, hardworking and paying attention to my friends.

  *Rewrite:* I try to be *honest, hardworking* and *attentive* to my friends.

  *Rationale:* What three qualities do "I" claim to have? I am hardworking, I am honest and I am attentive. The parallel structure uses three adjectives rather than two adjectives and an infinitive verb (the form of the verb that begins with *to*), as in the original sentence.

8. *Original:* The produce in that store is fresh, well displayed and they charge too much.

   *Rewrite:* The produce in that store is *fresh, well displayed,* and *too costly.*

   *Rationale:* What three words describe the produce in that store? Fresh, well displayed and too costly. Use these three adjectives to achieve parallelism.

# Sample Questions

The following sentences test correctness and effectiveness of expression. Part of each sentence or the entire sentence is underlined; beneath each sentence are five ways of phrasing the underlined material. Choice A repeats the original phrasing; the other four choices are different. If you think the original phrasing produces a better sentence than any of the alternatives, select choice A; if not, select one of the other choices.

In making your selection, follow the requirements of standard written English; that is, pay attention to grammar, choice of words, sentence construction, and punctuation. Your selection should result in the most effective sentence — clear and precise, without awkwardness or ambiguity.

**Example:**

Laura Ingalls Wilder published her first book <u>and she was sixty-five years old then</u>.

  (A)  and she was sixty-five years old then
  (B)  when she was sixty-five
  (C)  at age sixty-five years old
  (D)  upon the reaching of sixty-five years
  (E)  at the time when she was sixty-five      

---

1. Alice Walker, one of America's best-known <u>writers, she has published</u> both poetry and prose.

  (A)  writers, she has published
  (B)  writers, has published
  (C)  writers, and publishing
  (D)  writers since publishing
  (E)  writers when she published

2. Consumers are beginning to <u>take notice of electric cars</u> because they are quiet, <u>cause no air pollution, and gasoline is not used</u>.

  (A)  cause no air pollution, and gasoline is not used
  (B)  air pollution is not caused, and gasoline is not used
  (C)  cause no air pollution, and use no gasoline
  (D)  causing no air pollution and using no gasoline
  (E)  air pollution is not caused, and no gasoline is used

3. The <u>convenience and availability</u> of watercolor paint <u>account for its popularity</u> with amateur artists.

  (A)  account for its popularity
  (B)  account for their popularity
  (C)  accounts for its popularity
  (D)  is why it is popular
  (E)  are a reason for its popularity

# Answers and Explanations

1. Alice Walker, one of America's best-known <u>writers, she has published</u> both poetry and prose.

   (A) writers, she has published
   (B) writers, has published
   (C) writers, and publishing
   (D) writers since publishing
   (E) writers when she published

**Keep in Mind**

Restating the subject with a pronoun is a common mistake. Usually the pronoun is both unnecessary and distracting.

*Answer:* Choice (B) is the correct answer.

*Explanation:* This sentence describes Alice Walker, one of America's best-known writers, who has published both poetry and prose. Choice (B) is correct because it avoids the redundant pronoun error in the original sentence. Here's why each of the other choices is not the correct answer:

- Choice (A) is incorrect because the pronoun "she" is redundant. Simply dropping "she" will correct this problem.

- Choices (C), (D) and (E) are incorrect because they do not contain verb forms that produce grammatically complete sentences.

2. Consumers are beginning to take notice of electric cars because they are quiet, <u>cause no air pollution, and gasoline is not used</u>.

   (A) cause no air pollution, and gasoline is not used
   (B) air pollution is not caused, and gasoline is not used
   (C) cause no air pollution, and use no gasoline
   (D) causing no air pollution and using no gasoline
   (E) air pollution is not caused, and no gasoline is used

**Keep in Mind**

Parallelism is one sign of clear writing. When you see a pair or a series of items joined by *and* or *or*, make sure the grammatical structure is the same. The words, in most cases, should all be nouns, or all adjectives, or all verbs in the same tense.

*Answer:* Choice (C) is the correct answer.

*Explanation:* In this sentence, you must recognize that parts of a series separated by commas should parallel each other, as in the sentence produced by choice (C): Consumers are beginning to take notice of electric cars because they are quiet, cause no air pollution, and use no gasoline. Here's why each of the other choices is not the correct answer:

- In the original sentence and choice (A), the first two items in the series ("are quiet" and "cause") take the plural subject "they" and use active verbs, but the third item ("gasoline is not used") introduces a new subject and the passive voice. To follow the structure set forth by the phrase "they are quiet," the words "cause" and "use" — which also take "they" as their subject — should be used.

- Choices (B), (D) and (E) do not follow this parallel structure and so are incorrect.

3. The convenience and availability of watercolor paint <u>account for its popularity</u> with amateur artists.
   (A) account for its popularity
   (B) account for their popularity
   (C) accounts for its popularity
   (D) is why it is popular
   (E) are a reason for its popularity

*Answer:* The correct answer is (A).

*Explanation:* This sentence requires you to pay close attention to the plural subject. The original sentence is correct, so the answer is (A). Here's why each of the other choices is not the correct answer:

- In (B), the verb "account" correctly refers back to the plural subject "convenience and availability," but the plural pronoun "their" is incorrect — what is popular is "watercolor paint," not "convenience and availability."

- In (C) and (D), the verb is singular rather than plural.

- In (E), the singular noun "reason" does not agree with the plural subject.

> **Keep in Mind**
>
> Singular and plural parts of your sentences should match. If your subject is plural, your verb should also be plural, for example. You might mark the subject with an *S* or a *P* to remind yourself that it is singular or plural.

## Recap

1. Read the entire sentence before you look at the choices.

2. Remember that the right answer will result in the most effective sentence.

3. Read each choice along with the entire sentence; don't read the choices on their own.

4. Look for common problem areas in sentences, such as noun/verb agreement, parallelism, placement of modifiers and the use of relative clauses.

5. Read all five versions of the sentence aloud, if possible, while you're practicing.

6. Read more slowly than you normally do to help you pay closer attention.

7. Be sure that your subjects and verbs agree.

8. Mark each question that you don't answer in your test booklet, so you can easily return to it later.

# Practice Questions

The following sentences test correctness and effectiveness of expression. Part of each sentence or the entire sentence is underlined; beneath each sentence are five ways of phrasing the underlined material. Choice A repeats the original phrasing; the other four choices are different. If you think the original phrasing produces a better sentence than any of the alternatives, select choice A; if not, select one of the other choices.

In making your selection, follow the requirements of standard written English; that is, pay attention to grammar, choice of words, sentence construction, and punctuation. Your selection should result in the most effective sentence — clear and precise, without awkwardness or ambiguity.

**Example:**

Laura Ingalls Wilder published her first book <u>and she was sixty-five years old then</u>.

(A)   and she was sixty-five years old then
(B)   when she was sixty-five
(C)   at age sixty-five years old
(D)   upon the reaching of sixty-five years
(E)   at the time when she was sixty-five

---

1.  He arranged <u>the gems</u> on the counter, the sales assistant proceeded to tell us about the origins of each stone.

    (A)   He arranged the gems
    (B)   The gems, which were arranged
    (C)   The gems were first arranged
    (D)   After arranging the gems
    (E)   He, having arranged the gems

2.  Some of the Smithsonian Institution's most prized items, from Duke Ellington's musical transcripts to First Ladies' gowns, <u>coming from</u> unsolicited donations.

    (A)   coming from
    (B)   they come from
    (C)   they have come from
    (D)   came from
    (E)   which came from

3.  Brought to the United States at the age of thirteen to receive a Western education, <u>his first book discusses Lee Yan Phou's childhood in China</u>.

    (A)   his first book discusses Lee Yan Phou's childhood in China
    (B)   Lee Yan Phou's childhood in China is the subject of his first book
    (C)   the subject of his first book is Lee Yan Phou's childhood in China
    (D)   Lee Yan Phou discusses his childhood in China in his first book
    (E)   Lee Yan Phou, whose childhood was in China, discusses this in his first book

4.  Only since the publication of her first novel <u>Olivia has been considering</u> herself a genuine writer.

    (A)   Olivia has been considering
    (B)   Olivia considered
    (C)   has Olivia considered
    (D)   was Olivia considering
    (E)   could Olivia be able to

5. Scientists predict technological changes in the next <u>century, they will be as dramatic as was</u> the development of the transcontinental railroad in the last century.

   (A) century, they will be as dramatic as was
   (B) century, these will be as dramatic as
   (C) century; being as dramatic as was
   (D) century will be dramatic as is
   (E) century as dramatic as

6. Anita liked to watch <u>television, of which she found the science programs especially fascinating</u>.

   (A) television, of which she found the science programs especially fascinating
   (B) television; she found the science programs especially fascinating
   (C) television, and it was especially the science programs that were of fascination
   (D) television; the fascination of the science programs especially
   (E) television, especially fascinating to her were the science programs

7. Although gale force winds often pass through the Eiffel Tower, <u>causing it to sway no more</u> than four inches.

   (A) causing it to sway no more
   (B) and yet it sways no more
   (C) they do not cause it to sway more
   (D) and they do not cause it to sway
   (E) yet causing it to sway no more

8. <u>Underestimating its value, breakfast is a meal many people skip.</u>

   (A) Underestimating its value, breakfast is a meal many people skip.
   (B) Breakfast is skipped by many people because of their underestimating its value.
   (C) Many people, underestimating the value of breakfast, and skipping it.
   (D) Many people skip breakfast because they underestimate its value.
   (E) A meal skipped by many people underestimating its value is breakfast.

## Answer Key

1. D

2. D

3. D

4. C

5. E

6. B

7. C

8. D

 **Additional practice questions can be found in** *The Official SAT Online Course* **at www.collegeboard.org/satonlinecourse.**

# CHAPTER 11

# Identifying Sentence Errors

When you're writing and making revisions, being able to find mistakes in sentences is one of the most important skills you can have. Even writers who know the rules of good written English may need to correct mistakes while they're making revisions. To clearly express your written ideas, you must know grammar, usage, word choice and idioms.

The following box provides the directions and the example that will appear in the section on Identifying Sentence Errors.

---

The following sentences test your ability to recognize grammar and usage errors. Each sentence contains either a single error or no error at all. No sentence contains more than one error. The error, if there is one, is underlined and lettered. If the sentence contains an error, select the one underlined part that must be changed to make the sentence correct. If the sentence is correct, select choice E. In choosing answers, follow the requirements of standard written English.

**Example:**

The other delegates and him immediately
    A              B       C

accepted the resolution drafted by the
                          D

neutral states. No error
            E                    Ⓐ ● Ⓒ Ⓓ Ⓔ

---

Here's another example. This one includes an explanation to help you understand the reasoning behind the correct answer.

## EXAMPLE

In the following question, you are asked to identify the grammatical error.

> It is likely that the opening of the convention center,
>
> <u>previously</u> <u>set for</u> July 1, <u>would be</u> postponed
>   A       B            C
>
> <u>because of</u> the bricklayers' strike. <u>No error</u>
>   D                E

*Answer:* The correct answer is (C).

*Explanation:* Choice (C), "would be," is the wrong tense of the verb in this sentence. The sentence concerns when the convention center is going to open. This is a time in the future, either July 1 or later if there is a strike. Because the opening will definitely take place, the future tense, "will be," is needed. "Would be" (which is the conditional tense) indicates only that an event *might* happen.

## Approaches to Identifying Sentence Errors

The questions in this section are different from most other multiple-choice questions. For Identifying Sentence Errors, you will have to choose the answer that contains a *mistake.* Here are some approaches to try as you work through Identifying Sentence Errors.

▶ *Read each sentence quickly but carefully.* The error may be obvious as soon as you see it.

▶ *Consider each question as a cluster of true-false questions, each to be considered separately.* Only one can be false, and that is the one containing the error. If there are no false responses, the answer is (E) — no error.

▶ *Read aloud, if possible, during your practice sessions.* You won't be able to do this during the actual test, of course. If you read aloud, you may hear the error immediately. Keep in mind, however, that the rules for written English are stricter than those for everyday spoken English.

▶ *Examine the underlined choices A to D.* Consider which kind of correction may be needed for each one (and refer to the table in Chapter 8 on "Characteristics of Effective Writing").

▶ *Develop the habit of looking for the most common mistakes people make in grammar:* subject/verb agreement, pronoun agreement and adjective/adverb confusion.

▶ *Look for errors in idiom — words or phrases that are particular to our language because of what they mean when used together.* We say that we listen *to* someone, not listen *at* someone or *by* someone; a song is *by* a composer, not *from* a composer. We say at the top *of* the hill, not at the top *on* the hill.

▶ *Remember that some sentences have no error.* Don't spend time looking for what is not there. Mark (E), "No error," on your answer sheet if you believe the sentence is correct as written.

▶ *Correct errors even in questions for which you have only to identify the error.* As you practice, correcting the error may help you keep in mind the language principles.

▶ *Move quickly through questions about Identifying Sentence Errors.* The other kinds of questions — Improving Sentences (Chapter 10) and Improving Paragraphs (Chapter 12) — will likely take more time.

▶ *Mark questions in your test booklet that you've skipped.* Then you can return to them later.

# Writing Exercise: Avoid Dangling Participles

To improve your writing, make sure you avoid using participial phrases that have no subject; they are a frequent cause of confusion.

## *Quick Grammar Review: Participles*

Participles are verb forms that function as adjectives. In the present tense, participles always end in "-ing" (e.g., *laughing, falling, gusting*). In the sentence "The *laughing* child played with the *falling* leaves that the *gusting* breeze shook loose from the *quivering* branches," the italicized words are all present participles, and they describe nouns, which are underlined. These are the present participles of the verbs *laugh, fall, gust* and *quiver*.

In the past tense, participles often end in -ed, -en or -t (e.g., *cooked, washed; broken, written; spent, lost*), and some are irregular (e.g., *bought, wrung*). In the following sentences, the past participles are again italicized, and they describe nouns, which are again underlined:

- Raw vegetables are more nutritious than *cooked* ones.

- The newly *washed* car glistened in the afternoon sunshine.

- The jury had a hard time ignoring the *written* proof of the defendant's alibi.

- He had nothing to show for his road trip but receipts for all his *spent* money.

- *Lost* opportunities rarely come around a second time.

- You have to declare the value of all the *bought* goods you bring home from your trip.

- Tightly *wrung* laundry will dry faster but will need more ironing.

These are past participles of the verbs *cook, wash, write, spend, lose, buy* and *wring*.

### Quick Grammar Review: Participial Phrases

A group of words that begins with a participle is known as a participial phrase. Because a participle acts like an adjective, participial phrases are used to modify nouns. Because a participle comes from a verb, participial phrases need subjects. Read this sentence and see if you detect a problem in its clarity:

> Tourists see statues of many famous patriots walking along Boston's Freedom Trail

It appears that the statues are walking, not the tourists. In English, modifiers are usually placed as close as possible to the words they describe, so this sentence should read:

> Tourists walking along Boston's Freedom Trail see statues of many famous patriots.

### Example Exercise: Rewriting Sentences to Improve the Participial Phrase's Location

Revise each of the following sentences so that the participial phrase's location does not cause confusion. The first six are present participles; the last four are past participles.

1. I thought I heard a strange rattle driving my car.

*Rewrite:*

_____

_____

_____

2. Strumming on his guitar, we suddenly remembered where we had seen this folk singer before.

*Rewrite:*

_____

_____

_____

3.  I turned the corner and bumped into an elderly gentleman paying no attention to where I was going.

*Rewrite:*

_____

_____

_____

4.  Orbiting between Mars and Jupiter, research astronomers discovered a new group of asteroids.

*Rewrite:*

_____

_____

_____

5.  I saw a long line of traffic looking both ways before I tried to cross the street.

*Rewrite:*

_____

_____

_____

6.  The caterer served refreshments to the guests wearing a frilly white apron.

*Rewrite:*

_____

_____

_____

7.  Raised in an open field without any pesticides, I prefer vegetables and fruits.

*Rewrite:*

_____

_____

_____

8.  Cooked too long, she thought the pasta did not taste good any more.

*Rewrite:*

_____

_____

_____

9.  Spiced with Italian herbs, I had never tasted anything quite like Imelda's salad.

*Rewrite:*

_____

_____

_____

10. Wrapped in brightly colored paper, Mickey tore open the birthday present.

*Rewrite:*

_____

_____

_____

## POSSIBLE REWRITES THAT IMPROVE THE ORIGINAL SENTENCES

In the following rewritten sentences (others are possible), the participial phrase is italicized and the noun it describes is underlined. In each case, the participial phrase describes that noun and is located as close to it as the sentence will allow.

1.  *Original:* I thought I heard a strange rattle driving my car.

    *Rewrite:* *Driving my car,* <u>I</u> thought I heard a strange rattle.

    *Rationale:* The strange rattle was not driving the car. Relocating the participial phrase so it is next to the word *I* removes that confusion. The sentence "While I was driving my car, I thought I heard a strange rattle" is a perfectly good English sentence; it does not use a participial phrase.

2.  *Original:* Strumming on his guitar, we suddenly remembered where we had seen this folk singer before.

    *Rewrite:* *Hearing the folk singer strumming on his guitar,* <u>we</u> suddenly remembered where we had seen him before.

    *Rationale:* Whatever revised sentence you write, be sure that you do not make it sound like "we" were strumming on the guitar.

3. *Original:* I turned the corner and bumped into an elderly gentleman paying no attention to where I was going.

   *Rewrite:* *Paying no attention to where I was going,* I *turned the corner and bumped into an elderly gentleman.*

   *Rationale:* Who was paying no attention? It is not the elderly gentleman, so the participial phrase cannot be placed next to "gentleman."

4. *Original:* Orbiting between Mars and Jupiter, research astronomers discovered a new group of asteroids.

   *Rewrite:* Research astronomers discovered a new group of <u>asteroids</u> *orbiting between Mars and Jupiter.*

   *Rationale:* The original sentence says that the astronomers were orbiting between Mars and Jupiter. It's more likely that the asteroids were.

5. *Original:* I saw a long line of traffic looking both ways before I tried to cross the street.

   *Rewrite:* *Looking both ways before I tried to cross the street,* I *saw a long line* of traffic.

   *Rationale:* Is the traffic looking both ways? Place the participial phrase by the noun (in this case, pronoun) it actually describes.

6. *Original:* The caterer served refreshments to the guests wearing a frilly white apron.

   *Rewrite:* The <u>caterer</u>, *wearing a frilly white apron,* served refreshments to the guests.

   *Or:* *Wearing a frilly white apron,* the <u>caterer</u> served refreshments to the guests.

   *Rationale:* The original sentence makes it sound like only guests wearing frilly white aprons received refreshments. Probably the apron belonged to the caterer, so relocate the participial phrase to a position near the noun it describes.

7. *Original:* Raised in an open field without any pesticides, I prefer vegetables and fruits.

   *Rewrite:* I prefer <u>vegetables and fruits</u> *raised in an open field without any pesticides.*

   *Rationale:* It is not the subject "I" who was raised in a field, but the vegetables and fruits. Rephrase the sentence so that point is clear.

8. *Original:* Cooked too long, she thought the pasta did not taste good any more.

   *Rewrite:* She thought the <u>pasta</u>, *cooked too long,* did not taste good any more.

   *Rationale:* "She" was not cooked too long; the pasta was. Placing the participial phase next to "pasta" will correct that misstatement. You can also write, "Because the pasta was cooked too long, she thought it did not taste good any more." This is also accurate, but there is no participial phrase in this version.

9. *Original:* Spiced with Italian herbs, I had never tasted anything quite like Imelda's salad.

   *Rewrite:* I had never tasted anything quite like Imelda's <u>salad</u>, which was *spiced with Italian herbs.*

   *Rationale:* "I" am not spiced with Italian herbs, so the sentence needs rewriting. Place the descriptive participial phrase near the word it describes.

10 *Original:* Wrapped in brightly colored paper, Mickey tore open the birthday present.

   *Rewrite:* Mickey tore open the birthday <u>present</u> *wrapped in brightly colored paper.*

   *Rationale:* Although it is possible that Mickey was wrapped in brightly colored paper, it is much more likely that the birthday present was. Placing the participial phrase near "present" will make that clear.

In several of these examples, you might have revised the sentence and removed confusion by some means other than relocating the participial phrase. That's perfectly fine. The lesson here is to recognize when the participial phrase is poorly located and to take steps to correct the problem.

# Sample Questions

The following sentences test your ability to recognize grammar and usage errors. Each sentence contains either a single error or no error at all. No sentence contains more than one error. The error, if there is one, is underlined and lettered. If the sentence contains an error, select the one underlined part that must be changed to make the sentence correct. If the sentence is correct, select choice E. In choosing answers, follow the requirements of standard written English.

**Example:**

<u>The other</u> delegates and <u>him</u> <u>immediately</u>
    A                  B     C

accepted the resolution <u>drafted by</u> the
                           D

neutral states. <u>No error</u>
           E                    Ⓐ ● Ⓒ Ⓓ Ⓔ

1. The <u>bright</u> fiberglass sculptures of Luis Jimenez <u>has received</u> critical
      A                               B

   acclaim <u>not only</u> in his home state, New Mexico, but also <u>in</u> New York.
        C                              D

   <u>No error</u>
  E

2. <u>Even with</u> a calculator, you must have a basic <u>understanding of</u>
  A                             B

   mathematics if <u>one expects</u> to solve complex problems <u>correctly</u>. <u>No error</u>
          C                        D     E

3. People who dislike cats <u>sometimes</u> criticize them <u>for being</u> aloof and
            A                 B

   independent; people who are <u>fond of</u> cats often admire <u>them for</u> the same
                    C                   D

   qualities. <u>No error</u>
      E

4. The decision that <u>has just been</u> <u>agreed with</u> by the committee members
          A       B

   should serve as a basis <u>for their</u> work in the <u>years to come</u>. <u>No error</u>
            C            D     E

# Answers and Explanations

1. The bright fiberglass sculptures of Luis Jimenez has received
       A                                    B

   critical acclaim not only in his home state, New Mexico, but also in
                 C                              D

   New York. No error
           E

---

> **Keep in Mind**
>
> Read the entire sentence. The answer might be immediately apparent because the error is a common one of punctuation or grammar.

*Answer:* The correct answer is (B).

*Explanation:* The problem with this sentence lies in (B): the subject of the sentence, "sculptures," is plural and requires the plural verb "have received."

The other choices are all correct:

- The word "bright" in choice (A) is used properly as an adjective.

- In (C), "not only" is part of the combination "not only . . . but also."

- The preposition in (D), "in," begins a phrase that effectively parallels the preceding phrase "in his home state."

The best answer, then, is (B). The corrected sentence reads: "The bright fiberglass sculptures of Luis Jimenez have received critical acclaim not only in his home state, New Mexico, but also in New York."

2. Even with a calculator, you must have a basic understanding of
       A                                    B

   mathematics if one expects to solve complex problems correctly.
                 C                            D

   No error
     E

*Answer:* The correct answer is (C).

*Explanation:* The first part of the sentence addresses "you." Because this pronoun is not underlined, it cannot be changed, and subsequent pronouns must also use the second person. In (C), the third-person pronoun "one" is used incorrectly; choice (C) should be worded "you expect."

The other choices are all appropriate:

- Choice (A) introduces the conditional relationship set forth in the rest of the sentence.

- Choice (B) appropriately uses the preposition "of" with "understanding."

- The adverb "correctly" in (D) modifies the verb "solve."

The corrected sentence reads: "Even with a calculator, you must have a basic understanding of mathematics if you expect to solve complex problems correctly."

> **Keep in Mind**
>
> As you read a sentence, ask yourself if the error is obvious. If it isn't, consider the common problems: it's not subject/verb agreement (*you must have* is good) or adjective/adverb confusion (*correctly* is right, not *correct*). But the pronouns do not agree (you/one). Once again, the error is a common one.

3. People who dislike cats <u>sometimes</u> criticize them <u>for being</u> aloof and
                               A                          B

   independent; people who are <u>fond of</u> cats often admire <u>them</u> for the same
                                    C                        D

   qualities. <u>No error</u>
               E

*Answer:* The correct answer is (E).

*Explanation:* All of the underlined choices in this sentence are appropriate:

- The word "sometimes" in (A) properly modifies the verb "criticize."

- In (B), "being" is the verbal form that fits idiomatically with the phrase "criticize . . . for."

- The preposition "of" in (C) is appropriate to use after "fond."

- In (D), the plural pronoun, "them," is used appropriately to refer to "cats," and "for" is the correct preposition to use with the verb "admire."

> **Keep in Mind**
>
> If you can't find an error in a sentence, the correct answer may be (E), "No error."

Therefore, because all of the underlined parts of this sentence are correct, the best answer is (E), "No error."

4. The decision that <u>has just been</u> <u>agreed with</u> by the committee members
                                   A             B

   should serve as a basis <u>for their</u> work in the <u>years to come</u>. <u>No error</u>
                             C                    D       E

*Answer:* The correct answer is (B).

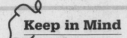

**Keep in Mind**

While practicing, read sentences aloud if you can. The error may then become obvious.

*Explanation:* The error is the preposition used in choice (B). In the context of this sentence, the correct idiomatic expression is "agreed to" rather than "agreed with." The other choices are correct:

- In (A), the present-perfect verb phrase is used appropriately to indicate an action that is completed in the present.

- In (C), "for" appropriately completes the expression "basis for," and "their" properly refers to the plural noun "members."

- Choice (D) properly expresses the time reference in the sentence.

The corrected sentence reads: "The decision that has just been agreed to by the committee members should serve as a basis for their work in the years to come."

# Recap

1. Look for the one underlined part of the sentence that must be changed to make the sentence correct.

2. Read each sentence quickly but carefully, and the error may become obvious.

3. Read aloud during your practice sessions if possible.

4. Examine the underlined choices A to D; then think of which correction may be needed for each.

5. Develop the habit of looking for the most common mistakes people make in punctuation, grammar and other areas.

6. Look for errors in idioms — that is, expressions whose meanings may not be clear from the individual words, but that mean something when used together.

7. Remember that some sentences have no error and that the correct answer may be (E), "No error."

8. Correct errors when you practice, even if you are asked only to identify the error.

9. Move quickly through questions about Identifying Sentence Errors, because the questions on Improving Sentences and Improving Paragraphs will probably take more time.

10. Mark questions in your test booklet that you've skipped so you can go back to them later.

# Practice Questions

The following sentences test your ability to recognize grammar and usage errors. Each sentence contains either a single error or no error at all. No sentence contains more than one error. The error, if there is one, is underlined and lettered. If the sentence contains an error, select the one underlined part that must be changed to make the sentence correct. If the sentence is correct, select choice E. In choosing answers, follow the requirements of standard written English.

**Example:**

The other delegates and him immediately
    A                B       C

accepted the resolution drafted by the
                             D

neutral states. No error
            E                              Ⓐ●ⒸⒹⒺ

---

1.  Since there is two pencils, a pad of paper, and a ruler on each desk, students
             A

    do not have to bring their own supplies. No error
        B      C       D           E

2.  Each time Caroline turns on her computer, she has to enter a company code, then
                                           A

    her initials, and then enters a password before she can begin working. No error
                       B        C           D          E

3.  Flints found in the region extending from the Nile Valley to the highlands of eastern
           A                                              B

    Iraq attests to the presence of people there as long ago as one hundred thousand
          C                               D

    years. No error
          E

4.  By virtue of its size and supersensitive electronics, modern radio telescopes are able
              A

    to gather more waves and discriminate among them with greater precision than
                          B         C                           D

    earlier versions could. No error
                      E

5.  Delgado's dilemma was like many other young writers: he had to choose between
                      A                                       B

    assured publication in a student magazine and probable rejection by a popular
                                           C        D

    magazine. No error
            E

6. Air pollution caused by industrial fumes <u>has been studied</u> for years, <u>but</u> only

                                              A                        B

   recently <u>has</u> the harmful effects of noise pollution <u>become</u> known. <u>No error</u>

           C                                    D            E

7. <u>No matter</u> how <u>cautious</u> snowmobiles <u>are</u> driven, they are capable <u>of damaging</u> the

     A                  B                   C                       D

   land over which they travel. <u>No error</u>

                              E

8. The starling is <u>such a</u> pest in rural areas that it <u>has become</u> necessary <u>to find ways</u> of

                A                            B                    C

   controlling the growth <u>of their</u> population. <u>No error</u>

                         D                   E

## Answer Key

1. A

2. B

3. C

4. A

5. A

6. C

7. B

8. D

**Additional practice questions can be found in _The Official SAT Online Course_ at www.collegeboard.org/satonlinecourse.**

# CHAPTER 12
# Improving Paragraphs

You will most likely be required to do a great amount of writing in college. That's the main reason the College Board added a writing section to the SAT in 2005.

The Improving Paragraphs questions call on all your skills in writing and revising. After you read a draft of a short essay, you will be asked to understand how the sentences and the paragraphs work together. You will have to make revisions by combining or deleting sentences and by altering structures within sentences. Though you may not realize it, that's the process you go through as you edit and revise your own essays until they're final.

The following box provides the directions for Improving Paragraphs questions that will appear on the test.

> **Directions:** The following passage is an early draft of an essay. Some parts of the passage need to be rewritten.
>
> Read the passage and select the best answers for the questions that follow. Some questions are about particular sentences or parts of sentences and ask you to improve sentence structure or word choice. Other questions ask you to consider organization and development. In choosing answers, follow the requirements of standard written English.

Here's an example of an improving paragraphs question.

### EXAMPLE

(1) At one point in the movie *Raiders of the Lost Ark*, the evil archaeologist Belloq shows the heroic Indiana Jones a cheap watch. (2) If the watch were to be buried in the desert for a thousand years and then dug up, Belloq says, it would be considered priceless. (3) I often think of the scene whenever I consider the record album–collecting phenomenon, it being one of the more remarkable aspects of popular culture in the United States. (4) Collecting record albums gives us a chance to make a low-cost investment that might pay dividends in the future.

(5) When my aunt collected them in the mid-sixties, nobody regarded them as investments. (6) A young fan shelled out dollar after dollar at the corner record store for no other reason than to assemble a complete collection of her favorite musical groups— in my aunt's case, the Beatles and the Supremes. (7) By committing so much of her allowance each week to the relentless pursuit of that one group not yet in her collection— the immortal Yardbirds, let us say—she was proving her loyalty to her superstars.

(8) The recording industry is a capitalist enterprise and so this hobby has become one. (9) Just as everyone has heard of the exorbitant prices being paid for the Beatles' first album in mint condition, so everyone is certain that a payoff is among each stack of old records. (10) But if that album was buried somewhere in my aunt's closet of dusty records, she never knew it. (11) Long before she learned it, she had thrown them out.

In the context of the first paragraph, which revision is most needed in sentence 3?

(A) Insert "As a matter of fact" at the beginning.
(B) Omit the words "it being".
(C) Omit the word "scene".
(D) Change the comma to a semicolon.
(E) Change "think" to "thought" and "consider" to "considered".

*Answer:* The correct answer is Choice (B).

*Explanation:* The words "it being" are unnecessary.

## Approaches to Improving Paragraphs

▶ *Read the essay thoroughly to determine its overall meaning before you look at the questions.* It's important to have a sense of the entire essay's organization and meaning before you deal with any changes. The essay is meant to be a draft, so there will be errors in it, but don't linger over those errors.

▶ *Read more slowly than you usually do, to help you pay closer attention.*

▶ *Try all of the options before you decide on your answer.* The directions tell you to choose the best answer. That means one may be satisfactory but not as good as another. Don't overlook any possibilities.

▶ *Make sure that your answer about a particular sentence or sentences makes sense in the context of the preceding and following sentences and of the passage as a whole.*

▶ *Use your test booklet to help you by marking each question that you don't answer.* Then you can easily find it later.

## Writing Exercise: Avoiding Wordiness

A great way to improve your writing is to simplify it. Why use lots of words when just one or two well-chosen words will convey exactly what you want to say?

Wordiness results from using unnecessary words and phrases and from adding empty expressions to a sentence. Unnecessary words are sometimes the result of redundancy, or surplus words. For example, expressions such as "two in number" are redundant because two *is* a number, so the phrase "in number" does not add any meaning to the sentence. Similarly, "sadly unhappy" is redundant. Finally, empty expressions, such as "if you know what I mean," add little to your writing except to fill up space — which should *not* be your goal. Eliminate those unnecessary words and phrases from your writing.

## Example Exercise: Rewriting Sentences to Avoid Wordiness

Here's some practice. Revise the following sentences so that no unneeded words remain:

1. Our most favorite balloons were those that were red in color.

*Rewrite:*

_____

_____

2. We put off until later in time the decision about whether or not the funny comedians would be appropriate and fitting for our evening of after-dinner entertainment performers.

*Rewrite:*

_____

_____

3. Snow continued to keep on falling, so we had to repeatedly shovel the sidewalk over and over again.

*Rewrite:*

_____

_____

4. Working so assiduously hard left her tired, fatigued, and exhausted; she could barely stay awake and avoid falling asleep.

*Rewrite:*

_____

_____

5. We considered his behavior rude, in the truest sense of the word.

*Rewrite:*

_____

_____

6. The driver witnessed a female person as she parked a blue-colored vehicle, exited out of it, and proceeded to make her way on foot in a northerly direction toward the blinking red light that was flashing on and off and on and off.

*Rewrite:*

_____

_____

7. The American War of Independence is principally the most important historic event that grade school children in elementary schools have to learn about and study.

*Rewrite:*

_____

_____

8. If you come to think about it, green vegetables ought to be a part of everyone's daily diet.

*Rewrite:*

_____

_____

_____

**POSSIBLE REWRITES THAT IMPROVE THE ORIGINAL SENTENCES**

Following are some suggested rewrites (though others are possible, too). The rationales show that many of the sentences displayed redundancy, or unnecessary repetition.

1. *Original:* Our most favorite balloons were those that were red in color.
   *Rewrite:* Our favorite balloons were red.
   *Or:* We like the red balloons best.
   *Rationale:* "Favorite" means the one most liked, so "most favorite" is redundant. And because red is a color, the words "in color" are unnecessary.

2. *Original:* We put off until later in time the decision about whether or not the funny comedians would be appropriate and fitting for our evening of after-dinner entertainment performers.
   *Rewrite:* We put off [or delayed] deciding whether the comedians would be appropriate for our after-dinner entertainment.
   *Rationale:* First of all, "later in time" is redundant in the same way "red in color" and "rainy weather" are. Second, unless they are not funny, we assume comedians *are* funny, so we don't have to say so. Third, "appropriate" and "fitting" are *two* words that say the same thing; we only need one. Finally, "entertainment performers" is also redundant, and because dinner *is* the evening meal, "after-dinner entertainment" already tells us that this is an evening event.

3. *Original:* Snow continued to keep on falling, so we had to repeatedly shovel the sidewalk over and over again.
   *Rewrite:* Snow kept on falling, so we had to shovel the sidewalk over and over.
   *Or:* Because it kept snowing, we had to shovel the sidewalk over and over.
   *Rationale:* "Continued to keep on" is redundant, as are "over and over again" and "repeatedly."

4. *Original:* Working so assiduously hard left her tired, fatigued, and exhausted; she could barely stay awake and avoid falling asleep.
   *Rewrite:* She was exhausted from working so hard, and she could hardly stay awake.
   *Or:* Because she worked herself into exhaustion, she could hardly stay awake.
   *Rationale:* "Assiduously" means "working hard," so "assiduously working hard" is redundant. "Tired," "fatigued" and "exhausted" all mean the same thing, as do "stay awake" and "avoid falling asleep."

5. *Original:* We considered his behavior rude, in the truest sense of the word.

    *Rewrite:* We considered him rude.

    *Rationale:* The word "behavior" is implied by the rest of the sentence, and the expression "in the truest sense of the word" does not add any meaning to the sentence. Why would a writer use a word in an untrue sense?

6. *Original:* The driver witnessed a female person as she parked a blue-colored vehicle, exited out of it, and proceeded to make her way on foot in a northerly direction toward the blinking red light that was flashing on and off and on and off.

    *Rewrite:* The driver saw a woman park a blue car, get out, and walk north toward the blinking red light.

    *Rationale:* "A female person" *is* a woman. "Blue-colored," like "red in color," is redundant. "Exited" means "went out." "Proceeded to make her way on foot" is a multiword version of "walked." "In a northerly direction" is more simply (and just as accurately) said by writing "north." "Blinking" is the same as "flashing on and off and on and off."

    It is true that, in another context, the expression "proceeded to make her way on foot" might be appropriate. If the writer were calling attention to the distinction between one mode of travel, for example, by bicycle or car, and foot travel, the phrase might tell something important. But in this simple sentence, there is no such need to make that distinction. Don't try to be fancy when being simple will do.

7. *Original:* The American War of Independence is principally the most important historic event that grade school children in elementary schools have to learn about and study.

    *Rewrite:* The American War of Independence is the most important historic event that elementary students have to study.

    *Rationale:* "Principally" means the same as "the most important." Grade school and elementary school are the same, so there is no need to say it twice. The same is true of "learn about" and "study."

8.. *Original:* If you come to think about it, green vegetables ought to be a part of everyone's daily diet.

    *Rewrite:* Everyone should eat green vegetables daily.

    *Rationale:* "If you come to think about it" is an empty expression, unnecessary for the meaning of the sentence. "Green vegetables ought to be a part of everyone's daily diet" is satisfactory. The other suggested answer, "Everyone should eat green vegetables daily," uses a different subject and verb, so it offers another good possible revision.

## ADDING DESCRIPTIVE WORDS THAT ARE *NOT* REDUNDANT

The previous exercise asked you to eliminate *unnecessary* words, words that are *repetitive* or words that *add nothing* to the sentence's meaning. If these sentences seem too simple, you can make them more interesting by adding descriptive details. For example, the first one could be revised in any of the following ways:

- "When we spent a day at the circus, our favorite balloons were red and star-shaped."

- "Our favorite balloons were red, but the kids in front of us liked the blue ones better."

- "Red balloons decorated with silver sparkles caught the sunshine the best, so we decided they were our favorites."

Now try improving the sentences by adding descriptive details.

1. *Original:* Our favorite balloons were red.

*Your rewrite:*

_____

_____

_____

2. *Original:* We did not go swimming because it rained.

*Your rewrite:*

_____

_____

_____

3. *Original:* We put off deciding whether the comedians would be appropriate for our after-dinner entertainment.

*Your rewrite:*

_____

_____

_____

4.  *Original:* Snow kept on falling, so we had to shovel the sidewalk over and over.

*Your rewrite:*

_____

_____

_____

5.  *Original:* She was exhausted from working so hard, and she could hardly stay awake.

*Your rewrite:*

_____

_____

_____

6.  *Original:* We considered him rude.

*Your rewrite:*

_____

_____

_____

7.  *Original:* The driver saw a woman park a blue car, get out, and walk north toward the blinking red light.

*Your rewrite:*

_____

_____

_____

_____

8. *Original:* The American War of Independence is the most important historic event that elementary students have to study.

*Your rewrite:*

_____

_____

_____

9. *Original:* Everyone should eat green vegetables daily.

*Your rewrite:*

_____

_____

_____

10. *Original:* My neighbor, Tony, is a doctor in a nearby hospital.

*Your rewrite:*

_____

_____

_____

Now that you've had some practice adding descriptive words, let's look at the sample questions from this section of the SAT.

# Sample Questions

**Directions:** The following passage is an early draft of an essay. Some parts of the passage need to be rewritten.

Read the passage and select the best answers for the questions that follow. Some questions are about particular sentences or parts of sentences and ask you to improve sentence structure or word choice. Other questions ask you to consider organization and development. In choosing answers, follow the requirements of standard written English.

---

**Questions 1-6 are based on the following passage.**

(1) My father has an exceptional talent. (2) The ability to understand people. (3) When I have a problem that I think no one else will understand, I take it to my father. (4) He listens intently, asks me some questions, and my feelings are seemingly known by him exactly. (5) Even my twin sister can talk to him more easily than to me. (6) Many people seem too busy to take the time to understand one another. (7) My father, by all accounts, sees taking time to listen as essential to any relationship, whether it involves family, friendship, or work.

(8) At work, my father's friends and work associates benefit from this talent. (9) His job requires him to attend social events and sometimes I go along. (10) I have watched him at dinner; his eyes are fixed on whoever is speaking, and he nods his head at every remark. (11) My father emerges from such a conversation with what I believe is a true sense of the speaker's meaning. (12) In the same way, we choose our friends.

(13) My father's ability to listen affects his whole life. (14) His ability allows him to form strong relationships with his coworkers and earns him lasting friendships. (15) It allows him to have open conversations with his children. (16) Furthermore, it has strengthened his relationship with my mother. (17) Certainly, his talent is one that I hope to develop as I mature.

1. Of the following, which is the best way to revise and combine sentences 1 and 2 (reproduced below) ?

   *My father has an exceptional talent. The ability to understand people.*

   (A) My father has an exceptional talent and the ability to understand people.
   (B) My father has an exceptional talent that includes the ability to understand people.
   (C) My father has an exceptional talent: the ability to understand people.
   (D) My father has an exceptional talent, it is his ability to understand people.
   (E) Despite my father's exceptional talent, he still has the ability to understand people.

2. Of the following, which is the best way to phrase sentence 4 (reproduced below) ?

   *He listens intently, asks me some questions, and my feelings are seemingly known by him exactly.*

   (A) (As it is now)
   (B) Listening intently, he will ask me some questions and then my exact feelings are seemingly known to him.
   (C) As he listens to me and asks me some questions, he seems to be knowing exactly my feelings.
   (D) He listened to me and asked me some questions, seeming to know exactly how I felt.
   (E) He listens intently, asks me some questions, and then seems to know exactly how I feel.

3. In sentence 7, the phrase *by all accounts* is best replaced by

   (A) however
   (B) moreover
   (C) to my knowledge
   (D) like my sister
   (E) but nevertheless

4. Which of the following sentences should be omitted to improve the unity of the second paragraph?

   (A) Sentence 8
   (B) Sentence 9
   (C) Sentence 10
   (D) Sentence 11
   (E) Sentence 12

5. In context, which of the following is the best way to phrase the underlined portion of sentence 16 (reproduced below) ?

   *Furthermore, it has strengthened his relationship with my mother.*

   (A) (As it is now)
   (B) Further strengthening
   (C) But it strengthens
   (D) However, he is strengthening
   (E) Considering this, he strengthens

6. A strategy that the writer uses within the third paragraph is to

   (A) make false assumptions and use exaggeration
   (B) include difficult vocabulary
   (C) repeat certain words and sentence patterns
   (D) argue in a tone of defiance
   (E) turn aside from the main subject

# Answers and Explanations

1. Of the following, which is the best way to revise and combine sentences 1 and 2 (reproduced below)?

   *My father has an exceptional talent. The ability to understand people.*

   (A)  My father has an exceptional talent and the ability to understand people.
   (B)  My father has an exceptional talent that includes the ability to understand people.
   (C)  My father has an exceptional talent. the ability to understand people.
   (D)  My father has an exceptional talent, it is his ability to understand people.
   (E)  Despite my father's exceptional talent, he still has the ability to understand people.

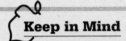

**Keep in Mind**

When you combine sentences, make sure that the relationship between them is clear.

*Answer:*  Choice (C) is correct.

*Explanation:*  The passage shows that the father's exceptional talent is his ability to understand people.  Because sentence 2 is a fragment, sentences 1 and 2 must be combined in a way that clearly indicates the correct relationship between the father's talent and ability. The use of a colon to join sentences 1 and 2 corrects the error of the original and signifies that the father's talent is his ability to understand people.

- Choice (A) is unsatisfactory because the passage suggests that the father's talent is his ability to understand people; his talent and his ability are not two separate things.

- Choice (B) is unsatisfactory because, as the passage shows, the father's talent does not include his ability to understand people; it is his ability to understand people.

- Choice (D) is unsatisfactory because it joins two independent thoughts with only a comma.

- Choice (E) is unsatisfactory because it contrasts the father's talent with his ability, when in fact, as the passage shows, they are the same thing.

2. Of the following, which is the best way to phrase sentence 4 (reproduced below)?

   *He listens intently, asks me some questions, and my feelings are seemingly known by him exactly.*

   (A)  (As it is now)
   (B)  Listening intently, he will ask me some questions and then my exact feelings are seemingly known to him.
   (C)  As he listens to me and asks me some questions, he seems to be knowing exactly my feelings.
   (D)  He listened to me and asked me some questions, seeming to know exactly how I felt.
   (E)  He listens intently, asks me some questions, and then seems to know exactly how I feel.

*Answer:* Choice (E) is correct.

*Explanation:* Sentence 4 should use a parallel construction of present-tense verbs to denote the series of events the father typically performs. This sentence properly follows sentence 3 by indicating, in a manner consistent with the rest of the paragraph, how the father typically responds to his child's problems.

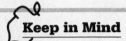

**Keep in Mind**

Don't reject a choice because the language is simple. Often the simplest expression of an idea is the clearest — and the best.

- Choice (A) is unsatisfactory because the sentence shifts unnecessarily from the active voice to the passive voice.

- Choice (B) is unsatisfactory because it awkwardly shifts the subject of the sentence from the father ("he") to the child's feelings.

- Choice (C) is unsatisfactory because it uses an improper verb form; "to know" is preferable to "to be knowing."

- Choice (D) is unsatisfactory because the sentence switches to the past tense; the context suggests that these are habitual, ongoing actions that require the present tense.

---

3. In sentence 7, the phrase *by all accounts* is best replaced by
   (A) however
   (B) moreover
   (C) to my knowledge
   (D) like my sister
   (E) but nevertheless

---

*Answer:* The correct answer is choice (A).

*Explanation:* Sentence 7 draws a contrast between the father and the people described in sentence 6. With the inclusion of the word "however," the sentence properly indicates that the father, unlike the busy people of sentence 6, is NOT too busy to spend time listening.

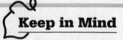

**Keep in Mind**

The revised sentence must make sense in the context of the passage as a whole.

- Choice (B) is unsatisfactory because the word "moreover" suggests that the thought about to be expressed supports and is consistent with the previous thought — but instead, sentence 7 draws a contrast with sentence 6.

- Choice (C) is unsatisfactory because the phrase "to my knowledge" is unnecessary; we know from the writer's use of the first person that these claims are a reflection of his or her knowledge.

■ Choice (D) is unsatisfactory because the subject of the paragraph is the father. It would be inappropriate at this point in the paragraph to introduce new information about the sister.

■ Choice (E) is unsatisfactory because the word "but" is unnecessary. The word "nevertheless" by itself would be sufficient to express the idea.

4. Which of the following sentences should be omitted to improve the unity of the second paragraph?
   (A) Sentence 8
   (B) Sentence 9
   (C) Sentence 10
   (D) Sentence 11
   (E) Sentence 12

*Answer:* Choice (E) is correct.

*Explanation:* Paragraph 2 continues the discussion of the father's ability to understand people by explaining how he utilizes this talent at work. Sentence 12 stands out from the paragraph because it introduces a new idea: how we choose our friends.

■ Choice (A) is unsatisfactory because sentence 8 introduces an idea — how the father uses his talent at work — that is supported in the following sentences.

■ Choice (B) is unsatisfactory because sentence 9 properly follows sentence 8 by explaining one aspect of the father's job.

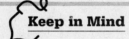

**Keep in Mind**

A concluding remark covers the entire essay, not just one part of it.

■ Choice (C) is unsatisfactory because the dinner discussed in sentence 10 is clearly one of the social events introduced in sentence 9.

■ Choice (D) is unsatisfactory because the phrase "such a conversation" in sentence 11 refers clearly to the previous sentence.

5. In context, which of the following is the best way to phrase the underlined portion of sentence 16 (reproduced below)?
   *Furthermore, it has strengthened his relationship with my mother.*
   (A) (As it is now)
   (B) Further strengthening
   (C) But it strengthens
   (D) However, he is strengthening
   (E) Considering this, he strengthens

*Answer:* Choice (A) is correct.

*Explanation:* The idea expressed in sentence 16 offers further support for the idea specified in sentence 13 and supported in sentences 14 and 15. The language of the sentence should indicate this.

The word "Furthermore" properly indicates that the information about the father's relationship with the mother offers further support for the statement made in sentence 13.

- Choice (B) is unsatisfactory because it creates a sentence fragment; the resulting sentence has no subject.

- Choice (C) is unsatisfactory because the word "But" indicates a contrast between the ideas expressed in sentences 15 and 16 where a contrast does not exist.

- Choice (D) is unsatisfactory because the word "However" indicates, illogically, that the strengthening of the father's relationship with the mother is somehow in contrast with the strengthening of his relationships with children and friends.

- Choice (E) is unsatisfactory because the phrase "Considering this" makes no sense in context. The resulting sentence implies that the strengthening of the relationship with the mother is separate from the father's ability to understand others, while the progression of support in the paragraph suggests the opposite.

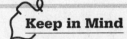

**Keep in Mind**

Adding material to an essay can be an excellent revision technique, as long as the new material is relevant and develops the ideas of the essay.

6. A strategy that the writer uses within the third paragraph is to
   (A) make false assumptions and use exaggeration
   (B) include difficult vocabulary
   (C) repeat certain words and sentence patterns
   (D) argue in a tone of defiance
   (E) turn aside from the main subject

*Answer:* Choice (C) is correct.

*Explanation:* The writer makes the point that the father's ability to understand people affects his whole life by specifying those particular areas of his life that have benefited. The writer emphasizes the point that the father's ability has benefited him in relationships with many different people (friends, co-workers, children, spouse) by utilizing a parallel structure in sentences 14, 15 and 16. The writer also repeats the words "ability" and "allows" and uses the same subject (the father's ability or talent) for each sentence in the paragraph.

- Choice (A) is unsatisfactory because nothing about this paragraph is exaggerated or shown to be false.

- Choice (B) is unsatisfactory because there is no evidence that vocabulary in the third paragraph is particularly difficult.

- Choice (D) is unsatisfactory because the tone of this paragraph is not defiant.

- Choice (E) is unsatisfactory because the paragraph continues the discussion of the main subject of the essay — the father's exceptional talent.

## Recap

1. Read the essay through to determine its overall meaning before you look at the questions.

2. Read more slowly than you usually do, to help you pay closer attention.

3. Make sure that your sentence revisions make sense in the context of the passage as a whole.

4. Don't reject a possible answer because the language is simple. Often, the simplest expression of an idea is the clearest and therefore the best answer.

5. Try *all* the suggestions before you decide on your answer.

6. Make sure that the relationship between the two sentences is clear when you combine sentences.

7. Remember that pronouns should always clearly refer back to a word or phrase.

8. Keep in mind that adding material to an essay can be an excellent revision technique, but the new material must be relevant and develop the ideas of the essay.

9. Use your test booklet to help you by marking each question that you don't answer. Then you can easily find it later.

# Practice Questions

**Directions:** The following passage is an early draft of an essay. Some parts of the passage need to be rewritten.

Read the passage and select the best answers for the questions that follow. Some questions are about particular sentences or parts of sentences and ask you to improve sentence structure or word choice. Other questions ask you to consider organization and development. In choosing answers, follow the requirements of standard written English.

---

**Questions 1-5 are based on the following passage.**

(1) I have just read an excellent book called "Having Our Say: The Delany Sisters' First 100 Years." (2) Usually I do not enjoy autobiographies. (3) I could hardly put this one down. (4) It is about Sadie Delany, who is 103 years old, and her "little" sister Bessie, she is 101.

(5) The sisters grew up in North Carolina in times that were not easy for African Americans. (6) Around 1916 they moved to New York City and went to Columbia University at their father's urging. (7) He tells them, "You are college material. (8) And if you don't go, shame on you!" (9) Sadie became a teacher and Bessie a dentist. (10) The second Black woman dentist in New York.

(11) They lived through an incredible amount of history. (12) For instance, Bessie participated in civil rights marches and protests in New York for decades, starting in the 1920s. (13) Imagine having people like Paul Robeson over to dinner!

(14) One aspect of the book that I especially liked was its humor; though Sadie is not as irreverent as Bessie, both are full of wisecracks. (15) The Delany sisters seem livelier than many twenty-year-olds. (16) They care deeply about what is going on around them — and they laugh at things whenever possible.

1. What is the best way to deal with sentence 3 (reproduced below)?

    *I could hardly put this one down.*

    (A) Leave it as it is.
    (B) Connect it to sentence 2 with the word "but".
    (C) Place it before sentence 2.
    (D) Change "this one" to "this autobiography".
    (E) Omit it.

2. In context, which is the best version of "He tells them" in sentence 7 (reproduced below)?

    *He tells them, "You are college material.*

    (A) (As it is now)
    (B) Their father tells them,
    (C) This is because he tells them,
    (D) He had told them,
    (E) His suggestion was:

3. Which of the following sentences is best to insert between sentences 12 and 13?

    (A) The two sisters also knew many famous figures personally.
    (B) Sadie usually did not march, but protested by other means.
    (C) Many young people seem to think this did not begin until the 1960s.
    (D) The last hundred years have seen many changes in civil rights laws.
    (E) Paul Robeson was a prominent singer, actor, and political activist.

4. In context, what is the best way to deal with sentence 14?

    (A) Move it to the beginning of the first paragraph.
    (B) Move it to the beginning of the second paragraph.
    (C) Start a new sentence after "irreverent" and delete "though".
    (D) Connect it to sentence 15 with a comma.
    (E) Follow it with an example.

5. Which of the following, if placed after sentence 16, would be the most effective concluding sentence for the essay?

(A) They eat healthy food and do yoga every day.
(B) Therefore, it is no small thing to survive past age 100.
(C) This book is a remarkable story made even better by the way it is told.
(D) Finally, young people should definitely communicate with their elders.
(E) Much as I enjoyed the rest of the book, the final chapter is my favorite.

**Questions 6-11 are based on the following passage.**

(1) Becoming the best is very difficult. (2) No matter if you are trying to become a better athlete, student, or musician. (3) If you want to be the best, sacrifices must be made by you. (4) You lose a lot of time that you would otherwise have for just relaxing. (5) This time could also have been spent exercising outdoors. (6) You must also be willing to cut down on time spent with family and friends. (7) If your goal is to become a fine jazz pianist, you must be willing to work hard.

(8) Many people think jazz musicians just sit down and play, this is a mistake. (9) Practicing demands many hours in a week. (10) Most of the exercises done are of repetition and become boring, but that is the price you must pay for success. (11) You must practice fingering techniques and learn about both classical and jazz harmonies and chords. (12) The reason you need to know about these harmonies is that so much of jazz involves improvisation, making up new sequences of notes to play. (13) You are not just playing notes that a composer wrote but are almost like a composer yourself. (14) Sometimes you will feel discouraged. (15) When you can play a classic like Dizzy Gillespie's "Manteca" the way it really should be played, the long hours and hard work seem worthwhile.

6. Of the following, which is the best way to write the underlined portion of sentences 1 and 2 (reproduced below)?

*Becoming the best is very difficult. No matter if you are trying to become a better athlete, student, or musician.*

(A) (As it is now)
(B) difficult, never mind if
(C) difficult, whether
(D) difficult. Regardless of whether
(E) difficult; whether or not

7. In context, which of the following is the best way to phrase the underlined portion of sentence 3 (reproduced below)?

*If you want to be the best, sacrifices must be made by you.*

(A) (As it is now)
(B) one must sacrifice some things
(C) you must make sacrifices
(D) one will have to make sacrifices
(E) sacrifices are necessary to make

8. Which of the following is the best way to revise and combine sentences 4 and 5 (reproduced below)?

   *You lose a lot of time that you would otherwise have for just relaxing. This time could also have been spent exercising outdoors.*

   (A) Time that could have been spent exercising outdoors or just to relax will be lost.
   (B) Spending time exercising outdoors or relaxation are things for which you will have less time.
   (C) You will have much less time for exercising outdoors or for just relaxing.
   (D) Sacrificing outdoor exercise and just relaxing, because you will not have time.
   (E) As examples of the things you will have to cut down on would be outdoor exercise or just relaxing.

9. Of the following, which would be the best way to revise the underlined portion of sentence 8 (reproduced below)?

   *Many people think jazz musicians just sit down and play, <u>this is a mistake</u>.*

   (A) and, this is a mistake however
   (B) this would be a mistake
   (C) what a mistake that would be
   (D) it is mistaken
   (E) but they are mistaken

10. In context, which of the following is the best way to phrase sentence 10 (reproduced below)?

    *Most of the exercises done are of repetition and become boring, but that is the price you must pay for success.*

    (A) (As it is now)
    (B) The price you must pay consists mostly of repetitious and boring exercises for success.
    (C) Doing repetitious and boring exercises; this is the price of success.
    (D) Repetition and boredom are the inevitable result when having done most of the exercises.
    (E) Doing repetitious and boring exercises is the price you must pay for success.

11. In context, which of the following is the best way to phrase the underlined portion of sentence 11 (reproduced below)?

    *<u>You must practice fingering techniques and learn</u> about both classical and jazz harmonies and chords.*

    (A) (As it is now)
    (B) You must practice fingering techniques and learning
    (C) One would practice techniques for fingering and learn
    (D) Fingering techniques must be practiced and learning
    (E) There must be practice of fingering techniques and you learn

## Answer Key

1. B
2. D
3. A
4. E
5. C
6. C
7. C
8. C
9. E
10. E
11. A

 Additional practice questions can be found in *The Official SAT Online Course* at www.collegeboard.org/satonlinecourse.

# CHAPTER 13

# Practice for the Writing Section

You can never practice too much. This chapter gives you additional practice in writing essays and answering questions. This chapter includes nine sample essays with scores ranging from 6 through 1. There are practice questions on improving sentences, identifying sentence errors and improving paragraphs. These are all in addition to the sample questions in Chapters 9, 10, 11 and 12.

 **Automated Score**

To receive an automated score for your response to this essay question, check out *The Official SAT Online Course* at www.collegeboard.org/ satonlinecourse.org.

## Practice for the Essay

The following is a typical essay prompt that you might find on the SAT. Follow the instructions and try writing an essay.

> Think carefully about the issue presented in the following excerpt and the assignment below.
>
> > Honesty is important, of course, but deception can actually make it easier for people to get along. In a recent study, for example, one out of every four of the lies told by participants was told solely for the benefit of another person. In fact, most lies are harmless social untruths in which people pretend to like someone or something more than they actually do ("Your muffins are the best!").
>
> Adapted from Allison Kornet, "The Truth About Lying"
>
> **Assignment:** Is deception ever justified? Plan and write an essay in which you develop your point of view on this issue. Support your position with reasoning and examples taken from your reading, studies, experience, or observations.

# Practice Questions: Improving Sentences

The following sentences test correctness and effectiveness of expression. Part of each sentence or the entire sentence is underlined; beneath each sentence are five ways of phrasing the underlined material. Choice A repeats the original phrasing; the other four choices are different. If you think the original phrasing produces a better sentence than any of the alternatives, select choice A; if not, select one of the other choices.

In making your selection, follow the requirements of standard written English; that is, pay attention to grammar, choice of words, sentence construction, and punctuation. Your selection should result in the most effective sentence — clear and precise, without awkwardness or ambiguity.

**Example:**

Laura Ingalls Wilder published her first book <u>and she was sixty-five years old then</u>.

(A)   and she was sixty-five years old then
(B)   when she was sixty-five
(C)   at age sixty-five years old
(D)   upon the reaching of sixty-five years
(E)   at the time when she was sixty-five

---

1.  To ensure that the bread will have the same consistency from batch to batch, <u>it is the quality control specialist who checks small random samples of dough from each lot</u>.

    (A)   it is the quality control specialist who checks small random samples of dough from each lot
    (B)   the quality control specialist checks small random samples of dough from each lot
    (C)   small random samples of dough are checked from each lot by the quality control specialist
    (D)   the quality control specialist checks samples of dough — small and randomly — from each lot
    (E)   the quality control specialist is the one checking small random samples from each lot of dough

2.  <u>Although Central Park in Manhattan is better known than Prospect Park in Brooklyn, the designer of both parks, Frederick Law Olmsted, preferred Prospect Park.</u>

    (A)   Although Central Park in Manhattan is better known than Prospect Park in Brooklyn, the designer of both parks, Frederick Law Olmsted, preferred Prospect Park.
    (B)   Central Park in Manhattan being better known than Prospect Park in Brooklyn, the designer of both, Frederick Law Olmsted, preferred the latter.
    (C)   Although not as well known as Central Park, Frederick Law Olmsted, who designed both parks, preferred Prospect Park.
    (D)   The designer of both Central Park and Prospect Park was Frederick Law Olmsted, he preferred Prospect Park.
    (E)   Although more people know about Manhattan's Central Park than Prospect Park in Brooklyn, Frederick Law Olmsted, having designed both, has preferred the latter.

3.  Growing up in a family where music was a daily part of life, Steve and Rick shared a determination <u>to become singing duos</u> known nationwide.

    (A)   to become singing duos
    (B)   to become a singing duo
    (C)   of becoming singing duos
    (D)   that they would become singing duos
    (E)   of becoming a singing duo

4. The bagpipe originated in ancient Sumer, <u>many people assume that it was</u> the Scottish Highlands.

    (A) many people assume that it was
    (B) many people assuming
    (C) not, as many people assume, in
    (D) not what many people assume
    (E) but many people assume it to be

5. Certain shipwrecks have a particular fascination for those people <u>which have a belief in finding the treasure in them</u>.

    (A) which have a belief in finding the treasure in them
    (B) that belief there is treasure to be found in them
    (C) who believe they hold treasure and that they can find it
    (D) who believe that there is treasure to be found in them
    (E) who believe about treasure to be found in them

6. Many of the instruments used in early operations of the United States Army Signal <u>Corps were adaptations of equipment used by the Plains Indians, particularly that of the heliograph</u>.

    (A) Corps were adaptations of equipment used by the Plains Indians, particularly that of the heliograph
    (B) Corps, there were adaptations of equipment used by the Plains Indians, particularly the heliograph
    (C) Corps, and in particular the heliograph, was an adaptation of equipment used by the Plains Indians
    (D) Corps, and in particular the heliograph, were adaptations of equipment used by the Plains Indians
    (E) Corps being adaptations, the heliograph in particular, of those used by Plains Indians

7. Marie and Pierre Curie discovered radium but refused to patent the process they <u>used nor otherwise profiting</u> from the commercial exploitation of radium.

    (A) used nor otherwise profiting
    (B) had used nor otherwise did they profit
    (C) have used or otherwise to have profited
    (D) used or otherwise profited
    (E) had used or otherwise to profit

8. <u>Many drivers violate traffic laws knowingly and openly, in other respects they are law-abiding citizens, however</u>.

    (A) Many drivers violate traffic laws knowingly and openly, in other respects they are law-abiding citizens, however.
    (B) Many drivers who are otherwise law-abiding citizens violate traffic laws knowingly and openly.
    (C) Many drivers violate traffic laws knowingly and openly and are otherwise law-abiding citizens.
    (D) Although otherwise law-abiding citizens, many drivers, however, violate traffic laws knowingly and openly.
    (E) Many drivers which violate traffic laws knowingly and openly are in other respects law-abiding citizens.

9. The primatologist has argued that sustained observation of a few animals <u>provides better behavioral data than does intermittent observation of many animals</u>.

    (A) provides better behavioral data than does intermittent observation of many animals
    (B) provides better behavioral data than many animals are observed intermittently
    (C) providing better behavioral data than does intermittent observation of many animals
    (D) do provide better behavioral data than intermittent observation of many animals do
    (E) in contrast to intermittent observation of many animals, provides better behavioral data

# Practice Questions:
# Identifying Sentence Errors

The following sentences test your ability to recognize grammar and usage errors. Each sentence contains either a single error or no error at all. No sentence contains more than one error. The error, if there is one, is underlined and lettered. If the sentence contains an error, select the one underlined part that must be changed to make the sentence correct. If the sentence is correct, select choice E. In choosing answers, follow the requirements of standard written English.

**Example:**

The other delegates and him immediately
   A             B       C

accepted the resolution drafted by the
                       D

neutral states. No error
          E                           Ⓐ ● Ⓒ Ⓓ Ⓔ

---

10. One challenge that writer Eleanor Wong Telemaque faced was how preserving her
                                                               A

    ethnic identity while becoming more accessible to readers who are accustomed to
                    B                   C                         D

    writers from other cultural backgrounds. No error
                                     E

11. Lions and tigers may be identical in size, but the tiger is the fiercer animal and the
                    A                   B             C

    lion the strongest. No error
         D        E

12. Ms. Jordan proudly demonstrated her company's most popular product, a watch that
             A         B

    flashes the time in lighted numerals when pressing a button. No error
                  C                   D           E

13. In the 1920s, much critical approval was given to a group of English writers
              A                   B

    known as the Bloomsbury group, the most famous of whom was Virginia Woolf.
     C                       D

    No error
     E

14. Maude Adams, after her spectacular triumph as the original Peter Pan, went about
                               A                              B

    heavy veiled and was accessible to only a handful of intimate friends. No error
     C                         D                      E

**15.** All states <u>impose</u> severe <u>penalties on</u> drivers who do not stop when <u>he or she is</u>
                 A                B                        C

     <u>involved</u> in accidents. <u>No error</u>
        D               E

**16.** If one is <u>interested in</u> <u>learning</u> <u>even more</u> about Zora Neale Hurston, <u>you should</u>
                 A         B    C                              D

     read Robert Hemenway's biography. <u>No error</u>
                                  E

**17.** If he <u>had begun</u> <u>earlier</u>, he might have succeeded <u>in finishing</u> the <u>extremely</u>
          A        B                          C         D

     complex project before the deadline. <u>No error</u>
                                  E

**18.** In the early twentieth century, new thinking <u>about</u> symbolism and the unconscious
                                           A

     <u>were</u> greatly inspired <u>by</u> the <u>writings of</u> Sigmund Freud and Carl Jung. <u>No error</u>
     B                  C        D                                E

# Practice Questions: Improving Paragraphs

**Directions:** The following passage is an early draft of an essay. Some parts of the passage need to be rewritten.

Read the passage and select the best answers for the questions that follow. Some questions are about particular sentences or parts of sentences and ask you to improve sentence structure or word choice. Other questions ask you to consider organization and development. In choosing answers, follow the requirements of standard written English.

**Questions 19–23 are based on the following passage.**

(1) Living in a city in central Alaska, I have become accustomed to extreme weather conditions, these are a part of living in a remote, northern region. (2) To us Alaskans, a 70 mph wind is something that messes up our hair. (3) Temperatures of 20 degrees Farenheit mean that we can take off our coats. (4) We are used to winter days with only 4 hours of sunlight, or summer baseball games that can start at 10:30 PM without artificial lighting. (5) Adjusting to such conditions is not too difficult. (6) But, Alaska's remote location creates challenging economic circumstances.

(7) Alaska is tremendously rich in natural resources, such as lumber, oil, and fish. (8) We must import processed goods from the lower forty-eight states. (9) Most goods are shipped all the way to the port of Anchorage; the cost is nearly triple that of sending goods from New York to Seattle by rail. (10) The state of Alaska is the number one harvester of seafood in the United States. (11) But processed seafood can be bought more inexpensively in the state of Washington because Alaska does not have enough fish processing plants of its own and so must ship a great deal of seafood to Seattle for processing. (12) Thus, the cost of long distance transportation drives up the price of the product.

(13) One solution that Alaskans definitely should consider is having built more local processing facilities. (14) After all, there is plenty of fish to keep them running. (15) Ultimately, this solution can benefit Alaskans by providing jobs, lower prices, and healthy competition.

19. In the context of the first paragraph, which of the following would be the best way to combine the underlined portions of sentences 5 and 6 (reproduced below)?

    *Adjusting to such conditions is not too <u>difficult. But, Alaska's remote location</u> creates challenging economic circumstances.*

    (A) difficult, and Alaska's remote location
    (B) difficult, but Alaska's remote location
    (C) difficult: the remote location of Alaska
    (D) difficult; indeed, its remote location
    (E) difficult, and the remoteness of our location

20. Which of the following would be the most logical insertion at the beginning of sentence 8?

    (A) In other words,
    (B) Not surprisingly,
    (C) Invariably,
    (D) Hence,
    (E) Unfortunately,

21. In context, which of the following sentences would best fit between sentences 10 and 11?

    (A) Many years ago the fishing was better than it is today.
    (B) I do not personally care for seafood.
    (C) Fishing can be a dangerous business because of the squalls that can blow up suddenly in this part of the world.
    (D) Our coastal waters contain an abundance of king crab, salmon, and other sea creatures.
    (E) Some fish nets drift out to sea.

22. In context, which of the following is the best way to phrase the underlined portion of sentence 13 (reproduced below)?

    *One solution that Alaskans definitely should consider is having built more local processing facilities.*

    (A) (As it is now)
    (B) is building more local processing facilities
    (C) is this: more local processing facilities should be built locally
    (D) is that more should be built locally
    (E) is that we should build more of them

23. The function of the third paragraph (sentences 13–15) is to

    (A) offer further evidence supporting the view presented in the first paragraph (sentences 1–6)
    (B) describe the result of problems listed in the second paragraph (sentences 7–12)
    (C) propose a way to remedy the situation described in the second paragraph
    (D) unify the essay by resolving a contradiction between the first and second paragraphs
    (E) end the essay with an ironic twist

# Answer Key

## *The Essay*

 **Automated Score**

**To receive an automated score for your response to this essay question, check out *The Official SAT Online Course* at www.collegeboard.org/ satonlinecourse.**

To prepare for the essay section, it is helpful to review sample essays written by other students and the explanations of the scores they received, ranging from 6 to 1.

Although all of the sample essays were *handwritten* by students, they are shown *typed* here, in bottom, for ease of reading. However, we are presenting one in handwriting to remind you that it is important to write legibly and clearly. The essays have been typed *exactly* as each student wrote his or her essay, without any corrections to spelling, punctuation, syntax or paragraph breaks.

The following is a sample prompt:

> Think carefully about the issue presented in the following excerpt and the assignment below.
>
> Honesty is important, of course, but deception can actually make it easier for people to get along. In a recent study, for example, one out of every four of the lies told by participants was told solely for the benefit of another person. In fact, most lies are harmless social untruths in which people pretend to like someone or something more than they actually do ("Your muffins are the best!").
>
> Adapted from Allison Kornet, "The Truth About Lying"
>
> **Assignment:** Is deception ever justified? Plan and write an essay in which you develop your point of view on this issue. Support your position with reasoning and examples taken from your reading, studies, experience, or observations.

*Essay #1: This essay received a score of 6.*

| Part A (Writing Sample) | Begin your composition on this side. If you need more space, continue on the reverse side. |
| --- | --- |

→ Deception is sometimes justified. When someone is trying to achieve an end, he or she must sometimes use deception as a means. On at least two occasions the Confederate Army used deception in an attempt to overthrow the more powerful Union Army. Also, in literature, Jay Gatsby uses deception to win over his true love.

→ In the first major battle of The Civil War, The First Battle of Bull Run, the Confederate Army gained a neat victory over the Union using deception. Although The Union appeared to be winning the battle General Stonewall Jackson was waiting with reserve troops. In fact, he surprised the overconfident Union army, and drove them back with his delayed attack. Had Stonewell Jackson not used deception, the South would not have won that important battle of the Civil War.

→ Deception was actually a major element in The South's overall war strategy. Since they lacked the resources and the manpower of the North, they had to make due with what They did have—cleverness. They used tactics such as fierce "rebel yelling" and false reports to make the North believe that There were more Confederate troops Than there actually were. General Mclellan of the North often hesitated to take action because he was always concerned about sending his men into certain death. The South's façade worked for some time, and they had the Union tricked out of attacking Them.

Continue on the reverse side if necessary.

*(continued)*

→ We also see the necessity of deception in F. Scott Fitzgerald's The Great Gatsby, when the protagonist uses the facade of his mansion and his parties to impress his love, Daisy. To him, his only goal in love is to win her over, which goal drives him to become wealthy and buy a huge mansion. He holds huge drinking parties merely for the sake of attracting Daisy to his house. ⊛ To him, deception is necessary, or else he could not procure true love for himself.

→ On many occasions, deception is necessary. The South had to deceive the North, and Gatsby had to deceive himself and Daisy. For deception to be justified by there must be some end that is necessary to achieve. However, deception must have a good cause. Enron's recent deception was unjustified, because their end was to steal and to embezzle. The Confederacy was defending its way of life, and Gatsby was in pursuit of true love. Although deception was justified in those cases, mendacity in general should not be encouraged. Lying and stealing are forms of deception that lack a just end. Therefore, deception can be sometimes justified, but at other times not. ⊛ Gatsby, however, does not fit into high saying he merely uses these things to attract Daisy]

## WHY ESSAY #1 RECEIVED A SCORE OF 6

This *outstanding* essay uses clearly appropriate examples to develop effectively the point of view that "For deception to be justified, there must be some end that is necessary to achieve." The writer demonstrates outstanding critical thinking by exploring two examples of outcomes that justified deception and one example of an outcome that did not justify deception:

- In paragraph 3, the writer describes how the Confederacy, lacking "the resources and the manpower of the North," was justifiably forced to rely on deception in order to "defend its way of life."

- Paragraph 4 provides the second example of justifiable deceit by discussing Jay Gatsby's use of deception in pursuit of true love.

- Paragraph 5 uses the recent Enron scandal as an example of deception that did not have "a good cause" and therefore was not justified.

This focused essay demonstrates clear coherence and exhibits skillful use of language. Consequently, the response demonstrates *clear and consistent mastery* and scored a 6.

**Essay #2: This essay also received a score of 6.**

"Honesty is always the best policy" may be a trite saying, but it holds an enormous amount of truth. Though deception often allows one to escape immediate repercussions, the truth will always emerge. In most situations, one will find that deception does not offer the same long-term benefits as honesty does.

Sometimes deception occurs in the form of white lies. For instance, my cousin Joanne was invited to her friend's wedding in Hawaii and she asked for my opinion on her dress. Her dress was a hideous creation; it looked like a mass of cabages sewn together. But I smiled and told Joanne that the dress was beautiful anyway. How could I ruin her excitement over the dress? Looking back at that 1 moment, I probably should have told her the truth, considering that the guests laughed at her. She had trusted me to give an honest, helpful opinion, but, instead, I led her to humiliation.

With regards to more serious matters, however, deception can lead to more dire consequences. Cheating on a test, for instance, may result in failure of a class or expulsion from school. My brother had helped his best friend cheat on a math test, but confessed the truth to the teacher immediately afterwards. The teacher only forced the two boys to retake the test because she appreciated their honesty. If my brother had not approached his teacher, he might have been kicked out of school. Furthermore, my brother's decision serves as an example of morality to his friend and other students. Thus, he saved his friend from more serious punishment, which would have been his justification for lying anyway.

Despite these advantages to telling the truth, deception can still be rather tempting. For instance, how can one explain the death of a relative to an innocent child? Is it justified to lie to him in order to protect him from the harshness of reality? Should a child learn about war? If one gives children sugar-coated versions of the truth, they may feel even greater shock when they discover the facts. Deception is often a kind, protective gesture, but truth can prepare a child for the future. If revealed gradually, truth offers valuable knowledge.

Thus, one can view deception as a sweet treat. It is like a cookie that satisfies hunger and gives immediate pleasure. However, the cookie will only cause poor health in the future. Similarly, deception appears to be a justifiable and sometimes even compassionate, but it only holds future problems.

## WHY ESSAY #2 RECEIVED A SCORE OF 6

In all ways, this well-organized and clearly focused essay demonstrates *clear and consistent mastery*. The writer demonstrates outstanding critical thinking by developing insightfully the main idea "that deception does not offer the same long-term benefits as honesty does," while also acknowledging and discussing the temptation to use deception "to escape immediate repercussions." Paragraphs 2 and 3 offer personal examples of instances when the use of deception led to unfortunate consequences. Paragraph 4 uses the example of protecting a child's innocence to describe a time when deception can be tempting.

Throughout this essay, the writer exhibits skillful use of language and demonstrates variety in sentence structure. Thus, this *outstanding* response scored a 6.

*Essay #3: This essay received a score of 5.*

In a world where horrific and negative incidents often occur the general public is often decieved. Some believe the shielding or twisting of certain information may be beneficial. However, as shown through major historical events, deception is never justifiable. Yellow journalism and the censorship of facts proves just this.

In the weeks previous to the Spanish-American war in the late 1800s, an arousing anger again spain was rising among the public. Advocates of war took the matter into their own hands and through yellow journalism, caused the war to break out. Hearst and Pulitzer used tainted information in their newspapers, assuring the public that Spain was brutal and cruel. When the American ship, The Maine mysteriously sunk in Havana Cuba, the newspapers fully blamed the Spanish of murdering American soldiers. A letter never meant for the public was published and the newspapers insisted that the letter was insulting McKinley. Soon the entire public was lied to and almost everyone encouraged war. The public was manipulated and decieved. They were tricked into war, and history has a large number of American and Spanish deaths which clearly show how truely harmful deception can be.

During the same period of time, as Americans yearned for imperialism, The Fillipino Insurection occured. As thousands of American soldiers became engaged in gorilla warfare, a large number of deaths occured. Back home, on United States soil, the American public wondered about the progress in this foreign land. they were lied to. Fearful that the fighting would become unpopular, imperialist politions told the public of great advancements and new territory and people conquered. As Americans and Fillipinos were being brutally slaughtered each day, censorship and deciet prevailed. By the time the truth was unvailed, the damage had already been done. The truth could have saved lives, resources, and dignity for the US, but it was sheilded

As shown through history, deception is never acceptable. Each person, regardless of political or social rank deserves the absolute truth on manners that greatly effect their lives.

## WHY ESSAY #3 RECEIVED A SCORE OF 5

This detailed essay uses examples of events in history to develop effectively the point of view that "deception is never justifiable." The writer displays strong critical thinking by describing two separate instances when the American public was led deceptively into supporting a war. The second paragraph describes how the media distorted the truth, provoking Americans into backing the Spanish-American War. In paragraph 3, the writer explores the use of "censorship and deciet" to maintain American support during the "Fillipino Insurection."

This response is focused, and the writer uses appropriate vocabulary and displays a progression of ideas. Thus, the essay demonstrates *reasonably consistent mastery* and scored a 5.

*Essay #4: This essay also received a score of 5.*

Deception, or the misrepresentation of true purposes, is a form of a lie. Although lieing might pose immediate benefits in the long-term, it simply creates problems. Thus, deception can never be justified.

Throughout literature, there are many instances of nefarious characters using deception. For example, in Macbeth by Shakespeare, the witches offer "half-truths" in the form of confusing and misleading riddles to Macbeth. Obviously, the witches are creatures of evil, intent on creating pain and wreaking havoc. The deceptive things the witches tell Macbeth drive him to do things he would not ordinarily do, such as kill the Duncan and Banquo. Through this and numerous other examples, it becomes apparent that deception and trickery are the tools of evil. Thus, by relation, deception is evil. How, then, can deception ever be justified as morally right?

In the folktale, The Boy Who Cried Wolf, a boy intentionally decieves others for his own amusement. However, when he seriously needs help and calls for it, no one will help him because they do not believe him. His previous deceptions have made him lose all credibility in the eyes of the townspeople. Had he not previously deceived them, surely they would help him now. This tale presents a strong message: deception can only cause trouble.

During The Watergate scandal, Nixon, among other things, deceived the American people. As an elected official, he was expected to uphold and maintain a standard of honesty. However, because he effectively lied in the manner he originally misrepresented the actions of his people in The Watergate incident, he committed an act of deception. Although the temporary rewards of this appealed to him, this was the easy (and incorrect) way out. Due to this deception, Nixon's image took a huge hit, and he ended up resigning the presidency of the United States. Effectively, deception led to the downfall of Richard Nixon.

This is why I believe deception can never be justified.

## WHY ESSAY #4 RECEIVED A SCORE OF 5

This well-organized and focused essay demonstrates *reasonably consistent mastery*. The writer develops effectively the point of view that "deception can never be justified" and demonstrates strong critical thinking by providing three appropriate examples to support this position:

- In the second paragraph, the writer provides evidence from the play *Macbeth* to illustrate the idea that because deception is evil, it cannot be "justified as morally right."

- Paragraph 3 uses the folktale *The Boy Who Cried Wolf* to show that deception leads to trouble.

- Paragraph 4 describes how Richard Nixon's deception of the American people eventually led to his downfall.

This response exhibits facility in the use of language, demonstrates variety in sentence structure and is generally free of errors. Therefore, this essay is categorized as *effective* and received a score of 5.

*Essay #5: This essay received a score of 4.*

"Ends justify the means." This quote signifies that in some cases, deception is justified. Deception occurs when a person's trust in others is taken advantge of. In special cases, this expiotation can be justified.

My best friend was turning 16 in 3 months when she revealed to me that she had never had a real birthday party before. Immediatly, I secretly began planning a suprise party in my head. I got excited just thinking about how suprised she was going to be.

For the next 3 months, almost everything that came out of my mouth was a lie. I didn't know all of her friends from outside of school, so I had to lie when she asked why I wanted to borrow her address book. "I lost mine and I want to copy the people from your book." She relucantly agreed, and although I felt a pang of guilt, I was able to create a complete guest list.

Thursday night I called her and pretended I was sick. All day Friday, instead of going to school, I had to get the cake, the balloons and other decorations. There was no way she could have suspected a suprise party if her best friend was sick.

The minute she walked into the room and saw all the people there for her birthday, she started crying with joy. Every lie and every deception had been justifed by the look on her face and the happiness in her eyes. Sometimes in life, the ends do justify the means.

**WHY ESSAY #5 RECEIVED A SCORE OF 4**

This generally focused essay demonstrates *adequate mastery*. The writer develops the point of view that "in some cases, deception is justified" by providing a personal, detailed example of an instance when the "ends do justify the means." By describing how the deception involved in planning a surprise party is justified by the ultimate happiness the friend feels because of the party, the writer demonstrates competent critical thinking.

The support is adequate and generally organized, exhibiting some coherence and progression of ideas. This response displays some variety in sentence structure and uses generally appropriate vocabulary. Thus, the essay is *competent* and scored a 4.

**Essay #6: This essay also received a score of 4.**

The use of deception is usually thought of as a bad thing. But there are times when deception is justified. In the cases of Holden Caufield and Abigail Williams their use of deception is acceptable because of the situations in which they are placed.

The main character of The Catcher in the Rye by J.D. Salinger, is Holden Caufield. Holden is a depressed character than ends up going crazy. In the weekend that the book takes place Holden is constantly using deception. He pretends to be older and more sufisticated than he really is. This is appropriate for him because he is trying to feel accepted in the predominantly adult atmosphere that he puts himself into. Holden wants to be smarter and better at everything than all the people he meets, so he acts that way. Even though Holden is using deception, he is using it to feel better about himself when he is at a very difficult part of his life. After being kicked out of four schools, having his brother die, and not having many friends Holdens use of deception is rightly justified.

Another character from a book that uses deception is Abigail Williams from The Crucible. Abigail is a orphan child who has stayed with many different families, none of which have liked her. Abigail is also in love with a man named John Proctor who does not love her back. Abigail uses deception to make her town of Salem Village think she sees witches. Abigail does this largely to get attention from the people who never gave it to her, and to get back at John Proctor for not loving her. Abigail ruins other peoples lives through deception to make herself feel better. Even though the deception is bad, it is justifiable in Abigails situation because of the harsh life she has lived.

As seen in the characters Holden Caufield and Abigail Williams, deception is sometimes justifiable. In both these characters cases it was becaus their lives were on a downward spiral and they were just trying to climb back up.

## WHY ESSAY #6 RECEIVED A SCORE OF 4

This *competent* essay develops the point of view that "there are times when deception is justified." The writer demonstrates competent critical thinking by providing two adequate examples from literature when the characters' use of deception was justified "becaus their lives were on a downward spiral and they were just trying to climb back up."

Evidence provided is generally organized and focused, demonstrating some coherence and progression of ideas. This writer uses generally appropriate vocabulary and displays some variety in sentence structure. Consequently, this response demonstrates *adequate mastery* and scored a 4.

**Essay #7: This essay received a score of 3.**

I believe that deception can be justified; it simply matters what the circumstances. Certainly it cannot hurt to compliment a friend on his new haircut, when personally you find it revolting. Such superficial deceptions occur in every day life, and cause no real harm. But in the larger sense, I feel deception can be separated into two categeries: the justifiable deception that one must use to gain advantage in a competitive field, and the unjustifiable deception one uses at the expense of others for his or her own personal gain.

The biggest news story today is that of the Enron bankruptcy. Granted, we do not yet know all the facts, but it is obvious that deception took place.* Heads of the company knowingly lied to their shareholders, encouraging them to buy more stock, while the heads themselves made millions by short-selling the plummeting stock. Thousands of workers lost their life-savings because of the company's deception.

*There is already evidence that several accounting documents were either shredded or covered up.

### WHY ESSAY #7 RECEIVED A SCORE OF 3

This limited essay demonstrates *developing mastery*. The writer offers a point of view ("I feel deception can be separated into two categeries: the justifiable deception that one must use to gain advantage in a competitive field, and the unjustifiable deception one uses at the expense of others for his or her own personal gain") but fails to provide adequate evidence to support this main idea.

By comparing a personal example of when deception is justified to the recent Enron scandal when deception caused harm to thousands of innocent people, the writer demonstrates some critical thinking. The writer displays a developing facility in the use of language. However, this response simply lacks the evidence to support the main idea or establish a progression of ideas. Therefore, the essay remains in the *inadequate* category and scored a 3.

*Essay #8: This essay received a score of 2.*

> In the late seventeen hundreds, the American colonies had entered a war for independence against the oppression of King George III. General George Washington, leader of the American troops, employed a young man to infiltrate the British lines in order to determine their army's position. The man was disguised as a school teacher and succesfully penatrated the British lines. After completing his mission and giving Washington the upper hand, he was betrayed, captured and killed. Thanks to the many men who offered their lives, and the cunning use of deception, America won that war for the freedom and liberty of her people.
>
> I agree that deception can sometimes be justified.

### WHY ESSAY #8 RECEIVED A SCORE OF 2

This sparse response demonstrates *little mastery*. The writer develops a point of view ("deception can sometimes be justified") that is seriously limited by providing only insufficient evidence to support this position. The response demonstrates weak critical thinking by offering the appropriate but brief example of Washington's use of secrecy to win "freedom and liberty" for the American people.

Although this response is focused, the writer fails to provide sufficient support to demonstrate a progression of ideas. Thus, the essay is *seriously limited* and scored a 2.

*Essay #9: This essay received a score of 1.*

Deception can sometimes be justified. Everything is sometimes always justified, even things you wouldn't think until you really looked into them.

One example that came to mind was how our world works and operates. If things were always unjustifiable, Then we wouldn't have that much freedon, would we. Like if someone was driving down the street and speeding. The police would pull him over give him/her a ticket, and their on their way. Instead of putting him/her in jail. Deception can work the same way.

The way the world operates is with people letting things slide a little.

### WHY ESSAY #9 RECEIVED A SCORE OF 1

This brief response demonstrates only *very little mastery*. Although there is a main idea present ("Deception can sometimes be justified"), the example of speeding offered as support is too unfocused to develop this point of view. Ideas are disorganized and unclear, resulting in a disjointed and incoherent essay.

Furthermore, the response demonstrates severe flaws in sentence structure. ("Like if someone was driving down the street and speeding." "Instead of putting him/her in jail.") Consequently, this essay is *fundamentally lacking* and received a score of 1.

### Automated Score

To receive an automated score for your essay response online, check out *The Official SAT Online Course* at www.collegeboard.org/satonlinecourse.

# Answer Key

## Improving Sentences

| | | | |
|---|---|---|---|
| 1. B | | 6. D | |
| 2. A | | 7. E | |
| 3. B | | 8. B | |
| 4. C | | 9. A | |
| 5. D | | | |

## Identifying Sentence Errors

| | | | |
|---|---|---|---|
| 10. A | | 15. C | |
| 11. D | | 16. D | |
| 12. D | | 17. E | |
| 13. E | | 18. B | |
| 14. C | | | |

## Improving Paragraphs

| | | | |
|---|---|---|---|
| 19. B | | 22. B | |
| 20. E | | 23. C | |
| 21. D | | | |

Additional practice questions can be found in *The Official SAT Online Course* at www.collegeboard.org/satonlinecourse.

# PART IV
# The Mathematics Section

# CHAPTER 14

# About the Mathematics Section

Just about every part of your life requires math skills, and math skills will be especially important for success in college. The questions on the SAT emphasize mathematical reasoning and evaluate how well you can think through math problems. You will need to know some specific math concepts and math skills. The mathematics section evaluates how well you use these concepts and skills to solve real-life math problems.

The mathematics section has the following questions:

- 44 multiple-choice questions

- 10 student-produced response questions, which require you to fill in a response

The mathematics section has four categories of questions:

1. Number and operations (reviewed in Chapter 15)

2. Algebra and functions (reviewed in Chapter 16)

3. Geometry and measurement (reviewed in Chapter 17)

4. Data analysis, statistics and probability (reviewed in Chapter 18)

## Mathematics Reference Information

The SAT mathematics section includes reference information. You may find these facts and formulas helpful as you answer some of the test questions, but don't let the reference information give you a false sense of security. It won't tell you how to solve math problems. To do well on the mathematics section, you have to be comfortable working with these facts and formulas. If you get a lot of practice using them *before* the test, you will be a lot more relaxed using them *during* the test.

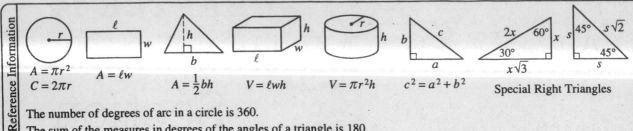

Reference Information

$A = \pi r^2$
$C = 2\pi r$

$A = \ell w$

$A = \frac{1}{2} bh$

$V = \ell wh$

$V = \pi r^2 h$

$c^2 = a^2 + b^2$

Special Right Triangles

The number of degrees of arc in a circle is 360.
The sum of the measures in degrees of the angles of a triangle is 180.

## *Example: Multiple Choice*

If $2x + 2x + 2x = 12$, what is the value of $2x - 1$ ?

(A) 2
(B) 3
(C) 4
(D) 5
(E) 6

*Answer:* The correct answer is (B).

Chapter 19 gives you ideas on answering specific kinds of multiple-choice questions.

## *Example: Student-Produced Response*

Student-produced response questions are *not* multiple choice. Instead, you must figure out the correct answer and fill it in on the answer sheet.

Student-produced response questions (also called *grid-in* questions) are solved just like any other math problems. Here's the same question presented above, but as a grid-in question.

If $2x + 2x + 2x = 12$, what is the value of $2x - 1$ ?

*Answer:* The answer is still 3, but instead of filling in choice (A), (B), (C), (D) or (E), you have to write "3" at the top of the grid and fill in the circle containing "3" below.

**Note:** *No question in this format has an answer that is negative, greater than 9999 or irrational because there is no way to grid this response.*

Specific ideas on completing student-produced response questions are presented in Chapter 20.

## Approaches to Mathematics Questions

▶ *Familiarize yourself with the directions ahead of time.* Also, learn how to complete the grids for student-produced response questions (see Chapter 20).

▶ *Ask yourself the following questions before you solve each problem:*
  - What is the question asking?
  - What do I know?

▶ *Limit your time on any one question.* All questions are worth the same number of points. If you need a lot of time to answer a question, go on to the next one. Later, you may have time to return to the question you skipped.

▶ *Keep in mind that questions are arranged from easy to hard.* Within any group of questions — for example, the multiple-choice questions — the easier ones come first and the questions become more difficult as you move along. If you find that the questions of one type are becoming too difficult, quickly read through the rest of the questions in that group to see if you can answer others. Then go on to the next group of questions in that section.

▶ *Don't make mistakes because of carelessness.* No matter how frustrated you are, don't pass over questions without at least reading them, and be sure to consider all the choices in each question. If you're careless, you could choose the wrong answers even on easy questions. Take each question as it comes and avoid careless mistakes by making sure you do the following:
  - Answer the question asked. For example, if the question asks for the area of a shaded region, don't give the area of the unshaded region.
  - Check that your answer makes sense. For example, is a discount higher than the original price? Is the average age of a high school student 56 years old? In both cases, obviously not — so think about your answer instead of just calculating automatically. Check your work from the beginning. If you can, use a different method from the one you used to get the answer. If you use the same method, you may make the same mistake twice.

▶ *Work out the problems in your test booklet.* You will not receive credit for anything written in the booklet, but you will be able to check your work easily later:
  - Draw figures to help you think through problems that involve geometric shapes, segment lengths, distances, proportions, sizes and so on.

- Mark key information on graphs, and add information to drawings and diagrams, as you work through the questions.

- Mark each question that you don't answer so that you can easily go back to it later.

▶ *Eliminate choices.* If you don't know the correct answer to a question, try eliminating wrong choices. It's sometimes easier to find the wrong answers than the correct one. On some questions, you can eliminate all the incorrect choices. Draw a line through each choice as you eliminate it until you have only the one correct answer left.

▶ *Make an educated guess whenever you can eliminate at least one answer choice.* On multiple-choice questions, if you can eliminate even one incorrect answer choice, you increase your chances of getting a question right. With each correct answer choice, you gain one point; if you leave the answer blank you get no points; if your answer is wrong you lose only one-fourth $\left(\frac{1}{4}\right)$ of a point.

▶ *Keep in mind that, on grid-in questions, you don't lose points for wrong answers.* Make an educated guess if you don't know the answer.

▶ *Always enter your answer by filling in the circles on the grid.* One of the most important rules to remember about grid-in questions is that *only answers entered on the grid are scored. Your handwritten answer at the top of the grid isn't scored.* However, writing your answer at the top of the grid may help you avoid gridding errors.

## Approaches to Finding the Right Answer

If you absolutely can't figure out how to approach a problem, you may find it helpful, when appropriate, to try to answer the question either by substituting numbers or by trying each of the answer choices to determine the answer. Note that these approaches are *quick fixes* as you prepare to take the SAT and don't help you *learn* what you need to know to solve problems. Also, keep in mind that these approaches sometimes take considerable time, so keep track of your time and remember to pace yourself.

▶ *Substitute numbers for variables.* Some questions use variables (indicated by letters) to represent the values you are asked to consider. You can sometimes approach these problems by substituting numbers for the variables. For example, consider the following question:

**Example**

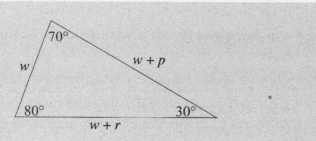

In the triangle above, which of the following must be true?

(A)  $p < r$
(B)  $p = r$
(C)  $p > r$
(D)  $p = 0$
(E)  $r = 0$

**How to solve:**  Because the question involves $p$ and $r$, try substituting a number for $w$. Then think about what you are given and what you know:

- Suppose $w = 3$.

- Then the side opposite the angle measuring 70° has length $3 + r$.

- The side opposite the angle measuring 80° has length $3 + p$.

- Because $70 < 80$, you know that $3 + r < 3 + p$.

- So $r < p$.

- The correct answer is (C).

▶ *Use each of the answer choices to help you solve a problem.*  Sometimes working through a question using the same format used in the answer choices will help you save time. For example, if the answer choices to a question are in the form of decimals, you may choose to do your work in decimals instead of fractions. This could save time because you won't have to convert your answer to a decimal. Also, some questions can be answered by working backward from the answer choices. This approach is often useful when the question includes a condition that you can express in the form of a formula — even a verbal one. (Keep in mind that this method can be time-consuming.) For example, look at the following multiple-choice question:

**Example**

If the product of three consecutive integers is equal to the middle integer, what is the LEAST of the three integers?

(A)   2
(B)   1
(C)   0
(D)  −1
(E)  −2

**How to solve:** Use the answer choices to figure out which choice satisfies the conditions of the question:

- Can the answer be (A)? If so, then it must be true that $2 \times 3 \times 4 = 3$ (the middle integer). Clearly, this is *not true*.

- Ask yourself the same question for the other choices.

- When you get to choice (D), the consecutive integers are −1, 0 and 1. The product of these three integers is 0, which is the middle integer.

- The correct answer is (D).

## Calculators Are Recommended

You should bring a calculator to use on the mathematics section of the SAT. Every question on the PSAT/NMSQT and the SAT can be solved without a calculator; however, using a calculator on some questions may be helpful to students. A scientific or graphing calculator is recommended. Using a calculator can help you avoid missing a question because of computation errors.

### *Bring Your Own Calculator*

You are expected to provide your own calculator.

You may *not* use any of the following:

- calculators that have QWERTY keypads (e.g., TI-92 Plus, Voyage 200) or have pen-input, stylus* or touch-screen capability

- calculators that have wireless, Bluetooth, cellular, audio/video recording and playing, camera or any other cell phone-type feature

- calculators that make noise or "talk," require an electrical outlet or use paper tape

- calculators that can access the Internet

*The use of the stylus with the Sharp EL-9600 calculator will not be permitted. The Sharp EL-9600 remains on the list of approved graphing calculators.

### *What to Keep in Mind When Using Calculators on the SAT*

1. Bring a calculator with you when you take the SAT, even if you're not sure that you will use it. Calculators will *not* be available at your test center.

2. Practice on the calculator you plan to use before the test so that you're used to it.

3. Remember that all questions on the test can be answered *without* a calculator. Complicated or tedious calculations won't be required.

4.  Don't buy an expensive, sophisticated calculator just for the test. If you already have one, though, that's fine.

5.  Don't try to use a calculator on every question. Before you start using the calculator, think through how you will solve each problem. Then decide whether to use the calculator.

6.  Use common sense. The calculator is meant to *help* you in problem solving, not to get in the way.

7.  Do *scratch work* in the test booklet before you use your calculator so that you'll get your thoughts down on paper quickly.

8.  Check that your calculator is *in good working order* and that its batteries (if needed) are *fresh*. If your calculator fails during the test, you'll need to complete the test without it.

## Recap

1. Familiarize yourself (ahead of time) with the directions and the reference information that will be on the SAT and that is shown at the beginning of this chapter.

2. Study the concepts and skills in Chapters 15 to 18, which cover mathematics reviews.

3. Bring a calculator that you know how to use — and don't forget fresh batteries.

4. Keep in mind that questions are arranged from easy to hard.

5. Pace yourself. Don't spend too much time on any one question.

6. Before you solve each problem, ask yourself: What is the question asking? What do I know?

7. Make notes in your test booklet:

   • Draw figures to help you think through problems with geometric shapes, distances, proportions and so on.

   • Write out calculations to check later.

   • For questions that contain figures, note any measurements or values you calculate right on the figure in the test booklet.

8. Use the answer choices to your advantage — for example, look at the form of the answer choices if you can't figure out how to approach a problem.

9. Substitute real numbers for variables, to make the problem more concrete.

10. Make an educated guess when you can eliminate at least one incorrect answer choice in a multiple-choice question.

11. Remember that figures that accompany questions are drawn to scale unless otherwise noted.

12. However, if you're told that a figure is *not* drawn to scale, remember that lengths and angles may *not* be shown accurately.

13. Don't panic when you're faced with special symbols: read the definition carefully and use it as your instruction for working out the answer.

14. Take each solution one step at a time. Some seemingly difficult questions are really just a series of easy questions.

15. Keep in mind that the answer sheet will be scored by a computer, so you will receive credit *only* if you fill in the circles correctly on the student-produced response questions. (Although it's not required, it's a good idea to write your answer in the boxes at the top of the column, to help you fill in the circles correctly.)

16. Avoid careless mistakes.

17. Answer the question asked.

18. Check that your answer makes sense.

19. If you have time to check your work, try to rework your calculations differently from the way you first did them.

# CHAPTER 15

# Number and Operations Review

## Concepts You Need to Know

Though you've been preparing for the mathematics section of the SAT all during your high school years, here's a chance to review what you know. For mathematics questions covering number and operations, you should be familiar with all of the following basic skills and concepts:

- Properties of integers

- Arithmetic word problems

- Number lines

- Squares and square roots

- Fractions and rational numbers

- Elementary number theory
  - Factors, multiples and remainders
  - Prime numbers

- Ratios, proportions and percents

- Sequences

- Sets (union, intersection, elements)

- Counting problems

- Logical reasoning

The SAT doesn't include

- Tedious or long computations

- Matrix operations

## Properties of Integers

You will need to know the following information for some questions in the mathematics section:

- Integers consist of the whole numbers and their negatives (including zero).

$$\ldots, -3, -2, -1, 0, 1, 2, 3, 4, \ldots$$

- Integers extend infinitely in both negative and positive directions.

The following are negative integers:

$$-4, -3, -2, -1$$

The following are positive integers:

$$1, 2, 3, 4$$

*The integer zero (0) is neither positive nor negative.*

### Odd Numbers

$$\ldots, -5, -3, -1, 1, 3, 5, \ldots$$

### Even Numbers

$$\ldots, -4, -2, 0, 2, 4, \ldots$$

*The integer zero (0) is an even number.*

### Consecutive Integers

Integers that follow in sequence, where the difference between two successive integers is 1, are consecutive integers. Here are three examples of some consecutive integers:

$$-1, 0, 1, 2, 3$$
$$1001, 1002, 1003, 1004$$
$$-14, -13, -12, -11$$

The following is an expression representing consecutive integers:

$$n, n + 1, n + 2, n + 3, \ldots, \text{ where } n \text{ is any integer.}$$

### Addition of Integers

$$\text{even} + \text{even} = \text{even}$$
$$\text{odd} + \text{odd} = \text{even}$$
$$\text{odd} + \text{even} = \text{odd}$$

Adding zero (0) to any number doesn't change the value:

$$8 + 0 = 8$$
$$-1 + 0 = -1$$

## Multiplication of Integers

$$\text{even} \times \text{even} = \text{even}$$
$$\text{odd} \times \text{odd} = \text{odd}$$
$$\text{odd} \times \text{even} = \text{even}$$

Multiplying any number by one (1) doesn't change the value:

$$3 \times 1 = 3$$
$$-10 \times 1 = -10$$

# Arithmetic Word Problems

The SAT often has arithmetic word problems that do not require you to write down an algebraic equation or expression. Such questions test your ability to apply correctly arithmetic operations in a problem situation. To solve these problems, you need to identify which quantities are being given, what is being asked for and which arithmetic operations must be applied to the given quantities to get the answer.

## Examples

### EXAMPLE 1

Ms. Griffen is making bags of Halloween treats. If she puts 3 treats in each bag, she will make 30 bags of treats and have no treats left over. If instead she puts 5 treats in each bag, how many bags of treats can she make?

**How to solve:** If Ms. Griffen puts 3 treats in each bag, she makes 30 bags of treats. There are $30 \times 3 = 90$ treats in the bags and none left over. Therefore, Ms. Griffen has a total of 90 treats.

If Ms. Griffen puts 5 treats in each bag, she can make $90 \div 5 = 18$ bags of treats.

### EXAMPLE 2

Jorge bought 5 pencils from the store. He gave the cashier a five-dollar bill and got back $0.75 in change. Jorge saw that he had gotten too much change, and he gave $0.25 back to the cashier. What was the price, in dollars, of each pencil?

**How to solve:** Jorge gave the cashier $5.00 for the 5 pencils, and he got $0.75 back. At this point, Jorge had paid $5.00 − 0.75 = $4.25. Then Jorge gave the cashier $0.25.

Therefore, Jorge paid a total of $4.25 + 0.25 = $4.50 for the 5 pencils. Each pencil cost $4.50 ÷ 5 = $0.90.

# Number Lines

A number line is used to graphically represent the relationships between numbers: integers, fractions or decimals.

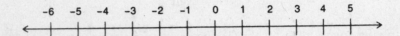

- Numbers on a number line always increase as you move to the right, and tick marks are always equally spaced.

- Negative numbers are always shown with a negative sign (–). For positive numbers, the plus sign (+) is usually not shown.

- Number lines are drawn to scale. You will be expected to make reasonable approximations of positions between labeled points on the line.

Number line questions generally require you to figure out the relationships among numbers placed on the line. Number line questions may ask:

- Where a number should be placed in relation to other numbers;

- The difference or product of two numbers;

- The lengths and the ratios of the lengths of line segments represented on the number line.

## Example

Here is an example of a number line question:

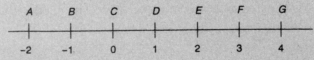

On the number line above, the ratio of *AC* to *AG* is equal to the ratio of *CD* to which of the following?

(A) *AD*
(B) *BD*
(C) *CG*
(D) *DF*
(E) *EG*

**How to solve:** In this question, the number line is used to determine lengths: $AC = 2$, $AG = 6$, $CD = 1$. Once you have these lengths, the question becomes a ratio and proportion problem.

- The ratio of *AC* to *AG* is 2 to 6.

- The ratio of *AC* to *AG* is equal to the ratio of *CD* to what?

- $\frac{2}{6} = \frac{1}{x}$

- $x = 3$

Now you have to go back to the number line to find which of the given segments has length 3. Because *AD* = 3, the answer is (A).

0.425           P        0.430

The number line shown above is from a question that appeared on the SAT. The question requires that you figure out the coordinate of point *P*, given that the tick marks are evenly spaced.

The units of measure are *thousandths*. (The distance between adjacent tick marks is 0.001.) Point *P* has coordinate 0.428 on this number line.

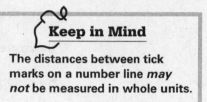

**Keep in Mind**

The distances between tick marks on a number line *may not* be measured in whole units.

## Squares and Square Roots

### *Squares of Integers*

Although you can always figure them out with paper and pencil or with your calculator, it's helpful if you know or at least can recognize the squares of integers between –12 and 12. Here they are:

| $x$ | 1 | 2 | 3 | 4 | 5 | 6 | 7 | 8 | 9 | 10 | 11 | 12 |
|-----|---|---|---|---|---|---|---|---|---|----|----|----|
| $x^2$ | 1 | 4 | 9 | 16 | 25 | 36 | 49 | 64 | 81 | 100 | 121 | 144 |

| $x$ | –1 | –2 | –3 | –4 | –5 | –6 | –7 | –8 | –9 | –10 | –11 | –12 |
|-----|----|----|----|----|----|----|----|----|----|-----|-----|-----|
| $x^2$ | 1 | 4 | 9 | 16 | 25 | 36 | 49 | 64 | 81 | 100 | 121 | 144 |

You can see, for example, that $5^2 = 25$ and $\sqrt{64} = 8$.

Your knowledge of common squares and square roots may speed up your solution to some math problems. The most common types of problems for which this knowledge will help you will be those involving:

- Factoring and/or simplifying expressions

- Problems involving the Pythagorean theorem ($a^2 + b^2 = c^2$)

- Areas of circles or squares

### *Squares of Fractions*

Remember that if a positive fraction with a value less than 1 is squared, the result is always smaller than the original fraction:

$$\text{If } 0 < n < 1$$
$$\text{Then } n^2 < n$$

Try it.

What are the values of the following fractions?

$$\left(\frac{2}{3}\right)^2$$

$$\left(\frac{1}{8}\right)^2$$

The answers are $\frac{4}{9}$ and $\frac{1}{64}$, respectively. Each of these is less than the original fraction. For example, $\frac{4}{9} < \frac{2}{3}$.

# Fractions and Rational Numbers

You should know how to do basic operations with fractions:

- Adding, subtracting, multiplying and dividing fractions

- Reducing to lowest terms

- Finding the least common denominator

- Expressing a value as a mixed number $\left(2\frac{1}{3}\right)$ and as an improper fraction $\left(\frac{7}{3}\right)$

- Working with complex fractions — ones that have fractions in their numerators or denominators

You should know that a *rational number* is a number that can be represented by a fraction whose numerator and denominator are both integers (and the denominator must be nonzero). The following are rational numbers:

$$\frac{1}{2}$$

$$\frac{15}{4} \text{ (or } 3\frac{3}{4}\text{)}$$

$$-\frac{12}{13}$$

$$\frac{5}{1} \text{ (or } 5\text{)}$$

As you can see from the last example, every integer is a rational number.

## Decimal Fraction Equivalents

You may have to work with decimal fraction equivalents. That is, you may have to be able to recognize common fractions as decimals and vice versa.

To change any fraction to a decimal, divide the numerator by the denominator.

Although you can figure out the decimal equivalent of any fraction (a calculator will help here), you'll be doing yourself a favor if you know the following:

| Fraction | $\frac{1}{4}$ | $\frac{1}{3}$ | $\frac{1}{2}$ | $\frac{2}{3}$ | $\frac{3}{4}$ |
|---|---|---|---|---|---|
| Decimal | 0.25 | $0.\overline{3}$* | 0.5 | $0.\overline{6}$* | 0.75 |

*The bar notation indicates that the 3 and the 6 repeat infinitely.

## Reciprocals

The reciprocal of a number is 1 divided by that number. For example, the reciprocal of 5 is $\frac{1}{5}$. Note that $5 \times \frac{1}{5} = 1$. The product of a number and its reciprocal is always 1.

Here is another example: The reciprocal of $\frac{2}{3}$ is 1 divided by $\frac{2}{3}$, which is equal to $\frac{3}{2}$. Note that you can find the reciprocal of any nonzero fraction by switching its numerator and denominator.

How do you find the reciprocal of $2\frac{1}{3}$? Write it as an improper fraction: $2\frac{1}{3} = \frac{7}{3}$. Now switch the numerator and denominator: the reciprocal of $2\frac{1}{3}$ is $\frac{3}{7}$.

You can also find the reciprocal of a negative number. For example, the reciprocal of $-2$ is $\frac{1}{-2} = -\frac{1}{2}$. Note that the reciprocal of a negative number is negative.

The number zero (0) has no reciprocal.

The number 1 is its own reciprocal. Also, the number $-1$ is its own reciprocal.

## Place Value and Scientific Notation

The number 123 can be written as $100 + 20 + 3$ or as $(1 \times 10^2) + (2 \times 10^1) + (3 \times 1)$. The digit 1 stands for 1 times 100; the digit 2 stands for 2 times 10; and the digit 3 stands for 3 times 1. We say these digits have the following *place values*:

> 1 is in the hundreds place.
> 2 is in the tens place.
> 3 is in the units (ones) place.

Every digit in a decimal number has a place value. The next places to the left of 123 are the thousands place, the ten-thousands place, the hundred-thousands place, the millions place and so on. Digits to the right of the decimal point also have place values. For example $0.56 = 0.5 + 0.06 = (5 \times 10^{-1}) + (6 \times 10^{-2})$; the digit 5 is in the tenths place, and the digit 6 is in the hundredths place.

Sometimes, using the concept of place value can let you write a very big or small number in a much shorter form. For example:

$$2,300,000,000,000 = 2.3 \times 10^{12}$$
$$0.0000000007 = 7 \times 10^{-10}$$

Because such numbers often occur in scientific calculations, writing a number as the product of a power of 10 and a number greater than or equal to 1 and less than 10 is called *scientific notation.*

# Elementary Number Theory

## *Factors, Multiples and Remainders*

On the SAT, you'll find questions that require you to understand and work with these three related concepts: factors, multiples and remainders.

### FACTORS

The factors of a number are positive integers that can be divided evenly into the number — that is, without remainder.

For instance, consider the number 24: The numbers 24, 12, 8, 6, 4, 3, 2 and 1 are all factors of the number 24. Each of these numbers can be divided evenly into 24 with no remainder.

The term *divisible by* means divisible by *without any remainder* or *with a remainder of zero.* For instance, 15 is divisible by 5 because 15 divided by 5 is 3 with a remainder of 0. But 15 is not divisible by 7 because 15 divided by 7 is 2 with a remainder of 1.

*Common factors:* Common factors are factors that two (or more) numbers have in common. For instance, 3 is a common factor of 12 and 18. The largest common factor of two (or more numbers) is called their *greatest common factor* (GCF). For example, 6 is the GCF of 12 and 18.

### MULTIPLES

The multiples of any given number are those numbers that can be divided by that given number *without a remainder.* You can find the multiples of a number by multiplying it by 1, 2, 3, 4 and so on. For instance, 8, 16, 24, 32, 40 and 48 are some of the multiples of 8.

Notice that the multiples of 8 are also multiples of 2 and 4 (factors of 8). Remember, the multiples of any number will always be multiples of all the factors of that number. For instance:

- The numbers 30, 45, 60 and 75 are all multiples of the number 15.

- Two factors of 15 are the numbers 3 and 5.

- That means that 30, 45, 60 and 75 are all multiples of 3 and 5.

*Common multiples:* Suppose you have two (or more) numbers. Any number that is a multiple of all the given numbers is called a *common multiple*. For instance, 48 and 96 are both common multiples of 8 and 12. The smallest multiple of two (or more) numbers is called their *least common multiple* (LCM). For example, 24 is the LCM of 8 and 12.

## Examples

### EXAMPLE 1

What is the *least* positive integer divisible by the numbers 2, 3, 4 and 5?

**How to solve:**

- To find *one example of* a number that is divisible by several other numbers, multiply those numbers together. You could multiply $2 \times 3 \times 4 \times 5$ and the result would be divisible by all those factors.

- But the question asks for the *least* positive number divisible by all four (in other words, the LCM of the four numbers). To find that, you have to eliminate any extra factors.

- Any number divisible by 4 will also be divisible by 2, so you can eliminate 2 from your initial multiplication. If you multiply $3 \times 4 \times 5$, you will get a smaller number than if you multiply $2 \times 3 \times 4 \times 5$, and the number will still be divisible by 2.

- Because the remaining factors (3, 4 and 5) have no common factors, the result of $3 \times 4 \times 5$ will give you the answer. So $3 \times 4 \times 5 = 60$ is the least positive integer divisible by 2, 3, 4 and 5.

### EXAMPLE 2

Which of the following could be the remainders when four consecutive positive integers are each divided by 3?

(A)  1, 2, 3, 1
(B)  1, 2, 3, 4
(C)  0, 1, 2, 3
(D)  0, 1, 2, 0
(E)  0, 2, 3, 0

**How to solve:**  Remember, the question asks only for the remainders.

- When you divide *any* positive integer by 3, the remainder must be less than or equal to 2.

- All the choices except (D) include remainders greater than 2, so (D) is the only possible correct choice. If the first and fourth of the consecutive integers are multiples of 3, the remainders will be 0, 1, 2 and 0.

Examining only the remainders of numbers is sometimes called *modular arithmetic.*

**EXAMPLE 3**

Does the equation $3x + 6y = 47$ have a solution in which $x$ and $y$ are both positive integers?

**How to solve:** Note that $3x + 6y = 3(x + 2y)$. Therefore, for any positive integers $x$ and $y$, the sum $3x + 6y = 3(x + 2y)$ is a multiple of 3. But 47 is not a multiple of 3. Therefore, no matter what positive integers you choose for $x$ and $y$, the sum will not be 47. Thus, the equation $3x + 6y = 47$ does *not* have a solution in which $x$ and $y$ are both positive integers.

This question is an example of a *Diophantine equation* — that is, it is an equation with integer coefficients for which you are seeking integer solutions.

## Prime Numbers

A prime number is a positive integer greater than 1 that has exactly two whole-number factors — itself and the number 1. The number 1 itself *is not* prime.

The first eight prime numbers are:

$$2, 3, 5, 7, 11, 13, 17, 19$$

(Note that 2 is the only even prime number.)

*Prime factors:* Prime factors are the factors of a number that are prime numbers. That is, the prime factors of a number cannot be factored further. For example, the prime factors of the number 24 are 2 and 3.

$$24 = 2 \times 2 \times 2 \times 3$$

# Ratios, Proportions and Percents

A *ratio* expresses a mathematical relationship between two quantities. Specifically, a ratio is a quotient of those quantities. The following are all relationships that can be expressed as ratios:

- My serving of pizza is $\frac{1}{4}$ of the whole pie.

- There are twice as many chocolate cookies as vanilla cookies in the cookie jar.

- My brother earns $5 for each $6 I earn.

The preceding ratios can be expressed in several different ways. They can be stated in words:

- The ratio of my serving of pizza to the whole pie is one to four.

- The ratio of chocolate to vanilla cookies is two to one.

- The ratio of my brother's earnings to mine is five to six.

They can be expressed as fractions:

- $\frac{1}{4}$

- $\frac{2}{1}$

- $\frac{5}{6}$

They can be expressed with a colon (:), as follows:

- 1:4

- 2:1

- 5:6

Or they can be expressed using the word *to*:

- 1 to 4

- 2 to 1

- 5 to 6

A *percent* (%) is a ratio in which the second quantity is 100: for example, I got 75 percent of all the questions right. (The ratio of questions I got right to all the questions is $\frac{75}{100}$.)

A *proportion* is an equation in which two ratios are set equal to each other. You may be asked to answer questions that require you to set up a proportion and solve it.

## Examples

### EXAMPLE 1

The weight of the tea in 100 identical tea bags is 8 ounces. What is the weight, in ounces, of the tea in 3 tea bags?

**How to solve:** You solve this problem using a proportion, which is two ratios set equal to each other. Start by setting up two ratios.

- The ratio of the tea in 3 tea bags to the tea in 100 tea bags is 3 to 100 (or $\frac{3}{100}$).

- Let $x$ equal the weight, in ounces, of the tea in 3 tea bags.

- The ratio of the weight of the tea in 3 tea bags to the weight of the tea in 100 tea bags is $x$ ounces to 8 ounces $\left(\frac{x}{8}\right)$.

The ratio of $x$ ounces to 8 ounces is equal to the ratio of 3 to 100:

$$\frac{x}{8} = \frac{3}{100}$$

$$100x = 24$$

$$x = \frac{24}{100} \text{ or } 0.24$$

Therefore the weight of the tea in 3 tea bags is 0.24 ounces.

### EXAMPLE 2

You may find questions that involve ratios in any of the following situations:

- Lengths of line segments

- Sizes of angles

- Areas and perimeters

- Rate/time/distance

- Numbers on a number line

You may be asked to combine ratios with other mathematical concepts. For instance:

> The ratio of the length of a rectangular floor to its width is 3:2. If the length of the floor is 12 meters, what is the perimeter of the floor, in meters?

**How to solve:** The ratio of the length to the width of the rectangle is 3:2, so set that ratio equal to the ratio of the actual measures of the sides of the rectangle:

$$\frac{3}{2} = \frac{\text{length}}{\text{width}}$$

$$\frac{3}{2} = \frac{12}{x}$$

$$3x = 24$$

$$x = 8 \text{ (the width)}$$

Now that you have the width of the rectangle, it is easy to find the perimeter: 2(length + width) = 2(12 + 8). The perimeter is 40 meters.

## Sequences

A sequence is an ordered list of numbers. Some sequences follow a specific pattern. For example, the sequence

$$3, 7, 11, 15, \ldots$$

follows the pattern *add 4*. That is, each term in the sequence is 4 more than the one before it. The first term is 3, the second term is 7 and, in general, if $n$ is a positive integer, the $n$th term in this sequence is $3 + 4(n - 1)$. The three dots ( ... ) indicate that this sequence goes on forever.

Not all sequences go on indefinitely. The sequence

$$2, 4, 6, \ldots, 22, 24$$

contains even numbers only through 24, where the sequence ends.

The mathematics section will include geometric sequences, which are sequences for which there is a constant ratio between consecutive terms. For example,

$$7, 21, 63, 189, \ldots$$

is a geometric sequence in which the first term is 7 and the constant ratio is 3. Note that $\frac{21}{7} = 3, \frac{63}{21} = 3$ and $\frac{189}{63} = 3$.

For any positive integer $n$, the $n$th term of this sequence is $7 \times 3^{n-1}$. These sequences have real-life applications, and there may be questions in the mathematics section using geometric sequences in contexts such as population growth. Because the $n$th term of geometric sequences can be written using exponential notation, the growth of such sequences is sometimes called *exponential growth*.

The mathematics section *does not* ask you to figure out the rule for determining the numbers in a sequence without giving the information in some way. For instance, in the preceding example, if you were given that the $n$th term of the sequence was $7 \times 3^{n-1}$, you may be asked to determine that each term after the first was 3 times the term before it. On the other hand, if you were given that the first term in the sequence was 7 and that each term after the first was 3 times the term before it, you might be asked to find that the $n$th term of the sequence was $7 \times 3^{n-1}$.

Number sequence questions might ask you for the following:

- The sum of certain terms in a sequence

- The average of certain terms in a sequence

- The value of a specific term in a sequence

## Sets (Union, Intersection, Elements)

A *set* is a collection of things, and the things are called *elements* or *members* of the set. Questions in the mathematics section might ask about the union of two sets (i.e., the set consisting of the elements that are in either set or both sets) or the intersection of two sets (i.e., the set consisting of the common elements). For example, if

$$\text{set } A = \{2, 4, 6, 8, 10\} \text{ and}$$
$$\text{set } B = \{8, 10, 12, 14\}$$

then the union of sets $A$ and $B$ would be

$$\{2, 4, 6, 8, 10, 12, 14\}$$

and the intersection of sets $A$ and $B$ would be $\{8, 10\}$.

# Counting Problems

Counting problems involve figuring out how many ways you can select or arrange members of groups, such as letters of the alphabet, numbers or menu selections.

## *Fundamental Counting Principle*

The fundamental counting principle is the principle by which you figure out how many possibilities there are for selecting members of different groups:

> If one event can happen in *n* ways, and a second, independent event can happen in *m* ways, the total ways in which the two events can happen is *n* times *m*.

For example:

> On a restaurant menu, there are three appetizers and four main courses. How many different dinners can be ordered if each dinner consists of one appetizer and one main course?

- The first event is the choice of appetizer, and there are three choices available.

- The second event is the choice of main course, and there are four main courses.

- The total number of different dinners is therefore $3 \times 4 = 12$.

This idea can be extended to more than two events. If you had two choices for beverage added to your choices for appetizer and main course, you would multiply the total by 2:

$$2 \times 3 \times 4 = 24$$

If you also had three choices for dessert, you would multiply by 3:

$$3 \times 2 \times 3 \times 4 = 72$$

## *Permutations and Combinations*

If you select member after member from the same group, the number of possible choices will decrease by 1 for each choice. Some counting problems involve *permutations*. A permutation of a set is a reordering of the elements in the set.

> A security system uses a four-letter password, but no letter can be used more than once. How many possible passwords are there?

- For the first letter, there are 26 possible choices — one for each letter of the alphabet.

- Because you cannot reuse any letters, there are only 25 choices for the second letter (26 minus the letter used in the first letter of the password).

- There are only 24 choices for the third letter, and only 23 choices for the fourth.

The total number of passwords will be $26 \times 25 \times 24 \times 23$.

If the order in which the members are chosen makes no difference, the counting problem involves *combinations*. For example:

There are 12 students in the school theater class. Two students will be responsible for finding the props needed for the skit the class is performing. How many different pairs of students can be chosen to find the props?

- The first student chosen can be any of the 12 students.

- The second student chosen can be any of the 11 remaining students.

- Suppose Amy and Juan are in the class. There are two ways Amy and Juan could be chosen: Amy first and Juan second, or Juan first and Amy second.

- To get the answer, you first multiply 12 by 11 to get the number of ways of choosing a pair of students, and then you divide by 2 because each pair of students can be chosen in two different ways. The answer is 66.

## Logical Reasoning

Some mathematics questions emphasize logical thinking. You have to figure out how to draw conclusions from a set of facts.

### *Example*

Here's an example:

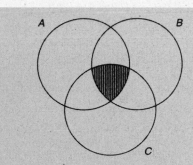

In the figure above, circular region $A$ represents the set of all numbers of the form $2m$, circular region $B$ represents the set of all numbers of the form $n^2$ and circular region $C$ represents the set of all numbers of the form $10^k$, where $m$, $n$ and $k$ are positive integers. Which of the following numbers belongs in the set represented by the shaded region?

(A)  2
(B)  4
(C)  10
(D)  25
(E)  100

**How to solve:** Answering this question correctly depends on understanding the logic of the figure.

- The question is asking about the shaded region.

- The shaded region is part of *all* of the circles.

- Therefore, any numbers in the shaded region have to obey the rules for *all* the circles:

   The rule for *A*: The numbers must be of the form 2*m*, which means that they must all be even numbers.

   And the rule for *B*: The numbers must be of the form $n^2$, which means that they must all be perfect squares.

   And the rule for *C*: The numbers must also be of the form $10^k$, which means they have to be some whole-number power of 10 (10, 100, 1,000, 10,000, etc.).

- When you realize that the numbers in the shaded area must obey *all* the individual rules, you have figured out the logic of the question, and the answer is easy. The only choice that obeys *all* the rules is 100. The answer is (E).

# CHAPTER 16
# Algebra and Functions Review

## Concepts You Need to Know

Many mathematics questions require a knowledge of algebra. This chapter gives you some further practice. You have to manipulate and solve a simple equation for an unknown, simplify and evaluate algebraic expressions, and use algebraic concepts in problem-solving situations.

For the mathematics questions covering algebra and functions content, you should be familiar with all of the following basic skills and topics:

- Operations on algebraic expressions

- Factoring

- Exponents

- Evaluating expressions with exponents and roots

- Solving equations
  - Determining if an equation has a solution
  - Solving for one variable in terms of another
  - Solving equations involving radical expressions

- Absolute value

- Direct translation into mathematical expressions

- Inequalities

- Systems of linear equations and inequalities

- Solving quadratic equations by factoring

- Rational equations and inequalities

- Direct and inverse variation

- Word problems

- Functions
  - Function notation and evaluation
  - Domain and range
  - Using new definitions
  - Functions as models
  - Linear functions: their equations and graphs
  - Quadratic functions: their equations and graphs
  - Qualitative behavior of graphs and functions
  - Translations and their effects on graphs of functions

The SAT does not include:

- Complex numbers

- Logarithms

- Trigonometry

## Operations on Algebraic Expressions

You will need to be able to apply the basic operations of arithmetic — addition, subtraction, multiplication and division — to algebraic expressions. For example:

$$4x + 5x = 9x$$
$$10z - 3y - (-2z) + 2y = 12z - y$$
$$(x + 3)(x - 2) = x^2 + x - 6$$
$$\frac{15xy}{3y} = 5x$$

## Factoring

The types of factoring included on the mathematics section are:

- Difference of two squares:
$$a^2 - b^2 = (a + b)(a - b)$$

- Finding common factors, as in:
$$x^2 + 2x = x(x + 2)$$
$$2x + 4y = 2(x + 2y)$$

- Factoring quadratics:

$$x^2 - 3x - 4 = (x - 4)(x + 1)$$

$$x^2 + 2x + 1 = (x + 1)(x + 1) = (x + 1)^2$$

You are not likely to find a question instructing you to "factor the following expression." However, you may see questions that ask you to evaluate or compare expressions that require factoring.

# Exponents

## Definitions

$$a^3 = a \cdot a \cdot a$$

$$p^{-4} = \frac{1}{p} \cdot \frac{1}{p} \cdot \frac{1}{p} \cdot \frac{1}{p} = \frac{1}{p^4}$$

$$x^0 = 1$$

$$x^{\frac{a}{b}} = \sqrt[b]{x^a} = \left(\sqrt[b]{x}\right)^a$$

and

$$y^{\frac{1}{2}} = \sqrt{y}$$

## Three Points to Remember

1. When multiplying expressions with the same base, add the exponents:

$$a^2 \cdot a^5 = (a \cdot a)(a \cdot a \cdot a \cdot a \cdot a)$$

$$= a^7$$

$$a^m \cdot a^n = a^{m+n}$$

   This rule also holds for exponents that are not positive integers:

$$t^5 \cdot t^{-2} = (t \cdot t \cdot t \cdot t \cdot t) \cdot \left(\frac{1}{t} \cdot \frac{1}{t}\right) = t^3$$

2. When dividing expressions with the same base, subtract exponents:

$$\frac{r^5}{r^3} = \frac{r \cdot r \cdot r \cdot r \cdot r}{r \cdot r \cdot r} = r^2$$

$$\frac{a^m}{a^n} = a^{m-n}$$

3. When a number raised to an exponent is raised to a second exponent, multiply the exponents:

$$(n^3)^6 = n^{3 \cdot 6} = n^{18}$$

$$(a^m)^n = a^{mn}$$

# Evaluating Expressions with Exponents and Roots

You will need to know how to evaluate expressions involving exponents and roots. For instance: If $y = 8$, what is $y^{\frac{2}{3}}$ ?

$$y^{\frac{2}{3}} = \sqrt[3]{8^2} = \sqrt[3]{64} = 4$$

Here is an example of how to work the reverse problem.

If $x^{\frac{3}{2}} = 64$, what is the value of $x$ ?

By the rules of exponents, $x^{\frac{3}{2}} = (x^3)^{\frac{1}{2}} = 64$.

Taking the cube root of both sides of this equation, you find $x^{\frac{1}{2}} = 4$.

Squaring both sides, you get $x = 16$.

# Solving Equations

Most of the equations that you will need to solve are linear equations. Equations that are not linear can usually be solved by factoring or by inspection.

## Working with "Unsolvable" Equations

At first, some equations may look like they can't be solved. You will find that although you can't solve the equation, you can answer the question. For instance:

If $a + b = 5$, what is the value of $2a + 2b$ ?

You can't solve the equation $a + b = 5$ for either $a$ or $b$. But you can answer the question:

- The question doesn't ask for the value of $a$ or $b$. It asks for the value of the entire quantity $2a + 2b$.

- $2a + 2b$ can be factored:

$$2a + 2b = 2(a + b)$$
$$a + b = 5$$

You are asked what 2 times $a + b$ is. That's $2(a + b) = 2 \times 5 = 10$.

## Solving for One Variable in Terms of Another

You may be asked to solve for one variable in terms of another. Again, you're not always going to be able to find a specific, numerical value for all of the variables. For example:

If $3x + y = z$, what is $x$ in terms of $y$ and $z$ ?

You aren't asked to find a numerical value for $x$. You are asked to manipulate the expression so that you can isolate $x$ (put it by itself) on one side of the equation. That equation will tell you what $x$ is in terms of the other variables:

- $3x + y = z$

- Subtract $y$ from each side of the equation.

$$3x = z - y$$

- Divide both sides by 3 to get $x$.

$$x = \frac{z - y}{3}$$

Then $x$ in terms of $y$ and $z$ is $\frac{z - y}{3}$.

### Solving Equations Involving Radical Expressions

The expression $5\sqrt{x}$ is a radical expression because it involves a root; in particular, the square root of $x$.

The equation $5\sqrt{x} + 14 - 29$ is a radical equation because it involves a radical expression. You can solve this equation:

$$5\sqrt{x} + 14 = 29$$
$$5\sqrt{x} = 15$$
$$\sqrt{x} = 3$$
$$x = 9$$

**Keep in Mind**

Be careful when solving radical equations such as $\sqrt{x} = 5$. There is *one* solution to this equation: 25. (However, there are *two* solutions to the equation $x^2 = 25$ : 5 and −5.)

## Absolute Value

Being familiar with both the concept and notation of absolute value will be helpful to you when solving the mathematics questions. The absolute value of a number is its distance from zero on the number line. The absolute value of the number $w$ is denoted $|w|$. For example, $|6.5| = 6.5$ and $|-32| = 32$. You can think of the absolute value of a number as the "size" of the number, disregarding whether it is positive or negative.

You may be asked to work with expressions and solve equations that involve absolute value. For example, you can solve the equation $|7 - t| = 10$ by thinking of it as either:

$$7 - t = 10$$

*or*

$$-(7 - t) = 10$$

In the first case:

$$7 - t = 10$$
$$-t = 3$$
$$t = -3$$

In the second case:

$$-(7 - t) = 10$$
$$-7 + t = 10$$
$$t = 17$$

So, $t = -3$ or $t = 17$.

# Direct Translation into Mathematical Expressions

Many word problems require you to translate the verbal description of a mathematical fact or relationship into mathematical terms.

Always read the word problem carefully and double-check that you have translated it exactly. For example:

"3 times the quantity $4x + 6$" translates to $3(4x + 6)$.

"A number $y$ decreased by 60" translates to $y - 60$.

"5 less than a number $k$" translates to $k - 5$.

"$x$ less than 5" translates to $5 - x$.

"20 divided by $n$" is $\dfrac{20}{n}$.

"20 divided into a number $y$" is $\dfrac{y}{20}$.

See the "Keep in Mind" ideas in the Word Problems section of this chapter.

> **Keep in Mind**
>
> Be especially careful with subtraction and division because the order of these operations is important.
>
> $5 - 3$ is not the same as $3 - 5$. Addition and multiplication are commutative, but subtraction and division are *not!*

# Inequalities

An inequality is a statement that one quantity is greater than or less than another. Inequalities are shown using four symbols:

- Greater than: >

$$5 > 3, \quad 1 > -2$$

- Greater than or equal to: ≥

$$\frac{7}{3} \geq 2, \quad 4 + 5 \geq 9$$

- Less than: <

$$0 < 1, \quad -7 < -6$$

- Less than or equal to: ≤

$$8 - 4 \leq 5, \quad \frac{5}{2} \leq 2.5$$

Most of the time, you can work with simple inequalities in exactly the same way you work with equalities. Consider the following:

$$2x + 1 > 11$$

If this were an equation, it would be pretty easy to solve:

$$2x + 1 = 11$$
$$2x = 11 - 1$$
$$2x = 10$$
$$x = 5$$

You can use a similar process to solve inequalities:

$$2x + 1 > 11$$
$$2x > 11 - 1$$
$$2x > 10$$
$$x > 5$$

> **Keep in Mind**
>
> Remember that multiplying or dividing both sides of an inequality by a negative number reverses the direction of the inequality:
>
> If $-x < 3$, then $x > -3$.

# Systems of Linear Equations and Inequalities

You may be asked to solve systems of two or more linear equations or inequalities. For example: For what values of $a$ and $b$ are the following equations both true?

$$a + 2b = 1$$
$$-3a - 8b = 1$$

You can solve this system of equations by eliminating one of the variables. Say you decide to eliminate $b$. Multiply both sides of the first equation by 4:

$$4a + 8b = 4$$
$$-3a - 8b = 1$$

Adding the two equations gives:

$$-3a - 1 = 4 - 4a$$
$$a = 5$$

Substituting $a = 5$ into the original equation gives $5 + 2b = 1$. You can solve this equation to find $b = -2$. The answer is that the first two equations are true if $a = 5$ and $b = -2$.

## Solving Quadratic Equations by Factoring

You may be asked to solve quadratic equations that can be factored. (You will not be expected to know the quadratic formula.)

For instance: For what values of $x$ is $x^2 - 10x + 20 = -4$?

Add 4 to both sides of the equation to get a standard quadratic equation: $x^2 - 10x + 24 = 0$. Now factor:

$$x^2 - 10x + 24 = 0$$
$$(x - 4)(x - 6) = 0$$

Therefore, either $x - 4 = 0$ or $x - 6 = 0$. The values $x = 4$ and $x = 6$ satisfy the original equation.

## Rational Equations and Inequalities

A rational algebraic expression is the quotient of two expressions. An example is

$$\frac{3y + 5}{y - 2}$$

You may be asked to solve equations or inequalities involving such expressions. For example: For what value of $x$ is the following equation true?

$$3 = \frac{x - 1}{2x + 3}$$

Multiplying both sides by $2x + 3$ gives

$$3(2x + 3) = x - 1$$
$$6x + 9 = x - 1$$
$$5x = -10$$
$$x = -2$$

## Direct and Inverse Variation

The quantities $x$ and $y$ are *directly proportional* if $y = kx$ for some constant $k$. For example: $x$ and $y$ are directly proportional. When the value $x$ is 10, $y$ is equal to –5. If $x = 3$, what is $y$?

Because $x$ and $y$ are directly proportional, $y = kx$ for some constant $k$. You know $y$ is –5 when $x$ is 10; you can use this to find $k$.

$$y = kx$$
$$-5 = k(10)$$
$$k = -\frac{1}{2}$$

So, the equation is $y = -\frac{1}{2}x$. When $x = 3$, you get $y = \left(-\frac{1}{2}\right)(3) = -\frac{3}{2}$.

The quantities $x$ and $y$ are *inversely proportional* if $y = \dfrac{k}{x}$ for some constant $k$. For example: If $xy = 4$, show that $x$ and $y$ are inversely proportional.

Divide both sides of the equation $xy = 4$ by $x$:

$$y = \frac{4}{x}$$

Therefore, $x$ and $y$ are inversely proportional, with $k = 4$.

# Word Problems

Some mathematics questions are presented as word problems. They require you to apply math skills to everyday situations. With word problems you have to:

- Read and interpret what is being asked.

- Determine what information you are given.

- Determine what information you need to know.

- Decide what mathematical skills or formulas you need to apply to find the answer.

- Work out the answer.

- Double-check to make sure the answer makes sense. When checking word problems, don't substitute your answer into *your* equations, because they may be wrong. Instead, check word problems by checking your answer with the original *words*.

## Translate as You Read

As you read word problems, translate the words into mathematical expressions and equations:

- When you read "Jane has three dollars more than Tom," translate to $J = T + 3$.

- When you read "the average (arithmetic mean) of the weights of three children is 80 pounds," translate to $\dfrac{a + b + c}{3} = 80$.

- When you read "Jane buys one clown fish and two guppies for \$3," translate to $c + 2g = 3$.

When you've finished reading the problem, you will have already translated it into mathematical expressions and equations. Table 16.1 will help you with some of the more common phrases and mathematical translations:

**Table 16.1** Mathematical Expressions

| Words | Symbol | Translation |
|---|---|---|
| *Is, was, has:* | = | |
| The number of days Jane worked is the number of days Tom worked. | = | $J = T$ |
| *More than, older than, farther than, greater than, sum of:* | + | Addition |
| Jane has 2 more dollars than Tom. | + | $J = 2 + T$ or $J = T + 2$ |
| Tom ran 10 miles farther than Jane. | | $T = 10 + J$ or $T = J + 10$ |
| The sum of two integers is 36. | | $x + y = 36$ |
| *Less than, difference, younger than, fewer:* | – | Subtraction |
| Tom has 5 fewer marbles than twice the number Jane has. | – | $T = 2J - 5$ (Don't make the "$5 - 2J$" mistake!) |
| The difference between Tom's height and Jane's height is 22 centimeters. | | $\left| T - J \right| = 22$ |
| *Of:* | × | Multiplication |
| 20% of Tom's socks are red. | % | $R = .2 \times T$ |
| Jane ate $\frac{3}{4}$ of the candy. | | $J = \frac{3}{4} \times C$ |
| *For, per:* | ratio | Division |
| Jane won 3 games for every 2 that Tom won. | ÷ | $\frac{J}{T} = \frac{3}{2}$ |
| 50 miles per hour | | 50 miles/hour |
| 2 bleeps per revolution | | 2 bleeps/revolution |

## Examples

Figuring out these problems takes more than just knowing all of the formulas. You have to think about what skills and tools you will apply to the questions in order to reason your way through to the correct answer.

### EXAMPLE 1

The price of a sweater went up 20% since last year. If last year's price was $x$, what is this year's price in terms of $x$?

**How to solve:**

- Last year's price = 100% of $x$

- This year's price is 100% of $x$ plus 20% of $x$.

$$x + 20\% \cdot x = x + 0.2x = 1.2x$$

## EXAMPLE 2

> One year ago, an average restaurant meal cost $12. Today, the average restaurant meal costs $15. By what percent has the cost of the average restaurant meal increased?

**How to solve:** You can figure percent increase by taking the difference in prices first and then expressing it as a percentage of the original price:

$$\$15 - \$12 = \$3 \text{ difference}$$

What percentage of the original price is $3?

$$\frac{3}{12} = \frac{x}{100}$$

$$12x = 300$$

$$x = 25$$

The cost increased by 25%.

Or you can figure what percent the new price is of the old price: 15 is what percent of 12?

$$15 = \left(\frac{x}{100}\right)12$$

$$\frac{15}{12} = \frac{x}{100}$$

$$x = 125$$

Therefore, 15 is 125 percent of 12.

This tells you what percent the current price ($15) is of the old price ($12). But the question asks for the percent increase, so you have to subtract 100 percent from 125 percent.

$$125\% - 100\% = 25\% \text{ increase}$$

## EXAMPLE 3

> The average height (arithmetic mean) of 4 members of a 6-person volleyball team is 175 cm. What does the average height in centimeters of the other 2 players have to be if the average height of the entire team equals 180 cm?

**How to solve:** Start with the formula for the average:

$$\frac{\text{Sum of values}}{\text{Number of values}} = \text{average}$$

Use what you know to find out the sum of the heights of the 4 members whose average is 175 cm.

$$\frac{\text{Sum of heights}}{4} = 175$$

$$\text{Sum of heights} = 4(175) = 700$$

The average of all 6 players is 180 cm.

$$\text{Average of 6 players' heights} = \frac{\text{sum of 4 players' heights} + \text{sum of 2 players' heights}}{6}$$

$$180 = \frac{700 + \text{sum of 2 players' heights}}{6}$$

$$1080 = 700 + \text{sum of 2 players' heights}$$
$$1080 - 700 = \text{sum of 2 players' heights}$$
$$380 = \text{sum of 2 players' heights}$$

What is the average of the heights of the 2 players?

$$\text{Average} = \frac{\text{sum}}{\text{number of players}}$$

$$\text{Average} = \frac{380}{2}$$

$$= 190 \text{ cm}$$

## EXAMPLE 4

A car traveling at an average rate of 55 kilometers per hour made a trip in 6 hours. If it had traveled at an average rate of 50 kilometers per hour, the trip would have taken how many *minutes* longer?

**How to solve:**

- How long was the trip?

$$\text{Distance} = \text{rate} \times \text{time}$$
$$\text{Distance} = 55 \text{ kph} \times 6 \text{ hours}$$
$$\text{Distance} = 330 \text{ km}$$

- How long does the 330-kilometer trip take if the car is traveling at 50 kilometers per hour?

$$\text{Time} = \frac{\text{distance}}{\text{rate}}$$
$$\text{Time} = \frac{330 \text{ km}}{50 \text{ kph}}$$
$$\text{Time} = 6\frac{3}{5} \text{ hours}$$

- What does the question ask? The difference *in minutes* between the two trips.

$$\text{Difference} = \frac{3}{5} \text{ hour}$$

$$\text{Difference} = x \text{ minutes}$$

$$\frac{3}{5} = \frac{x}{60}$$

$$5x = 180$$
$$x = 36 \text{ minutes}$$

## Examples

The test may include questions that involve quantities that are directly proportional to each other and quantities that are inversely proportional to each other. Look at the next two examples:

### EXAMPLE 1

> The number of juice packs that Rambling Pines Day Camp buys each day is directly proportional to the number of children at the camp that day. If the camp bought 150 juice boxes yesterday for 60 children, how many juice boxes will they buy today for 52 children?

**How to solve:** If two quantities $x$ and $y$ are directly proportional (another way to say this is that one varies directly with the other), then there is a constant $k$ for which $y = kx$. In this case, the number of juice boxes varies directly with the number of children. There are 150 juice boxes when there are 60 children:

$$150 = k(60)$$

You can solve for $k$ to get

$$k = \frac{5}{2}$$

What does the question ask? How many juice boxes for 52 children?

$$k \times 52 = \frac{5}{2} \times 52 = 5 \times 26 = 130$$

The camp will buy 130 juice boxes for 52 children.

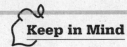

**Keep in Mind**

Recall that two quantities $x$ and $y$ are inversely proportional if there is a nonzero constant $k$ for which $y = \frac{k}{x}$.

### EXAMPLE 2

> If $c$ and $d$ are inversely proportional and $c = 10$ when $d = 6$, what is $d$ when $c = 30$?

**How to solve:** The quantities $c$ and $d$ are inversely proportional, so

$$d = \frac{k}{c}$$

for some constant $k$.

Because $c = 10$ when $d = 6$, you get

$$6 = \frac{k}{10},$$

and so $k = 60$.

You now can find $d$ when $c = 30$:

$$d = \frac{60}{30} = 2$$

So $d = 2$ when $c = 30$.

# Functions

## Function Notation and Evaluation

A function can be thought of as a rule or formula that tells how to associate the elements in one set (the *domain*) with the elements in another set (the *range*). For example, the squaring function can be thought of as the rule "take the square of $x$" or as the rule $x^2$.

You should be familiar with function notation. The squaring function can be written in function notation as $f(x) = x^2$. Function notation lets you write complicated functions much more easily. For example, you can write that the function $g$ is defined by $g(x) = 3^x + \dfrac{1}{x}$. Then $g(2) = 3^2 + \dfrac{1}{2} = 9\dfrac{1}{2}$.

## Domain and Range

- The *domain* of a function is the set of all the values for which the function is defined.

- The *range* of a function is the set of all values that are the output, or result, of applying the function.

**EXAMPLE**

What are the domain and range of $f(x) = 1 + \sqrt{x}$ ?

**How to solve:** The domain of $f$ is the set of all values of $x$ for which the formula $1 + \sqrt{x}$ is defined. This formula makes sense if $x$ is zero or a positive number. But if $x$ is negative, $f$ is not defined, the square root of a negative number is not a real number. Therefore, the domain of $f(x) = 1 + \sqrt{x}$ is all nonnegative numbers $x$.

What is the range of $f$? In other words, what is the set of all possible values of $f(x) = 1 + \sqrt{x}$ ? A square root is always nonnegative, so every value of $f$ must be at least 1. The question now remains: Is every number $r \geq 1$ equal to $f(s)$ for some $s$ ? Let's try a value, say $r = 9$.

$$f(s) = 1 + \sqrt{s} = 9$$
$$\sqrt{s} = 8$$
$$s = 64$$

You can see that for any $r \geq 1$, you can find $s$ such that $r = f(s)$ :

$$f(s) = 1 + \sqrt{s} = r$$
$$\sqrt{s} = r - 1$$
$$s = (r - 1)^2$$

So, the range of $f$ is all numbers greater than or equal to 1.

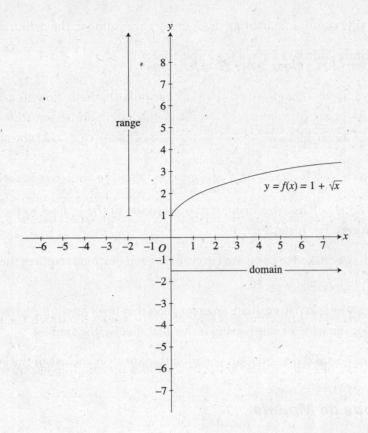

$$y = f(x) = 1 + \sqrt{x}$$

## Using New Definitions

For functions, especially those involving more than one variable, a special symbol is sometimes introduced and defined.

These symbols generally have unusual looking signs (☆, ✱, §) so you won't confuse them with standard mathematical symbols.

The key to these questions is to make sure that you read the definition carefully. A typical special symbol question might look something like this:

Let 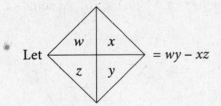 $= wy - xz$

where $w$, $x$, $y$ and $z$ are integers.

What is the value of 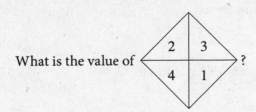 ?

To answer this question, substitute the numbers according to the definition:

- Substitute 2 for $w$, 3 for $x$, 4 for $z$ and 1 for $y$.

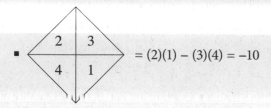 $= (2)(1) - (3)(4) = -10$

Some questions will ask you to apply the definition of the symbol to more complicated situations. For instance:

- You may be asked to compare two values, each of which requires the use of the symbol.

- You may be asked to evaluate an expression that involves multiplying, dividing, adding, squaring or subtracting terms that involve the symbol.

- You may be asked to solve an equation that involves the use of the symbol.

## Functions as Models

Functions can be used as models of real-life situations. Here is an example:

The temperature in City $X$ is $W(t)$ degrees Fahrenheit $t$ hours after sundown at 5:00 p.m. The function $W(t)$ is given by

$$W(t) = 0.1 \, (400 - 40t + t^2) \text{ for } 0 \le t \le 12$$

You can draw a graph of this function:

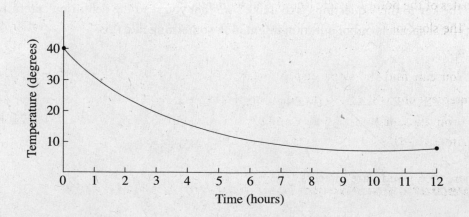

## Linear Functions: Their Equations and Graphs

You may be asked to answer questions involving linear equations and their graphs. Therefore, you will need to understand the concepts of slope and intercepts:

$y = mx + b$, where $m$ and $b$ are constants, is a linear function, and the graph of $y = mx + b$ in the $xy$-plane is a line with slope $m$ and $y$-intercept $b$.

For example:

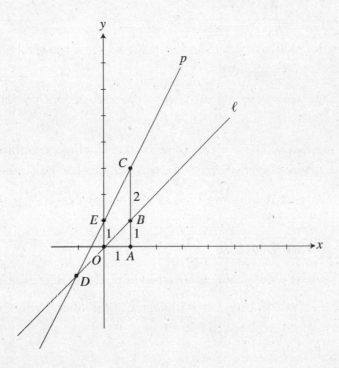

In the figure above, points $A$, $B$ and $C$ lie on a vertical line segment that intersects line $\ell$ at $B$ and line $p$ at $C$. $OA = 1$, $OE = 1$, $BA = 1$ and $BC = 2$. What are the coordinates of the point $D$ where lines $\ell$ and $p$ intersect?

The slope of $\ell$ is $\dfrac{BA}{OA} = 1$. Because $\ell$ passes through the origin, its equation is $y = x$.

You can find the slope of $p$ in a few ways. For instance, it is $\dfrac{BC}{EB} = 2$. The $y$-intercept of $p$ is 1, and so the equation of $p$ is $y = 2x + 1$.

From the equations of lines $\ell$ and $p$, you can see their intersection at $D$ has coordinates $(-1, -1)$.

## Quadratic Functions: Their Equations and Graphs

You may be asked to answer questions involving quadratic equations and their graphs. You will need to be able to identify some of the basic features of the graph of a quadratic equation, such as its highest or lowest point, its zeros and its direction.

For example, which of the following could be the graph of $y = -x^2 - 1$ ?

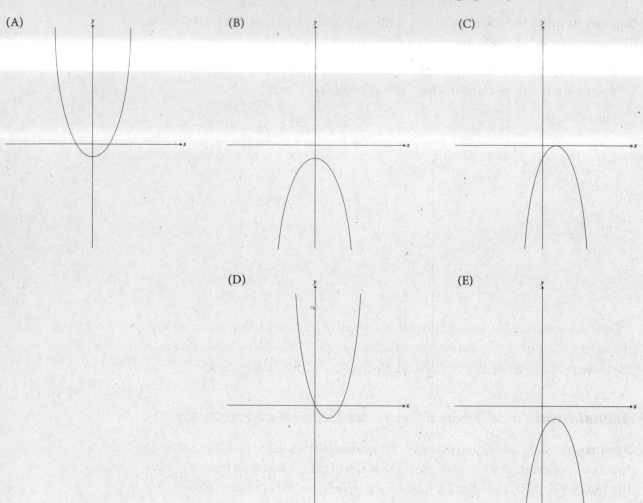

(A)       (B)       (C)

(D)       (E)

Because the square of any number is nonnegative, $-x^2 - 1$ must always be a negative number. This eliminates all choices except (B) and (E). The largest value of $y$ must occur when $x = 0$. This eliminates (E). The correct answer is (B).

## Qualitative Behavior of Graphs and Functions

You will need to understand how the properties of a function and its graph are related. For example, the zeros of the function $f$ are given by the points where the graph of $f(x)$ in the $xy$-plane intersects the $x$-axis. Or you could be asked a question such as the following: The graphs of $y = f(x)$ and $y = 2$ are shown below. (Note that the domain of the function $f$ is the interval from $x = -3$ to $x = 4$ .) For how many values of $x$ does $f(x) = 2$ ?

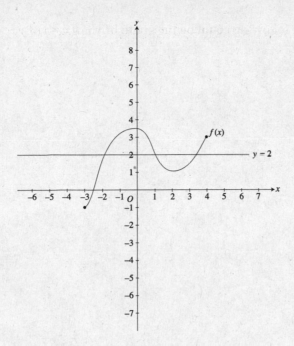

The value of $f(x)$ equals 2 exactly when the graph of $y = f(x)$ has height 2. This graph has height 2 at the points where it intersects the line $y = 2$. The figure shows that there are three points of intersection, so you know that $f(x) = 2$ for three values of $x$.

## Translations and Their Effects on Graphs of Functions

You may be asked questions on the effects of simple translations on the graph of a function. For example, if you are given the graph of $g(x)$, you should be able to identify the graph of $g(x + 3)$. For example: The graph of $y = f(x)$ is shown below.

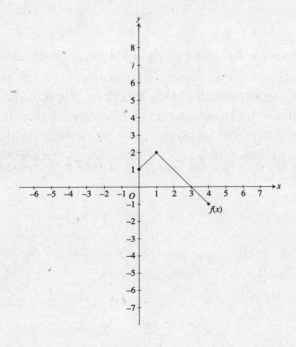

Which of the following could be the graph of $y = f(x - 1)$ ?

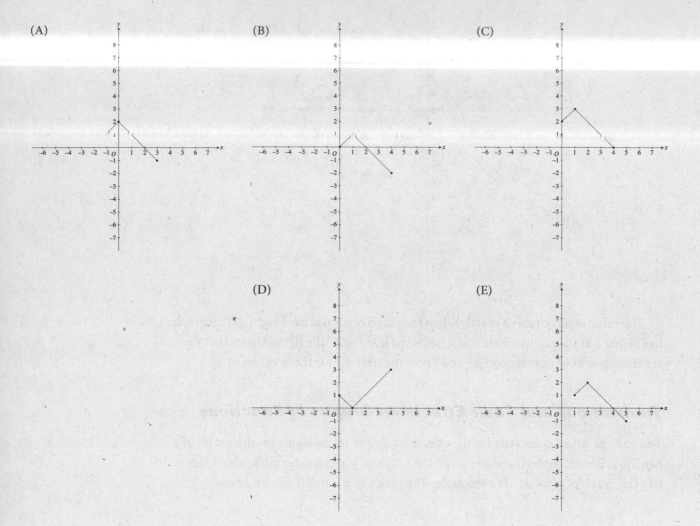

The graph of $y = f(x - 1)$ is the graph of $y = f(x)$ shifted 1 unit to the right. The correct choice is (E).

You can also check the values of the functions at specific points. The original graph shows that $f(3) = 0$. Therefore, the graph of $y = f(x - 1)$ must contain the point $(4, 0)$. Only the graphs in (C) and (E) contain $(4, 0)$. But $f(0) = 1$. Therefore, the graph of $y = f(x - 1)$ must contain the point $(1, 1)$; the graph in (C) doesn't contain $(1, 1)$, so the correct answer is (E).

# CHAPTER 17

# Geometry and Measurement Review

## Concepts You Need to Know

For the mathematics questions covering geometry and measurement concepts, you should be familiar with all of the following basic skills, topics and formulas:

- Geometric notation

- Points and lines

- Angles in the plane

- Triangles (including special triangles)
  - Equilateral triangles
  - Isosceles triangles
  - Right triangles and the Pythagorean theorem
  - 30°-60°-90° triangles
  - 45°-45°-90° triangles
  - 3-4-5 triangles
  - Congruent triangles
  - Similar triangles
  - The triangle inequality

- Quadrilaterals
  - Parallelograms
  - Rectangles
  - Squares

- Areas and perimeters
  - Areas of squares and rectangles
  - Perimeters of squares and rectangles
  - Area of triangles
  - Area of parallelograms

  - Other polygons
    - Angles in a polygon
    - Perimeter
    - Area

  - Circles
    - Diameter
    - Radius
    - Arc
    - Tangent to a circle
    - Circumference
    - Area

  - Solid geometry
    - Solid figures and volumes
    - Surface area

  - Geometric perception

  - Coordinate geometry
    - Slopes, parallel lines and perpendicular lines
    - The midpoint formula
    - The distance formula

  - Transformations

The SAT doesn't include:

  - Formal geometric proofs

  - Trigonometry

  - Radian measure

# Geometric Notation

You will need to be able to recognize and use geometric notation for points and lines, line segments, rays, angles and their measures, and lengths.

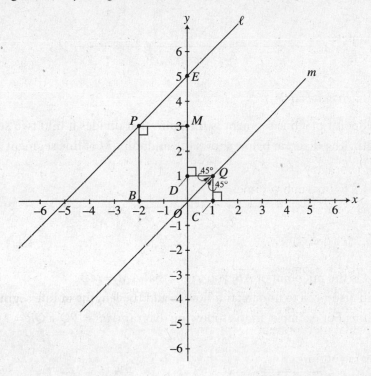

In the figure above, the *xy*-coordinate plane has origin *O*. The values of *x* on the horizontal *x*-axis increase as you move to the right, and the values of *y* on the vertical *y*-axis increase as you move up. Line $\ell$ contains point *P*, which has coordinates (−2, 3), and point *E*, which has coordinates (0, 5). Line *m* passes through the origin *O* (0, 0) and the point *Q* (1, 1).

Lines $\ell$ and *m* are parallel — they never meet. This is written $\ell \parallel m$.

You will also need to know the meaning of the following notation:

| | |
|---|---|
| $\overleftrightarrow{PE}$ | the line containing the points *P* and *E* (this is the same as line $\ell$) |
| $\overline{PE}$ | the line segment with endpoints *P* and *E* |
| $PE$ | the length of the line segment $\overline{PE}$ (you can write PE = $2\sqrt{2}$) |
| $\overrightarrow{PE}$ | the ray starting at *P* and extending infinitely in the direction of *E* |
| $\overrightarrow{EP}$ | the ray starting at *E* and extending infinitely in the direction of *P* |
| $\angle DOC$ | the angle formed by $\overrightarrow{OD}$ and $\overrightarrow{OC}$ |
| $m\angle DOC$ | the measure of $\angle DOC$ (you can write $m\angle DOC$ = 90°) |
| $\triangle OQC$ | the triangle with vertices *O*, *C* and *Q* |
| $BPMO$ | the quadrilateral with vertices *B*, *P*, *M* and *O* |
| $\overline{BP} \perp \overline{PM}$ | the relation that $\overline{BP}$ is perpendicular to $\overline{PM}$ (you should also recognize that the small square within $\angle BPM$ means this is a right angle) |

# Points and Lines

There is a unique line that contains any two distinct points. Therefore, in the following diagram, line $\ell$ is the only line that contains both point $A$ and point $B$.

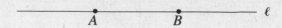

The midpoint of a line segment is the point that divides it into two segments of equal length. The diagram below shows the midpoint $M$ of line segment $\overline{AB}$.

Because $M$ is the midpoint of $\overline{AB}$, you know that $AM = MB$.

You will also need to understand how to add the lengths of line segments along the same line. For example, in the following diagram, $PR = PQ + QR = 2 + 3 = 5$.

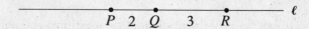

You may also be given the lengths of line segments along a common line and be asked a question that requires you to find the order of points along the line.

### Example

Points $E$, $F$ and $G$ all lie on line $m$, with $E$ to the left of $F$. $EF = 10$, $FG = 8$ and $EG > FG$. What is $EG$?

**How to solve:** You can start to solve the problem by drawing the following diagram of $E$ and $F$ on $m$.

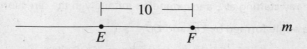

The diagram uses the given information that $E$ is to the left of $F$ and that $EF = 10$. Now the question is where to place point $G$ on $m$. You are given that $FG = 8$, but is $G$ to the left or to the right of $F$?

Try putting $G$ to the left of $F$. Using $FG = 8$, you get the following diagram.

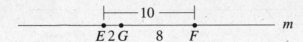

In the diagram, $EG = 2$. But you are given that $EG$ must be greater than $FG$, and in the diagram, $EG < FG$. Therefore, $G$ cannot be to the left of $F$.

This means $G$ must be to the right of $F$, as shown below.

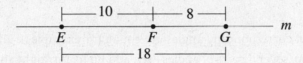

Now $EG > FG$, as required. Therefore, this diagram shows the correct order of points $E$, $F$, and $G$ along line $m$, and $EG = 18$.

## Angles in the Plane

In order to work through some of the mathematics questions, you will need to know the basic facts about the angles formed in a plane by lines, line segments and rays.

- *Vertical angles and supplementary angles.* Two opposite angles formed by two intersecting lines are called *vertical angles.*

Vertical angles have the same measure. In the figure above, $y = 115$ and $x = 65$.

Note that any pair of angles next to each other in the figure have measures that add up to 180°. (This is the measure of a *straight angle*, the angle formed by a straight line.) Two angles whose measures have a sum of 180° are called *supplementary angles.*

■ *Parallel lines.* When a line intersects a pair of parallel lines, the eight angles formed are related in several ways.

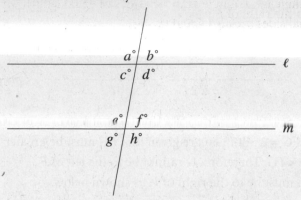

The measures of corresponding angles are equal; for example, *a* and *e* are equal, as are *d* and *h*. Also, several pairs of angles each add up to a straight angle; for example, $d + f = 180$ and $a + g = 180$. Finally, alternate interior angles have equal measures; in the figure, *c* and *f* are equal, as are *d* and *e*.

■ *Right angles, perpendicular lines, and complementary angles.* A *right angle* is an angle with a measure of 90°. If two lines intersect and one of the four angles formed is a right angle, the lines are *perpendicular*. In this case, all four angles that are formed are right angles. Two angles whose measures have a sum of 90° are called *complementary angles.*

# Triangles (Including Special Triangles)

The sum of the measures of the angles in any triangle is 180°.

## Equilateral Triangles

The three sides of an equilateral triangle (*a, b, c*) are equal in length. The three angles are also equal, and they each measure 60° ($x = y = z = 60$).

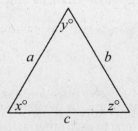

### Isosceles Triangles

An isosceles triangle is a triangle with two sides of equal length ($m = n$). The angles opposite the equal sides are also equal ($x = y$).

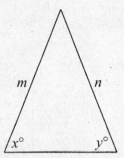

## Right Triangles and the Pythagorean Theorem

A right triangle is a triangle with a right angle. (Note that the other two angles in a right triangle are complementary angles.) You can get a lot of information from figures that contain right triangles. This information frequently involves the Pythagorean theorem: The square of the length of the hypotenuse of a right triangle is equal to the sum of the squares of the lengths of the other two sides.

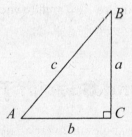

The hypotenuse is the longest side of the triangle and is opposite the right angle. The other two sides are usually referred to as *legs*. In the figure above:

- $\overline{AB}$ is the hypotenuse with length $c$.

- $\overline{BC}$ and $\overline{AC}$ are the two legs, with lengths $a$ and $b$, respectively.

- The Pythagorean theorem leads to the equation:

$$a^2 + b^2 = c^2$$

- If you know the lengths of any two sides, you can use the Pythagorean theorem to find the length of the third side.

### 30°-60°-90° *Triangles*

The lengths of the sides of a 30°-60°-90° triangle are in the ratio of $1 : \sqrt{3} : 2$, as shown in the figure:

- Short leg $= x$

- Long leg $= x\sqrt{3}$

- Hypotenuse $= 2x$

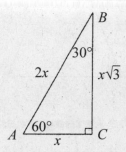

If you know the lengths of any one side, you can find the lengths of the other two sides.

For instance, if you know the length of the short leg is 1, then the length of the hypotenuse is 2, and the Pythagorean theorem gives you the length of the longer leg:

$$c^2 = a^2 + b^2$$
$$c = 2, b = 1$$
$$2^2 = a^2 + 1$$
$$4 = a^2 + 1$$
$$3 = a^2$$
$$\sqrt{3} = a$$

### 45°-45°-90° *Triangles*

The lengths of the sides of a 45°-45°-90° triangle are in the ratio of $1 : 1 : \sqrt{2}$, as shown in the figure below. To verify this ratio when the equal sides are of length 1, apply the Pythagorean theorem to find the length of the hypotenuse:

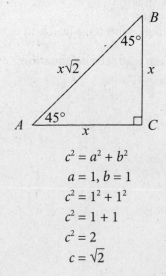

$$c^2 = a^2 + b^2$$
$$a = 1, b = 1$$
$$c^2 = 1^2 + 1^2$$
$$c^2 = 1 + 1$$
$$c^2 = 2$$
$$c = \sqrt{2}$$

## 3-4-5 Triangles

The sides of a 3-4-5 right triangle are in the ratio of 3:4:5. For example, in the figure below, if $x = 2$, the sides of the triangle have lengths 6, 8 and 10. It is easy to use the Pythagorean theorem to verify this:

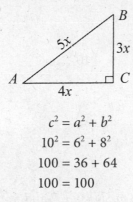

$$c^2 = a^2 + b^2$$
$$10^2 = 6^2 + 8^2$$
$$100 = 36 + 64$$
$$100 = 100$$

## Congruent Triangles

*Congruent triangles* are triangles that have the same size and shape.

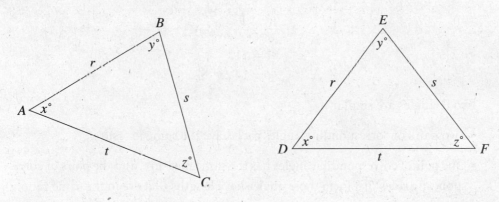

In the figure, each side of $\triangle ABC$ has the same length as the corresponding side of $\triangle DEF$.

$$AB = DE = r$$
$$BC = EF = s$$
$$CA = FD = t$$

Each angle of $\triangle ABC$ is also equal to its corresponding angle in $\triangle DEF$.

Two triangles are congruent if any of the following is true:

- Each pair of corresponding sides has the same length.

- Two pairs of corresponding sides each have the same length, and the angles formed by these sides have the same measure.

- One pair of corresponding sides has the same length, and two pairs of corresponding angles each have the same measure.

### Similar Triangles

*Similar triangles* have the same shape. Each corresponding pair of angles has the same measure.

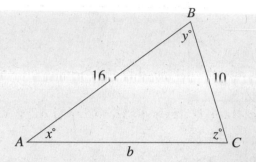
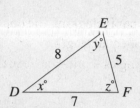

In the figure, $m\angle A = m\angle D$, $m\angle B = m\angle E$ and $m\angle C = m\angle F$. An important fact about similar triangles is that the ratio of the lengths of any pair of corresponding sides is the same. (In other words, the lengths of corresponding sides are in proportion.) For example, in the figure $\frac{16}{8} = \frac{10}{5}$. We can also find $b$ in the figure:

$$\frac{16}{8} = \frac{b}{7}$$
$$8b = 112$$
$$b = 14$$

Two triangles are similar if

- Two pairs of corresponding angles each have the same measure.

- One pair of corresponding angles has the same measure, and the pairs of corresponding sides that form those angles have lengths that are in the same ratio.

### The Triangle Inequality

The triangle inequality is an important fact about triangles. It states that the sum of the lengths of any two sides of a triangle is greater than the length of the third side.

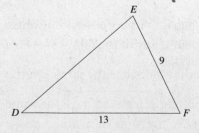

In the figure, for example, $9 + 13 > DE$. Therefore, you know $DE$ must be less than 22.

# Quadrilaterals

In some special quadrilaterals — parallelograms, rectangles and squares — there are relationships among the angles and sides that can help you solve geometry problems.

### *Parallelograms*

In a parallelogram, the opposite angles are of equal measure and the opposite sides are of equal length.

Angles *A* and *C* are equal, and angles *B* and *D* are equal. *AB* = *CD* and *AD* = *BC* .

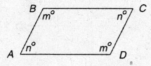

### *Rectangles*

A rectangle is a special case of a parallelogram. In rectangles, all the angles are right angles.

### *Squares*

A square is a special case of a rectangle in which the lengths of all the sides are equal.

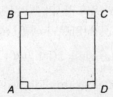

Notice that if you know the length of any side of a square, you also know the length of a diagonal.

A diagonal makes two 45°-45°-90° triangles with the sides of the square. You can figure out the lengths of the sides from the length of a diagonal or the length of a diagonal from the length of a side.

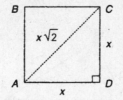

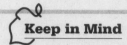
**Keep in Mind**

Remember the reference information. Formulas for areas of common figures are given in the reference material that is printed in the test booklet.

# Areas and Perimeters

## Areas of Rectangles and Squares

The formula for the area of any rectangle is:

$$\text{Area} = \text{length} \times \text{width}$$

Because all sides of a square are equal, the length and width are often both referred to as the length of a side, *s*. So, the area of a square can be written as:

$$\text{Area} = s^2$$

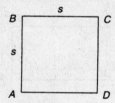

## Perimeters of Rectangles and Squares

The perimeter of a polygon is the sum of the lengths of its sides. Because the opposite sides of rectangles are equal, the formula for the perimeter of a rectangle is:

$$\text{Perimeter of a rectangle} = 2(\text{length} + \text{width}) = 2(\ell + w)$$

The same is true for any parallelogram. For a square, it's even easier. Because all four sides of a square are equal, the perimeter of a square is:

$$\text{Perimeter of a square} = 4(\text{length of any side}) = 4s$$

## Area of Triangles

The area of a triangle is:

$$A = \left(\frac{1}{2}\right) bh$$

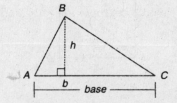

- *b* is the base.

- *h* is the height, a perpendicular segment drawn from a vertex of the triangle to the base.

## Area of Parallelograms

To find the area of a parallelogram, you drop a perpendicular — segment *BE* in the figure shown below. This makes a right triangle, *ABE* .

If you take this triangle away from the parallelogram and add it to the other side (Δ*DCF*), you have a rectangle with the same area as the original parallelogram.

The area of the rectangle is length × width.

The width of this rectangle is the same as the height of the parallelogram, so the formula for the area of a parallelogram is:

$$\text{Area} = \text{length} \times \text{height}$$

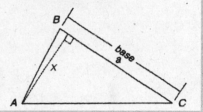

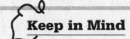

**Keep in Mind**

You can start with any vertex of the triangle. The side opposite the vertex you choose becomes the base and the perpendicular line from that vertex to the segment becomes the height. For instance, the area of the triangle in the figure could be calculated using point *A* as the vertex instead of point *B*.

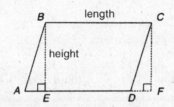

# Other Polygons

Occasionally, a question will ask you to work with polygons other than triangles and quadrilaterals. A *regular polygon* is a polygon whose sides all have the same length and whose angles all have the same measure. Here are a few other things to remember about other polygons.

## Angles in a Polygon

You can figure out the total number of degrees in the interior angles of most polygons by dividing the polygon into triangles:

- From any vertex, divide the polygon into as many nonoverlapping triangles as possible. Use only straight lines. Make sure that all the space inside the polygon is divided into triangles.

- Count the triangles. In this figure, there are four triangles.

- There is a total of 180° in the angles of each triangle, so multiply the number of triangles by 180. The product will be the sum of the angles in the polygon (720° in the hexagon shown below).

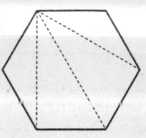

| Sides | Interior Angle Sum |
|-------|--------------------|
| 3 | 180° |
| 4 | 360° |
| 5 | 540° |
| 6 | 720° |
| . | |
| . | |
| . | |
| $n$ | $180(n - 2)$ |

## *Example*

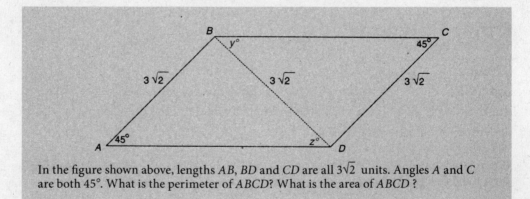

In the figure shown above, lengths $AB$, $BD$ and $CD$ are all $3\sqrt{2}$ units. Angles $A$ and $C$ are both 45°. What is the perimeter of $ABCD$? What is the area of $ABCD$?

**How to solve:** You are asked for the perimeter and the area of the figure. For the perimeter you will need to know the lengths of $\overline{BC}$ and $\overline{AD}$. For the area you will also need to know the heights of $\triangle ABD$ and $\triangle BCD$.

### PERIMETER

- You are given the lengths of 3 line segments, all of which are the same: $3\sqrt{2}$.

- You are given two angles, both of which have the same measure: 45°.

- $\triangle ABD$ is a triangle with two equal sides.

- $\triangle BCD$ is a triangle with two equal sides.

- Therefore, they are both isosceles triangles.

- The measure of angle $C$ is 45°, so $y = 45$, because angles opposite equal sides are equal.

- In the same way, you can show that $z = 45$.

- Both triangles are 45°-45°-90° triangles.

- You can figure out the lengths of $\overline{AD}$ and $\overline{BC}$ by the Pythagorean theorem:

$$AD^2 = (3\sqrt{2})^2 + (3\sqrt{2})^2 = 36, \text{ so } AD = 6$$

- Do the same for the length of $\overline{BC}$ to find that $BC = 6$.

- You can now add up the lengths of the sides to get the perimeter:

$$2(6 + 3\sqrt{2}) = 12 + 6\sqrt{2}.$$

## AREA

- $ABCD$ is a parallelogram. You know this because both sets of opposite sides are equal: $AB = CD$ and $AD = BC$.

- That means that you can use the formula for the area of a parallelogram: area = length × height.

- To find the height, drop a perpendicular from $B$.

- That creates another 45°-45°-90° triangle whose hypotenuse is $\overline{AB}$.

- The ratio of the sides of a 45°-45°-90° triangle is 1:1:$\sqrt{2}$.

- From that ratio, you know the height of the figure is 3.

- With the height, you can then calculate the area: $3 \times 6 = 18$.

If you label everything you figure out as you go along, you will end up with a figure that looks like the one below.

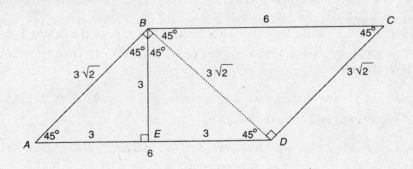

# Circles

### Diameter

The diameter of a circle is a line segment that passes through the center and has its endpoints on the circle. All diameters of the same circle have equal lengths.

### Radius

The radius of a circle is a line segment extending from the center of the circle to a point on the circle. In the figure shown below, $\overline{OB}$ and $\overline{OA}$ are radii.

All radii of the same circle have equal lengths, and the radius is half the diameter. In the figure, $OB = OA$.

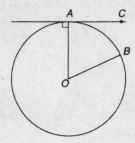

### Arc

An arc is a part of a circle. In the figure above, the points on the circle from $A$ to $B$ form an arc. An arc can be measured in degrees or in units of length.

If you form an angle by drawing radii from the ends of the arc to the center of the circle, the number of degrees in the arc (arc $AB$ in the figure) equals the number of degrees in the angle formed by the two radii at the center of the circle ($\angle AOB$), called the *central angle*.

### Tangent to a Circle

A tangent to a circle is a line that intersects the circle at exactly one point. In the figure, line $\overleftrightarrow{AC}$ is a tangent. A tangent to a circle is always perpendicular to the radius that contains the one point of the line that touches the circle. In this case, $\overline{OA} \perp \overleftrightarrow{AC}$.

### Circumference

The circumference is the distance around a circle, and it is equal to $\pi$ times the diameter, $d$ (or $\pi$ times twice the radius, $r$).

$$\text{Circumference} = \pi d$$
$$\text{Circumference} = 2\pi r$$

If the diameter is 16, the circumference is $16\pi$. If the radius is 3, the circumference is $2(3)\pi$, or $6\pi$.

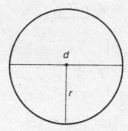

## Area

The area of a circle is equal to $\pi$ times the square of the radius.

$$\text{Area} = \pi r^2$$

## Example

> In the figure shown below, $A$ is the center of a circle whose area is $25\pi$. $B$ and $C$ are points on the circle. The measure of angle $ACB$ is $45°$. What is the length of line segment $BC$?
>
>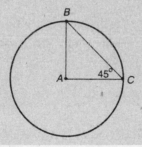

**How to solve:**

- Point $A$ is the center of the circle.

- That makes both $\overline{AB}$ and $\overline{AC}$ radii, which means that they have equal length.

- Because $AB = AC$, $\triangle ABC$ is an isosceles triangle. The angle opposite $\overline{AB}$ has a measure of $45°$.

- That means the angle opposite the other equal side is also $45°$.

- The remaining angle is $90°$.

- The area of the circle is $25\pi$.

- The formula for the area of a circle is $\pi r^2$. You can use that formula to figure out the length of the radius, $r$.

- That length, $r$, is also the length of the legs of the triangle whose hypotenuse ($\overline{BC}$) has the length you are trying to figure out.

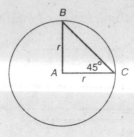

What is the value of $r$ ?

$$\text{Area} = \pi r^2$$
$$25\pi = \pi r^2$$
$$25 = r^2$$
$$5 = r$$

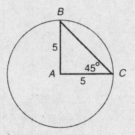

Figuring out the final answer to the problem is a simple matter of working through the Pythagorean theorem or remembering that the ratio of the sides of 45°-45°-90° triangles is 1:1:$\sqrt{2}$. The answer is 5$\sqrt{2}$.

# Solid Geometry

## Solid Figures and Volumes

You may be asked questions about the basic types of solids: cubes, rectangular solids, prisms, cylinders, cones, spheres and pyramids. You will be given the formulas for the volume of a rectangular solid and a right circular cylinder in the Reference Information box in the SAT. You are not expected to memorize complicated formulas involving solids, but you may be asked questions that require logic and applying your knowledge in new ways.

*Cubes and rectangular solids.* The simplest type of solid is a cube. Every edge of a cube has the same length. If the edge length of a cube is $s$, then the volume of the cube is $s^3$.

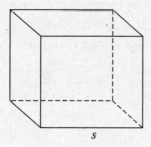

Note that the dashed lines indicate edges of the cubes that are hidden from your view. Remember, on the SAT, *you will be told if a figure does not lie in a plane.* Just because you see a dashed line in a figure does not mean it is a solid.

In a rectangular solid, the length, width and height may be different.

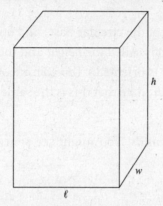

The volume is given by the formula $V = \ell wh$.

**Prisms and cylinders.** A rectangular solid is one example of a right prism, which is a solid in which two congruent polygons are joined by rectangular faces that are perpendicular to the polygons. The congruent polygons are called the *bases* of the prism, and the length of an edge joining the polygons is called the *height,* even if the prism is not standing on its base.

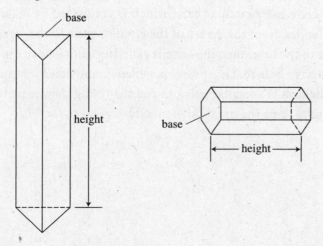

A prism may be named after its polygonal base: for example, *triangular* prism, *hexagonal* prism.

The volume of a prism is given by the product of its height and the area of its base. You should also be familiar with a right circular cylinder, a solid in which two congruent circles are joined by a curved surface that meets the circles at a right angle.

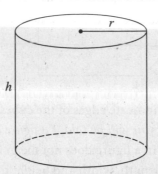

In the figure, $r$ is the radius of the circular base, and $h$ is the height of the cylinder. (As with a prism, this length is called the *height* and the circles are called the *bases*, no matter how the cylinder is oriented.) The volume of a right circular cylinder is given by the formula $V = \pi r^2 h$; note that this is the same as the area of the base times the height.

*Spheres, cones and pyramids.* You might see spheres, cones or pyramids in a question.

Sphere          Cone          Pyramid

A sphere is the solid analogue of a circle. All radii of a sphere are equal.

A circular cone has a circular base, which is connected by a curved surface to its vertex. If the line from the vertex of the circular cone to the center of its base is perpendicular to the base, then the cone is called a *right circular cone.*

A pyramid has a base that is a polygon, which is connected by triangular faces to its vertex. If the base is a regular polygon and the triangular faces are all congruent isosceles triangles, then the pyramid is called a *regular pyramid.*

### Surface Area

If you make cuts in a solid that allow you to open it up to form a plane figure, the result is called a *net* of the solid. A solid may have many different nets. The figure below shows one net for a cube.

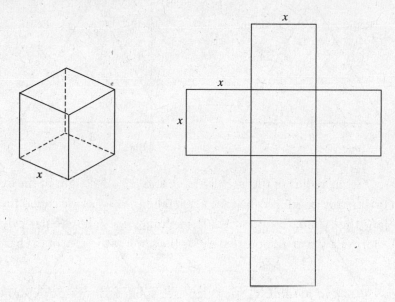

Sometimes, you can find the surface area of a solid by working with one of its nets. For example, from the net of the cube with edge length $x$, you can see its surface consists of six squares, each with side $x$. The surface area of the cube is the sum of the areas of these six squares, which is $6x^2$.

## Geometric Perception

The SAT may ask you questions that require you to visualize a plane figure or a solid from different views or orientations. These are questions in geometric perception.

For example:

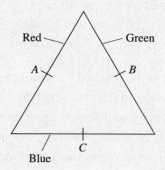

The wire frame above is made of three wires permanently joined together: a red wire, a blue wire and a green wire. Three beads, labeled $A$, $B$ and $C$, are attached to the frame so that each of them can move all around the frame. However, none of the beads can be taken off the frame, nor can they be moved past one another. Which of the following configurations cannot be reached by sliding the beads around the frame or changing the position of the frame?

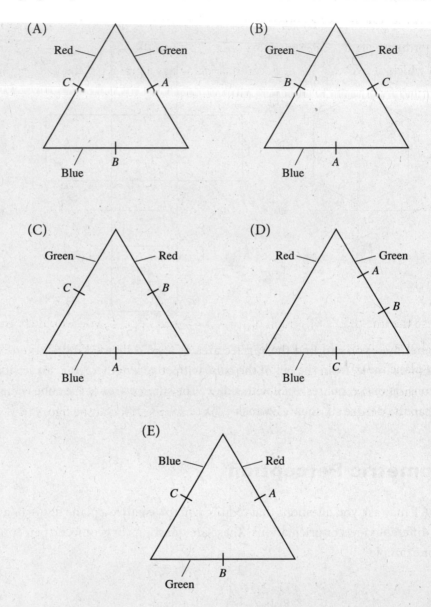

(A)   Red — Green   C   A   B   Blue

(B)   Green — Red   B   C   A   Blue

(C)   Green — Red   C   B   A   Blue

(D)   Red — Green   A   B   C   Blue

(E)   Blue — Red   C   A   B   Green

The configuration in (A) can be reached by sliding each bead clockwise to the next wire piece. The configuration in (C) can be reached by sliding each bead counterclockwise to the next wire piece and then flipping the frame over. The configuration in (D) is reached simply by sliding bead *A* clockwise to the green wire. The configuration in (E) comes from turning the wire frame a third of a revolution clockwise.

The configuration in (B) cannot be reached no matter how you slide the beads or rotate and flip the frame. The correct answer is (B).

# Coordinate Geometry

## Slopes, Parallel Lines and Perpendicular Lines

Some of the geometry questions on the test will involve points, lines and figures in the coordinate plane. For example, you may be given the equation $y = \frac{1}{2}x + 2$ and be asked which of five lines in the coordinate plane has a graph parallel to the graph of that equation. Two of the choices might look like this:

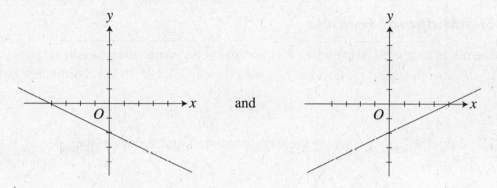

and

Because the line that is the graph of $y = \frac{1}{2}x + 2$ has slope $\frac{1}{2}$, you would choose the second of the choices above because the slope of the line in that figure is $\frac{1}{2}$. Lines in the $xy$-plane are parallel exactly when their slopes are equal.

You should also know the following fact about slopes: Two lines are perpendicular when the product of their slopes is $-1$. For example, look at the figure below:

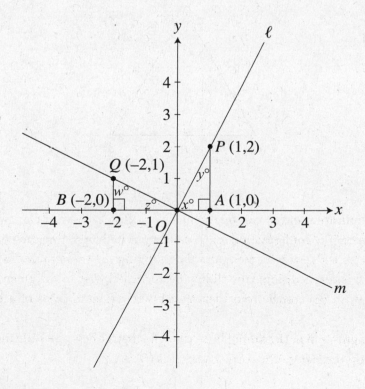

Line $\ell$ is the graph of $y = 2x$. It has slope 2 and passes through $P\,(1, 2)$. Line $m$ is the graph of the equation $y = -\frac{1}{2}x$. It has slope $-\frac{1}{2}$ and passes through $Q\,(-2, 1)$. The product of the slopes of lines $\ell$ and $m$ is $-1$. Therefore, it should be true that lines $\ell$ and $m$ are perpendicular.

Triangles $OBQ$ and $PAO$ are congruent, so $x = w$. You know $z + w = 90$, so you can conclude that $z + x = 90$. That implies $\angle QOP$ is a right angle. So lines $\ell$ and $m$ are indeed perpendicular.

## The Midpoint Formula

You might also be asked to find the midpoint of line segments in the coordinate plane. If $\overline{AB}$ has endpoints $A\,(3, 4)$ and $B\,(7, 8)$, then the midpoint of $\overline{AB}$ has coordinates

$$\left( \frac{3 + 7}{2}, \frac{4 + 8}{2} \right) = (5, 6)$$

The midpoint $(x_m, y_m)$ is simply the average of the $x$'s and average of the $y$'s:

$$\frac{x_1 + x_2}{2} = x_m \qquad \frac{y_1 + y_2}{2} = y_m$$

## The Distance Formula

In the coordinate plane, the Pythagorean theorem can be used to find the distance between any two points. For example, you can find the distance between $A\,(1, 2)$ and $B\,(4, 6)$, as indicated in the figure below:

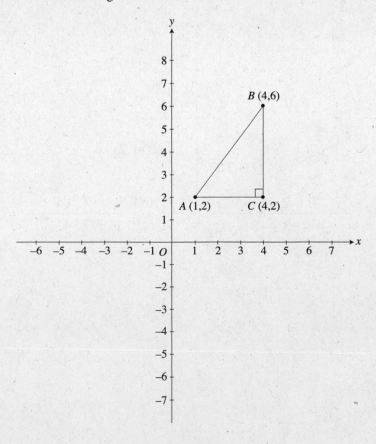

Clearly, $\triangle ABC$ is a right triangle, $AC = 3$, and $CB = 4$. Applying the Pythagorean theorem:

$$AB^2 = 3^2 + 4^2$$
$$AB^2 = 25$$
$$AB = 5$$

In general, if $(x_1, y_1)$ and $(x_2, y_2)$ are two points in the coordinate plane, the distance between them is given by the formula:

$$d = \sqrt{(x_2 - x_1)^2 + (y_2 - y_1)^2}$$

# Transformations

Understanding the concepts of simple geometric transformations — translations, rotations and reflections — will help you work through some of the mathematics questions.

A *translation* moves a shape without any rotation or reflection. For example, the square on the left has been translated 2 units up (that is, in the positive $y$-direction) to get the square on the right.

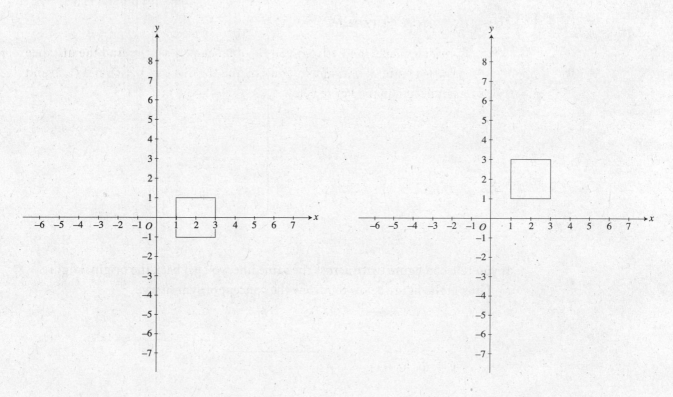

*Rotating* an object means turning it around a point, which is called the *center of rotation*. For example, when the clock face on the left is rotated 90° counterclockwise, the result is the clock face on the right:

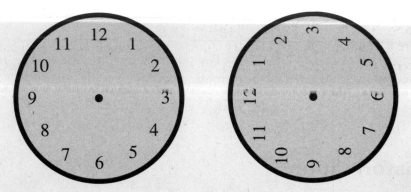

To *reflect* an object means to produce its mirror image with respect to a line, which is called the *line of reflection*. The figure below shows a triangle reflected across the line ℓ. A mirror image is produced on the other side of the line.

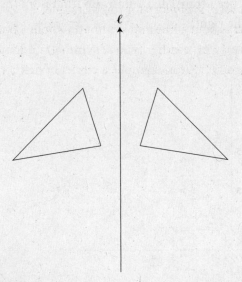

If you reflect a figure twice across the same line, you get back the original figure. Look at the figure below to review the concept of symmetry:

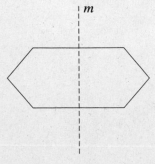

The dashed line *m* divides the hexagon into two halves. If the left half is reflected across line *m*, the result is the right half — and vice versa. In other words, if you reflect the hexagon across line $m$, the result is the same hexagon. The hexagon is said to be symmetrical about the line $m$, and $m$ is called a *line of symmetry* for the hexagon.

A geometric figure may have more than one line of symmetry (for example, a rectangle), or it may have no lines of symmetry.

There is another type of symmetry. Look at the rectangle below, with point $P$ at its center:

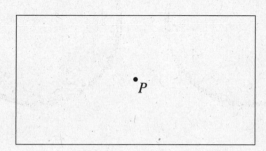

If you rotate the rectangle 180° (clockwise or counterclockwise) around $P$, then the result is the same rectangle. The rectangle is said to be symmetric around the point $P$, and $P$ is called a *point of symmetry* for the rectangle.

Note that symmetry about a line and symmetry about a point are different properties. A given figure may have either type of symmetry and not the other, or it may have both types of symmetry (for example, a circle) or neither type.

# CHAPTER 18

# Data Analysis, Statistics and Probability Review

## Concepts You Need to Know

For the mathematics questions covering data analysis, statistics and probability concepts, you should be familiar with all of the following basic skills and topics:

- Data interpretation

- Statistics
  - Arithmetic mean
  - Median
  - Mode
  - Weighted average
  - Average of algebraic expressions
  - Using averages to find missing numbers

- Elementary probability

- Geometric probability

The SAT doesn't include

- Computation of standard deviation

## Data Interpretation

Your primary task in these questions is to interpret information in graphs, tables or charts, and then compare quantities, recognize trends and changes in the data, or perform calculations based on the information you have found. You should be able to understand information presented in a table or in various types of graphs.

## *Circle Graphs (Pie Charts)*

MUNICIPAL EXPENSES FOR THE TOWN OF WESTON IN 2004

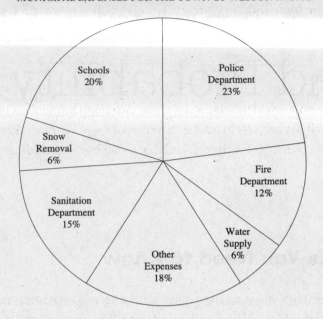

The pie chart above shows the percentages of its total expenditures that Weston spends on various types of expenses. Suppose you are given that Weston's total expenses in 2004 were $10 million, and you are asked for the amount of money spent on the police department and fire department combined. You can see that together these two categories account for 23% + 12% = 35% of the town's expenses. Therefore, Weston spends 35% of $10 million = $3.5 million on the police and fire departments combined.

## *Line Graphs*

Information can be displayed in a line graph. Below is an example of a double line graph that shows the high and low temperatures in Weston for the first seven days of February.

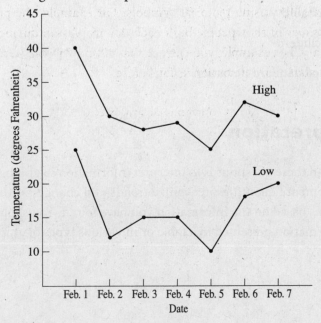

From the graph you can see, for example, that on February 5 the high was 25 degrees Fahrenheit and the low was 10 degrees Farenheit. So you also know that the difference between the high and low temperatures on that day was 15 degrees Fahrenheit.

## Bar Graphs

Bar graphs can also be used to present data. The bar graph below shows the amount of snow that fell each day in Weston for the first seven days of February. For example, you can see that no snow fell on February 2 and that 6 inches of snow fell the next day.

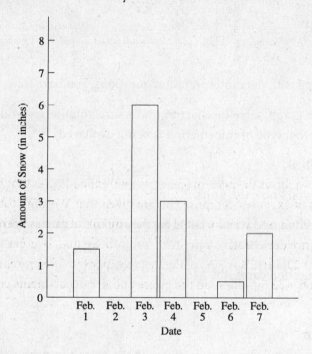

## Pictographs

A pictograph presents data using pictorial symbols. For example, the pictograph below shows the number of snowpeople built each day in Weston during the first seven days of February. For example, you can see that 40 snowpeople were built on February 7 and that about 25 were built the day before.

| Date | Number of Snowpeople |
|---|---|
| February 1 | ☃ ☃ ☃ |
| February 2 | ☃ |
| February 3 | ☃ ☃ ☃ ☃ ☃ |
| February 4 | ☃ ☃ ☃ ☃ ☃ ☃ |
| February 5 | ☃ ☃ ☃ |
| February 6 | ☃ ☃ ☃ |
| February 7 | ☃ ☃ ☃ ☃ |

☃ = 10 snowpeople

There is another type of graph you may see on the SAT: a scatterplot. Scatterplots will be discussed a little later in this chapter.

The questions you are asked may require you to do more than read the data presented in a graph or chart. A question on a graph like the one shown below might require you to identify specific pieces of information (data), compare data from different parts of the graph and manipulate the data.

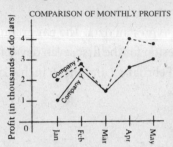

When working with data interpretation questions, you have to:

- Look at the graph, table or chart to make sure you understand it. Make sure you know what type of information is being displayed.

- Read the labels.

- Make sure you know the units.

- Make sure you understand what is happening to the data as you move through the table, graph or chart.

- Read the question carefully.

## Examples

The graph below shows profits over time. The greater the profits, the higher the point on the vertical axis will be. (Each tick mark on the vertical axis is another $1,000.) As you move to the right along the horizontal axis, months are passing.

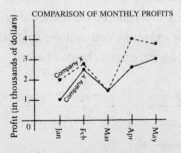

1. In what month or months did each company make the greatest profit?

**How to solve:** Follow the line labeled Company $X$ to its highest point. Then check the month at the bottom of the graph. Follow the same procedure for Company $Y$.

For Company X, the greatest profit was made in April.

For Company Y, the greatest profit was made in May.

2. Between which two consecutive months did each company show the greatest increase in profit?

**How to solve:** The increase (or decrease) in profit is shown by the steepness, or *slope*, of the graph.

For Company X, it's easy to see that the biggest jump occurred between March and April.

For Company Y, you have to be a little more careful. The biggest increase in profits occurred between January and February. You know this because the slope of the line connecting January and February is the steepest. The increase between January and February is about $1,500, which is greater than the increase for any other pair of consecutive months.

3. In what month did the profits of the two companies show the greatest difference?

**How to solve:** To figure this out, you have to compare one company to the other, month by month. The month in which the points are farthest apart is the one in which there is the greatest difference between the two companies. The distance between the two graph points is greatest in April.

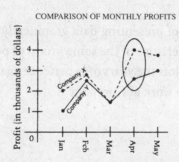

COMPARISON OF MONTHLY PROFITS

4. If the rate of increase or decrease for each company continues for the next six months at the same rate shown between April and May, which company would have higher profits at the end of that time?

**How to solve:** This question is asking you to look at the graph and project changes into the future. To project changes, extend the lines between April and May for each company. The lines cross pretty quickly — well before six more months have passed. So the answer is that Company Y would have higher profit in six months if the rates of change from month to month stay the same as they were between April and May.

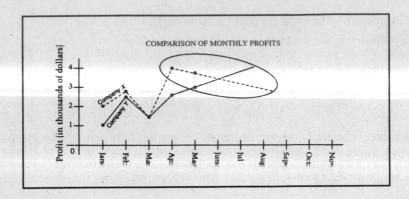

*From graph to table.* The same information presented in the profit chart could be presented in a profit table, which might look something like this:

| | PROFIT (IN DOLLARS) | | | | |
|---|---|---|---|---|---|
| | Jan | Feb | Mar | Apr | May |
| Company X | 2,000 | 2,750 | 1,500 | 4,000 | 3,750 |
| Company Y | 1,000 | 2,500 | 1,500 | 2,500 | 3,000 |

With a table it's a little harder to make the comparisons and see the trends. But the table is much more precise. The graph does not show the exact numbers the way the table does.

*Scatterplots.* One way of presenting data graphically is a scatterplot. A scatterplot compares two characteristics of the same group of people or things. For example, the scatterplot below plots the years of experience against the weekly salaries for each of 20 salespeople who work at Company X.

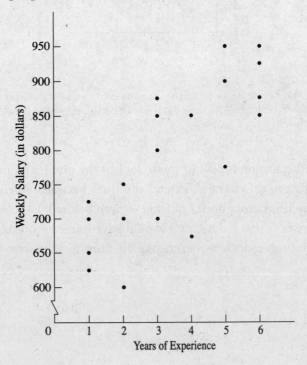

From the scatterplot, you can see many things. For example:

- There are 20 salespeople: 4 with one year of experience, 3 with two years, 4 with three years, 2 with four years, 3 with five years and 4 with six years.

- The median level of experience is 3 years. There are three modes for experience level: 1 year, 3 years and 6 years.

- Salary tends to increase with experience.

- Three people make $700 a week and 3 others make $850 a week. These are the two modes for salary level.

- The middle two salaries are $775 and $800. Therefore, the median of the salaries is $787.50.

If you do not know what a median or a mode is, you can learn about them in the next section.

# Statistics

## Arithmetic Mean

Arithmetic mean is what is usually thought of when talking about averages. If you want to know the arithmetic mean of a list of values, the formula is:

$$\frac{\text{The sum of a list of values}}{\text{The number of values in the list}}$$

For example, if there are three children, aged 6, 7 and 11, the arithmetic mean of their ages is:

$$\frac{6 + 7 + 11}{3} = \frac{24}{3}$$

or 8 years.

## Median

The median is the middle value of a list when the numbers are in order. To find the median, place the values in ascending (or descending) order and select the middle value. For instance, what is the median of the following values?

$$200, 2, 667, 19, 4, 309, 44, 6, 1$$

- Place the values in ascending order:

$$1, 2, 4, 6, 19, 44, 200, 309, 667$$

- Select the value in the middle.

- There are nine values listed. The middle value is the fifth.

- The median of these values is 19.

### THE MEDIAN OF A LIST WITH AN EVEN NUMBER OF VALUES

When the number of values in a list is an even number, the median is the average (arithmetic mean) of the two middle values when the numbers are placed in order. For example, the median of 3, 7, 10, 20 is

$$\frac{7 + 10}{2} = 8.5$$

## Mode

The mode of a list of values is the value or values that appear the greatest number of times. Consider the following list:

$$1, 5, 5, 7, 89, 4, 100, 276, 89, 4, 89, 1, 8$$

- The number 89 appears three times, which is more times than any other number appears.

- The mode of this list is 89.

### MULTIPLE MODES

It is possible to have more than one mode in a list of numbers:

$$1, 5, 5, 7, 276, 4, 10004, 89, 4, 276, 1, 8$$

In the list above, there are four modes: 1, 4, 5 and 276.

## Weighted Average

A weighted average is the average of two or more groups that do not all have the same number of members. For instance:

Fifteen members of a class had an average (arithmetic mean) SAT math score of 500. The remaining 10 members of the class had an average of 550. What is the average score of the entire class?

You can't simply take the average of 500 and 550, because there are more students with 500s than with 550s. The correct average has to be weighted toward the group with the greater number.

> **Keep in Mind**
>
> A calculator may help you find the answer to this question more quickly.

To find a weighted average, multiply each individual average by its weighting factor. The weighting factor is the number of values that correspond to a particular average. In this problem, you multiply each average by the number of students that corresponds to that average. Then you divide by the total number of students involved:

$$\frac{(500 \times 15) + (550 \times 10)}{25} = 520$$

Thus the average score for the entire class is 520.

## Average of Algebraic Expressions

Algebraic expressions can be averaged in the same way as any other values:

What is the average (arithmetic mean) of $3x + 1$ and $x - 3$ ?

There are two expressions, $3x + 1$ and $x - 3$, to be averaged. Find the sum of the expressions and divide by the number of expressions:

$$\frac{(3x + 1) + (x - 3)}{2} = \frac{4x - 2}{2} = 2x - 1$$

## Using Averages to Find Missing Numbers

You can use simple algebra in the basic average formula to find missing values when the average is given:

- The basic average formula is:

$$\frac{\text{The sum of a list of values}}{\text{The number of values in the list}} = \text{average}$$

- If you have the average and the number of values, you can figure out the sum of the values:

$$\text{Average} \times \text{number of values} = \text{sum of values}$$

## Example

Try putting this knowledge to work with a typical question on averages:

The average (arithmetic mean) of a list of 10 numbers is 15. If one of the numbers is removed, the average of the remaining numbers is 14. What is the number that was removed?

**How to solve:**

- You know the average and the number of values in the list, so you can figure out the sum of all the values in the list.

- The difference between the sum before you remove the number and after you remove the number will give you the value of the number you removed.

- The sum of all the values when you start out is the average times the number of values: $10 \times 15 = 150$.

- The sum of the values after you remove a number is $9 \times 14 = 126$.

- The difference between the sums is $150 - 126 = 24$.

- You only removed one number, so that number is 24.

# Probability

Some questions in the mathematics section will involve elementary probability. You may be asked, for example, to find the probability of choosing an even number at random from the set:

$$\{6, 13, 5, 7, 2, 9\}$$

Because there are 6 numbers in the set and 2 of them are even, the probability of choosing an even number at random is 2 out of 6, or $\frac{2}{6} = \frac{1}{3}$.

Remember: The probability of an event is a number between 0 and 1, inclusive. If an event is certain, it has probability 1. If an event is impossible (i.e., it cannot occur), it has probability 0.

## Independent/Dependent Events

You may be asked to find the probability that two (or more) events will both occur. To answer such a question, you need to understand the difference between independent and dependent events.

Two events are *independent* if the outcome of either event has no effect on the other. For example, if you toss a penny, it has probability $\frac{1}{2}$ of landing heads. If you then toss a nickel, it has probability $\frac{1}{2}$ of landing heads. Neither event affects the probability of the other.

To find the probability of two or more independent events occurring together, you multiply together the probabilities of the individual events. For example, in the previous situation, the probability of the penny landing heads *and* the nickel landing heads is $\frac{1}{2} \times \frac{1}{2} = \frac{1}{4}$.

Two events need not be independent. For example, if you toss a fair coin, the probability that it lands tails is $\frac{1}{2}$ and the probability it lands heads is $\frac{1}{2}$. But these are *not* independent events — if the coin lands heads, it cannot land tails at the same time! If the outcome of one event affects the probability of another event, the events are called *dependent* events. You must use logical reasoning to help figure out probabilities involving dependent events.

Here's an example:

On Monday, Anderson High School's basketball team will play the team from Baker High School. On Wednesday, Baker's team will play the team from Cole High School. On Friday, Cole will play Anderson. In each game, either team has a 50 percent chance of winning.

(a) What is the probability that Anderson will win both its games?
(b) What is the probability that Baker will lose both its games?
(c) What is the probability that Anderson will win both its games and Baker will lose both its games?

**How to solve:**

(a) The probability that the team from Anderson High School will win on Monday against Baker is $\frac{1}{2}$. The probability they will win on Friday against Cole's team is also $\frac{1}{2}$. These two games are independent events. The probability that Anderson will win both games is therefore $\frac{1}{2} \times \frac{1}{2} = \frac{1}{4}$.

(b) The probability that Baker will lose its game against Anderson on Monday is the same as the probability that Anderson will win: $\frac{1}{2}$. The probability that Baker will lose on Wednesday against Cole is also $\frac{1}{2}$. These two games are independent events. The probability that Baker will lose both games is therefore $\frac{1}{2} \times \frac{1}{2} = \frac{1}{4}$.

(c) In (a), you found that the probability that Anderson will win both games is $\frac{1}{4}$. In (b), you found that the probability that Baker will lose both games is $\frac{1}{4}$. Can you multiply $\frac{1}{4}$ by $\frac{1}{4}$ to find the probability that Anderson will win both its games and Baker will lose both its games? The answer is *no*. Because Anderson plays Baker on Monday, the event that Anderson wins both its games and the event that Baker loses both its games are *dependent* events. You must analyze the situation logically to answer (c).

If Anderson wins both its games, that means that Anderson defeats Baker on Monday and Anderson defeats Cole on Friday. So you already know Baker has lost one of its games. For Baker to lose both its games, Cole must defeat Baker on Wednesday. So the results of the three games must be as follows:

Monday: Anderson wins its game with Baker.

Wednesday: Cole wins its game with Baker.

Friday: Anderson wins its game with Cole.

The results of these games *are* independent events. Each outcome has probability $\frac{1}{2}$ of occurring, so the probability that the three games will have the above results is $\frac{1}{2} \times \frac{1}{2} \times \frac{1}{2} = \frac{1}{8}$.

Therefore the answer to (c) is that the probability Anderson will win both its games and Baker will lose both its games is $\frac{1}{8}$.

## *Geometric Probability*

Some probability questions in the mathematics section may involve geometric figures. For example, you may be given a figure like this

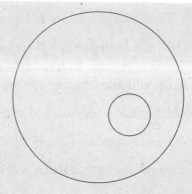

and be told that the large circle has radius 8 and the small circle has radius 2. If a point is chosen at random from the large circle, what is the probability that the point chosen will be in the small circle?

- The area of the large circle is $64\pi$.

- The area of the small circle is $4\pi$.

$$\frac{\text{Area of the small circle}}{\text{Area of the large circle}} = \frac{4\pi}{64\pi} = \frac{4}{64} = \frac{1}{16}$$

So the probability of choosing a point from the small circle is $\frac{1}{16}$.

# CHAPTER 19

# Multiple-Choice Questions

The SAT mathematics section includes 44 multiple-choice questions and covers the content you reviewed in Chapters 15 to 18: number and operations; algebra and functions; geometry and measurement; and data analysis, statistics and probability. You may find a calculator helpful on some problems, but none of the problems requires the use of one. While you're doing the sample questions in this chapter, practice using the calculator you plan to take to the test. It is important that you be familiar with your own calculator and know when it can be helpful to you.

## Approaches to Multiple-Choice Questions

▶ *Ask yourself the following questions before you solve each problem:*

1. What is the question asking?
2. What do I know?

▶ *Once you've answered the preceding questions, do the following:*

- Answer the question asked.
- Check that your answer makes sense.
- Check your work from the beginning. If you can, use a different method from the one you used to get the answer. If you use the same method, you may make the same mistake again.

▶ *Work the problems in your test booklet.* You will not receive credit for anything written in the booklet, but you will be able to check your work if you have time. Here are some suggestions on how to use your test booklet:

- Draw figures to help you think through problems that involve geometric shapes, segment lengths, distances, proportions, sizes and so on.

- Mark key information on graphs and add information to drawings and diagrams as you work through the problems.

- Mark each question that you don't answer so that you can easily go back to it later.

- When you're working on a question, draw a line through each choice you eliminate.

▶ *Substitute numbers.* Some questions use variables (indicated by letters) to represent the values you are asked to consider. You can make the problem more concrete by substituting numbers for the variables.

- Use common sense when picking numbers to substitute.

- Substitute numbers that are easy to work with.

▶ *Substitute in the answer choices.* Sometimes you can find the correct answer by working backward. Try substituting in the answer choices to see which one works. When substituting in the answer choices, start with choice (C). If the choices are numbers, they are usually listed in order from lowest to highest value or highest to lowest. If (C) turns out to be too high, you may not have to try out the larger numbers, and if (C) is too low, you don't have to try out the smaller numbers. However, keep in mind that this method may be time-consuming, and it may be quicker and easier to just work through the problem from the beginning.

▶ *Make an educated guess when you can eliminate at least one answer choice.* On multiple-choice questions, if you can eliminate even one incorrect answer choice, you increase your chances of getting a question right. With each correct answer, you gain one point; if you leave the answer blank, you do not receive any points; but if your answer is wrong, you lose only one-fourth $\left(\frac{1}{4}\right)$ of a point.

# Sample Questions

**Directions:** For this section, solve each problem and decide which is the best of the choices given. Fill in the corresponding circle on the answer sheet. You may use any available space for scratchwork.

Notes

1. The use of a calculator is permitted.

2. All numbers used are real numbers.

3. Figures that accompany problems in this test are intended to provide information useful in solving the problems.

   They are drawn as accurately as possible EXCEPT when it is stated in a specific problem that the figure is not drawn to scale. All figures lie in a plane unless otherwise indicated.

4. Unless otherwise specified, the domain of any function $f$ is assumed to be the set of all real numbers $x$ for which $f(x)$ is a real number.

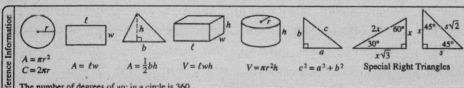

$A = \pi r^2$
$C = 2\pi r$    $A = \ell w$    $A = \frac{1}{2}bh$    $V = \ell wh$    $V = \pi r^2 h$    $c^2 = a^2 + b^2$    **Special Right Triangles**

The number of degrees of arc in a circle is 360.
The sum of the measures in degrees of the angles of a triangle is 180.

1. $\dfrac{1}{2} \cdot \dfrac{2x}{3} \cdot \dfrac{3}{4} \cdot \dfrac{4}{5y} \cdot \dfrac{5}{6} \cdot \dfrac{6}{7} =$

(A) $\dfrac{x}{7y}$

(B) $\dfrac{3x}{7y}$

(C) $\dfrac{21}{27} \cdot xy$

(D) $\dfrac{6x}{7}$

(E) $\dfrac{7y}{8x}$

**2.** If $\frac{x}{3} = x^2$, the value of $x$ can be which of the following?

   I. $-\frac{1}{3}$

   II.  0

   III.  $\frac{1}{3}$

(A) I only
(B) II only
(C) III only
(D) II and III only
(E) I, II, and III

---

**3.** All numbers divisible by both 4 and 15 are also divisible by which of the following?

(A)  6
(B)  8
(C)  18
(D)  24
(E)  45

---

**4.** If United States imports increased 20 percent and exports decreased 10 percent during a certain year, the ratio of imports to exports at the end of the year was how many times the ratio at the beginning of the year?

(A) $\frac{12}{11}$

(B) $\frac{4}{3}$

(C) $\frac{11}{8}$

(D) $\frac{3}{2}$

(E) 2

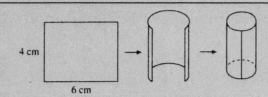

**5.** The figure above shows how a rectangular piece of paper is rolled into the shape of a cylinder. If it is assumed that the 4-centimeter sides of the rectangle meet with no overlap, what is the area, in square centimeters, of the base of the cylinder?

(A) $16\pi$

(B) $9\pi$

(C) $4\pi$

(D) $\dfrac{9}{\pi}$

(E) $\dfrac{4}{\pi}$

**6.** The odometer of a new automobile functions improperly and registers only 2 miles for every 3 miles driven. If the odometer indicates 48 miles, how many miles has the automobile actually been driven?

(A) 144
(B) 72
(C) 64
(D) 32
(E) 24

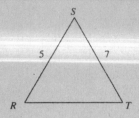

**Note:** Figure not drawn to scale.

7. If the perimeter of $\triangle RST$ above is 3 times the length of $\overline{RS}$, then $RT =$

(A)  3
(B)  5
(C)  8
(D)  9
(E)  10

8. $A$, $B$, $C$ and $D$ are points on a line, with $D$ the midpoint of $\overline{BC}$. The lengths of $\overline{AB}$, $\overline{AC}$ and $\overline{BC}$ are 10, 2 and 12, respectively. What is the length of $\overline{AD}$?

(A)  2
(B)  4
(C)  6
(D)  10
(E)  12

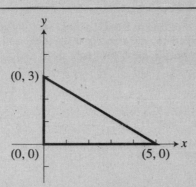

**9.** What is the area of the triangle in the figure above?

(A) 4.0
(B) 7.5
(C) 8.0
(D) 8.5
(E) 15.0

**10.**
$$A - \{3,\ 6,\ 9\}$$
$$B = \{5,\ 7,\ 9\}$$
$$C = \{7,\ 8,\ 9\}$$

If three <u>different</u> numbers are selected, one from each of the sets shown above, what is the greatest sum that these three numbers could have?

(A) 22
(B) 23
(C) 24
(D) 25
(E) 27

**11.** Let the symbol $\textcircled{x}$ represent the number of different pairs of positive integers whose product is $x$. For example, $\textcircled{16} = 3$, because there are 3 different pairs of positive integers whose product is 16:

$$16 \times 1, 8 \times 2 \text{ and } 4 \times 4.$$

What does $\textcircled{36}$ equal?

(A)   5
(B)   6
(C)   8
(D)  10
(E)  12

12. Several people are standing in a straight line. Starting at one end of the line, Bill is counted as the 5th person, and starting at the other end, he is counted as the 12th person. How many people are in the line?

(A) 15
(B) 16
(C) 17
(D) 18
(E) 19

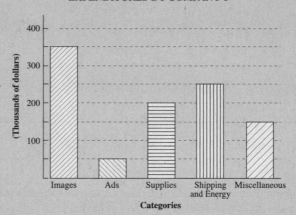

EXPENDITURES BY COMPANY Y

13. In the graph above, the total expenditures by Company Y were $1,000,000. If each of the following pie charts represents the total expenditures of Company Y, in which of the charts does the shaded region best represent the expenditures other than shipping and energy?

(A)
(B)
(C)
(D)
(E)

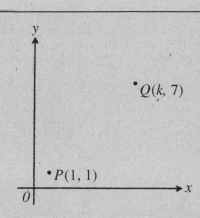

**14.** In the figure above, the slope of the line through points $P$ and $Q$ is $\frac{3}{2}$. What is the value of $k$ ?

(A) 4
(B) 5
(C) 6
(D) 7
(E) 8

**15.** In the $xy$-plane, point $R$ (2, 3) and point $S$ (5, 6) are two vertices of triangle $RST$. If the sum of the slopes of the sides of the triangle is 1, which of the following angles could be a right angle?

      I. $\angle R$
     II. $\angle S$
   III. $\angle T$

(A) None
(B) I only
(C) III only
(D) I and II only
(E) I, II, and III

16. For pumpkin carving, Mr. Sephera will not use pumpkins that weigh less than 2 pounds or more than 10 pounds. If $x$ represents the weight of a pumpkin, in pounds, he will <u>not</u> use, which of the following inequalities represents all possible values of $x$?

(A) $|x - 2| > 10$

(B) $|x - 4| > 6$

(C) $|x - 5| > 5$

(D) $|x - 6| > 4$

(E) $|x - 10| > 4$

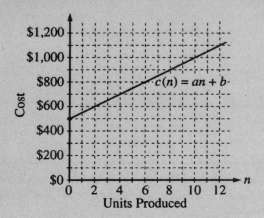

17. The cost, in dollars, of producing $n$ units of a certain product is given by the function $c$ as $c(n) = an + b$, where $a$ and $b$ are positive constants. The graph of $c$ is given above. Which of the following functions, $f$, represents the average (arithmetic mean) cost per unit, in dollars, when $n$ units are produced?

(A) $f(n) = 50 + \dfrac{50}{n}$

(B) $f(n) = 50 + \dfrac{500}{n}$

(C) $f(n) = 500 + 50n$

(D) $f(n) = 500 + \dfrac{50}{n}$

(E) $f(n) = 500 + \dfrac{500}{n}$

18. For all positive values of $x$, the function $f$ is defined by $f(x) = x^3 - x^{-2}$. Of the following, which is the best approximation of $f(x)$ for values of $x$ greater than 1,000?

    (A) $x^3$
    (B) $x^4$
    (C) $x^5$
    (D) $x^6$
    (E) $x^9$

# Answers and Explanations

1. $\dfrac{1}{2} \cdot \dfrac{2x}{3} \cdot \dfrac{3}{4} \cdot \dfrac{4}{5y} \cdot \dfrac{5}{6} \cdot \dfrac{6}{7} =$

   (A) $\dfrac{x}{7y}$

   (D) $\dfrac{3x}{7y}$

   (C) $\dfrac{21}{27} \cdot xy$

   (D) $\dfrac{6x}{7}$

   (E) $\dfrac{7y}{8x}$

**Keep in Mind**

If you have a question in which all of the fractions are being multiplied, canceling may be a possibility.

*Answer:* The correct answer is (A).

*Explanation:* In this question, all the fractions are being multiplied, so canceling is a possibility. The denominators cancel diagonally with the numerators that follow.

- The 2 from $\dfrac{1}{2}$ cancels with the 2 from $\dfrac{2}{3}$.

- The 3 from $\dfrac{2}{3}$ cancels with the 3 from $\dfrac{3}{4}$.

- And so on, right down to the equal sign.

$$\dfrac{1}{2} \cdot \dfrac{2}{3} \cdot \dfrac{3}{4} \cdot \dfrac{4}{5} \cdot \dfrac{5}{6} \cdot \dfrac{6}{7} \cdot \dfrac{x}{y}$$

Note that the $x$ in the numerator and the $y$ in the denominator can be rearranged as $\dfrac{x}{y}$. After you have canceled everything that can be canceled, you are left with the fraction $\dfrac{1}{7} \cdot \dfrac{x}{y} = \dfrac{x}{7y}$.

2. If $\dfrac{x}{3} = x^2$, the value of $x$ can be which of the following?

   I. $-\dfrac{1}{3}$

   II. $0$

   III. $\dfrac{1}{3}$

   (A) I only
   (B) II only
   (C) III only
   (D) II and III only
   (E) I, II, and III

*Answer:* The correct answer is (D).

*Explanation:* Question 2 uses what is referred to as the Roman numeral answer format. This format is used in both the mathematics and critical reading questions. The way to approach these is to work on each Roman numeral as a separate and independent true-false question. Once you have decided (and marked) each Roman numeral as true or false, it's easy to find the correct answer.

To answer this question, let's look at each of the three possible values.

### ROMAN NUMERAL I: CAN THE VALUE OF $x$ BE $-\frac{1}{3}$?

You could test this answer by substituting $-\frac{1}{3}$ for $x$ in the equation and seeing whether the result is true. But you can also reason this question out without substituting numbers:

- $x^2$ has to be a positive number because any nonzero number squared is positive.

- If $x$ were negative, $\frac{x}{3}$ would be negative.

- So $\frac{x}{3}$ is negative and $x^2$ is positive.

- Therefore, $x$ cannot be $-\frac{1}{3}$.

Mark Roman numeral I with an F for false.

> **Keep in Mind**
>
> When you're checking the values of expressions, remember the rules for multiplying positive and negative numbers:
> $$(+)(+) = (+)$$
> $$(-)(+) = (-)$$
> $$(-)(-) = (+)$$

### ROMAN NUMERAL II: CAN THE VALUE OF $x$ BE 0?

This is a very easy substitution to make:

$$\frac{x}{3} = x^2$$

$$\frac{0}{3} = 0^2 = 0$$

Roman numeral II is true, so mark it with a T for true.

### ROMAN NUMERAL III: CAN THE VALUE OF $x$ BE $\frac{1}{3}$?

Substitute $\frac{1}{3}$ for $x$ :

$$\text{If } x = \frac{1}{3}, \frac{x}{3} = \frac{1}{9} .$$

$$\text{Also, } x^2 = \left(\frac{1}{3}\right)^2 = \frac{1}{9} .$$

Roman numeral III is true, so mark it with a T for true.

> **Keep in Mind**
>
> Remember the approaches to Roman numeral format answers:
> - Take each Roman numeral statement as a separate true/false question.
> - Mark each Roman numeral with a T for true or an F for false as you evaluate it.
> - Look for the answer that matches your Ts and Fs.

### CHECK THE ANSWERS

You now know whether each of the Roman numeral statements is true or false:

- I is false.

- II is true.

- III is true.

Find the answer that says only II and III are true, choice (D).

3. All numbers divisible by both 4 and 15 are also divisible by which of the following?

   (A)  6
   (B)  8
   (C)  18
   (D)  24
   (E)  45

*Answer:* The correct answer is (A).

*Explanation:* One way to solve this problem is to first find a number that is divisible by both 4 and 15. "Divisible by" means that the remainder is zero after the division. For example, 8 is divisible by 4, but it is not divisible by 3. One such number is 60. Now check each choice to see if 60 is divisible by that choice; 60 is divisible by choice (A) but is not divisible by any of the other choices. The answer must be (A).

4. If United States imports increased 20 percent and exports decreased 10 percent during a certain year, the ratio of imports to exports at the end of the year was how many times the ratio at the beginning of the year?

   (A)  $\dfrac{12}{11}$

   (B)  $\dfrac{4}{3}$

   (C)  $\dfrac{11}{8}$

   (D)  $\dfrac{3}{2}$

   (E)  2

*Answer:* The correct answer is (B).

*Explanation:* To solve this problem, express what you know in mathematical terms:

- State the ratio of imports to exports as $\dfrac{I}{E}$.

- At the end of the year, imports were up by 20 percent. So imports at the end of the year can be expressed as 100 percent of beginning-of-the-year imports *plus* 20 percent:

$$100\% \text{ of } I + 20\% \text{ of } I = I + 0.2I = 1.2I$$

- At the end of the year, exports were down by 10 percent. So exports at the end of the year can be expressed as 100 percent of beginning-of-the-year exports *minus* 10 percent:

$$100\% \text{ of } E - 10\% \text{ of } E = 90\% \text{ of } E = 0.9E$$

■ Express the ratio of imports to exports at the end of the year:

$$\frac{1.2I}{0.9E} = \frac{12}{9} \cdot \frac{I}{E}$$

■ Reduce the fraction:

$$\frac{12}{9} = \frac{4}{3}$$

■ The ratio of imports to exports at the end of the year was $\frac{4}{3}$ times the ratio at the beginning of the year:

$$\frac{1.2I}{0.9E} = \frac{4}{3} \cdot \frac{I}{E}$$

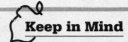

**Keep in Mind**

*Read word problems carefully.*
- *"x is n times y"* does not mean the same thing as *"x is n times greater than y."*
- *"x is n times y"* means $x = ny$.
- *"x is n times greater than y"* means $x = y + ny$.
  For example: 120 is $\frac{4}{3}$ times 90 ($120 = \frac{4}{3} \cdot 90$), but 120 is $\frac{1}{3}$ greater than 90 ($120 = 90 + \frac{1}{3} \cdot 90$).

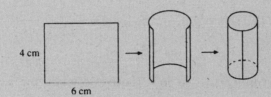

5. The figure above shows how a rectangular piece of paper is rolled into the shape of a cylinder. If it is assumed that the 4-centimeter sides of the rectangle meet with no overlap, what is the area, in square centimeters, of the base of the cylinder?

 (A) $16\pi$

 (B) $9\pi$

 (C) $4\pi$

 (D) $\dfrac{9}{\pi}$

 (E) $\dfrac{4}{\pi}$

*Answer:* The correct answer is (D).

*Explanation:* To solve this problem, follow these three steps:

1. Ask yourself: what do you know?

2. Then ask: are there any formulas that will solve the problem?

3. Finally, apply the formula to get the answer.

**WHAT DO YOU KNOW?**

■ You know the circumference of the circle.

■ Label the middle and the right-hand figures in the diagram.

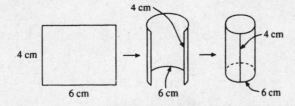

Notice that the 4-centimeter sides meet to form the seam in the cylinder and the 6-centimeter sides curl around to become the top and bottom of the cylinder.

- So the circumference of the circle is 6 centimeters.

### ARE THERE ANY FORMULAS THAT WILL SOLVE THE PROBLEM?

The question has now become a rather simple one. You know the circumference of the circle, and you have to figure out the area.

- You need to calculate the area, and you can get there in two steps.

  1. Relate the radius to the circumference by the formula:

$$\text{Circumference} = 2\pi r$$

  2. Relate the area to the radius by the formula:

$$\text{Area} = \pi r^2$$

- You know the circumference, so start there and work toward the area. The radius $r$ is the common term in the two formulas, so start by solving for $r$.

### APPLY THE FORMULA TO GET THE ANSWER

$$\text{Circumference} = 2\pi r$$

$$6 = 2\pi r$$

$$\frac{6}{2\pi} = r$$

$$\frac{3}{\pi} = r$$

> ### Keep in Mind
>
> Label diagrams and figures with the information you have. This often reveals key information that you need to answer the question.

Now use the value for $r$ in the formula for the area.

$$A = \pi r^2$$

$$r = \frac{3}{\pi}$$

$$A = \pi \left(\frac{3}{\pi}\right)^2$$

$$A = \pi \left(\frac{9}{\pi^2}\right)$$

$$A = \frac{9}{\pi}$$

---

6. The odometer of a new automobile functions improperly and registers only 2 miles for every 3 miles driven. If the odometer indicates 48 miles, how many miles has the automobile actually been driven?

   (A) 144
   (B) 72
   (C) 64
   (D) 32
   (E) 24

---

*Answer:* The correct answer is (B).

*Explanation:* In this problem you are told that the odometer registers only 2 miles for every 3 miles driven. So the ratio of miles registered to miles driven is 2 to 3, or $\frac{2}{3}$. This can be expressed as

$$\frac{2 \text{ miles registered}}{3 \text{ miles driven}} = \frac{48 \text{ miles registered}}{x \text{ miles driven}}$$

If the odometer indicates 48 miles, the actual miles can be found using the above relationship, as follows:

$$\frac{2}{3} = \frac{48}{x}$$

$$2x = 144$$

$$x = 72$$

If the odometer indicates 48 miles, the actual number of miles driven is 72.

## HOW TO AVOID ERRORS WHEN WORKING WITH PROPORTIONS

The most important thing with proportions is to be consistent in the way you set them up. There are several correct ways to set up a proportion, but if you mix up the terms, you will not get the correct answer. For instance, if you put the registered mileage in the numerator of one ratio but the actual mileage in the numerator of the other ratio, you will come up with a wrong answer:

$$\frac{3}{2} = \frac{48}{x}$$

$$3x = 96$$

$$x = \frac{96}{3} = 32 \text{ miles}$$

But this answer is wrong, which you should realize if you do a "make-sense" check, as described in the next section.

## MAKE A "DOES-IT-MAKE-SENSE?" CHECK

When you arrive at an answer to a word problem, check to see whether it makes sense. The question states that the actual mileage is greater than the registered mileage, so the actual mileage has to be a number larger than 48.

Your check should warn you not to choose the incorrect answer, (D) 32, that was obtained by setting up the wrong proportion.

**Keep in Mind**

A quick "make-sense" check before you start working on a question can help you eliminate some of the answers right away. If you realize that the actual mileage has to be greater than the registered mileage, you can eliminate answers (D) and (E) immediately.

## PUT IN THE UNITS OF MEASUREMENT

One way to help you set up proportions correctly and to avoid mixing up the terms is to put in the units of measurement. For example:

If 10 cans of peas cost $4.80, how much will 7 cans cost at this rate?

$$\frac{\$4.80}{10 \text{ cans}} = \frac{\$x}{7 \text{ cans}}$$

Note that dollars are in the numerators of both ratios, and cans are in the denominators of both ratios. To solve for $x$:

$$4.80 \cdot 7 = 10x$$
$$33.60 = 10x$$
$$3.36 = x$$

So 7 cans will cost $3.36.

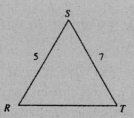

**Note:** Figure not drawn to scale.

7. If the perimeter of $\triangle RST$ above is 3 times the length of $\overline{RS}$, then $RT =$

   (A)   3
   (B)   5
   (C)   8
   (D)   9
   (E)  10

*Answer:* The correct answer is (A).

"Note: Figure not drawn to scale" means that the points and angles are in their relative positions, but the lengths of the sides and the sizes of the angles may not be as pictured.

*Explanation:* To solve this problem, again, first ask yourself what you already know, and then express the problem using an equation.

## WHAT DO YOU KNOW?

- The perimeter of the triangle is the sum of the lengths of the 3 sides.

- The question states that the perimeter is 3 times the length of $\overline{RS}$.

- $\overline{RS}$ is 5 units long.

- $\overline{ST}$ is 7 units long.

**EXPRESS THE PROBLEM USING AN EQUATION**

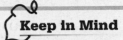

- The perimeter is equal to 3 times the length of $\overline{RS}$.

- That means that the perimeter is 3 times 5, or 15.

- So $5 + 7 + RT = 15$, or $RT = 3$.

8. $A$, $B$, $C$ and $D$ are points on a line, with $D$ the midpoint of $\overline{BC}$. The lengths of $\overline{AB}$, $\overline{AC}$ and $\overline{BC}$ are 10, 2 and 12, respectively. What is the length of $\overline{AD}$?

   (A)  2
   (B)  4
   (C)  6
   (D)  10
   (E)  12

*Answer:* The correct answer is (B).

*Explanation:* The key to this question lies in not jumping to incorrect conclusions. The question names the points on a line. It gives you a variety of information about the points. The one thing it does not do is tell you the order in which the points fall.

Many students assume that the order of the points is $A$, then $B$, then $C$, then $D$. As you will see, if you try to locate the points in this order, you will be unable to answer the question.

**WHAT IS THE QUESTION ASKING?**

The question asks for the length of $\overline{AD}$. In order to find this length, you have to establish the relative positions of the four points on the line.

**WHAT DO YOU KNOW?**

Try to draw the figure. You might be tempted to locate point $A$ first. Unfortunately, you don't have enough information about $A$, yet, to place it.

- You can place $B$, $C$ and $D$ because $D$ is the midpoint of $\overline{BC}$.

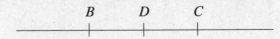

- You know the lengths of three of the line segments:

$$AB = 10$$
$$AC = 2$$
$$BC = 12$$

- Because you know where $\overline{BC}$ is, you can label the length of $\overline{BC}$.

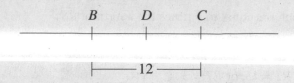

### BUILD THE FIGURE, ADDING WHAT YOU KNOW AND WHAT YOU CAN FIGURE OUT

Because $D$ is the midpoint of $\overline{BC}$, you know that $\overline{BD}$ and $\overline{DC}$ are each 6 units long.

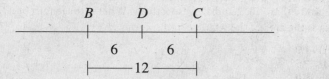

Where can you place point $A$?

- It has to be 2 units from $C$, because $AC = 2$.

- It also has to be 10 units from $B$, because $AB = 10$.

- So the only location for $A$ is between $B$ and $C$, but closer to $C$.

- Place point $A$ and mark the distances.

It is now an easy matter to figure out the answer to the question:

- $DC$ is 6 units.

- $A$ is 2 units closer to $D$ than $C$ is to $D$, so $AD$ is 4 units.

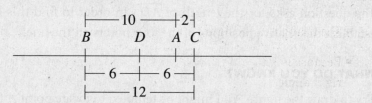

---

### ◊ Keep in Mind

**If you have time, always check that the picture you have drawn is consistent with the information given in the problem. Also check that you answered the question. Check:**

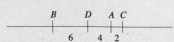

- *A, B, C* and *D* are on the line.
- *D* is the midpoint of $\overline{BC}$.
- *AB* = 10, *AC* = 2 and *BC* = 12.
- *AD* = 4.

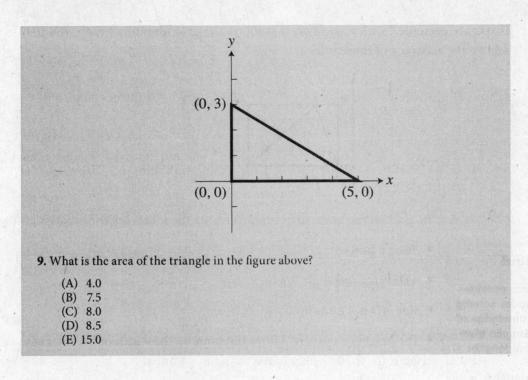

**9.** What is the area of the triangle in the figure above?

    (A)  4.0
    (B)  7.5
    (C)  8.0
    (D)  8.5
    (E) 15.0

*Answer:* The correct answer is (B).

*Explanation:* The figure provides all the information you need to answer the question.

### WHAT IS THE QUESTION ASKING?

You are asked to figure out the area of a triangle that is defined by three points on a coordinate plane.

### WHAT DO YOU KNOW?

- The triangle in the figure is a right triangle with the right angle at the lower left.

- Because it is a right triangle, its base and height are the two sides that form the right angle.

- The area of a triangle is $\frac{1}{2}bh$, where $b$ is the length of the base and $h$ is the height.

- The base of the triangle extends from point $(0, 0)$ to point $(5, 0)$, so $b = 5$.

- The height of the triangle extends from point $(0, 0)$ to point $(0, 3)$, so $h = 3$.

$$\text{Area} = \frac{1}{2}bh$$

$$= \frac{1}{2}(5)(3)$$

$$= \frac{1}{2}(15)$$

$$= 7.5$$

If you are presented with a question that shows the grid lines of a graph, you may rely on the accuracy of those lines.

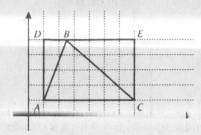

You can use the grid on the graph above to determine the following information:

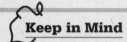
- $\overline{AC}$ is 6 units long.

- $ADEC$ is a rectangle.

- Side $\overline{AD}$ is 4 units long.

- The height of triangle $ABC$ is the same as the width of the rectangle ($ADEC$), so the height of the triangle is 4 units.

- The area of the triangle is $\frac{1}{2}$ the area of the rectangle.

- The area of a rectangle = width × length = $AD \times AC = 4 \times 6 = 24$ square units.

- The area of the triangle = $\frac{1}{2}$(base × height) = $\frac{1}{2}(AC \times AD) = \frac{1}{2}(6 \times 4)$ = 12 square units.

$$A = \{3, \ 6, \ 9\}$$
$$B = \{5, \ 7, \ 9\}$$
$$C = \{7, \ 8, \ 9\}$$

**10.** If three <u>different</u> numbers are selected, one from each of the sets shown above, what is the greatest sum that these three numbers could have?

(A) 22
(B) 23
(C) 24
(D) 25
(E) 27

*Answer:* The correct answer is (C).

*Explanation:* This question challenges your ability to reason with numbers. In other words, it is more a question of logic than of arithmetic.

**WHAT IS THE QUESTION ASKING?**

The question asks what is the largest sum you can get if you choose one number from each set and add those numbers together. Each number you select must be *different*, so you *cannot* take the largest number, 9, from each set, add the nines together and come up with choice (E) 27.

## WHAT DO YOU KNOW?

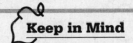

- The number 9 is the largest number in each set.

- You can only take one 9. This means that you will have to take the second-largest or third-largest number from two of the sets.

## MAKE YOUR SELECTIONS

- The second-largest number in set *A* is 6, which is smaller than the second-largest number in sets *B* and *C*, so select 9 from set *A* .

- The other two choices are now easy. Take the largest numbers available from sets *B* and *C* .

- The greatest sum is $9 + 7 + 8 = 24$.

---

11. Let the symbol Ⓧ represent the number of different pairs of positive integers whose product is *x*. For example, ⑯ = 3, because there are 3 different pairs of positive integers whose product is 16:

$$16 \times 1, 8 \times 2 \text{ and } 4 \times 4$$

What does ㊱ equal?

- (A)   5
- (B)   6
- (C)   8
- (D)   10
- (E)   12

---

*Answer:* The correct answer is (A).

*Explanation:* Most SAT mathematics sections have at least one question involving a newly defined symbol. Sometimes there will be an easy question, like this one, followed by a more difficult one in which you might have to use the new symbol in an equation.

To answer these questions, you have to read the definition of the special symbol carefully and follow the instructions. *It is not expected that you have ever seen the new symbol before.*

The question asks you to figure out how many different pairs of positive integers can be multiplied together to give you the number in the circle.

### Keep in Mind

When you're faced with a special symbol, read the definition
carefully and use it as your
instruction for working out the
answer.

## PUT THE SPECIAL SYMBOL TO WORK

- To figure out ⑤, list the pairs of positive integers whose product is 36:

$$1 \times 36$$
$$2 \times 18$$
$$3 \times 12$$
$$4 \times 9$$
$$6 \times 6$$

- Count up the pairs. The answer is 5.

12. Several people are standing in a straight line. Starting at one end of the line, Bill is counted as the 5th person, and starting at the other end, he is counted as the 12th person. How many people are in the line?
    (A) 15
    (B) 16
    (C) 17
    (D) 18
    (E) 19

*Answer:* The correct answer is (B).

### Keep in Mind

Problems like this one focus on
your ability to reason logically.
There's nothing wrong with
drawing a figure using dots to
represent the people in line.
Just make sure that you follow
the instructions carefully when
you draw your figure.

*Explanation:* You can answer this question by careful reasoning, or you can draw it out and count. Either way, be careful that you don't leave Bill out or count him twice.

## WHAT DO YOU KNOW?

- Bill is the 5th person from one end of the line.

- Bill is the 12th person from the other end.

## USING LOGIC TO SOLVE THE PROBLEM

- If Bill is the 5th person from one end of the line, there are 4 people (not counting Bill) between him and that end of the line.

- If Bill is the 12th person from the other end of the line, there are 11 people (not counting Bill) between him and that end of the line.

- The sum of 4 people between Bill and one end plus 11 people between Bill and the other end equals 15 people. Then you have to add in Bill. So, there are 16 people in line.

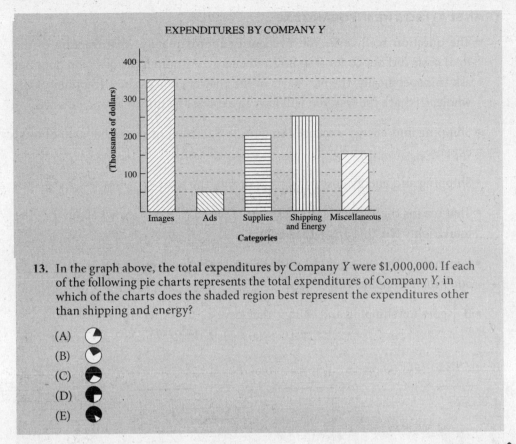

EXPENDITURES BY COMPANY Y

13. In the graph above, the total expenditures by Company *Y* were $1,000,000. If each of the following pie charts represents the total expenditures of Company *Y*, in which of the charts does the shaded region best represent the expenditures other than shipping and energy?

(A)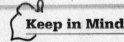

(B)

(C)

(D)

(E)

*Answer:* The correct answer is (D)

*Explanation:* In this question you have to interpret information from one type of graph (bar graph) and translate that information into another type of graph (pie chart). Questions that involve interpreting data presented on graphs or in tables will be common on the SAT.

> **Keep in Mind**
>
> If you are presented with a math question that shows the grid lines of a graph, you may rely on the accuracy of those lines.

## WHAT IS THE QUESTION ASKING?

The question asks you to identify the pie chart that shows all of Company *Y*'s expenses other than shipping and energy. That "Miscellaneous" category is important. It's easy to overlook.

## WHAT DO YOU KNOW?

All you need to know to answer the question is the amount of money spent on shipping and energy and the total expenses for the company.

- You are given the total expenses: $1,000,000. (You also could have figured that total from the graph by adding all the expenses from the individual categories.)

- The graph shows you that the expenditures for shipping and energy amount to $250,000.

### TRANSLATING THE INFORMATION

- The question really asks you to identify approximately what fraction of the total costs did not go for shipping and energy. Although the question does not ask this specifically, the pie charts in the answer choices show fractions of the whole, so that's the way you will have to express the information you have.

- Shipping and energy expenses amount to $250,000 of the $1,000,000 of total expenses.

- Shipping and energy cost $\frac{\$250,000}{\$1,000,000}$ or $\frac{1}{4}$ of the total.

- That means the answer is (B) because the pie chart in (B) shows about $\frac{1}{4}$ of the total, right? No, this answer is wrong.

- Remember, the question asks which pie chart "best represents expenditures *other than* shipping and energy."

- If $\frac{1}{4}$ goes for shipping and energy, that leaves $\frac{3}{4}$ for other things.

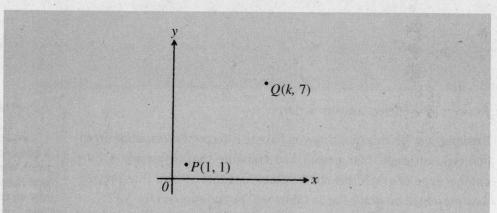

14. In the figure above, the slope of the line through points $P$ and $Q$ is $\frac{3}{2}$. What is the value of $k$ ?

   (A) 4
   (B) 5
   (C) 6
   (D) 7
   (E) 8

**Answer:** The correct answer is (B).

**Explanation:** Your ability to answer this question depends on knowing and being able to apply the definition of *slope*. The *slope* of a line in the *xy*-coordinate plane is:

$$\frac{\text{The change in } y \text{ between any two points on the line}}{\text{The change in } x \text{ between the same points on the line}}$$

The question asks for the value of $k$, which is the $x$ coordinate of point $Q$.

## WHAT DO YOU KNOW?

- The slope of the line that goes through $P$ and $Q$ is $\frac{3}{2}$.

- That means for every 3 units that $y$ changes, $x$ will change 2 units.

- The coordinates of $P$ are $(1, 1)$.

- The coordinates of $Q$ are $(k, 7)$.

- The change in the value of $y$ between $P$ and $Q$ is 6 units $(7 - 1 = 6)$.

## APPLY WHAT YOU KNOW

- $y$ changes 6 units between the two points.

- That means that $x$ will change 4 units, since for every 3 units that $y$ changes, $x$ changes 2 units.

- The $x$ coordinate of point $P$ is 1.

- The $x$ coordinate of point $Q$ will be $1 + 4 = 5$.

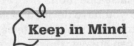

**Keep in Mind**

Remember to check that your answer fits the conditions of the problem.
- If $k = 5$, then point $Q$ has coordinates $(5, 7)$.
- Is the slope of the line through the points $P$ $(1,1)$ and $Q$ $(5, 7)$ equal to $\frac{3}{2}$?

Yes, $\frac{7-1}{5-1} = \frac{6}{4} = \frac{3}{2}$.

---

**15.** In the $xy$-plane, point $R$ $(2, 3)$ and point $S$ $(5, 6)$ are two vertices of triangle $RST$. If the sum of the slopes of the sides of the triangle is 1, which of the following angles could be a right angle?

     I.    $\angle R$
    II.   $\angle S$
   III.  $\angle T$

(A) None
(B) I only
(C) III only
(D) I and II only
(E) I, II, and III

*Answer:* The correct answer is (A).

*Explanation:* Given the coordinates of points $R$ and $S$, the slope of $\overline{RS}$ is $\frac{6-3}{5-2} = \frac{3}{3} = 1$. If $\angle R$ is a right angle, then $\overline{RS}$ and $\overline{RT}$ would be perpendicular. The slope of $\overline{RT}$ would be $-1$ because the slopes of $\overline{RT}$ and $\overline{RS}$ would have to be negative reciprocals of each other. Because it is given that the sum of the slopes of $\overline{RS}$, $\overline{ST}$ and $\overline{RT}$ is 1, the slope of $\overline{ST}$ would have to be 1. Then $\overline{RS}$ and $\overline{ST}$ would have the same slope, which means that they would be parallel, or that points $R$, $S$ and $T$ would be collinear. Neither of these is possible if $RST$ is a triangle.

Similarly, if $\angle S$ is a right angle, then the slope of $\overline{ST}$ would be $-1$. Because the sum of the slopes of $\overline{RS}$, $\overline{ST}$ and $\overline{RT}$ is 1, the slope of $\overline{RT}$ would have to be 1. Then $\overline{RS}$ and $\overline{RT}$ would have the same slope, which means that they would be parallel, or that points $R$, $S$ and $T$ would be collinear. Neither of these is possible if $RST$ is a triangle.

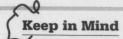

**Keep in Mind**

In questions with three Roman numeral choices, consider each of I, II and III separately.
- Consider each as a separate true-false question.
- After you have decided which are true and which are false, you can answer the question

If $\angle T$ is a right angle, let the slope of $\overline{RT}$ be $k$. The slope of $\overline{ST}$ would have to be $-\frac{1}{k}$. Because the sum of the slopes of the three sides of triangle $RST$ is 1, the sum of the slopes of $\overline{ST}$ and $\overline{RT}$ will be zero, so that $k - \frac{1}{k} = 0$ or $k = \frac{1}{k}$. Solving this equation for $k$ yields $k = \pm 1$. In either case, the result is that one of the two sides would again be parallel to $\overline{RS}$, or points $R$, $S$ and $T$ would be collinear. Neither of these is possible if $RST$ is a triangle.

16. For pumpkin carving, Mr. Sephera will not use pumpkins that weigh less than 2 pounds or more than 10 pounds. If $x$ represents the weight of a pumpkin, in pounds, he will <u>not</u> use, which of the following inequalities represents all possible values of $x$?

    (A) $|x - 2| > 10$

    (B) $|x - 4| > 6$

    (C) $|x - 5| > 5$

    (D) $|x - 6| > 4$

    (E) $|x - 10| > 4$

*Answer:* The correct answer is (D).

*Explanation:* If $x$ represents the weight of the pumpkins Mr. Sephera will not use, then $x < 2$ or $x > 10$. This is represented graphically as follows:

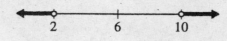

Because 6 is midway between 2 and 10, each point in the solution is more than 4 units from 6. This is equivalent to the statement $|x - 6| > 4$.

    Another way to solve the problem is to rewrite both $x < 2$ and $x > 10$. Algebraically, the expression $x < 2$ is equivalent to $-x > -2$ or $-x + 6 > 4$ or $-(x - 6) > 4$. The expression $x > 10$ is equivalent to $x - 6 > 4$. Combining the two expressions yields $|x - 6| > 4$.

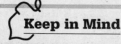

**Keep in Mind**

Remember $|a| > 4$ means that either $a > 4$ or $-a > 4$.
  Check your answer:
- $|x - 6| > 4$ means that either $x - 6 > 4$ or $-(x - 6) > 4$.
- If $x - 6 > 4$, then $x > 10$.
- If $-(x - 6) > 4$, then $-x + 6 > 4$, so $-x > -2$, and $x < 2$.
- Because Mr. Sephera will not use pumpkins that weigh more than 10 pounds or less than 2 pounds, $|x - 6| > 4$ is the correct answer.

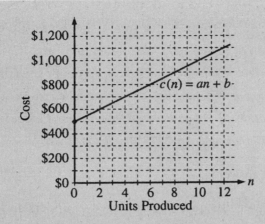

17. The cost, in dollars, of producing $n$ units of a certain product is given by the function $c$ as $c(n) = an + b$, where $a$ and $b$ are positive constants. The graph of $c$ is given above. Which of the following functions, $f$, represents the average (arithmetic mean) cost per unit, in dollars, when $n$ units are produced?

(A) $f(n) = 50 + \dfrac{50}{n}$

(B) $f(n) = 50 + \dfrac{500}{n}$

(C) $f(n) = 500 + 50n$

(D) $f(n) = 500 + \dfrac{50}{n}$

(E) $f(n) = 500 + \dfrac{500}{n}$

*Answer:* The correct answer is (B).

*Explanation:* To solve this problem, start by finding the values of $a$ and $b$. Because $c$ is a linear function, $a$ is the slope of the line and $b$ is the $y$-intercept. The $y$-intercept of the line is 500 because the line contains the point $(0, 500)$. To find the slope, take any two points on the line and the slope is $\dfrac{\text{change in } y}{\text{change in } x}$. Two such points are $(0, 500)$ and $(12, 1100)$. The slope of the line is $\dfrac{1100 - 500}{12 - 0} = \dfrac{600}{12} = 50$. Because $a = 50$ and $b = 500$, the cost to produce $n$ units of the product is given by $c(n) = 50n + 500$. The average cost per unit is the total cost divided by the number of units produced, or $f(n) = \dfrac{c(n)}{n} = \dfrac{50n + 500}{n} = 50 + \dfrac{500}{n}$.

> **Keep in Mind**
>
> - If the function $g$ is given by $g(x) = ax + b$, for constants $a$ and $b$, then $g$ is a linear function.
> - The graph of $g$ in the $xy$-plane is a line.
> - The slope of the graph of $g$ is $a$.
> - The $y$-intercept (i.e., the point where the line crosses the $y$-axis) is $(0, b)$.

18. For all positive values of $x$, the function $f$ is defined by $f(x) = x^3 - x^{-2}$. Of the following, which is the best approximation of $f(x)$ for values of $x$ greater than 1,000?

   (A) $x^3$
   (B) $x^4$
   (C) $x^5$
   (D) $x^6$
   (E) $x^9$

*Answer:* The correct answer is (A).

*Explanation:* To answer this question, you need to understand the notation $x^{-2}$. In general, $x^{-m}$ means $\frac{1}{x^m}$. Because $x^{-2}$ is equivalent to $\frac{1}{x^2}$, the definition of $f$ can be rewritten as $f(x) = x^3 - \frac{1}{x^2}$. For large values of $x$, the value of $x^2$ is very large; therefore the value of $\frac{1}{x^2}$ is very small, but greater than 0. For example, when $x = 10$, $\frac{1}{x^2} = \frac{1}{100}$, and when $x = 30$, $\frac{1}{x^2} = \frac{1}{900}$. If you keep trying larger and larger values of $x$, you can probably convince yourself that $\frac{1}{x^2}$ is a very small positive number for all $x$ values greater than 1,000. For large values of $x$, $x^3$ is very large. For large values of $x$, the value of $f(x)$ is $x^3$ minus a very small positive number. This means that for $x > 1,000$, $f(x)$ is just a bit less than $x^3$. Of the answer choices given, $x^3$ is the best approximation of $f(x)$ for large values of $x$.

> ### Keep in Mind
>
> - Remember that $x^{-1} = \frac{1}{x}$.
> - If $x$ is positive, then as $x$ becomes larger, $\frac{1}{x}$ becomes closer to 0.
> - In general, $x^{-m} = \frac{1}{x^m}$.
> - If $x$ is positive, and $m$ is a positive integer, then as $x$ becomes larger, $x^{-m}$ becomes closer to 0.

# Recap

1. Ask yourself these questions before you solve each problem: What is the question asking? What do I know?

2. Answer the question that is asked.

3. Check that your answer makes sense.

4. Check your work from the beginning.

5. Work the problems in your test booklet.

6. Draw figures and lines to help you think through problems.

7. Mark key information on graphs and add information to drawings and diagrams.

8. Mark each question that you don't answer so you can return to it later.

9. Draw a line through each choice you eliminate.

10. Make problems more concrete by substituting numbers for the variables.

11. Work backward and substitute the answer choices to see which one works.

12. Make an educated guess when you can eliminate at least one answer choice.

13. If you have a question in which a group of fractions is being multiplied, canceling may be a possibility.

14. When you're checking the values of expressions, remember the rules for multiplying positive and negative numbers.

15. Consider each Roman numeral answer choice as a separate true-false question.

16. Read word problems carefully.

17. Label diagrams and figures with the information you have.

18. If a figure is not given, draw the lines and figures that are described in a question.

19. Check that the picture you have drawn is consistent with the information given in the problem.

20. Find information about lengths and angles from your knowledge of the coordinate system.

21. Check that your answer observes the conditions of a problem.

*(continued)*

# CHAPTER 19

22. When faced with a special symbol, read the definition carefully.

23. Make sure that you follow the instructions carefully when you draw figures to help you solve logic problems.

24. Rely on the accuracy of the grid lines shown in a graph.

# Practice Questions

**Directions:** For this section, solve each problem and decide which is the best of the choices given. Fill in the corresponding circle on the answer sheet. You may use any available space for scratchwork.

---

Notes

1. The use of a calculator is permitted.

2. All numbers used are real numbers.

3. Figures that accompany problems in this test are intended to provide information useful in solving the problems.

    They are drawn as accurately as possible EXCEPT when it is stated in a specific problem that the figure is not drawn to scale. All figures lie in a plane unless otherwise indicated.

4. Unless otherwise specified, the domain of any function $f$ is assumed to be the set of all real numbers $x$ for which $f(x)$ is a real number.

---

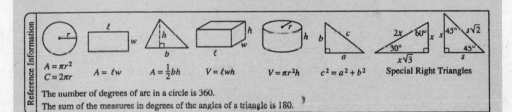

$A = \pi r^2$
$C = 2\pi r$ $\quad A = \ell w \quad A = \frac{1}{2}bh \quad V = \ell wh \quad V = \pi r^2 h \quad c^2 = a^2 + b^2 \quad$ **Special Right Triangles**

The number of degrees of arc in a circle is 360.
The sum of the measures in degrees of the angles of a triangle is 180.

---

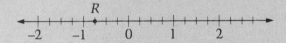

1. On the number line above, what number is the coordinate of point $R$ ?

(A) $-1\frac{3}{4}$

(B) $-1\frac{1}{4}$

(C) $-\frac{3}{4}$

(D) $-\frac{1}{3}$

(E) $-\frac{1}{4}$

2. If a certain number is doubled and the result is increased by 7, the number obtained is 19. What is the original number?

(A)  2.5
(B)  6
(C)  13
(D)  16.5
(E)  24

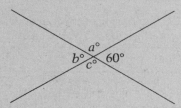

3. For the two intersecting lines above, which of the following must be true?

I.    $a > c$
II.   $a = 2b$
III.  $a + 60 = b + c$

(A)  I only
(B)  II only
(C)  I and II only
(D)  II and III only
(E)  I, II, and III

4. Three consecutive integers are listed in increasing order. If their sum is 102, what is the second integer in the list?

(A)  28
(B)  29
(C)  33
(D)  34
(E)  35

**5.** If 10,000 microns = 1 centimeter and 100,000,000 angstrom units = 1 centimeter, how many angstrom units equal 1 micron?

(A) 0.000000000001
(B) 0.0001
(C) 10,000
(D) 100,000
(E) 1,000,000,000,000

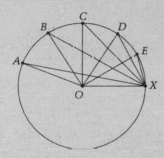

**6.** In the figure above, $\overline{OX}$ is a radius of the circle with center $O$. Which of the following triangles has the <u>least</u> area?

(A) $\triangle AOX$
(B) $\triangle BOX$
(C) $\triangle COX$
(D) $\triangle DOX$
(E) $\triangle EOX$

**7.** If the product of five integers is negative, then, at most, how many of the five integers could be negative?

(A) One
(B) Two
(C) Three
(D) Four
(E) Five

8. If $x - 7 = 2y$ and $x = 5 + 3y$, what is the value of $y$ ?

    (A)  −5
    (B)  −2
    (C)   2
    (D)   5
    (E)  12

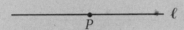

9. In the figure above, if two points $S$ and $T$ are to be placed on line $\ell$ on opposite sides of point $P$ so that $2SP = PT$, what will be the value of $\dfrac{ST}{PT}$ ?

    (A)  $\dfrac{2}{1}$

    (B)  $\dfrac{3}{2}$

    (C)  $\dfrac{2}{3}$

    (D)  $\dfrac{1}{2}$

    (E)  $\dfrac{1}{3}$

$$f(x) = (x + 1)^{\frac{3}{4}}$$

10. For the function $f$, defined above, what are all the values of $x$ for which $f(x)$ is a real number?

    (A)  All real numbers
    (B)  $x \geq -1$
    (C)  $x \geq 0$
    (D)  $x \geq \dfrac{3}{4}$
    (E)  $x \geq 1$

11. There are $g$ gallons of paint available to paint a house. After $n$ gallons have been used, then, in terms of $g$ and $n$, what percent of the paint has <u>not</u> been used?

   (A) $\dfrac{100n}{g}\%$

   (B) $\dfrac{g}{100n}\%$

   (C) $\dfrac{100g}{n}\%$

   (D) $\dfrac{g}{100\,(g-n)}\%$

   (E) $\dfrac{100\,(g-n)}{g}\%$

12. If $x$ is an integer and $2 < x < 7$, how many different triangles are there with sides of lengths 2, 7 and $x$ ?

   (A) One
   (B) Two
   (C) Three
   (D) Four
   (E) Five

13. If $2\left|x+3\right| = 4$ and $\dfrac{\left|y+1\right|}{3} = 2$, then $\left|x+y\right|$ could equal each of the following

   EXCEPT

   (A)   0
   (B)   4
   (C)   8
   (D)  10
   (E)  12

**14.** If $a > b$ and $a(b - a) = 0$, which of the following must be true?

      I.    $a = 0$
      II.   $b < 0$
      III.  $a - b > 0$

(A)  I only
(B)  II only
(C)  III only
(D)  I and II only
(E)  I, II, and III

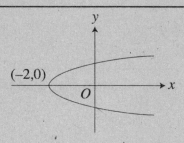

**15.** The graph above is a parabola that is symmetric about the $x$-axis. Which of the following could be an equation of the parabola?

(A)  $x = y^2 - 2$
(B)  $x = -y^2 - 2$
(C)  $x = (y - 2)^2$
(D)  $x = (y - \sqrt{2})^2$
(E)  $x = -(y - \sqrt{2})^2$

## Answer Key

1. C
2. B
3. D
4. D
5. C
6. A
7. E
8. C
9. B
10. B
11. E
12. A
13. D
14. E
15. A

 **Additional practice questions can be found in** *The Official SAT Online Course* **at www.collegeboard.org/satonlinecourse.**

# CHAPTER 20

# Student-Produced Response Questions

On the SAT, you will find 10 student-produced response or grid-in questions. These questions require the same math skills and reasoning abilities as the multiple-choice math questions. In fact, many student-produced response questions are similar to multiple-choice questions. The big difference: no answers are provided. You must work out each problem yourself and enter your answer onto a special math grid. Use the sample grids at the end of this chapter to practice gridding techniques.

## Guidelines for Completing the Grid

Become very familiar with the guidelines for answering and gridding student-produced response questions. You can save time and improve your confidence by knowing the rules before the test.

### Calculators May Help Here

If you are asked to calculate the answer of a grid-in problem, be careful to check your work. Without answers to choose from, you may make careless mistakes. That's why it is a good idea to use a calculator for this section.

### Practicing with the Grid

Before the test, practice completing the grids. You don't have to write your answer in the boxes above the grid, but it's a good idea to do so to avoid errors. Remember that only the answers you put in the grid will be scored. Be careful to mark no more than one circle in any column because answer sheets are machine scored and you will receive credit only if the circles are filled in correctly.

### Positive Numbers and Zero Only

The grid can only hold four places and can accommodate only positive numbers and zero. It is not possible to grid a negative number of any type. If you obtain a negative answer for a student-produced response question, you will know that you have made a mistake. *Rework the problem.*

### Place Answer in Any Column

Don't worry about which column to use when you begin writing the answer. As long as the answer is gridded completely, you will receive credit. For example, 156 can be gridded as shown below; both answers are correct.

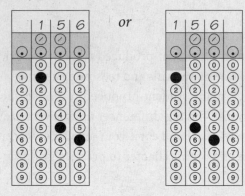

### Integers

You can grid one-, two-, three- or four-digit positive integers or zero as follows.

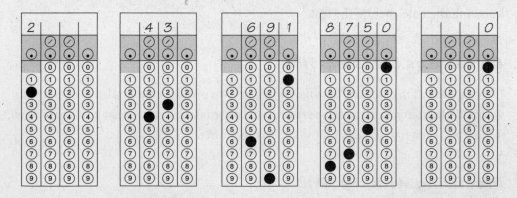

### Decimals and Fractions

The grids include decimal points (.) and fraction lines (/) so that you can enter answers both in decimal and fraction form. You can grid your answer as a decimal or a fraction.

### Decimal Points

If the answer is 0, grid it in column 2, 3 or 4. Zero has been omitted from column 1 to encourage you to grid the most accurate values for rounded answers. For example, an answer of $\frac{1}{8}$ could also be gridded as .125 but not as 0.12, which is less accurate.

### No Mixed Numbers

You can grid both proper and improper fractions. However, it is not possible to grid mixed numbers. If your answer is a mixed number, convert it to an improper fraction or to a decimal. For example, if you get the answer $2\frac{3}{4}$, grid $\frac{11}{4}$ or 2.75, as shown.

The fraction line appears in the first shaded row of circles.

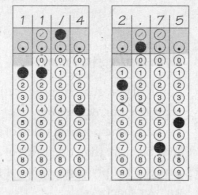

If you grid $2\frac{3}{4}$, the scoring machine will read the answer as $\frac{23}{4}$, which is wrong.

### Repeating Decimals

If the answer you are gridding is a repeating decimal, you must grid the most accurate possible decimal. The easiest way to follow the rule for repeating decimals is to completely fill the grid with the answer. If you obtain a decimal answer with more digits than the grid can accommodate, it may be either rounded or truncated, but it must fill the entire grid. For example, if you obtain an answer such as 0.6666..., you should record your result as .666 or .667. A less accurate value such as .66 or .67 will be scored as incorrect.

$9/11 = .81\overline{81}$     $1/6 = .16\overline{6}$     $2/3 = .6\overline{6}$     $51/2 = 5.5$

| . | 8 | 1 | 8 |
|---|---|---|---|

.81 or .82 will not be correct

.166 will also be correct. But, .16 or .17 will not be correct.

.666 will also be correct. But, .6, .7, .66 or .67 will not be.

(NOT a repeating decimal.)

## Important

Remember, *only the answer entered on the grid, and not the answer handwritten at the top of the grid, is scored.* You must decide whether to first write your answer in at the top of the grid and then transfer it to the grid, or to transfer your answer directly from notes in your test booklet or in your head to the grid. You might practice both approaches and see which one works best for you. You want to make sure you enter your answer correctly. While it might be more time-consuming to first write your answer in at the top of the grid, you may find this approach helps you avoid errors.

## Multiple Answers

Some of the student-produced response questions may have more than one correct answer. These questions may say something like, "What is one possible value of *x*?" This wording indicates that there may be more than one value of *x* that is correct. Under these circumstances, simply choose one of the possible answers to grid on your answer sheet.

## There Is No Penalty for Wrong Answers

On student-produced response questions, unlike multiple-choice questions, no points are subtracted for wrong answers. Feel comfortable gridding whatever answer you get without fear that it may subtract from your final score if it is wrong.

# Sample Questions

For Student-Produced Response questions 1–9, use the grids at the bottom of the answer sheet page.

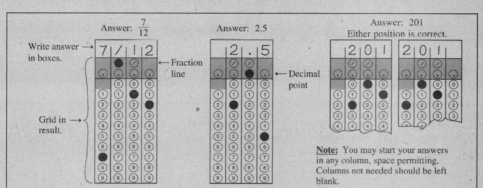

- Mark no more than one circle in any column.

- Because the answer sheet will be machine-scored, **you will receive credit only if the circles are filled in correctly.**

- Although not required, it is suggested that you write your answer in the boxes at the top of the columns to help you fill in the circles accurately.

- Some problems may have more than one correct answer. In such cases, grid only one answer.

- No question has a negative answer.

- **Mixed numbers** such as $3\frac{1}{2}$ must be gridded as 3.5 or 7/2. (If $3|1|/|2$ is gridded, it will be interpreted as $\frac{31}{2}$, not $3\frac{1}{2}$.)

- **Decimal Answers:** If you obtain a decimal answer with more digits than the grid can accommodate, it may be either rounded or truncated, but it must fill the entire grid. For example, if you obtain an answer such as 0.6666..., you should record your result as .666 or .667. **A less accurate value such as .66 or .67 will be scored as incorrect.**

Acceptable ways to grid $\frac{2}{3}$ are:

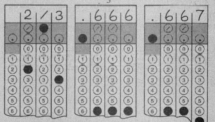

**Note:** You may start your answers in any column, space permitting. Columns not needed should be left blank.

---

1. In a restaurant where the sales tax on a $4.00 lunch is $0.24, what will be the sales tax due, in dollars, on a $15.00 dinner? (Disregard the $ sign when gridding your answer. For example, if the answer is $1.37, mark 1.37 on the grid.)

2. A team has won 60 percent of the 20 games it has played so far this season. If the team plays a total of 50 games all season and wins 80 percent of the remaining games, how many games will the team win for the entire season?

3. If $n$ is a two-digit number that can be expressed as the product of two consecutive even integers, what is one possible value of $n$?

4. If the ratio of $a$ to $b$ is $\frac{7}{3}$, what is the ratio of $2a$ to $b$ ?

5. If the population of a town doubles every 10 years, the population in the year $X + 100$ will be how many times the population in the year $X$ ?

| Number of Donuts | Total Price |
|:---:|:---:|
| 1 | $ 0.40 |
| Box of 6 | $ 1.89 |
| Box of 12 | $ 3.59 |

**6.** According to the information in the table above, what would be the least amount of money needed, in dollars, to purchase exactly 21 donuts? (Disregard the $ sign when gridding your answer. For example, if the answer is $1.37, mark 1.37 on the grid.)

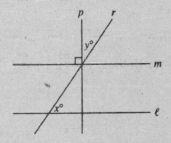

**Note:** Figure not drawn to scale.

**7.** In the figure above, line $m$ is parallel to line $\ell$ and is perpendicular to line $p$. If $x = y$, what is the value of $x$ ?

**8.** If $\frac{x}{2} = y$ and $2y = y$, what is the value of $x$ ?

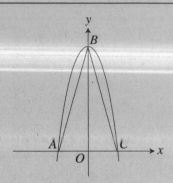

9. The figure above shows the graph of $y = k - x^2$, where $k$ is a constant. If the area of $\triangle ABC$ is 64, what is the value of $k$ ?

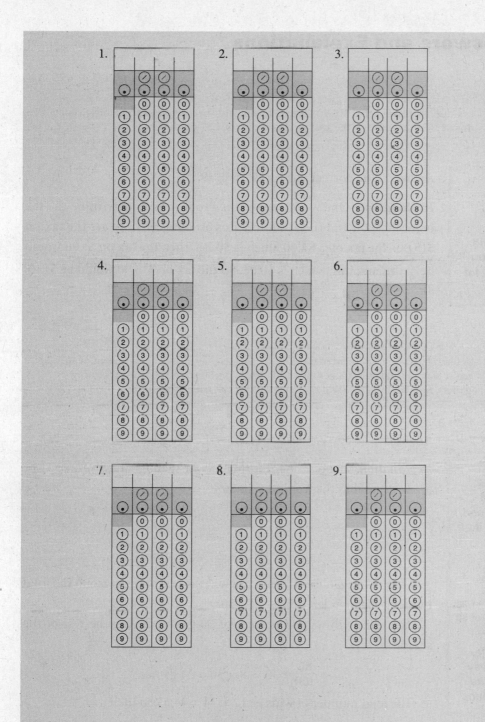

# Answers and Explanations

1. In a restaurant where the sales tax on a $4.00 lunch is $0.24, what will be the sales tax due, in dollars, on a $15.00 dinner? (Disregard the $ sign when gridding your answer. For example, if the answer is $1.37, mark 1.37 on the grid.)

---

**Keep in Mind**

Do not grid zeros before the decimal point. For example, don't try to grid 0.90; just grid .90 or .9. The question asks for the number of dollars, so 90 for 90 cents would be wrong.

---

*Answer:* The correct answer is .90 or .9.

*Explanation:* One way to solve this problem is to determine the tax on each $1.00 and then multiply this amount by 15 to get the tax on $15.00. The tax on a $4.00 lunch is $0.24. Then the tax on $1.00 would be $\frac{1}{4}$ this amount, which is $0.06. So the tax on $15.00 would be $15 × .06 = $0.90.

---

2. A team has won 60 percent of the 20 games it has played so far this season. If the team plays a total of 50 games all season and wins 80 percent of the remaining games, how many games will the team win for the entire season?

---

**Keep in Mind**

When working problems, especially student-produced response problems, it is a good idea to check your answers if you have time.
For example:

| | Games Played | Games Won |
|---|---|---|
| So far: | 20 | 12 = 60% of 20 |
| Remaining: | 30 | 24 = 80% of 30 |
| Total: | 50 | 36 |

You don't have to use a table, but you should find some way to check that your answer fits the information in the problem.

---

*Answer:* The correct answer is 36.

*Explanation:* Express the information in mathematical terms: How many games has the team won so far?

$$60\% \text{ of } 20 \text{ games} =$$

$$\frac{60}{100} \times 20 = .6 \times 20 = 12 \text{ games}$$

How many games will the team win the rest of the season? The total number of games left is 50 − 20 = 30.

The team will win 80 percent of 30 games during the rest of the season.

$$\frac{80}{100} \times 30 = .8 \times 30 = 24 \text{ games}$$

The total number of wins is: 12 + 24 = 36. Grid in 36.

---

3. If *n* is a two-digit number that can be expressed as the product of two consecutive even integers, what is one possible value of *n*?

---

*Answer:* There are three acceptable correct answers: 24, 48 and 80. You have to find only one.

*Explanation:* Although there are several values for *n* that will work, you have to find only one.

## FOLLOW THE INSTRUCTIONS

- *n* is the product of two consecutive even integers. In other words, the question tells you to multiply consecutive even integers.

- *n* is also a two-digit number.

## TRY SOME VALUES

Start with two small consecutive even integers, 2 and 4.

- $2 \times 4 = 8$

- 8 is not a two-digit number, so *n* cannot be 8.

Try the next two consecutive even integers, 4 and 6.

- $4 \times 6 = 24$

- 24 is a two-digit number.

- 24 is the product of two consecutive even integers.

Therefore, 24 is an acceptable value for *n*. Grid in 24.

## OTHER CORRECT ANSWERS

The other possible values are 48 ($6 \times 8$) and 80 ($8 \times 10$). You can grid in any one of these three values and get credit for answering the question correctly.

---

**4.** If the ratio of *a* to *b* is $\frac{7}{3}$, what is the ratio of 2*a* to *b* ?

*Answer:* The correct answer is $\frac{14}{3}$, 4.66 or 4.67.

*Explanation:* This question requires that you know how to work with ratios.

## EXPRESS THE RATIO

The ratio of *a* to *b* can be written as $\frac{a}{b}$.

The ratio of *a* to *b* is $\frac{7}{3}$, which can be expressed as $\frac{a}{b} = \frac{7}{3}$.

$$\text{If } \frac{a}{b} = \frac{7}{3}, \text{ then } 2\frac{a}{b} = 2\left(\frac{7}{3}\right) = \frac{14}{3}.$$

Grid in the answer $\frac{14}{3}$ as 14/3.

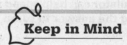

**5.** If the population of a town doubles every 10 years, the population in the year $X + 100$ will be how many times the population in the year $X$ ?

*Answer:* The correct answer is 1024.

*Explanation:* Express the population growth in mathematical terms. Each time the population doubles, multiply it by 2. Let $p$ represent the population in year $X$.

- In 10 years, the population increases from $p$ to $2p$.

- In 10 more years, it increases to $2(2p)$.

- In 10 more years, it increases to $2[2(2p)]$, and so on for 100 years.

This repeated doubling can be expressed by using powers of 2:

- Another way to express $2(2)$ is $2^2$.

- So a population of $2(2p) = (2^2)p$.

- In 10 more years, the population is $2(2^2)p$, or $(2^3)p$.

- In 10 more years, the population is $2(2^3)p$, or $(2^4)p$, etc.

## HOW MANY GROWTH CYCLES ARE THERE?

- The population doubles (is raised to another power of 2) every 10 years.

- This goes on for 100 years.

- So there are $\frac{100}{10} = 10$ cycles.

- The population increases to $2^{10}$ times what it was in year $X$.

## FIGURE OUT THE ANSWER

**Keep in Mind**

A calculator can help speed up getting the answer to some questions.

You can multiply ten 2s, but this invites error. You may want to use your calculator to find $2^{10}$. Some calculators have an exponent key that allows you to find $y^x$ directly. If your calculator does not have this feature, you can still quickly get the value of $2^{10}$ on your calculator as follows.

$$2^5 = 2 \times 2 \times 2 \times 2 \times 2 = 32$$

$$2^{10} = 2^5 \times 2^5 = 32 \times 32 = 1024$$

Grid in the answer, 1024.

| Number of Donuts | Total Price |
| --- | --- |
| 1 | $ 0.40 |
| Box of 6 | $ 1.89 |
| Box of 12 | $ 3.59 |

**6.** According to the information in the table above, what would be the least amount of money needed, in dollars, to purchase exactly 21 donuts? (Disregard the $ sign when gridding your answer. For example, if the answer is $1.37, mark 1.37 on the grid.)

*Answer:* The correct answer is $6.68.

*Explanation:*

### WHAT DO YOU KNOW?

- You can save money by purchasing donuts by the box. A box of 6 donuts costs $1.89, but 6 individual donuts cost $2.40.

- You can save more money by purchasing the larger box. A box of 12 donuts costs $3.59, but 2 boxes of 6 donuts cost 2($1.89) = $3.78.

- The question says you have to buy exactly 21 donuts.

### USE YOUR HEAD

You want to buy as few individual donuts as you can. You want to buy as many donuts in large boxes as you can. You cannot buy 2 boxes of 12 because that would put you over the 21-donut limit. So start with 1 box of 12 donuts.

- Mark down 12 donuts, so you can keep track as you add more donuts.

- Mark down $3.59, so you can keep track as you spend more money.

You have 12 donuts, so there are 9 left to buy. You can save money by buying a box of 6 donuts.

- Add 6 to your donut total.

- Add $1.89 to your money total.

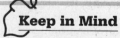

**Keep in Mind**

When you're working out an answer, jot down your calculations in the space provided in your test booklet.

You now have 18 donuts, which means you will have to buy 3 individual donuts.

- Add 3 to your donut total. You now have exactly 21 donuts.

- Add 3 × $.40 = $1.20 to your money total.

- Add up the dollar figures: $3.59 + $1.89 + $1.20 = $6.68.

Grid in 6.68. Remember to disregard the $ sign.

*Note:* Do not grid 668 without the decimal mark — it will be interpreted as

$668!

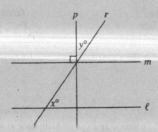

**Note:** Figure not drawn to scale.

7. In the figure above, line $m$ is parallel to line $\ell$ and is perpendicular to line $p$. If $x = y$, what is the value of $x$?

---

*Answer:* The correct answer is 45.

*Explanation:* This question requires that you use your knowledge of lines, angles and triangles to calculate values for parts of the figure that are not labeled. As you work on the question, remember:

- It's helpful to label parts of the figure as you work.

- Use what you know about parallel lines, vertical angles, and special types of triangles and their properties.

### WHAT DO YOU KNOW?

- Lines $\ell$ and $m$ are parallel.

- Line $p$ is perpendicular to line $m$.

- $x = y$

### WHAT CAN YOU FIGURE OUT FROM THE FIGURE?

You can use the parallel lines in the figure to label another angle that has measure $x°$ because corresponding angles are congruent.

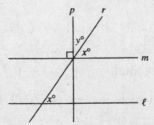

Because line $p$ is perpendicular to line $m$, $x° + y° = 90°$. You are told that $x = y$. Therefore,

$$x° + x° = 90°$$
$$2x = 90$$
$$x = 45$$

Grid the answer, 45. Disregard the degree symbol (°).

8. If $\frac{x}{2} = y$ and $2y = y$, what is the value of $x$?

*Answer:* The correct answer is 0.

*Explanation:* This is another question that takes some reasoning in addition to some simple mathematical manipulation.

### LOOK AT THE EQUATIONS

The second equation may look a little unusual to you:

$$2y = y$$

If $2y = y$, then $y = 0$. Therefore:

$$2y = 0$$

$$\frac{x}{2} = y = 0$$

$$x = 0$$

Grid in the answer, 0.

> **Keep in Mind**
>
> To grid zero, just enter 0 in a single column (any column where 0 appears). Leave the other three columns blank.

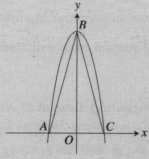

9. The figure above shows the graph of $y = k - x^2$, where $k$ is a constant. If the area of $\triangle ABC$ is 64, what is the value of $k$?

*Answer:* The correct answer is 16.

*Explanation:* The area of $\triangle ABC$ is equal to $\frac{1}{2}(AC)(OB)$, which is equivalent to $(OC)(OB)$ because the parabola is symmetric about the $y$-axis and $\frac{1}{2}AC = OC$. So you know that $(OC)(OB) = 64$. Because the length of $\overline{OB}$ can be determined from the $y$-intercept of the graph of $y = k - x^2$, it follows that $OB = k$. Similarly, the length of $\overline{OC}$ can be determined from the $x$-intercepts of the parabola. To find the $x$-intercepts, set $y = k - x^2 = 0$. Solving this equation for $x$ gives the two intercepts $x = \pm\sqrt{k}$, which correspond to the point $A$ $(-\sqrt{k}, 0)$ and the point $C$ $(\sqrt{k}, 0)$. Therefore, $OC = \sqrt{k}$, and you can now substitute into the equation $(OC)(OB) = 64$ to get that $(\sqrt{k})(k) = 64$. But since $(\sqrt{k})(k) = k^{\frac{1}{2}}k = k^{\frac{3}{2}}$, it follows that $k^{\frac{3}{2}} = 64$, and you can now solve this equation for $k$ by raising both sides to the two-thirds power. Therefore, $k = (64)^{\frac{2}{3}} = (\sqrt[3]{64})^2 = 4^2 = 16$.

## Recap

1. Remember that only the answer *entered* on the grid is scored; the answer that is *handwritten* on the top of the grid is *not* scored.

2. Don't grid zeros before the decimal point.

3. Take each question one step at a time because some questions that seem difficult are just a series of easy questions.

4. Think about what you need to know in order to answer a question.

5. Make sure you answer the question that has been asked.

6. Double-check your answers, especially on grid-in questions, if you have time.

7. Remember that some questions have more than one correct answer; you can grid any of the correct answers and get full credit.

8. State an answer as a fraction or a decimal: You can grid $\frac{1}{2}$ as $\frac{1}{2}$ or .5.

9. Write mixed numbers as improper fractions. For example, $1\frac{3}{5}$ is $\frac{8}{5}$. The grid-reading system cannot distinguish between $1\frac{3}{5}$ and $\frac{13}{5}$.

10. Grid as much of a repeating decimal as will fit in the grid. You may need to round a repeating decimal, but round only the last digit: grid $\frac{2}{3}$ as $\frac{2}{3}$, .666 or .667. Do not grid the value $\frac{2}{3}$ as .67 or .66.

11. Use a calculator to help speed up getting an answer.

12. Jot down your calculations in your test booklet.

13. Write relevant facts (about angles, lengths of sides, etc.) on figures as you pick up more information.

14. Look for special properties that may help you answer questions.

15. Grid zero by entering 0 in a single column (any column where 0 appears).

# Practice Questions — Student-Produced Response Questions

For Student-Produced Response questions 1–8, use the grids at the bottom of the answer sheet page.

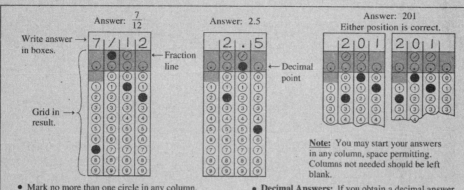

- Mark no more than one circle in any column.

- Because the answer sheet will be machine-scored, **you will receive credit only if the circles are filled in correctly.**

- Although not required, it is suggested that you write your answer in the boxes at the top of the columns to help you fill in the circles accurately.

- Some problems may have more than one correct answer. In such cases, grid only one answer.

- No question has a negative answer.

- **Mixed numbers** such as $3\frac{1}{2}$ must be gridded as

$3.5$ or $7/2$. (If [3 1 / 2] is gridded, it will be

interpreted as $\frac{31}{2}$, not $3\frac{1}{2}$.)

- **Decimal Answers:** If you obtain a decimal answer with more digits than the grid can accommodate, it may be either rounded or truncated, but it must fill the entire grid. For example, if you obtain an answer such as 0.6666...., you should record your result as .666 or .667. **A less accurate value such as .66 or .67 will be scored as incorrect.**

Acceptable ways to grid $\frac{2}{3}$ are:

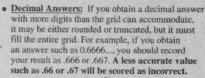

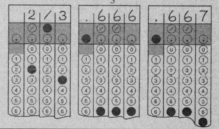

**Note:** You may start your answers in any column, space permitting. Columns not needed should be left blank.

---

1. In 2 weeks, 550 cartons of juice were sold in the school cafeteria. At this rate, how many cartons of juice would one expect to be sold in 5 weeks?

---

2. For what integer value of $x$ is $3x + 5 > 11$ and $x - 3 < 1$?

**3.** The number 0.008 is equivalent to the ratio of 8 to what number?

| $x$ | 4 | 9 | 36 |
|---|---|---|---|
| $y$ | 1 | | 3 |

**4.** If $y$ is directly proportional to the square root of $x$, what is the missing value of $y$ in the table above?

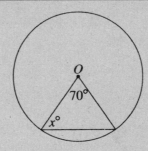

**5.** In the figure above, if $O$ is the center of the circle, what is the value of $x$ ?

**6.** The average (arithmetic mean) of 4 numbers is greater than 7 and less than 11. What is one possible number that could be the sum of these 4 numbers?

7. A line $\ell$ with a slope of $\frac{1}{4}$ passes through the points $(0, \frac{1}{2})$ and $(4, y)$. What is the value of $y$ ?

$$\sqrt{x^2 - t^2} = 2t - x$$

8. If $x$ and $t$ are positive numbers that satisfy the equation above, what is the value of $\frac{x}{t}$ ?

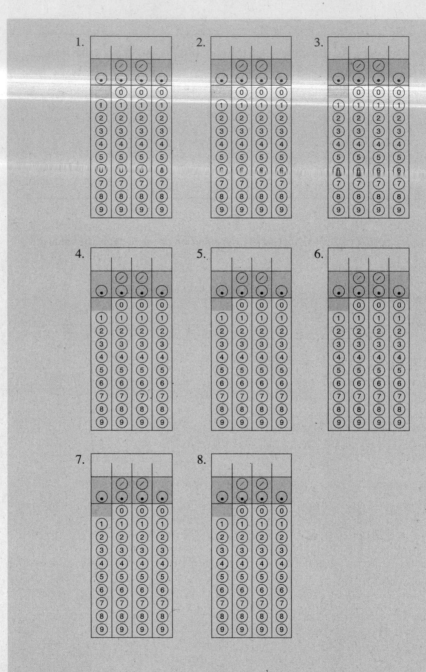

## Answer Key

1. 1375

2. 3

3. 1000

4. 3/2 or 1.5

5. 55

6. $28 < x < 44$

7. 3/2 or 1.5

8. 5/4 or 1.25

 **Additional practice questions can be found in** *The Official SAT Online Course* **at www.collegeboard.org/satonlinecourse.**

# CHAPTER 21
# Practice for the Mathematics Section

The questions in this chapter give you a chance to practice the approaches you've learned so far. Use the approaches on the questions in this chapter before you take the practice tests in the last section of this book. This chapter will give you practice on different types of math questions that are on the SAT.

# Multiple-Choice Questions

This section contains two types of questions. For questions 1–12, solve each problem and decide which is the best of the choices given. Fill in the corresponding circle on the answer sheet. You may use any available space for scratchwork.

---

Notes

1. The use of a calculator is permitted.

2. All numbers used are real numbers.

3. Figures that accompany problems in this test are intended to provide information useful in solving the problems.

   They are drawn as accurately as possible EXCEPT when it is stated in a specific problem that the figure is not drawn to scale. All figures lie in a plane unless otherwise indicated.

4. Unless otherwise specified, the domain of any function $f$ is assumed to be the set of all real numbers $x$ for which $f(x)$ is a real number.

---

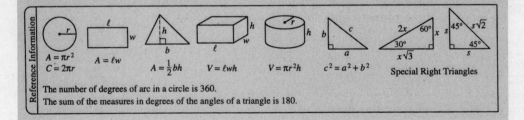

$A = \pi r^2$
$C = 2\pi r$

$A = \ell w$

$A = \frac{1}{2} bh$

$V = \ell wh$

$V = \pi r^2 h$

$c^2 = a^2 + b^2$

Special Right Triangles

The number of degrees of arc in a circle is 360.
The sum of the measures in degrees of the angles of a triangle is 180.

---

CABLE TELEVISION SUBSCRIBERS IN
TOWN $T$ BY REGION

= 1,000 subscribers

| Region $M$ | |
| Region $N$ | |
| Region $O$ | |
| Region $P$ | |

1. If the four regions shown in the graph above are the only regions in Town $T$, the total of which two regions accounts for exactly 70 percent of all cable television subscribers in Town $T$?

   (A) Regions $M$ and $N$
   (B) Regions $M$ and $O$
   (C) Regions $N$ and $O$
   (D) Regions $N$ and $P$
   (E) Regions $O$ and $P$

2. If $x^2 = k$, where $x$ and $k$ are integers, which of the following could be the value of $k$?

    (A)  3
    (B)  6
    (C)  9
    (D) 12
    (E) 15

3. For which of the following graphs of $f$ does $f(x) = f(-x)$ for all values of $x$ shown?

(A)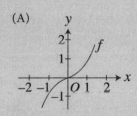

(B)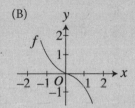

(C)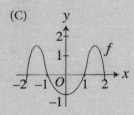

(D)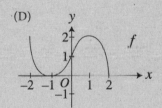

(E)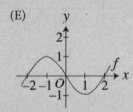

4. A class has twice as many boys as girls. The students in the class stand in one line, with a girl at the front of the line. Which of the following must be true?

    (A)  The last person in line is a girl.
    (B)  The last person in line is a boy.
    (C)  There are more girls than boys in the class.
    (D)  There are at least two girls standing next to each other.
    (E)  There are at least two boys standing next to each other.

5. Which of the following is an equation of the line that has a *y*-intercept of 2 and an *x*-intercept of 3?

(A)  −2*x* + 3*y* = 4
(B)  −2*x* + 3*y* = 6
(C)   2*x* + 3*y* = 4
(D)   2*x* + 3*y* = 6
(E)   3*x* + 2*y* = 6

6. In a certain game, each of 5 players received a score between 0 and 100, inclusive. If their average (arithmetic mean) score was 80, what is the greatest possible number of the 5 players who could have received a score of 50?

(A)  None
(B)  One
(C)  Two
(D)  Three
(E)  Four

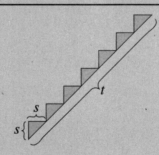

7. On the staircase shown above, both the depth and the height of each step are *s*, and each step forms a right angle. What is the value of *t* in terms of *s* ?

(A)  10*s*
(B)  14*s*
(C)  7*s*$\sqrt{2}$
(D)  7*s*$\sqrt{3}$
(E)  2*s*$^2$

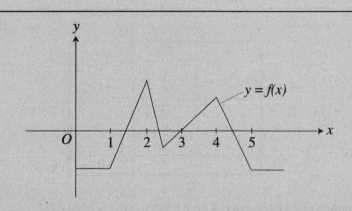

8. The figure above shows a portion of the graph of the function $f$. If $f(x + 5) = f(x)$ for all values of $x$, then $f(x) = 0$ for how many different values of $x$ between 0 and 12?

    (A) Eight
    (B) Nine
    (C) Tcn
    (D) Eleven
    (E) Twelve

9. The sum of four consecutive odd integers $w$, $x$, $y$ and $z$ is 24. What is the median of the set $\{w, x, y, z, 24\}$?

    (A)    3
    (B)    5
    (C)    7
    (D)    9
    (E)    24

| x | f(x) | g(x) |
|---|------|------|
| 0 | 5 | 2 |
| 1 | 0 | 4 |
| 2 | 2 | 3 |
| 3 | 4 | 1 |
| 4 | 1 | 5 |
| 5 | 3 | 0 |

10. According to the table above, if $k = f(3)$, what is the value of $g(k)$ ?

   (A) 1
   (B) 2
   (C) 3
   (D) 4
   (E) 5

11. In a certain school, there are $k$ classes with $n$ students in each class. If a total of $p$ pencils are distributed equally among these students, how many pencils are there for each student?

   (A) $\dfrac{p}{kn}$

   (B) $\dfrac{kn}{p}$

   (C) $\dfrac{kp}{n}$

   (D) $\dfrac{np}{k}$

   (E) $npk$

12. In the figure above, the four circles have the same center and their radii are 1, 2, 3 and 4, respectively. What is the ratio of the area of the small shaded ring to the area of the large shaded ring?

   (A)  1:2
   (B)  1:4
   (C)  3:5
   (D)  3:7
   (E)  5:7

# Student-Produced Response Questions

For Student-Produced Response questions 1–8, use the grids at the bottom of the answer sheet page.

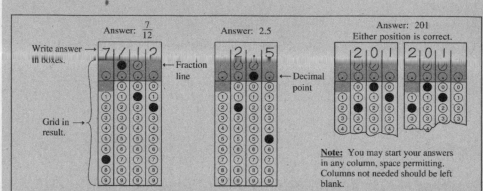

- Mark no more than one circle in any column.

- Because the answer sheet will be machine-scored, **you will receive credit only if the circles are filled in correctly.**

- Although not required, it is suggested that you write your answer in the boxes at the top of the columns to help you fill in the circles accurately.

- Some problems may have more than one correct answer. In such cases, grid only one answer.

- No question has a negative answer.

- **Mixed numbers** such as $3\frac{1}{2}$ must be gridded as 3.5 or 7/2. (If $\boxed{3\,1/2}$ is gridded, it will be interpreted as $\frac{31}{2}$, not $3\frac{1}{2}$.)

- **Decimal Answers:** If you obtain a decimal answer with more digits than the grid can accommodate, it may be either rounded or truncated, but it must fill the entire grid. For example, if you obtain an answer such as 0.6666..., you should record your result as .666 or .667. **A less accurate value such as .66 or .67 will be scored as incorrect.**

Acceptable ways to grid $\frac{2}{3}$ are:

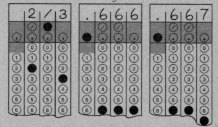

**Note:** You may start your answers in any column, space permitting. Columns not needed should be left blank.

---

1. A store has 660 books in stock. If 30 percent of these books are on sale, how many books are <u>not</u> on sale?

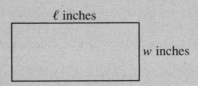

**Note:** Figure not drawn to scale.

2. The perimeter of the rectangle above is $p$ inches and the area of the rectangle is 36 square inches. If $\ell$ and $w$ are integers, what is one possible value of $p$ ?

3. If $x + \dfrac{1}{x} = 2$, what is the value of $x^2 + \dfrac{1}{x^2}$ ?

4. If $\dfrac{1}{4}$ of $\dfrac{4}{3}$ is subtracted from 2, what is the resulting value?

5. Tim wrote a seven-digit phone number on a piece of paper. He later tore the paper accidentally and the last two digits were lost. What is the maximum number of arrangements of two digits, using the digits 0 through 9, that he could use in attempting to reconstruct the correct phone number?

6. If the slope of the line that passes through the points $(a, 0)$ and $(1, -2)$ is $\frac{1}{2}$, what is the value of $a$ ?

7. One adult and 10 children are in an elevator. If the adult's weight is 4 times the average (arithmetic mean) weight of the children, then the adult's weight is what fraction of the total weight of the 11 people in the elevator?

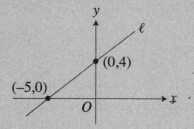

8. The figure above shows line $\ell$ in the $xy$-coordinate plane. Line $m$ (not shown) is obtained by horizontally translating each point on line $\ell$ 2 units to the left. If the equation of $m$ is $y = \frac{4}{5}x + k$, what is the value of $k$?

1.

2.

3.

4.

5.

6.

7.

8.

# Answer Key

## *Multiple-Choice Questions*

1. A
2. C
3. C
4. E
5. D
6. C
7. C
8. B
9. C
10. E
11. A
12. D

## *Student-Produced Response Questions (Grid-ins)*

1. 462
2. 24, 26, 30, 40 or 74
3. 2
4. 5/3, 1.66 or 1.67
5. 100
6. 5
7. 2/7, .285 or .286
8. 28/5 or 5.6

 **Additional practice questions can be found in *The Official SAT Online Course* at www.collegeboard.org/satonlinecourse.**

# PART V

# 10 Official Practice Tests with Answer Keys

## Taking the Practice Tests

Part V offers 10 practice tests for the SAT. Each version includes only 9 of the 10 sections in the actual test. The variable sections have been omitted. You'll get the most out of the practice tests if you take them under conditions that are as close as possible to those of the real test:

- Leave yourself 3 hours and 20 minutes to complete each sample test. (The actual test is 3 hours and 45 minutes. The omitted variable section is 25 minutes.)

- Sit at a desk or table cleared of any other papers or books. Items such as dictionaries, books, or notes won't be allowed when you take the actual SAT.

- For the math questions, use the calculator that you plan to use on the test.

- Set a timer or use a watch or clock to time yourself on each section.

- Tear out or make a copy of the 8-page practice answer sheet located just before each practice test and fill it in just as you will on the day of the actual test.

- When you complete a practice test, use the corresponding answer key, scoring instructions, scoring worksheet, and conversion tables to determine your score ranges.

 *After you complete each test:*

- Use this book to its full potential! Get exclusive access answer explanations, free practice score reports and free sample student essays to help you score your essay in the Book Owners' Area at www.collegeboard.org/satstudyguide.

- Want more practice? Get 10 more official practice tests, auto essay scoring and lesson plans from the test maker by subscribing to *The Official SAT Online Course*. As a book owner, you're entitled to a $10 discount. Sign up at www.collegeboard.org/satstudyguide.

# SAT Practice Test #1

## After this test:

- Use this book to its full potential! Get exclusive access answer explanations, free practice score reports and free sample student essays to help you score your essay in the Book Owners' Area at www.collegeboard.org/satstudyguide.

- Want more practice? Get 10 more official practice tests, auto essay scoring and lesson plans from the test maker by subscribing to *The Official SAT Online Course*. As a book owner, you're entitled to a $10 discount. Sign up at www.collegeboard.org/satstudyguide.

*Note:* Section 4, the variable section, has been omitted from this practice test.

YOUR NAME (PRINT) _____

                   LAST                              FIRST               MI

TEST CENTER _____

               NUMBER           NAME OF TEST CENTER          ROOM NUMBER

# SAT Reasoning Test — General Directions

## Timing

- You will have 3 hours and 45 minutes to work on this test.
- There are ten separately timed sections:
  - ▶ One 25-minute essay
  - ▶ Six other 25-minute sections
  - ▶ Two 20-minute sections
  - ▶ One 10-minute section
- You may work on only one section at a time.
- The supervisor will tell you when to begin and end each section.
- If you finish a section before time is called, check your work on that section. You may NOT turn to any other section.
- Work as rapidly as you can without losing accuracy. Don't waste time on questions that seem too difficult for you.

## Marking Answers

- Be sure to mark your answer sheet properly.

COMPLETE MARK ●    EXAMPLES OF INCOMPLETE MARKS

- You must use a No. 2 pencil.
- Carefully mark only one answer for each question.
- Make sure you fill the entire circle darkly and completely.
- Do not make any stray marks on your answer sheet.
- If you erase, do so completely. Incomplete erasures may be scored as intended answers.
- Use only the answer spaces that correspond to the question numbers.

## Using Your Test Book

- You may use the test book for scratchwork, but you will not receive credit for anything written there.
- After time has been called, you may not transfer answers to your answer sheet or fill in circles.
- You may not fold or remove pages or portions of a page from this book, or take the book or answer sheet from the testing room.

## Scoring

- For each correct answer, you receive one point.
- For questions you omit, you receive no points.
- For a wrong answer to a multiple-choice question, you lose one-fourth of a point.
  - ▶ If you can eliminate one or more of the answer choices as wrong, you increase your chances of choosing the correct answer and earning one point.
  - ▶ If you can't eliminate any choice, move on. You can return to the question later if there is time.
- For a wrong answer to a student-produced response ("grid-in") math question, you don't lose any points.
- Multiple-choice and student-produced response questions are machine scored.
- The essay is scored on a 1 to 6 scale by two different readers. The total essay score is the sum of the two readers' scores.
- Off-topic essays, blank essays, and essays written in ink will receive a score of zero.

**IMPORTANT:** The codes below are unique to your test book. Copy them on your answer sheet in boxes 8 and 9 and <u>fill in the corresponding circles exactly as shown.</u>

**9   TEST FORM** (Copy from back of test book.)

**8   FORM CODE** (Copy and grid as on back of test book.)

The passages for this test have been adapted from published material. The ideas contained in them do not necessarily represent the opinions of the College Board.

## DO NOT OPEN THIS BOOK UNTIL THE SUPERVISOR TELLS YOU TO DO SO.

# SAT Reasoning Test™

**MARKS MUST BE COMPLETE**

COMPLETE MARK ●  EXAMPLES OF INCOMPLETE MARKS

*You must use a No. 2 pencil. Do not use a mechanical pencil. It is very important that you fill in the entire circle darkly and completely. If you change your response, erase as completely as possible. Incomplete marks or erasures may affect your score. It is very important that you follow these instructions when filling out your answer sheet.*

**1 Your Name:**
(Print)

Last _____ First _____ M.I. _____

I agree to the conditions on the back of the SAT Reasoning Test™ booklet. I also agree to use only a No. 2 pencil to complete my answer sheet.

Signature: _____ Date: ___ / ___ / ___

**Home Address:**
(Print) _____ Number and Street ___ City ___ State ___ Zip Code

**Home Phone:** ( ) _____ **Center:** _____
(Print) ___ (Print) ___ City ___ State/Country

**2 YOUR NAME**

Last Name (First 6 Letters) | First Name (First 4 Letters) | Mid. Init.

**3 DATE OF BIRTH**

| MONTH | DAY | YEAR |
|-------|-----|------|
| Jan | | |
| Feb | | |
| Mar | | |
| Apr | | |
| May | | |
| Jun | | |
| Jul | | |
| Aug | | |
| Sep | | |
| Oct | | |
| Nov | | |
| Dec | | |

**5 SEX**
○ Female ○ Male

**6 REGISTRATION NUMBER**
(Copy from Admission Ticket.)

○ I turned in my registration form today.

**Important:** Fill in items 8 and 9 exactly as shown on the back of test book.

**9 TEST FORM**
(Copy from back of test book.)

**8 FORM CODE**
(Copy and grid as on back of test book.)

**10 TEST BOOK SERIAL NUMBER**
(Copy from front of test book.)

**11 TEST CENTER**
(Supplied by Test Center Supervisor)

**4 ZIP CODE**

**7 SOCIAL SECURITY NUMBER**

**FOR OFFICIAL USE ONLY**
0 1 2 3 4 5 6
0 1 2 3 4 5 6
0 1 2 3 4 5 6

00272-36390 • NS75E4600 • Printed in U.S.A.
732652

**PLEASE DO NOT WRITE IN THIS AREA**

**SERIAL #**

381

**SECTION 1**

○ I prefer NOT to grant the College Board the right to use, reproduce, or publish my essay for any purpose beyond the assessment of my writing skills, even though my name will not be used in any way in conjunction with my essay. I understand that I am free to mark this circle with no effect on my score.

*IMPORTANT:* **USE A NO. 2 PENCIL. DO NOT WRITE OUTSIDE THE BORDER!**
Words written outside the essay box or written in ink **WILL NOT APPEAR** in the copy sent to be scored, and your score will be affected.

**Begin your essay on this page. If you need more space, continue on the next page.**

**Page 2**
Continue on the next page, if necessary.

**Continuation of ESSAY Section 1 from previous page. Write below only if you need more space.**
***IMPORTANT:*** **DO NOT START on this page—if you do, your essay may appear blank and your score may be affected.**

**Page 3**

**PLEASE DO NOT WRITE IN THIS AREA**

**SERIAL #**

1

1

**COMPLETE MARK** ●  **EXAMPLES OF INCOMPLETE MARKS** Ⓐ ⊗ ⊖ Ⓓ / ⊘ ⊜ ⊛

You must use a No. 2 pencil and marks must be complete. Do not use a mechanical pencil. It is very important that you fill in the entire circle darkly and completely. If you change your response, erase as completely as possible. Incomplete marks or erasures may affect your score.

## SECTION 2

1 Ⓐ Ⓑ Ⓒ Ⓓ Ⓔ    11 Ⓐ Ⓑ Ⓒ Ⓓ Ⓔ    21 Ⓐ Ⓑ Ⓒ Ⓓ Ⓔ    31 Ⓐ Ⓑ Ⓒ Ⓓ Ⓔ
2 Ⓐ Ⓑ Ⓒ Ⓓ Ⓔ    12 Ⓐ Ⓑ Ⓒ Ⓓ Ⓔ    22 Ⓐ Ⓑ Ⓒ Ⓓ Ⓔ    32 Ⓐ Ⓑ Ⓒ Ⓓ Ⓔ
3 Ⓐ Ⓑ Ⓒ Ⓓ Ⓔ    13 Ⓐ Ⓑ Ⓒ Ⓓ Ⓔ    23 Ⓐ Ⓑ Ⓒ Ⓓ Ⓔ    33 Ⓐ Ⓑ Ⓒ Ⓓ Ⓔ
4 Ⓐ Ⓑ Ⓒ Ⓓ Ⓔ    14 Ⓐ Ⓑ Ⓒ Ⓓ Ⓔ    24 Ⓐ Ⓑ Ⓒ Ⓓ Ⓔ    34 Ⓐ Ⓑ Ⓒ Ⓓ Ⓔ
5 Ⓐ Ⓑ Ⓒ Ⓓ Ⓔ    15 Ⓐ Ⓑ Ⓒ Ⓓ Ⓔ    25 Ⓐ Ⓑ Ⓒ Ⓓ Ⓔ    35 Ⓐ Ⓑ Ⓒ Ⓓ Ⓔ
6 Ⓐ Ⓑ Ⓒ Ⓓ Ⓔ    16 Ⓐ Ⓑ Ⓒ Ⓓ Ⓔ    26 Ⓐ Ⓑ Ⓒ Ⓓ Ⓔ    36 Ⓐ Ⓑ Ⓒ Ⓓ Ⓔ
7 Ⓐ Ⓑ Ⓒ Ⓓ Ⓔ    17 Ⓐ Ⓑ Ⓒ Ⓓ Ⓔ    27 Ⓐ Ⓑ Ⓒ Ⓓ Ⓔ    37 Ⓐ Ⓑ Ⓒ Ⓓ Ⓔ
8 Ⓐ Ⓑ Ⓒ Ⓓ Ⓔ    18 Ⓐ Ⓑ Ⓒ Ⓓ Ⓔ    28 Ⓐ Ⓑ Ⓒ Ⓓ Ⓔ    38 Ⓐ Ⓑ Ⓒ Ⓓ Ⓔ
9 Ⓐ Ⓑ Ⓒ Ⓓ Ⓔ    19 Ⓐ Ⓑ Ⓒ Ⓓ Ⓔ    29 Ⓐ Ⓑ Ⓒ Ⓓ Ⓔ    39 Ⓐ Ⓑ Ⓒ Ⓓ Ⓔ
10 Ⓐ Ⓑ Ⓒ Ⓓ Ⓔ   20 Ⓐ Ⓑ Ⓒ Ⓓ Ⓔ    30 Ⓐ Ⓑ Ⓒ Ⓓ Ⓔ    40 Ⓐ Ⓑ Ⓒ Ⓓ Ⓔ

## SECTION 3

1 Ⓐ Ⓑ Ⓒ Ⓓ Ⓔ    11 Ⓐ Ⓑ Ⓒ Ⓓ Ⓔ    21 Ⓐ Ⓑ Ⓒ Ⓓ Ⓔ    31 Ⓐ Ⓑ Ⓒ Ⓓ Ⓔ
2 Ⓐ Ⓑ Ⓒ Ⓓ Ⓔ    12 Ⓐ Ⓑ Ⓒ Ⓓ Ⓔ    22 Ⓐ Ⓑ Ⓒ Ⓓ Ⓔ    32 Ⓐ Ⓑ Ⓒ Ⓓ Ⓔ
3 Ⓐ Ⓑ Ⓒ Ⓓ Ⓔ    13 Ⓐ Ⓑ Ⓒ Ⓓ Ⓔ    23 Ⓐ Ⓑ Ⓒ Ⓓ Ⓔ    33 Ⓐ Ⓑ Ⓒ Ⓓ Ⓔ
4 Ⓐ Ⓑ Ⓒ Ⓓ Ⓔ    14 Ⓐ Ⓑ Ⓒ Ⓓ Ⓔ    24 Ⓐ Ⓑ Ⓒ Ⓓ Ⓔ    34 Ⓐ Ⓑ Ⓒ Ⓓ Ⓔ
5 Ⓐ Ⓑ Ⓒ Ⓓ Ⓔ    15 Ⓐ Ⓑ Ⓒ Ⓓ Ⓔ    25 Ⓐ Ⓑ Ⓒ Ⓓ Ⓔ    35 Ⓐ Ⓑ Ⓒ Ⓓ Ⓔ
6 Ⓐ Ⓑ Ⓒ Ⓓ Ⓔ    16 Ⓐ Ⓑ Ⓒ Ⓓ Ⓔ    26 Ⓐ Ⓑ Ⓒ Ⓓ Ⓔ    36 Ⓐ Ⓑ Ⓒ Ⓓ Ⓔ
7 Ⓐ Ⓑ Ⓒ Ⓓ Ⓔ    17 Ⓐ Ⓑ Ⓒ Ⓓ Ⓔ    27 Ⓐ Ⓑ Ⓒ Ⓓ Ⓔ    37 Ⓐ Ⓑ Ⓒ Ⓓ Ⓔ
8 Ⓐ Ⓑ Ⓒ Ⓓ Ⓔ    18 Ⓐ Ⓑ Ⓒ Ⓓ Ⓔ    28 Ⓐ Ⓑ Ⓒ Ⓓ Ⓔ    38 Ⓐ Ⓑ Ⓒ Ⓓ Ⓔ
9 Ⓐ Ⓑ Ⓒ Ⓓ Ⓔ    19 Ⓐ Ⓑ Ⓒ Ⓓ Ⓔ    29 Ⓐ Ⓑ Ⓒ Ⓓ Ⓔ    39 Ⓐ Ⓑ Ⓒ Ⓓ Ⓔ
10 Ⓐ Ⓑ Ⓒ Ⓓ Ⓔ   20 Ⓐ Ⓑ Ⓒ Ⓓ Ⓔ    30 Ⓐ Ⓑ Ⓒ Ⓓ Ⓔ    40 Ⓐ Ⓑ Ⓒ Ⓓ Ⓔ

**CAUTION** Grid answers in the section below for SECTION 2 or SECTION 3 only if directed to do so in your test book.

## Student-Produced Responses

ONLY ANSWERS THAT ARE GRIDDED WILL BE SCORED. YOU WILL NOT RECEIVE CREDIT FOR ANYTHING WRITTEN IN THE BOXES.

Qualty Assurance Mark ●

9   10   11   12   13

*(Grid-in response boxes with digits 0–9 for each column)*

14   15   16   17   18

*(Grid-in response boxes with digits 0–9 for each column)*

COMPLETE MARK ● EXAMPLES OF INCOMPLETE MARKS

You must use a No. 2 pencil and marks must be complete. Do not use a mechanical pencil. It is very important that you fill in the entire circle darkly and completely. If you change your response, erase as completely as possible. Incomplete marks or erasures may affect your score.

**SECTION 4**

| 1 | A B C D E | 11 | A B C D E | 21 | A B C D E | 31 | A B C D E |
| 2 | A B C D E | 12 | A B C D E | 22 | A B C D E | 32 | A B C D E |
| 3 | A B C D E | 13 | A B C D E | 23 | A B C D E | 33 | A B C D E |
| 4 | A B C D E | 14 | A B C D E | 24 | A B C D E | 34 | A B C D E |
| 5 | A B C D E | 15 | A B C D E | 25 | A B C D E | 35 | A B C D E |
| 6 | A B C D E | 16 | A B C D E | 26 | A B C D E | 36 | A B C D E |
| 7 | A B C D E | 17 | A B C D E | 27 | A B C D E | 37 | A B C D E |
| 8 | A B C D E | 18 | A B C D E | 28 | A B C D E | 38 | A B C D E |
| 9 | A B C D E | 19 | A B C D E | 29 | A B C D E | 39 | A B C D E |
| 10 | A B C D E | 20 | A B C D E | 30 | A B C D E | 40 | A B C D E |

**SECTION 5**

| 1 | A B C D E | 11 | A B C D E | 21 | A B C D E | 31 | A B C D E |
| 2 | A B C D E | 12 | A B C D E | 22 | A B C D E | 32 | A B C D E |
| 3 | A B C D E | 13 | A B C D E | 23 | A B C D E | 33 | A B C D E |
| 4 | A B C D E | 14 | A B C D E | 24 | A B C D E | 34 | A B C D E |
| 5 | A B C D E | 15 | A B C D E | 25 | A B C D E | 35 | A B C D E |
| 6 | A B C D E | 16 | A B C D E | 26 | A B C D E | 36 | A B C D E |
| 7 | A B C D E | 17 | A B C D E | 27 | A B C D E | 37 | A B C D E |
| 8 | A B C D E | 18 | A B C D E | 28 | A B C D E | 38 | A B C D E |
| 9 | A B C D E | 19 | A B C D E | 29 | A B C D E | 39 | A B C D E |
| 10 | A B C D E | 20 | A B C D E | 30 | A B C D E | 40 | A B C D E |

**CAUTION** Grid answers in the section below for SECTION 4 or SECTION 5 only if directed to do so in your test book.

**Student-Produced Responses** ONLY ANSWERS THAT ARE GRIDDED WILL BE SCORED. YOU WILL NOT RECEIVE CREDIT FOR ANYTHING WRITTEN IN THE BOXES.

Quality Assurance Mark

9 10 11 12 13

14 15 16 17 18

COMPLETE MARK ●

EXAMPLES OF INCOMPLETE MARKS

You must use a No. 2 pencil and marks must be complete. Do not use a mechanical pencil. It is very important that you fill in the entire circle darkly and completely. If you change your response, erase as completely as possible. Incomplete marks or erasures may affect your score.

## SECTION 6

| 1 (A)(B)(C)(D)(E) | 11 (A)(B)(C)(D)(E) | 21 (A)(B)(C)(D)(E) | 31 (A)(B)(C)(D)(E) |
| 2 (A)(B)(C)(D)(E) | 12 (A)(B)(C)(D)(E) | 22 (A)(B)(C)(D)(E) | 32 (A)(B)(C)(D)(E) |
| 3 (A)(B)(C)(D)(E) | 13 (A)(B)(C)(D)(E) | 23 (A)(B)(C)(D)(E) | 33 (A)(B)(C)(D)(E) |
| 4 (A)(B)(C)(D)(E) | 14 (A)(B)(C)(D)(E) | 24 (A)(B)(C)(D)(E) | 34 (A)(B)(C)(D)(E) |
| 5 (A)(B)(C)(D)(E) | 15 (A)(B)(C)(D)(E) | 25 (A)(B)(C)(D)(E) | 35 (A)(B)(C)(D)(E) |
| 6 (A)(B)(C)(D)(E) | 16 (A)(B)(C)(D)(E) | 26 (A)(B)(C)(D)(E) | 36 (A)(B)(C)(D)(E) |
| 7 (A)(B)(C)(D)(E) | 17 (A)(B)(C)(D)(E) | 27 (A)(B)(C)(D)(E) | 37 (A)(B)(C)(D)(E) |
| 8 (A)(B)(C)(D)(E) | 18 (A)(B)(C)(D)(E) | 28 (A)(B)(C)(D)(E) | 38 (A)(B)(C)(D)(E) |
| 9 (A)(B)(C)(D)(E) | 19 (A)(B)(C)(D)(E) | 29 (A)(B)(C)(D)(E) | 39 (A)(B)(C)(D)(E) |
| 10 (A)(B)(C)(D)(E) | 20 (A)(B)(C)(D)(E) | 30 (A)(B)(C)(D)(E) | 40 (A)(B)(C)(D)(E) |

## SECTION 7

| 1 (A)(B)(C)(D)(E) | 11 (A)(B)(C)(D)(E) | 21 (A)(B)(C)(D)(E) | 31 (A)(B)(C)(D)(E) |
| 2 (A)(B)(C)(D)(E) | 12 (A)(B)(C)(D)(E) | 22 (A)(B)(C)(D)(E) | 32 (A)(B)(C)(D)(E) |
| 3 (A)(B)(C)(D)(E) | 13 (A)(B)(C)(D)(E) | 23 (A)(B)(C)(D)(E) | 33 (A)(B)(C)(D)(E) |
| 4 (A)(B)(C)(D)(E) | 14 (A)(B)(C)(D)(E) | 24 (A)(B)(C)(D)(E) | 34 (A)(B)(C)(D)(E) |
| 5 (A)(B)(C)(D)(E) | 15 (A)(B)(C)(D)(E) | 25 (A)(B)(C)(D)(E) | 35 (A)(B)(C)(D)(E) |
| 6 (A)(B)(C)(D)(E) | 16 (A)(B)(C)(D)(E) | 26 (A)(B)(C)(D)(E) | 36 (A)(B)(C)(D)(E) |
| 7 (A)(B)(C)(D)(E) | 17 (A)(B)(C)(D)(E) | 27 (A)(B)(C)(D)(E) | 37 (A)(B)(C)(D)(E) |
| 8 (A)(B)(C)(D)(E) | 18 (A)(B)(C)(D)(E) | 28 (A)(B)(C)(D)(E) | 38 (A)(B)(C)(D)(E) |
| 9 (A)(B)(C)(D)(E) | 19 (A)(B)(C)(D)(E) | 29 (A)(B)(C)(D)(E) | 39 (A)(B)(C)(D)(E) |
| 10 (A)(B)(C)(D)(E) | 20 (A)(B)(C)(D)(E) | 30 (A)(B)(C)(D)(E) | 40 (A)(B)(C)(D)(E) |

**CAUTION** Grid answers in the section below for SECTION 6 or SECTION 7 only if directed to do so in your test book.

**Student-Produced Responses** ONLY ANSWERS THAT ARE GRIDDED WILL BE SCORED. YOU WILL NOT RECEIVE CREDIT FOR ANYTHING WRITTEN IN THE BOXES.

9    10    11    12    13

Quality Assurance Mark

14    15    16    17    18

Page 6

PLEASE DO NOT WRITE IN THIS AREA

SERIAL #

COMPLETE MARK ● EXAMPLES OF INCOMPLETE MARKS

**You must use a No. 2 pencil and marks must be complete. Do not use a mechanical pencil.** *It is very important that you fill in the entire circle darkly and completely. If you change your response, erase as completely as possible. Incomplete marks or erasures may affect your score.*

## SECTION 8

| | | | |
|---|---|---|---|
| 1 (A)(B)(C)(D)(E) | 11 (A)(B)(C)(D)(E) | 21 (A)(B)(C)(D)(E) | 31 (A)(B)(C)(D)(E) |
| 2 (A)(B)(C)(D)(E) | 12 (A)(B)(C)(D)(E) | 22 (A)(B)(C)(D)(E) | 32 (A)(B)(C)(D)(E) |
| 3 (A)(B)(C)(D)(E) | 13 (A)(B)(C)(D)(E) | 23 (A)(B)(C)(D)(E) | 33 (A)(B)(C)(D)(E) |
| 4 (A)(B)(C)(D)(E) | 14 (A)(B)(C)(D)(E) | 24 (A)(B)(C)(D)(E) | 34 (A)(B)(C)(D)(E) |
| 5 (A)(B)(C)(D)(E) | 15 (A)(B)(C)(D)(E) | 25 (A)(B)(C)(D)(E) | 35 (A)(B)(C)(D)(E) |
| 6 (A)(B)(C)(D)(E) | 16 (A)(B)(C)(D)(E) | 26 (A)(B)(C)(D)(E) | 36 (A)(B)(C)(D)(E) |
| 7 (A)(B)(C)(D)(E) | 17 (A)(B)(C)(D)(E) | 27 (A)(B)(C)(D)(E) | 37 (A)(B)(C)(D)(E) |
| 8 (A)(B)(C)(D)(E) | 18 (A)(B)(C)(D)(E) | 28 (A)(B)(C)(D)(E) | 38 (A)(B)(C)(D)(E) |
| 9 (A)(B)(C)(D)(E) | 19 (A)(B)(C)(D)(E) | 29 (A)(B)(C)(D)(E) | 39 (A)(B)(C)(D)(E) |
| 10 (A)(B)(C)(D)(E) | 20 (A)(B)(C)(D)(E) | 30 (A)(B)(C)(D)(E) | 40 (A)(B)(C)(D)(E) |

## SECTION 9

| | | | |
|---|---|---|---|
| 1 (A)(B)(C)(D)(E) | 11 (A)(B)(C)(D)(E) | 21 (A)(B)(C)(D)(E) | 31 (A)(B)(C)(D)(E) |
| 2 (A)(B)(C)(D)(E) | 12 (A)(B)(C)(D)(E) | 22 (A)(B)(C)(D)(E) | 32 (A)(B)(C)(D)(E) |
| 3 (A)(B)(C)(D)(E) | 13 (A)(B)(C)(D)(E) | 23 (A)(B)(C)(D)(E) | 33 (A)(B)(C)(D)(E) |
| 4 (A)(B)(C)(D)(E) | 14 (A)(B)(C)(D)(E) | 24 (A)(B)(C)(D)(E) | 34 (A)(B)(C)(D)(E) |
| 5 (A)(B)(C)(D)(E) | 15 (A)(B)(C)(D)(E) | 25 (A)(B)(C)(D)(E) | 35 (A)(B)(C)(D)(E) |
| 6 (A)(B)(C)(D)(E) | 16 (A)(B)(C)(D)(E) | 26 (A)(B)(C)(D)(E) | 36 (A)(B)(C)(D)(E) |
| 7 (A)(B)(C)(D)(E) | 17 (A)(B)(C)(D)(E) | 27 (A)(B)(C)(D)(E) | 37 (A)(B)(C)(D)(E) |
| 8 (A)(B)(C)(D)(E) | 18 (A)(B)(C)(D)(E) | 28 (A)(B)(C)(D)(E) | 38 (A)(B)(C)(D)(E) |
| 9 (A)(B)(C)(D)(E) | 19 (A)(B)(C)(D)(E) | 29 (A)(B)(C)(D)(E) | 39 (A)(B)(C)(D)(E) |
| 10 (A)(B)(C)(D)(E) | 20 (A)(B)(C)(D)(E) | 30 (A)(B)(C)(D)(E) | 40 (A)(B)(C)(D)(E) |

Quality
Assurance
Mark

## SECTION 10

| | | | |
|---|---|---|---|
| 1 (A)(B)(C)(D)(E) | 11 (A)(B)(C)(D)(E) | 21 (A)(B)(C)(D)(E) | 31 (A)(B)(C)(D)(E) |
| 2 (A)(B)(C)(D)(E) | 12 (A)(B)(C)(D)(E) | 22 (A)(B)(C)(D)(E) | 32 (A)(B)(C)(D)(E) |
| 3 (A)(B)(C)(D)(E) | 13 (A)(B)(C)(D)(E) | 23 (A)(B)(C)(D)(E) | 33 (A)(B)(C)(D)(E) |
| 4 (A)(B)(C)(D)(E) | 14 (A)(B)(C)(D)(E) | 24 (A)(B)(C)(D)(E) | 34 (A)(B)(C)(D)(E) |
| 5 (A)(B)(C)(D)(E) | 15 (A)(B)(C)(D)(E) | 25 (A)(B)(C)(D)(E) | 35 (A)(B)(C)(D)(E) |
| 6 (A)(B)(C)(D)(E) | 16 (A)(B)(C)(D)(E) | 26 (A)(B)(C)(D)(E) | 36 (A)(B)(C)(D)(E) |
| 7 (A)(B)(C)(D)(E) | 17 (A)(B)(C)(D)(F) | 27 (A)(B)(C)(D)(E) | 37 (A)(B)(C)(D)(E) |
| 8 (A)(B)(C)(D)(E) | 18 (A)(B)(C)(D)(E) | 28 (A)(B)(C)(D)(E) | 38 (A)(B)(C)(D)(E) |
| 9 (A)(D)(D)(D)(E) | 19 (A)(B)(C)(D)(E) | 29 (A)(B)(C)(D)(E) | 39 (A)(B)(C)(D)(E) |
| 10 (A)(B)(C)(D)(E) | 20 (A)(B)(C)(D)(E) | 30 (A)(B)(C)(D)(E) | 40 (A)(B)(C)(D)(E) |

**1**

## SPECIAL QUESTIONS

1 Ⓐ Ⓑ Ⓒ Ⓓ Ⓔ Ⓕ Ⓖ Ⓗ Ⓘ Ⓙ
2 Ⓐ Ⓑ Ⓒ Ⓓ Ⓔ Ⓕ Ⓖ Ⓗ Ⓘ Ⓙ
3 Ⓐ Ⓑ Ⓒ Ⓓ Ⓔ Ⓕ Ⓖ Ⓗ Ⓘ Ⓙ
4 Ⓐ Ⓑ Ⓒ Ⓓ Ⓔ Ⓕ Ⓖ Ⓗ Ⓘ Ⓙ
5 Ⓐ Ⓑ Ⓒ Ⓓ Ⓔ Ⓕ Ⓖ Ⓗ Ⓘ Ⓙ
6 Ⓐ Ⓑ Ⓒ Ⓓ Ⓔ Ⓕ Ⓖ Ⓗ Ⓘ Ⓙ
7 Ⓐ Ⓑ Ⓒ Ⓓ Ⓔ Ⓕ Ⓖ Ⓗ Ⓘ Ⓙ
8 Ⓐ Ⓑ Ⓒ Ⓓ Ⓔ Ⓕ Ⓖ Ⓗ Ⓘ Ⓙ

**PLEASE DO NOT WRITE IN THIS AREA**

◉ ○ ○ ○ ○ ○ ○ ○ ○ ○ ○ ○ ○ ○ ○ ○ ○ ○ ○ ○ ○ ○ ○ ○ ○ ○ ○     **SERIAL #**

1 ESSAY  ESSAY 1

Unauthorized copying or reuse of
any part of this page is illegal.

**ESSAY**
Time — 25 minutes

---

### Turn to page 2 of your answer sheet to write your ESSAY.

---

The essay gives you an opportunity to show how effectively you can develop and express ideas. You should, therefore, take care to develop your point of view, present your ideas logically and clearly, and use language precisely.

Your essay must be written on the lines provided on your answer sheet—you will receive no other paper on which to write. You will have enough space if you write on every line, avoid wide margins, and keep your handwriting to a reasonable size. Remember that people who are not familiar with your handwriting will read what you write. Try to write or print so that what you are writing is legible to those readers.

**Important Reminders:**

- **A pencil is required for the essay.** An essay written in ink will receive a score of zero.
- **Do not write your essay in your test book.** You will receive credit only for what you write on your answer sheet.
- **An off-topic essay will receive a score of zero.**
- **If your essay does not reflect your original and individual work, your test scores may be canceled.**

You have twenty-five minutes to write an essay on the topic assigned below.

---

Think carefully about the issue presented in the following excerpt and the assignment below.

> Sometimes it is necessary to challenge what people in authority claim to be true. Although some respect for authority is, no doubt, necessary in order for any group or organization to function, questioning the people in charge—even if they are experts or leaders in their fields—makes us better thinkers. It forces all concerned to defend old ideas and decisions and to consider new ones. Sometimes it can even correct old errors in thought and put an end to wrong actions.

**Assignment:** Is it important to question the ideas and decisions of people in positions of authority? Plan and write an essay in which you develop your point of view on this issue. Support your position with reasoning and examples taken from your reading, studies, experience, or observations.

---

BEGIN WRITING YOUR ESSAY ON PAGE 2 OF THE ANSWER SHEET.

---

**If you finish before time is called, you may check your work on this section only.
Do not turn to any other section in the test.**

## SECTION 2
Time — 25 minutes
24 Questions

---

**Turn to Section 2 (page 4) of your answer sheet to answer the questions in this section.**

---

**Directions:** For each question in this section, select the best answer from among the choices given and fill in the corresponding circle on the answer sheet.

---

Each sentence below has one or two blanks, each blank indicating that something has been omitted. Beneath the sentence are five words or sets of words labeled A through E. Choose the word or set of words that, when inserted in the sentence, <u>best</u> fits the meaning of the sentence as a whole.

**Example:**

Hoping to ------- the dispute, negotiators proposed a compromise that they felt would be ------- to both labor and management.

(A) enforce . . useful
(B) end . . divisive
(C) overcome . . unattractive
(D) extend . . satisfactory
(E) resolve . . acceptable

(A) (B) (C) (D) ●

1. Aleksandr Solzhenitsyn's ------- proved keenest when he accurately predicted that his books would someday appear in his native Russia.

   (A) foresight    (B) nostalgia    (C) folly
       (D) despair    (E) artistry

2. The simple and direct images in Dorothea Lange's photographs provide ------- reflection of a bygone social milieu.

   (A) an intricate    (B) a candid
       (C) an ostentatious    (D) a fictional
           (E) a convoluted

3. Kate's impulsive nature and sudden whims led her friends to label her -------.

   (A) capricious    (B) bombastic    (C) loquacious
       (D) dispassionate    (E) decorous

4. Neurosurgeon Alexa Canady maintained that choosing a career was a visceral decision rather than ------- judgment; that is, it was not so much rational as -------.

   (A) an emotional . . intellectual
   (B) a chance . . random
   (C) an intuitive . . impulsive
   (D) a deliberate . . instinctive
   (E) an intentional . . logical

5. Creative business stratagems frequently become ------- as a result of -------, their versatility and adaptability destroyed by their transformation into rigid policies.

   (A) streamlined . . infighting
   (B) mitigated . . jingoism
   (C) ossified . . bureaucratization
   (D) politicized . . innovation
   (E) venerable . . legislation

---

**GO ON TO THE NEXT PAGE** ⇨

The passages below are followed by questions based on their content; questions following a pair of related passages may also be based on the relationship between the paired passages. Answer the questions on the basis of what is stated or implied in the passages and in any introductory material that may be provided.

**Questions 6-7 are based on the following passage.**

Whistling and moaning, a 50-mile-an-hour wind whipped among the telescope domes atop Kitt Peak. A few feet below, turning gray in the dusk, slid a river of clouds that had been rising and dropping all day. High above,
*Line*
5 comet Hale-Bopp hung like a feathery fishing lure, its tail curving off a bit, as if blown to the side by the punishing wind. One by one, stars winked on in a darkening sky. Nearby, wild horses wandered past. They never glanced skyward at the gossamer swath of Hale-Bopp nor at the
10 wondrous spectacle that is the night sky on a clear night, comet or no.

It felt good to be human.

6. In line 12, the author implies that being "human" includes

(A) making occasional mistakes
(B) enjoying the company of others
(C) reflecting on past experiences
(D) appreciating nature's beauty
(E) seeking joy through simplicity

7. The rhetorical device primarily featured in this passage is

(A) appeal to emotion
(B) metaphorical language
(C) extended analogy
(D) flashback
(E) irony

**Questions 8-9 are based on the following passage.**

In 1843 Augusta Ada King published an influential set of notes describing Charles Babbage's conception of an "analytical engine"—the first design for an automatic computer. King's notes, which included her program for
*Line*
5 computing a series of figures called Bernoulli numbers, established her importance in computer science. However, her fascinating life and lineage (she was the daughter of the flamboyant poet Lord Byron)—and her role as a female pioneer in her field—have turned her into an
10 icon. She has inspired biographies, plays, novels, and even a feature film. And whereas many women have helped to advance computer science, only King has had a computer language named after her: Ada.

8. The passage is primarily concerned with

(A) explaining Augusta Ada King's interest in computer science
(B) providing a character analysis of Augusta Ada King
(C) summarizing how and why Augusta Ada King is celebrated
(D) tracing the development of the modern-day computer
(E) encouraging more women to pursue careers in computer science

9. The author of the passage would most likely disagree with which of the following statements about Augusta Ada King?

(A) Her family history plays no part in the fascination she arouses.
(B) Her contributions to computer science were markedly original.
(C) Interest in her has spread throughout popular culture.
(D) She was well known in the field of computer science long after she had completed her work.
(E) Her life was remarkable even apart from her contributions to computer science.

**GO ON TO THE NEXT PAGE**

**Questions 10-15 are based on the following passage.**

*The following passage is adapted from a 1999 memoir. The author, the son of a Black American woman and a Congolese man, has lived in both the United States and Africa: he was raised in Boston, Massachusetts, and Dar es Salaam, Tanzania. Here, he offers his views on the historical relationship between Black Americans and Black Africans.*

A Kikongo proverb states, "A tree cannot stand without its roots." It seems such obvious wisdom now, a well-worn cliché in our era in which everything truly insightful has
Line already been said. But all clichés derive their endurance
5 from their truth, and my ancestors who coined this adage were sending a clear and powerful message to their descendants: a people cannot flourish without their life-giving foundations in the past. The ties between those who came before and those who live now must be
10 maintained and nurtured if a people is to survive. It's a truth that my grandmother understood when she made a point of directing me to "tell the others" about her. And it's a truth that has been well recognized by successive generations of Black people in America. Another Kikongo
15 proverb reminds us that "one can only steal a sleeping baby: once awake, she will look for her parents." This is a maxim that conveys the seemingly instinctive pull of one's heritage, our inborn curiosity in our origins, the quest we all share for self-identification and self-
20 knowledge.
    Black Americans have managed to sustain links with the continent of their origin, against tremendous odds. Through ingenuity and dogged determination, in calculated symbolism and unwitting remembrance, for over 300 years
25 Black Americans have kept various ties to Africa intact. The bond has frayed and stretched, it has become twisted and contorted, but through it all, it has not been broken. And for as long as Black people in America have reached back to Africa to offer and receive reassurance, reaffir-
30 mation, fraternity, and strength, Africans have reached to Black people in the Americas, "those who were taken," for the same reasons.
    We have sought to understand each other ever since we were separated so long ago. For centuries, we have
35 gazed at one another across the transatlantic divide like a child seeing itself in the mirror for the first time. And, unable for so long to reach behind the glass and touch the strangely familiar face we saw staring back, we filled in all that we did not know with all that we could imagine.
40    When we finally met, in Africa and America, we were sometimes disappointed. Shadowy imaginings do not usually hold up in the light of real experience. We

wondered if we hadn't been mistaken, if the kinship we could feel more than describe was really there, if the roots
45 that had once bound us together had not already withered and died. But time and again we were reminded of what we shared. Africa has left her mark on all of us. And when we have reached out to one another through literature, politics, music, and religion, whenever we've made contact, the
50 world has been forced to take note.

**10.** The primary purpose of this passage is to

(A) show the impact Black Americans have had on African societies
(B) discuss Africans' efforts to embrace American culture
(C) point out the ambivalent feelings one community has for another
(D) emphasize the significance of an ongoing relationship
(E) examine the cultural ties between two nations

**11.** The "message" (line 6) is best characterized as

(A) veiled criticism
(B) cautionary advice
(C) a questionable proposition
(D) a nostalgic recollection
(E) an optimistic prediction

**12.** The proverb in lines 15-16 primarily serves to

(A) offer insight into young children's behavior
(B) emphasize the vulnerability of children
(C) show people's inherent interest in their history
(D) demonstrate the complexity of familial relations
(E) warn those who seek to undermine the family

**13.** In context, "Shadowy" (line 41) primarily serves to suggest something

(A) gloomy
(B) secret
(C) sinister
(D) concealed
(E) unsubstantiated

**GO ON TO THE NEXT PAGE**

**14.** In lines 42-50 ("We wondered . . . note"), there is a shift in feeling from

(A) fear to courage
(B) anger to forgiveness
(C) uncertainty to despair
(D) regret to determination
(E) doubt to pride

**15.** The author primarily makes use of which of the following to convey his point?

(A) Hypothetical scenarios
(B) Broad generalizations
(C) Historical facts
(D) Personal anecdotes
(E) Scholarly analyses

**GO ON TO THE NEXT PAGE**

**Questions 16-24 are based on the following passages.**

*The following passages, adapted from books published in 1992 and 2001, respectively, discuss a famous painting by Renaissance artist Leonardo da Vinci (1452-1519).*

### Passage 1

It hung in Napoleon's bedroom until moving to the Louvre in 1804. It caused traffic jams in New York for seven weeks as 1.6 million people jostled to see it. In
Line Tokyo viewers were allowed ten seconds each. The
5 object of all this attention was the world's most famous portrait, the *Mona Lisa*.

Historically, its subject was nobody special, probably the wife of a Florentine merchant named Giocondo. But her portrait set the standard for High Renaissance paintings
10 in many important ways. The use of perspective, which creates the illusion of depth behind Mona Lisa's head, and triangular composition established the importance of geometry in painting. It diverged from the stiff, profile portraits that had been the norm by displaying the subject
15 in a relaxed, natural, three-quarter pose.

One of the first easel paintings intended to be framed and hung on a wall, the *Mona Lisa* fully realized the potential of the new oil medium. Instead of proceeding from outlined figures, as painters did before, Leonardo
20 modeled features through light and shadow. Starting with dark undertones, he built the illusion of three-dimensional features through layers and layers of thin, transparent glazes. This technique rendered the whole, as Leonardo said, "without lines or borders, in the man-
25 ner of smoke." His colors ranged from light to dark in a continuous gradation of subtle tones, without crisp separating edges. The forms seemed to emerge from, and melt into, shadows.

And then there's that famous smile . . .

### Passage 2

30 Why is the *Mona Lisa* the best-known painting in the entire world? A small glimpse at even some of its subject's features—her eyes, or perhaps just her hands—brings instant recognition even to those who have no taste or passion for painting. Art historians, poets, and admirers
35 have tried to explain the commanding place that the *Mona Lisa* has in our cultural life with reference to qualities intrinsic to the work. There is something, they argue, *inside* the painting that speaks to us all, that unleashes feelings, emotion, and recognition.
40 This idea originated at the beginning of the nineteenth century, though it had precedents. It is still the position of many art critics.

Art historian Kenneth Clarke, for example, writing in 1973, could not accept that the *Mona Lisa* was famous
45 for reasons other than its inner qualities. There are millions of people, he explained, who know the name of only one

picture—the *Mona Lisa*. This, he argues, is not simply due to an accident of accumulated publicity. It means that this strange image strikes at the subconscious with
50 a force that is extremely rare in an individual work of art.

Clarke's conception of art history is now regarded as somewhat old-fashioned. This is not the case with the "postmodern" Paul Barolsky, who in 1994, seeking to explain what it is about the *Mona Lisa* that "holds us
55 in thrall," pointed to Leonardo's remarkable technique, which creates a sense of texture and depth. The painter, he added, rendered the "inwardness of the sitter, the sense . . . of her mind or soul."

I think one should avoid succumbing to the charm
60 of a myth, to the idea that inside every masterpiece that has remained alive for centuries something imponderable speaks to us. It is of course intensely pleasurable to imagine that, as we face the products of Leonardo, Raphael, and other great artists of bygone ages, armed with nothing but
65 our "innate" sensibility, a mysterious yet almost palpable contact is established. But like most historians, I start with the assumption that the renown of a masterpiece rests on a sequence of events and historical agencies (people, institutions, processes) working in a largely unplanned
70 manner for different ends. Such forces have turned the *Mona Lisa* into the best-known painting in the world. Whether the *Mona Lisa* "deserves" this position is a judgment I happily leave to the reader.

16. Both passages call attention to which aspect of the *Mona Lisa* ?

(A) Its subject's mysterious smile
(B) Its subject's identity
(C) Its popular appeal
(D) Its influence on artists
(E) Its deteriorating condition

17. The author of Passage 2 would most likely regard the phenomena described in lines 1-6 in Passage 1 ("It hung . . . *Mona Lisa*") as

(A) circumstances that may themselves have contributed to the renown of the *Mona Lisa*
(B) occurrences that fundamentally distort the true importance of the *Mona Lisa*
(C) incidents that cause art enthusiasts undue annoyance
(D) events that are not worthy of the consideration of art critics
(E) facts that have proved inconvenient for many art historians

**GO ON TO THE NEXT PAGE**

18. The observations in lines 7-10 ("Historically . . . ways") establish a contrast between a woman's

   (A) unremarkable appearance and her portrait's astonishing beauty
   (B) humble origins and her portrait's monetary value
   (C) untimely demise and her portrait's immortality
   (D) lack of charisma and her portrait's universal allure
   (E) ordinary status and her portrait's aesthetic significance

19. The quotation from Leonardo in lines 24-25 primarily serves to

   (A) defend a methodology
   (B) characterize an effect
   (C) criticize a technique
   (D) downplay an accomplishment
   (E) acknowledge an influence

20. Which of Mona Lisa's features would the author of Passage 1 most likely add to those mentioned in Passage 2, line 32 ?

   (A) Her mouth
   (B) Her hair
   (C) Her nose
   (D) Her chin
   (E) Her profile

21. In line 41, "position" most nearly means

   (A) rank
   (B) role
   (C) policy
   (D) view
   (E) location

22. Both the author of Passage 1 and Paul Barolsky (line 53, Passage 2) make which of the following points about the *Mona Lisa* ?

   (A) It tends to elicit idiosyncratic responses from viewers.
   (B) It is unduly revered by much of the general public.
   (C) It has influenced many generations of artists.
   (D) It was the first oil painting intended to be framed and hung.
   (E) It gives the appearance of having three dimensions.

23. The author of Passage 2 uses quotation marks in line 65 primarily to

   (A) label a revolutionary movement
   (B) refer to an overused technique in art
   (C) emphasize the symbolic meaning of a term
   (D) highlight the importance of a finding
   (E) imply skepticism about a theory

24. Which statement best characterizes the different ways in which the authors of Passage 1 and Passage 2 approach the *Mona Lisa* ?

   (A) The first stresses the unique smile in the portrait, while the second focuses on other mysterious qualities of its subject.
   (B) The first emphasizes its striking appearance, while the second examines the background of its creator.
   (C) The first focuses on its stylistic innovations, while the second seeks to account for its cultural preeminence.
   (D) The first speculates about the life of its subject, while the second argues that historical interpretations are irrelevant.
   (E) The first alludes to its societal importance, while the second debates its artistic merits.

# STOP

**If you finish before time is called, you may check your work on this section only.**
**Do not turn to any other section in the test.**

## SECTION 3
### Time — 25 minutes
### 20 Questions

---

**Turn to Section 3 (page 4) of your answer sheet to answer the questions in this section.**

---

**Directions:** For this section, solve each problem and decide which is the best of the choices given. Fill in the corresponding circle on the answer sheet. You may use any available space for scratchwork.

**Reference Information**

          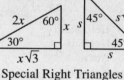

$A = \pi r^2$
$C = 2\pi r$
$A = \ell w$
$A = \frac{1}{2}bh$
$V = \ell wh$
$V = \pi r^2 h$
$c^2 = a^2 + b^2$
Special Right Triangles

The number of degrees of arc in a circle is 360.
The sum of the measures in degrees of the angles of a triangle is 180.

---

**1.** If $x = 4$, which of the following is greatest in value?

(A) $(x + 1)(x + 2)$
(B) $(x + 1)(x - 1)$
(C) $(x - 2)(x + 2)$
(D) $(x - 2)(x + 1)$
(E) $(x - 4)(x + 4)$

**2.** Trains $A$, $B$, and $C$ passed through a station at different speeds. Train $A$'s speed was 3 times Train $B$'s speed, and Train $C$'s speed was twice Train $A$'s. What was Train $C$'s speed, in miles per hour, if Train $B$'s speed was 7 miles per hour?

(A) 14
(B) 21
(C) 28
(D) 35
(E) 42

---

**GO ON TO THE NEXT PAGE**

**3.** If the average (arithmetic mean) of $x$, $5x$, and $6x$ is 8, what is the value of $x$?

(A) 1
(B) 2
(C) 3
(D) 4
(E) 5

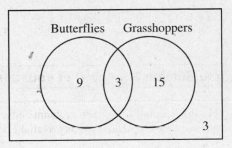

**5.** The Venn diagram above shows the distribution of 30 science students who studied butterflies, grasshoppers, both, or neither. What percent of the students studied butterflies only?

(A) 10%
(B) 20%
(C) 30%
(D) 40%
(E) 50%

No two points on the graph
have the same $x$-coordinate.

**4.** Which of the following graphs has the property stated above?

(A)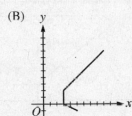

(B)

(C)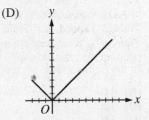

(D)

(E)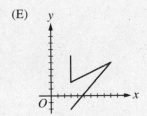

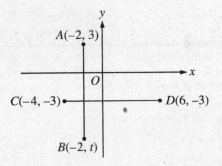

**6.** In the figure above, $AB = CD$. What is the value of $t$?

(A)  2
(B)  −2
(C)  −7
(D)  −10
(E)  −12

**GO ON TO THE NEXT PAGE**

7. If $3x^2 = 4y = 12$, what is the value of $x^2y$ ?

   (A) 48
   (B) 36
   (C) 24
   (D) 12
   (E) 6

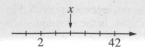

9. In the figure above, tick marks are equally spaced on the number line. What is the value of $x$ ?

   (A) 4
   (B) 6
   (C) 10
   (D) 18
   (E) 22

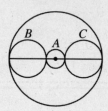

8. In the figure above, the circles are tangent as shown and the center of circle $A$ is also the center of the largest circle. If the radius of circle $A$ is 2, the radius of circle $B$ is 4, and the radius of circle $C$ is 4, what is the radius of the largest circle?

   (A) 4
   (B) 5
   (C) 6
   (D) 10
   (E) 20

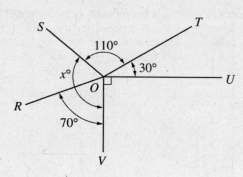

10. In the figure above, what is the value of $x$ ?

   (A) 110
   (B) 120
   (C) 130
   (D) 140
   (E) 150

**GO ON TO THE NEXT PAGE**

**11.** When the positive integer $k$ is divided by 7, the remainder is 6. What is the remainder when $k + 2$ is divided by 7 ?

(A) 0
(B) 1
(C) 2
(D) 3
(E) 4

| Depth (in feet) | Pressure (in psi) |
|-----------------|-------------------|
| 0 | 14.7 |
| 15 | 21.375 |
| 30 | 28.05 |
| 45 | 34.725 |

**12.** The chart above shows the pressure as a function of the depth for every 15 feet of descent into the ocean. If the pressure increases at a constant rate for every foot of descent, which of the following graphs describes the given data?

(A)
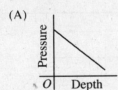

(B)
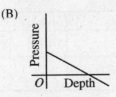

(C)
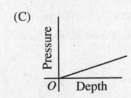

(D)
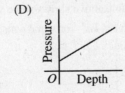

(E)
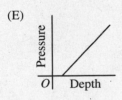

**13.** The first term of a sequence of numbers is 1. If each term after the first is the product of $-2$ and the preceding term, what is the sixth term of the sequence?

(A) 64
(B) 32
(C) 16
(D) $-16$
(E) $-32$

**14.** If $(2x - 5)(2x + 5) = 5$, what is the value of $4x^2$ ?

(A) $-30$
(B) $-20$
(C) 10
(D) 20
(E) 30

**GO ON TO THE NEXT PAGE**

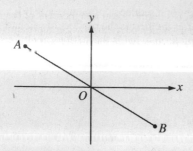

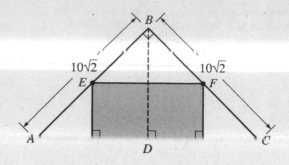

15. The coordinates of point $A$ in the figure above are $(p, r)$, where $|p| > |r|$. Which of the following could be the slope of $\overline{AB}$ ?

(A) $-2$

(B) $-\dfrac{1}{2}$

(C) $0$

(D) $\dfrac{2}{3}$

(E) $\dfrac{5}{2}$

17. In right triangle $ABC$ above, $\overline{EF} \parallel \overline{AC}$, and $F$ is the midpoint of $\overline{BC}$. What is the area of the shaded rectangular region?

(A) 25
(B) $25\sqrt{2}$
(C) 50
(D) $50\sqrt{2}$
(E) 100

16. If $3a + 4b = b$, which of the following must equal $6a + 6b$ ?

(A) 0
(B) 12
(C) $2b$
(D) $12b$
(E) $6b - 8$

| $x$ | $-1$ | $0$ | $1$ |
|-----|------|-----|-----|
| $f(x)$ | $\dfrac{1}{8}$ | $\dfrac{1}{2}$ | $2$ |

18. The table above shows some values for the function $f$. If $f(x) = ka^x$ for some constants $k$ and $a$, what is the value of $a$ ?

(A) $\dfrac{1}{2}$

(B) $\dfrac{1}{4}$

(C) $2$

(D) $4$

(E) $16$

GO ON TO THE NEXT PAGE

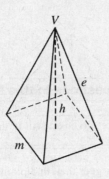

V

e

h

m

Note: Figure not drawn to scale.

19. The pyramid shown above has altitude $h$ and a square base of side $m$. The four edges that meet at $V$, the vertex of the pyramid, each have length $e$. If $e = m$, what is the value of $h$ in terms of $m$?

(A) $\dfrac{m}{\sqrt{2}}$

(B) $\dfrac{m\sqrt{3}}{2}$

(C) $m$

(D) $\dfrac{2m}{\sqrt{3}}$

(E) $m\sqrt{2}$

20. A salesperson's commission is $k$ percent of the selling price of a car. Which of the following represents the commission, in dollars, on 2 cars that sold for $14,000 each?

(A) $280k$

(B) $7,000k$

(C) $28,000k$

(D) $\dfrac{14,000}{100 + 2k}$

(E) $\dfrac{28,000 + k}{100}$

# STOP

**If you finish before time is called, you may check your work on this section only.**
**Do not turn to any other section in the test.**

## SECTION 5
### Time — 25 minutes
### 24 Questions

**Turn to Section 5 (page 5) of your answer sheet to answer the questions in this section.**

**Directions:** For each question in this section, select the best answer from among the choices given and fill in the corresponding circle on the answer sheet.

Each sentence below has one or two blanks, each blank indicating that something has been omitted. Beneath the sentence are five words or sets of words labeled A through E. Choose the word or set of words that, when inserted in the sentence, best fits the meaning of the sentence as a whole.

**Example:**

Hoping to ------- the dispute, negotiators proposed a compromise that they felt would be ------- to both labor and management.

(A) enforce . . useful
(B) end . . divisive
(C) overcome . . unattractive
(D) extend . . satisfactory
(E) resolve . . acceptable

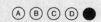

1. Known for her -------, Miranda eagerly welcomes anyone into her home.

   (A) cowardice  (B) prudence  (C) hospitality
   (D) aloofness  (E) loyalty

2. Not surprisingly, supporters of the governor's plan to set aside land for a forest preserve were disappointed when a court decision ------- the plan.

   (A) applauded  (B) derailed  (C) acknowledged
   (D) permitted  (E) anticipated

3. Because playing a musical instrument increases brain activity, it is sometimes used as a ------- to promote learning in children.

   (A) condition  (B) highlight  (C) stimulus
   (D) dictum  (E) respite

4. The ambassador argues that, in diplomacy, there is a subtle but important difference between a country's showing a willingness to ------- and a too-obvious readiness to make -------.

   (A) negotiate . . concessions
   (B) antagonize . . friends
   (C) surrender . . enemies
   (D) dominate . . inquiries
   (E) equivocate . . denunciations

5. The dancer's performing style was ------- and -------, with each move taken from another artist, and poorly executed at that.

   (A) rousing . . memorable
   (B) pedestrian . . evolving
   (C) chaotic . . unprecedented
   (D) derivative . . inept
   (E) spontaneous . . graceless

6. Lewis Latimer's inexpensive method of producing carbon filaments ------- the nascent electric industry by making electric lamps commercially -------.

   (A) cheapened . . affordable
   (B) transformed . . viable
   (C) revolutionized . . prohibitive
   (D) provoked . . improbable
   (E) stimulated . . inaccessible

7. After winning the award, Phillip adopted a haughty pose, treating even his best friends in a ------- manner.

   (A) cryptic  (B) judicious  (C) jubilant
   (D) supercilious  (E) pugnacious

8. The general was so widely suspected of ------- during the war that his name eventually became synonymous with disloyalty.

   (A) belligerence  (B) indigence  (C) perfidy
   (D) aspersion  (E) tenacity

**GO ON TO THE NEXT PAGE**

The passages below are followed by questions based on their content; questions following a pair of related passages may also be based on the relationship between the paired passages. Answer the questions on the basis of what is stated or implied in the passages and in any introductory material that may be provided.

**Questions 9-12 are based on the following passages.**

**Passage 1**

Foraging near the hut that he built himself, cultivating beans whose properties invited speculation, gazing into the depths of Walden Pond, Henry David Thoreau epitomizes
*Line* a long-standing American worship of nature. Generations
5 of teachers have assigned Thoreau's book *Walden* (1854), which recounts his experiment in living in solitary harmony with nature, as an illustration of the intensity with which nineteenth-century America protested the intrusion into pastoral harmony of the forces of industrialization and
10 urbanization. In this sense, *Walden* is revered as a text of regret, a lament for a world passing out of existence.

**Passage 2**

Although Thoreau, in *Walden*, was sometimes ambivalent about the mechanization that he saw around him, at other times he was downright enthusiastic, as in
15 his response to the railroad: "When I hear the iron horse make the hills echo with his snort like thunder, shaking the earth with his feet, and breathing fire and smoke from his nostrils, . . . it seems as if the earth had got a race now worthy to inhabit it." At Walden Pond, civilization and
20 industrialization no longer seemed threatening. Providing a full record of Thoreau's purposeful energy, *Walden* demonstrates that the power unleashed by the machine is not that different from the power required to transform the wilderness into a productive garden.

9. The author of Passage 2 and the "teachers" mentioned in line 5, Passage 1, would probably disagree regarding which of the following about *Walden* ?

(A) The extent to which *Walden* presents nature as being threatened
(B) The extent to which *Walden* successfully recounts Thoreau's experiment in solitary living
(C) The extent to which *Walden* has been considered an important work of literature
(D) Whether *Walden* recognizes the spread of industrialization and urbanization
(E) Whether the power of the machine was a topic central to *Walden*

10. Passage 1 suggests that Thoreau would most likely agree that the "power unleashed by the machine" (line 22, Passage 2) was

(A) kept in check by comparable forces in nature
(B) largely destructive of nature's tranquility
(C) exaggerated by those who did not seek out nature
(D) necessary to transform nature into something productive
(E) less threatening to one who lived close to nature

11. The author of Passage 1 would most likely argue that the enthusiasm referred to in line 14, Passage 2, is

(A) supportive of the idea that *Walden* expresses regret about industrialization
(B) a response that would have resonated with nineteenth-century Americans
(C) a characteristic of Thoreau's that is often emphasized by teachers
(D) an attitude that derives from Thoreau's experiment in solitary living
(E) atypical of Thoreau's perceived attitude toward mechanization

12. The author of Passage 1 would probably agree with which of the following statements about the interpretation of *Walden* offered in Passage 2 ?

(A) It exaggerates the destructive power of the machine.
(B) It is overly influenced by the long-standing American worship of nature.
(C) It is not representative of the way *Walden* is often taught in schools.
(D) It overlooks Thoreau's enthusiasm in *Walden* for the railroad.
(E) It is more in accord with the way *Walden* was generally understood in Thoreau's time than it is currently.

**GO ON TO THE NEXT PAGE**

**Questions 13-24 are based on the following passage.**

*This passage is adapted from a book published in 1994.*

As a scientist, I find that only one vision of the city really gets my hackles up—the notion that a city is somehow "unnatural," a blemish on the face of nature.

Line
5   The argument goes like this: Cities remove human beings from their natural place in the world. They are a manifestation of the urge to conquer nature rather than to live in harmony with it. Therefore, we should abandon both our cities and our technologies and return to an earlier, happier state of existence, one that presum-
10 ably would include many fewer human beings than now inhabit our planet.

There is an important hidden assumption behind this attitude, one that needs to be brought out and examined if only because it is so widely held today. This is the
15 assumption that nature, left to itself, will find a state of equilibrium (a "balance of nature") and that the correct role for humanity is to find a way to fit into that balance. If you think this way, you are likely to feel that all of human history since the Industrial (if not the Agricultural)
20 Revolution represents a wrong turning—a blind alley, something like the failed Soviet experiment in central planning. Cities, and particularly the explosive postwar growth of suburbs ("urban sprawl"), are agencies that destroy the balance of nature, and hence are evil presences
25 on the planet.

What bothers me about this point of view is that it implies that human beings, in some deep sense, are not part of nature. "Nature," to many environmental thinkers, is what happens when there are no people around. As soon
30 as we show up and start building towns and cities, "nature" stops and something infinitely less worthwhile starts.

It seems to me that we should begin our discussion of cities by recognizing that they aren't unnatural, any more than beaver dams or anthills are unnatural. Beavers, ants,
35 and human beings are all part of the web of life that exists on our planet. As part of their survival strategy, they alter their environments and build shelters. There is nothing "unnatural" about this.

Nor is there anything unnatural about downtown areas.
40 Yes, in the town the soil has been almost completely covered by concrete, buildings, and asphalt: often there is no grass or undisturbed soil to be seen anywhere. But this isn't really unnatural. There are plenty of places in nature where there is no soil at all—think of cliffsides in the
45 mountains or along the ocean. From our point of view, the building of Manhattan simply amounted to the exchange of a forest for a cliffside ecosystem.*

Look at the energy sources of the downtown ecosystem. There is, of course, sunlight to provide warmth. In addition,
50 there is a large amount of human-made detritus that can serve as food for animals: hamburger buns, apple cores,

and partially filled soft drink containers. All of these can and do serve as food sources. Indeed, urban yellow jackets seem to find sugar-rich soft drink cans an excellent source
55 of "nectar" for their honey—just notice them swarming around waste containers during the summer.

A glimpse of downtown, in fact, illustrates that the city can be thought of as a natural system on at least three different levels. At the most obvious level, although we
60 don't normally think in these terms, a city is an ecosystem, much as a salt marsh or a forest is. A city operates in pretty much the same way as any other ecosystem, with its own peculiar collection of flora and fauna. This way of looking at cities has recently received the ultimate academic
65 accolade—the creation of a subfield of science, called "urban ecology," devoted to understanding it.

At a somewhat deeper level, a natural ecosystem like a forest is a powerful metaphor to aid in understanding how cities work. Both systems grow and evolve, and both
70 require a larger environment to supply them with materials and to act as a receptacle for waste. Both require energy from outside sources to keep them functioning, and both have a life cycle—birth, maturity, and death.

Finally, our cities are like every other natural system
75 in that, at bottom, they operate according to a few well-defined laws of nature. There is, for example, a limit to how high a tree can grow, set by several factors including the kinds of forces that exist between atoms in wood. There is also a limit to how high a wood (or stone or steel)
80 building can be built—a limit that is influenced by those same interatomic forces.

So let me state this explicitly: *A city is a natural system, and we can study it in the same way we study other natural systems and how they got to be the way they are.*

\* An ecosystem is defined as all plants and animals that live in a place, along with their physical surroundings.

**13.** In line 1, "vision" most nearly means

(A) fantasy
(B) illusion
(C) prophecy
(D) conception
(E) apparition

**GO ON TO THE NEXT PAGE**

14. The author would most likely describe the "happier state" (line 9) as a

(A) satisfactory solution
(B) stroke of luck
(C) complicated arrangement
(D) false supposition
(E) bittersweet memory

15. According to the author, those who "think this way" (line 18) view the Industrial Revolution as

(A) an example of an important human achievement
(B) an instance of technology's double-edged potential
(C) an era when cities became successfully self-sufficient
(D) a time when social distinctions became easier to transcend
(E) the beginning of a harmful trend in human history

16. The author would most likely characterize the views of the "thinkers" referred to in line 28 as

(A) carefully reasoned
(B) thought-provoking
(C) unintelligible
(D) inconclusive
(E) erroneous

17. The author compares cities to beaver dams and anthills (lines 33-36) in order to

(A) explain how some ecological systems work
(B) suggest that all three are the products of natural impulses
(C) assert that all three are ultimately detrimental to nature
(D) point out that different species flourish in different environments
(E) call attention to particular obstacles facing cities today

18. The author's attitude toward the "downtown ecosystem" (line 48) is best described as one of

(A) regret
(B) frustration
(C) ambivalence
(D) unconcern
(E) appreciation

19. The three levels discussed in lines 57-81 ("A glimpse . . . forces") serve primarily to

(A) present several arguments in support of a fundamental claim
(B) organize the author's opinions from most to least important
(C) illustrate a process of reasoning from initial assertion to ultimate conclusion
(D) group hypotheses that address two opposing principles
(E) compare alternative theories proposed by the scientific community

20. In line 63, "peculiar" most nearly means

(A) eccentric
(B) abnormal
(C) rare
(D) distinctive
(E) significant

21. The author's attitude toward the "subfield" (line 65) is best characterized as one of

(A) approval
(B) curiosity
(C) uncertainty
(D) surprise
(E) dismay

22. The discussion of the forest ecosystem in lines 67-73 ("At a . . . death") is best characterized as

(A) a defense
(B) a concession
(C) a comparison
(D) an exception
(E) an allusion

**GO ON TO THE NEXT PAGE**

23. The discussion of limits in lines 74-81 suggests that

   (A) cities have the ability to change and grow
   (B) cities are often larger than they need to be
   (C) cities must be self-regulating in order to survive
   (D) human efforts to conquer nature tend to backfire
   (E) natural principles significantly affect human endeavors

24. The final paragraph primarily serves to

   (A) restate the elements of a dilemma
   (B) summarize the author's evidence
   (C) heighten an emotional impact
   (D) suggest a focus for further research
   (E) emphasize the author's position

## STOP

**If you finish before time is called, you may check your work on this section only.**
**Do not turn to any other section in the test.**

**SECTION 6**
Time — 25 minutes
35 Questions

**Turn to Section 6 (page 6) of your answer sheet to answer the questions in this section.**

**Directions:** For each question in this section, select the best answer from among the choices given and fill in the corresponding circle on the answer sheet.

The following sentences test correctness and effectiveness of expression. Part of each sentence or the entire sentence is underlined; beneath each sentence are five ways of phrasing the underlined material. Choice A repeats the original phrasing; the other four choices are different. If you think the original phrasing produces a better sentence than any of the alternatives, select choice A; if not, select one of the other choices.

In making your selection, follow the requirements of standard written English; that is, pay attention to grammar, choice of words, sentence construction, and punctuation. Your selection should result in the most effective sentence—clear and precise, without awkwardness or ambiguity.

EXAMPLE:

Laura Ingalls Wilder published her first book and she was sixty-five years old then.

(A) and she was sixty-five years old then
(B) when she was sixty-five
(C) at age sixty-five years old
(D) upon the reaching of sixty-five years
(E) at the time when she was sixty-five

1. A recent report indicates that sleep-deprived drivers caused more than 100,000 accidents last year, they fall asleep at the wheel.

   (A) year, they fall
   (B) year, and they fall
   (C) year by falling
   (D) year and falling
   (E) year, they were falling

2. The depths of the Arctic Ocean are hard to study, mainly because the icy surface is being difficult to penetrate using current techniques.

   (A) to study, mainly because the icy surface is being
   (B) to study as a result of the icy surface, mainly, is
   (C) to study, mainly because the icy surface is
   (D) studying, mainly from the icy surface being
   (E) studying, mainly resulting from the icy surface being

3. Several of the forest fires that occurred last summer which were because people are careless.

   (A) which were because people are careless
   (B) were caused by human carelessness
   (C) because people are careless
   (D) are because of human carelessness
   (E) happened from people being careless

4. Dr. Chien-Shiung Wu has disproved a widely accepted theory of physics when she showed that identical nuclear particles do not always act alike.

   (A) has disproved
   (B) having disproved
   (C) disproved
   (D) disproves
   (E) disproving

5. We generally think of Canada as the northern neighbor of the United States, and more than half of the states extend farther north than Canada's southernmost point.

   (A) States, and more than half of the states extend
   (B) States, and it is the case that more than half of the states extend
   (C) States, but more than half of the states extending
   (D) States, whereas more than half of the states are extending
   (E) States; however, more than half of the states extend

**GO ON TO THE NEXT PAGE**

**6.** The three volumes of memoirs by Wole Soyinka <u>begin with his childhood in a Nigerian village and culminate</u> with his years at the University of Ibadan, one of the best universities in West Africa.

 (A) begin with his childhood in a Nigerian village and culminate
 (B) that begin with his childhood in a Nigerian village and culminate
 (C) have begun with his childhood in a Nigerian village and culminating
 (D) beginning with his childhood in a Nigerian village and culminating
 (E) are begun as a child in a Nigerian village and culminate

**7.** <u>Dressed in a crisp, clean uniform, it reflected the efficient manner of the tour guide</u> as she distributed maps for a walking tour of central Canberra.

 (A) Dressed in a crisp, clean uniform, it reflected the efficient manner of the tour guide
 (B) Dressed in a crisp, clean uniform, the efficient manner of the tour guide was reflected
 (C) Dressed in a crisp, clean uniform that reflected the efficient manner of the tour guide
 (D) The crisp, clean uniform of the tour guide reflected her efficient manner
 (E) The crisp, clean uniform of the tour guide, a reflection of her efficient manner

**8.** A cure for some kinds of cancer, <u>scientists believe, may be</u> found within the next decade.

 (A) scientists believe, may be
 (B) scientists believe they may be
 (C) being maybe, in the belief of some scientists,
 (D) there are some scientists who believe it may be
 (E) which, some scientists believe, may be

**9.** A review of the composer's new symphony called it confusing because of its unusual <u>structure, and its melodious final movement makes it elegant</u>.

 (A) structure, and its melodious final movement makes it elegant
 (B) structure, although elegant by having its melodious final movement
 (C) structure, and it is elegant with its melodious final movement
 (D) structure while having a melodious final movement that made it elegant
 (E) structure but elegant because of its melodious final movement

**10.** <u>By building new windmill farms, consumption of fossil fuels are reduced, and tons of carbon dioxide emissions are kept</u> out of the atmosphere.

 (A) By building new windmill farms, consumption of fossil fuels are reduced, and tons of carbon dioxide emissions are kept
 (B) By building new windmill farms, it reduces consumption of fossil fuels, and tons of carbon dioxide emissions are kept
 (C) Building new windmill farms reduces fossil fuel consumption and keeps tons of carbon dioxide emissions
 (D) When new windmill farms are built, they reduce fossil fuel consumption, and it keeps tons of carbon dioxide emissions
 (E) New windmill farms, when built, reduce fossil fuel consumption, and also tons of carbon dioxide emissions are kept

**11.** The famous battle depicted in the film *Braveheart* took place in northern England, <u>and many people assume that it was</u> the Scottish Highlands.

 (A) and many people assume that it was
 (B) many people assuming
 (C) but many people assume it to be
 (D) not what many people assume
 (E) not, as many people assume, in

GO ON TO THE NEXT PAGE

The following sentences test your ability to recognize grammar and usage errors. Each sentence contains either a single error or no error at all. No sentence contains more than one error. The error, if there is one, is underlined and lettered. If the sentence contains an error, select the one underlined part that must be changed to make the sentence correct. If the sentence is correct, select choice E. In choosing answers, follow the requirements of standard written English.

EXAMPLE:

$\underset{\text{A}}{\underline{\text{The other}}}$ delegates and $\underset{\text{B}}{\underline{\text{him}}}$ $\underset{\text{C}}{\underline{\text{immediately}}}$
accepted the resolution $\underset{\text{D}}{\underline{\text{drafted by}}}$ the
neutral states. $\underset{\text{E}}{\underline{\text{No error}}}$

Ⓐ ● Ⓒ Ⓓ Ⓔ

**12.** Interested $\underset{\text{A}}{\underline{\text{in studying}}}$ insects and their effects
on agriculture, Larissa and Tariq plan $\underset{\text{B}}{\underline{\text{to become}}}$
$\underset{\text{C}}{\underline{\text{an entomologist}}}$ and then $\underset{\text{D}}{\underline{\text{return to help}}}$ the
farmers in their small town. $\underset{\text{E}}{\underline{\text{No error}}}$

**13.** $\underset{\text{A}}{\underline{\text{From}}}$ about A.D. 700 to 1600, sculptors $\underset{\text{B}}{\underline{\text{created}}}$
$\underset{\text{C}}{\underline{\text{nearly}}}$ 1,000 colossal rock statues on
the $\underset{\text{D}}{\underline{\text{remote}}}$ and tiny Easter Island. $\underset{\text{E}}{\underline{\text{No error}}}$

**14.** Because our casserole was smelling $\underset{\text{A}}{\underline{\text{surprisingly badly}}}$
as it baked, the food science teacher came over to ask
$\underset{\text{B}}{\underline{\text{us what}}}$ $\underset{\text{C}}{\underline{\text{we had put}}}$ $\underset{\text{D}}{\underline{\text{in it}}}$. $\underset{\text{E}}{\underline{\text{No error}}}$

**15.** Jerome often referred $\underset{\text{A}}{\underline{\text{to}}}$ art history textbooks
$\underset{\text{B}}{\underline{\text{while he}}}$ was sculpting; whenever he learned
a new method in art class, he $\underset{\text{C}}{\underline{\text{seeks out}}}$ the work
of sculptors who $\underset{\text{D}}{\underline{\text{had used it}}}$ in the past. $\underset{\text{E}}{\underline{\text{No error}}}$

**16.** As he $\underset{\text{A}}{\underline{\text{eagerly}}}$ awaited the interview $\underset{\text{B}}{\underline{\text{for}}}$ the job,
Miguel $\underset{\text{C}}{\underline{\text{thought it wise}}}$ $\underset{\text{D}}{\underline{\text{suppressing}}}$ his nervousness
and to display a calm he did not feel. $\underset{\text{E}}{\underline{\text{No error}}}$

**17.** $\underset{\text{A}}{\underline{\text{According to}}}$ educational statistics, the average
age of college students $\underset{\text{B}}{\underline{\text{has risen}}}$ $\underset{\text{C}}{\underline{\text{quite noticeable}}}$
$\underset{\text{D}}{\underline{\text{over the past}}}$ 25 years. $\underset{\text{E}}{\underline{\text{No error}}}$

**18.** Neither the koala bear $\underset{\text{A}}{\underline{\text{or}}}$ the red panda $\underset{\text{B}}{\underline{\text{belongs to}}}$ the
bear family; the koala is a marsupial, and the red panda
$\underset{\text{C}}{\underline{\text{is}}}$ thought to be $\underset{\text{D}}{\underline{\text{related to}}}$ the raccoon. $\underset{\text{E}}{\underline{\text{No error}}}$

**19.** Before $\underset{\text{A}}{\underline{\text{boarding}}}$, passengers $\underset{\text{B}}{\underline{\text{must purchase}}}$
$\underset{\text{C}}{\underline{\text{his or her}}}$ tickets in the main concourse of
the bus terminal $\underset{\text{D}}{\underline{\text{because}}}$ tickets are not sold
on the bus. $\underset{\text{E}}{\underline{\text{No error}}}$

**GO ON TO THE NEXT PAGE** ⟹

**20.** According to some demographers, the number of
       A

United States citizens aged 65 or older is likely
                   B    C

to rise to 87 million by 2050. No error
  D                    E

**21.** When they were asked to compare Norman
          A

Rockwell's paintings to painter Robert Rauschenberg,
            B

the students entered into a prolonged discussion
          C     D

about the representation of reality in art. No error
                     E

**22.** Contrary to what many people believe, heat lightning
     A

is not lightning caused by heat; it is ordinary lightning
  B

that occurs at too great a distance for its accompanying
         C

thunder to be audible. No error
      D      E

**23.** The grooved and barbed spears of the box jellyfish,

each trailed by a poison thread, is released when
 A    B          C    D

the animal is threatened. No error
           E

**24.** The derelict old house across from the warehouses
          A

and the even more decrepit one just beside them
     B         C

have been placed on the list of historic landmarks.
    D

No error
  E

**25.** As their brains mature neurologically , infants
  A         B

become more capable to distinguish the shapes and
          C

textures of the objects around them . No error
          D     E

**26.** Home of the world's largest chocolate-manufacturing
     A

plant, Hershey, Pennsylvania, was originally known as
               B

Derry Church, but its name was changed in 1906

to honor one of their most famous residents.
  C        D

No error
  E

**27.** The valuable stringed instruments in this display,
          A

all more than 300 years old, were carefully crafted
     B

by artisans famous in their day but long since
     C               D

forgotten. No error
      E

**28.** The regularly scheduled conference between my tutor
     A

and me is set for Friday, but my low grades in
    B  C

chemistry requires me to arrange an earlier meeting.
      D

No error
  E

**29.** There is probably no story more dramatic
  A    B         C

than baseball's great hitter and right fielder,
      D

Hank Aaron. No error
       E

**GO ON TO THE NEXT PAGE** ⟹

**Directions:** The following passage is an early draft of an essay. Some parts of the passage need to be rewritten.

Read the passage and select the best answers for the questions that follow. Some questions are about particular sentences or parts of sentences and ask you to improve sentence structure or word choice. Other questions ask you to consider organization and development. In choosing answers, follow the requirements of standard written English.

**Questions 30-35 refer to the following passage.**

(1) A castle is not the same thing as a palace, though some people use the terms "castle" and "palace" interchangeably. (2) Castles are fortified dwellings, built by feudal lords of the Middle Ages. (3) Their stone walls, moats, iron gates, and drawbridges were designed to ward off marauding plunderers and hostile armies. (4) Small windows in castle walls allowed archers to shoot at intruders from positions of comparative safety. (5) But even welcomed guests would have found castles less than inviting. (6) In royal palaces there were to be found many comforts that medieval castles did not offer. (7) These had dark dungeons and damp, drafty living quarters instead.

(8) Though castles were made obsolete by the invention of the cannon in the fourteenth century, many survive to the present day as fascinating relics of a bygone era. (9) These structures, which were designed to keep people at a distance, now attract visitors from all over the world. (10) There are scores of medieval castles located throughout Europe. (11) Some, like Eilean Donan Castle and the Château de Chambonneau, are well-maintained tourist attractions. (12) In one Welsh village, the decaying remnants of a castle sit beside cozy brick houses on an ordinary street.

30. Of the following, which would most improve the first paragraph (sentences 1-7) ?

(A) Providing a brief summary of medieval history
(B) Tracing the origin of the word "castle"
(C) Explaining more fully what a palace is
(D) Placing sentence 7 immediately after sentence 1
(E) Deleting sentence 3

31. Which of the following sentences, if inserted immediately after sentence 3, would most effectively link sentences 3 and 4 ?

(A) These walls were built by laborers known as "serfs."
(B) Drawbridges had been in use since ancient times.
(C) Those who defied such obstacles did so at their peril.
(D) Under feudalism, all land was considered property of the king.
(E) Still, not all visitors came with hostile intentions.

32. In context, which of the following is the best way to combine sentences 6 and 7 (reproduced below) ?

*In royal palaces there were to be found many comforts that medieval castles did not offer. These had dark dungeons and damp, drafty living quarters instead.*

(A) Because medieval castles had dark dungeons and damp, drafty living quarters, royal palaces offered many more comforts than could be found there.
(B) Lacking many comforts compared to royal palaces, medieval castles instead offered dark dungeons and damp, drafty living quarters.
(C) While medieval castles offered only dark dungeons and damp, drafty living quarters, many comforts were to be found in royal palaces.
(D) Unlike medieval castles, royal palaces offered many comforts not found in dark dungeons and damp, drafty living quarters.
(E) With their dark dungeons and damp, drafty living quarters, medieval castles offered few of the comforts to be found in royal palaces.

33. Which of the following would most appropriately be inserted at the beginning of sentence 9 ?

(A) Actually,
(B) Basically,
(C) Ironically,
(D) By contrast,
(E) In retrospect,

**GO ON TO THE NEXT PAGE**

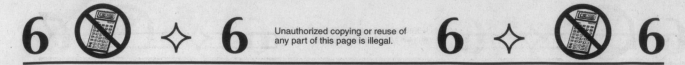
**34.** Which of the following sentences would best be inserted between sentences 11 and 12 ?

   (A) But not all castles can be considered obsolete.

   (B) Elsewhere, the environment may be a factor.

   (C) However, many travelers prefer to avoid such "tourist traps."

   (D) Others crumble away in relative obscurity.

   (E) Besides, appearances are often misleading.

**35.** Which of the following sentences would most effectively be placed after sentence 12 ?

   (A) In the final analysis, palaces are actually little more than luxurious castles.

   (B) There, medieval austerity stands in bold relief against a background of modern comfort.

   (C) The decline of the castle's importance as an architectural form coincided with the transformation of medieval society.

   (D) In the United States, imposing structures like Hearst's Castle are not really castles in the strictest sense of the word.

   (E) Eilean Donan Castle was named for a 7th-century saint who lived as a hermit in the Scottish Highlands.

# STOP

**If you finish before time is called, you may check your work on this section only.**
**Do not turn to any other section in the test.**

412

## SECTION 7
### Time — 25 minutes
### 18 Questions

**Turn to Section 7 (page 6) of your answer sheet to answer the questions in this section.**

**Directions:** This section contains two types of questions. You have 25 minutes to complete both types. For questions 1-8, solve each problem and decide which is the best of the choices given. Fill in the corresponding circle on the answer sheet. You may use any available space for scratchwork.

Notes

1. The use of a calculator is permitted.
2. All numbers used are real numbers.
3. Figures that accompany problems in this test are intended to provide information useful in solving the problems. They are drawn as accurately as possible EXCEPT when it is stated in a specific problem that the figure is not drawn to scale. All figures lie in a plane unless otherwise indicated.
4. Unless otherwise specified, the domain of any function $f$ is assumed to be the set of all real numbers $x$ for which $f(x)$ is a real number.

Reference Information

$A = \pi r^2$
$C = 2\pi r$

$A = \ell w$

$A = \frac{1}{2}bh$

$V = \ell w h$

$V = \pi r^2 h$

$c^2 = a^2 + b^2$

Special Right Triangles

The number of degrees of arc in a circle is 360.
The sum of the measures in degrees of the angles of a triangle is 180.

---

### NEW HOMES IN CITYVILLE

1961–1970 ⌂⌂
1971–1980 ⌂⌂⌂⌂
1981–1990 ⌂⌂⌂⌂⌂⌂⌂⌂
1991–2000 ⌂⌂⌂⌂⌂⌂⌂⌂⌂⌂⌂⌂⌂⌂

Each ⌂ represents 2,000 homes.

1. The pictogram above shows the number of new homes built in Cityville for each of four different time periods from 1961 through 2000. How many new homes were built from 1961 through 1990?

(A)    14
(B)    30
(C) 16,000
(D) 20,000
(E) 28,000

---

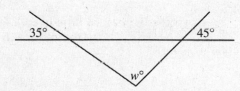

2. What is the value of $w$ in the figure above?

(A)    90
(B)   100
(C)   110
(D)   135
(E)   145

**GO ON TO THE NEXT PAGE**

3. A restaurant has 19 tables that can seat a total of
84 people. Some of the tables seat 4 people and the
others seat 5 people. How many tables seat 5 people?

(A) 4
(B) 5
(C) 6
(D) 7
(E) 8

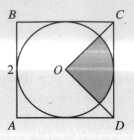

5. In the figure above, the circle with center $O$ is
inscribed in square $ABCD$. What is the area of the
shaded portion of the circle?

(A) $\dfrac{\pi}{4}$

(B) $\dfrac{\pi}{2}$

(C) $\pi$

(D) $\dfrac{3\pi}{2}$

(E) $2\pi$

4. If $a = 4$, which of the following is equivalent to
$am^2 + am + a$ ?

(A) $4(m^3 + 1)$
(B) $4(m + 1)^2$
(C) $4(m^2 + m)$
(D) $4(m^2 + m + 1)$
(E) $4(4m^2 + m + 1)$

GO ON TO THE NEXT PAGE

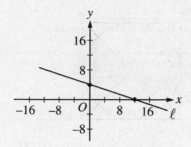

**6.** In the $xy$-plane above, the equation of line $\ell$ is $x + 3y = 12$. Which of the following is an equation of a line that is perpendicular to line $\ell$ ?

(A)  $y = x + 2$

(B)  $y = -3x + 2$

(C)  $y = 3x - 6$

(D)  $y = \dfrac{1}{3}x + 6$

(E)  $y = -\dfrac{1}{2}x - 3$

**7.** Two sides of a triangle each have length 5. All of the following could be the length of the third side EXCEPT

(A)  1
(B)  3
(C)  4
(D)  $\sqrt{50}$ (approximately 7.07)
(E)  10

**8.** In an election, 2.8 million votes were cast and each vote was for either Candidate I or Candidate II. Candidate I received 28,000 more votes than Candidate II. What percent of the 2.8 million votes were cast for Candidate I ?

(A)  50.05%
(B)  50.1%
(C)  50.5%
(D)  51%
(E)  55%

**GO ON TO THE NEXT PAGE**

**Directions:** For Student-Produced Response questions 9-18, use the grids at the bottom of the answer sheet page on which you have answered questions 1-8.

Each of the remaining 10 questions requires you to solve the problem and enter your answer by marking the circles in the special grid, as shown in the examples below. You may use any available space for scratchwork.

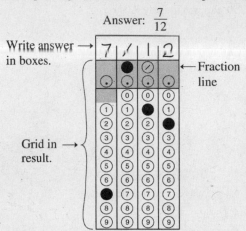

Answer: $\frac{7}{12}$      Answer: 2.5      Answer: 201
Either position is correct.

Write answer → in boxes.    ← Fraction line

← Decimal point

Grid in → result.

**Note:** You may start your answers in any column, space permitting. Columns not needed should be left blank.

- Mark no more than one circle in any column.

- Because the answer sheet will be machine-scored, **you will receive credit only if the circles are filled in correctly.**

- Although not required, it is suggested that you write your answer in the boxes at the top of the columns to help you fill in the circles accurately.

- Some problems may have more than one correct answer. In such cases, grid only one answer.

- No question has a negative answer.

- **Mixed numbers** such as $3\frac{1}{2}$ must be gridded as

  3.5 or 7/2. (If 3|1|/|2 is gridded, it will be

  interpreted as $\frac{31}{2}$, not $3\frac{1}{2}$.)

- **Decimal Answers:** If you obtain a decimal answer with more digits than the grid can accommodate, it may be either rounded or truncated, but it must fill the entire grid. For example, if you obtain an answer such as 0.6666..., you should record your result as .666 or .667. **A less accurate value such as .66 or .67 will be scored as incorrect.**

Acceptable ways to grid $\frac{2}{3}$ are:

---

**9.** If $\sqrt{2p} = \sqrt{18}$, what is the value of $p$ ?

**10.** When 1.783 is rounded to the nearest whole number, the result is how much greater than when 1.783 is rounded to the nearest tenth?

GO ON TO THE NEXT PAGE →

**7**

Unauthorized copying or reuse of
any part of this page is illegal.

**7**

**11.** Samantha is packing for a trip. Of the towels in the closet, 6 are brown. She will randomly pick one of the towels to pack. If the probability is $\frac{2}{5}$ that the towel she will pick is brown, how many towels are in the closet?

**12.** Five different points $A$, $B$, $C$, $D$, and $E$ lie on a line in that order. The length of $\overline{AD}$ is 4.5 and the length of $\overline{BE}$ is 3.5. If the length of $\overline{CD}$ is 2, what is one possible value for the length of $\overline{BC}$?

**13.** In the 30-day month of April, for every three days it rained, there were two days it did not rain. The number of days in April on which it rained was how much greater than the number of days on which it did not rain?

**14.** Each term of a certain sequence is greater than the term before it. The difference between any two consecutive terms in the sequence is always the same number. If the third and sixth terms of the sequence are 17 and 77, respectively, what is the eighth term?

**GO ON TO THE NEXT PAGE**

$$|x - 3| = \frac{1}{2}$$

**15.** What is the least value of $x$ that satisfies the equation above?

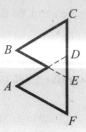

Note: Figure not drawn to scale.

**17.** The flag shown above is made of overlapping equilateral triangles $ADF$ and $BCE$. Because ribbon is to be sewn around the entire outer edge, it is necessary to know the perimeter of the flag. If $\overline{CD}$, $\overline{DE}$, and $\overline{EF}$ each have length 10 inches, what is the length, in inches, of the perimeter shown in bold?

**16.** A four-digit integer, $WXYZ$, in which $W$, $X$, $Y$, and $Z$ each represent a different digit, is formed according to the following rules.

1. $X = W + Y + Z$
2. $W = Y + 1$
3. $Z = W - 5$

What is the four-digit integer?

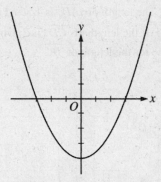

**18.** The graph above shows the function $g$, where $g(x) = k(x + 3)(x - 3)$ for some constant $k$. If $g(a - 1.2) = 0$ and $a > 0$, what is the value of $a$?

# STOP

**If you finish before time is called, you may check your work on this section only.**
**Do not turn to any other section in the test.**

## SECTION 8

Time — 20 minutes
16 Questions

**Turn to Section 8 (page 7) of your answer sheet to answer the questions in this section.**

**Directions:** For this section, solve each problem and decide which is the best of the choices given. Fill in the corresponding circle on the answer sheet. You may use any available space for scratchwork.

Notes

1. The use of a calculator is permitted.
2. All numbers used are real numbers.
3. Figures that accompany problems in this test are intended to provide information useful in solving the problems. They are drawn as accurately as possible EXCEPT when it is stated in a specific problem that the figure is not drawn to scale. All figures lie in a plane unless otherwise indicated.
4. Unless otherwise specified, the domain of any function $f$ is assumed to be the set of all real numbers $x$ for which $f(x)$ is a real number.

Reference Information

$A = \pi r^2$
$C = 2\pi r$

$A = \ell w$

$A = \frac{1}{2}bh$

$V = \ell w h$

$V = \pi r^2 h$

$c^2 = a^2 + b^2$

Special Right Triangles

The number of degrees of arc in a circle is 360.
The sum of the measures in degrees of the angles of a triangle is 180.

ART AWARDS

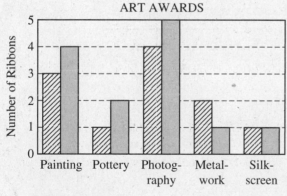

▨ Prize Ribbons

▨ Honorable Mention Ribbons

1. According to the chart above, how many honorable mention ribbons were awarded altogether?

(A) 5
(B) 8
(C) 11
(D) 13
(E) 24

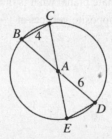

2. In the figure above, point $A$ is the center of the circle and segments $\overline{BD}$ and $\overline{CE}$ are diameters. Which of the following statements is true?

(A) $CA > 6$
(B) $ED > 4$
(C) $BA < 4$
(D) $CA = 4$
(E) $ED = 4$

**GO ON TO THE NEXT PAGE** ⇨

3. For positive integers $a$, $b$, and $c$, let $\begin{array}{|c|}\hline a \\ \hline b \\ \hline c \\ \hline\end{array}$ be defined

   by $\begin{array}{|c|}\hline a \\ \hline b \\ \hline c \\ \hline\end{array} = a^b - ac + c$. What is the value of $\begin{array}{|c|}\hline 5 \\ \hline 2 \\ \hline 6 \\ \hline\end{array}$ ?

   (A)   1
   (B)   11
   (C)   16
   (D)   21
   (E)   31

4. In the $xy$-coordinate plane, what is the area of
   the square with opposite vertices at $(-2, -2)$
   and $(2, 2)$ ?

   (A)   4
   (B)   8
   (C)   16
   (D)   32
   (E)   64

5. The four children in the Speer family are Owen,
   Chadd, Steph, and Daria. Chadd is neither the youngest
   nor the oldest. Daria is one of the two older children.
   Steph is the youngest child. Owen is often taken care
   of by his older brother and sister. Who is the oldest
   child?

   (A)   Chadd
   (B)   Daria
   (C)   Owen
   (D)   Steph
   (E)   It cannot be determined from the information
          given.

**GO ON TO THE NEXT PAGE**

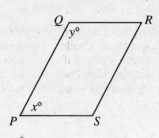

6. If $\overline{QR} \parallel \overline{PS}$ in the figure above, what is the value of $2(x + y)$?

(A) 90
(B) 120
(C) 180
(D) 270
(E) 360

7. The average (arithmetic mean) of three positive numbers, $x$, $y$, and $z$, is 12. When the greatest of these numbers is subtracted from the sum of the other two, the result is 4. If $x < y < z$, which of the following pairs of equations could correctly express the information above?

(A) $x + y + z = 36$
   $x + y - z = 4$

(B) $x + y + z = 36$
   $x + y - z = 8$

(C) $x + y + z = 24$
   $x + y - z = 4$

(D) $x + y + z = 24$
   $x + y - z = 8$

(E) $x + y + z = 36$
   $xy - z = 4$

**GO ON TO THE NEXT PAGE**

8. If $x$ and $y$ are positive integers and $3^{2x} \cdot 3^{2y} = 81$, what is the value of $x + y$?

(A) $\dfrac{3}{2}$

(B) 2

(C) 4

(D) $\dfrac{81}{2}$

(E) 81

10. If $k = \dfrac{x}{3}$ and $x \neq 0$, what does $3x$ equal in terms of $k$?

(A) $k$

(B) $9k$

(C) $\dfrac{9}{k}$

(D) $\dfrac{k}{9}$

(E) $\dfrac{k}{3}$

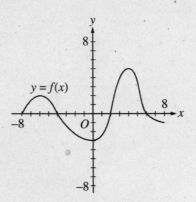

9. The figure above shows the graph of $y = f(x)$ from $x = -8$ to $x = 8$. For what value of $x$ in this interval does the function $f$ attain its maximum value?

(A) 2
(B) 4
(C) 5
(D) 6
(E) 8

**GO ON TO THE NEXT PAGE**

**11.** A cube has 2 faces painted black and the remaining faces painted white. The total area of the white faces is 64 square inches. What is the volume of the cube, in cubic inches?

(A) 64
(B) 125
(C) 128
(D) 216
(E) 256

**12.** The letters $v$, $w$, $x$, and $y$ represent numbers as shown on the number line above. Which of the following expressions has the least value?

(A) $v + y$
(B) $v + x$
(C) $w + x$
(D) $v - w$
(E) $y - x$

3, 4, 6, 7, 10, 12

**13.** The number $n$ is to be added to the list above. If $n$ is an integer, which of the following could be the median of the new list of seven numbers?

I. 6

II. $6\frac{1}{2}$

III. 7

(A) I only
(B) II only
(C) III only
(D) I and III only
(E) I, II, and III

**GO ON TO THE NEXT PAGE**

423

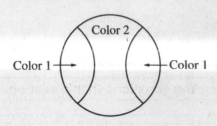

14. As shown above, a certain design is to be painted using 2 different colors. If 5 different colors are available for the design, how many differently painted designs are possible?

(A) 10
(B) 20
(C) 25
(D) 60
(E) 120

15. If the length of a rectangle is increased by 30% and the width of the same rectangle is decreased by 30%, what is the effect on the area of the rectangle?

(A) It is increased by 60%.
(B) It is increased by 30%.
(C) It is unchanged.
(D) It is decreased by 15%.
(E) It is decreased by 9%.

$$n(t) = \frac{t^2}{2} - 20t + k$$

16. There was a 100-day period when the number of bees in a certain hive could be modeled by the function $n$ above. In the function, $k$ is a constant and $n(t)$ represents the number of bees on day number $t$ for $0 \le t \le 99$. On what number day was the number of bees in the hive the same as it was on day number 10 ?

(A) 20
(B) 30
(C) 40
(D) 50
(E) 60

**STOP**

If you finish before time is called, you may check your work on this section only.
Do not turn to any other section in the test.

## SECTION 9
### Time — 20 minutes
### 19 Questions

**Turn to Section 9 (page 7) of your answer sheet to answer the questions in this section.**

**Directions:** For each question in this section, select the best answer from among the choices given and fill in the corresponding circle on the answer sheet.

Each sentence below has one or two blanks, each blank indicating that something has been omitted. Beneath the sentence are five words or sets of words labeled A through E. Choose the word or set of words that, when inserted in the sentence, <u>best</u> fits the meaning of the sentence as a whole.

**Example:**

Hoping to ------- the dispute, negotiators proposed a compromise that they felt would be ------- to both labor and management.

(A) enforce . . useful
(B) end . . divisive
(C) overcome . . unattractive
(D) extend . . satisfactory
(E) resolve . . acceptable

(A) (B) (C) (D) ●

1. The prose of Richard Wright's autobiographical *Black Boy* (1945) is -------, free of stylistic tricks or evasiveness.

   (A) imprecise   (B) straightforward   (C) deficient
   (D) obtrusive   (E) elliptical

2. It seemed from the size of the crowd, which was -------, and the resonance of its cheers, which were -------, that the team was experiencing a resurgence of popularity.

   (A) vast . . hollow
   (B) sparse . . thunderous
   (C) enormous . . deafening
   (D) unimpressive . . muted
   (E) negligible . . rousing

3. Evidence that the universe is expanding ------- our perception of the cosmos and thus caused a ------- in astronomical thinking.

   (A) advanced . . setback
   (B) altered . . revolution
   (C) contradicted . . truce
   (D) reinforced . . crisis
   (E) halted . . breakthrough

4. Although the theory that widespread lead poisoning contributed to the decline of the Roman Empire has gained -------, the evidence is still -------.

   (A) credence . . irrefutable
   (B) disrepute . . dubious
   (C) acceptance . . convincing
   (D) momentum . . systematic
   (E) currency . . inconclusive

5. The fashion designer favored fabrics that were so ------- as to be virtually transparent.

   (A) palpable   (B) diaphanous   (C) variegated
   (D) luxurious   (E) anomalous

6. Professor Williams disdained tradition: she regularly attacked cherished beliefs and institutions, earning a reputation as -------.

   (A) an egalitarian   (B) a dowager
   (C) a dilettante   (D) an iconoclast
   (E) a purveyor

**GO ON TO THE NEXT PAGE**

The passage below is followed by questions based on its content. Answer the questions on the basis of what is <u>stated</u> or <u>implied</u> in the passage and in any introductory material that may be provided.

**Questions 7-19 are based on the following passage.**

*This passage, taken from an early nineteenth-century novel, presents two characters—Shirley Keeldar, a young woman of twenty-one who has inherited a fortune and land in Yorkshire, England, and Mr. Sympson, the uncle who was her guardian until she reached adulthood.*

Miss Keeldar and her uncle had characters that would not harmonize,—that never had harmonized. He was irritable, and she was spirited; he was despotic,
Line and she liked freedom; he was worldly, and she, perhaps,
5 romantic.

Not without purpose had he come down to Yorkshire: his mission was clear, and he intended to discharge it conscientiously: he anxiously desired to have his niece married; to make for her a suitable match; give her in
10 charge to a proper husband, and wash his hands of her for ever.

The misfortune was, from infancy upwards, Shirley and he had disagreed on the meaning of the words "suitable" and "proper." She never yet had accepted
15 his definition; and it was doubtful whether, in the most important step of her life, she would consent to accept it.

The trial soon came.

Mr. Wynne announced to Mr. Sympson that his family wished to arrange a marriage between his son, Samuel
20 Fawthrop Wynne, and Miss Keeldar.

"Decidedly suitable! Most proper!" pronounced Mr. Sympson. "A fine unencumbered estate; real substance; good connections. *It must be done*!"

He sent for his niece to the oak-parlor; he shut
25 himself up there with her alone; he communicated the offer; he gave his opinion; he claimed her consent.

It was withheld.

"No: I shall not marry Samuel Fawthrop Wynne."

"I ask why? I must have a reason. In all respects
30 he is more than worthy of you."

She stood on the hearth; she was pale as the white marble slab and cornice behind her; her eyes flashed large, dilated, unsmiling.

"And *I* ask in what sense that young man is worthy
35 of *me*?"

"He has twice your money,—twice your common sense;—equal connections,—equal respectability."

"Had he my money counted five score times, I would take no vow to love him."

40 "Please to state your objections."

"He has run a course of despicable, commonplace profligacy. Accept that as the first reason why I spurn him."

"Miss Keeldar, you shock me!"

45 "That conduct alone sinks him in a gulf of immeasurable inferiority. His intellect reaches no standard I can esteem:—there is a second stumbling block. His views are narrow; his feelings are blunt; his tastes are coarse; his manners vulgar."

50 "The man is a respectable, wealthy man. To refuse him is presumption on your part."

"I refuse, point-blank! Cease to annoy me with the subject: I forbid it!"

"Is it your intention ever to marry, or do you prefer
55 celibacy?"

"I deny your right to claim an answer to that question."

"May I ask if you expect some man of title—some peer of the realm—to demand your hand?"

"I doubt if the peer breathes on whom I would
60 confer it."

"Were there insanity in the family, I should believe you mad. Your eccentricity and conceit touch the verge of frenzy."

"Perhaps, ere I have finished, you will see me over-
65 leap it."

"I anticipate no less. Frantic and impracticable girl! Take warning! I dare you to sully our name by a misalliance!"

"*Our* name! Am *I* called Sympson?"

70 "God be thanked that you are not! But be on your guard!—I will not be trifled with!"

"What, in the name of common law and common sense, would you, or could you do, if my pleasure led me to a choice you disapprove?"

75 "Take care! take care!" (warning her with voice and hand that trembled alike.)

"Why? What shadow of power have *you* over me? Why should I fear you?"

"Take care, madam!"

80 "Scrupulous care I will take, Mr. Sympson. Before I marry, I am resolved to esteem—to admire—to *love*."

**GO ON TO THE NEXT PAGE**

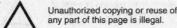  
"Preposterous stuff! indecorous! unwomanly!"

"To love with my whole heart. I know I speak
85 in an unknown tongue; but I feel indifferent whether
I am comprehended or not."

"And if this love of yours should fall on a beggar?"

"On a beggar it will never fall. Mendicancy is
not estimable."

90 "On a low clerk, a play-actor, a play-writer,
or—or—"

"Take courage, Mr. Sympson! Or what?"

"Any literary scrub, or shabby, whining artist."

"For the scrubby, shabby, whining, I have no taste:
95 for literature and the arts, I have. And there I wonder
how your Fawthrop Wynne would suit me? He cannot write a note without orthographical errors; he
reads only a sporting paper; he was the booby of
Stilbro' grammar school!"

100 "Unladylike language! To what will she come?"
He lifted hands and eyes toward the heavens.

"Never to the altar with Sam Wynne."

"To what will she come? Why are not the laws
more stringent, that I might compel her to hear reason?"

105 "Console yourself, uncle. Were Britain a serfdom,
and you the czar, you could not *compel* me to this
step. *I* will write to Mr. Wynne. Give yourself no
further trouble on the subject."

**7.** The episode presented in the passage is best
described as a

(A) setback in an otherwise warm family
relationship

(B) disappointment experienced by a young
and ambitious woman

(C) confrontation between people whose
differences seem irreconcilable

(D) collaboration between two individuals
whose goals are similar

(E) conversation about the need for unity
within an extended family

**8.** In context, the contrasts in lines 3-5 suggest that
Miss Keeldar is "perhaps, romantic" in that she

(A) seems attractive and mysterious to others

(B) is overly concerned with finding a good
husband

(C) has passionate and unconventional ideas
about life

(D) prefers to read books and poetry about love

(E) is the subject of fancifully exaggerated stories

**9.** The list in lines 8-11 ("he anxiously . . . ever")
suggests that Mr. Sympson is primarily motivated by

(A) anticipation of a project on which he
and his niece can collaborate

(B) eagerness to help his niece realize her
ambitious goals

(C) apprehension about his family's tarnished
reputation

(D) frustration with the limited opportunities
available to his niece

(E) impatience to free himself of a perceived
family responsibility

**10.** Mr. Sympson's comments in lines 22-23 ("A fine . . .
connections") indicate that a marriage is suitable
when it

(A) meets the emotional needs of both partners

(B) promises to benefit the local community

(C) has the approval of all family members

(D) involves formal ceremonies and celebrations

(E) brings social and financial advantages

**11.** Miss Keeldar's first objection to Mr. Wynne
(lines 41-43) is that he

(A) wastes his time in reckless, undignified
pursuits

(B) expresses no regret for damage caused
by his actions

(C) fails to treat others with the respect they
deserve

(D) is dependent on his family for financial
support

(E) lacks the imagination and sensitivity
of an artist

**12.** Miss Keeldar responds to the question posed
in lines 54-55 by doing which of the following?

(A) Denying the accusation that she is secretly
engaged

(B) Challenging the idea that she must address
the question

(C) Correcting the exaggerations implicit in the
question

(D) Contradicting her earlier claim of complete
independence

(E) Asserting her right to live without marrying

**GO ON TO THE NEXT PAGE**

13. The passage as a whole suggests that the implied threat in lines 70-71 ("But be . . . with") is,

   (A) implausible, because Miss Keeldar can outwit Mr. Sympson
   (B) serious, because Miss Keeldar's decisions must be approved by Mr. Sympson
   (C) misleading, because Mr. Sympson is genuinely concerned about Miss Keeldar's happiness
   (D) baseless, because Mr. Sympson has no real power over Miss Keeldar
   (E) absurd, because Miss Keeldar herself is trying to intimidate Mr. Sympson

14. In lines 80-82 ("Scrupulous . . . *love*"), Miss Keeldar deflects the warning from Mr. Sympson by

   (A) deliberately misunderstanding his meaning
   (B) scornfully turning the blame back on him
   (C) childishly mocking the tone of his comment
   (D) lamenting his failure to sympathize with her
   (E) justifying her previously sensible behavior

15. Miss Keeldar uses the expression "an unknown tongue" (line 85) to suggest that Mr. Sympson is

   (A) mistrustful of anything new and unfamiliar
   (B) ignorant of Wynne's reputation in the community
   (C) inclined to speak in an obscure manner
   (D) incapable of understanding her sentiments
   (E) unwilling to acknowledge their family's mistakes

16. Mr. Sympson poses the question in line 100 ("To . . . come") as a

   (A) warning about financial losses
   (B) prediction of a bleak future
   (C) confession of his own relief
   (D) plea for an unexpected diversion
   (E) condemnation of conventional lifestyles

17. Miss Keeldar responds to the question in line 100 ("To . . . come") as if it were an

   (A) unreasonable request for an explanation
   (B) appeal to her sense of fair play
   (C) inquiry about her future course of action
   (D) expression of moral uncertainty
   (E) attempt to understand her family's history

18. Her remarks to Mr. Sympson indicate that Miss Keeldar views love as a

   (A) natural consequence of prolonged companionship
   (B) crucial prerequisite for a satisfactory marriage
   (C) desirable element in an independent woman's daily life
   (D) fortunate accident that sometimes results from marriage
   (E) sentimental delusion that is potentially harmful

19. Miss Keeldar and Mr. Sympson would most likely agree on which point?

   (A) She must seek marriage with an aristocratic man.
   (B) She should feel honored by the attentions of the Wynne family.
   (C) She needs to become more mature before she marries.
   (D) She must not act against her most deeply held beliefs.
   (E) She should not marry a man who is both poor and undignified.

# STOP

**If you finish before time is called, you may check your work on this section only.**
**Do not turn to any other section in the test.**

10  10

Unauthorized copying or reuse of
any part of this page is illegal.

## SECTION 10
Time — 10 minutes
14 Questions

**Turn to Section 10 (page 7) of your answer sheet to answer the questions in this section.**

**Directions:** For each question in this section, select the best answer from among the choices given and fill in the corresponding circle on the answer sheet.

The following sentences test correctness and effectiveness of expression. Part of each sentence or the entire sentence is underlined; beneath each sentence are five ways of phrasing the underlined material. Choice A repeats the original phrasing; the other four choices are different. If you think the original phrasing produces a better sentence than any of the alternatives, select choice A; if not, select one of the other choices.

In making your selection, follow the requirements of standard written English; that is, pay attention to grammar, choice of words, sentence construction, and punctuation. Your selection should result in the most effective sentence—clear and precise, without awkwardness or ambiguity.

EXAMPLE:

Laura Ingalls Wilder published her first book and she was sixty-five years old then.

(A) and she was sixty-five years old then
(B) when she was sixty-five
(C) at age sixty-five years old
(D) upon the reaching of sixty-five years
(E) at the time when she was sixty-five

1. There <u>is many challenges associated</u> with starting one's own business.

(A) is many challenges associated
(B) is many challenges to associate
(C) is many challenges associating
(D) are many challenges associated
(E) are many challenges which associate

2. The watercolors <u>it has on display by the museum represent the era when</u> Japan's emergence from feudalism and isolation inspired its artists to explore new themes and techniques.

(A) it has on display by the museum represent the era when
(B) that it, the museum, is displaying represents the era of
(C) on display at the museum represent the era when
(D) displayed at the museum representing the era when
(E) being displayed at the museum represents the era while

3. The origins of the Teapot Dome scandal <u>can be traced to the presidency of</u> Theodore Roosevelt, William Howard Taft, and Woodrow Wilson.

(A) can be traced to the presidency of
(B) can be traced to the presidencies of
(C) happened in the presidency of
(D) happening during the presidencies of
(E) that happened in the presidency of

4. When Sheila and Lucy visited the restaurant, <u>she noticed that the menu had changed</u> and that their favorite dish was no longer offered.

(A) she noticed that the menu had changed
(B) she notices that the menu has changed
(C) Sheila has noticed the menu changed
(D) Sheila had noticed the menu changing
(E) Sheila noticed that the menu had changed

**GO ON TO THE NEXT PAGE**

5. Carried by the strong, dry winds of the stratosphere, the 1980 eruption of Mount Saint Helens caused dust that crossed the United States in three days and circled the globe in two weeks.

   (A) the 1980 eruption of Mount Saint Helens caused dust that
   (B) Mount Saint Helens' eruption in 1980 caused dust that
   (C) dust from the 1980 eruption of Mount Saint Helens
   (D) dust from the 1980 eruption of Mount Saint Helens that
   (E) there was dust from the 1980 eruption of Mount Saint Helens and it

6. The new regulations have so complicated the process of formulating a school budget to where no one on the Board of Education is eager to undertake the task.

   (A) budget to where
   (B) budget, therefore
   (C) budget, even
   (D) budget as
   (E) budget that

7. The shift from traditional to cosmetic dentistry is because adults are getting fewer cavities and becoming more vain.

   (A) is because adults are getting fewer cavities and becoming
   (B) is because of adults getting fewer cavities and their becoming
   (C) is caused from adults getting fewer cavities and in addition become
   (D) is occurring because adults are getting fewer cavities and becoming
   (E) occurs because of adults getting fewer cavities and become

8. If asked to name a musical group with broad and lasting appeal, the Beatles would be the choice for many, no matter what kinds of music are actually preferred.

   (A) the Beatles would be the choice for many, no matter what kinds of music are actually preferred
   (B) the Beatles will be chosen by many people, no matter what kinds of music they actually prefer
   (C) the choice for many people, whatever kinds of music they actually prefer, would be the Beatles
   (D) many, who actually preferred different kinds of music, choose the Beatles
   (E) many people, no matter what kinds of music they actually prefer, would choose the Beatles

9. In 1972, to reduce pollution in the Great Lakes, limits having been set by the United States and Canada on the amount of phosphorus that could be discharged into Lakes Erie and Ontario.

   (A) limits having been set by the United States and Canada
   (B) limits set by the United States and Canada
   (C) limits have been set by the United States and Canada
   (D) the United States and Canada have set limits
   (E) the United States and Canada set limits

10. Ruben Blades, already certified as a lawyer in his native country of Panama, supported himself by singing salsa while pursuing an advanced degree in international law at Harvard University.

    (A) Blades, already certified as a lawyer
    (B) Blades, already being a certified lawyer
    (C) Blades, already certified for being a lawyer
    (D) Blades was already certified as a lawyer
    (E) Blades is certified as a lawyer already

**GO ON TO THE NEXT PAGE**

11. The newspaper business in the United States faces a <u>challenge, being that it must reconcile the high-minded goal of informing readers with the commercial one of making money</u>.

   (A) challenge, being that it must reconcile the high-minded goal of informing readers with the commercial one of making money
   (B) challenge of it reconciling the high-minded goal of informing readers with the commercial one of making money
   (C) challenge; as such it must reconcile the high-minded goal of informing readers with the commercial one of making money
   (D) challenge because it must reconcile the high-minded goal of informing readers with the commercial one of making money
   (E) challenge; since it has the high-minded goal of informing readers with the commercial one of making money being reconciled

12. All species of sea turtles are endangered because <u>of overharvesting of adults, their eggs being disturbed, and destruction of nesting habitats</u>.

   (A) of overharvesting of adults, their eggs being disturbed, and destruction of nesting habitats
   (B) of the adults being overharvested, their eggs disturbed, and destroying nesting habitats
   (C) the overharvesting of adults, disturbance of their eggs, and destruction of nesting habitats
   (D) the adults are overharvested, their eggs are disturbed, and their nesting habitats are destroyed
   (E) being overharvested as adults, their eggs being disturbed, and destruction of nesting habitats

13. Although the exact cause of type 2 diabetes is unknown, experts say that for some people improper diet and lack of <u>exercise contributes</u> to the onset of the disease.

   (A) exercise contributes
   (B) exercise, they contribute
   (C) exercise contribute
   (D) exercise, contributing
   (E) exercise has been contributing

14. Acquaintances of Alexei have commented that he is at once annoying because of his unpredictability <u>but his imagination is still a delight</u>.

   (A) but his imagination is still a delight
   (B) although he is delightfully imaginative
   (C) and he is delightful in his imagination too
   (D) while being imaginative and they are delighted
   (E) and delightful because of his imagination

# STOP

**If you finish before time is called, you may check your work on this section only.**
**Do not turn to any other section in the test.**

# Correct Answers and Difficulty Levels
## SAT Practice Test #1

## Critical Reading

### Section 2

| COR. ANS. | DIFF. LEV. | COR. ANS. | DIFF. LEV. |
|---|---|---|---|
| 1. A | 1 | 13. E | 4 |
| 2. B | 3 | 14. E | 2 |
| 3. A | 5 | 15. B | 5 |
| 4. D | 4 | 16. C | 2 |
| 5. C | 5 | 17. A | 3 |
| 6. D | 1 | 18. E | 3 |
| 7. B | 3 | 19. B | 3 |
| 8. C | 3 | 20. A | 3 |
| 9. A | 3 | 21. D | 3 |
| 10. D | 4 | 22. E | 4 |
| 11. B | 3 | 23. E | 4 |
| 12. C | 3 | 24. C | 4 |

Number correct _____

Number incorrect _____

### Section 5

| COR. ANS. | DIFF. LEV. | COR. ANS. | DIFF. LEV. |
|---|---|---|---|
| 1. C | 1 | 13. D | 2 |
| 2. B | 1 | 14. D | 4 |
| 3. C | 1 | 15. E | 1 |
| 4. A | 3 | 16. E | 5 |
| 5. D | 3 | 17. B | 3 |
| 6. B | 4 | 18. E | 3 |
| 7. D | 5 | 19. A | 4 |
| 8. C | 5 | 20. D | 3 |
| 9. A | 4 | 21. A | 3 |
| 10. B | 3 | 22. C | 2 |
| 11. E | 4 | 23. E | 3 |
| 12. C | 5 | 24. E | 3 |

Number correct _____

Number incorrect _____

### Section 9

| COR. ANS. | DIFF. LEV. | COR. ANS. | DIFF. LEV. |
|---|---|---|---|
| 1. B | 1 | 11. A | 4 |
| 2. C | 1 | 12. B | 3 |
| 3. B | 2 | 13. D | 3 |
| 4. E | 4 | 14. A | 5 |
| 5. B | 5 | 15. D | 2 |
| 6. D | 5 | 16. B | 3 |
| 7. C | 2 | 17. C | 3 |
| 8. C | 2 | 18. B | 3 |
| 9. E | 2 | 19. E | 3 |
| 10. E | 1 | | |

Number correct _____

Number incorrect _____

## Mathematics

### Section 3

| COR. ANS. | DIFF. LEV. | COR. ANS. | DIFF. LEV. |
|---|---|---|---|
| 1. A | 1 | 11. B | 3 |
| 2. E | 1 | 12. D | 3 |
| 3. B | 1 | 13. E | 3 |
| 4. D | 2 | 14. E | 3 |
| 5. C | 1 | 15. B | 3 |
| 6. C | 2 | 16. A | 3 |
| 7. D | 2 | 17. C | 4 |
| 8. D | 2 | 18. D | 4 |
| 9. D | 3 | 19. A | 5 |
| 10. C | 2 | 20. A | 5 |

Number correct _____

Number incorrect _____

### Section 7

| Multiple-Choice Questions | | | Student-Produced Response Questions | | |
|---|---|---|---|---|---|
| COR. ANS. | DIFF. LEV. | | COR. ANS. | | DIFF. LEV. |
| 1. E | 1 | | 9. | 9 | 1 |
| 2. B | 1 | | 10. | .2 or 1/5 | 2 |
| 3. E | 2 | | 11. | 15 | 2 |
| 4. D | 2 | | 12. | 0<x<1.5 or 0<x<3/2 | 3 |
| 5. A | 3 | | 13. | 6 | 3 |
| 6. C | 3 | | 14. | 117 | 4 |
| 7. E | 3 | | 15. | 2.5 or 5/2 | 3 |
| 8. C | 5 | | 16. | 5940 | 4 |
| | | | 17. | 90 | 4 |
| | | | 18. | 4.2 or 21/5 | 5 |

Number correct _____

Number incorrect _____

Number correct (9-18) _____

### Section 8

| COR. ANS. | DIFF. LEV. | COR. ANS. | DIFF. LEV. |
|---|---|---|---|
| 1. D | 1 | 9. B | 3 |
| 2. E | 1 | 10. B | 3 |
| 3. A | 1 | 11. A | 3 |
| 4. C | 2 | 12. B | 4 |
| 5. B | 1 | 13. D | 3 |
| 6. E | 3 | 14. B | 4 |
| 7. A | 3 | 15. E | 5 |
| 8. B | 3 | 16. B | 4 |

Number correct _____

Number incorrect _____

## Writing

### Section 6

| COR. ANS. | DIFF. LEV. | COR. ANS. | DIFF. LEV. | COR. ANS. | DIFF. LEV. | COR. ANS. | DIFF. LEV. |
|---|---|---|---|---|---|---|---|
| 1. C | 1 | 10. C | 3 | 19. C | 3 | 28. D | 4 |
| 2. C | 1 | 11. E | 5 | 20. E | 3 | 29. D | 5 |
| 3. B | 1 | 12. C | 2 | 21. B | 3 | 30. C | 2 |
| 4. C | 1 | 13. E | 2 | 22. E | 3 | 31. C | 3 |
| 5. E | 2 | 14. A | 1 | 23. C | 3 | 32. E | 5 |
| 6. A | 2 | 15. C | 2 | 24. E | 4 | 33. C | 2 |
| 7. D | 2 | 16. D | 3 | 25. C | 3 | 34. D | 3 |
| 8. A | 3 | 17. C | 3 | 26. D | 4 | 35. B | 4 |
| 9. E | 3 | 18. A | 3 | 27. E | 5 | | |

Number correct _____

Number incorrect _____

### Section 10

| COR. ANS. | DIFF. LEV. | COR. ANS. | DIFF. LEV. | COR. ANS. | DIFF. LEV. |
|---|---|---|---|---|---|
| 1. D | 1 | 6. E | 3 | 11. D | 3 |
| 2. C | 1 | 7. D | 2 | 12. D | 4 |
| 3. B | 3 | 8. E | 3 | 13. C | 4 |
| 4. E | 2 | 9. E | 3 | 14. E | 5 |
| 5. C | 3 | 10. A | 3 | | |

Number correct _____

Number incorrect _____

NOTE: Difficulty levels are estimates of question difficulty for a reference group of college-bound seniors. Difficulty levels range from 1 (easiest) to 5 (hardest).

# The SAT Scoring Process

**Scoring.** The computer compares the circle filled in for each question with the correct response. Each correct answer receives one point; omitted questions do not affect your score. For each wrong answer to a multiple-choice question, one-fourth of a point is subtracted to correct for random guessing. The SAT critical reading section has 67 questions. If, for example, a student has 44 right, 20 wrong, and 3 omitted, the resulting raw score is determined as follows:

$$44 \text{ right} - \frac{20 \text{ wrong}}{4} = 44 - 5 = 39 \text{ raw score points}$$

Obtaining raw scores frequently involves the rounding of fractions to the nearest whole number. For example, a raw score of 39.25 is rounded to 39, the nearest whole number. A raw score of 39.50 is rounded upward to 40. **For the WRITING SECTION**, your essay raw score counts approximately 30% and your multiple-choice raw score counts approximately 70%.

**Converting to reported scaled score.** Raw scores are then placed on the College Board scale of 200 to 800 through a process that adjusts scores to account for minor differences in difficulty among different versions of the test. This process, known as equating, is performed so that a student's reported score is not affected by the version of the test taken or by the abilities of the group with whom the student takes the test. As a result of placing SAT scores on the College Board scale, scores earned by students at different times can be compared. For example, an SAT critical reading score of 400 on a test taken at one administration indicates the same level of developed critical reading ability as a 400 score obtained on a different version of the test taken at another time.

# How to Score Practice Test #1

## SAT Critical Reading Sections 2, 5, and 9

**Step A:** Count the number of correct answers for *Section 2* and record the number in the space provided on the Scoring Worksheet. Then do the same for the incorrect answers. (Do not count omitted answers.)

**Step B:** Count the number of correct answers and the number of incorrect answers for *Section 5* and record the numbers in the spaces provided on the Scoring Worksheet. (Do not count omitted answers.)

**Step C:** Count the number of correct answers and the number of incorrect answers for *Section 9* and record the numbers in the spaces provided on the Scoring Worksheet. (Do not count omitted answers.)

**Step D:** Total the number of correct responses. Total the number of incorrect responses. Enter the resulting figures on the Scoring Worksheet. To determine A, use the formula:

$$\text{Number correct} - \frac{\text{Number incorrect}}{4} = A$$

**Step E:** To obtain B, your Rounded Critical Reading Raw Score, round A to the nearest whole number. (For example, any number from 44.50 to 45.49 rounds to 45.) Enter the resulting figure on the Scoring Worksheet.

**Step F:** To find your Critical Reading Scaled Score, look up the Total Rounded Raw Score you obtained in step E in the Critical Reading Conversion Table (Table 1). Enter this score in the box on the Scoring Worksheet.

## SAT Mathematics Sections 3, 7, and 8

**Step A:** Count the number of correct answers and the number of incorrect answers for *Section 3* and record the numbers in the spaces provided on the Scoring Worksheet. (Do not count omitted answers.)

**Step B:** Count the number of correct answers and the number of incorrect answers for the multiple-choice questions (*questions 1 through 8*) in *Section 7* and record the numbers in the spaces provided on the Scoring Worksheet. (Do not count omitted answers.)

**Step C:** Count the number of correct answers for the student-produced response questions (*questions 9 through 18*) in *Section 7* and record the number in the space provided on the Scoring Worksheet.

**Step D:** Count the number of correct answers and the number of incorrect answers for *Section 8* and record the numbers in the spaces provided on the Scoring Worksheet. (Do not count omitted answers.)

**Step E:** Total the number of correct responses. Total the number of incorrect responses. Enter the resulting figures on the Scoring Worksheet. To determine A, use the formula:

$$\text{Number correct} - \frac{\text{Number incorrect}}{4} = A$$

**Step F:** To obtain B, your Mathematics Rounded Raw Score, round A to the nearest whole number. (For example, any number from 44.50 to 45.49 rounds to 45.) Enter the resulting figure on the Scoring Worksheet.

**Step G:** To find your Mathematics Scaled Score, use the Mathematics Conversion Table (Table 2) to look up the Total Rounded Raw Score you obtained in step F. Enter this score in the box on the Scoring Worksheet.

## SAT Writing Sections 1, 6, and 10

**Step A:** Enter your Essay Score for Section 1 in the box on the Scoring Worksheet. Multiply your score by 2. (Keep in mind that on the actual SAT, two readers will read your essay and you will receive a total score of 0 to 12 on your score report.) For help scoring your essay see page 105.

**Step B:** Count the number of correct answers and the number of incorrect answers for *Section 6* and record the numbers in the spaces provided on the Scoring Worksheet. (Do not count omitted answers.)

**Step C:** Count the number of correct answers and the number of incorrect answers for *Section 10* and record the numbers in the spaces provided on the Scoring Worksheet. (Do not count omitted answers.)

**Step D:** Total the number of correct responses. Total the number of incorrect responses. Enter the resulting figure on the Scoring Worksheet. To determine A, use the formula:

$$\text{Number correct} - \frac{\text{Number incorrect}}{4} = A$$

**Step E:** To obtain B, your Writing Multiple-Choice (MC) Rounded Raw Score, round A to the nearest whole number. (For example, any number from 44.50 to 45.49 rounds to 45.) Enter the resulting figure on the Scoring Worksheet.

**Step F:** To find your overall Writing Scaled Score, use Table 3. Look up the Total MC Rounded Raw Score you obtained in Step E in the left side of Table 3 and the Essay Score entered in Step A across the top of the table. Enter this score in the box on the Scoring Worksheet.

**Step G:** To find your Writing MC Subscore, look up the Total MC Rounded Raw Score you obtained in Step E on the Writing Multiple-Choice Conversion Table (Table 4). Enter this score in the box on the Scoring Worksheet.

**Note:** For the **WRITING SECTION**, your Essay Raw Score counts approximately 30% and your Multiple-Choice Raw Score counts approximately 70%.

# SAT Practice Test #1 Scoring Worksheet

**SAT Critical Reading Section**

A. Section 2:

         _____         _____
         no. correct                 no. incorrect
    +                                +

B. Section 5:

         _____         _____
         no. correct                 no. incorrect
    +                                +

C. Section 9:

         _____         _____
         no. correct                 no. incorrect
    =                                =

D. Total Unrounded Raw Score

         _____     –  ( _____ ÷ 4)  = _____
         no. correct                 no. incorrect            A

E. Total Rounded Raw Score
   (Rounded to nearest whole number)

                                            _____
                                                B

F. Critical Reading Scaled Score
   (See Table 1)

Critical
Reading Scaled
Score

**SAT Mathematics Section**

A. Section 3:

         _____         _____
         no. correct                 no. incorrect
    +                                +

B. Section 7:
   Questions 1-8

         _____         _____
         no. correct                 no. incorrect
    +

C. Section 7:
   Questions 9-18

         _____
         no. correct
    +                                +

D. Section 8:

         _____         _____
         no. correct                 no. incorrect
    =                                =

E. Total Unrounded Raw Score

         _____      ( _____ ÷ 4)  = _____
         no. correct                 no. incorrect            A

F. Total Rounded Raw Score
   (Rounded to nearest whole number)

                                            _____
                                                B

G. Mathematics Scaled Score
   (See Table 2)

Mathematics
Scaled
Score

**SAT Writing Section**

A. Section 1:

Essay Score ×2

B. Section 6:

_____      _____
no. correct          no. incorrect

+                 +

C. Section 10:

_____      _____
no. correct          no. incorrect

=                 =

D. Total MC Unrounded Raw Score

_____     ( _____ ÷ 4)   =   _____
no. correct          no. incorrect             A

E. Total MC Rounded Raw Score
   (Rounded to nearest whole number)

_____
B

F. Writing Scaled Score
   (See Table 3)

Writing Scaled Score

G. Writing MC Subscore
   (See Table 4)

Writing MC Subscore

| Table 1. Critical Reading Conversion Table | | | |
|---|---|---|---|
| Raw Score | Scaled Score | Raw Score | Scaled Score |
| 67 | 800 | 31 | 510 |
| 66 | 800 | 30 | 500 |
| 65 | 800 | 29 | 490 |
| 64 | 800 | 28 | 490 |
| 63 | 780 | 27 | 480 |
| 62 | 770 | 26 | 480 |
| 61 | 750 | 25 | 470 |
| 60 | 740 | 24 | 460 |
| 59 | 720 | 23 | 460 |
| 58 | 710 | 22 | 450 |
| 57 | 700 | 21 | 440 |
| 56 | 690 | 20 | 440 |
| 55 | 680 | 19 | 430 |
| 54 | 670 | 18 | 430 |
| 53 | 660 | 17 | 420 |
| 52 | 650 | 16 | 410 |
| 51 | 640 | 15 | 410 |
| 50 | 630 | 14 | 400 |
| 49 | 630 | 13 | 390 |
| 48 | 620 | 12 | 380 |
| 47 | 610 | 11 | 380 |
| 46 | 600 | 10 | 370 |
| 45 | 600 | 9 | 360 |
| 44 | 590 | 8 | 350 |
| 43 | 580 | 7 | 340 |
| 42 | 580 | 6 | 330 |
| 41 | 570 | 5 | 320 |
| 40 | 560 | 4 | 310 |
| 39 | 560 | 3 | 300 |
| 38 | 550 | 2 | 280 |
| 37 | 540 | 1 | 270 |
| 36 | 540 | 0 | 250 |
| 35 | 530 | -1 | 230 |
| 34 | 530 | -2 | 210 |
| 33 | 520 | -3 and below | 200 |
| 32 | 510 | | |

| Table 2. Mathematics Conversion Table | | | |
|---|---|---|---|
| Raw Score | Scaled Score | Raw Score | Scaled Score |
| 54 | 800 | 25 | 500 |
| 53 | 800 | 24 | 490 |
| 52 | 770 | 23 | 490 |
| 51 | 750 | 22 | 480 |
| 50 | 730 | 21 | 470 |
| 49 | 710 | 20 | 460 |
| 48 | 700 | 19 | 450 |
| 47 | 690 | 18 | 440 |
| 46 | 680 | 17 | 430 |
| 45 | 670 | 16 | 420 |
| 44 | 660 | 15 | 420 |
| 43 | 650 | 14 | 410 |
| 42 | 650 | 13 | 400 |
| 41 | 640 | 12 | 390 |
| 40 | 630 | 11 | 380 |
| 39 | 620 | 10 | 370 |
| 38 | 610 | 9 | 350 |
| 37 | 600 | 8 | 340 |
| 36 | 590 | 7 | 330 |
| 35 | 590 | 6 | 320 |
| 34 | 580 | 5 | 300 |
| 33 | 570 | 4 | 290 |
| 32 | 560 | 3 | 270 |
| 31 | 550 | 2 | 260 |
| 30 | 540 | 1 | 240 |
| 29 | 540 | 0 | 220 |
| 28 | 530 | -1 and below | 200 |
| 27 | 520 | | |
| 26 | 510 | | |

# Table 3. Writing Conversion Table

| Writing MC Raw Score | Essay Raw Score | | | | | | | | | | | |
|---|---|---|---|---|---|---|---|---|---|---|---|---|
| | 12 | 11 | 10 | 9 | 8 | 7 | 6 | 5 | 4 | 3 | 2 | 0 |
| 49 | 800 | 800 | 800 | 800 | 770 | 760 | 740 | 730 | 710 | 700 | 680 | 670 |
| 48 | 800 | 800 | 790 | 770 | 750 | 730 | 710 | 700 | 680 | 670 | 650 | 640 |
| 47 | 790 | 770 | 760 | 740 | 720 | 700 | 690 | 670 | 660 | 640 | 630 | 620 |
| 46 | 770 | 750 | 740 | 720 | 700 | 680 | 670 | 650 | 640 | 620 | 610 | 600 |
| 45 | 760 | 740 | 730 | 710 | 690 | 670 | 650 | 640 | 620 | 610 | 590 | 590 |
| 44 | 740 | 720 | 710 | 690 | 670 | 650 | 640 | 620 | 610 | 590 | 580 | 570 |
| 43 | 730 | 710 | 700 | 680 | 660 | 640 | 620 | 610 | 600 | 580 | 570 | 560 |
| 42 | 720 | 700 | 690 | 670 | 650 | 630 | 610 | 600 | 580 | 570 | 550 | 550 |
| 41 | 710 | 690 | 670 | 660 | 630 | 620 | 600 | 590 | 570 | 560 | 540 | 530 |
| 40 | 690 | 680 | 660 | 650 | 620 | 610 | 590 | 570 | 560 | 540 | 530 | 520 |
| 39 | 680 | 670 | 650 | 640 | 610 | 600 | 580 | 560 | 550 | 530 | 520 | 510 |
| 38 | 670 | 660 | 640 | 630 | 600 | 590 | 570 | 550 | 540 | 530 | 510 | 500 |
| 37 | 670 | 650 | 630 | 620 | 590 | 580 | 560 | 550 | 530 | 520 | 500 | 490 |
| 36 | 660 | 640 | 630 | 610 | 590 | 570 | 550 | 540 | 520 | 510 | 490 | 490 |
| 35 | 650 | 630 | 620 | 600 | 580 | 560 | 540 | 530 | 510 | 500 | 480 | 480 |
| 34 | 640 | 620 | 610 | 590 | 570 | 550 | 530 | 520 | 510 | 490 | 480 | 470 |
| 33 | 630 | 610 | 600 | 580 | 560 | 540 | 530 | 510 | 500 | 480 | 470 | 460 |
| 32 | 620 | 600 | 590 | 580 | 550 | 530 | 520 | 500 | 490 | 470 | 460 | 450 |
| 31 | 620 | 600 | 590 | 570 | 550 | 530 | 510 | 500 | 480 | 470 | 450 | 440 |
| 30 | 610 | 590 | 580 | 560 | 540 | 520 | 500 | 490 | 480 | 460 | 450 | 440 |
| 29 | 600 | 580 | 570 | 550 | 530 | 510 | 500 | 480 | 470 | 450 | 440 | 430 |
| 28 | 590 | 580 | 560 | 550 | 520 | 510 | 490 | 470 | 460 | 450 | 430 | 420 |
| 27 | 590 | 570 | 560 | 540 | 520 | 500 | 480 | 470 | 450 | 440 | 430 | 420 |
| 26 | 580 | 560 | 550 | 530 | 510 | 490 | 480 | 460 | 450 | 430 | 420 | 410 |
| 25 | 570 | 560 | 540 | 530 | 500 | 490 | 470 | 450 | 440 | 420 | 410 | 400 |
| 24 | 570 | 550 | 540 | 520 | 500 | 480 | 460 | 450 | 440 | 420 | 410 | 400 |
| 23 | 560 | 540 | 530 | 510 | 490 | 470 | 460 | 440 | 430 | 410 | 400 | 390 |
| 22 | 560 | 540 | 520 | 510 | 480 | 470 | 450 | 440 | 420 | 410 | 390 | 380 |
| 21 | 550 | 530 | 520 | 500 | 480 | 460 | 440 | 430 | 420 | 400 | 390 | 380 |
| 20 | 540 | 520 | 510 | 490 | 470 | 450 | 440 | 420 | 410 | 390 | 380 | 370 |
| 19 | 540 | 520 | 510 | 490 | 470 | 450 | 430 | 420 | 400 | 390 | 370 | 370 |
| 18 | 530 | 510 | 500 | 480 | 460 | 440 | 430 | 410 | 400 | 380 | 370 | 360 |
| 17 | 520 | 500 | 490 | 480 | 450 | 430 | 420 | 400 | 390 | 370 | 360 | 350 |
| 16 | 520 | 500 | 490 | 470 | 450 | 430 | 410 | 400 | 380 | 370 | 350 | 350 |
| 15 | 510 | 490 | 480 | 460 | 440 | 420 | 410 | 390 | 380 | 360 | 350 | 340 |
| 14 | 500 | 490 | 470 | 460 | 430 | 420 | 400 | 390 | 370 | 360 | 340 | 330 |
| 13 | 500 | 480 | 470 | 450 | 430 | 410 | 390 | 380 | 370 | 350 | 340 | 330 |
| 12 | 490 | 470 | 460 | 440 | 420 | 400 | 390 | 370 | 360 | 340 | 330 | 320 |
| 11 | 480 | 470 | 450 | 440 | 410 | 400 | 380 | 370 | 350 | 340 | 320 | 310 |
| 10 | 480 | 460 | 450 | 430 | 410 | 390 | 370 | 360 | 350 | 330 | 320 | 310 |
| 9 | 470 | 450 | 440 | 420 | 400 | 380 | 370 | 350 | 340 | 320 | 310 | 300 |
| 8 | 460 | 440 | 430 | 420 | 390 | 370 | 360 | 340 | 330 | 310 | 300 | 290 |
| 7 | 460 | 440 | 420 | 410 | 390 | 370 | 350 | 340 | 320 | 310 | 290 | 280 |
| 6 | 450 | 430 | 420 | 400 | 380 | 360 | 340 | 330 | 310 | 300 | 280 | 280 |
| 5 | 440 | 420 | 410 | 390 | 370 | 350 | 330 | 320 | 310 | 290 | 280 | 270 |
| 4 | 430 | 410 | 400 | 380 | 360 | 340 | 320 | 310 | 300 | 280 | 270 | 260 |
| 3 | 420 | 400 | 390 | 370 | 350 | 330 | 310 | 300 | 280 | 270 | 250 | 250 |
| 2 | 400 | 390 | 370 | 360 | 330 | 320 | 300 | 280 | 270 | 250 | 240 | 230 |
| 1 | 390 | 370 | 360 | 340 | 320 | 300 | 290 | 270 | 260 | 240 | 230 | 220 |
| 0 | 370 | 360 | 340 | 330 | 300 | 290 | 270 | 250 | 240 | 220 | 210 | 200 |
| -1 | 360 | 340 | 330 | 310 | 290 | 270 | 250 | 240 | 220 | 210 | 200 | 200 |
| -2 | 340 | 320 | 310 | 290 | 270 | 250 | 230 | 220 | 200 | 200 | 200 | 200 |
| -3 | 310 | 300 | 280 | 270 | 240 | 230 | 210 | 200 | 200 | 200 | 200 | 200 |
| -4 and below | 310 | 290 | 280 | 260 | 240 | 220 | 200 | 200 | 200 | 200 | 200 | 200 |

## Table 4. Writing Multiple-Choice Conversion Table

| Raw Score | Scaled Score | Raw Score | Scaled Score |
|---|---|---|---|
| 49 | 80 | 22 | 47 |
| 48 | 79 | 21 | 46 |
| 47 | 76 | 20 | 46 |
| 46 | 73 | 19 | 45 |
| 45 | 71 | 18 | 44 |
| 44 | 70 | 17 | 43 |
| 43 | 68 | 16 | 43 |
| 42 | 67 | 15 | 42 |
| 41 | 65 | 14 | 41 |
| 40 | 64 | 13 | 40 |
| 39 | 63 | 12 | 39 |
| 38 | 62 | 11 | 39 |
| 37 | 60 | 10 | 38 |
| 36 | 59 | 9 | 37 |
| 35 | 58 | 8 | 36 |
| 34 | 57 | 7 | 35 |
| 33 | 56 | 6 | 34 |
| 32 | 55 | 5 | 33 |
| 31 | 54 | 4 | 32 |
| 30 | 54 | 3 | 30 |
| 29 | 53 | 2 | 29 |
| 28 | 52 | 1 | 27 |
| 27 | 51 | 0 | 25 |
| 26 | 50 | -1 | 23 |
| 25 | 49 | -2 | 21 |
| 24 | 49 | -3 and below | 20 |
| 23 | 48 | | |

# SAT Practice Test #2

 **After this test:**

- Use this book to its full potential! Get exclusive access answer explanations, free practice score reports and free sample student essays to help you score your essay in the Book Owners' Area at www.collegeboard.org/satstudyguide.

- Want more practice? Get 10 more official practice tests, auto essay scoring and lesson plans from the test maker by subscribing to *The Official SAT Online Course*. As a book owner, you're entitled to a $10 discount. Sign up at www.collegeboard.org/satstudyguide.

*Note:* Section 3, the variable section, has been omitted from this practice test.

YOUR NAME (PRINT) _____

LAST          FIRST          MI

TEST CENTER _____

NUMBER      NAME OF TEST CENTER      ROOM NUMBER

# SAT Reasoning Test — General Directions

### Timing

- You will have 3 hours and 45 minutes to work on this test.
- There are ten separately timed sections:
  - ▶ One 25-minute essay
  - ▶ Six other 25-minute sections
  - ▶ Two 20-minute sections
  - ▶ One 10-minute section
- You may work on only one section at a time.
- The supervisor will tell you when to begin and end each section.
- If you finish a section before time is called, check your work on that section. You may NOT turn to any other section.
- Work as rapidly as you can without losing accuracy. Don't waste time on questions that seem too difficult for you.

### Marking Answers

- Be sure to mark your answer sheet properly.

COMPLETE MARK ●     EXAMPLES OF INCOMPLETE MARKS ⊘⊗⊖◐ ◑⌀⍉⊛

- You must use a No. 2 pencil.
- Carefully mark only one answer for each question.
- Make sure you fill the entire circle darkly and completely.
- Do not make any stray marks on your answer sheet.
- If you erase, do so completely. Incomplete erasures may be scored as intended answers.
- Use only the answer spaces that correspond to the question numbers.

### Using Your Test Book

- You may use the test book for scratchwork, but you will not receive credit for anything written there.
- After time has been called, you may not transfer answers to your answer sheet or fill in circles.
- You may not fold or remove pages or portions of a page from this book, or take the book or answer sheet from the testing room.

### Scoring

- For each correct answer, you receive one point.
- For questions you omit, you receive no points.
- For a wrong answer to a multiple-choice question, you lose one-fourth of a point.
  - ▶ If you can eliminate one or more of the answer choices as wrong, you increase your chances of choosing the correct answer and earning one point.
  - ▶ If you can't eliminate any choice, move on. You can return to the question later if there is time.
- For a wrong answer to a student-produced response ("grid-in") math question, you don't lose any points.
- Multiple-choice and student-produced response questions are machine scored.
- The essay is scored on a 1 to 6 scale by two different readers. The total essay score is the sum of the two readers' scores.
- Off-topic essays, blank essays, and essays written in ink will receive a score of zero.

**IMPORTANT:** The codes below are unique to your test book. Copy them on your answer sheet in boxes 8 and 9 and fill in the corresponding circles exactly as shown.

**9**   **TEST FORM** (Copy from back of test book.)

**8**   **FORM CODE** (Copy and grid as on back of test book.)

A B C D E F G H I J K L M N O P Q R S T U V W X Y Z / 0 1 2 3 4 5 6 7 8 9

The passages for this test have been adapted from published material.
The ideas contained in them do not necessarily represent the opinions of the College Board.

## DO NOT OPEN THIS BOOK UNTIL THE SUPERVISOR TELLS YOU TO DO SO.

CollegeBoard SAT

# SAT Reasoning Test™

**MARKS MUST BE COMPLETE**

COMPLETE MARK ●

EXAMPLES OF INCOMPLETE MARKS Ⓐ⊗⊖ⓒ ⊘⊘⊘⊗

*You must use a No. 2 pencil. Do not use a mechanical pencil. It is very important that you fill in the entire circle darkly and completely. If you change your response, erase as completely as possible. Incomplete marks or erasures may affect your score. It is very important that you follow these instructions when filling out your answer sheet.*

**1** Your Name:
(Print)
_____
Last                    First                    M.I.

I agree to the conditions on the back of the SAT Reasoning Test™ booklet. I also agree to use only a No. 2 pencil to complete my answer sheet.

Signature: _____ Date: __/__/__

Home Address: _____
(Print)          Number and Street          City          State          Zip Code
Home Phone: ( ) _____ Center: _____
(Print)                                        (Print)          City          State/Country

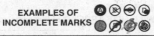

**2** YOUR NAME

Last Name (First 6 Letters)    First Name (First 4 Letters)    Mid. Init.

**3** DATE OF BIRTH

| MONTH | DAY | YEAR |
| --- | --- | --- |
| ○ Jan | | |
| ○ Feb | 0 0 | 0 |
| ○ Mar | 1 1 | 1 |
| ○ Apr | 2 2 | 2 |
| ○ May | 3 3 | 3 |
| ○ Jun | 4 | 4 |
| ○ Jul | 5 5 | 5 |
| ○ Aug | 6 6 | 6 |
| ○ Sep | 7 7 | 7 |
| ○ Oct | 8 8 | 8 |
| ○ Nov | 9 9 | 9 |
| ○ Dec | | |

**5** SEX
○ Female   ○ Male

**Important:** Fill in items 8 and 9 exactly as shown on the back of test book.

**9** TEST FORM
(Copy from back of test book.)

**6** REGISTRATION NUMBER
(Copy from Admission Ticket.)

○ I turned in my registration form today.

**8** FORM CODE
(Copy and grid as on back of test book.)

**10** TEST BOOK SERIAL NUMBER
(Copy from front of test book.)

**4** ZIP CODE

**7** SOCIAL SECURITY NUMBER

**11** TEST CENTER
(Supplied by Test Center Supervisor.)

FOR OFFICIAL USE ONLY
0 1 2 3 4 5 6
0 1 2 3 4 5 6
0 1 2 3 4 5 6

00272-36390 • NS75E4600 • Printed in U.S.A.
732652

PLEASE DO NOT WRITE IN THIS AREA

**SERIAL #**

**SECTION 1**

2

*IMPORTANT:* **USE A NO. 2 PENCIL. DO NOT WRITE OUTSIDE THE BORDER!**
Words written outside the essay box or written in ink **WILL NOT APPEAR** in the copy sent to be scored, and your score will be affected.

**Begin your essay on this page. If you need more space, continue on the next page.**

Continuation of ESSAY Section 1 from previous page. Write below only if you need more space.
IMPORTANT: DO NOT START on this page—if you do, your essay may appear blank and your score may be affected.

2

Page 3

| COMPLETE MARK ● | EXAMPLES OF INCOMPLETE MARKS Ⓐ Ⓧ ⊖ Ⓓ Ⓒ ⊘ ⊘ ⊛ | You must use a No. 2 pencil and marks must be complete. Do not use a mechanical pencil. It is very important that you fill in the entire circle darkly and completely. If you change your response, erase as completely as possible. Incomplete marks or erasures may affect your score. |

**SECTION 2**

1 Ⓐ Ⓑ Ⓒ Ⓓ Ⓔ  11 Ⓐ Ⓑ Ⓒ Ⓓ Ⓔ  21 Ⓐ Ⓑ Ⓒ Ⓓ Ⓔ  31 Ⓐ Ⓑ Ⓒ Ⓓ Ⓔ
2 Ⓐ Ⓑ Ⓒ Ⓓ Ⓔ  12 Ⓐ Ⓑ Ⓒ Ⓓ Ⓔ  22 Ⓐ Ⓑ Ⓒ Ⓓ Ⓔ  32 Ⓐ Ⓑ Ⓒ Ⓓ Ⓔ
3 Ⓐ Ⓑ Ⓒ Ⓓ Ⓔ  13 Ⓐ Ⓑ Ⓒ Ⓓ Ⓔ  23 Ⓐ Ⓑ Ⓒ Ⓓ Ⓔ  33 Ⓐ Ⓑ Ⓒ Ⓓ Ⓔ
4 Ⓐ Ⓑ Ⓒ Ⓓ Ⓔ  14 Ⓐ Ⓑ Ⓒ Ⓓ Ⓔ  24 Ⓐ Ⓑ Ⓒ Ⓓ Ⓔ  34 Ⓐ Ⓑ Ⓒ Ⓓ Ⓔ
5 Ⓐ Ⓑ Ⓒ Ⓓ Ⓔ  15 Ⓐ Ⓑ Ⓒ Ⓓ Ⓔ  25 Ⓐ Ⓑ Ⓒ Ⓓ Ⓔ  35 Ⓐ Ⓑ Ⓒ Ⓓ Ⓔ
6 Ⓐ Ⓑ Ⓒ Ⓓ Ⓔ  16 Ⓐ Ⓑ Ⓒ Ⓓ Ⓔ  26 Ⓐ Ⓑ Ⓒ Ⓓ Ⓔ  36 Ⓐ Ⓑ Ⓒ Ⓓ Ⓔ
7 Ⓐ Ⓑ Ⓒ Ⓓ Ⓔ  17 Ⓐ Ⓑ Ⓒ Ⓓ Ⓔ  27 Ⓐ Ⓑ Ⓒ Ⓓ Ⓔ  37 Ⓐ Ⓑ Ⓒ Ⓓ Ⓔ
8 Ⓐ Ⓑ Ⓒ Ⓓ Ⓔ  18 Ⓐ Ⓑ Ⓒ Ⓓ Ⓔ  28 Ⓐ Ⓑ Ⓒ Ⓓ Ⓔ  38 Ⓐ Ⓑ Ⓒ Ⓓ Ⓔ
9 Ⓐ Ⓑ Ⓒ Ⓓ Ⓔ  19 Ⓐ Ⓑ Ⓒ Ⓓ Ⓔ  29 Ⓐ Ⓑ Ⓒ Ⓓ Ⓔ  39 Ⓐ Ⓑ Ⓒ Ⓓ Ⓔ
10 Ⓐ Ⓑ Ⓒ Ⓓ Ⓔ  20 Ⓐ Ⓑ Ⓒ Ⓓ Ⓔ  30 Ⓐ Ⓑ Ⓒ Ⓓ Ⓔ  40 Ⓐ Ⓑ Ⓒ Ⓓ Ⓔ

**SECTION 3**

1 Ⓐ Ⓑ Ⓒ Ⓓ Ⓔ  11 Ⓐ Ⓑ Ⓒ Ⓓ Ⓔ  21 Ⓐ Ⓑ Ⓒ Ⓓ Ⓔ  31 Ⓐ Ⓑ Ⓒ Ⓓ Ⓔ
2 Ⓐ Ⓑ Ⓒ Ⓓ Ⓔ  12 Ⓐ Ⓑ Ⓒ Ⓓ Ⓔ  22 Ⓐ Ⓑ Ⓒ Ⓓ Ⓔ  32 Ⓐ Ⓑ Ⓒ Ⓓ Ⓔ
3 Ⓐ Ⓑ Ⓒ Ⓓ Ⓔ  13 Ⓐ Ⓑ Ⓒ Ⓓ Ⓔ  23 Ⓐ Ⓑ Ⓒ Ⓓ Ⓔ  33 Ⓐ Ⓑ Ⓒ Ⓓ Ⓔ
4 Ⓐ Ⓑ Ⓒ Ⓓ Ⓔ  14 Ⓐ Ⓑ Ⓒ Ⓓ Ⓔ  24 Ⓐ Ⓑ Ⓒ Ⓓ Ⓔ  34 Ⓐ Ⓑ Ⓒ Ⓓ Ⓔ
5 Ⓐ Ⓑ Ⓒ Ⓓ Ⓔ  15 Ⓐ Ⓑ Ⓒ Ⓓ Ⓔ  25 Ⓐ Ⓑ Ⓒ Ⓓ Ⓔ  35 Ⓐ Ⓑ Ⓒ Ⓓ Ⓔ
6 Ⓐ Ⓑ Ⓒ Ⓓ Ⓔ  16 Ⓐ Ⓑ Ⓒ Ⓓ Ⓔ  26 Ⓐ Ⓑ Ⓒ Ⓓ Ⓔ  36 Ⓐ Ⓑ Ⓒ Ⓓ Ⓔ
7 Ⓐ Ⓑ Ⓒ Ⓓ Ⓔ  17 Ⓐ Ⓑ Ⓒ Ⓓ Ⓔ  27 Ⓐ Ⓑ Ⓒ Ⓓ Ⓔ  37 Ⓐ Ⓑ Ⓒ Ⓓ Ⓔ
8 Ⓐ Ⓑ Ⓒ Ⓓ Ⓔ  18 Ⓐ Ⓑ Ⓒ Ⓓ Ⓔ  28 Ⓐ Ⓑ Ⓒ Ⓓ Ⓔ  38 Ⓐ Ⓑ Ⓒ Ⓓ Ⓔ
9 Ⓐ Ⓑ Ⓒ Ⓓ Ⓔ  19 Ⓐ Ⓑ Ⓒ Ⓓ Ⓔ  29 Ⓐ Ⓑ Ⓒ Ⓓ Ⓔ  39 Ⓐ Ⓑ Ⓒ Ⓓ Ⓔ
10 Ⓐ Ⓑ Ⓒ Ⓓ Ⓔ  20 Ⓐ Ⓑ Ⓒ Ⓓ Ⓔ  30 Ⓐ Ⓑ Ⓒ Ⓓ Ⓔ  40 Ⓐ Ⓑ Ⓒ Ⓓ Ⓔ

**CAUTION** Grid answers in the section below for SECTION 2 or SECTION 3 only if directed to do so in your test book.

**Student-Produced Responses** ONLY ANSWERS THAT ARE GRIDDED WILL BE SCORED. YOU WILL NOT RECEIVE CREDIT FOR ANYTHING WRITTEN IN THE BOXES.

Quality Assurance Mark ●

9  10  11  12  13

(grid-in answer boxes with digits 0–9)

14  15  16  17  18

(grid-in answer boxes with digits 0–9)

COMPLETE MARK ● EXAMPLES OF INCOMPLETE MARKS Ⓐ Ⓧ ⊖ Ⓓ ⊘ ⊘ ⊘

You must use a No. 2 pencil and marks must be complete. *Do not use a mechanical pencil. It is very important that you fill in the entire circle darkly and completely. If you change your response, erase as completely as possible. Incomplete marks or erasures may affect your score.*

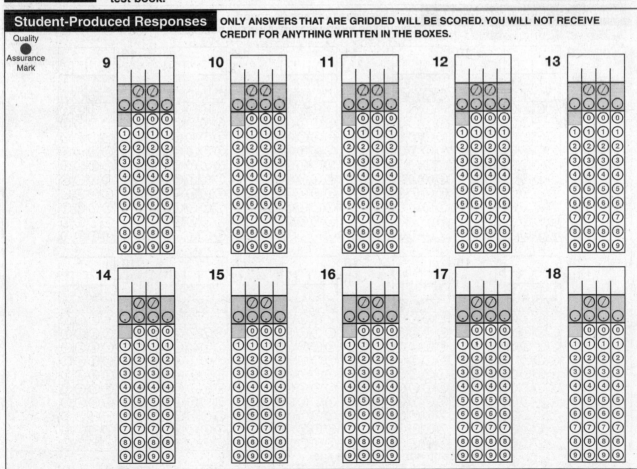

**SECTION 4**

1 Ⓐ Ⓑ Ⓒ Ⓓ Ⓔ
2 Ⓐ Ⓑ Ⓒ Ⓓ Ⓔ
3 Ⓐ Ⓑ Ⓒ Ⓓ Ⓔ
4 Ⓐ Ⓑ Ⓒ Ⓓ Ⓔ
5 Ⓐ Ⓑ Ⓒ Ⓓ Ⓔ
6 Ⓐ Ⓑ Ⓒ Ⓓ Ⓔ
7 Ⓐ Ⓑ Ⓒ Ⓓ Ⓔ
8 Ⓐ Ⓑ Ⓒ Ⓓ Ⓔ
9 Ⓐ Ⓑ Ⓒ Ⓓ Ⓔ
10 Ⓐ Ⓑ Ⓒ Ⓓ Ⓔ

11 Ⓐ Ⓑ Ⓒ Ⓓ Ⓔ
12 Ⓐ Ⓑ Ⓒ Ⓓ Ⓔ
13 Ⓐ Ⓑ Ⓒ Ⓓ Ⓔ
14 Ⓐ Ⓑ Ⓒ Ⓓ Ⓔ
15 Ⓐ Ⓑ Ⓒ Ⓓ Ⓔ
16 Ⓐ Ⓑ Ⓒ Ⓓ Ⓔ
17 Ⓐ Ⓑ Ⓒ Ⓓ Ⓔ
18 Ⓐ Ⓑ Ⓒ Ⓓ Ⓔ
19 Ⓐ Ⓑ Ⓒ Ⓓ Ⓔ
20 Ⓐ Ⓑ Ⓒ Ⓓ Ⓔ

21 Ⓐ Ⓑ Ⓒ Ⓓ Ⓔ
22 Ⓐ Ⓑ Ⓒ Ⓓ Ⓔ
23 Ⓐ Ⓑ Ⓒ Ⓓ Ⓔ
24 Ⓐ Ⓑ Ⓒ Ⓓ Ⓔ
25 Ⓐ Ⓑ Ⓒ Ⓓ Ⓔ
26 Ⓐ Ⓑ Ⓒ Ⓓ Ⓔ
27 Ⓐ Ⓑ Ⓒ Ⓓ Ⓔ
28 Ⓐ Ⓑ Ⓒ Ⓓ Ⓔ
29 Ⓐ Ⓑ Ⓒ Ⓓ Ⓔ
30 Ⓐ Ⓑ Ⓒ Ⓓ Ⓔ

31 Ⓐ Ⓑ Ⓒ Ⓓ Ⓔ
32 Ⓐ Ⓑ Ⓒ Ⓓ Ⓔ
33 Ⓐ Ⓑ Ⓒ Ⓓ Ⓔ
34 Ⓐ Ⓑ Ⓒ Ⓓ Ⓔ
35 Ⓐ Ⓑ Ⓒ Ⓓ Ⓔ
36 Ⓐ Ⓑ Ⓒ Ⓓ Ⓔ
37 Ⓐ Ⓑ Ⓒ Ⓓ Ⓔ
38 Ⓐ Ⓑ Ⓒ Ⓓ Ⓔ
39 Ⓐ Ⓑ Ⓒ Ⓓ Ⓔ
40 Ⓐ Ⓑ Ⓒ Ⓓ Ⓔ

**SECTION 5**

1 Ⓐ Ⓑ Ⓒ Ⓓ Ⓔ
2 Ⓐ Ⓑ Ⓒ Ⓓ Ⓔ
3 Ⓐ Ⓑ Ⓒ Ⓓ Ⓔ
4 Ⓐ Ⓑ Ⓒ Ⓓ Ⓔ
5 Ⓐ Ⓑ Ⓒ Ⓓ Ⓔ
6 Ⓐ Ⓑ Ⓒ Ⓓ Ⓔ
7 Ⓐ Ⓑ Ⓒ Ⓓ Ⓔ
8 Ⓐ Ⓑ Ⓒ Ⓓ Ⓔ
9 Ⓐ Ⓑ Ⓒ Ⓓ Ⓔ
10 Ⓐ Ⓑ Ⓒ Ⓓ Ⓔ

11 Ⓐ Ⓑ Ⓒ Ⓓ Ⓔ
12 Ⓐ Ⓑ Ⓒ Ⓓ Ⓔ
13 Ⓐ Ⓑ Ⓒ Ⓓ Ⓔ
14 Ⓐ Ⓑ Ⓒ Ⓓ Ⓔ
15 Ⓐ Ⓑ Ⓒ Ⓓ Ⓔ
16 Ⓐ Ⓑ Ⓒ Ⓓ Ⓕ
17 Ⓐ Ⓑ Ⓒ Ⓓ Ⓔ
18 Ⓐ Ⓑ Ⓒ Ⓓ Ⓔ
19 Ⓐ Ⓑ Ⓒ Ⓓ Ⓔ
20 Ⓐ Ⓑ Ⓒ Ⓓ Ⓔ

21 Ⓐ Ⓑ Ⓒ Ⓓ Ⓔ
22 Ⓐ Ⓑ Ⓒ Ⓓ Ⓔ
23 Ⓐ Ⓑ Ⓒ Ⓓ Ⓔ
24 Ⓐ Ⓑ Ⓒ Ⓓ Ⓔ
25 Ⓐ Ⓑ Ⓒ Ⓓ Ⓔ
26 Ⓐ Ⓑ Ⓒ Ⓓ Ⓔ
27 Ⓐ Ⓑ Ⓒ Ⓓ Ⓔ
28 Ⓐ Ⓑ Ⓒ Ⓓ Ⓔ
29 Ⓐ Ⓑ Ⓒ Ⓓ Ⓔ
30 Ⓐ Ⓑ Ⓒ Ⓓ Ⓔ

31 Ⓐ Ⓑ Ⓒ Ⓓ Ⓔ
32 Ⓐ Ⓑ Ⓒ Ⓓ Ⓔ
33 Ⓐ Ⓑ Ⓒ Ⓓ Ⓔ
34 Ⓐ Ⓑ Ⓒ Ⓓ Ⓔ
35 Ⓐ Ⓑ Ⓒ Ⓓ Ⓔ
36 Ⓐ Ⓑ Ⓒ Ⓓ Ⓔ
37 Ⓐ Ⓑ Ⓒ Ⓓ Ⓔ
38 Ⓐ Ⓑ Ⓒ Ⓓ Ⓔ
39 Ⓐ Ⓑ Ⓒ Ⓓ Ⓔ
40 Ⓐ Ⓑ Ⓒ Ⓓ Ⓔ

**CAUTION** Grid answers in the section below for SECTION 4 or SECTION 5 only if directed to do so in your test book.

**Student-Produced Responses** ONLY ANSWERS THAT ARE GRIDDED WILL BE SCORED. YOU WILL NOT RECEIVE CREDIT FOR ANYTHING WRITTEN IN THE BOXES.

Quality Assurance Mark ●

9 10 11 12 13

14 15 16 17 18

Page 5

COMPLETE MARK ●    EXAMPLES OF INCOMPLETE MARKS

You must use a No. 2 pencil and marks must be complete. Do not use a mechanical pencil. It is very important that you fill in the entire circle darkly and completely. If you change your response, erase as completely as possible. Incomplete marks or erasures may affect your score.

**SECTION 6**

| | | | |
|---|---|---|---|
| 1 (A)(B)(C)(D)(E) | 11 (A)(B)(C)(D)(E) | 21 (A)(B)(C)(D)(E) | 31 (A)(B)(C)(D)(E) |
| 2 (A)(B)(C)(D)(E) | 12 (A)(B)(C)(D)(E) | 22 (A)(B)(C)(D)(E) | 32 (A)(B)(C)(D)(E) |
| 3 (A)(B)(C)(D)(E) | 13 (A)(B)(C)(D)(E) | 23 (A)(B)(C)(D)(E) | 33 (A)(B)(C)(D)(E) |
| 4 (A)(B)(C)(D)(E) | 14 (A)(B)(C)(D)(E) | 24 (A)(B)(C)(D)(E) | 34 (A)(B)(C)(D)(E) |
| 5 (A)(B)(C)(D)(E) | 15 (A)(B)(C)(D)(E) | 25 (A)(B)(C)(D)(E) | 35 (A)(B)(C)(D)(E) |
| 6 (A)(B)(C)(D)(E) | 16 (A)(B)(C)(D)(E) | 26 (A)(B)(C)(D)(E) | 36 (A)(B)(C)(D)(E) |
| 7 (A)(B)(C)(D)(E) | 17 (A)(B)(C)(D)(E) | 27 (A)(B)(C)(D)(E) | 37 (A)(B)(C)(D)(E) |
| 8 (A)(B)(C)(D)(E) | 18 (A)(B)(C)(D)(E) | 28 (A)(B)(C)(D)(E) | 38 (A)(B)(C)(D)(E) |
| 9 (A)(B)(C)(D)(E) | 19 (A)(B)(C)(D)(E) | 29 (A)(B)(C)(D)(E) | 39 (A)(B)(C)(D)(E) |
| 10 (A)(B)(C)(D)(E) | 20 (A)(B)(C)(D)(E) | 30 (A)(B)(C)(D)(E) | 40 (A)(B)(C)(D)(E) |

**SECTION 7**

| | | | |
|---|---|---|---|
| 1 (A)(B)(C)(D)(E) | 11 (A)(B)(C)(D)(E) | 21 (A)(B)(C)(D)(E) | 31 (A)(B)(C)(D)(E) |
| 2 (A)(B)(C)(D)(E) | 12 (A)(B)(C)(D)(E) | 22 (A)(B)(C)(D)(E) | 32 (A)(B)(C)(D)(E) |
| 3 (A)(B)(C)(D)(E) | 13 (A)(B)(C)(D)(E) | 23 (A)(B)(C)(D)(E) | 33 (A)(B)(C)(D)(E) |
| 4 (A)(B)(C)(D)(E) | 14 (A)(B)(C)(D)(E) | 24 (A)(B)(C)(D)(E) | 34 (A)(B)(C)(D)(E) |
| 5 (A)(B)(C)(D)(E) | 15 (A)(B)(C)(D)(E) | 25 (A)(B)(C)(D)(E) | 35 (A)(B)(C)(D)(E) |
| 6 (A)(B)(C)(D)(E) | 16 (A)(B)(C)(D)(E) | 26 (A)(B)(C)(D)(E) | 36 (A)(B)(C)(D)(E) |
| 7 (A)(B)(C)(D)(E) | 17 (A)(B)(C)(D)(E) | 27 (A)(B)(C)(D)(E) | 37 (A)(B)(C)(D)(E) |
| 8 (A)(B)(C)(D)(E) | 18 (A)(B)(C)(D)(E) | 28 (A)(B)(C)(D)(E) | 38 (A)(B)(C)(D)(E) |
| 9 (A)(B)(C)(D)(E) | 19 (A)(B)(C)(D)(E) | 29 (A)(B)(C)(D)(E) | 39 (A)(B)(C)(D)(E) |
| 10 (A)(B)(C)(D)(E) | 20 (A)(B)(C)(D)(E) | 30 (A)(B)(C)(D)(E) | 40 (A)(B)(C)(D)(E) |

**CAUTION**    Grid answers in the section below for SECTION 6 or SECTION 7 only if directed to do so in your test book.

**Student-Produced Responses**    ONLY ANSWERS THAT ARE GRIDDED WILL BE SCORED. YOU WILL NOT RECEIVE CREDIT FOR ANYTHING WRITTEN IN THE BOXES.

Quality Assurance Mark

9   10   11   12   13

14   15   16   17   18

PLEASE DO NOT WRITE IN THIS AREA

SERIAL #

2

**SECTION 8**

| | | | | |
|---|---|---|---|
| 1 Ⓐ Ⓑ Ⓒ Ⓓ Ⓔ | 11 Ⓐ Ⓑ Ⓒ Ⓓ Ⓔ | 21 Ⓐ Ⓑ Ⓒ Ⓓ Ⓔ | 31 Ⓐ Ⓑ Ⓒ Ⓓ Ⓔ |
| 2 Ⓐ Ⓑ Ⓒ Ⓓ Ⓔ | 12 Ⓐ Ⓑ Ⓒ Ⓓ Ⓔ | 22 Ⓐ Ⓑ Ⓒ Ⓓ Ⓔ | 32 Ⓐ Ⓑ Ⓒ Ⓓ Ⓔ |
| 3 Ⓐ Ⓑ Ⓒ Ⓓ Ⓔ | 13 Ⓐ Ⓑ Ⓒ Ⓓ Ⓔ | 23 Ⓐ Ⓑ Ⓒ Ⓓ Ⓔ | 33 Ⓐ Ⓑ Ⓒ Ⓓ Ⓔ |
| 4 Ⓐ Ⓑ Ⓒ Ⓓ Ⓔ | 14 Ⓐ Ⓑ Ⓒ Ⓓ Ⓔ | 24 Ⓐ Ⓑ Ⓒ Ⓓ Ⓔ | 34 Ⓐ Ⓑ Ⓒ Ⓓ Ⓔ |
| 5 Ⓐ Ⓑ Ⓒ Ⓓ Ⓔ | 15 Ⓐ Ⓑ Ⓒ Ⓓ Ⓔ | 25 Ⓐ Ⓑ Ⓒ Ⓓ Ⓔ | 35 Ⓐ Ⓑ Ⓒ Ⓓ Ⓔ |
| 6 Ⓐ Ⓑ Ⓒ Ⓓ Ⓔ | 16 Ⓐ Ⓑ Ⓒ Ⓓ Ⓔ | 26 Ⓐ Ⓑ Ⓒ Ⓓ Ⓔ | 36 Ⓐ Ⓑ Ⓒ Ⓓ Ⓔ |
| 7 Ⓐ Ⓑ Ⓒ Ⓓ Ⓔ | 17 Ⓐ Ⓑ Ⓒ Ⓓ Ⓔ | 27 Ⓐ Ⓑ Ⓒ Ⓓ Ⓔ | 37 Ⓐ Ⓑ Ⓒ Ⓓ Ⓔ |
| 8 Ⓐ Ⓑ Ⓒ Ⓓ Ⓔ | 18 Ⓐ Ⓑ Ⓒ Ⓓ Ⓔ | 28 Ⓐ Ⓑ Ⓒ Ⓓ Ⓔ | 38 Ⓐ Ⓑ Ⓒ Ⓓ Ⓔ |
| 9 Ⓐ Ⓑ Ⓒ Ⓓ Ⓔ | 19 Ⓐ Ⓑ Ⓒ Ⓓ Ⓔ | 29 Ⓐ Ⓑ Ⓒ Ⓓ Ⓔ | 39 Ⓐ Ⓑ Ⓒ Ⓓ Ⓔ |
| 10 Ⓐ Ⓑ Ⓒ Ⓓ Ⓔ | 20 Ⓐ Ⓑ Ⓒ Ⓓ Ⓔ | 30 Ⓐ Ⓑ Ⓒ Ⓓ Ⓔ | 40 Ⓐ Ⓑ Ⓒ Ⓓ Ⓔ |

**SECTION 9**

| | | | | |
|---|---|---|---|
| 1 Ⓐ Ⓑ Ⓒ Ⓓ Ⓔ | 11 Ⓐ Ⓑ Ⓒ Ⓓ Ⓔ | 21 Ⓐ Ⓑ Ⓒ Ⓓ Ⓔ | 31 Ⓐ Ⓑ Ⓒ Ⓓ Ⓔ |
| 2 Ⓐ Ⓑ Ⓒ Ⓓ Ⓔ | 12 Ⓐ Ⓑ Ⓒ Ⓓ Ⓕ | 22 Ⓐ Ⓑ Ⓒ Ⓓ Ⓔ | 32 Ⓐ Ⓑ Ⓒ Ⓓ Ⓔ |
| 3 Ⓐ Ⓑ Ⓒ Ⓓ Ⓔ | 13 Ⓐ Ⓑ Ⓒ Ⓓ Ⓔ | 23 Ⓐ Ⓑ Ⓒ Ⓓ Ⓔ | 33 Ⓐ Ⓑ Ⓒ Ⓓ Ⓔ |
| 4 Ⓐ Ⓑ Ⓒ Ⓓ Ⓔ | 14 Ⓐ Ⓑ Ⓒ Ⓓ Ⓔ | 24 Ⓐ Ⓑ Ⓒ Ⓓ Ⓔ | 34 Ⓐ Ⓑ Ⓒ Ⓓ Ⓔ |
| 5 Ⓐ Ⓑ Ⓒ Ⓓ Ⓔ | 15 Ⓐ Ⓑ Ⓒ Ⓓ Ⓔ | 25 Ⓐ Ⓑ Ⓒ Ⓓ Ⓕ | 35 Ⓐ Ⓑ Ⓒ Ⓓ Ⓕ |
| 6 Ⓐ Ⓑ Ⓒ Ⓓ Ⓔ | 16 Ⓐ Ⓑ Ⓒ Ⓓ Ⓔ | 26 Ⓐ Ⓑ Ⓒ Ⓤ Ⓔ | 36 Ⓐ Ⓑ Ⓒ Ⓓ Ⓔ |
| 7 Ⓐ Ⓑ Ⓒ Ⓓ Ⓔ | 17 Ⓐ Ⓑ Ⓒ Ⓓ Ⓔ | 27 Ⓐ Ⓑ Ⓒ Ⓓ Ⓔ | 37 Ⓐ Ⓑ Ⓒ Ⓓ Ⓔ |
| 8 Ⓐ Ⓑ Ⓒ Ⓓ Ⓔ | 18 Ⓐ Ⓑ Ⓒ Ⓓ Ⓔ | 28 Ⓐ Ⓑ Ⓒ Ⓓ Ⓔ | 38 Ⓐ Ⓑ Ⓒ Ⓓ Ⓔ |
| 9 Ⓐ Ⓑ Ⓒ Ⓓ Ⓔ | 19 Ⓐ Ⓑ Ⓒ Ⓓ Ⓔ | 29 Ⓐ Ⓑ Ⓒ Ⓓ Ⓔ | 39 Ⓐ Ⓑ Ⓒ Ⓓ Ⓔ |
| 10 Ⓐ Ⓑ Ⓒ Ⓓ Ⓔ | 20 Ⓐ Ⓑ Ⓒ Ⓓ Ⓔ | 30 Ⓐ Ⓑ Ⓒ Ⓓ Ⓔ | 40 Ⓐ Ⓑ Ⓒ Ⓓ Ⓔ |

Quality
●
Assurance
Mark

**SECTION 10**

| | | | | |
|---|---|---|---|
| 1 Ⓐ Ⓑ Ⓒ Ⓓ Ⓔ | 11 Ⓐ Ⓑ Ⓒ Ⓓ Ⓔ | 21 Ⓐ Ⓑ Ⓒ Ⓓ Ⓔ | 31 Ⓐ Ⓑ Ⓒ Ⓓ Ⓔ |
| 2 Ⓐ Ⓑ Ⓒ Ⓓ Ⓔ | 12 Ⓐ Ⓑ Ⓒ Ⓓ Ⓔ | 22 Ⓐ Ⓑ Ⓒ Ⓓ Ⓔ | 32 Ⓐ Ⓑ Ⓒ Ⓓ Ⓔ |
| 3 Ⓐ Ⓑ Ⓒ Ⓓ Ⓔ | 13 Ⓐ Ⓑ Ⓒ Ⓓ Ⓔ | 23 Ⓐ Ⓑ Ⓒ Ⓓ Ⓔ | 33 Ⓐ Ⓑ Ⓒ Ⓓ Ⓔ |
| 4 Ⓐ Ⓑ Ⓒ Ⓓ Ⓔ | 14 Ⓐ Ⓑ Ⓒ Ⓓ Ⓔ | 24 Ⓐ Ⓑ Ⓒ Ⓓ Ⓔ | 34 Ⓐ Ⓑ Ⓒ Ⓓ Ⓔ |
| 5 Ⓐ Ⓑ Ⓒ Ⓓ Ⓔ | 15 Ⓐ Ⓑ Ⓒ Ⓓ Ⓔ | 25 Ⓐ Ⓑ Ⓒ Ⓓ Ⓔ | 35 Ⓐ Ⓑ Ⓒ Ⓓ Ⓔ |
| 6 Ⓐ Ⓑ Ⓒ Ⓓ Ⓔ | 16 Ⓐ Ⓑ Ⓒ Ⓓ Ⓔ | 26 Ⓐ Ⓑ Ⓒ Ⓓ Ⓔ | 36 Ⓐ Ⓑ Ⓒ Ⓓ Ⓔ |
| 7 Ⓐ Ⓑ Ⓒ Ⓓ Ⓔ | 17 Ⓐ Ⓑ Ⓒ Ⓓ Ⓔ | 27 Ⓐ Ⓑ Ⓒ Ⓓ Ⓔ | 37 Ⓐ Ⓑ Ⓒ Ⓓ Ⓔ |
| 8 Ⓐ Ⓑ Ⓒ Ⓓ Ⓔ | 18 Ⓐ Ⓑ Ⓒ Ⓓ Ⓔ | 28 Ⓐ Ⓑ Ⓒ Ⓓ Ⓔ | 38 Ⓐ Ⓑ Ⓒ Ⓓ Ⓔ |
| 9 Ⓐ Ⓑ Ⓒ Ⓓ Ⓔ | 19 Ⓐ Ⓑ Ⓒ Ⓓ Ⓔ | 29 Ⓐ Ⓑ Ⓒ Ⓓ Ⓔ | 39 Ⓐ Ⓑ Ⓒ Ⓓ Ⓔ |
| 10 Ⓐ Ⓑ Ⓒ Ⓓ Ⓔ | 20 Ⓐ Ⓑ Ⓒ Ⓓ Ⓔ | 30 Ⓐ Ⓑ Ⓒ Ⓓ Ⓔ | 40 Ⓐ Ⓑ Ⓒ Ⓓ Ⓔ |

**Page 7**

449

**2**

## CERTIFICATION STATEMENT

Copy the statement below (do not print) and sign your name as you would an official document.

I hereby agree to the conditions set forth online at www.collegeboard.org and/or in the SAT® Registration Booklet and certify that I am the person whose name and address appear on this answer sheet.

_____

_____

_____

_____

By signing below, I agree not to share any specific test questions or essay topics with anyone by any form of communication, including, but not limited to: email, text messages, or use of the Internet.

Signature _____     Date _____

## SPECIAL QUESTIONS

1 (A)(B)(C)(D)(E)(F)(G)(H)(I)(J)
2 (A)(B)(C)(D)(E)(F)(G)(H)(I)(J)
3 (A)(B)(C)(D)(E)(F)(G)(H)(I)(J)
4 (A)(B)(C)(D)(E)(F)(G)(H)(I)(J)
5 (A)(B)(C)(D)(E)(F)(G)(H)(I)(J)
6 (A)(B)(C)(D)(E)(F)(G)(H)(I)(J)
7 (A)(B)(C)(D)(E)(F)(G)(H)(I)(J)
8 (A)(B)(C)(D)(E)(F)(G)(H)(I)(J)

**Page 8**

## ESSAY
### Time — 25 minutes

---

| **Turn to page 2 of your answer sheet to write your ESSAY.** |
| --- |

The essay gives you an opportunity to show how effectively you can develop and express ideas. You should, therefore, take care to develop your point of view, present your ideas logically and clearly, and use language precisely.

Your essay must be written on the lines provided on your answer sheet—you will receive no other paper on which to write. You will have enough space if you write on every line, avoid wide margins, and keep your handwriting to a reasonable size. Remember that people who are not familiar with your handwriting will read what you write. Try to write or print so that what you are writing is legible to those readers.

**Important Reminders:**

- **A pencil is required for the essay.** An essay written in ink will receive a score of zero.
- **Do not write your essay in your test book.** You will receive credit only for what you write on your answer sheet.
- **An off-topic essay will receive a score of zero.**
- **If your essay does not reflect your original and individual work, your test scores may be canceled.**

You have twenty-five minutes to write an essay on the topic assigned below.

---

Think carefully about the issue presented in the following excerpt and the assignment below.

> Many people believe that our government should do more to solve our problems. After all, how can one individual create more jobs or make roads safer or improve the schools or help to provide any of the other benefits that we have come to enjoy? And yet expecting that the government—rather than individuals—should always come up with the solutions to society's ills may have made us less self-reliant, undermining our independence and self-sufficiency.

**Assignment:**  Should people take more responsibility for solving problems that affect their communities or the nation in general? Plan and write an essay in which you develop your point of view on this issue. Support your position with reasoning and examples taken from your reading, studies, experience, or observations.

Yes

---

BEGIN WRITING YOUR ESSAY ON PAGE 2 OF THE ANSWER SHEET.

- Impact you already
- Make their own choice
- things

---

**If you finish before time is called, you may check your work on this section only.**
**Do not turn to any other section in the test.**

## SECTION 2
### Time — 25 minutes
### 20 Questions

**Turn to Section 2 (page 4) of your answer sheet to answer the questions in this section.**

**Directions:** For this section, solve each problem and decide which is the best of the choices given. Fill in the corresponding circle on the answer sheet. You may use any available space for scratchwork.

Notes

1. The use of a calculator is permitted.
2. All numbers used are real numbers.
3. Figures that accompany problems in this test are intended to provide information useful in solving the problems. They are drawn as accurately as possible EXCEPT when it is stated in a specific problem that the figure is not drawn to scale. All figures lie in a plane unless otherwise indicated.
4. Unless otherwise specified, the domain of any function $f$ is assumed to be the set of all real numbers $x$ for which $f(x)$ is a real number.

Reference Information

$A = \pi r^2$
$C = 2\pi r$
$A = \ell w$
$A = \frac{1}{2}bh$
$V = \ell wh$
$V = \pi r^2 h$
$c^2 = a^2 + b^2$
Special Right Triangles

The number of degrees of arc in a circle is 360.
The sum of the measures in degrees of the angles of a triangle is 180.

1, 4, 10, $t$, 46, …

**1.** In the sequence above, the first term is 1 and each term after the first is 2 more than twice the previous term. What is the value of $t$ ?

(A) 12
(B) 14
(C) 20
(D) 22
(E) 24

**2.** A machine can fill 24 cartons in 1 hour. At this rate, how many cartons can the machine fill in 5 minutes?

(A) Two
(B) Three
(C) Five
(D) Six
(E) Eight

**GO ON TO THE NEXT PAGE**

**Questions 3-4 refer to the following graph.**

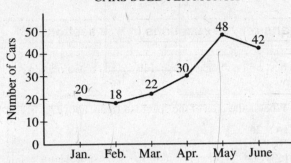

CARS SOLD PER MONTH

The line graph above shows the number of cars Cathy sold in each of the first six months of 2003.

3. Cathy sold how many more cars in the month of May than in the months of January and February combined?

   (A) 10
   (B) 15
   (C) 20
   (D) 25
   (E) 30

4. If the car sales data from these six months were illustrated by a circle graph, what would be the measure of the central angle of the sector that represents the month of April?

   (A) 30°
   (B) 54°
   (C) 60°
   (D) 108°
   (E) 120°

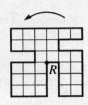

5. If the figure above were rotated counterclockwise 90° about point $R$, which of the following would be the result?

   (A)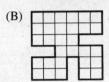

   (B)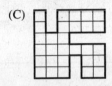

   (C)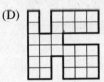

   (D)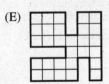

   (E)

GO ON TO THE NEXT PAGE

**6.** If 3 more than twice a number is equal to 10, what is 4 times the number?

(A)  $3\frac{1}{2}$

(B)  7

(C)  $10\frac{1}{2}$

(D)  14

(E)  $17\frac{1}{2}$

$3 + 2x = 10$

$2x = 7$

$x = \left(\frac{7}{2}\right) + 2 \leq 14$

$a,\ 2a,\ 4a,\ 8a$

**7.** If  $a \leq 0$ , which of the four numbers above is the greatest?

(A)  $a$
(B)  $2a$
(C)  $4a$
(D)  $8a$
(E)  It cannot be determined from the information given.

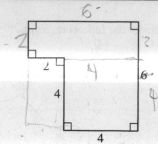

6

2

2    4    6

4    4

4

**8.** What is the area of the six-sided figure above?

(A)  26
(B)  28
(C)  30
(D)  34
(E)  40

$12 + 16$

$28$

**9.** If  $(x - 2)^2 = 25$  and  $x < 0$ , what is the value of  $x$ ?

(A)  −23
(B)  −7
(C)  −5
(D)  −3
(E)  −2

$x - 2 = -5$

$x = -3$

GO ON TO THE NEXT PAGE

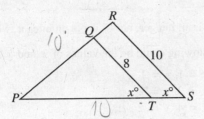

**10.** In the figure above, what is the value of $\dfrac{PT}{PS}$ ?

(A) $\dfrac{1}{5}$

(B) $\dfrac{1}{4}$

(C) $\dfrac{2}{5}$

(D) $\dfrac{1}{2}$

(E) $\dfrac{4}{5}$

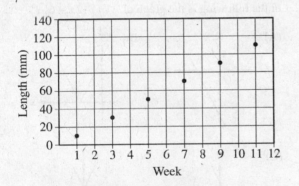

**11.** A biology teacher graphed the length of a fish over time, and the results are shown above. If $L$ represents the length of the fish in millimeters and $W$ represents the number of the week, which of the following equations best describes the data shown?

(A) $L = W$
(B) $L = 10$
(C) $L = W + 10$
(D) $L = 10W$
(E) $L = 10W + 10$

5, 6, 5, 6, 7, 5, 5, $n$, 6

**12.** For the numbers listed above, the only mode is 5 and the median is 6. Each of the following could be the value of $n$ EXCEPT

(A) 6
(B) 7
(C) 8
(D) 9
(E) 10

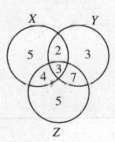

**13.** In the Venn diagram above, the number in each region indicates how many elements are in that region. How many elements are in the intersection of sets $Y$ and $Z$ ?

(A) 3
(B) 7
(C) 10
(D) 16
(E) 25

**GO ON TO THE NEXT PAGE**

**14.** If $m = t^3$ for any positive integer $t$, and if $w = m^2 + m$, what is $w$ in terms of $t$ ?

(A) $t^2 + t$

(B) $t^3$

(C) $t^3 + t$

(D) $t^5 + t^3$

(E) $t^6 + t^3$

$w = (t^3)^2 + m$

$w = t^6 + t^3$

$= t$

**15.** For all positive integers $x$, let $x\blacktriangle$ be defined to be $(x - 1)(x + 1)$. Which of the following is equal to $6\blacktriangle - 5\blacktriangle$ ?

$x = +1, -1$

(A) $2\blacktriangle + 1\blacktriangle$

(B) $3\blacktriangle + 2\blacktriangle$

(C) $4\blacktriangle + 3\blacktriangle$

(D) $5\blacktriangle + 4\blacktriangle$

(E) $6\blacktriangle + 5\blacktriangle$

$(6x - 6)(5x + 5)$

**16.** If $\dfrac{x^2}{y}$ is an integer, but $\dfrac{x}{y}$ is not an integer, which of the following could be the values of $x$ and $y$ ?

(A) $x = 1, y = 1$

(B) $x = 3, y = 2$

(C) $x = 4, y = 2$

(D) $x = 6, y = 4$

(E) $x = 9, y = 3$

$\dfrac{9}{2}$

$\dfrac{36}{4} = 9$

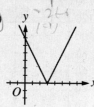

**17.** The equation of the line above is $y = -2x + 6$. Which of the following is the graph of $y = |-2x + 6|$ ?

(A)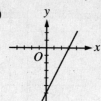

(B)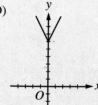

(C)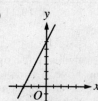

(D)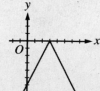

(E)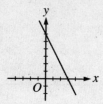

**GO ON TO THE NEXT PAGE**

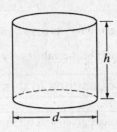

**18.** The right circular cylinder above has diameter $d$ and height $h$. Of the following expressions, which represents the volume of the smallest rectangular box that completely contains the cylinder?

(A)  $dh$

(B)  $d^2h$

(C)  $dh^2$

(D)  $d^2h^2$

(E)  $(d+h)^2$

**19.** The square of $x$ is equal to 4 times the square of $y$. If $x$ is 1 more than twice $y$, what is the value of $x$?

(A)  4

(B)  $-\dfrac{1}{2}$

(C)  $-\dfrac{1}{4}$

(D)  $\dfrac{1}{4}$

(E)  $\dfrac{1}{2}$

**20.** In the $xy$-coordinate plane, lines $\ell$ and $q$ are perpendicular. If line $\ell$ contains the points $(0, 0)$ and $(2, 1)$, and line $q$ contains the points $(2, 1)$ and $(0, t)$, what is the value of $t$?

(A)  $-3$

(B)  $-2$

(C)  $2$

(D)  $3$

(E)  $5$

**STOP**

If you finish before time is called, you may check your work on this section only.
Do not turn to any other section in the test.

# SECTION 4
## Time — 25 minutes
## 25 Questions

**Turn to Section 4 (page 5) of your answer sheet to answer the questions in this section.**

**Directions:** For each question in this section, select the best answer from among the choices given and fill in the corresponding circle on the answer sheet.

---

Each sentence below has one or two blanks, each blank indicating that something has been omitted. Beneath the sentence are five words or sets of words labeled A through E. Choose the word or set of words that, when inserted in the sentence, best fits the meaning of the sentence as a whole.

**Example:**

Hoping to ------- the dispute, negotiators proposed a compromise that they felt would be ------- to both labor and management.

(A) enforce . . useful
(B) end . . divisive
(C) overcome . . unattractive
(D) extend . . satisfactory
(E) resolve . . acceptable

(A) (B) (C) (D) ●

---

1. The movie's plot was -------: once you knew what befell the hero, you could ------- the fate of the villain.

   (A) convincing . . misinterpret
   (B) misleading . . anticipate
   (C) predictable . . foresee
   (D) ironic . . endorse
   (E) spellbinding . . ignore

2. A certain additive put in gasoline to reduce air pollution is actually ------- groundwater, a finding that shows that even the most well-intentioned fixes can sometimes -------.

   (A) liquefying . . founder
   (B) contaminating . . backfire
   (C) purifying . . boomerang
   (D) saturating . . reciprocate
   (E) polluting . . prevail

3. The biologist's description of the wolf pack was truly -------, devoid of any emotion or personal prejudice.

   (A) dispassionate    (B) insubstantial    (C) esoteric
   (D) capricious    (E) indignant

4. No longer considered -------, the belief that all of Puerto Rico's indigenous Taino people perished centuries ago appears to be a ------- now that modern Taino descendants have come forward.

   (A) conclusive . . reality
   (B) tenable . . misconception
   (C) mythical . . possibility
   (D) erroneous . . delusion
   (E) hypothetical . . digression

5. Although easily angered by our mischievous behavior, our mother could be immediately ------- by our expressions of remorse.

   (A) substantiated    (B) impugned    (C) protected
   (D) united    (E) mollified

6. Scientists wonder what to do with the dead satellites, jettisoned rockets, drifting paint flecks, and other ------- orbiting Earth.

   (A) flotsam    (B) reconnaissance    (C) decimation
   (D) raiment    (E) sustenance

7. Although aging brings about profound physiological changes, it does not often alter an individual's -------: an irascible thirty year old will probably still be ------- at seventy.

   (A) disposition . . cantankerous
   (B) anatomy . . churlish
   (C) outlook . . benevolent
   (D) personality . . laconic
   (E) stature . . robust

8. The commentator characterized the electorate as ------- because it was unpredictable and given to constantly shifting moods.

   (A) mercurial    (B) corrosive    (C) disingenuous
   (D) implacable    (E) phlegmatic

**GO ON TO THE NEXT PAGE**

The passages below are followed by questions based on their content; questions following a pair of related passages may also be based on the relationship between the paired passages. Answer the questions on the basis of what is <u>stated</u> or <u>implied</u> in the passages and in any introductory material that may be provided.

**Questions 9-12 are based on the following passages.**

**Passage 1**

Just how overcrowded is Earth anyway? Certainly the world is filled with empty places. A flight almost anywhere reveals vast expanses of unoccupied land. Cities cover only a small percentage of Earth. Indeed, when we look at the
*Line*
5  world's population relative to the land available, we find out just how *under*populated the world is. A noted economist recently put Earth's population in perspective by asking what would happen if the world's six billion people were put into the land area of Texas. His answer:
10  each person would have an area equal to the floor space of a typical U.S. home. And he further notes that some cities in the United States contain enough land area to provide standing room for the entire global population.

**Passage 2**

The idea that the number of people per square mile is a
15  key determinant of population pressure is as widespread as it is wrong. The key issue in judging overpopulation is not how many people can fit into any given space but whether Earth can supply the population's long-term requirement for food, water, and other resources. Most of the "empty"
20  land in the United States, for example, either grows the food essential to our well-being or supplies us with raw materials. Densely populated countries and cities can be crowded only because the rest of the world is not.

9. The author of Passage 2 would most likely criticize the author of Passage 1 for

(A) using incorrect data to support a flawed conclusion
(B) severely overstating the extent of a global problem
(C) recommending a course of action that might have damaging effects
(D) focusing on the wrong factor in considering an issue
(E) allowing personal prejudice to interfere with scientific inquiry

10. The tone of the first sentence of Passage 2 is best characterized as

(A) wistful
(B) dismayed
(C) emphatic
(D) ambivalent
(E) apologetic

11. It can be inferred from the use of quotation marks in line 19 that the author of Passage 2 would most likely

(A) criticize Passage 1 for overstating the nature of a problem
(B) take issue with Passage 1 for failing to acknowledge a change in population patterns
(C) disagree with the characterization in Passage 1 of certain regions
(D) endorse the solution to a problem advanced in Passage 1
(E) concur with a specific theory briefly mentioned in Passage 1

12. Both authors acknowledge which of the following points?

(A) Earth contains a great deal of unoccupied land.
(B) Estimates of Earth's population are not reliable.
(C) Technology is transforming empty spaces into productive land.
(D) Nonscientists do not appreciate the dangers of overpopulation.
(E) Earth's population is outstripping available resources.

**GO ON TO THE NEXT PAGE**

**Questions 13-25 are based on the following passage.**

*This passage is excerpted from a novel published in 1970. As the passage begins, four men are looking at a map in preparation for a canoe trip.*

It unrolled slowly, forced to show its colors, curling and snapping back whenever one of us turned loose. The whole land was very tense until we put our four steins on
Line its corners and laid the river out to run for us through the
5 mountains 150 miles north. Lewis' hand took a pencil and marked out a small strong X in a place where some of the green bled away and the paper changed with high ground, and began to work downstream, northeast to southwest through the printed woods. I watched the hand rather
10 than the location, for it seemed to have power over the terrain, and when it stopped for Lewis' voice to explain something, it was as though all streams everywhere quit running, hanging silently where they were to let the point be made. The pencil turned over and pretended to sketch
15 in with the eraser an area that must have been around fifty miles long, through which the river hooked and cramped.

"When they take another survey and rework the map," Lewis said, "all this in here will be blue. The dam at Aintry has already been started, and when it's finished next spring
20 the river will back up fast. This whole valley will be under water. But right now it's wild. And I *mean* wild; it looks like something up in Alaska. We really ought to go up there before the real estate people get hold of it and make it over into one of their heavens."

25 I leaned forward and concentrated down into the invisible shape he had drawn, trying to see the changes that would come, the nighttime rising of dammed water bringing a new lake up with its choice lots, its marinas and beer cans, and also trying to visualize the land as
30 Lewis said it was at that moment, unvisited and free. I breathed in and out once, consciously; my body, particularly the back and arms, felt ready for something like this. I looked around the bar and then back into the map, picking up the river where we would enter it. A little way
35 to the southwest the paper blanched.

"Does this mean it's higher here?" I asked.

"Yes," Lewis said, looking quickly at me to see if I saw he was being tolerant.

Ah, he's going to turn this into something, I thought.
40 A lesson. A moral. A life principle. A Way.

"It must run through a gorge or something" was all he said though. "But we can get through that in a day, easy. And the water should be good, in that part especially."

I didn't have much idea what good meant in the way
45 of river water, but for it to seem good to Lewis it would have to meet some very definite standards. The way he went about things was strictly his own; that was mainly what he liked about doing them. He liked particularly to take some extremely specialized and difficult form
50 of sport—usually one he could do by himself—and evolve a personal approach to it which he could then expound. I had been through this with him in fly casting, in archery and weight lifting and spelunking, in all of which he had developed complete mystiques. Now it
55 was canoeing. I settled back and came out of the map.

Bobby Trippe was there, across from me. He had smooth thin hair and a high pink complexion. I knew him least well of the others at the table, but I liked him a good deal, even so. He was pleasantly cynical
60 and gave me the impression that he shared some kind of understanding with me that neither of us was to take Lewis too seriously.

"They tell me that this is the kind of thing that gets hold of middle-class householders every once in a while,"
65 Bobby said. "But most of them just lie down till the feeling passes."

"And when most of them lie down they're at Woodlawn* before they think about getting up," Lewis said.

* A cemetery.

**13.** In lines 1-5 ("It unrolled . . . north"), the map is described as if it were

(A) invaluable
(B) animate
(C) cryptic
(D) antiquated
(E) erroneous

**14.** Lines 9-14 ("I watched . . . made") primarily serve to

(A) recount an anecdote
(B) offer an example
(C) note an impression
(D) make a prediction
(E) advance a theory

GO ON TO THE NEXT PAGE

**15.** In lines 9-14 ("I watched . . . made"), the narrator suggests that Lewis' hand is

(A) deft
(B) languid
(C) resilient
(D) omnipotent
(E) expressive

**16.** In line 13, "hanging" most nearly means

(A) flowing
(B) drooping
(C) inclining
(D) unfinished
(E) suspended

**17.** In line 22, "Alaska" serves as an example of a place that is

(A) distant
(B) immense
(C) scenic
(D) cold
(E) undeveloped

**18.** Lewis' attitude toward the "real estate people" (line 23) is best described as

(A) contemptuous
(B) envious
(C) furious
(D) puzzled
(E) intrigued

**19.** Lewis' use of the word "heavens" (line 24) is best characterized as

(A) appreciative
(B) deceitful
(C) tentative
(D) defensive
(E) ironic

**20.** In lines 25-30 ("I leaned . . . free"), the narrator reacts to Lewis' suggestion by

(A) visualizing an unlikely series of events
(B) imagining two radically different states
(C) considering a problem and its proposed solution
(D) weighing the pros and cons of a course of action
(E) reflecting on how the past shapes the future

**21.** The narrator's reference to his "back and arms" (line 32) primarily serves to

(A) suggest a sense of physical anticipation
(B) emphasize his insecurity about his athletic abilities
(C) indicate a feeling of intense discomfort
(D) express pride in his personal appearance
(E) call attention to his success in previous contests of strength

**22.** In line 34, "picking up" most nearly means

(A) locating
(B) acquiring
(C) learning
(D) claiming
(E) gathering

**23.** In lines 39-40 ("Ah . . . Way"), the narrator suggests that Lewis is sometimes

(A) whimsical
(B) callous
(C) remiss
(D) didactic
(E) impetuous

**GO ON TO THE NEXT PAGE**

4  4

Unauthorized copying or reuse of
any part of this page is illegal.

**24.** The narrative in lines 46-54 ("The way . . . mystiques")
suggests that Lewis prefers sports that

(A) do not require special equipment
(B) are inherently competitive
(C) allow room for individual expression
(D) demand great strength but little skill
(E) pose few risks to beginners

**25.** In context, Bobby's remarks in lines 63-66 ("They . . .
passes") are best characterized as

(A) explicit criticism
(B) veiled malice
(C) dry humor
(D) frank confession
(E) factual observation

# STOP

**If you finish before time is called, you may check your work on this section only.
Do not turn to any other section in the test.**

5 ▭ ▭ 5 ▭ ▭ 5 ▭ 5

Unauthorized copying or reuse of any part of this page is illegal.

## SECTION 5
**Time — 25 minutes**
**18 Questions**

**Turn to Section 5 (page 5) of your answer sheet to answer the questions in this section.**

**Directions:** This section contains two types of questions. You have 25 minutes to complete both types. For questions 1-8, solve each problem and decide which is the best of the choices given. Fill in the corresponding circle on the answer sheet. You may use any available space for scratchwork.

Notes

1. The use of a calculator is permitted.
2. All numbers used are real numbers.
3. Figures that accompany problems in this test are intended to provide information useful in solving the problems. They are drawn as accurately as possible EXCEPT when it is stated in a specific problem that the figure is not drawn to scale. All figures lie in a plane unless otherwise indicated.
4. Unless otherwise specified, the domain of any function $f$ is assumed to be the set of all real numbers $x$ for which $f(x)$ is a real number.

Reference Information

$A = \pi r^2$
$C = 2\pi r$     $A = \ell w$     $A = \frac{1}{2}bh$     $V = \ell wh$     $V = \pi r^2 h$     $c^2 = a^2 + b^2$     Special Right Triangles

The number of degrees of arc in a circle is 360.
The sum of the measures in degrees of the angles of a triangle is 180.

---

**1.** If $3x = 0$, what is the value of $1 + x + x^2$ ?

(A) $\dfrac{7}{9}$

(B) $1$

(C) $\dfrac{13}{9}$    $x < 0$

(D) $7$

(E) $13$

**2.** The diameter of circle $A$ is 3 times the diameter of circle $B$. What is the ratio of the radius of circle $A$ to the radius of circle $B$ ?

(A) $9 : 1$
(B) $6 : 1$
(C) $3 : 4$
(D) $3 : 2$
(E) $3 : 1$

**GO ON TO THE NEXT PAGE**

463

**3.** $N$ is a set of numbers whose average (arithmetic mean) is 3. $M$ is a set that is generated by doubling each number in $N$. What is the average of the numbers in set $M$?

(A) $\frac{1}{3}$

(B) 2

(C) 3

(D) 6

(E) 9

**4.** If $P$, $R$, and $T$ are digits in the positive three-digit integer $PRT$, what is the decimal equivalent of $PRT \times 10^{-2}$ ?

(A) 0.0$PRT$

(B) 0.$PRT$

(C) $P.RT$

(D) $PR.T$

(E) $PR,T$00

**5.** If $k + n < k$, which of the following must be true?

(A) $k > 0$

(B) $k = 0$

(C) $k < 0$

(D) $n > 0$

(E) $n < 0$

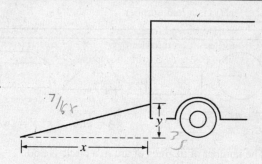

Note: Figure not drawn to scale.

**6.** A ramp is extended from a truck to the ground, as shown in the figure above. The ramp has a slope of $\frac{7}{16}$. If $y$ is 3.5 feet, what is $x$, in feet?

(A) 8

(B) 12.5

(C) 20

(D) 24.5

(E) 32

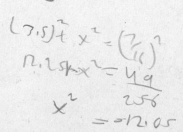

GO ON TO THE NEXT PAGE

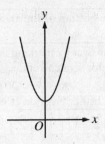

**7.** The graph above is a parabola whose equation is

$y = ax^2 + 2$, where $a$ is a constant. If $y = \dfrac{a}{3}x^2 + 2$

is graphed on the same axes, which of the following

best describes the resulting graph as compared with

the graph above?

(A) It will be narrower.
(B) It will be wider.
(C) It will be moved to the left.
(D) It will be moved to the right.
(E) It will be moved 3 units downward.

**8.** Meredith has a red hat, a blue hat, and a white hat. She also has three sweaters—one red, one blue, and one white—and three pairs of jeans—one red, one blue, and one white. Meredith wants to wear a red, white, and blue outfit consisting of one hat, one sweater, and one pair of jeans. How many different possibilities does she have?

(A) 3
(B) 6
(C) 9
(D) 12
(E) 27

**GO ON TO THE NEXT PAGE**

5 ☐ 5 ☐ 5 ☐ 5 ☐ 5

Unauthorized copying or reuse of
any part of this page is illegal.

**Directions:** For Student-Produced Response questions 9-18, use the grids at the bottom of the answer sheet page on which you have answered questions 1-8.

Each of the remaining 10 questions requires you to solve the problem and enter your answer by marking the circles in the special grid, as shown in the examples below. You may use any available space for scratchwork.

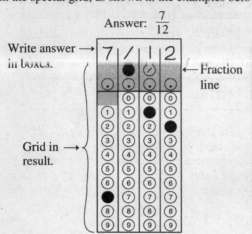

Answer: $\frac{7}{12}$

Write answer → in boxes.

← Fraction line

Grid in → result.

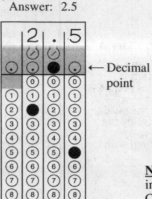

Answer: 2.5

← Decimal point

Answer: 201
Either position is correct.

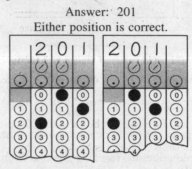

**Note:** You may start your answers in any column, space permitting. Columns not needed should be left blank.

- Mark no more than one circle in any column.

- Because the answer sheet will be machine-scored, **you will receive credit only if the circles are filled in correctly.**

- Although not required, it is suggested that you write your answer in the boxes at the top of the columns to help you fill in the circles accurately.

- Some problems may have more than one correct answer. In such cases, grid only one answer.

- No question has a negative answer.

- **Mixed numbers** such as $3\frac{1}{2}$ must be gridded as

  3.5 or 7/2. (If | 3 | 1 | / | 2 | is gridded, it will be

  interpreted as $\frac{31}{2}$, not $3\frac{1}{2}$.)

- **Decimal Answers:** If you obtain a decimal answer with more digits than the grid can accommodate, it may be either rounded or truncated, but it must fill the entire grid. For example, if you obtain an answer such as 0.6666..., you should record your result as .666 or .667. **A less accurate value such as .66 or .67 will be scored as incorrect.**

Acceptable ways to grid $\frac{2}{3}$ are:

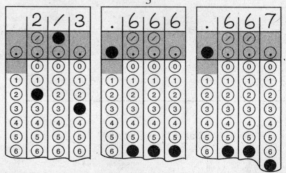

9. When twice a certain number is increased by 5, the result is 14. What is the number?

$$2x + 5 = 14$$
$$2x = 9$$
$$x = \frac{9}{2}$$

10. In the figure above, $\ell \parallel m$ and $y = 3x$. What is the value of $y$?

$6x = 360$
$\frac{360}{2}$
$x = 180$
$x = 30$

$y = 3(30)$

$y = 90$

$x = 60$

$y = 3(30)$

**GO ON TO THE NEXT PAGE** →

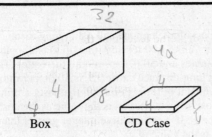

Box          CD Case

**11.** The inside dimensions of the rectangular box shown above are 4 inches by 4 inches by 8 inches. What is the maximum number of CD cases like the one shown that will fit inside the box if each CD case has outside dimensions of 4 inches by 4 inches by $\frac{1}{4}$ inch?

**12.** If $\dfrac{3x+y}{y} = \dfrac{6}{5}$, what is the value of $\dfrac{x}{y}$ ?

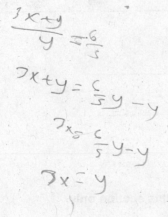

PROFITS OF CERTAIN STORES

|         | Year 1   | Year 2   |
|---------|----------|----------|
| Store A | $ 5,000  | $ 6,200  |
| Store B | 6,000    | 7,350    |
| Store C | 10,000   | 12,700   |
| TOTAL   | $21,000  | $26,250  |

**13.** The table above lists the profits of 3 stores in 2 consecutive years. What was the average (arithmetic mean) increase in profit, in dollars, for these 3 stores from year 1 to year 2 ? (Disregard the $ sign when gridding your answer.)

$$f(x) = |3x - 17|$$

**14.** For the function defined above, what is one possible value of $a$ for which $f(a) < a$ ?

**GO ON TO THE NEXT PAGE**

15. From a jar containing 50 pieces of candy, of which 25 are red and 25 are green, Ari has taken 3 red and 4 green pieces. He takes an additional 13 pieces from the jar. What is the least number of these additional pieces that must be red in order for Ari to have more red candies than green candies among all the pieces he has taken?

16. A positive integer is said to be "tri-factorable" if it is the product of three consecutive integers. How many positive integers less than 1,000 are tri-factorable?

17. The cost of a telephone call using long-distance carrier $A$ is $1.00 for any time up to and including 20 minutes and $0.07 per minute thereafter. The cost using long-distance carrier $B$ is $0.06 per minute for any amount of time. For a call that lasts $t$ minutes, the cost using carrier $A$ is the same as the cost using carrier $B$. If $t$ is a positive integer greater than 20, what is the value of $t$?

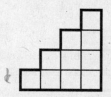

18. The figure above shows an arrangement of 10 squares, each with side of length $k$ inches. The perimeter of the figure is $p$ inches. The area of the figure is $a$ square inches. If $p = a$, what is the value of $k$?

# STOP

**If you finish before time is called, you may check your work on this section only.**
**Do not turn to any other section in the test.**

## SECTION 6
### Time — 25 minutes
### 35 Questions

**Turn to Section 6 (page 6) of your answer sheet to answer the questions in this section.**

**Directions:** For each question in this section, select the best answer from among the choices given and fill in the corresponding circle on the answer sheet.

The following sentences test correctness and effectiveness of expression. Part of each sentence or the entire sentence is underlined; beneath each sentence are five ways of phrasing the underlined material. Choice A repeats the original phrasing; the other four choices are different. If you think the original phrasing produces a better sentence than any of the alternatives, select choice A; if not, select one of the other choices.

In making your selection, follow the requirements of standard written English; that is, pay attention to grammar, choice of words, sentence construction, and punctuation. Your selection should result in the most effective sentence—clear and precise, without awkwardness or ambiguity.

EXAMPLE:

Laura Ingalls Wilder published her first book
and she was sixty-five years old then.

- (A) and she was sixty-five years old then
- (B) when she was sixty-five
- (C) at age sixty-five years old
- (D) upon the reaching of sixty-five years
- (E) at the time when she was sixty-five

Ⓐ ● Ⓒ Ⓓ Ⓔ

1. Confident that she was fully prepared, Ellen decided to spend the night before the recital reading and relaxing but not to be practicing.

   - (A) but not to be practicing
   - (B) and not for practicing
   - (C) more than to practice
   - (D) rather than practicing
   - (E) rather than having practiced

2. Sir Ronald Ross, winner of the 1902 Nobel Prize for Physiology or Medicine, and who identified the *Anopheles* mosquito as the transmitter of human malaria.

   - (A) and who identified
   - (B) he has identified
   - (C) and he has identified
   - (D) and who is identifying
   - (E) identified

3. Traveling through Yosemite, the scenery of waterfalls and granite peaks, which we photographed, was beautiful.

   - (A) the scenery of waterfalls and granite peaks, which we photographed, was beautiful
   - (B) the waterfalls and granite peaks were the beautiful scenery we photographed
   - (C) we photographed the beautiful scenery of waterfalls and granite peaks
   - (D) we photographed the scenery of waterfalls and granite peaks, being beautiful
   - (E) what we photographed was the beautiful scenery of waterfalls and granite peaks

4. The poet Firdawsi composed the Iranian national epic *Shah-nameh* in 1010 with his purpose being to recount the history of the Persian kings.

   - (A) with his purpose being to recount
   - (B) and his purpose was recounting
   - (C) to recount
   - (D) thus recounted
   - (E) he recounted

**GO ON TO THE NEXT PAGE**

5. As a choreographer, Judith <u>Jamison has enriched the world of dance, she uses as her work's inspiration</u> African American culture.

(A) Jamison has enriched the world of dance, she uses as her work's inspiration
(B) Jamison has enriched the world of dance with works inspired by
(C) Jamison, who has enriched the world of dance by works whose inspirations are
(D) Jamison, enriching the world of dance, with works inspired by
(E) Jamison enriches the world of dance through works that had the inspiration of

6. Leslie Marmon Silko has said that <u>her writing, which was powerfully influenced by storytellers in her family</u> but that the landscape of her childhood also shaped her vision and provided stories.

(A) her writing, which was powerfully influenced by storytellers in her family
(B) her writing, powerfully influenced by family storytellers
(C) family storytellers powerfully influenced her writing
(D) storytellers in the family being powerful influences on her writing
(E) powerfully influential in her writing was family storytellers

7. <u>Finding the Baltimore waterfront fascinating, all that there was to see was thoroughly explored by Antonio.</u>

(A) Finding the Baltimore waterfront fascinating, all that there was to see was thoroughly explored by Antonio.
(B) Antonio found the Baltimore waterfront fascinating, he thoroughly explored all that there was to see.
(C) Finding the Baltimore waterfront fascinating, Antonio thoroughly explored all that there was to see.
(D) The Baltimore waterfront is fascinating and is why Antonio thoroughly explored all that there was to see.
(E) The Baltimore waterfront can be found fascinating, and this made Antonio explore all that there was to see.

8. In the 100-yard relay our team impressed the crowd, with each <u>of the members shaving</u> several seconds off her own best time.

(A) of the members shaving
(B) of the members had shaved
(C) of the members was shaving
(D) who had been shaving
(E) who shaved

9. <u>Because of their ability to eat large numbers of insects, some people are building bat houses in their backyards.</u>

(A) Because of their ability to eat large numbers of insects, some people are building bat houses in their backyards.
(B) They have the ability to eat large numbers of insects, so some people are building bat houses in their backyards.
(C) Because bats can eat large numbers of insects, bat houses are being built in their backyards by some people.
(D) Some people are building bat houses in their backyards because bats can eat large numbers of insects.
(E) Bats can eat large numbers of insects, because of this some people are building bat houses in their backyards.

10. <u>For all their talk</u> about ecology, major companies have so far spent very little to fight pollution.

(A) For all their talk
(B) In spite of the fact of their having talked
(C) Besides their having talked
(D) In addition to their talking
(E) Although there is talk between one and the other

11. The survival of many species of marine life may depend on both the enforcement of waste-disposal regulations <u>and the education of the public</u> about the fragility of ocean resources.

(A) and the education of the public
(B) educating the public
(C) and the public being educated
(D) along with the education of the public
(E) in combination with public education

**GO ON TO THE NEXT PAGE**

The following sentences test your ability to recognize grammar and usage errors. Each sentence contains either a single error or no error at all. No sentence contains more than one error. The error, if there is one, is underlined and lettered. If the sentence contains an error, select the one underlined part that must be changed to make the sentence correct. If the sentence is correct, select choice E. In choosing answers, follow the requirements of standard written English.

EXAMPLE:

The other delegates and him immediately
A                         B         C
accepted the resolution drafted by the
                                D
neutral states. No error
                     E

Ⓐ ● Ⓞ Ⓓ Ⓔ

12. Hearing the unexpected loud noise, Cindy, Leroy, and
    A
me were so startled that we almost jumped
B      C
out of our seats. No error
              D          E

13. Many admire Louisa May Alcott for her

detailed descriptions of nineteenth-century domestic
              A
life in novels such as *Little Women*, but few have read
              B                              C
the lurid thrillers she writes early in her career.
                         D

No error
    E

14. According to some critics, the title character of

the Greek tragedy *Oedipus Rex* saw himself
                                    A
as the savior of his people and believing
         B                          C
erroneously that he could do no wrong. No error
                         D              E

15. Unlike Thomas, neither Leslie or her younger
    A                              B
brother Philip has an interest in a career in law.
                    C              D

No error
    E

16. One subject of Felipe Alfau's second novel, published
         A
more than 40 years after it has been written, is the
    B                         C         D
illusory nature of the passage of time. No error
                                            E

17. Joining a grassroots movement against inhumane

working conditions, some consumers in the United

States have stopped buying products from countries
      A
in which workers are essentially a slave laborer.
    B                  C              D
No error
    E

18. As the mayor was evaluating the proposed tax, he was
                    A
less interested in the revenue it would generate than in
                                    B
whether they would disproportionately affect certain
         C              D
income groups. No error
                  E

19. Eating garlic has long been regarded as a means
                    A                  B
of warding off malaise, and scientific research

has shown that it does have some therapeutic
    C              D
value. No error
         E

GO ON TO THE NEXT PAGE ⟩

20. Although the night shift is <u>fully staffed</u>, the managers
A

always <u>holds us</u> responsible for <u>that shift's</u> work if
B C

<u>it</u> is not finished when we arrive in the morning.
D

<u>No error</u>
E

21. Members of the Alvin Ailey Dance Company <u>have</u>
A

once again <u>shown how</u> the combination of strength
B

and <u>being agile</u> <u>can produce</u> beautiful movements.
C D

<u>No error</u>
E

22. Anne Tyler's novel *The Accidental Tourist* <u>features</u>
A

a character <u>whose</u> obsession <u>with saving</u> time and
B C

money <u>are</u> absurd, yet somehow plausible. <u>No error</u>
D E

23. At the conclusion of the novel *The Great Gatsby*,

Nick Carraway, a young Midwesterner recently

<u>arrived to</u> New York, <u>moodily</u> <u>watches</u> the blinking
A B C

green light at the <u>tip of</u> Long Island. <u>No error</u>
D E

24. <u>Despite</u> the efforts of the publicity subcommittee,
A

<u>hardly anyone</u> attended the workshop that <u>had been</u>
B C

planned <u>so painstakingly</u>. <u>No error</u>
D E

25. Peter's <u>seemingly effortless</u> flights, <u>achieved through</u>
A B

the use of sophisticated technical equipment,

<u>continues</u> to delight those <u>who</u> see the play
C D

*Peter Pan*. <u>No error</u>
E

26. Mediators were standing by, prepared <u>to intervene in</u>
A

the labor dispute <u>even though</u> both sides <u>had refused</u>
B C

earlier offers <u>for</u> assistance. <u>No error</u>
D E

27. According to some theorists, <u>what</u> <u>any</u> particular bird
A B

can eat could change <u>with even</u> <u>the slightest</u> variation
C D

in the shape of its beak. <u>No error</u>
E

28. Neither Ms. Perez <u>nor</u> Ms. Tanaka <u>believes</u> that
A B

watching as much television as <u>her</u> son Sam does
C

<u>will lead</u> to anything productive. <u>No error</u>
D E

29. An amateur potter <u>herself</u>, the accountant offered
A

<u>to help</u> the artist with his business accounts, com-
B

plicated <u>as they were</u> <u>by</u> his unusual system of record
C D

keeping. <u>No error</u>
E

**GO ON TO THE NEXT PAGE** ⇨

**Directions:** The following passage is an early draft of an essay. Some parts of the passage need to be rewritten.

Read the passage and select the best answers for the questions that follow. Some questions are about particular sentences or parts of sentences and ask you to improve sentence structure or word choice. Other questions ask you to consider organization and development. In choosing answers, follow the requirements of standard written English.

**Questions 30-35 are based on the following passage.**

(1) Many critics consider modern film remakes of classical works disrespectful and a waste of time and money. (2) A recent version of Shakespeare's *Romeo and Juliet* drew harsh reviews from purists, they are people who expect filmmakers to follow the original text exactly. (3) The only positive ones expressed relief that Shakespeare was not around to feel the insult. (4) Wouldn't he be horrified to see his play open with a gang shoot-out at a gas station? (5) And *Clueless*, a remake of Jane Austen's 1815 novel *Emma*. (6) Imagine equating flirtation in a Southern California high school with dignified courtship in a nineteenth-century English country estate.

(7) I see nothing wrong with creative remakes. (8) After all, didn't Shakespeare borrow freely from other writers' plots? (9) For example, his *Romeo and Juliet* is borrowed from a myth popularized by the Roman poet Ovid. (10) And as for being insulted, Shakespeare would have starved if he had written only about genteel topics. (11) No doubt he would recognize the swaggering teenagers in the movie, they would be distant relatives of his own warring characters. (12) Austen will see traces of her characters in the frivolous, money-conscious society of *Clueless*. (13) The movie's main character is preoccupied with appearances, and it would make her feel right at home in the England mocked by Austen.

(14) The themes of the great classics are timeless, so we should not let these works become fossils.

30. Which of the following is the best version of the underlined portion of sentence 2 (reproduced below)?

*A recent version of Shakespeare's* Romeo and Juliet *drew harsh reviews from* purists, they are people who expect *filmmakers to follow the original text exactly.*

(A) (as it is now)
(B) purists; they were people who expected
(C) purists in expecting
(D) purists. These expected
(E) purists, those who expect

31. In context, which of the following is the best word to use instead of "ones" in sentence 3?

(A) scenes
(B) instances
(C) reviews
(D) remakes
(E) sections

32. In context, which of the following is the best version of the underlined portion of sentence 5 (reproduced below)?

*And* Clueless, *a remake of Jane Austen's 1815 novel* Emma.

(A) (As it is now)
(B) *Clueless* is a
(C) Another supposed outrage is *Clueless*, a
(D) We can also take offense at *Clueless*, a
(E) Yet consider *Clueless*, which is a

33. An important strategy used in the first paragraph is to

(A) elaborate on a view that contrasts with the essay's argument
(B) use descriptive detail to animate a personal experience
(C) provide a thoughtful, objective analysis of modern criticism
(D) introduce an unconventional approach to writing fiction
(E) reveal the sense of playfulness implicit in much film criticism

**34.** Which of the following is the best version of the underlined portion of sentence 11 (reproduced below) ?

*No doubt he would recognize the swaggering teenagers in the movie, they would be distant relatives of his own warring characters.*

(A) (as it is now)
(B) movie, they are
(C) movie; they were
(D) movie for being
(E) movie as

**35.** In context, which of the following is the best way to revise the underlined portion of sentence 12 (reproduced below) ?

*Austen will see traces of her characters in the frivolous, money-conscious society of* Clueless.

(A) Austen could have seen
(B) Austen, too, would see
(C) However, Austen might have seen
(D) In addition to this, Austen would see
(E) Likewise, Austen can see

# STOP

**If you finish before time is called, you may check your work on this section only.
Do not turn to any other section in the test.**

## SECTION 7
Time — 25 minutes
24 Questions

**Turn to Section 7 (page 6) of your answer sheet to answer the questions in this section.**

**Directions:** For each question in this section, select the best answer from among the choices given and fill in the corresponding circle on the answer sheet.

---

Each sentence below has one or two blanks, each blank indicating that something has been omitted. Beneath the sentence are five words or sets of words labeled A through E. Choose the word or set of words that, when inserted in the sentence, best fits the meaning of the sentence as a whole.

**Example:**

Hoping to ------- the dispute, negotiators proposed a compromise that they felt would be ------- to both labor and management.

(A) enforce . . useful
(B) end . . divisive
(C) overcome . . unattractive
(D) extend . . satisfactory
(E) resolve . . acceptable

Ⓐ Ⓑ Ⓒ Ⓓ ●

1. Geoffrey's corrupt dealings earned him such disgrace that any possibility of his being reelected to the city council was completely -------.

(A) ensured     (B) approved     (C) belittled
(D) eliminated     (E) defended

2. Although the editors were reputed to be very -------, the uneven quality of the material they put into the anthology suggests they were too -------.

(A) amateurish . . professional
(B) lax . . harsh
(C) selective . . inclusive
(D) judgmental . . discriminating
(E) sensitive . . insightful

3. The professor's presentation was both ------- and -------: though brief, it was instructive.

(A) verbose . . mundane
(B) concise . . elaborate
(C) comprehensive . . edifying
(D) succinct . . enlightening
(E) provocative . . technical

4. With its large circulation, *Essence* magazine has enjoyed ------- only recently challenged by new publications aggressively seeking female African American readers.

(A) an aggregation     (B) an inclination
(C) a prognosis     (D) a retrenchment
(E) a preeminence

5. The judge's published opinions, though sophisticated and subtle, were undeniably -------: they left no doubt of her intentions.

(A) unequivocal     (B) effusive     (C) incorrigible
(D) tenuous     (E) ineffable

**GO ON TO THE NEXT PAGE**

7

Unauthorized copying or reuse of
any part of this page is illegal.

7

Each passage below is followed by questions based on its content. Answer the questions on the basis of what is <u>stated</u> or <u>implied</u> in each passage and in any introductory material that may be provided.

**Questions 6-7 are based on the following passage.**

Properly speaking, a movement is a continuous, collective effort to bring about fundamental social reform. It is a collaborative rather than an individ-
*Line* ualistic enterprise. No matter how many factions
5 are involved, there is always a common objective. The Black freedom struggle of the 1960's was such an effort. Its objective was to transform the manner in which Black Americans in the United States were viewed and treated. And Black writers and artists,
10 as a vital sector of the movement, sought to trans-form the manner in which Black Americans were represented or portrayed in literature and the arts.

**6.** The first sentence of the passage ("Properly speaking . . . reform") primarily serves to

(A) present a controversial opinion
(B) question the effectiveness of a process
(C) provide an example of an abstract idea
(D) define the meaning of a term
(E) offer a solution to a problem

**7.** The passage indicates that Black writers and artists were most important to the freedom struggle in that they

(A) promoted freedom of artistic expression for Black Americans
(B) attempted to alter the way Black people were depicted in the arts
(C) created powerful protest art that documented the Black struggle
(D) were a cohesive group that opposed excessive individualism
(E) prescribed a course of action to help ensure social justice

**Questions 8-9 are based on the following passage.**

As a slang word, "cool" has stayed cool far longer than most such words. One of the main characteristics of slang is the continual renewal of its vocabulary:
*Line* in order for slang to feel slangy, it has to have a feeling
5 of novelty. Slang expressions meaning the same thing as "cool," like "groovy," "hep," "far-out," "rad," and "tubular," have for the most part not had the staying power of "cool." In general, there is no intrinsic reason why one word stays alive and others get consigned to
10 the scrap heap of linguistic history, but slang terms, like fashion designs, are rarely "in" for long. The jury is still out on how long "def" and "phat" will survive.

**8.** The primary purpose of the passage is to

(A) address a pressing question
(B) define an unusual expression
(C) note the durability of a term
(D) oppose a particular use of language
(E) challenge a linguistic theory

**9.** In line 11, "fashion designs" serve as an example of something

(A) provocative
(B) ephemeral
(C) pretentious
(D) esoteric
(E) exotic

**GO ON TO THE NEXT PAGE**

**Questions 10-15 are based on the following passage.**

*This passage was adapted from a 1995 book about astronomy.*

Apart from the Moon and occasional comets and asteroids, Venus is often our nearest neighbor. Its orbit brings it closer to Earth than any other planet—only
Line 26 million miles away at certain times. Despite that
5 proximity, for a long time it was generally termed "the planet of mystery." This is because the atmosphere of Venus is so dense and so cloud-laden that its surface is permanently hidden from sight.

The first attempt to learn more about Venus was to
10 analyze its upper atmosphere using spectroscopic methods. In size and mass, Venus is almost the equal of Earth, and its gravitational field is only slightly weaker than ours, so that logically it might be expected to have the same kind of atmosphere—but this is emphatically not so. Scientists
15 found that the main constituent of its atmosphere is carbon dioxide. Since this is a heavy gas that would be expected to sink, it was reasonable to assume that carbon dioxide made up most of the atmosphere down to ground level. Carbon dioxide acts in the manner of a greenhouse, trapping
20 the Sun's heat, so it followed that Venus was likely to be a very torrid sort of world.

Yet opinions differed. According to one theory, the clouds contained a great deal of water. It was even claimed that the surface might be largely ocean covered, in which
25 case the atmospheric carbon dioxide would have fouled the water and produced seas of soda water. Another intriguing theory made Venus very similar to the Earth of over 200 million years ago. There would be marshes, luxuriant vegetation of the fern and horsetail variety, and primitive
30 life-forms such as giant dragonflies. If so, then Venus might presumably evolve the same way Earth has done.

In 1962 the American probe Mariner 2 bypassed Venus at less than 22,000 miles and gave us our first reliable information. The surface proved to be very hot
35 indeed; we now know that the maximum temperature is almost 500°C. The atmosphere really is almost pure carbon dioxide, and those shining clouds are rich in sulfuric acid. All ideas of a pleasant, oceanic Venus had to be abandoned. In 1975 Venera 9, a Russian automatic lander, visited Venus
40 and sent back pictures direct from the surface. The scene— a rocky, scorched landscape—could hardly be more hostile. Subsequent probes have confirmed this impression.

Why is Venus so unlike Earth? The answer can only lie in its lesser distance from the Sun. It seems that in the early
45 days of the solar system the Sun was less luminous than it is now, in which case Venus and Earth may have started to evolve along the same lines, but when the Sun became more powerful the whole situation changed. Earth, at 93 million miles, was just out of harm's way, but Venus,
50 at 67 million, was not. The water in oceans vaporized, the carbonates were driven out of the rocks, and in a relatively short time on the cosmic scale, Venus was transformed from a potentially life-bearing world into the inferno of today.

**10.** The primary purpose of the passage is to

  (A) criticize the lack of research on a topic of mystery
  (B) speculate about life on another world
  (C) lament the demise of a compelling theory
  (D) illustrate the principles of planetary research
  (E) discuss attempts to understand an astronomical enigma

**11.** The statement in lines 11-14 ("In size . . . so") functions primarily to

  (A) dismiss a plausible supposition
  (B) mock an outrageous claim
  (C) bolster an accepted opinion
  (D) summarize a particular experiment
  (E) undermine a controversial hypothesis

**12.** The primary purpose of the third paragraph (lines 22-31) is to

  (A) provide evidence in support of a controversial theory
  (B) challenge two popular misconceptions about Venus
  (C) show why a particular hypothesis was misguided
  (D) suggest that Venus has been romanticized throughout history
  (E) present two distinct theories about Venus

**GO ON TO THE NEXT PAGE**

7 7

Unauthorized copying or reuse of
any part of this page is illegal.

**13.** In order for the hypothesis in lines 28-30 ("There would . . . dragonflies") to be correct, which statement could NOT be true of conditions on Venus?

(A) The environment is generally warm and humid.
(B) The atmosphere is pure carbon dioxide.
(C) It is possible for evolutionary change to occur.
(D) There is enough light for photosynthesis to occur.
(E) Creatures are able to fly with ease.

**14.** The statement in lines 32-34 ("In 1962 . . . information") suggests that the

(A) quality of the data surprised the scientists
(B) evidence collected earlier was relatively untrustworthy
(C) records had been lost for a long time before scientists rediscovered them
(D) probe allowed scientists to formulate a completely new theory
(E) data confirmed an obscure and implausible theory

**15.** The tone of the statement in lines 43-44 ("The answer . . . Sun") is best described as

(A) regretful
(B) guarded
(C) skeptical
(D) decisive
(E) amused

**GO ON TO THE NEXT PAGE**

**Questions 16-24 are based on the following passage.**

*This passage has been adapted from a memoir published in 1999. The year is 1961; the author, then a young girl, has just moved to New York City with her family.*

New York was darker than I expected, and, in spite of the cleansing rain, dirtier. Used to the sensual curves of Puerto Rico, my eyes had to adjust to the regular,
Line
5 aggressive two-dimensionality of Brooklyn. Raindrops pounded the hard streets, captured the dim silver glow of street lamps, bounced against sidewalks in glistening sparks, then disappeared like tiny ephemeral jewels, into the darkness. Mami and Tata* teased that I was disillu-sioned because the streets were not paved with gold. But
10 I had no such vision of New York. I was disappointed by the darkness and fixed my hopes on the promise of light deep within the sparkling raindrops.

Two days later, I leaned against the wall of our apart-ment building on McKibbin Street wondering where
15 New York ended and the rest of the world began. It was hard to tell. There was no horizon in Brooklyn. Everywhere I looked, my eyes met a vertical maze of gray and brown straight-edged buildings with sharp corners and deep shadows. Every few blocks there was
20 a cement playground surrounded by chain-link fence. And in between, weedy lots mounded with garbage and rusting cars.

A girl came out of the building next door, a jump rope in her hand. She appraised me shyly; I pretended
25 to ignore her. She stepped on the rope, stretched the ends overhead as if to measure their length, and then began to skip, slowly, grunting each time she came down on the sidewalk. Swish splat grunt swish, she turned her back to me; swish splat grunt swish, she faced me again and
30 smiled. I smiled back, and she hopped over.

"¿Tú eres hispana?" she asked, as she whirled the rope in lazy arcs.

"No, I'm Puerto Rican."

"Same thing. Puerto Rican, Hispanic. That's what we
35 are here." She skipped a tight circle, stopped abruptly, and shoved the rope in my direction. "Want a turn?"

"Sure." I hopped on one leg, then the other. "So, if you're Puerto Rican, they call you Hispanic?"

"Yeah. Anybody who speaks Spanish."
40 I jumped a circle, as she had done, but faster. "You mean, if you speak Spanish, you're Hispanic?"

"Well, yeah. No . . . I mean your parents have to be Puerto Rican or Cuban or something."

I whirled the rope to the right, then the left, like
45 a boxer. "Okay, your parents are Cuban, let's say, and you're born here, but you don't speak Spanish. Are you Hispanic?"

She bit her lower lip. "I guess so," she finally said. "It has to do with being from a Spanish country. I mean,
50 you or your parents, like, even if you don't speak Spanish, you're Hispanic, you know?" She looked at me uncertainly. I nodded and returned her rope.

But I didn't know. I'd always been Puerto Rican, and it hadn't occurred to me that in Brooklyn I'd be someone
55 else.

Later, I asked, "Are we Hispanics, Mami?"

"Yes, because we speak Spanish."

"But a girl said you don't have to speak the language to be Hispanic."
60 She scrunched her eyes. "What girl? Where did you meet a girl?"

"Outside. She lives in the next building."

"Who said you could go out to the sidewalk? This isn't Puerto Rico. *Algo te puede suceder.*"
65 "Something could happen to you" was a variety of dangers outside the locked doors of our apartment. I listened to Mami's lecture with downcast eyes and the necessary, respectful expression of humility. But inside, I quaked. Two days in New York, and I'd
70 already become someone else. It wasn't hard to imagine that greater dangers lay ahead.

* The narrator's mother and grandmother

16. In line 3, "regular" most nearly means

(A) customary
(B) agreeable
(C) unvarying
(D) recurring
(E) average

17. Lines 4-8 ("Raindrops . . . darkness") are particularly notable for their

(A) despairing mood
(B) vivid imagery
(C) humorous wordplay
(D) nostalgic atmosphere
(E) abstract language

**GO ON TO THE NEXT PAGE**

7

Unauthorized copying or reuse of
any part of this page is illegal.

7

18. In lines 8-9, Mami and Tata imply that the narrator

   (A) faced economic barriers
   (B) exhibited driving ambitions
   (C) believed in miraculous transformations
   (D) was ruled by greedy impulses
   (E) harbored unrealistic expectations

19. The second paragraph (lines 13-22) suggests that
the narrator experienced Brooklyn as

   (A) mysterious and unknowable
   (B) uniform and oppressive
   (C) orderly and appealing
   (D) drab yet multifaceted
   (E) menacing yet alluring

20. Which of the following best describes the initial
interaction of the "girl" (line 23) and the narrator?

   (A) Neither was in a mood to meet someone new.
   (B) Neither wanted to show her fear of the other.
   (C) They acted as if they already knew each other.
   (D) They studied each other suspiciously.
   (E) They cautiously took note of each other.

21. The exchange between the narrator and the girl
(lines 31-52) is best described as

   (A) a debate over the power of language to
       shape personality
   (B) a discussion of the value of using ethnic
       labels to characterize people
   (C) an exchange of strategies for survival
       in a mystifying culture
   (D) an attempt to identify the criteria that
       determine an ethnic label
   (E) an effort to reconcile group identity
       with personal autonomy

22. The paragraph in lines 53-55 ("But I . . . else")
suggests that, for the narrator, being considered
Hispanic represents

   (A) the end of childhood as she has known it
   (B) the loss of her former identity
   (C) a restriction to be overcome
   (D) an opportunity for self-redefinition
   (E) an unavoidable result of emigration

23. The mother refers to "Puerto Rico" (line 64)
in order to impress upon the narrator that

   (A) nostalgia for one's birthplace can be
       a distraction
   (B) New Yorkers are indifferent to cultural
       backgrounds
   (C) newcomers must embrace New York
       if they are to flourish
   (D) life was more restricted in Puerto Rico
   (E) different rules apply to life in New York

24. The narrator's mood at the conclusion of the passage
is best described as one of

   (A) apathy and sullenness
   (B) anger and bewilderment
   (C) defeat and resignation
   (D) fearfulness and uncertainty
   (E) resentment and defiance

# STOP

**If you finish before time is called, you may check your work on this section only.**
**Do not turn to any other section in the test.**

## SECTION 8
**Time — 20 minutes**
**16 Questions**

Turn to Section 8 (page 7) of your answer sheet to answer the questions in this section.

**Directions:** For this section, solve each problem and decide which is the best of the choices given. Fill in the corresponding circle on the answer sheet. You may use any available space for scratchwork.

**1.** If a film takes 90 minutes to show, what fraction of the film is completed 15 minutes after it begins?

(A) $\frac{1}{9}$

(B) $\frac{1}{6}$

(C) $\frac{1}{5}$

(D) $\frac{1}{4}$

(E) $\frac{1}{3}$

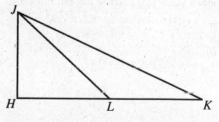

**2.** In $\triangle HJK$ above, $\angle JHK$ is a right angle. Which of the following lengths is greatest?

(A) $HJ$
(B) $HK$
(C) $HL$
(D) $JK$
(E) $JL$

GO ON TO THE NEXT PAGE

| $n$ | 1 | 2 | 3 | 4 | 5 | 6 |
|------|---|----|----|---|----|----|
| $f(n)$ | 7 | 13 | 19 | $p$ | 31 | 37 |

**3.** The table above defines a linear function. What is the value of $p$ ?

(A) 21
(B) 23
(C) 25
(D) 27
(E) 29

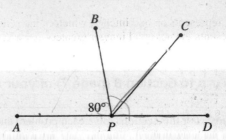

**5.** In the figure above, $P$ lies on $\overline{AD}$ and $\overline{PC}$ bisects $\angle BPD$. What is the measure of $\angle CPD$ ?

(A) 40°
(B) 50°
(C) 60°
(D) 70°
(E) 80°

**4.** Charlie has built houses for 5 years less than twice as long as Maly has. If Maly has built houses for $n$ years, which of the following expressions represents the number of years that Charlie has built houses?

(A) $n - 5$
(B) $n + 5$
(C) $2n - 5$
(D) $2n + 5$
(E) $5 - 2n$

**GO ON TO THE NEXT PAGE**

**6.** If $x$ represents an odd integer, which of the following represents the next odd integer greater than $x$ ?

(A) $x - 1$
(B) $x + 1$
(C) $x + 2$
(D) $x + 3$
(E) $2x - 1$

**8.** A box contains wood beads, red glass beads, and blue glass beads. The number of glass beads is 4 times the number of wood beads. If one bead is to be chosen at random from the box, the probability that a red glass bead will be chosen is 3 times the probability that a blue glass bead will be chosen. If there are 12 red glass beads in the box, what is the total number of beads in the box?

(A) 20
(B) 45
(C) 48
(D) 60
(E) 90

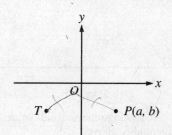

**7.** In the figure above, point $T$ is the same distance from $O$ as point $P$ is from $O$. Which of the following could be the coordinates of point $T$ ?

(A) $(-a, b)$
(B) $(a, -b)$
(C) $(-b, -a)$
(D) $(-b, a)$
(E) $(b, a)$

GO ON TO THE NEXT PAGE

**8** ○ ○ ○ ○ ○ ○ **8**

Unauthorized copying or reuse of
any part of this page is illegal.

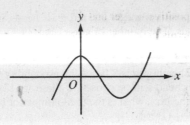

**9.** Which of the following graphs is the reflection
of the graph above about the $x$-axis?

(A)

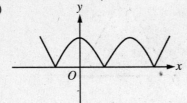

(B)

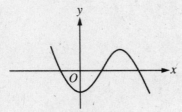

(C)

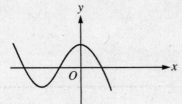

(D)

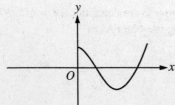

(E)

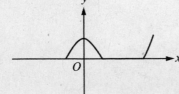

**10.** If $(x + y)^2 = 100$ and $(x - y)^2 = 16$, what is the
value of $xy$ ?

(A)  6
(B)  10
(C)  21
(D)  25
(E)  29

$-1 \le 4x - 5$

**11.** Which of the following represents all values of $x$ that
satisfy the inequality above?

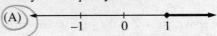

(A)

(B)

(C)

(D)

(E)

**GO ON TO THE NEXT PAGE**

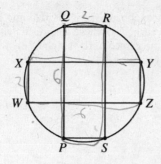

**12.** In the figure above, rectangles *PQRS* and *WXYZ* each have perimeter 12 and are inscribed in the circle. How many other rectangles with perimeter 12 can be inscribed in the circle?

(A) One
(B) Two
(C) Three
(D) Four
(E) More than four

**13.** If $n$ is a positive integer and $2^n + 2^{n+1} = k$, what is $2^{n+2}$ in terms of $k$?

(A) $\dfrac{k-1}{2}$

(B) $\dfrac{4k}{3}$

(C) $2k$

(D) $2k+1$

(E) $k^2$

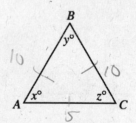

Note: Figure not drawn to scale.

**14.** The triangle above is isosceles and $AB > AC$. Which of the following must be FALSE?

(A) $AB = BC$
(B) $BC = AC$
(C) $x = y$
(D) $x = z$
(E) $y = z$

**GO ON TO THE NEXT PAGE**

485

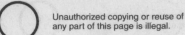  

TOM'S TRIP EXPENSES

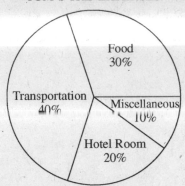

15. The graph above shows the distribution of Tom's
$240 trip expenses. The amount Tom paid for the
hotel room was only part of the total hotel room cost,
because he shared the cost of the room equally with
3 other people. What was the total cost of the hotel
room?

(A)  $20
(B)  $80
(C)  $144
(D)  $192
(E)  $240

16. On a square gameboard that is divided into $n$ rows
of $n$ squares each, $k$ of these squares lie along the
boundary of the gameboard. Which of the following
is a possible value for $k$ ?

(A)  10
(B)  25
(C)  34
(D)  42
(E)  52

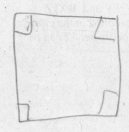

# STOP

**If you finish before time is called, you may check your work on this section only.**
**Do not turn to any other section in the test.**

## SECTION 9
Time — 20 minutes
18 Questions

**Turn to Section 9 (page 7) of your answer sheet to answer the questions in this section.**

**Directions:** For each question in this section, select the best answer from among the choices given and fill in the corresponding circle on the answer sheet.

Each sentence below has one or two blanks, each blank indicating that something has been omitted. Beneath the sentence are five words or sets of words labeled A through E. Choose the word or set of words that, when inserted in the sentence, best fits the meaning of the sentence as a whole.

**Example:**

Hoping to ------- the dispute, negotiators proposed a compromise that they felt would be ------- to both labor and management.

(A) enforce . . useful
(B) end . . divisive
(C) overcome . . unattractive
(D) extend . . satisfactory
(E) resolve . . acceptable            Ⓐ Ⓑ Ⓒ Ⓓ ●

1. Many paintings of the American Southwest convey a feeling of isolation and loneliness that mirrors the ------- landscape they depict.

(A) lush    (B) sprawling    (C) desolate
(D) gaudy    (E) monumental

2. Only recently created, this orchid is a _____, a plant produced by deliberately crossbreeding two different varieties of flowers.

(A) misnomer    (B) hybrid    (C) vector
(D) curative    (E) precursor

3. The pharmaceutical company insisted that its testing of new drugs was quite -------, more rigorous than the industry standard.

(A) stringent    (B) dispersive    (C) conditional
(D) recessive    (E) obtrusive

4. Freedom of expression is not necessarily a ------- force: communities that encourage it often feel less threatened by social unrest than do those in which dissent is -------.

(A) revolutionary . . promoted
(B) positive . . prohibited
(C) successful . . protested
(D) divisive . . restricted
(E) militant . . fostered

5. Thomas Hardy's novels are described as ------- because of their preoccupation with daily life in rural and agricultural settings.

(A) bucolic    (B) prolific    (C) lugubrious
(D) sundry    (E) metaphorical

6. Some skeptics consider the Search for Extraterrestrial Intelligence (SETI) to be -------, even foolish; others go so far as to accuse SETI scientists of outright ------- in applying skewed data.

(A) misguided . . remonstrance
(B) absurd . . erudition
(C) plausible . . lassitude
(D) painstaking . . fabrication
(E) wrongheaded . . chicanery

**GO ON TO THE NEXT PAGE**

The two passages below are followed by questions based on their content and on the relationship between the two passages. Answer the questions on the basis of what is <u>stated</u> or <u>implied</u> in the passages and in any introductory material that may be provided.

**Questions 7-18 are based on the following passages.**

*Passage 1 was adapted from a well-known 1953 study of comic books. Passage 2 was adapted from a 1965 analysis of the major comic books of the 1940's and 1950's.*

### Passage 1

I have found the effect of comic books to be first of all anti-educational. They interfere with education in the larger sense. For children, education is not merely a
*Line* question of learning, but is a part of mental health. They
5 do not "learn" only in school; they learn also during play, from entertainment, and in social life with adults and with other children. To take large chunks of time out of a child's life—time during which he or she is not positively, that is, educationally, occupied—means to interfere with healthful
10 mental growth.

To make a sharp distinction between entertainment and learning is poor pedagogy, and even worse psychology. A great deal of learning comes in the form of entertainment, and a great deal of entertainment painlessly teaches
15 important things. By no stretch of critical standards can the text in comics qualify as literature, or the drawings as art. Children spend an enormous amount of time on comic books, but their gain is nil. They do not learn how to read a serious book or magazine. They
20 do not gain a true picture of the West from the "Westerns." They do not learn about any normal aspects of sex, love, or life. I have known many adults who have treasured throughout their lives some of the books they read as children. I have never come across any adult or adoles-
25 cent who had outgrown comic book reading who would ever dream of keeping any of these "books" for any sentimental or other reason. In other words, children spend a large amount of their time and money on these publications and have nothing positive to show for it.
30 And since almost all good children's reading has some educational value, comics by their very nature are not only non-educational; they are anti-educational. They fail to teach anything that might be useful to a child; they do suggest many things that are harmful.

### Passage 2

35 Surprisingly, there *are* old comic book fans, a small army of them: adults wearing school ties and tweeds, teaching in universities, writing ad copy, writing for chic magazines, writing novels—who continue to be addicts, who save old comic books, buy them, trade them, who
40 publish mimeographed "fanzines," strange little publi- cations deifying what is looked back on as "the golden age of comic books." Ruined by the critics. Ruined by growing up.

The charges against comic books in the 1950's—that
45 they were participating factors in juvenile delinquency, that they were, in general, a corrupting influence, glori- fying crime and depravity—can only, in all fairness, be answered: "But of course. Why else read them?"

Comic books, first of all, are junk. To accuse them
50 of being what they are is to make no accusation at all: there is no such thing as *uncorrupt* junk or *moral* junk or *educational* junk—though attempts at the latter have, from time to time, been foisted upon us. But education is not the purpose of junk (which is one reason why half-
55 hearted attempts to bring reality or literature to comic books invariably look embarrassing.) Junk is there to entertain on the basest, most compromised of levels. It finds the lowest common denominator and proceeds from there. A good many readers, when challenged, will
60 say defiantly: "I know it's junk, but I like it." Which is the whole point about junk. It is there to be nothing else but liked. Junk is a second-class citizen of the arts, a status of which we and it are constantly aware. There are certain privileges inherent in second-class citizenship. Irresponsi-
65 bility is one. Not being taken seriously is another. Junk can get away with doing or saying anything because, by its very appearance, it is already in disgrace.

What critics of comic books dismiss is the more posi- tive side of junk, their *underground* antisocial influence.
70 Children are bombarded with hard work, labeled *education*. They rise at the same time or earlier than their parents, start work without office chatter, go till noon without coffee breaks, have waxed milk for lunch, then back at the desk until three o'clock. And always at someone else's conveni-
75 ence. It should come as no surprise, then, that within this shifting hodgepodge of external pressures, children, simply to stay sane, must go underground. Have a place to hide where they cannot be got at by grownups. A relief zone. And the basic sustenance for this relief was, in my day,
80 comic books.

With them we were able to roam free, disguised in cos- tume, committing the greatest of feats—and the worst of sins. And, in every instance, getting away with them. For a little while, at least, it was our show. For a little while, at
85 least, we were the bosses. Psychically renewed, we could then return aboveground and put up with another couple of days of victimization.

**GO ON TO THE NEXT PAGE**

7. Both authors would most likely agree that comic books

(A) impair social development
(B) could benefit from self-regulation
(C) have no educational value
(D) are obtained too easily
(E) are garishly amusing

8. In line 4, "question" most nearly means

(A) matter
(B) request
(C) objection
(D) possibility
(E) doubt

9. The author of Passage 1 criticizes those who would "make a sharp distinction" (line 11) because the author believes that

(A) the best educators are also entertainers of a sort
(B) without entertainment little learning takes place
(C) entertainment and learning are closely interrelated
(D) reading comic books may inspire children to create their own comic works
(E) effective textbooks often adopt certain humorous techniques

10. In lines 18-22, the three sentences beginning with "They" primarily serve to

(A) lament students' lack of interest in traditional learning
(B) condemn those who profit by pandering to children
(C) enumerate the failings of the educational system
(D) indicate ways in which children are shortchanged
(E) specify how comic books might be improved

11. In response to the claim made in lines 24-27 of Passage 1 ("I have . . . reason"), the author of Passage 2 would most likely assert that

(A) adolescents tend to be passionate about their dislikes as well as their likes
(B) comic books are not intended to provide lifelong entertainment
(C) collectible pop-culture items are now displayed in museums
(D) the sentimental value of comic books cannot be logically explained
(E) many adults eagerly read and collect comic books

12. The argument from Passage 2 that best refutes the statement in lines 27-29 of Passage 1 ("In . . . it") is that comic books

(A) do not cost much compared to other amusements
(B) openly acknowledge their true purpose
(C) help children cope with the stresses of their world
(D) cannot be appreciated by someone who lacks a sense of humor
(E) have never been proven to distract children from homework

13. In line 40, quotation marks are used to

(A) underscore a traditional definition
(B) set off a specialized term
(C) attribute a novel concept
(D) mock a flawed hypothesis
(E) support a challenging assertion

14. It can be inferred that the author of Passage 2 considers "attempts at the latter" (line 52) to have been

(A) unpolished products
(B) unpopular changes
(C) misunderstood creations
(D) ill-conceived failures
(E) foolish imitations

GO ON TO THE NEXT PAGE

**15.** In line 57, "compromised" most nearly means

(A) settled
(B) endangered
(C) combined
(D) reconciled
(E) degraded

**16.** In lines 68-87 ("What . . . victimization"), the author of Passage 2 argues that the fantasy world of comic books

(A) taps into the repressed fears of every child
(B) fails to stand up to extended critical scrutiny
(C) appeals to adults who cultivate childlike wonder
(D) has a therapeutic effect on young readers
(E) inspires many children to learn to write well

**17.** The author of Passage 1 would most likely regard lines 81-83, Passage 2 ("With . . . them"), as evidence of the

(A) students' inability to read demanding fiction
(B) schools' failure to monitor student activities
(C) need to combine education with entertainment
(D) hackneyed narratives found in comic books
(E) potentially harmful influence of comic books

**18.** Compared to the tone of Passage 2, that of Passage 1 is more

(A) conversational
(B) facetious
(C) severe
(D) sarcastic
(E) analytical

**STOP**
**If you finish before time is called, you may check your work on this section only.**
**Do not turn to any other section in the test.**

## SECTION 10
### Time — 10 minutes
### 14 Questions

**Turn to Section 10 (page 7) of your answer sheet to answer the questions in this section.**

**Directions:** For each question in this section, select the best answer from among the choices given and fill in the corresponding circle on the answer sheet.

The following sentences test correctness and effectiveness of expression. Part of each sentence or the entire sentence is underlined; beneath each sentence are five ways of phrasing the underlined material. Choice A repeats the original phrasing; the other four choices are different. If you think the original phrasing produces a better sentence than any of the alternatives, select choice A; if not, select one of the other choices.

In making your selection, follow the requirements of standard written English; that is, pay attention to grammar, choice of words, sentence construction, and punctuation. Your selection should result in the most effective sentence—clear and precise, without awkwardness or ambiguity.

EXAMPLE:

Laura Ingalls Wilder published her first book <u>and she was sixty-five years old then</u>.

(A) and she was sixty-five years old then
(B) when she was sixty-five
(C) at age sixty-five years old
(D) upon the reaching of sixty-five years
(E) at the time when she was sixty-five

1. Mr. Lee and his grandchildren practiced traditional Chinese calligraphy together so that the children <u>would be knowing</u> an art cherished by earlier generations of their family.

   (A) would be knowing
   (B) would know
   (C) will know
   (D) were known to
   (E) will be knowing

2. <u>Isabel Allende, the author of *The House of the Spirits,* currently resides in California, but she was raised in Chile, being born in Peru first.</u>

   (A) Isabel Allende, the author of *The House of the Spirits,* currently resides in California, but she was raised in Chile, being born in Peru first.
   (B) Being raised in Chile, after being born in Peru, Isabel Allende, now residing in California, wrote *The House of the Spirits.*
   (C) Born in Peru and raised in Chile, Isabel Allende, the author of *The House of the Spirits,* now resides in California.
   (D) Although now in California, Isabel Allende was born in Peru and raised in Chile, she is the author of *The House of the Spirits.*
   (E) Raised in Chile, and now she resides in California, Isabel Allende, a Peruvian, is the author of *The House of the Spirits.*

3. Although women in the Wyoming territory voted as early as 1869, <u>suffrage for women throughout the United States not being established</u> until ratification of the Nineteenth Amendment in 1920.

   (A) suffrage for women throughout the United States not being established
   (B) suffrage for women throughout the United States which had not been established
   (C) suffrage for women throughout the United States was not established
   (D) it did not establish suffrage for women throughout the United States
   (E) throughout the United States, suffrage for women was not being established

4. Bees must leave the safety of the hive to forage for food many times a <u>day, they are risking being eaten</u> by any of a multitude of predators.

   (A) day, they are risking being eaten
   (B) day at the risk of being eaten
   (C) day risking them to be eaten
   (D) day; the risk is to be eaten
   (E) day; likewise, they risk being eaten

**GO ON TO THE NEXT PAGE**

5. It took the Museum of Modern Art in New York half a century of creative and persistent effort <u>and it acquired the outstanding Picasso collection</u>.

   (A) and it acquired the outstanding Picasso collection
   (B) before their outstanding Picasso collection being acquired
   (C) and finally they had an outstanding Picasso collection there
   (D) but finally an outstanding Picasso collection was acquired at last
   (E) to acquire its outstanding Picasso collection

6. <u>An artist who explores Mexican cultural themes, the art of Maria Elena is world renowned.</u>

   (A) An artist who explores Mexican cultural themes, the art of Maria Elena is world renowned.
   (B) To explore Mexican cultural themes, the work of artist Maria Elena is world-renowned art.
   (C) Artist Maria Elena has explored Mexican cultural themes, the art of which is world renowned.
   (D) An artist who has explored Mexican cultural themes, Maria Elena's art is world renowned.
   (E) Maria Elena is a world-renowned artist whose art explores Mexican cultural themes.

7. The prevailing attitude in seventeenth-century England was that schools and universities <u>should teach nothing that would</u> discredit the established religion or the authority of kings and magistrates.

   (A) should teach nothing that would
   (B) should teach nothing that will
   (C) are to teach nothing that would
   (D) should only teach that which will not
   (E) shall teach nothing that will

8. During a conference with Pravika's parents, the teacher mentioned that Pravika had demonstrated <u>considerable ability in math and to learn</u> foreign languages.

   (A) considerable ability in math and to learn
   (B) considerable ability in math and that she could do it well in
   (C) ability that was considerable in math as well as in learning
   (D) considerable ability in math and in
   (E) considerable ability to learn math and in

9. <u>Through his novels Thomas Wolfe reveals to us both the pain and</u> the beauty of his boyhood in the American South.

   (A) Through his novels Thomas Wolfe reveals to us both the pain and
   (B) By means of Thomas Wolfe's novels, which reveal to us both the pain and
   (C) Not only the pain is revealed to us in Thomas Wolfe's novels but he also describes
   (D) Thomas Wolfe, through the medium of his novels, reveals to us both the pain with
   (E) As a novelist, Thomas Wolfe thus revealing to us the pain and

10. <u>Because many Szechuan recipes require for one to cook without there having to be interruptions,</u> it is a good idea to measure all ingredients in advance.

    (A) Because many Szechuan recipes require for one to cook without there having to be interruptions,
    (B) Because many Szechuan recipes require that one cook without interruption,
    (C) Being that many Szechuan recipes require you to cook and not be interrupted,
    (D) Many Szechuan recipes require that one cook without interruption and
    (E) When following many Szechuan recipes it is advisable for one to cook without interruptions and therefore

11. A mixture of jazz and classical idioms, the music of Gershwin was more innovative <u>than most of his contemporaries</u>.

    (A) than most of his contemporaries
    (B) than most of his contemporaries were
    (C) than were most of his contemporaries
    (D) than that of most of his contemporaries
    (E) than most of his contemporaries, as far as music is concerned

12. On October 13, 1955, at the Six Gallery in San Francisco, Allen Ginsberg read his poem *Howl,* <u>being the inauguration of both</u> a new style in poetry and the Beat movement.

    (A) *Howl,* being the inauguration of both
    (B) *Howl,* both inaugurated
    (C) *Howl,* it was the inauguration of both
    (D) *Howl,* whose inauguration of both
    (E) *Howl,* thus inaugurating both

**GO ON TO THE NEXT PAGE** ⟩

10 • • 10

Unauthorized copying or reuse of
any part of this page is illegal.

**13.** Indicating their desire to extend free enterprise, <u>Canadians elected a member of the Progressive Conservative Party, Kim Campbell, as Prime Minister</u> in 1993.

(A) Canadians elected a member of the Progressive Conservative Party, Kim Campbell, as Prime Minister

(B) Canadians' election of a member of the Progressive Conservative Party as Prime Minister was Kim Campbell

(C) Kim Campbell of the Progressive Conservative Party was elected Prime Minister of Canada

(D) the Progressive Conservative Party's Kim Campbell was elected Prime Minister of Canadians

(E) a member of the Progressive Conservative Party, Kim Campbell, was elected by Canadians as Prime Minister

**14.** Researchers tend to praise studies that agree with their own <u>conclusions, and it is rare for kindness to be shown</u> to contrary theories.

(A) conclusions, and it is rare for kindness to be shown

(B) conclusions, and kindness being rarely shown

(C) conclusions, and they rarely show kindness

(D) conclusions, they are rarely kind

(E) conclusions, although rarely showing kindness

# STOP

**If you finish before time is called, you may check your work on this section only.
Do not turn to any other section in the test.**

# Correct Answers and Difficulty Levels
## SAT Practice Test #2

## Critical Reading

| Section 4 | | | | Section 7 | | | | Section 9 | | | |
|---|---|---|---|---|---|---|---|---|---|---|---|
| **COR. ANS.** | **DIFF. LEV.** | **COR. ANS.** | **DIFF. LEV.** | **COR. ANS.** | **DIFF. LEV.** | **COR. ANS.** | **DIFF. LEV.** | **COR. ANS.** | **DIFF. LEV.** | **COR. ANS.** | **DIFF. LEV.** |
| 1. C | 1 | 14. C | 2 | 1. D | 1 | 13. B | 2 | 1. C | 2 | 10. D | 3 |
| 2. B | 1 | 15. D | 4 | 2. C | 3 | 14. B | 4 | 2. B | 1 | 11. E | 4 |
| 3. A | 3 | 16. E | 3 | 3. D | 5 | 15. D | 3 | 3. A | 3 | 12. C | 3 |
| 4. B | 3 | 17. E | 3 | 4. E | 4 | 16. C | 4 | 4. D | 4 | 13. B | 3 |
| 5. E | 3 | 18. A | 3 | 5. A | 3 | 17. B | 2 | 5. A | 5 | 14. D | 4 |
| 6. A | 5 | 19. E | 4 | 6. D | 2 | 18. E | 2 | 6. E | 5 | 15. E | 4 |
| 7. A | 5 | 20. B | 3 | 7. B | 2 | 19. B | 3 | 7. C | 1 | 16. D | 2 |
| 8. A | 5 | 21. A | 2 | 8. C | 2 | 20. E | 3 | 8. A | 2 | 17. E | 3 |
| 9. D | 3 | 22. A | 1 | 9. B | 5 | 21. D | 3 | 9. C | 3 | 18. C | 4 |
| 10. C | 5 | 23. D | 5 | 10. E | 4 | 22. B | 3 | | | | |
| 11. D | 0 | 24. C | 3 | 11. A | 2 | 23. E | 2 | | | | |
| 12. A | 2 | 25. C | 3 | 12. E | 3 | 24. D | 3 | | | | |
| 13. B | 3 | | | | | | | | | | |

Number correct _____        Number correct _____        Number correct _____

Number incorrect _____        Number incorrect _____        Number incorrect _____

## Mathematics

### Section 2

| COR. ANS. | DIFF. LEV. | COR. ANS. | DIFF. LEV. |
|---|---|---|---|
| 1. D | 1 | 11. D | 2 |
| 2. A | 1 | 12. A | 3 |
| 3. A | 1 | 13. C | 3 |
| 4. C | 3 | 14. E | 3 |
| 5. D | 2 | 15. B | 4 |
| 6. D | 2 | 16. D | 3 |
| 7. A | 2 | 17. B | 3 |
| 8. B | 2 | 18. B | 4 |
| 9. D | 2 | 19. E | 4 |
| 10. E | 3 | 20. E | 5 |

### Section 5

**Multiple-Choice Questions**

| COR. ANS. | DIFF. LEV. |
|---|---|
| 1. B | 1 |
| 2. E | 1 |
| 3. D | 2 |
| 4. C | 2 |
| 5. E | 2 |
| 6. A | 3 |
| 7. B | 3 |
| 8. B | 4 |

**Student-Produced Response Questions**

| COR. ANS. | DIFF. LEV. |
|---|---|
| 9. 9/2 or 4.5 | 2 |
| 10. 135 | 3 |
| 11. 32 | 2 |
| 12. 1/15, .066 or .067 | 4 |
| 13. 1750 | 3 |
| 14. $4.25<x<8.5$ or $17/4<x<17/2$ | 3 |
| 15. 8 | 3 |
| 16. 9 | 4 |
| 17. 40 | 4 |
| 18. 8/5 or 1.6 | 5 |

### Section 8

| COR. ANS. | DIFF. LEV. | COR. ANS. | DIFF. LEV. |
|---|---|---|---|
| 1. B | 1 | 9. A | 2 |
| 2. D | 1 | 10. C | 3 |
| 3. C | 1 | 11. A | 3 |
| 4. C | 2 | 12. E | 4 |
| 5. B | 2 | 13. B | 4 |
| 6. C | 2 | 14. E | 5 |
| 7. A | 3 | 15. D | 5 |
| 8. A | 3 | 16. E | 5 |

Number correct _____        Number correct _____        Number correct (9-18) _____        Number correct _____

Number incorrect _____        Number incorrect _____        Number incorrect _____

## Writing

### Section 6

| COR. ANS. | DIFF. LEV. | COR. ANS. | DIFF. LEV. | COR. ANS. | DIFF. LEV. | COR. ANS. | DIFF. LEV. |
|---|---|---|---|---|---|---|---|
| 1. D | 1 | 10. A | 4 | 19. E | 2 | 28. C | 5 |
| 2. E | 1 | 11. A | 4 | 20. B | 3 | 29. E | 5 |
| 3. C | 1 | 12. B | 1 | 21. C | 3 | 30. E | 3 |
| 4. C | 2 | 13. D | 1 | 22. D | 3 | 31. C | 2 |
| 5. B | 1 | 14. C | 3 | 23. A | 3 | 32. C | 3 |
| 6. C | 2 | 15. B | 3 | 24. E | 3 | 33. A | 4 |
| 7. C | 3 | 16. C | 2 | 25. C | 4 | 34. E | 3 |
| 8. A | 1 | 17. D | 3 | 26. D | 5 | 35. B | 4 |
| 9. D | 3 | 18. C | 3 | 27. E | 4 | | |

### Section 10

| COR. ANS. | DIFF. LEV. | COR. ANS. | DIFF. LEV. | COR. ANS. | DIFF. LEV. |
|---|---|---|---|---|---|
| 1. B | 1 | 6. E | 1 | 11. D | 4 |
| 2. C | 1 | 7. A | 3 | 12. E | 3 |
| 3. C | 1 | 8. D | 3 | 13. A | 3 |
| 4. B | 2 | 9. A | 2 | 14. C | 3 |
| 5. E | 1 | 10. B | 3 | | |

Number correct _____        Number correct _____

Number incorrect _____        Number incorrect _____

**NOTE:** Difficulty levels are estimates of question difficulty for a reference group of college-bound seniors. Difficulty levels range from 1 (easiest) to 5 (hardest).

# The SAT Scoring Process

**Scoring.** The computer compares the circle filled in for each question with the correct response. Each correct answer receives one point; omitted questions do not affect your score. For each wrong answer to a multiple-choice question, one-fourth of a point is subtracted to correct for random guessing. The SAT critical reading section has 67 questions. If, for example, a student has 44 right, 20 wrong, and 3 omitted, the resulting raw score is determined as follows:

$$44 \text{ right} - \frac{20 \text{ wrong}}{4} = 44 - 5 = 39 \text{ raw score points}$$

Obtaining raw scores frequently involves the rounding of fractions to the nearest whole number. For example, a raw score of 39.25 is rounded to 39, the nearest whole number. A raw score of 39.50 is rounded upward to 40. **For the WRITING SECTION**, your essay raw score counts approximately 30% and your multiple-choice raw score counts approximately 70%.

**Converting to reported scaled score.** Raw scores are then placed on the College Board scale of 200 to 800 through a process that adjusts scores to account for minor differences in difficulty among different versions of the test. This process, known as equating, is performed so that a student's reported score is not affected by the version of the test taken or by the abilities of the group with whom the student takes the test. As a result of placing SAT scores on the College Board scale, scores earned by students at different times can be compared. For example, an SAT critical reading score of 400 on a test taken at one administration indicates the same level of developed critical reading ability as a 400 score obtained on a different version of the test taken at another time.

# How to Score Practice Test #2

## SAT Critical Reading Sections 4, 7, and 9

**Step A:** Count the number of correct answers for *Section 4* and record the number in the space provided on the Scoring Worksheet. Then do the same for the incorrect answers. (Do not count omitted answers.)

**Step B:** Count the number of correct answers and the number of incorrect answers for *Section 7* and record the numbers in the spaces provided on the Scoring Worksheet. (Do not count omitted answers.)

**Step C:** Count the number of correct answers and the number of incorrect answers for *Section 9* and record the numbers in the spaces provided on the Scoring Worksheet. (Do not count omitted answers.)

**Step D:** Total the number of correct responses. Total the number of incorrect responses. Enter the resulting figures on the Scoring Worksheet. To determine A, use the formula:

$$\text{Number correct} - \frac{\text{Number incorrect}}{4} = A$$

**Step E:** To obtain B, your Rounded Critical Reading Raw Score, round A to the nearest whole number. (For example, any number from 44.50 to 45.49 rounds to 45.) Enter the resulting figure on the Scoring Worksheet.

**Step F:** To find your Critical Reading Scaled Score, look up the Total Rounded Raw Score you obtained in step E in the Critical Reading Conversion Table (Table 1). Enter this score in the box on the Scoring Worksheet.

## SAT Mathematics Sections 2, 5, and 8

**Step A:** Count the number of correct answers and the number of incorrect answers for *Section 2* and record the numbers in the spaces provided on the Scoring Worksheet. (Do not count omitted answers.)

**Step B:** Count the number of correct answers and the number of incorrect answers for the multiple-choice questions (*questions 1 through 8*) in *Section 5* and record the numbers in the spaces provided on the Scoring Worksheet. (Do not count omitted answers.)

**Step C:** Count the number of correct answers for the student-produced response questions (*questions 9 through 18*) in *Section 5* and record the number in the space provided on the Scoring Worksheet.

**Step D:** Count the number of correct answers and the number of incorrect answers for *Section 8* and record the numbers in the spaces provided on the Scoring Worksheet. (Do not count omitted answers.)

**Step E:** Total the number of correct responses. Total the number of incorrect responses. Enter the resulting figures on the Scoring Worksheet. To determine A, use the formula:

$$\text{Number correct} - \frac{\text{Number incorrect}}{4} = A$$

**Step F:** To obtain B, your Mathematics Rounded Raw Score, round A to the nearest whole number. (For example, any number from 44.50 to 45.49 rounds to 45.) Enter the resulting figure on the Scoring Worksheet.

**Step G:** To find your Mathematics Scaled Score, use the Mathematics Conversion Table (Table 2) to look up the Total Rounded Raw Score you obtained in step F. Enter this score in the box on the Scoring Worksheet.

## SAT Writing Sections 1, 6, and 10

**Step A:** Enter your Essay Score for *Section 1* in the box on the Scoring Worksheet. Multiply your score by 2. (Keep in mind that on the actual SAT, two readers will read your essay and you will receive a total score of 0 to 12 on your score report.) For help scoring your essay see page 105.

**Step B:** Count the number of correct answers and the number of incorrect answers for *Section 6* and record the numbers in the spaces provided on the Scoring Worksheet. (Do not count omitted answers.)

**Step C:** Count the number of correct answers and the number of incorrect answers for *Section 10* and record the numbers in the spaces provided on the Scoring Worksheet. (Do not count omitted answers.)

**Step D:** Total the number of correct responses. Total the number of incorrect responses. Enter the resulting figure on the Scoring Worksheet. To determine A, use the formula:

$$\text{Number correct} - \frac{\text{Number incorrect}}{4} = A$$

**Step E:** To obtain B, your Writing Multiple-Choice (MC) Rounded Raw Score, round A to the nearest whole number. (For example, any number from 44.50 to 45.49 rounds to 45.) Enter the resulting figure on the Scoring Worksheet.

**Step F:** To find your overall Writing Scaled Score, use Table 3. Look up the Total MC Rounded Raw Score you obtained in Step E in the left side of Table 3 and the Essay Score entered in Step A across the top of the table. Enter this score in the box on the Scoring Worksheet.

**Step G:** To find your Writing MC Subscore, look up the Total MC Rounded Raw Score you obtained in Step E on the Writing Multiple-Choice Conversion Table (Table 4). Enter this score in the box on the Scoring Worksheet.

**Note:** For the **WRITING SECTION**, your Essay Raw Score counts approximately 30% and your Multiple-Choice Raw Score counts approximately 70%.

# SAT Practice Test #2 Scoring Worksheet

**SAT Critical Reading Section**

A. Section 4:

_____ _____
no. correct        no. incorrect

+                              +

B. Section 7:

_____ _____
no. correct        no. incorrect

+                              +

C. Section 9:

_____ _____
no. correct        no. incorrect

=                              =

D. Total Unrounded Raw Score

_____  – ( _____ ÷ 4)  = _____
no. correct              no. incorrect                      A

E. Total Rounded Raw Score          _____
   (Rounded to nearest whole number)              B

F. Critical Reading Scaled Score
   (See Table 1)

Critical
Reading Scaled
Score

**SAT Mathematics Section**

A. Section 2:

_____ _____
no. correct        no. incorrect

+                              +

B. Section 5:
   Questions 1-8

_____ _____
no. correct        no. incorrect

+

C. Section 5:
   Questions 9-18

_____
no. correct

+                              +

D. Section 8:

_____ _____
no. correct        no. incorrect

=                              =

E. Total Unrounded Raw Score

_____  ( _____ ÷ 4)  = _____
no. correct              no. incorrect                      A

F. Total Rounded Raw Score          _____
   (Rounded to nearest whole number)              B

G. Mathematics Scaled Score
   (See Table 2)

Mathematics
Scaled
Score

**SAT Writing Section**

A. Section 1:

☐ Essay Score  ×2

B. Section 6: _____    _____
                   no. correct         no. incorrect

+                                +

C. Section 10: _____    _____
                   no. correct         no. incorrect

=                                =

D. Total MC Unrounded Raw Score   _____ − (_____ ÷ 4) − _____
                                      no. correct         no. incorrect            A

E. Total MC Rounded Raw Score                                       _____
   (Rounded to nearest whole number)                                      B

F. Writing Scaled Score
   (See Table 3)

☐

Writing Scaled
Score

G. Writing MC Subscore
   (See Table 4)

☐

Writing MC
Subscore

| Table 1. Critical Reading Conversion Table | | | |
|---|---|---|---|
| Raw Score | Scaled Score | Raw Score | Scaled Score |
| 67 | 800 | 30 | 500 |
| 66 | 800 | 29 | 490 |
| 65 | 800 | 28 | 490 |
| 64 | 800 | 27 | 480 |
| 63 | 780 | 26 | 470 |
| 62 | 760 | 25 | 470 |
| 61 | 750 | 24 | 460 |
| 60 | 740 | 23 | 460 |
| 59 | 720 | 22 | 450 |
| 58 | 710 | 21 | 450 |
| 57 | 700 | 20 | 440 |
| 56 | 690 | 19 | 430 |
| 55 | 680 | 18 | 430 |
| 54 | 670 | 17 | 420 |
| 53 | 660 | 16 | 420 |
| 52 | 650 | 15 | 410 |
| 51 | 640 | 14 | 400 |
| 50 | 640 | 13 | 400 |
| 49 | 630 | 12 | 390 |
| 48 | 620 | 11 | 380 |
| 47 | 610 | 10 | 380 |
| 46 | 600 | 9 | 370 |
| 45 | 600 | 8 | 360 |
| 44 | 590 | 7 | 350 |
| 43 | 580 | 6 | 340 |
| 42 | 570 | 5 | 330 |
| 41 | 570 | 4 | 320 |
| 40 | 560 | 3 | 310 |
| 39 | 550 | 2 | 300 |
| 38 | 550 | 1 | 280 |
| 37 | 540 | 0 | 270 |
| 36 | 530 | -1 | 250 |
| 35 | 530 | -2 | 230 |
| 34 | 520 | -3 | 210 |
| 33 | 520 | -4 and below | 200 |
| 32 | 510 | | |
| 31 | 500 | | |

| Table 2. Mathematics Conversion Table | | | |
|---|---|---|---|
| Raw Score | Scaled Score | Raw Score | Scaled Score |
| 54 | 800 | 24 | 490 |
| 53 | 780 | 23 | 480 |
| 52 | 760 | 22 | 470 |
| 51 | 740 | 21 | 460 |
| 50 | 720 | 20 | 460 |
| 49 | 710 | 19 | 450 |
| 48 | 700 | 18 | 440 |
| 47 | 690 | 17 | 430 |
| 46 | 680 | 16 | 420 |
| 45 | 670 | 15 | 410 |
| 44 | 660 | 14 | 410 |
| 43 | 650 | 13 | 400 |
| 42 | 640 | 12 | 390 |
| 41 | 640 | 11 | 380 |
| 40 | 630 | 10 | 370 |
| 39 | 620 | 9 | 360 |
| 38 | 610 | 8 | 350 |
| 37 | 600 | 7 | 340 |
| 36 | 590 | 6 | 330 |
| 35 | 580 | 5 | 310 |
| 34 | 570 | 4 | 300 |
| 33 | 560 | 3 | 280 |
| 32 | 560 | 2 | 270 |
| 31 | 550 | 1 | 250 |
| 30 | 540 | 0 | 230 |
| 29 | 530 | -1 | 210 |
| 28 | 520 | -2 | 200 |
| 27 | 510 | -3 | 200 |
| 26 | 500 | -4 and below | 200 |
| 25 | 500 | | |

## Table 3. Writing Conversion Table

| Writing MC Raw Score | Essay Raw Score | | | | | | | | | | | |
|---|---|---|---|---|---|---|---|---|---|---|---|---|
| | 12 | 11 | 10 | 9 | 8 | 7 | 6 | 5 | 4 | 3 | 2 | 0 |
| 49 | 800 | 800 | 800 | 800 | 790 | 760 | 750 | 730 | 720 | 700 | 680 | 680 |
| 48 | 800 | 800 | 790 | 770 | 750 | 730 | 710 | 690 | 680 | 660 | 650 | 650 |
| 47 | 800 | 780 | 760 | 750 | 720 | 700 | 690 | 670 | 660 | 640 | 620 | 620 |
| 46 | 780 | 760 | 750 | 730 | 700 | 680 | 670 | 650 | 640 | 620 | 600 | 600 |
| 45 | 760 | 750 | 730 | 710 | 690 | 670 | 650 | 630 | 620 | 600 | 590 | 590 |
| 44 | 740 | 730 | 710 | 700 | 670 | 650 | 630 | 620 | 610 | 590 | 570 | 570 |
| 43 | 730 | 720 | 700 | 680 | 660 | 640 | 620 | 610 | 590 | 570 | 560 | 560 |
| 42 | 720 | 700 | 690 | 670 | 650 | 630 | 610 | 590 | 580 | 560 | 540 | 540 |
| 41 | 710 | 690 | 680 | 660 | 630 | 610 | 600 | 580 | 570 | 550 | 530 | 530 |
| 40 | 700 | 680 | 660 | 650 | 620 | 600 | 590 | 570 | 560 | 540 | 520 | 520 |
| 39 | 680 | 670 | 650 | 640 | 610 | 590 | 570 | 560 | 550 | 530 | 510 | 510 |
| 38 | 670 | 660 | 640 | 630 | 600 | 580 | 560 | 550 | 540 | 520 | 500 | 500 |
| 37 | 660 | 650 | 630 | 620 | 590 | 570 | 550 | 540 | 530 | 510 | 490 | 490 |
| 36 | 650 | 640 | 620 | 610 | 580 | 560 | 540 | 530 | 520 | 500 | 480 | 480 |
| 35 | 650 | 630 | 610 | 600 | 570 | 550 | 540 | 520 | 510 | 490 | 470 | 470 |
| 34 | 640 | 620 | 610 | 590 | 560 | 540 | 530 | 510 | 500 | 480 | 460 | 460 |
| 33 | 630 | 610 | 600 | 580 | 560 | 530 | 520 | 500 | 490 | 470 | 450 | 450 |
| 32 | 620 | 610 | 590 | 570 | 550 | 530 | 510 | 490 | 480 | 460 | 450 | 450 |
| 31 | 610 | 600 | 580 | 560 | 540 | 520 | 500 | 490 | 470 | 450 | 440 | 440 |
| 30 | 600 | 590 | 570 | 560 | 530 | 510 | 490 | 480 | 460 | 450 | 430 | 430 |
| 29 | 600 | 580 | 560 | 550 | 520 | 500 | 490 | 470 | 460 | 440 | 420 | 420 |
| 28 | 590 | 570 | 560 | 540 | 520 | 490 | 480 | 460 | 450 | 430 | 410 | 410 |
| 27 | 580 | 570 | 550 | 530 | 510 | 490 | 470 | 450 | 440 | 420 | 410 | 410 |
| 26 | 570 | 560 | 540 | 530 | 500 | 480 | 460 | 450 | 430 | 410 | 400 | 400 |
| 25 | 570 | 550 | 540 | 520 | 490 | 470 | 460 | 440 | 430 | 410 | 390 | 390 |
| 24 | 560 | 550 | 530 | 510 | 490 | 470 | 450 | 430 | 420 | 400 | 380 | 380 |
| 23 | 550 | 540 | 520 | 500 | 480 | 460 | 440 | 430 | 410 | 390 | 380 | 380 |
| 22 | 540 | 530 | 510 | 500 | 470 | 450 | 430 | 420 | 410 | 390 | 370 | 370 |
| 21 | 540 | 520 | 510 | 490 | 470 | 440 | 430 | 410 | 400 | 380 | 360 | 360 |
| 20 | 530 | 520 | 500 | 480 | 460 | 440 | 420 | 410 | 390 | 370 | 360 | 360 |
| 19 | 520 | 510 | 490 | 480 | 450 | 430 | 410 | 400 | 390 | 370 | 350 | 350 |
| 18 | 520 | 500 | 490 | 470 | 450 | 430 | 410 | 390 | 380 | 360 | 340 | 340 |
| 17 | 510 | 500 | 480 | 460 | 440 | 420 | 400 | 390 | 370 | 350 | 340 | 340 |
| 16 | 510 | 490 | 470 | 460 | 430 | 410 | 400 | 380 | 370 | 350 | 330 | 330 |
| 15 | 500 | 490 | 470 | 450 | 430 | 410 | 390 | 370 | 360 | 340 | 320 | 320 |
| 14 | 490 | 480 | 460 | 440 | 420 | 400 | 380 | 370 | 350 | 330 | 320 | 320 |
| 13 | 490 | 470 | 460 | 440 | 410 | 390 | 380 | 360 | 350 | 330 | 310 | 310 |
| 12 | 480 | 470 | 450 | 430 | 410 | 390 | 370 | 350 | 340 | 320 | 310 | 310 |
| 11 | 470 | 460 | 440 | 420 | 400 | 380 | 360 | 350 | 330 | 310 | 300 | 300 |
| 10 | 470 | 450 | 440 | 420 | 390 | 370 | 360 | 340 | 330 | 310 | 290 | 290 |
| 9 | 460 | 450 | 430 | 410 | 390 | 370 | 350 | 330 | 320 | 300 | 280 | 280 |
| 8 | 450 | 440 | 420 | 400 | 380 | 360 | 340 | 330 | 310 | 290 | 280 | 280 |
| 7 | 440 | 430 | 410 | 400 | 370 | 350 | 330 | 320 | 300 | 290 | 270 | 270 |
| 6 | 430 | 420 | 400 | 390 | 360 | 340 | 320 | 310 | 300 | 280 | 260 | 260 |
| 5 | 430 | 410 | 390 | 380 | 350 | 330 | 320 | 300 | 290 | 270 | 250 | 250 |
| 4 | 420 | 400 | 380 | 370 | 340 | 320 | 310 | 290 | 280 | 260 | 240 | 240 |
| 3 | 400 | 390 | 370 | 360 | 330 | 310 | 290 | 280 | 270 | 250 | 230 | 230 |
| 2 | 390 | 380 | 360 | 340 | 320 | 300 | 280 | 260 | 250 | 230 | 220 | 220 |
| 1 | 370 | 360 | 340 | 330 | 300 | 280 | 260 | 250 | 240 | 220 | 200 | 200 |
| 0 | 360 | 340 | 330 | 310 | 280 | 260 | 250 | 230 | 220 | 200 | 200 | 200 |
| -1 | 340 | 320 | 310 | 290 | 260 | 240 | 230 | 210 | 200 | 200 | 200 | 200 |
| -2 | 310 | 300 | 280 | 270 | 240 | 220 | 200 | 200 | 200 | 200 | 200 | 200 |
| -3 and below | 310 | 300 | 280 | 260 | 240 | 220 | 200 | 200 | 200 | 200 | 200 | 200 |

## Table 4. Writing Multiple-Choice Conversion Table

| Raw Score | Scaled Score | Raw Score | Scaled Score |
|-----------|--------------|-----------|--------------|
| 49 | 80 | 23 | 46 |
| 48 | 78 | 22 | 45 |
| 47 | 75 | 21 | 44 |
| 46 | 73 | 20 | 44 |
| 45 | 71 | 19 | 43 |
| 44 | 69 | 18 | 42 |
| 43 | 68 | 17 | 41 |
| 42 | 66 | 16 | 41 |
| 41 | 65 | 15 | 40 |
| 40 | 63 | 14 | 39 |
| 39 | 62 | 13 | 38 |
| 38 | 61 | 12 | 37 |
| 37 | 60 | 11 | 37 |
| 36 | 58 | 10 | 36 |
| 35 | 57 | 9 | 35 |
| 34 | 56 | 8 | 34 |
| 33 | 55 | 7 | 33 |
| 32 | 54 | 6 | 32 |
| 31 | 53 | 5 | 31 |
| 30 | 52 | 4 | 30 |
| 29 | 51 | 3 | 28 |
| 28 | 50 | 2 | 27 |
| 27 | 50 | 1 | 25 |
| 26 | 49 | 0 | 23 |
| 25 | 48 | -1 and below | 20 |
| 24 | 47 | | |

# SAT Practice Test #3

 **After this test:**

- Use this book to its full potential! Get exclusive access answer explanations, free practice score reports and free sample student essays to help you score your essay in the Book Owners' Area at www.collegeboard.org/satstudyguide.

- Want more practice? Get 10 more official practice tests, auto essay scoring and lesson plans from the test maker by subscribing to *The Official SAT Online Course*. As a book owner, you're entitled to a $10 discount. Sign up at www.collegeboard.org/satstudyguide.

*Note:* Section 3, the variable section, has been omitted from this practice test.

YOUR NAME (PRINT) _____

LAST                                    FIRST                          MI

TEST CENTER _____

NUMBER          NAME OF TEST CENTER                          ROOM NUMBER

# SAT Reasoning Test — General Directions

## Timing

- You will have 3 hours and 45 minutes to work on this test.
- There are ten separately timed sections:
  - ► One 25-minute essay
  - ► Six other 25-minute sections
  - ► Two 20-minute sections
  - ► One 10-minute section
- You may work on only one section at a time.
- The supervisor will tell you when to begin and end each section.
- If you finish a section before time is called, check your work on that section. You may NOT turn to any other section.
- Work as rapidly as you can without losing accuracy. Don't waste time on questions that seem too difficult for you.

## Marking Answers

- Be sure to mark your answer sheet properly.

**COMPLETE MARK** ●    **EXAMPLES OF INCOMPLETE MARKS** ⊗ ⊖ ◑

- You must use a No. 2 pencil.
- Carefully mark only one answer for each question.
- Make sure you fill the entire circle darkly and completely.
- Do not make any stray marks on your answer sheet.
- If you erase, do so completely. Incomplete erasures may be scored as intended answers.
- Use only the answer spaces that correspond to the question numbers.

## Using Your Test Book

- You may use the test book for scratchwork, but you will not receive credit for anything written there.
- After time has been called, you may not transfer answers to your answer sheet or fill in circles.
- You may not fold or remove pages or portions of a page from this book, or take the book or answer sheet from the testing room.

## Scoring

- For each correct answer, you receive one point.
- For questions you omit, you receive no points.
- For a wrong answer to a multiple-choice question, you lose one-fourth of a point.
  - ► If you can eliminate one or more of the answer choices as wrong, you increase your chances of choosing the correct answer and earning one point.
  - ► If you can't eliminate any choice, move on. You can return to the question later if there is time.
- For a wrong answer to a student-produced response ("grid-in") math question, you don't lose any points.
- Multiple-choice and student-produced response questions are machine scored.
- The essay is scored on a 1 to 6 scale by two different readers. The total essay score is the sum of the two readers' scores.
- Off-topic essays, blank essays, and essays written in ink will receive a score of zero.

**IMPORTANT:** The codes below are unique to your test book. Copy them on your answer sheet in boxes 8 and 9 and fill in the corresponding circles exactly as shown.

**9 | TEST FORM**
(Copy from back of test book.)

**8 | FORM CODE**
(Copy and grid as on back of test book.)

The passages for this test have been adapted from published material. The ideas contained in them do not necessarily represent the opinions of the College Board.

# DO NOT OPEN THIS BOOK UNTIL THE SUPERVISOR TELLS YOU TO DO SO.

# CollegeBoard SAT

# SAT Reasoning Test™

| MARKS MUST BE COMPLETE | | You must use a No. 2 pencil. Do not use a mechanical pencil. It is very important that you fill in the entire circle darkly and completely. If you change your response, erase as completely as possible. Incomplete marks or erasures may affect your score. It is very important that you follow these instructions when filling out your answer sheet. |
|---|---|---|
| COMPLETE MARK ● | EXAMPLES OF INCOMPLETE MARKS 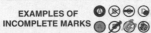 | |

**1** Your Name:
(Print)

Last _____ First _____ M.I. _____

I agree to the conditions on the back of the SAT Reasoning Test™ booklet. I also agree to use only a No. 2 pencil to complete my answer sheet.

Signature: _____ Date: ___ / ___ / ___

Home Address: _____
(Print)    Number and Street    City    State    Zip Code

Home Phone: ( ) _____ Center: _____
(Print)    (Print)    City    State/Country

**2** YOUR NAME
Last Name (First 6 Letters)  First Name (First 4 Letters)  Mid. Init.

**3** DATE OF BIRTH
MONTH  DAY  YEAR
Jan, Feb, Mar, Apr, May, Jun, Jul, Aug, Sep, Oct, Nov, Dec

**5** SEX
○ Female  ○ Male

**6** REGISTRATION NUMBER
(Copy from Admission Ticket.)
○ I turned in my registration form today.

**Important:** Fill in items 8 and 9 exactly as shown on the back of test book.

**8** FORM CODE
(Copy and grid as on back of test book.)

**9** TEST FORM
(Copy from back of test book.)

**10** TEST BOOK SERIAL NUMBER
(Copy from front of test book.)

**11** TEST CENTER
(Supplied by Test Center Supervisor.)

**4** ZIP CODE

**7** SOCIAL SECURITY NUMBER

FOR OFFICIAL USE ONLY
0 1 2 3 4 5 6
0 1 2 3 4 5 6
0 1 2 3 4 5 6

00272-36390 • NS75E4600 • Printed in U.S.A.
732652
172625-001:654321    ISD5960

PLEASE DO NOT WRITE IN THIS AREA

SERIAL #

**SECTION 1**

**Begin your essay on this page. If you need more space, continue on the next page.**

**SECTION 2**

1 Ⓐ Ⓑ Ⓒ Ⓓ Ⓔ   11 Ⓐ Ⓑ Ⓒ Ⓓ Ⓔ   21 Ⓐ Ⓑ Ⓒ Ⓓ Ⓔ   31 Ⓐ Ⓑ Ⓒ Ⓓ Ⓔ
2 Ⓐ Ⓑ Ⓒ Ⓓ Ⓔ   12 Ⓐ Ⓑ Ⓒ Ⓓ Ⓔ   22 Ⓐ Ⓑ Ⓒ Ⓓ Ⓔ   32 Ⓐ Ⓑ Ⓒ Ⓓ Ⓔ
3 Ⓐ Ⓑ Ⓒ Ⓓ Ⓔ   13 Ⓐ Ⓑ Ⓒ Ⓓ Ⓔ   23 Ⓐ Ⓑ Ⓒ Ⓓ Ⓔ   33 Ⓐ Ⓑ Ⓒ Ⓓ Ⓔ
4 Ⓐ Ⓑ Ⓒ Ⓓ Ⓔ   14 Ⓐ Ⓑ Ⓒ Ⓓ Ⓔ   24 Ⓐ Ⓑ Ⓒ Ⓓ Ⓔ   34 Ⓐ Ⓑ Ⓒ Ⓓ Ⓔ
5 Ⓐ Ⓑ Ⓒ Ⓓ Ⓔ   15 Ⓐ Ⓑ Ⓒ Ⓓ Ⓔ   25 Ⓐ Ⓑ Ⓒ Ⓓ Ⓔ   35 Ⓐ Ⓑ Ⓒ Ⓓ Ⓔ
6 Ⓐ Ⓑ Ⓒ Ⓓ Ⓔ   16 Ⓐ Ⓑ Ⓒ Ⓓ Ⓔ   26 Ⓐ Ⓑ Ⓒ Ⓓ Ⓔ   36 Ⓐ Ⓑ Ⓒ Ⓓ Ⓔ
7 Ⓐ Ⓑ Ⓒ Ⓓ Ⓔ   17 Ⓐ Ⓑ Ⓒ Ⓓ Ⓔ   27 Ⓐ Ⓑ Ⓒ Ⓓ Ⓔ   37 Ⓐ Ⓑ Ⓒ Ⓓ Ⓔ
8 Ⓐ Ⓑ Ⓒ Ⓓ Ⓔ   18 Ⓐ Ⓑ Ⓒ Ⓓ Ⓔ   28 Ⓐ Ⓑ Ⓒ Ⓓ Ⓔ   38 Ⓐ Ⓑ Ⓒ Ⓓ Ⓔ
9 Ⓐ Ⓑ Ⓒ Ⓓ Ⓔ   19 Ⓐ Ⓑ Ⓒ Ⓓ Ⓔ   29 Ⓐ Ⓑ Ⓒ Ⓓ Ⓔ   39 Ⓐ Ⓑ Ⓒ Ⓓ Ⓔ
10 Ⓐ Ⓑ Ⓒ Ⓓ Ⓔ   20 Ⓐ Ⓑ Ⓒ Ⓓ Ⓔ   30 Ⓐ Ⓑ Ⓒ Ⓓ Ⓔ   40 Ⓐ Ⓑ Ⓒ Ⓓ Ⓔ

**SECTION 3**

1 Ⓐ Ⓑ Ⓒ Ⓓ Ⓔ   11 Ⓐ Ⓑ Ⓒ Ⓓ Ⓔ   21 Ⓐ Ⓑ Ⓒ Ⓓ Ⓔ   31 Ⓐ Ⓑ Ⓒ Ⓓ Ⓔ
2 Ⓐ Ⓑ Ⓒ Ⓓ Ⓔ   12 Ⓐ Ⓑ Ⓒ Ⓓ Ⓔ   22 Ⓐ Ⓑ Ⓒ Ⓓ Ⓔ   32 Ⓐ Ⓑ Ⓒ Ⓓ Ⓔ
3 Ⓐ Ⓑ Ⓒ Ⓓ Ⓔ   13 Ⓐ Ⓑ Ⓒ Ⓓ Ⓔ   23 Ⓐ Ⓑ Ⓒ Ⓓ Ⓔ   33 Ⓐ Ⓑ Ⓒ Ⓓ Ⓔ
4 Ⓐ Ⓑ Ⓒ Ⓓ Ⓔ   14 Ⓐ Ⓑ Ⓒ Ⓓ Ⓔ   24 Ⓐ Ⓑ Ⓒ Ⓓ Ⓔ   34 Ⓐ Ⓑ Ⓒ Ⓓ Ⓔ
5 Ⓐ Ⓑ Ⓒ Ⓓ Ⓔ   15 Ⓐ Ⓑ Ⓒ Ⓓ Ⓔ   25 Ⓐ Ⓑ Ⓒ Ⓓ Ⓔ   35 Ⓐ Ⓑ Ⓒ Ⓓ Ⓔ
6 Ⓐ Ⓑ Ⓒ Ⓓ Ⓔ   16 Ⓐ Ⓑ Ⓒ Ⓓ Ⓔ   26 Ⓐ Ⓑ Ⓒ Ⓓ Ⓔ   36 Ⓐ Ⓑ Ⓒ Ⓓ Ⓔ
7 Ⓐ Ⓑ Ⓒ Ⓓ Ⓔ   17 Ⓐ Ⓑ Ⓒ Ⓓ Ⓔ   27 Ⓐ Ⓑ Ⓒ Ⓓ Ⓔ   37 Ⓐ Ⓑ Ⓒ Ⓓ Ⓔ
8 Ⓐ Ⓑ Ⓒ Ⓓ Ⓔ   18 Ⓐ Ⓑ Ⓒ Ⓓ Ⓔ   28 Ⓐ Ⓑ Ⓒ Ⓓ Ⓔ   38 Ⓐ Ⓑ Ⓒ Ⓓ Ⓔ
9 Ⓐ Ⓑ Ⓒ Ⓓ Ⓔ   19 Ⓐ Ⓑ Ⓒ Ⓓ Ⓔ   29 Ⓐ Ⓑ Ⓒ Ⓓ Ⓔ   39 Ⓐ Ⓑ Ⓒ Ⓓ Ⓔ
10 Ⓐ Ⓑ Ⓒ Ⓓ Ⓔ   20 Ⓐ Ⓑ Ⓒ Ⓓ Ⓔ   30 Ⓐ Ⓑ Ⓒ Ⓓ Ⓔ   40 Ⓐ Ⓑ Ⓒ Ⓓ Ⓔ

**CAUTION** Grid answers in the section below for SECTION 2 or SECTION 3 only if directed to do so in your test book.

**Student-Produced Responses** ONLY ANSWERS THAT ARE GRIDDED WILL BE SCORED. YOU WILL NOT RECEIVE CREDIT FOR ANYTHING WRITTEN IN THE BOXES.

Quality Assurance Mark

Grids numbered 9, 10, 11, 12, 13, 14, 15, 16, 17, 18 — each with digit columns 0–9.

Page 4

508

**SECTION 4**

| 1 Ⓐ Ⓑ Ⓒ Ⓓ Ⓔ | 11 Ⓐ Ⓑ Ⓒ Ⓓ Ⓔ | 21 Ⓐ Ⓑ Ⓒ Ⓓ Ⓔ | 31 Ⓐ Ⓑ Ⓒ Ⓓ Ⓔ |
| 2 Ⓐ Ⓑ Ⓒ Ⓓ Ⓔ | 12 Ⓐ Ⓑ Ⓒ Ⓓ Ⓔ | 22 Ⓐ Ⓑ Ⓒ Ⓓ Ⓔ | 32 Ⓐ Ⓑ Ⓒ Ⓓ Ⓔ |
| 3 Ⓐ Ⓑ Ⓒ Ⓓ Ⓔ | 13 Ⓐ Ⓑ Ⓒ Ⓓ Ⓔ | 23 Ⓐ Ⓑ Ⓒ Ⓓ Ⓔ | 33 Ⓐ Ⓑ Ⓒ Ⓓ Ⓔ |
| 4 Ⓐ Ⓑ Ⓒ Ⓓ Ⓔ | 14 Ⓐ Ⓑ Ⓒ Ⓓ Ⓔ | 24 Ⓐ Ⓑ Ⓒ Ⓓ Ⓔ | 34 Ⓐ Ⓑ Ⓒ Ⓓ Ⓔ |
| 5 Ⓐ Ⓑ Ⓒ Ⓓ Ⓔ | 15 Ⓐ Ⓑ Ⓒ Ⓓ Ⓔ | 25 Ⓐ Ⓑ Ⓒ Ⓓ Ⓔ | 35 Ⓐ Ⓑ Ⓒ Ⓓ Ⓔ |
| 6 Ⓐ Ⓑ Ⓒ Ⓓ Ⓔ | 16 Ⓐ Ⓑ Ⓒ Ⓓ Ⓔ | 26 Ⓐ Ⓑ Ⓒ Ⓓ Ⓔ | 36 Ⓐ Ⓑ Ⓒ Ⓓ Ⓔ |
| 7 Ⓐ Ⓑ Ⓒ Ⓓ Ⓔ | 17 Ⓐ Ⓑ Ⓒ Ⓓ Ⓔ | 27 Ⓐ Ⓑ Ⓒ Ⓓ Ⓔ | 37 Ⓐ Ⓑ Ⓒ Ⓓ Ⓔ |
| 8 Ⓐ Ⓑ Ⓒ Ⓓ Ⓔ | 18 Ⓐ Ⓑ Ⓒ Ⓓ Ⓔ | 28 Ⓐ Ⓑ Ⓒ Ⓓ Ⓔ | 38 Ⓐ Ⓑ Ⓒ Ⓓ Ⓔ |
| 9 Ⓐ Ⓑ Ⓒ Ⓓ Ⓔ | 19 Ⓐ Ⓑ Ⓒ Ⓓ Ⓔ | 29 Ⓐ Ⓑ Ⓒ Ⓓ Ⓔ | 39 Ⓐ Ⓑ Ⓒ Ⓓ Ⓔ |
| 10 Ⓐ Ⓑ Ⓒ Ⓓ Ⓔ | 20 Ⓐ Ⓑ Ⓒ Ⓓ Ⓔ | 30 Ⓐ Ⓑ Ⓒ Ⓓ Ⓔ | 40 Ⓐ Ⓑ Ⓒ Ⓓ Ⓔ |

**SECTION 5**

| 1 Ⓐ Ⓑ Ⓒ Ⓓ Ⓔ | 11 Ⓐ Ⓑ Ⓒ Ⓓ Ⓔ | 21 Ⓐ Ⓑ Ⓒ Ⓓ Ⓔ | 31 Ⓐ Ⓑ Ⓒ Ⓓ Ⓔ |
| 2 Ⓐ Ⓑ Ⓒ Ⓓ Ⓔ | 12 Ⓐ Ⓑ Ⓒ Ⓓ Ⓔ | 22 Ⓐ Ⓑ Ⓒ Ⓓ Ⓔ | 32 Ⓐ Ⓑ Ⓒ Ⓓ Ⓔ |
| 3 Ⓐ Ⓑ Ⓒ Ⓓ Ⓔ | 13 Ⓐ Ⓑ Ⓒ Ⓓ Ⓔ | 23 Ⓐ Ⓑ Ⓒ Ⓓ Ⓔ | 33 Ⓐ Ⓑ Ⓒ Ⓓ Ⓔ |
| 4 Ⓐ Ⓑ Ⓒ Ⓓ Ⓔ | 14 Ⓐ Ⓑ Ⓒ Ⓓ Ⓔ | 24 Ⓐ Ⓑ Ⓒ Ⓓ Ⓔ | 34 Ⓐ Ⓑ Ⓒ Ⓓ Ⓔ |
| 5 Ⓐ Ⓑ Ⓒ Ⓓ Ⓔ | 15 Ⓐ Ⓑ Ⓒ Ⓓ Ⓔ | 25 Ⓐ Ⓑ Ⓒ Ⓓ Ⓔ | 35 Ⓐ Ⓑ Ⓒ Ⓓ Ⓔ |
| 6 Ⓐ Ⓑ Ⓒ Ⓓ Ⓔ | 16 Ⓐ Ⓑ Ⓒ Ⓓ Ⓔ | 26 Ⓐ Ⓑ Ⓒ Ⓓ Ⓔ | 36 Ⓐ Ⓑ Ⓒ Ⓓ Ⓔ |
| 7 Ⓐ Ⓑ Ⓒ Ⓓ Ⓔ | 17 Ⓐ Ⓑ Ⓒ Ⓓ Ⓔ | 27 Ⓐ Ⓑ Ⓒ Ⓓ Ⓔ | 37 Ⓐ Ⓑ Ⓒ Ⓓ Ⓔ |
| 8 Ⓐ Ⓑ Ⓒ Ⓓ Ⓔ | 18 Ⓐ Ⓑ Ⓒ Ⓓ Ⓔ | 28 Ⓐ Ⓑ Ⓒ Ⓓ Ⓔ | 38 Ⓐ Ⓑ Ⓒ Ⓓ Ⓔ |
| 9 Ⓐ Ⓑ Ⓒ Ⓓ Ⓔ | 19 Ⓐ Ⓑ Ⓒ Ⓓ Ⓔ | 29 Ⓐ Ⓑ Ⓒ Ⓓ Ⓔ | 39 Ⓐ Ⓑ Ⓒ Ⓓ Ⓔ |
| 10 Ⓐ Ⓑ Ⓒ Ⓓ Ⓔ | 20 Ⓐ Ⓑ Ⓒ Ⓓ Ⓔ | 30 Ⓐ Ⓑ Ⓒ Ⓓ Ⓔ | 40 Ⓐ Ⓑ Ⓒ Ⓓ Ⓔ |

**CAUTION**  Grid answers in the section below for SECTION 4 or SECTION 5 only if directed to do so in your test book.

**Student-Produced Responses**  ONLY ANSWERS THAT ARE GRIDDED WILL BE SCORED. YOU WILL NOT RECEIVE CREDIT FOR ANYTHING WRITTEN IN THE BOXES.

Quality Assurance Mark ●

Grid questions: 9, 10, 11, 12, 13, 14, 15, 16, 17, 18 — each with standard student-produced response grid (fraction bar, decimal point, digits 0–9).

**SECTION 6**

| | | | |
|---|---|---|---|
| 1 Ⓐ Ⓑ Ⓒ Ⓓ Ⓔ | 11 Ⓐ Ⓑ Ⓒ Ⓓ Ⓔ | 21 Ⓐ Ⓑ Ⓒ Ⓓ Ⓔ | 31 Ⓐ Ⓑ Ⓒ Ⓓ Ⓔ |
| 2 Ⓐ Ⓑ Ⓒ Ⓓ Ⓔ | 12 Ⓐ Ⓑ Ⓒ Ⓓ Ⓔ | 22 Ⓐ Ⓑ Ⓒ Ⓓ Ⓔ | 32 Ⓐ Ⓑ Ⓒ Ⓓ Ⓔ |
| 3 Ⓐ Ⓑ Ⓒ Ⓓ Ⓔ | 13 Ⓐ Ⓑ Ⓒ Ⓓ Ⓔ | 23 Ⓐ Ⓑ Ⓒ Ⓓ Ⓔ | 33 Ⓐ Ⓑ Ⓒ Ⓓ Ⓔ |
| 4 Ⓐ Ⓑ Ⓒ Ⓓ Ⓔ | 14 Ⓐ Ⓑ Ⓒ Ⓓ Ⓔ | 24 Ⓐ Ⓑ Ⓒ Ⓓ Ⓔ | 34 Ⓐ Ⓑ Ⓒ Ⓓ Ⓔ |
| 5 Ⓐ Ⓑ Ⓒ Ⓓ Ⓔ | 15 Ⓐ Ⓑ Ⓒ Ⓓ Ⓔ | 25 Ⓐ Ⓑ Ⓒ Ⓓ Ⓔ | 35 Ⓐ Ⓑ Ⓒ Ⓓ Ⓔ |
| 6 Ⓐ Ⓑ Ⓒ Ⓓ Ⓔ | 16 Ⓐ Ⓑ Ⓒ Ⓓ Ⓔ | 26 Ⓐ Ⓑ Ⓒ Ⓓ Ⓔ | 36 Ⓐ Ⓑ Ⓒ Ⓓ Ⓔ |
| 7 Ⓐ Ⓑ Ⓒ Ⓓ Ⓔ | 17 Ⓐ Ⓑ Ⓒ Ⓓ Ⓔ | 27 Ⓐ Ⓑ Ⓒ Ⓓ Ⓔ | 37 Ⓐ Ⓑ Ⓒ Ⓓ Ⓔ |
| 8 Ⓐ Ⓑ Ⓒ Ⓓ Ⓔ | 18 Ⓐ Ⓑ Ⓒ Ⓓ Ⓔ | 28 Ⓐ Ⓑ Ⓒ Ⓓ Ⓔ | 38 Ⓐ Ⓑ Ⓒ Ⓓ Ⓔ |
| 9 Ⓐ Ⓑ Ⓒ Ⓓ Ⓔ | 19 Ⓐ Ⓑ Ⓒ Ⓓ Ⓔ | 29 Ⓐ Ⓑ Ⓒ Ⓓ Ⓔ | 39 Ⓐ Ⓑ Ⓒ Ⓓ Ⓔ |
| 10 Ⓐ Ⓑ Ⓒ Ⓓ Ⓔ | 20 Ⓐ Ⓑ Ⓒ Ⓓ Ⓔ | 30 Ⓐ Ⓑ Ⓒ Ⓓ Ⓔ | 40 Ⓐ Ⓑ Ⓒ Ⓓ Ⓔ |

**SECTION 7**

| | | | |
|---|---|---|---|
| 1 Ⓐ Ⓑ Ⓒ Ⓓ Ⓔ | 11 Ⓐ Ⓑ Ⓒ Ⓓ Ⓔ | 21 Ⓐ Ⓑ Ⓒ Ⓓ Ⓔ | 31 Ⓐ Ⓑ Ⓒ Ⓓ Ⓔ |
| 2 Ⓐ Ⓑ Ⓒ Ⓓ Ⓔ | 12 Ⓐ Ⓑ Ⓒ Ⓓ Ⓔ | 22 Ⓐ Ⓑ Ⓒ Ⓓ Ⓔ | 32 Ⓐ Ⓑ Ⓒ Ⓓ Ⓔ |
| 3 Ⓐ Ⓑ Ⓒ Ⓓ Ⓔ | 13 Ⓐ Ⓑ Ⓒ Ⓓ Ⓔ | 23 Ⓐ Ⓑ Ⓒ Ⓓ Ⓔ | 33 Ⓐ Ⓑ Ⓒ Ⓓ Ⓔ |
| 4 Ⓐ Ⓑ Ⓒ Ⓓ Ⓔ | 14 Ⓐ Ⓑ Ⓒ Ⓓ Ⓔ | 24 Ⓐ Ⓑ Ⓒ Ⓓ Ⓔ | 34 Ⓐ Ⓑ Ⓒ Ⓓ Ⓔ |
| 5 Ⓐ Ⓑ Ⓒ Ⓓ Ⓔ | 15 Ⓐ Ⓑ Ⓒ Ⓓ Ⓔ | 25 Ⓐ Ⓑ Ⓒ Ⓓ Ⓔ | 35 Ⓐ Ⓑ Ⓒ Ⓓ Ⓔ |
| 6 Ⓐ Ⓑ Ⓒ Ⓓ Ⓔ | 16 Ⓐ Ⓑ Ⓒ Ⓓ Ⓔ | 26 Ⓐ Ⓑ Ⓒ Ⓓ Ⓔ | 36 Ⓐ Ⓑ Ⓒ Ⓓ Ⓔ |
| 7 Ⓐ Ⓑ Ⓒ Ⓓ Ⓔ | 17 Ⓐ Ⓑ Ⓒ Ⓓ Ⓔ | 27 Ⓐ Ⓑ Ⓒ Ⓓ Ⓔ | 37 Ⓐ Ⓑ Ⓒ Ⓓ Ⓔ |
| 8 Ⓐ Ⓑ Ⓒ Ⓓ Ⓔ | 18 Ⓐ Ⓑ Ⓒ Ⓓ Ⓔ | 28 Ⓐ Ⓑ Ⓒ Ⓓ Ⓔ | 38 Ⓐ Ⓑ Ⓒ Ⓓ Ⓔ |
| 9 Ⓐ Ⓑ Ⓒ Ⓓ Ⓔ | 19 Ⓐ Ⓑ Ⓒ Ⓓ Ⓔ | 29 Ⓐ Ⓑ Ⓒ Ⓓ Ⓔ | 39 Ⓐ Ⓑ Ⓒ Ⓓ Ⓔ |
| 10 Ⓐ Ⓑ Ⓒ Ⓓ Ⓔ | 20 Ⓐ Ⓑ Ⓒ Ⓓ Ⓔ | 30 Ⓐ Ⓑ Ⓒ Ⓓ Ⓔ | 40 Ⓐ Ⓑ Ⓒ Ⓓ Ⓔ |

**CAUTION** Grid answers in the section below for SECTION 6 or SECTION 7 only if directed to do so in your test book.

**Student-Produced Responses** ONLY ANSWERS THAT ARE GRIDDED WILL BE SCORED. YOU WILL NOT RECEIVE CREDIT FOR ANYTHING WRITTEN IN THE BOXES.

Quality Assurance Mark

Grid-in response boxes numbered 9, 10, 11, 12, 13, 14, 15, 16, 17, 18, each with digits 0–9.

Page 6

PLEASE DO NOT WRITE IN THIS AREA

SERIAL #

510

**SECTION 8**

1 Ⓐ Ⓑ Ⓒ Ⓓ Ⓔ
2 Ⓐ Ⓑ Ⓒ Ⓓ Ⓔ
3 Ⓐ Ⓑ Ⓒ Ⓓ Ⓔ
4 Ⓐ Ⓑ Ⓒ Ⓓ Ⓔ
5 Ⓐ Ⓑ Ⓒ Ⓓ Ⓔ
6 Ⓐ Ⓑ Ⓒ Ⓓ Ⓔ
7 Ⓐ Ⓑ Ⓒ Ⓓ Ⓔ
8 Ⓐ Ⓑ Ⓒ Ⓓ Ⓔ
9 Ⓐ Ⓑ Ⓒ Ⓓ Ⓔ
10 Ⓐ Ⓑ Ⓒ Ⓓ Ⓔ

11 Ⓐ Ⓑ Ⓒ Ⓓ Ⓔ
12 Ⓐ Ⓑ Ⓒ Ⓓ Ⓔ
13 Ⓐ Ⓑ Ⓒ Ⓓ Ⓔ
14 Ⓐ Ⓑ Ⓒ Ⓓ Ⓔ
15 Ⓐ Ⓑ Ⓒ Ⓓ Ⓔ
16 Ⓐ Ⓑ Ⓒ Ⓓ Ⓔ
17 Ⓐ Ⓑ Ⓒ Ⓓ Ⓔ
18 Ⓐ Ⓑ Ⓒ Ⓓ Ⓔ
19 Ⓐ Ⓑ Ⓒ Ⓓ Ⓔ
20 Ⓐ Ⓑ Ⓒ Ⓓ Ⓔ

21 Ⓐ Ⓑ Ⓒ Ⓓ Ⓔ
22 Ⓐ Ⓑ Ⓒ Ⓓ Ⓔ
23 Ⓐ Ⓑ Ⓒ Ⓓ Ⓔ
24 Ⓐ Ⓑ Ⓒ Ⓓ Ⓔ
25 Ⓐ Ⓑ Ⓒ Ⓓ Ⓔ
26 Ⓐ Ⓑ Ⓒ Ⓓ Ⓔ
27 Ⓐ Ⓑ Ⓒ Ⓓ Ⓔ
28 Ⓐ Ⓑ Ⓒ Ⓓ Ⓔ
29 Ⓐ Ⓑ Ⓒ Ⓓ Ⓔ
30 Ⓐ Ⓑ Ⓒ Ⓓ Ⓔ

31 Ⓐ Ⓑ Ⓒ Ⓓ Ⓔ
32 Ⓐ Ⓑ Ⓒ Ⓓ Ⓔ
33 Ⓐ Ⓑ Ⓒ Ⓓ Ⓔ
34 Ⓐ Ⓑ Ⓒ Ⓓ Ⓔ
35 Ⓐ Ⓑ Ⓒ Ⓓ Ⓔ
36 Ⓐ Ⓑ Ⓒ Ⓓ Ⓔ
37 Ⓐ Ⓑ Ⓒ Ⓓ Ⓔ
38 Ⓐ Ⓑ Ⓒ Ⓓ Ⓔ
39 Ⓐ Ⓑ Ⓒ Ⓓ Ⓔ
40 Ⓐ Ⓑ Ⓒ Ⓓ Ⓔ

**SECTION 9**

1 Ⓐ Ⓑ Ⓒ Ⓓ Ⓔ
2 Ⓐ Ⓑ Ⓒ Ⓓ Ⓔ
3 Ⓐ Ⓑ Ⓒ Ⓓ Ⓔ
4 Ⓐ Ⓑ Ⓒ Ⓓ Ⓔ
5 Ⓐ Ⓑ Ⓒ Ⓓ Ⓔ
6 Ⓐ Ⓑ Ⓒ Ⓓ Ⓔ
7 Ⓐ Ⓑ Ⓒ Ⓓ Ⓔ
8 Ⓐ Ⓑ Ⓒ Ⓓ Ⓔ
9 Ⓐ Ⓑ Ⓒ Ⓓ Ⓔ
10 Ⓐ Ⓑ Ⓒ Ⓓ Ⓔ

11 Ⓐ Ⓑ Ⓒ Ⓓ Ⓔ
12 Ⓐ Ⓑ Ⓒ Ⓓ Ⓔ
13 Ⓐ Ⓑ Ⓒ Ⓓ Ⓔ
14 Ⓐ Ⓑ Ⓒ Ⓓ Ⓔ
15 Ⓐ Ⓑ Ⓒ Ⓓ Ⓔ
16 Ⓐ Ⓑ Ⓒ Ⓓ Ⓔ
17 Ⓐ Ⓑ Ⓒ Ⓓ Ⓔ
18 Ⓐ Ⓑ Ⓒ Ⓓ Ⓔ
19 Ⓐ Ⓑ Ⓒ Ⓓ Ⓔ
20 Ⓐ Ⓑ Ⓒ Ⓓ Ⓔ

21 Ⓐ Ⓑ Ⓒ Ⓓ Ⓔ
22 Ⓐ Ⓑ Ⓒ Ⓓ Ⓔ
23 Ⓐ Ⓑ Ⓒ Ⓓ Ⓔ
24 Ⓐ Ⓑ Ⓒ Ⓓ Ⓔ
25 Ⓐ Ⓑ Ⓒ Ⓓ Ⓔ
26 Ⓐ Ⓑ Ⓒ Ⓓ Ⓔ
27 Ⓐ Ⓑ Ⓒ Ⓓ Ⓔ
28 Ⓐ Ⓑ Ⓒ Ⓓ Ⓔ
29 Ⓐ Ⓑ Ⓒ Ⓓ Ⓔ
30 Ⓐ Ⓑ Ⓒ Ⓓ Ⓔ

31 Ⓐ Ⓑ Ⓒ Ⓓ Ⓔ
32 Ⓐ Ⓑ Ⓒ Ⓓ Ⓔ
33 Ⓐ Ⓑ Ⓒ Ⓓ Ⓔ
34 Ⓐ Ⓑ Ⓒ Ⓓ Ⓔ
35 Ⓐ Ⓑ Ⓒ Ⓓ Ⓔ
36 Ⓐ Ⓑ Ⓒ Ⓓ Ⓔ
37 Ⓐ Ⓑ Ⓒ Ⓓ Ⓔ
38 Ⓐ Ⓑ Ⓒ Ⓓ Ⓔ
39 Ⓐ Ⓑ Ⓒ Ⓓ Ⓔ
40 Ⓐ Ⓑ Ⓒ Ⓓ Ⓔ

Quality Assurance Mark ●

**SECTION 10**

1 Ⓐ Ⓑ Ⓒ Ⓓ Ⓔ
2 Ⓐ Ⓑ Ⓒ Ⓓ Ⓔ
3 Ⓐ Ⓑ Ⓒ Ⓓ Ⓔ
4 Ⓐ Ⓑ Ⓒ Ⓓ Ⓔ
5 Ⓐ Ⓑ Ⓒ Ⓓ Ⓔ
6 Ⓐ Ⓑ Ⓒ Ⓓ Ⓔ
7 Ⓐ Ⓑ Ⓒ Ⓓ Ⓔ
8 Ⓐ Ⓑ Ⓒ Ⓓ Ⓔ
9 Ⓐ Ⓑ Ⓒ Ⓓ Ⓔ
10 Ⓐ Ⓑ Ⓒ Ⓓ Ⓔ

11 Ⓐ Ⓑ Ⓒ Ⓓ Ⓔ
12 Ⓐ Ⓑ Ⓒ Ⓓ Ⓔ
13 Ⓐ Ⓑ Ⓒ Ⓓ Ⓔ
14 Ⓐ Ⓑ Ⓒ Ⓓ Ⓔ
15 Ⓐ Ⓑ Ⓒ Ⓓ Ⓔ
16 Ⓐ Ⓑ Ⓒ Ⓓ Ⓔ
17 Ⓐ Ⓑ Ⓒ Ⓓ Ⓔ
18 Ⓐ Ⓑ Ⓒ Ⓓ Ⓔ
19 Ⓐ Ⓑ Ⓒ Ⓓ Ⓔ
20 Ⓐ Ⓑ Ⓒ Ⓓ Ⓔ

21 Ⓐ Ⓑ Ⓒ Ⓓ Ⓔ
22 Ⓐ Ⓑ Ⓒ Ⓓ Ⓔ
23 Ⓐ Ⓑ Ⓒ Ⓓ Ⓔ
24 Ⓐ Ⓑ Ⓒ Ⓓ Ⓔ
25 Ⓐ Ⓑ Ⓒ Ⓓ Ⓔ
26 Ⓐ Ⓑ Ⓒ Ⓓ Ⓔ
27 Ⓐ Ⓑ Ⓒ Ⓓ Ⓔ
28 Ⓐ Ⓑ Ⓒ Ⓓ Ⓔ
29 Ⓐ Ⓑ Ⓒ Ⓓ Ⓔ
30 Ⓐ Ⓑ Ⓒ Ⓓ Ⓔ

31 Ⓐ Ⓑ Ⓒ Ⓓ Ⓔ
32 Ⓐ Ⓑ Ⓒ Ⓓ Ⓔ
33 Ⓐ Ⓑ Ⓒ Ⓓ Ⓔ
34 Ⓐ Ⓑ Ⓒ Ⓓ Ⓔ
35 Ⓐ Ⓑ Ⓒ Ⓓ Ⓔ
36 Ⓐ Ⓑ Ⓒ Ⓓ Ⓔ
37 Ⓐ Ⓑ Ⓒ Ⓓ Ⓔ
38 Ⓐ Ⓑ Ⓒ Ⓓ Ⓔ
39 Ⓐ Ⓑ Ⓒ Ⓓ Ⓔ
40 Ⓐ Ⓑ Ⓒ Ⓓ Ⓔ

3

## CERTIFICATION STATEMENT

Copy the statement below (do not print) and sign your name as you would an official document.

I hereby agree to the conditions set forth online at www.collegeboard.org and/or in the SAT® Registration Booklet and certify that I am the person whose name and address appear on this answer sheet.

_____

_____

_____

_____

By signing below, I agree not to share any specific test questions or essay topics with anyone by any form of communication, including, but not limited to: email, text messages, or use of the Internet.

Signature _____  /  Date _____

## SPECIAL QUESTIONS

1 Ⓐ Ⓑ Ⓒ Ⓓ Ⓔ Ⓕ Ⓖ Ⓗ Ⓘ Ⓙ
2 Ⓐ Ⓑ Ⓒ Ⓓ Ⓔ Ⓕ Ⓖ Ⓗ Ⓘ Ⓙ
3 Ⓐ Ⓑ Ⓒ Ⓓ Ⓔ Ⓕ Ⓖ Ⓗ Ⓘ Ⓙ
4 Ⓐ Ⓑ Ⓒ Ⓓ Ⓔ Ⓕ Ⓖ Ⓗ Ⓘ Ⓙ
5 Ⓐ Ⓑ Ⓒ Ⓓ Ⓔ Ⓕ Ⓖ Ⓗ Ⓘ Ⓙ
6 Ⓐ Ⓑ Ⓒ Ⓓ Ⓔ Ⓕ Ⓖ Ⓗ Ⓘ Ⓙ
7 Ⓐ Ⓑ Ⓒ Ⓓ Ⓔ Ⓕ Ⓖ Ⓗ Ⓘ Ⓙ
8 Ⓐ Ⓑ Ⓒ Ⓓ Ⓔ Ⓕ Ⓖ Ⓗ Ⓘ Ⓙ

PLEASE DO NOT WRITE IN THIS AREA

◻○○○○○○○○○○○○○○○○○○○○○○○○○○○○○  **SERIAL #**

## ESSAY
### Time — 25 minutes

The essay gives you an opportunity to show how effectively you can develop and express ideas. You should, therefore, take care to develop your point of view, present your ideas logically and clearly, and use language precisely.

Your essay must be written on the lines provided on your answer sheet—you will receive no other paper on which to write. You will have enough space if you write on every line, avoid wide margins, and keep your handwriting to a reasonable size. Remember that people who are not familiar with your handwriting will read what you write. Try to write or print so that what you are writing is legible to those readers.

**Important Reminders:**

- **A pencil is required for the essay.** An essay written in ink will receive a score of zero.
- **Do not write your essay in your test book.** You will receive credit only for what you write on your answer sheet.
- **An off-topic essay will receive a score of zero.**
- **If your essay does not reflect your original and individual work, your test scores may be canceled.**

You have twenty-five minutes to write an essay on the topic assigned below.

*[handwritten: such as tech Have access to new things — enriches your understanding of things such as environment — Opens many doors to education]*

Think carefully about the issue presented in the following excerpt and the assignment below.

> Knowledge is power. In agriculture, medicine, and industry, for example, knowledge has liberated us from hunger, disease, and tedious labor. Today, however, our knowledge has become so powerful that it is beyond our control. We know how to do many things, but we do not know where, when, or even whether this know-how should be used.

**Assignment:** Can knowledge be a burden rather than a benefit? Plan and write an essay in which you develop your point of view on this issue. Support your position with reasoning and examples taken from your reading, studies, experience, or observations.

BEGIN WRITING YOUR ESSAY ON PAGE 2 OF THE ANSWER SHEET.

*[handwritten: Although some people think knowledge is burden, knowledge is truly beneficial because]*

**If you finish before time is called, you may check your work on this section only.**
**Do not turn to any other section in the test.**

*[handwritten: Opens doors to future]*

## SECTION 2
Time — 25 minutes
20 Questions

**Turn to Section 2 (page 4) of your answer sheet to answer the questions in this section.**

**Directions:** For this section, solve each problem and decide which is the best of the choices given. Fill in the corresponding circle on the answer sheet. You may use any available space for scratchwork.

**Notes**

1. The use of a calculator is permitted.
2. All numbers used are real numbers.
3. Figures that accompany problems in this test are intended to provide information useful in solving the problems. They are drawn as accurately as possible EXCEPT when it is stated in a specific problem that the figure is not drawn to scale. All figures lie in a plane unless otherwise indicated.
4. Unless otherwise specified, the domain of any function $f$ is assumed to be the set of all real numbers $x$ for which $f(x)$ is a real number.

**Reference Information**

$A = \pi r^2$
$C = 2\pi r$
$A = \ell w$
$A = \frac{1}{2}bh$
$V = \ell wh$
$V = \pi r^2 h$
$c^2 = a^2 + b^2$
Special Right Triangles

The number of degrees of arc in a circle is 360.
The sum of the measures in degrees of the angles of a triangle is 180.

---

**1.** If $y = x - 5$ and $20y - 5y = 15$, what is the value of $x$ ?

(A) 6
(B) 9
(C) 12
(D) 15
(E) 18

**2.** There are exactly 9 buttons in a bag. There are 4 blue buttons and 3 red buttons, and the rest are yellow. If one button is drawn at random from the bag, what is the probability that the button is yellow?

(A) $\frac{1}{9}$

(B) $\frac{1}{7}$

(C) $\frac{2}{9}$

(D) $\frac{2}{7}$

(E) $\frac{1}{3}$

**GO ON TO THE NEXT PAGE**

**3.** Which figure below, when placed together with the figure above, will make a complete circular disc with no overlap and no spaces?

(A)

(B)

(C)

(D)

(E)

ICE-CREAM SALES BY FLAVOR

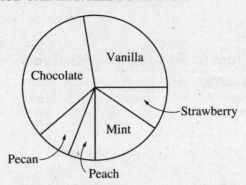

**4.** According to the circle graph above, how many of the ice-cream flavors individually represent less than 25 percent of the total sales?

(A) One
(B) Two
(C) Three
(D) Four
(E) Five

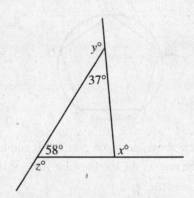

**5.** In the figure above, what is the value of $x + y + z$ ?

(A) 85
(B) 170
(C) 180
(D) 255
(E) 360

GO ON TO THE NEXT PAGE

**6.** If $6x + 4 = 7$, what is the value of $6x - 4$ ?

(A)   $-7$
(B)   $-1$
(C)   $1$
(D)   $7$
(E)   $8$

**8.** Tick marks are equally spaced on the number line above. Which of the lettered points has a coordinate equal to $\left(-\dfrac{1}{2}\right)^2$ ?

(A)   $A$
(B)   $B$
(C)   $C$
(D)   $D$
(E)   $E$

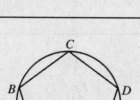

**7.** In the circle above, pentagon $ABCDE$ is equilateral. What is the ratio of the length of arc $\overset{\frown}{ABC}$ to the length of arc $\overset{\frown}{AEC}$ ?

(A)   1 to 2
(B)   2 to 3
(C)   2 to 5
(D)   3 to 5
(E)   4 to 5

**9.** If $t > w$, how much greater is the sum of $s$ and $t$ than the sum of $s$ and $w$ ?

(A)   $s - t$
(B)   $2s - w$
(C)   $t - w$
(D)   $t + w$
(E)   $2s - t - w$

**GO ON TO THE NEXT PAGE** ⇨

$$P(t) = 3{,}000 \cdot 2^{\frac{t}{4}}$$

**10.** Some organisms are being cultured in a biology lab. The population, $P$, of the organisms in the culture $t$ days after the culture began is modeled by the function above. By how many organisms does the population increase from $t = 4$ to $t = 16$ ?

(A)  6,000
(B)  24,000
(C)  36,000
(D)  42,000
(E)  48,000

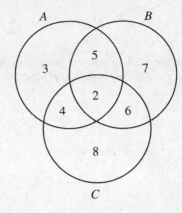

**12.** The figure above is a Venn diagram that represents sets $A$, $B$, and $C$. The number in each region indicates how many elements are in that region. How many elements are common to sets $A$ and $B$ ?

(A)  27
(B)  17
(C)  10
(D)  7
(E)  5

**11.** If the average (arithmetic mean) of 3, $s$, and $t$ is 5, what is the value of $s + t$ ?

(A)   2
(B)   4
(C)   6
(D)  10
(E)  12

**13.** State University plans on accepting a total of 1,000 students for next year's class. Of the 800 students accepted so far, 60 percent are female and 40 percent are male. How many of the remaining students to be accepted must be male in order for half of the total number of students accepted to be male?

(A)  100
(B)  120
(C)  160
(D)  180
(E)  200

**GO ON TO THE NEXT PAGE**

2 □ □ □ □ □ □ 2

Unauthorized copying or reuse of
any part of this page is illegal.

$$t^2 - k^2 < 6$$
$$t + k > 4$$

**14.** If $t$ and $k$ are positive integers in the inequalities above and $t > k$, what is the value of $t$ ?

(A) 1
(B) 2
(C) 3
(D) 4
(E) 5

| $x$ | $f(x)$ |
|-----|--------|
| 2 | −1 |
| 3 | 0 |
| 4 | 2 |
| 5 | −3 |
| 6 | 4 |
| 7 | 5 |
| 8 | 6 |

**16.** Several values of the function $f$ are shown above. The function $g$ is defined by $g(x) = f(3x + 1)$. What is the value of $g(2)$ ?

(A) −5
(B) −1
(C) 0
(D) 2
(E) 4

**15.** Which of the following is equivalent to $\frac{1}{2}$ of 23 percent of 618 ?

(A) 23% of 309

(B) 23% of $\dfrac{309}{2}$

(C) $22\dfrac{1}{2}\%$ of 618

(D) $\dfrac{23}{2}\%$ of 309

(E) $\dfrac{23}{2} \times 618$

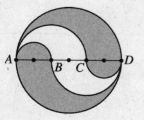

**17.** Semicircular arcs $\overset{\frown}{AB}$, $\overset{\frown}{AC}$, $\overset{\frown}{BD}$, and $\overset{\frown}{CD}$ divide the circle above into regions. The points shown along the diameter $\overline{AD}$ divide it into 6 equal parts. If $AD = 6$, what is the total area of the shaded regions?

(A) $4\pi$
(B) $5\pi$
(C) $6\pi$
(D) $12\pi$
(E) $24\pi$

**GO ON TO THE NEXT PAGE**

**18.** Any 2 points determine a line. If there are 6 points in a plane, no 3 of which lie on the same line, how many lines are determined by pairs of these 6 points?

(A)  15
(B)  18
(C)  20
(D)  30
(E)  36

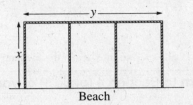

Beach

**20.** At a beach, a rectangular swimming area with dimensions $x$ and $y$ meters and a total area of 4,000 square meters is marked off on three sides with rope, as shown above, and bounded on the fourth side by the beach. Additionally, rope is used to divide the area into three smaller rectangular sections. In terms of $y$, what is the total length, in meters, of the rope that is needed both to bound the three sides of the area and to divide it into sections?

(A)  $y + \dfrac{4,000}{y}$

(B)  $y + \dfrac{16,000}{y}$

(C)  $y + \dfrac{16,000}{3y}$

(D)  $3y + \dfrac{8,000}{3y}$

(E)  $3y + \dfrac{16,000}{3y}$

**19.** A certain function $f$ has the property that

$f(x + y) = f(x) + f(y)$ for all values of $x$ and $y$. Which of the following statements must be true when $a = b$ ?

  I.  $f(a + b) = 2f(a)$

  II.  $f(a + b) = [f(a)]^2$

  III.  $f(b) + f(b) = f(2a)$

(A)  None
(B)  I only
(C)  I and III only
(D)  II and III only
(E)  I, II, and III

# STOP

**If you finish before time is called, you may check your work on this section only.**
**Do not turn to any other section in the test.**

4

Unauthorized copying or reuse of any part of this page is illegal.

4

## SECTION 4
### Time — 25 minutes
### 24 Questions

**Turn to Section 4 (page 5) of your answer sheet to answer the questions in this section.**

**Directions:** For each question in this section, select the best answer from among the choices given and fill in the corresponding circle on the answer sheet.

Each sentence below has one or two blanks, each blank indicating that something has been omitted. Beneath the sentence are five words or sets of words labeled A through E. Choose the word or set of words that, when inserted in the sentence, best fits the meaning of the sentence as a whole.

**Example:**

Hoping to ------- the dispute, negotiators proposed a compromise that they felt would be ------- to both labor and management.

(A) enforce . . useful
(B) end . . divisive
(C) overcome . . unattractive
(D) extend . . satisfactory
(E) resolve . . acceptable

1. Extensive travel afforded Langston Hughes a ------- perspective, but it was Harlem that served as the creative ------- for his writing.

    (A) cosmopolitan . . defense
    (B) worldly . . inspiration
    (C) moral . . obligation
    (D) stunted . . condition
    (E) limited . . center

2. One requirement of timeless art is that it deepen and ------- our awareness, not that it merely confirm what we already know.

    (A) hinder    (B) reconcile    (C) control
       (D) soothe    (E) extend

3. Despairing that the performance of the chief executive would ever improve, the corporation's board of directors took decisive action and ------- him.

    (A) coddled    (B) taunted    (C) prodded
       (D) ousted    (E) chided

4. The discovery of the fossil was ------- and -------, surprising scientists and undermining accepted theories about plant distribution.

    (A) exhilarating . . banal
    (B) shocking . . prophetic
    (C) startling . . revolutionary
    (D) appalling . . groundbreaking
    (E) unanticipated . . irrelevant

5. Citing the ------- of the Asian American community, the scholar argued that Asian Americans constituted the region's fastest-growing minority population.

    (A) digression    (B) proximity    (C) expansion
       (D) stabilization    (E) correlation

6. Far from being -------, bears in some national parks are surprisingly ------- when approached by humans; still, visitors must exercise caution.

    (A) benign . . cantankerous
    (B) reticent . . bellicose
    (C) complacent . . docile
    (D) aggressive . . placid
    (E) playful . . frisky

7. Before becoming a stockbroker, Victoria Woodhull had a career as a -------, someone believed to have insights about events beyond ordinary human perception.

    (A) mentor    (B) profiteer    (C) counterfeiter
       (D) clairvoyant    (E) propagandist

8. The judges for the chili competition were -------, noting subtle differences between dishes that most people would not detect.

    (A) obscure    (B) deferential    (C) discriminating
       (D) sanctimonious    (E) unrelenting

**GO ON TO THE NEXT PAGE**

The passages below are followed by questions based on their content; questions following a pair of related passages may also be based on the relationship between the paired passages. Answer the questions on the basis of what is <u>stated</u> or <u>implied</u> in the passages and in any introductory material that may be provided.

**Questions 9-12 are based on the following passages.**

**Passage 1**

A reform movement in journalism is afoot in newsrooms and boardrooms across the country. Industry organizations are launching initiatives, offering training, and fostering
Line new ways of thinking about news coverage and its effects.
5 The goals are to reinstill journalism's core values, regain credibility, and generally better the media's performance. What really is wrong with journalism? Lack of accuracy and fairness, too much sensationalism and bias are all components of the problem, but the number one issue is
10 that "people distrust our motives," said Tom Rosenstiel, founding director of the Project for Excellence in Journalism, who hopes to get more journalists thinking about standards.

**Passage 2**

Conditions for journalism have never been better:
15 robust media profits, strong legal protections, and sophisticated technology. Yet there is an influential movement, representing the consensus of the profession's elite, dedicated to convincing us that all is not well. Bill Kovach and Tom Rosenstiel, arguably the two most
20 prominent media critics in America, are the go-to people if you need a quotation lamenting the sensationalism of television newscasts or other media ills. Their recent book *The Elements of Journalism* suggests that unless a certain "theory of news" is adhered to, the United States might be
25 *annihilated*. Such factually uncluttered hyperbole does not merely invite a certain awe but also quite plausibly violates their number one axiom: "journalism's first obligation is to the truth."

9. Which best describes the relationship between Passage 1 and Passage 2 ?

(A) Passage 1 describes a particular campaign for change, whereas Passage 2 challenges the necessity of that change.
(B) Passage 1 describes the causes of sensationalism in journalism, whereas Passage 2 explores its effects.
(C) Passage 1 praises an individual's influence on journalism, whereas Passage 2 questions that individual's contributions.
(D) Passage 1 suggests that journalism is evolving, whereas Passage 2 argues that it is stagnating.
(E) Passage 1 defines the purpose of journalism, whereas Passage 2 examines journalism's impact on society.

10. Unlike Passage 1, Passage 2 alludes to journalism's

(A) core values
(B) specific critics
(C) complex history
(D) sensationalistic tendencies
(E) economic well-being

11. The author of Passage 2 would most likely characterize the "initiatives" mentioned in line 3 of Passage 1 as

(A) timely
(B) rational
(C) indecipherable
(D) unwarranted
(E) equivocal

12. Lines 25-28 in Passage 2 ("Such . . . truth' ") serve primarily to

(A) assuage the concerns of readers
(B) speculate about an outcome
(C) exaggerate the depth of a problem
(D) define a technical term
(E) highlight an irony

**GO ON TO THE NEXT PAGE**

**Questions 13-24 are based on the following passage.**

*This passage is adapted from a 1996 book on sleep research.*

To conduct some forms of sleep research, we have to find a way to track sleepiness over the day. Some people might believe that measuring sleepiness is a fairly trivial
Line task. Couldn't you, for instance, simply count the number
5 of times a person yawns during any given hour or so?

In most people's minds, yawning—that slow, exaggerated mouth opening with the long, deep inhalation of air, followed by a briefer exhalation—is the most obvious sign of sleepiness. It is a common behavior shared
10 by many animals, including our pet dogs and cats but also crocodiles, snakes, birds, and even some fish. It is certainly true that sleepy people tend to yawn more than wide-awake people. It is also true that people who say they are bored by what is happening at the moment will tend to yawn more
15 frequently. However, whether yawning is a sign that you are getting ready for sleep or that you are successfully fighting off sleep is not known. Simply stretching your body, as you might do if you have been sitting in the same position for a long period of time, will often trigger a yawn.
20 Unfortunately, yawns don't just indicate sleepiness. In some animals, yawning is a sign of stress. When a dog trainer sees a dog yawning in a dog obedience class, it is usually a sign that the animal is under a good deal of pressure. Perhaps the handler is pushing too hard or moving
25 too fast for the dog to feel in control of the situation. A moment or two of play and then turning to another activity is usually enough to banish yawning for quite a while.

Yawning can also be a sign of stress in humans. Once,
30 when observing airborne troops about to take their first parachute jump, I noticed that several of the soldiers were sitting in the plane and yawning. It was 10 A.M., just after a coffee break, and I doubted that they were tired; I knew for a fact that they were far too nervous to be bored. When I
35 asked about this, the officer in charge laughed and said it was really quite a common behavior, especially on the first jump.

There is also a social aspect to yawning. Psychologists have placed actors in crowded rooms and auditoriums and
40 had them deliberately yawn. Within moments, there is usually an increase in yawning by everyone else in the room. Similarly, people who watch films or videos of others yawning are more likely to yawn. Even just reading about yawning tends to stimulate people to yawn.
45 The truth of the matter is that we really don't know what purpose yawning serves. Scientists originally thought that the purpose of yawning was to increase the amount of oxygen in the blood or to release some accumulated carbon dioxide. We now know that this is not true, since increasing
50 the concentration of carbon dioxide in the air seems not to

make people more likely to yawn but to make them breathe faster to try to bring in more oxygen. On the other hand, breathing 100 percent pure oxygen does not seem to reduce the likelihood of yawning.
55 Since yawning seems to be associated with a lot more than the need for sleep, we obviously have to find some other measure of sleepiness. Some researchers have simply tried to ask people how sleepy they feel at any time using some sort of self-rating scale. There are, however,
60 problems with getting people to make these types of judgments. Sometimes people simply lie to the researchers when asked about how sleepy they are. This occurs because in many areas of society admitting that one is fatigued and sleepy is considered a mark of weakness or lack of
65 ambition and drive. In other instances, people may admit they need four cups of coffee to make it through the morning, but it may never occur to them that this might be due to the fact that they are so sleepy that they need stimulation from caffeine to be able to do their required
70 tasks. For these reasons, many researchers have developed an alternate method to determine how sleepy a person is. It is based upon a simple definition of sleep need: The greater your sleep need, or the sleepier you are, the faster you will fall asleep if given the opportunity to do so.

13. The question in lines 4-5 is based on which of the following assumptions?

(A) Direct observation is the only reliable method of conducting sleep research.
(B) People will yawn most frequently in the moments before they fall asleep.
(C) There is a direct correlation between yawning and sleepiness.
(D) Yawning is a behavior over which individuals exert little conscious control.
(E) Conducting sleep research is a time-consuming process.

14. The comment between the dashes in lines 6-8 primarily serves to

(A) clarify a claim
(B) define a term
(C) note a qualification
(D) offer a humorous aside
(E) voice a personal insight

15. The author uses which of the following in the fourth paragraph (lines 29-37) ?

(A) Understatement
(B) Personification
(C) Analogy
(D) Metaphor
(E) Anecdote

**GO ON TO THE NEXT PAGE**

**16.** The author mentions the "coffee break" (line 33) to emphasize that a

(A) brief respite was sorely needed
(B) given attitude was inappropriate
(C) specific response was understandable
(D) particular action was unnecessary
(E) certain behavior was unexpected

**17.** The discussion of the "social aspect" (line 38) most directly demonstrates

(A) the power of suggestion
(B) a need for personal accountability
(C) a link between personality and behavior
(D) the psychological cost of conformity
(E) the desire for companionship

**18.** Which of the following, if true, would most directly disprove what "Scientists originally thought" (line 46) ?

(A) Carbon dioxide does not affect people's breathing rates.
(B) Yawning does not reduce the need for sleep, though it may make a person feel less tired.
(C) Because yawning brings more air into the lungs, it can increase the rate at which oxygen is absorbed.
(D) People do not tend to yawn much at high altitudes, where oxygen levels in the air are low.
(E) People often yawn more after exercise, when carbon dioxide levels in the blood are marginally higher.

**19.** Lines 55-57 ("Since . . . sleepiness") primarily serve to

(A) introduce a lighthearted digression
(B) provide a transition to a new subject
(C) offer evidence in support of a prior claim
(D) acknowledge a drawback to an approach advocated in the previous paragraph
(E) return the discussion to a problem mentioned earlier in the passage

**20.** In line 65, "drive" most nearly means

(A) propulsion
(B) instinct
(C) campaign
(D) vitality
(E) momentum

**21.** The author mentions the "other instances" (line 65) primarily to make the point that people

(A) are often intentionally deceptive about their sleep needs
(B) may not be accurate judges of their own sleepiness
(C) frequently do not experience a restful night of sleep
(D) may sometimes use stimulants like caffeine rather than feel tired
(E) are often afraid that exhaustion will interfere with their job performance

**22.** Which of the following, if true, would most effectively undermine the "simple definition" (line 72) ?

(A) When people are being watched by researchers, they may show different sleep patterns.
(B) When people are extremely sleepy, they may have difficulty falling asleep.
(C) Some people have the ability to go without sleep for very long periods of time.
(D) Some people yawn whether they are tired or not.
(E) Some people rarely yawn, no matter how tired they are.

**GO ON TO THE NEXT PAGE**

23. All of the following cases of yawning can be accounted for in the passage EXCEPT:

(A) A student yawns during a lecture on a boring subject.

(B) A musician yawns before taking the stage for a very important performance.

(C) An airplane pilot yawns to clear her ears during takeoff.

(D) A person at a party yawns after those around him begin yawning.

(E) A researcher yawns while reading a scientific article about yawning.

24. The passage as a whole is best characterized as

(A) informative
(B) confessional
(C) philosophical
(D) humorous
(E) argumentative

# STOP

**If you finish before time is called, you may check your work on this section only.**
**Do not turn to any other section in the test.**

## SECTION 5
Time — 25 minutes
18 Questions

**Turn to Section 5 (page 5) of your answer sheet to answer the questions in this section.**

**Directions:** This section contains two types of questions. You have 25 minutes to complete both types. For questions 1-8, solve each problem and decide which is the best of the choices given. Fill in the corresponding circle on the answer sheet. You may use any available space for scratchwork.

**Notes**

1. The use of a calculator is permitted.

2. All numbers used are real numbers.

3. Figures that accompany problems in this test are intended to provide information useful in solving the problems. They are drawn as accurately as possible EXCEPT when it is stated in a specific problem that the figure is not drawn to scale. All figures lie in a plane unless otherwise indicated.

4. Unless otherwise specified, the domain of any function $f$ is assumed to be the set of all real numbers $x$ for which $f(x)$ is a real number.

**Reference Information**

$A = \pi r^2$
$C = 2\pi r$
$A = \ell w$
$A = \frac{1}{2}bh$
$V = \ell w h$
$V = \pi r^2 h$
$c^2 = a^2 + b^2$
Special Right Triangles

The number of degrees of arc in a circle is 360.
The sum of the measures in degrees of the angles of a triangle is 180.

1. Fred, Norman, and Dave own a total of 128 comic books. If Dave owns 44 of them, what is the average (arithmetic mean) number of comic books owned by Fred and Norman?

   (A) 42
   (B) 44
   (C) 46
   (D) 48
   (E) 50

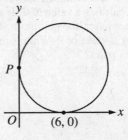

2. In the $xy$-coordinate system above, the circle is tangent to the $x$-axis and the $y$-axis. What are the coordinates of point $P$ ?

   (A) $(0, 3)$
   (B) $(0, 6)$
   (C) $(3, 0)$
   (D) $(3, 3)$
   (E) $(6, 6)$

**GO ON TO THE NEXT PAGE**

**525**

3. A hotel charges a service fee of $1.00 per day to use its copy machine. In addition, there is a charge of $0.10 per copy made. Which of the following represents the total charge, in dollars, to use this copy machine to make $n$ copies in one day?

(A) $0.90n$
(B) $1.10n$
(C) $1.00 + 10n$
(D) $1.00 + 0.10n$
(E) $1.00 + 0.10 + n$

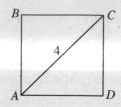

5. What is the area of square $ABCD$ above?

(A)  8
(B)  12
(C)  16
(D)  20
(E)  24

aa bc
ab aa
ac ba

4. In the six pairs of letters shown above, if $a$ is paired with itself, the pair has a value of 2. If $a$ appears in a pair with another letter, the pair has a value of 1. All other pairs have a value of 0. What is the sum of the values of the six pairs?

(A)  6
(B)  7
(C)  8
(D)  10
(E)  12

**GO ON TO THE NEXT PAGE**

**6.** If $x \neq 0$ and $x$ is inversely proportional to $y$, which of the following is directly proportional to $\dfrac{1}{x^2}$ ?

(A) $-\dfrac{1}{y^2}$

(B) $\dfrac{1}{y^2}$

(C) $\dfrac{1}{y}$

(D) $y$

(E) $y^2$

**7.** Point $A$ is a vertex of an 8-sided polygon. The polygon has 8 sides of equal length and 8 angles of equal measure. When all possible diagonals are drawn from point $A$ in the polygon, how many triangles are formed?

(A) Four
(B) Five
(C) Six
(D) Seven
(E) Eight

$$(x - 8)(x - k) = x^2 - 5kx + m$$

**8.** In the equation above, $k$ and $m$ are constants. If the equation is true for all values of $x$, what is the value of $m$ ?

(A) 8
(B) 16
(C) 24
(D) 32
(E) 40

**GO ON TO THE NEXT PAGE**

**Directions:** For Student-Produced Response questions 9-18, use the grids at the bottom of the answer sheet page on which you have answered questions 1-8.

Each of the remaining 10 questions requires you to solve the problem and enter your answer by marking the circles in the special grid, as shown in the examples below. You may use any available space for scratchwork.

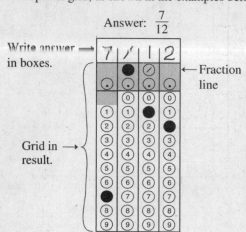

Answer: $\frac{7}{12}$

Write answer in boxes. → Fraction line

Grid in → result.

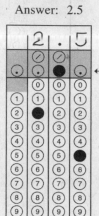

Answer: 2.5

← Decimal point

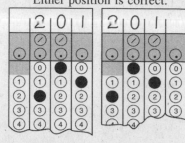

Answer: 201
Either position is correct.

- Mark no more than one circle in any column.

- Because the answer sheet will be machine-scored, **you will receive credit only if the circles are filled in correctly.**

- Although not required, it is suggested that you write your answer in the boxes at the top of the columns to help you fill in the circles accurately.

- Some problems may have more than one correct answer. In such cases, grid only one answer.

- No question has a negative answer.

- **Mixed numbers** such as $3\frac{1}{2}$ must be gridded as 3.5 or 7/2. (If $\boxed{3\,|\,1\,/\,2}$ is gridded, it will be interpreted as $\frac{31}{2}$, not $3\frac{1}{2}$.)

**Note:** You may start your answers in any column, space permitting. Columns not needed should be left blank.

- **Decimal Answers:** If you obtain a decimal answer with more digits than the grid can accommodate, it may be either rounded or truncated, but it must fill the entire grid. For example, if you obtain an answer such as 0.6666..., you should record your result as .666 or .667. **A less accurate value such as .66 or .67 will be scored as incorrect.**

Acceptable ways to grid $\frac{2}{3}$ are:

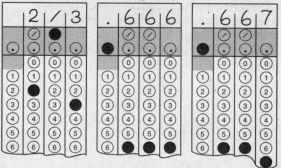

---

**9.** Flying at a constant speed, a bird traveled 62 miles in 4 hours. At this rate, how many miles did the bird travel in 3 hours?

**10.** Points $Q$, $R$, $S$, and $T$ lie on a circle with center $P$. If the radius of the circle is 1, what is the value of $PQ + PR + PS + PT$?

GO ON TO THE NEXT PAGE

**11.** If $10^{ab} = 10,000$, where $a$ and $b$ are positive integers, what is one possible value of $a$?

FEMALE AND MALE STUDENTS AT
CENTRAL HIGH SCHOOL, 1990–1999

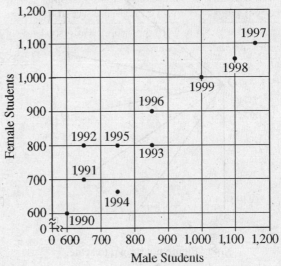

**13.** The scatterplot above shows the number of male and female students at Central High School from 1990 to 1999. In which one of the years shown was the absolute value of the difference between the numbers of male and female students greatest?

**12.** In the $xy$-plane, the line $2x - 3y = c$ passes through point $(5, -1)$. What is the value of $c$?

**14.** Five times a number is the same as the number added to five. What is the number?

GO ON TO THE NEXT PAGE

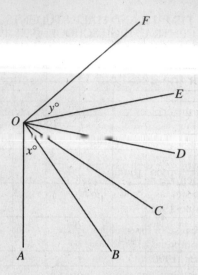

Note: Figure not drawn to scale.

**15.** In the figure above, six segments intersect at $O$; $\overline{OD}$ bisects $\angle AOF$, $\overline{OC}$ bisects $\angle AOE$, and $\overline{OB}$ bisects $\angle AOD$. If $x = 40$ and $y = 30$, what is the measure of $\angle BOE$ ? (Disregard the degree symbol when gridding your answer.)

---

1, 2, 2, 3, 3, 3, 4, 4, 4, 4, . . .

**16.** All positive integers appear in the sequence above, and each positive integer $k$ appears in the sequence $k$ times. In the sequence, each term after the first is greater than or equal to each of the terms before it. If the integer 12 first appears in the sequence as the $n$th term, what is the value of $n$ ?

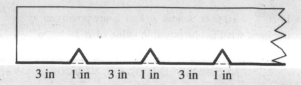

3 in    1 in    3 in    1 in    3 in    1 in

**17.** One end of an 80-inch-long paper strip is shown in the figure above. The notched edge, shown in bold, was formed by removing an equilateral triangle from the end of each 4-inch length on one edge of the paper strip. What is the total length, in inches, of the bold notched edge on the 80-inch paper strip?

---

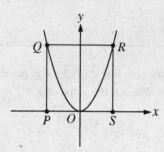

**18.** In the figure above, $PQRS$ is a square and points $Q$, $R$, and $O$ lie on the graph of $y = ax^2$, where $a$ is a constant. If the area of the square is 64, what is the value of $a$ ?

# STOP

**If you finish before time is called, you may check your work on this section only.**
**Do not turn to any other section in the test.**

## SECTION 6
### Time — 25 minutes
### 35 Questions

**Turn to Section 6 (page 6) of your answer sheet to answer the questions in this section.**

**Directions:** For each question in this section, select the best answer from among the choices given and fill in the corresponding circle on the answer sheet.

---

The following sentences test correctness and effectiveness of expression. Part of each sentence or the entire sentence is underlined; beneath each sentence are five ways of phrasing the underlined material. Choice A repeats the original phrasing; the other four choices are different. If you think the original phrasing produces a better sentence than any of the alternatives, select choice A; if not, select one of the other choices.

In making your selection, follow the requirements of standard written English; that is, pay attention to grammar, choice of words, sentence construction, and punctuation. Your selection should result in the most effective sentence—clear and precise, without awkwardness or ambiguity.

EXAMPLE:

Laura Ingalls Wilder published her first book <u>and she was sixty five years old then</u>.

(A) and she was sixty-five years old then
(B) when she was sixty-five
(C) at age sixty-five years old
(D) upon the reaching of sixty-five years
(E) at the time when she was sixty-five

Ⓐ ● Ⓒ Ⓓ Ⓔ

1. <u>Norman Rockwell was an illustrator and painter that was able to make a living at it.</u>

(A) Norman Rockwell was an illustrator and painter that was able to make a living at it.
(B) Norman Rockwell was able to make a living as an illustrator and painter.
(C) An illustrator and painter, Norman Rockwell was able to make a living at it.
(D) Able to make a living from them, Norman Rockwell illustrated and painted.
(E) By illustrating and painting was how Norman Rockwell was able to make a living.

2. <u>Because of repeatedly asking in vain for a comprehensive health-care plan,</u> the employees called in sick as a protest against their employer's stubbornness.

(A) Because of repeatedly asking in vain for a comprehensive health-care plan,
(B) After repeatedly asking in vain for a comprehensive health-care plan,
(C) They have repeatedly asked in vain for a comprehensive health-care plan, then
(D) Repeatedly asking in vain for a comprehensive health-care plan, finally
(E) While they repeatedly ask in vain for a comprehensive health-care plan,

3. In the tennis match Martina Hingis took advantage of Venus Williams' error and tied the <u>score; however, Williams fought back to take</u> the lead again.

(A) score; however, Williams fought back to take the lead again
(B) score; Williams, though, fought back again took the lead
(C) score; however, Williams fighting back to take the lead again
(D) score, along with Williams fighting back to take the lead again
(E) score; in fact, Williams fought back to take the lead again

4. Nursing and physical therapy <u>are an example of health-care fields that</u> have shortages in staffing.

(A) are an example of health-care fields that
(B) are examples of health-care fields that
(C) are examples where health-care fields
(D) exemplifies a health-care field that
(E) exemplify health-care fields where they

**GO ON TO THE NEXT PAGE** ➡

5. Alice Guy Blaché, an early filmmaker, introduced close-ups and double <u>exposures, also she set</u> cars on fire, used rats in special effects sequences, and ran film backward.

   (A) exposures, also she set
   (B) exposures, and also she sets
   (C) exposures, she set
   (D) exposures, she also set
   (E) exposures by her setting

6. The company maintains computer systems for small <u>businesses, plus it will manage</u> their payroll accounts.

   (A) businesses, plus it will manage
   (B) businesses, in addition it will manage
   (C) businesses and manages
   (D) businesses, and, additionally, they also manage
   (E) businesses, it manages

7. Studying dance for many years, practicing difficult steps every day, and <u>frequent performances has enabled the young dancer</u> to secure the leading role in the spring production.

   (A) frequent performances has enabled the young dancer
   (B) frequent performances would have enabled the young dancer
   (C) frequently performing, the young dancer being enabled
   (D) frequent performing, these enabled the young dancer
   (E) performing frequently enabled the young dancer

8. Though now one of the most famous abstract artists, <u>critics once ridiculed Jackson Pollock</u> for his technique of splattering paint on canvases.

   (A) critics once ridiculed Jackson Pollock
   (B) critics once were ridiculing Jackson Pollock
   (C) Jackson Pollock once ridiculed by critics
   (D) Jackson Pollock was once ridiculed by critics
   (E) Jackson Pollock, having once been ridiculed by critics

9. Legendary nineteenth-century endurance rider Frank T. Hopkins, who rode an American mustang to victory in a 3,000-mile race across the Arabian Desert, <u>and</u> the hero of the Disney movie *Hidalgo*.

   (A) and
   (B) and who has become
   (C) also has become
   (D) is
   (E) having been

10. To introduce itself to a wider audience, the little-known band <u>sold its CD's cheaply</u> to enthusiastic fans, who in turn shared the music with friends.

    (A) sold its CD's cheaply
    (B) sold their CD's cheaply
    (C) sells its CD's at a low price
    (D) prices their CD's low for to sell
    (E) will sell its CD's at a cheap price

11. Twice as many bird species inhabit Ecuador <u>as in</u> North America.

    (A) as in
    (B) as inhabit
    (C) instead of in
    (D) when compared to
    (E) than

**GO ON TO THE NEXT PAGE** ⇒

The following sentences test your ability to recognize grammar and usage errors. Each sentence contains either a single error or no error at all. No sentence contains more than one error. The error, if there is one, is underlined and lettered. If the sentence contains an error, select the one underlined part that must be changed to make the sentence correct. If the sentence is correct, select choice E. In choosing answers, follow the requirements of standard written English.

EXAMPLE:

$\underline{\text{The other}}$ delegates and $\underline{\text{him}}$ $\underline{\text{immediately}}$
   A            B       C

accepted the resolution $\underline{\text{drafted by}}$ the
                     D

neutral states. $\underline{\text{No error}}$
         E

(A) ● (C) (D) (E)

**12.** Of the hundreds of warm-water coral species,

$\underline{\text{only a few}}$ $\underline{\text{are highly prized}}$ for use in
  A        B

jewelry $\underline{\text{because of their}}$ beauty, luster, and
           C

$\underline{\text{they are hard}}$. $\underline{\text{No error}}$
  D       E

**13.** Because of its innovativeness $\underline{\text{and its}}$ effective
                 A

presentation, Mary's science project $\underline{\text{received}}$ more
                   B

judges' votes $\underline{\text{at the exhibit}}$ than $\underline{\text{did Jim}}$. $\underline{\text{No error}}$
      C          D     E

**14.** Mr. Johnson's assumption that a teenager had robbed

his house $\underline{\text{being unfounded}}$, $\underline{\text{for}}$ the witnesses
         A        B

described the person they $\underline{\text{had seen}}$ fleeing
                C

$\underline{\text{as a woman}}$ in her 40s. $\underline{\text{No error}}$
  D            E

**15.** Waterways close to land $\underline{\text{poses}}$ challenges
              A

to navigation that $\underline{\text{differ}}$ $\underline{\text{greatly from}}$ $\underline{\text{those}}$
          B    C     D

posed by the open seas. $\underline{\text{No error}}$
             E

**16.** $\underline{\text{During}}$ my $\underline{\text{most recent}}$ trip, I $\underline{\text{came across}}$
  A      B          C

a wonderful antique store $\underline{\text{wandering}}$ in
              D

the old quarter of the city. $\underline{\text{No error}}$
              E

**17.** It is difficult to predict $\underline{\text{what kinds}}$ of books $\underline{\text{will be}}$
              A        B

popular in the years ahead, because tastes change

and topics either get overexplored $\underline{\text{and}}$ lose $\underline{\text{their}}$
                C     D

relevance. $\underline{\text{No error}}$
     E

GO ON TO THE NEXT PAGE →

18. As children mature, they develop <u>an independence</u>
    A                                B
that their parents, who <u>have been</u> responsible for them
                          C
since they were born, often find difficult <u>to accept</u>.
                                              D
<u>No error</u>
    E

19. Horse psychology, a science that investigates

the <u>reasons for</u> the behavior of horses, <u>help</u>
        A                                      B
trainers both motivate <u>their charges</u> <u>and prevent</u>
                            C                    D
problems. <u>No error</u>
              E

20. <u>To an Iranian,</u> only a salt desert truly merits the name
        A
"desert," <u>for other types</u> of deserts can be sown with
              B
dates, figs, and pistachios <u>and it can be watered</u> by
                                      C
sprinklers or <u>by ancient</u> subterranean canals called
                  D
*qanats*. <u>No error</u>
              E

21. Ms. Kovak proudly displayed <u>her research group's</u>
                                        A
<u>most ingenious invention</u>, a vacuum cleaner
            B
<u>that empties its own</u> dust bag when
            C
<u>pressing a button</u>. <u>No error</u>
        D              E

22. Famous for <u>their</u> sticky feet, the gecko <u>can</u> <u>run up</u>
                  A                                  B      C
walls and across ceilings as well as <u>hang</u> from a
                                          D
surface by its toes. <u>No error</u>
                        E

23. Both her work on community service projects and

her dedication <u>to learning</u> <u>has gained</u> Ms. Stevens
                    A              B
the <u>respect of</u> the <u>entire</u> faculty. <u>No error</u>
        C              D                    E

24. After the uprising of October 10, 1911, that <u>has led</u>
                                                    A
to <u>the establishment of</u> a Chinese republic, many
        B
Chinese Americans decided to return to China <u>in</u>
                                                  C
hopes of a bright future <u>there</u>. <u>No error</u>
                            D          E

25. At the art show, Amy <u>enjoyed looking at</u> her friend
                              A
Mark's innovative paintings, <u>which she</u> thought
                                  B
were <u>more original</u> <u>than</u> the other artists. <u>No error</u>
        C              D                          E

GO ON TO THE NEXT PAGE

26. Traffic was heavy, so by the time Brianne finally

    $\underset{A}{\underline{\text{arrived at}}}$ the theater, we $\underset{B}{\underline{\text{waited}}}$ for her for an hour,

    $\underset{C}{\underline{\text{missing}}}$ the $\underset{D}{\underline{\text{entire}}}$ first act of the play. $\underset{E}{\underline{\text{No error}}}$

27. Although its reputation is not $\underset{A}{\underline{\text{as good as}}}$ it $\underset{B}{\underline{\text{once was}}}$,

    the university is still proud of $\underset{C}{\underline{\text{their}}}$ productive,

    intelligent graduates, many of whom have gone

    on $\underset{D}{\underline{\text{to earn}}}$ national recognition. $\underset{E}{\underline{\text{No error}}}$

28. $\underset{A}{\underline{\text{Although}}}$ familiar to us $\underset{B}{\underline{\text{from representations}}}$

    in ancient art, war chariots are rare museum artifacts

    $\underset{C}{\underline{\text{because by}}}$ the sixth century B.C. they were

    $\underset{D}{\underline{\text{no longer}}}$ used in battle. $\underset{E}{\underline{\text{No error}}}$

29. A volunteer organization, the Covington Soup Kitchen

    $\underset{A}{\underline{\text{has been feeding}}}$ needy families $\underset{B}{\underline{\text{since 1977}}}$, annually

    distributing $\underset{C}{\underline{\text{nearly}}}$ a million pounds of food

    $\underset{D}{\underline{\text{each year}}}$. $\underset{E}{\underline{\text{No error}}}$

---

**Directions:** The following passage is an early draft of an essay. Some parts of the passage need to be rewritten.

Read the passage and select the best answers for the questions that follow. Some questions are about particular sentences or parts of sentences and ask you to improve sentence structure or word choice. Other questions ask you to consider organization and development. In choosing answers, follow the requirements of standard written English.

**Questions 30-35 refer to the following passage.**

(1) Seeds of Peace Camp in Otisfield, Maine, is unlike any other camp in the world. (2) Due to the fact of bringing together teenagers from opposite sides of conflicts all over the globe. (3) At Seeds of Peace the campers, who have been taught to hate the enemy, learn to see that the enemy has a name and a face. (4) When they learn to get along on an individual basis, they start to question calling someone "enemy."

(5) During each three-week session, young people who are enemies in their home countries eat and play together, share bunkhouses, and cope with the homesickness they have in common. (6) Guided by specially trained counselors, the youngsters engage in daily, structured conversations called "coexistence sessions." (7) These conversations are often emotional but therapeutic. (8) The campers live side by side from the moment of their arrival.

(9) John Wallach, an award-winning journalist who covered conflicts in the Middle East for two decades, founded Seeds of Peace in 1993. (10) He chose the campsite because it is a beautiful natural setting far from the places of conflict. (11) Countries may select their campers but cannot pay for the camp. (12) The camp remains unaffiliated with any nation, organization, or peace group. (13) It is financed by private fund-raising efforts.

(14) According to Wallach, "If you begin to know your enemy, if you begin to understand your enemy, it's inevitable that you will begin to feel some empathy." (15) He believed that peace has to start among the young, being that the hatred of the adults in the campers' homelands is very deeply ingrained.

GO ON TO THE NEXT PAGE ⟩

30. In context, what is the best revision of sentence 2 (reproduced below) ?

    *Due to the fact of bringing together teenagers from opposite sides of conflicts all over the globe.*

    (A) Due to the camp's bringing together teenagers all over the globe from opposite sides of conflicts.
    (B) They brought together teenagers from opposite sides of conflicts from all over the globe.
    (C) All over the globe, teenagers are brought together from opposite sides of conflicts by Seeds of Peace Camp.
    (D) Teenagers are brought together by it from opposite sides of conflicts all over the globe.
    (E) It brings together teenagers from opposite sides of conflicts all over the globe.

31. Paragraph one would best be improved by the addition of

    (A) a quotation about the beauty of the camp from a former camper
    (B) examples of the native countries of the various campers
    (C) the names of chief staff members of the camp
    (D) a description of a typical day at camp
    (E) a reference to other efforts to promote peace

32. Where is the best place for sentence 8 ?

    (A) (Where it is now)
    (B) After sentence 1
    (C) At the end of the first paragraph (after sentence 4)
    (D) At the beginning of the second paragraph (before sentence 5)
    (E) After sentence 15

33. In context, which version of sentences 11 and 12 best combines them into a single sentence?

    (A) Countries may select their campers but cannot pay for the camp, which remains unaffiliated with any nation, organization, or peace group.
    (B) Unaffiliated with any nation, organization, or peace group, countries may select their campers but cannot pay for the camp.
    (C) Countries may select their campers, in addition, they cannot pay for the camp, which remains unaffiliated with any nation, organization, or peace group.
    (D) Countries cannot pay for the camp although they may select their campers, the camp remains unaffiliated with any nation, organization, or peace group.
    (E) It remains unaffiliated with any nation, organization, or peace group, and although countries may select their campers, they cannot pay for the camp.

34. Which of the following revisions is most needed in sentence 15 (reproduced below) ?

    *He believed that peace has to start among the young, being that the hatred of the adults in the campers' homelands is very deeply ingrained.*

    (A) Insert "Furthermore" at the beginning.
    (B) Add "people" after "young".
    (C) Change "being that" to "since".
    (D) Change "adults" to "elders".
    (E) Change "is" to "are".

35. Which of the following, if placed after sentence 15, would be the most effective concluding sentence for the essay?

    (A) Seeds of Peace is an outstanding example of Maine's many summer camps.
    (B) There is a great need for international understanding and cooperation today.
    (C) Only camps like Seeds of Peace make world peace a reality.
    (D) An interesting fact is that prospective campers must undergo a competitive selection process, including writing an essay.
    (E) Thanks to Wallach's convictions, over 2,000 campers are now helping to sow the seeds of peace around the world.

## STOP

**If you finish before time is called, you may check your work on this section only.**
**Do not turn to any other section in the test.**

## SECTION 7
Time — 25 minutes
24 Questions

**Turn to Section 7 (page 6) of your answer sheet to answer the questions in this section.**

**Directions:** For each question in this section, select the best answer from among the choices given and fill in the corresponding circle on the answer sheet.

---

Each sentence below has one or two blanks, each blank indicating that something has been omitted. Beneath the sentence are five words or sets of words labeled A through E. Choose the word or set of words that, when inserted in the sentence, <u>best</u> fits the meaning of the sentence as a whole.

**Example:**

Hoping to ------- the dispute, negotiators proposed a compromise that they felt would be ------- to both labor and management.

(A) enforce . . useful
(B) end . . divisive
(C) overcome . . unattractive
(D) extend . . satisfactory
(E) resolve . . acceptable   Ⓐ Ⓑ Ⓒ Ⓓ ●

---

1. Although the archaeologist ------- the symbols on the cave wall, she was unable to ------- them because they were too faint.

   (A) replicated . . ignore
   (B) perused . . discard
   (C) obliterated . . translate
   (D) recollected . . conceal
   (E) scrutinized . . decipher

2. Popular interest in music performed by folk singer Jean Ritchie acted as a ------- because it ------- a wider interest in the music of Ritchie's native Kentucky.

   (A) deterrent . . launched
   (B) panacea . . overcame
   (C) barrier . . awakened
   (D) catalyst . . stirred
   (E) provocation . . mitigated

3. Oceanographers have identified more than 50 "dead zones" around the world: areas of sea that various forms of pollution have rendered ------- life.

   (A) conducive to     (B) invaluable to
   (C) imperative to     (D) indistinguishable from
   (E) bereft of

4. The few female physicians practicing at the end of the nineteenth century might be considered ------- because they constituted a very small percentage of all physicians.

   (A) miscreants     (B) revisionists     (C) anomalies
   (D) pacifists     (E) extremists

5. Rose smiled approvingly but gave neither written nor spoken permission to proceed with the project: her consent, in short, was -------.

   (A) tacit     (B) fervent     (C) unqualified
   (D) impetuous     (E) conditional

**GO ON TO THE NEXT PAGE**

537

The passages below are followed by questions based on their content; questions following a pair of related passages may also be based on the relationship between the paired passages. Answer the questions on the basis of what is <u>stated</u> or <u>implied</u> in the passages and in any introductory material that may be provided.

**Questions 6-7 are based on the following passage.**

Poetry discovered me when I was four or five. My mother wrote a poem for me, and I had to recite it in church. Soon I was writing my own poems. This was *Line* during a time when my primary artistic expression
5 was drawing, usually with crayons. We also called it "coloring." Since my command of the crayon was greater than my command of writing, in a sense my drawings became my poems. Then at about the age of twelve—while still drawing and now painting with
10 a passion—I seriously (too seriously!) committed myself to writing poetry. I wanted to be a Renaissance artist: write, paint, compose music, invent things.

**6.** In lines 6-8 ("Since . . . poems"), the author suggests that drawing and writing were

(A) talents that were not generally encouraged by adults
(B) activities that served the same desire for self-expression
(C) accomplishments that gave pleasure to others
(D) abilities that had already been developed to the limit of the author's talent
(E) hobbies that would be supplanted as the author grew to adulthood

**7.** In the passage, the author's childhood wish "to be a Renaissance artist" (lines 11-12) is best understood as

(A) an early sign of artistic ability
(B) a common goal of young people
(C) a naïve and grandiose ambition
(D) the beginning of an arduous and painful apprenticeship
(E) the spark that initiated a devotion to the visual arts

**Questions 8-9 are based on the following passage.**

The Second World War was a watershed event for all Americans. It brought the Great Depression to an end and marked the beginning of significant socioeconomic and *Line* political changes for women and racial minorities. Chinese
5 American women played an important role in these long-term changes.
　Galvanized by motives ranging from Chinese nationalism to American patriotism and feminism, Chinese American women initiated an outpouring of
10 highly organized activities in such areas as fund-raising, propaganda, civil defense, and Red Cross work. While some women in San Francisco's Chinatown enlisted in the armed services, many others went to work in businesses outside their neighborhood and in defense industries for
15 the first time.

**8.** The primary purpose of the passage is to

(A) highlight the contributions of San Francisco's Chinatown to the war effort
(B) describe the different jobs held by women during the Second World War
(C) explain how the Second World War helped to end the Great Depression
(D) discuss the impact of the Second World War on Chinese American women
(E) highlight the influence of feminism on Chinese American women

**9.** Which best characterizes the relationship between the first paragraph and the second paragraph?

(A) The first paragraph relates an anecdote that illustrates a generalization made in the second paragraph.
(B) The first paragraph presents a claim that is supported in the second paragraph.
(C) The paragraphs offer different explanations for the same phenomenon.
(D) The second paragraph digresses from the topic discussed in the first paragraph.
(E) The second paragraph challenges the validity of the argument made in the first paragraph.

**GO ON TO THE NEXT PAGE**

**Questions 10-14 are based on the following passage.**

*This passage is adapted from a novel set in London in the 1870's.*

All along the burnished footpaths of Greek Street,
the shopkeepers are out already, the second wave of early
risers. Of course they regard themselves as the first wave.
Line The grim procession of factory workers less than an hour
5 ago might as well have happened in another country in
another age. Welcome to the real world.

Getting up as early as the shopkeepers do is, in their
view, stoic heroism beyond the understanding of lazier
mortals. Not that they are cruel, these industrious men. It's
10 just that the shopkeepers of Greek Street care nothing about
the shadowy creatures who actually manufacture the goods
that they sell. The world has outgrown its quaint rural
intimacies, and now it's the modern age: an order is put in
for fifty cakes of Coal Tar Soap, and a few days later, a cart
15 arrives and the order is delivered. How that soap came to
exist is no question for a modern man. Everything in this
world issues fully formed from a benign monster called
manufacture; a never-ending stream of objects—of
graded quality, of perfect uniformity—from behind
20 veils of smoke.

You may point out that the clouds of smut from the
factory chimneys of Hammersmith and Lambeth blacken
all the city alike, a humbling reminder of where the
cornucopia really comes from. But humility is not a trait
25 for the modern man, and filthy air is quite good enough
for breathing; its only disadvantage is the film of muck
that accumulates on shop windows.

But what use is there, the shopkeepers sigh, in nostalgia
for past times? The machine age has come, the world will
30 never be clean again, but oh: what compensation!

Already they're working up a sweat, their only sweat
for the day, as they labor to open their shops. They ease the
tainted frost from the windows with sponges of lukewarm
water and sweep the slush into the gutter with stiff brooms.
35 Standing on their toes, stretching their arms, they strip off
the shutters, panels, iron bars and stanchions that have kept
their goods safe another night. All along the street, keys
rattle in keyholes as each shop's ornate metal clothing is
stripped away.

40 The men are in a hurry now, in case someone with
money should come along and choose a wide-open shop
over a half-open one. Passers-by are few and often strange
at this hour of the morning, but all types may stray into
Greek Street and there's no telling who'll spend.

10. The shopkeepers' attitude toward the workers who
are described in lines 4-6 is best characterized as

(A) ambivalent
(B) dismissive
(C) combative
(D) fearful
(E) suspicious

11. In line 13, "an order" most nearly means

(A) a command from a military authority
(B) an instruction to provide something
(C) an established system of organization
(D) a customary procedure
(E) a logical arrangement

**GO ON TO THE NEXT PAGE**

**12.** The author uses the phrase "benign monster" (line 17) in order to

(A) criticize the greed of the merchants on Greek Street

(B) evoke sympathy for the fate of the factory workers

(C) characterize the process by which modern goods are created

(D) suggest that consistency is not always an outcome of mass production

(E) emphasize the many hardships of life on Greek Street

**13.** The "compensation" referred to in line 30 is best understood as the

(A) economic costs of a polluted environment

(B) ability of merchants to market goods effectively

(C) lucrative profits that manufacturers glean from shopkeepers

(D) awareness that present success will not make up for past failure

(E) financial benefits that come with industrialization

**14.** In the final paragraph, the shopkeepers can best be described as

(A) frantic about the delivery of their goods

(B) elated about their abundant profits

(C) eager for the arrival of customers

(D) nonchalant about their success as merchants

(E) suspicious of the neighboring shopkeepers

GO ON TO THE NEXT PAGE

**Questions 15-24 are based on the following passages.**

*The following passages were adapted from articles published in 1999 and 2000, respectively.*

### Passage 1

In 1929 a teenager named Ridgely Whiteman wrote to the Smithsonian Institution in Washington, D.C., about what he called warheads that he had found near Clovis, New Mexico. These "warheads" were actually spear points,
5 elegantly chipped to sharpness on both edges and finished off with a groove, or flute, down the center of each side. Eventually, such fluted points turned up in the oldest archaeological excavations elsewhere in North America.

Stone cannot be carbon-dated, but the dating of organic
10 material found with these tools showed that the people who used them were in America no earlier than about 13,500 years ago. The story most archaeologists built on these ancient tools was of a people they nicknamed Clovis, who came into North America via Siberia, moved
15 south through an ice-free corridor, then dispersed, their descendants occupying North and South America within a thousand years. Since their tools were often found with the bones of mammoths and other large creatures, scientists usually described the Clovis people as big-
20 game hunters. As late as 1996 a prominent archaeologist, Frederick Hadleigh West, could state that "Clovis is taken to be the basal, the founding, population for the Americas." But in the past decade such certainty has been dramatically shaken.

25 The most straightforward challenge to the old story is the matter of time. The era in which the Clovis people lived is limited by a time barrier that stops about 13,500 years ago: there is geologic evidence that an ice-free corridor between Siberia and North America would not have been
30 open much before then. But in 1997 a blue-ribbon panel of archaeologists visited a site in Chile called Monte Verde and agreed that people had lived there at least 14,500 years ago, about 1,000 years before the first sign of Clovis people in North America. Acceptance of the Monte Verde date not
35 only broke the time barrier but also focused new interest on other sites that may have even earlier dates.

### Passage 2

One of the biggest barriers to accepting pre-Clovis sites has been geographic. During the most recent ice age, the New World was pretty much closed to pedestrian traffic:
40 the northwest corridor in Canada would have been covered with ice. Though ancient humans might have mastered prehistoric crampons,* mastodons almost certainly did not, and finding food and shelter under those circumstances would have been difficult at best. But the latest idea
45 circulating among archaeologists and anthropologists has people ditching their crampons and spears for skin-covered boats. Maybe the first Americans came not by land but by sea, hugging the ice-age coast.

When the seafaring theory was proposed in the mid-
50 1970's, it sank for lack of evidence. But as the time line for New World occupation has changed, the theory seems downright sensible, if not quite provable. The Pacific Rim has vast resources of salmon and sea mammals, and people need only the simplest of tools to exploit them: nets, weirs,
55 clubs, knives. Whereas ancient landlubbers would have had to reinvent their means of hunting, foraging, and housing as they passed through different terrains, ancient mariners could have had smooth sailing through relatively unchanging coastal environments. And recent geologic
60 studies show that even when glaciers stretched down into North America, there were thawed pockets of coastline in northwest North America where people could take refuge and gather provisions. "Most archaeologists have a continental mind-set," says anthropologist Robson
65 Bonnichsen, "but the peopling of the Americas is likely to be tied very much to the development and spread of maritime adaptation."

---

* spiked devices attached to boots to prevent slippage when climbing on ice

**15.** Both authors agree on which of the following points?

(A) A maritime environment would have presented unique challenges to early Americans.
(B) The first Americans most likely subsisted on mastodons and other big game.
(C) Overland travel to the New World would have been difficult during the most recent ice age.
(D) It may never be definitively determined when America was initially settled.
(E) The Clovis people were most likely the first Americans.

**16.** In lines 5-6, "finished off" most nearly means

(A) defeated
(B) terminated
(C) completed
(D) disposed of
(E) consumed totally

**17.** The quotation in lines 21-22 serves primarily to

(A) provide concrete evidence
(B) discredit a widely shared assumption
(C) support a provocative claim
(D) offer an opposing viewpoint
(E) summarize a common understanding

**GO ON TO THE NEXT PAGE** →

7  7

Unauthorized copying or reuse of
any part of this page is illegal.

18. In line 33, "sign" most nearly means

    (A) omen
    (B) symbol
    (C) gesture
    (D) indication
    (E) figure

19. The author of Passage 2 would most likely claim that the information presented in lines 25-36 of Passage 1

    (A) validates the notion that the peopling of America occurred shortly after the most recent ice age
    (B) adds credibility to the theory that the first Americans may have arrived by boat
    (C) indicates that overland travel to the New World was not possible
    (D) demonstrates that early Americans must have relied on the sea for sustenance
    (E) reveals that archaeologists can differ over even the most basic facts

20. Which of the following, if found on the west coast of America, would best support the "latest idea" (line 44) ?

    (A) Primitive fishing hooks dating back 9,000 years
    (B) Simple cooking tools dating back 11,000 years
    (C) Stone arrowheads dating back 13,000 years
    (D) Crude boat anchors dating back 15,000 years
    (E) Fossilized mastodon bones dating back 17,000 years

21. The author of Passage 2 implies that the findings of the "geologic studies" (lines 59-60) are

    (A) proof that a particular theory is correct
    (B) virtually certain to be verified independently
    (C) characteristic of, though not essential to, an experimental approach
    (D) critical of, though not opposed to, a specific hypothesis
    (E) grounds for granting increased plausibility to a particular theory

22. Which of the following can be found in both passages?

    I. A theory about how people originally traveled to America
    II. An exact date the Americas were initially settled
    III. Reference to possible sources of food for early Americans

    (A) I only
    (B) II only
    (C) I and III only
    (D) II and III only
    (E) I, II, and III

23. Both passages make use of which of the following?

    (A) Political allusion
    (B) Direct quotation
    (C) Rhetorical questioning
    (D) Personal anecdote
    (E) Extended metaphor

24. Which best describes the relationship between the two passages?

    (A) Passage 2 disproves a hypothesis that is debated in some detail in Passage 1.
    (B) Passage 2 examines the implications of using a term that is defined in Passage 1.
    (C) Passage 2 traces the origins of an ancient technology that is discussed in Passage 1.
    (D) Passage 2 presents a theory that may help explain a finding mentioned in Passage 1.
    (E) Passage 2 describes an archaeological discovery that verifies the central claim made in Passage 1.

# STOP

**If you finish before time is called, you may check your work on this section only.**
**Do not turn to any other section in the test.**

## SECTION 8
### Time — 20 minutes
### 16 Questions

**Turn to Section 8 (page 7) of your answer sheet to answer the questions in this section.**

**Directions:** For this section, solve each problem and decide which is the best of the choices given. Fill in the corresponding circle on the answer sheet. You may use any available space for scratchwork.

**Notes**

1. The use of a calculator is permitted.
2. All numbers used are real numbers.
3. Figures that accompany problems in this test are intended to provide information useful in solving the problems. They are drawn as accurately as possible EXCEPT when it is stated in a specific problem that the figure is not drawn to scale. All figures lie in a plane unless otherwise indicated.
4. Unless otherwise specified, the domain of any function $f$ is assumed to be the set of all real numbers $x$ for which $f(x)$ is a real number.

**Reference Information**

$A = \pi r^2$
$C = 2\pi r$ $A = \ell w$ $A = \frac{1}{2}bh$ $V = \ell wh$ $V = \pi r^2 h$ $c^2 = a^2 + b^2$ Special Right Triangles

The number of degrees of arc in a circle is 360.
The sum of the measures in degrees of the angles of a triangle is 180.

---

1. If $\frac{3}{4}$ of a number is 18, what is $\frac{1}{4}$ of the number?

(A) $\frac{3}{2}$

(B) $\frac{9}{2}$

(C) 6

(D) 12

(E) 24

2. For all integers $k$, let $k*$ be defined by $k* = k(k - 1)$. What is the value of $5*$ ?

(A) 9
(B) 20
(C) 24
(D) 25
(E) 30

**GO ON TO THE NEXT PAGE**

8

Unauthorized copying or reuse of
any part of this page is illegal.

8

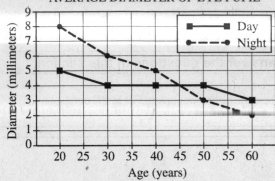

AVERAGE DIAMETER OF EYE PUPIL

3. The graph above shows the effect of aging on the diameter of the eye pupil. Based on the graph, what is the best estimate of the age at which the average diameter of the eye pupil during the day will equal the average diameter of the eye pupil at night?

(A)  20
(B)  30
(C)  35
(D)  45
(E)  60

4. On each of the days Monday through Friday, Toni spent 1 hour commuting to work and 1 hour commuting back home. What fraction of the total number of hours in these five days did she spend commuting?

(A)  $\dfrac{1}{12}$

(B)  $\dfrac{1}{24}$

(C)  $\dfrac{5}{12}$

(D)  $\dfrac{5}{24}$

(E)  $\dfrac{10}{168}$

5. If $\sqrt{3} = x + 1$, what is the value of $(x + 1)^2$ ?

(A)  $\sqrt{2}$
(B)  $\sqrt{3}$
(C)  3
(D)  9
(E)  16

GO ON TO THE NEXT PAGE

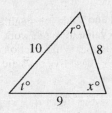

**6.** Which of the following must be true about $t$, $r$, and $x$ in the figure above?

(A) $t < r < x$
(B) $t < x < r$
(C) $r < t < x$
(D) $x < t < r$
(E) $x < r < t$

**7.** If $|6 - 5y| > 20$, which of the following is a possible value of $y$?

(A) $-3$
(B) $-1$
(C) $1$
(D) $3$
(E) $5$

**8.** The legs of right triangle $ABC$ have lengths 3 and 4. What is the perimeter of a right triangle with each side twice the length of its corresponding side in $\triangle ABC$?

(A) 8
(B) 14
(C) 16
(D) 24
(E) 48

NUMBER OF CAR RENTAL LOCATIONS

| Company | United States Locations | Foreign Locations |
|---------|------------------------|-------------------|
| A | 1,400 | 4,000 |
| B | 1,300 | 3,300 |
| C | 1,012 | 3,618 |
| D | 1,242 | 2,268 |
| E | 762 | 2,100 |

**9.** The table above shows the number of car rental locations for five car rental companies. For which of the five companies is the ratio of the number of foreign locations to the number of United States locations the greatest?

(A) $A$
(B) $B$
(C) $C$
(D) $D$
(E) $E$

**GO ON TO THE NEXT PAGE**

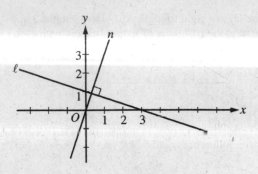

**10.** In the $xy$-coordinate plane above, line $n$ is perpendicular to line $\ell$. What is the slope of line $n$ ?

(A)  $-3$

(B)  $-\dfrac{1}{3}$

(C)  $\dfrac{1}{3}$

(D)  $2$

(E)  $3$

**11.** If $k$ is a constant and $2x + 5 = 3kx + 5$ for all values of $x$, what is the value of $k$ ?

(A)  $5$

(B)  $3$

(C)  $2$

(D)  $\dfrac{3}{2}$

(E)  $\dfrac{2}{3}$

**GO ON TO THE NEXT PAGE**

**12.** The sum of eleven different integers is zero. What is the least number of these integers that <u>must</u> be positive?

(A) None
(B) One
(C) Five
(D) Six
(E) Ten

**13.** In a certain game, each token has one of three possible values: 1 point, 5 points, or 10 points. How many different combinations of these token values are worth a total of 17 points?

(A) Two
(B) Three
(C) Four
(D) Five
(E) Six

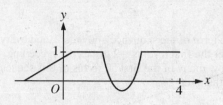

**14.** The graph of $y = f(x)$ is shown above. Which of the following could be the graph of $y = 2f(x)$ ?

(A)

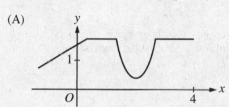

(B)

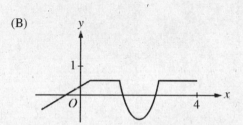

(C)

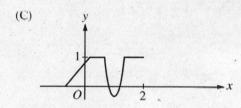

(D)

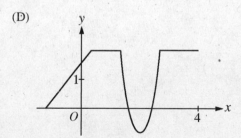

(E)

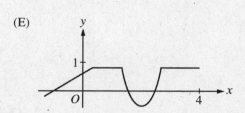

**GO ON TO THE NEXT PAGE**

**8** ○ ○ ○ Unauthorized copying or reuse of any part of this page is illegal. ○ ○ ○ **8**

2, −4, 8, ...

15. The first term of the sequence above is 2, and every term after the first term is −2 times the preceding term. How many of the first 50 terms of this sequence are less than 100 ?

(A) 22
(B) 25
(C) 28
(D) 30
(E) 37

16. A cube with volume 8 cubic centimeters is inscribed in a sphere so that each vertex of the cube touches the sphere. What is the length of the diameter, in centimeters, of the sphere?

(A) 2

(B) $\sqrt{6}$ (approximately 2.45)

(C) 2.5

(D) $2\sqrt{3}$ (approximately 3.46)

(E) 4

# STOP
**If you finish before time is called, you may check your work on this section only.**
**Do not turn to any other section in the test.**

## SECTION 9
Time — 20 minutes
19 Questions

---

**Turn to Section 9 (page 7) of your answer sheet to answer the questions in this section.**

---

**Directions:** For each question in this section, select the best answer from among the choices given and fill in the corresponding circle on the answer sheet.

---

Each sentence below has one or two blanks, each blank indicating that something has been omitted. Beneath the sentence are five words or sets of words labeled A through E. Choose the word or set of words that, when inserted in the sentence, best fits the meaning of the sentence as a whole.

**Example:**

Hoping to ------- the dispute, negotiators proposed a compromise that they felt would be ------- to both labor and management.

(A) enforce . . useful
(B) end . . divisive
(C) overcome . . unattractive
(D) extend . . satisfactory
(E) resolve . . acceptable            Ⓐ Ⓑ Ⓒ Ⓓ ●

1. Paradoxically, during the French Revolution, the very leaders who proclaimed ------- philosophies sometimes also engaged in ------- practices.

   (A) regal . . imperial
   (B) simplistic . . neutral
   (C) liberating . . repressive
   (D) totalitarian . . absolutist
   (E) scandalous . . compromised

2. Despite his brilliant career, Gerald was plagued by doubts and could not ------- his feelings of -------.

   (A) imagine . . worthlessness
   (B) reconcile . . superiority
   (C) embrace . . insecurity
   (D) dispel . . inferiority
   (E) fathom . . levity

3. Jane was both ------- and -------: she was blatantly proud and offensively bold.

   (A) haughty . . impudent
   (B) irresolute . . insolent
   (C) presumptuous . . loquacious
   (D) arrogant . . articulate
   (E) reverential . . contemptuous

4. New Zealand and Spain can accurately be described as ------- because they are diametrically opposite one another on the globe.

   (A) satellites    (B) antipodes    (C) reversals
        (D) bifurcations    (E) dichotomies

5. Ken took his ------- obligations seriously, patiently caring for his mother throughout her long recuperation.

   (A) filial    (B) symbiotic    (C) avuncular
        (D) convivial    (E) funerary

6. The sound produced by the youth orchestra was so ------- that even its least experienced members were abashed.

   (A) cacophonous    (B) syncopated    (C) harmonic
        (D) collaborative    (E) mellifluous

**GO ON TO THE NEXT PAGE** ⟩

The passage below is followed by questions based on its content. Answer the questions on the basis of what is <u>stated</u> or <u>implied</u> in the passage and in any introductory material that may be provided.

**Questions 7-19 are based on the following passage.**

*This passage is adapted from a 1998 memoir in which the author recalls her childhood in Chicago in the 1960's.*

A trip to the library was like a great excursion to a different country. To get there, we had to walk a mile. But the distance between where we lived and where we
*Line* were going was much greater. To get there we traveled
5 beyond the usual parameters of school and church and the shopping strip we frequented, into the manicured lawns and gardens of Hyde Park. I loved the walk as much as the destination itself. In the middle of the anger that was my home and the upheaval of a changing world in which
10 it seemed I had no place, our semimonthly excursions to the library were a piece of perfection. I had around me at one time all the people I loved best—my mother and brothers and sister—and all the things I loved best— quiet, space, and books.
15 We went to the T. B. Blackstone Library, not far from Lake Michigan. You could easily miss the building if you didn't know what you were looking for. But once you were inside, you could never mistake it for anything else. We passed through two sets of heavy brass doors to the
20 lobby of the library, a great domed entrance with a ceiling adorned with what I used to imagine were the angels of books. They were great gilded figures armed with harps and with scrolls and other instruments of learning.
If we turned right, we could see an alcove with tables;
25 this led, in turn, to a spacious reading room adorned with a gigantic and ancient globe that sat in front of the largest windows. At some point during every visit, I found my way into that room to touch the globe, to finger the ridges and the painted canvas already frayed and separating from
30 its sphere. I liked to look at Africa, with the coded colors of the different countries like the Belgian Congo and Rhodesia, and try to remember which countries were fighting to be free just as we were struggling for civil rights. I had heard Daddy talking about the struggle,
35 arguing with the television as someone discussed it on a news show. And I had seen pictures on the news of people gathered together marching. But I didn't really know anything about Africa except what I saw in the Tarzan movies, which I watched a lot, but thought were
40 really strange. (Why did that White man live in a tree?)
I read a lot of books about mythology, and then about science: not the missiles and spaceships Brother preferred, but the birds and the bees—literally. I brought home a giant book of birds and searched the skies and trees for
45 anything other than robins and pigeons. And I read about

bees because I liked the idea that all of them listened to the queen and couldn't go on without her. I went through a phase of loving books with practical science experiments and used up a whole bottle of white vinegar by pouring it
50 on the sides of our apartment building to prove that it was constructed of limestone.
One Saturday, as I wandered through the young adult section, I saw a title: *Little Women,* by Louisa May Alcott. I could tell from looking at the shelf that she'd written
55 a lot of books, but I didn't know anything about her. I had learned from experience that titles weren't everything. A book that sounded great on the shelf could be dull once you got it home, and every bad book I brought home meant one less book to read until we went back in two weeks. So
60 I sat in a chair near the shelves to skim the first paragraphs:

"Christmas won't be Christmas without
any presents," grumbled Jo, lying on the rug.
"It's so dreadful to be poor!" sighed Meg,
looking down at her old dress.
65 "I don't think it's fair for some girls to have
plenty of pretty things, and other girls nothing
at all," added little Amy, with an injured sniff.
"We've got Father and Mother and each
other," said Beth contentedly from her corner.

70 It was a good thing I'd already decided on some other books to take home, because I didn't look through the rest of the section that day. I read and read and read *Little Women* until it was time to walk home, and, except for a few essential interruptions like sleeping and eating,
75 I would not put it down until the end. Even the freedom to watch weekend television held no appeal for me in the wake of Alcott's story. It was about girls, for one thing, girls who could almost be like me, especially Jo. It seemed to me a shame that she wasn't Black; then our similarity
80 would be complete. She loved to read, she loved to make up plays, she hated acting ladylike, she had a dreadful temper. I had found a kindred spirit.

**7.** The author viewed the "semimonthly excursions" (line 10) with

(A) apprehension
(B) detachment
(C) resentment
(D) pride
(E) delight

**GO ON TO THE NEXT PAGE** ⇨

**8.** In lines 16-18 ("You could . . . else"), the author distinguishes between

(A) general and particular impressions
(B) objective and subjective experiences
(C) external and internal appearances
(D) public and private observations
(E) true and false assumptions

**9.** The tone of the statement in lines 17-18 ("But once . . . else") is one of

(A) arrogance
(B) foreboding
(C) conviction
(D) diffidence
(E) sarcasm

**10.** The author's reaction to the "ceiling" (line 20) conveys her

(A) aspirations of becoming a novelist
(B) distaste for religious imagery
(C) puzzlement about artistic symbolism
(D) reverence for the library's educational offerings
(E) discomfort in the presence of high culture

**11.** For the author, to "look at Africa" on the globe (line 30) served as a reminder of

(A) an American movement for social change
(B) a personal experience abroad
(C) the diversity of cultures around the world
(D) the ethnic diversity of her neighborhood
(E) the influence of African politics on America

**12.** What does the description in lines 34-36 ("I had . . . show") suggest about the author's father?

(A) He was uncomfortable discussing politics with his children.
(B) He did not approve of most television news coverage.
(C) He had strong feelings about the Civil Rights movement.
(D) He generally had a pessimistic worldview.
(E) He was an outspoken public advocate for equal rights.

**13.** The author refers to "Tarzan movies" in line 39 to demonstrate that, as a child, she had

(A) no concerns about the authenticity of most films
(B) a preference for watching movies rather than reading books
(C) a fascination with movie actors
(D) limited knowledge about Africa
(E) little interest in fictional characters

**14.** The primary purpose of the fourth paragraph (lines 41-51) is to

(A) contrast the books about mythology and science that the author had been reading
(B) discuss why the author enjoyed books that were about birds and bees
(C) characterize the author's reading interests during a particular period of time
(D) distinguish between books preferred by the author and those preferred by her brother
(E) provide several examples of practical science experiments that the author conducted

**15.** Lines 52-60 ("One Saturday . . . paragraphs") suggest that the author accepted which of the following generalizations about books?

(A) Books seem duller when read in libraries than when read at home.
(B) Interesting books are often very dull in their first few paragraphs.
(C) Novels are usually more interesting than nonfiction works.
(D) Book titles can sometimes be misleading.
(E) Books are rarely as interesting as their titles.

**16.** The author uses an extended quote in lines 61-69 ("Christmas . . . corner") as part of a larger attempt to

(A) convey the impact of an unexpected discovery
(B) illustrate the suddenness of a decision
(C) simulate a child's misconceptions
(D) criticize the artificiality of the "young adult" classification
(E) describe a young reader's sense of history

GO ON TO THE NEXT PAGE

17. In line 65, "fair" most nearly means

   (A) comely
   (B) temperate
   (C) equitable
   (D) auspicious
   (E) mediocre

18. The description in lines 70-75 ("It was . . . end") suggests that the author found *Little Women* to be

   (A) bewildering
   (B) unremarkable
   (C) hilarious
   (D) profound
   (E) captivating

19. The list in lines 80-82 ("She loved . . . temper") serves primarily to

   (A) support a hypothesis
   (B) challenge an interpretation
   (C) emphasize an inconsistency
   (D) substantiate a comparison
   (E) develop a critique

# STOP

**If you finish before time is called, you may check your work on this section only.**
**Do not turn to any other section in the test.**

10 10

Unauthorized copying or reuse of
any part of this page is illegal.

**SECTION 10**
Time — 10 minutes
14 Questions

Turn to Section 10 (page 7) of your answer sheet to answer the questions in this section.

**Directions:** For each question in this section, select the best answer from among the choices given and fill in the corresponding circle on the answer sheet.

The following sentences test correctness and effectiveness of expression. Part of each sentence or the entire sentence is underlined; beneath each sentence are five ways of phrasing the underlined material. Choice A repeats the original phrasing; the other four choices are different. If you think the original phrasing produces a better sentence than any of the alternatives, select choice A; if not, select one of the other choices.

In making your selection, follow the requirements of standard written English; that is, pay attention to grammar, choice of words, sentence construction, and punctuation. Your selection should result in the most effective sentence—clear and precise, without awkwardness or ambiguity.

EXAMPLE:

Laura Ingalls Wilder published her first book
and she was sixty-five years old then.

(A) and she was sixty-five years old then
(B) when she was sixty-five
(C) at age sixty-five years old
(D) upon the reaching of sixty-five years
(E) at the time when she was sixty-five

1. Wa Nu assured the worried members of her group that they would finish the project on time.

(A) assured the worried members of her group that they would finish the project on time
(B) assured them of finishing the project on time, the members of her group were worried
(C) assured that the project would be finished on time to the worried members of her group
(D) assuring the worried members of her group that they would finish the project on time
(E) assures the worried members of her group, they would finish the project on time

2. Richard Rodriguez pointed out that Mission San Luis Rey, a Spanish church with an Arabic dome getting its name to honor a French king.

(A) Mission San Luis Rey, a Spanish church with an Arabic dome getting its name to honor a French king
(B) Mission San Luis Rey, a Spanish church with an Arabic dome, was named in honor of a French king
(C) Mission San Luis Rey's being a Spanish church with an Arabic dome got named in honor of a French king
(D) they named Mission San Luis Rey, a Spanish church in honor of a French king that had an Arabic dome
(E) the name of Mission San Luis Rey having been a Spanish church with an Arabic dome honoring a French king

3. Joan feeling tired and frustrated, and she was able to finish her painting before the light faded.

(A) Joan feeling tired and frustrated, and
(B) Joan felt tired and frustrated,
(C) Although Joan felt tired and frustrated,
(D) Despite Joan felt tired and frustrated,
(E) Nevertheless, Joan felt tired and frustrated,

4. Men and women leave the village before sunrise to hike four miles up steep, precarious trails to the forests, to be returning by late afternoon with 70-pound loads of firewood on their backs.

(A) forests, to be returning by late afternoon
(B) forests, and it is late afternoon that they return
(C) forests, they return by late afternoon
(D) forests and return by late afternoon
(E) forests to have returned by late afternoon

GO ON TO THE NEXT PAGE

5. The Poetry Book Society is an organization in London that <u>provides information and guidance for all lovers of contemporary poetry and giving them discounts on books of poetry</u>.

   (A) provides information and guidance for all lovers of contemporary poetry and giving them discounts on books of poetry
   (D) provides information, guidance, and the getting of discounts on books of poetry for all lovers of contemporary poetry
   (C) not only provides information and guidance for lovers of contemporary poetry but also gives them discounts on books of poetry
   (D) has been providing information and guidance for lovers of contemporary poetry and were giving discounts on books of poetry
   (E) are providing information and guidance for all lovers of contemporary poetry and having given them discounts on books of poetry

6. During the American Civil War, American Red Cross founder Clara Barton ministered to soldiers on the <u>battlefields, at Antietam, so close was she to the actual fighting</u> that a bullet pierced her sleeve.

   (A) battlefields, at Antietam, so close was she to the actual fighting
   (B) battlefields, she was at Antietam so close to the actual fighting
   (C) battlefields, being so close to the actual fighting at Antietam so
   (D) battlefields; at Antietam, she was so close to the actual fighting
   (E) battlefields; she was at Antietam so close to the actual fighting so

7. <u>Because their flight was missed, the bride's parents ran</u> frantically to another part of the airport to catch another plane that might still arrive in time for the wedding.

   (A) Because their flight was missed, the bride's parents ran
   (B) Because the bride's parents missed their flight, they had to run
   (C) The bride's parents had missed their flight, thus, finally, running
   (D) The bride's parents had missed their flight, then they ran
   (E) Their flight was missed, which eventually caused the bride's parents to run

8. Buffalo herds, which once thrived in the Great Plains of North America, trampled vegetation, <u>and future plant growth was aided by this by returning nutrients</u> to the soil.

   (A) and future plant growth was aided by this by returning nutrients
   (B) future plant growth was thereby aided and nutrients returned
   (C) thereby aiding future plant growth by returning nutrients
   (D) thereby an aid to future plant growth returned nutrients
   (E) but this aided future plant growth and nutrients were returned

9. The students criticized the administration for failing either to renovate the old dormitories <u>nor replace</u> them with new buildings.

   (A) nor replace
   (B) nor replacing
   (C) nor did they replace
   (D) or by replacing
   (E) or to replace

10. <u>Because insufficient funding causes the failure of many new businesses is the reason why</u> Tamar and Robert waited to open their coffee shop until they had enough money.

    (A) Because insufficient funding causes the failure of many new businesses is the reason why
    (B) Because insufficient funding causes the failure of many new businesses,
    (C) Insufficient funding causes the failure of many new businesses is the reason why
    (D) As a result of insufficient funding causing the failure of many new businesses;
    (E) The fact of insufficient funding is causing many new businesses to fail is why

11. <u>Theodore Roosevelt was not just a great reformer; he was also a great president.</u>

    (A) Theodore Roosevelt was not just a great reformer; he was also a great president.
    (B) Theodore Roosevelt was not just a great reformer, and also a great president.
    (C) Theodore Roosevelt was not just a great reformer; but also a great president.
    (D) Great not just as a reformer, but Theodore Roosevelt was also a great president.
    (E) Not just as a reformer, Theodore Roosevelt was also a great president.

GO ON TO THE NEXT PAGE ▷

12. Jesse Jackson's Rainbow PUSH <u>Coalition was established</u> to encourage diverse populations to become socially and politically active, was created in 1996 by the merging of two groups Jackson had previously founded.

   (A) Coalition was established
   (B) Coalition is established
   (C) Coalition, establishing
   (D) Coalition, which being established
   (E) Coalition, established

13. In the novel, Jane Eyre must make many difficult choices, <u>like when she forces</u> herself to leave the house of Mr. Rochester, the married man she loves.

   (A) like when she forces
   (B) and, as an example, when she forces
   (C) for example, by forcing
   (D) as exemplified by when she forces
   (E) including forcing

14. Nicknamed the supergrain of the future, quinoa is a complete <u>protein, one that contains all the necessary amino acids and is</u> high in fiber.

   (A) protein, one that contains all the necessary amino acids and is
   (B) protein, it contains all the necessary amino acids and is
   (C) protein, and containing all the necessary amino acids in addition to being
   (D) protein that contained all the necessary amino acids and also is
   (E) protein; thus, containing all the necessary amino acids and being also

## STOP
**If you finish before time is called, you may check your work on this section only.**
**Do not turn to any other section in the test.**

# Correct Answers and Difficulty Levels
## SAT Practice Test #3

## Critical Reading

| | Section 4 | | | | | Section 7 | | | | | Section 9 | | | |
|---|---|---|---|---|---|---|---|---|---|---|---|---|---|---|
| | COR. ANS. | DIFF. LEV. | | COR. ANS. | DIFF. LEV. | COR. ANS. | DIFF. LEV. | | COR. ANS. | DIFF. LEV. | COR. ANS. | DIFF. LEV. | | COR. ANS. | DIFF. LEV. |
| 1. | B | 1 | 13. | C | 3 | 1. E 3 | | 13. C 2 | | | 1. C 3 | | 11. A 3 | |
| 2. | E | 1 | 14. | B | 3 | 2. D 3 | | 14. C 2 | | | 2. D 3 | | 12. C 2 | |
| 3. | D | 2 | 15. | E | 3 | 3. E 4 | | 15. C 5 | | | 3. A 4 | | 13. D 1 | |
| 4. | C | 3 | 16. | E | 3 | 4. C 4 | | 16. C 1 | | | 4. B 4 | | 14. C 2 | |
| 5. | C | 1 | 17. | A | 4 | 5. A 5 | | 17. E 5 | | | 5. A 4 | | 15. D 1 | |
| 6. | D | 3 | 18. | D | 4 | 6. B 2 | | 18. D 1 | | | 6. A 5 | | 16. A 3 | |
| 7. | D | 3 | 19. | E | 4 | 7. C 5 | | 19. B 4 | | | 7. E 2 | | 17. C 2 | |
| 8. | C | 5 | 20. | D | 4 | 8. D 2 | | 20. D 3 | | | 8. C 2 | | 18. E 1 | |
| 9. | A | 3 | 21. | B | 4 | 9. B 2 | | 21. E 3 | | | 9. C 4 | | 19. D 2 | |
| 10. | E | 5 | 22. | D | 3 | 10. B 3 | | 22. C 3 | | | 10. D 3 | | | |
| 11. | D | 4 | 23. | C | 3 | 11. B 2 | | 23. B 3 | | | | | | |
| 12. | E | 3 | 24. | A | 3 | 12. C 3 | | 24. D 4 | | | | | | |

Section 4: Number correct ___  Number incorrect ___

Section 7: Number correct ___  Number incorrect ___

Section 9: Number correct ___  Number incorrect ___

## Mathematics

### Section 2

| | COR. ANS. | DIFF. LEV. | | COR. ANS. | DIFF. LEV. |
|---|---|---|---|---|---|
| 1. | A | 1 | 11. | E | 3 |
| 2. | C | 1 | 12. | D | 3 |
| 3. | B | 1 | 13. | D | 3 |
| 4. | D | 2 | 14. | C | 3 |
| 5. | E | 2 | 15. | A | 3 |
| 6. | B | 2 | 16. | A | 4 |
| 7. | B | 2 | 17. | C | 4 |
| 8. | D | 2 | 18. | A | 4 |
| 9. | C | 3 | 19. | C | 4 |
| 10. | D | 3 | 20. | B | 5 |

Number correct ___  Number incorrect ___

### Section 5

**Multiple-Choice Questions**

| | COR. ANS. | DIFF. LEV. |
|---|---|---|
| 1. | A | 1 |
| 2. | B | 1 |
| 3. | D | 1 |
| 4. | B | 1 |
| 5. | A | 4 |
| 6. | E | 3 |
| 7. | C | 4 |
| 8. | B | 5 |

Number correct ___  Number incorrect ___

**Student-Produced Response Questions**

| | COR. ANS. | DIFF. LEV. |
|---|---|---|
| 9. | 93/2 or 46.5 | 1 |
| 10. | 4 | 2 |
| 11. | 1,2 or 4 | 2 |
| 12. | 13 | 3 |
| 13. | 1992 | 2 |
| 14. | 5/4 or 1.25 | 3 |
| 15. | 90 | 4 |
| 16. | 67 | 4 |
| 17. | 100 | 4 |
| 18. | 1/2 or .5 | 4 |

Number correct (9-18) ___

### Section 8

| | COR. ANS. | DIFF. LEV. | | COR. ANS. | DIFF. LEV. |
|---|---|---|---|---|---|
| 1. | C | 1 | 9. | C | 3 |
| 2. | B | 2 | 10. | E | 3 |
| 3. | D | 1 | 11. | E | 3 |
| 4. | A | 2 | 12. | B | 3 |
| 5. | C | 2 | 13. | E | 4 |
| 6. | A | 2 | 14. | D | 3 |
| 7. | A | 2 | 15. | C | 4 |
| 8. | D | 2 | 16. | D | 5 |

Number correct ___  Number incorrect ___

## Writing Multiple-Choice

### Section 6

| | COR. ANS. | DIFF. LEV. | | COR. ANS. | DIFF. LEV. | | COR. ANS. | DIFF. LEV. | | COR. ANS. | DIFF. LEV. |
|---|---|---|---|---|---|---|---|---|---|---|---|
| 1. | B | 1 | 10. | A | 5 | 19. | B | 3 | 28. | E | 4 |
| 2. | B | 1 | 11. | B | 5 | 20. | C | 3 | 29. | D | 5 |
| 3. | A | 1 | 12. | D | 1 | 21. | D | 3 | 30. | E | 3 |
| 4. | B | 1 | 13. | D | 1 | 22. | A | 5 | 31. | B | 3 |
| 5. | D | 2 | 14. | A | 2 | 23. | B | 4 | 32. | D | 3 |
| 6. | C | 3 | 15. | A | 3 | 24. | A | 3 | 33. | A | 4 |
| 7. | E | 2 | 16. | D | 3 | 25. | D | 4 | 34. | C | 4 |
| 8. | D | 2 | 17. | C | 2 | 26. | B | 3 | 35. | E | 3 |
| 9. | D | 3 | 18. | E | 2 | 27. | C | 4 | | | |

Number correct ___  Number incorrect ___

### Section 10

| | COR. ANS. | DIFF. LEV. | | COR. ANS. | DIFF. LEV. | | COR. ANS. | DIFF. LEV. |
|---|---|---|---|---|---|---|---|---|
| 1. | A | 1 | 6. | D | 2 | 11. | A | 3 |
| 2. | B | 1 | 7. | B | 2 | 12. | E | 5 |
| 3. | C | 1 | 8. | C | 3 | 13. | E | 4 |
| 4. | D | 2 | 9. | E | 3 | 14. | A | 5 |
| 5. | C | 1 | 10. | B | 3 | | | |

Number correct ___  Number incorrect ___

**NOTE:** Difficulty levels are estimates of question difficulty for a reference group of college-bound seniors. Difficulty levels range from 1 (easiest) to 5 (hardest).

# The SAT Scoring Process

**Scoring.** The computer compares the circle filled in for each question with the correct response. Each correct answer receives one point; omitted questions do not affect your score. For each wrong answer to a multiple-choice question, one-fourth of a point is subtracted to correct for random guessing. The SAT critical reading section has 67 questions. If, for example, a student has 44 right, 20 wrong, and 3 omitted, the resulting raw score is determined as follows:

$$44 \text{ right} - \frac{20 \text{ wrong}}{4} = 44 - 5 = 39 \text{ raw score points}$$

Obtaining raw scores frequently involves the rounding of fractions to the nearest whole number. For example, a raw score of 39.25 is rounded to 39, the nearest whole number. A raw score of 39.50 is rounded upward to 40. **For the WRITING SECTION**, your essay raw score counts approximately 30% and your multiple-choice raw score counts approximately 70%.

**Converting to reported scaled score.** Raw scores are then placed on the College Board scale of 200 to 800 through a process that adjusts scores to account for minor differences in difficulty among different versions of the test. This process, known as equating, is performed so that a student's reported score is not affected by the version of the test taken or by the abilities of the group with whom the student takes the test. As a result of placing SAT scores on the College Board scale, scores earned by students at different times can be compared. For example, an SAT critical reading score of 400 on a test taken at one administration indicates the same level of developed critical reading ability as a 400 score obtained on a different version of the test taken at another time.

# How to Score Practice Test #3

## SAT Critical Reading Sections 4, 7, and 9

**Step A:** Count the number of correct answers for *Section 4* and record the number in the space provided on the Scoring Worksheet. Then do the same for the incorrect answers. (Do not count omitted answers.)

**Step B:** Count the number of correct answers and the number of incorrect answers for *Section 7* and record the numbers in the spaces provided on the Scoring Worksheet. (Do not count omitted answers.)

**Step C:** Count the number of correct answers and the number of incorrect answers for *Section 9* and record the numbers in the spaces provided on the Scoring Worksheet. (Do not count omitted answers.)

**Step D:** Total the number of correct responses. Total the number of incorrect responses. Enter the resulting figures on the Scoring Worksheet. To determine A, use the formula:

$$\text{Number correct} - \frac{\text{Number incorrect}}{4} = A$$

**Step E:** To obtain B, your Rounded Critical Reading Raw Score, round A to the nearest whole number. (For example, any number from 44.50 to 45.49 rounds to 45.) Enter the resulting figure on the Scoring Worksheet.

**Step F:** To find your Critical Reading Scaled Score, look up the Total Rounded Raw Score you obtained in step E in the Critical Reading Conversion Table (Table 1). Enter this score in the box on the Scoring Worksheet.

## SAT Mathematics Sections 2, 5, and 8

**Step A:** Count the number of correct answers and the number of incorrect answers for *Section 2* and record the numbers in the spaces provided on the Scoring Worksheet. (Do not count omitted answers.)

**Step B:** Count the number of correct answers and the number of incorrect answers for the multiple-choice questions *(questions 1 through 8)* in *Section 5* and record the numbers in the spaces provided on the Scoring Worksheet. (Do not count omitted answers.)

**Step C:** Count the number of correct answers for the student-produced response questions *(questions 9 through 18)* in *Section 5* and record the number in the space provided on the Scoring Worksheet.

**Step D:** Count the number of correct answers and the number of incorrect answers for *Section 8* and record the numbers in the spaces provided on the Scoring Worksheet. (Do not count omitted answers.)

**Step E:** Total the number of correct responses. Total the number of incorrect responses. Enter the resulting figures on the Scoring Worksheet. To determine A, use the formula:

$$\text{Number correct} - \frac{\text{Number incorrect}}{4} = A$$

**Step F:** To obtain B, your Mathematics Rounded Raw Score, round A to the nearest whole number. (For example, any number from 44.50 to 45.49 rounds to 45.) Enter the resulting figure on the Scoring Worksheet.

**Step G:** To find your Mathematics Scaled Score, use the Mathematics Conversion Table (Table 2) to look up the Total Rounded Raw Score you obtained in step F. Enter this score in the box on the Scoring Worksheet.

## SAT Writing Sections 1, 6, and 10

**Step A:** Enter your Essay Score for *Section 1* in the box on the Scoring Worksheet. Multiply your score by 2. (Keep in mind that on the actual SAT, two readers will read your essay and you will receive a total score of 0 to 12 on your score report.) For help scoring your essay see page 105.

**Step B:** Count the number of correct answers and the number of incorrect answers for *Section 6* and record the numbers in the spaces provided on the Scoring Worksheet. (Do not count omitted answers.)

**Step C:** Count the number of correct answers and the number of incorrect answers for *Section 10* and record the numbers in the spaces provided on the Scoring Worksheet. (Do not count omitted answers.)

**Step D:** Total the number of correct responses. Total the number of incorrect responses. Enter the resulting figure on the Scoring Worksheet. To determine A, use the formula:

$$\text{Number correct} - \frac{\text{Number incorrect}}{4} = A$$

**Step E:** To obtain B, your Writing Multiple-Choice (MC) Rounded Raw Score, round A to the nearest whole number. (For example, any number from 44.50 to 45.49 rounds to 45.) Enter the resulting figure on the Scoring Worksheet.

**Step F:** To find your overall Writing Scaled Score, use Table 3. Look up the Total MC Rounded Raw Score you obtained in Step E in the left side of Table 3 and the Essay Score entered in Step A across the top of the table. Enter this score in the box on the Scoring Worksheet.

**Step G:** To find your Writing MC Subscore, look up the Total MC Rounded Raw Score you obtained in Step E on the Writing Multiple-Choice Conversion Table (Table 4). Enter this score in the box on the Scoring Worksheet.

**Note:** For the **WRITING SECTION**, your Essay Raw Score counts approximately 30% and your Multiple-Choice Raw Score counts approximately 70%.

# SAT Practice Test #3 Scoring Worksheet

**SAT Critical Reading Section**

A. Section 4:

_____       _____
no. correct            no. incorrect

+                      +

B. Section 7:

_____       _____
no. correct            no. incorrect

+                      +

C. Section 9:

_____       _____
no. correct            no. incorrect

=                      =

D. Total Unrounded Raw Score

_____   –   ( _____ ÷ 4)  =  _____
no. correct            no. incorrect                    A

E. Total Rounded Raw Score
   (Rounded to nearest whole number)                    _____
                                                              B

F. Critical Reading Scaled Score
   (See Table 1)

[ _____ ]

Critical
Reading Scaled
Score


**SAT Mathematics Section**

A. Section 2:

_____       _____
no. correct            no. incorrect

+                      +

B. Section 5:
   Questions 1-8

_____       _____
no. correct            no. incorrect

+

C. Section 5:
   Questions 9-18

_____
no. correct

+                      +

D. Section 8:

_____       _____
no. correct            no. incorrect

–                      =

E. Total Unrounded Raw Score

_____   ( _____ ÷ 4)  =  _____
no. correct            no. incorrect                    A

F. Total Rounded Raw Score
   (Rounded to nearest whole number)                    _____
                                                              B

G. Mathematics Scaled Score
   (See Table 2)

[ _____ ]

Mathematics
Scaled
Score

## SAT Writing Section

A. Section 1:

$\boxed{\phantom{XXXXX}}$

Essay Score $\times 2$

B. Section 6:

_____   _____
no. correct        no. incorrect

$+$                $+$

C. Section 10:

_____   _____
no. correct        no. incorrect

$=$                $=$

D. Total MC Unrounded Raw Score   _____ $-$ ( _____ $\div 4$ ) $=$ _____
                                   no. correct        no. incorrect              A

E. Total MC Rounded Raw Score                                                    _____
   (Rounded to nearest whole number)                                             B

F. Writing Scaled Score
   (See Table 3)

$\boxed{\phantom{XXXXX}}$

Writing Scaled
Score

G. Writing MC Subscore
   (See Table 4)

$\boxed{\phantom{XXXXX}}$

Writing MC
Subscore

| Table 1. Critical Reading Conversion Table | | | |
|---|---|---|---|
| Raw Score | Scaled Score | Raw Score | Scaled Score |
| 67 | 800 | 31 | 500 |
| 66 | 800 | 30 | 490 |
| 65 | 800 | 29 | 490 |
| 64 | 780 | 28 | 480 |
| 63 | 760 | 27 | 480 |
| 62 | 740 | 26 | 470 |
| 61 | 730 | 25 | 470 |
| 60 | 720 | 24 | 460 |
| 59 | 700 | 23 | 450 |
| 58 | 690 | 22 | 450 |
| 57 | 680 | 21 | 440 |
| 56 | 670 | 20 | 440 |
| 55 | 660 | 19 | 430 |
| 54 | 650 | 18 | 420 |
| 53 | 640 | 17 | 420 |
| 52 | 630 | 16 | 410 |
| 51 | 630 | 15 | 400 |
| 50 | 620 | 14 | 400 |
| 49 | 610 | 13 | 390 |
| 48 | 600 | 12 | 380 |
| 47 | 600 | 11 | 370 |
| 46 | 590 | 10 | 370 |
| 45 | 580 | 9 | 360 |
| 44 | 580 | 8 | 350 |
| 43 | 570 | 7 | 340 |
| 42 | 560 | 6 | 330 |
| 41 | 560 | 5 | 320 |
| 40 | 550 | 4 | 310 |
| 39 | 550 | 3 | 300 |
| 38 | 540 | 2 | 290 |
| 37 | 530 | 1 | 270 |
| 36 | 530 | 0 | 260 |
| 35 | 520 | -1 | 240 |
| 34 | 520 | -2 | 220 |
| 33 | 510 | -3 and below | 200 |
| 32 | 510 | | |

| Table 2. Mathematics Conversion Table | | | |
|---|---|---|---|
| Raw Score | Scaled Score | Raw Score | Scaled Score |
| 54 | 800 | 25 | 490 |
| 53 | 800 | 24 | 480 |
| 52 | 770 | 23 | 470 |
| 51 | 750 | 22 | 460 |
| 50 | 730 | 21 | 450 |
| 49 | 720 | 20 | 450 |
| 48 | 700 | 19 | 440 |
| 47 | 690 | 18 | 430 |
| 46 | 680 | 17 | 420 |
| 45 | 670 | 16 | 410 |
| 44 | 660 | 15 | 410 |
| 43 | 650 | 14 | 400 |
| 42 | 640 | 13 | 390 |
| 41 | 630 | 12 | 380 |
| 40 | 620 | 11 | 370 |
| 39 | 610 | 10 | 360 |
| 38 | 600 | 9 | 350 |
| 37 | 590 | 8 | 340 |
| 36 | 580 | 7 | 330 |
| 35 | 570 | 6 | 320 |
| 34 | 570 | 5 | 310 |
| 33 | 560 | 4 | 300 |
| 32 | 550 | 3 | 280 |
| 31 | 540 | 2 | 260 |
| 30 | 530 | 1 | 250 |
| 29 | 520 | 0 | 230 |
| 28 | 510 | -1 | 210 |
| 27 | 500 | -2 and below | 200 |
| 26 | 490 | | |

# Table 3. Writing Conversion Table

| Writing MC Raw Score | Essay Raw Score | | | | | | | | | | | |
|---|---|---|---|---|---|---|---|---|---|---|---|---|
| | 12 | 11 | 10 | 9 | 8 | 7 | 6 | 5 | 4 | 3 | 2 | 0 |
| 49 | 800 | 800 | 800 | 800 | 790 | 770 | 750 | 740 | 730 | 710 | 700 | 680 |
| 48 | 800 | 800 | 790 | 770 | 750 | 730 | 710 | 700 | 690 | 670 | 660 | 640 |
| 47 | 790 | 780 | 760 | 750 | 720 | 700 | 690 | 670 | 660 | 650 | 630 | 620 |
| 46 | 770 | 760 | 740 | 730 | 710 | 680 | 670 | 650 | 640 | 630 | 620 | 600 |
| 45 | 760 | 750 | 730 | 710 | 690 | 670 | 650 | 640 | 630 | 610 | 600 | 580 |
| 44 | 750 | 730 | 710 | 700 | 680 | 660 | 640 | 620 | 610 | 600 | 590 | 570 |
| 43 | 730 | 720 | 700 | 680 | 660 | 640 | 630 | 610 | 600 | 590 | 570 | 560 |
| 42 | 720 | 710 | 690 | 670 | 650 | 630 | 620 | 600 | 590 | 580 | 560 | 540 |
| 41 | 710 | 700 | 680 | 660 | 640 | 620 | 600 | 590 | 580 | 570 | 550 | 530 |
| 40 | 700 | 690 | 670 | 650 | 630 | 610 | 590 | 580 | 570 | 560 | 540 | 520 |
| 39 | 690 | 680 | 660 | 640 | 620 | 600 | 590 | 570 | 560 | 550 | 530 | 510 |
| 38 | 680 | 670 | 650 | 630 | 610 | 590 | 580 | 560 | 550 | 540 | 520 | 510 |
| 37 | 670 | 660 | 640 | 630 | 600 | 580 | 570 | 550 | 540 | 530 | 510 | 500 |
| 36 | 670 | 650 | 630 | 620 | 600 | 580 | 560 | 540 | 530 | 520 | 510 | 490 |
| 35 | 660 | 640 | 630 | 610 | 590 | 570 | 550 | 540 | 530 | 510 | 500 | 480 |
| 34 | 650 | 640 | 620 | 600 | 580 | 560 | 540 | 530 | 520 | 500 | 490 | 470 |
| 33 | 640 | 630 | 610 | 590 | 570 | 550 | 540 | 520 | 510 | 500 | 480 | 460 |
| 32 | 630 | 620 | 600 | 590 | 560 | 540 | 530 | 510 | 500 | 490 | 480 | 460 |
| 31 | 630 | 610 | 590 | 580 | 560 | 540 | 520 | 510 | 500 | 480 | 470 | 450 |
| 30 | 620 | 610 | 590 | 570 | 550 | 530 | 510 | 500 | 490 | 480 | 460 | 440 |
| 29 | 610 | 600 | 580 | 560 | 540 | 520 | 510 | 490 | 480 | 470 | 450 | 440 |
| 28 | 600 | 590 | 570 | 560 | 540 | 510 | 500 | 480 | 470 | 460 | 450 | 430 |
| 27 | 600 | 580 | 570 | 550 | 530 | 510 | 490 | 480 | 470 | 450 | 440 | 420 |
| 26 | 590 | 580 | 560 | 540 | 520 | 500 | 480 | 470 | 460 | 450 | 430 | 410 |
| 25 | 580 | 570 | 550 | 530 | 510 | 490 | 480 | 460 | 450 | 440 | 420 | 410 |
| 24 | 580 | 560 | 540 | 530 | 510 | 490 | 470 | 450 | 440 | 430 | 420 | 400 |
| 23 | 570 | 550 | 540 | 520 | 500 | 480 | 460 | 450 | 440 | 420 | 410 | 390 |
| 22 | 560 | 550 | 530 | 510 | 490 | 470 | 460 | 440 | 430 | 420 | 400 | 380 |
| 21 | 550 | 540 | 520 | 510 | 480 | 460 | 450 | 430 | 420 | 410 | 400 | 380 |
| 20 | 550 | 530 | 510 | 500 | 480 | 460 | 440 | 430 | 420 | 400 | 390 | 370 |
| 19 | 540 | 530 | 510 | 490 | 470 | 450 | 430 | 420 | 410 | 400 | 380 | 360 |
| 18 | 530 | 520 | 500 | 480 | 460 | 440 | 430 | 410 | 400 | 390 | 370 | 360 |
| 17 | 520 | 510 | 490 | 480 | 460 | 430 | 420 | 400 | 390 | 380 | 370 | 350 |
| 16 | 520 | 500 | 490 | 470 | 450 | 430 | 410 | 400 | 390 | 370 | 360 | 340 |
| 15 | 510 | 500 | 480 | 460 | 440 | 420 | 400 | 390 | 380 | 370 | 350 | 330 |
| 14 | 500 | 490 | 470 | 450 | 430 | 410 | 400 | 380 | 370 | 360 | 340 | 330 |
| 13 | 500 | 480 | 460 | 450 | 430 | 410 | 390 | 370 | 360 | 350 | 340 | 320 |
| 12 | 490 | 470 | 460 | 440 | 420 | 400 | 380 | 370 | 360 | 340 | 330 | 310 |
| 11 | 480 | 470 | 450 | 430 | 410 | 390 | 370 | 360 | 350 | 340 | 320 | 300 |
| 10 | 470 | 460 | 440 | 420 | 400 | 380 | 370 | 350 | 340 | 330 | 310 | 300 |
| 9 | 460 | 450 | 430 | 420 | 390 | 370 | 360 | 340 | 330 | 320 | 310 | 290 |
| 8 | 460 | 440 | 420 | 410 | 390 | 370 | 350 | 330 | 320 | 310 | 300 | 280 |
| 7 | 450 | 430 | 420 | 400 | 380 | 360 | 340 | 330 | 320 | 300 | 290 | 270 |
| 6 | 440 | 420 | 410 | 390 | 370 | 350 | 330 | 320 | 310 | 290 | 280 | 260 |
| 5 | 430 | 420 | 400 | 380 | 360 | 340 | 320 | 310 | 300 | 280 | 270 | 250 |
| 4 | 420 | 400 | 390 | 370 | 350 | 330 | 310 | 300 | 290 | 270 | 260 | 240 |
| 3 | 410 | 390 | 380 | 360 | 340 | 320 | 300 | 290 | 280 | 260 | 250 | 230 |
| 2 | 400 | 380 | 360 | 350 | 330 | 310 | 290 | 270 | 260 | 250 | 240 | 220 |
| 1 | 380 | 370 | 350 | 330 | 310 | 290 | 280 | 260 | 250 | 240 | 220 | 200 |
| 0 | 370 | 350 | 330 | 320 | 300 | 280 | 260 | 240 | 230 | 220 | 210 | 200 |
| -1 | 350 | 330 | 320 | 300 | 280 | 260 | 240 | 230 | 220 | 200 | 200 | 200 |
| -2 | 330 | 320 | 300 | 280 | 260 | 240 | 230 | 210 | 200 | 200 | 200 | 200 |
| -3 and below | 310 | 300 | 280 | 260 | 240 | 220 | 210 | 200 | 200 | 200 | 200 | 200 |

## Table 4. Writing Multiple-Choice Conversion Table

| Raw Score | Scaled Score | Raw Score | Scaled Score |
|---|---|---|---|
| 49 | 80 | 22 | 47 |
| 48 | 78 | 21 | 46 |
| 47 | 75 | 20 | 45 |
| 46 | 73 | 19 | 45 |
| 45 | 71 | 18 | 44 |
| 44 | 69 | 17 | 43 |
| 43 | 68 | 16 | 42 |
| 42 | 66 | 15 | 41 |
| 41 | 65 | 14 | 40 |
| 40 | 64 | 13 | 39 |
| 39 | 63 | 12 | 38 |
| 38 | 62 | 11 | 37 |
| 37 | 61 | 10 | 36 |
| 36 | 60 | 9 | 35 |
| 35 | 59 | 8 | 34 |
| 34 | 58 | 7 | 33 |
| 33 | 57 | 6 | 32 |
| 32 | 56 | 5 | 31 |
| 31 | 55 | 4 | 30 |
| 30 | 54 | 3 | 29 |
| 29 | 53 | 2 | 27 |
| 28 | 52 | 1 | 25 |
| 27 | 52 | 0 | 24 |
| 26 | 51 | -1 | 22 |
| 25 | 50 | -2 and below | 20 |
| 24 | 49 | | |
| 23 | 48 | | |

# SAT Practice Test #4

 **After this test:**

- Use this book to its full potential! Get exclusive access answer explanations, free practice score reports and free sample student essays to help you score your essay in the Book Owners' Area at www.collegeboard.org/satstudyguide.

- Want more practice? Get 10 more official practice tests, auto essay scoring and lesson plans from the test maker by subscribing to *The Official SAT Online Course*. As a book owner, you're entitled to a $10 discount. Sign up at www.collegeboard.org/satstudyguide.

*Note:* Section 4, the variable section, has been omitted from this practice test.

# SAT Reasoning Test — General Directions

### Timing

- You will have 3 hours and 45 minutes to work on this test.
- There are ten separately timed sections:
  - ► One 25-minute essay
  - ► Six other 25-minute sections
  - ► Two 20-minute sections
  - ► One 10-minute section
- You may work on only one section at a time.
- The supervisor will tell you when to begin and end each section.
- If you finish a section before time is called, check your work on that section. You may NOT turn to any other section.
- Work as rapidly as you can without losing accuracy. Don't waste time on questions that seem too difficult for you.

### Marking Answers

- Be sure to mark your answer sheet properly.

COMPLETE MARK ●    EXAMPLES OF INCOMPLETE MARKS

- You must use a No. 2 pencil.
- Carefully mark only one answer for each question.
- Make sure you fill the entire circle darkly and completely.
- Do not make any stray marks on your answer sheet.
- If you erase, do so completely. Incomplete erasures may be scored as intended answers.
- Use only the answer spaces that correspond to the question numbers.

### Using Your Test Book

- You may use the test book for scratchwork, but you will not receive credit for anything written there.
- After time has been called, you may not transfer answers to your answer sheet or fill in circles.
- You may not fold or remove pages or portions of a page from this book, or take the book or answer sheet from the testing room.

### Scoring

- For each correct answer, you receive one point.
- For questions you omit, you receive no points.
- For a wrong answer to a multiple-choice question, you lose one-fourth of a point.
  - ► If you can eliminate one or more of the answer choices as wrong, you increase your chances of choosing the correct answer and earning one point.
  - ► If you can't eliminate any choice, move on. You can return to the question later if there is time.
- For a wrong answer to a student-produced response ("grid-in") math question, you don't lose any points.
- Multiple-choice and student-produced response questions are machine scored.
- The essay is scored on a 1 to 6 scale by two different readers. The total essay score is the sum of the two readers' scores.
- Off-topic essays, blank essays, and essays written in ink will receive a score of zero.

IMPORTANT: The codes below are unique to your test book. Copy them on your answer sheet in boxes 8 and 9 and fill in the corresponding circles exactly as shown.

**9   TEST FORM**
(Copy from back of test book.)

**8   FORM CODE**
(Copy and grid as on back of test book.)

The passages for this test have been adapted from published material.
The ideas contained in them do not necessarily represent the opinions of the College Board.

## DO NOT OPEN THIS BOOK UNTIL THE SUPERVISOR TELLS YOU TO DO SO.

**CollegeBoard** SAT

# SAT Reasoning Test™

*You must use a No. 2 pencil. Do not use a mechanical pencil. It is very important that you fill in the entire circle darkly and completely. If you change your response, erase as completely as possible. Incomplete marks or erasures may affect your score. It is very important that you follow these instructions when filling out your answer sheet.*

**1** | **Your Name:**
(Print)

Last _____ First _____ M.I. _____

I agree to the conditions on the back of the SAT Reasoning Test™ booklet. I also agree to use only a No. 2 pencil to complete my answer sheet.

Signature: _____ Date: __ / __ / __

**Home Address:**
(Print)
Number and Street _____ City _____ State _____ Zip Code

**Home Phone:** ( ) _____ **Center:**
(Print)
(Print) _____ City _____ State/Country

**2 YOUR NAME**

Last Name (First 6 Letters) | First Name (First 4 Letters) | Mid. Init.

**3 DATE OF BIRTH**

| MONTH | DAY | YEAR |
|---|---|---|
| Jan | | |
| Feb | 0 0 | 0 |
| Mar | 1 1 | 1 |
| Apr | 2 2 | 2 |
| May | 3 3 | 3 |
| Jun | 4 | 4 |
| Jul | 5 5 | 5 |
| Aug | 6 6 | 6 |
| Sep | 7 7 | 7 |
| Oct | 8 8 | 8 |
| Nov | 9 9 | 9 |
| Dec | | |

**5 SEX**

◯ Female ◯ Male

**6 REGISTRATION NUMBER**
(Copy from Admission Ticket.)

◯ I turned in my registration form today.

**Important:** Fill in items 8 and 9 exactly as shown on the back of test book.

**8 FORM CODE**
(Copy and grid as on back of test book.)

**9 TEST FORM**
(Copy from back of test book.)

**10 TEST BOOK SERIAL NUMBER**
(Copy from front of test book.)

**4 ZIP CODE**

**7 SOCIAL SECURITY NUMBER**

**11 TEST CENTER**
(Supplied by Test Center Supervisor.)

**FOR OFFICIAL USE ONLY**
0 1 2 3 4 5 6
0 1 2 3 4 5 6
0 1 2 3 4 5 6

00272-36390 • NS75E4600 • Printed in U.S.A.
732652

**PLEASE DO NOT WRITE IN THIS AREA**

**SERIAL #**

567

**SECTION 1**

*IMPORTANT:* **USE A NO. 2 PENCIL. DO NOT WRITE OUTSIDE THE BORDER!**
Words written outside the essay box or written in ink **WILL NOT APPEAR** in the copy sent to be scored, and your score will be affected.

**Begin your essay on this page. If you need more space, continue on the next page.**

4

Page 2                                                      Continue on the next page, if necessary.

Page 3

SERIAL #

4

## SECTION 2

1 Ⓐ Ⓑ Ⓒ Ⓓ Ⓔ
2 Ⓐ Ⓑ Ⓒ Ⓓ Ⓔ
3 Ⓐ Ⓑ Ⓒ Ⓓ Ⓔ
4 Ⓐ Ⓑ Ⓒ Ⓓ Ⓔ
5 Ⓐ Ⓑ Ⓒ Ⓓ Ⓔ
6 Ⓐ Ⓑ Ⓒ Ⓓ Ⓔ
7 Ⓐ Ⓑ Ⓒ Ⓓ Ⓔ
8 Ⓐ Ⓑ Ⓒ Ⓓ Ⓔ
9 Ⓐ Ⓑ Ⓒ Ⓓ Ⓔ
10 Ⓐ Ⓑ Ⓒ Ⓓ Ⓔ

11 Ⓐ Ⓑ Ⓒ Ⓓ Ⓔ
12 Ⓐ Ⓑ Ⓒ Ⓓ Ⓔ
13 Ⓐ Ⓑ Ⓒ Ⓓ Ⓔ
14 Ⓐ Ⓑ Ⓒ Ⓓ Ⓔ
15 Ⓐ Ⓑ Ⓒ Ⓓ Ⓔ
16 Ⓐ Ⓑ Ⓒ Ⓓ Ⓔ
17 Ⓐ Ⓑ Ⓒ Ⓓ Ⓔ
18 Ⓐ Ⓑ Ⓒ Ⓓ Ⓔ
19 Ⓐ Ⓑ Ⓒ Ⓓ Ⓔ
20 Ⓐ Ⓑ Ⓒ Ⓓ Ⓔ

21 Ⓐ Ⓑ Ⓒ Ⓓ Ⓔ
22 Ⓐ Ⓑ Ⓒ Ⓓ Ⓔ
23 Ⓐ Ⓑ Ⓒ Ⓓ Ⓔ
24 Ⓐ Ⓑ Ⓒ Ⓓ Ⓔ
25 Ⓐ Ⓑ Ⓒ Ⓓ Ⓔ
26 Ⓐ Ⓑ Ⓒ Ⓓ Ⓔ
27 Ⓐ Ⓑ Ⓒ Ⓓ Ⓔ
28 Ⓐ Ⓑ Ⓒ Ⓓ Ⓔ
29 Ⓐ Ⓑ Ⓒ Ⓓ Ⓔ
30 Ⓐ Ⓑ Ⓒ Ⓓ Ⓔ

31 Ⓐ Ⓑ Ⓒ Ⓓ Ⓔ
32 Ⓐ Ⓑ Ⓒ Ⓓ Ⓔ
33 Ⓐ Ⓑ Ⓒ Ⓓ Ⓔ
34 Ⓐ Ⓑ Ⓒ Ⓓ Ⓔ
35 Ⓐ Ⓑ Ⓒ Ⓓ Ⓔ
36 Ⓐ Ⓑ Ⓒ Ⓓ Ⓔ
37 Ⓐ Ⓑ Ⓒ Ⓓ Ⓔ
38 Ⓐ Ⓑ Ⓒ Ⓓ Ⓔ
39 Ⓐ Ⓑ Ⓒ Ⓓ Ⓔ
40 Ⓐ Ⓑ Ⓒ Ⓓ Ⓔ

## SECTION 3

(1–40, Ⓐ Ⓑ Ⓒ Ⓓ Ⓔ)

**CAUTION** Grid answers in the section below for SECTION 2 or SECTION 3 only if directed to do so in your test book.

### Student-Produced Responses

ONLY ANSWERS THAT ARE GRIDDED WILL BE SCORED. YOU WILL NOT RECEIVE CREDIT FOR ANYTHING WRITTEN IN THE BOXES.

Quality Assurance Mark

(Grid-in response boxes numbered 9–18)

Page 4

570

**SECTION 4**

| | | | |
|---|---|---|---|
| 1 ⒶⒷⒸⒹⒺ | 11 ⒶⒷⒸⒹⒺ | 21 ⒶⒷⒸⒹⒺ | 31 ⒶⒷⒸⒹⒺ |
| 2 ⒶⒷⒸⒹⒺ | 12 ⒶⒷⒸⒹⒺ | 22 ⒶⒷⒸⒹⒺ | 32 ⒶⒷⒸⒹⒺ |
| 3 ⒶⒷⒸⒹⒺ | 13 ⒶⒷⒸⒹⒺ | 23 ⒶⒷⒸⒹⒺ | 33 ⒶⒷⒸⒹⒺ |
| 4 ⒶⒷⒸⒹⒺ | 14 ⒶⒷⒸⒹⒺ | 24 ⒶⒷⒸⒹⒺ | 34 ⒶⒷⒸⒹⒺ |
| 5 ⒶⒷⒸⒹⒺ | 15 ⒶⒷⒸⒹⒺ | 25 ⒶⒷⒸⒹⒺ | 35 ⒶⒷⒸⒹⒺ |
| 6 ⒶⒷⒸⒹⒺ | 16 ⒶⒷⒸⒹⒺ | 26 ⒶⒷⒸⒹⒺ | 36 ⒶⒷⒸⒹⒺ |
| 7 ⒶⒷⒸⒹⒺ | 17 ⒶⒷⒸⒹⒺ | 27 ⒶⒷⒸⒹⒺ | 37 ⒶⒷⒸⒹⒺ |
| 8 ⒶⒷⒸⒹⒺ | 18 ⒶⒷⒸⒹⒺ | 28 ⒶⒷⒸⒹⒺ | 38 ⒶⒷⒸⒹⒺ |
| 9 ⒶⒷⒸⒹⒺ | 19 ⒶⒷⒸⒹⒺ | 29 ⒶⒷⒸⒹⒺ | 39 ⒶⒷⒸⒹⒺ |
| 10 ⒶⒷⒸⒹⒺ | 20 ⒶⒷⒸⒹⒺ | 30 ⒶⒷⒸⒹⒺ | 40 ⒶⒷⒸⒹⒺ |

**SECTION 5**

| | | | |
|---|---|---|---|
| 1 ⒶⒷⒸⒹⒺ | 11 ⒶⒷⒸⒹⒺ | 21 ⒶⒷⒸⒹⒺ | 31 ⒶⒷⒸⒹⒺ |
| 2 ⒶⒷⒸⒹⒺ | 12 ⒶⒷⒸⒹⒺ | 22 ⒶⒷⒸⒹⒺ | 32 ⒶⒷⒸⒹⒺ |
| 3 ⒶⒷⒸⒹⒺ | 13 ⒶⒷⒸⒹⒺ | 23 ⒶⒷⒸⒹⒺ | 33 ⒶⒷⒸⒹⒺ |
| 4 ⒶⒷⒸⒹⒺ | 14 ⒶⒷⒸⒹⒺ | 24 ⒶⒷⒸⒹⒺ | 34 ⒶⒷⒸⒹⒺ |
| 5 ⒶⒷⒸⒹⒺ | 15 ⒶⒷⒸⒹⒺ | 25 ⒶⒷⒸⒹⒺ | 35 ⒶⒷⒸⒹⒺ |
| 6 ⒶⒷⒸⒹⒺ | 16 ⒶⒷⒸⒹⒺ | 26 ⒶⒷⒸⒹⒺ | 36 ⒶⒷⒸⒹⒺ |
| 7 ⒶⒷⒸⒹⒺ | 17 ⒶⒷⒸⒹⒺ | 27 ⒶⒷⒸⒹⒺ | 37 ⒶⒷⒸⒹⒺ |
| 8 ⒶⒷⒸⒹⒺ | 18 ⒶⒷⒸⒹⒺ | 28 ⒶⒷⒸⒹⒺ | 38 ⒶⒷⒸⒹⒺ |
| 9 ⒶⒷⒸⒹⒺ | 19 ⒶⒷⒸⒹⒺ | 29 ⒶⒷⒸⒹⒺ | 39 ⒶⒷⒸⒹⒺ |
| 10 ⒶⒷⒸⒹⒺ | 20 ⒶⒷⒸⒹⒺ | 30 ⒶⒷⒸⒹⒺ | 40 ⒶⒷⒸⒹⒺ |

**CAUTION**    Grid answers in the section below for SECTION 4 or SECTION 5 only if directed to do so in your test book.

**Student-Produced Responses**    ONLY ANSWERS THAT ARE GRIDDED WILL BE SCORED. YOU WILL NOT RECEIVE CREDIT FOR ANYTHING WRITTEN IN THE BOXES.

Quality Assurance Mark ●

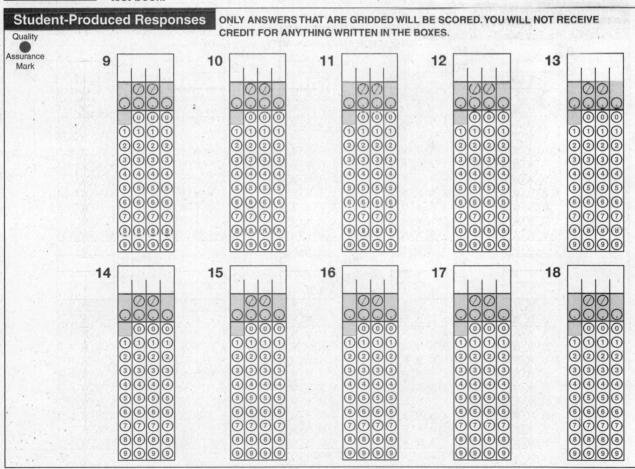

**SECTION 6**

| 1 Ⓐ Ⓑ Ⓒ Ⓓ Ⓔ | 11 Ⓐ Ⓑ Ⓒ Ⓓ Ⓔ | 21 Ⓐ Ⓑ Ⓒ Ⓓ Ⓔ | 31 Ⓐ Ⓑ Ⓒ Ⓓ Ⓔ |
| 2 Ⓐ Ⓑ Ⓒ Ⓓ Ⓔ | 12 Ⓐ Ⓑ Ⓒ Ⓓ Ⓔ | 22 Ⓐ Ⓑ Ⓒ Ⓓ Ⓔ | 32 Ⓐ Ⓑ Ⓒ Ⓓ Ⓔ |
| 3 Ⓐ Ⓑ Ⓒ Ⓓ Ⓔ | 13 Ⓐ Ⓑ Ⓒ Ⓓ Ⓔ | 23 Ⓐ Ⓑ Ⓒ Ⓓ Ⓔ | 33 Ⓐ Ⓑ Ⓒ Ⓓ Ⓔ |
| 4 Ⓐ Ⓑ Ⓒ Ⓓ Ⓔ | 14 Ⓐ Ⓑ Ⓒ Ⓓ Ⓔ | 24 Ⓐ Ⓑ Ⓒ Ⓓ Ⓔ | 34 Ⓐ Ⓑ Ⓒ Ⓓ Ⓔ |
| 5 Ⓐ Ⓑ Ⓒ Ⓓ Ⓔ | 15 Ⓐ Ⓑ Ⓒ Ⓓ Ⓔ | 25 Ⓐ Ⓑ Ⓒ Ⓓ Ⓔ | 35 Ⓐ Ⓑ Ⓒ Ⓓ Ⓔ |
| 6 Ⓐ Ⓑ Ⓒ Ⓓ Ⓔ | 16 Ⓐ Ⓑ Ⓒ Ⓓ Ⓔ | 26 Ⓐ Ⓑ Ⓒ Ⓓ Ⓔ | 36 Ⓐ Ⓑ Ⓒ Ⓓ Ⓔ |
| 7 Ⓐ Ⓑ Ⓒ Ⓓ Ⓔ | 17 Ⓐ Ⓑ Ⓒ Ⓓ Ⓔ | 27 Ⓐ Ⓑ Ⓒ Ⓓ Ⓔ | 37 Ⓐ Ⓑ Ⓒ Ⓓ Ⓔ |
| 8 Ⓐ Ⓑ Ⓒ Ⓓ Ⓔ | 18 Ⓐ Ⓑ Ⓒ Ⓓ Ⓔ | 28 Ⓐ Ⓑ Ⓒ Ⓓ Ⓔ | 38 Ⓐ Ⓑ Ⓒ Ⓓ Ⓔ |
| 9 Ⓐ Ⓑ Ⓒ Ⓓ Ⓔ | 19 Ⓐ Ⓑ Ⓒ Ⓓ Ⓔ | 29 Ⓐ Ⓑ Ⓒ Ⓓ Ⓔ | 39 Ⓐ Ⓑ Ⓒ Ⓓ Ⓔ |
| 10 Ⓐ Ⓑ Ⓒ Ⓓ Ⓔ | 20 Ⓐ Ⓑ Ⓒ Ⓓ Ⓔ | 30 Ⓐ Ⓑ Ⓒ Ⓓ Ⓔ | 40 Ⓐ Ⓑ Ⓒ Ⓓ Ⓔ |

**SECTION 7**

| 1 Ⓐ Ⓑ Ⓒ Ⓓ Ⓔ | 11 Ⓐ Ⓑ Ⓒ Ⓓ Ⓔ | 21 Ⓐ Ⓑ Ⓒ Ⓓ Ⓔ | 31 Ⓐ Ⓑ Ⓒ Ⓓ Ⓔ |
| 2 Ⓐ Ⓑ Ⓒ Ⓓ Ⓔ | 12 Ⓐ Ⓑ Ⓒ Ⓓ Ⓔ | 22 Ⓐ Ⓑ Ⓒ Ⓓ Ⓔ | 32 Ⓐ Ⓑ Ⓒ Ⓓ Ⓔ |
| 3 Ⓐ Ⓑ Ⓒ Ⓓ Ⓔ | 13 Ⓐ Ⓑ Ⓒ Ⓓ Ⓔ | 23 Ⓐ Ⓑ Ⓒ Ⓓ Ⓔ | 33 Ⓐ Ⓑ Ⓒ Ⓓ Ⓔ |
| 4 Ⓐ Ⓑ Ⓒ Ⓓ Ⓔ | 14 Ⓐ Ⓑ Ⓒ Ⓓ Ⓔ | 24 Ⓐ Ⓑ Ⓒ Ⓓ Ⓔ | 34 Ⓐ Ⓑ Ⓒ Ⓓ Ⓔ |
| 5 Ⓐ Ⓑ Ⓒ Ⓓ Ⓔ | 15 Ⓐ Ⓑ Ⓒ Ⓓ Ⓔ | 25 Ⓐ Ⓑ Ⓒ Ⓓ Ⓔ | 35 Ⓐ Ⓑ Ⓒ Ⓓ Ⓔ |
| 6 Ⓐ Ⓑ Ⓒ Ⓓ Ⓔ | 16 Ⓐ Ⓑ Ⓒ Ⓓ Ⓔ | 26 Ⓐ Ⓑ Ⓒ Ⓓ Ⓔ | 36 Ⓐ Ⓑ Ⓒ Ⓓ Ⓔ |
| 7 Ⓐ Ⓑ Ⓒ Ⓓ Ⓔ | 17 Ⓐ Ⓑ Ⓒ Ⓓ Ⓔ | 27 Ⓐ Ⓑ Ⓒ Ⓓ Ⓔ | 37 Ⓐ Ⓑ Ⓒ Ⓓ Ⓔ |
| 8 Ⓐ Ⓑ Ⓒ Ⓓ Ⓔ | 18 Ⓐ Ⓑ Ⓒ Ⓓ Ⓔ | 28 Ⓐ Ⓑ Ⓒ Ⓓ Ⓔ | 38 Ⓐ Ⓑ Ⓒ Ⓓ Ⓔ |
| 9 Ⓐ Ⓑ Ⓒ Ⓓ Ⓔ | 19 Ⓐ Ⓑ Ⓒ Ⓓ Ⓔ | 29 Ⓐ Ⓑ Ⓒ Ⓓ Ⓔ | 39 Ⓐ Ⓑ Ⓒ Ⓓ Ⓔ |
| 10 Ⓐ Ⓑ Ⓒ Ⓓ Ⓔ | 20 Ⓐ Ⓑ Ⓒ Ⓓ Ⓔ | 30 Ⓐ Ⓑ Ⓒ Ⓓ Ⓔ | 40 Ⓐ Ⓑ Ⓒ Ⓓ Ⓔ |

**CAUTION** Grid answers in the section below for SECTION 6 or SECTION 7 only if directed to do so in your test book.

**Student-Produced Responses** ONLY ANSWERS THAT ARE GRIDDED WILL BE SCORED. YOU WILL NOT RECEIVE CREDIT FOR ANYTHING WRITTEN IN THE BOXES.

9   10   11   12   13

Quality Assurance Mark

14   15   16   17   18

Page 6

PLEASE DO NOT WRITE IN THIS AREA

SERIAL #

572

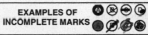

| COMPLETE MARK ● | EXAMPLES OF INCOMPLETE MARKS | You must use a No. 2 pencil and marks must be complete. Do not use a mechanical pencil. It is very important that you fill in the entire circle darkly and completely. If you change your response, erase as completely as possible. Incomplete marks or erasures may affect your score. |

**SECTION 8**

1 Ⓐ Ⓑ Ⓒ Ⓓ Ⓔ   11 Ⓐ Ⓑ Ⓒ Ⓓ Ⓔ   21 Ⓐ Ⓑ Ⓒ Ⓓ Ⓔ   31 Ⓐ Ⓑ Ⓒ Ⓓ Ⓔ
2 Ⓐ Ⓑ Ⓒ Ⓓ Ⓔ   12 Ⓐ Ⓑ Ⓒ Ⓓ Ⓔ   22 Ⓐ Ⓑ Ⓒ Ⓓ Ⓔ   32 Ⓐ Ⓑ Ⓒ Ⓓ Ⓔ
3 Ⓐ Ⓑ Ⓒ Ⓓ Ⓔ   13 Ⓐ Ⓑ Ⓒ Ⓓ Ⓔ   23 Ⓐ Ⓑ Ⓒ Ⓓ Ⓔ   33 Ⓐ Ⓑ Ⓒ Ⓓ Ⓔ
4 Ⓐ Ⓑ Ⓒ Ⓓ Ⓔ   14 Ⓐ Ⓑ Ⓒ Ⓓ Ⓔ   24 Ⓐ Ⓑ Ⓒ Ⓓ Ⓔ   34 Ⓐ Ⓑ Ⓒ Ⓓ Ⓔ
5 Ⓐ Ⓑ Ⓒ Ⓓ Ⓔ   15 Ⓐ Ⓑ Ⓒ Ⓓ Ⓔ   25 Ⓐ Ⓑ Ⓒ Ⓓ Ⓔ   35 Ⓐ Ⓑ Ⓒ Ⓓ Ⓔ
6 Ⓐ Ⓑ Ⓒ Ⓓ Ⓔ   16 Ⓐ Ⓑ Ⓒ Ⓓ Ⓔ   26 Ⓐ Ⓑ Ⓒ Ⓓ Ⓔ   36 Ⓐ Ⓑ Ⓒ Ⓓ Ⓔ
7 Ⓐ Ⓑ Ⓒ Ⓓ Ⓔ   17 Ⓐ Ⓑ Ⓒ Ⓓ Ⓔ   27 Ⓐ Ⓑ Ⓒ Ⓓ Ⓔ   37 Ⓐ Ⓑ Ⓒ Ⓓ Ⓔ
8 Ⓐ Ⓑ Ⓒ Ⓓ Ⓔ   18 Ⓐ Ⓑ Ⓒ Ⓓ Ⓔ   28 Ⓐ Ⓑ Ⓒ Ⓓ Ⓔ   38 Ⓐ Ⓑ Ⓒ Ⓓ Ⓔ
9 Ⓐ Ⓑ Ⓒ Ⓓ Ⓔ   19 Ⓐ Ⓑ Ⓒ Ⓓ Ⓔ   29 Ⓐ Ⓑ Ⓒ Ⓓ Ⓔ   39 Ⓐ Ⓑ Ⓒ Ⓓ Ⓔ
10 Ⓐ Ⓑ Ⓒ Ⓓ Ⓔ   20 Ⓐ Ⓑ Ⓒ Ⓓ Ⓔ   30 Ⓐ Ⓑ Ⓒ Ⓓ Ⓔ   40 Ⓐ Ⓑ Ⓒ Ⓓ Ⓔ

**SECTION 9**

1 Ⓐ Ⓑ Ⓒ Ⓓ Ⓔ   11 Ⓐ Ⓑ Ⓒ Ⓓ Ⓔ   21 Ⓐ Ⓑ Ⓒ Ⓓ Ⓔ   31 Ⓐ Ⓑ Ⓒ Ⓓ Ⓔ
2 Ⓐ Ⓑ Ⓒ Ⓓ Ⓔ   12 Ⓐ Ⓑ Ⓒ Ⓓ Ⓔ   22 Ⓐ Ⓑ Ⓒ Ⓓ Ⓕ   32 Ⓐ Ⓑ Ⓒ Ⓓ Ⓔ
3 Ⓐ Ⓑ Ⓒ Ⓓ Ⓔ   13 Ⓐ Ⓑ Ⓒ Ⓓ Ⓔ   23 Ⓐ Ⓑ Ⓒ Ⓓ Ⓔ   33 Ⓐ Ⓑ Ⓒ Ⓓ Ⓔ
4 Ⓐ Ⓑ Ⓒ Ⓓ Ⓔ   14 Ⓐ Ⓑ Ⓒ Ⓓ Ⓔ   24 Ⓐ Ⓑ Ⓒ Ⓓ Ⓔ   34 Ⓐ Ⓑ Ⓒ Ⓓ Ⓔ
5 Ⓐ Ⓑ Ⓒ Ⓓ Ⓔ   15 Ⓐ Ⓑ Ⓒ Ⓓ Ⓔ   25 Ⓐ Ⓑ Ⓒ Ⓓ Ⓔ   35 Ⓐ Ⓑ Ⓒ Ⓓ Ⓔ
6 Ⓐ Ⓑ Ⓒ Ⓓ Ⓕ   16 Ⓐ Ⓑ Ⓒ Ⓓ Ⓔ   26 Ⓐ Ⓑ Ⓒ Ⓓ Ⓔ   36 Ⓐ Ⓑ Ⓒ Ⓓ Ⓔ
7 Ⓐ Ⓑ Ⓒ Ⓓ Ⓔ   17 Ⓐ Ⓑ Ⓒ Ⓓ Ⓔ   27 Ⓐ Ⓑ Ⓒ Ⓓ Ⓔ   37 Ⓐ Ⓑ Ⓒ Ⓓ Ⓔ
8 Ⓐ Ⓑ Ⓒ Ⓓ Ⓔ   18 Ⓐ Ⓑ Ⓒ Ⓓ Ⓔ   28 Ⓐ Ⓑ Ⓒ Ⓓ Ⓔ   38 Ⓐ Ⓑ Ⓒ Ⓓ Ⓔ
9 Ⓐ Ⓑ Ⓒ Ⓓ Ⓔ   19 Ⓐ Ⓑ Ⓒ Ⓓ Ⓔ   29 Ⓐ Ⓑ Ⓒ Ⓓ Ⓔ   39 Ⓐ Ⓑ Ⓒ Ⓓ Ⓔ
10 Ⓐ Ⓑ Ⓒ Ⓓ Ⓔ   20 Ⓐ Ⓑ Ⓒ Ⓓ Ⓔ   30 Ⓐ Ⓑ Ⓒ Ⓓ Ⓔ   40 Ⓐ Ⓑ Ⓒ Ⓓ Ⓔ

Quality
●
Assurance
Mark

**SECTION 10**

1 Ⓐ Ⓑ Ⓒ Ⓓ Ⓔ   11 Ⓐ Ⓑ Ⓒ Ⓓ Ⓔ   21 Ⓐ Ⓑ Ⓒ Ⓓ Ⓔ   31 Ⓐ Ⓑ Ⓒ Ⓓ Ⓔ
2 Ⓐ Ⓑ Ⓒ Ⓓ Ⓔ   12 Ⓐ Ⓑ Ⓒ Ⓓ Ⓔ   22 Ⓐ Ⓑ Ⓒ Ⓓ Ⓔ   32 Ⓐ Ⓑ Ⓒ Ⓓ Ⓔ
3 Ⓐ Ⓑ Ⓒ Ⓓ Ⓔ   13 Ⓐ Ⓑ Ⓒ Ⓓ Ⓔ   23 Ⓐ Ⓑ Ⓒ Ⓓ Ⓔ   33 Ⓐ Ⓑ Ⓒ Ⓓ Ⓔ
4 Ⓐ Ⓑ Ⓒ Ⓓ Ⓔ   14 Ⓐ Ⓑ Ⓒ Ⓓ Ⓔ   24 Ⓐ Ⓑ Ⓒ Ⓓ Ⓔ   34 Ⓐ Ⓑ Ⓒ Ⓓ Ⓔ
5 Ⓐ Ⓑ Ⓒ Ⓓ Ⓔ   15 Ⓐ Ⓑ Ⓒ Ⓓ Ⓔ   25 Ⓐ Ⓑ Ⓒ Ⓓ Ⓔ   35 Ⓐ Ⓑ Ⓒ Ⓓ Ⓔ
6 Ⓐ Ⓑ Ⓒ Ⓓ Ⓔ   16 Ⓐ Ⓑ Ⓒ Ⓓ Ⓔ   26 Ⓐ Ⓑ Ⓒ Ⓓ Ⓔ   36 Ⓐ Ⓑ Ⓒ Ⓓ Ⓔ
7 Ⓐ Ⓑ Ⓒ Ⓓ Ⓔ   17 Ⓐ Ⓑ Ⓒ Ⓓ Ⓔ   27 Ⓐ Ⓑ Ⓒ Ⓓ Ⓔ   37 Ⓐ Ⓑ Ⓒ Ⓓ Ⓔ
8 Ⓐ Ⓑ Ⓒ Ⓓ Ⓔ   18 Ⓐ Ⓑ Ⓒ Ⓓ Ⓔ   28 Ⓐ Ⓑ Ⓒ Ⓓ Ⓔ   38 Ⓐ Ⓑ Ⓒ Ⓓ Ⓔ
9 Ⓐ Ⓑ Ⓒ Ⓓ Ⓔ   19 Ⓐ Ⓑ Ⓒ Ⓓ Ⓔ   29 Ⓐ Ⓑ Ⓒ Ⓓ Ⓔ   39 Ⓐ Ⓑ Ⓒ Ⓓ Ⓔ
10 Ⓐ Ⓑ Ⓒ Ⓓ Ⓔ   20 Ⓐ Ⓑ Ⓒ Ⓓ Ⓔ   30 Ⓐ Ⓑ Ⓒ Ⓓ Ⓔ   40 Ⓐ Ⓑ Ⓒ Ⓓ Ⓔ

4

## CERTIFICATION STATEMENT

Copy the statement below (do not print) and sign your name as you would an official document.

I hereby agree to the conditions set forth online at www.collegeboard.org and/or in the SAT® Registration Booklet and certify that I am the person whose name and address appear on this answer sheet.

_____

_____

_____

_____

By signing below, I agree not to share any specific test questions or essay topics with anyone by any form of communication, including, but not limited to: email, text messages, or use of the Internet.

Signature _____   Date _____

4

## SPECIAL QUESTIONS

1 Ⓐ Ⓑ Ⓒ Ⓓ Ⓔ Ⓕ Ⓖ Ⓗ Ⓘ Ⓙ
2 Ⓐ Ⓑ Ⓒ Ⓓ Ⓔ Ⓕ Ⓖ Ⓗ Ⓘ Ⓙ
3 Ⓐ Ⓑ Ⓒ Ⓓ Ⓔ Ⓕ Ⓖ Ⓗ Ⓘ Ⓙ
4 Ⓐ Ⓑ Ⓒ Ⓓ Ⓔ Ⓕ Ⓖ Ⓗ Ⓘ Ⓙ
5 Ⓐ Ⓑ Ⓒ Ⓓ Ⓔ Ⓕ Ⓖ Ⓗ Ⓘ Ⓙ
6 Ⓐ Ⓑ Ⓒ Ⓓ Ⓔ Ⓕ Ⓖ Ⓗ Ⓘ Ⓙ
7 Ⓐ Ⓑ Ⓒ Ⓓ Ⓔ Ⓕ Ⓖ Ⓗ Ⓘ Ⓙ
8 Ⓐ Ⓑ Ⓒ Ⓓ Ⓔ Ⓕ Ⓖ Ⓗ Ⓘ Ⓙ

**Page 8**

## ESSAY
### Time — 25 minutes

---

**Turn to page 2 of your answer sheet to write your ESSAY.**

---

The essay gives you an opportunity to show how effectively you can develop and express ideas. You should, therefore, take care to develop your point of view, present your ideas logically and clearly, and use language precisely.

Your essay must be written on the lines provided on your answer sheet—you will receive no other paper on which to write. You will have enough space if you write on every line, avoid wide margins, and keep your handwriting to a reasonable size. Remember that people who are not familiar with your handwriting will read what you write. Try to write or print so that what you are writing is legible to those readers.

**Important Reminders:**

- **A pencil is required for the essay.** An essay written in ink will receive a score of zero.
- **Do not write your essay in your test book.** You will receive credit only for what you write on your answer sheet.
- **An off-topic essay will receive a score of zero.**
- **If your essay does not reflect your original and individual work, your test scores may be canceled.**

You have twenty-five minutes to write an essay on the topic assigned below.

---

Think carefully about the issue presented in the following excerpt and the assignment below.

> Technology promises to make our lives easier, freeing up time for leisure pursuits. But the rapid pace of technological innovation and the split second processing capabilities of computers that can work virtually nonstop have made all of us feel rushed. We have adopted the relentless pace of the very machines that were supposed to simplify our lives, with the result that, whether at work or play, people do not feel like their lives have changed for the better.
>
> Adapted from Karen Finucan, "Life in the Fast Lane"

**Assignment:** Do changes that make our lives easier not necessarily make them better? Plan and write an essay in which you develop your point of view on this issue. Support your position with reasoning and examples taken from your reading, studies, experience, or observations.

---

BEGIN WRITING YOUR ESSAY ON PAGE 2 OF THE ANSWER SHEET.

**If you finish before time is called, you may check your work on this section only.
Do not turn to any other section in the test.**

## SECTION 2
Time — 25 minutes
24 Questions

**Turn to Section 2 (page 4) of your answer sheet to answer the questions in this section.**

**Directions:** For each question in this section, select the best answer from among the choices given and fill in the corresponding circle on the answer sheet.

---

Each sentence below has one or two blanks, each blank indicating that something has been omitted. Beneath the sentence are five words or sets of words labeled A through E. Choose the word or set of words that, when inserted in the sentence, best fits the meaning of the sentence as a whole.

**Example:**

Hoping to ------- the dispute, negotiators proposed a compromise that they felt would be ------- to both labor and management.

(A) enforce . . useful
(B) end . . divisive
(C) overcome . . unattractive
(D) extend . . satisfactory
(E) resolve . . acceptable

---

1. To avoid being -------, composer Stephen Sondheim strives for an element of surprise in his songs.

   (A) erratic (B) informal (C) elaborate
   (D) predictable (E) idiosyncratic

2. Because the pandas had already been weakened by disease and drought, a harsh winter would have had ------- consequences for them.

   (A) preventive (B) regressive (C) catastrophic
   (D) unforeseen (E) moderate

3. For many of the villagers, marriage was a practical -------, one not necessarily ------- of love but nevertheless grounded largely in economic advantage.

   (A) arrangement . . devoid
   (B) entertainment . . disparaging
   (C) attitude . . consisting
   (D) bargain . . worthy
   (E) misfortune . . trusting

4. Maggie is a procrastinator, naturally inclined to ------- and to ------- discussions.

   (A) meddle . . scoff at
   (B) temporize . . prolong
   (C) misbehave . . disrupt
   (D) sneer . . terminate
   (E) withdraw . . intrude in

5. Just as glass windows offer buildings both light and insulation, certain atmospheric gases ------- incoming sunlight and ------- heat radiated from the ground, preventing warmth from escaping.

   (A) conduct . . release
   (B) deflect . . transmit
   (C) admit . . contain
   (D) absorb . . dispense
   (E) resist . . trap

6. The speaker, praised for her style yet ridiculed for her vacuity, often moved naive listeners with ------- alone and led them to believe that her speech had -------.

   (A) reason . . dalliance
   (B) infelicity . . conviction
   (C) rhetoric . . substance
   (D) pragmatism . . futility
   (E) boorishness . . integrity

7. The actor was noted for his ------- behavior: he quickly became irritated if his every whim was not immediately satisfied.

   (A) fastidious (B) sedulous (C) vindictive
   (D) petulant (E) mercenary

8. Hayley Mills's films have been called -------, although most of them are not so sentimental as to deserve that description.

   (A) treacly (B) cursory (C) prosaic
   (D) meticulous (E) consecrated

---

**GO ON TO THE NEXT PAGE**

Unauthorized copying or reuse of
any part of this page is illegal.

The passages below are followed by questions based on their content; questions following a pair of related passages may also be based on the relationship between the paired passages. Answer the questions on the basis of what is <u>stated</u> or <u>implied</u> in the passages and in any introductory material that may be provided.

**Questions 9-10 are based on the following passage.**

That nineteenth-century French novelist Honoré
de Balzac could be financially wise in his fiction while
losing all his money in life was an irony duplicated in
other matters. For instance, the very women who had
*Line*
5 been drawn to him by the penetrating intuition of
the female heart that he showed in his novels were
appalled to discover how insensitive and awkward the
real man could be. It seems the true source of creation
for Balzac was not sensitivity but *imagination*. Balzac's
10 fiction originally sprang from an intuition he first discovered as a wretched little school boy locked in a dark
closet of his boarding school:  life is a prison, and only
imagination can open its doors.

9. The example in lines 4-8 primarily suggests that

(A) Balzac's work was not especially popular
  among female readers
(B) Balzac could not write convincingly about
  financial matters
(C) Balzac's insights into character were not
  evident in his everyday life
(D) people who knew Balzac personally could
  not respect him as an artist
(E) readers had unreasonable expectations
  of Balzac the man

10. The author mentions Balzac's experience as
a schoolboy in order to

(A) explain why Balzac was unable to conduct
  his financial affairs properly
(B) point out a possible source of Balzac's
  powerful imagination
(C) exonerate the boarding school for Balzac's
  lackluster performance
(D) foster the impression that Balzac was an
  unruly student
(E) depict the conditions of boarding school
  life during Balzac's youth

**Questions 11-12 are based on the following passage.**

Dr. Jane Wright insisted in later years that her
father, surgeon Louis Wright, never pressured her
to study medicine; indeed he warned her how hard
becoming a doctor would be. His very fame, within
*Line*
5 and beyond the African American community, made
her training harder in some ways. "His being so good
really makes it very difficult," Wright told an inter-
viewer soon after she graduated from medical school
in 1945. "Everyone knows who Papa is."

11. The passage suggests that Jane Wright's medical
training was made more difficult because

(A) her father warned her not to study medicine
(B) her father flaunted his success
(C) she did not spend adequate time studying
(D) she shared her father's desire for fame
(E) she was inevitably compared to her father

12. The passage is primarily concerned with Jane Wright's

(A) views of the medical profession
(B) childhood recollections
(C) perception of her father as a role model
(D) reluctance to collaborate with her father
(E) gratitude for her father's encouragement

**GO ON TO THE NEXT PAGE**

**Questions 13-24 are based on the following passages.**

*The following two passages consider the experiences of middle-class women in nineteenth-century England under the reign of Queen Victoria (1837-1901). Passage 1 is from a work of social history; Passage 2 is from a study of travel writing.*

**Passage 1**

In nineteenth-century England, middle-class women were usually assigned domestic roles and faced severely limited professional career options. Of course, one can
Line point to England's monarch, Queen Victoria, as a famous
5 example of a woman at work, and millions of working-class women worked for wages in factories and private homes, on farms, and in stores and markets. But aristocrats were often exempt from societal strictures that bound the middle class, and working-class women were usually
10 looked down on as not being "respectable" for their efforts as workers. As the nineteenth century progressed, it was assumed that a woman engaged in business was a woman without either her own inheritance or a man to support her. Middle-class women already shared with upper-middle-
15 class men the societal stumbling blocks to active pursuit of business, which included the feeling that labor was demeaning and not suitable for those with aspirations to gentility. But unlike a man, whose self-worth rose through his economic exertions, a woman who did likewise risked
20 opprobrium for herself and possibly shame for those around her. Inequality in the working world made it exceedingly difficult for a middle-class woman to support herself on her own, let alone support dependents. Thus, at a time when occupation was becoming a core element in masculine
25 identity, any position for middle-class women other than in relation to men was considered anomalous. In the 1851 census, the Registrar General introduced a new fifth class of workers, exclusively made up of women:

The fifth class comprises large numbers of the population
30 that have no occupation; but it requires no argument to prove that the wife, the mother, the mistress of an English family—fills offices and discharges duties of no ordinary importance; or that children are or should be occupied in filial or household duties, and in the task
35 of education, either at home or at school.

This conception of women had been developing over a long period. For example, in the late seventeenth century, trade tokens used by local shopkeepers and small masters in family businesses carried the initials of the man's and the
40 woman's first names and the couple's surname, but by the late eighteenth century, only the initials of the male proprietor were retained. This serves to confirm the view of one Victorian man, born in 1790, that whereas his mother had confidently joined in the family auctioneering business,
45 the increased division of the sexes had seen the withdrawal of women from business life.

Marriage became, more than ever, the only career option offering economic prosperity for women; in business, women appear only as faint shadows behind the scenes.
50 The absence of women in business and financial records makes our knowledge of what middle-class women actually did and how they survived economically quite fragmentary. What we do know is that women's ability to survive economically on their own became increasingly difficult in
55 the course of the nineteenth century.

**Passage 2**

In the second half of the nineteenth century in England, under the rule of Queen Victoria, because of the long peace and the increasing prosperity, more and more women found themselves able to travel to Europe unescorted. With the
60 increase in travel came an increase in the number of guidebooks, collections of travel hints, and diaries by travelers—many of which were written by or directed to women.

Although nineteenth-century women traveled for a variety
65 of reasons, ranging from a desire to do scientific research to involvement in missionary work, undoubtedly a major incentive was the desire to escape from domestic confinement and the social restrictions imposed on the Victorian female in Britain. As Dorothy Middleton observes, "Travel
70 was an individual gesture of the housebound, man-dominated Victorian woman." The "caged birds" of the Victorian parlor found their wings and often took flight in other lands. In a less constrained environment they achieved physical and psychological freedom and some measure of
75 autonomy. In *Celebrated Women Travelers of the Nineteenth Century* (1883), Davenport Adams comments: "Fettered as women are in European countries by restraints, obligations, and responsibilities, which are too often arbitrary and artificial . . . it is natural enough that when the opportunity
80 offers, they should hail even a temporary emancipation through travel."

By the latter part of the nineteenth century, women travelers began to be singled out as exemplars of the new social and political freedom and prowess of women.
85 Ironically, Mary Kingsley and other women travelers were opposed to or simply uninterested in the late Victorian campaigns to extend women's political rights. Thus, when Mary Kingsley returned from West Africa in 1895, she was chagrined to discover that she was being hailed as a "new
90 woman" because of her travels. Despite her often out-spoken distaste for the "new women" agitating for greater freedom, the travel books that she and others had written still suggested, as Paul Fussell has argued, "an implicit celebration of freedom."

**GO ON TO THE NEXT PAGE**

2  2

Unauthorized copying or reuse of any part of this page is illegal.

**13.** Lines 18-21 suggest that for Victorian middle-class women, "self-worth" and "economic exertions" were thought to be

(A) mutually exclusive
(B) constantly evolving
(C) the two keys to success
(D) essential to finding a husband
(E) easy to achieve

**14.** In line 24, "occupation" most nearly means

(A) military conquest
(B) pleasant diversion
(C) vocation
(D) settlement
(E) political repression

**15.** The author of Passage 1 considers trade tokens (lines 37-38) as evidence against the prevalence of a fifth class in the seventeenth century because they

(A) served as legal currency
(B) were issued to both middle-class and working-class women
(C) helped neutralize gender stereotypes of the day
(D) failed to identify women by their names and positions
(E) identified men and women as partners in business

**16.** All of the following are referred to in Passage 1 as evidence of women's diminished social status in Victorian England EXCEPT the

(A) disparity between men's and women's career opportunities
(B) shame risked by women who wished to enter commerce
(C) exclusion of women's initials from trade tokens
(D) influence of the queen
(E) absence of financial records documenting women's activity

**17.** Which statement about British society, if true, would most directly support the view described in lines 42-46 ?

(A) Seventeenth-century women workers could raise their status by assuming greater responsibilities.
(B) Women wrote more novels in the early nineteenth century than they did in the early eighteenth century.
(C) Women and girls worked in factories throughout the nineteenth century.
(D) The practice of married couples jointly running businesses died out in the early nineteenth century.
(E) In the seventeenth century, formal academic institutions were closed to women.

**18.** In context, "hail" (line 80) most nearly means

(A) call out to
(B) gesture to
(C) come from
(D) welcome
(E) summon

**19.** In Passage 2, Mary Kingsley's attitude toward women's rights campaigns (lines 85-90) suggests

(A) a single-minded dedication to equality between the sexes
(B) a way in which dedication to one cause can lead to antagonism toward another
(C) a striking inconsistency between her identity as a British citizen and her identity as a woman
(D) an understanding of the link between women's struggle for freedom and the struggles of other groups
(E) a contradiction between her personal motives and the way her actions are interpreted

**20.** According to Passage 2, nineteenth-century British women were motivated to travel by which of the following?

I. Educational pursuits
II. Humanitarian concerns
III. Entrepreneurial interests

(A) I only
(B) III only
(C) I and II only
(D) I and III only
(E) II and III only

**21.** Which British traveler of the Victorian era would best illustrate the argument made in Passage 2 ?

(A) A middle-class woman who tours Greece and Egypt to examine ancient ruins.
(B) An aristocratic woman who lives in the Asian capital where her father is the British ambassador.
(C) A young woman and her husband, both missionaries, who relocate permanently in a distant country.
(D) A nursemaid who accompanies an aristocratic family to its new home in New York City.
(E) A young girl from a poor family who is sent by relatives to make her fortune in Australia.

**GO ON TO THE NEXT PAGE**

2  2

Unauthorized copying or reuse of
any part of this page is illegal.

**22.** The "fifth class" (line 29) in Passage 1 is most like which group in Passage 2 ?

(A) Women who worked as missionaries
(B) The "caged birds" (line 71)
(C) The "new woman" (lines 89-90)
(D) Dorothy Middleton and Mary Kingsley
(E) Davenport Adams and Paul Fussell

**23.** Passage 1 and Passage 2 share a general tone of

(A) affectionate nostalgia
(B) analytical detachment
(C) personal regret
(D) righteous indignation
(E) open hostility

**24.** The information in Passage 1 supports which assumption about the women described in Passage 2 ?

(A) They were discouraged from pursuing careers in their native country.
(B) They sought to establish new businesses in foreign countries.
(C) They traveled with children and other family members.
(D) They were universally admired by British women from every class of society.
(E) They were committed advocates of social reform.

# STOP

**If you finish before time is called, you may check your work on this section only.**
**Do not turn to any other section in the test.**

## SECTION 3
### Time — 25 minutes
### 20 Questions

**Turn to Section 3 (page 4) of your answer sheet to answer the questions in this section.**

**Directions:** For this section, solve each problem and decide which is the best of the choices given. Fill in the corresponding circle on the answer sheet. You may use any available space for scratchwork.

Notes

1. The use of a calculator is permitted.
2. All numbers used are real numbers.
3. Figures that accompany problems in this test are intended to provide information useful in solving the problems. They are drawn as accurately as possible EXCEPT when it is stated in a specific problem that the figure is not drawn to scale. All figures lie in a plane unless otherwise indicated.
4. Unless otherwise specified, the domain of any function $f$ is assumed to be the set of all real numbers $x$ for which $f(x)$ is a real number.

Reference Information

$A = \pi r^2$
$C = 2\pi r$
$A = \ell w$
$A = \frac{1}{2}bh$
$V = \ell w h$
$V = \pi r^2 h$
$c^2 = a^2 + b^2$
Special Right Triangles

The number of degrees of arc in a circle is 360.
The sum of the measures in degrees of the angles of a triangle is 180.

---

**1.** If $3b + 1 < 10$, which of the following CANNOT be the value of $b$ ?

(A)  $-1$
(B)  $0$
(C)  $1$
(D)  $2$
(E)  $3$

**2.** If $2^{4x} = 16$, then $x =$

(A)  $1$
(B)  $2$
(C)  $4$
(D)  $8$
(E)  $12$

**3.** How much greater than $r - 2$ is $r + 5$ ?

(A)  $2$
(B)  $3$
(C)  $5$
(D)  $6$
(E)  $7$

**GO ON TO THE NEXT PAGE**

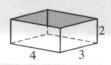

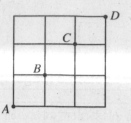

4. If the rectangular box with no lid shown above is cut along the vertical edges and flattened, which of the following figures best represents the result?

(A)

(B)
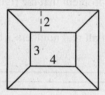

(C)
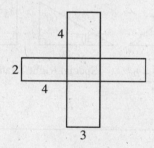

(D)
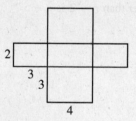

(E)
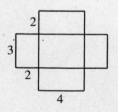

5. In the figure above, a path from point $A$ to point $D$ is determined by moving upward or to the right along the grid lines. How many different paths can be drawn from $A$ to $D$ that do not include either $B$ or $C$?

(A) Two
(B) Four
(C) Six
(D) Eight
(E) Sixteen

6. If $\frac{3}{7}$ of $n$ is 42, what is $\frac{5}{7}$ of $n$?

(A) 70
(B) 45
(C) 30
(D) 18
(E) 10

**GO ON TO THE NEXT PAGE**

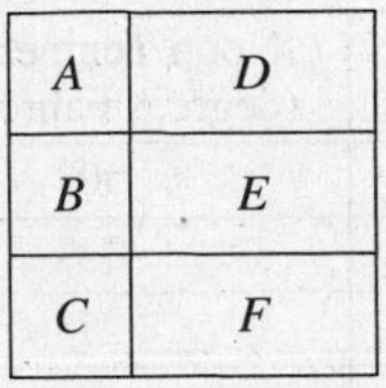

| A | D |
|---|---|
| B | E |
| C | F |

**7.** The figure above shows the top view of an open square box that is divided into 6 compartments with walls of equal height. Each of the rectangles $D$, $E$, and $F$ has twice the area of each of the equal squares $A$, $B$, and $C$. When a marble is dropped into the box at random, it falls into one of the compartments. What is the probability that it will fall into compartment $F$?

(A) $\dfrac{1}{12}$

(B) $\dfrac{1}{8}$

(C) $\dfrac{1}{6}$

(D) $\dfrac{2}{11}$

(E) $\dfrac{2}{9}$

**8.** If $a$ and $b$ are odd integers, which of the following must also be an odd integer?

    I. $(a + 1)b$
    II. $(a + 1) + b$
    III. $(a + 1) - b$

(A) I only
(B) II only
(C) III only
(D) I and II
(E) II and III

5.101001000100001 . . .

**9.** The decimal number above consists of only 1's and 0's to the right of the decimal point. The first 1 is followed by one 0, the second 1 is followed by two 0's, the third 1 is followed by three 0's, and so on. What is the total number of 0's between the 98th and the 101st 1 in this decimal number?

(A) 288
(B) 291
(C) 294
(D) 297
(E) 300

**10.** If $f(x) = \dfrac{3 - 2x^2}{x}$ for all nonzero $x$, then $f(2) =$

(A) $\dfrac{11}{2}$

(B) $\dfrac{7}{2}$

(C) $-\dfrac{1}{2}$

(D) $-\dfrac{5}{2}$

(E) $-7$

**GO ON TO THE NEXT PAGE**

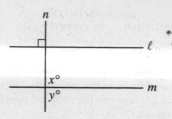

Note: Figure not drawn to scale.

11. In the figure above, $\ell \perp n$ and $x > 90$. Which of the following must be true?

(A) $y < 90$
(B) $y > 90$
(C) $y = 90$
(D) $n \perp m$
(E) $\ell \parallel m$

12. In the $xy$-plane, the line with equation $y = 5x - 10$ crosses the $x$-axis at the point with coordinates $(a, b)$. What is the value of $a$?

(A) $-10$
(B) $-2$
(C) $0$
(D) $2$
(E) $5$

| City | Noon Temperature (degrees Fahrenheit) |
|------|---------------------------------------|
| A | 50° |
| B | 33° |
| C | 27° |
| D | $t°$ |
| E | 68° |
| F | 44° |
| G | 40° |

13. The table above shows the noon temperatures for seven cities designated $A$ through $G$. If the median noon temperature of these cities is 40°F, then the noon temperature for City $D$ could be any of the following EXCEPT

(A) 29°F
(B) 35°F
(C) 39°F
(D) 40°F
(E) 42°F

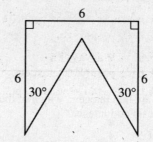

14. What is the perimeter of the figure above?

(A) 24
(B) 25
(C) 28
(D) 30
(E) 36

GO ON TO THE NEXT PAGE

15. If $m$ is the greatest prime factor of 38 and $n$ is the greatest prime factor of 100, what is the value of $m + n$?

(A)   7
(B)   12
(C)   24
(D)   29
(E)   44

16. Line $\ell$ has a positive slope and passes through the point $(0, 0)$. If line $k$ is perpendicular to line $\ell$, which of the following must be true?

(A)   Line $k$ passes through the point $(0, 0)$.
(B)   Line $k$ has a positive slope.
(C)   Line $k$ has a negative slope.
(D)   Line $k$ has a positive $x$-intercept.
(E)   Line $k$ has a negative $y$-intercept.

17. Let the operation $\Upsilon$ be defined by $a \mathbin{\Upsilon} b = \dfrac{a + b}{a - b}$ for all numbers $a$ and $b$, where $a \neq b$.
If $1 \mathbin{\Upsilon} 2 = 2 \mathbin{\Upsilon} x$, what is the value of $x$?

(A)   4
(B)   3
(C)   2
(D)   1
(E)   0

18. During a sale, a customer can buy one shirt for $x$ dollars. Each additional shirt the customer buys costs $z$ dollars less than the first shirt. For example, the cost of the second shirt is $x - z$ dollars. Which of the following represents the customer's cost, in dollars, for $n$ shirts bought during this sale?

(A)   $x + (n - 1)(x - z)$

(B)   $x + n(x - z)$

(C)   $n(x - z)$

(D)   $\dfrac{x + (x - z)}{n}$

(E)   $(x - z) + \dfrac{(x - z)}{n}$

GO ON TO THE NEXT PAGE

585

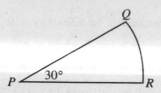

**19.** In the figure above, $QR$ is the arc of a circle with center $P$. If the length of arc $QR$ is $6\pi$, what is the area of sector $PQR$ ?

(A) $108\pi$
(B) $72\pi$
(C) $54\pi$
(D) $36\pi$
(E) $9\pi$

**20.** There are 75 more women than men enrolled in Linden College. If there are $n$ men enrolled, then, in terms of $n$, what percent of those enrolled are men?

(A) $\dfrac{n}{n+75}\%$

(B) $\dfrac{n}{2n+75}\%$

(C) $\dfrac{n}{100(2n+75)}\%$

(D) $\dfrac{100n}{n+75}\%$

(E) $\dfrac{100n}{2n+75}\%$

# STOP

**If you finish before time is called, you may check your work on this section only.**
**Do not turn to any other section in the test.**

5  5

Unauthorized copying or reuse of
any part of this page is illegal.

5  5

## SECTION 5
Time — 25 minutes
24 Questions

**Turn to Section 5 (page 5) of your answer sheet to answer the questions in this section.**

**Directions:** For each question in this section, select the best answer from among the choices given and fill in the corresponding circle on the answer sheet.

Each sentence below has one or two blanks, each blank indicating that something has been omitted. Beneath the sentence are five words or sets of words labeled A through E. Choose the word or set of words that, when inserted in the sentence, <u>best</u> fits the meaning of the sentence as a whole.

**Example:**

Hoping to ------- the dispute, negotiators proposed a compromise that they felt would be ------- to both labor and management.

(A) enforce . . useful
(B) end . . divisive
(C) overcome . . unattractive
(D) extend . . satisfactory
(E) resolve . . acceptable

1. Predictably, detail-oriented workers are ------- keeping track of the myriad particulars of a situation.

(A) remiss in    (B) adept at
 (C) humorous about    (D) hesitant about
   (E) contemptuous of

2. The controversial tax fueled a sustained ------- that could not be ------- by the Prime Minister's impassioned speeches.

(A) rebellion . . challenged
(B) interrogation . . fortified
(C) conflagration . . fostered
(D) denial . . restrained
(E) uprising . . quelled

3. Inbreeding can promote the expression of ------- genes, those that make an animal subject to disease or impair reproductive efficiency.

(A) ineffable    (B) articulated    (C) consummate
 (D) presumptive    (E) deleterious

4. The doctor ------- so frequently on disease-prevention techniques that his colleagues accused him of -------.

(A) vacillated . . inconsistency
(B) sermonized . . fidelity
(C) wavered . . steadfastness
(D) experimented . . inflexibility
(E) relied . . negligence

5. A judicious biography must be ------- representation that depicts both the strengths and the weaknesses of the subject, avoiding the two extremes of ------- and indictment.

(A) a polarized . . vindication
(B) an imaginative . . discernment
(C) a holistic . . censure
(D) a complimentary . . animosity
(E) an equitable . . eulogy

**GO ON TO THE NEXT PAGE**

587

The passages below are followed by questions based on their content; questions following a pair of related passages may also be based on the relationship between the paired passages. Answer the questions on the basis of what is <u>stated</u> or <u>implied</u> in the passages and in any introductory material that may be provided.

**Questions 6-9 are based on the following passages.**

**Passage 1**

Farm families are able to achieve efficiency only through a brutal work schedule that few people could tolerate. "The farm family does physically demanding *Line* work and highly stressful work at least 14 hours a day
5 (often at least 18 hours a day during harvest season), 7 days a week, 365 days a year, without a scheduled vacation or weekends off," wrote Minnesota politician and farm alumnus Darrell McKigney. "The farmer must endure all of this without . . . any of the benefits that most
10 United States labor unions demand." A dairy farmer, for instance, cannot just take off for a two-week vacation and not milk the cows. "Farmers lose perspective on the other things in life," one psychologist has written. "The farm literally consumes them."

**Passage 2**

15 Americans have distanced themselves from the ethics and morals of food production, except where it serves them to think nostalgically about family farms as the source of our better values. Little wonder that a poll taken by *The New York Times* finds a majority
20 of Americans seeing farm life as superior to any other kind of life in this country. As consumers, Americans have enjoyed relatively inexpensive food. What will happen if family farms disappear? What will we do without family farmers to watch over the system for
25 us, to be our dupes, and to create that pleasant situation through their own great discomfort?

6. Unlike Passage 2, Passage 1 is primarily concerned with the

   (A) ethical implications of food production
   (B) harsh working conditions on many farms
   (C) need for farmers to form a labor union
   (D) plentiful and varied food available in the United States
   (E) beliefs of many Americans regarding farm life

7. Both passages serve to discourage the

   (A) reliance on polls for accurate information
   (B) desire of many farmers to take annual vacations
   (C) tendency of Americans to buy inexpensive foods
   (D) romanticization of farm life by nonfarmers
   (E) rise in price of home-grown produce

8. The author of Passage 1 would most likely assert which of the following about the "majority" (line 19, Passage 2)?

   (A) They would be bored by the routine chores that are performed on a farm.
   (B) They have little understanding of the realities of farm life.
   (C) They admire the efficiency of the average family farm.
   (D) They wish to improve the arduous life of many farmers.
   (E) They are impressed by the current research on economical food production.

9. Unlike the author of Passage 2, the author of Passage 1 does which of the following?

   (A) Explains a study.
   (B) Offers a solution.
   (C) Argues a position.
   (D) Discusses a phenomenon.
   (E) Quotes an authority.

**GO ON TO THE NEXT PAGE**

**Questions 10-15 are based on the following passage.**

*This excerpt from a novel by a Chinese American author is about a Chinese American woman named June. During a family dinner party attended by some of June's Chinese American friends, Waverly, a tax attorney, discusses an advertisement that June wrote for her.*

Waverly laughed in a lighthearted way. "I mean, really, June." And then she started in a deep television-announcer voice: "*Three* benefits, *three* needs, *three* reasons to buy . . .
Line Satisfaction *guaranteed . . . .*"
5     She said this in such a funny way that everybody thought it was a good joke and laughed. And then, to make matters worse, I heard my mother saying to Waverly: "True, one can't teach style. June is not sophisticated like you. She must have been born this way."
10     I was surprised at myself, how humiliated I felt. I had been outsmarted by Waverly once again, and now betrayed by my own mother.

   . . . . . . . . . . . . . . . . . . . . . . . . . . . . . . . . . . . . . . . . . . .

    Five months ago, some time after the dinner, my mother gave me my "life's importance," a jade pendant on a gold
15 chain. The pendant was not a piece of jewelry I would have chosen for myself. It was almost the size of my little finger, a mottled green and white color, intricately carved. To me, the whole effect looked wrong: too large, too green, too garishly ornate. I stuffed the necklace in my lacquer box
20 and forgot about it.
    But these days, I think about my life's importance. I wonder what it means, because my mother died three months ago, six days before my thirty-sixth birthday. And she's the only person I could have asked to tell me
25 about life's importance, to help me understand my grief.
    I now wear that pendant every day. I think the carvings mean something, because shapes and details, which I never seem to notice until after they're pointed out to me, always mean something to Chinese people. I know I could ask
30 Auntie Lindo, Auntie An-mei, or other Chinese friends, but I also know they would tell me a meaning that is different from what my mother intended. What if they tell me this curving line branching into three oval shapes is a pomegranate and that my mother was wishing me fertility
35 and posterity? What if my mother really meant the carvings were a branch of pears to give me purity and honesty?
    And because I think about this all the time, I always notice other people wearing these same jade pendants —not the flat rectangular medallions or the round white
40 ones with holes in the middle but ones like mine, a two-inch oblong of bright apple green. It's as though we were all sworn to the same secret covenant, so secret we don't even know what we belong to. Last weekend, for example, I saw a bartender wearing one. As I fingered mine, I asked
45 him, "Where'd you get yours?"

"My mother gave it to me," he said.
    I asked him why, which is a nosy question that only one Chinese person can ask another; in a crowd of Caucasians, two Chinese people are already like family.
50     "She gave it to me after I got divorced. I guess my mother's telling me I'm still worth something."
    And I knew by the wonder in his voice that he had no idea what the pendant really meant.

**10.** In lines 1-4, Waverly characterizes June's advertisement as being

(A) unsophisticated and heavy-handed
(B) somber and convoluted
(C) clear and concise
(D) humorous and effective
(E) clever and lively

**11.** In the context of the passage, the statement "I was surprised at myself" (line 10) suggests that June

(A) had been unaware of the extent of her emotional vulnerability
(B) was exasperated that she allowed Waverly to embarrass her in public
(C) was amazed that she could dislike anyone so much
(D) had not realized that her mother admired her friend Waverly
(E) felt guilty about how much she resented her own mother

**12.** June's observation in lines 10-11 ("I had . . . again") suggests that

(A) June had expected Waverly to insult her
(B) June had hoped to embarrass Waverly this time
(C) Waverly had a private understanding with June's mother
(D) Waverly had made June feel inadequate on previous occasions
(E) Waverly was a more talented writer than June was

**13.** For June, a significant aspect of what happened at the dinner party is that

(A) her mother had taken great pains to make Waverly feel welcome
(B) her mother had criticized her for arguing with Waverly
(C) her mother had sided against her in front of family and friends
(D) Waverly had angered June's mother
(E) Waverly had lied to June's mother

**GO ON TO THE NEXT PAGE** ⇨

**14.** The description of June's encounter with the bartender primarily serves to suggest that

(A) the relationship of mother and son is different from that of mother and daughter
(B) June is not the only one who ponders the meaning of a jade pendant
(C) a jade pendant symbolizes the mystery of life and death
(D) June finally understands the true meaning of her jade pendant
(E) strangers are easier to talk to than family members and friends

**15.** The passage indicates that the act of giving a jade pendant can best be described as

(A) a widely observed tradition
(B) a mother's plea for forgiveness
(C) an example of a mother's extravagance
(D) an unprecedented act of generosity
(E) an unremarkable event in June's life

**GO ON TO THE NEXT PAGE**

**Questions 16-24 are based on the following passage.**

*This passage is from a book of nature writing published in 1991.*

In North America, bats fall into mainly predictable categories: they are nocturnal, eat insects, and are rather small. But winging through their lush, green-black world, *Line* tropical bats are more numerous and have more exotic
5 habits than do temperate species. Some of them feed on nectar that bat-pollinated trees have evolved to profit from their visits. Carnivorous bats like nothing better than a local frog, lizard, fish, or bird, which they pluck from the foliage or a moonlit pond. Of course, some bats are vampires and
10 dine on blood. In the movies, vampires are rather showy, theatrical types, but vampire bats rely on stealth and small, pinprick incisions made by razory, triangular front teeth. Sleeping livestock are their usual victims, and they take care not to wake them. First, they make the classic incisions
15 shaped like quotation marks; then, with saliva full of anti-coagulants so that the victim's blood will flow nicely, they quietly lap their fill. Because this anticoagulant is not toxic to humans, vampire bats may one day play an important role in the treatment of heart patients—that is, if we can
20 just get over our phobia about them. Having studied them intimately, I now know that bats are sweet-tempered, useful, and fascinating creatures. The long-standing fear that many people have about bats tells us less about bats than about human fear.
25 Things that live by night live outside the realm of "normal" time. Chauvinistic about our human need to wake by day and sleep by night, we come to associate night dwellers with people up to no good, people who have the jump on the rest of us and are defying nature, defying their
30 circadian rhythms.* Also, night is when we dream, and so we picture the bats moving through a dreamtime, in which reality is warped. After all, we do not see very well at night; we do not need to. But that makes us nearly defense-less after dark. Although we are accustomed to mastering
35 our world by day, in the night we become vulnerable as prey. Thinking of bats as masters of the night threatens the safety we daily take for granted. Though we are at the top of our food chain, if we had to live alone in the rain forest, say, and protect ourselves against roaming predators, we
40 would live partly in terror, as our ancestors did. Our sense of safety depends on predictability, so anything living outside the usual rules we suspect to be an outlaw, a ghoul.
Bats have always figured as frightening or supernatural creatures in the mythology, religion, and superstition of
45 peoples everywhere. Finnish peasants once believed that their souls rose from their bodies while they slept and flew around the countryside as bats, then returned to them by morning. Ancient Egyptians prized bat parts as medicine for a variety of diseases. Perhaps the most mystical, ghoul-
50 ish, and intimate relationship between bats and humans occurred among the Maya about two thousand years ago.

Zotzilaha Chamalcán, their bat god, had a human body but the stylized head and wings of a bat. His image appears often on their altars, pottery, gold ornaments, and stone
55 pillars. One especially frightening engraving shows the bat god with outstretched wings and a question-mark nose, its tongue wagging with hunger, as it holds a human corpse in one hand and the human's heart in the other. A number of other Central American cultures raised the bat to the ulti-
60 mate height: as god of death and the underworld. But it was Bram Stoker's riveting novel *Dracula* that turned small, furry mammals into huge, bloodsucking monsters in the minds of English-speaking people. If vampires were semihuman, then they could fascinate with their conniving
65 cruelty, and thus a spill of horror books began to appear about the human passions of vampires.

---

\* Circadian rhythms are patterns of daily change within one's body that are determined by the time of day or night.

**16.** The author's main point in the passage is that

(A) there are only a few kinds of bats
(B) humans are especially vulnerable to nocturnal predators
(C) bat saliva may have medicinal uses
(D) only myth and literature have depicted the true nature of the bat
(E) our perception of bats has its basis in human psychology

**17.** As used in line 14, "classic" most nearly means

(A) literary
(B) enduring
(C) elegant
(D) well-known
(E) significant

**18.** The discussion of vampire bats in the first paragraph (lines 1-24) primarily suggests that

(A) vampire bats are potentially useful creatures
(B) movies about vampires are based only on North American bats
(C) most tropical bats are not carnivorous
(D) the saliva of vampire bats is more toxic than commonly supposed
(E) scientists know very little about the behavior of most bats

**GO ON TO THE NEXT PAGE** →

**19.** In line 26, the quotation marks around the word "normal" serve to

(A) emphasize the individuality of the author's writing
(B) criticize the human obsession with time
(C) emphasize the limitations of a point of view
(D) demonstrate the author's agreement with the common use of the word
(E) indicate that this word would be stressed if it were spoken out loud

**20.** Which of the following assertions detracts LEAST from the author's argument in the second paragraph (lines 25-42) ?

(A) Many people work at night and sleep during the day.
(B) Owls, which hunt at night, do not arouse our fear.
(C) Most dangerous predators hunt during the day.
(D) Some cultures associate bats with positive qualities.
(E) Some dream imagery has its source in the dreamer's personal life.

**21.** The examples cited in the third paragraph (lines 43-66) are primarily drawn from

(A) anthropology
(B) autobiography
(C) fiction
(D) psychiatry
(E) biology

**22.** The author develops the third paragraph (lines 43-66) by presenting

(A) different sides of a single issue
(B) details that culminate in truth
(C) a thesis followed by specific illustrations
(D) a common argument followed by a refutation of it
(E) a common opinion and the reasons it is held

**23.** The practices of which group mentioned in the last paragraph best substantiate the claim that bats are "useful" (line 21)?

(A) Finnish peasants
(B) Ancient Egyptians
(C) Ancient Maya
(D) A number of Central American cultures
(E) English-speaking people

**24.** The reference to Stoker's work in lines 60-66 extends the author's idea that

(A) bats are sweet-tempered creatures
(B) our fear of bats reveals more about us than about bats
(C) humans have always been curious about nocturnal creatures
(D) bats can see better than humans at night
(E) bats appear as supernatural creatures even in the folklore of distant nations

# STOP

**If you finish before time is called, you may check your work on this section only.**
**Do not turn to any other section in the test.**

## SECTION 6
**Time — 25 minutes**
**18 Questions**

---

**Turn to Section 6 (page 6) of your answer sheet to answer the questions in this section.**

---

**Directions:** This section contains two types of questions. You have 25 minutes to complete both types. For questions 1-8, solve each problem and decide which is the best of the choices given. Fill in the corresponding circle on the answer sheet. You may use any available space for scratchwork.

**Notes**

1. The use of a calculator is permitted.

2. All numbers used are real numbers.

3. Figures that accompany problems in this test are intended to provide information useful in solving the problems. They are drawn as accurately as possible EXCEPT when it is stated in a specific problem that the figure is not drawn to scale. All figures lie in a plane unless otherwise indicated.

4. Unless otherwise specified, the domain of any function $f$ is assumed to be the set of all real numbers $x$ for which $f(x)$ is a real number.

**Reference Information**

    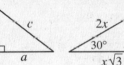 

$A = \pi r^2$
$C = 2\pi r$     $A = \ell w$     $A = \frac{1}{2}bh$     $V = \ell wh$     $V = \pi r^2 h$     $c^2 = a^2 + b^2$     Special Right Triangles

The number of degrees of arc in a circle is 360.
The sum of the measures in degrees of the angles of a triangle is 180.

---

$$\frac{3 + \diamond}{2} = 7\frac{1}{2}$$

**1.** What number, when used in place of ◇ above, makes the statement true?

(A)  4
(B)  5
(C)  9
(D)  12
(E)  15

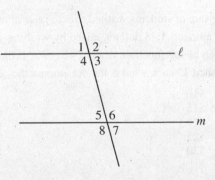

**2.** In the figure above, if $\ell \parallel m$, then the sum of the measures of angles 2 and 4 must equal the sum of the measures of which of the following pairs of angles?

(A)  5 and 6
(B)  5 and 7
(C)  6 and 7
(D)  6 and 8
(E)  7 and 8

**GO ON TO THE NEXT PAGE** ⟶

**6** ◇ ◇ **6**

Unauthorized copying or reuse of
any part of this page is illegal.

**6** ◇ ◇ **6**

## PRESTON CITY WORKFORCE

|       | Employed | Unemployed | Total  |
|-------|----------|------------|--------|
| Men   | 27,000   |            |        |
| Women |          |            | 21,500 |
| Total | 48,000   |            | 50,500 |

3. The table above, describing the Preston City workforce, is partially filled in. Based on the information in the table, how many women in the Preston City workforce are unemployed?

(A)   500
(B) 1,000
(C) 1,500
(D) 2,000
(E) 2,500

4. A group of students washed cars to raise money. The net amount $A$, in dollars, raised by washing $k$ cars is given by the function $A(k) = 4k - 30$. If the group washed 15 cars, what is the net amount they raised?

(A) $10
(B) $15
(C) $20
(D) $25
(E) $30

5. If $xr = v$, $v = kr$, and $rv \neq 0$, which of the following is equal to $k$ ?

(A)  1

(B)  $\dfrac{1}{x}$

(C)  $x - 1$

(D)  $x$

(E)  $x + 1$

6. The eggs in a certain basket are either white or brown. If the ratio of the number of white eggs to the number of brown eggs is $\dfrac{2}{3}$, each of the following could be the number of eggs in the basket EXCEPT

(A) 10
(B) 12
(C) 15
(D) 30
(E) 60

**GO ON TO THE NEXT PAGE** ⇨

7. If $18\sqrt{18} = r\sqrt{t}$, where $r$ and $t$ are positive integers and $r > t$, which of the following could be the value of $rt$ ?

(A)  18
(B)  36
(C)  108
(D)  162
(E)  324

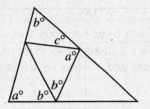

8. In the figure above, what is the value of $c$ in terms of $a$ and $b$ ?

(A)  $a + 3b - 180$
(B)  $2a + 2b - 180$
(C)  $180 - a - b$
(D)  $360 - a - b$
(E)  $360 - 2a - 3b$

GO ON TO THE NEXT PAGE

**Directions:** For Student-Produced Response questions 9-18, use the grids at the bottom of the answer sheet page on which you have answered questions 1-8.

Each of the remaining 10 questions requires you to solve the problem and enter your answer by marking the circles in the special grid, as shown in the examples below. You may use any available space for scratchwork.

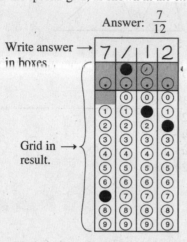

Answer: $\frac{7}{12}$

Write answer → in boxes.

Fraction line

Grid in → result.

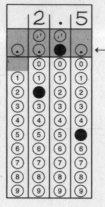

Answer: 2.5

← Decimal point

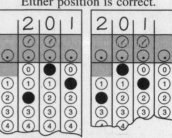

Answer: 201
Either position is correct.

**Note:** You may start your answers in any column, space permitting. Columns not needed should be left blank.

- Mark no more than one circle in any column.

- Because the answer sheet will be machine-scored, **you will receive credit only if the circles are filled in correctly.**

- Although not required, it is suggested that you write your answer in the boxes at the top of the columns to help you fill in the circles accurately.

- Some problems may have more than one correct answer. In such cases, grid only one answer.

- No question has a negative answer.

- **Mixed numbers** such as $3\frac{1}{2}$ must be gridded as 3.5 or 7/2. (If $3|1|/|2$ is gridded, it will be interpreted as $\frac{31}{2}$, not $3\frac{1}{2}$.)

- **Decimal Answers:** If you obtain a decimal answer with more digits than the grid can accommodate, it may be either rounded or truncated, but it must fill the entire grid. For example, if you obtain an answer such as 0.6666..., you should record your result as .666 or .667. **A less accurate value such as .66 or .67 will be scored as incorrect.**

Acceptable ways to grid $\frac{2}{3}$ are:

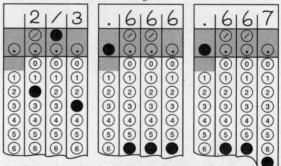

---

9.  If $t^3 = 351$, what is the value of $4t^3$ ?

10. What is the coordinate of the point on a number line that is exactly halfway between the points with coordinates 53 and 62 ?

**GO ON TO THE NEXT PAGE** →

**11.** A certain triangle has two angles that have the same measure. If the lengths of two of the sides of the triangle are 50 and 30, what is the <u>least</u> possible value for the perimeter of the triangle?

**12.** If $x^2 - y^2 = 77$ and $x + y = 11$, what is the value of $x$ ?

**13.** Tameka cut a circular pizza into wedge-shaped pieces, one of which is shown above. The tip of each piece is at the center of the pizza and the angle at the tip is always greater than 20°, but less than 30°. What is one possible value for the number of pieces into which the pizza is cut?

$$a, 3a, \ldots$$

**14.** The first term in the sequence above is $a$, and each term after the first is 3 times the preceding term. If the sum of the first 5 terms is 605, what is the value of $a$ ?

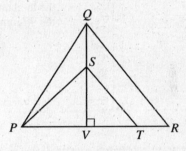

Note: Figure not drawn to scale.

**15.** In $\triangle PQR$ above, $\dfrac{QS}{QV} = \dfrac{1}{3}$ and $\dfrac{PT}{PR} = \dfrac{3}{4}$. What is the value of the fraction $\dfrac{\text{area } \triangle PST}{\text{area } \triangle PQR}$ ?

**16.** Let the function $h$ be defined by $h(x) = 14 + \dfrac{x^2}{4}$. If $h(2m) = 9m$, what is one possible value of $m$ ?

GO ON TO THE NEXT PAGE ⟶

## INVENTORY OF CLOCKS AND FREQUENCY OF CHIMES

| | Number of Clocks | Chimes $n$ Times on the $n$th Hour | Chimes Once on the Hour | Chimes Once on the Half Hour |
|---|---|---|---|---|
| Type $A$ | 10 | ✓ | | ✓ |
| Type $B$ | 5 | ✓ | | |
| Type $C$ | 3 | | ✓ | ✓ |

**17.** A merchant sells three types of clocks that chime as indicated by the check marks in the table above. What is the total number of chimes of the inventory of clocks in the 90-minute period from 7:15 to 8:45 ?

**18.** If the 5 cards shown above are placed in a row so that ▨ is never at either end, how many different arrangements are possible?

# STOP

**If you finish before time is called, you may check your work on this section only.
Do not turn to any other section in the test.**

# SECTION 7
### Time — 25 minutes
### 35 Questions

**Turn to Section 7 (page 6) of your answer sheet to answer the questions in this section.**

**Directions:** For each question in this section, select the best answer from among the choices given and fill in the corresponding circle on the answer sheet.

The following sentences test correctness and effectiveness of expression. Part of each sentence or the entire sentence is underlined; beneath each sentence are five ways of phrasing the underlined material. Choice A repeats the original phrasing; the other four choices are different. If you think the original phrasing produces a better sentence than any of the alternatives, select choice A; if not, select one of the other choices.

In making your selection, follow the requirements of standard written English; that is, pay attention to grammar, choice of words, sentence construction, and punctuation. Your selection should result in the most effective sentence—clear and precise, without awkwardness or ambiguity.

EXAMPLE:

Laura Ingalls Wilder published her first book and she was sixty-five years old then.

(A) and she was sixty-five years old then
(B) when she was sixty-five
(C) at age sixty-five years old
(D) upon the reaching of sixty-five years
(E) at the time when she was sixty-five

1. In a recent year, more tourists from the United States visited museums in Great Britain than Canada.

(A) Canada
(B) Canada did
(C) compared to Canada's
(D) Canadian ones
(E) in Canada

2. Conners, a publishing and media services company, is acquiring Dispatch Education, it manufactures school uniforms.

(A) Dispatch Education, it manufactures
(B) Dispatch Education, which manufactures
(C) Dispatch Education, manufacturing
(D) Dispatch Education; it is manufacturing
(E) Dispatch Education; for the manufacturing of

3. The campus newspaper does not print as much world news as does my hometown.

(A) as does my hometown
(B) as does my hometown newspaper
(C) compared to what my hometown does
(D) like my hometown newspaper does
(E) like the one in my hometown does

4. During the labor dispute, barrels of potatoes were emptied across the highway, and they thereby blocked it to all traffic.

(A) highway, and they thereby blocked it to all traffic
(B) highway and therefore blocking it to all traffic
(C) highway, by which all traffic was therefore blocked
(D) highway, and therefore this had all traffic blocked
(E) highway, thereby blocking all traffic

5. Having thought the problem through with some care, that the committee did not understand her solution frustrated the chairperson extremely.

(A) that the committee did not understand her solution frustrated the chairperson extremely
(B) the chairperson's extreme frustration resulted from the committee not understanding her solution
(C) the chairperson's frustration at the committee's failing to understand her solution was extreme
(D) the chairperson was extremely frustrated by the committee's failure to understand her solution
(E) the committee's failing to understand her solution was an extreme frustration to the chairperson

GO ON TO THE NEXT PAGE

6. The main reasons students give for failing to participate in the political process <u>is that they have demanding assignments and work at</u> part-time jobs.

(A) is that they have demanding assignments and work at

(B) are demanding assignments and they work at

(C) are that they have demanding assignments and that they work at

(D) is having demanding assignments and having to work at

(E) are demanding assignments, in addition to working at

7. Archaeologists say that the Pueblo village of Acoma, <u>which is 7,500 feet above sea level and 400 feet above</u> the valley floor, is the oldest continuously inhabited spot in the United States.

(A) which is 7,500 feet above sea level and 400 feet above

(B) located 7,500 feet high above sea level while having measured 400 feet above

(C) with a height 7,500 feet above sea level as well as 400 feet above that of

(D) 7,500 feet higher than sea level, and it ascends 400 feet above

(E) being 7,500 feet above sea level and 400 feet high measured from that of

8. <u>Returning to Dayville after ten years, the small town seemed much livelier to Margo</u> than it had been when she was growing up there.

(A) Returning to Dayville after ten years, the small town seemed much livelier to Margo

(B) Having returned to Dayville after ten years, it seemed a much livelier town to Margo

(C) After Margo returned to Dayville in ten years, the small town seems much livelier

(D) Margo returned to Dayville after ten years, the small town was seemingly much livelier

(E) When Margo returned to Dayville after ten years, the small town seemed much livelier to her

9. <u>Having command of pathos, tragedy, as well as humor,</u> George Eliot is considered to be a great English novelist.

(A) Having command of pathos, tragedy, as well as humor

(B) Having command of pathos, tragedy, and her humorous side

(C) By being in command of both pathos and tragedy and also humor

(D) With her command of pathos and tragedy and being humorous

(E) Because of her command of pathos, tragedy, and humor

10. Richard Wright moved many times in his life, <u>moving from the South first he went to the North, then eventually to France from the United States</u>.

(A) moving from the South first he went to the North, then eventually to France from the United States

(B) the first move he made was from the South to the North and eventually from the United States to France

(C) first from the South to the North and eventually from the United States to France

(D) moving first from the South, he came to the North and eventually to France

(E) first from the South he moved to the North and ended up in France after leaving the United States

11. Though heavily dependent on the government for business and <u>information while universities supply the space research center with talent, as a corporation it remains</u> independent of both.

(A) information while universities supply the space research center with talent, as a corporation it remains

(B) information and on talent by universities, the space research center, a corporation

(C) information and on universities for talent, the space research center is a corporation

(D) information, universities supply the space research center with talent, but it is a corporation

(E) information, universities supply the space research center with talent, while it remains a corporation

**GO ON TO THE NEXT PAGE**

The following sentences test your ability to recognize grammar and usage errors. Each sentence contains either a single error or no error at all. No sentence contains more than one error. The error, if there is one, is underlined and lettered. If the sentence contains an error, select the one underlined part that must be changed to make the sentence correct. If the sentence is correct, select choice E. In choosing answers, follow the requirements of standard written English.

EXAMPLE:

The other delegates and him immediately
  A           B   C

accepted the resolution drafted by the
                 D

neutral states. No error
          E

Ⓐ ● Ⓒ Ⓓ Ⓔ

12. Fourteen years after the Galileo space probe was
          A

launched from the space shuttle Atlantis, the mission

was purposely ended when the Galileo disintegrates
           B          C

in the dense atmosphere of the planet Jupiter.
  D

No error
  E

13. The labor union is negotiating a contract with
         A

the hospital that will satisfy the demands of
       B   C

the workers and be acceptable to all levels of
          D

management. No error
      E

14. Many professional athletes are motivated by either
           A

personal pride and love of their sport, but some seem
       B         C

interested only in money. No error
      D    E

15. Even though only parts of clay vessels may be
  A              B

recovered, these pottery shards are invaluable to
            C

the archaeologist because it is virtually indestructible.
          D

No error
  E

16. Along the curve of islands known as the Florida Keys
  A

lies a reef of living coral, the only one of a kind in
  B          C     D

the continental United States. No error
      E

17. Paule Marshall, whose Barbadian background
      A

has influenced her writing, describes many details
  B         C

of life in the Caribbean Islands vividly in her novels
          D

and short stories. No error
      E

18. Because he is absent when his rivals voted against
      A            B

his proposal, Selby is worried about missing future
        C     D

meetings of the board of directors. No error
      E

19. In those cities in which public transportation
    A    B

is adequate, fewer traffic problems occur and

pedestrians are rarely involved in accidents.
    C     D

No error
  E

**GO ON TO THE NEXT PAGE**

7 7

Unauthorized copying or reuse of any part of this page is illegal.

20. Social scientists <u>agree that</u> a system <u>for exchanging</u>
                A                    B

goods and services is <u>not only</u> present but also
                      C

<u>of necessity</u> in all societies. <u>No error</u>
       D                    E

21. The report Alexander <u>is discussing</u>, a report
                       A

prepared jointly by <u>he</u> and the committee,
                 B

does not <u>take into account</u> the socioeconomic
             C

status <u>of those interviewed</u>. <u>No error</u>
          D           E

22. It is <u>far easier</u> to ride a bicycle <u>than explaining</u> in
          A                B

words <u>exactly how</u> a bicycle <u>is ridden</u>. <u>No error</u>
        C            D     E

23. Jorge wanted, <u>for the most part</u>, to travel around
                A

the world <u>after graduation</u>, but sometimes he
           B

<u>thought about</u> <u>taking a job</u> at his mother's company
     C      D

instead. <u>No error</u>
        E

24. <u>Since some</u> people are <u>convinced that</u> dowsing,
     A              B

a method of finding underground water with a

Y-shaped stick, is effective, but others condemn

the procedure <u>as</u> <u>mere superstition</u>. <u>No error</u>
         C     D     E

25. Intense preoccupation <u>on</u> technique <u>appears to be</u>
                 A          B

<u>the one</u> trait that great pianists <u>have in</u> common.
    C                 D

<u>No error</u>
   E

26. Apparently <u>impressed with</u> our plans, the foundation
         A

awarded <u>Carlos and I</u> a grant <u>to establish</u> a network
         B           C

of community centers <u>throughout</u> the city. <u>No error</u>
              D         E

27. <u>Also supported</u> by the commission <u>was</u> the proposed
     A                  B

health clinics and the proposed <u>center</u> to distribute
                    C

information <u>on job-training</u> opportunities. <u>No error</u>
          D           E

28. The quality of multivitamin tablets <u>is determined</u>
                        A

by <u>how long</u> <u>its</u> potency <u>can be protected</u> by
     B   C        D

the manufacturer's coating material. <u>No error</u>
                     E

29. The research study <u>reveals</u> startling proof of a
              A

<u>constant</u> changing seafloor that <u>comprises</u> the
    B                C

major <u>part of</u> the underwater landscape. <u>No error</u>
     D               E

**GO ON TO THE NEXT PAGE**

**Directions:** The following passage is an early draft of an essay. Some parts of the passage need to be rewritten.

Read the passage and select the best answers for the questions that follow. Some questions are about particular sentences or parts of sentences and ask you to improve sentence structure or word choice. Other questions ask you to consider organization and development. In choosing answers, follow the requirements of standard written English.

**Questions 30-35 are based on following passage.**

(1) Employers must be aware of their employees and the variety of situations that arise in the workplace. (2) Employers should become familiar with the demands a worker faces. (3) But he or she too should also assume responsibility.

(4) Some workplace problems are caused by the employer's insufficient attention to the needs of the workers. (5) One familiar situation is the concern of the boss for the customer's satisfaction above all else. (6) Often unreasonable demands are made on an employee to satisfy the customers. (7) This results from an employer's lack of consideration for employees. (8) Workers often become resentful of an employer who is unconcerned about their needs. (9) Sometimes the employer does not listen fully to suggestions from employees this can make workers feel undervalued.

(10) Many times employers must deal with an employee who ties up the phone for hours or has friends who continually drop by during working hours. (11) If workers would take more responsibility, then maybe an employer would be a little more easily tempted to promote them.

(12) There are many problems to be solved in the workplace. (13) In order to achieve a happy balance between boss and employee, the job of a worker should be clearly defined. (14) Employers should listen to workers' ideas about improving working conditions.

30. Which of the following, if inserted before sentence 1, would make a good introduction to the essay?

(A) To avoid problems in the workplace, one must first recognize the variety of workplaces that exist.
(B) Many employees do not feel free to communicate with their employers, which can cause difficulties.
(C) Some employers have tried to respect their employees.
(D) Communication between an employer and employees is necessary for maintaining good working conditions.
(E) In the future, relations between employers and employees will be different from what they are now.

31. In context, which of the following is the best way to revise and combine sentences 2 and 3 (reproduced below)?

*Employers should become familiar with the demands a worker faces. But he or she too should also assume responsibility.*

(A) When employers become familiar with the demands placed on their workers, they would also assume responsibility.
(B) Employers ought to become familiar with the demands their workers face, but workers, too, must assume responsibility for their jobs.
(C) Employers who have familiarity with the demands their workers face also need to take responsibility for them.
(D) Those employees whose employers are familiar with their demands need to take responsibility for their jobs.
(E) Employees and employers, familiar with the demands of the workplace, must also assume responsibility for them.

**GO ON TO THE NEXT PAGE** ⟩

**32.** In context, the underlined portion of sentence 7 (reproduced below) could best be revised in which of the following ways? .

*This results from an employer's lack of consideration for employees.*

  (A) In contrast is
  (B) With unreasonable demands, they show
  (C) This concern illustrates
  (D) Such a distorted view shows
  (E) Such treatment demonstrates

**33.** Which of the following is the best version of the underlined portion of sentence 9 (reproduced below) ?

*Sometimes the employer does not listen fully to suggestions of employees this can make workers feel undervalued.*

  (A) (As it is now)
  (B) When sometimes they do not listen fully to suggestions from employees, this can make
  (C) Because the employers had not listened fully to suggestions from employees, they made
  (D) An employer who does not listen closely to suggestions of employees, making
  (E) Sometimes an employer does not listen closely to suggestions from employees, making

**34.** Which of the following sentences, if inserted before sentence 10, would best improve the third paragraph?

  (A) The role of technology in the workplace is also important.
  (B) The success of any business depends on effective communication with customers.
  (C) Sometimes employers have legitimate complaints about their employees.
  (D) It is difficult to tell whether certain problems are caused by employees or employers.
  (E) Employees rarely complain without good reason.

**35.** Which of the following would make the most logical final sentence for the essay?

  (A) Responsibility for removal of safety hazards from the workplace lies with the employer.
  (B) For most employers, open communication with employees seems somewhat difficult.
  (C) The challenge of technology offers new opportunities for opening up communication in the workplace.
  (D) Without clearly assigned duties, workers tend to lose their motivation.
  (E) Employers and employees should work together to improve conditions in the workplace.

# STOP

**If you finish before time is called, you may check your work on this section only.
Do not turn to any other section in the test.**

## SECTION 8
### Time — 20 minutes
### 19 Questions

**Turn to Section 8 (page 7) of your answer sheet to answer the questions in this section.**

**Directions:** For each question in this section, select the best answer from among the choices given and fill in the corresponding circle on the answer sheet.

Each sentence below has one or two blanks, each blank indicating that something has been omitted. Beneath the sentence are five words or sets of words labeled A through E. Choose the word or set of words that, when inserted in the sentence, <u>best</u> fits the meaning of the sentence as a whole.

**Example:**

Hoping to ------- the dispute, negotiators proposed a compromise that they felt would be ------- to both labor and management.

(A) enforce . . useful
(B) end . . divisive
(C) overcome . . unattractive
(D) extend . . satisfactory
(E) resolve . . acceptable     ⒶⒷⒸⒹ●

1. Though Luis eagerly sought her -------, he subsequently chose not to heed that advice.

    (A) secretiveness     (B) cooperation
       (C) understanding     (D) counsel
          (E) concord

2. As a young physics instructor, Richard Feynman discovered that he had the gift of sharing his ------- his subject and making that excitement -------.

    (A) passion for . . contagious
    (B) knowledge of . . inaudible
    (C) contempt for . . praiseworthy
    (D) propensity for . . futile
    (E) commitment to . . impersonal

3. As ------- as the disintegration of the Roman Empire must have seemed, that disaster nevertheless presented some ------- aspects.

    (A) momentous . . formidable
    (B) decisive . . unavoidable
    (C) unexpected . . ambiguous
    (D) advantageous . . beneficial
    (E) catastrophic . . constructive

4. The beauty of Mount McKinley is usually cloaked: clouds ------- the summit nine days out of ten.

    (A) release     (B) elevate     (C) entangle
       (D) shroud     (E) attain

5. Madame C. J. Walker introduced her first hair-care product just as demand was reaching its peak; this ------- marketing made her a millionaire.

    (A) opportune     (B) instantaneous
       (C) intermittent     (D) dubious
          (E) extravagant

6. A scientist should not automatically reject folkways that might at first seem silly or superstitious; scientific qualifications are not a license for -------, nor do they ------- prejudice or bias.

    (A) experimentation . . eliminate
    (B) arrogance . . pursue
    (C) humility . . advocate
    (D) smugness . . legitimate
    (E) rigidity . . console

**GO ON TO THE NEXT PAGE**

The passage below is followed by questions based on its content. Answer the questions on the basis of what is <u>stated</u> or <u>implied</u> in the passage and in any introductory material that may be provided.

**Questions 7-19 are based on the following passage.**

*Since the advent of television, social commentators have been evaluating its role in a modern society. In the following excerpt from an essay published in 1992, a German social commentator offers a pointed evaluation of the evaluators.*

"Television makes you stupid."

Virtually all current theories of the medium come down to this simple statement. As a rule, this conclusion is deliv-

*Line*
5  ered with a melancholy undertone. Four principal theories can be distinguished.

The manipulation thesis points to an ideological dimension. It sees in television above all an instrument of political domination. The medium is understood as a neutral vessel, which pours out opinions over a public

10  thought of as passive. Seduced, unsuspecting viewers are won over by the wire-pullers, without ever realizing what is happening to them.

The imitation thesis argues primarily in moral terms. According to it, television consumption leads above all

15  to moral dangers. Anyone who is exposed to the medium becomes habituated to libertinism, irresponsibility, crime, and violence. The private consequences are blunted, callous, and obstinate individuals; the public consequences are the loss of social virtues and general moral decline.

20  This form of critique draws, as is obvious at first glance, on traditional, bourgeois sources. The motifs that recur in this thesis can be identified as far back as the eighteenth century in the vain warnings that early cultural criticism sounded against the dangers of reading novels.

25  More recent is the simulation thesis. According to it, the viewer is rendered incapable of distinguishing between reality and fiction. The primary reality is rendered unrecognizable or replaced by a secondary, phantomlike reality.

All of these converge in the stupefaction thesis.

30  According to it, watching television not only undermines the viewers' ability to criticize and differentiate, along with the moral and political fiber of their being, but also impairs their overall ability to perceive. Television produces, therefore, a new type of human being, who can, according to

35  taste, be imagined as a zombie or a mutant.

All these theories are rather unconvincing. Their authors consider proof to be superfluous. Even the minimal criterion of plausibility does not worry them at all. To mention just one example, no one has yet succeeded in putting before

40  us even a single viewer who was incapable of telling the difference between a family quarrel in the current soap opera and one at his or her family's breakfast table. This doesn't seem to bother the advocates of the simulation thesis.

45  Another common feature of the theories is just as curious but has even more serious consequences. Basically, the viewers appear as defenseless victims, the programmers as crafty criminals. This polarity is maintained with great seriousness: manipulators and manipulated, actors and

50  imitators, simulants and simulated, stupefiers and stupefied face one another in a fine symmetry.

The relationship of the theorists themselves to television raises some important questions. Either the theorists make no use of television at all (in which case they do not know

55  what they are talking about) or they subject themselves to it, and then the question arises—through what miracle is the theorist able to escape the alleged effects of television? Unlike everyone else, the theorist has remained completely intact morally, can distinguish in a sovereign manner

60  between deception and reality, and enjoys complete immunity in the face of the idiocy that he or she sorrowfully diagnoses in the rest of us. Or could—fatal loophole in the dilemma—the theories themselves be symptoms of a universal stupefaction?

65  One can hardly say that these theorists have failed to have any effect. It is true that their influence on what is actually broadcast is severely limited, which may be considered distressing or noted with gratitude, depending on one's mood. On the other hand, they have found ready

70  listeners among politicians. That is not surprising, for the conviction that one is dealing with millions of idiots "out there in the country" is part of the basic psychological equipment of the professional politician. One might have second thoughts about the theorists' influence when one

75  watches how the veterans of televised election campaigns fight each other for every single minute when it comes to displaying their limousine, their historic appearance before the guard of honor, their hairstyle on the platform, and above all their speech organs. The number of broadcast

80  minutes, the camera angles, and the level of applause are registered with a touching enthusiasm. The politicians have been particularly taken by the good old manipulation thesis.

**7.** In line 11, the term "wire-pullers" refers to the

(A) bland technicians who staff television studios
(B) shadowy molders of public opinion
(C) self-serving critics of television
(D) hack writers who recycle old concepts
(E) slick advertisers of consumer goods

GO ON TO THE NEXT PAGE ⟩

8. As used in line 14, "consumption" most nearly means

(A) destruction
(B) viewing
(C) erosion
(D) purchasing
(E) obsession

9. The reference to the eighteenth century in lines 21-24 conveys what impression about cultural critiques based on moral grounds?

(A) They are part of a tradition dating back to early civilization.
(B) They were the main preoccupation of that era's social commentators.
(C) They were once persuasive but now go mostly unheeded.
(D) They are no more valid today than they were in those years.
(E) They continue to appeal to people having no real understanding of art.

10. The author makes the comparison to the novel in lines 21-24 in order to

(A) point out television's literary origins
(B) underscore the general decline of culture
(C) emphasize television's reliance on visual imagery
(D) expose narrow-minded resistance to new forms of expression
(E) attack the cultural shortcomings of television producers

11. The terms "primary" (line 27) and "secondary" (line 28) are used to refer to the distinction between

(A) an ideal democracy and our political system
(B) natural objects and human artifacts
(C) the everyday world and its fictional counterpart
(D) the morality of the elite and that of the populace
(E) the world view of scientists and that of mystics

12. Advocates of the simulation thesis might best respond to the criticism in lines 37-44 by pointing out that the author

(A) trivializes their theory by applying it too literally
(B) concentrates excessively on a relatively insignificant point
(C) is not a psychologist and so cannot properly evaluate their argument
(D) attacks their theory in order to bolster one of the other three theories
(E) fails to consider the impact of television on popular culture

13. The author's attitude toward the evaluators of television can be best described as

(A) intrigued
(B) scornful
(C) equivocal
(D) indulgent
(E) nonchalant

14. The author responds to the four theories of television primarily by

(A) offering contrary evidence
(B) invoking diverse authorities
(C) adding historical perspective
(D) blurring the line between the manipulator and the manipulated
(E) implying that no reasonable person could take them seriously

15. According to the passage, most current evaluations of television are based on which of the following assumptions about viewers?

I. Viewers are mostly interested in comedy programs.
II. Viewers never engage their analytical faculties.
III. Viewers see political content where there is none.

(A) I only
(B) II only
(C) I and II only
(D) II and III only
(E) I, II, and III

16. In mapping out categories of theories about television, the author uses which of the following?

(A) Earnest reevaluation
(B) Incredulous analysis of academic documentation
(C) Somber warnings about the future
(D) Intentional falsification of data
(E) Description tinged with irony

17. In line 59, "sovereign" is best understood to mean

(A) excellent
(B) opulent
(C) elitist
(D) absolute
(E) oppressive

**GO ON TO THE NEXT PAGE**

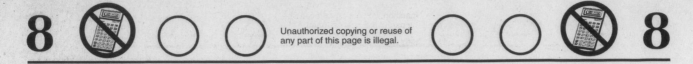

**18.** The "fatal loophole" (line 62) is best summarized by which of the following statements?

(A) Theorists are conspiring with the politicians.
(B) Theorists are themselves victims of television.
(C) All human beings occasionally behave like zombies and mutants.
(D) Even serious thinkers need mindless entertainment occasionally.
(E) Theorists have disregarded the enjoyment that television provides.

**19.** In the last paragraph, the author's attitude toward politicians is primarily one of

(A) humorous contempt
(B) outraged embarrassment
(C) worried puzzlement
(D) relieved resignation
(E) begrudging sympathy

# STOP
**If you finish before time is called, you may check your work on this section only.**
**Do not turn to any other section in the test.**

## SECTION 9
### Time — 20 minutes
### 16 Questions

---

**Turn to Section 9 (page 7) of your answer sheet to answer the questions in this section.**

---

**Directions:** For this section, solve each problem and decide which is the best of the choices given. Fill in the corresponding circle on the answer sheet. You may use any available space for scratchwork.

Notes

1. The use of a calculator is permitted.
2. All numbers used are real numbers.
3. Figures that accompany problems in this test are intended to provide information useful in solving the problems. They are drawn as accurately as possible EXCEPT when it is stated in a specific problem that the figure is not drawn to scale. All figures lie in a plane unless otherwise indicated.
4. Unless otherwise specified, the domain of any function $f$ is assumed to be the set of all real numbers $x$ for which $f(x)$ is a real number.

Reference Information

     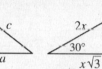 

$A = \pi r^2$
$C = 2\pi r$
$A = \ell w$
$A = \frac{1}{2}bh$
$V = \ell wh$
$V = \pi r^2 h$
$c^2 = a^2 + b^2$
Special Right Triangles

The number of degrees of arc in a circle is 360.
The sum of the measures in degrees of the angles of a triangle is 180.

---

1. There is the same number of boys and girls on a school bus when it departs from school. At the first stop, 4 boys get off the bus and nobody gets on. After the first stop, there are twice as many girls as boys on the bus. How many girls are on the bus?

   (A) 4
   (B) 6
   (C) 8
   (D) 12
   (E) 16

2. Which of the following is the graph of a linear function with a negative slope and a positive $y$-intercept?

   (A)

   (B)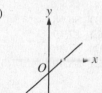

   (C)

   (D)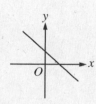

   (E)

GO ON TO THE NEXT PAGE

**609**

**Questions 3-4 refer to the following price list.**

| Number of Donuts | Total Price |
|---|---|
| 1 | $0.40 |
| Box of 6 | $1.89 |
| Box of 12 | $3.59 |

3. Of the following, which is the closest approximation of the cost per donut when one purchases a box of 6 ?

(A) $0.20
(B) $0.30
(C) $0.40
(D) $0.50
(E) $0.60

4. What would be the <u>least</u> amount of money needed to purchase exactly 21 donuts?

(A) $5.88
(B) $6.68
(C) $7.19
(D) $7.38
(E) $8.40

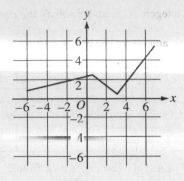

5. The figure above shows the graph of the function $h$. Which of the following is closest to $h(5)$ ?

(A) 1
(B) 2
(C) 3
(D) 4
(E) 5

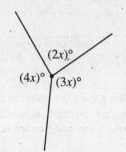

Note: Figure not drawn to scale.

6. In the figure above, three line segments meet at a point to form three angles. What is the value of $x$ ?

(A) 20
(B) 36
(C) 40
(D) 45
(E) 60

GO ON TO THE NEXT PAGE

7. Positive integers $x$, $y$, and $z$ satisfy the equations $x^{-\frac{1}{2}} = \frac{1}{3}$ and $y^z = 16$. If $z > y$, what is the value of $x + z$ ?

(A)  5
(B)  7
(C)  11
(D)  13
(E)  15

8. In the semicircle above, the center is at $(4, 0)$. Which of the following are $x$-coordinates of two points on this semicircle whose $y$-coordinates are equal?

(A)  1 and 6
(B)  1 and 8
(C)  2 and 6
(D)  2 and 8
(E)  3 and 6

9. If $p$ is an integer and 3 is the remainder when $2p + 7$ is divided by 5, then $p$ could be

(A)  2
(B)  3
(C)  4
(D)  5
(E)  6

10. Stacy noted that she is both the 12th tallest and the 12th shortest student in her class. If everyone in the class is of a different height, how many students are in the class?

(A)  22
(B)  23
(C)  24
(D)  25
(E)  34

GO ON TO THE NEXT PAGE

11. The quadratic function $g$ is given by $g(x) = ax^2 + bx + c$, where $a$ and $c$ are negative constants. Which of the following could be the graph of $g$?

(A)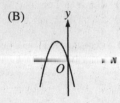

(B)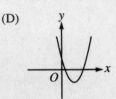

(C)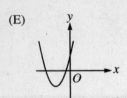

(D)

(E)

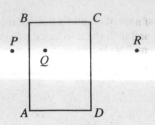

Note: Figure not drawn to scale.

12. In the figure above, $ABCD$ is a rectangle with $BC = 4$ and $AB = 6$. Points $P$, $Q$, and $R$ are different points on a line (not shown) that is parallel to $\overline{AD}$. Points $P$ and $Q$ are symmetric about line $AB$ and points $Q$ and $R$ are symmetric about line $CD$. What is the length of $\overline{PR}$?

(A)  6
(B)  8
(C)  10
(D)  12
(E)  20

GO ON TO THE NEXT PAGE

13. The price of a telephone was first increased by 10 percent and then the new price was decreased by 25 percent. The final price was what percent of the initial price?

(A) 78%
(B) 80%
(C) 82.5%
(D) 85%
(E) 87.5%

14. When the number $w$ is multiplied by 4, the result is the same as when 4 is added to $w$. What is the value of $3w$?

(A) $\dfrac{3}{4}$

(B) 1

(C) $\dfrac{4}{3}$

(D) 3

(E) 4

15. The lengths of the sides of a right triangle are consecutive even integers, and the length of the shortest side is $x$. Which of the following equations could be used to find $x$?

(A) $x + x + 1 = x + 2$
(B) $x^2 + (x + 1)^2 = (x + 2)^2$
(C) $x^2 + (x + 2)^2 = (x + 4)^2$
(D) $x + x + 2 = x + 4$
(E) $x^2 = (x + 2)(x + 4)$

16. If $x$ is an integer greater than 1 and if $y = x + \dfrac{1}{x}$, which of the following must be true?

  I. $y \neq x$
  II. $y$ is an integer.
  III. $xy > x^2$

(A) I only
(B) III only
(C) I and II only
(D) I and III only
(E) I, II, and III

## STOP
If you finish before time is called, you may check your work on this section only.
Do not turn to any other section in the test.

**10**  **10**

Unauthorized copying or reuse of
any part of this page is illegal.

## SECTION 10
Time — 10 minutes
14 Questions

---

**Turn to Section 10 (page 7) of your answer sheet to answer the questions in this section.**

---

**Directions:** For each question in this section, select the best answer from among the choices given and fill in the corresponding circle on the answer sheet.

---

The following sentences test correctness and effectiveness of expression. Part of each sentence or the entire sentence is underlined; beneath each sentence are five ways of phrasing the underlined material. Choice A repeats the original phrasing; the other four choices are different. If you think the original phrasing produces a better sentence than any of the alternatives, select choice A; if not, select one of the other choices.

In making your selection, follow the requirements of standard written English; that is, pay attention to grammar, choice of words, sentence construction, and punctuation. Your selection should result in the most effective sentence—clear and precise, without awkwardness or ambiguity.

EXAMPLE:

Laura Ingalls Wilder published her first book
and she was sixty-five years old then.

(A) and she was sixty-five years old then
(B) when she was sixty-five
(C) at age sixty-five years old
(D) upon the reaching of sixty-five years
(E) at the time when she was sixty-five

1. In scenarios reminiscent of the old science fiction movie *Fantastic Voyage*, medical researchers hope exploring the body with miniature robots sent into the bloodstream.

(A) hope exploring
(B) hope to explore
(C) hope it can explore
(D) have hopes to explore
(E) are having hopes of exploring

2. H. Ford Douglas, one of the few Black soldiers in White regiments during the early part of the Civil War, and eventually to recruit and command his own unit.

(A) and eventually to recruit and command his own unit
(B) eventually recruited and commanded his own unit
(C) he eventually recruited and commanded his own unit
(D) he eventually had his own unit that he recruited and commanded
(E) having eventually recruited and commanded his own unit

3. Ignorance is not equivalent to stupidity, for ignorance can often be corrected while stupidity cannot.

(A) for ignorance can often be corrected while stupidity cannot
(B) since you can often correct ignorance while the same is not true about stupidity
(C) because it can be corrected and the other cannot
(D) because of its correctible nature
(E) because the two differ regarding correctibility

4. Journalists should present a balanced view of the news but with their goal to stir discussion and unsettle complacent thinkers.

(A) with their goal to stir
(B) should also stir
(C) aiming at the same time to stir
(D) also trying to stir
(E) its goal should also be in stirring

**GO ON TO THE NEXT PAGE**

**10**  🚫

Unauthorized copying or reuse of
any part of this page is illegal.

🚫  **10**

5. The ancient Spartans tested the endurance of potential <u>warriors, devised</u> various ordeals, including one that required them to run bare-legged through fields of stinging nettles.

(A) warriors, devised
(B) warriors devising
(C) warriors; and devised
(D) warriors by devising
(E) warriors with the devising of

6. The lawyers representing the parking-lot operators asserted <u>as to the defensibility of their practices as legal and ethical</u>.

(A) as to the defensibility of their practices as legal and ethical
(B) as to their practices and their defensibility on legal and ethical grounds
(C) that their practices, that is the operators, are defensible in legal terms as well as ethics
(D) that in regards to defensibility their practices are legally and ethically defensible
(E) that the practices of the operators are legally and ethically defensible

7. Toni Morrison was honored by Harvard University not only as a great novelist but also <u>she wrote eloquently of the history</u> of African American culture.

(A) she wrote eloquently of the history
(B) having written an eloquent history
(C) writing eloquently about the history
(D) being an eloquent historian
(E) as an eloquent historian

8. <u>Although Central Park in Manhattan is better known than Prospect Park in Brooklyn, the designer of both parks, Frederick Law Olmsted, preferred Prospect Park.</u>

(A) Although Central Park in Manhattan is better known than Prospect Park in Brooklyn, the designer of both parks, Frederick Law Olmsted, preferred Prospect Park.
(B) Central Park in Manhattan being better known than Prospect Park in Brooklyn, the designer of both, Frederick Law Olmsted, preferred the latter.
(C) Although not as well known as Central Park, Frederick Law Olmsted, he designed both parks, preferred Prospect Park.
(D) The designer of both Central Park and Prospect Park was Frederick Law Olmsted, he preferred Prospect Park.
(E) Although more people know about Manhattan's Central Park than Prospect Park in Brooklyn, Frederick Law Olmsted, having designed both, has preferred the latter.

9. Because Uranus is nearly three billion kilometers from the Sun and is enveloped by a thick methane cloud <u>layer, this blocks almost all solar radiation</u>.

(A) layer, this blocks almost all solar radiation
(B) layer, this accounts for its receiving almost no solar radiation
(C) layer is the reason why it receives almost no solar radiation
(D) layer, almost no solar radiation reaches the planet
(E) layer, it blocks almost all solar radiation from reaching the planet

**GO ON TO THE NEXT PAGE** ⟩

**10.** Lacking good instruction, <u>my mistakes in creating a graph to illustrate historical trends were numerous</u>.

  (A)  my mistakes in creating a graph to illustrate historical trends were numerous

  (B)  I made numerous mistakes in creating a graph to illustrate historical trends

  (C)  there were numerous mistakes in the graph I created to illustrate historical trends

  (D)  I created a graph to illustrate historical trends with numerous mistakes

  (E)  the graph I made for illustrating historical trends had numerous mistakes

**11.** It is a myth that mathematicians are <u>so absorbed with abstractions and thus</u> have no practical interests.

  (A)  so absorbed with abstractions and thus

  (B)  absorbed by abstractions and therefore

  (C)  so absorbed in abstractions that they

  (D)  absorbed in so much abstraction that they

  (E)  too abstract, and so they

**12.** By simply entering an Internet website or calling a toll-free number, <u>a catalog order can be placed</u> for almost anything from cheesecakes to fully equipped desktop computers.

  (A)  a catalog order can be placed

  (B)  by placing a catalog order

  (C)  they will place your catalog order

  (D)  you can place a catalog order

  (E)  your catalog order can be placed

**13.** Some people believe that one day <u>we will establish not only bases on the Moon, but also a landing on Neptune will occur</u>.

  (A)  we will establish not only bases on the Moon, but also a landing on Neptune will occur

  (B)  not only bases on the Moon will be established, but also a landing on Neptune will be made

  (C)  we will not only establish bases on the Moon but also land on Neptune

  (D)  we will not only establish bases on the Moon, but we will land on Neptune in addition

  (E)  we will not only establish bases on the Moon, but we will land on Neptune

**14.** The city is populated by many people who, although their common language is English, <u>the languages at home range from speaking Armenian to Zapotec</u>.

  (A)  the languages at home range from speaking Armenian to Zapotec

  (B)  speaking at home is in languages ranging from Armenian to Zapotec

  (C)  the languages range from Armenian to Zapotec at home

  (D)  speak languages at home that range from Armenian to Zapotec

  (E)  they are speaking languages at home ranging from Armenian to Zapotec

# STOP

**If you finish before time is called, you may check your work on this section only.**
**Do not turn to any other section in the test.**

# Correct Answers and Difficulty Levels
## SAT Practice Test #4

## CRITICAL READING

### Section 2
#### Multiple-Choice Questions

| Correct Answer | Difficulty Level | | Correct Answer | Difficulty Level |
|---|---|---|---|---|
| 1 D | E | 13 | A | M |
| 2 C | E | 14 | C | M |
| 3 A | M | 15 | E | M |
| 4 B | M | 16 | D | M |
| 5 C | M | 17 | D | M |
| 6 C | M | 18 | D | M |
| 7 D | H | 19 | E | M |
| 8 A | H | 20 | C | M |
| 9 C | H | 21 | A | M |
| 10 B | M | 22 | B | M |
| 11 E | E | 23 | B | H |
| 12 C | E | 24 | A | M |

Number correct _____

Number incorrect _____

### Section 5
#### Multiple-Choice Questions

| Correct Answer | Difficulty Level | | Correct Answer | Difficulty Level |
|---|---|---|---|---|
| 1 B | M | 13 | C | E |
| 2 E | M | 14 | B | M |
| 3 E | H | 15 | A | M |
| 4 A | H | 16 | E | M |
| 5 E | H | 17 | D | E |
| 6 B | E | 18 | A | E |
| 7 D | M | 19 | C | M |
| 8 B | M | 20 | E | H |
| 9 A | M | 21 | A | M |
| 10 A | M | 22 | C | M |
| 11 A | M | 23 | B | M |
| 12 D | M | 24 | B | M |

Number correct _____

Number incorrect _____

### Section 8
#### Multiple-Choice Questions

| Correct Answer | Difficulty Level | | Correct Answer | Difficulty Level |
|---|---|---|---|---|
| 1 D | E | 11 | C | E |
| 2 A | M | 12 | A | M |
| 3 E | M | 13 | B | M |
| 4 D | M | 14 | E | H |
| 5 A | M | 15 | B | M |
| 6 D | H | 16 | E | M |
| 7 B | M | 17 | D | M |
| 8 B | E | 18 | B | M |
| 9 D | M | 19 | A | M |
| 10 D | M | | | |

Number correct _____

Number incorrect _____

## MATHEMATICS

### Section 3
#### Multiple-Choice Questions

| Correct Answer | Difficulty Level | | Correct Answer | Difficulty Level |
|---|---|---|---|---|
| 1 E | E | 11 | A | M |
| 2 A | E | 12 | D | M |
| 3 E | E | 13 | E | M |
| 4 E | E | 14 | D | M |
| 5 B | E | 15 | C | M |
| 6 A | E | 16 | C | M |
| 7 E | M | 17 | A | M |
| 8 E | M | 18 | A | H |
| 9 D | M | 19 | A | H |
| 10 D | M | 20 | E | H |

Number correct _____

Number incorrect _____

### Section 6

#### Multiple-Choice Questions

| Correct Answer | Difficulty Level |
|---|---|
| 1 D | E |
| 2 D | E |
| 3 A | E |
| 4 E | E |
| 5 D | M |
| 6 B | M |
| 7 C | M |
| 8 E | H |

#### Student-Produced Response Questions

| Correct Answer | Difficulty Level |
|---|---|
| 9 | 1404 | E |
| 10 | 57.5 | E |
| 11 | 110 | M |
| 12 | 9 | M |
| 13 | 13, 14, 15, 16, 17 | M |
| 14 | 5 | M |
| 15 | 1/2, .5 | M |
| 16 | 2, 7 | H |
| 17 | 149 | H |
| 18 | 72 | H |

Number correct _____

Number correct (9-18) _____

Number incorrect _____

### Section 9
#### Multiple-Choice Questions

| Correct Answer | Difficulty Level | | Correct Answer | Difficulty Level |
|---|---|---|---|---|
| 1 C | E | 9 | B | M |
| 2 D | E | 10 | B | M |
| 3 B | E | 11 | A | M |
| 4 B | E | 12 | B | M |
| 5 C | E | 13 | C | M |
| 6 C | M | 14 | E | M |
| 7 D | M | 15 | C | M |
| 8 C | M | 16 | D | H |

Number correct _____

Number incorrect _____

## WRITING

### Essay

Essay Score* (0-6) _____

### Section 7
#### Multiple-Choice Questions

| Correct Answer | Difficulty Level | | Correct Answer | Difficulty Level |
|---|---|---|---|---|
| 1 E | E | 19 | E | E |
| 2 B | E | 20 | D | M |
| 3 B | E | 21 | B | M |
| 4 E | E | 22 | B | M |
| 5 D | M | 23 | E | M |
| 6 C | E | 24 | A | M |
| 7 A | E | 25 | A | M |
| 8 E | E | 26 | B | M |
| 9 E | M | 27 | B | M |
| 10 C | M | 28 | C | H |
| 11 C | M | 29 | B | H |
| 12 E | E | 30 | D | E |
| 13 E | E | 31 | E | M |
| 14 B | E | 32 | E | M |
| 15 D | E | 33 | E | M |
| 16 D | E | 34 | C | M |
| 17 E | M | 35 | E | E |
| 18 A | E | | | |

Number correct _____

Number incorrect _____

### Section 10
#### Multiple-Choice Questions

| Correct Answer | Difficulty Level |
|---|---|
| 1 | B | E |
| 2 | B | E |
| 3 | A | M |
| 4 | B | E |
| 5 | D | E |
| 6 | E | E |
| 7 | E | E |
| 8 | A | M |
| 9 | D | M |
| 10 | B | M |
| 11 | C | M |
| 12 | D | M |
| 13 | C | M |
| 14 | D | H |

Number correct _____

Number incorrect _____

**NOTE:** Difficulty levels are E (easy), M (medium), and H (hard).

* To score your essay, use the SAT scoring guide in Chapter 9 and the free sample essays available online at www.collegeboard.org/satonlinecourse.
  On practice tests 4-10, your essay score should range from 0 to 6. (Keep in mind that on the actual SAT, your essay will be read by two readers and you will receive a score of 0 to 12 on your score report.)

# The SAT Scoring Process

**Scoring.** The computer compares the circle filled in for each question with the correct response. Each correct answer receives one point; omitted questions do not affect your score. For each wrong answer to a multiple-choice question, one-fourth of a point is subtracted to correct for random guessing. The SAT critical reading section has 67 questions. If, for example, a student has 44 right, 20 wrong, and 3 omitted, the resulting raw score is determined as follows:

$$44 \text{ right} - \frac{20 \text{ wrong}}{4} = 44 - 5 = 39 \text{ raw score points}$$

Obtaining raw scores frequently involves the rounding of fractions to the nearest whole number. For example, a raw score of 39.25 is rounded to 39, the nearest whole number. A raw score of 39.50 is rounded upward to 40. **For the WRITING SECTION**, your essay raw score counts approximately 30% and your multiple-choice raw score counts approximately 70%.

**Converting to reported scaled score.** Raw scores are then placed on the College Board scale of 200 to 800 through a process that adjusts scores to account for minor differences in difficulty among different versions of the test. This process, known as equating, is performed so that a student's reported score is not affected by the version of the test taken or by the abilities of the group with whom the student takes the test. As a result of placing SAT scores on the College Board scale, scores earned by students at different times can be compared. For example, an SAT critical reading score of 400 on a test taken at one administration indicates the same level of developed critical reading ability as a 400 score obtained on a different version of the test taken at another time.

**Note:** Since this test has not been previously administered, score ranges are provided for each possible raw score.

## How to Score Practice Test #4

### SAT Critical Reading Sections 2, 5, and 8

**Step A:** Count the number of correct answers for *Section 2* and record the number in the space provided on the Scoring Worksheet. Then do the same for the incorrect answers. (Do not count omitted answers.)

**Step B:** Count the number of correct answers and the number of incorrect answers for *Section 5* and record the numbers in the spaces provided on the Scoring Worksheet. (Do not count omitted answers.)

**Step C:** Count the number of correct answers and the number of incorrect answers for *Section 8* and record the numbers in the spaces provided on the Scoring Worksheet. (Do not count omitted answers.)

**Step D:** Total the number of correct responses. Total the number of incorrect responses. Enter the resulting figures on the Scoring Worksheet. To determine A, use the formula:

$$\text{Number correct} - \frac{\text{Number incorrect}}{4} = A$$

**Step E:** To obtain B, your Rounded Critical Reading Raw Score, round A to the nearest whole number. (For example, any number from 44.50 to 45.49 rounds to 45.) Enter the resulting figure on the Scoring Worksheet.

**Step F:** To find your Critical Reading Scaled Score Range, look up the Total Rounded Raw Score you obtained in step E in the Critical Reading Conversion Table (Table 1). Enter this range in the box on the Scoring Worksheet.

### SAT Mathematics Sections 3, 6, and 9

**Step A:** Count the number of correct answers and the number of incorrect answers for *Section 3* and record the numbers in the spaces provided on the Scoring Worksheet. (Do not count omitted answers.)

**Step B:** Count the number of correct answers and the number of incorrect answers for the multiple-choice questions (*questions 1 through 8*) in *Section 6* and record the numbers in the spaces provided on the Scoring Worksheet. (Do not count omitted answers.)

**Step C:** Count the number of correct answers for the student-produced response questions (*questions 9 through 18*) in *Section 6* and record the number in the space provided on the Scoring Worksheet.

**Step D:** Count the number of correct answers and the number of incorrect answers for *Section 9* and record the numbers in the spaces provided on the Scoring Worksheet. (Do not count omitted answers.)

**Step E:** Total the number of correct responses. Total the number of incorrect responses. Enter the resulting figures on the Scoring Worksheet. To determine A, use the formula:

$$\text{Number correct} - \frac{\text{Number incorrect}}{4} = A$$

**Step F:** To obtain B, your Mathematics Rounded Raw Score, round A to the nearest whole number. (For example, any number from 44.50 to 45.49 rounds to 45.) Enter the resulting figure on the Scoring Worksheet.

**Step G:** To find your Mathematics Scaled Score Range, use the Mathematics Conversion Table (Table 2) to look up the Total Rounded Raw Score you obtained in step F. Enter this range in the box on the Scoring Worksheet.

## SAT Writing Sections 1, 7, and 10

**Step A:** Enter your Essay Score for *Section 1* in the box on the Scoring Worksheet. (On this practice test, your essay score should range from 0 to 6. Keep in mind that on the actual SAT, two readers will read your essay and you will receive a total score of 0 to 12 on your score report.)

**Step B:** Count the number of correct answers and the number of incorrect answers for *Section 7* and record the numbers in the spaces provided on the Scoring Worksheet. (Do not count omitted answers.)

**Step C:** Count the number of correct answers and the number of incorrect answers for *Section 10* and record the numbers in the spaces provided on the Scoring Worksheet. (Do not count omitted answers.)

**Step D:** Total the number of correct responses. Total the number of incorrect responses. Enter the resulting figure on the Scoring Worksheet. To determine A, use the formula:

$$\text{Number correct} - \frac{\text{Number incorrect}}{4} = A$$

**Step E:** To obtain B, your Writing Multiple-Choice (MC) Rounded Raw Score, round A to the nearest whole number. (For example, any number from 44.50 to 45.49 rounds to 45.) Enter the resulting figure on the Scoring Worksheet.

**Step F:** To find your overall Writing Scaled Score Range, use Table 3. Look up the Total MC Rounded Raw Score you obtained in Step E in the left side of Table 3 and the Essay Score entered in Step A across the top of the table. Enter this range in the box on the Scoring Worksheet.

**Step G:** To find your Writing MC Subscore Range, look up the Total MC Rounded Raw Score you obtained in Step E on the Writing Multiple-Choice Conversion Table (Table 4). Enter this range in the box on the Scoring Worksheet.

**Note:** For the **WRITING SECTION**, your Essay Raw Score counts approximately 30% and your Multiple-Choice Raw Score counts approximately 70%.

# SAT Practice Test #4 Scoring Worksheet

## SAT Critical Reading Section

A. Section 2: _____    _____
                 no. correct             no. incorrect
                  +                     +

B. Section 5: _____    _____
                 no. correct             no. incorrect
                  +                     +

C. Section 8: _____    _____
                 no. correct             no. incorrect
                  =                     =

D. Total Unrounded Raw Score    _____  –  (_____ ÷ 4)  =  _____
                                   no. correct                  no. incorrect          A

E. Total Rounded Raw Score
   (Rounded to nearest whole number)
                                                              B

F. Critical Reading Scaled Score Range
   (See Table 1)

                                                 [    –    ]

Critical
Reading Scaled
Score Range

## SAT Mathematics Section

A. Section 3: _____    _____
                 no. correct             no. incorrect
                  +                     +

B. Section 6: _____    _____
   Questions 1-8       no. correct             no. incorrect
                  +                     +

C. Section 6: _____    _____
   Questions 9-18      no. correct
                  +                     +

D. Section 9: _____    _____
                 no. correct             no. incorrect
                  =                     =

E. Total Unrounded Raw Score    _____  –  (_____ ÷ 4)  =  _____
                                   no. correct                  no. incorrect          A

F. Total Rounded Raw Score
   (Rounded to nearest whole number)
                                                                B

G. Mathematics Scaled Score Range
   (See Table 2)

                                                   [    –    ]

Mathematics
Scaled
Score Range

## SAT Writing Section

**A. Section 1:**

Essay Score

**B. Section 7:**

_____   _____
no. correct           no. incorrect

+                          +

**C. Section 10:**

_____   _____
no. correct           no. incorrect

=                          =

**D. Total MC Unrounded Raw Score**

_____ – (_____ ÷ 4)  =  _____
no. correct              no. incorrect                              A

**E. Total MC Rounded Raw Score**
  (Rounded to nearest whole number)

_____
B

**F. Writing Scaled Score Range**
  (See Table 3)

Writing Scaled
Score Range

**G. Writing MC Subscore Range**
  (See Table 4)

Writing MC
Subscore Range

| Table 1. Critical Reading Conversion Table | | | |
|---|---|---|---|
| Raw Score | Scaled Score | Raw Score | Scaled Score |
| 67 | 800 | 30 | 470-530 |
| 66 | 770-800 | 29 | 470-530 |
| 65 | 740-800 | 28 | 460-520 |
| 64 | 720-800 | 27 | 450-510 |
| 63 | 700-800 | 26 | 450-510 |
| 62 | 690-790 | 25 | 440-500 |
| 61 | 670-770 | 24 | 440-500 |
| 60 | 660-760 | 23 | 430-490 |
| 59 | 660-740 | 22 | 420-480 |
| 58 | 650-730 | 21 | 420-480 |
| 57 | 640-720 | 20 | 410-470 |
| 56 | 630-710 | 19 | 400-460 |
| 55 | 630-710 | 18 | 400-460 |
| 54 | 620-700 | 17 | 390-450 |
| 53 | 610-690 | 16 | 380-440 |
| 52 | 600-680 | 15 | 380-440 |
| 51 | 610-670 | 14 | 370-430 |
| 50 | 600-660 | 13 | 360-420 |
| 49 | 590-650 | 12 | 350-410 |
| 48 | 580-640 | 11 | 350-410 |
| 47 | 580-640 | 10 | 340-400 |
| 46 | 570-630 | 9 | 330-390 |
| 45 | 560-620 | 8 | 310-390 |
| 44 | 560-620 | 7 | 300-380 |
| 43 | 550-610 | 6 | 290-370 |
| 42 | 550-610 | 5 | 270-370 |
| 41 | 540-600 | 4 | 260-360 |
| 40 | 530-590 | 3 | 250-350 |
| 39 | 530-590 | 2 | 230-330 |
| 38 | 520-580 | 1 | 220-320 |
| 37 | 510-570 | 0 | 200-290 |
| 36 | 510-570 | -1 | 200-290 |
| 35 | 500-560 | -2 | 200-270 |
| 34 | 500-560 | -3 | 200-250 |
| 33 | 490-550 | -4 | 200-230 |
| 32 | 480-540 | -5 | 200-210 |
| 31 | 480-540 | -6 and below | 200 |

| Table 2. Mathematics Conversion Table | | | |
|---|---|---|---|
| Raw Score | Scaled Score | Raw Score | Scaled Score |
| 54 | 800 | 23 | 460-520 |
| 53 | 750-800 | 22 | 450-510 |
| 52 | 720-800 | 21 | 440-500 |
| 51 | 700-780 | 20 | 430-490 |
| 50 | 690-770 | 19 | 430-490 |
| 49 | 680-740 | 18 | 420-480 |
| 48 | 670-730 | 17 | 410-470 |
| 47 | 660-720 | 16 | 400-460 |
| 46 | 640-700 | 15 | 400-460 |
| 45 | 630-690 | 14 | 390-450 |
| 44 | 620-680 | 13 | 380-440 |
| 43 | 620-680 | 12 | 360-440 |
| 42 | 610-670 | 11 | 350-430 |
| 41 | 600-660 | 10 | 340-420 |
| 40 | 580-660 | 9 | 330-430 |
| 39 | 570-650 | 8 | 320-420 |
| 38 | 560-640 | 7 | 310-410 |
| 37 | 550-630 | 6 | 290-390 |
| 36 | 550-630 | 5 | 280-380 |
| 35 | 540-620 | 4 | 270-370 |
| 34 | 530-610 | 3 | 260-360 |
| 33 | 520-600 | 2 | 240-340 |
| 32 | 520-600 | 1 | 230-330 |
| 31 | 520-580 | 0 | 210-310 |
| 30 | 510-570 | -1 | 200-290 |
| 29 | 500-560 | -2 | 200-270 |
| 28 | 490-550 | -3 | 200-250 |
| 27 | 490-550 | -4 | 200-230 |
| 26 | 480-540 | -5 | 200-210 |
| 25 | 470-530 | -6 and below | 200 |
| 24 | 460-520 | | |

| MC Raw Score | Essay Score | | | | | | |
|---|---|---|---|---|---|---|---|
| | 0 | 1 | 2 | 3 | 4 | 5 | 6 |
| 49 | 650-690 | 670-720 | 690-740 | 710-770 | 750-800 | 780-800 | 800 |
| 48 | 630-690 | 640-720 | 660-740 | 690-770 | 720-800 | 760-800 | 780-800 |
| 47 | 600-690 | 620-720 | 640-740 | 660-770 | 700-800 | 730-800 | 760-800 |
| 46 | 580-690 | 600-720 | 620-740 | 650-770 | 680-800 | 710-800 | 740-800 |
| 45 | 570-690 | 580-720 | 600-740 | 630-770 | 670-800 | 700-800 | 730-800 |
| 44 | 560-680 | 570-710 | 590-730 | 620-760 | 660-790 | 690-800 | 720-800 |
| 43 | 540-660 | 560-690 | 580-710 | 610-740 | 640-780 | 670-800 | 700-800 |
| 42 | 530-660 | 550-690 | 570-700 | 600-730 | 630-770 | 660-800 | 690-800 |
| 41 | 530-650 | 540-680 | 560-700 | 590-720 | 620-760 | 660-790 | 680-800 |
| 40 | 520-640 | 530-670 | 550-690 | 580-710 | 620-750 | 630-780 | 660-800 |
| 39 | 510-630 | 520-660 | 540-680 | 570-710 | 610-740 | 640-770 | 670-800 |
| 38 | 500-620 | 520-650 | 540-670 | 560-700 | 600-730 | 630-770 | 660-790 |
| 37 | 490-610 | 510-640 | 530-660 | 560-690 | 590-720 | 620-760 | 650-780 |
| 36 | 480-600 | 500-630 | 520-650 | 550-680 | 580-720 | 610-750 | 640-770 |
| 35 | 480-590 | 490-620 | 510-640 | 540-670 | 570-710 | 610-740 | 640-770 |
| 34 | 470-590 | 480-620 | 500-630 | 530-660 | 570-700 | 600-730 | 630-760 |
| 33 | 460-580 | 470-610 | 490-630 | 520-650 | 560-690 | 590-720 | 620-750 |
| 32 | 450-570 | 470-600 | 490-620 | 510-640 | 550-680 | 580-710 | 610-740 |
| 31 | 440-560 | 460-590 | 480-610 | 510-640 | 540-670 | 570-700 | 600-730 |
| 30 | 430-550 | 450-580 | 470-600 | 500-630 | 530-660 | 560-700 | 590-720 |
| 29 | 430-540 | 440-570 | 460-590 | 490-620 | 520-650 | 560-690 | 590-710 |
| 28 | 420-530 | 430-560 | 450-580 | 480-610 | 520-650 | 550-680 | 580-700 |
| 27 | 410-520 | 420-550 | 440-570 | 470-600 | 510-640 | 540-670 | 570-700 |
| 26 | 400-520 | 420-550 | 430-560 | 460-590 | 500-630 | 530-660 | 560-690 |
| 25 | 390-510 | 410-540 | 430-560 | 450-580 | 490-620 | 520-650 | 550-680 |
| 24 | 380-500 | 400-530 | 420-550 | 450-570 | 480-610 | 510-640 | 540-670 |
| 23 | 370-490 | 390-520 | 410-540 | 440-570 | 470-600 | 500-630 | 530-660 |
| 22 | 370-480 | 380-510 | 400-530 | 430-560 | 460-590 | 500-630 | 520-650 |
| 21 | 370-480 | 380-510 | 400-530 | 430-560 | 460-590 | 500-630 | 520-650 |
| 20 | 360-470 | 370-500 | 390-520 | 420-550 | 460-580 | 490-620 | 520-640 |
| 19 | 350-460 | 360-490 | 380-510 | 410-540 | 450-580 | 480-610 | 510-630 |
| 18 | 340-450 | 350-480 | 370-500 | 400-530 | 440-570 | 470-600 | 500-630 |
| 17 | 330-450 | 350-480 | 360-490 | 390-520 | 430-560 | 460-590 | 490-620 |
| 16 | 320-440 | 340-470 | 360-490 | 390-510 | 420-550 | 450-580 | 480-610 |
| 15 | 310-430 | 330-460 | 350-480 | 380-510 | 410-540 | 440-570 | 470-600 |
| 14 | 300-420 | 320-450 | 340-470 | 370-500 | 400-530 | 430-560 | 460-590 |
| 13 | 300-410 | 310-440 | 330-460 | 360-490 | 390-520 | 430-560 | 450-580 |
| 12 | 290-400 | 300-430 | 320-450 | 350-480 | 390-510 | 420-550 | 450-570 |
| 11 | 280-390 | 290-420 | 310-440 | 340-470 | 380-510 | 410-540 | 440-570 |
| 10 | 270-390 | 280-420 | 300-430 | 330-460 | 370-500 | 400-530 | 430-560 |
| 9 | 260-380 | 280-410 | 290-430 | 320-450 | 360-490 | 390-520 | 420-550 |
| 8 | 250-370 | 270-400 | 290-420 | 320-450 | 350-480 | 380-510 | 410-540 |
| 7 | 240-360 | 260-390 | 280-410 | 310-440 | 340-470 | 370-510 | 400-530 |
| 6 | 230-350 | 250-380 | 270-400 | 300-430 | 330-460 | 360-500 | 390-520 |
| 5 | 230-340 | 240-370 | 260-390 | 290-420 | 320-460 | 360-490 | 380-520 |
| 4 | 220-340 | 230-370 | 250-380 | 280-410 | 320-450 | 350-480 | 380-510 |
| 3 | 210-330 | 220-360 | 240-380 | 270-400 | 310-440 | 340-470 | 370-500 |
| 2 | 200-320 | 210-350 | 230-370 | 260-400 | 300-430 | 330-460 | 360-490 |
| 1 | 200-300 | 200-330 | 220-350 | 250-380 | 280-410 | 310-450 | 340-470 |
| 0 | 200-290 | 200-320 | 210-340 | 240-370 | 270-410 | 300-440 | 330-470 |
| -1 | 200-280 | 200-310 | 200-330 | 220-350 | 250-390 | 290-420 | 310-450 |
| -2 | 200-260 | 200-290 | 200-310 | 200-340 | 240-370 | 270-410 | 300-430 |
| -3 | 200-240 | 200-270 | 200-290 | 200-320 | 240-360 | 270-390 | 300-420 |
| -4 | 200-230 | 200-260 | 200-280 | 200-300 | 240-340 | 270-370 | 300-400 |
| -5 | 200 | 200-230 | 200-250 | 200-280 | 240-320 | 270-350 | 300-370 |
| -6 | 200 | 200-220 | 200-240 | 200-270 | 240-310 | 270-340 | 300-370 |
| -7 | 200 | 200-220 | 200-230 | 200-260 | 240-300 | 270-330 | 300-360 |
| -8 | 200 | 200-210 | 200-230 | 200-250 | 240-290 | 270-320 | 300-350 |
| -9 | 200 | 200-210 | 200-230 | 200-250 | 240-290 | 270-320 | 300-350 |
| -10 | 200 | 200-210 | 200-230 | 200-250 | 240-290 | 270-320 | 300-350 |
| -11 | 200 | 200-210 | 200-230 | 200-250 | 240-290 | 270-320 | 300-350 |
| -12 | 200 | 200-210 | 200-230 | 200-250 | 240-290 | 270-320 | 300-350 |

**Table 3. Writing Conversion Table**

## Table 4. Writing Multiple-Choice Conversion Table

| Raw Score | Scaled Score | Raw Score | Scaled Score |
|---|---|---|---|
| 49 | 78-80 | 21 | 46-56 |
| 48 | 77-80 | 20 | 45-55 |
| 47 | 74-80 | 19 | 44-54 |
| 46 | 72-80 | 18 | 43-53 |
| 45 | 70-80 | 17 | 42-52 |
| 44 | 69-79 | 16 | 41-51 |
| 43 | 67-77 | 15 | 40-50 |
| 42 | 66-76 | 14 | 39-49 |
| 41 | 65-75 | 13 | 38-48 |
| 40 | 64-74 | 12 | 37-47 |
| 39 | 63-73 | 11 | 36-46 |
| 38 | 62-72 | 10 | 35-45 |
| 37 | 61-71 | 9 | 34-44 |
| 36 | 60-70 | 8 | 33-43 |
| 35 | 59-69 | 7 | 32-42 |
| 34 | 58-68 | 6 | 31-41 |
| 33 | 57-67 | 5 | 30-40 |
| 32 | 56-66 | 4 | 29-39 |
| 31 | 55-65 | 3 | 28-38 |
| 30 | 54-64 | 2 | 27-37 |
| 29 | 53-63 | 1 | 25-35 |
| 28 | 52-62 | 0 | 24-34 |
| 27 | 51-61 | -1 | 22-32 |
| 26 | 50-60 | -2 | 20-30 |
| 25 | 49-59 | -3 | 20-28 |
| 24 | 48-58 | -4 | 20-26 |
| 23 | 47-57 | -5 | 20-23 |
| 22 | 46-56 | -6 and below | 20-22 |

# SAT Practice Test #5

## After this test:

- Use this book to its full potential! Get exclusive access answer explanations, free practice score reports and free sample student essays to help you score your essay in the Book Owners' Area at www.collegeboard.org/satstudyguide.

- Want more practice? Get 10 more official practice tests, auto essay scoring and lesson plans from the test maker by subscribing to *The Official SAT Online Course*. As a book owner, you're entitled to a $10 discount. Sign up at www.collegeboard.org/satstudyguide.

*Note:* Section 5, the variable section, has been omitted from this practice test.

# SAT Reasoning Test — General Directions

## Timing

- You will have 3 hours and 45 minutes to work on this test.
- There are ten separately timed sections:
  - ► One 25-minute essay
  - ► Six other 25-minute sections
  - ► Two 20-minute sections
  - ► One 10-minute section
- You may work on only one section at a time.
- The supervisor will tell you when to begin and end each section.
- If you finish a section before time is called, check your work on that section. You may NOT turn to any other section.
- Work as rapidly as you can without losing accuracy. Don't waste time on questions that seem too difficult for you.

## Marking Answers

- Be sure to mark your answer sheet properly.

COMPLETE MARK ●    EXAMPLES OF INCOMPLETE MARKS

- You must use a No. 2 pencil.
- Carefully mark only one answer for each question.
- Make sure you fill the entire circle darkly and completely.
- Do not make any stray marks on your answer sheet.
- If you erase, do so completely. Incomplete erasures may be scored as intended answers.
- Use only the answer spaces that correspond to the question numbers.

## Using Your Test Book

- You may use the test book for scratchwork, but you will not receive credit for anything written there.
- After time has been called, you may not transfer answers to your answer sheet or fill in circles.
- You may not fold or remove pages or portions of a page from this book, or take the book or answer sheet from the testing room.

## Scoring

- For each correct answer, you receive one point.
- For questions you omit, you receive no points.
- For a wrong answer to a multiple-choice question, you lose one-fourth of a point.
  - ► If you can eliminate one or more of the answer choices as wrong, you increase your chances of choosing the correct answer and earning one point.
  - ► If you can't eliminate any choice, move on. You can return to the question later if there is time.
- For a wrong answer to a student-produced response ("grid-in") math question, you don't lose any points.
- Multiple-choice and student-produced response questions are machine scored.
- The essay is scored on a 1 to 6 scale by two different readers. The total essay score is the sum of the two readers' scores.
- Off-topic essays, blank essays, and essays written in ink will receive a score of zero.

The passages for this test have been adapted from published material. The ideas contained in them do not necessarily represent the opinions of the College Board.

## DO NOT OPEN THIS BOOK UNTIL THE SUPERVISOR TELLS YOU TO DO SO.

# SAT Reasoning Test™

**MARKS MUST BE COMPLETE**

COMPLETE MARK ●

EXAMPLES OF INCOMPLETE MARKS Ⓐ Ⓧ ⊖ Ⓟ / Ⓐ Ⓐ Ⓐ

You must use a **No. 2 pencil. Do not use a mechanical pencil.** It is very important that you fill in the entire circle darkly and completely. If you change your response, erase as completely as possible. Incomplete marks or erasures may affect your score. It is very important that you follow these instructions when filling out your answer sheet.

**1  Your Name:**
(Print)

Last | First | M.I.

I agree to the conditions on the back of the SAT Reasoning Test™ booklet. I also agree to use only a No. 2 pencil to complete my answer sheet.

Signature: _____  Date: __ / __ / __

Home Address: _____
(Print)   Number and Street | City | State | Zip Code

Home Phone: ( )   Center: _____
(Print)   (Print)   City   State/Country

---

**2  YOUR NAME**

Last Name (First 6 Letters) | First Name (First 4 Letters) | Mid. Init.

**3  DATE OF BIRTH**

MONTH | DAY | YEAR

○ Jan
○ Feb
○ Mar
○ Apr
○ May
○ Jun
○ Jul
○ Aug
○ Sep
○ Oct
○ Nov
○ Dec

**5  SEX**

○ Female   ○ Male

**6  REGISTRATION NUMBER**
(Copy from Admission Ticket.)

○ I turned in my registration form today.

**7  SOCIAL SECURITY NUMBER**

**4  ZIP CODE**

**Important:** Fill in items 8 and 9 exactly as shown on the back of test book.

**8  FORM CODE**
(Copy and grid as on back of test book.)

**9  TEST FORM**
(Copy from back of test book.)

**10  TEST BOOK SERIAL NUMBER**
(Copy from front of test book.)

**11  TEST CENTER**
(Supplied by Test Center Supervisor.)

**FOR OFFICIAL USE ONLY**
0 1 2 3 4 5 6
0 1 2 3 4 5 6
0 1 2 3 4 5 6

00272-36390 • NS75E4600 • Printed in U.S.A.
732652

172625-001:654321   ISD5960

**PLEASE DO NOT WRITE IN THIS AREA**   **SERIAL #**

5

629

# SECTION 1

**IMPORTANT:** USE A NO. 2 PENCIL. DO NOT WRITE OUTSIDE THE BORDER!
Words written outside the essay box or written in ink **WILL NOT APPEAR** in the copy sent to be scored, and your score will be affected.

Begin your essay on this page. If you need more space, continue on the next page.

5

Page 3

**SECTION 2**

1 Ⓐ Ⓑ Ⓒ Ⓓ Ⓔ    11 Ⓐ Ⓑ Ⓒ Ⓓ Ⓔ    21 Ⓐ Ⓑ Ⓒ Ⓓ Ⓔ    31 Ⓐ Ⓑ Ⓒ Ⓓ Ⓔ
2 Ⓐ Ⓑ Ⓒ Ⓓ Ⓔ    12 Ⓐ Ⓑ Ⓒ Ⓓ Ⓔ    22 Ⓐ Ⓑ Ⓒ Ⓓ Ⓔ    32 Ⓐ Ⓑ Ⓒ Ⓓ Ⓔ
3 Ⓐ Ⓑ Ⓒ Ⓓ Ⓔ    13 Ⓐ Ⓑ Ⓒ Ⓓ Ⓔ    23 Ⓐ Ⓑ Ⓒ Ⓓ Ⓔ    33 Ⓐ Ⓑ Ⓒ Ⓓ Ⓔ
4 Ⓐ Ⓑ Ⓒ Ⓓ Ⓔ    14 Ⓐ Ⓑ Ⓒ Ⓓ Ⓔ    24 Ⓐ Ⓑ Ⓒ Ⓓ Ⓔ    34 Ⓐ Ⓑ Ⓒ Ⓓ Ⓔ
5 Ⓐ Ⓑ Ⓒ Ⓓ Ⓔ    15 Ⓐ Ⓑ Ⓒ Ⓓ Ⓔ    25 Ⓐ Ⓑ Ⓒ Ⓓ Ⓔ    35 Ⓐ Ⓑ Ⓒ Ⓓ Ⓔ
6 Ⓐ Ⓑ Ⓒ Ⓓ Ⓔ    16 Ⓐ Ⓑ Ⓒ Ⓓ Ⓔ    26 Ⓐ Ⓑ Ⓒ Ⓓ Ⓔ    36 Ⓐ Ⓑ Ⓒ Ⓓ Ⓔ
7 Ⓐ Ⓑ Ⓒ Ⓓ Ⓔ    17 Ⓐ Ⓑ Ⓒ Ⓓ Ⓔ    27 Ⓐ Ⓑ Ⓒ Ⓓ Ⓔ    37 Ⓐ Ⓑ Ⓒ Ⓓ Ⓔ
8 Ⓐ Ⓑ Ⓒ Ⓓ Ⓔ    18 Ⓐ Ⓑ Ⓒ Ⓓ Ⓔ    28 Ⓐ Ⓑ Ⓒ Ⓓ Ⓔ    38 Ⓐ Ⓑ Ⓒ Ⓓ Ⓔ
9 Ⓐ Ⓑ Ⓒ Ⓓ Ⓔ    19 Ⓐ Ⓑ Ⓒ Ⓓ Ⓔ    29 Ⓐ Ⓑ Ⓒ Ⓓ Ⓔ    39 Ⓐ Ⓑ Ⓒ Ⓓ Ⓔ
10 Ⓐ Ⓑ Ⓒ Ⓓ Ⓔ    20 Ⓐ Ⓑ Ⓒ Ⓓ Ⓔ    30 Ⓐ Ⓑ Ⓒ Ⓓ Ⓔ    40 Ⓐ Ⓑ Ⓒ Ⓓ Ⓔ

**SECTION 3**

1 Ⓐ Ⓑ Ⓒ Ⓓ Ⓔ    11 Ⓐ Ⓑ Ⓒ Ⓓ Ⓔ    21 Ⓐ Ⓑ Ⓒ Ⓓ Ⓔ    31 Ⓐ Ⓑ Ⓒ Ⓓ Ⓔ
2 Ⓐ Ⓑ Ⓒ Ⓓ Ⓔ    12 Ⓐ Ⓑ Ⓒ Ⓓ Ⓔ    22 Ⓐ Ⓑ Ⓒ Ⓓ Ⓔ    32 Ⓐ Ⓑ Ⓒ Ⓓ Ⓔ
3 Ⓐ Ⓑ Ⓒ Ⓓ Ⓔ    13 Ⓐ Ⓑ Ⓒ Ⓓ Ⓔ    23 Ⓐ Ⓑ Ⓒ Ⓓ Ⓔ    33 Ⓐ Ⓑ Ⓒ Ⓓ Ⓔ
4 Ⓐ Ⓑ Ⓒ Ⓓ Ⓔ    14 Ⓐ Ⓑ Ⓒ Ⓓ Ⓔ    24 Ⓐ Ⓑ Ⓒ Ⓓ Ⓔ    34 Ⓐ Ⓑ Ⓒ Ⓓ Ⓔ
5 Ⓐ Ⓑ Ⓒ Ⓓ Ⓔ    15 Ⓐ Ⓑ Ⓒ Ⓓ Ⓔ    25 Ⓐ Ⓑ Ⓒ Ⓓ Ⓔ    35 Ⓐ Ⓑ Ⓒ Ⓓ Ⓔ
6 Ⓐ Ⓑ Ⓒ Ⓓ Ⓔ    16 Ⓐ Ⓑ Ⓒ Ⓓ Ⓔ    26 Ⓐ Ⓑ Ⓒ Ⓓ Ⓔ    36 Ⓐ Ⓑ Ⓒ Ⓓ Ⓔ
7 Ⓐ Ⓑ Ⓒ Ⓓ Ⓔ    17 Ⓐ Ⓑ Ⓒ Ⓓ Ⓔ    27 Ⓐ Ⓑ Ⓒ Ⓓ Ⓔ    37 Ⓐ Ⓑ Ⓒ Ⓓ Ⓔ
8 Ⓐ Ⓑ Ⓒ Ⓓ Ⓔ    18 Ⓐ Ⓑ Ⓒ Ⓓ Ⓔ    28 Ⓐ Ⓑ Ⓒ Ⓓ Ⓔ    38 Ⓐ Ⓑ Ⓒ Ⓓ Ⓔ
9 Ⓐ Ⓑ Ⓒ Ⓓ Ⓔ    19 Ⓐ Ⓑ Ⓒ Ⓓ Ⓔ    29 Ⓐ Ⓑ Ⓒ Ⓓ Ⓔ    39 Ⓐ Ⓑ Ⓒ Ⓓ Ⓔ
10 Ⓐ Ⓑ Ⓒ Ⓓ Ⓔ    20 Ⓐ Ⓑ Ⓒ Ⓓ Ⓔ    30 Ⓐ Ⓑ Ⓒ Ⓓ Ⓔ    40 Ⓐ Ⓑ Ⓒ Ⓓ Ⓔ

**CAUTION**  Grid answers in the section below for SECTION 2 or SECTION 3 only if directed to do so in your test book.

**Student-Produced Responses**  ONLY ANSWERS THAT ARE GRIDDED WILL BE SCORED. YOU WILL NOT RECEIVE CREDIT FOR ANYTHING WRITTEN IN THE BOXES.

Quality Assurance Mark ●

9    10    11    12    13

14    15    16    17    18

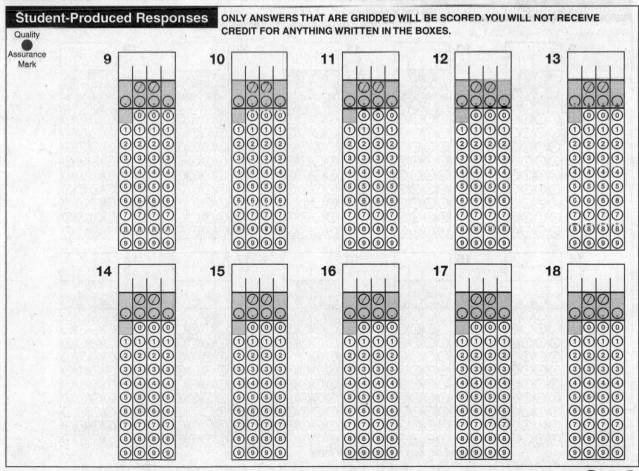

**SECTION 4**

1 Ⓐ Ⓑ Ⓒ Ⓓ Ⓔ   11 Ⓐ Ⓑ Ⓒ Ⓓ Ⓔ   21 Ⓐ Ⓑ Ⓒ Ⓓ Ⓔ   31 Ⓐ Ⓑ Ⓒ Ⓓ Ⓔ
2 Ⓐ Ⓑ Ⓒ Ⓓ Ⓔ   12 Ⓐ Ⓑ Ⓒ Ⓓ Ⓔ   22 Ⓐ Ⓑ Ⓒ Ⓓ Ⓔ   32 Ⓐ Ⓑ Ⓒ Ⓓ Ⓔ
3 Ⓐ Ⓑ Ⓒ Ⓓ Ⓔ   13 Ⓐ Ⓑ Ⓒ Ⓓ Ⓔ   23 Ⓐ Ⓑ Ⓒ Ⓓ Ⓔ   33 Ⓐ Ⓑ Ⓒ Ⓓ Ⓔ
4 Ⓐ Ⓑ Ⓒ Ⓓ Ⓔ   14 Ⓐ Ⓑ Ⓒ Ⓓ Ⓔ   24 Ⓐ Ⓑ Ⓒ Ⓓ Ⓔ   34 Ⓐ Ⓑ Ⓒ Ⓓ Ⓔ
5 Ⓐ Ⓑ Ⓒ Ⓓ Ⓔ   15 Ⓐ Ⓑ Ⓒ Ⓓ Ⓔ   25 Ⓐ Ⓑ Ⓒ Ⓓ Ⓔ   35 Ⓐ Ⓑ Ⓒ Ⓓ Ⓔ
6 Ⓐ Ⓑ Ⓒ Ⓓ Ⓔ   16 Ⓐ Ⓑ Ⓒ Ⓓ Ⓔ   26 Ⓐ Ⓑ Ⓒ Ⓓ Ⓔ   36 Ⓐ Ⓑ Ⓒ Ⓓ Ⓔ
7 Ⓐ Ⓑ Ⓒ Ⓓ Ⓔ   17 Ⓐ Ⓑ Ⓒ Ⓓ Ⓔ   27 Ⓐ Ⓑ Ⓒ Ⓓ Ⓔ   37 Ⓐ Ⓑ Ⓒ Ⓓ Ⓔ
8 Ⓐ Ⓑ Ⓒ Ⓓ Ⓔ   18 Ⓐ Ⓑ Ⓒ Ⓓ Ⓔ   28 Ⓐ Ⓑ Ⓒ Ⓓ Ⓔ   38 Ⓐ Ⓑ Ⓒ Ⓓ Ⓔ
9 Ⓐ Ⓑ Ⓒ Ⓓ Ⓔ   19 Ⓐ Ⓑ Ⓒ Ⓓ Ⓔ   29 Ⓐ Ⓑ Ⓒ Ⓓ Ⓔ   39 Ⓐ Ⓑ Ⓒ Ⓓ Ⓔ
10 Ⓐ Ⓑ Ⓒ Ⓓ Ⓔ  20 Ⓐ Ⓑ Ⓒ Ⓓ Ⓔ   30 Ⓐ Ⓑ Ⓒ Ⓓ Ⓔ   40 Ⓐ Ⓑ Ⓒ Ⓓ Ⓔ

**SECTION 5**

1 Ⓐ Ⓑ Ⓒ Ⓓ Ⓔ   11 Ⓐ Ⓑ Ⓒ Ⓓ Ⓔ   21 Ⓐ Ⓑ Ⓒ Ⓓ Ⓔ   31 Ⓐ Ⓑ Ⓒ Ⓓ Ⓔ
2 Ⓐ Ⓑ Ⓒ Ⓓ Ⓔ   12 Ⓐ Ⓑ Ⓒ Ⓓ Ⓔ   22 Ⓐ Ⓑ Ⓒ Ⓓ Ⓔ   32 Ⓐ Ⓑ Ⓒ Ⓓ Ⓔ
3 Ⓐ Ⓑ Ⓒ Ⓓ Ⓔ   13 Ⓐ Ⓑ Ⓒ Ⓓ Ⓔ   23 Ⓐ Ⓑ Ⓒ Ⓓ Ⓔ   33 Ⓐ Ⓑ Ⓒ Ⓓ Ⓔ
4 Ⓐ Ⓑ Ⓒ Ⓓ Ⓔ   14 Ⓐ Ⓑ Ⓒ Ⓓ Ⓔ   24 Ⓐ Ⓑ Ⓒ Ⓓ Ⓔ   34 Ⓐ Ⓑ Ⓒ Ⓓ Ⓔ
5 Ⓐ Ⓑ Ⓒ Ⓓ Ⓔ   15 Ⓐ Ⓑ Ⓒ Ⓓ Ⓔ   25 Ⓐ Ⓑ Ⓒ Ⓓ Ⓔ   35 Ⓐ Ⓑ Ⓒ Ⓓ Ⓔ
6 Ⓐ Ⓑ Ⓒ Ⓓ Ⓔ   16 Ⓐ Ⓑ Ⓒ Ⓓ Ⓔ   26 Ⓐ Ⓑ Ⓒ Ⓓ Ⓔ   36 Ⓐ Ⓑ Ⓒ Ⓓ Ⓔ
7 Ⓐ Ⓑ Ⓒ Ⓓ Ⓔ   17 Ⓐ Ⓑ Ⓒ Ⓓ Ⓔ   27 Ⓐ Ⓑ Ⓒ Ⓓ Ⓔ   37 Ⓐ Ⓑ Ⓒ Ⓓ Ⓔ
8 Ⓐ Ⓑ Ⓒ Ⓓ Ⓔ   18 Ⓐ Ⓑ Ⓒ Ⓓ Ⓔ   28 Ⓐ Ⓑ Ⓒ Ⓓ Ⓔ   38 Ⓐ Ⓑ Ⓒ Ⓓ Ⓔ
9 Ⓐ Ⓑ Ⓒ Ⓓ Ⓔ   19 Ⓐ Ⓑ Ⓒ Ⓓ Ⓔ   29 Ⓐ Ⓑ Ⓒ Ⓓ Ⓔ   39 Ⓐ Ⓑ Ⓒ Ⓓ Ⓔ
10 Ⓐ Ⓑ Ⓒ Ⓓ Ⓔ  20 Ⓐ Ⓑ Ⓒ Ⓓ Ⓔ   30 Ⓐ Ⓑ Ⓒ Ⓓ Ⓔ   40 Ⓐ Ⓑ Ⓒ Ⓓ Ⓔ

**CAUTION** Grid answers in the section below for SECTION 4 or SECTION 5 only if directed to do so in your test book.

**Student-Produced Responses** ONLY ANSWERS THAT ARE GRIDDED WILL BE SCORED. YOU WILL NOT RECEIVE CREDIT FOR ANYTHING WRITTEN IN THE BOXES.

Quality Assurance Mark

Page 5

633

**SECTION 6**

1 Ⓐ Ⓑ Ⓒ Ⓓ Ⓔ   11 Ⓐ Ⓑ Ⓒ Ⓓ Ⓔ   21 Ⓐ Ⓑ Ⓒ Ⓓ Ⓔ   31 Ⓐ Ⓑ Ⓒ Ⓓ Ⓔ
2 Ⓐ Ⓑ Ⓒ Ⓓ Ⓔ   12 Ⓐ Ⓑ Ⓒ Ⓓ Ⓔ   22 Ⓐ Ⓑ Ⓒ Ⓓ Ⓔ   32 Ⓐ Ⓑ Ⓒ Ⓓ Ⓔ
3 Ⓐ Ⓑ Ⓒ Ⓓ Ⓔ   13 Ⓐ Ⓑ Ⓒ Ⓓ Ⓔ   23 Ⓐ Ⓑ Ⓒ Ⓓ Ⓔ   33 Ⓐ Ⓑ Ⓒ Ⓓ Ⓔ
4 Ⓐ Ⓑ Ⓒ Ⓓ Ⓔ   14 Ⓐ Ⓑ Ⓒ Ⓓ Ⓔ   24 Ⓐ Ⓑ Ⓒ Ⓓ Ⓔ   34 Ⓐ Ⓑ Ⓒ Ⓓ Ⓔ
5 Ⓐ Ⓑ Ⓒ Ⓓ Ⓔ   15 Ⓐ Ⓑ Ⓒ Ⓓ Ⓔ   25 Ⓐ Ⓑ Ⓒ Ⓓ Ⓔ   35 Ⓐ Ⓑ Ⓒ Ⓓ Ⓔ
6 Ⓐ Ⓑ Ⓒ Ⓓ Ⓔ   16 Ⓐ Ⓑ Ⓒ Ⓓ Ⓔ   26 Ⓐ Ⓑ Ⓒ Ⓓ Ⓔ   36 Ⓐ Ⓑ Ⓒ Ⓓ Ⓔ
7 Ⓐ Ⓑ Ⓒ Ⓓ Ⓔ   17 Ⓐ Ⓑ Ⓒ Ⓓ Ⓔ   27 Ⓐ Ⓑ Ⓒ Ⓓ Ⓔ   37 Ⓐ Ⓑ Ⓒ Ⓓ Ⓔ
8 Ⓐ Ⓑ Ⓒ Ⓓ Ⓔ   18 Ⓐ Ⓑ Ⓒ Ⓓ Ⓔ   28 Ⓐ Ⓑ Ⓒ Ⓓ Ⓔ   38 Ⓐ Ⓑ Ⓒ Ⓓ Ⓔ
9 Ⓐ Ⓑ Ⓒ Ⓓ Ⓔ   19 Ⓐ Ⓑ Ⓒ Ⓓ Ⓔ   29 Ⓐ Ⓑ Ⓒ Ⓓ Ⓔ   39 Ⓐ Ⓑ Ⓒ Ⓓ Ⓔ
10 Ⓐ Ⓑ Ⓒ Ⓓ Ⓔ  20 Ⓐ Ⓑ Ⓒ Ⓓ Ⓔ   30 Ⓐ Ⓑ Ⓒ Ⓓ Ⓔ   40 Ⓐ Ⓑ Ⓒ Ⓓ Ⓔ

**SECTION 7**

1 Ⓐ Ⓑ Ⓒ Ⓓ Ⓔ   11 Ⓐ Ⓑ Ⓒ Ⓓ Ⓔ   21 Ⓐ Ⓑ Ⓒ Ⓓ Ⓔ   31 Ⓐ Ⓑ Ⓒ Ⓓ Ⓔ
2 Ⓐ Ⓑ Ⓒ Ⓓ Ⓔ   12 Ⓐ Ⓑ Ⓒ Ⓓ Ⓔ   22 Ⓐ Ⓑ Ⓒ Ⓓ Ⓔ   32 Ⓐ Ⓑ Ⓒ Ⓓ Ⓔ
3 Ⓐ Ⓑ Ⓒ Ⓓ Ⓔ   13 Ⓐ Ⓑ Ⓒ Ⓓ Ⓔ   23 Ⓐ Ⓑ Ⓒ Ⓓ Ⓔ   33 Ⓐ Ⓑ Ⓒ Ⓓ Ⓔ
4 Ⓐ Ⓑ Ⓒ Ⓓ Ⓔ   14 Ⓐ Ⓑ Ⓒ Ⓓ Ⓔ   24 Ⓐ Ⓑ Ⓒ Ⓓ Ⓔ   34 Ⓐ Ⓑ Ⓒ Ⓓ Ⓔ
5 Ⓐ Ⓑ Ⓒ Ⓓ Ⓔ   15 Ⓐ Ⓑ Ⓒ Ⓓ Ⓔ   25 Ⓐ Ⓑ Ⓒ Ⓓ Ⓔ   35 Ⓐ Ⓑ Ⓒ Ⓓ Ⓔ
6 Ⓐ Ⓑ Ⓒ Ⓓ Ⓔ   16 Ⓐ Ⓑ Ⓒ Ⓓ Ⓔ   26 Ⓐ Ⓑ Ⓒ Ⓓ Ⓔ   36 Ⓐ Ⓑ Ⓒ Ⓓ Ⓔ
7 Ⓐ Ⓑ Ⓒ Ⓓ Ⓔ   17 Ⓐ Ⓑ Ⓒ Ⓓ Ⓔ   27 Ⓐ Ⓑ Ⓒ Ⓓ Ⓔ   37 Ⓐ Ⓑ Ⓒ Ⓓ Ⓔ
8 Ⓐ Ⓑ Ⓒ Ⓓ Ⓔ   18 Ⓐ Ⓑ Ⓒ Ⓓ Ⓔ   28 Ⓐ Ⓑ Ⓒ Ⓓ Ⓔ   38 Ⓐ Ⓑ Ⓒ Ⓓ Ⓔ
9 Ⓐ Ⓑ Ⓒ Ⓓ Ⓔ   19 Ⓐ Ⓑ Ⓒ Ⓓ Ⓔ   29 Ⓐ Ⓑ Ⓒ Ⓓ Ⓔ   39 Ⓐ Ⓑ Ⓒ Ⓓ Ⓔ
10 Ⓐ Ⓑ Ⓒ Ⓓ Ⓔ  20 Ⓐ Ⓑ Ⓒ Ⓓ Ⓔ   30 Ⓐ Ⓑ Ⓒ Ⓓ Ⓔ   40 Ⓐ Ⓑ Ⓒ Ⓓ Ⓔ

**CAUTION** Grid answers in the section below for SECTION 6 or SECTION 7 only if directed to do so in your test book.

**Student-Produced Responses** ONLY ANSWERS THAT ARE GRIDDED WILL BE SCORED. YOU WILL NOT RECEIVE CREDIT FOR ANYTHING WRITTEN IN THE BOXES.

Quality Assurance Mark

9   10   11   12   13

14   15   16   17   18

Page 6

PLEASE DO NOT WRITE IN THIS AREA

SERIAL #

5

634

**SECTION 8**

| | | | |
|---|---|---|---|
| 1 Ⓐ Ⓑ Ⓒ Ⓓ Ⓔ | 11 Ⓐ Ⓑ Ⓒ Ⓓ Ⓔ | 21 Ⓐ Ⓑ Ⓒ Ⓓ Ⓔ | 31 Ⓐ Ⓑ Ⓒ Ⓓ Ⓔ |
| 2 Ⓐ Ⓑ Ⓒ Ⓓ Ⓔ | 12 Ⓐ Ⓑ Ⓒ Ⓓ Ⓔ | 22 Ⓐ Ⓑ Ⓒ Ⓓ Ⓔ | 32 Ⓐ Ⓑ Ⓒ Ⓓ Ⓔ |
| 3 Ⓐ Ⓑ Ⓒ Ⓓ Ⓔ | 13 Ⓐ Ⓑ Ⓒ Ⓓ Ⓔ | 23 Ⓐ Ⓑ Ⓒ Ⓓ Ⓔ | 33 Ⓐ Ⓑ Ⓒ Ⓓ Ⓔ |
| 4 Ⓐ Ⓑ Ⓒ Ⓓ Ⓔ | 14 Ⓐ Ⓑ Ⓒ Ⓓ Ⓔ | 24 Ⓐ Ⓑ Ⓒ Ⓓ Ⓔ | 34 Ⓐ Ⓑ Ⓒ Ⓓ Ⓔ |
| 5 Ⓐ Ⓑ Ⓒ Ⓓ Ⓔ | 15 Ⓐ Ⓑ Ⓒ Ⓓ Ⓔ | 25 Ⓐ Ⓑ Ⓒ Ⓓ Ⓔ | 35 Ⓐ Ⓑ Ⓒ Ⓓ Ⓔ |
| 6 Ⓐ Ⓑ Ⓒ Ⓓ Ⓔ | 16 Ⓐ Ⓑ Ⓒ Ⓓ Ⓔ | 26 Ⓐ Ⓑ Ⓒ Ⓓ Ⓔ | 36 Ⓐ Ⓑ Ⓒ Ⓓ Ⓔ |
| 7 Ⓐ Ⓑ Ⓒ Ⓓ Ⓔ | 17 Ⓐ Ⓑ Ⓒ Ⓓ Ⓔ | 27 Ⓐ Ⓑ Ⓒ Ⓓ Ⓔ | 37 Ⓐ Ⓑ Ⓒ Ⓓ Ⓔ |
| 8 Ⓐ Ⓑ Ⓒ Ⓓ Ⓔ | 18 Ⓐ Ⓑ Ⓒ Ⓓ Ⓔ | 28 Ⓐ Ⓑ Ⓒ Ⓓ Ⓔ | 38 Ⓐ Ⓑ Ⓒ Ⓓ Ⓔ |
| 9 Ⓐ Ⓑ Ⓒ Ⓓ Ⓔ | 19 Ⓐ Ⓑ Ⓒ Ⓓ Ⓔ | 29 Ⓐ Ⓑ Ⓒ Ⓓ Ⓔ | 39 Ⓐ Ⓑ Ⓒ Ⓓ Ⓔ |
| 10 Ⓐ Ⓑ Ⓒ Ⓓ Ⓔ | 20 Ⓐ Ⓑ Ⓒ Ⓓ Ⓔ | 30 Ⓐ Ⓑ Ⓒ Ⓓ Ⓔ | 40 Ⓐ Ⓑ Ⓒ Ⓓ Ⓔ |

**SECTION 9**

| | | | |
|---|---|---|---|
| 1 Ⓐ Ⓑ Ⓒ Ⓓ Ⓔ | 11 Ⓐ Ⓑ Ⓒ Ⓓ Ⓔ | 21 Ⓐ Ⓑ Ⓒ Ⓓ Ⓔ | 31 Ⓐ Ⓑ Ⓒ Ⓓ Ⓔ |
| 2 Ⓐ Ⓑ Ⓒ Ⓓ Ⓔ | 12 Ⓐ Ⓑ Ⓒ Ⓓ Ⓔ | 22 Ⓐ Ⓑ Ⓒ Ⓓ Ⓔ | 32 Ⓐ Ⓑ Ⓒ Ⓓ Ⓔ |
| 3 Ⓐ Ⓑ Ⓒ Ⓓ Ⓔ | 13 Ⓐ Ⓑ Ⓒ Ⓓ Ⓔ | 23 Ⓐ Ⓑ Ⓒ Ⓓ Ⓔ | 33 Ⓐ Ⓑ Ⓒ Ⓓ Ⓔ |
| 4 Ⓐ Ⓑ Ⓒ Ⓓ Ⓔ | 14 Ⓐ Ⓑ Ⓒ Ⓓ Ⓔ | 24 Ⓐ Ⓑ Ⓒ Ⓓ Ⓔ | 34 Ⓐ Ⓑ Ⓒ Ⓓ Ⓔ |
| 5 Ⓐ Ⓑ Ⓒ Ⓓ Ⓔ | 15 Ⓐ Ⓑ Ⓒ Ⓓ Ⓔ | 25 Ⓐ Ⓑ Ⓒ Ⓓ Ⓔ | 35 Ⓐ Ⓑ Ⓒ Ⓓ Ⓔ |
| 6 Ⓐ Ⓑ Ⓒ Ⓓ Ⓔ | 16 Ⓐ Ⓑ Ⓒ Ⓓ Ⓔ | 26 Ⓐ Ⓑ Ⓒ Ⓓ Ⓔ | 36 Ⓐ Ⓑ Ⓒ Ⓓ Ⓔ |
| 7 Ⓐ Ⓑ Ⓒ Ⓓ Ⓔ | 17 Ⓐ Ⓑ Ⓒ Ⓓ Ⓔ | 27 Ⓐ Ⓑ Ⓒ Ⓓ Ⓔ | 37 Ⓐ Ⓑ Ⓒ Ⓓ Ⓔ |
| 8 Ⓐ Ⓑ Ⓒ Ⓓ Ⓔ | 18 Ⓐ Ⓑ Ⓒ Ⓓ Ⓔ | 28 Ⓐ Ⓑ Ⓒ Ⓓ Ⓔ | 38 Ⓐ Ⓑ Ⓒ Ⓓ Ⓔ |
| 9 Ⓐ Ⓑ Ⓒ Ⓓ Ⓔ | 19 Ⓐ Ⓑ Ⓒ Ⓓ Ⓔ | 29 Ⓐ Ⓑ Ⓒ Ⓓ Ⓔ | 39 Ⓐ Ⓑ Ⓒ Ⓓ Ⓔ |
| 10 Ⓐ Ⓑ Ⓒ Ⓓ Ⓔ | 20 Ⓐ Ⓑ Ⓒ Ⓓ Ⓔ | 30 Ⓐ Ⓑ Ⓒ Ⓓ Ⓔ | 40 Ⓐ Ⓑ Ⓒ Ⓓ Ⓔ |

Quality ● Assurance Mark

**SECTION 10**

| | | | |
|---|---|---|---|
| 1 Ⓐ Ⓑ Ⓒ Ⓓ Ⓔ | 11 Ⓐ Ⓑ Ⓒ Ⓓ Ⓔ | 21 Ⓐ Ⓑ Ⓒ Ⓓ Ⓔ | 31 Ⓐ Ⓑ Ⓒ Ⓓ Ⓔ |
| 2 Ⓐ Ⓑ Ⓒ Ⓓ Ⓔ | 12 Ⓐ Ⓑ Ⓒ Ⓓ Ⓔ | 22 Ⓐ Ⓑ Ⓒ Ⓓ Ⓔ | 32 Ⓐ Ⓑ Ⓒ Ⓓ Ⓔ |
| 3 Ⓐ Ⓑ Ⓒ Ⓓ Ⓔ | 13 Ⓐ Ⓑ Ⓒ Ⓓ Ⓔ | 23 Ⓐ Ⓑ Ⓒ Ⓓ Ⓔ | 33 Ⓐ Ⓑ Ⓒ Ⓓ Ⓔ |
| 4 Ⓐ Ⓑ Ⓒ Ⓓ Ⓔ | 14 Ⓐ Ⓑ Ⓒ Ⓓ Ⓔ | 24 Ⓐ Ⓑ Ⓒ Ⓓ Ⓔ | 34 Ⓐ Ⓑ Ⓒ Ⓓ Ⓔ |
| 5 Ⓐ Ⓑ Ⓒ Ⓓ Ⓔ | 15 Ⓐ Ⓑ Ⓒ Ⓓ Ⓔ | 25 Ⓐ Ⓑ Ⓒ Ⓓ Ⓔ | 35 Ⓐ Ⓑ Ⓒ Ⓓ Ⓔ |
| 6 Ⓐ Ⓑ Ⓒ Ⓓ Ⓔ | 16 Ⓐ Ⓑ Ⓒ Ⓓ Ⓔ | 26 Ⓐ Ⓑ Ⓒ Ⓓ Ⓔ | 36 Ⓐ Ⓑ Ⓒ Ⓓ Ⓔ |
| 7 Ⓐ Ⓑ Ⓒ Ⓓ Ⓔ | 17 Ⓐ Ⓑ Ⓒ Ⓓ Ⓔ | 27 Ⓐ Ⓑ Ⓒ Ⓓ Ⓔ | 37 Ⓐ Ⓑ Ⓒ Ⓓ Ⓔ |
| 8 Ⓐ Ⓑ Ⓒ Ⓓ Ⓔ | 18 Ⓐ Ⓑ Ⓒ Ⓓ Ⓔ | 28 Ⓐ Ⓑ Ⓒ Ⓓ Ⓔ | 38 Ⓐ Ⓑ Ⓒ Ⓓ Ⓔ |
| 9 Ⓐ Ⓑ Ⓒ Ⓓ Ⓔ | 19 Ⓐ Ⓑ Ⓒ Ⓓ Ⓔ | 29 Ⓐ Ⓑ Ⓒ Ⓓ Ⓔ | 39 Ⓐ Ⓑ Ⓒ Ⓓ Ⓔ |
| 10 Ⓐ Ⓑ Ⓒ Ⓓ Ⓔ | 20 Ⓐ Ⓑ Ⓒ Ⓓ Ⓔ | 30 Ⓐ Ⓑ Ⓒ Ⓓ Ⓔ | 40 Ⓐ Ⓑ Ⓒ Ⓓ Ⓔ |

**5**

## SPECIAL QUESTIONS

1 Ⓐ Ⓑ Ⓒ Ⓓ Ⓔ Ⓕ Ⓖ Ⓗ Ⓘ Ⓙ
2 Ⓐ Ⓑ Ⓒ Ⓓ Ⓔ Ⓕ Ⓖ Ⓗ Ⓘ Ⓙ
3 Ⓐ Ⓑ Ⓒ Ⓓ Ⓔ Ⓕ Ⓖ Ⓗ Ⓘ Ⓙ
4 Ⓐ Ⓑ Ⓒ Ⓓ Ⓔ Ⓕ Ⓖ Ⓗ Ⓘ Ⓙ
5 Ⓐ Ⓑ Ⓒ Ⓓ Ⓔ Ⓕ Ⓖ Ⓗ Ⓘ Ⓙ
6 Ⓐ Ⓑ Ⓒ Ⓓ Ⓔ Ⓕ Ⓖ Ⓗ Ⓘ Ⓙ
7 Ⓐ Ⓑ Ⓒ Ⓓ Ⓔ Ⓕ Ⓖ Ⓗ Ⓘ Ⓙ
8 Ⓐ Ⓑ Ⓒ Ⓓ Ⓔ Ⓕ Ⓖ Ⓗ Ⓘ Ⓙ

Page 8

## ESSAY
### Time — 25 minutes

---

**Turn to page 2 of your answer sheet to write your ESSAY.**

---

The essay gives you an opportunity to show how effectively you can develop and express ideas. You should, therefore, take care to develop your point of view, present your ideas logically and clearly, and use language precisely.

Your essay must be written on the lines provided on your answer sheet—you will receive no other paper on which to write. You will have enough space if you write on every line, avoid wide margins, and keep your handwriting to a reasonable size. Remember that people who are not familiar with your handwriting will read what you write. Try to write or print so that what you are writing is legible to those readers.

**Important Reminders:**

- **A pencil is required for the essay.** An essay written in ink will receive a score of zero.
- **Do not write your essay in your test book.** You will receive credit only for what you write on your answer sheet.
- **An off-topic essay will receive a score of zero.**
- **If your essay does not reflect your original and individual work, your test scores may be canceled.**

You have twenty-five minutes to write an essay on the topic assigned below.

---

Think carefully about the issue presented in the following excerpt and the assignment below.

> A mistakenly cynical view of human behavior holds that people are primarily driven by selfish motives: the desire for wealth, for power, or for fame. Yet history gives us many examples of individuals who have sacrificed their own welfare for a cause or a principle that they regarded as more important than their own lives. Conscience—that powerful inner voice that tells us what is right and what is wrong—can be a more compelling force than money, power, or fame.

**Assignment:** Is conscience a more powerful motivator than money, fame, or power? Plan and write an essay in which you develop your point of view on this issue. Support your position with reasoning and examples taken from your reading, studies, experience, or observations.

---

BEGIN WRITING YOUR ESSAY ON PAGE 2 OF THE ANSWER SHEET.

**If you finish before time is called, you may check your work on this section only.**
**Do not turn to any other section in the test.**

## SECTION 2
### Time — 25 minutes
### 20 Questions

**Turn to Section 2 (page 4) of your answer sheet to answer the questions in this section.**

**Directions:** For this section, solve each problem and decide which is the best of the choices given. Fill in the corresponding circle on the answer sheet. You may use any available space for scratchwork.

**Notes**

1. The use of a calculator is permitted.
2. All numbers used are real numbers.
3. Figures that accompany problems in this test are intended to provide information useful in solving the problems. They are drawn as accurately as possible EXCEPT when it is stated in a specific problem that the figure is not drawn to scale. All figures lie in a plane unless otherwise indicated.
4. Unless otherwise specified, the domain of any function $f$ is assumed to be the set of all real numbers $x$ for which $f(x)$ is a real number.

**Reference Information**

   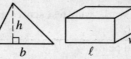    

$A = \pi r^2$
$C = 2\pi r$    $A = \ell w$    $A = \frac{1}{2}bh$    $V = \ell wh$    $V = \pi r^2 h$    $c^2 = a^2 + b^2$    Special Right Triangles

The number of degrees of arc in a circle is 360.
The sum of the measures in degrees of the angles of a triangle is 180.

---

**1.** If $3x + 9 = 5x + 1$, what is the value of $x$ ?

(A) 1
(B) 2
(C) 3
(D) 4
(E) 8

$$7, 15, 31, 63, \ldots$$

**2.** The first term in the sequence above is 7, and each term after the first is determined by multiplying the preceding term by $m$ and then adding $p$. What is the value of $m$ ?

(A) 1
(B) 2
(C) 3
(D) 4
(E) 9

**GO ON TO THE NEXT PAGE**

**T-SHIRTS**

| Color | Size |
|-------|------|
| Red | Small |
| White | Medium |
| Blue | Large |
|  | Extra-large |

**3.** The tables above show the different colors and sizes of T-shirts that are available at Independence High School. How many different combinations of color and size are possible?

(A) 7
(B) 12
(C) 15
(D) 25
(E) 64

**4.** For which of the following functions is $f(-3) > f(3)$

(A) $f(x) = 4x^2$

(B) $f(x) = 4$

(C) $f(x) = \dfrac{4}{x}$

(D) $f(x) = 4x^3$

(E) $f(x) = x^4 + 4$

**5.** The force required to stretch a spring beyond its natural length is proportional to how far the spring is being stretched. If a force of 15 pounds stretches a spring 8 centimeters beyond its natural length, what force, in pounds, is needed to stretch this spring 20 centimeters beyond its natural length?

(A) 23
(B) 27
(C) 30.5
(D) 35
(E) 37.5

**6.** If $Y$ is the midpoint of $\overline{XZ}$, which of the following must be true?

 I. $YZ = \dfrac{1}{2} XZ$

 II. $\dfrac{1}{2} XZ = 2XY$

 III. $2XY = XZ$

(A) I only
(B) II only
(C) III only
(D) I and II
(E) I and III

GO ON TO THE NEXT PAGE

7. If $2r = 5s$ and $5s = 6t$, what does $r$ equal in terms of $t$ ?

   (A) $\dfrac{12}{25}t$

   (B) $\dfrac{6}{5}t$

   (C) $3t$

   (D) $15t$

   (E) $30t$

8. A total of $k$ passengers went on a bus trip. Each of the $n$ buses that were used to transport the passengers could seat a maximum of $x$ passengers. If one bus had 3 empty seats and the remaining buses were filled, which of the following expresses the relationship among $n$, $x$, and $k$ ?

   (A) $nx - 3 = k$
   (B) $nx + 3 = k$
   (C) $n + x + 3 = k$
   (D) $nk = x + 3$
   (E) $nk = x - 3$

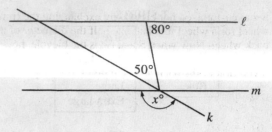

9. In the figure above, line $\ell$ is parallel to line $m$. What is the value of $x$ ?

   (A) 150
   (B) 140
   (C) 130
   (D) 110
   (E) 100

$$3x^2 < (3x)^2$$

10. For what value of $x$ is the statement above FALSE?

   (A) $-3$

   (B) $0$

   (C) $\dfrac{1}{3}$

   (D) $1$

   (E) For no value of $x$

**GO ON TO THE NEXT PAGE**

11. Senai customized her bicycle by exchanging the front wheel for a wheel that had one half the diameter of the back wheel. Now when Senai rides the bicycle, how many revolutions does the front wheel make for each revolution of the back wheel?

(A) 8

(B) 4

(C) 2

(D) $\frac{1}{2}$

(E) $\frac{1}{4}$

12. A list of numbers consists of $p$ positive and $n$ negative numbers. If a number is picked at random from this list, the probability that the number is positive is $\frac{3}{5}$. What is the value of $\frac{n}{p}$ ?

(A) $\frac{3}{8}$

(B) $\frac{5}{8}$

(C) $\frac{2}{3}$

(D) $\frac{3}{2}$

(E) $\frac{8}{3}$

13. The total daily cost $c$, in dollars, of producing $x$ units of a certain product is given by the function $c(x) = \frac{600\,x - 200}{x} + k$, where $k$ is a constant and $x \leq 100$. If 20 units were produced yesterday for a total cost of \$640, what is the value of $k$ ?

(A) 40
(B) 50
(C) 60
(D) 590
(E) 600

14. For how many ordered pairs of positive integers $(x, y)$ is $2x + 3y < 6$ ?

(A) One
(B) Two
(C) Three
(D) Five
(E) Seven

GO ON TO THE NEXT PAGE

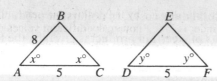

Note: Figures not drawn to scale.

**15.** If $y = 60$ in $\triangle DEF$ above, how much greater is the perimeter of $\triangle ABC$ than the perimeter of $\triangle DEF$?

(A) 0
(B) 3
(C) 6
(D) 8
(E) 9

**16.** If $x$ and $y$ are positive consecutive odd integers, where $y > x$, which of the following is equal to $y^2 - x^2$?

(A) $2x$
(B) $4x$
(C) $2x + 2$
(D) $2x + 4$
(E) $4x + 4$

**17.** In the $xy$-plane, line $\ell$ passes through the origin and is perpendicular to the line $4x + y = k$, where $k$ is a constant. If the two lines intersect at the point $(t, t + 1)$, what is the value of $t$?

(A) $-\dfrac{4}{3}$

(B) $-\dfrac{5}{4}$

(C) $\dfrac{3}{4}$

(D) $\dfrac{5}{4}$

(E) $\dfrac{4}{3}$

**18.** If the average (arithmetic mean) of $x$ and $y$ is $k$, which of the following is the average of $x$, $y$, and $z$?

(A) $\dfrac{2k + z}{3}$

(B) $\dfrac{2k + z}{2}$

(C) $\dfrac{k + z}{3}$

(D) $\dfrac{k + z}{2}$

(E) $\dfrac{2(k + z)}{3}$

GO ON TO THE NEXT PAGE

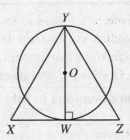

**19.** In the figure above, $\triangle XYZ$ is equilateral, with side of length 2. If $WY$ is a diameter of the circle with center $O$, then the area of the circle is

(A) $\dfrac{\sqrt{3}\pi}{4}$

(B) $\dfrac{2\pi}{3}$

(C) $\dfrac{3\pi}{4}$

(D) $\pi$

(E) $\dfrac{3\pi}{2}$

**20.** When 15 is divided by the positive integer $k$, the remainder is 3. For how many different values of $k$ is this true?

(A) One
(B) Two
(C) Three
(D) Four
(E) Five

## STOP

**If you finish before time is called, you may check your work on this section only.**
**Do not turn to any other section in the test.**

## SECTION 3
### Time — 25 minutes
### 24 Questions

Turn to Section 3 (page 4) of your answer sheet to answer the questions in this section.

**Directions:** For each question in this section, select the best answer from among the choices given and fill in the corresponding circle on the answer sheet.

Each sentence below has one or two blanks, each blank indicating that something has been omitted. Beneath the sentence are five words or sets of words labeled A through E. Choose the word or set of words that, when inserted in the sentence, best fits the meaning of the sentence as a whole.

**Example:**

Hoping to ------- the dispute, negotiators proposed a compromise that they felt would be ------- to both labor and management.

(A) enforce . . useful
(B) end . . divisive
(C) overcome . . unattractive
(D) extend . . satisfactory
(E) resolve . . acceptable        Ⓐ Ⓑ Ⓒ Ⓓ ●

1. For a long time, most doctors maintained that taking massive doses of vitamins was relatively harmless; now, however, some are warning that excessive dosages can be -------.

   (A) healthy    (B) expensive    (C) wasteful
       (D) toxic    (E) inane

2. In Jamaica Kincaid's novel *Lucy*, the West Indian heroine ------- her employers' world, critically examining its assumptions and values.

   (A) idealizes    (B) avoids    (C) beautifies
       (D) scrutinizes    (E) excludes

3. The frequent name changes that the country has undergone ------- the political turbulence that has attended its recent history.

   (A) argue against    (B) contrast with
       (C) testify to    (D) jeopardize
           (E) sustain

4. Brachiopods, clamlike bivalves of prehistoric times, were one of the most ------- forms of life on the Earth: more than 30,000 species have been ------- from fossil records.

   (A) plentiful . . subtracted
   (B) ornate . . retrieved
   (C) multifarious . . catalogued
   (D) scarce . . extracted
   (E) anachronistic . . extrapolated

5. Some interactive computer games are so elaborately contrived and require such ------- strategies that only the most ------- player can master them.

   (A) byzantine . . adroit
   (B) nefarious . . conscientious
   (C) devious . . lackadaisical
   (D) onerous . . slipshod
   (E) predictable . . compulsive

**GO ON TO THE NEXT PAGE**

Each passage below is followed by questions based on its content. Answer the questions on the basis of what is <u>stated</u> or <u>implied</u> in each passage and in any introductory material that may be provided.

**Questions 6-7 are based on the following passage.**

The critic Edmund Wilson was not a self-conscious letter writer or one who tried to sustain studied mannerisms. Nor did he resort to artifice or entangle himself in
*Line* circumlocutions. The young, middle-aged, and old Wilson
5 speaks directly through his letters, which are informal for the most part and which undisguisedly reflect his changing moods. On occasion—in response, perhaps, to the misery of a friend or a public outrage or a personal challenge—he can become eloquent, even passionate, but that is not his
10 prevailing tone.

6. Based on the information in the passage, Wilson's letters can best be described as

    (A) cynical
    (B) spontaneous
    (C) critical
    (D) preachy
    (E) witty

7. The reference to the "young, middle-aged, and old Wilson" (line 4) serves to suggest the

    (A) multifaceted nature of Wilson's literary persona
    (B) maturity Wilson displayed even as a youth
    (C) effect aging had on Wilson's temperament
    (D) longevity of Wilson's literary career
    (E) consistency of Wilson's letter-writing style

**Questions 8-9 are based on the following passage.**

The belief that it is harmful to the Black community for authors to explore the humanity of our leaders can have troubling effects. At the least, it promotes the belief
*Line* that our heroes have to be perfect to be useful. At worst,
5 it censors our full investigation of Black life. If our paintings of that life are stock and cramped, their colors drab and predictable, the representations of our culture are likely to be untrue. They will not capture the breadth and complexity of Black identity.

8. The passage implies that Black leaders have sometimes been portrayed as being

    (A) overly sentimental
    (B) deeply complex
    (C) above reproach
    (D) without regret
    (E) beyond understanding

9. In context, the "paintings" (lines 5-6) are best understood as a reference to

    (A) realistic sculptures
    (B) historical biographies
    (C) whimsical novels
    (D) political cartoons
    (E) colorful theorems

**GO ON TO THE NEXT PAGE**

**Questions 10-18 are based on the following passage.**

*The following passage was written by a physicist in 1986.*

When astronomers point their telescopes to the nearest galaxy, Andromeda, they see it as it was two million years ago. That's about the time *Australopithecus** was basking
Line in the African sun. This little bit of time travel is possible
5 because light takes two million years to make the trip from there to here. Too bad we couldn't turn things around and observe Earth from some cozy planet in Andromeda.

But looking at light from distant objects isn't real time travel, the in-the-flesh participation in past and future found
10 in literature. Ever since I've been old enough to read science fiction, I've dreamed of time traveling. The possibilities are staggering. You could take medicine back to fourteenth-century Europe and stop the spread of plague, or you could travel to the twenty-third century, where people take their
15 annual holidays in space stations.

Being a scientist myself, I know that time travel is quite unlikely according to the laws of physics. For one thing, there would be a causality violation. If you could travel backward in time, you could alter a chain of events
20 with the knowledge of how they would have turned out. Cause would no longer always precede effect. For example, you could prevent your parents from ever meeting. Contemplating the consequences of that will give you a headache, and science fiction writers for decades have
25 delighted in the paradoxes that can arise from traveling through time.

Physicists are, of course, horrified at the thought of causality violation. Differential equations for the way things should behave under a given set of forces and
30 initial conditions would no longer be valid, since what happens in one instant would not necessarily determine what happens in the next. Physicists do rely on a determin-istic universe in which to operate, and time travel would almost certainly put them and most other scientists
35 permanently out of work.

Still, I dream of time travel. There is something very personal about time. When the first mechanical clocks were invented, marking off time in crisp, regular inter-vals, it must have surprised people to discover that time
40 flowed outside their own mental and physiological pro-cesses. Body time flows at its own variable rate, oblivious to the most precise clocks in the laboratory. In fact, the human body contains its own exquisite timepieces, all with their separate rhythms. There are the alpha waves in the
45 brain; another clock is the heart. And all the while tick the mysterious, ruthless clocks that regulate aging.

Recently, I found my great-grandfather's favorite pipe. Papa Joe, as he was called, died more than seventy years ago, long before I was born. There are few surviving photo-
50 graphs or other memorabilia of Papa Joe. But I do have his

pipe, which had been tucked away in a drawer somewhere for years and was in good condition when I found it. I ran a pipe cleaner through it, filled it with some tobacco I had on hand, and settled down to read and smoke. After a cou-
55 ple of minutes, the most wonderful and foreign blend of smells began wafting from the pipe. All the different occa-sions when Papa Joe had lit his pipe, all the different places he had been that I will never know—all had been locked up in that pipe and now poured out into the room. I was
60 vaguely aware that something had got delightfully twisted in time for a moment, skipped upward on the page. There *is* a kind of time travel to be had, if you don't insist on how it happens.

\* An extinct humanlike primate

**10.** The author mentions *Australopithecus* in line 3 in order to

(A) note an evolutionary progression in the physical world
(B) dramatize how different Earth was two million years ago
(C) commend the superior work of astronomers in isolating a moment early in time
(D) establish a link between the length of time that Africa has been inhabited and the discovery of the Andromeda galaxy
(E) emphasize the relatively long period of human life compared to the age of the universe

**11.** The statement in lines 6-7 ("Too bad . . . Andromeda") suggests that

(A) scientists would like to observe events that occurred on Earth in the distant past
(B) there may be planets in Andromeda that are reachable through space travel
(C) the study of Andromeda would offer inter-esting comparisons to planet Earth
(D) a planet in Andromeda will be a likely observation point for Earth in the future
(E) Andromeda is much older than Earth

**12.** The author mentions "plague" (line 13) and "space stations" (line 15) primarily to

(A) give an example of the themes of novels about time travel
(B) suggest contrasting views of the future
(C) scoff at the scientific consequences of time travel
(D) give examples of the subjects that scientists are interested in
(E) suggest why time travel is such a fascinating topic

**GO ON TO THE NEXT PAGE**

13. The author introduces the third paragraph with the words "Being a scientist" in order to

(A) explain an intense personal interest in the topic
(B) lend an air of authority to the discussion of time travel
(C) suggest why certain forms of literature are so appealing
(D) provoke those who defend science fiction
(E) help illustrate the term "causality violation"

14. In discussing causality violations (lines 16-35), the author addresses concerns about all of the following EXCEPT

(A) anticipatory knowledge of events
(B) the belief in a deterministic universe
(C) the mechanics of space travel
(D) cause-and-effect relationships
(E) differential equations based on known forces

15. Which of the following, if true, would undermine the validity of the author's assumption about the impact of mechanical clocks ("When the first . . . the laboratory") in lines 37-42 ?

(A) People were oblivious to time on a physical level before clocks were invented.
(B) People have always perceived time as composed of discrete, uniform intervals.
(C) Concern about time was unnecessary until clocks were invented.
(D) Mental and physiological processes are very predictable.
(E) Body time does not move at a constant rate.

16. The author mentions the brain and the heart (lines 44-45) in order to

(A) demonstrate the rhythmical qualities of timepieces
(B) explain the historical significance of mechanical clocks
(C) emphasize how the two organs interact to regulate internal rhythms
(D) illustrate the body's different internal clocks
(E) demystify the precision of organic processes

17. The author uses the word "ruthless" (line 46) to suggest that

(A) people are bewildered by the prospect of aging
(B) the human body has mysterious capacities
(C) some people age more rapidly than others do
(D) people's sense of time changes as they age
(E) the process of aging is relentless

18. The author mentions that "something . . . skipped upward on the page" (lines 60-61) to suggest that

(A) he reread a portion of the page
(B) his vision was affected by the smoke
(C) he traveled back in time in his imagination
(D) his reading reminded him of Papa Joe
(E) he believes that reading is the best way to recreate the past

**GO ON TO THE NEXT PAGE** ➡

**Questions 19-24 are based on the following passage.**

*The following passage is an excerpt from a book about twentieth-century developments in art. The author refers here to the modern art that emerged shortly after the turn of the century. Many people found this art shocking.*

If the new art is not accessible to everyone, which
certainly seems to be the case, this implies that its impulses
are not of a generically human kind. It is an art not for
*Line* people in general but for a special class who may not be
5   better but who are evidently different.
    Before we go further, one point must be clarified. What
is it that the majority of people call aesthetic pleasure?
What happens in their minds when they "like" a work of
art; for example, a play? The answer is easy. They like a
10  play when they become interested in the human destinies
that are represented, when the love and hatred, the joys and
sorrows of the dramatic personages so move them that they
participate in it all as though it were happening in real life.
And they call a work "good" if it succeeds in creating the
15  illusion necessary to make the imaginary personages appear
like living persons. In poetry the majority of people seek
the passion and pain of the human being behind the poet.
Paintings attract them if they find in them figures of men or
women it would be interesting to meet.
20      It thus appears that to the majority of people aesthetic
pleasure means a state of mind that is essentially
indistinguishable from their ordinary behavior. It differs
merely in accidental qualities, being perhaps less utilitarian,
more intense, and free from painful consequences. But the
25  object toward which their attention and, consequently, all
their other mental activities are directed is the same as in
daily life:  people and passions. When forced to consider
artistic forms proper—for example, in some surrealistic or
abstract art—most people will only tolerate them if they do
30  not interfere with their perception of human forms and
fates. As soon as purely aesthetic elements predominate
and the story of John and Susie grows elusive, most people
feel out of their depth and are at a loss as to what to make
of the scene, the book, or the painting. A work of art
35  vanishes from sight for a beholder who seeks in that work
of art nothing but the moving fate of John and Susie or
Tristan and Isolde.* Unaccustomed to behaving in any
mode except the practical one in which feelings are aroused
and emotional involvement ensues, most people are unsure
40  how to respond to a work that does not invite sentimental
intervention.
    Now this is a point that has to be made perfectly clear.
Neither grieving nor rejoicing at such human destinies as
those presented by a work of art begins to define true
45  artistic pleasure; indeed, preoccupation with the human
content of the work is in principle incompatible with
aesthetic enjoyment proper.

* Tristan and Isolde were star-crossed lovers in a medieval romance.

19. The passage is primarily concerned with the

    (A) lives artists lead as opposed to the ones they
        imagine
    (B) emotional impact of a painting's subject matter
    (C) nature of the pleasure that most people find in a
        work of art
    (D) wide variety of responses that audiences have to
        different works of art
    (E) contrast between the formal elements of the new
        art and those of the old

20. As used in line 18, "figures" most nearly means

    (A) crude images
    (B) abstractions
    (C) representations
    (D) numbers
    (E) famous persons

21. It is most likely that "the story of John and Susie"
    (line 32) refers to

    (A) a fictional work that the author will proceed to
        critique
    (B) a typical narrative of interpersonal relationships
    (C) an account of an affair in the form of a mystery
    (D) a legendary couple that has fascinated artists
        through the ages
    (E) a cryptic chronicle of renowned historical
        personages

22. The author suggests that the majority of people resist
    modern art because they

    (A) consider modern artists to be elitist
    (B) are too influenced by critics to view the art on its
        own merits
    (C) are annoyed by its social message
    (D) find in it little of human interest to engage them
    (E) find it too difficult to guess at the artist's source
        of inspiration

**GO ON TO THE NEXT PAGE**

23. The author's attitude toward the majority of people can best be described as

    (A) genuinely puzzled
    (B) aggressively hostile
    (C) solemnly respectful
    (D) generally indifferent
    (E) condescendingly tolerant

24. The author's assumption in the final paragraph (lines 42-47) is that

    (A) aesthetic pleasure is a response to the purely artistic elements in a work of art
    (B) aesthetic enjoyment of a work of art must focus on the artist's intentions as much as on the artist's actual accomplishments
    (C) responses to a work of art vary and cannot be easily defined
    (D) the evocation of emotional responses by a traditional work of art depends on the moral conventions of the artist's society
    (E) the majority of people trying to interpret a work of art will concentrate on the artistic technique

# STOP

**If you finish before time is called, you may check your work on this section only.**
**Do not turn to any other section in the test.**

## SECTION 4
**Time — 25 minutes**
**18 Questions**

**Turn to Section 4 (page 5) of your answer sheet to answer the questions in this section.**

**Directions:** This section contains two types of questions. You have 25 minutes to complete both types. For questions 1-8, solve each problem and decide which is the best of the choices given. Fill in the corresponding circle on the answer sheet. You may use any available space for scratchwork.

Notes

1. The use of a calculator is permitted.
2. All numbers used are real numbers.
3. Figures that accompany problems in this test are intended to provide information useful in solving the problems. They are drawn as accurately as possible EXCEPT when it is stated in a specific problem that the figure is not drawn to scale. All figures lie in a plane unless otherwise indicated.
4. Unless otherwise specified, the domain of any function $f$ is assumed to be the set of all real numbers $x$ for which $f(x)$ is a real number.

Reference Information

$A = \pi r^2$
$C = 2\pi r$

$A = \ell w$

$A = \frac{1}{2}bh$

$V = \ell w h$

$V = \pi r^2 h$

$c^2 = a^2 + b^2$

Special Right Triangles

The number of degrees of arc in a circle is 360.
The sum of the measures in degrees of the angles of a triangle is 180.

---

**1.** If $s + t = 3$, what is the value of $s + t - 6$ ?

(A)  −3
(B)  0
(C)  3
(D)  6
(E)  9

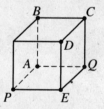

**2.** On the cube in the figure above, each of the following points is the same distance from $P$ as it is from $Q$ EXCEPT

(A)  $A$
(B)  $B$
(C)  $C$
(D)  $D$
(E)  $E$

**GO ON TO THE NEXT PAGE**

## FRAUD ON THE INTERNET

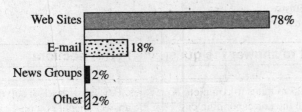

Web Sites 78%
E-mail 18%
News Groups 2%
Other 2%

**3.** The bar graph above shows where fraud is committed on the Internet. Which of the following circle graphs most accurately displays the same data?

(A)

(B)

(C)

(D)

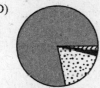

(E)

**4.** The numerator of a certain fraction is 5 less than the denominator. If the fraction is equal to $\frac{3}{4}$, what is the denominator of this fraction?

(A) 8
(B) 12
(C) 16
(D) 20
(E) 24

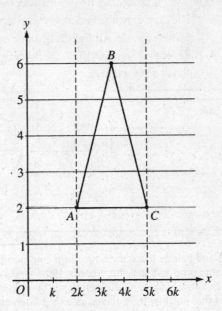

**5.** In the figure above, the scale on the $x$-axis is different from the scale on the $y$-axis. If the area of $\triangle ABC$ is 18, what is the value of $k$?

(A) $\frac{3}{10}$

(B) $\frac{3}{4}$

(C) $\frac{6}{5}$

(D) $\frac{3}{2}$

(E) 3

**GO ON TO THE NEXT PAGE**

**6.** If $m$ and $k$ are positive and $10m^2 k^{-1} = 100m$, what is $m^{-1}$ in terms of $k$?

(A) $\dfrac{k}{10}$

(B) $\dfrac{k}{90}$

(C) $\dfrac{\sqrt{k}}{10}$

(D) $\dfrac{1}{10k}$

(E) $\dfrac{1}{90k}$

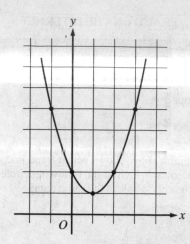

**8.** The figure above shows the graph of a quadratic function $f$ that has a minimum at the point $(1, 1)$. If $f(b) = f(3)$, which of the following could be the value of $b$?

(A) $-3$
(B) $-2$
(C) $-1$
(D) $1$
(E) $5$

**7.** Edna and Nancy leave the house of a common friend at the same time and walk for 4 hours. Edna walks due east at the average rate of 4 kilometers per hour and Nancy walks due north at the average rate of 3 kilometers per hour. What is the straight-line distance between them, in kilometers, at the end of the 4 hours?

(A) 4
(B) 5
(C) 12
(D) 16
(E) 20

**GO ON TO THE NEXT PAGE**

Unauthorized copying or reuse of any part of this page is illegal.

**Directions:** For Student-Produced Response questions 9-18, use the grids at the bottom of the answer sheet page on which you have answered questions 1-8.

Each of the remaining 10 questions requires you to solve the problem and enter your answer by marking the circles in the special grid, as shown in the examples below. You may use any available space for scratchwork.

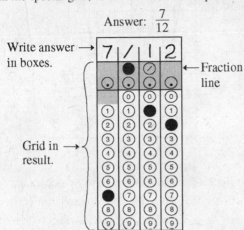

Answer: $\frac{7}{12}$

Write answer in boxes. → ← Fraction line

Grid in → result.

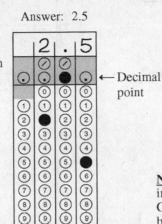

Answer: 2.5

← Decimal point

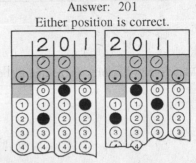

Answer: 201
Either position is correct.

**Note:** You may start your answers in any column, space permitting. Columns not needed should be left blank.

- Mark no more than one circle in any column.

- Because the answer sheet will be machine-scored, **you will receive credit only if the circles are filled in correctly.**

- Although not required, it is suggested that you write your answer in the boxes at the top of the columns to help you fill in the circles accurately.

- Some problems may have more than one correct answer. In such cases, grid only one answer.

- No question has a negative answer.

- **Mixed numbers** such as $3\frac{1}{2}$ must be gridded as 3.5 or 7/2. (If $3\ |\ 1\ /\ 2$ is gridded, it will be interpreted as $\frac{31}{2}$, not $3\frac{1}{2}$.)

- **Decimal Answers:** If you obtain a decimal answer with more digits than the grid can accommodate, it may be either rounded or truncated, but it must fill the entire grid. For example, if you obtain an answer such as 0.6666..., you should record your result as .666 or .667. **A less accurate value such as .66 or .67 will be scored as incorrect.**

Acceptable ways to grid $\frac{2}{3}$ are:

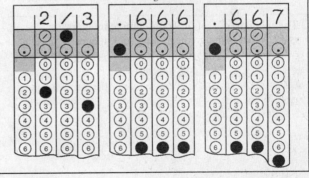

**9.** A family of 5 is planning a 4-day camping trip. Each person will need to bring 1 bottle of water for each day of the trip. If the water is sold only in 3-bottle packages, how many packages must the family buy for the trip?

$$|10 - k| = 3$$
$$|k - 5| = 8$$

**10.** What is the value of $k$ that satisfies both equations above?

**GO ON TO THE NEXT PAGE** →

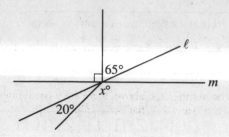

**11.** What is the value of $x$ in the figure above?

**12.** The median of a set of 9 consecutive integers is 42. What is the greatest of these 9 integers?

**13.** Let the function $f$ be defined by $f(x) = x + 1$. If $2f(p) = 20$, what is the value of $f(3p)$?

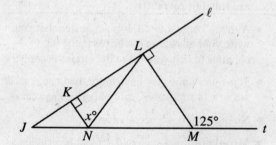

**14.** In the figure above, $\overline{KN} \perp \overline{JL}$ and $\overline{LM} \perp \overline{JL}$. If the lengths of $\overline{LN}$ and $\overline{LM}$ are equal, what is the value of $x$?

**GO ON TO THE NEXT PAGE**

15. A measuring cup contains $\frac{1}{5}$ of a cup of orange juice.

    It is then filled to the 1 cup mark with a mixture that contains equal amounts of orange, grapefruit, and pineapple juices. What fraction of the final mixture is orange juice?

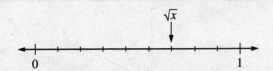

17. On the number line above, there are 9 equal intervals between 0 and 1. What is the value of $x$?

16. If $a + 2b$ is equal to 125 percent of $4b$, what is the value of $\frac{a}{b}$?

18. In the $xy$-coordinate plane, the distance between point $B(10, 18)$ and point $A(x, 3)$ is 17. What is one possible value of $x$?

# STOP
If you finish before time is called, you may check your work on this section only.
Do not turn to any other section in the test.

## SECTION 6
### Time — 25 minutes
### 35 Questions

**Turn to Section 6 (page 5) of your answer sheet to answer the questions in this section.**

**Directions:** For each question in this section, select the best answer from among the choices given and fill in the corresponding circle on the answer sheet.

The following sentences test correctness and effectiveness of expression. Part of each sentence or the entire sentence is underlined; beneath each sentence are five ways of phrasing the underlined material. Choice A repeats the original phrasing; the other four choices are different. If you think the original phrasing produces a better sentence than any of the alternatives, select choice A; if not, select one of the other choices.

In making your selection, follow the requirements of standard written English; that is, pay attention to grammar, choice of words, sentence construction, and punctuation. Your selection should result in the most effective sentence—clear and precise, without awkwardness or ambiguity.

EXAMPLE:

Laura Ingalls Wilder published her first book and she was sixty-five years old then.

(A) and she was sixty-five years old then
(B) when she was sixty-five
(C) at age sixty-five years old
(D) upon the reaching of sixty-five years
(E) at the time when she was sixty-five

1. The delegates coming this far, they did not want to return without accomplishing something.

(A) The delegates coming this far, they
(B) Coming this far, the delegates felt they
(C) Having come this far, the delegates
(D) To come this far, the delegates
(E) The delegates came this far, so that they

2. After marching for four hours in temperatures exceeding ninety degrees, the band members were as soaked as if marching through a rainstorm.

(A) if marching
(B) having marched
(C) if from marching
(D) if they had marched
(E) if they would have marched

3. The harmful effects of smoking on the vascular system is increasingly well documented.

(A) is increasingly well documented
(B) is more and more documented
(C) are increasingly well documented
(D) are increasing in better documentation
(E) has increased in better documentation

4. The issue the council debated, which was whether repeal of rent control will improve housing or just increase profits for landlords.

(A) debated, which was whether repeal of rent control will improve
(B) debated was if they would repeal rent control would this improve
(C) debated was that repeal of rent control would result in improved
(D) debated was will repealing rent control mean improvement in
(E) debated was whether repeal of rent control would improve

**GO ON TO THE NEXT PAGE**

**5.** American journalist <u>Harriet Quimby, the first woman to pilot a plane across the English Channel, doing it</u> just nine years after the Wright brothers' first powered flight.

(A) Harriet Quimby, the first woman to pilot a plane across the English Channel, doing it

(B) Harriet Quimby the first woman who piloted a plane across the English Channel, and who did so

(C) Harriet Quimby became the first woman to have piloted a plane across the English Channel and did it

(D) Harriet Quimby became the first woman to pilot a plane across the English Channel, accomplishing this feat

(E) Harriet Quimby was the first woman piloting a plane across the English Channel, the feat was accomplished

**6.** Naomi and Charles will represent Ammonton High in the debating <u>contest, their work in this having been excellent this year</u>.

(A) contest, their work in this having been excellent this year

(B) contest; they have done excellent work this year in this

(C) contest, for this year they have done excellent work in this

(D) contest, for their work as public speakers has been excellent this year

(E) contest; their work as public speakers having been excellent this year

**7.** The poem's colorful images and its verbal wit <u>give the reader pleasure</u>.

(A) give the reader pleasure

(B) please the one who is reading

(C) gives pleasure to the one who reads it

(D) give one pleasure in the reading of it

(E) gives one pleasure in reading it

**8.** <u>Being as she is a gifted storyteller</u>, Linda Goss is an expert at describing people and places.

(A) Being as she is a gifted storyteller

(B) In being a gifted storyteller

(C) A gifted storyteller

(D) Although she is a gifted storyteller

(E) Telling stories giftedly

**9.** <u>Although the English artist William Blake never having painted portraits, he regarded them</u> as merely mechanical reproductions that, despite their popularity, lacked true creativity.

(A) Although the English artist William Blake never having painted portraits, he regarded them

(B) The English artist William Blake never painted portraits, he regarded them

(C) Never having painted a portrait, they were regarded by the English artist William Blake

(D) The English artist William Blake never painted portraits; however, regarding them

(E) The English artist William Blake never painted portraits because he regarded them

**10.** The heat was already <u>overwhelming and lasted a week, which duration made it seem</u> sheer torture.

(A) overwhelming and lasted a week, which duration made it seem

(B) overwhelming, and because of lasting a week, it made it seem

(C) overwhelming and lasted the duration of a week to make it to seem

(D) overwhelming, and its lasting a week made it seem

(E) overwhelming and, by lasting a week, making it seem

**11.** The reason first novels are so often their writers' best work <u>is that it draws upon</u> all the experiences of childhood.

(A) is that it draws upon

(B) is that these first efforts draw upon

(C) is because of these first efforts drawing from

(D) is because of them drawing upon

(E) is their drawing from

**GO ON TO THE NEXT PAGE** ⟶

The following sentences test your ability to recognize grammar and usage errors. Each sentence contains either a single error or no error at all. No sentence contains more than one error. The error, if there is one, is underlined and lettered. If the sentence contains an error, select the one underlined part that must be changed to make the sentence correct. If the sentence is correct, select choice E. In choosing answers, follow the requirements of standard written English.

EXAMPLE:

The other delegates and him immediately
  A              B        C
accepted the resolution drafted by the
                          D
neutral states. No error
                   E

Ⓐ ● Ⓒ Ⓓ Ⓔ

12. Directed by George Wolfe, the Broadway musical

_Bring in 'Da Noise, Bring in 'Da Funk_ telling  how
                                          A      B

tap dancing evolved from the African American
              C

experience in the decades following the Civil War.
              D

No error
  E

13. The question of whether certain chemical fertilizers
                        A

are a curse or are they a blessing is  still being
                B                 C      D

debated. No error
            E

14. People which need immediate reeducation for
            A

employment are  impatient with the prolonged
            B        C

debate over funding for the new national program.
    D

No error
  E

15. The thoughtful student wonders what

Patrick Henry meant  when he talked about liberty
        A                  B

because most of the members of the House of
  C

Burgesses then having been slaveholders. No error
                D                          E

16. One challenge that writer Eleanor Wong Telemaque

faced was how preserving her ethnic identity
              A

while becoming more accessible to readers who
      B                   C

are not accustomed to writers from other cultural
          D

backgrounds. No error
                E

17. No one objects to his company, even though he has
          A

made insulting remarks about almost every member
                        B          C

of the group, when he is a remarkably witty man.
            D

No error
  E

**GO ON TO THE NEXT PAGE**

18. Just how critical an improved balance of trade is to
    A                                              B
    a healthy economy has never been more clearer than
                       C              D
    it is now. No error
                 E

19. Critics contend that reforms in welfare
             A
    has not managed to bring the high percentage
    B
    of our nation's children living in poverty the
    economic security that they need to thrive .
                           C         D
    No error
    E

20. Crabs living in polluted waters will come
           A
    in contact with large numbers of disease-causing
    B
    microorganisms because it feeds by filtering
                           C       D
    nutrients from water. No error
                          E

21. The new system, which uses remote cameras
                         A
    in the catching of speeding motorists ,
    B               C
    may undermine the police department's authority.
    D
    No error
    E

22. Although the politician was initially very sensitive to
                                A
    be criticized by the press, he quickly became more
    B                           C
    confident about responding to reporters' sometimes
                     D
    pointed questions. No error
                       E

23. Although Pre-Raphaelite artists advocated the close
    A
    study of nature , their paintings sometimes seem
          B          C
    elaborately artificial to modern viewers. No error
    D                                        E

24. Lions and tigers may be identical in size, but the
                      A                       B
    tiger is the fiercer animal and the lion the strongest .
           C                               D
    No error
    E

25. The decline in science education during the
    period had two causes: less funding for scientific
           A                   B
    research with a decrease in jobs related to space and
             C                     D
    defense. No error
             E

GO ON TO THE NEXT PAGE

26. The number of awards given  $\underline{\text{this year}}$  to biochemists
   A

   $\underline{\text{accentuate}}$  the  $\underline{\text{significant gains}}$  being  $\underline{\text{made in}}$  the
   B            C                              D

   study of the chemistry of living organisms.  $\underline{\text{No error}}$
   E

27. The novel *Pride and Prejudice* by Jane Austen

   $\underline{\text{was once}}$  more  $\underline{\text{widely read}}$  and was  $\underline{\text{more popular}}$
   A                B                        C

   in high schools in the United States

   $\underline{\text{than Charlotte Brontë}}$ .  $\underline{\text{No error}}$
   D                            E

28. $\underline{\text{Until it}}$  can be replaced by a  $\underline{\text{faster}}$ , more efficient,
   A                               B

   and more economical means of transportation, trucks

   $\underline{\text{will carry most}}$  of the freight  $\underline{\text{within and through}}$
   C                                    D

   metropolitan areas.  $\underline{\text{No error}}$
   E

29. $\underline{\text{Nearly all}}$  of the editors of the magazine
   A

   $\underline{\text{agree}}$  that of the two articles  $\underline{\text{to be published}}$ ,
   B                              C

   Fujimura's is the  $\underline{\text{more exciting}}$ .  $\underline{\text{No error}}$
   D                    E

**Directions:** The following passage is an early draft of an essay. Some parts of the passage need to be rewritten.

Read the passage and select the best answers for the questions that follow. Some questions are about particular sentences or parts of sentences and ask you to improve sentence structure or word choice. Other questions ask you to consider organization and development. In choosing answers, follow the requirements of standard written English.

**Questions 30-35 are based on the following passage.**

(1) This summer I felt as if I were listening in on the Middle Ages with a hidden microphone. (2) No, there were no microphones in those days. (3) But there were letters, and sometimes these letters speak to me like voices from very long ago.

(4) A book I found contained selected letters from five generations of a family. (5) The Pastons, who lived in a remote part of England over 500 years ago.

(6) Getting anywhere in the Middle Ages was really hard, with deep rivers and few bridges and sudden snowstorms coming on in the empty lands between settlements. (7) An earl rebelled in London, so that a messenger rode for days to tell the distant head of the Paston family of a feared civil war.

(8) Through the letters a modern reader can sense their anxieties about rebellious sons and daughters, belligerent neighbors, outbreaks of plague, and shortages of certain foods and textiles. (9) Unbelievably, there is a 1470 love letter. (10) The man who wrote it ends "I beg you, let no one see this letter. (11) As soon as you have read it, burn it, for I would not want anyone to see it." (12) I was sitting on the front porch with bare feet on the hottest afternoon in July and I read that with a shiver. (13) I had been part of a centuries-old secret.

**GO ON TO THE NEXT PAGE**

**30.** The best way to describe the relationship of sentence 2 to sentence 1 is that sentence 2

   (A) anticipates a reader's possible response to sentence 1
   (B) provides historical background for sentence 1
   (C) repeats the idea presented in sentence 1
   (D) introduces a contrasting view of sentence 1
   (E) corrects an inaccuracy stated in sentence 1

**31.** Which of the following sentences would be most logical to insert before sentence 4 ?

   (A) I first came across these letters while browsing in a library.
   (B) No, I am not dreaming; I have been reading them.
   (C) On the contrary, microphones are a recent invention.
   (D) Obviously, a library can open the door to mystery.
   (E) However, letters are not the oldest form of communication.

**32.** In context, which is the best version of the underlined portions of sentences 4 and 5 (reproduced below) ?

*A book I found contained selected letters from five generations of a family. The Pastons, who lived in a remote part of England over 500 years ago.*

   (A) (as it is now)
   (B) a family. The Pastons, living
   (C) a family; it was the Pastons living
   (D) the Paston family, who lived
   (E) the family named Paston and living

**33.** In context, which of the following is the best version of the underlined portion of sentence 7 (reproduced below) ?

*An earl rebelled in London, so that a messenger rode for days to tell the distant head of the Paston family of a feared civil war.*

   (A) (As it is now)
   (B) An earl had rebelled in London, so
   (C) For example, with a rebelling earl in London
   (D) While an earl rebels in London,
   (E) Once, when an earl rebelled in London,

**34.** In context, which is the best revision to make to sentence 8 (reproduced below) ?

*Through the letters a modern reader can sense their anxieties about rebellious sons and daughters, belligerent neighbors, outbreaks of plague, and shortages of certain foods and textiles.*

   (A) Insert "one's reading of" after "Through".
   (B) Change "their" to "the Pastons' ".
   (C) Change "sense" to "record".
   (D) Delete some of the examples.
   (E) Insert "etc." after "textiles".

**35.** All of the following strategies are used by the writer of the passage EXCEPT

   (A) background explanation
   (B) imaginative description
   (C) rhetorical questions
   (D) personal narration
   (E) direct quotation

## STOP

**If you finish before time is called, you may check your work on this section only.**
**Do not turn to any other section in the test.**

## SECTION 7
Time — 25 minutes
24 Questions

Turn to Section 7 (page 6) of your answer sheet to answer the questions in this section.

**Directions:** For each question in this section, select the best answer from among the choices given and fill in the corresponding circle on the answer sheet.

Each sentence below has one or two blanks, each blank indicating that something has been omitted. Beneath the sentence are five words or sets of words labeled A through E. Choose the word or set of words that, when inserted in the sentence, best fits the meaning of the sentence as a whole.

**Example:**

Hoping to ------- the dispute, negotiators proposed a compromise that they felt would be ------- to both labor and management.

(A) enforce . . useful
(B) end . . divisive
(C) overcome . . unattractive
(D) extend . . satisfactory
(E) resolve . . acceptable          Ⓐ Ⓑ Ⓒ Ⓓ ●

1. Commerce on the remote island was conducted exclusively by -------, exchanging goods for goods.

    (A) credit    (B) loan    (C) faith
        (D) patronage    (E) barter

2. The existence of environmental contamination is no longer a point of -------; government, industry, and the public agree that it is a serious problem.

    (A) concern    (B) cooperation    (C) urgency
        (D) relevance    (E) dispute

3. In rock climbing, survival depends as much on ,
the ability to perceive without conscious reasoning, as on physical strength.

    (A) autonomy    (B) incoherence    (C) intuition
        (D) sophistry    (E) receptivity

4. Using computer labs to ------- classroom instruction is most effective when the curriculum ------- lab exercises and classroom teaching in a coordinated manner.

    (A) supplement . . integrates
    (B) substantiate . . undermines
    (C) remedy . . compromises
    (D) disparage . . reinforces
    (E) foster . . curtails

5. Many ------- of the style of painting exemplified by Marcel Duchamp's work focused on Duchamp's *Nude Descending a Staircase* as the ------- of what they detested about modern art.

    (A) critics . . epitome
    (B) proponents . . realization
    (C) advocates . . embodiment
    (D) debunkers . . rejection
    (E) belittlers . . reversal

6. Colonial American playwright Mercy Otis Warren was known for her political -------: her keen judgment and insight were widely acknowledged.

    (A) partisanship    (B) intemperance    (C) acumen
        (D) irreverence    (E) interest

7. Johnson's writing is considered ------- and ------- because it is filled with obscure references and baffling digressions.

    (A) deceiving . . ingenuous
    (B) arcane . . abstruse
    (C) spare . . didactic
    (D) lucid . . definitive
    (E) concise . . esoteric

8. Because the congresswoman has been so openhanded with many of her constituents, it is difficult to reconcile this ------- with her private -------.

    (A) selfishness . . inattention
    (B) insolence . . virtue
    (C) magnanimity . . pettiness
    (D) opportunism . . ambition
    (E) solicitousness . . generosity

GO ON TO THE NEXT PAGE ▷

The passages below are followed by questions based on their content; questions following a pair of related passages may also be based on the relationship between the paired passages. Answer the questions on the basis of what is <u>stated</u> or <u>implied</u> in the passages and in any introductory material that may be provided.

**Questions 9-12 are based on the following passages.**

**Passage 1**

What accounts for the inexorable advance of the giant sports utility vehicle (SUV) into our lives? Why do we want high-clearance trucks with four-wheel drive and front bumpers as big as battering rams? A large part of
Line
5 the answer lies in the fake Western names so many of them carry. No one much cares about what those names denote (lakes, frontier towns, mountain ranges); what matters is their connotations of rugged individualism, mastery over the wilderness, cowboy endurance. The
10 names simply magnify the appeal of these vehicles that are the Frankensteinian concoctions of our private anxieties and desires.

**Passage 2**

When a major manufacturer launched an SUV named for an Alaskan mountain, an auto-trade publication dis-
15 cussed the subtleties of its name. It proposed that even though most buyers will never venture into territory any less trampled than the parking lot of the local shopping mall, the important goal of the marketing hype is to plant the image in customers' minds that they can conquer
20 rugged terrain. Perhaps we're trying to tame a different kind of wilderness. Indeed, in an age when many who can afford to do so live in limited-access communities in houses guarded by sophisticated surveillance systems, the SUV is the perfect transportation shelter to protect us
25 from fears both real and imagined.

9. Passage 1 and Passage 2 both support which of the following generalizations about buyers of SUVs?

(A) They intend to drive them on rough terrain.
(B) They wish to live in mountainous regions.
(C) They are wealthier than most other car buyers.
(D) They are influenced by marketing strategies.
(E) They are insecure about their social status.

10. Which of the following aspects of SUVs is addressed in Passage 1 but <u>not</u> in Passage 2 ?

(A) Their imposing bulk
(B) Their escalating cost
(C) The psychology of their owners
(D) Their environmental impact
(E) The significance of their names

11. Which of the following in Passage 1 exemplifies the "subtleties" mentioned in Passage 2, line 15 ?

(A) "inexorable advance" (line 1)
(B) "battering rams" (line 4)
(C) "lakes, frontier towns, mountain ranges" (line 7)
(D) "connotations" (line 8)
(E) "Frankensteinian concoctions" (line 11)

12. Passage 1 and the article cited in Passage 2 both indicate that the imagery used to market SUVs is intended to

(A) appeal to drivers' primitive instincts
(B) stir yearnings for a simpler way of life
(C) engender feelings of power and control
(D) evoke the beauty of unspoiled nature
(E) create an aura of nonconformity

**GO ON TO THE NEXT PAGE**

**Questions 13-24 are based on the following passages.**

*These two passages discuss different aspects of the impact of the First World War (1914-1918) on British people and society. Passage 1 is from a book that examines the depiction of the war in literature, letters, and newspapers; Passage 2 is from a book that examines the differences between men's and women's experiences of war.*

### Passage 1

Even if the civilian population at home had wanted to know the realities of the war, they couldn't have without experiencing them: its conditions were too novel, its indus-
Line trialized ghastliness too unprecedented. The war would
5 have been simply unbelievable. From the very beginning a fissure was opening between the army and the civilians.

The causes of civilian incomprehension were numerous. Few soldiers wrote the truth in letters home for fear of causing needless uneasiness. If they did ever write the
10 truth, it was excised by company officers, who censored all outgoing mail. The press was under rigid censorship throughout the war. Only correspondents willing to file wholesome, optimistic copy were permitted to visit France, and even they were seldom allowed near the battlefields of
15 the front line. Typical of these reporters was George Adam, Paris correspondent of the *Times*. His *Behind the Scenes at the Front*, published in 1915, exudes cheer, as well as warm condescension, toward the common British soldier, whom he depicts as well fed, warm, safe, and happy—better off,
20 indeed, than at home.

Lord Northcliffe, the publisher of the *Times*, eventually assumed full charge of government propaganda. It is no surprise to find Northcliffe's *Times* on July 3, 1916, reporting the first day's attack during the battle of the Somme* with
25 an airy confidence which could not help but deepen the division between those on the spot and those at home. "Sir Douglas Haig telephoned last night," says the *Times*, "that the general situation was favorable." It soon ascends to the rhetoric of heroic romance: "There is a fair field . . . and
30 we have elected to fight out our quarrel with the Germans and to give them as much battle as they want." No wonder communication failed between the troops and those who could credit prose like that as factual testimony.

* The British army had nearly 60,000 casualties, the largest number for any single day in the army's history.

### Passage 2

The First World War is a classic case of the dissonance
35 between official, male-centered history and unofficial female history. Not only did the apocalyptic events of this war have very different *meanings* for men and women, such events were in fact very different for men and women, a point understood almost at once by an involved contemporary
40 like Vera Brittain. She noted about her relationship with her soldier fiancé that the war put a "barrier of indescribable experience between men and women whom they loved. Sometimes (I wrote at the time) I fear that even if he gets through, what he has experienced out there may change his
45 ideas and tastes utterly."

The nature of the barrier thrust between Vera Brittain and her fiancé, however, may have been even more complex than she herself realized, for the impediment preventing a marriage of their true minds was constituted not only by *his*
50 altered experience but by *hers*. Specifically, as young men became increasingly alienated from their pre-war selves, increasingly immured in the muck and blood of the battlefields, increasingly abandoned by the civilization of which they had ostensibly been heirs, women seemed to become,
55 as if by some uncanny swing of history's pendulum, ever more powerful. As nurses, as munitions workers, as bus drivers, as soldiers in the agricultural "land army," even as wives and mothers, these formerly subservient creatures began to loom larger. A visitor to London observed in
60 1918 that "England was a world of women—women in uniforms."

The wartime poems, stories, and memoirs by women sometimes subtly, sometimes explicitly explore the political and economic revolution by which the First World War
65 at least temporarily dispossessed male citizens of the primacy that had always been their birthright, while permanently granting women access to both the votes and the professions that they had never before possessed. Similarly, a number of these women writers covertly or overtly cele-
70 brated the release of female desires and powers which that revolution made possible, as well as the reunion (or even reunification) of women which was a consequence of such liberated energies.

Their enthusiasm, which might otherwise seem like
75 morbid gloating, was explained by Virginia Woolf, a writer otherwise known for her pacifist sympathies:

*How . . . can we explain that amazing outburst in August 1914, when the daughters of educated men . . . rushed into hospitals . . . drove lorries, worked in fields*
80 *and munitions factories, and used all their immense stores of charm . . . to persuade young men that to fight was heroic . . . ? So profound was (woman's) unconscious loathing for the education of the private house that she would undertake any task, however menial, exercise any*
85 *fascination, however fatal, that enabled her to escape. Thus consciously she desired "our splendid Empire"; unconsciously she desired our splendid war.*

**GO ON TO THE NEXT PAGE**

**13.** Passage 2 is unlike Passage 1 in that Passage 2

(A) describes war as dehumanizing
(B) endorses the official view of the war
(C) discusses war in terms of how it affects women
(D) tries to identify the root causes of the conflict
(E) criticizes the censorship of information about the war

**14.** The "fissure" (line 6) was primarily caused by the

(A) civilians' ignorance about the soldiers' experience
(B) discrepancy between the experiences of men and of women
(C) behavior of the officers who led the battles
(D) guilt that civilians felt about sending young men off to war
(E) special privileges granted to war correspondents

**15.** The footnote about the battle of the Somme adds information that

(A) shows how history has been rewritten to glorify the war
(B) trivializes the dangers faced by most of the soldiers
(C) emphasizes the inaccuracy of the published reports
(D) suggests that the costs of war outweighed its benefits
(E) offers a journalist's personal reflection on the war

**16.** In Passage 1, the author suggests that the attitudes of "those at home" (line 26) were strongly influenced by

(A) the government's inadequate control over propaganda
(B) the lack of opportunities for soldiers to write home
(C) the disparity between men's and women's views of war
(D) efforts of pacifists to end the war
(E) censored reports from the press

**17.** In line 33, "credit" most nearly means

(A) award
(B) believe
(C) enter
(D) supply
(E) enrich

**18.** In Passage 2, the author mentions Vera Brittain (line 40) primarily to

(A) support an argument by quoting material written at the time of the war
(B) present an example of the kind of powers women gained during the war
(C) describe how a writer manipulated the facts about the war
(D) discuss the wartime literature produced by women
(E) dispute recent historians' views of the war

**19.** In line 58, the reference to "wives and mothers" most directly implies the author's assumption that

(A) families prospered more when women became head of the household
(B) soldiers were unaware of the fundamental change taking place in society
(C) women embraced their chance to work outside the home
(D) women were anxious about fulfilling family responsibilities
(E) women in domestic roles had previously exercised little authority

**20.** In line 64, the "revolution" refers to

(A) women's literary output during the war
(B) women's pursuit of rights previously unavailable to them
(C) the change that men underwent after experiencing war
(D) the redistribution of power from the upper to the middle class
(E) the growing equalization of men's and women's wages

**21.** The author of Passage 2 implies that women's enthusiasm "might . . . seem like morbid gloating" (lines 74-75) because

(A) women's progress caused the deterioration of men's status
(B) women achieved recognition as the real peace-makers in the war
(C) women boasted that the war would be lost without them
(D) women celebrated the fact that they did not have to fight in the war
(E) women were enjoying power while men were in battle

**GO ON TO THE NEXT PAGE**

7 7

Unauthorized copying or reuse of
any part of this page is illegal.

22. In lines 84-85, the discussion of women's involvement with "menial" tasks and "fatal" fascinations primarily serves to emphasize the

(A) far-reaching consequences of women's roles during wartime
(B) extent to which women felt stifled in their traditional roles
(C) contrast between how women idealized war and what it was really like
(D) desire by women to escape the horrors of war
(E) risks that women took to fight in the war

23. What do *Behind the Scenes at the Front* (lines 16-17) and "wartime poems, stories and memoirs" (line 62) have in common?

(A) Both caused needless uneasiness among civilians.
(B) Both deliberately reflected the views of the government.
(C) Both changed the status quo for women in wartime Britain.
(D) Both encouraged writers to take their craft more seriously.
(E) Neither focused on the realities of the battlefield.

24. Which of the following statements about the effect of the First World War is supported by both passages?

(A) Officers resented the government's complacency.
(B) Women gained independence in postwar Britain.
(C) Soldiers felt isolated from parts of civilian society.
(D) Writers failed in their attempts to describe the atrocities of war.
(E) War proved an undesirable way to resolve the European conflict.

## STOP

**If you finish before time is called, you may check your work on this section only.**
**Do not turn to any other section in the test.**

## SECTION 8
**Time — 20 minutes**
**16 Questions**

---

**Turn to Section 8 (page 7) of your answer sheet to answer the questions in this section.**

---

**Directions:** For this section, solve each problem and decide which is the best of the choices given. Fill in the corresponding circle on the answer sheet. You may use any available space for scratchwork.

---

Notes

1. The use of a calculator is permitted.

2. All numbers used are real numbers.

3. Figures that accompany problems in this test are intended to provide information useful in solving the problems. They are drawn as accurately as possible EXCEPT when it is stated in a specific problem that the figure is not drawn to scale. All figures lie in a plane unless otherwise indicated.

4. Unless otherwise specified, the domain of any function $f$ is assumed to be the set of all real numbers $x$ for which $f(x)$ is a real number.

---

Reference Information

 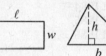 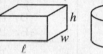 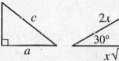

$A = \pi r^2$
$C = 2\pi r$

$A = \ell w$

$A = \frac{1}{2}bh$

$V = \ell wh$

$V = \pi r^2 h$

$c^2 = a^2 + b^2$

Special Right Triangles

The number of degrees of arc in a circle is 360.
The sum of the measures in degrees of the angles of a triangle is 180.

---

**1.** If $E$ is the set of even integers, $P$ is the set of positive integers, and $F$ is the set of integers less than 5, which of the following integers will be in all three sets?

(A)  6
(B)  4
(C)  1
(D)  0
(E)  −2

**2.** If $8 + \sqrt{k} = 15$, then $k =$

(A)   7
(B)   49
(C)  529
(D)  $\sqrt{7}$
(E)  $\sqrt{23}$

**GO ON TO THE NEXT PAGE**

**3.** In a poll, 35 people were in favor of building a new library, 14 people were against it, and 1 person had no opinion. What fraction of those polled were in favor of building a new library?

(A) $\frac{7}{10}$

(B) $\frac{2}{3}$

(C) $\frac{3}{7}$

(D) $\frac{1}{3}$

(E) $\frac{3}{10}$

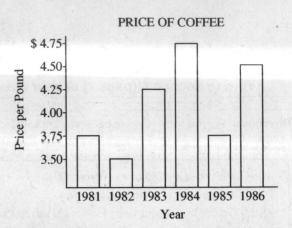

PRICE OF COFFEE

**5.** According to the graph above, between which two consecutive years was there the greatest change in the price of coffee?

(A) 1981 and 1982
(B) 1982 and 1983
(C) 1983 and 1984
(D) 1984 and 1985
(E) 1985 and 1986

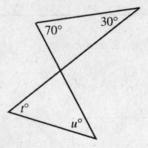

**4.** In the figure above, what is the value of $t + u$ ?

(A)  80
(B)  90
(C) 100
(D) 110
(E) 120

**GO ON TO THE NEXT PAGE**

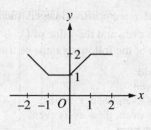

6. The graph of $y = g(x)$ is shown above. If $g(k) = 1$, which of the following is a possible value of $k$?

(A) $-1.5$
(B) $-0.5$
(C) $1$
(D) $1.5$
(E) $2$

7. If $a$, $b$, and $c$ are different positive integers and $2^a \cdot 2^b \cdot 2^c = 64$, then $2^a + 2^b + 2^c =$

(A) 14
(B) 17
(C) 21
(D) 28
(E) 34

8. In the $xy$-plane, the center of a circle has coordinates $(3, -7)$. If one endpoint of a diameter of the circle is $(-2, -7)$, what are the coordinates of the other endpoint of this diameter?

(A) $(-7, -7)$
(B) $(-2, -2)$
(C) $(3, -2)$
(D) $(8, -2)$
(E) $(8, -7)$

9. A regulation for riding a certain amusement park ride requires that a child be between 30 inches and 50 inches tall. Which of the following inequalities can be used to determine whether or not a child's height $h$ satisfies the regulation for this ride?

(A) $|h - 10| < 50$
(B) $|h - 20| < 40$
(C) $|h - 30| < 20$
(D) $|h - 40| < 10$
(E) $|h - 45| < 5$

10. A right circular cylinder with radius 5 and height 4 has volume $v$. In terms of $v$, what is the volume of a right circular cylinder with radius 5 and height 8?

(A) $v + 4$
(B) $2v$
(C) $4v$
(D) $6v$
(E) $8v$

**GO ON TO THE NEXT PAGE**

**11.** If $k$, $n$, and $r$ are integers, let $k \blacklozenge (n, r)$ be defined to be true only if $n < k < r$. If $-2 \blacklozenge (n, 0)$ is true, which of the following could be a possible value of $n$ ?

    I.  $-3$
   II.  $-1$
  III.   $3$

(A) I only
(B) III only
(C) I and II
(D) I and III
(E) II and III

**12.** If 20 percent of $x$ equals 80 percent of $y$, which of the following expresses $y$ in terms of $x$ ?

(A)  $y = 16\%$ of $x$
(B)  $y = 25\%$ of $x$
(C)  $y = 60\%$ of $x$
(D)  $y = 100\%$ of $x$
(E)  $y = 400\%$ of $x$

**13.** If $x$, $y$, and $z$ are positive integers such that the value of $x + y$ is even and the value of $(x + y)^2 + x + z$ is odd, which of the following must be true?

(A)  $x$ is odd.
(B)  $x$ is even.
(C)  If $z$ is even, then $x$ is odd.
(D)  If $z$ is even, then $xy$ is even.
(E)  $xy$ is even.

**14.** If $0 < x < 1$, which of the following statements must be true?

    I.  $x^2 > x^3$

   II.  $x > \dfrac{x}{2}$

  III.  $x > x^3$

(A) I only
(B) II only
(C) I and II only
(D) I and III only
(E) I, II, and III

**GO ON TO THE NEXT PAGE**

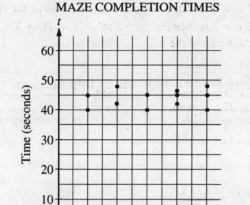

MAZE COMPLETION TIMES

**15.** Doug's biology experiment involved timing 12 hamsters in a maze. Each hamster received at least one practice before being timed. The scatterplot above shows the time each hamster took to complete the maze and the corresponding number of practices that each hamster received. Based on the data, which of the following functions best models the relationship between $t$, the number of seconds to complete the maze, and $p$, the number of practices?

(A)  $t(p) = 44$

(B)  $t(p) = p$

(C)  $t(p) = 44p$

(D)  $t(p) = \dfrac{p}{44}$

(E)  $t(p) = p + 44$

**16.** The pattern shown above is composed of rectangles. This pattern is used repeatedly to completely cover a rectangular region 12$L$ units long and 10$L$ units wide. How many rectangles of dimension $L$ by $W$ are needed?

(A)   30
(B)   36
(C)   100
(D)   150
(E)   180

# STOP

**If you finish before time is called, you may check your work on this section only.**
**Do not turn to any other section in the test.**

## SECTION 9
### Time — 20 minutes
### 19 Questions

**Turn to Section 9 (page 7) of your answer sheet to answer the questions in this section.**

**Directions.** For each question in this section, select the best answer from among the choices given and fill in the corresponding circle on the answer sheet.

Each sentence below has one or two blanks, each blank indicating that something has been omitted. Beneath the sentence are five words or sets of words labeled A through E. Choose the word or set of words that, when inserted in the sentence, best fits the meaning of the sentence as a whole.

**Example:**

Hoping to ------- the dispute, negotiators proposed a compromise that they felt would be ------- to both labor and management.

(A) enforce . . useful
(B) end . . divisive
(C) overcome . . unattractive
(D) extend . . satisfactory
(E) resolve . . acceptable

Ⓐ Ⓑ Ⓒ Ⓓ ●

1. As sea urchins are becoming scarcer, divers are ------- to more dangerous depths to retrieve them, ------- the potential for diving injuries.

(A) swimming . . lessening
(B) descending . . increasing
(C) removing . . avoiding
(D) returning . . seeing
(E) climbing . . creating

2. Anne mentioned John's habitual boasting about his wardrobe as an example of his ------- ways.

(A) erratic    (B) egotistical    (C) flexible
(D) tactful    (E) inconspicuous

3. His peers respected him because he was both ------- and -------: steadfast in his beliefs and tactful in his negotiations.

(A) resourceful . . courteous
(B) tenacious . . manipulative
(C) determined . . demonstrative
(D) resolute . . diplomatic
(E) outspoken . . indiscriminate

4. Considering that many women had little control over their own lives in medieval England, Margery Kempe's fifteenth-century autobiography demonstrates a remarkable degree of -------.

(A) consecration    (B) rationalism
(C) autonomy    (D) effacement
(E) simplicity

5. Following the decree banning ------- acts, suspected ------- could be forcibly detained without the filing of formal charges.

(A) rebellious . . conformists
(B) apolitical . . loyalists
(C) seditious . . insurrectionists
(D) subversive . . nonpartisans
(E) supportive . . opponents

6. By portraying a wide spectrum of characters in his one-man show, John Leguizamo provides a ------- to the theater's tendency to offer a limited range of roles to Latino actors.

(A) corrective    (B) tribute    (C) corollary
(D) stimulus    (E) precursor

**GO ON TO THE NEXT PAGE**

The passage below is followed by questions based on its content. Answer the questions on the basis of what is stated or implied in the passage and in any introductory material that may be provided.

**Questions 7-19 are based on the following passage.**

*The following passage, set in the early 1970's, is from a 1992 novel. The principal characters, Virginia and Clayton, are two cellists in a college orchestra.*

She'd met lots of crazy musicians, but no one like Clayton. He was as obsessed as the others, but he had a quirky sense of humor, a slow ironic counterpoint to his
Line own beliefs. And he didn't look quite like anyone else.
5 He wore his hair parted dangerously near the middle and combed it in little ripples like Cab Calloway,[1] though sometimes he let it fly up a bit at the ends in deference to the campus pressure for Afros. His caramel-colored skin darkened to toffee under fluorescent light but sometimes
10 took on a golden sheen, especially in the vertical shafts of sunlight that poured into his favorite practice room where she'd often peek in on him—an uncanny complexion, as if the shades swirled just under the surface.
Virginia's friends gave her advice on how to get him.
15 "You two can play hot duets together," they giggled.
As it turned out, she didn't have to plan a thing. She was reading one afternoon outside the Fine Arts Building when the day suddenly turned cold. If she went back to the dorm for a sweater, she'd be late for orchestra rehearsal. So she
20 stuck it out until a few minutes before rehearsal at four. By that time, her fingers were so stiff she had to run them under hot water to loosen them up. Then she hurried to the cello room, where all the instruments were lined up like novitiates;[2] she felt a strange reverence every time she
25 stepped across the threshold into its cool serenity. There they stood, obedient yet voluptuous in their molded cases. In the dim light their plump forms looked sadly human, as if they were waiting for something better to come along but knew it wouldn't.
30 Virginia grabbed her cello and was halfway down the hall when she realized she'd forgotten to leave her books behind. She decided against turning back and continued to the basement, where the five-till-four pandemonium was breaking loose. Clayton was stuffing his books into his
35 locker.
"Hey, Clayton, how's it going?"
As if it were routine, he took her books and wedged them in next to his. They started toward the orchestra hall. Virginia cast a surreptitious glance upward; five minutes
40 to four or not, Clayton was not rushing. His long, gangling frame seemed to be held together by molasses; he moved deliberately, negotiating the crush while humming a tricky passage from Schumann,[3] sailing above the mob.
After rehearsal she reminded him that her books were in
45 his locker.

"I think I'll go practice," he said. "Would you like to listen?"
"I'll miss dinner," she replied, and was about to curse herself for her honesty when he said, "I have cheese and
50 soup back at the fraternity house, if you don't mind the walk."
The walk was twenty minutes of agonizing bliss, with the wind off the lake whipping her blue, and Clayton too involved with analyzing the orchestra's horn section to
55 notice. When they reached the house, a brick building with a crumbling porch and weeds cracking the front path, she was nearly frozen through. He heated up a can of soup, and plunked the cheese down in the center of the dinette table.
"It's not much," he apologized, but she was thinking
60 *A loaf of bread, a jug of wine,*[4] and felt sated before lifting the first spoonful. The house was rented to Alpha Phi Alpha, one of three Black fraternities on campus. It had a musty tennis-shoes-and-ripe-laundry smell. Books and jackets were strewn everywhere, dishes piled in the sink.
65 "When did you begin playing?" she asked.
"I began late, I'm afraid," Clayton replied. "Ninth grade. But I felt at home immediately. With the music, I mean. The instrument took a little longer. Everyone said I was too tall to be a cellist." He grimaced.
70 Virginia watched him as he talked. He was the same golden brown as the instrument, and his mustache followed the lines of the cello's scroll.
"So what did you do?" she asked.
"Whenever my height came up, I would say, 'Remember
75 the bumblebee.' "
"What do bumblebees have to do with cellos?"
"The bumblebee, aerodynamically speaking, is too large for flight. But the bee has never heard of aerodynamics, so it flies in spite of the laws of gravity. I merely wrapped my
80 legs and arms around the cello and kept playing."
Music was the only landscape in which he seemed at ease. In that raunchy kitchen, elbows propped on either side of the cooling soup, he was fidgety, even a little awkward. But when he sat up behind his instrument, he had the irresistible
85 beauty of someone who had found his place.

[1] American jazz musician and bandleader (1907-1994)
[2] Persons who have entered a religious order but have not yet taken final vows
[3] German composer (1810-1856)
[4] A reference to Edward Fitzgerald's "A jug of wine, a loaf of bread, and thou," a line from *The Rubaiyat of Omar Khayyam*

**GO ON TO THE NEXT PAGE**

7. The passage is best described as

   (A) a social commentary on classical musicians in the early 1970's
   (B) a nostalgic depiction of students in college orchestras
   (C) a story of how one individual inspired many others
   (D) an introduction to a character through the perspective of another character
   (E) an illustration of a strained but enduring relationship

8. The references to "fluorescent light" (line 9) and "sunlight" (line 11) suggest the

   (A) way that Clayton's demeanor brightened when Virginia was nearby
   (B) contrast between Clayton's restraint and Virginia's passion
   (C) attentiveness with which Virginia regarded Clayton
   (D) monotony of Clayton's everyday routine
   (E) superficiality of Clayton's beauty

9. The imagery in lines 12-13 ("as if . . . surface") conveys which of the following about Clayton?

   (A) His complicated nature
   (B) His erratic reactions
   (C) His unseemly complacency
   (D) His passionate loyalty
   (E) His tendency to argue

10. As contrasted with the language in the opening paragraph, the advice offered by Virginia's friends (lines 14-15) functions primarily to

    (A) break the mood of abstracted musing
    (B) introduce an element of foreboding
    (C) poke fun at the pretensions of romantic music
    (D) contradict Virginia's opinion of Clayton
    (E) counter Clayton's offbeat sense of humor

11. As described in lines 22-25, the atmosphere in the cello room is most nearly one of

    (A) creativity
    (B) emptiness
    (C) urgency
    (D) sanctity
    (E) accomplishment

12. In line 42, "crush" most nearly means

    (A) pressure
    (B) crowd
    (C) power
    (D) infatuation
    (E) critical condition

13. In lines 12-13, the reference to Clayton's humming creates an impression that he is

    (A) uncomfortable with making conversation
    (B) amused by the plight of other musicians
    (C) unaware of his effect on other people
    (D) compelled to show off his talent
    (E) immersed in his private world

14. In the context of the passage, Clayton's statement in line 46 ("I think . . . practice") emphasizes his

    (A) need to make a dramatic first impression
    (B) willingness to disrupt a fixed routine
    (C) consuming interest in music
    (D) distaste for competition
    (E) insecurity around other musicians

15. In line 52, the phrase "agonizing bliss" suggests that Virginia's pleasure is tempered by

    (A) Clayton's cold manner
    (B) Clayton's visible uneasiness
    (C) her physical discomfort
    (D) her overriding self-consciousness
    (E) her sense that the happiness would be short-lived

16. In lines 59-61, Virginia's reaction to the meal most directly suggests that she

    (A) was contented enough without the food
    (B) was amused by Clayton's attempts at hospitality
    (C) was suddenly aware of the chaos in the fraternity kitchen
    (D) felt guilty about making Clayton uneasy
    (E) did not find the atmosphere conducive to romance

17. The description in lines 70-72 emphasizes how

    (A) strikingly Clayton resembles famous musicians
    (B) awkwardly Clayton behaves in social situations
    (C) profoundly Clayton is affected by music
    (D) closely Virginia associates Clayton with his cello
    (E) strongly Virginia identifies with Clayton's situation

GO ON TO THE NEXT PAGE

**18.** In referring to the bumblebee (lines 77-80), Clayton conveys his

(A) superstitious nature
(B) cunning instincts
(C) frail pride
(D) resolute determination
(E) volatile temperament

**19.** In lines 82-85, the descriptions of Clayton in the kitchen and Clayton behind his instrument present a contrast between his

(A) chaos and organization
(B) mediocrity and excellence
(C) pretension and genuineness
(D) laziness and dedication
(E) clumsiness and gracefulness

# STOP

**If you finish before time is called, you may check your work on this section only.**
**Do not turn to any other section in the test.**

# 10  10

Unauthorized copying or reuse of
any part of this page is illegal.

## SECTION 10
Time — 10 minutes
14 Questions

Turn to Section 10 (page 7) of your answer sheet to answer the questions in this section.

**Directions:** For each question in this section, select the best answer from among the choices given and fill in the corresponding circle on the answer sheet.

The following sentences test correctness and effectiveness of expression. Part of each sentence or the entire sentence is underlined; beneath each sentence are five ways of phrasing the underlined material. Choice A repeats the original phrasing; the other four choices are different. If you think the original phrasing produces a better sentence than any of the alternatives, select choice A; if not, select one of the other choices.

In making your selection, follow the requirements of standard written English; that is, pay attention to grammar, choice of words, sentence construction, and punctuation. Your selection should result in the most effective sentence—clear and precise, without awkwardness or ambiguity.

EXAMPLE:

Laura Ingalls Wilder published her first book
and she was sixty-five years old then.

(A)  and she was sixty-five years old then
(B)  when she was sixty-five
(C)  at age sixty-five years old
(D)  upon the reaching of sixty-five years
(E)  at the time when she was sixty-five

1. At Versailles after the First World War, the Allies believed they had drafted a treaty that <u>would have ensured permanent peace</u>.

   (A)  would have ensured permanent peace
   (B)  would ensure permanent peace
   (C)  had ensured permanent peace
   (D)  will ensure permanent peace
   (E)  ensures permanent peace

2. The new bird <u>sanctuary, consisting of one hundred acres of unspoiled tideland, and is protected by the state</u>.

   (A)  sanctuary, consisting of one hundred acres of unspoiled tideland, and is protected by the state
   (B)  sanctuary is protected by the state, it consists of one hundred acres of unspoiled tideland
   (C)  sanctuary, consisting of one hundred acres of unspoiled tideland, is protected by the state
   (D)  sanctuary is protected by the state consisting of one hundred acres of unspoiled tideland
   (E)  sanctuary to consist of one hundred acres of unspoiled tideland and to be protected by the state

3. Most people know about calories and nutrition, but they do not use this knowledge to lose weight <u>permanently and keep it off</u>.

   (A)  permanently and keep it off
   (B)  permanent and have it stay off
   (C)  and have it be off permanently
   (D)  and make it permanent
   (E)  and keep it off permanently

4. No sooner had Andrea del Sarto traveled to France to work for the French king <u>but his wife persuaded him to return</u> to Italy.

   (A)  but his wife persuaded him to return
   (B)  but his wife had him persuaded into returning
   (C)  than he was persuaded by his wife that he will return
   (D)  but he was persuaded by his wife into returning
   (E)  than his wife persuaded him to return

**GO ON TO THE NEXT PAGE**

5. During the 1980's and early 1990's, one reason highways in the United States became safer than <u>ever, the use of seat belts increased to about 67 percent nationwide</u>.

   (A) ever, the use of seat belts increased to about 67 percent nationwide
   (B) ever, nationwide, the use of seat belts increased to about 67 percent
   (C) ever, there was a nationwide increase in seat belt use to 67 percent
   (D) ever since they increased seat belt use to 67 percent nationwide
   (E) ever was that the use of seat belts nationwide increased to about 67 percent

6. Chaplin will not be remembered for espousing radical causes <u>any more than they will remember Wayne</u> for endorsing conservative political candidates.

   (A) any more than they will remember Wayne
   (B) as will Wayne not be remembered
   (C) any more than Wayne will be remembered
   (D) just as they will not remember Wayne
   (E) no more than Wayne will be remembered

7. Civil rights leader and author W. E. B. Du Bois was interested in drama because he believed that <u>if you represented historical events on stage it</u> could have a greater, more lasting effect than any exhibit or lecture.

   (A) if you represented historical events on stage it
   (B) with the events of history represented on stage they
   (C) events which were represented historically on stage
   (D) by representing historical events on stage
   (E) representing historical events on stage

8. Many colleges are adopting work-study <u>programs, which offer practical advantages to both the students and</u> the institutions.

   (A) programs, which offer practical advantages to both the students and
   (B) programs, which offers practical advantages to both the students and
   (C) programs, which offer both practical advantages to the students plus
   (D) programs; it offers practical advantages to both the students as well as
   (E) programs; this offers practical advantages both to the students and

9. One of the first people to recognize the talent of Langston Hughes, <u>Jessie Fauset, was an editor at *Crisis* magazine, publishing</u> Hughes's poetry in 1921.

   (A) Jessie Fauset, was an editor at *Crisis* magazine, publishing
   (B) Jessie Fauset who edited *Crisis* magazine and published
   (C) Jessie Fauset edited *Crisis* magazine who published
   (D) Jessie Fauset, an editor at *Crisis* magazine, published
   (E) the editor, Jessie Fauset, published at *Crisis* magazine

10. <u>Until being widely hunted for its</u> ivory and blubber in the eighteenth century, walruses were plentiful in the waters of the northeastern United States.

    (A) Until being widely hunted for its
    (B) Before having been widely hunted for its
    (C) Up to them being widely hunted for their
    (D) Until they were widely hunted for their
    (E) Before they have been widely hunted for their

11. Jesse passed the California bar examination last year, <u>and he has been practicing law in California ever since</u>.

    (A) and he has been practicing law in California ever since
    (B) since that time he has practiced law there
    (C) where ever since he practices law
    (D) he has been practicing law in California since then
    (E) and since then is practicing law there

12. Persuading even the queasiest of readers to spend hours learning about an extravagant variety of invertebrates, <u>the effect of Richard Conniff's *Spineless Wonders* is to render the repulsive beautiful</u>.

    (A) the effect of Richard Conniff's *Spineless Wonders* is to render the repulsive beautiful
    (B) Richard Conniff renders the repulsive beautiful in *Spineless Wonders*
    (C) the effect of *Spineless Wonders*, by Richard Conniff, is to render the repulsive beautiful
    (D) Richard Conniff has had the effect of rendering the repulsive beautiful in *Spineless Wonders*
    (E) *Spineless Wonders*, by Richard Conniff, has effect in rendering the repulsive beautiful

**GO ON TO THE NEXT PAGE**

**10**

Unauthorized copying or reuse of
any part of this page is illegal.

 **10**

13. Most drivers <u>know not only that excessive speeding on highways wastes</u> gasoline, but also that it is dangerous.

   (A) know not only that excessive speeding on
       highways wastes

   (B) know that excessive speeding on highways could
       be wasteful of

   (C) are knowledgeable that excessive speeding on
       highways not only wastes

   (D) have known that excessive speeding on highways
       wastes not only

   (E) know that excessive speeding on highways not
       only by itself can waste

14. Walt Disney's first success was his third Mickey Mouse film, in which Disney produced a cartoon with <u>sound, and Mickey was made to talk</u>.

   (A) sound, and Mickey was made to talk

   (B) sound and making Mickey talk

   (C) sound, with the result being Mickey talking

   (D) sound in where Mickey talks

   (E) sound and made Mickey talk

# STOP

**If you finish before time is called, you may check your work on this section only.**
**Do not turn to any other section in the test.**

# Correct Answers and Difficulty Levels
## SAT Practice Test #5

## CRITICAL READING

### Section 3
#### Multiple-Choice Questions

| Correct Answer | Difficulty Level | Correct Answer | Difficulty Level |
|---|---|---|---|
| 1 D | E | 13 B | M |
| 2 D | E | 14 C | M |
| 3 C | M | 15 B | H |
| 4 C | M | 16 D | E |
| 5 A | H | 17 E | E |
| 6 B | M | 18 C | E |
| 7 E | M | 19 C | M |
| 8 C | H | 20 C | E |
| 9 B | M | 21 B | M |
| 10 B | M | 22 D | M |
| 11 A | E | 23 E | H |
| 12 E | M | 24 A | M |

Number correct _____

Number incorrect _____

### Section 7
#### Multiple-Choice Questions

| Correct Answer | Difficulty Level | Correct Answer | Difficulty Level |
|---|---|---|---|
| 1 E | E | 13 C | E |
| 2 E | E | 14 A | E |
| 3 C | E | 15 C | M |
| 4 A | E | 16 E | M |
| 5 A | M | 17 B | M |
| 6 C | H | 18 A | M |
| 7 B | M | 19 E | M |
| 8 C | H | 20 B | E |
| 9 D | E | 21 E | M |
| 10 A | M | 22 B | M |
| 11 D | H | 23 E | E |
| 12 C | M | 24 C | M |

Number correct _____

Number incorrect _____

### Section 9
#### Multiple-Choice Questions

| Correct Answer | Difficulty Level | Correct Answer | Difficulty Level |
|---|---|---|---|
| 1 B | E | 11 D | M |
| 2 B | E | 12 B | H |
| 3 D | M | 13 E | M |
| 4 C | M | 14 C | M |
| 5 C | H | 15 C | M |
| 6 A | H | 16 A | M |
| 7 A | M | 17 D | E |
| 8 C | M | 18 D | E |
| 9 A | M | 19 E | M |
| 10 A | M | | |

Number correct _____

Number incorrect _____

## MATHEMATICS

### Section 2
#### Multiple-Choice Questions

| Correct Answer | Difficulty Level | Correct Answer | Difficulty Level |
|---|---|---|---|
| 1 D | E | 11 C | M |
| 2 B | E | 12 C | M |
| 3 B | E | 13 B | M |
| 4 D | E | 14 A | M |
| 5 E | E | 15 C | M |
| 6 E | E | 16 E | M |
| 7 C | M | 17 A | M |
| 8 A | M | 18 A | H |
| 9 A | M | 19 C | H |
| 10 B | M | 20 C | H |

Number correct _____

Number incorrect _____

### Section 4

| Multiple-Choice Questions | | Student-Produced Response Questions | |
|---|---|---|---|
| Correct Answer | Difficulty Level | Correct Answer | Difficulty Level |
| 1 A | E | 9 7 | E |
| 2 C | E | 10 13 | E |
| 3 D | E | 11 135 | M |
| 4 D | E | 12 46 | M |
| 5 E | M | 13 28 | M |
| 6 D | H | 14 70 | M |
| 7 E | M | 15 7/15, .466, .467 | M |
| 8 C | H | 16 3 | H |
| | | 17 4/9, .444 | H |
| | | 18 2, 18 | H |

Number correct _____

Number incorrect _____

Number correct (9-18) _____

### Section 8
#### Multiple-Choice Questions

| Correct Answer | Difficulty Level | Correct Answer | Difficulty Level |
|---|---|---|---|
| 1 B | E | 9 D | M |
| 2 B | E | 10 B | M |
| 3 A | E | 11 A | M |
| 4 C | E | 12 B | M |
| 5 D | E | 13 C | M |
| 6 B | M | 14 E | M |
| 7 A | M | 15 A | H |
| 8 E | M | 16 E | H |

Number correct _____

Number incorrect _____

## WRITING

### Essay

Essay Score* (0-6) _____

### Section 6
#### Multiple-Choice Questions

| Correct Answer | Difficulty Level | Correct Answer | Difficulty Level |
|---|---|---|---|
| 1 C | E | 19 B | E |
| 2 D | E | 20 C | E |
| 3 C | M | 21 B | M |
| 4 E | M | 22 B | M |
| 5 D | M | 23 E | M |
| 6 D | M | 24 D | M |
| 7 A | M | 25 C | M |
| 8 C | M | 26 B | M |
| 9 E | M | 27 D | M |
| 10 D | M | 28 A | H |
| 11 B | H | 29 E | H |
| 12 B | E | 30 A | M |
| 13 B | E | 31 A | E |
| 14 A | E | 32 D | E |
| 15 D | E | 33 E | M |
| 16 A | E | 34 B | M |
| 17 D | E | 35 C | E |
| 18 D | E | | |

Number correct _____

Number incorrect _____

### Section 10
#### Multiple-Choice Questions

| Correct Answer | Difficulty Level |
|---|---|
| 1 B | E |
| 2 C | E |
| 3 E | M |
| 4 E | M |
| 5 E | M |
| 6 C | M |
| 7 E | M |
| 8 A | M |
| 9 D | M |
| 10 A | M |
| 11 A | M |
| 12 B | M |
| 13 A | M |
| 14 E | M |

Number correct _____

Number incorrect _____

**NOTE:** Difficulty levels are E (easy), M (medium), and H (hard).

* To score your essay, use the SAT scoring guide in Chapter 9 and the free sample essays available online at www.collegeboard.org/satonlinecourse. On this practice test, your essay score should range from 0 to 6. (Keep in mind that on the actual SAT, your essay will be read by two readers and you will receive a score of 0 to 12 on your score report.)

# The SAT Scoring Process

**Scoring.** The computer compares the circle filled in for each question with the correct response. Each correct answer receives one point; omitted questions do not affect your score. For each wrong answer to a multiple-choice question, one-fourth of a point is subtracted to correct for random guessing. The SAT critical reading section has 67 questions. If, for example, a student has 44 right, 20 wrong, and 3 omitted, the resulting raw score is determined as follows:

$$44 \text{ right} - \frac{20 \text{ wrong}}{4} = 44 - 5 = 39 \text{ raw score points}$$

Obtaining raw scores frequently involves the rounding of fractions to the nearest whole number. For example, a raw score of 39.25 is rounded to 39, the nearest whole number. A raw score of 39.50 is rounded upward to 40. **For the WRITING SECTION**, your essay raw score counts approximately 30% and your multiple-choice raw score counts approximately 70%.

**Converting to reported scaled score.** Raw scores are then placed on the College Board scale of 200 to 800 through a process that adjusts scores to account for minor differences in difficulty among different versions of the test. This process, known as equating, is performed so that a student's reported score is not affected by the version of the test taken or by the abilities of the group with whom the student takes the test. As a result of placing SAT scores on the College Board scale, scores earned by students at different times can be compared. For example, an SAT critical reading score of 400 on a test taken at one administration indicates the same level of developed critical reading ability as a 400 score obtained on a different version of the test taken at another time.

**Note:** Since this test has not been previously administered, score ranges are provided for each possible raw score.

# How to Score Practice Test #5

## SAT Critical Reading Sections 3, 7, and 9

**Step A:** Count the number of correct answers for *Section 3* and record the number in the space provided on the Scoring Worksheet. Then do the same for the incorrect answers. (Do not count omitted answers.)

**Step B:** Count the number of correct answers and the number of incorrect answers for *Section 7* and record the numbers in the spaces provided on the Scoring Worksheet. (Do not count omitted answers.)

**Step C:** Count the number of correct answers and the number of incorrect answers for *Section 9* and record the numbers in the spaces provided on the Scoring Worksheet. (Do not count omitted answers.)

**Step D:** Total the number of correct responses. Total the number of incorrect responses. Enter the resulting figures on the Scoring Worksheet. To determine A, use the formula:

$$\text{Number correct} - \frac{\text{Number incorrect}}{4} = A$$

**Step E:** To obtain B, your Rounded Critical Reading Raw Score, round A to the nearest whole number. (For example, any number from 44.50 to 45.49 rounds to 45.) Enter the resulting figure on the Scoring Worksheet.

**Step F:** To find your Critical Reading Scaled Score Range, look up the Total Rounded Raw Score you obtained in step E in the Critical Reading Conversion Table (Table 1). Enter this range in the box on the Scoring Worksheet.

## SAT Mathematics Sections 2, 4, and 8

**Step A:** Count the number of correct answers and the number of incorrect answers for *Section 2* and record the numbers in the spaces provided on the Scoring Worksheet. (Do not count omitted answers.)

**Step B:** Count the number of correct answers and the number of incorrect answers for the multiple-choice questions (*questions 1 through 8*) in *Section 4* and record the numbers in the spaces provided on the Scoring Worksheet. (Do not count omitted answers.)

**Step C:** Count the number of correct answers for the student-produced response questions (*questions 9 through 18*) in *Section 4* and record the number in the space provided on the Scoring Worksheet.

**Step D:** Count the number of correct answers and the number of incorrect answers for *Section 8* and record the numbers in the spaces provided on the Scoring Worksheet. (Do not count omitted answers.)

**Step E:** Total the number of correct responses. Total the number of incorrect responses. Enter the resulting figures on the Scoring Worksheet. To determine A, use the formula:

$$\text{Number correct} - \frac{\text{Number incorrect}}{4} = A$$

**Step F:** To obtain B, your Mathematics Rounded Raw Score, round A to the nearest whole number. (For example, any number from 44.50 to 45.49 rounds to 45.) Enter the resulting figure on the Scoring Worksheet.

**Step G:** To find your Mathematics Scaled Score Range, use the Mathematics Conversion Table (Table 2) to look up the Total Rounded Raw Score you obtained in step F. Enter this range in the box on the Scoring Worksheet.

## SAT Writing Sections 1, 6, and 10

**Step A:** Enter your Essay Score for *Section 1* in the box on the Scoring Worksheet. (On this practice test, your essay score should range from 0 to 6. Keep in mind that on the actual SAT, two readers will read your essay and you will receive a total score of 0 to 12 on your score report.)

**Step B:** Count the number of correct answers and the number of incorrect answers for *Section 6* and record the numbers in the spaces provided on the Scoring Worksheet. (Do not count omitted answers.)

**Step C:** Count the number of correct answers and the number of incorrect answers for *Section 10* and record the numbers in the spaces provided on the Scoring Worksheet. (Do not count omitted answers.)

**Step D:** Total the number of correct responses. Total the number of incorrect responses. Enter the resulting figure on the Scoring Worksheet. To determine A, use the formula:

$$\text{Number correct} - \frac{\text{Number incorrect}}{4} = A$$

**Step E:** To obtain B, your Writing Multiple-Choice (MC) Rounded Raw Score, round A to the nearest whole number. (For example, any number from 44.50 to 45.49 rounds to 45.) Enter the resulting figure on the Scoring Worksheet.

**Step F:** To find your overall Writing Scaled Score Range, use Table 3. Look up the Total MC Rounded Raw Score you obtained in Step E in the left side of Table 3 and the Essay Score entered in Step A across the top of the table. Enter this range in the box on the Scoring Worksheet.

**Step G:** To find your Writing MC Subscore Range, look up the Total MC Rounded Raw Score you obtained in Step E on the Writing Multiple-Choice Conversion Table (Table 4). Enter this range in the box on the Scoring Worksheet.

**Note:** For the **WRITING SECTION**, your Essay Raw Score counts approximately 30% and your Multiple-Choice Raw Score counts approximately 70%.

# SAT Practice Test #5 Scoring Worksheet

## SAT Critical Reading Section

A. Section 3:
        _____      _____
        no. correct         no. incorrect
        +              + 

B. Section 7:
        _____      _____
        no. correct         no. incorrect
        +              + 

C. Section 9:
        _____      _____
        no. correct         no. incorrect
        =              = 

D. Total Unrounded Raw Score
        _____ − ( _____ ÷ 4) = _____
        no. correct         no. incorrect         A

E. Total Rounded Raw Score
   (Rounded to nearest whole number)
                                             _____
                                             B

F. Critical Reading Scaled Score Range
   (See Table 1)

                                            ┌──────────┐
                                             │    −    │
                                               └──────────┘

Critical
Reading Scaled
Score Range

## SAT Mathematics Section

A. Section 2:
        _____      _____
        no. correct         no. incorrect
        +              + 

B. Section 4:
   Questions 1-8
        _____      _____
        no. correct         no. incorrect
        +              + 

C. Section 4:
   Questions 9-18
        _____
        no. correct
        +              + 

D. Section 8:
        _____      _____
        no. correct         no. incorrect
        =              = 

E. Total Unrounded Raw Score
        _____ − ( _____ ÷ 4) = _____
        no. correct         no. incorrect         A

F. Total Rounded Raw Score
   (Rounded to nearest whole number)
                                             _____
                                             B

G. Mathematics Scaled Score Range
   (See Table 2)

                                             ┌──────────┐
                                             │    −    │
                                             └──────────┘

Mathematics
Scaled
Score Range

**SAT Writing Section**

A. Section 1:

Essay Score

B. Section 6:

_____     _____
no. correct          no. incorrect

\+                    \+

C. Section 10:

_____     _____
no. correct          no. incorrect

=                    =

D. Total MC Unrounded Raw Score

_____  −  ( _____ ÷ 4)  =  _____
no. correct            no. incorrect                      A

E. Total MC Rounded Raw Score
   (Rounded to nearest whole number)

_____
B

F. Writing Scaled Score Range
   (See Table 3)

_____ − _____

Writing Scaled
Score Range

G. Writing MC Subscore Range
   (See Table 4)

_____ − _____

Writing MC
Subscore Range

| Table 1. Critical Reading Conversion Table | | | |
|---|---|---|---|
| Raw Score | Scaled Score | Raw Score | Scaled Score |
| 67 | 800 | 30 | 470-530 |
| 66 | 770-800 | 29 | 470-530 |
| 65 | 740-800 | 28 | 460-520 |
| 64 | 720-800 | 27 | 450-510 |
| 63 | 700-800 | 26 | 450-510 |
| 62 | 690-790 | 25 | 440-500 |
| 61 | 670-770 | 24 | 440-500 |
| 60 | 660-760 | 23 | 430-490 |
| 59 | 660-740 | 22 | 420-480 |
| 58 | 650-730 | 21 | 420-480 |
| 57 | 640-720 | 20 | 410-470 |
| 56 | 630-710 | 19 | 400-460 |
| 55 | 630-710 | 18 | 400-460 |
| 54 | 620-700 | 17 | 390-450 |
| 53 | 610-690 | 16 | 380-440 |
| 52 | 600-680 | 15 | 380-440 |
| 51 | 610-670 | 14 | 370-430 |
| 50 | 600-660 | 13 | 360-420 |
| 49 | 590-650 | 12 | 350-410 |
| 48 | 580-640 | 11 | 350-410 |
| 47 | 580-640 | 10 | 340-400 |
| 46 | 570-630 | 9 | 330-390 |
| 45 | 560-620 | 8 | 310-390 |
| 44 | 560-620 | 7 | 300-380 |
| 43 | 550-610 | 6 | 290-370 |
| 42 | 550-610 | 5 | 270-370 |
| 41 | 540-600 | 4 | 260-360 |
| 40 | 530-590 | 3 | 250-350 |
| 39 | 530-590 | 2 | 230-330 |
| 38 | 520-580 | 1 | 220-320 |
| 37 | 510-570 | 0 | 200-290 |
| 36 | 510-570 | -1 | 200-290 |
| 35 | 500-560 | -2 | 200-270 |
| 34 | 500-560 | -3 | 200-250 |
| 33 | 490-550 | -4 | 200-230 |
| 32 | 480-540 | -5 | 200-210 |
| 31 | 480-540 | -6 and below | 200 |

| Table 2. Mathematics Conversion Table | | | |
|---|---|---|---|
| Raw Score | Scaled Score | Raw Score | Scaled Score |
| 54 | 800 | 23 | 460-520 |
| 53 | 750-800 | 22 | 450-510 |
| 52 | 720-800 | 21 | 440-500 |
| 51 | 700-780 | 20 | 430-490 |
| 50 | 690-770 | 19 | 430-490 |
| 49 | 680-740 | 18 | 420-480 |
| 48 | 670-730 | 17 | 410-470 |
| 47 | 660-720 | 16 | 400-460 |
| 46 | 640-700 | 15 | 400-460 |
| 45 | 630-690 | 14 | 390-450 |
| 44 | 620-680 | 13 | 380-440 |
| 43 | 620-680 | 12 | 360-440 |
| 42 | 610-670 | 11 | 350-430 |
| 41 | 600-660 | 10 | 340-420 |
| 40 | 580-660 | 9 | 330-430 |
| 39 | 570-650 | 8 | 320-420 |
| 38 | 560-640 | 7 | 310-410 |
| 37 | 550-630 | 6 | 290-390 |
| 36 | 550-630 | 5 | 280-380 |
| 35 | 540-620 | 4 | 270-370 |
| 34 | 530-610 | 3 | 260-360 |
| 33 | 520-600 | 2 | 240-340 |
| 32 | 520-600 | 1 | 230-330 |
| 31 | 520-580 | 0 | 210-310 |
| 30 | 510-570 | -1 | 200-290 |
| 29 | 500-560 | -2 | 200-270 |
| 28 | 490-550 | -3 | 200-250 |
| 27 | 490-550 | -4 | 200-230 |
| 26 | 480-540 | -5 | 200-210 |
| 25 | 470-530 | -6 and below | 200 |
| 24 | 460-520 | | |

| MC Raw Score | Essay Score | | | | | | |
|---|---|---|---|---|---|---|---|
| | 0 | 1 | 2 | 3 | 4 | 5 | 6 |
| 49 | 650-690 | 670-720 | 690-740 | 710-770 | 750-800 | 780-800 | 800 |
| 48 | 630-690 | 640-720 | 660-740 | 690-770 | 720-800 | 760-800 | 780-800 |
| 47 | 600-690 | 620-720 | 640-740 | 660-770 | 700-800 | 730-800 | 760-800 |
| 46 | 580-690 | 600-720 | 620-740 | 650-770 | 680-800 | 710-800 | 740-800 |
| 45 | 570-690 | 580-720 | 600-740 | 630-770 | 670-800 | 700-800 | 730-800 |
| 44 | 560-680 | 570-710 | 590-730 | 620-760 | 660-790 | 690-800 | 720-800 |
| 43 | 540-660 | 560-690 | 580-710 | 610-740 | 640-780 | 670-800 | 700-800 |
| 42 | 530-660 | 550-690 | 570-700 | 600-730 | 630-770 | 660-800 | 690-800 |
| 41 | 530-650 | 540-680 | 560-700 | 590-720 | 620-760 | 660-790 | 680-800 |
| 40 | 520-640 | 530-670 | 550-690 | 580-710 | 620-750 | 650-780 | 680-800 |
| 39 | 510-630 | 520-660 | 540-680 | 570-710 | 610-740 | 640-770 | 670-800 |
| 38 | 500-620 | 520-650 | 540-670 | 560-700 | 600-730 | 630-770 | 660-790 |
| 37 | 490-610 | 510-640 | 530-660 | 560-690 | 590-720 | 620-760 | 650-780 |
| 36 | 480-600 | 500-630 | 520-650 | 550-680 | 580-720 | 610-750 | 640-770 |
| 35 | 480-590 | 490-620 | 510-640 | 540-670 | 570-710 | 610-740 | 640-770 |
| 34 | 470-590 | 480-620 | 500-630 | 530-660 | 570-700 | 600-730 | 630-760 |
| 33 | 460-580 | 470-610 | 490-630 | 520-650 | 560-690 | 590-720 | 620-750 |
| 32 | 450-570 | 470-600 | 490-620 | 510-640 | 550-680 | 580-710 | 610-740 |
| 31 | 440-560 | 460-590 | 480-610 | 510-640 | 540-670 | 570-700 | 600-730 |
| 30 | 430-550 | 450-580 | 470-600 | 500-630 | 530-660 | 560-700 | 590-720 |
| 29 | 430-540 | 440-570 | 460-590 | 490-620 | 520-650 | 560-690 | 590-710 |
| 28 | 420-530 | 430-560 | 450-580 | 480-610 | 520-650 | 550-680 | 580-700 |
| 27 | 410-520 | 420-550 | 440-570 | 470-600 | 510-640 | 540-670 | 570-700 |
| 26 | 400-520 | 420-550 | 430-560 | 460-590 | 500-630 | 530-660 | 560-690 |
| 25 | 390-510 | 410-540 | 430-560 | 450-580 | 490-620 | 520-650 | 550-680 |
| 24 | 380-500 | 400-530 | 420-550 | 450-570 | 480-610 | 510-640 | 540-670 |
| 23 | 370-490 | 390-520 | 410-540 | 440-570 | 470-600 | 500-630 | 530-660 |
| 22 | 370-480 | 380-510 | 400-530 | 430-560 | 460-590 | 500-630 | 520-650 |
| 21 | 370-480 | 380-510 | 400-530 | 430-560 | 460-590 | 500-630 | 520-650 |
| 20 | 360-470 | 370-500 | 390-520 | 420-550 | 460-580 | 490-620 | 520-640 |
| 19 | 350-460 | 360-490 | 380-510 | 410-540 | 450-580 | 480-610 | 510-630 |
| 18 | 340-450 | 350-480 | 370-500 | 400-530 | 440-570 | 470-600 | 500-630 |
| 17 | 330-450 | 350-480 | 360-490 | 390-520 | 430-560 | 460-590 | 490-620 |
| 16 | 320-440 | 340-470 | 360-490 | 390-510 | 420-550 | 450-580 | 480-610 |
| 15 | 310-430 | 330-460 | 350-480 | 380-510 | 410-540 | 440-570 | 470-600 |
| 14 | 300-420 | 320-450 | 340-470 | 370-500 | 400-530 | 430-560 | 460-590 |
| 13 | 300-410 | 310-440 | 330-460 | 360-490 | 390-520 | 430-560 | 450-580 |
| 12 | 290-400 | 300-430 | 320-450 | 350-480 | 390-510 | 420-550 | 450-570 |
| 11 | 280-390 | 290-420 | 310-440 | 340-470 | 380-510 | 410-540 | 440-570 |
| 10 | 270-390 | 280-420 | 300-430 | 330-460 | 370-500 | 400-530 | 430-560 |
| 9 | 260-380 | 280-410 | 290-430 | 320-450 | 360-490 | 390-520 | 420-550 |
| 8 | 250-370 | 270-400 | 290-420 | 320-450 | 350-480 | 380-510 | 410-540 |
| 7 | 240-360 | 260-390 | 280-410 | 310-440 | 340-470 | 370-510 | 400-530 |
| 6 | 230-350 | 250-380 | 270-400 | 300-430 | 330-460 | 360-500 | 390-520 |
| 5 | 230-340 | 240-370 | 260-390 | 290-420 | 320-460 | 360-490 | 380-520 |
| 4 | 220-340 | 230-370 | 250-380 | 280-410 | 320-450 | 350-480 | 380-510 |
| 3 | 210-330 | 220-360 | 240-380 | 270-400 | 310-440 | 340-470 | 370-500 |
| 2 | 200-320 | 210-350 | 230-370 | 260-400 | 300-430 | 330-460 | 360-490 |
| 1 | 200-300 | 200-330 | 220-350 | 250-380 | 280-410 | 310-450 | 340-470 |
| 0 | 200-290 | 200-320 | 210-340 | 240-370 | 270-410 | 300-440 | 330-470 |
| -1 | 200-280 | 200-310 | 200-330 | 220-350 | 250-390 | 290-420 | 310-450 |
| -2 | 200-260 | 200-290 | 200-310 | 200-340 | 240-370 | 270-410 | 300-430 |
| -3 | 200-240 | 200-270 | 200-290 | 200-320 | 240-360 | 270-390 | 300-420 |
| -4 | 200-230 | 200-260 | 200-280 | 200-300 | 240-340 | 270-370 | 300-400 |
| -5 | 200 | 200-230 | 200-250 | 200-280 | 240-320 | 270-350 | 300-370 |
| -6 | 200 | 200-220 | 200-240 | 200-270 | 240-310 | 270-340 | 300-370 |
| -7 | 200 | 200-220 | 200-230 | 200-260 | 240-300 | 270-330 | 300-360 |
| -8 | 200 | 200-210 | 200-230 | 200-250 | 240-290 | 270-320 | 300-350 |
| -9 | 200 | 200-210 | 200-230 | 200-250 | 240-290 | 270-320 | 300-350 |
| -10 | 200 | 200-210 | 200-230 | 200-250 | 240-290 | 270-320 | 300-350 |
| -11 | 200 | 200-210 | 200-230 | 200-250 | 240-290 | 270-320 | 300-350 |
| -12 | 200 | 200-210 | 200-230 | 200-250 | 240-290 | 270-320 | 300-350 |

Table 3. Writing Conversion Table

## Table 4.  Writing Multiple-Choice Conversion Table

| Raw Score | Scaled Score | Raw Score | Scaled Score |
|---|---|---|---|
| 49 | 78-80 | 21 | 46-56 |
| 48 | 77-80 | 20 | 45-55 |
| 47 | 74-80 | 19 | 44-54 |
| 46 | 72-80 | 18 | 43-53 |
| 45 | 70-80 | 17 | 42-52 |
| 44 | 69-79 | 16 | 41-51 |
| 43 | 67-77 | 15 | 40-50 |
| 42 | 66-76 | 14 | 39-49 |
| 41 | 65-75 | 13 | 38-48 |
| 40 | 64-74 | 12 | 37-47 |
| 39 | 63-73 | 11 | 36-46 |
| 38 | 62-72 | 10 | 35-45 |
| 37 | 61-71 | 9 | 34-44 |
| 36 | 60-70 | 8 | 33-43 |
| 35 | 59-69 | 7 | 32-42 |
| 34 | 58-68 | 6 | 31-41 |
| 33 | 57-67 | 5 | 30-40 |
| 32 | 56-66 | 4 | 29-39 |
| 31 | 55-65 | 3 | 28-38 |
| 30 | 54-64 | 2 | 27-37 |
| 29 | 53-63 | 1 | 25-35 |
| 28 | 52-62 | 0 | 24-34 |
| 27 | 51-61 | -1 | 22-32 |
| 26 | 50-60 | -2 | 20-30 |
| 25 | 49-59 | 3 | 20-28 |
| 24 | 48-58 | -4 | 20-26 |
| 23 | 47-57 | -5 | 20-23 |
| 22 | 46-56 | -6 and below | 20-22 |

# SAT Practice Test #6

 **After this test:**

- Use this book to its full potential! Get exclusive access answer explanations, free practice score reports and free sample student essays to help you score your essay in the Book Owners' Area at www.collegeboard.org/satstudyguide.

- Want more practice? Get 10 more official practice tests, auto essay scoring and lesson plans from the test maker by subscribing to *The Official SAT Online Course.* As a book owner, you're entitled to a $10 discount. Sign up at www.collegeboard.org/satstudyguide.

6

*Note:* Section 5, the variable section, has been omitted from this practice test.

# SAT Reasoning Test — General Directions

### Timing

- You will have 3 hours and 45 minutes to work on this test.
- There are ten separately timed sections:
  - ▶ One 25-minute essay
  - ▶ Six other 25-minute sections
  - ▶ Two 20-minute sections
  - ▶ One 10-minute section
- You may work on only one section at a time.
- The supervisor will tell you when to begin and end each section.
- If you finish a section before time is called, check your work on that section. You may NOT turn to any other section.
- Work as rapidly as you can without losing accuracy. Don't waste time on questions that seem too difficult for you.

### Marking Answers

- Be sure to mark your answer sheet properly.

COMPLETE MARK ●    EXAMPLES OF INCOMPLETE MARKS ◑ ⊗ ⊖ ◐ ⊙ ⊘ ◓ ◒

- You must use a No. 2 pencil.
- Carefully mark only one answer for each question.
- Make sure you fill the entire circle darkly and completely.
- Do not make any stray marks on your answer sheet.
- If you erase, do so completely. Incomplete erasures may be scored as intended answers.
- Use only the answer spaces that correspond to the question numbers.

### Using Your Test Book

- You may use the test book for scratchwork, but you will not receive credit for anything written there.
- After time has been called, you may not transfer answers to your answer sheet or fill in circles.
- You may not fold or remove pages or portions of a page from this book, or take the book or answer sheet from the testing room.

### Scoring

- For each correct answer, you receive one point.
- For questions you omit, you receive no points.
- For a wrong answer to a multiple-choice question, you lose one-fourth of a point.
  - ▶ If you can eliminate one or more of the answer choices as wrong, you increase your chances of choosing the correct answer and earning one point.
  - ▶ If you can't eliminate any choice, move on. You can return to the question later if there is time.
- For a wrong answer to a student-produced response ("grid-in") math question, you don't lose any points.
- Multiple-choice and student-produced response questions are machine scored.
- The essay is scored on a 1 to 6 scale by two different readers. The total essay score is the sum of the two readers' scores.
- Off-topic essays, blank essays, and essays written in ink will receive a score of zero.

The passages for this test have been adapted from published material. The ideas contained in them do not necessarily represent the opinions of the College Board.

**IMPORTANT:** The codes below are unique to your test book. Copy them on your answer sheet in boxes 8 and 9 and fill in the corresponding circles exactly as shown.

**9   TEST FORM** (Copy from back of test book.)

**8   FORM CODE** (Copy and grid as on back of test book.)

## DO NOT OPEN THIS BOOK UNTIL THE SUPERVISOR TELLS YOU TO DO SO.

6

# SAT Reasoning Test™

You must use a No. 2 pencil. Do not use a mechanical pencil. It is very important that you fill in the entire circle darkly and completely. If you change your response, erase as completely as possible. Incomplete marks or erasures may affect your score. It is very important that you follow these instructions when filling out your answer sheet.

**1** Your Name:
(Print)

Last                                    First                                    M.I.

I agree to the conditions on the back of the SAT Reasoning Test™ booklet. I also agree to use only a No. 2 pencil to complete my answer sheet.

Signature:                                                                Date:      /      /

Home Address:
(Print)                    Number and Street              City                    State        Zip Code

Home Phone: (      )              Center:
(Print)                                      (Print)          City              State/Country

**2** YOUR NAME

Last Name (First 6 Letters)    First Name (First 4 Letters)    Mid. Init.

**3** DATE OF BIRTH

| MONTH | DAY | YEAR |
|-------|-----|------|
| Jan | | |
| Feb | 0 0 | U |
| Mar | 1 1 | 1 |
| Apr | 2 2 | 2 |
| May | 3 3 | 3 |
| Jun | 4 | 4 |
| Jul | 5 5 | 5 |
| Aug | 6 6 | 6 |
| Sep | 7 7 | 7 |
| Oct | 8 8 | 8 |
| Nov | 9 9 | 9 |
| Dec | | |

**5** SEX

○ Female   ○ Male

**6** REGISTRATION NUMBER
(Copy from Admission Ticket.)

○ I turned in my registration form today.

**4** ZIP CODE

**7** SOCIAL SECURITY NUMBER

**Important:** Fill in items 8 and 9 exactly as shown on the back of test book.

**9** TEST FORM
(Copy from back of test book.)

**8** FORM CODE
(Copy and grid as on back of test book.)

**10** TEST BOOK SERIAL NUMBER
(Copy from front of test book.)

**11** TEST CENTER
(Supplied by Test Center Supervisor.)

6

PLEASE DO NOT WRITE IN THIS AREA

SERIAL #

## SECTION 1

○ I prefer NOT to grant the College Board the right to use, reproduce, or publish my essay for any purpose beyond the assessment of my writing skills, even though my name will not be used in any way in conjunction with my essay. I understand that I am free to mark this circle with no effect on my score.

***IMPORTANT:*** **USE A NO. 2 PENCIL. DO NOT WRITE OUTSIDE THE BORDER!**
Words written outside the essay box or written in ink **WILL NOT APPEAR** in the copy sent to be scored, and your score will be affected.

**Begin your essay on this page. If you need more space, continue on the next page.**

6

6

SERIAL #

COMPLETE MARK ●    EXAMPLES OF ⓐ Ⓑ̶ ⊖ ⓓ
INCOMPLETE MARKS ● ∅ ⊘ ⊛

You must use a No. 2 pencil and marks must be complete. Do not use a mechanical pencil. It is very important that you fill in the entire circle darkly and completely. If you change your response, erase as completely as possible. Incomplete marks or erasures may affect your score.

## SECTION 2

| 1 Ⓐ Ⓑ Ⓒ Ⓓ Ⓔ | 11 Ⓐ Ⓑ Ⓒ Ⓓ Ⓔ | 21 Ⓐ Ⓑ Ⓒ Ⓓ Ⓔ | 31 Ⓐ Ⓑ Ⓒ Ⓓ Ⓔ |
| 2 Ⓐ Ⓑ Ⓒ Ⓓ Ⓔ | 12 Ⓐ Ⓑ Ⓒ Ⓓ Ⓔ | 22 Ⓐ Ⓑ Ⓒ Ⓓ Ⓔ | 32 Ⓐ Ⓑ Ⓒ Ⓓ Ⓔ |
| 3 Ⓐ Ⓑ Ⓒ Ⓓ Ⓔ | 13 Ⓐ Ⓑ Ⓒ Ⓓ Ⓔ | 23 Ⓐ Ⓑ Ⓒ Ⓓ Ⓔ | 33 Ⓐ Ⓑ Ⓒ Ⓓ Ⓔ |
| 4 Ⓐ Ⓑ Ⓒ Ⓓ Ⓔ | 14 Ⓐ Ⓑ Ⓒ Ⓓ Ⓔ | 24 Ⓐ Ⓑ Ⓒ Ⓓ Ⓔ | 34 Ⓐ Ⓑ Ⓒ Ⓓ Ⓔ |
| 5 Ⓐ Ⓑ Ⓒ Ⓓ Ⓔ | 15 Ⓐ Ⓑ Ⓒ Ⓓ Ⓔ | 25 Ⓐ Ⓑ Ⓒ Ⓓ Ⓔ | 35 Ⓐ Ⓑ Ⓒ Ⓓ Ⓔ |
| 6 Ⓐ Ⓑ Ⓒ Ⓓ Ⓔ | 16 Ⓐ Ⓑ Ⓒ Ⓓ Ⓔ | 26 Ⓐ Ⓑ Ⓒ Ⓓ Ⓔ | 36 Ⓐ Ⓑ Ⓒ Ⓓ Ⓔ |
| 7 Ⓐ Ⓑ Ⓒ Ⓓ Ⓔ | 17 Ⓐ Ⓑ Ⓒ Ⓓ Ⓔ | 27 Ⓐ Ⓑ Ⓒ Ⓓ Ⓔ | 37 Ⓐ Ⓑ Ⓒ Ⓓ Ⓔ |
| 8 Ⓐ Ⓑ Ⓒ Ⓓ Ⓔ | 18 Ⓐ Ⓑ Ⓒ Ⓓ Ⓔ | 28 Ⓐ Ⓑ Ⓒ Ⓓ Ⓔ | 38 Ⓐ Ⓑ Ⓒ Ⓓ Ⓔ |
| 9 Ⓐ Ⓑ Ⓒ Ⓓ Ⓔ | 19 Ⓐ Ⓑ Ⓒ Ⓓ Ⓔ | 29 Ⓐ Ⓑ Ⓒ Ⓓ Ⓔ | 39 Ⓐ Ⓑ Ⓒ Ⓓ Ⓔ |
| 10 Ⓐ Ⓑ Ⓒ Ⓓ Ⓔ | 20 Ⓐ Ⓑ Ⓒ Ⓓ Ⓔ | 30 Ⓐ Ⓑ Ⓒ Ⓓ Ⓔ | 40 Ⓐ Ⓑ Ⓒ Ⓓ Ⓔ |

## SECTION 3

| 1 Ⓐ Ⓑ Ⓒ Ⓓ Ⓔ | 11 Ⓐ Ⓑ Ⓒ Ⓓ Ⓔ | 21 Ⓐ Ⓑ Ⓒ Ⓓ Ⓔ | 31 Ⓐ Ⓑ Ⓒ Ⓓ Ⓔ |
| 2 Ⓐ Ⓑ Ⓒ Ⓓ Ⓔ | 12 Ⓐ Ⓑ Ⓒ Ⓓ Ⓔ | 22 Ⓐ Ⓑ Ⓒ Ⓓ Ⓔ | 32 Ⓐ Ⓑ Ⓒ Ⓓ Ⓔ |
| 3 Ⓐ Ⓑ Ⓒ Ⓓ Ⓔ | 13 Ⓐ Ⓑ Ⓒ Ⓓ Ⓔ | 23 Ⓐ Ⓑ Ⓒ Ⓓ Ⓔ | 33 Ⓐ Ⓑ Ⓒ Ⓓ Ⓔ |
| 4 Ⓐ Ⓑ Ⓒ Ⓓ Ⓔ | 14 Ⓐ Ⓑ Ⓒ Ⓓ Ⓔ | 24 Ⓐ Ⓑ Ⓒ Ⓓ Ⓔ | 34 Ⓐ Ⓑ Ⓒ Ⓓ Ⓔ |
| 5 Ⓐ Ⓑ Ⓒ Ⓓ Ⓔ | 15 Ⓐ Ⓑ Ⓒ Ⓓ Ⓔ | 25 Ⓐ Ⓑ Ⓒ Ⓓ Ⓔ | 35 Ⓐ Ⓑ Ⓒ Ⓓ Ⓔ |
| 6 Ⓐ Ⓑ Ⓒ Ⓓ Ⓔ | 16 Ⓐ Ⓑ Ⓒ Ⓓ Ⓔ | 26 Ⓐ Ⓑ Ⓒ Ⓓ Ⓔ | 36 Ⓐ Ⓑ Ⓒ Ⓓ Ⓔ |
| 7 Ⓐ Ⓑ Ⓒ Ⓓ Ⓔ | 17 Ⓐ Ⓑ Ⓒ Ⓓ Ⓔ | 27 Ⓐ Ⓑ Ⓒ Ⓓ Ⓔ | 37 Ⓐ Ⓑ Ⓒ Ⓓ Ⓔ |
| 8 Ⓐ Ⓑ Ⓒ Ⓓ Ⓔ | 18 Ⓐ Ⓑ Ⓒ Ⓓ Ⓔ | 28 Ⓐ Ⓑ Ⓒ Ⓓ Ⓔ | 38 Ⓐ Ⓑ Ⓒ Ⓓ Ⓔ |
| 9 Ⓐ Ⓑ Ⓒ Ⓓ Ⓔ | 19 Ⓐ Ⓑ Ⓒ Ⓓ Ⓔ | 29 Ⓐ Ⓑ Ⓒ Ⓓ Ⓔ | 39 Ⓐ Ⓑ Ⓒ Ⓓ Ⓔ |
| 10 Ⓐ Ⓑ Ⓒ Ⓓ Ⓔ | 20 Ⓐ Ⓑ Ⓒ Ⓓ Ⓔ | 30 Ⓐ Ⓑ Ⓒ Ⓓ Ⓔ | 40 Ⓐ Ⓑ Ⓒ Ⓓ Ⓔ |

**CAUTION** Grid answers in the section below for SECTION 2 or SECTION 3 only if directed to do so in your test book.

## Student-Produced Responses

ONLY ANSWERS THAT ARE GRIDDED WILL BE SCORED. YOU WILL NOT RECEIVE CREDIT FOR ANYTHING WRITTEN IN THE BOXES.

Quality Assurance Mark ●

9   10   11   12   13

14   15   16   17   18

Page 4

694

## SECTION 4

| 1 ⒶⒷⒸⒹⒺ | 11 ⒶⒷⒸⒹⒺ | 21 ⒶⒷⒸⒹⒺ | 31 ⒶⒷⒸⒹⒺ |
| 2 ⒶⒷⒸⒹⒺ | 12 ⒶⒷⒸⒹⒺ | 22 ⒶⒷⒸⒹⒺ | 32 ⒶⒷⒸⒹⒺ |
| 3 ⒶⒷⒸⒹⒺ | 13 ⒶⒷⒸⒹⒺ | 23 ⒶⒷⒸⒹⒺ | 33 ⒶⒷⒸⒹⒺ |
| 4 ⒶⒷⒸⒹⒺ | 14 ⒶⒷⒸⒹⒺ | 24 ⒶⒷⒸⒹⒺ | 34 ⒶⒷⒸⒹⒺ |
| 5 ⒶⒷⒸⒹⒺ | 15 ⒶⒷⒸⒹⒺ | 25 ⒶⒷⒸⒹⒺ | 35 ⒶⒷⒸⒹⒺ |
| 6 ⒶⒷⒸⒹⒺ | 16 ⒶⒷⒸⒹⒺ | 26 ⒶⒷⒸⒹⒺ | 36 ⒶⒷⒸⒹⒺ |
| 7 ⒶⒷⒸⒹⒺ | 17 ⒶⒷⒸⒹⒺ | 27 ⒶⒷⒸⒹⒺ | 37 ⒶⒷⒸⒹⒺ |
| 8 ⒶⒷⒸⒹⒺ | 18 ⒶⒷⒸⒹⒺ | 28 ⒶⒷⒸⒹⒺ | 38 ⒶⒷⒸⒹⒺ |
| 9 ⒶⒷⒸⒹⒺ | 19 ⒶⒷⒸⒹⒺ | 29 ⒶⒷⒸⒹⒺ | 39 ⒶⒷⒸⒹⒺ |
| 10 ⒶⒷⒸⒹⒺ | 20 ⒶⒷⒸⒹⒺ | 30 ⒶⒷⒸⒹⒺ | 40 ⒶⒷⒸⒹⒺ |

## SECTION 5

| 1 ⒶⒷⒸⒹⒺ | 11 ⒶⒷⒸⒹⒺ | 21 ⒶⒷⒸⒹⒺ | 31 ⒶⒷⒸⒹⒺ |
| 2 ⒶⒷⒸⒹⒺ | 12 ⒶⒷⒸⒹⒺ | 22 ⒶⒷⒸⒹⒺ | 32 ⒶⒷⒸⒹⒺ |
| 3 ⒶⒷⒸⒹⒺ | 13 ⒶⒷⒸⒹⒺ | 23 ⒶⒷⒸⒹⒺ | 33 ⒶⒷⒸⒹⒺ |
| 4 ⒶⒷⒸⒹⒺ | 14 ⒶⒷⒸⒹⒺ | 24 ⒶⒷⒸⒹⒺ | 34 ⒶⒷⒸⒹⒺ |
| 5 ⒶⒷⒸⒹⒺ | 15 ⒶⒷⒸⒹⒺ | 25 ⒶⒷⒸⒹⒺ | 35 ⒶⒷⒸⒹⒺ |
| 6 ⒶⒷⒸⒹⒺ | 16 ⒶⒷⒸⒹⒺ | 26 ⒶⒷⒸⒹⒺ | 36 ⒶⒷⒸⒹⒺ |
| 7 ⒶⒷⒸⒹⒺ | 17 ⒶⒷⒸⒹⒺ | 27 ⒶⒷⒸⒹⒺ | 37 ⒶⒷⒸⒹⒺ |
| 8 ⒶⒷⒸⒹⒺ | 18 ⒶⒷⒸⒹⒺ | 28 ⒶⒷⒸⒹⒺ | 38 ⒶⒷⒸⒹⒺ |
| 9 ⒶⒷⒸⒹⒺ | 19 ⒶⒷⒸⒹⒺ | 29 ⒶⒷⒸⒹⒺ | 39 ⒶⒷⒸⒹⒺ |
| 10 ⒶⒷⒸⒹⒺ | 20 ⒶⒷⒸⒹⒺ | 30 ⒶⒷⒸⒹⒺ | 40 ⒶⒷⒸⒹⒺ |

**CAUTION** Grid answers in the section below for SECTION 4 or SECTION 5 only if directed to do so in your test book.

## Student-Produced Responses

ONLY ANSWERS THAT ARE GRIDDED WILL BE SCORED. YOU WILL NOT RECEIVE CREDIT FOR ANYTHING WRITTEN IN THE BOXES.

Quality Assurance Mark ●

Grids 9, 10, 11, 12, 13, 14, 15, 16, 17, 18

## SECTION 6

1 Ⓐ Ⓑ Ⓒ Ⓓ Ⓔ
2 Ⓐ Ⓑ Ⓒ Ⓓ Ⓔ
3 Ⓐ Ⓑ Ⓒ Ⓓ Ⓔ
4 Ⓐ Ⓑ Ⓒ Ⓓ Ⓔ
5 Ⓐ Ⓑ Ⓒ Ⓓ Ⓔ
6 Ⓐ Ⓑ Ⓒ Ⓓ Ⓔ
7 Ⓐ Ⓑ Ⓒ Ⓓ Ⓔ
8 Ⓐ Ⓑ Ⓒ Ⓓ Ⓔ
9 Ⓐ Ⓑ Ⓒ Ⓓ Ⓔ
10 Ⓐ Ⓑ Ⓒ Ⓓ Ⓔ

11 Ⓐ Ⓑ Ⓒ Ⓓ Ⓔ
12 Ⓐ Ⓑ Ⓒ Ⓓ Ⓔ
13 Ⓐ Ⓑ Ⓒ Ⓓ Ⓔ
14 Ⓐ Ⓑ Ⓒ Ⓓ Ⓔ
15 Ⓐ Ⓑ Ⓒ Ⓓ Ⓔ
16 Ⓐ Ⓑ Ⓒ Ⓓ Ⓔ
17 Ⓐ Ⓑ Ⓒ Ⓓ Ⓔ
18 Ⓐ Ⓑ Ⓒ Ⓓ Ⓔ
19 Ⓐ Ⓑ Ⓒ Ⓓ Ⓔ
20 Ⓐ Ⓑ Ⓒ Ⓓ Ⓔ

21 Ⓐ Ⓑ Ⓒ Ⓓ Ⓔ
22 Ⓐ Ⓑ Ⓒ Ⓓ Ⓔ
23 Ⓐ Ⓑ Ⓒ Ⓓ Ⓔ
24 Ⓐ Ⓑ Ⓒ Ⓓ Ⓔ
25 Ⓐ Ⓑ Ⓒ Ⓓ Ⓔ
26 Ⓐ Ⓑ Ⓒ Ⓓ Ⓔ
27 Ⓐ Ⓑ Ⓒ Ⓓ Ⓔ
28 Ⓐ Ⓑ Ⓒ Ⓓ Ⓔ
29 Ⓐ Ⓑ Ⓒ Ⓓ Ⓔ
30 Ⓐ Ⓑ Ⓒ Ⓓ Ⓔ

31 Ⓐ Ⓑ Ⓒ Ⓓ Ⓔ
32 Ⓐ Ⓑ Ⓒ Ⓓ Ⓔ
33 Ⓐ Ⓑ Ⓒ Ⓓ Ⓔ
34 Ⓐ Ⓑ Ⓒ Ⓓ Ⓔ
35 Ⓐ Ⓑ Ⓒ Ⓓ Ⓔ
36 Ⓐ Ⓑ Ⓒ Ⓓ Ⓔ
37 Ⓐ Ⓑ Ⓒ Ⓓ Ⓔ
38 Ⓐ Ⓑ Ⓒ Ⓓ Ⓔ
39 Ⓐ Ⓑ Ⓒ Ⓓ Ⓔ
40 Ⓐ Ⓑ Ⓒ Ⓓ Ⓔ

## SECTION 7

1 Ⓐ Ⓑ Ⓒ Ⓓ Ⓔ
2 Ⓐ Ⓑ Ⓒ Ⓓ Ⓔ
3 Ⓐ Ⓑ Ⓒ Ⓓ Ⓔ
4 Ⓐ Ⓑ Ⓒ Ⓓ Ⓔ
5 Ⓐ Ⓑ Ⓒ Ⓓ Ⓔ
6 Ⓐ Ⓑ Ⓒ Ⓓ Ⓔ
7 Ⓐ Ⓑ Ⓒ Ⓓ Ⓔ
8 Ⓐ Ⓑ Ⓒ Ⓓ Ⓔ
9 Ⓐ Ⓑ Ⓒ Ⓓ Ⓔ
10 Ⓐ Ⓑ Ⓒ Ⓓ Ⓔ

11 Ⓐ Ⓑ Ⓒ Ⓓ Ⓔ
12 Ⓐ Ⓑ Ⓒ Ⓓ Ⓔ
13 Ⓐ Ⓑ Ⓒ Ⓓ Ⓔ
14 Ⓐ Ⓑ Ⓒ Ⓓ Ⓔ
15 Ⓐ Ⓑ Ⓒ Ⓓ Ⓔ
16 Ⓐ Ⓑ Ⓒ Ⓓ Ⓔ
17 Ⓐ Ⓑ Ⓒ Ⓓ Ⓔ
18 Ⓐ Ⓑ Ⓒ Ⓓ Ⓔ
19 Ⓐ Ⓑ Ⓒ Ⓓ Ⓔ
20 Ⓐ Ⓑ Ⓒ Ⓓ Ⓔ

21 Ⓐ Ⓑ Ⓒ Ⓓ Ⓔ
22 Ⓐ Ⓑ Ⓒ Ⓓ Ⓔ
23 Ⓐ Ⓑ Ⓒ Ⓓ Ⓔ
24 Ⓐ Ⓑ Ⓒ Ⓓ Ⓔ
25 Ⓐ Ⓑ Ⓒ Ⓓ Ⓔ
26 Ⓐ Ⓑ Ⓒ Ⓓ Ⓔ
27 Ⓐ Ⓑ Ⓒ Ⓓ Ⓔ
28 Ⓐ Ⓑ Ⓒ Ⓓ Ⓔ
29 Ⓐ Ⓑ Ⓒ Ⓓ Ⓔ
30 Ⓐ Ⓑ Ⓒ Ⓓ Ⓔ

31 Ⓐ Ⓑ Ⓒ Ⓓ Ⓔ
32 Ⓐ Ⓑ Ⓒ Ⓓ Ⓔ
33 Ⓐ Ⓑ Ⓒ Ⓓ Ⓔ
34 Ⓐ Ⓑ Ⓒ Ⓓ Ⓔ
35 Ⓐ Ⓑ Ⓒ Ⓓ Ⓔ
36 Ⓐ Ⓑ Ⓒ Ⓓ Ⓔ
37 Ⓐ Ⓑ Ⓒ Ⓓ Ⓔ
38 Ⓐ Ⓑ Ⓒ Ⓓ Ⓔ
39 Ⓐ Ⓑ Ⓒ Ⓓ Ⓔ
40 Ⓐ Ⓑ Ⓒ Ⓓ Ⓔ

**CAUTION** Grid answers in the section below for SECTION 6 or SECTION 7 only if directed to do so in your test book.

## Student-Produced Responses

ONLY ANSWERS THAT ARE GRIDDED WILL BE SCORED. YOU WILL NOT RECEIVE CREDIT FOR ANYTHING WRITTEN IN THE BOXES.

Quality Assurance Mark ●

9 10 11 12 13

14 15 16 17 18

Page 6

PLEASE DO NOT WRITE IN THIS AREA

SERIAL #

696

**SECTION 8**

| 1 | Ⓐ Ⓑ Ⓒ Ⓓ Ⓔ | 11 | Ⓐ Ⓑ Ⓒ Ⓓ Ⓔ | 21 | Ⓐ Ⓑ Ⓒ Ⓓ Ⓔ | 31 | Ⓐ Ⓑ Ⓒ Ⓓ Ⓔ |
| 2 | Ⓐ Ⓑ Ⓒ Ⓓ Ⓔ | 12 | Ⓐ Ⓑ Ⓒ Ⓓ Ⓔ | 22 | Ⓐ Ⓑ Ⓒ Ⓓ Ⓔ | 32 | Ⓐ Ⓑ Ⓒ Ⓓ Ⓔ |
| 3 | Ⓐ Ⓑ Ⓒ Ⓓ Ⓔ | 13 | Ⓐ Ⓑ Ⓒ Ⓓ Ⓔ | 23 | Ⓐ Ⓑ Ⓒ Ⓓ Ⓔ | 33 | Ⓐ Ⓑ Ⓒ Ⓓ Ⓔ |
| 4 | Ⓐ Ⓑ Ⓒ Ⓓ Ⓔ | 14 | Ⓐ Ⓑ Ⓒ Ⓓ Ⓔ | 24 | Ⓐ Ⓑ Ⓒ Ⓓ Ⓔ | 34 | Ⓐ Ⓑ Ⓒ Ⓓ Ⓔ |
| 5 | Ⓐ Ⓑ Ⓒ Ⓓ Ⓔ | 15 | Ⓐ Ⓑ Ⓒ Ⓓ Ⓔ | 25 | Ⓐ Ⓑ Ⓒ Ⓓ Ⓔ | 35 | Ⓐ Ⓑ Ⓒ Ⓓ Ⓔ |
| 6 | Ⓐ Ⓑ Ⓒ Ⓓ Ⓔ | 16 | Ⓐ Ⓑ Ⓒ Ⓓ Ⓔ | 26 | Ⓐ Ⓑ Ⓒ Ⓓ Ⓔ | 36 | Ⓐ Ⓑ Ⓒ Ⓓ Ⓔ |
| 7 | Ⓐ Ⓑ Ⓒ Ⓓ Ⓔ | 17 | Ⓐ Ⓑ Ⓒ Ⓓ Ⓔ | 27 | Ⓐ Ⓑ Ⓒ Ⓓ Ⓔ | 37 | Ⓐ Ⓑ Ⓒ Ⓓ Ⓔ |
| 8 | Ⓐ Ⓑ Ⓒ Ⓓ Ⓔ | 18 | Ⓐ Ⓑ Ⓒ Ⓓ Ⓔ | 28 | Ⓐ Ⓑ Ⓒ Ⓓ Ⓔ | 38 | Ⓐ Ⓑ Ⓒ Ⓓ Ⓔ |
| 9 | Ⓐ Ⓑ Ⓒ Ⓓ Ⓔ | 19 | Ⓐ Ⓑ Ⓒ Ⓓ Ⓔ | 29 | Ⓐ Ⓑ Ⓒ Ⓓ Ⓔ | 39 | Ⓐ Ⓑ Ⓒ Ⓓ Ⓔ |
| 10 | Ⓐ Ⓑ Ⓒ Ⓓ Ⓔ | 20 | Ⓐ Ⓑ Ⓒ Ⓓ Ⓔ | 30 | Ⓐ Ⓑ Ⓒ Ⓓ Ⓔ | 40 | Ⓐ Ⓑ Ⓒ Ⓓ Ⓔ |

**SECTION 9**

| 1 | Ⓐ Ⓑ Ⓒ Ⓓ Ⓔ | 11 | Ⓐ Ⓑ Ⓒ Ⓓ Ⓔ | 21 | Ⓐ Ⓑ Ⓒ Ⓓ Ⓔ | 31 | Ⓐ Ⓑ Ⓒ Ⓓ Ⓔ |
| 2 | Ⓐ Ⓑ Ⓒ Ⓓ Ⓔ | 12 | Ⓐ Ⓑ Ⓒ Ⓓ Ⓔ | 22 | Ⓐ Ⓑ Ⓒ Ⓓ Ⓔ | 32 | Ⓐ Ⓑ Ⓒ Ⓓ Ⓔ |
| 3 | Ⓐ Ⓑ Ⓒ Ⓓ Ⓔ | 13 | Ⓐ Ⓑ Ⓒ Ⓓ Ⓔ | 23 | Ⓐ Ⓑ Ⓒ Ⓓ Ⓔ | 33 | Ⓐ Ⓑ Ⓒ Ⓓ Ⓔ |
| 4 | Ⓐ Ⓑ Ⓒ Ⓓ Ⓔ | 14 | Ⓐ Ⓑ Ⓒ Ⓓ Ⓔ | 24 | Ⓐ Ⓑ Ⓒ Ⓓ Ⓔ | 34 | Ⓐ Ⓑ Ⓒ Ⓓ Ⓔ |
| 5 | Ⓐ Ⓑ Ⓒ Ⓓ Ⓔ | 15 | Ⓐ Ⓑ Ⓒ Ⓓ Ⓔ | 25 | Ⓐ Ⓑ Ⓒ Ⓓ Ⓔ | 35 | Ⓐ Ⓑ Ⓒ Ⓓ Ⓔ |
| 6 | Ⓐ Ⓑ Ⓒ Ⓓ Ⓔ | 16 | Ⓐ Ⓑ Ⓒ Ⓓ Ⓔ | 26 | Ⓐ Ⓑ Ⓒ Ⓓ Ⓔ | 36 | Ⓐ Ⓑ Ⓒ Ⓓ Ⓔ |
| 7 | Ⓐ Ⓑ Ⓒ Ⓓ Ⓔ | 17 | Ⓐ Ⓑ Ⓒ Ⓓ Ⓔ | 27 | Ⓐ Ⓑ Ⓒ Ⓓ Ⓔ | 37 | Ⓐ Ⓑ Ⓒ Ⓓ Ⓔ |
| 8 | Ⓐ Ⓑ Ⓒ Ⓓ Ⓔ | 18 | Ⓐ Ⓑ Ⓒ Ⓓ Ⓔ | 28 | Ⓐ Ⓑ Ⓒ Ⓓ Ⓔ | 38 | Ⓐ Ⓑ Ⓒ Ⓓ Ⓔ |
| 9 | Ⓐ Ⓑ Ⓒ Ⓓ Ⓔ | 19 | Ⓐ Ⓑ Ⓒ Ⓓ Ⓔ | 29 | Ⓐ Ⓑ Ⓒ Ⓓ Ⓔ | 39 | Ⓐ Ⓑ Ⓒ Ⓓ Ⓔ |
| 10 | Ⓐ Ⓑ Ⓒ Ⓓ Ⓔ | 20 | Ⓐ Ⓑ Ⓒ Ⓓ Ⓔ | 30 | Ⓐ Ⓑ Ⓒ Ⓓ Ⓔ | 40 | Ⓐ Ⓑ Ⓒ Ⓓ Ⓔ |

Quality
●
Assurance
Mark

**SECTION 10**

| 1 | Ⓐ Ⓑ Ⓒ Ⓓ Ⓔ | 11 | Ⓐ Ⓑ Ⓒ Ⓓ Ⓔ | 21 | Ⓐ Ⓑ Ⓒ Ⓓ Ⓔ | 31 | Ⓐ Ⓑ Ⓒ Ⓓ Ⓔ |
| 2 | Ⓐ Ⓑ Ⓒ Ⓓ Ⓔ | 12 | Ⓐ Ⓑ Ⓒ Ⓓ Ⓔ | 22 | Ⓐ Ⓑ Ⓒ Ⓓ Ⓔ | 32 | Ⓐ Ⓑ Ⓒ Ⓓ Ⓔ |
| 3 | Ⓐ Ⓑ Ⓒ Ⓓ Ⓔ | 13 | Ⓐ Ⓑ Ⓒ Ⓓ Ⓔ | 23 | Ⓐ Ⓑ Ⓒ Ⓓ Ⓔ | 33 | Ⓐ Ⓑ Ⓒ Ⓓ Ⓔ |
| 4 | Ⓐ Ⓑ Ⓒ Ⓓ Ⓔ | 14 | Ⓐ Ⓑ Ⓒ Ⓓ Ⓔ | 24 | Ⓐ Ⓑ Ⓒ Ⓓ Ⓔ | 34 | Ⓐ Ⓑ Ⓒ Ⓓ Ⓔ |
| 5 | Ⓐ Ⓑ Ⓒ Ⓓ Ⓔ | 15 | Ⓐ Ⓑ Ⓒ Ⓓ Ⓔ | 25 | Ⓐ Ⓑ Ⓒ Ⓓ Ⓔ | 35 | Ⓐ Ⓑ Ⓒ Ⓓ Ⓔ |
| 6 | Ⓐ Ⓑ Ⓒ Ⓓ Ⓔ | 16 | Ⓐ Ⓑ Ⓒ Ⓓ Ⓔ | 26 | Ⓐ Ⓑ Ⓒ Ⓓ Ⓔ | 36 | Ⓐ Ⓑ Ⓒ Ⓓ Ⓔ |
| 7 | Ⓐ Ⓑ Ⓒ Ⓓ Ⓔ | 17 | Ⓐ Ⓑ Ⓒ Ⓓ Ⓔ | 27 | Ⓐ Ⓑ Ⓒ Ⓓ Ⓔ | 37 | Ⓐ Ⓑ Ⓒ Ⓓ Ⓔ |
| 8 | Ⓐ Ⓑ Ⓒ Ⓓ Ⓔ | 18 | Ⓐ Ⓑ Ⓒ Ⓓ Ⓔ | 28 | Ⓐ Ⓑ Ⓒ Ⓓ Ⓔ | 38 | Ⓐ Ⓑ Ⓒ Ⓓ Ⓔ |
| 9 | Ⓐ Ⓑ Ⓒ Ⓓ Ⓔ | 19 | Ⓐ Ⓑ Ⓒ Ⓓ Ⓔ | 29 | Ⓐ Ⓑ Ⓒ Ⓓ Ⓔ | 39 | Ⓐ Ⓑ Ⓒ Ⓓ Ⓔ |
| 10 | Ⓐ Ⓑ Ⓒ Ⓓ Ⓔ | 20 | Ⓐ Ⓑ Ⓒ Ⓓ Ⓔ | 30 | Ⓐ Ⓑ Ⓒ Ⓓ Ⓔ | 40 | Ⓐ Ⓑ Ⓒ Ⓓ Ⓔ |

6

**Page 7**

**6**

## SPECIAL QUESTIONS

1 (A) (B) (C) (D) (E) (F) (G) (H) (I) (J)
2 (A) (B) (C) (D) (E) (F) (G) (H) (I) (J)
3 (A) (B) (C) (D) (E) (F) (G) (H) (I) (J)
4 (A) (B) (C) (D) (E) (F) (G) (H) (I) (J)
5 (A) (B) (C) (D) (E) (F) (G) (H) (I) (J)
6 (A) (B) (C) (D) (E) (F) (G) (H) (I) (J)
7 (A) (B) (C) (D) (E) (F) (G) (H) (I) (J)
8 (A) (B) (C) (D) (E) (F) (G) (H) (I) (J)

**Page 8**

## ESSAY
### Time — 25 minutes

---

### Turn to page 2 of your answer sheet to write your ESSAY.

---

The essay gives you an opportunity to show how effectively you can develop and express ideas. You should, therefore, take care to develop your point of view, present your ideas logically and clearly, and use language precisely.

Your essay must be written on the lines provided on your answer sheet—you will receive no other paper on which to write. You will have enough space if you write on every line, avoid wide margins, and keep your handwriting to a reasonable size. Remember that people who are not familiar with your handwriting will read what you write. Try to write or print so that what you are writing is legible to those readers.

**Important Reminders:**

- **A pencil is required for the essay.** An essay written in ink will receive a score of zero.
- **Do not write your essay in your test book.** You will receive credit only for what you write on your answer sheet.
- **An off-topic essay will receive a score of zero.**
- **If your essay does not reflect your original and individual work, your test scores may be canceled.**

You have twenty-five minutes to write an essay on the topic assigned below.

---

Think carefully about the issue presented in the following excerpt and the assignment below.

> The old saying, "be careful what you wish for," may be an appropriate warning. The drive to achieve a particular goal can dangerously narrow one's perspective and encourage the fantasy that success in one endeavor will solve all of life's difficulties. In fact, success can sometimes have unexpected consequences. Those who propel themselves toward the achievement of one goal often find that their lives are worse once "success" is achieved than they were before.

**Assignment:** Can success be disastrous? Plan and write an essay in which you develop your point of view on this issue. Support your position with reasoning and examples taken from your reading, studies, experience, or observations.

---

BEGIN WRITING YOUR ESSAY ON PAGE 2 OF THE ANSWER SHEET.

---

**If you finish before time is called, you may check your work on this section only.**
**Do not turn to any other section in the test.**

Unauthorized copying or reuse of
any part of this page is illegal.

## SECTION 2
Time — 25 minutes
20 Questions

**Turn to Section 2 (page 4) of your answer sheet to answer the questions in this section.**

**Directions:** For this section, solve each problem and decide which is the best of the choices given. Fill in the corresponding circle on the answer sheet. You may use any available space for scratchwork.

Notes

1. The use of a calculator is permitted.
2. All numbers used are real numbers.
3. Figures that accompany problems in this test are intended to provide information useful in solving the problems. They are drawn as accurately as possible EXCEPT when it is stated in a specific problem that the figure is not drawn to scale. All figures lie in a plane unless otherwise indicated.
4. Unless otherwise specified, the domain of any function $f$ is assumed to be the set of all real numbers $x$ for which $f(x)$ is a real number.

Reference Information

$A = \pi r^2$
$C = 2\pi r$  $\quad A = \ell w \quad A = \frac{1}{2}bh \quad V = \ell wh \quad V = \pi r^2 h \quad c^2 = a^2 + b^2$  **Special Right Triangles**

The number of degrees of arc in a circle is 360.
The sum of the measures in degrees of the angles of a triangle is 180.

1. When Ms. Yun arrived at the grocery store, there were 5 packages of hot dog rolls left on the shelf. One package contained 12 rolls, and each of the others contained 8 rolls. If Ms. Yun bought all 5 packages, how many hot dog rolls did she purchase at the store?

(A) 32
(B) 36
(C) 44
(D) 48
(E) 52

2. $A$, $B$, and $C$ are points on a line in that order. If $AB = 30$ and $BC$ is 20 more than $AB$, what does $AC$ equal?

(A) 50
(B) 60
(C) 70
(D) 80
(E) 90

3. If $x + 3 = a$, then $2x + 6 =$

(A) $a + 3$
(B) $a + 6$
(C) $2a$
(D) $2a + 3$
(E) $2a + 6$

**GO ON TO THE NEXT PAGE**

**Questions 4-5 refer to the following graph.**

### TEST SCORES OF FIVE STUDENTS

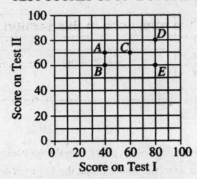

**4.** For which student was the change in scores from test I to test II the greatest?

(A) *A*
(B) *B*
(C) *C*
(D) *D*
(E) *E*

**5.** What was the average (arithmetic mean) of the scores of the 5 students on test II ?

(A) 60
(B) 65
(C) 68
(D) 70
(E) 72

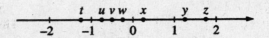

**6.** On the number line above, *t*, *u*, *v*, *w*, *x*, *y*, and *z* are coordinates of the indicated points. Which of the following is closest in value to $|u + v|$ ?

(A) *t*
(B) *w*
(C) *x*
(D) *y*
(E) *z*

**7.** If $x = \dfrac{1}{2}$, what is the value of $\dfrac{1}{x} + \dfrac{1}{x - 1}$ ?

(A) −4
(B) 0
(C) 1
(D) 2
(E) 3

**GO ON TO THE NEXT PAGE**

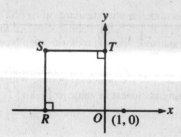

**8.** In the figure above, $RS = ST$ and the coordinates of $S$ are $(k, 3)$. What is the value of $k$?

(A) $-3$

(B) $-\sqrt{3}$

(C) $0$

(D) $\sqrt{3}$

(E) $3$

| $x$ | 0 | 1 | 2 | 3 |
|------|---|---|---|----|
| $f(x)$ | 1 | 2 | 5 | 10 |

**9.** The table above gives values of the quadratic function $f$ for selected values of $x$. Which of the following defines $f$?

(A) $f(x) = x^2 + 1$

(B) $f(x) = x^2 + 2$

(C) $f(x) = 2x^2 - 2$

(D) $f(x) = 2x^2 - 1$

(E) $f(x) = 2x^2 + 1$

**10.** How old was a person exactly 1 year ago if exactly $x$ years ago the person was $y$ years old?

(A) $y - 1$

(B) $y - x - 1$

(C) $x - y - 1$

(D) $y + x + 1$

(E) $y + x - 1$

**Z W Y X**

**11.** The sequence above may be changed in either of two ways. Either two adjacent letters may be interchanged or the entire sequence may be reversed. What is the least number of such changes needed to put the letters into alphabetical order from left to right?

(A) 2

(B) 3

(C) 4

(D) 5

(E) 6

**12.** How many cubical blocks, each with edges of length 4 centimeters, are needed to fill a rectangular box that has inside dimensions 20 centimeters by 24 centimeters by 32 centimeters?

(A) 38

(B) 96

(C) 192

(D) 240

(E) 384

**GO ON TO THE NEXT PAGE**

**13.** If $0 < n < 1$, which of the following gives the correct ordering of $\sqrt{n}$, $n$, and $n^2$ ?

(A) $\sqrt{n} < n < n^2$

(B) $\sqrt{n} < n^2 < n$

(C) $n < \sqrt{n} < n^2$

(D) $n < n^2 < \sqrt{n}$

(E) $n^2 < n < \sqrt{n}$

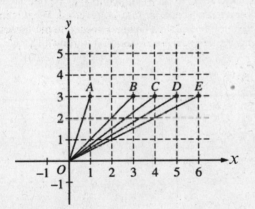

**14.** In the figure above, what is the median of the slopes of $\overline{OA}$, $\overline{OB}$, $\overline{OC}$, $\overline{OD}$, and $\overline{OE}$ ?

(A) $\dfrac{4}{3}$

(B) $1$

(C) $\dfrac{3}{4}$

(D) $\dfrac{3}{5}$

(E) $\dfrac{1}{2}$

**15.** When it is noon eastern standard time (EST) in New York City, it is 9:00 A.M. Pacific standard time (PST) in San Francisco. A plane took off from New York City at noon EST and arrived in San Francisco at 4:00 P.M. PST on the same day. If a second plane left San Francisco at noon PST and took exactly the same amount of time for the trip, what was the plane's arrival time (EST) in New York City?

(A) 10:00 P.M. EST
(B) 9:00 P.M. EST
(C) 7:00 P.M. EST
(D) 6:00 P.M. EST
(E) 4:00 P.M. EST

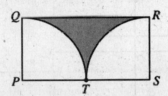

**16.** In rectangle *PQRS* above, arcs *QT* and *RT* are quarter circles with centers at *P* and *S*, respectively. If the radius of each quarter circle is 1, what is the area of the shaded region?

(A) $1 - \dfrac{\pi}{4}$

(B) $2 - \dfrac{\pi}{2}$

(C) $2 - \dfrac{\pi}{4}$

(D) $\dfrac{\pi}{4}$

(E) $\dfrac{2}{3}$

**GO ON TO THE NEXT PAGE**

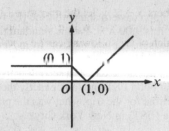

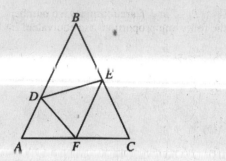

Note: Figure not drawn to scale.

17. The graph of $y = f(x)$ is shown above. Which of the following could be the graph of $y = f(x + 2)$ ?

(A)

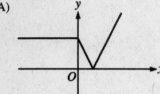

(B)

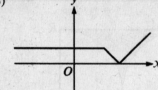

(C)

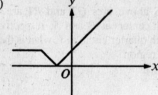

(D)

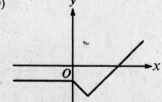

(E)

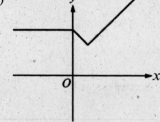

18. In the figure above, $AB = BC$ and $DE = EF = DF$. If the measure of $\angle ABC$ is 30° and the measure of $\angle BDE$ is 50°, what is the measure of $\angle DFA$ ?

(A) 30°
(B) 35°
(C) 40°
(D) 45°
(E) 50°

GO ON TO THE NEXT PAGE

**19.** If $a$, $b$, $c$, and $f$ are four nonzero numbers, then all of the following proportions are equivalent EXCEPT

(A) $\dfrac{a}{f} = \dfrac{b}{c}$

(B) $\dfrac{f}{c} = \dfrac{b}{a}$

(C) $\dfrac{c}{a} = \dfrac{f}{b}$

(D) $\dfrac{a}{c} = \dfrac{b}{f}$

(E) $\dfrac{af}{bc} = \dfrac{1}{1}$

**20.** For all numbers $x$ and $y$, let the operation $\square$ be defined by $x \square y = xy - y$. If $a$ and $b$ are positive integers, which of the following can be equal to zero?

   I. $a \square b$
   II. $(a + b) \square b$
   III. $a \square (a + b)$

(A) I only
(B) II only
(C) III only
(D) I and II
(E) I and III

# STOP

**If you finish before time is called, you may check your work on this section only.**
**Do not turn to any other section in the test.**

## SECTION 3
Time — 25 minutes
24 Questions

**Turn to Section 3 (page 4) of your answer sheet to answer the questions in this section.**

**Directions:** For each question in this section, select the best answer from among the choices given and fill in the corresponding circle on the answer sheet.

---

Each sentence below has one or two blanks, each blank indicating that something has been omitted. Beneath the sentence are five words or sets of words labeled A through E. Choose the word or set of words that, when inserted in the sentence, best fits the meaning of the sentence as a whole.

**Example:**

Hoping to ------- the dispute, negotiators proposed a compromise that they felt would be ------- to both labor and management.

(A) enforce . . useful
(B) end . . divisive
(C) overcome . . unattractive
(D) extend . . satisfactory
(E) resolve . . acceptable

Ⓐ Ⓑ Ⓒ Ⓓ ●

---

1. The rebels saw the huge statue of the dictator as ------- of the totalitarian regime and swiftly toppled the monument.

(A) an indictment    (B) an illusion    (C) a copy
(D) a symbol    (E) a mockery

2. Residents of the isolated island were forced to master the art of navigation, becoming the ocean's most ------- sailors.

(A) adept    (B) temperamental    (C) congenial
(D) vulnerable    (E) reclusive

3. The spotted bowerbird has a ------- for amassing the bright shiny objects it needs for decorating its bower: it will enter houses to ------- cutlery, coins, thimbles, nails, screws, even car keys.

(A) knack . . assess
(B) penchant . . pilfer
(C) purpose . . dispense
(D) predilection . . disturb
(E) remedy . . raid

4. Not only was the science of Hildegard of Bingen ------- her theology, but her religious visions helped give her scientific works ------- by winning her the support of medieval church authorities.

(A) inseparable from . . legitimacy
(B) unconcerned with . . prestige
(C) derived from . . profundity
(D) related to . . accuracy
(E) diminished by . . detachment

5. Opponents of the research institute label it ------- anachronism; its scholars, they allege, have ------- rivaling those of pre-Revolutionary French nobility.

(A) an elitist . . perquisites
(B) a monarchical . . tribulations
(C) an irreproachable . . luxuries
(D) a reprehensible . . afflictions
(E) a commendable . . privileges

---

**GO ON TO THE NEXT PAGE** ▷

The passages below are followed by questions based on their content; questions following a pair of related passages may also be based on the relationship between the paired passages. Answer the questions on the basis of what is <u>stated</u> or <u>implied</u> in the passages and in any introductory material that may be provided.

**Questions 6-9 are based on the following passages.**

**Passage 1**

The eighteenth-century botanist Carolus Linnaeus' enormous and essential contribution to natural history was to devise a system of classification whereby any
Line plant or animal could be identified and slotted into
5 an overall plan. Yet Linnaeus himself would probably have been the first to admit that classification is only a tool, and not the ultimate purpose, of biological inquiry. Unfortunately, this truth was not apparent to his immediate successors, who for the next hundred
10 years were to concern themselves almost exclusively with classification.

**Passage 2**

I am a heretic about Linnaeus. I do not dispute the value of the tool he gave natural science, but I am wary about the change it has effected on humans' relationship
15 to the world. From Linnaeus on, much of science has been devoted to sorting masses into individual entities and arranging the entities neatly. The cost of having so successfully itemized and pigeonholed nature is to limit certain possibilities of seeing and apprehending. For
20 example, the modern human thinks that he or she can best understand a tree (or a species of tree) by examining a single tree. But trees are not intended to grow in isolation. They are social creatures, and their society in turn supports other species of plants, insects, birds, mammals, and micro-
25 organisms, all of which make up the whole experience of the woods.

6. Compared to the author of Passage 2, the author of Passage 1 regards Linnaeus with more

(A) cynicism
(B) bafflement
(C) appreciation
(D) nostalgia
(E) resentment

7. Unlike the author of Passage 1, the author of Passage 2 makes use of

(A) scientific data
(B) literary allusion
(C) historical research
(D) personal voice
(E) direct citation

8. Both passages emphasize which of the following aspects of Linnaeus' work?

(A) The extent to which it contributed to natural science
(B) The way in which it limits present-day science
(C) The degree to which it revived interest in biology
(D) The decisiveness with which it settled scientific disputes
(E) The kinds of scientific discoveries on which it built

9. The author of Passage 1 would most likely respond to the opening of Passage 2 (lines 12-17) by arguing that the author of Passage 2 has

(A) demonstrated that Linnaeus should be better known as a scientist than he currently is
(B) minimized the achievements of those scientists who built on Linnaeus' work
(C) refused to appreciate the importance of proper classification to scientific progress
(D) failed to distinguish the ideas of Linnaeus from those of his followers
(E) misunderstood Linnaeus' primary contribution to natural history

**GO ON TO THE NEXT PAGE**

**Questions 10-15 are based on the following passage.**

*The following is an excerpt from a translation of a novel written in Spanish by an author from Colombia. In a fanciful manner, the novelist portrays the townspeople of an isolated village.*

Dazzled by so many and such marvelous inventions, the people of Macondo did not know where their amazement began. They stayed up all night looking at the pale electric
*Line* bulbs fed by the electric plant that Aureliano Triste had
5 brought back when the train made its second trip, and it took time and effort for them to grow accustomed to its obsessive noise.

They became indignant over the living images that the prosperous merchant Bruno Crespi projected on the screen
10 in the theater with the lion-head ticket windows, for the character who had died and was buried in one film, and for whose misfortune tears of affliction had been shed, would reappear alive and transformed into an Arab sheik in the next one. The audience, who paid two cents apiece to share
15 the difficulties of the actors, would not tolerate such an outlandish fraud and they broke up the seats. The mayor, at the urging of Bruno Crespi, explained in a proclamation that the cinema was a machine of illusions that did not merit the emotional outbursts of the audience. With that
20 discouraging explanation many felt that they had been the victims of some new trickery and they decided not to return to the movies, considering that they already had too many troubles of their own to weep over the acted-out misfortunes of imaginary beings.

25 Something similar happened with cylinder phonographs brought from France and intended as a substitute for the antiquated hand organs used by the band of musicians. For a time the phonograph records had serious effects on the livelihood of the musicians. At first curiosity increased the
30 business on the street where they were sold and there was even word of respectable persons who disguised themselves as workers in order to observe the novelty of the phonograph at firsthand, but from so much and such close observation they soon reached the conclusion that it was
35 not an enchanted mill as everyone had thought and as some had said, but a mechanical trick that could not be compared with something so moving, so human, and so full of everyday truth as a band of musicians. It was such a serious disappointment that when phonographs became so popular
40 that there was one in every house they were not considered objects for amusement for adults but as something good for children to take apart.

On the other hand, when someone from the town had the opportunity to test the crude reality of the telephone
45 installed in the railroad station, which was thought to be a rudimentary version of the phonograph because of its crank, even the most incredulous were upset. It was as if God had decided to put to the test every capacity for surprise and was keeping the inhabitants of Macondo in a
50 permanent alternation between excitement and disappointment, doubt and revelation, to such an extreme that no one knew for certain where the limits of reality lay.

10. The word "obsessive" (line 7) most nearly means

(A) enthusiastic
(B) persistent
(C) obvious
(D) infatuated
(E) hardworking

11. The "fraud" (line 16) that upset the citizens of Macondo was related to the

(A) excessive charge for admission
(B) outlandish adventures of the characters on the screen
(C) fact that the events depicted on the screen did not actually occur
(D) types of difficulties the actors faced
(E) implausible plots of the stories that were told

12. The citizens lost interest in their phonographs because

(A) the machines lacked the heart and soul of true musicians
(B) few people were able to operate them
(C) the machines were too difficult to observe firsthand
(D) many musicians lost their jobs because of them
(E) the children were breaking them faster than they were made

13. The citizens of Macondo were distressed by the arrival of the telephone because they

(A) did not know where it had come from
(B) had expected a more socially beneficial invention
(C) could envision the changes it would bring to daily village life
(D) no longer felt able to make the usual assumptions about their world
(E) were fearful that it would have serious effects on their continued employment

**GO ON TO THE NEXT PAGE** →

**14.** The aspect of the new inventions that most disappointed the citizens was that these inventions

(A) were not all fashioned with a crank
(B) did not have any real educational value
(C) were not at all what they seemed to be
(D) were meant purely for entertainment
(E) were so intricate they were difficult to operate

**15.** The major purpose of the passage is to

(A) illustrate the influence the distinguished residents of Macondo had on the other citizens
(B) describe the new scientific inventions that were introduced to Macondo
(C) depict a diverse crowd reacting in unison to a magical performance
(D) describe the people's responses to the influx of technical advances
(E) delineate old-fashioned ideas about the virtue of nature over technology

GO ON TO THE NEXT PAGE

**Questions 16-24 are based on the following passage.**

*This passage is by a choreographer who worked with the influential dancer and choreographer Martha Graham (1894-1991). It focuses on the use of space and gesture in dance.*

I am not an adept aesthetician, and I could not presume
to analyze Martha's sense of design or approach toward
design. But I believe she dealt with the elements of line and
*Line* direction with the instincts of a mathematician or physicist,
5 adding to each their emotional relations. For example, a
straight line rarely, if ever, occurs in nature, but it does
occur in art, and it is used in art with various telling
effects. Direction works similar magic. An approaching
body produces one kind of emotional line, a receding or
10 departing body another; the meeting of two forces produces
visual, kinesthetic, and emotional effects, with a world of
suggestibility around them like a penumbra that evokes
many ideas and emotions whenever these forms are manipulated. Basic human gestures assume, therefore, an almost
15 mystic power. The simple maneuver of turning the face
away, for example, removes personality, relationship. Not
only that, it seems to alter the relation of the individual to
present time and present place, to make here-and-now
other-where and other-time. It also shifts the particular
20 personality to the general and the symbolic. This is the
power of the human face and the human regard, and the
meeting of the eyes is probably as magic a connection as
can be made on this earth, equal to any amount of electrical
shock or charge. It represents the heart of dynamism, life
25 itself. The loss of that regard reduces all connections to
nothingness and void.

"Turning one's back" has become a common figure of
speech. It means withholding approval, disclaiming, negat-
ing; and, in fact, in common conduct the physical turning
30 of the back is equated with absolute negation and insult.
No back is turned on a royal personage or a figure of high
respect. This is linked with the loss of visual contact and
regard. One cuts dead by not meeting the eyes.

We know much about emotional symbols. Those used
35 by the medieval and Renaissance painters were understood
by the scholars and artists of the time—but, more wonderful, they mean to us today spontaneously just what they
meant then; they seem to be permanent. We dream, Jung*
tells us, in terms and symbols of classic mythology. And
40 since, according to Jung, all people share a "collective
unconscious," people from disparate traditions nonetheless
dream in the same terms. Is it not also likely, then, that
certain space relations, rhythms, and stresses have psychological significance, that some of these patterns are
45 universal and the key to emotional response, that their
deviations and modifications can be meaningful to artists
in terms of their own life experiences and that these over-
tones are grasped by spectators without conscious analysis?

These matters are basic to our well-being as land and air
50 animals. As plants will turn to sunlight or rocks or moisture
according to their nature, so we bend toward or escape
from spatial arrangements according to our emotional
needs. Look around any restaurant and see how few people
will sit at a center table unless the sides are filled up. Yet
55 monarchs of old always dined dead center and many times
in public.

The individual as a personality, then, has a particular
code in space and rhythm, evolved from his or her life
history and from the history of the human race. It is just
60 the manipulation of these suggestions through time-space
that is the material of choreography.

*A Swiss psychologist (1875-1961)

**16.** The first two sentences (lines 1-5) are characterized, respectively, by

(A) disclaimer and assertion
(B) invocation and definition
(C) apology and confession
(D) authority and hypothesis
(E) rebuttal and analysis

**17.** In lines 5-6, the statement "a straight line rarely, if ever, occurs in nature" emphasizes the author's recognition of the

(A) choreographer's need for spectacular effects
(B) choreographer's use of mathematical forms
(C) choreographer's estrangement from nature
(D) impossibility of performing certain choreographed motions
(E) universality of geometrical forms

**18.** By saying that the meeting of two forces produces effects that have "a world of suggestibility around them" (lines 11-12), the author means that the physical event

(A) provokes unwarranted suspicions
(B) reveals the motives of the artist
(C) acts on the gullibility of the audience
(D) lulls the audience into complacent acceptance
(E) evokes a vast number of associations

**19.** The author's main point about "human gestures" (line 14) is that they

(A) are not subject to an individual's control
(B) are difficult to analyze without scientific terminology
(C) provoke different responses in people
(D) carry powerful, universally understood messages
(E) evolve with changes in cultural hierarchy

**GO ON TO THE NEXT PAGE**

20. The author mentions "the meeting of the eyes" (lines 21-22) to suggest the

(A) effect that rank or status has on gestural meaning
(B) difficulty of controlling emotional symbols
(C) degree to which body language is not a function of personality
(D) extent of the power of individual human contact
(E) nature of artistically pleasing events

21. The author suggests which of the following about the work of "medieval and Renaissance painters" (line 35) ?

(A) It was influenced by its royal patronage.
(B) It was conceived more spontaneously than is modern art.
(C) It should be cherished for its unique symbolism.
(D) It contains symbols that are immediately accessible to contemporary viewers.
(E) It is an unsophisticated version of symbolism developed later by choreographers.

22. As used in line 43, "stresses" most nearly means

(A) emphases
(B) loads
(C) anxieties
(D) influences
(E) sounds

23. As used in line 48, "grasped" most nearly means

(A) adhered to
(B) seized on
(C) controlled
(D) held
(E) understood

24. The author suggests that people in a restaurant (lines 53-54) are expressing their emotional need for

(A) unhindered interaction
(B) relative privacy
(C) respect from strangers
(D) approval from others
(E) reclusive isolation

# STOP

**If you finish before time is called, you may check your work on this section only.**
**Do not turn to any other section in the test.**

711

**4** □ □ □ □ □    □ □ □ □ **4**

Unauthorized copying or reuse of any part of this page is illegal.

## SECTION 4
### Time — 25 minutes
### 18 Questions

**Turn to Section 4 (page 5) of your answer sheet to answer the questions in this section.**

**Directions:** This section contains two types of questions. You have 25 minutes to complete both types. For questions 1-8, solve each problem and decide which is the best of the choices given. Fill in the corresponding circle on the answer sheet. You may use any available space for scratchwork.

**Notes**

1. The use of a calculator is permitted.
2. All numbers used are real numbers.
3. Figures that accompany problems in this test are intended to provide information useful in solving the problems. They are drawn as accurately as possible EXCEPT when it is stated in a specific problem that the figure is not drawn to scale. All figures lie in a plane unless otherwise indicated.
4. Unless otherwise specified, the domain of any function $f$ is assumed to be the set of all real numbers $x$ for which $f(x)$ is a real number.

**Reference Information**

    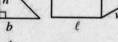   

$A = \pi r^2$
$C = 2\pi r$       $A = \ell w$       $A = \frac{1}{2}bh$       $V = \ell wh$       $V = \pi r^2 h$       $c^2 = a^2 + b^2$       Special Right Triangles

The number of degrees of arc in a circle is 360.
The sum of the measures in degrees of the angles of a triangle is 180.

1. If $x - y = 8$, $y = 3z$, and $z = 2$, what is the value of $x$?

   (A)  −14
   (B)  −2
   (C)   2
   (D)   3
   (E)  14

2. Todd is older than Marta but younger than Susan. If $t$, $m$, and $s$ represent the ages, in years, of Todd, Marta, and Susan, respectively, which of the following is true?

   (A)  $m < t < s$
   (B)  $s < m < t$
   (C)  $s < t < m$
   (D)  $t < m < s$
   (E)  $t < s < m$

**GO ON TO THE NEXT PAGE**

3. If the areas of two regions are equal and the sum of the areas of the regions is 5, what is the average (arithmetic mean) of the areas of the two regions?

(A)  0

(B)  $\dfrac{5}{2}$

(C)  $\dfrac{5}{4}$

(D)  5

(E)  10

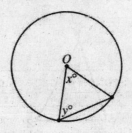

Note: Figure not drawn to scale.

5. In the figure above, point $O$ is the center of the circle. If $x = 40$, what is the value of $y$?

(A)  40
(B)  50
(C)  60
(D)  70
(E)  80

4. Let $S$ be the set of all integers that can be written as $n^2 + 1$, where $n$ is a nonzero integer. Which of the following integers is in $S$?

(A)  16
(B)  28
(C)  35
(D)  39
(E)  50

6. A "simple square" is any integer greater than 1 that has only three positive integer factors—itself, its square root, and 1. Which of the following is a simple square?

(A)  121
(B)  100
(C)  81
(D)  64
(E)  33

GO ON TO THE NEXT PAGE

713

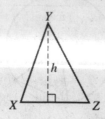

7. In $\triangle XYZ$ above, $XZ$ is $\frac{6}{7}$ of $h$, the length of the altitude. What is the area of $\triangle XYZ$ in terms of $h$ ?

(A) $\dfrac{h^2}{3}$

(B) $\dfrac{3h^2}{7}$

(C) $\dfrac{3h}{7}$

(D) $\dfrac{6h^2}{7}$

(E) $\dfrac{12h^2}{7}$

8. If $a$ and $b$ are positive integers and $\left(a^{\frac{1}{2}}\, b^{\frac{1}{3}}\right)^6 = 432$, what is the value of $ab$ ?

(A) 6
(B) 12
(C) 18
(D) 24
(E) 36

**GO ON TO THE NEXT PAGE**

Unauthorized copying or reuse of any part of this page is illegal.

**Directions:** For Student-Produced Response questions 9-18, use the grids at the bottom of the answer sheet page on which you have answered questions 1-8.

Each of the remaining 10 questions requires you to solve the problem and enter your answer by marking the circles in the special grid, as shown in the examples below. You may use any available space for scratchwork.

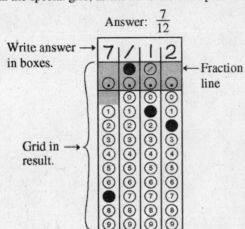

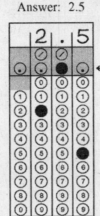

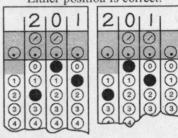

Answer: 201
Either position is correct.

**Note:** You may start your answers in any column, space permitting. Columns not needed should be left blank.

- Mark no more than one circle in any column.

- Because the answer sheet will be machine-scored, **you will receive credit only if the circles are filled in correctly.**

- Although not required, it is suggested that you write your answer in the boxes at the top of the columns to help you fill in the circles accurately.

- Some problems may have more than one correct answer. In such cases, grid only one answer.

- No question has a negative answer.

- **Mixed numbers** such as $3\frac{1}{2}$ must be gridded as

  3.5 or 7/2. (If ⬛3⬜1⬜/⬜2 is gridded, it will be

  interpreted as $\frac{31}{2}$, not $3\frac{1}{2}$.)

- **Decimal Answers:** If you obtain a decimal answer with more digits than the grid can accommodate, it may be either rounded or truncated, but it must fill the entire grid. For example, if you obtain an answer such as 0.6666..., you should record your result as .666 or .667. **A less accurate value such as .66 or .67 will be scored as incorrect.**

Acceptable ways to grid $\frac{2}{3}$ are:

---

9. What is the greatest three-digit integer that has a factor of 10 ?

10. A recipe for chili for 20 people requires 4 pounds of beans. At this rate, how many pounds of beans are required to make chili for 150 people?

**GO ON TO THE NEXT PAGE** ⇒

**11.** When the positive <u>even</u> integer $n$ is increased by 50 percent of itself, the result is between 10 and 20. What is one possible value of $n$ ?

**12.** The perimeter of a rectangular plot of land is 250 meters. If the length of one side of the plot is 40 meters, what is the area of the plot, in square meters?

**13.** A school ordered $600 worth of lightbulbs. Some of the lightbulbs cost $1 each and the others cost $2 each. If twice as many $1 bulbs as $2 bulbs were ordered, how many lightbulbs were ordered altogether?

**14.** If $4(x + y)(x - y) = 40$ and $x - y = 20$, what is the value of $x + y$ ?

**GO ON TO THE NEXT PAGE**

15. In a rectangular coordinate system, the center of a circle has coordinates (5, 12), and the circle touches the x-axis at one point only. What is the radius of the circle?

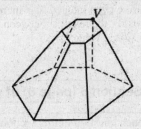

17. The three-dimensional figure above has two parallel bases and 18 edges. Line segments are to be drawn connecting vertex V with each of the other 11 vertices in the figure. How many of these segments will <u>not</u> lie on an edge of the figure?

### BRIDGETON VOTER REGISTRATION DATA

|  | Voting-Age Population | Number of Registered Voters |
|---|---|---|
| Men | 1,200 | 1,000 |
| Women | 1,300 | 1,200 |

16. The table above gives the voter registration data for the town of Bridgeton at the time of a recent election. In the election, 40 percent of the voting-age population actually voted. If the turnout for an election is defined to be the fraction

$$\frac{\text{number who actually voted}}{\text{number of registered voters}},$$

what was the turnout for this election?

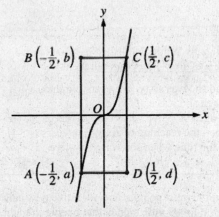

<u>Note</u>: Figure not drawn to scale.

18. In the figure above, ABCD is a rectangle. Points A and C lie on the graph of $y = px^3$, where p is a constant. If the area of ABCD is 4, what is the value of p?

# STOP

If you finish before time is called, you may check your work on this section only.
Do not turn to any other section in the test.

## SECTION 6
### Time — 25 minutes
### 35 Questions

**Turn to Section 6 (page 6) of your answer sheet to answer the questions in this section.**

**Directions:** For each question in this section, select the best answer from among the choices given and fill in the corresponding circle on the answer sheet.

The following sentences test correctness and effectiveness of expression. Part of each sentence or the entire sentence is underlined; beneath each sentence are five ways of phrasing the underlined material. Choice A repeats the original phrasing; the other four choices are different. If you think the original phrasing produces a better sentence than any of the alternatives, select choice A; if not, select one of the other choices.

In making your selection, follow the requirements of standard written English; that is, pay attention to grammar, choice of words, sentence construction, and punctuation. Your selection should result in the most effective sentence—clear and precise, without awkwardness or ambiguity.

EXAMPLE:

Laura Ingalls Wilder published her first book and she was sixty-five years old then.

(A) and she was sixty-five years old then
(B) when she was sixty-five
(C) at age sixty-five years old
(D) upon the reaching of sixty-five years
(E) at the time when she was sixty-five

Ⓐ ● Ⓒ Ⓓ Ⓔ

1. One of the most popular and attractive new cars <u>were available for so little money that people thought something was</u> wrong.

(A) were available for so little money that people thought something was
(B) was available for so little money that people thought something were
(C) was available for so little money that people thought something has gone
(D) was available for so little money that people thought something was
(E) was selling for very little money, so people thought of it as something was

2. The tornado ripped through the central part of town, toppling small buildings, uprooting trees, and <u>power lines were snapped</u>.

(A) power lines were snapped
(B) power lines snapping
(C) snapping power lines
(D) snapped power lines
(E) power lines snapped

3. As I entered the Pantheon, a building that has existed in Rome since ancient times, my brother <u>is turning to me to whisper</u> that the great rotunda of the Pantheon was a haven of peace and harmony.

(A) is turning to me to whisper
(B) turned to me and whispered
(C) turns to me and is whispering
(D) turns and also whispers to me
(E) would turn and whisper to me

4. No one is <u>more sorrier than me</u> that you missed the awards ceremony.

(A) more sorrier than me
(B) sorrier than I
(C) more sorry like myself
(D) as sorry like I am
(E) sorrier but me

5. Many people were alarmed by the Supreme Court ruling that gave judges discretionary power to determine <u>about closing trials</u> to the public.

(A) about closing trials
(B) whether he or she ought to close trials
(C) whether trials should be closed
(D) if he or she should close trials
(E) the closing of trials, if they wish

**GO ON TO THE NEXT PAGE** →

6. The mountain's summit having been reached, the weary climbers gazed down upon a scene of indescribable grandeur.

   (A) The mountain's summit having been reached
   (B) The summit of the mountain being reached
   (C) At the mountain's summit, when they reached it
   (D) When they reached the mountain's summit
   (E) When having reached the mountain's summit

7. Whether the ancient Egyptians actually sailed or did not to South America remains uncertain, but Heyerdahl's Ra II expedition demonstrated that they could have done so.

   (A) Whether the ancient Egyptians actually sailed or did not
   (B) Whether in actuality the ancient Egyptians sailed or did not
   (C) The actuality of the sailing by the ancient Egyptians
   (D) That the ancient Egyptians actually sailed
   (E) The ancient Egyptians, their actual sailing

8. In 1969 Baldwin High School defeated Ross Academy in the district's first televised quiz bowl game, even so, they did not win again until 1983.

   (A) game, even so, they
   (B) game, so they
   (C) game, they
   (D) game; as a result, it
   (E) game, but it

9. Isolated by the sea, the aboriginal peoples of Australia had developed a unique culture long before the arrival of Europeans.

   (A) had developed a unique culture
   (B) had a unique culture and it developed
   (C) having developed a unique culture
   (D) have a unique culture, it developed
   (E) have a unique culture; development was

10. Although criticized by a few for her daredevil aviation escapades, most people viewed Amelia Earhart as a skillful pilot.

    (A) most people viewed Amelia Earhart as a skillful pilot
    (B) most people viewed Amelia Earhart to be a skillful pilot
    (C) a skillful pilot was what most people viewed Amelia Earhart as
    (D) Amelia Earhart was viewed by most people as a skillful pilot
    (E) Amelia Earhart, a skillful pilot in the view of most people

11. Among the Inuit peoples of arctic Canada, poetry contests are held to settle conflicts that might otherwise be disruptive to families and communities.

    (A) that might otherwise be disruptive to families and communities
    (B) that otherwise, to families and communities, were disrupting them
    (C) and they are otherwise disruptive to families and communities
    (D) by which families and communities were otherwise being disrupted
    (E) whereby families and communities that might otherwise be disrupted are not

GO ON TO THE NEXT PAGE

The following sentences test your ability to recognize grammar and usage errors. Each sentence contains either a single error or no error at all. No sentence contains more than one error. The error, if there is one, is underlined and lettered. If the sentence contains an error, select the one underlined part that must be changed to make the sentence correct. If the sentence is correct, select choice E. In choosing answers, follow the requirements of standard written English.

EXAMPLE:

The other delegates and him immediately
     A                     B        C
accepted the resolution drafted by the
                               D
neutral states. No error
                    E

Ⓐ ● Ⓒ Ⓓ Ⓔ

12. Brand-name prescription drugs are often more
                                        A
    familiar to consumers than generic drugs, but the
              B
    latter are not nearly as expensive than brand-name
                  C                    D
    drugs. No error
           E

13. In 1508, the Spanish explorer Juan Ponce de Leon—
    A
    the same Ponce de Leon who later would seek
         B                          C
    the fountain of youth—landed on Puerto Rico

    accompanied by a small force. No error
        D                          E

14. Because they painted scenes of life as ordinary
    A
    people lived it, rather than scenes from myths,
           B           C
    many nineteenth-century American artists differed

    from earlier times. No error
        D              E

15. Few issues of public policy are as likely to provoke
                                A       B
    widespread interest as that involving possible
                            C
    danger to the health or safety of children. No error
        D                                       E

16. The young fish were very tiny, yet each of them ate
                    A                          B
    many times its own weight in solid food every day.
              C          D
    No error
    E

17. In the opinion of the lecturer, a background in the
    A                                B
    history of the Middle Ages is not a condition necessary

    in the enjoyment of medieval literature. No error
    C              D                          E

18. Driving less frequently is one way to save energy;
            A
    to turn off all appliances when they are not being
        B                        C
    used is another. No error
        D            E

19. After Gertrude Ederle had swam the English Channel,
                              A
    she was celebrated as the first woman ever
        B
    to accomplish the feat. No error
    C            D          E

GO ON TO THE NEXT PAGE ▷

**20.** When a government agency encouraged the use
      A

of high-grade recycled office paper, they helped
                          B

increase the availability of writing paper and
                 C

envelopes made from recycled paper. No error
              D                        E

**21.** Malaria, a disease which has been almost completely
                              A

eradicated in the United States, is still a threat
                              B

of travelers in some foreign countries. No error
    C          D                          E

**22.** If I am reading the editorial correct, the mayor is
      A                          B

deliberately avoiding any discussion of the tax-reform
              C

bill until after the November elections. No error
         D                                E

**23.** The Papago Indians of southern Arizona take

justifiable pride in their traditional craft of
            A      B

basket-weaving, an art that has brought them
                          C

fame throughout the Southwest. No error
         D                        E

**24.** The record left by fossils, the ancient remains of plants

and animals, provide scientists with their primary
              A                B

source of information about prehistoric life.
    C                  D

No error
    E

**25.** The exchange between the teacher and the student

promotes learning far different from that which
    A                  B

results as the student listens but does not participate.
        C                          D

No error
    E

**26.** Studying the language and culture of a foreign
      A

country is highly recommended to the tourist
                      B

who expect to learn from his or her vacation
        C              D

abroad. No error
            E

**27.** For we students, concern about impending
        A                          B

tuition hikes was even more acute than
                          C

apprehension about final exams. No error
            D                        E

**28.** The jury took offense at the prosecutor's mocking
              A

tone but could deny neither the accuracy of the
              B                C

charges or the seriousness of the crime. No error
            D                                E

**29.** Available through the school's guidance office

is a job directory and a list of job referral centers
    A

that provide information for students in need of
    B              C                  D

employment. No error
              E

**GO ON TO THE NEXT PAGE**

**Directions:** The following passage is an early draft of an essay. Some parts of the passage need to be rewritten.

Read the passage and select the best answers for the questions that follow. Some questions are about particular sentences or parts of sentences and ask you to improve sentence structure or word choice. Other questions ask you to consider organization and development. In choosing answers, follow the requirements of standard written English.

**Questions 30-35 are based on the following passage.**

(1) I have started to wonder if there is a skunk sharing my family's home. (2) Although I've never seen one in our yard in the daytime, several times recently, around midnight, I have sniffed that familiar odor through the open bedroom window. (3) While usually unable to locate the source of it, even on a moonlit night. (4) However, twice, I got to the window in time to glimpse an indistinct black-and-white bundle scooting across the yard, heading away from the front corner of the house. (5) Whatever it is, it seemed that the creature has a burrow under our front porch.

(6) Sometime, probably in daylight, when I've gathered my courage and put on a gas mask, maybe I'll crawl under there for the purpose of looking around visually. (7) But what if it really is a skunk? (8) I know that a skunk's Latin name is Mephitis mephitis, and that skunks should not be confused with polecats. (9) Getting in a skunk's way, these facts will not help you much. (10) Welcome to Aromaville! (11) Evicting a skunk is probably not a pleasant task.

(12) Maybe it's not all that important to know for sure if it's a skunk. (13) In fact, maybe the best solution would be if we simply moved away.

30. In context, which of the following is the best version of the underlined portion of sentence 3 (reproduced below)?

    *While usually unable to locate the source of it*, even on a moonlit night.

    (A) (As it is now)
    (B) Usually, however, I have been unable to locate its source
    (C) Usually, though, the source could not have been located
    (D) Having been unable, usually, to locate its source
    (E) Without being able to locate its source

31. Of the following, which is the best version of the underlined portion of sentence 5 below?

    *Whatever it is, it seemed that the creature has* a burrow under our front porch.

    (A) (As it is now)
    (B) In spite of what it is, it seems that the creature has
    (C) The creature, whatever it was, seemingly having
    (D) It would seem, whatever it is, that it would have
    (E) Whatever the creature is, it seems to have

32. In the first paragraph (sentences 1-5), the author is primarily

    (A) informing the reader about the behavior of skunks
    (B) providing examples to argue a point
    (C) ridiculing those who dislike skunks
    (D) relating a story about personal experiences
    (E) casting doubt on a common misconception

33. Of the following, which is the best way to revise and combine the underlined portions of sentences 8 and 9 (reproduced below)?

    *I know that a skunk's Latin name is* Mephitis mephitis, *and that skunks should not be confused with polecats. Getting in a skunk's way, these facts will not help you much.*

    (A) polecats, but getting in the way of a skunk
    (B) polecats, but if you get in a skunk's way
    (C) polecats; consequently, if you get in a skunk's way
    (D) polecats; then, to get in the way of a skunk
    (E) polecats: getting in a skunk's way

**GO ON TO THE NEXT PAGE**

**34.** Which of the following should be done with sentence 11 (reproduced below)?

*Evicting a skunk is probably not a pleasant task.*

(A) Insert the word "Definitely" at the beginning.
(B) Delete it; the point has already been made.
(C) Move it to the end of the essay as a summary statement.
(D) Move it to the end of paragraph 1 (after sentence 5).
(E) Move it to the beginning of the essay as an introduction.

**35.** The primary effect of the final paragraph (sentences 12 and 13) is to

(A) continue the essay's tone of playful humor
(B) summarize the ideas introduced in the preceding paragraph
(C) give an example to prove the point of the first paragraph
(D) use persuasion to change the reader's opinion
(E) explain contradictions within the essay

# STOP
**If you finish before time is called, you may check your work on this section only.**
**Do not turn to any other section in the test.**

723

## SECTION 7
### Time — 25 minutes
### 24 Questions

**Turn to Section 7 (page 6) of your answer sheet to answer the questions in this section.**

**Directions:** For each question in this section, select the best answer from among the choices given and fill in the corresponding circle on the answer sheet.

Each sentence below has one or two blanks, each blank indicating that something has been omitted. Beneath the sentence are five words or sets of words labeled A through E. Choose the word or set of words that, when inserted in the sentence, best fits the meaning of the sentence as a whole.

**Example:**

Hoping to ------- the dispute, negotiators proposed a compromise that they felt would be ------- to both labor and management.

(A) enforce . . useful
(B) end . . divisive
(C) overcome . . unattractive
(D) extend . . satisfactory
(E) resolve . . acceptable

Ⓐ Ⓑ Ⓒ Ⓓ ●

1. O'Leary tolerates worms and snakes but is ------- about insects: he has an exaggerated fear of them.

(A) agnostic    (B) eclectic    (C) empiric
(D) phobic    (E) quixotic

2. The challenge facing public health officials is to ------- an outbreak of disease and then ------- that school-children are immunized.

(A) foster . . provide
(B) predict . . allege
(C) sustain . . question
(D) effect . . ascertain
(E) anticipate . . ensure

3. Guests at the party found the general merriment infectious and were won over by the party's -------.

(A) presumption    (B) gaiety
(C) conspicuousness    (D) unexpectedness
(E) brevity

4. Demagogues do not deserve full blame for last summer's public hysteria: although they turned the mood to their political advantage, they did not actually ------- it.

(A) oppose    (B) subdue    (C) create
(D) postpone    (E) confirm

5. Orangutans are ------- apes: they typically conduct most of their lives up in the trees of tropical rain forests.

(A) indigenous    (B) transitory    (C) recessive
(D) pliant    (E) arboreal

6. Since establishing the Children's Defense Fund in 1973, Marian Wright Edelman has been an ------- advocate, steadfast and constant.

(A) unwitting    (B) unswerving    (C) inhibiting
(D) elusive    (E) antagonistic

7. The author ------- the last act of her play to appease those critics who ------- the work for its brevity.

(A) eliminated . . extolled
(B) condensed . . censured
(C) expanded . . disparaged
(D) intensified . . glorified
(E) rearranged . . endorsed

8. The editorial claimed that the gubernatorial candidate lacked worldly wisdom and that this ------- would likely be his undoing.

(A) naïveté    (B) furtiveness    (C) venality
(D) indecisiveness    (E) sarcasm

**GO ON TO THE NEXT PAGE**

7  7

Unauthorized copying or reuse of
any part of this page is illegal.

The passages below are followed by questions based on their content; questions following a pair of related passages may also be based on the relationship between the paired passages. Answer the questions on the basis of what is stated or implied in the passages and in any introductory material that may be provided.

**Questions 9-10 are based on the following passage.**

When the tide was in and the water rose up to within a foot of the lawn, we children boasted that we could fish out of our bedroom windows. This was not quite true. But
*Line* it was true that, from our front lawn, the house was full of
5 waves. When the tide was up and the sun was shining, the white front of the house was in movement with reflected waves. The tall windows became so solid in color and form, gold and blue, that the house seemed to be full of sea; until, of course, one turned round and saw the real
10 sea, so miraculously real that it startled.

9. What does the narrator mean by the comment "the house was full of waves" (lines 4-5) ?

   (A) The house was decorated with a nautical theme.
   (B) The children enjoyed drawing pictures of the sea.
   (C) The house mirrored the movements of the sea.
   (D) The basement of the house sometimes filled with water.
   (E) The house appeared as if it had been damaged by the sea.

10. In context, the tone of lines 5-10 ("When . . . startled") is best described as one of

    (A) awe and fear
    (B) mischief and curiosity
    (C) sadness and confusion
    (D) wonder and delight
    (E) uncertainty and impatience

**Questions 11-12 are based on the following passage.**

Recently excavated artifacts from Pakistan have inspired a reevaluation of one of the great early urban cultures—the enigmatic Indus Valley civilization, one of the four great
*Line* early Old World state-cultures, along with Mesopotamia,
5 Egypt, and China's Yellow River civilization. Much less is known about the Indus civilization than these other states because linguists have yet to decipher the Harappan script found on recovered objects. Attempting to understand these vanished people and their social structures, my colleagues
10 and I have drawn clues from the miscellaneous objects we uncover and sites we excavate. In this effort, the Harappan writings have not been totally useless; we have gleaned insights by examining the context of the writing's use.

11. A major assumption of the passage is that

    (A) the spot within an excavated site where an object is found is a clue to its social significance
    (B) it is a great help in understanding a civilization to be able to decode its language
    (C) there are similarities among the social structures of ancient urban civilizations
    (D) an effective archaeologist should learn the language of the civilization being studied
    (E) ancient languages are all very difficult to decipher

12. The author's tone in the final sentence is best described as

    (A) frustrated
    (B) resigned
    (C) ambivalent
    (D) somewhat encouraged
    (E) unshakably confident

GO ON TO THE NEXT PAGE

7 7

Unauthorized copying or reuse of
any part of this page is illegal.

**Questions 13-24 are based on the following passages.**

*These two passages, written in the 1990's, address the ways in which environmental concerns have been made public.*

**Passage 1**

There is nothing wrong with attempting to make the often difficult and complex findings of science available to a wider audience, but environmental popularizers often
Line present a one-sided picture and hide important scientific
5 disagreements on issues relevant to environmental quality. The zeal to draw firm conclusions from the results of scientific research frequently prompts speculative matters to be left out or presented with greater authority than they deserve. The partisanship implicit in these failures is most
10 often excused by the originality of the author's perspective on the subject or a passionate commitment to do good. How could one regret the "minor" confusions that might arise from such noble impulses?

But using one-sided and incomplete accounts of the state
15 of scientific knowledge has led to projections, predictions, and warnings that, not surprisingly, have been falsified by events. No one knows what the future holds. But reports that Lake Erie and the oceans would be dead by now were surely greatly exaggerated. The United States is wracked
20 neither by food riots nor a great epidemic of pesticide-induced cancers. Birds continue to sing in the mornings, and they do not have to face the rigors of either an ice age caused by humans or a global warming caused by the heat of increased energy production and consumption. With
25 what confidence should we look upon the projected horrors of global warming, rain forest destruction, or toxic waste, given the record of the past?

This failure of prophecy may be an intellectual weakness, yet prophecy continues because it provides the popularizers
30 with a profound rhetorical strength: it releases the power of fear. The central role of this sentiment in political rhetoric has long been understood. Arousing fear, though, is not always easy. Even as far back as Aristotle, it was observed that we fear things less the more distant they are. Hence
35 when Churchill sought to rouse the British, he brought the Germans to the beaches, landing grounds, fields, streets, and hills of "our island." So, too, to arouse fears the popularizers have to present pictures of imminent calamities that could befall their relatively comfortable and well-off
40 readers. Environmental disasters like endemic waterborne disease due to inadequate sewage treatment in faraway nations do not fit this category. The prospect of my getting skin cancer due to ozone depletion does. Without such immediacy, one could only arouse a sentiment like com-
45 passion, which is not as strong as fear.

**Passage 2**

Few ideas are more deeply entrenched in our political culture than that of impending ecological doom. Beginning in 1962, when Rachel Carson warned readers that pollution was a threat to all life on the planet, pessimistic appraisals
50 of the health of the environment have been issued with increasing urgency. And yet, thanks in large part to her warnings, a powerful political movement was born and a series of landmark environmental bills became law: the Clean Air Act (1970), the Clean Water Act (1972), and
55 the Endangered Species Act (1973). These laws and their equivalents in Western Europe, along with a vast array of private efforts, have been a stunning success. In both the United States and Europe, environmental trends are, for the most part, positive; and environmental regulations, far from
60 being burdensome and expensive, have proved to be strikingly effective, have cost less than was anticipated, and have made the economies of the countries that have put them into effect stronger, not weaker.

Nevertheless, the vocabulary of environmentalism has
65 continued to be dominated by images of futility, crisis, and decline. In 1988, Thomas Berry, an essayist popular among ecologists, wrote that "the planet cannot long endure present modes of human exploitation." In 1990, Gaylord Nelson, the former senator from Wisconsin who was a prime mover
70 behind the first Earth Day in 1970, said that environmental problems "are a greater threat to Earth's life-sustaining systems than a nuclear war." And in 1993 Vice President Al Gore said that the planet now was suffering "grave and perhaps irreparable damage." But, at least insofar as the
75 Western world is concerned, this line of thought is an anachronism, rendered obsolete by its own success. Nor are environmentalists the only people reluctant to acknowledge the good news; advocates at both ends of the political spectrum, each side for its own reasons, seem to have
80 tacitly agreed to play it down. The Left is afraid of the environmental good news because it undercuts stylish pessimism; the Right is afraid of the good news because it shows that government regulations might occasionally amount to something other than wickedness incarnate, and
85 actually produce benefits at an affordable cost.

This is a bad bargain—for liberals especially. Their philosophy is under siege on many fronts—crime, welfare, medical care, and education, among others. So why not trumpet the astonishing, and continuing, record of success
90 in environmental protection?

**13.** In line 14, "state" most nearly means

(A) rank
(B) excitement
(C) territory
(D) government
(E) condition

GO ON TO THE NEXT PAGE

7 7

Unauthorized copying or reuse of
any part of this page is illegal.

**14.** The author of Passage 1 indicates that "food riots" (line 20) and "pesticide-induced cancers" (lines 20-21) are

(A) problems the nation will ultimately encounter
(B) problems facing underdeveloped areas of the world
(C) among the predictions of environmental popularizers
(D) among the consequences of global warming
(E) potential results of the pollution of lakes and oceans

**15.** The term "rigors" in line 22 refers to the

(A) efforts needed for environmental cleanup
(B) stringent regulations put in place since 1970
(C) moralistic attitudes of many environmental popularizers
(D) projected consequences of environmental decline
(E) ability of nature to recover from environmental abuse

**16.** The author of Passage 1 uses the example in lines 42-43 ("The prospect . . . does") to

(A) describe a personal experience
(B) imply that the subject should not be frightening
(C) elicit sympathy from the reader
(D) demonstrate a psychological fact
(E) emphasize the prevalence of a crisis

**17.** The first paragraph of Passage 2 (lines 46-63) presents

(A) an elaborate speculation
(B) a historical summary
(C) a list of sources
(D) an introductory aside
(E) a scientific theory

**18.** In Passage 2, the phrase "rendered . . . success" (line 76) indicates that

(A) the desires of environmentalists have changed over the years
(B) the success of the environmental movement has frightened conservative politicians
(C) the accomplishments of the environmental movement have made its public pronouncements irrelevant
(D) environmentalists often appear old-fashioned in a world primarily concerned with technology
(E) environmentalism plays on the political concerns of both liberals and conservatives

**19.** The phrase "wickedness incarnate" (line 84) is used to

(A) cast aspersions on bureaucratic ineptitude
(B) parody the language used by people with certain political leanings
(C) convey humorously a deep longing of the author
(D) rail against blatant polluters of the environment
(E) suggest the quasi-religious underpinnings of environmentalism

**20.** The attitudes toward environmentalism of the authors of Passage 1 and Passage 2, respectively, are

(A) outrage and resentful disappointment
(B) skepticism and qualified admiration
(C) indifference and urgent concern
(D) alarm and grudging acceptance
(E) open-mindedness and staunch advocacy

**21.** What would the author of Passage 2 most likely say about the sort of reports mentioned in lines 17-19 of Passage 1 ?

(A) They were unethical attempts to manipulate public opinion.
(B) They reflected the scientific uncertainty of their era.
(C) They seem quite naïve in retrospect.
(D) They served a purpose in their time.
(E) They are needed today more than ever.

**22.** The author of Passage 1 would most likely argue that the "line of thought" (line 75) illustrated in Passage 2 was

(A) once original but is now trite
(B) once wholly based on science but is now driven by politics
(C) in no way meant to be taken literally
(D) of no significance to faraway nations
(E) of dubious validity from the beginning

GO ON TO THE NEXT PAGE

23. How would the author of Passage 1 be most likely to answer the question posed at the end of Passage 2 ?

(A) Because good news is less of a stimulus to action than are dire warnings

(B) Because environmentalists fear alienating either the Left or the Right

(C) Because environmentalists themselves are divided about whether their task has been accomplished

(D) Because boasting is still considered inappropriate by the liberal elite

(E) Because laypersons lack the training to evaluate the environmental record

24. The authors of Passage 1 and Passage 2 agree that

(A) the state of the environment continues to worsen

(B) the environmental movement lacks political influence

(C) most of the information citizens receive about the environment is overly technical

(D) spokespeople for the environmental movement are not sufficiently knowledgeable

(E) the environmental movement employs exaggerated rhetoric

# STOP

**If you finish before time is called, you may check your work on this section only.**
**Do not turn to any other section in the test.**

**SECTION 8**
Time — 20 minutes
16 Questions

**Turn to Section 8 (page 7) of your answer sheet to answer the questions in this section.**

**Directions:** For this section, solve each problem and decide which is the best of the choices given. Fill in the corresponding circle on the answer sheet. You may use any available space for scratchwork.

Notes

1. The use of a calculator is permitted.
2. All numbers used are real numbers.
3. Figures that accompany problems in this test are intended to provide information useful in solving the problems. They are drawn as accurately as possible EXCEPT when it is stated in a specific problem that the figure is not drawn to scale. All figures lie in a plane unless otherwise indicated.
4. Unless otherwise specified, the domain of any function $f$ is assumed to be the set of all real numbers $x$ for which $f(x)$ is a real number.

Reference Information

$A = \pi r^2$
$C = 2\pi r$

$A = \ell w$

$A = \frac{1}{2}bh$

$V = \ell wh$

$V = \pi r^2 h$

$c^2 = a^2 + b^2$

**Special Right Triangles**

The number of degrees of arc in a circle is 360.
The sum of the measures in degrees of the angles of a triangle is 180.

---

1. If $3(n - 4) = 18$, what is the value of $n$ ?

(A) $\dfrac{14}{3}$

(B) $\dfrac{22}{3}$

(C) 6

(D) 10

(E) 22

---

2. For a class ring, each senior can choose from 4 types of stones and 3 types of metals. How many combinations of a stone and a metal are there?

(A) 7
(B) 8
(C) 10
(D) 12
(E) 16

---

**GO ON TO THE NEXT PAGE**

The sum of $3a$ and the square root of $b$ is equal to the square of the sum of $a$ and $b$.

3. Which of the following is an expression for the statement above?

(A) $3a + b^2 = \sqrt{a + b}$

(B) $3a + \sqrt{b} = (a + b)^2$

(C) $3a + \sqrt{b} = a^2 + b^2$

(D) $\sqrt{3a + b} = a^2 + b^2$

(E) $\sqrt{3a} + \sqrt{b} = (a + b)^2$

4. Kerry has a cordless telephone receiver that can operate within a range of 1,000 feet from the telephone's base. Kerry takes the receiver from the base and walks 800 feet due north. From that point she walks due east and stops at the maximum range of the receiver. In which of the following directions can Kerry walk and still be within the range of the receiver?

 I. Due north
 II. Due south
 III. Due west

(A) II only
(B) III only
(C) I and II
(D) I and III
(E) II and III

5. If $\dfrac{x}{4} = \dfrac{2x}{a}$ and $x \neq 0$, what is the value of $a$ ?

(A) 8

(B) 4

(C) 2

(D) $\dfrac{1}{2}$

(E) $\dfrac{1}{4}$

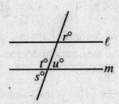

Note: Figure not drawn to scale.

6. In the figure above, $\ell \parallel m$ and $r = 50$. What is the value of $s + t + u$ ?

(A) 230
(B) 240
(C) 250
(D) 270
(E) 310

**GO ON TO THE NEXT PAGE** →

7. In the $xy$-coordinate plane, line $\ell$ is perpendicular to the $y$-axis and passes through the point $(5, -3)$. Which of the following is an equation of line $\ell$ ?

(A) $x = 0$
(B) $x = 5$
(C) $y = -3$
(D) $y + 3 = x + 5$
(E) $y - 3 = x + 5$

8. The total daily profit $p$, in dollars, from producing and selling $x$ units of a certain product is given by the function $p(x) = 17x - (10x + b)$, where $b$ is a constant. If 300 units were produced and sold yesterday for a total profit of $1,900, what is the value of $b$ ?

(A) $-200$
(B) $-100$
(C) $\phantom{0}0$
(D) $\phantom{0}100$
(E) $\phantom{0}200$

9. The number that results when an integer is multiplied by itself CANNOT end in which of the following digits?

(A) 1
(B) 4
(C) 5
(D) 6
(E) 8

10. A bag contains only red marbles, blue marbles, and yellow marbles. The probability of randomly selecting a red marble from this bag is $\dfrac{1}{4}$, and the probability of randomly selecting a blue marble is $\dfrac{1}{6}$. Which of the following could be the total number of marbles in the bag?

(A) 10
(B) 12
(C) 18
(D) 20
(E) 30

**GO ON TO THE NEXT PAGE**

11. When the sum of a list of prices is divided by the average (arithmetic mean) of the prices, the result is $k$. What does $k$ represent?

   (A) The sum of the prices
   (B) Half of the sum of the prices
   (C) The average of the prices
   (D) The number of prices
   (E) Half of the number of prices

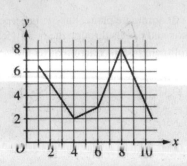

13. The graph of $y = g(x)$ is shown above. If $g(2) = k$, which of the following could be the value of $g(k)$ ?

   (A) 2
   (B) 2.5
   (C) 3
   (D) 3.5
   (E) 5

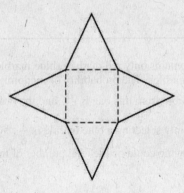

12. If the area of the square in the figure above is 81 and the perimeter of each of the 4 triangles is 30, what is the perimeter of the figure outlined by the solid line?

   (A) 36
   (B) 72
   (C) 80
   (D) 84
   (E) 120

14. If $0 \leq x \leq 8$ and $-1 \leq y \leq 3$, which of the following gives the set of all possible values of $xy$ ?

   (A) $xy = 4$
   (B) $0 \leq xy \leq 24$
   (C) $-1 \leq xy \leq 11$
   (D) $-1 \leq xy \leq 24$
   (E) $-8 \leq xy \leq 24$

**GO ON TO THE NEXT PAGE**

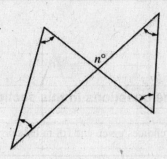

**15.** In the figure above, what is the sum, in terms of $n$, of the degree measures of the four angles marked with arrows?

(A) $n$
(B) $2n$
(C) $180 - n$
(D) $360 - n$
(E) $360 - 2n$

**16.** After the first term, each term in a sequence is 3 greater than $\frac{1}{3}$ of the preceding term. If $t$ is the first term of the sequence and $t \neq 0$, what is the ratio of the second term to the first term?

(A) $\dfrac{t + 9}{3}$

(B) $\dfrac{t + 3}{3}$

(C) $\dfrac{t + 9}{3t}$

(D) $\dfrac{t + 3}{3t}$

(E) $\dfrac{9 - 2t}{3}$

# STOP

**If you finish before time is called, you may check your work on this section only.**
**Do not turn to any other section in the test.**

733

## SECTION 9
**Time — 20 minutes**
**19 Questions**

**Turn to Section 9 (page 7) of your answer sheet to answer the questions in this section.**

**Directions:** For each question in this section, select the best answer from among the choices given and fill in the corresponding circle on the answer sheet.

Each sentence below has one or two blanks, each blank indicating that something has been omitted. Beneath the sentence are five words or sets of words labeled A through E. Choose the word or set of words that, when inserted in the sentence, <u>best</u> fits the meaning of the sentence as a whole.

**Example:**

Hoping to ------- the dispute, negotiators proposed a compromise that they felt would be ------- to both labor and management.

(A) enforce . . useful
(B) end . . divisive
(C) overcome . . unattractive
(D) extend . . satisfactory
(E) resolve . . acceptable     Ⓐ Ⓑ Ⓒ Ⓓ ●

1. In the 1960's Americans ------- Jean Toomer's 1923 book *Cane* when an interest in Black culture ------- many of them to read the classics of Black fiction.

   (A) neglected . . coerced
   (B) rediscovered . . inspired
   (C) limited . . required
   (D) collected . . allowed
   (E) circulated . . disinclined

2. In addition to ------- stacks of résumés and references, some employers want to ------- the hiring process by employing graphologists to study applicants' handwriting for character analysis.

   (A) evaluating . . supplement
   (B) envisioning . . circumvent
   (C) ignoring . . depersonalize
   (D) ameliorating . . revisit
   (E) condoning . . belabor

3. Tame koala bears handled by tourists are -------, but wild koalas are hard to control and typically require two people to hold them.

   (A) mischievous     (B) gluttonous     (C) supple
   (D) adroit     (E) docile

4. Ms. Rivers gave a performance of noteworthy -------: her piano repertoire ranged from classical music to jazz.

   (A) intensity     (B) precision     (C) scope
   (D) polish     (E) duration

5. The skepticism of some ancient philosophers ------- and helps to elucidate varieties of nihilism that appeared in the early nineteenth century.

   (A) suppresses     (B) disseminates
   (C) undermines     (D) confounds
   (E) foreshadows

6. Some critics of congressional proceedings contend that important debates on issues are marred by a ------- of denunciations and accusations that precludes ------- discourse.

   (A) repertory . . expendable
   (B) paucity . . meaningful
   (C) barrage . . libelous
   (D) rehash . . repetitive
   (E) cacophony . . orderly

**GO ON TO THE NEXT PAGE** ▷

The passage below is followed by questions based on its content. Answer the questions on the basis of what is <u>stated</u> or <u>implied</u> in the passage and in any introductory material that may be provided.

**Questions 7-19 are based on the following passage.**

*Frederick Douglass (1817-1895), who escaped from slavery, became an author and publisher and was internationally known for his instrumental role in the abolitionist movement.*

In spite of the ridicule that various newspapers aimed at the women's movement, Frederick Douglass continued to lend it his active support. Indeed, few women's rights conventions were held during the 1850's at which Douglass
Line
5   was not a featured speaker and whose proceedings were not fully reported in his paper. Invariably, the notice would be accompanied by an editorial comment hailing the meeting and expressing the editor's hope that it "will have a powerful effect on the public's mind." In 1853, when Douglass
10  was considering changing the name of his newspaper, he rejected the proposed title, *The Brotherhood*, because it "implied the exclusion of the sisterhood." He called it *Frederick Douglass' Paper*, and underneath the title were the words "All Rights For All!"
15  Because women were not permitted to speak at mass meetings of state temperance associations,[1] women in New York formed the Woman's State Temperance Society, with Elizabeth Cady Stanton as president. Douglass supported the society but took issue with the move led by secretary
20  Amelia Bloomer to limit to women the right to hold its offices. He aligned himself with Stanton and Susan B. Anthony in opposing this as a violation of "the principle of human equality"—a violation, in short, of men's rights. Douglass felt that by excluding men from office the society
25  would lose supporters in the battle against those in the temperance movement who wished to deny women equal rights. How, he asked, could women effectively contend for equality in the movement when they denied it to men? In June 1853, the society accepted the logic of this position
30  and admitted men to office.
Douglass learned much from women with whom he associated at the national and state women's rights conventions. At one time, he had entertained serious doubts about wives being given the right to share equally with their
35  husbands the disposition of property, since "the husband labors hard" while the wife might not be earning money. But his discussions with pioneers of the women's rights movement convinced him that even though wives were not paid for their domestic labors, their work was as important
40  to the family as that of their husbands. Once convinced, he acted. He wrote the call for the 1853 convention in Rochester, New York, which demanded not only that women be paid equally with men for their work, but also that women, including married women, have equal rights
45  with men in the ownership and disposition of property. In his newspaper that year, Douglass urged state legislation calling for passage of a law requiring equality in "the holding, and division of real and personal property."

On one issue, however, Douglass refused to budge.
50  He was critical of women's rights leaders who addressed audiences from which Black people were barred. His particular target was Lucy Stone. Douglass often praised this abolitionist and veteran fighter for equal rights for women, but he criticized her for not having canceled a
55  lecture in 1853 at Philadelphia's Music Hall when she discovered that Black people would be excluded. Later, he was more severe when he learned that she had invited Senator Stephen A. Douglas of Illinois, one of the architects of the infamous Fugitive Slave Act of 1850,[2] to join
60  the women who were to meet in Chicago in 1859 to publicize the women's rights cause. Frederick Douglass bluntly accused Stone of willingness to advance women's rights on the back of "the defenceless slave woman" who "has also to bear the ten thousand wrongs of slavery in addition to
65  the common wrongs of woman."
Douglass' disputes with some of the women's rights leaders went beyond the question of their appearance before segregated audiences. Women like Stanton and Anthony were close to abolitionist William Lloyd Garrison.
70  When Douglass split with Garrison over the latter's reliance on words and "moral suasion" as the major route to abolition, as well as over Garrison's opposition to antislavery political action, some women's rights leaders grew cool toward Douglass.
75  Although Susan B. Anthony had sided with Garrison, she solicited Douglass' support in her campaign against capital punishment. She circulated a petition for a meeting in 1858 to protest an impending execution and to support a law making life imprisonment the punishment for capital
80  crimes. Long an opponent of capital punishment, Douglass signed the petition, prepared a set of resolutions on the issue, and agreed to take over for the scheduled chair, who had been intimidated by mob violence. Douglass' conduct won over even those women who had allied themselves
85  with Anthony and Garrison.
Thus, on the eve of the Civil War, Douglass' relationship with the women's movement was once again cordial. Although this situation was to change after the war, Douglass' influence had helped the women's rights
90  movement become more sensitive to the issue of prejudice against Black Americans.

[1] Temperance associations were groups that advocated laws to control the use of alcoholic beverages.

[2] The Fugitive Slave Act of 1850 authorized slaveholders to reclaim runaway slaves.

**GO ON TO THE NEXT PAGE**

7. The passage provides the most information about Douglass'

(A) loyalty to old friends
(B) refusal to change old ideas
(C) fluent writing style
(D) political activism
(E) tactful rhetoric

8. In context, the word "hailing" (line 7) most nearly means

(A) pouring down on
(B) audibly greeting
(C) summoning
(D) originating
(E) praising

9. The discussion of the naming of Douglass' newspaper (lines 9-14) suggests that Douglass was

(A) very effective at persuading others to adopt his point of view
(B) more committed to women's rights than he was to other reform movements
(C) concerned that his paper not receive the same kind of ridicule that women's rights publications had
(D) a reformer who recognized the similarity among the goals of different causes
(E) eager to publicize the recent successes of the women's rights movement

10. The passage suggests that Stanton and Anthony prevailed against Bloomer (lines 21-30) because their position

(A) defied the male status quo
(B) asserted women's political rights
(C) opposed Douglass' ideas
(D) was recognized as being politically wise
(E) had financial consequences

11. The discussion of Douglass' position on property rights for women (lines 33-48) suggests that Douglass

(A) was extremely adept at political negotiation
(B) was flexible enough to change his views
(C) sided with women's rights leaders on this issue so that they would support him on abolition
(D) believed that causes should be tackled one at a time
(E) believed that state laws could be easily changed

12. In context, the phrase "disposition of" (line 45) most nearly means

(A) exploration of
(B) safeguarding of
(C) control over
(D) characteristics of
(E) payment for

13. In lines 49-65, the passage mainly suggests which of the following about Lucy Stone?

(A) She allowed one of the two causes she endorsed to supersede the other.
(B) Her courageous actions consistently won Frederick Douglass' respect.
(C) She was willing to compromise for the sake of abolition.
(D) She and Stephen Douglas had little in common politically.
(E) Her political inexperience contributed to certain errors in judgment.

14. Douglass probably believed that using Stephen A. Douglas to publicize women's rights amounted to

(A) allowing men to influence women's associations
(B) supporting the repeal of the Fugitive Slave Act of 1850
(C) contradicting the philosophy of temperance
(D) inadvertently sacrificing the gains that women had made
(E) tacitly exploiting Black women who were slaves

15. Douglass probably regarded the technique of "moral suasion" (line 71) as

(A) suitable for only the capital-punishment cause
(B) preferable to lengthy political debate
(C) less desirable than direct action
(D) too closely associated with the temperance movement
(E) too subtle for most mass meetings

16. Women's rights leaders most likely "grew cool toward Douglass" (lines 73-74) because they

(A) were experiencing dissension among their ranks
(B) preferred Garrison's political approach
(C) strongly favored the use of civil disobedience
(D) felt that Douglass had not been contributing actively to their movement
(E) realized that Douglass had stopped publicizing their concerns

**GO ON TO THE NEXT PAGE**

17. As presented in the passage, Douglass' views coincided most consistently with those of

    (A) Stephen A. Douglas
    (B) William Lloyd Garrison
    (C) Amelia Bloomer
    (D) Lucy Stone
    (E) Susan B. Anthony

18. The author apparently believes which of the following about the interaction between the abolitionist and the women's rights movements?

    (A) It helped both groups broaden their perspectives in spite of frequent friction between them.
    (B) It seemed to many to be productive but actually caused both groups to make their goals too general.
    (C) It was natural, since both groups got their start at the same time.
    (D) It was rewarding for members of both groups but made both less popular with the public.
    (E) It was politically expedient for both groups in spite of their reluctance to work together.

19. According to the passage, Douglass most consistently opposed

    (A) using the press to criticize the women's and abolitionist movements
    (B) allowing men to hold office in women's state temperance associations
    (C) pay scales that were higher for men than for women
    (D) neglecting the rights of other groups while furthering the rights of women
    (E) property laws that gave men more rights than they gave women

# STOP

**If you finish before time is called, you may check your work on this section only.
Do not turn to any other section in the test.**

**10**  **10**

Unauthorized copying or reuse of
any part of this page is illegal.

## SECTION 10

Time — 10 minutes
14 Questions

---

**Turn to Section 10 (page 7) of your answer sheet to answer the questions in this section.**

---

**Directions:** For each question in this section, select the best answer from among the choices given and fill in the corresponding circle on the answer sheet.

---

The following sentences test correctness and effectiveness of expression. Part of each sentence or the entire sentence is underlined; beneath each sentence are five ways of phrasing the underlined material. Choice A repeats the original phrasing; the other four choices are different. If you think the original phrasing produces a better sentence than any of the alternatives, select choice A; if not, select one of the other choices.

In making your selection, follow the requirements of standard written English; that is, pay attention to grammar, choice of words, sentence construction, and punctuation. Your selection should result in the most effective sentence—clear and precise, without awkwardness or ambiguity.

EXAMPLE:

Laura Ingalls Wilder published her first book
and she was sixty-five years old then.

(A) and she was sixty-five years old then
(B) when she was sixty-five
(C) at age sixty-five years old
(D) upon the reaching of sixty-five years
(E) at the time when she was sixty-five

1. For as many as twenty years and more Joseph Conrad lived the life of a sailor.

 (A) For as many as twenty years and more
 (B) For not much more than about twenty years
 (C) For a little over twenty years and more
 (D) For twenty years and then some
 (E) For more than twenty years

2. The duties of a firefighter are often as dangerous as a police officer.

 (A) as a police officer
 (B) as those of a police officer
 (C) like a police officer
 (D) such as a police officer
 (E) like a police officer's

3. Pearl Buck, one of the most popular writers of her day, winning the Nobel Prize in Literature in 1938 for her novels about China.

 (A) day, winning the Nobel Prize in Literature in 1938 for her novels about China
 (B) day, winning the Nobel Prize in Literature, which she won in 1938 for her novels about China
 (C) day, and she won the Nobel Prize in Literature in 1938 for her novels about China
 (D) day, won the Nobel Prize in Literature in 1938 for her novels about China
 (E) day, her novels about China bringing her the Nobel Prize in Literature in 1938

4. The first world computer chess championship, held in Stockholm, was won by a Russian computer program called Kaissa, and there were four Kaissa victories and no defeats.

 (A) Kaissa, and there were four Kaissa victories and no defeats
 (B) Kaissa, which had four victories and no defeats
 (C) Kaissa, having four victories and with no defeats
 (D) Kaissa, which was victorious four times and no defeats
 (E) Kaissa; it was won by four victories and no defeats

**GO ON TO THE NEXT PAGE** ▷

**10**

Unauthorized copying or reuse of
any part of this page is illegal.

**10**

5. Anyone who <u>has high motivation or is reasonably
intelligent</u> can learn to play a competent game of chess.

   (A) has high motivation or is reasonably intelligent
   (B) has either high motivation or else intelligence in
   reasonable amounts
   (C) is highly motivated or who has reasonable
   intelligence instead
   (D) is highly motivated or reasonably intelligent
   (E) has high motivation or else reasonable amounts of
   intelligence

6. Although Jonathan is very much interested in
Mexican culture, <u>he does not speak Spanish
and has never visited Mexico.</u>

   (A) he does not speak Spanish and has never
   visited Mexico
   (B) it is without being able to speak Spanish
   or having visited Mexico
   (C) he does not speak Spanish and has never
   visited there
   (D) he does not speak Spanish nor has he ever
   visited there
   (E) it is without speaking Spanish nor having
   visited there

7. <u>The more you eat of convenience foods,</u> the more our
taste buds will prefer chemical flavors to natural ones.

   (A) The more you eat of convenience foods
   (B) The more we eat convenience foods
   (C) The more convenience foods are eaten
   (D) As the use of convenience foods increases
   (E) As people eat more convenience foods

8. <u>Having Florence Nightingale as their leader</u> and a
growing awareness of the need for cleanliness helped
to bring about the establishment of standards of
hygiene in hospitals.

   (A) Having Florence Nightingale as their leader
   (B) Having the leadership of Florence Nightingale's
   (C) Florence Nightingale as their leader
   (D) To be led by Florence Nightingale
   (E) The leadership of Florence Nightingale

9. An expedition was sent in 1949 to check <u>a Turkish
villager's reporting</u> he had seen the remains of Noah's
ark on Mount Ararat.

   (A) a Turkish villager's reporting
   (B) the report of a Turkish villager that
   (C) the reporting of a Turkish villager
   (D) that a Turkish villager who reported
   (E) the Turkish villager report saying

10. Many communities in my state are forming
neighborhood watch <u>programs, for it will deter</u>
criminals.

   (A) programs, for it will deter
   (B) programs, in which it will deter
   (C) programs that will deter
   (D) programs for the deterrence of
   (E) programs being able to deter

11. Friends of Dreiser reported that he was fired from his
first job <u>for the reason that his news stories were
sympathetic always for the poor.</u>

   (A) for the reason that his news stories were
   sympathetic always for the poor
   (B) since his news stories for the poor that were
   always sympathetic
   (C) because his sympathy to the poor was always in
   his news stories
   (D) the fact being that his news stories were always
   sympathetic about the poor
   (E) because his news stories were always sympathetic
   to the poor

12. An article suggests that *The Great Gatsby* was not
read during the <u>1930's, the reason was that the novel
described a lifestyle made extinct and frivolous</u> by
the current Great Depression.

   (A) 1930's, the reason was that the novel described
   a lifestyle made extinct and frivolous
   (B) 1930's, it is describing a lifestyle that was made
   an extinct and frivolous one
   (C) 1930's; describing a lifestyle made extinct and
   frivolous
   (D) 1930's because the novel described a lifestyle
   made extinct and frivolous
   (E) 1930's because its description had been of
   an extinct and frivolous lifestyle, caused by

**GO ON TO THE NEXT PAGE**

13. Computers compiling statistics for scientists have supplied a deluge of information, and it has changed the way that research is conducted.

   (A)  a deluge of information, and it has
   (B)  a great deal of information, and that is
   (C)  so much information; it is, therefore
   (D)  so much information that they have
   (E)  so much information, which they have been

14. Of all the states represented at the conference, the governor of Missouri was the only one to present plans for enforcing the new regulations.

   (A)  the governor of Missouri was the only one to present
   (B)  making the governor from Missouri the only one to present
   (C)  Missouri's governor only presented
   (D)  Missouri's governor presented the only
   (E)  Missouri was the only one whose governor presented

# STOP

**If you finish before time is called, you may check your work on this section only.**
**Do not turn to any other section in the test.**

# Correct Answers and Difficulty Levels
## SAT Practice Test #6

## CRITICAL READING

### Section 3
#### Multiple-Choice Questions

| Correct Answer | Difficulty Level | Correct Answer | Difficulty Level |
|---|---|---|---|
| 1 D | M | 13 D | M |
| 2 A | M | 14 C | M |
| 3 B | M | 15 D | E |
| 4 A | M | 16 A | M |
| 5 A | H | 17 A | H |
| 6 C | M | 18 E | M |
| 7 D | H | 19 D | M |
| 8 A | H | 20 D | M |
| 9 D | H | 21 D | M |
| 10 B | E | 22 A | M |
| 11 C | M | 23 E | E |
| 12 A | E | 24 B | M |

Number correct _____

Number incorrect _____

### Section 7
#### Multiple-Choice Questions

| Correct Answer | Difficulty Level | Correct Answer | Difficulty Level |
|---|---|---|---|
| 1 D | E | 13 E | M |
| 2 E | E | 14 E | M |
| 3 B | M | 15 D | M |
| 4 C | M | 16 D | H |
| 5 E | M | 17 B | M |
| 6 B | M | 18 C | M |
| 7 C | M | 19 B | H |
| 8 A | M | 20 D | M |
| 9 C | E | 21 D | H |
| 10 D | M | 22 E | H |
| 11 B | M | 23 A | M |
| 12 D | E | 24 E | M |

Number correct _____

Number incorrect _____

### Section 9
#### Multiple-Choice Questions

| Correct Answer | Difficulty Level | Correct Answer | Difficulty Level |
|---|---|---|---|
| 1 B | E | 11 B | M |
| 2 A | E | 12 C | E |
| 3 E | M | 13 A | M |
| 4 C | M | 14 E | M |
| 5 E | H | 15 C | M |
| 6 E | H | 16 B | M |
| 7 D | E | 17 E | M |
| 8 E | M | 18 A | M |
| 9 D | M | 19 D | M |
| 10 D | M | | |

Number correct _____

Number incorrect _____

## MATHEMATICS

### Section 2
#### Multiple-Choice Questions

| Correct Answer | Difficulty Level | Correct Answer | Difficulty Level |
|---|---|---|---|
| 1 C | E | 11 B | M |
| 2 D | E | 12 D | M |
| 3 C | E | 13 E | M |
| 4 A | E | 14 C | M |
| 5 C | E | 15 A | M |
| 6 D | M | 16 B | M |
| 7 B | E | 17 C | M |
| 8 A | M | 18 B | H |
| 9 A | M | 19 A | H |
| 10 E | M | 20 E | H |

Number correct _____

Number incorrect _____

### Section 4
#### Multiple-Choice Questions

| Correct Answer | Difficulty Level |
|---|---|
| 1 E | E |
| 2 A | E |
| 3 B | E |
| 4 E | M |
| 5 D | M |
| 6 A | M |
| 7 B | M |
| 8 B | H |

#### Student-Produced Response Questions

| Correct Answer | Difficulty Level |
|---|---|
| 9 990 | M |
| 10 30 | E |
| 11 8,10, 12 | M |
| 12 3400 | M |
| 13 450 | M |
| 14 1/2, .5 | M |
| 15 12 | M |
| 16 5/11, .454, .455 | M |
| 17 8 | H |
| 18 16 | H |

Number correct (9-18) _____

Number incorrect _____

### Section 8
#### Multiple-Choice Questions

| Correct Answer | Difficulty Level | Correct Answer | Difficulty Level |
|---|---|---|---|
| 1 D | E | 9 E | M |
| 2 D | E | 10 B | M |
| 3 B | E | 11 D | M |
| 4 E | E | 12 D | M |
| 5 A | E | 13 B | M |
| 6 A | M | 14 E | H |
| 7 C | M | 15 B | H |
| 8 E | M | 16 C | H |

Number correct _____

Number incorrect _____

## WRITING

### Essay

Essay Score* (0-6) _____

### Section 6
#### Multiple-Choice Questions

| Correct Answer | Difficulty Level | Correct Answer | Difficulty Level |
|---|---|---|---|
| 1 D | E | 19 A | E |
| 2 C | E | 20 B | E |
| 3 B | M | 21 C | M |
| 4 C | M | 22 B | M |
| 5 C | E | 23 B | E |
| 6 D | E | 24 A | M |
| 7 D | M | 25 C | M |
| 8 E | M | 26 C | M |
| 9 A | M | 27 A | E |
| 10 A | M | 28 D | M |
| 11 A | E | 29 A | M |
| 12 D | E | 30 B | M |
| 13 E | E | 31 E | E |
| 14 D | E | 32 D | M |
| 15 C | M | 33 B | E |
| 16 E | E | 34 B | M |
| 17 C | E | 35 A | M |
| 18 B | E | | |

Number correct _____

Number incorrect _____

### Section 10
#### Multiple-Choice Questions

| Correct Answer | Difficulty Level |
|---|---|
| 1 E | E |
| 2 B | E |
| 3 D | E |
| 4 B | E |
| 5 D | E |
| 6 A | E |
| 7 B | M |
| 8 E | M |
| 9 B | M |
| 10 C | E |
| 11 E | M |
| 12 D | M |
| 13 D | M |
| 14 E | M |

Number correct _____

Number incorrect _____

**NOTE:** Difficulty levels are E (easy), M (medium), and H (hard).

* To score your essay, use the SAT scoring guide in Chapter 9 and the free sample essays available online at www.collegeboard.org/satonlinecourse. On this practice test, your essay score should range from 0 to 6. (Keep in mind that on the actual SAT, your essay will be read by two readers and you will receive a score of 0 to 12 on your score report.)

# The SAT Scoring Process

**Scoring.** The computer compares the circle filled in for each question with the correct response. Each correct answer receives one point; omitted questions do not affect your score. For each wrong answer to a multiple-choice question, one-fourth of a point is subtracted to correct for random guessing. The SAT critical reading section has 67 questions. If, for example, a student has 44 right, 20 wrong, and 3 omitted, the resulting raw score is determined as follows:

$$44 \text{ right} - \frac{20 \text{ wrong}}{4} = 44 - 5 = 39 \text{ raw score points}$$

Obtaining raw scores frequently involves the rounding of fractions to the nearest whole number. For example, a raw score of 39.25 is rounded to 39, the nearest whole number. A raw score of 39.50 is rounded upward to 40. **For the WRITING SECTION**, your essay raw score counts approximately 30% and your multiple-choice raw score counts approximately 70%.

**Converting to reported scaled score.** Raw scores are then placed on the College Board scale of 200 to 800 through a process that adjusts scores to account for minor differences in difficulty among different versions of the test. This process, known as equating, is performed so that a student's reported score is not affected by the version of the test taken or by the abilities of the group with whom the student takes the test. As a result of placing SAT scores on the College Board scale, scores earned by students at different times can be compared. For example, an SAT critical reading score of 400 on a test taken at one administration indicates the same level of developed critical reading ability as a 400 score obtained on a different version of the test taken at another time.

**Note:** Since this test has not been previously administered, score ranges are provided for each possible raw score.

# How to Score Practice Test #6

## SAT Critical Reading Sections 3, 7, and 9

**Step A:** Count the number of correct answers for *Section 3* and record the number in the space provided on the Scoring Worksheet. Then do the same for the incorrect answers. (Do not count omitted answers.)

**Step B:** Count the number of correct answers and the number of incorrect answers for *Section 7* and record the numbers in the spaces provided on the Scoring Worksheet. (Do not count omitted answers.)

**Step C:** Count the number of correct answers and the number of incorrect answers for *Section 9* and record the numbers in the spaces provided on the Scoring Worksheet. (Do not count omitted answers.)

**Step D:** Total the number of correct responses. Total the number of incorrect responses. Enter the resulting figures on the Scoring Worksheet. To determine A, use the formula:

$$\text{Number correct} - \frac{\text{Number incorrect}}{4} = A$$

**Step E:** To obtain B, your Rounded Critical Reading Raw Score, round A to the nearest whole number. (For example, any number from 44.50 to 45.49 rounds to 45.) Enter the resulting figure on the Scoring Worksheet.

**Step F:** To find your Critical Reading Scaled Score Range, look up the Total Rounded Raw Score you obtained in step E in the Critical Reading Conversion Table (Table 1). Enter this range in the box on the Scoring Worksheet.

## SAT Mathematics Sections 2, 4, and 8

**Step A:** Count the number of correct answers and the number of incorrect answers for *Section 2* and record the numbers in the spaces provided on the Scoring Worksheet. (Do not count omitted answers.)

**Step B:** Count the number of correct answers and the number of incorrect answers for the multiple-choice questions (*questions 1 through 8*) in *Section 4* and record the numbers in the spaces provided on the Scoring Worksheet. (Do not count omitted answers.)

**Step C:** Count the number of correct answers for the student-produced response questions (*questions 9 through 18*) in *Section 4* and record the number in the space provided on the Scoring Worksheet.

**Step D:** Count the number of correct answers and the number of incorrect answers for *Section 8* and record the numbers in the spaces provided on the Scoring Worksheet. (Do not count omitted answers.)

**Step E:** Total the number of correct responses. Total the number of incorrect responses. Enter the resulting figures on the Scoring Worksheet. To determine A, use the formula:

$$\text{Number correct} - \frac{\text{Number incorrect}}{4} = A$$

**Step F:** To obtain B, your Mathematics Rounded Raw Score, round A to the nearest whole number. (For example, any number from 44.50 to 45.49 rounds to 45.) Enter the resulting figure on the Scoring Worksheet.

**Step G:** To find your Mathematics Scaled Score Range, use the Mathematics Conversion Table (Table 2) to look up the Total Rounded Raw Score you obtained in step F. Enter this range in the box on the Scoring Worksheet.

## SAT Writing Sections 1, 6, and 10

**Step A:** Enter your Essay Score for *Section 1* in the box on the Scoring Worksheet. (On this practice test, your essay score should range from 0 to 6. Keep in mind that on the actual SAT, two readers will read your essay and you will receive a total score of 0 to 12 on your score report.)

**Step B:** Count the number of correct answers and the number of incorrect answers for *Section 6* and record the numbers in the spaces provided on the Scoring Worksheet. (Do not count omitted answers.)

**Step C:** Count the number of correct answers and the number of incorrect answers for *Section 10* and record the numbers in the spaces provided on the Scoring Worksheet. (Do not count omitted answers.)

**Step D:** Total the number of correct responses. Total the number of incorrect responses. Enter the resulting figure on the Scoring Worksheet. To determine A, use the formula:

$$\text{Number correct} - \frac{\text{Number incorrect}}{4} = A$$

**Step E:** To obtain B, your Writing Multiple-Choice (MC) Rounded Raw Score, round A to the nearest whole number. (For example, any number from 44.50 to 45.49 rounds to 45.) Enter the resulting figure on the Scoring Worksheet.

**Step F:** To find your overall Writing Scaled Score Range, use Table 3. Look up the Total MC Rounded Raw Score you obtained in Step E in the left side of Table 3 and the Essay Score entered in Step A across the top of the table. Enter this range in the box on the Scoring Worksheet.

**Step G:** To find your Writing MC Subscore Range, look up the Total MC Rounded Raw Score you obtained in Step E on the Writing Multiple-Choice Conversion Table (Table 4). Enter this range in the box on the Scoring Worksheet.

**Note:** For the **WRITING SECTION**, your Essay Raw Score counts approximately 30% and your Multiple-Choice Raw Score counts approximately 70%.

# SAT Practice Test #6 Scoring Worksheet

**SAT Critical Reading Section**

A. Section 3:

|  | no. correct |  | no. incorrect |
|---|---|---|---|
| + |  | + |  |

B. Section 7:

|  | no. correct |  | no. incorrect |
|---|---|---|---|
| + |  | + |  |

C. Section 9:

|  | no. correct |  | no. incorrect |
|---|---|---|---|
| = |  | = |  |

D. Total Unrounded Raw Score

_____ − (_____ ÷ 4) = _____
no. correct     no. incorrect      A

E. Total Rounded Raw Score
(Rounded to nearest whole number)

_____
B

F. Critical Reading Scaled Score Range
(See Table 1)

[     –     ]

Critical
Reading Scaled
Score Range

**SAT Mathematics Section**

A. Section 2:

|  | no. correct |  | no. incorrect |
|---|---|---|---|
| I |  | + |  |

B. Section 4:
Questions 1-8

|  | no. correct |  | no. incorrect |
|---|---|---|---|
| + |  | + |  |

C. Section 4:
Questions 9-18

|  | no. correct |  | no. incorrect |
|---|---|---|---|
| = |  | + |  |

D. Section 8:

|  | no. correct |  | no. incorrect |
|---|---|---|---|
| = |  | = |  |

E. Total Unrounded Raw Score

_____ − (_____ ÷ 4) = _____
no. correct     no. incorrect      A

F. Total Rounded Raw Score
(Rounded to nearest whole number)

_____
B

G. Mathematics Scaled Score Range
(See Table 2)

[     –     ]

Mathematics
Scaled
Score Range

## SAT Writing Section

A. Section 1:

B. Section 6:

$$\underline{\hspace{3cm}} \atop \text{no. correct} \qquad + \qquad \underline{\hspace{3cm}} \atop \text{no. incorrect}$$

C. Section 10:

$$\underline{\hspace{3cm}} \atop \text{no. correct} \qquad + \qquad \underline{\hspace{3cm}} \atop \text{no. incorrect}$$

$$= \qquad\qquad\qquad =$$

D. Total MC Unrounded Raw Score

$$\underline{\hspace{3cm}} \atop \text{no. correct} \quad - \quad (\underline{\hspace{3cm}} \atop \text{no. incorrect} \div 4) \quad = \quad \underline{\hspace{3cm}} \atop A$$

E. Total MC Rounded Raw Score
   (Rounded to nearest whole number)

$$\underline{\hspace{3cm}} \atop B$$

F. Writing Scaled Score Range
   (See Table 3)

G. Writing MC Subscore Range
   (See Table 4)

Essay Score

Writing Scaled
Score Range

Writing MC
Subscore Range

| Table 1. Critical Reading Conversion Table | | | |
|---|---|---|---|
| Raw Score | Scaled Score | Raw Score | Scaled Score |
| 67 | 800 | 30 | 470-530 |
| 66 | 770-800 | 29 | 470-530 |
| 65 | 740-800 | 28 | 460-520 |
| 64 | 720-800 | 27 | 450-510 |
| 63 | 700-800 | 26 | 450-510 |
| 62 | 690-790 | 25 | 440-500 |
| 61 | 670-770 | 24 | 440-500 |
| 60 | 660-760 | 23 | 430-490 |
| 59 | 660-740 | 22 | 420-480 |
| 58 | 650-730 | 21 | 420-480 |
| 57 | 640-720 | 20 | 410-470 |
| 56 | 630-710 | 19 | 400-460 |
| 55 | 630-710 | 18 | 400-460 |
| 54 | 620-700 | 17 | 390-450 |
| 53 | 610-690 | 16 | 380-440 |
| 52 | 600-680 | 15 | 380-440 |
| 51 | 610-670 | 14 | 370-430 |
| 50 | 600-660 | 13 | 360-420 |
| 49 | 590-650 | 12 | 350-410 |
| 48 | 580-640 | 11 | 350-410 |
| 47 | 580-640 | 10 | 340-400 |
| 46 | 570-630 | 9 | 330-390 |
| 45 | 560-620 | 8 | 310-390 |
| 44 | 560-620 | 7 | 300-380 |
| 43 | 550-610 | 6 | 290-370 |
| 42 | 550-610 | 5 | 270-370 |
| 41 | 540-600 | 4 | 260-360 |
| 40 | 530-590 | 3 | 250-350 |
| 39 | 530-590 | 2 | 230-330 |
| 38 | 520-580 | 1 | 220-320 |
| 37 | 510-570 | 0 | 200-290 |
| 36 | 510-570 | -1 | 200-290 |
| 35 | 500-560 | -2 | 200-270 |
| 34 | 500-560 | -3 | 200-250 |
| 33 | 490-550 | -4 | 200-230 |
| 32 | 480-540 | -5 | 200-210 |
| 31 | 480-540 | -6 and below | 200 |

| Table 2. Mathematics Conversion Table | | | |
|---|---|---|---|
| Raw Score | Scaled Score | Raw Score | Scaled Score |
| 54 | 800 | 23 | 460-520 |
| 53 | 750-800 | 22 | 450-510 |
| 52 | 720-800 | 21 | 440-500 |
| 51 | 700-780 | 20 | 430-490 |
| 50 | 690-770 | 19 | 430-490 |
| 49 | 680-740 | 18 | 420-480 |
| 48 | 670-730 | 17 | 410-470 |
| 47 | 660-720 | 16 | 400-460 |
| 46 | 640-700 | 15 | 400-460 |
| 45 | 630-690 | 14 | 390-450 |
| 44 | 620-680 | 13 | 380-440 |
| 43 | 620-680 | 12 | 360-440 |
| 42 | 610-670 | 11 | 350-430 |
| 41 | 600-660 | 10 | 340-420 |
| 40 | 580-660 | 9 | 330-430 |
| 39 | 570-650 | 8 | 320-420 |
| 38 | 560-640 | 7 | 310-410 |
| 37 | 550-630 | 6 | 290-390 |
| 36 | 550-630 | 5 | 280-380 |
| 35 | 540-620 | 4 | 270-370 |
| 34 | 530-610 | 3 | 260-360 |
| 33 | 520-600 | 2 | 240-340 |
| 32 | 520-600 | 1 | 230-330 |
| 31 | 520-580 | 0 | 210-310 |
| 30 | 510-570 | -1 | 200-290 |
| 29 | 500-560 | -2 | 200-270 |
| 28 | 490-550 | -3 | 200-250 |
| 27 | 490-550 | -4 | 200-230 |
| 26 | 480-540 | -5 | 200-210 |
| 25 | 470-530 | -6 and below | 200 |
| 24 | 460-520 | | |

| | | | | | | | |
|---|---|---|---|---|---|---|---|
| **Table 3. Writing Conversion Table** | | | | | | | |
| **MC Raw** | **Essay Score** | | | | | | |
| **Score** | **0** | **1** | **2** | **3** | **4** | **5** | **6** |
| 49 | 650-690 | 670-720 | 690-740 | 710-770 | 750-800 | 780-800 | 800 |
| 48 | 630-690 | 640-720 | 660-740 | 690-770 | 720-800 | 760-800 | 780-800 |
| 47 | 600-690 | 620-720 | 640-740 | 660-770 | 700-800 | 730-800 | 760-800 |
| 46 | 580-690 | 600-720 | 620-740 | 650-770 | 680-800 | 710-800 | 740-800 |
| 45 | 570-690 | 580-720 | 600-740 | 630-770 | 670-800 | 700-800 | 730-800 |
| 44 | 560-680 | 570-710 | 590-730 | 620-760 | 660-790 | 690-800 | 720-800 |
| 43 | 540-660 | 560-690 | 580-710 | 610-740 | 640-780 | 670-800 | 700-800 |
| 42 | 530-660 | 550-690 | 570-700 | 600-730 | 630-770 | 660-800 | 690-800 |
| 41 | 530-650 | 540-680 | 560-700 | 590-720 | 620-760 | 660-790 | 680-800 |
| 40 | 520-640 | 530-670 | 550-690 | 580-710 | 620-750 | 650-780 | 680-800 |
| 39 | 510-630 | 520-660 | 540-680 | 570-710 | 610-740 | 640-770 | 670-800 |
| 38 | 500-620 | 520-650 | 540-670 | 560-700 | 600-730 | 630-770 | 660-790 |
| 37 | 490-610 | 510-640 | 530-660 | 560-690 | 590-720 | 620-760 | 650-780 |
| 36 | 480-600 | 500-630 | 520-650 | 550-680 | 580-720 | 610-750 | 640-770 |
| 35 | 480-590 | 490-620 | 510-640 | 540-670 | 570-710 | 610-740 | 640-770 |
| 34 | 470-590 | 480-620 | 500-630 | 530-660 | 570-700 | 600-730 | 630-760 |
| 33 | 460-580 | 470-610 | 490-630 | 520-650 | 560-690 | 590-720 | 620-750 |
| 32 | 450-570 | 470-600 | 490-620 | 510-640 | 550-680 | 580-710 | 610-740 |
| 31 | 440-560 | 460-590 | 480-610 | 510-640 | 540-670 | 570-700 | 600-730 |
| 30 | 430-550 | 450-580 | 470-600 | 500-630 | 530-660 | 560-700 | 590-720 |
| 29 | 430-540 | 440-570 | 460-590 | 490-620 | 520-650 | 560-690 | 590-710 |
| 28 | 420-530 | 430-560 | 450-580 | 480-610 | 520-650 | 550-680 | 580-700 |
| 27 | 410-520 | 420-550 | 440-570 | 470-600 | 510-640 | 540-670 | 570-700 |
| 26 | 400-520 | 420-550 | 430-560 | 460-590 | 500-630 | 530-660 | 560-690 |
| 25 | 390-510 | 410-540 | 430-560 | 450-580 | 490-620 | 520-650 | 550-680 |
| 24 | 380-500 | 400-530 | 420-550 | 450-570 | 480-610 | 510-640 | 540-670 |
| 23 | 370-490 | 390-520 | 410-540 | 440-570 | 470-600 | 500-630 | 530-660 |
| 22 | 370-480 | 380-510 | 400-530 | 430-560 | 460-590 | 500-630 | 520-650 |
| 21 | 370-480 | 380-510 | 400-530 | 430-560 | 460-590 | 500-630 | 520-650 |
| 20 | 360-470 | 370-500 | 390-520 | 420-550 | 460-580 | 490-620 | 520-640 |
| 19 | 350-460 | 360-490 | 380-510 | 410-540 | 450-580 | 480-610 | 510-630 |
| 18 | 340-450 | 350-480 | 370-500 | 400-530 | 440-570 | 470-600 | 500-630 |
| 17 | 330-450 | 350-480 | 360-490 | 390-520 | 430-560 | 460-590 | 490-620 |
| 16 | 320-440 | 340-470 | 360-490 | 390-510 | 420-550 | 450-580 | 480-610 |
| 15 | 310-430 | 330-460 | 350-480 | 380-510 | 410-540 | 440-570 | 470-600 |
| 14 | 300-420 | 320-450 | 340-470 | 370-500 | 400-530 | 430-560 | 460-590 |
| 13 | 300-410 | 310-440 | 330-460 | 360-490 | 390-520 | 430-560 | 450-580 |
| 12 | 290-400 | 300-430 | 320-450 | 350-480 | 390-510 | 420-550 | 450-570 |
| 11 | 280-390 | 290-420 | 310-440 | 340-470 | 380-510 | 410-540 | 440-570 |
| 10 | 270-390 | 280-420 | 300-430 | 330-460 | 370-500 | 400-530 | 430-560 |
| 9 | 260-380 | 280-410 | 290-430 | 320-450 | 360-490 | 390-520 | 420-550 |
| 8 | 250-370 | 270-400 | 290-420 | 320-450 | 350-480 | 380-510 | 410-540 |
| 7 | 240-360 | 260-390 | 280-410 | 310-440 | 340-470 | 370-510 | 400-530 |
| 6 | 230-350 | 250-380 | 270-400 | 300-430 | 330-460 | 360-500 | 390-520 |
| 5 | 230-340 | 240-370 | 260-390 | 290-420 | 320-460 | 360-490 | 380-520 |
| 4 | 220-340 | 230-370 | 250-380 | 280-410 | 320-450 | 350-480 | 380-510 |
| 3 | 210-330 | 220-360 | 240-380 | 270-400 | 310-440 | 340-470 | 370-500 |
| 2 | 200-320 | 210-350 | 230-370 | 260-400 | 300-430 | 330-460 | 360-490 |
| 1 | 200-300 | 200-330 | 220-350 | 250-380 | 280-410 | 310-450 | 340-470 |
| 0 | 200-290 | 200-320 | 210-340 | 240-370 | 270-410 | 300-440 | 330-470 |
| -1 | 200-280 | 200-310 | 200-330 | 220-350 | 250-390 | 290-420 | 310-450 |
| -2 | 200-260 | 200-290 | 200-310 | 200-340 | 240-370 | 270-410 | 300-430 |
| -3 | 200-240 | 200-270 | 200-290 | 200-320 | 240-360 | 270-390 | 300-420 |
| -4 | 200-230 | 200-260 | 200-280 | 200-300 | 240-340 | 270-370 | 300-400 |
| -5 | 200 | 200-230 | 200-250 | 200-280 | 240-320 | 270-350 | 300-370 |
| -6 | 200 | 200-220 | 200-240 | 200-270 | 240-310 | 270-340 | 300-370 |
| -7 | 200 | 200-220 | 200-230 | 200-260 | 240-300 | 270-330 | 300-360 |
| -8 | 200 | 200-210 | 200-230 | 200-250 | 240-290 | 270-320 | 300-350 |
| -9 | 200 | 200-210 | 200-230 | 200-250 | 240-290 | 270-320 | 300-350 |
| -10 | 200 | 200-210 | 200-230 | 200-250 | 240-290 | 270-320 | 300-350 |
| -11 | 200 | 200-210 | 200-230 | 200-250 | 240-290 | 270-320 | 300-350 |
| -12 | 200 | 200-210 | 200-230 | 200-250 | 240-290 | 270-320 | 300-350 |

## Table 4. Writing Multiple-Choice Conversion Table

| Raw Score | Scaled Score | Raw Score | Scaled Score |
|-----------|--------------|-----------|--------------|
| 49 | 78-80 | 21 | 46-56 |
| 48 | 77-80 | 20 | 45-55 |
| 47 | 74-80 | 19 | 44-54 |
| 46 | 72-80 | 18 | 43-53 |
| 45 | 70-80 | 17 | 42-52 |
| 44 | 69-79 | 16 | 41-51 |
| 43 | 67-77 | 15 | 40-50 |
| 42 | 66-76 | 14 | 39-49 |
| 41 | 65-75 | 13 | 38-48 |
| 40 | 64-74 | 12 | 37-47 |
| 39 | 63-73 | 11 | 36-46 |
| 38 | 62-72 | 10 | 35-45 |
| 37 | 61-71 | 9 | 34-44 |
| 36 | 60-70 | 8 | 33-43 |
| 35 | 59-69 | 7 | 32-42 |
| 34 | 58-68 | 6 | 31-41 |
| 33 | 57-67 | 5 | 30-40 |
| 32 | 56-66 | 4 | 29-39 |
| 31 | 55-65 | 3 | 28-38 |
| 30 | 54-64 | 2 | 27-37 |
| 29 | 53-63 | 1 | 25-35 |
| 28 | 52-62 | 0 | 24-34 |
| 27 | 51-61 | -1 | 22-32 |
| 26 | 50-60 | -2 | 20-30 |
| 25 | 49-59 | -3 | 20-28 |
| 24 | 48-58 | -4 | 20-26 |
| 23 | 47-57 | -5 | 20-23 |
| 22 | 46-56 | -6 and below | 20-22 |

# SAT Practice Test #7

 **After this test:**

- Use this book to its full potential! Get exclusive access answer explanations, free practice score reports and free sample student essays to help you score your essay in the Book Owners' Area at www.collegeboard.org/satstudyguide.

- Want more practice? Get 10 more official practice tests, auto essay scoring and lesson plans from the test maker by subscribing to *The Official SAT Online Course*. As a book owner, you're entitled to a $10 discount. Sign up at www.collegeboard.org/satstudyguide.

*Note:* Section 6, the variable section, has been omitted from this practice test.

# SAT Reasoning Test — General Directions

### Timing

- You will have 3 hours and 45 minutes to work on this test.
- There are ten separately timed sections:
  - ▶ One 25-minute essay
  - ▶ Six other 25-minute sections
  - ▶ Two 20-minute sections
  - ▶ One 10-minute section
- You may work on only one section at a time.
- The supervisor will tell you when to begin and end each section.
- If you finish a section before time is called, check your work on that section. You may NOT turn to any other section.
- Work as rapidly as you can without losing accuracy. Don't waste time on questions that seem too difficult for you.

### Marking Answers

- Be sure to mark your answer sheet properly.

    **COMPLETE MARK** ●      **EXAMPLES OF**
                             **INCOMPLETE MARKS**

- You must use a No. 2 pencil.
- Carefully mark only one answer for each question.
- Make sure you fill the entire circle darkly and completely.
- Do not make any stray marks on your answer sheet.
- If you erase, do so completely. Incomplete erasures may be scored as intended answers.
- Use only the answer spaces that correspond to the question numbers.

### Using Your Test Book

- You may use the test book for scratchwork, but you will not receive credit for anything written there.
- After time has been called, you may not transfer answers to your answer sheet or fill in circles.
- You may not fold or remove pages or portions of a page from this book, or take the book or answer sheet from the testing room.

### Scoring

- For each correct answer, you receive one point.
- For questions you omit, you receive no points.
- For a wrong answer to a multiple-choice question, you lose one-fourth of a point.
  - ▶ If you can eliminate one or more of the answer choices as wrong, you increase your chances of choosing the correct answer and earning one point.
  - ▶ If you can't eliminate any choice, move on. You can return to the question later if there is time.
- For a wrong answer to a student-produced response ("grid-in") math question, you don't lose any points.
- Multiple-choice and student-produced response questions are machine scored.
- The essay is scored on a 1 to 6 scale by two different readers. The total essay score is the sum of the two readers' scores.
- Off-topic essays, blank essays, and essays written in ink will receive a score of zero.

The passages for this test have been adapted from published material.
The ideas contained in them do not necessarily represent the opinions of the College Board.

**IMPORTANT:** The codes below are unique to your test book. Copy them on your answer sheet in boxes 8 and 9 and <u>fill in the corresponding circles exactly as shown.</u>

**9 | TEST FORM**
(Copy from back of test book.)

**8 | FORM CODE**
(Copy and grid as on back of test book.)

## DO NOT OPEN THIS BOOK UNTIL THE SUPERVISOR TELLS YOU TO DO SO.

**CollegeBoard** SAT

# SAT Reasoning Test™

**1** **Your Name:**
(Print)

Last                                    First                                    M.I.

**I agree to the conditions on the back of the SAT Reasoning Test™ booklet. I also agree to use only a No. 2 pencil to complete my answer sheet.**

Signature: _____    Date: __ / __ / __

**Home Address:**
(Print)
Number and Street          City          State     Zip Code

**Home Phone:** ( )          **Center:**
(Print)                      (Print)      City          State/Country

**2 YOUR NAME**

Last Name (First 6 Letters)    First Name (First 4 Letters)    Mid. Init.

**3 DATE OF BIRTH**

MONTH | DAY | YEAR
Jan, Feb, Mar, Apr, May, Jun, Jul, Aug, Sep, Oct, Nov, Dec

**5 SEX**
○ Female   ○ Male

**6 REGISTRATION NUMBER**
(Copy from Admission Ticket.)
○ I turned in my registration form today.

**Important:** Fill in items 8 and 9 exactly as shown on the back of test book.

**9 TEST FORM**
(Copy from back of test book.)

**8 FORM CODE**
(Copy and grid as on back of test book.)

**10 TEST BOOK SERIAL NUMBER**
(Copy from front of test book.)

**11 TEST CENTER**
(Supplied by Test Center Supervisor.)

**4 ZIP CODE**

**7 SOCIAL SECURITY NUMBER**

**PLEASE DO NOT WRITE IN THIS AREA**                    **SERIAL #**

7

753

**Begin your essay on this page. If you need more space, continue on the next page.**

7

**Page 2**

Continue on the next page, if necessary.

754

Page 3

**SECTION 2**

| 1 Ⓐ Ⓑ Ⓒ Ⓓ Ⓔ | 11 Ⓐ Ⓑ Ⓒ Ⓓ Ⓔ | 21 Ⓐ Ⓑ Ⓒ Ⓓ Ⓔ | 31 Ⓐ Ⓑ Ⓒ Ⓓ Ⓔ |
| 2 Ⓐ Ⓑ Ⓒ Ⓓ Ⓔ | 12 Ⓐ Ⓑ Ⓒ Ⓓ Ⓔ | 22 Ⓐ Ⓑ Ⓒ Ⓓ Ⓔ | 32 Ⓐ Ⓑ Ⓒ Ⓓ Ⓔ |
| 3 Ⓐ Ⓑ Ⓒ Ⓓ Ⓔ | 13 Ⓐ Ⓑ Ⓒ Ⓓ Ⓔ | 23 Ⓐ Ⓑ Ⓒ Ⓓ Ⓔ | 33 Ⓐ Ⓑ Ⓒ Ⓓ Ⓔ |
| 4 Ⓐ Ⓑ Ⓒ Ⓓ Ⓔ | 14 Ⓐ Ⓑ Ⓒ Ⓓ Ⓔ | 24 Ⓐ Ⓑ Ⓒ Ⓓ Ⓔ | 34 Ⓐ Ⓑ Ⓒ Ⓓ Ⓔ |
| 5 Ⓐ Ⓑ Ⓒ Ⓓ Ⓔ | 15 Ⓐ Ⓑ Ⓒ Ⓓ Ⓔ | 25 Ⓐ Ⓑ Ⓒ Ⓓ Ⓔ | 35 Ⓐ Ⓑ Ⓒ Ⓓ Ⓔ |
| 6 Ⓐ Ⓑ Ⓒ Ⓓ Ⓔ | 16 Ⓐ Ⓑ Ⓒ Ⓓ Ⓔ | 26 Ⓐ Ⓑ Ⓒ Ⓓ Ⓔ | 36 Ⓐ Ⓑ Ⓒ Ⓓ Ⓔ |
| 7 Ⓐ Ⓑ Ⓒ Ⓓ Ⓔ | 17 Ⓐ Ⓑ Ⓒ Ⓓ Ⓔ | 27 Ⓐ Ⓑ Ⓒ Ⓓ Ⓔ | 37 Ⓐ Ⓑ Ⓒ Ⓓ Ⓔ |
| 8 Ⓐ Ⓑ Ⓒ Ⓓ Ⓔ | 18 Ⓐ Ⓑ Ⓒ Ⓓ Ⓔ | 28 Ⓐ Ⓑ Ⓒ Ⓓ Ⓔ | 38 Ⓐ Ⓑ Ⓒ Ⓓ Ⓔ |
| 9 Ⓐ Ⓑ Ⓒ Ⓓ Ⓔ | 19 Ⓐ Ⓑ Ⓒ Ⓓ Ⓔ | 29 Ⓐ Ⓑ Ⓒ Ⓓ Ⓔ | 39 Ⓐ Ⓑ Ⓒ Ⓓ Ⓔ |
| 10 Ⓐ Ⓑ Ⓒ Ⓓ Ⓔ | 20 Ⓐ Ⓑ Ⓒ Ⓓ Ⓔ | 30 Ⓐ Ⓑ Ⓒ Ⓓ Ⓔ | 40 Ⓐ Ⓑ Ⓒ Ⓓ Ⓔ |

**SECTION 3**

| 1 Ⓐ Ⓑ Ⓒ Ⓓ Ⓔ | 11 Ⓐ Ⓑ Ⓒ Ⓓ Ⓔ | 21 Ⓐ Ⓑ Ⓒ Ⓓ Ⓔ | 31 Ⓐ Ⓑ Ⓒ Ⓓ Ⓔ |
| 2 Ⓐ Ⓑ Ⓒ Ⓓ Ⓔ | 12 Ⓐ Ⓑ Ⓒ Ⓓ Ⓔ | 22 Ⓐ Ⓑ Ⓒ Ⓓ Ⓔ | 32 Ⓐ Ⓑ Ⓒ Ⓓ Ⓔ |
| 3 Ⓐ Ⓑ Ⓒ Ⓓ Ⓔ | 13 Ⓐ Ⓑ Ⓒ Ⓓ Ⓔ | 23 Ⓐ Ⓑ Ⓒ Ⓓ Ⓔ | 33 Ⓐ Ⓑ Ⓒ Ⓓ Ⓔ |
| 4 Ⓐ Ⓑ Ⓒ Ⓓ Ⓔ | 14 Ⓐ Ⓑ Ⓒ Ⓓ Ⓔ | 24 Ⓐ Ⓑ Ⓒ Ⓓ Ⓔ | 34 Ⓐ Ⓑ Ⓒ Ⓓ Ⓔ |
| 5 Ⓐ Ⓑ Ⓒ Ⓓ Ⓔ | 15 Ⓐ Ⓑ Ⓒ Ⓓ Ⓔ | 25 Ⓐ Ⓑ Ⓒ Ⓓ Ⓔ | 35 Ⓐ Ⓑ Ⓒ Ⓓ Ⓔ |
| 6 Ⓐ Ⓑ Ⓒ Ⓓ Ⓔ | 16 Ⓐ Ⓑ Ⓒ Ⓓ Ⓔ | 26 Ⓐ Ⓑ Ⓒ Ⓓ Ⓔ | 36 Ⓐ Ⓑ Ⓒ Ⓓ Ⓔ |
| 7 Ⓐ Ⓑ Ⓒ Ⓓ Ⓔ | 17 Ⓐ Ⓑ Ⓒ Ⓓ Ⓔ | 27 Ⓐ Ⓑ Ⓒ Ⓓ Ⓔ | 37 Ⓐ Ⓑ Ⓒ Ⓓ Ⓔ |
| 8 Ⓐ Ⓑ Ⓒ Ⓓ Ⓔ | 18 Ⓐ Ⓑ Ⓒ Ⓓ Ⓔ | 28 Ⓐ Ⓑ Ⓒ Ⓓ Ⓔ | 38 Ⓐ Ⓑ Ⓒ Ⓓ Ⓔ |
| 9 Ⓐ Ⓑ Ⓒ Ⓓ Ⓔ | 19 Ⓐ Ⓑ Ⓒ Ⓓ Ⓔ | 29 Ⓐ Ⓑ Ⓒ Ⓓ Ⓔ | 39 Ⓐ Ⓑ Ⓒ Ⓓ Ⓔ |
| 10 Ⓐ Ⓑ Ⓒ Ⓓ Ⓔ | 20 Ⓐ Ⓑ Ⓒ Ⓓ Ⓔ | 30 Ⓐ Ⓑ Ⓒ Ⓓ Ⓔ | 40 Ⓐ Ⓑ Ⓒ Ⓓ Ⓔ |

**CAUTION**    Grid answers in the section below for SECTION 2 or SECTION 3 only if directed to do so in your test book.

**Student-Produced Responses**    ONLY ANSWERS THAT ARE GRIDDED WILL BE SCORED. YOU WILL NOT RECEIVE CREDIT FOR ANYTHING WRITTEN IN THE BOXES.

Quality Assurance Mark ●

9    10    11    12    13

14    15    16    17    18

Page 4

756

## SECTION 4

1 Ⓐ Ⓑ Ⓒ Ⓓ Ⓔ   11 Ⓐ Ⓑ Ⓒ Ⓓ Ⓔ   21 Ⓐ Ⓑ Ⓒ Ⓓ Ⓔ   31 Ⓐ Ⓑ Ⓒ Ⓓ Ⓔ
2 Ⓐ Ⓑ Ⓒ Ⓓ Ⓔ   12 Ⓐ Ⓑ Ⓒ Ⓓ Ⓔ   22 Ⓐ Ⓑ Ⓒ Ⓓ Ⓔ   32 Ⓐ Ⓑ Ⓒ Ⓓ Ⓔ
3 Ⓐ Ⓑ Ⓒ Ⓓ Ⓔ   13 Ⓐ Ⓑ Ⓒ Ⓓ Ⓔ   23 Ⓐ Ⓑ Ⓒ Ⓓ Ⓔ   33 Ⓐ Ⓑ Ⓒ Ⓓ Ⓔ
4 Ⓐ Ⓑ Ⓒ Ⓓ Ⓔ   14 Ⓐ Ⓑ Ⓒ Ⓓ Ⓔ   24 Ⓐ Ⓑ Ⓒ Ⓓ Ⓔ   34 Ⓐ Ⓑ Ⓒ Ⓓ Ⓔ
5 Ⓐ Ⓑ Ⓒ Ⓓ Ⓔ   15 Ⓐ Ⓑ Ⓒ Ⓓ Ⓔ   25 Ⓐ Ⓑ Ⓒ Ⓓ Ⓔ   35 Ⓐ Ⓑ Ⓒ Ⓓ Ⓔ
6 Ⓐ Ⓑ Ⓒ Ⓓ Ⓔ   16 Ⓐ Ⓑ Ⓒ Ⓓ Ⓔ   26 Ⓐ Ⓑ Ⓒ Ⓓ Ⓔ   36 Ⓐ Ⓑ Ⓒ Ⓓ Ⓔ
7 Ⓐ Ⓑ Ⓒ Ⓓ Ⓔ   17 Ⓐ Ⓑ Ⓒ Ⓓ Ⓔ   27 Ⓐ Ⓑ Ⓒ Ⓓ Ⓔ   37 Ⓐ Ⓑ Ⓒ Ⓓ Ⓔ
8 Ⓐ Ⓑ Ⓒ Ⓓ Ⓔ   18 Ⓐ Ⓑ Ⓒ Ⓓ Ⓔ   28 Ⓐ Ⓑ Ⓒ Ⓓ Ⓔ   38 Ⓐ Ⓑ Ⓒ Ⓓ Ⓔ
9 Ⓐ Ⓑ Ⓒ Ⓓ Ⓔ   19 Ⓐ Ⓑ Ⓒ Ⓓ Ⓔ   29 Ⓐ Ⓑ Ⓒ Ⓓ Ⓔ   39 Ⓐ Ⓑ Ⓒ Ⓓ Ⓔ
10 Ⓐ Ⓑ Ⓒ Ⓓ Ⓔ   20 Ⓐ Ⓑ Ⓒ Ⓓ Ⓔ   30 Ⓐ Ⓑ Ⓒ Ⓓ Ⓔ   40 Ⓐ Ⓑ Ⓒ Ⓓ Ⓔ

## SECTION 5

1 Ⓐ Ⓑ Ⓒ Ⓓ Ⓔ   11 Ⓐ Ⓑ Ⓒ Ⓓ Ⓔ   21 Ⓐ Ⓑ Ⓒ Ⓓ Ⓔ   31 Ⓐ Ⓑ Ⓒ Ⓓ Ⓔ
2 Ⓐ Ⓑ Ⓒ Ⓓ Ⓔ   12 Ⓐ Ⓑ Ⓒ Ⓓ Ⓔ   22 Ⓐ Ⓑ Ⓒ Ⓓ Ⓔ   32 Ⓐ Ⓑ Ⓒ Ⓓ Ⓔ
3 Ⓐ Ⓑ Ⓒ Ⓓ Ⓔ   13 Ⓐ Ⓑ Ⓒ Ⓓ Ⓔ   23 Ⓐ Ⓑ Ⓒ Ⓓ Ⓔ   33 Ⓐ Ⓑ Ⓒ Ⓓ Ⓔ
4 Ⓐ Ⓑ Ⓒ Ⓓ Ⓔ   14 Ⓐ Ⓑ Ⓒ Ⓓ Ⓔ   24 Ⓐ Ⓑ Ⓒ Ⓓ Ⓔ   34 Ⓐ Ⓑ Ⓒ Ⓓ Ⓔ
5 Ⓐ Ⓑ Ⓒ Ⓓ Ⓔ   15 Ⓐ Ⓑ Ⓒ Ⓓ Ⓔ   25 Ⓐ Ⓑ Ⓒ Ⓓ Ⓔ   35 Ⓐ Ⓑ Ⓒ Ⓓ Ⓔ
6 Ⓐ Ⓑ Ⓒ Ⓓ Ⓔ   16 Ⓐ Ⓑ Ⓒ Ⓓ Ⓔ   26 Ⓐ Ⓑ Ⓒ Ⓓ Ⓔ   36 Ⓐ Ⓑ Ⓒ Ⓓ Ⓔ
7 Ⓐ Ⓑ Ⓒ Ⓓ Ⓔ   17 Ⓐ Ⓑ Ⓒ Ⓓ Ⓔ   27 Ⓐ Ⓑ Ⓒ Ⓓ Ⓔ   37 Ⓐ Ⓑ Ⓒ Ⓓ Ⓔ
8 Ⓐ Ⓑ Ⓒ Ⓓ Ⓔ   18 Ⓐ Ⓑ Ⓒ Ⓓ Ⓔ   28 Ⓐ Ⓑ Ⓒ Ⓓ Ⓔ   38 Ⓐ Ⓑ Ⓒ Ⓓ Ⓔ
9 Ⓐ Ⓑ Ⓒ Ⓓ Ⓔ   19 Ⓐ Ⓑ Ⓒ Ⓓ Ⓔ   29 Ⓐ Ⓑ Ⓒ Ⓓ Ⓔ   39 Ⓐ Ⓑ Ⓒ Ⓓ Ⓔ
10 Ⓐ Ⓑ Ⓒ Ⓓ Ⓔ   20 Ⓐ Ⓑ Ⓒ Ⓓ Ⓔ   30 Ⓐ Ⓑ Ⓒ Ⓓ Ⓔ   40 Ⓐ Ⓑ Ⓒ Ⓓ Ⓔ

**CAUTION** Grid answers in the section below for SECTION 4 or SECTION 5 only if directed to do so in your test book.

## Student-Produced Responses

ONLY ANSWERS THAT ARE GRIDDED WILL BE SCORED. YOU WILL NOT RECEIVE CREDIT FOR ANYTHING WRITTEN IN THE BOXES.

Quality Assurance Mark ●

9   10   11   12   13

14   15   16   17   18

## SECTION 6

1 Ⓐ Ⓑ Ⓒ Ⓓ Ⓔ
2 Ⓐ Ⓑ Ⓒ Ⓓ Ⓔ
3 Ⓐ Ⓑ Ⓒ Ⓓ Ⓔ
4 Ⓐ Ⓑ Ⓒ Ⓓ Ⓔ
5 Ⓐ Ⓑ Ⓒ Ⓓ Ⓔ
6 Ⓐ Ⓑ Ⓒ Ⓓ Ⓔ
7 Ⓐ Ⓑ Ⓒ Ⓓ Ⓔ
8 Ⓐ Ⓑ Ⓒ Ⓓ Ⓔ
9 Ⓐ Ⓑ Ⓒ Ⓓ Ⓔ
10 Ⓐ Ⓑ Ⓒ Ⓓ Ⓔ

11 Ⓐ Ⓑ Ⓒ Ⓓ Ⓔ
12 Ⓐ Ⓑ Ⓒ Ⓓ Ⓔ
13 Ⓐ Ⓑ Ⓒ Ⓓ Ⓔ
14 Ⓐ Ⓑ Ⓒ Ⓓ Ⓔ
15 Ⓐ Ⓑ Ⓒ Ⓓ Ⓔ
16 Ⓐ Ⓑ Ⓒ Ⓓ Ⓔ
17 Ⓐ Ⓑ Ⓒ Ⓓ Ⓔ
18 Ⓐ Ⓑ Ⓒ Ⓓ Ⓔ
19 Ⓐ Ⓑ Ⓒ Ⓓ Ⓔ
20 Ⓐ Ⓑ Ⓒ Ⓓ Ⓔ

21 Ⓐ Ⓑ Ⓒ Ⓓ Ⓔ
22 Ⓐ Ⓑ Ⓒ Ⓓ Ⓔ
23 Ⓐ Ⓑ Ⓒ Ⓓ Ⓔ
24 Ⓐ Ⓑ Ⓒ Ⓓ Ⓔ
25 Ⓐ Ⓑ Ⓒ Ⓓ Ⓔ
26 Ⓐ Ⓑ Ⓒ Ⓓ Ⓔ
27 Ⓐ Ⓑ Ⓒ Ⓓ Ⓔ
28 Ⓐ Ⓑ Ⓒ Ⓓ Ⓔ
29 Ⓐ Ⓑ Ⓒ Ⓓ Ⓔ
30 Ⓐ Ⓑ Ⓒ Ⓓ Ⓔ

31 Ⓐ Ⓑ Ⓒ Ⓓ Ⓔ
32 Ⓐ Ⓑ Ⓒ Ⓓ Ⓔ
33 Ⓐ Ⓑ Ⓒ Ⓓ Ⓔ
34 Ⓐ Ⓑ Ⓒ Ⓓ Ⓔ
35 Ⓐ Ⓑ Ⓒ Ⓓ Ⓔ
36 Ⓐ Ⓑ Ⓒ Ⓓ Ⓔ
37 Ⓐ Ⓑ Ⓒ Ⓓ Ⓔ
38 Ⓐ Ⓑ Ⓒ Ⓓ Ⓔ
39 Ⓐ Ⓑ Ⓒ Ⓓ Ⓔ
40 Ⓐ Ⓑ Ⓒ Ⓓ Ⓔ

## SECTION 7

1 Ⓐ Ⓑ Ⓒ Ⓓ Ⓔ
2 Ⓐ Ⓑ Ⓒ Ⓓ Ⓔ
3 Ⓐ Ⓑ Ⓒ Ⓓ Ⓔ
4 Ⓐ Ⓑ Ⓒ Ⓓ Ⓔ
5 Ⓐ Ⓑ Ⓒ Ⓓ Ⓔ
6 Ⓐ Ⓑ Ⓒ Ⓓ Ⓔ
7 Ⓐ Ⓑ Ⓒ Ⓓ Ⓔ
8 Ⓐ Ⓑ Ⓒ Ⓓ Ⓔ
9 Ⓐ Ⓑ Ⓒ Ⓓ Ⓔ
10 Ⓐ Ⓑ Ⓒ Ⓓ Ⓔ

11 Ⓐ Ⓑ Ⓒ Ⓓ Ⓔ
12 Ⓐ Ⓑ Ⓒ Ⓓ Ⓔ
13 Ⓐ Ⓑ Ⓒ Ⓓ Ⓔ
14 Ⓐ Ⓑ Ⓒ Ⓓ Ⓔ
15 Ⓐ Ⓑ Ⓒ Ⓓ Ⓔ
16 Ⓐ Ⓑ Ⓒ Ⓓ Ⓔ
17 Ⓐ Ⓑ Ⓒ Ⓓ Ⓔ
18 Ⓐ Ⓑ Ⓒ Ⓓ Ⓔ
19 Ⓐ Ⓑ Ⓒ Ⓓ Ⓔ
20 Ⓐ Ⓑ Ⓒ Ⓓ Ⓔ

21 Ⓐ Ⓑ Ⓒ Ⓓ Ⓔ
22 Ⓐ Ⓑ Ⓒ Ⓓ Ⓔ
23 Ⓐ Ⓑ Ⓒ Ⓓ Ⓔ
24 Ⓐ Ⓑ Ⓒ Ⓓ Ⓔ
25 Ⓐ Ⓑ Ⓒ Ⓓ Ⓔ
26 Ⓐ Ⓑ Ⓒ Ⓓ Ⓔ
27 Ⓐ Ⓑ Ⓒ Ⓓ Ⓔ
28 Ⓐ Ⓑ Ⓒ Ⓓ Ⓔ
29 Ⓐ Ⓑ Ⓒ Ⓓ Ⓔ
30 Ⓐ Ⓑ Ⓒ Ⓓ Ⓔ

31 Ⓐ Ⓑ Ⓒ Ⓓ Ⓔ
32 Ⓐ Ⓑ Ⓒ Ⓓ Ⓔ
33 Ⓐ Ⓑ Ⓒ Ⓓ Ⓔ
34 Ⓐ Ⓑ Ⓒ Ⓓ Ⓔ
35 Ⓐ Ⓑ Ⓒ Ⓓ Ⓔ
36 Ⓐ Ⓑ Ⓒ Ⓓ Ⓔ
37 Ⓐ Ⓑ Ⓒ Ⓓ Ⓔ
38 Ⓐ Ⓑ Ⓒ Ⓓ Ⓔ
39 Ⓐ Ⓑ Ⓒ Ⓓ Ⓔ
40 Ⓐ Ⓑ Ⓒ Ⓓ Ⓔ

**CAUTION** Grid answers in the section below for SECTION 6 or SECTION 7 only if directed to do so in your test book.

**Student-Produced Responses** ONLY ANSWERS THAT ARE GRIDDED WILL BE SCORED. YOU WILL NOT RECEIVE CREDIT FOR ANYTHING WRITTEN IN THE BOXES.

Quality Assurance Mark ●

9 10 11 12 13

14 15 16 17 18

Page 6

PLEASE DO NOT WRITE IN THIS AREA

SERIAL #

758

**SECTION 8**

| 1 | Ⓐ Ⓑ Ⓒ Ⓓ Ⓔ | 11 | Ⓐ Ⓑ Ⓒ Ⓓ Ⓔ | 21 | Ⓐ Ⓑ Ⓒ Ⓓ Ⓔ | 31 | Ⓐ Ⓑ Ⓒ Ⓓ Ⓔ |
| 2 | Ⓐ Ⓑ Ⓒ Ⓓ Ⓔ | 12 | Ⓐ Ⓑ Ⓒ Ⓓ Ⓔ | 22 | Ⓐ Ⓑ Ⓒ Ⓓ Ⓔ | 32 | Ⓐ Ⓑ Ⓒ Ⓓ Ⓔ |
| 3 | Ⓐ Ⓑ Ⓒ Ⓓ Ⓔ | 13 | Ⓐ Ⓑ Ⓒ Ⓓ Ⓔ | 23 | Ⓐ Ⓑ Ⓒ Ⓓ Ⓔ | 33 | Ⓐ Ⓑ Ⓒ Ⓓ Ⓔ |
| 4 | Ⓐ Ⓑ Ⓒ Ⓓ Ⓔ | 14 | Ⓐ Ⓑ Ⓒ Ⓓ Ⓔ | 24 | Ⓐ Ⓑ Ⓒ Ⓓ Ⓔ | 34 | Ⓐ Ⓑ Ⓒ Ⓓ Ⓔ |
| 5 | Ⓐ Ⓑ Ⓒ Ⓓ Ⓔ | 15 | Ⓐ Ⓑ Ⓒ Ⓓ Ⓔ | 25 | Ⓐ Ⓑ Ⓒ Ⓓ Ⓔ | 35 | Ⓐ Ⓑ Ⓒ Ⓓ Ⓔ |
| 6 | Ⓐ Ⓑ Ⓒ Ⓓ Ⓔ | 16 | Ⓐ Ⓑ Ⓒ Ⓓ Ⓔ | 26 | Ⓐ Ⓑ Ⓒ Ⓓ Ⓔ | 36 | Ⓐ Ⓑ Ⓒ Ⓓ Ⓔ |
| 7 | Ⓐ Ⓑ Ⓒ Ⓓ Ⓔ | 17 | Ⓐ Ⓑ Ⓒ Ⓓ Ⓔ | 27 | Ⓐ Ⓑ Ⓒ Ⓓ Ⓔ | 37 | Ⓐ Ⓑ Ⓒ Ⓓ Ⓔ |
| 8 | Ⓐ Ⓑ Ⓒ Ⓓ Ⓔ | 18 | Ⓐ Ⓑ Ⓒ Ⓓ Ⓔ | 28 | Ⓐ Ⓑ Ⓒ Ⓓ Ⓔ | 38 | Ⓐ Ⓑ Ⓒ Ⓓ Ⓔ |
| 9 | Ⓐ Ⓑ Ⓒ Ⓓ Ⓔ | 19 | Ⓐ Ⓑ Ⓒ Ⓓ Ⓔ | 29 | Ⓐ Ⓑ Ⓒ Ⓓ Ⓔ | 39 | Ⓐ Ⓑ Ⓒ Ⓓ Ⓔ |
| 10 | Ⓐ Ⓑ Ⓒ Ⓓ Ⓔ | 20 | Ⓐ Ⓑ Ⓒ Ⓓ Ⓔ | 30 | Ⓐ Ⓑ Ⓒ Ⓓ Ⓔ | 40 | Ⓐ Ⓑ Ⓒ Ⓓ Ⓔ |

**SECTION 9**

| 1 | Ⓐ Ⓑ Ⓒ Ⓓ Ⓔ | 11 | Ⓐ Ⓑ Ⓒ Ⓓ Ⓔ | 21 | Ⓐ Ⓑ Ⓒ Ⓓ Ⓔ | 31 | Ⓐ Ⓑ Ⓒ Ⓓ Ⓔ |
| 2 | Ⓐ Ⓑ Ⓒ Ⓓ Ⓔ | 12 | Ⓐ Ⓑ Ⓒ Ⓓ Ⓔ | 22 | Ⓐ Ⓑ Ⓒ Ⓓ Ⓔ | 32 | Ⓐ Ⓑ Ⓒ Ⓓ Ⓔ |
| 3 | Ⓐ Ⓑ Ⓒ Ⓓ Ⓔ | 13 | Ⓐ Ⓑ Ⓒ Ⓓ Ⓔ | 23 | Ⓐ Ⓑ Ⓒ Ⓓ Ⓔ | 33 | Ⓐ Ⓑ Ⓒ Ⓓ Ⓔ |
| 4 | Ⓐ Ⓑ Ⓒ Ⓓ Ⓔ | 14 | Ⓐ Ⓑ Ⓒ Ⓓ Ⓔ | 24 | Ⓐ Ⓑ Ⓒ Ⓓ Ⓔ | 34 | Ⓐ Ⓑ Ⓒ Ⓓ Ⓔ |
| 5 | Ⓐ Ⓑ Ⓒ Ⓓ Ⓔ | 15 | Ⓐ Ⓑ Ⓒ Ⓓ Ⓔ | 25 | Ⓐ Ⓑ Ⓒ Ⓓ Ⓔ | 35 | Ⓐ Ⓑ Ⓒ Ⓓ Ⓔ |
| 6 | Ⓐ Ⓑ Ⓒ Ⓓ Ⓔ | 16 | Ⓐ Ⓑ Ⓒ Ⓓ Ⓔ | 26 | Ⓐ Ⓑ Ⓒ Ⓓ Ⓔ | 36 | Ⓐ Ⓑ Ⓒ Ⓓ Ⓔ |
| 7 | Ⓐ Ⓑ Ⓒ Ⓓ Ⓔ | 17 | Ⓐ Ⓑ Ⓒ Ⓓ Ⓔ | 27 | Ⓐ Ⓑ Ⓒ Ⓓ Ⓔ | 37 | Ⓐ Ⓑ Ⓒ Ⓓ Ⓔ |
| 8 | Ⓐ Ⓑ Ⓒ Ⓓ Ⓔ | 18 | Ⓐ Ⓑ Ⓒ Ⓓ Ⓔ | 28 | Ⓐ Ⓑ Ⓒ Ⓓ Ⓔ | 38 | Ⓐ Ⓑ Ⓒ Ⓓ Ⓔ |
| 9 | Ⓐ Ⓑ Ⓒ Ⓓ Ⓔ | 19 | Ⓐ Ⓑ Ⓒ Ⓓ Ⓔ | 29 | Ⓐ Ⓑ Ⓒ Ⓓ Ⓔ | 39 | Ⓐ Ⓑ Ⓒ Ⓓ Ⓔ |
| 10 | Ⓐ Ⓑ Ⓒ Ⓓ Ⓔ | 20 | Ⓐ Ⓑ Ⓒ Ⓓ Ⓔ | 30 | Ⓐ Ⓑ Ⓒ Ⓓ Ⓔ | 40 | Ⓐ Ⓑ Ⓒ Ⓓ Ⓔ |

Quality ● Assurance Mark

**SECTION 10**

| 1 | Ⓐ Ⓑ Ⓒ Ⓓ Ⓔ | 11 | Ⓐ Ⓑ Ⓒ Ⓓ Ⓔ | 21 | Ⓐ Ⓑ Ⓒ Ⓓ Ⓔ | 31 | Ⓐ Ⓑ Ⓒ Ⓓ Ⓔ |
| 2 | Ⓐ Ⓑ Ⓒ Ⓓ Ⓔ | 12 | Ⓐ Ⓑ Ⓒ Ⓓ Ⓔ | 22 | Ⓐ Ⓑ Ⓒ Ⓓ Ⓔ | 32 | Ⓐ Ⓑ Ⓒ Ⓓ Ⓔ |
| 3 | Ⓐ Ⓑ Ⓒ Ⓓ Ⓔ | 13 | Ⓐ Ⓑ Ⓒ Ⓓ Ⓔ | 23 | Ⓐ Ⓑ Ⓒ Ⓓ Ⓔ | 33 | Ⓐ Ⓑ Ⓒ Ⓓ Ⓔ |
| 4 | Ⓐ Ⓑ Ⓒ Ⓓ Ⓔ | 14 | Ⓐ Ⓑ Ⓒ Ⓓ Ⓔ | 24 | Ⓐ Ⓑ Ⓒ Ⓓ Ⓔ | 34 | Ⓐ Ⓑ Ⓒ Ⓓ Ⓔ |
| 5 | Ⓐ Ⓑ Ⓒ Ⓓ Ⓔ | 15 | Ⓐ Ⓑ Ⓒ Ⓓ Ⓔ | 25 | Ⓐ Ⓑ Ⓒ Ⓓ Ⓔ | 35 | Ⓐ Ⓑ Ⓒ Ⓓ Ⓔ |
| 6 | Ⓐ Ⓑ Ⓒ Ⓓ Ⓔ | 16 | Ⓐ Ⓑ Ⓒ Ⓓ Ⓔ | 26 | Ⓐ Ⓑ Ⓒ Ⓓ Ⓔ | 36 | Ⓐ Ⓑ Ⓒ Ⓓ Ⓔ |
| 7 | Ⓐ Ⓑ Ⓒ Ⓓ Ⓔ | 17 | Ⓐ Ⓑ Ⓒ Ⓓ Ⓔ | 27 | Ⓐ Ⓑ Ⓒ Ⓓ Ⓔ | 37 | Ⓐ Ⓑ Ⓒ Ⓓ Ⓔ |
| 8 | Ⓐ Ⓑ Ⓒ Ⓓ Ⓔ | 18 | Ⓐ Ⓑ Ⓒ Ⓓ Ⓔ | 28 | Ⓐ Ⓑ Ⓒ Ⓓ Ⓔ | 38 | Ⓐ Ⓑ Ⓒ Ⓓ Ⓔ |
| 9 | Ⓐ Ⓑ Ⓒ Ⓓ Ⓔ | 19 | Ⓐ Ⓑ Ⓒ Ⓓ Ⓔ | 29 | Ⓐ Ⓑ Ⓒ Ⓓ Ⓔ | 39 | Ⓐ Ⓑ Ⓒ Ⓓ Ⓔ |
| 10 | Ⓐ Ⓑ Ⓒ Ⓓ Ⓔ | 20 | Ⓐ Ⓑ Ⓒ Ⓓ Ⓔ | 30 | Ⓐ Ⓑ Ⓒ Ⓓ Ⓔ | 40 | Ⓐ Ⓑ Ⓒ Ⓓ Ⓔ |

## CERTIFICATION STATEMENT

Copy the statement below (do not print) and sign your name as you would an official document.

I hereby agree to the conditions set forth online at www.collegeboard.org and/or in the SAT® Registration Booklet and certify that I am the person whose name and address appear on this answer sheet.

_____

_____

_____

_____

By signing below, I agree not to share any specific test questions or essay topics with anyone by any form of communication, including, but not limited to: email, text messages, or use of the Internet.

Signature _____     Date _____

## SPECIAL QUESTIONS

1 Ⓐ Ⓑ Ⓒ Ⓓ Ⓔ Ⓕ Ⓖ Ⓗ Ⓘ Ⓙ
2 Ⓐ Ⓑ Ⓒ Ⓓ Ⓔ Ⓕ Ⓖ Ⓗ Ⓘ Ⓙ
3 Ⓐ Ⓑ Ⓒ Ⓓ Ⓔ Ⓕ Ⓖ Ⓗ Ⓘ Ⓙ
4 Ⓐ Ⓑ Ⓒ Ⓓ Ⓔ Ⓕ Ⓖ Ⓗ Ⓘ Ⓙ
5 Ⓐ Ⓑ Ⓒ Ⓓ Ⓔ Ⓕ Ⓖ Ⓗ Ⓘ Ⓙ
6 Ⓐ Ⓑ Ⓒ Ⓓ Ⓔ Ⓕ Ⓖ Ⓗ Ⓘ Ⓙ
7 Ⓐ Ⓑ Ⓒ Ⓓ Ⓔ Ⓕ Ⓖ Ⓗ Ⓘ Ⓙ
8 Ⓐ Ⓑ Ⓒ Ⓓ Ⓔ Ⓕ Ⓖ Ⓗ Ⓘ Ⓙ

7

**Page 8**

## ESSAY
### Time — 25 minutes

**Turn to page 2 of your answer sheet to write your ESSAY.**

The essay gives you an opportunity to show how effectively you can develop and express ideas. You should, therefore, take care to develop your point of view, present your ideas logically and clearly, and use language precisely.

Your essay must be written on the lines provided on your answer sheet—you will receive no other paper on which to write. You will have enough space if you write on every line, avoid wide margins, and keep your handwriting to a reasonable size. Remember that people who are not familiar with your handwriting will read what you write. Try to write or print so that what you are writing is legible to those readers.

**Important Reminders:**

- **A pencil is required for the essay.** An essay written in ink will receive a score of zero.
- **Do not write your essay in your test book.** You will receive credit only for what you write on your answer sheet.
- **An off-topic essay will receive a score of zero.**
- **If your essay does not reflect your original and individual work, your test scores may be canceled.**

You have twenty-five minutes to write an essay on the topic assigned below.

Think carefully about the issue presented in the following excerpt and the assignment below.

> A better understanding of other people contributes to the development of moral virtues. We shall be both kinder and fairer in our treatment of others if we understand them better. Understanding ourselves and understanding others are connected, since as human beings we all have things in common.
>
> Adapted from Anne Sheppard, *Aesthetics: An Introduction to the Philosophy of Art*

**Assignment:** Do we need other people in order to understand ourselves? Plan and write an essay in which you develop your point of view on this issue. Support your position with reasoning and examples taken from your reading, studies, experience, or observations.

BEGIN WRITING YOUR ESSAY ON PAGE 2 OF THE ANSWER SHEET.

**If you finish before time is called, you may check your work on this section only.
Do not turn to any other section in the test.**

## SECTION 2
### Time — 25 minutes
### 24 Questions

---

**Turn to Section 2 (page 4) of your answer sheet to answer the questions in this section.**

---

**Directions:** For each question in this section, select the best answer from among the choices given and fill in the corresponding circle on the answer sheet.

---

Each sentence below has one or two blanks, each blank indicating that something has been omitted. Beneath the sentence are five words or sets of words labeled A through E. Choose the word or set of words that, when inserted in the sentence, <u>best</u> fits the meaning of the sentence as a whole.

**Example:**

Hoping to ------- the dispute, negotiators proposed a compromise that they felt would be ------- to both labor and management.

(A) enforce . . useful
(B) end . . divisive
(C) overcome . . unattractive
(D) extend . . satisfactory
(E) resolve . . acceptable

1. Like many other groups of people in the United States who have needed laws to ------- equal rights, Americans with disabilities have had to ------- legislation addressing their concerns.

(A) guarantee . . lobby for
(B) preclude . . enact
(C) ascertain . . consolidate
(D) compound . . contend with
(E) suppress . . ratify

2. The café attracts a ------- clientele: a startlingly heterogeneous group of people collects there.

(A) motley    (B) callous    (C) languid
(D) mysterious    (E) humane

3. The second edition of the textbook provides ------- footnotes; since the first edition, the editors have apparently ------- a great deal of background data.

(A) meager . . accumulated
(B) illegible . . clarified
(C) copious . . amassed
(D) voluminous . . excised
(E) monotonous . . embellished

4. Professor Fernandez has been ------- about most of the purportedly humanitarian aspects of the colonial government and has insisted that its actions were, on the contrary, -------.

(A) dubious . . self-serving
(B) enthusiastic . . contemptible
(C) disparaging . . sporadic
(D) excited . . gratuitous
(E) disillusioned . . benevolent

5. Concrete is ------- of many materials, a composite of rocks, pebbles, sand, and cement.

(A) a conflagration    (B) a distillation
(C) a concordance    (D) an aberration
(E) an amalgamation

---

**GO ON TO THE NEXT PAGE** ⇨

Unauthorized copying or reuse of
any part of this page is illegal.

Each passage below is followed by questions based on its content. Answer the questions on the basis of what is <u>stated</u> or <u>implied</u> in each passage and in any introductory material that may be provided.

**Questions 6-7 are based on the following passage.**

Choice of language frequently plays a significant role in the development of the Hispanic American writer's voice and message. "I lack language," wrote Cherrie
*Line* Moraga, author of *Loving in the War Years: lo que*
5 *nunca pasó por sus labios*. The use of two languages in the title itself expresses the difficulty that the author perceives in narrating personal experience in one language when one has lived in another.

6. The author cites Moraga's book primarily in order to

(A) emphasize the challenges that some Hispanic American writers face in getting their work published
(B) celebrate the achievements of a young Hispanic American novelist
(C) demonstrate the expressiveness of a writer who has mastered several languages
(D) confirm that American writers are exploring new artistic approaches
(E) illustrate a dilemma that Hispanic American writers often face

7. Which of the following situations is most analogous to the problem presented in the passage?

(A) A Hispanic American artist living in Chile has difficulty selling his paintings.
(B) A Cherokee columnist assumes that readers of national newspapers are unfamiliar with Native American cultures.
(C) An African American novelist draws upon the historical past of African Americans to bring nuance to her work.
(D) A Russian novelist, living in the United States, finds it difficult to articulate insights in American English.
(E) An Asian American journalist attempts to write essays for both Japanese and American audiences.

**Questions 8-9 are based on the following passage.**

The science fiction masterpiece *2001: A Space Odyssey* will probably be remembered best for the finely honed portrait of HAL, the Heuristically pro-
*Line* grammed ALgorithmic computer that could not only
5 reason but also experience human feelings and anxiety. Surprisingly, perhaps, computers have in some ways surpassed writer Arthur C. Clarke's and film director Stanley Kubrick's vision of computing technology at the turn of the millennium. Today's computers are
10 vastly smaller and more portable than HAL and use software interfaces that forgo the type of manual controls found on the spaceship that carried HAL.

8. The author's attitude toward the "portrait" (line 3) is best characterized as one of

(A) resentment
(B) appreciation
(C) confusion
(D) awe
(E) derision

9. In the last sentence, the reference to "software interfaces" and "manual controls" provides an example of the

(A) superiority of current computers to those envisioned by Clarke and Kubrick
(B) amazing ability of Clarke and Kubrick to envision certain aspects of the future
(C) many ways that computers like HAL could be accessed by human beings
(D) consistent attempts by computer programmers to override certain software
(E) deficiencies of current computers attempting to simulate human intelligence and emotions

**GO ON TO THE NEXT PAGE**

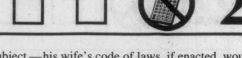
**Questions 10-16 are based on the following passage.**

*In this passage, the author discusses the question of women's rights during the Revolutionary War period.*

Among the founding fathers, there was no controversy
or debate on the definition of a voter as male. The United
States Constitution embodied the patriarchal assumption,
*Line* shared by the entire society, that women could not partici-
5 pate in government. It was felt necessary by the founders
to define the status of indentured servants, slaves, and
American Indians in regard to voting rights, but there
was no need felt even to mention, much less to explain
or justify, that while women were to be counted among
10 "the whole number of free persons" in each state for purposes of representation, they had no right to vote or to be
elected to public office. The issue of the civil and political
status of women never entered the debate.

Yet women in large numbers had been involved in polit-
15 ical actions in the American Revolution and had begun to
define themselves differently than had their mothers and
grandmothers. At the very least, they had found ways of
exerting influence on political events by fund-raising, tea
boycotts, and actions against profiteering merchants.
20 Loyalist women (those that sided with the British) made
political claims when they argued for their property rights
independent of those of their husbands or when they protested against various wartime atrocities. Several influential
female members of elite families privately raised the issue
25 of women's rights as citizens. Unbidden and without a
recognized public forum, and emboldened by the revolutionary rhetoric and the language of democracy, women
began to reinterpret their own status. Like the slaves,
women took literally the preamble of the Declaration
30 of Independence, which states that all men are created
equal. The institution of slavery was hotly contested by
the founding fathers and highly controversial. But unlike
slaves, women were not defined as being even problematic
in the debate.

35 The well-known exchange of private letters between
John Adams and his wife Abigail sharply exemplifies the
limits of consciousness on this issue of women's rights.
Here was a well-matched and loving couple, but unusual
in the wife's political interest and involvement. In 1776,
40 Abigail Adams urged her husband, in a letter, to "remember
the ladies" in his work on the legal code for the new republic, reminding him that wives needed protection against the
"naturally tyrannical" tendencies of their husbands. Abigail's
language was appropriate to women's subordinate status in
45 marriage and society—she asked for men's chivalrous
protection from the excesses of other men. Chiding his wife
for being "saucy," he trivialized her argument by claiming
that men were, in practice, "the subjects. We have only the
name of masters." A problem outside of definition and
50 discourse could not be taken seriously. And yet, for an
instant, John Adams allowed himself to think seriously

on this subject—his wife's code of laws, if enacted, would
lead to social disorder: "Depend upon it, we know better
than to repeal our Masculine systems."
55 Here we see, in its extreme manifestation, the impact
on history of men's power to define. Having established
patriarchy as the foundation of family and the state, men
viewed it as immutable and made it the very definition of
social order. To challenge it was seen as both ludicrous and
60 profoundly threatening.

**10.** The author most likely includes the quotation from the
United States Constitution in line 10 in order to

(A) point out the incongruity of women being characterized as free while having no political rights
(B) demonstrate that women were in fact free, while
servants, slaves, and American Indians were not
(C) suggest that women could be appointed as representatives but could not vote
(D) illustrate the difficult task of ensuring equitable
political representation
(E) explain how women could be represented in
government without being considered free
citizens

**11.** The author specifies "fund-raising, tea boycotts, and
actions against profiteering merchants" in lines 18-19
in order to

(A) prove that women altered the course of the
American Revolution through their activities
(B) demonstrate how women protested male
dominance
(C) point out the only activities available to women
during this period
(D) indicate that women only engaged in political
activities that directly affected their households
(E) give examples of political activities undertaken by
women during the Revolutionary War

**12.** The author mentions "Loyalist women" (line 20) to
demonstrate that

(A) women who demanded property rights during
the American Revolution were not considered
disloyal
(B) women on both sides of the American Revolution
engaged in political activities
(C) Loyalist women were more vocal about their
political views than other women
(D) Loyalist women were noted for their tea boycotts
and fund-raising
(E) Loyalist women tended to be more socially influential than those that supported the revolution

**GO ON TO THE NEXT PAGE** ⟩

13. The author describes John and Abigail Adams as "a well-matched and loving couple" (line 38) to point out that

(A) the couple fundamentally agreed on political issues
(B) the couple were compatible until Abigail Adams became outspoken in her political views
(C) even compatible marriage partners did not agree on issues involving women's rights
(D) contrary to public belief, John and Abigail Adams were a happily married couple
(E) most married partners do not agree on issues that involve conflicts between men and women

14. In line 43, "naturally" is closest in meaning to

(A) appropriately
(B) authentically
(C) thoroughly
(D) innately
(E) unsurprisingly

15. The author uses the phrase "for an instant" (lines 50-51) in order to

(A) point out John Adams' desire for an immediate solution to a pressing issue
(B) suggest disapproval of any amount of time devoted to such an insignificant issue
(C) indicate that John Adams glimpsed his wife's point despite his cultural limitations
(D) express approval for John Adams' swift response to a crucial issue
(E) show outrage at John Adams' outright dismissal of Abigail Adams' request

16. In the final sentence, the author's characterization of the challenge to the social order serves to

(A) suggest that such a challenge was in the militant spirit of the Founding Fathers
(B) express ambivalence toward the political assumptions of the Founding Fathers
(C) show the author's disapproval of such an ill-fated effort
(D) indicate that the men of the era both ridiculed and feared a change in the social order
(E) imply that women of the era recognized the futility of their efforts to gain their rights

GO ON TO THE NEXT PAGE ▷

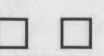
**Questions 17-24 are based on the following passage.**

*The following is excerpted from an essay written in 1995 to acquaint a general audience with new developments in research on play among animals.*

Consider the puppy. At only three weeks of age, this tiny ball of fur has already begun gnawing, pawing, and tugging at its littermates. At four to five weeks, its antics
Line rival those of a rambunctious child, chasing and wrestling
5  with its siblings at all hours of the day and night.

Such behavior is not unusual among social mammals. From human children to whales to sewer rats, many groups of mammals and even some birds play for a significant fraction of their youth. Brown bear cubs, like puppies and
10 kittens, stalk and wrestle with one another in imaginary battles. Deer play tag, chasing and fleeing from one another. Wolves play solitary games with rocks and sticks. Chimpanzees tickle one another.

However fascinating these displays of youthful exu-
15 berance may be, play among animals was ignored by scientists for most of this century. Biologists assumed that this seemingly purposeless activity had little effect on animal development, was not a distinct form of behavior, and was too nebulous a concept either to define or to study.
20 Even the term "play" caused problems for researchers, because it suggests that watching animals goof off is not an activity for serious scientists.

But a steady accumulation of evidence over the past two decades now suggests that play is a distinct form of
25 behavior with an important role in the social, physical, and mental development of many animals. In one study, kittens, mice, and rats were found to play the most at ages when permanent changes were occurring in their muscle fiber and the parts of their brains regulating movement. Kittens were
30 most playful between 4 and 20 weeks of age; rats, from 12 to 50 days; and mice, from 15 to 29 days. Development at those ages is comparable to that of a two-year-old human infant. At these precise times in the development of these animals, muscle fibers differentiate and the connections
35 to areas of the brain regulating movement are made. Such changes apparently are not unique to kittens, mice, and rats, but apply to mammals in general.

Thus, research on play has given biologists an important tool with which to probe the development of the brain and
40 motor systems of animals. The study on rats, kittens, and mice may, for instance, provide a physiological explanation for why infant animals employ in their play the same kinds of behavior that they will later use as adults. By stalking and capturing imaginary prey over and over again, a kitten
45 builds its muscle and brain connections in a way that allows it to perform those actions later in life.

Play may also provide insight into the social develop-ment of animals. When the rough-and-tumble of play ends traumatically with a yelp or a shriek, young animals may
50 be learning the limits of their strength and how to control themselves among others. Those are essential lessons for an animal living in a close-knit group. Perhaps, some scientists

guess, as mammals gathered into social groups, play took on the function of socializing members of the group. Not
55 everyone agrees with this theory, though. Another expla-nation is that play may not have evolved to confer any advantage but is simply a consequence of higher cognitive abilities or an abundance of nutrition and parental care.

Why did play evolve? No one knows for certain, but
60 after ten years of studying brown bears of Alaska, biolo-gist Robert Fagen has his own opinion. "Why do people dance?" he asks. "Why do birds sing? For the bears, we're becoming increasingly convinced that aesthetic factors are primary." Sometimes, that is, animals play simply for the
65 fun of it.

17. In line 4, "rival" is closest in meaning to

(A) mock
(B) dispute
(C) nearly equal
(D) play with
(E) contend against

18. In the second paragraph (lines 6-13), the references to animals primarily serve to

(A) suggest that animal play can be difficult to study
(B) prove a controversial point about animal behavior
(C) contrast with a previous description of animal play
(D) emphasize physical similarities between animals and humans
(E) show the variety of animal play

19. The findings of "one study" (line 26) primarily support which of the following claims?

(A) Play is difficult to study because it takes so many forms.
(B) Most animal species tend to begin playing as they approach adulthood.
(C) Play is a key factor in the social organization of some animal groups.
(D) Researchers do not always recognize behavioral similarities among diverse species.
(E) Research into play may help us understand animals' physiological development.

**GO ON TO THE NEXT PAGE**

**2**  **2**

Unauthorized copying or reuse of
any part of this page is illegal.

**20.** The principle illustrated in lines 43-46 ("By stalking . . . life") is best conveyed by which additional example?

(A) Some puppies play only with their siblings.
(B) A toddler prefers to play with one particular toy.
(C) A lion is trained to jump through a hoop.
(D) Young monkeys chase each other up and down a tree.
(E) Certain species of birds migrate south every fall.

**21.** Which would be most likely to learn the "essential lessons" mentioned in line 51 ?

(A) A class setting out on a field trip
(B) A young athlete playing on a soccer team
(C) A small child attempting to roller-skate
(D) A bear defending its young
(E) A kitten playing with a ball of string

**22.** The "theory" (line 55) and the "opinion" (line 61) differ primarily about whether

(A) animals enjoy playing
(B) play occurs mainly among social animals
(C) animals learn to play by watching one another
(D) play serves a useful purpose
(E) play is pleasurable to watch

**23.** The discussion of Robert Fagen's work (lines 59-65) serves to

(A) strengthen an argument with corroborating evidence
(B) show that varying explanations may be logically related
(C) illustrate the resistance of conservative scientists to new ideas
(D) demonstrate how a widely held belief loses credibility as new findings emerge
(E) expand the discussion to include a different type of explanation

**24.** In lines 61-64, Fagen compares bears playing to people dancing in order to suggest that both activities

(A) have little practical function
(B) involve peer groups in shared physical activity
(C) promote physical coordination
(D) are often observed in younger animals
(E) are commonly associated with social development

## STOP

**If you finish before time is called, you may check your work on this section only.**
**Do not turn to any other section in the test.**

## SECTION 3
### Time — 25 minutes
### 18 Questions

**Turn to Section 3 (page 4) of your answer sheet to answer the questions in this section.**

**Directions:** This section contains two types of questions. You have 25 minutes to complete both types. For questions 1-8, solve each problem and decide which is the best of the choices given. Fill in the corresponding circle on the answer sheet. You may use any available space for scratchwork.

**Notes**

1. The use of a calculator is permitted.
2. All numbers used are real numbers.
3. Figures that accompany problems in this test are intended to provide information useful in solving the problems. They are drawn as accurately as possible EXCEPT when it is stated in a specific problem that the figure is not drawn to scale. All figures lie in a plane unless otherwise indicated.
4. Unless otherwise specified, the domain of any function $f$ is assumed to be the set of all real numbers $x$ for which $f(x)$ is a real number.

**Reference Information**

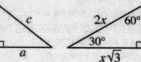

$A = \pi r^2$
$C = 2\pi r$
$A = \ell w$
$A = \frac{1}{2}bh$
$V = \ell wh$
$V = \pi r^2 h$
$c^2 = a^2 + b^2$
**Special Right Triangles**

The number of degrees of arc in a circle is 360.
The sum of the measures in degrees of the angles of a triangle is 180.

1. According to a certain recipe, 25 pounds of flour are needed to make 300 rolls. At this rate, how many pounds of flour are needed to make 12 rolls?

(A) 1
(B) 2
(C) 3
(D) 4
(E) 6

2. If $xy = 10$, what is the value of $2 \cdot \dfrac{x}{y} \cdot y^2$ ?

(A) 5
(B) 8
(C) 10
(D) 12
(E) 20

**GO ON TO THE NEXT PAGE**

768

3 3 3 3 3 3 3 3

Unauthorized copying or reuse of
any part of this page is illegal.

3. If $x + y = 30$ and $x > 8$, then which of the
following must be true?

(A) $y > 0$
(B) $y < 22$
(C) $y = 22$
(D) $y > 22$
(E) $x < 30$

$P(3, 2)$
$Q(7, 2)$
$R(7, 4)$

4. The coordinates of points $P$, $Q$, and $R$ in the $xy$-plane
are given above. What is the perimeter of $\triangle PQR$ ?

(A) 12
(B) 14
(C) $6 + \sqrt{20}$ (approximately 10.47)
(D) $6 + \sqrt{32}$ (approximately 11.66)
(E) $\sqrt{164}$ (approximately 12.81)

$8, 17, 26, 35, 44, \ldots$

5. The first 5 terms in a sequence are shown above. Each
term after the first is found by adding 9 to the term
immediately preceding it. Which term in this sequence
is equal to $8 + (26 - 1)9$ ?

(A) The 8th
(B) The 9th
(C) The 25th
(D) The 26th
(E) The 27th

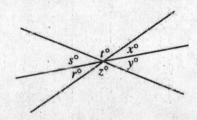

6. Three lines intersect in a point as shown in the figure
above. Which of the following pairs of angle measures is
NOT sufficient for determining all six angle measures?

(A) $t$ and $z$
(B) $t$ and $y$
(C) $s$ and $x$
(D) $r$ and $t$
(E) $r$ and $s$

GO ON TO THE NEXT PAGE

7. The sum of two numbers that differ by 1 is $t$. In terms of $t$, what is the value of the greater of the two numbers?

(A) $\dfrac{t-1}{2}$

(B) $\dfrac{t}{2}$

(C) $\dfrac{t+1}{2}$

(D) $\dfrac{t}{2}+1$

(E) $\dfrac{2t-1}{2}$

**NUMBER OF SIBLINGS PER STUDENT IN A PRESCHOOL CLASS**

| Number of Siblings | Number of Students |
|---|---|
| 0 | 3 |
| 1 | 6 |
| 2 | 2 |
| 3 | 1 |

8. The table above shows how many students in a class of 12 preschoolers had 0, 1, 2, or 3 siblings. Later, a new student joined the class, and the average (arithmetic mean) number of siblings per student became equal to the median number of siblings per student. How many siblings did the new student have?

(A) 0
(B) 1
(C) 2
(D) 3
(E) 4

GO ON TO THE NEXT PAGE

**Directions:** For Student-Produced Response questions 9-18, use the grids at the bottom of the answer sheet page on which you have answered questions 1-8.

Each of the remaining 10 questions requires you to solve the problem and enter your answer by marking the circles in the special grid, as shown in the examples below. You may use any available space for scratchwork.

Answer: $\frac{7}{12}$

Answer: 2.5

Answer: 201
Either position is correct.

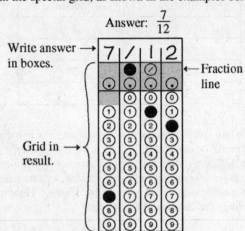

Write answer → in boxes.

← Fraction line

Grid in → result.

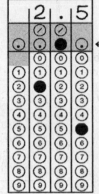

← Decimal point

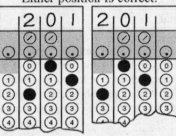

**Note:** You may start your answers in any column, space permitting. Columns not needed should be left blank.

- Mark no more than one circle in any column.

- Because the answer sheet will be machine-scored, **you will receive credit only if the circles are filled in correctly.**

- Although not required, it is suggested that you write your answer in the boxes at the top of the columns to help you fill in the circles accurately.

- Some problems may have more than one correct answer. In such cases, grid only one answer.

- No question has a negative answer.

- **Mixed numbers** such as $3\frac{1}{2}$ must be gridded as

  3.5 or 7/2. (If $3\ 1\ /\ 2$ is gridded, it will be

  interpreted as $\frac{31}{2}$, not $3\frac{1}{2}$.)

- **Decimal Answers:** If you obtain a decimal answer with more digits than the grid can accommodate, it may be either rounded or truncated, but it must fill the entire grid. For example, if you obtain an answer such as 0.6666..., you should record your result as .666 or .667. **A less accurate value such as .66 or .67 will be scored as incorrect.**

Acceptable ways to grid $\frac{2}{3}$ are:

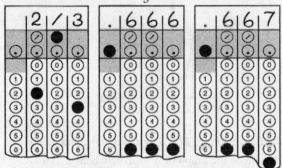

---

9. If $2(x - 3) = 8$, what does $\dfrac{x - 3}{x + 3}$ equal?

10. When twice a number is decreased by 3, the result is 253. What is the number?

**GO ON TO THE NEXT PAGE** →

771

OUTDOOR SNEAKER COMPANY'S
JULY PRODUCTION

|        | High-tops | Low-tops | Total  |
|--------|-----------|----------|--------|
| White  | 3,600     |          |        |
| Black  |           | 1,500    |        |
| Total  |           | 5,500    | 10,000 |

11. Outdoor Sneaker Company manufactures only white sneakers and black sneakers, both of which are available as either high-tops or low-tops. On the basis of the information in the table above, how many black sneakers did Outdoor Sneaker Company manufacture in July?

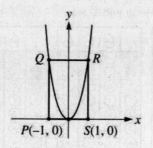

12. In the figure above, *PQRS* is a rectangle, and points *Q* and *R* lie on the graph of $y = ax^2$, where *a* is a constant. If the perimeter of *PQRS* is 10, what is the value of *a* ?

13. If $ab + b = a + 2c$, what is the value of *b* when $a = 2$ and $c = 3$ ?

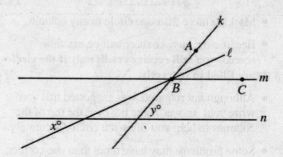

**Note: Figure not drawn to scale.**

14. In the figure above, $m \parallel n$ and $\ell$ bisects $\angle ABC$. If $45 < y < 55$, what is one possible value for *x* ?

⟶ **GO ON TO THE NEXT PAGE**

**15.** The Acme Plumbing Company will send a team of 3 plumbers to work on a certain job. The company has 4 experienced plumbers and 4 trainees. If a team consists of 1 experienced plumber and 2 trainees, how many different such teams are possible?

**Note: Figure not drawn to scale.**

**16.** The figure above consists of two circles that have the same center. If the shaded area is $64\pi$ square inches and the smaller circle has a radius of 6 inches, what is the radius, in inches, of the larger circle?

**17.** If $p$, $r$, and $s$ are three different prime numbers greater than 2, and $n = p \times r \times s$, how many positive factors, including 1 and $n$, does $n$ have?

$$h(t) = c - (d - 4t)^2$$

**18.** At time $t = 0$, a ball was thrown upward from an initial height of 6 feet. Until the ball hit the ground, its height, in feet, after $t$ seconds was given by the function $h$ above, in which $c$ and $d$ are positive constants. If the ball reached its maximum height of 106 feet at time $t = 2.5$, what was the height, in feet, of the ball at time $t = 1$ ?

# STOP

**If you finish before time is called, you may check your work on this section only.**
**Do not turn to any other section in the test.**

## SECTION 4
### Time — 25 minutes
### 35 Questions

---

**Turn to Section 4 (page 5) of your answer sheet to answer the questions in this section.**

---

**Directions:** For each question in this section, select the best answer from among the choices given and fill in the corresponding circle on the answer sheet.

---

The following sentences test correctness and effectiveness of expression. Part of each sentence or the entire sentence is underlined; beneath each sentence are five ways of phrasing the underlined material. Choice A repeats the original phrasing; the other four choices are different. If you think the original phrasing produces a better sentence than any of the alternatives, select choice A; if not, select one of the other choices.

In making your selection, follow the requirements of standard written English; that is, pay attention to grammar, choice of words, sentence construction, and punctuation. Your selection should result in the most effective sentence—clear and precise, without awkwardness or ambiguity.

EXAMPLE:

Laura Ingalls Wilder published her first book <u>and she was sixty-five years old then</u>.

(A) and she was sixty-five years old then
(B) when she was sixty-five
(C) at age sixty-five years old
(D) upon the reaching of sixty-five years
(E) at the time when she was sixty-five

(A) ● (C) (D) (E)

1. <u>Mr. Chung would like to retire, but retirement is unable to be afforded by him.</u>

(A) Mr. Chung would like to retire, but retirement is unable to be afforded by him.
(B) Mr. Chung would like to retire, but he cannot afford to do so.
(C) Mr. Chung would like to retire, but he is unable to afford that.
(D) Retirement is what Mr. Chung would like to do, but he cannot afford it.
(E) Retirement appeals to Mr. Chung, but he cannot afford stopping working.

2. The Ussuri tiger, a relative of the Bengal tiger, has been described as <u>the strongest tiger and also the most peaceful of them</u>.

(A) the strongest tiger and also the most peaceful of them
(B) not only the strongest tiger, but also more peaceful than any
(C) the strongest tiger at the same time as it is the most peaceful tiger
(D) at once the strongest and also the most peaceful of them
(E) the strongest and yet the most peaceful of tigers

3. Like most new residents, <u>the town's winding streets confused the Curtis family</u> for a day or two.

(A) the town's winding streets confused the Curtis family
(B) the winding streets of the town confusing the Curtis family
(C) the Curtis family was confused by the town's winding streets
(D) the Curtis family, who found the town's winding streets confusing
(E) there were winding streets in the town which confused the Curtis family

4. The city of Houston, Texas, <u>is about sixty miles inland, while being</u> the third largest foreign-trade port in the United States.

(A) is about sixty miles inland, while being
(B) although about sixty miles inland, is
(C) being located about sixty miles inland makes it
(D) which is about sixty miles inland, although it is
(E) whose location is about sixty miles inland, makes it

GO ON TO THE NEXT PAGE

5. Great literature, such as the Greek tragedies or the novels of Jane Austen, endures <u>by their speaking directly and freshly</u> to each new generation of readers.

   (A) by their speaking directly and freshly
   (B) by its speaking direct and fresh
   (C) because it speaks directly and freshly
   (D) because of speaking direct and fresh
   (E) since they speak with directness and freshness

6. The services of architect I.M. Pei are always very much in demand <u>considering that his buildings combine both beauty and an affordable price</u>.

   (A) considering that his buildings combine both beauty and an affordable price
   (B) considering that his buildings combine both beauty and affordability
   (C) because his buildings combine beauty and affordability
   (D) because his buildings will combine not only beauty but also an affordable price
   (E) being that his buildings will combine both beauty and affordability

7. <u>The tragic story of Paolo and Francesca was the subject of a poem and a symphony, being popular throughout the nineteenth century.</u>

   (A) The tragic story of Paolo and Francesca was the subject of a poem and a symphony, being popular throughout the nineteenth century.
   (B) The tragic story of Paolo and Francesca was popular throughout the nineteenth century, where it is being made the subject of a poem and a symphony.
   (C) The tragic story of Paolo and Francesca was popular throughout the nineteenth century, when it was the subject of both a poem and a symphony.
   (D) Paolo and Francesca, whose tragic story was the subject of a popular poem and symphony throughout the nineteenth century.
   (E) Being the subject of a poem and a symphony, the tragic story of Paolo and Francesca having been popular throughout the nineteenth century.

8. <u>C.G. Jung, a Swiss psychologist, whose renown as a pioneer</u> in the field of psychoanalysis almost equals that of Sigmund Freud.

   (A) C.G. Jung, a Swiss psychologist, whose renown as a pioneer
   (B) C.G. Jung, who was a Swiss psychologist and whose renown as a pioneer
   (C) A Swiss with renown as a psychological pioneer, C.G. Jung
   (D) C.G. Jung was a Swiss psychologist whose renown as a pioneer
   (E) A Swiss, C.G. Jung who was a psychological pioneer and whose renown

9. Many people think taxes are too <u>high, consequently, some of those people do not report</u> all the money they earn.

   (A) high, consequently, some of those people do not report
   (B) high, therefore, some of those people do not report
   (C) high; consequently, some do not report
   (D) high, some people do not report
   (E) high, and therefore not reporting

10. Just as Ireland has produced many famous writers and the Netherlands an abundance of famous painters, <u>so Finland has provided a large number of famous architects</u>.

    (A) so Finland has provided a large number of famous architects
    (B) Finland provides famous architects, and by large numbers
    (C) Finland's contribution is to provide famous architects in a large number
    (D) and so then, for Finland, a large number of famous architects is provided
    (E) and like them Finland has provided a large number of famous architects

11. Readers of the novice writer's recent book have said that it is at once frustrating because of its chaotic structure <u>but its originality is still a delight</u>.

    (A) but its originality is still a delight
    (B) although it is delightfully original
    (C) and it is delightful in its originality
    (D) while being so original as to delight them
    (E) and delightful because of its originality

**GO ON TO THE NEXT PAGE**

The following sentences test your ability to recognize grammar and usage errors. Each sentence contains either a single error or no error at all. No sentence contains more than one error. The error, if there is one, is underlined and lettered. If the sentence contains an error, select the one underlined part that must be changed to make the sentence correct. If the sentence is correct, select choice E. In choosing answers, follow the requirements of standard written English.

EXAMPLE:

The other delegates and him immediately
 A              B        C
accepted the resolution drafted by the
                          D
neutral states. No error
                   E

Ⓐ ● Ⓒ Ⓓ Ⓔ

---

**12.** Much of the success of Frank Capra and George
        A
Stevens as a director of motion pictures can be
        B
attributed to the technical work of talented film
     C            D
editors. No error
          E

**13.** It was fortunate that Ms. Seward attended the
       A
committee meeting, for only she was able to examine
                              B          C
the problem calm and thoughtfully. No error
             D                      E

**14.** My colleague and myself received an award for our
                       A              B
paper on the accuracy with which a polygraph
                        C
measures physiological processes. No error
     D                             E

**15.** A lack of job opportunities for recent graduates
        A
restricts their independence, often forcing them
         B                           C
to remain at home or else they move back home.
                    D
No error
 E

**16.** Marathon racing, a challenging test of endurance,

has become increasingly popular among amateur
    A           B              C
athletes in the last few years. No error
               D                 E

**17.** Crossing and recrossing the stream, stepping on or
        A
over slippery rocks, and following a trail that grew
                          B              C
steeper and steeper, the hikers soon realized

how challenging their day would be. No error
    D                                 E

**18.** Though best known as a jazz vocalist, he
              A
also enjoyed gospel music, whereby he told his
     B                       C
manager that he wanted to make a recording of his
                                  D
favorite gospel songs. No error
                        E

**19.** In the foothills of that large mountain range is
                                                  A
the sources of a river whose course was not
                        B
fully mapped until this century. No error
     C        D                   E

GO ON TO THE NEXT PAGE →

4  4

Unauthorized copying or reuse of any part of this page is illegal.

**20.** In 1850 Jim Beckwourth, a Black American explorer,

discovered in the mountains of the Sierra Nevada
    A     B

a pass soon becoming an important gateway to
       C              D

California gold-rush country. No error
                   E

**21.** Because the flood has made the bridge inaccessible to
                                  A

automobiles and pedestrians alike , we had rented
                   B       C

a small boat to reach the island. No error
         D           E

**22.** The Mount Isa mine complex is one of
                    A

the most highly mechanized in the world,
         B

plus being the largest single industrial
   C       D

enterprise in Queensland. No error
              E

**23.** Although one likes to believe that your own
    A        B         C

children are beautiful, intelligent, and well behaved,

what one believes is not always the case. No error
                  D      E

**24.** The warning in the plays is clear: unless we restore
                A        B

the integrity of the family , all traditional values
            C

will disappear . No error
   D       E

**25.** As a student becomes familiar with both early
                A

and contemporary Native American literature, one
                          B

may notice that traditional stories have influenced
    C                   D

recent ones. No error
         E

**26.** John Edgar Wideman is regarded to be one of
                   A    B

the most talented writers of the late twentieth century

and is often compared to such literary giants as
           C                 D

Ralph Ellison and Richard Wright. No error
                      E

**27.** Mastery of cardiopulmonary resuscitation techniques
      A

are mandatory for firefighters and police officers
 B     C

as well as rescue squad volunteers. No error
   D                 E

**28.** In the United States, the industrial use of plastics is
  A                      B       C

greater than steel , aluminum, and copper combined.
      D

No error
 E

**29.** The dolls in the collection, all more than two hundred
                    A   B

years old, had been carefully carved for children
                 C

long since gone. No error
   D        E

**GO ON TO THE NEXT PAGE**

**Directions:** The following passage is an early draft of an essay. Some parts of the passage need to be rewritten.

Read the passage and select the best answers for the questions that follow. Some questions are about particular sentences or parts of sentences and ask you to improve sentence structure or word choice. Other questions ask you to consider organization and development. In choosing answers, follow the requirements of standard written English.

**Questions 30-35 are based on the following essay, a response to an assignment to write about a historical figure one would like to meet.**

(1) What person from the past would I most like to meet? (2) Not a famous or powerful person; I would prefer meeting a really good observer who lived in a faraway place at a dramatic moment in time. (3) Nancy Gardner Prince, a young African American woman who went to live at the imperial Russian court in 1824. (4) Some of the most famous events in Russian history took place then, there was a time when people challenged the government, fought hardly for social reforms, risking being defeated and punished. (5) Nancy Gardner Prince was right there in Saint Petersburg. (6) Anyone can read about this period, but I would love to listen to that woman who was born and raised in Massachusetts who heard the rumors and felt the unrest.

(7) Her ability to speak several languages enabled her to gather stories from eyewitnesses of major events like the uprising of December 1825. (8) She shared in the hope and sadness of those long-ago people. (9) We know that she tried to learn about everything she found—I believe she would have much to say about the many countries she lived in. (10) For nine years she worked and moved through all levels of society, from meeting with the empress on charitable projects to fostering poor children. (11) Talking to Nancy Prince would be just great.

**30.** In context, which of the following is the best phrase to insert at the beginning of sentence 3 ?

(A) That one is
(B) My choice would be
(C) In any case, that would be
(D) An excellent observer,
(E) Nevertheless, I have chosen

**31.** In context, which of the following revisions would NOT improve sentence 4 (reproduced below) ?

*Some of the most famous events in Russian history took place then, there was a time when people challenged the government, fought hardly for social reforms, risking being defeated and punished.*

(A) Begin with "I should explain".
(B) Change "then, there" to "then. It".
(C) Delete the comma after "government" and insert "and".
(D) Change "hardly" to "passionately".
(E) Change "being defeated and punished" to "defeat and punishment".

**32.** Sentence 5 in the passage is best described as

(A) introducing a new topic
(B) providing an additional example
(C) emphasizing a major point
(D) linking two contrasting discussions
(E) presenting a personal opinion

**33.** In context, which revision appropriately shortens sentence 6 (reproduced below) ?

*Anyone can read about this period, but I would love to listen to that woman who was born and raised in Massachusetts who heard the rumors and felt the unrest.*

(A) Change "Anyone can read" to "Read".
(B) Change "this period" to "this".
(C) Change "I would love to listen" to "to listen".
(D) Change "who was born and raised in" to "from".
(E) Delete "and felt the unrest".

GO ON TO THE NEXT PAGE

**34.** Which of the following is the best sentence to insert at the beginning of the second paragraph?

(A) The journey from Massachusetts had been long.

(B) In 1824 Saint Petersburg was a turbulent city.

(C) Russian history has fascinated me for years.

(D) Unfortunately, Prince faced harsh winters in Saint Petersburg.

(E) Prince was an ideal observer in several ways.

**35.** In context, which of the following revisions would NOT improve sentence 9 (reproduced below) ?

*We know that she tried to learn about everything she found—I believe she would have much to say about the many countries she lived in.*

(A) Delete "We know that".

(B) Delete "I believe".

(C) Change "found" to "encountered".

(D) Change the dash to a semicolon.

(E) Change "much" to "tons of things".

## STOP

**If you finish before time is called, you may check your work on this section only.
Do not turn to any other section in the test.**

## SECTION 5
Time — 25 minutes
24 Questions

**Turn to Section 5 (page 5) of your answer sheet to answer the questions in this section.**

**Directions:** For each question in this section, select the best answer from among the choices given and fill in the corresponding circle on the answer sheet.

Each sentence below has one or two blanks, each blank indicating that something has been omitted. Beneath the sentence are five words or sets of words labeled A through E. Choose the word or set of words that, when inserted in the sentence, best fits the meaning of the sentence as a whole.

**Example:**

Hoping to ------- the dispute, negotiators proposed a compromise that they felt would be ------- to both labor and management.

(A) enforce . . useful
(B) end . . divisive
(C) overcome . . unattractive
(D) extend . . satisfactory
(E) resolve . . acceptable    Ⓐ Ⓑ Ⓒ Ⓓ ●

1. The depiction of the ------- wolf is largely a misconception; wolves are ------- creatures that prefer to run in packs.

   (A) howling . . noisy
   (B) maternal . . shy
   (C) lone . . social
   (D) vicious . . dangerous
   (E) hungry . . famished

2. Jazz pioneer Louis Armstrong is renowned for his improvisations on the trumpet; his innovations as a vocalist are equally -------.

   (A) obscure    (B) severe    (C) conventional
      (D) erroneous    (E) noteworthy

3. Andrew's hunch that Ms. Smith would lose the election was ------- when her opponent won in a landslide, proving Andrew's ------- to be correct.

   (A) compromised . . prediction
   (B) rejected . . insolence
   (C) substantiated . . endorsement
   (D) confirmed . . intuition
   (E) belied . . retraction

4. The medicine does have a salutary effect by ------- pain, even if recent studies prove that it cannot eliminate such discomfort entirely.

   (A) alleviating    (B) distracting    (C) revitalizing
      (D) eradicating    (E) augmenting

5. The intern was almost too -------; he felt the suffering of his patients as if it were his own.

   (A) candid    (B) disarming    (C) empathetic
      (D) insightful    (E) hysterical

6. As the charismatic speaker left the podium, she was surrounded by ------- of zealous supporters who ------- our attempts to approach her.

   (A) an entourage . . interfered with
   (B) a debacle . . concurred with
   (C) a faction . . pertained to
   (D) a dearth . . intercepted
   (E) a coalition . . encompassed

7. Sally was a lighthearted and even-tempered woman; she had none of her sister's -------.

   (A) affluence    (B) affability    (C) equanimity
      (D) resilience    (E) truculence

8. Because postmodernist critics often rely on ------- language, their prose frequently seems ------- to nonspecialists who fail to comprehend its meaning.

   (A) accessible . . abstruse
   (B) arcane . . unequivocal
   (C) esoteric . . impenetrable
   (D) hackneyed . . exotic
   (E) lucid . . grating

**GO ON TO THE NEXT PAGE** →

The passages below are followed by questions based on their content; questions following a pair of related passages may also be based on the relationship between the paired passages. Answer the questions on the basis of what is stated or implied in the passages and in any introductory material that may be provided.

**Questions 9-12 are based on the following passages.**

**Passage 1**

When children are first born, they know nothing of the world beyond themselves. Almost immediately they are presented with rattles, dolls, or other playthings that will become their constant companions and, in some sense, their
*Line*
5   mentors. In nearly every imaginable situation, children are accompanied by toys that perform the vital role of reducing a complex universe of human culture to terms that they can readily apprehend. It is not that children are unable to grasp such things on their own. Rather, toys furnish a playground
10  where rehearsals for reality can proceed without constraint or self-consciousness, allowing children an opportunity to exercise their inherent capacities for learning and assimilation.

**Passage 2**

I can't dispute that children might learn something
15  from their toys. What I do dispute, however, are the grandiose conclusions that the so-called "experts" have drawn from that simple fact. Some have gone so far as to claim that toys are critical to teaching children about their cultures, maintaining that, without toys, children
20  would have difficulty adjusting to the ways of the world. Hogwash! Children play with toys to have fun, not to create some sort of cultural microcosm. Perhaps those who speculate about the profound significance of child-hood recreation should spend more time playing with
25  toys and less time writing about them.

9. Both passages are concerned with the

(A) distinction between play and reality
(B) role of toys in children's lives
(C) validity of expert opinions
(D) transition from childhood to maturity
(E) different ways that toys reflect human culture

10. The author of Passage 2 would most probably consider the last sentence of Passage 1 to be

(A) accurate but misleading
(B) unnecessarily cautious
(C) too vague to verify or dispute
(D) uncharacteristically perceptive
(E) exaggerated and pretentious

11. Compared to the tone of Passage 1, the tone of Passage 2 is more

(A) scholarly
(B) disdainful
(C) apologetic
(D) sentimental
(E) somber

12. The last line of Passage 2 suggests that the author of Passage 1 has

(A) treated a serious subject lightly
(B) utilized a stilted writing style
(C) never observed children at play
(D) lost touch with childhood realities
(E) falsified crucial evidence

**GO ON TO THE NEXT PAGE**

**Questions 13-24 are based on the following passages.**

*The following passages consider the experience of listening to recorded books. Passage 1 is from a 1994 collection of essays on reading in the electronic age. Passage 2 is from a 1998 essay by a teacher of writing and literature who is legally blind.*

### Passage 1

When we read with our eyes, we hear the words in the theater of our auditory inwardness. The voice we conjure up is our own—it is the sound-print of the self. Bringing *Line* this voice to life via the book is one of the subtler aspects
5 of the reading magic, but hearing a book in the voice of another amounts to a silencing of that self—it is an act of vocal tyranny. The listener is powerless against the taped voice, not at all in the position of my five-year-old daughter, who admonishes me continually, "Don't read it
10 like that, Dad." With the audio book, everything—pace, timbre, inflection—is determined for the captive listener. The collaborative component is gone; one simply receives.

Both the reader's inner voice and the writer's literary or stylistic voice are, obviously, sexed. When I read a male
15 writer, I simply adjust my vocalization to the tone of the text; when I read a woman, I don't attempt an impersonation, but I am aware that my voicing is a form of translation. But when I listened to a cassette of John Cheever's stories read by an expressive female voice, I just couldn't take it.
20 Midway through "The Enormous Radio" I had to pop the tape from the machine to keep her from wreaking havoc on my sense of Cheever. Cheever's prose is as imprinted with his gender as Virginia Woolf's is with hers. Nor could I get past the bright vigor of the performing voice; I missed the
25 dark notes, the sense of pooling shadows that has always accompanied my readings of the man.

Sometimes, to be sure, the fit is excellent—either because the reader achieves the right neutrality, allowing the voice to become a clear medium for the text, or because
30 the interpretation somehow accords with my own expectations. Then, too, I have had the pleasure of hearing an author rendering his or her own work. Indeed, listening to certain re-mastered recordings of the "greats," I have experienced the skin-prickling illusion of proximity (I am actually
35 listening to James Joyce . . .). The author can open up a work in ways that no other reader can. At moments like these I find myself wavering, questioning the fixity of my assumptions.

### Passage 2

For better or worse, listening to an audio book almost
40 always feels like a shared experience. I feel myself not merely a passive audience but engaged in a kind of exchange. Readers are not reading to me; we are reading together. I have a sense of continuous back-and-forth commentary, where I bounce my ideas off the readers'
45 ideas, or what I perceive as their ideas from their intonations, mistakes, involuntary grunts, and sighs. This is precisely what alarms the sighted reader who thinks of reading as a private and intensely personal act, a solo flight with no copilot to look over your shoulder, make snide
50 comments, or gush about the view. But I can't help myself. This way of thinking about reading comes from the habit of listening to people I know read aloud to me. When my husband reads to me, usually a big novel or epic, the text becomes a topic of conversation throughout the day. The
55 initial impressions one has during the course of reading, the ideas one revises or rejects as reading continues, become our mutual property. We share the process of reading, a real-time event in the intimate space where ideas take shape.

60 I require my writing students to turn in taped readings of their work. This is not only a convenience that allows me to return their work as quickly as a sighted teacher would. But reading their work aloud also makes the students more conscious of flaws in their prose. Frequently, I notice, they
65 feel compelled to speak to me at the end of the tape, particularly after reading a longer piece of work. "I tried to do it another way first, but I think this works better," they say. "Reading it over, I see the ending is kind of abrupt." I don't discount the possibility that these outpourings are staged
70 pleas for me to go easy on them. But I also think there is something about having just read aloud for an extended time that makes them drop their guard. I sense they are not so much speaking to me as thinking aloud. I feel myself briefly invited into the mysterious space between the writer
75 and the text. I imagine them sitting alone, in the circle of light cast by a solitary reading lamp. The text lies in their laps. Or they read it off the computer screen, their reading punctuated by an occasional tap-tap-tap of the scroll command. Outside the circle of light, in the general darkness,
80 I hover, a receiving presence.

13. Compared to the author of Passage 2, the author of Passage 1 shows a greater concern about the

(A) creation of genuine dialogue between lovers of great books
(B) limited availability of recorded books
(C) problems inherent in listening to a writer's interpretation of his or her own work
(D) difficulty of imagining a distinctive voice when one reads silently
(E) particular gender of speakers, listeners, and writers

**GO ON TO THE NEXT PAGE**

**14.** The author of Passage 1 notes his daughter's admonition (lines 9-10) primarily to

(A) acknowledge the tendency of adults to read aloud without sufficient expression
(B) caution the reader against indulging precocious children
(C) offer an example of active participation
(D) stress the importance of reading to children
(E) recount his daughter's achievements with pride

**15.** The statement in lines 13-14 ("Both . . . sexed") primarily indicates that the author of Passage 1 believes that

(A) gender can create particular stylistic problems for a writer
(B) people prefer to read novels written by authors of their own gender
(C) readers and writers are often interested in discussions of romantic love
(D) gender usually shapes an individual's use of language
(E) a reader will experience difficulty expressing his or her inner voice

**16.** Which hypothetical situation involves the same "form of translation" (line 17) discussed by the author of Passage 1?

(A) A feminist scholar studies a novel written by a woman during the nineteenth century.
(B) An artist who has always painted in oils decides to attempt a landscape in watercolors.
(C) A tourist has difficulty understanding speakers of a regional dialect.
(D) A father revises a traditional fairy tale in order to include his daughter in the plot.
(E) A song written by a woman and normally performed by a female vocalist is sung by a man.

**17.** In line 29, "clear medium" refers to situations in which

(A) the voice of the audio-book speaker does not interfere with the listener's enjoyment
(B) a person enjoys listening to an audio book more than reading silently
(C) an audio book leads to a greater appreciation of a writer's intent than a printed book does
(D) the gender of an author cannot easily be determined
(E) the listener's tastes do not color his or her response to a book

**18.** In Passage 1, the discussion about writers reading their own works (lines 31-38) serves primarily to

(A) reiterate the author's opposition to audio-book speakers
(B) introduce a particular instance that challenges the main argument of the passage
(C) offer a note of irony in an otherwise serious discussion
(D) pay tribute to those writers the author has particularly enjoyed reading
(E) shift the discussion from listening to audio books to producing them

**19.** The author of Passage 1 would most likely interpret the "exchange" described in lines 42-46 of Passage 2 as being

(A) disturbing, because speakers of audio books enunciate words in a peculiar manner
(B) one-sided, since the listener cannot communicate directly with the speaker
(C) enjoyable, since the listener can hear a book while performing a monotonous chore
(D) disheartening, because fewer and fewer people are discovering the pleasure of silent reading
(E) inspiring, because it will encourage more people to enjoy classic works

**GO ON TO THE NEXT PAGE** →

5 5 5 5

Unauthorized copying or reuse of
any part of this page is illegal.

20. The author of Passage 2 mentions "intonations, mistakes, involuntary grunts, and sighs" (lines 45-46) in order to

(A) imply that some audio-book readers have surprisingly poor speaking skills
(B) assert that listening to audio books is enjoyable regardless of the reader's speaking ability
(C) argue that a speaker's vocal inflections can obscure the author's intended meaning
(D) indicate that her ideas are considered idiosyncratic by some
(E) suggest that unconscious expressions often betray one's true opinions

21. In Passage 2, the author's reasons for setting the requirement described in lines 60-61 are best characterized as both

(A) rigorous and presumptuous
(B) pragmatic and pedagogical
(C) capricious and creative
(D) provocative and unprecedented
(E) arbitrary and idiosyncratic

22. In lines 66-68, the author of Passage 2 uses quotations to demonstrate that

(A) beginning writers make fairly predictable errors
(B) students tend to be overly critical of their own work
(C) students know more about writing than one would expect
(D) reading aloud makes students more aware of their prose
(E) reading aloud can be challenging for writers of all abilities

23. The author of Passage 2 uses the term "staged pleas" (lines 69-70) in order to

(A) illustrate the dramatic quality of her students' readings
(B) underscore the high standards she sets for her students' work
(C) suggest that there might be an opportunistic motive for her students' behavior
(D) congratulate herself on devising a useful technique for teaching writing
(E) mock her students' efforts to earn high grades without hard work

24. How do the examples of the daughter in Passage 1 (lines 8-10) and the husband in Passage 2 (lines 52-54) primarily function in their respective passages?

(A) The first is offered to illustrate the naïvete of a child, whereas the second demonstrates the sophistication of an adult.
(B) The first introduces a humorous moment, whereas the second emphasizes the seriousness of a problem.
(C) The first contrasts with the notion of a passive experience, whereas the second exemplifies a shared activity.
(D) The first represents a burdensome responsibility, whereas the second depicts an enjoyable interaction.
(E) The first captures a spontaneous emotion, whereas the second illustrates intellectual objectivity.

# STOP

**If you finish before time is called, you may check your work on this section only.
Do not turn to any other section in the test.**

## SECTION 7
### Time — 25 minutes
### 20 Questions

**Turn to Section 7 (page 6) of your answer sheet to answer the questions in this section.**

**Directions:** For this section, solve each problem and decide which is the best of the choices given. Fill in the corresponding circle on the answer sheet. You may use any available space for scratchwork.

**Notes**

1. The use of a calculator is permitted.
2. All numbers used are real numbers.
3. Figures that accompany problems in this test are intended to provide information useful in solving the problems. They are drawn as accurately as possible EXCEPT when it is stated in a specific problem that the figure is not drawn to scale. All figures lie in a plane unless otherwise indicated.
4. Unless otherwise specified, the domain of any function $f$ is assumed to be the set of all real numbers $x$ for which $f(x)$ is a real number.

**Reference Information**

$A = \pi r^2$
$C = 2\pi r$
$A = \ell w$
$A = \frac{1}{2}bh$
$V = \ell wh$
$V = \pi r^2 h$
$c^2 = a^2 + b^2$
Special Right Triangles

The number of degrees of arc in a circle is 360.
The sum of the measures in degrees of the angles of a triangle is 180.

---

**1.** If $k$ is a positive integer divisible by 3, and if $k < 60$, what is the greatest possible value of $k$?

(A) 55
(B) 56
(C) 57
(D) 58
(E) 59

**2.** The letter H is symmetric with respect to two different lines, as shown by the dotted lines in the figure above. Which of the following letters is symmetric with respect to at least two different lines?

(A) K

(B) L

(C) M

(D) X

(E) Y

**GO ON TO THE NEXT PAGE**

7

Unauthorized copying or reuse of
any part of this page is illegal.

7

3. Bobby receives $2 for each chore he does during the week, plus a weekly allowance of $10. If Bobby receives no other money, which of the following expressions represents the total dollar amount Bobby receives for a week in which he has done $n$ chores?

(A) $10 + n$
(B) $(10 + 2)n$
(C) $10n + 2$
(D) $10 + 2n$
(E) $(10 + n)2$

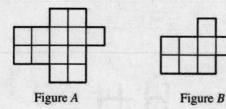

Figure A        Figure B

4. The smallest squares in Figure $A$ and Figure $B$ are all equal in size. If the area of Figure $A$ is 26 square centimeters, what is the area of Figure $B$ ?

(A) 12 sq cm
(B) 14 sq cm
(C) 16 sq cm
(D) 18 sq cm
(E) 20 sq cm

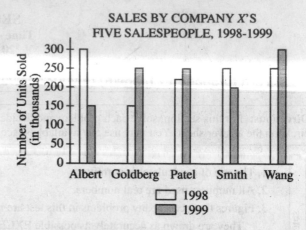

SALES BY COMPANY $X$'S
FIVE SALESPEOPLE, 1998-1999

☐ 1998
▨ 1999

5. According to the graph above, which salesperson had the greatest increase in the number of units sold from 1998 to 1999 ?

(A) Albert
(B) Goldberg
(C) Patel
(D) Smith
(E) Wang

6. If the average (arithmetic mean) of 6, 6, 12, 16, and $x$ is equal to $x$, what is the value of $x$ ?

(A) 6
(B) 8
(C) 9
(D) 10
(E) 11

**GO ON TO THE NEXT PAGE**

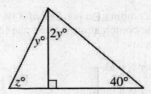

**7.** In the figure above, what is the value of $z$ ?

(A) 55
(B) 60
(C) 65
(D) 70
(E) 75

**8.** A computer program randomly selects a positive two-digit integer. If the integer selected is odd, twice that integer is printed. If the integer selected is even, the integer itself is printed. If the integer printed is 26, which of the following could have been the integer selected?

   I. 13
  II. 26
 III. 52

(A) I only
(B) II only
(C) I and II only
(D) I and III only
(E) I, II, and III

**9.** How many seconds are there in $m$ minutes and $s$ seconds?

(A) $60m + s$

(B) $m + 60s$

(C) $60(m + s)$

(D) $\dfrac{m + s}{60}$

(E) $\dfrac{m}{60} + s$

**10.** If $(2x - 2)(2 - x) = 0$, what are all the possible values of $x$ ?

(A) 0 only
(B) 1 only
(C) 2 only
(D) 1 and 2 only
(E) 0, 1, and 2

**GO ON TO THE NEXT PAGE**

Unauthorized copying or reuse of
any part of this page is illegal.

**11.** If $x^3 = y^9$, what is $x$ in terms of $y$ ?

(A) $\sqrt{y}$

(B) $y^2$

(C) $y^3$

(D) $y^6$

(E) $y^{12}$

**13.** Kyle's lock combination consists of 3 two-digit numbers. The combination satisfies the three conditions below.

- One number is odd.

- One number is a multiple of 5.

- One number is the day of the month of Kyle's birthday.

If each number satisfies **exactly** one of the conditions, which of the following could be the combination to the lock?

(A) 14-20-13

(B) 14-25-13

(C) 15-18-16

(D) 20-15-20

(E) 34-30-21

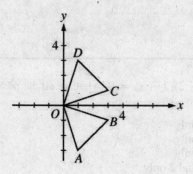

**12.** In the $xy$-coordinate system above, which of the following line segments has a slope of $-1$ ?

(A) $\overline{OA}$

(B) $\overline{OB}$

(C) $\overline{OC}$

(D) $\overline{OD}$

(E) $\overline{DC}$

$$\sqrt{x+9} = x - 3$$

**14.** For all values of $x$ greater than 3, the equation above is equivalent to which of the following?

(A) $x = x^2$

(B) $x = x^2 + 18$

(C) $x = x^2 - 6x$

(D) $x = x^2 - 6x + 9$

(E) $x = x^2 - 6x + 18$

**GO ON TO THE NEXT PAGE**

**7**

Unauthorized copying or reuse of
any part of this page is illegal.

**7**

**15.** How many integers in the set of all integers from
1 to 100, inclusive, are <u>not</u> the square of an integer?

(A) 19
(B) 50
(C) 81
(D) 89
(E) 90

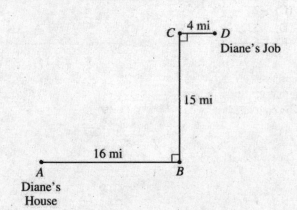

*C* 4 mi *D*
    Diane's Job

15 mi

16 mi

*A*        *B*
Diane's
House

**16.** The figure above shows the route of Diane's trip
from her house to her job. Diane travels 16 miles
from *A* to *B*, 15 miles from *B* to *C*, and 4 miles
from *C* to *D*. If she were able to travel from *A*
to *D* directly, how much shorter, in miles, would
the trip be?

(A)   5
(B)   8
(C)  10
(D)  11
(E)  15

**17.** One circle has a radius of $\frac{1}{2}$ and another circle has a
radius of 1. What is the ratio of the area of the larger
circle to the area of the smaller circle?

(A) 2 : 1
(B) 3 : 1
(C) 3 : 2
(D) 4 : 1
(E) 5 : 2

**18.** If the sum of the consecutive integers from −22
to *x*, inclusive, is 72, what is the value of *x* ?

(A) 23
(B) 25
(C) 50
(D) 75
(E) 94

GO ON TO THE NEXT PAGE

7 | 7

Unauthorized copying or reuse of
any part of this page is illegal.

19. If $k$, $n$, $x$, and $y$ are positive numbers satisfying
$x^{-\frac{4}{3}} = k^{-2}$ and $y^{\frac{4}{3}} = n^2$, what is $(xy)^{-\frac{2}{3}}$ in
terms of $n$ and $k$ ?

(A) $\dfrac{1}{nk}$

(B) $\dfrac{n}{k}$

(C) $\dfrac{k}{n}$

(D) $nk$

(E) $1$

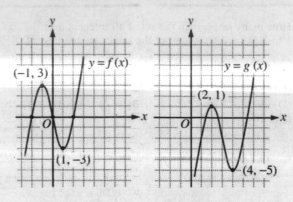

20. The figures above show the graphs of the functions $f$
and $g$. The function $f$ is defined by $f(x) = x^3 - 4x$.
The function $g$ is defined by $g(x) = f(x + h) + k$,
where $h$ and $k$ are constants. What is the value
of $hk$ ?

(A) $-6$
(B) $-3$
(C) $-2$
(D) $3$
(E) $6$

## STOP

**If you finish before time is called, you may check your work on this section only.
Do not turn to any other section in the test.**

**8**

Unauthorized copying or reuse of
any part of this page is illegal.

 **8**

## SECTION 8
### Time — 20 minutes
### 19 Questions

**Turn to Section 8 (page 7) of your answer sheet to answer the questions in this section.**

**Directions:** For each question in this section, select the best answer from among the choices given and fill in the corresponding circle on the answer sheet.

Each sentence below has one or two blanks, each blank indicating that something has been omitted. Beneath the sentence are five words or sets of words labeled A through E. Choose the word or set of words that, when inserted in the sentence, best fits the meaning of the sentence as a whole.

**Example:**

Hoping to ------- the dispute, negotiators proposed a compromise that they felt would be ------- to both labor and management.

(A) enforce . . useful
(B) end . . divisive
(C) overcome . . unattractive
(D) extend . . satisfactory
(E) resolve . . acceptable

Ⓐ Ⓑ Ⓒ Ⓓ ●

1. Eduardo was ------- to find that the editorial he had written was ------- by several typographical errors.

(A) dismayed . . authenticated
(B) overjoyed . . exacerbated
(C) intrigued . . enveloped
(D) prepared . . enhanced
(E) embarrassed . . marred

2. In order to ------- the loss of natural wetlands used by migrating snow geese, conservationists in the 1960's and 1970's ------- wetland refuges in the northern prairies.

(A) standardize . . ignored
(B) offset . . surrendered
(C) explain . . dismantled
(D) compensate for . . established
(E) account for . . administered

3. Frequently used as a spice, ginger also has ------- properties: it can be used to help treat coughs, colds, and upset stomachs.

(A) timeworn    (B) invariable    (C) edible
(D) curative    (E) descriptive

4. The scientific organization ------- the newspaper for prominently covering the predictions of a psychic while ------- to report on a major research conference.

(A) celebrated . . failing
(B) promoted . . refusing
(C) denounced . . neglecting
(D) spurned . . hastening
(E) honored . . opting

5. The colors and patterns on butterflies' wings may seem merely -------, but they are actually ------- the survival of these insects, enabling them to attract mates and to hide from predators.

(A) artificial . . dependent on
(B) unique . . unnecessary to
(C) decorative . . instrumental in
(D) beautiful . . results of
(E) unrelated . . precursors of

6. A discerning publishing agent can ------- promising material from a mass of submissions, separating the good from the bad.

(A) supplant    (B) dramatize    (C) finagle
(D) winnow    (E) overhaul

**GO ON TO THE NEXT PAGE**

791

The passage below is followed by questions based on its content. Answer the questions on the basis of what is <u>stated</u> or <u>implied</u> in the passage and in any introductory material that may be provided.

**Questions 7-19 are based on the following passage.**

*The following passage is from a novel set at the imaginary Jocelyn College in 1950.*

When Henry Mulcahy, a middle-aged instructor of literature at Jocelyn College, Jocelyn, Pennsylvania, unfolded the president's letter and became aware of its
*Line* contents, he gave a sudden sharp cry of impatience and
5 irritation, as if such interruptions could positively be brooked no longer. This was the last straw. How was he expected to take care of forty students if other demands on his attention were continually being put in the way? On the surface of his mind, this vagrant grievance kept playing.
10 Meanwhile, he had grown pale and his hands were trembling with anger and a strange sort of exultation. "Your appointment will not be continued beyond the current academic year. . . ." He sprang to his feet and mimed the sentence aloud, triumphantly, in inverted commas, bringing the
15 whole force of his personality to bear on this specimen or exhibit of the incredible.

He had guessed long ago that Hoar meant to dismiss him, but he was amazed, really amazed (he repeated the word to himself) that the man should have given himself
20 away by an action as overt as this one. As an intellectual, he felt stunned not so much by the moral insensitiveness of the president's move as by the transparency of it. You do not fire a person who has challenged you openly at faculty meetings, who has fought, despite you and your cabal, for a
25 program of salary increases and a lightening of the teaching load, who has not feared to point to waste and mismanagement concealed by those in high places, who dared to call only last week (yes, fantastic as it seemed, this was the background of the case) for an investigation of the Buildings
30 and Grounds Department and begged the dietitian to *unscramble*, if she would be so good, for her colleagues, the history of the twenty thousand eggs. . . . A condolatory smile, capping this enumeration, materialized on his lips; the letter was so inconsonant with the simplest precepts
35 of strategy that it elicited a kind of pity, mingled with contempt and dry amusement.

Still, the triteness of the attempt, the tedium of it, tried forbearance to the limit; at a progressive college, surely, one had the right to expect something better than what
40 one was used to at Dudley or Wilkins State, and the very element of repetition gave the whole affair an unwarranted and unreal character, as of some tawdry farce seriously reenacted. He had been in the academic harness long enough, he should have thought (and the files in the college office
45 could testify), to anticipate anything, yet some unseen tendril of trust, he now remarked with a short harsh laugh, must have spiraled out from his heart and clung to the president's person, or simply to the idea of decency, for him now to feel this new betrayal so keenly.

50 For the truth was, as Mulcahy had to acknowledge, pacing up and down his small office, that in spite of all the evidence he had been given of the president's unremitting hatred, he found himself hurt by the letter—wounded, to be honest, not only in his self-esteem but in some tenderer place, in
55 that sense of contract between people that transcends personal animosities and factional differences, that holds the individual distinct from the deed and maintains even in the fieriest opposition the dream of final agreement and concord. He had not known, in short, that the president disliked him
60 so flatly. It was the usual mistake of a complex intelligence in assessing a simple intelligence, of an imagination that is capable of seeing and feeling on many levels at once, as opposed to an administrative mentality that feels operationally, through acts. Like most people of literary sensibility, he had
65 been unprepared, when it came down to it, for the obvious: a blunt, naked wielding of power. And the fact that he had *thought* himself prepared, he bitterly reflected, was precisely a measure of the abyss between the Maynard Hoars of this world and the Mulcahys.

70 The anomalies of the situation afforded him a gleam of pleasure—to a person of superior intellect, the idea that he or she has been weak or a fool in comparison with an inferior adversary is fraught with moral comedy and sardonic philosophic applications. He sat down at his desk, popped a
75 peppermint into his mouth, and began to laugh softly at the ironies of his biography: Henry Mulcahy, called Hen by his friends, forty-one years old, the only Ph.D. in the literature department, contributor to such prestigious magazines as the *Nation* and the *Kenyon Review*, Rhodes
80 scholar, Guggenheim fellow, father of four, fifteen years teaching experience, yet having the salary and rank of only instructor—an "unfortunate" personality in the lexicon of department heads, but in the opinion of a number of his colleagues the cleverest man at Jocelyn and the victim,
85 here as elsewhere, of that ferocious envy of mediocrity for excellence that is the ruling passion of all systems of jobholders.

7. The passage is narrated from the point of view of

   (A) Henry Mulcahy
   (B) an observer who does not know Mulcahy initially but who learns about him during the course of the passage
   (C) an observer who has only partial knowledge of Mulcahy
   (D) an observer who knows all about Mulcahy and his thoughts
   (E) an administrator at Jocelyn College

**GO ON TO THE NEXT PAGE** ⟶

**8.** The mention of the "transparency" (line 22) of President Hoar's move implies that Mulcahy views the president's decision as a

(A) vindictive and unwise action
(B) timid and hesitant rebuke
(C) necessary enforcement of Jocelyn's stated policies
(D) step that was not motivated by any personal considerations
(E) choice that was painful and difficult to make

**9.** The issues that Mulcahy has fought for at Jocelyn are listed (lines 22-32) in order to point out that they

(A) elicited a sympathetic response from the college faculty
(B) prove that Jocelyn is a poorly run college
(C) are criticisms raised by President Hoar in his letter to Mulcahy
(D) deal with theoretical issues that most people cannot understand
(E) represent a wide range of topics, from the trivial to the serious

**10.** Mulcahy most likely regards the choice of the word *"unscramble"* (line 31) as

(A) an imitation of the literal-minded diction of the dietitian
(B) a euphemism for a harsher word
(C) a witty and amusing play on words
(D) an example of how administrators like President Hoar abuse language
(E) a scholarly word that is in keeping with the mood of faculty meetings

**11.** In context, Mulcahy's "condolatory smile" (lines 32-33) is most probably an expression of both

(A) cynical skepticism and comical self-pity
(B) sincere compassion and whimsical delight
(C) profound surprise and delighted appreciation
(D) bitter disappointment and sly criticism
(E) condescending sympathy and amused scorn

**12.** Mulcahy apparently believes that he is being dismissed from Jocelyn College because he

(A) is outspoken in his criticism of the way the college is run
(B) has not continued to do research in his field
(C) is not as dedicated to the students as the other faculty members are
(D) made fun of the college president at a faculty meeting
(E) is resented by other professors who are jealous of his academic achievements

**13.** In context, the term "progressive college" (line 38) suggests that the college is

(A) successful and respected
(B) liberal and experimental
(C) eager to increase enrollment
(D) steadily improving in quality
(E) oriented toward the sciences

**14.** The passage suggests that Dudley and Wilkins State (line 40) are colleges that

(A) are best known for their drama courses
(B) are less progressive than Jocelyn
(C) have better academic programs than Jocelyn
(D) have been trying to imitate Jocelyn
(E) are smaller than Jocelyn

**15.** In the context of the passage, one who "holds the individual distinct from the deed" (lines 56-57) can be expected to

(A) forgive someone, even though that person has been malicious
(B) praise someone, even when that person is wrong
(C) promote someone, even though that person may not be qualified
(D) disagree with someone's actions without attacking that person's character
(E) understand someone's motives without revealing that knowledge to the person's enemies

**16.** In line 60, "flatly" most nearly means

(A) evenly
(B) tautly
(C) shallowly
(D) unemphatically
(E) unequivocally

**17.** The phrase "ironies of his biography" (line 76) refers to Mulcahy's belief that

(A) he has not received the recognition and rewards that he deserves
(B) he has been more active later in his academic career than at its beginning
(C) he is ridiculed by his friends despite his impressive academic achievements
(D) his personal life is not as satisfying as his professional career
(E) his personality is not suited to his scholarly pursuits

**GO ON TO THE NEXT PAGE**

18. The passage suggests that Mulcahy's main shortcoming is that

   (A) his devotion to literature takes precedence over his loyalty to college administrators
   (B) he allows himself to be intimidated by his peers
   (C) he is too idealistic and self-sacrificing in his dedication to teaching and research
   (D) because of his superior education and academic honors, he is arrogant to his students
   (E) despite his intelligence, he is naïve about the politics of college administration

19. Mulcahy apparently attributes his difficulties at Jocelyn to the

   (A) extraordinary amount of time that he has to spend with his students
   (B) fact that he is too modest to tell others of his academic accomplishments
   (C) distaste he has for making himself appear competent at the expense of others
   (D) resentment of those whom he judges to be less intelligent than he is
   (E) length and nature of his academic experience, which has alerted him to the flaws of others

# STOP

**If you finish before time is called, you may check your work on this section only.**
**Do not turn to any other section in the test.**

## SECTION 9
### Time — 20 minutes
### 16 Questions

**Turn to Section 9 (page 7) of your answer sheet to answer the questions in this section.**

**Directions:** For this section, solve each problem and decide which is the best of the choices given. Fill in the corresponding circle on the answer sheet. You may use any available space for scratchwork.

Reference Information

   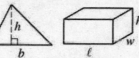   

$A = \pi r^2$
$C = 2\pi r$

$A = \ell w$ $A = \frac{1}{2}bh$ $V = \ell wh$ $V = \pi r^2 h$ $c^2 = a^2 + b^2$ Special Right Triangles

The number of degrees of arc in a circle is 360.
The sum of the measures in degrees of the angles of a triangle is 180.

---

1. If 6 cars out of 10 on an assembly line are red, what is the probability that a car selected at random from the assembly line will be red?

   (A) $\frac{2}{3}$

   (B) $\frac{3}{5}$

   (C) $\frac{1}{2}$

   (D) $\frac{2}{5}$

   (E) $\frac{1}{6}$

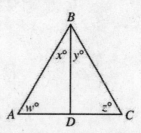

Note: Figure not drawn to scale.

2. If $AB = BC$ and $\overline{BD}$ bisects $\overline{AC}$ in the figure above, which of the following CANNOT be concluded?

   (A) $w = x$

   (B) $w = z$

   (C) $x = y$

   (D) $AD = DC$

   (E) $\overline{BD} \perp \overline{AC}$

**GO ON TO THE NEXT PAGE**

795

3. If 30 percent of $m$ is 40, what is 15 percent of $m$ ?

   (A) 15
   (B) 20
   (C) 25
   (D) 30
   (E) 35

4. If $n$ is any negative number, which of the following must be positive?

   (A) $\dfrac{n}{2}$

   (B) $2n$

   (C) $n + 2$

   (D) $n - 2$

   (E) $2 - n$

5. The ratio 1.2 to 1 is equal to which of the following ratios?

   (A) 1 to 2
   (B) 12 to 1
   (C) 5 to 6
   (D) 6 to 5
   (E) 6 to 50

6. The legend of a certain pictograph shows = 5 million new homes. Approximately how many new homes are represented by the symbols ?

   (A) 3.5 million
   (B) 10.5 million
   (C) 15.5 million
   (D) 17.5 million
   (E) 35 million

**GO ON TO THE NEXT PAGE**

7. If $a$ and $b$ are positive integers and $a^2 - b^2 = 7$, what is the value of $a$?

(A) 3
(B) 4
(C) 5
(D) 6
(E) 7

9. A number $n$ is increased by 5 and the result is multiplied by 5. This result is decreased by 5. Finally, that result is divided by 5. In terms of $n$, what is the final result?

(A) $n - 5$
(B) $n - 1$
(C) $n$
(D) $n + 4$
(E) $5(n + 5)$

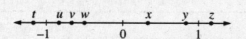

8. On the number line above, which of the following corresponds to $|u - w|$?

(A) $t$
(B) $v$
(C) $x$
(D) $y$
(E) $z$

10. Phillip used four pieces of masking tape, each 6 inches long, to put up each of his posters. Phillip had a 300-foot roll of masking tape when he started. If no tape was wasted, which of the following represents the number of <u>feet</u> of masking tape that was left on the roll after he put up $n$ posters? (12 inches = 1 foot)

(A) $300 - 6n$

(B) $300 - 2n$

(C) $300 - n$

(D) $300 - \dfrac{1}{2}n$

(E) $300 - \dfrac{1}{4}n$

GO ON TO THE NEXT PAGE

11. In the *xy*-coordinate plane, line *m* is the reflection of line $\ell$ about the *x*-axis. If the slope of line *m* is $-\dfrac{4}{5}$, what is the slope of line $\ell$ ?

    (A) $\dfrac{5}{4}$

    (B) $\dfrac{4}{5}$

    (C) $\dfrac{1}{5}$

    (D) $-\dfrac{4}{5}$

    (E) $-\dfrac{5}{4}$

12. If $n = 3p$, for what value of $p$ is $n = p$ ?

    (A) 0

    (B) $\dfrac{1}{3}$

    (C) 1

    (D) 3

    (E) $n$ can never equal $p$.

**GO ON TO THE NEXT PAGE**

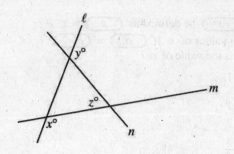

Note: Figure not drawn to scale.

13. In the figure above, if $z = 30$, what is the value of $x + y$ ?

(A) 60
(B) 150
(C) 180
(D) 210
(E) 330

14. If the function $f$ is defined by $f(x) = x^2 + bx + c$, where $b$ and $c$ are positive constants, which of the following could be the graph of $f$ ?

(A)

(B)

(C)

(D)

(E)

**GO ON TO THE NEXT PAGE**

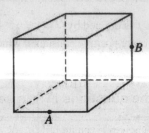

15. The cube shown above has edges of length 2, and A and B are midpoints of two of the edges. What is the length of $\overline{AB}$ (not shown) ?

(A) $\sqrt{2}$

(B) $\sqrt{3}$

(C) $\sqrt{5}$

(D) $\sqrt{6}$

(E) $\sqrt{10}$

16. Let $\boxed{x}$ be defined as $\boxed{x} = x^2 - x$ for all values of $x$. If $\boxed{a} = \boxed{a-2}$, what is the value of $a$ ?

(A) 1

(B) $\dfrac{1}{2}$

(C) $\dfrac{3}{2}$

(D) $\dfrac{6}{5}$

(E) 3

**S T O P**

If you finish before time is called, you may check your work on this section only.
Do not turn to any other section in the test.

**10**  **10**

Unauthorized copying or reuse of
any part of this page is illegal.

# SECTION 10
Time — 10 minutes
14 Questions

**Turn to Section 10 (page 7) of your answer sheet to answer the questions in this section.**

**Directions:** For each question in this section, select the best answer from among the choices given and fill in the corresponding circle on the answer sheet.

The following sentences test correctness and effectiveness of expression. Part of each sentence or the entire sentence is underlined; beneath each sentence are five ways of phrasing the underlined material. Choice A repeats the original phrasing; the other four choices are different. If you think the original phrasing produces a better sentence than any of the alternatives, select choice A; if not, select one of the other choices.

In making your selection, follow the requirements of standard written English; that is, pay attention to grammar, choice of words, sentence construction, and punctuation. Your selection should result in the most effective sentence—clear and precise, without awkwardness or ambiguity.

EXAMPLE:

Laura Ingalls Wilder published her first book
and she was sixty-five years old then.

(A) and she was sixty-five years old then
(B) when she was sixty-five
(C) at age sixty-five years old
(D) upon the reaching of sixty-five years
(E) at the time when she was sixty-five

Ⓐ ● Ⓒ Ⓓ Ⓔ

1. Before signing up for next year's courses, the students' schedules must be approved by their advisers.

   (A) the students' schedules must be approved by their advisers
   (B) the students must have their schedules approved by their advisers
   (C) their advisers must approve the schedule of each student
   (D) the schedules of students must be approved, and by their advisers
   (E) approval of each one's schedule must be given by their advisers

2. Although its being factual in content, the televised biography of Queen Elizabeth I did not seem credible.

   (A) Although its being factual in content
   (B) Despite its factual content
   (C) Whereas it was factual in content
   (D) Its contents being factual
   (E) Even though factual contents were there

3. We do not have absolute personal freedom because what anyone does would have an effect on other people's lives.

   (A) freedom because what anyone does would have an effect on other people's lives
   (B) freedom because it has an effect on the lives of other people
   (C) freedom because what we do affects other people
   (D) freedom, and the reason is the effect our actions have on other people
   (E) freedom, our actions having an effect on other people

4. The information age has ushered children into a global society, this situation causing educators to lament a lack of texts that explain the diversity of cultures.

   (A) this situation causing educators to lament
   (B) which is the cause of educators lamenting
   (C) this causing educators' laments over
   (D) a situation causing educators to lament
   (E) and with it educators' lament at

**GO ON TO THE NEXT PAGE**

10  10

Unauthorized copying or reuse of
any part of this page is illegal.

**5.** One result of the fire department's new contract
is that they can no longer offer overtime pay on
weekends

(A) One result of the fire department's new contract
is that they can no longer offer overtime pay
on weekends.
(B) As one result of its new contract, the fire
department can no longer offer overtime pay
on weekends.
(C) One result of the fire department's new contract
is that overtime pay on weekends can no longer
be offered to them.
(D) The fire department's new contract results in their
no longer being able to offer them overtime pay
on weekends.
(E) One result of the fire department's new contract
are that offering overtime pay on weekends is
no longer possible.

**6.** Anita liked to watch television, of which she found the
science programs especially fascinating.

(A) television, of which she found the science
programs especially fascinating
(B) television; she found the science programs
especially fascinating
(C) television, and it was especially the science
programs that were of fascination
(D) television; the fascination of the science programs
especially
(E) television, especially fascinating to her were the
science programs

**7.** Poet Anne Spencer initially allowed very little of her
work to be published because her exacting standards
caused her to doubt that her poems were good enough
to share with others.

(A) because her exacting standards caused her to
doubt
(B) her standards being exacting, she doubted
(C) because of her standards being exacting, which
she doubted
(D) from having exacting standards causing her to
doubt
(E) having exacting standards causing her doubting

**8.** It is hard for some young people to believe that women
were at one time not admitted to some colleges, but they
have since become coeducational.

(A) colleges, but they have since become coeducational
(B) colleges, but they are now coeducational
(C) colleges, and have since become coeducational
(D) colleges that have since become coeducational
(E) colleges, since becoming coeducational

**9.** The Navajo migrated from Canada to the southwestern United States at the same time as the Apache,
and they speak an Apachean language.

(A) The Navajo migrated from Canada to the
southwestern United States at the same time as
the Apache, and they
(B) The Navajo, who migrated from Canada to the
southwestern United States at the same time as
the Apache,
(C) Migrating from Canada to the southwestern
United States at the same time were the Navajo
and the Apache, and they
(D) The Navajo migrated from Canada to the
southwestern United States with the Apache and
this is why they
(E) A migration from Canada to the southwestern
United States at the same time with the Apache,
the Navajo

**10.** Arelia believes that cloth draped over hills is an art
form that cannot last long enough as a work of art
either to please or influence future generations.

(A) cannot last long enough as a work of art either to
please or influence future generations
(B) cannot last long enough as a work of art, for ages
to come neither pleasing or influencing future
generations
(C) is not a lasting work of art that for ages to come
will either please or influence future generations
(D) is not a lasting work of art that will remain for
ages pleasing and influencing future generations
(E) will not last long enough either to please or to
influence future generations

**GO ON TO THE NEXT PAGE**

11. The price of gold has been influenced by continued inflation and <u>because people have lost faith</u> in the dollar.

    (A) because people have lost faith
    (B) because of the loss of faith
    (C) by people which have lost faith
    (D) losing faith
    (E) loss of faith

12. Giraffes born with very long necks were able to stay alive when food was scarce <u>and were therefore able to pass this desirable trait on to their offspring</u>.

    (A) and were therefore able to pass this desirable trait on to their offspring
    (B) and this desirable trait was passed on as a result to its offspring
    (C) so that their offspring could have this desirable trait passed to them
    (D) so, therefore, this desirable trait would be inherited by their offspring
    (E) and therefore have this desirable trait inherited in their offspring

13. <u>If we compare the number of alligators with the Gila monster over time, we see that the alligator is</u> in decline.

    (A) If we compare the number of alligators with the Gila monster over time, we see that the alligator is
    (B) Comparing the number of alligators and the Gila monster, we see that alligators are
    (C) In comparison with Gila monsters, the number of alligators are
    (D) To compare the alligator with Gila monsters is to show that it is
    (E) A comparison over time of the numbers of alligators and Gila monsters shows that alligators are

14. Many of the instruments used in early operations of the United States Army Signal <u>Corps were adaptations of equipment used by the Plains Indians, particularly that of the heliograph</u>.

    (A) Corps were adaptations of equipment used by the Plains Indians, particularly that of the heliograph
    (B) Corps, there were adaptations of equipment used by the Plains Indians, particularly the heliograph
    (C) Corps, and in particular the heliograph, was an adaptation of equipment used by the Plains Indians
    (D) Corps, particularly the heliograph, were adaptations of equipment used by Plains Indians
    (E) Corps being adaptations, the heliograph in particular, of those used by Plains Indians

# STOP

**If you finish before time is called, you may check your work on this section only.
Do not turn to any other section in the test.**

# Correct Answers and Difficulty Levels
## SAT Practice Test #7

## CRITICAL READING

### Section 2
#### Multiple-Choice Questions

| Correct Answer | Difficulty Level | | Correct Answer | Difficulty Level |
|---|---|---|---|---|
| 1 A | E | 13 | C | E |
| 2 A | M | 14 | D | M |
| 3 C | M | 15 | C | E |
| 4 A | H | 16 | D | M |
| 5 E | H | 17 | C | M |
| 6 E | M | 18 | E | M |
| 7 D | M | 19 | E | M |
| 8 B | M | 20 | D | M |
| 9 A | E | 21 | B | M |
| 10 A | E | 22 | D | E |
| 11 E | M | 23 | E | M |
| 12 B | M | 24 | A | M |

Number correct _____

Number incorrect _____

### Section 5
#### Multiple-Choice Questions

| Correct Answer | Difficulty Level | | Correct Answer | Difficulty Level |
|---|---|---|---|---|
| 1 C | E | 13 | E | M |
| 2 E | E | 14 | C | H |
| 3 D | E | 15 | D | M |
| 4 A | E | 16 | E | M |
| 5 C | E | 17 | A | M |
| 6 A | E | 18 | B | M |
| 7 E | H | 19 | B | M |
| 8 C | H | 20 | B | M |
| 9 B | E | 21 | B | H |
| 10 E | M | 22 | | F |
| 11 B | E | 23 | C | M |
| 12 D | M | 24 | C | M |

Number correct _____

Number incorrect _____

### Section 8
#### Multiple-Choice Questions

| Correct Answer | Difficulty Level | | Correct Answer | Difficulty Level |
|---|---|---|---|---|
| 1 E | E | 11 | E | H |
| 2 D | E | 12 | A | E |
| 3 D | E | 13 | B | H |
| 4 C | E | 14 | B | E |
| 5 C | E | 15 | D | M |
| 6 D | H | 16 | E | H |
| 7 D | E | 17 | A | M |
| 8 A | E | 18 | D | M |
| 9 E | M | 19 | D | H |
| 10 C | M | | | |

Number correct _____

Number incorrect _____

## MATHEMATICS

### Section 3
#### Multiple-Choice Questions

| Correct Answer | Difficulty Level |
|---|---|
| 1 A | E |
| 2 E | E |
| 3 B | E |
| 4 C | M |
| 5 D | M |
| 6 A | M |
| 7 C | M |
| 8 A | H |

### Section 3
#### Student-Produced Response Questions

| Correct Answer | Difficulty Level |
|---|---|
| 9 2/5, .4 | E |
| 10 128 | E |
| 11 2400 | E |
| 12 3 | M |
| 13 8/3, 2.66, 2.67 | M |
| 14 22.5<x<27.5, 45/2<x<55/2 | M |
| 15 24 | H |
| 16 10 | H |
| 17 8 | H |
| 18 70 | H |

Number correct _____

Number correct (9-18) _____

Number incorrect _____

### Section 7
#### Multiple-Choice Questions

| Correct Answer | Difficulty Level | | Correct Answer | Difficulty Level |
|---|---|---|---|---|
| 1 C | E | 11 | C | M |
| 2 D | E | 12 | E | M |
| 3 D | E | 13 | A | M |
| 4 C | E | 14 | C | M |
| 5 B | E | 15 | E | M |
| 6 D | E | 16 | E | M |
| 7 C | E | 17 | D | M |
| 8 C | M | 18 | B | H |
| 9 A | M | 19 | A | H |
| 10 D | M | 20 | E | H |

Number correct _____

Number incorrect _____

### Section 9
#### Multiple-Choice Questions

| Correct Answer | Difficulty Level | | Correct Answer | Difficulty Level |
|---|---|---|---|---|
| 1 B | E | 9 | D | M |
| 2 A | E | 10 | B | M |
| 3 B | E | 11 | B | M |
| 4 E | E | 12 | A | M |
| 5 D | E | 13 | D | M |
| 6 D | M | 14 | E | M |
| 7 B | M | 15 | D | H |
| 8 C | M | 16 | C | H |

Number correct _____

Number incorrect _____

## WRITING

### Essay

Essay Score* (0-6) _____

### Section 4
#### Multiple-Choice Questions

| Correct Answer | Difficulty Level | | Correct Answer | Difficulty Level |
|---|---|---|---|---|
| 1 B | E | 19 | A | E |
| 2 E | E | 20 | C | E |
| 3 C | E | 21 | C | E |
| 4 B | E | 22 | C | E |
| 5 C | M | 23 | C | M |
| 6 C | M | 24 | C | M |
| 7 C | M | 25 | B | M |
| 8 D | M | 26 | A | M |
| 9 C | M | 27 | B | M |
| 10 E | E | 28 | D | M |
| 11 A | H | 29 | E | H |
| 12 B | E | 30 | B | M |
| 13 D | E | 31 | A | M |
| 14 A | E | 32 | C | M |
| 15 D | E | 33 | D | M |
| 16 E | E | 34 | E | M |
| 17 E | E | 35 | E | M |
| 18 C | E | | | |

Number correct _____

Number incorrect _____

### Section 10
#### Multiple-Choice Questions

| | Correct Answer | Difficulty Level |
|---|---|---|
| 1 | B | E |
| 2 | B | E |
| 3 | C | M |
| 4 | D | M |
| 5 | B | M |
| 6 | B | M |
| 7 | A | M |
| 8 | D | M |
| 9 | B | M |
| 10 | E | M |
| 11 | E | M |
| 12 | A | M |
| 13 | E | M |
| 14 | D | M |

Number correct _____

Number incorrect _____

**NOTE:** Difficulty levels are E (easy), M (medium), and H (hard).

* To score your essay, use the SAT scoring guide in Chapter 9 and the free sample essays available online at www.collegeboard.org/satonlinecourse. On this practice test, your essay score should range from 0 to 6. (Keep in mind that on the actual SAT, your essay will be read by two readers and you will receive a score of 0 to 12 on your score report.)

# The SAT Scoring Process

**Scoring.** The computer compares the circle filled in for each question with the correct response. Each correct answer receives one point; omitted questions do not affect your score. For each wrong answer to a multiple-choice question, one-fourth of a point is subtracted to correct for random guessing. The SAT critical reading section has 67 questions. If, for example, a student has 44 right, 20 wrong, and 3 omitted, the resulting raw score is determined as follows:

$$44 \text{ right} - \frac{20 \text{ wrong}}{4} = 44 - 5 = 39 \text{ raw score points}$$

Obtaining raw scores frequently involves the rounding of fractions to the nearest whole number. For example, a raw score of 39.25 is rounded to 39, the nearest whole number. A raw score of 39.50 is rounded upward to 40. **For the WRITING SECTION**, your essay raw score counts approximately 30% and your multiple-choice raw score counts approximately 70%.

**Converting to reported scaled score.** Raw scores are then placed on the College Board scale of 200 to 800 through a process that adjusts scores to account for minor differences in difficulty among different versions of the test. This process, known as equating, is performed so that a student's reported score is not affected by the version of the test taken or by the abilities of the group with whom the student takes the test. As a result of placing SAT scores on the College Board scale, scores earned by students at different times can be compared. For example, an SAT critical reading score of 400 on a test taken at one administration indicates the same level of developed critical reading ability as a 400 score obtained on a different version of the test taken at another time.

**Note:** Since this test has not been previously administered, score ranges are provided for each possible raw score.

# How to Score Practice Test #7

## SAT Critical Reading Sections 2, 5, and 8

**Step A:** Count the number of correct answers for *Section 2* and record the number in the space provided on the Scoring Worksheet. Then do the same for the incorrect answers. (Do not count omitted answers.)

**Step B:** Count the number of correct answers and the number of incorrect answers for *Section 5* and record the numbers in the spaces provided on the Scoring Worksheet. (Do not count omitted answers.)

**Step C:** Count the number of correct answers and the number of incorrect answers for *Section 8* and record the numbers in the spaces provided on the Scoring Worksheet. (Do not count omitted answers.)

**Step D:** Total the number of correct responses. Total the number of incorrect responses. Enter the resulting figures on the Scoring Worksheet. To determine A, use the formula:

$$\text{Number correct} - \frac{\text{Number incorrect}}{4} = A$$

**Step E:** To obtain B, your Rounded Critical Reading Raw Score, round A to the nearest whole number. (For example, any number from 44.50 to 45.49 rounds to 45.) Enter the resulting figure on the Scoring Worksheet.

**Step F:** To find your Critical Reading Scaled Score Range, look up the Total Rounded Raw Score you obtained in step E in the Critical Reading Conversion Table (Table 1). Enter this range in the box on the Scoring Worksheet.

## SAT Mathematics Sections 3, 7, and 9

**Step A:** Count the number of correct answers and the number of incorrect answers for the multiple choice questions (*questions 1 through 8*) in *Section 3* and record the numbers in the spaces provided on the Scoring Worksheet. (Do not count omitted answers.)

**Step B:** Count the number of correct answers for the student-produced response questions (*questions 9 through 18*) in *Section 3* and record the number in the space provided on the Scoring Worksheet.

**Step C:** Count the number of correct answers and the number of incorrect answers for *Section 7* and record the number in the space provided on the Scoring Worksheet. (Do not count omitted answers.)

**Step D:** Count the number of correct answers and the number of incorrect answers for *Section 9* and record the numbers in the spaces provided on the Scoring Worksheet. (Do not count omitted answers.)

**Step E:** Total the number of correct responses. Total the number of incorrect responses. Enter the resulting figures on the Scoring Worksheet. To determine A, use the formula:

$$\text{Number correct} - \frac{\text{Number incorrect}}{4} = A$$

**Step F:** To obtain B, your Mathematics Rounded Raw Score, round A to the nearest whole number. (For example, any number from 44.50 to 45.49 rounds to 45.) Enter the resulting figure on the Scoring Worksheet.

**Step G:** To find your Mathematics Scaled Score Range, use the Mathematics Conversion Table (Table 2) to look up the Total Rounded Raw Score you obtained in step F. Enter this range in the box on the Scoring Worksheet.

### SAT Writing Sections 1, 4, and 10

**Step A:** Enter your Essay Score for *Section 1* in the box on the Scoring Worksheet. (On this practice test, your essay score should range from 0 to 6. Keep in mind that on the actual SAT, two readers will read your essay and you will receive a total score of 0 to 12 on your score report.) For help scoring your essay see page 105.

**Step B:** Count the number of correct answers and the number of incorrect answers for *Section 4* and record the numbers in the spaces provided on the Scoring Worksheet. (Do not count omitted answers.)

**Step C:** Count the number of correct answers and the number of incorrect answers for *Section 10* and record the numbers in the spaces provided on the Scoring Worksheet. (Do not count omitted answers.)

**Step D:** Total the number of correct responses. Total the number of incorrect responses. Enter the resulting figure on the Scoring Worksheet. To determine A, use the formula:

$$\text{Number correct} - \frac{\text{Number incorrect}}{4} = A$$

**Step E:** To obtain B, your Writing Multiple-Choice (MC) Rounded Raw Score, round A to the nearest whole number. (For example, any number from 44.50 to 45.49 rounds to 45.) Enter the resulting figure on the Scoring Worksheet.

**Step F:** To find your overall Writing Scaled Score Range, use Table 3. Look up the Total MC Rounded Raw Score you obtained in Step E in the left side of Table 3 and the Essay Score entered in Step A across the top of the table. Enter this range in the box on the Scoring Worksheet.

**Step G:** To find your Writing MC Subscore Range, look up the Total MC Rounded Raw Score you obtained in Step E on the Writing Multiple-Choice Conversion Table (Table 4). Enter this range in the box on the Scoring Worksheet.

**Note:** For the **WRITING SECTION**, your Essay Raw Score counts approximately 30% and your Multiple-Choice Raw Score counts approximately 70%.

# SAT Practice Test #7 Scoring Worksheet

**SAT Critical Reading Section**

A. Section 2:

+ _____ no. correct    + _____ no. incorrect

B. Section 5:

+ _____ no. correct    + _____ no. incorrect

C. Section 8:

= _____ no. correct    = _____ no. incorrect

D. Total Unrounded Raw Score

_____ no. correct − (_____ no. incorrect ÷ 4) = _____ A

E. Total Rounded Raw Score
   (Rounded to nearest whole number)

_____ B

F. Critical Reading Scaled Score Range
   (See Table 1)

```
┌──────────────┐
│      _       │
└──────────────┘
```
Critical
Reading Scaled
Score Range

**SAT Mathematics Section**

A. Section 3:
   Questions 1-8

+ _____ no. correct    _____ no. incorrect

B. Section 3:
   Questions 9-18

+ _____ no. correct    + _____

C. Section 7:

= _____ no. correct    = _____ no. incorrect

D. Section 9:

= _____ no. correct    = _____ no. incorrect

E. Total Unrounded Raw Score

_____ no. correct − (_____ no. incorrect ÷ 4) = _____ A

F. Total Rounded Raw Score
   (Rounded to nearest whole number)

_____ B

G. Mathematics Scaled Score Range
   (See Table 2)

```
┌──────────────┐
│      _       │
└──────────────┘
```
Mathematics
Scaled
Score Range

**SAT Writing Section**

A. Section 1:

| | |
|---|---|
| | Essay Score |

B. Section 4: _____        _____
                   no. correct            no. incorrect

                        +                        +

C. Section 10: _____        _____
                     no. correct            no. incorrect

                        =                        =

D. Total MC Unrounded Raw Score   _____   ( _____ ÷ 4)  = _____
                                        no. correct        no. incorrect              A

E. Total MC Rounded Raw Score                                              _____
   (Rounded to nearest whole number)                                            B

F. Writing Scaled Score Range
   (See Table 3)

| |
|---|
| – |

Writing Scaled
Score Range

G. Writing MC Subscore Range
   (See Table 4)

| |
|---|
| – |

Writing MC
Subscore Range

| Table 1. Critical Reading Conversion Table | | | |
|---|---|---|---|
| Raw Score | Scaled Score | Raw Score | Scaled Score |
| 67 | 800 | 30 | 470-530 |
| 66 | 770-800 | 29 | 470-530 |
| 65 | 740-800 | 28 | 460-520 |
| 64 | 720-800 | 27 | 450-510 |
| 63 | 700-800 | 26 | 450-510 |
| 62 | 690-790 | 25 | 440-500 |
| 61 | 670-770 | 24 | 440-500 |
| 60 | 660-760 | 23 | 430-490 |
| 59 | 660-740 | 22 | 420-480 |
| 58 | 650-730 | 21 | 420-480 |
| 57 | 640-720 | 20 | 410-470 |
| 56 | 630-710 | 19 | 400-460 |
| 55 | 630-710 | 18 | 400-460 |
| 54 | 620-700 | 17 | 390-450 |
| 53 | 610-690 | 16 | 380-440 |
| 52 | 600-680 | 15 | 380-440 |
| 51 | 610-670 | 14 | 370-430 |
| 50 | 600-660 | 13 | 360-420 |
| 49 | 590-650 | 12 | 350-410 |
| 48 | 580-640 | 11 | 350-410 |
| 47 | 580-640 | 10 | 340-400 |
| 46 | 570-630 | 9 | 330-390 |
| 45 | 560-620 | 8 | 310-390 |
| 44 | 560-620 | 7 | 300-380 |
| 43 | 550-610 | 6 | 290-370 |
| 42 | 550-610 | 5 | 270-370 |
| 41 | 540-600 | 4 | 260-360 |
| 40 | 530-590 | 3 | 250-350 |
| 39 | 530-590 | 2 | 230-330 |
| 38 | 520-580 | 1 | 220-320 |
| 37 | 510-570 | 0 | 200-290 |
| 36 | 510-570 | -1 | 200-290 |
| 35 | 500-560 | -2 | 200-270 |
| 34 | 500-560 | -3 | 200-250 |
| 33 | 490-550 | -4 | 200-230 |
| 32 | 480-540 | -5 | 200-210 |
| 31 | 480-540 | -6 and below | 200 |

| Table 2. Mathematics Conversion Table | | | |
|---|---|---|---|
| Raw Score | Scaled Score | Raw Score | Scaled Score |
| 54 | 800 | 23 | 460-520 |
| 53 | 750-800 | 22 | 450-510 |
| 52 | 720-800 | 21 | 440-500 |
| 51 | 700-780 | 20 | 430-490 |
| 50 | 690-770 | 19 | 430-490 |
| 49 | 680-740 | 18 | 420-480 |
| 48 | 670-730 | 17 | 410-470 |
| 47 | 660-720 | 16 | 400-460 |
| 46 | 640-700 | 15 | 400-460 |
| 45 | 630-690 | 14 | 390-450 |
| 44 | 620-680 | 13 | 380-440 |
| 43 | 620-680 | 12 | 360-440 |
| 42 | 610-670 | 11 | 350-430 |
| 41 | 600-660 | 10 | 340-420 |
| 40 | 580-660 | 9 | 330-430 |
| 39 | 570-650 | 8 | 320-420 |
| 38 | 560-640 | 7 | 310-410 |
| 37 | 550-630 | 6 | 290-390 |
| 36 | 550-630 | 5 | 280-380 |
| 35 | 540-620 | 4 | 270-370 |
| 34 | 530-610 | 3 | 260-360 |
| 33 | 520-600 | 2 | 240-340 |
| 32 | 520-600 | 1 | 230-330 |
| 31 | 520-580 | 0 | 210-310 |
| 30 | 510-570 | -1 | 200-290 |
| 29 | 500-560 | -2 | 200-270 |
| 28 | 490-550 | -3 | 200-250 |
| 27 | 490-550 | -4 | 200-230 |
| 26 | 480-540 | -5 | 200-210 |
| 25 | 470-530 | -6 and below | 200 |
| 24 | 460-520 | | |

## Table 3. Writing Conversion Table

| MC Raw Score | Essay Score | | | | | | |
|---|---|---|---|---|---|---|---|
| | 0 | 1 | 2 | 3 | 4 | 5 | 6 |
| 49 | 650-690 | 670-720 | 690-740 | 710-770 | 750-800 | 780-800 | 800 |
| 48 | 630-690 | 640-720 | 660-740 | 690-770 | 720-800 | 760-800 | 780-800 |
| 47 | 600-690 | 620-720 | 640-740 | 660-770 | 700-800 | 730-800 | 760-800 |
| 46 | 580-690 | 600-720 | 620-740 | 650-770 | 680-800 | 710-800 | 740-800 |
| 45 | 570-690 | 580-720 | 600-740 | 630-770 | 670-800 | 700-800 | 730-800 |
| 44 | 560-680 | 570-710 | 590-730 | 620-760 | 660-790 | 690-800 | 720-800 |
| 43 | 540-660 | 560-690 | 580-710 | 610-740 | 640-780 | 670-800 | 700-800 |
| 42 | 530-660 | 550-690 | 570-700 | 600-730 | 630-770 | 660-800 | 690-800 |
| 41 | 530-650 | 540-680 | 560-700 | 590-720 | 620-760 | 660-790 | 680-800 |
| 40 | 520-640 | 530-670 | 550-690 | 580-710 | 620-750 | 650-780 | 680-800 |
| 39 | 510-630 | 520-660 | 540-680 | 570-710 | 610-740 | 640-770 | 670-800 |
| 38 | 500-620 | 520-650 | 540-670 | 560-700 | 600-730 | 630-770 | 660-790 |
| 37 | 490-610 | 510-640 | 530-660 | 560-690 | 590-720 | 620-760 | 650-780 |
| 36 | 480-600 | 500-630 | 520-650 | 550-680 | 580-720 | 610-750 | 640-770 |
| 35 | 480-590 | 490-620 | 510-640 | 540-670 | 570-710 | 610-740 | 640-770 |
| 34 | 470-590 | 480-620 | 500-630 | 530-660 | 570-700 | 600-730 | 630-760 |
| 33 | 460-580 | 470-610 | 490-630 | 520-650 | 560-690 | 590-720 | 620-750 |
| 32 | 450-570 | 470-600 | 490-620 | 510-640 | 550-680 | 580-710 | 610-740 |
| 31 | 440-560 | 460-590 | 480-610 | 510-640 | 540-670 | 570-700 | 600-730 |
| 30 | 430-550 | 450-580 | 470-600 | 500-630 | 530-660 | 560-700 | 590-720 |
| 29 | 430-540 | 440-570 | 460-590 | 490-620 | 520-650 | 560-690 | 590-710 |
| 28 | 420-530 | 430-560 | 450-580 | 480-610 | 520-650 | 550-680 | 580-700 |
| 27 | 410-520 | 420-550 | 440-570 | 470-600 | 510-640 | 540-670 | 570-700 |
| 26 | 400-520 | 420-550 | 430-560 | 460-590 | 500-630 | 530-660 | 560-690 |
| 25 | 390-510 | 410-540 | 430-560 | 450-580 | 490-620 | 520-650 | 550-680 |
| 24 | 380-500 | 400-530 | 420-550 | 450-570 | 480-610 | 510-640 | 540-670 |
| 23 | 370-490 | 390-520 | 410-540 | 440-570 | 470-600 | 500-630 | 530-660 |
| 22 | 370-480 | 380-510 | 400-530 | 430-560 | 460-590 | 500-630 | 520-650 |
| 21 | 370-480 | 380-510 | 400-530 | 430-560 | 460-590 | 500-630 | 520-650 |
| 20 | 360-470 | 370-500 | 390-520 | 420-550 | 460-580 | 490-620 | 520-640 |
| 19 | 350-460 | 360-490 | 380-510 | 410-540 | 450-580 | 480-610 | 510-630 |
| 18 | 340-450 | 350-480 | 370-500 | 400-530 | 440-570 | 470-600 | 500-630 |
| 17 | 330-450 | 350-480 | 360-490 | 390-520 | 430-560 | 460-590 | 490-620 |
| 16 | 320-440 | 340-470 | 360-490 | 390-510 | 420-550 | 450-580 | 480-610 |
| 15 | 310-430 | 330-460 | 350-480 | 380-510 | 410-540 | 440-570 | 470-600 |
| 14 | 300-420 | 320-450 | 340-470 | 370-500 | 400-530 | 430-560 | 460-590 |
| 13 | 300-410 | 310-440 | 330-460 | 360-490 | 390-520 | 430-560 | 450-580 |
| 12 | 290-400 | 300-430 | 320-450 | 350-480 | 390-510 | 420-550 | 450-570 |
| 11 | 280-390 | 290-420 | 310-440 | 340-470 | 380-510 | 410-540 | 440-570 |
| 10 | 270-390 | 280-420 | 300-430 | 330-460 | 370-500 | 400-530 | 430-560 |
| 9 | 260-380 | 280-410 | 290-430 | 320-450 | 360-490 | 390-520 | 420-550 |
| 8 | 250-370 | 270-400 | 290-420 | 320-450 | 350-480 | 380-510 | 410-540 |
| 7 | 240-360 | 260-390 | 280-410 | 310-440 | 340-470 | 370-510 | 400-530 |
| 6 | 230-350 | 250-380 | 270-400 | 300-430 | 330-460 | 360-500 | 390-520 |
| 5 | 230-340 | 240-370 | 260-390 | 290-420 | 320-460 | 360-490 | 380-520 |
| 4 | 220-340 | 230-370 | 250-380 | 280-410 | 320-450 | 350-480 | 380-510 |
| 3 | 210-330 | 220-360 | 240-380 | 270-400 | 310-440 | 340-470 | 370-500 |
| 2 | 200-320 | 210-350 | 230-370 | 260-400 | 300-430 | 330-460 | 360-490 |
| 1 | 200-300 | 200-330 | 220-350 | 250-380 | 280-410 | 310-450 | 340-470 |
| 0 | 200-290 | 200-320 | 210-340 | 240-370 | 270-410 | 300-440 | 330-470 |
| -1 | 200-280 | 200-310 | 200-330 | 220-350 | 250-390 | 290-420 | 310-450 |
| -2 | 200-260 | 200-290 | 200-310 | 200-340 | 240-370 | 270-410 | 300-430 |
| -3 | 200-240 | 200-270 | 200-290 | 200-320 | 240-360 | 270-390 | 300-420 |
| -4 | 200-230 | 200-260 | 200-280 | 200-300 | 240-340 | 270-370 | 300-400 |
| -5 | 200 | 200-230 | 200-250 | 200-280 | 240-320 | 270-350 | 300-370 |
| -6 | 200 | 200-220 | 200-240 | 200-270 | 240-310 | 270-340 | 300-370 |
| -7 | 200 | 200-220 | 200-230 | 200-260 | 240-300 | 270-330 | 300-360 |
| -8 | 200 | 200-210 | 200-230 | 200-250 | 240-290 | 270-320 | 300-350 |
| -9 | 200 | 200-210 | 200-230 | 200-250 | 240-290 | 270-320 | 300-350 |
| -10 | 200 | 200-210 | 200-230 | 200-250 | 240-290 | 270-320 | 300-350 |
| -11 | 200 | 200-210 | 200-230 | 200-250 | 240-290 | 270-320 | 300-350 |
| -12 | 200 | 200-210 | 200-230 | 200-250 | 240-290 | 270-320 | 300-350 |

| Table 4. Writing Multiple-Choice Conversion Table | | | |
|---|---|---|---|
| Raw Score | Scaled Score | Raw Score | Scaled Score |
| 49 | 78-80 | 21 | 46-56 |
| 48 | 77-80 | 20 | 45-55 |
| 47 | 74-80 | 19 | 44-54 |
| 46 | 72-80 | 18 | 43-53 |
| 45 | 70-80 | 17 | 42-52 |
| 44 | 69-79 | 16 | 41-51 |
| 43 | 67-77 | 15 | 40-50 |
| 42 | 66-76 | 14 | 39-49 |
| 41 | 65-75 | 13 | 38-48 |
| 40 | 64-74 | 12 | 37-47 |
| 39 | 63-73 | 11 | 36-46 |
| 38 | 62-72 | 10 | 35-45 |
| 37 | 61-71 | 9 | 34-44 |
| 36 | 60-70 | 8 | 33-43 |
| 35 | 59-69 | 7 | 32-42 |
| 34 | 58-68 | 6 | 31-41 |
| 33 | 57-67 | 5 | 30-40 |
| 32 | 56-66 | 4 | 29-39 |
| 31 | 55-65 | 3 | 28-38 |
| 30 | 54-64 | 2 | 27-37 |
| 29 | 53-63 | 1 | 25-35 |
| 28 | 52-62 | 0 | 24-34 |
| 27 | 51-61 | -1 | 22-32 |
| 26 | 50-60 | -2 | 20-30 |
| 25 | 49-59 | -3 | 20-28 |
| 24 | 48-58 | -4 | 20-26 |
| 23 | 47-57 | -5 | 20-23 |
| 22 | 46-56 | -6 and below | 20-22 |

# SAT Practice Test #8

 **After this test:**

- Use this book to its full potential! Get exclusive access answer explanations, free practice score reports and free sample student essays to help you score your essay in the Book Owners' Area at www.collegeboard.org/satstudyguide.

- Want more practice? Get 10 more official practice tests, auto essay scoring and lesson plans from the test maker by subscribing to *The Official SAT Online Course*. As a book owner, you're entitled to a $10 discount. Sign up at www.collegeboard.org/satstudyguide.

8

*Note:* Section 6, the variable section, has been omitted from this practice test.

# SAT Reasoning Test — General Directions

### Timing

- You will have 3 hours and 45 minutes to work on this test.
- There are ten separately timed sections:
  - ▶ One 25-minute essay
  - ▶ Six other 25-minute sections
  - ▶ Two 20-minute sections
  - ▶ One 10-minute section
- You may work on only one section at a time.
- The supervisor will tell you when to begin and end each section.
- If you finish a section before time is called, check your work on that section. You may NOT turn to any other section.
- Work as rapidly as you can without losing accuracy. Don't waste time on questions that seem too difficult for you.

### Marking Answers

- Be sure to mark your answer sheet properly.

  COMPLETE MARK  ●     EXAMPLES OF      ⬤⊗⊖◖
                       INCOMPLETE MARKS  ◔⊘⊙⊚

- You must use a No. 2 pencil.
- Carefully mark only one answer for each question.
- Make sure you fill the entire circle darkly and completely.
- Do not make any stray marks on your answer sheet.
- If you erase, do so completely. Incomplete erasures may be scored as intended answers.
- Use only the answer spaces that correspond to the question numbers.

### Using Your Test Book

- You may use the test book for scratchwork, but you will not receive credit for anything written there.
- After time has been called, you may not transfer answers to your answer sheet or fill in circles.
- You may not fold or remove pages or portions of a page from this book, or take the book or answer sheet from the testing room.

### Scoring

- For each correct answer, you receive one point.
- For questions you omit, you receive no points.
- For a wrong answer to a multiple-choice question, you lose one-fourth of a point.
  - ▶ If you can eliminate one or more of the answer choices as wrong, you increase your chances of choosing the correct answer and earning one point.
  - ▶ If you can't eliminate any choice, move on. You can return to the question later if there is time.
- For a wrong answer to a student-produced response ("grid-in") math question, you don't lose any points.
- Multiple-choice and student-produced response questions are machine scored.
- The essay is scored on a 1 to 6 scale by two different readers. The total essay score is the sum of the two readers' scores.
- Off-topic essays, blank essays, and essays written in ink will receive a score of zero.

The passages for this test have been adapted from published material.
The ideas contained in them do not necessarily represent the opinions of the College Board.

**DO NOT OPEN THIS BOOK UNTIL THE SUPERVISOR TELLS YOU TO DO SO.**

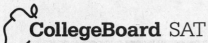

# SAT Reasoning Test™

*You must use a No. 2 pencil. Do not use a mechanical pencil. It is very important that you fill in the entire circle darkly and completely. If you change your response, erase as completely as possible. Incomplete marks or erasures may affect your score. It is very important that you follow these instructions when filling out your answer sheet.*

**1** **Your Name:**
(Print)

Last                    First                    M.I.

I agree to the conditions on the back of the SAT Reasoning Test™ booklet. I also agree to use only a No. 2 pencil to complete my answer sheet.

Signature: _____  Date: __/__/__

**Home Address:**
(Print)
Number and Street      City      State    Zip Code
**Home Phone:** ( )
(Print)          Center: _____  City      State/Country
(Print)

**2** **YOUR NAME**
Last Name (First 6 Letters) | First Name (First 4 Letters) | Mid. Init.

**3** **DATE OF BIRTH**
MONTH | DAY | YEAR
○ Jan
○ Feb
○ Mar
○ Apr
○ May
○ Jun
○ Jul
○ Aug
○ Sep
○ Oct
○ Nov
○ Dec

**5** **SEX**
○ Female ○ Male

**6** **REGISTRATION NUMBER**
(Copy from Admission Ticket.)
○ I turned in my registration form today.

**Important:** Fill in items 8 and 9 exactly as shown on the back of test book.

**9** **TEST FORM**
(Copy from back of test book.)

**8** **FORM CODE**
(Copy and grid as on back of test book.)

**10** **TEST BOOK SERIAL NUMBER**
(Copy from front of test book.)

**4** **ZIP CODE**

**7** **SOCIAL SECURITY NUMBER**

**11** **TEST CENTER**
(Supplied by Test Center Supervisor.)

**FOR OFFICIAL USE ONLY**
⓪①②③④⑤⑥
⓪①②③④⑤⑥
⓪①②③④⑤⑥

00272-36390 • NS75E4600 • Printed in U.S.A.
732652

**PLEASE DO NOT WRITE IN THIS AREA**          **SERIAL #**

815

**SECTION 1**

*IMPORTANT:* **USE A NO. 2 PENCIL. DO NOT WRITE OUTSIDE THE BORDER!**
Words written outside the essay box or written in ink **WILL NOT APPEAR** in the copy sent to be scored, and your score will be affected.

**Begin your essay on this page. If you need more space, continue on the next page.**

Page 3

SERIAL #

**SECTION 2**

1 Ⓐ Ⓑ Ⓒ Ⓓ Ⓔ
2 Ⓐ Ⓑ Ⓒ Ⓓ Ⓔ
3 Ⓐ Ⓑ Ⓒ Ⓓ Ⓔ
4 Ⓐ Ⓑ Ⓒ Ⓓ Ⓔ
5 Ⓐ Ⓑ Ⓒ Ⓓ Ⓔ
6 Ⓐ Ⓑ Ⓒ Ⓓ Ⓔ
7 Ⓐ Ⓑ Ⓒ Ⓓ Ⓔ
8 Ⓐ Ⓑ Ⓒ Ⓓ Ⓔ
9 Ⓐ Ⓑ Ⓒ Ⓓ Ⓔ
10 Ⓐ Ⓑ Ⓒ Ⓓ Ⓔ

11 Ⓐ Ⓑ Ⓒ Ⓓ Ⓔ
12 Ⓐ Ⓑ Ⓒ Ⓓ Ⓔ
13 Ⓐ Ⓑ Ⓒ Ⓓ Ⓔ
14 Ⓐ Ⓑ Ⓒ Ⓓ Ⓔ
15 Ⓐ Ⓑ Ⓒ Ⓓ Ⓔ
16 Ⓐ Ⓑ Ⓒ Ⓓ Ⓔ
17 Ⓐ Ⓑ Ⓒ Ⓓ Ⓔ
18 Ⓐ Ⓑ Ⓒ Ⓓ Ⓔ
19 Ⓐ Ⓑ Ⓒ Ⓓ Ⓔ
20 Ⓐ Ⓑ Ⓒ Ⓓ Ⓔ

21 Ⓐ Ⓑ Ⓒ Ⓓ Ⓔ
22 Ⓐ Ⓑ Ⓒ Ⓓ Ⓔ
23 Ⓐ Ⓑ Ⓒ Ⓓ Ⓔ
24 Ⓐ Ⓑ Ⓒ Ⓓ Ⓔ
25 Ⓐ Ⓑ Ⓒ Ⓓ Ⓔ
26 Ⓐ Ⓑ Ⓒ Ⓓ Ⓔ
27 Ⓐ Ⓑ Ⓒ Ⓓ Ⓔ
28 Ⓐ Ⓑ Ⓒ Ⓓ Ⓔ
29 Ⓐ Ⓑ Ⓒ Ⓓ Ⓔ
30 Ⓐ Ⓑ Ⓒ Ⓓ Ⓔ

31 Ⓐ Ⓑ Ⓒ Ⓓ Ⓔ
32 Ⓐ Ⓑ Ⓒ Ⓓ Ⓔ
33 Ⓐ Ⓑ Ⓒ Ⓓ Ⓔ
34 Ⓐ Ⓑ Ⓒ Ⓓ Ⓔ
35 Ⓐ Ⓑ Ⓒ Ⓓ Ⓔ
36 Ⓐ Ⓑ Ⓒ Ⓓ Ⓔ
37 Ⓐ Ⓑ Ⓒ Ⓓ Ⓔ
38 Ⓐ Ⓑ Ⓒ Ⓓ Ⓔ
39 Ⓐ Ⓑ Ⓒ Ⓓ Ⓔ
40 Ⓐ Ⓑ Ⓒ Ⓓ Ⓔ

**SECTION 3**

1 Ⓐ Ⓑ Ⓒ Ⓓ Ⓔ
2 Ⓐ Ⓑ Ⓒ Ⓓ Ⓔ
3 Ⓐ Ⓑ Ⓒ Ⓓ Ⓔ
4 Ⓐ Ⓑ Ⓒ Ⓓ Ⓔ
5 Ⓐ Ⓑ Ⓒ Ⓓ Ⓔ
6 Ⓐ Ⓑ Ⓒ Ⓓ Ⓔ
7 Ⓐ Ⓑ Ⓒ Ⓓ Ⓔ
8 Ⓐ Ⓑ Ⓒ Ⓓ Ⓔ
9 Ⓐ Ⓑ Ⓒ Ⓓ Ⓔ
10 Ⓐ Ⓑ Ⓒ Ⓓ Ⓔ

11 Ⓐ Ⓑ Ⓒ Ⓓ Ⓔ
12 Ⓐ Ⓑ Ⓒ Ⓓ Ⓔ
13 Ⓐ Ⓑ Ⓒ Ⓓ Ⓔ
14 Ⓐ Ⓑ Ⓒ Ⓓ Ⓔ
15 Ⓐ Ⓑ Ⓒ Ⓓ Ⓔ
16 Ⓐ Ⓑ Ⓒ Ⓓ Ⓔ
17 Ⓐ Ⓑ Ⓒ Ⓓ Ⓔ
18 Ⓐ Ⓑ Ⓒ Ⓓ Ⓔ
19 Ⓐ Ⓑ Ⓒ Ⓓ Ⓔ
20 Ⓐ Ⓑ Ⓒ Ⓓ Ⓔ

21 Ⓐ Ⓑ Ⓒ Ⓓ Ⓔ
22 Ⓐ Ⓑ Ⓒ Ⓓ Ⓔ
23 Ⓐ Ⓑ Ⓒ Ⓓ Ⓔ
24 Ⓐ Ⓑ Ⓒ Ⓓ Ⓔ
25 Ⓐ Ⓑ Ⓒ Ⓓ Ⓔ
26 Ⓐ Ⓑ Ⓒ Ⓓ Ⓔ
27 Ⓐ Ⓑ Ⓒ Ⓓ Ⓔ
28 Ⓐ Ⓑ Ⓒ Ⓓ Ⓔ
29 Ⓐ Ⓑ Ⓒ Ⓓ Ⓔ
30 Ⓐ Ⓑ Ⓒ Ⓓ Ⓔ

31 Ⓐ Ⓑ Ⓒ Ⓓ Ⓔ
32 Ⓐ Ⓑ Ⓒ Ⓓ Ⓔ
33 Ⓐ Ⓑ Ⓒ Ⓓ Ⓔ
34 Ⓐ Ⓑ Ⓒ Ⓓ Ⓔ
35 Ⓐ Ⓑ Ⓒ Ⓓ Ⓔ
36 Ⓐ Ⓑ Ⓒ Ⓓ Ⓔ
37 Ⓐ Ⓑ Ⓒ Ⓓ Ⓔ
38 Ⓐ Ⓑ Ⓒ Ⓓ Ⓔ
39 Ⓐ Ⓑ Ⓒ Ⓓ Ⓔ
40 Ⓐ Ⓑ Ⓒ Ⓓ Ⓔ

**CAUTION**    Grid answers in the section below for SECTION 2 or SECTION 3 only if directed to do so in your test book.

**Student-Produced Responses**    ONLY ANSWERS THAT ARE GRIDDED WILL BE SCORED. YOU WILL NOT RECEIVE CREDIT FOR ANYTHING WRITTEN IN THE BOXES.

Quality Assurance Mark ●

9, 10, 11, 12, 13 — gridded response grids (0–9)

14, 15, 16, 17, 18 — gridded response grids (0–9)

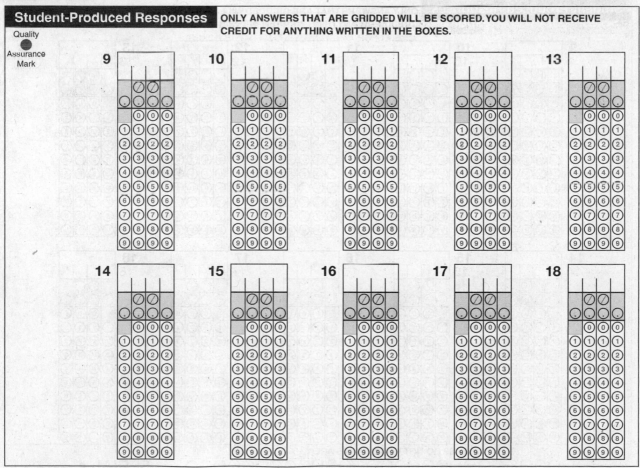

**SECTION 4**

| 1 Ⓐ Ⓑ Ⓒ Ⓓ Ⓔ | 11 Ⓐ Ⓑ Ⓒ Ⓓ Ⓔ | 21 Ⓐ Ⓑ Ⓒ Ⓓ Ⓔ | 31 Ⓐ Ⓑ Ⓒ Ⓓ Ⓔ |
| 2 Ⓐ Ⓑ Ⓒ Ⓓ Ⓔ | 12 Ⓐ Ⓑ Ⓒ Ⓓ Ⓔ | 22 Ⓐ Ⓑ Ⓒ Ⓓ Ⓔ | 32 Ⓐ Ⓑ Ⓒ Ⓓ Ⓔ |
| 3 Ⓐ Ⓑ Ⓒ Ⓓ Ⓔ | 13 Ⓐ Ⓑ Ⓒ Ⓓ Ⓔ | 23 Ⓐ Ⓑ Ⓒ Ⓓ Ⓔ | 33 Ⓐ Ⓑ Ⓒ Ⓓ Ⓔ |
| 4 Ⓐ Ⓑ Ⓒ Ⓓ Ⓔ | 14 Ⓐ Ⓑ Ⓒ Ⓓ Ⓔ | 24 Ⓐ Ⓑ Ⓒ Ⓓ Ⓔ | 34 Ⓐ Ⓑ Ⓒ Ⓓ Ⓔ |
| 5 Ⓐ Ⓑ Ⓒ Ⓓ Ⓔ | 15 Ⓐ Ⓑ Ⓒ Ⓓ Ⓔ | 25 Ⓐ Ⓑ Ⓒ Ⓓ Ⓔ | 35 Ⓐ Ⓑ Ⓒ Ⓓ Ⓔ |
| 6 Ⓐ Ⓑ Ⓒ Ⓓ Ⓔ | 16 Ⓐ Ⓑ Ⓒ Ⓓ Ⓔ | 26 Ⓐ Ⓑ Ⓒ Ⓓ Ⓔ | 36 Ⓐ Ⓑ Ⓒ Ⓓ Ⓔ |
| 7 Ⓐ Ⓑ Ⓒ Ⓓ Ⓔ | 17 Ⓐ Ⓑ Ⓒ Ⓓ Ⓔ | 27 Ⓐ Ⓑ Ⓒ Ⓓ Ⓔ | 37 Ⓐ Ⓑ Ⓒ Ⓓ Ⓔ |
| 8 Ⓐ Ⓑ Ⓒ Ⓓ Ⓔ | 18 Ⓐ Ⓑ Ⓒ Ⓓ Ⓔ | 28 Ⓐ Ⓑ Ⓒ Ⓓ Ⓔ | 38 Ⓐ Ⓑ Ⓒ Ⓓ Ⓔ |
| 9 Ⓐ Ⓑ Ⓒ Ⓓ Ⓔ | 19 Ⓐ Ⓑ Ⓒ Ⓓ Ⓔ | 29 Ⓐ Ⓑ Ⓒ Ⓓ Ⓔ | 39 Ⓐ Ⓑ Ⓒ Ⓓ Ⓔ |
| 10 Ⓐ Ⓑ Ⓒ Ⓓ Ⓔ | 20 Ⓐ Ⓑ Ⓒ Ⓓ Ⓔ | 30 Ⓐ Ⓑ Ⓒ Ⓓ Ⓔ | 40 Ⓐ Ⓑ Ⓒ Ⓓ Ⓔ |

**SECTION 5**

| 1 Ⓐ Ⓑ Ⓒ Ⓓ Ⓔ | 11 Ⓐ Ⓑ Ⓒ Ⓓ Ⓔ | 21 Ⓐ Ⓑ Ⓒ Ⓓ Ⓔ | 31 Ⓐ Ⓑ Ⓒ Ⓓ Ⓔ |
| 2 Ⓐ Ⓑ Ⓒ Ⓓ Ⓔ | 12 Ⓐ Ⓑ Ⓒ Ⓓ Ⓔ | 22 Ⓐ Ⓑ Ⓒ Ⓓ Ⓔ | 32 Ⓐ Ⓑ Ⓒ Ⓓ Ⓔ |
| 3 Ⓐ Ⓑ Ⓒ Ⓓ Ⓔ | 13 Ⓐ Ⓑ Ⓒ Ⓓ Ⓔ | 23 Ⓐ Ⓑ Ⓒ Ⓓ Ⓔ | 33 Ⓐ Ⓑ Ⓒ Ⓓ Ⓔ |
| 4 Ⓐ Ⓑ Ⓒ Ⓓ Ⓔ | 14 Ⓐ Ⓑ Ⓒ Ⓓ Ⓔ | 24 Ⓐ Ⓑ Ⓒ Ⓓ Ⓔ | 34 Ⓐ Ⓑ Ⓒ Ⓓ Ⓔ |
| 5 Ⓐ Ⓑ Ⓒ Ⓓ Ⓔ | 15 Ⓐ Ⓑ Ⓒ Ⓓ Ⓔ | 25 Ⓐ Ⓑ Ⓒ Ⓓ Ⓔ | 35 Ⓐ Ⓑ Ⓒ Ⓓ Ⓔ |
| 6 Ⓐ Ⓑ Ⓒ Ⓓ Ⓔ | 16 Ⓐ Ⓑ Ⓒ Ⓓ Ⓔ | 26 Ⓐ Ⓑ Ⓒ Ⓓ Ⓔ | 36 Ⓐ Ⓑ Ⓒ Ⓓ Ⓔ |
| 7 Ⓐ Ⓑ Ⓒ Ⓓ Ⓔ | 17 Ⓐ Ⓑ Ⓒ Ⓓ Ⓔ | 27 Ⓐ Ⓑ Ⓒ Ⓓ Ⓔ | 37 Ⓐ Ⓑ Ⓒ Ⓓ Ⓔ |
| 8 Ⓐ Ⓑ Ⓒ Ⓓ Ⓔ | 18 Ⓐ Ⓑ Ⓒ Ⓓ Ⓔ | 28 Ⓐ Ⓑ Ⓒ Ⓓ Ⓔ | 38 Ⓐ Ⓑ Ⓒ Ⓓ Ⓔ |
| 9 Ⓐ Ⓑ Ⓒ Ⓓ Ⓔ | 19 Ⓐ Ⓑ Ⓒ Ⓓ Ⓔ | 29 Ⓐ Ⓑ Ⓒ Ⓓ Ⓔ | 39 Ⓐ Ⓑ Ⓒ Ⓓ Ⓔ |
| 10 Ⓐ Ⓑ Ⓒ Ⓓ Ⓔ | 20 Ⓐ Ⓑ Ⓒ Ⓓ Ⓔ | 30 Ⓐ Ⓑ Ⓒ Ⓓ Ⓔ | 40 Ⓐ Ⓑ Ⓒ Ⓓ Ⓔ |

**CAUTION**    Grid answers in the section below for SECTION 4 or SECTION 5 only if directed to do so in your test book.

**Student-Produced Responses**    ONLY ANSWERS THAT ARE GRIDDED WILL BE SCORED. YOU WILL NOT RECEIVE CREDIT FOR ANYTHING WRITTEN IN THE BOXES.

Quality Assurance Mark ●

**SECTION 6**

| | | | |
|---|---|---|---|
| 1 Ⓐ Ⓑ Ⓒ Ⓓ Ⓔ | 11 Ⓐ Ⓑ Ⓒ Ⓓ Ⓔ | 21 Ⓐ Ⓑ Ⓒ Ⓓ Ⓔ | 31 Ⓐ Ⓑ Ⓒ Ⓓ Ⓔ |
| 2 Ⓐ Ⓑ Ⓒ Ⓓ Ⓔ | 12 Ⓐ Ⓑ Ⓒ Ⓓ Ⓔ | 22 Ⓐ Ⓑ Ⓒ Ⓓ Ⓔ | 32 Ⓐ Ⓑ Ⓒ Ⓓ Ⓔ |
| 3 Ⓐ Ⓑ Ⓒ Ⓓ Ⓔ | 13 Ⓐ Ⓑ Ⓒ Ⓓ Ⓔ | 23 Ⓐ Ⓑ Ⓒ Ⓓ Ⓔ | 33 Ⓐ Ⓑ Ⓒ Ⓓ Ⓔ |
| 4 Ⓐ Ⓑ Ⓒ Ⓓ Ⓔ | 14 Ⓐ Ⓑ Ⓒ Ⓓ Ⓔ | 24 Ⓐ Ⓑ Ⓒ Ⓓ Ⓔ | 34 Ⓐ Ⓑ Ⓒ Ⓓ Ⓔ |
| 5 Ⓐ Ⓑ Ⓒ Ⓓ Ⓔ | 15 Ⓐ Ⓑ Ⓒ Ⓓ Ⓔ | 25 Ⓐ Ⓑ Ⓒ Ⓓ Ⓔ | 35 Ⓐ Ⓑ Ⓒ Ⓓ Ⓔ |
| 6 Ⓐ Ⓑ Ⓒ Ⓓ Ⓔ | 16 Ⓐ Ⓑ Ⓒ Ⓓ Ⓔ | 26 Ⓐ Ⓑ Ⓒ Ⓓ Ⓔ | 36 Ⓐ Ⓑ Ⓒ Ⓓ Ⓔ |
| 7 Ⓐ Ⓑ Ⓒ Ⓓ Ⓔ | 17 Ⓐ Ⓑ Ⓒ Ⓓ Ⓔ | 27 Ⓐ Ⓑ Ⓒ Ⓓ Ⓔ | 37 Ⓐ Ⓑ Ⓒ Ⓓ Ⓔ |
| 8 Ⓐ Ⓑ Ⓒ Ⓓ Ⓔ | 18 Ⓐ Ⓑ Ⓒ Ⓓ Ⓔ | 28 Ⓐ Ⓑ Ⓒ Ⓓ Ⓔ | 38 Ⓐ Ⓑ Ⓒ Ⓓ Ⓔ |
| 9 Ⓐ Ⓑ Ⓒ Ⓓ Ⓔ | 19 Ⓐ Ⓑ Ⓒ Ⓓ Ⓔ | 29 Ⓐ Ⓑ Ⓒ Ⓓ Ⓔ | 39 Ⓐ Ⓑ Ⓒ Ⓓ Ⓔ |
| 10 Ⓐ Ⓑ Ⓒ Ⓓ Ⓔ | 20 Ⓐ Ⓑ Ⓒ Ⓓ Ⓔ | 30 Ⓐ Ⓑ Ⓒ Ⓓ Ⓔ | 40 Ⓐ Ⓑ Ⓒ Ⓓ Ⓔ |

**SECTION 7**

| | | | |
|---|---|---|---|
| 1 Ⓐ Ⓑ Ⓒ Ⓓ Ⓔ | 11 Ⓐ Ⓑ Ⓒ Ⓓ Ⓔ | 21 Ⓐ Ⓑ Ⓒ Ⓓ Ⓔ | 31 Ⓐ Ⓑ Ⓒ Ⓓ Ⓔ |
| 2 Ⓐ Ⓑ Ⓒ Ⓓ Ⓔ | 12 Ⓐ Ⓑ Ⓒ Ⓓ Ⓔ | 22 Ⓐ Ⓑ Ⓒ Ⓓ Ⓔ | 32 Ⓐ Ⓑ Ⓒ Ⓓ Ⓔ |
| 3 Ⓐ Ⓑ Ⓒ Ⓓ Ⓔ | 13 Ⓐ Ⓑ Ⓒ Ⓓ Ⓔ | 23 Ⓐ Ⓑ Ⓒ Ⓓ Ⓔ | 33 Ⓐ Ⓑ Ⓒ Ⓓ Ⓔ |
| 4 Ⓐ Ⓑ Ⓒ Ⓓ Ⓔ | 14 Ⓐ Ⓑ Ⓒ Ⓓ Ⓔ | 24 Ⓐ Ⓑ Ⓒ Ⓓ Ⓔ | 34 Ⓐ Ⓑ Ⓒ Ⓓ Ⓔ |
| 5 Ⓐ Ⓑ Ⓒ Ⓓ Ⓔ | 15 Ⓐ Ⓑ Ⓒ Ⓓ Ⓔ | 25 Ⓐ Ⓑ Ⓒ Ⓓ Ⓔ | 35 Ⓐ Ⓑ Ⓒ Ⓓ Ⓔ |
| 6 Ⓐ Ⓑ Ⓒ Ⓓ Ⓔ | 16 Ⓐ Ⓑ Ⓒ Ⓓ Ⓔ | 26 Ⓐ Ⓑ Ⓒ Ⓓ Ⓔ | 36 Ⓐ Ⓑ Ⓒ Ⓓ Ⓔ |
| 7 Ⓐ Ⓑ Ⓒ Ⓓ Ⓔ | 17 Ⓐ Ⓑ Ⓒ Ⓓ Ⓔ | 27 Ⓐ Ⓑ Ⓒ Ⓓ Ⓔ | 37 Ⓐ Ⓑ Ⓒ Ⓓ Ⓔ |
| 8 Ⓐ Ⓑ Ⓒ Ⓓ Ⓔ | 18 Ⓐ Ⓑ Ⓒ Ⓓ Ⓔ | 28 Ⓐ Ⓑ Ⓒ Ⓓ Ⓔ | 38 Ⓐ Ⓑ Ⓒ Ⓓ Ⓔ |
| 9 Ⓐ Ⓑ Ⓒ Ⓓ Ⓔ | 19 Ⓐ Ⓑ Ⓒ Ⓓ Ⓔ | 29 Ⓐ Ⓑ Ⓒ Ⓓ Ⓔ | 39 Ⓐ Ⓑ Ⓒ Ⓓ Ⓔ |
| 10 Ⓐ Ⓑ Ⓒ Ⓓ Ⓔ | 20 Ⓐ Ⓑ Ⓒ Ⓓ Ⓔ | 30 Ⓐ Ⓑ Ⓒ Ⓓ Ⓔ | 40 Ⓐ Ⓑ Ⓒ Ⓓ Ⓔ |

**CAUTION** Grid answers in the section below for SECTION 6 or SECTION 7 only if directed to do so in your test book.

**Student-Produced Responses** ONLY ANSWERS THAT ARE GRIDDED WILL BE SCORED. YOU WILL NOT RECEIVE CREDIT FOR ANYTHING WRITTEN IN THE BOXES.

Quality Assurance Mark

9 · 10 · 11 · 12 · 13 · 14 · 15 · 16 · 17 · 18

(grid fields 0–9 for each response)

Page 6

PLEASE DO NOT WRITE IN THIS AREA

SERIAL #

820

**SECTION 8**

| 1 Ⓐ Ⓑ Ⓒ Ⓓ Ⓔ | 11 Ⓐ Ⓑ Ⓒ Ⓓ Ⓔ | 21 Ⓐ Ⓑ Ⓒ Ⓓ Ⓔ | 31 Ⓐ Ⓑ Ⓒ Ⓓ Ⓔ |
| 2 Ⓐ Ⓑ Ⓒ Ⓓ Ⓔ | 12 Ⓐ Ⓑ Ⓒ Ⓓ Ⓔ | 22 Ⓐ Ⓑ Ⓒ Ⓓ Ⓔ | 32 Ⓐ Ⓑ Ⓒ Ⓓ Ⓔ |
| 3 Ⓐ Ⓑ Ⓒ Ⓓ Ⓔ | 13 Ⓐ Ⓑ Ⓒ Ⓓ Ⓔ | 23 Ⓐ Ⓑ Ⓒ Ⓓ Ⓔ | 33 Ⓐ Ⓑ Ⓒ Ⓓ Ⓔ |
| 4 Ⓐ Ⓑ Ⓒ Ⓓ Ⓔ | 14 Ⓐ Ⓑ Ⓒ Ⓓ Ⓔ | 24 Ⓐ Ⓑ Ⓒ Ⓓ Ⓔ | 34 Ⓐ Ⓑ Ⓒ Ⓓ Ⓔ |
| 5 Ⓐ Ⓑ Ⓒ Ⓓ Ⓔ | 15 Ⓐ Ⓑ Ⓒ Ⓓ Ⓔ | 25 Ⓐ Ⓑ Ⓒ Ⓓ Ⓔ | 35 Ⓐ Ⓑ Ⓒ Ⓓ Ⓔ |
| 6 Ⓐ Ⓑ Ⓒ Ⓓ Ⓔ | 16 Ⓐ Ⓑ Ⓒ Ⓓ Ⓔ | 26 Ⓐ Ⓑ Ⓒ Ⓓ Ⓔ | 36 Ⓐ Ⓑ Ⓒ Ⓓ Ⓔ |
| 7 Ⓐ Ⓑ Ⓒ Ⓓ Ⓔ | 17 Ⓐ Ⓑ Ⓒ Ⓓ Ⓔ | 27 Ⓐ Ⓑ Ⓒ Ⓓ Ⓔ | 37 Ⓐ Ⓑ Ⓒ Ⓓ Ⓔ |
| 8 Ⓐ Ⓑ Ⓒ Ⓓ Ⓔ | 18 Ⓐ Ⓑ Ⓒ Ⓓ Ⓔ | 28 Ⓐ Ⓑ Ⓒ Ⓓ Ⓔ | 38 Ⓐ Ⓑ Ⓒ Ⓓ Ⓔ |
| 9 Ⓐ Ⓑ Ⓒ Ⓓ Ⓔ | 19 Ⓐ Ⓑ Ⓒ Ⓓ Ⓔ | 29 Ⓐ Ⓑ Ⓒ Ⓓ Ⓔ | 39 Ⓐ Ⓑ Ⓒ Ⓓ Ⓔ |
| 10 Ⓐ Ⓑ Ⓒ Ⓓ Ⓔ | 20 Ⓐ Ⓑ Ⓒ Ⓓ Ⓔ | 30 Ⓐ Ⓑ Ⓒ Ⓓ Ⓔ | 40 Ⓐ Ⓑ Ⓒ Ⓓ Ⓔ |

**SECTION 9**

| 1 Ⓐ Ⓑ Ⓒ Ⓓ Ⓔ | 11 Ⓐ Ⓑ Ⓒ Ⓓ Ⓔ | 21 Ⓐ Ⓑ Ⓒ Ⓓ Ⓔ | 31 Ⓐ Ⓑ Ⓒ Ⓓ Ⓔ |
| 2 Ⓐ Ⓑ Ⓒ Ⓓ Ⓔ | 12 Ⓐ Ⓑ Ⓒ Ⓓ Ⓔ | 22 Ⓐ Ⓑ Ⓒ Ⓓ Ⓔ | 32 Ⓐ Ⓑ Ⓒ Ⓓ Ⓔ |
| 3 Ⓐ Ⓑ Ⓒ Ⓓ Ⓔ | 13 Ⓐ Ⓑ Ⓒ Ⓓ Ⓔ | 23 Ⓐ Ⓑ Ⓒ Ⓓ Ⓔ | 33 Ⓐ Ⓑ Ⓒ Ⓓ Ⓔ |
| 4 Ⓐ Ⓑ Ⓒ Ⓓ Ⓔ | 14 Ⓐ Ⓑ Ⓒ Ⓓ Ⓔ | 24 Ⓐ Ⓑ Ⓒ Ⓓ Ⓔ | 34 Ⓐ Ⓑ Ⓒ Ⓓ Ⓔ |
| 5 Ⓐ Ⓑ Ⓒ Ⓓ Ⓔ | 15 Ⓐ Ⓑ Ⓒ Ⓓ Ⓔ | 25 Ⓐ Ⓑ Ⓒ Ⓓ Ⓔ | 35 Ⓐ Ⓑ Ⓒ Ⓓ Ⓔ |
| 6 Ⓐ Ⓑ Ⓒ Ⓓ Ⓔ | 16 Ⓐ Ⓑ Ⓒ Ⓓ Ⓔ | 26 Ⓐ Ⓑ Ⓒ Ⓓ Ⓔ | 36 Ⓐ Ⓑ Ⓒ Ⓓ Ⓔ |
| 7 Ⓐ Ⓑ Ⓒ Ⓓ Ⓔ | 17 Ⓐ Ⓑ Ⓒ Ⓓ Ⓔ | 27 Ⓐ Ⓑ Ⓒ Ⓓ Ⓔ | 37 Ⓐ Ⓑ Ⓒ Ⓓ Ⓔ |
| 8 Ⓐ Ⓑ Ⓒ Ⓓ Ⓔ | 18 Ⓐ Ⓑ Ⓒ Ⓓ Ⓔ | 28 Ⓐ Ⓑ Ⓒ Ⓓ Ⓔ | 38 Ⓐ Ⓑ Ⓒ Ⓓ Ⓔ |
| 9 Ⓐ Ⓑ Ⓒ Ⓓ Ⓔ | 19 Ⓐ Ⓑ Ⓒ Ⓓ Ⓔ | 29 Ⓐ Ⓑ Ⓒ Ⓓ Ⓔ | 39 Ⓐ Ⓑ Ⓒ Ⓓ Ⓔ |
| 10 Ⓐ Ⓑ Ⓒ Ⓓ Ⓔ | 20 Ⓐ Ⓑ Ⓒ Ⓓ Ⓔ | 30 Ⓐ Ⓑ Ⓒ Ⓓ Ⓔ | 40 Ⓐ Ⓑ Ⓒ Ⓓ Ⓔ |

Quality
●
Assurance
Mark

**SECTION 10**

| 1 Ⓐ Ⓑ Ⓒ Ⓓ Ⓔ | 11 Ⓐ Ⓑ Ⓒ Ⓓ Ⓔ | 21 Ⓐ Ⓑ Ⓒ Ⓓ Ⓔ | 31 Ⓐ Ⓑ Ⓒ Ⓓ Ⓔ |
| 2 Ⓐ Ⓑ Ⓒ Ⓓ Ⓔ | 12 Ⓐ Ⓑ Ⓒ Ⓓ Ⓔ | 22 Ⓐ Ⓑ Ⓒ Ⓓ Ⓔ | 32 Ⓐ Ⓑ Ⓒ Ⓓ Ⓔ |
| 3 Ⓐ Ⓑ Ⓒ Ⓓ Ⓔ | 13 Ⓐ Ⓑ Ⓒ Ⓓ Ⓔ | 23 Ⓐ Ⓑ Ⓒ Ⓓ Ⓔ | 33 Ⓐ Ⓑ Ⓒ Ⓓ Ⓔ |
| 4 Ⓐ Ⓑ Ⓒ Ⓓ Ⓔ | 14 Ⓐ Ⓑ Ⓒ Ⓓ Ⓔ | 24 Ⓐ Ⓑ Ⓒ Ⓓ Ⓔ | 34 Ⓐ Ⓑ Ⓒ Ⓓ Ⓔ |
| 5 Ⓐ Ⓑ Ⓒ Ⓓ Ⓔ | 15 Ⓐ Ⓑ Ⓒ Ⓓ Ⓔ | 25 Ⓐ Ⓑ Ⓒ Ⓓ Ⓔ | 35 Ⓐ Ⓑ Ⓒ Ⓓ Ⓔ |
| 6 Ⓐ Ⓑ Ⓒ Ⓓ Ⓔ | 16 Ⓐ Ⓑ Ⓒ Ⓓ Ⓔ | 26 Ⓐ Ⓑ Ⓒ Ⓓ Ⓔ | 36 Ⓐ Ⓑ Ⓒ Ⓓ Ⓔ |
| 7 Ⓐ Ⓑ Ⓒ Ⓓ Ⓔ | 17 Ⓐ Ⓑ Ⓒ Ⓓ Ⓔ | 27 Ⓐ Ⓑ Ⓒ Ⓓ Ⓔ | 37 Ⓐ Ⓑ Ⓒ Ⓓ Ⓔ |
| 8 Ⓐ Ⓑ Ⓒ Ⓓ Ⓔ | 18 Ⓐ Ⓑ Ⓒ Ⓓ Ⓔ | 28 Ⓐ Ⓑ Ⓒ Ⓓ Ⓔ | 38 Ⓐ Ⓑ Ⓒ Ⓓ Ⓔ |
| 9 Ⓐ Ⓑ Ⓒ Ⓓ Ⓔ | 19 Ⓐ Ⓑ Ⓒ Ⓓ Ⓔ | 29 Ⓐ Ⓑ Ⓒ Ⓓ Ⓔ | 39 Ⓐ Ⓑ Ⓒ Ⓓ Ⓔ |
| 10 Ⓐ Ⓑ Ⓒ Ⓓ Ⓔ | 20 Ⓐ Ⓑ Ⓒ Ⓓ Ⓔ | 30 Ⓐ Ⓑ Ⓒ Ⓓ Ⓔ | 40 Ⓐ Ⓑ Ⓒ Ⓓ Ⓔ |

8

## CERTIFICATION STATEMENT

Copy the statement below (do not print) and sign your name as you would an official document.

I hereby agree to the conditions set forth online at www.collegeboard.org and/or in the SAT® Registration Booklet and certify that I am the person whose name and address appear on this answer sheet.

_____

_____

_____

_____

By signing below, I agree not to share any specific test questions or essay topics with anyone by any form of communication, including, but not limited to: email, text messages, or use of the Internet.

Signature _____     Date _____

## SPECIAL QUESTIONS

1 Ⓐ Ⓑ Ⓒ Ⓓ Ⓔ Ⓕ Ⓖ Ⓗ Ⓘ Ⓙ
2 Ⓐ Ⓑ Ⓒ Ⓓ Ⓔ Ⓕ Ⓖ Ⓗ Ⓘ Ⓙ
3 Ⓐ Ⓑ Ⓒ Ⓓ Ⓔ Ⓕ Ⓖ Ⓗ Ⓘ Ⓙ
4 Ⓐ Ⓑ Ⓒ Ⓓ Ⓔ Ⓕ Ⓖ Ⓗ Ⓘ Ⓙ
5 Ⓐ Ⓑ Ⓒ Ⓓ Ⓔ Ⓕ Ⓖ Ⓗ Ⓘ Ⓙ
6 Ⓐ Ⓑ Ⓒ Ⓓ Ⓔ Ⓕ Ⓖ Ⓗ Ⓘ Ⓙ
7 Ⓐ Ⓑ Ⓒ Ⓓ Ⓔ Ⓕ Ⓖ Ⓗ Ⓘ Ⓙ
8 Ⓐ Ⓑ Ⓒ Ⓓ Ⓔ Ⓕ Ⓖ Ⓗ Ⓘ Ⓙ

8

PLEASE DO NOT WRITE IN THIS AREA

Ⓞ ◯ ◯ ◯ ◯ ◯ ◯ ◯ ◯ ◯ ◯ ◯ ◯ ◯ ◯ ◯ ◯ ◯ ◯ ◯ ◯ ◯ ◯ ◯ ◯ ◯ ◯ ◯ ◯ ◯ ◯     **SERIAL #**

822

## ESSAY
Time — 25 minutes

---

**Turn to page 2 of your answer sheet to write your ESSAY.**

---

The essay gives you an opportunity to show how effectively you can develop and express ideas. You should, therefore, take care to develop your point of view, present your ideas logically and clearly, and use language precisely.

Your essay must be written on the lines provided on your answer sheet—you will receive no other paper on which to write. You will have enough space if you write on every line, avoid wide margins, and keep your handwriting to a reasonable size. Remember that people who are not familiar with your handwriting will read what you write. Try to write or print so that what you are writing is legible to those readers.

**Important Reminders:**

- **A pencil is required for the essay.** An essay written in ink will receive a score of zero.
- **Do not write your essay in your test book.** You will receive credit only for what you write on your answer sheet.
- **An off-topic essay will receive a score of zero.**
- **If your essay does not reflect your original and individual work, your test scores may be canceled.**

You have twenty-five minutes to write an essay on the topic assigned below.

---

Think carefully about the issue presented in the following excerpt and the assignment below.

> There is, of course, no legitimate branch of science that enables us to predict the future accurately. Yet the degree of change in the world is so overwhelming and so promising that the future, I believe, is far brighter than anyone has contemplated since the end of the Second World War.
>
> Adapted from Allan E. Goodman, *A Brief History of the Future: The United States in a Changing World Order*

**Assignment:** Is the world changing for the better? Plan and write an essay in which you develop your point of view on this issue. Support your position with reasoning and examples taken from your reading, studies, experience, or observations.

---

BEGIN WRITING YOUR ESSAY ON PAGE 2 OF THE ANSWER SHEET.

---

**If you finish before time is called, you may check your work on this section only.**
**Do not turn to any other section in the test.**

**2**

Unauthorized copying or reuse of
any part of this page is illegal.

**2**

## SECTION 2
### Time — 25 minutes
### 24 Questions

---

**Turn to Section 2 (page 4) of your answer sheet to answer the questions in this section.**

---

**Directions:** For each question in this section, select the best answer from among the choices given and fill in the corresponding circle on the answer sheet.

---

Each sentence below has one or two blanks, each blank indicating that something has been omitted. Beneath the sentence are five words or sets of words labeled A through E. Choose the word or set of words that, when inserted in the sentence, <u>best</u> fits the meaning of the sentence as a whole.

**Example:**

Hoping to ------- the dispute, negotiators proposed a compromise that they felt would be ------- to both labor and management.

(A) enforce . . useful
(B) end . . divisive
(C) overcome . . unattractive
(D) extend . . satisfactory
(E) resolve . . acceptable

1. Residents of the secluded island fear that -------
   commercial development will ------- their quiet
   way of life.

   (A) widespread . . reinforce
   (B) waning . . harm
   (C) diminishing . . reform
   (D) encroaching . . disturb
   (E) further . . aid

2. Though it is often exclusively ------- Brazil, the
   Amazon jungle actually ------- parts of eight other
   South American countries.

   (A) protected by . . threatens
   (B) located in . . bypasses
   (C) limited to . . touches
   (D) surrounded by . . borders
   (E) associated with . . covers

3. Sandra Gilbert and Susan Gubar's recent book presents
   a ------- of detail, providing far more information than
   one can easily digest.

   (A) modicum     (B) discrepancy     (C) surfeit
       (D) deficit     (E) juxtaposition

4. More ------- than her predecessor, Superintendent
   Reynolds would, many predicted, have a far less
   ------- term of office.

   (A) phlegmatic . . apathetic
   (B) conciliatory . . confrontational
   (C) empathetic . . compassionate
   (D) vigilant . . reputable
   (E) penurious . . frugal

5. Galloping technological progress has made consumers
   -------: advances undreamed of a generation ago are so
   common that they seem humdrum.

   (A) flabbergasted     (B) miffed     (C) jaded
       (D) wary     (E) embittered

**GO ON TO THE NEXT PAGE**

The passages below are followed by questions based on their content; questions following a pair of related passages may also be based on the relationship between the paired passages. Answer the questions on the basis of what is <u>stated</u> or <u>implied</u> in the passages and in any introductory material that may be provided.

**Questions 6-9 are based on the following passages.**

**Passage 1**

Does science fiction serve a useful purpose? I cannot see much justice in the repeated claims that it sugars the pill of a scientific education: most of the science is wrong anyway, and its amount is such that one might as well be

Line 5 reading Westerns in the hope of finding out about ranching methods. Science fiction's most important use, I submit, is as a means of dramatizing social inquiry, of providing a fictional mode in which cultural tendencies can be isolated and judged. Many a trend hound would be surprised and

10 perhaps mortified to discover how many of his or her cherished insights are common ground in science fiction.

**Passage 2**

Much of the science in science fiction is hokum; some of it is totally wrong. But beneath all the surface trickery of science fiction, there is a general respect for science and

15 some appreciation of its methodology, which is probably more important than the facts that can be found in a textbook. And because science fiction combines scientific elements with stories involving people and relationships, the genre serves as a link between the culture of the

20 humanities and arts on the one hand, and of science and technology on the other. Younger readers of science fiction, not firmly fixed in either culture, absorb both scientific and humanistic elements from their readings. Thereafter, neither culture can be quite so strange.

6. Both passages express the view that science fiction is

   (A) predictably insightful
   (B) chillingly realistic
   (C) artistically pleasing
   (D) socially useful
   (E) widely understood

7. Both passages suggest that science fiction

   (A) can motivate people to pursue a scientific education
   (B) can provide a bridge between the worlds of art and science
   (C) is more appealing to children than it is to adults
   (D) intentionally glosses over the difficult challenges that scientists face
   (E) does not attempt to reflect scientific reality with rigorous exactness

8. The author of Passage 2 would most likely respond to lines 3-6 in Passage 1 ("most of . . . methods") by

   (A) claiming that the literary merits of science fiction transcend its scientific fallacies
   (B) arguing that science fiction portrays science more accurately than is generally understood
   (C) asserting that science fiction, despite its factual inaccuracies, values scientific thought
   (D) pointing out that science fiction has increased in popularity despite its factual distortions
   (E) suggesting that more people trained as scientists should attempt to write science fiction

9. The attitude of each author toward the genre of science fiction might best be described as

   (A) unabashed admiration
   (B) qualified appreciation
   (C) open amusement
   (D) veiled distaste
   (E) utter contempt

**GO ON TO THE NEXT PAGE**

**Questions 10-14 are based on the following passage.**

*This passage, about animal perception, was adapted from an essay by a writer who trains animals.*

Anyone who trains animals recognizes that human and animal perceptual capacities are different. For most humans, seeing is believing, although we do occasionally brood about
*Line* whether we can believe our eyes. The other senses are largely
5  ancillary; most of us do not know how we might go about either doubting or believing our noses. But for dogs, scenting is believing. A dog's nose is to ours as the wrinkled surface of our complex brain is to the surface of an egg. A dog who did comparative psychology might easily worry about our
10  consciousness or lack thereof, just as we worry about the consciousness of a squid.

We who take sight for granted can draw pictures of scent, but we have no language for doing it the other way about, no way to represent something visually familiar by means
15  of actual scent. Most humans cannot know, with their limited noses, what they can imagine about being deaf, blind, mute, or paralyzed. The sighted can, for example, speak of a blind person as "in the darkness," but there is no corollary expression for what it is that we are in relationship to scent. If we
20  tried to coin words, we might come up with something like "scent-blind." But what would it mean? It couldn't have the sort of meaning that "color-blind" and "tone-deaf" do, because most of us have experienced what "tone" and "color" mean in those expressions, but we don't know
25  what "scent" means in the expression "scent-blind." Scent for many of us can be only a theoretical, technical expression that we use because our grammar requires that we have a noun to go in the sentences we are prompted to utter about animals' tracking. We don't have a sense
30  of scent. What we do have is a sense of smell—for Thanksgiving dinner and skunks and a number of things we call chemicals.

So if Fido and I are sitting on the terrace, admiring the view, we inhabit worlds with radically different principles
35  of phenomenology. Say that the wind is to our backs. Our world lies all before us, within a 180 degree angle. The dog's—well, we don't know, do we?

He sees roughly the same things that I see but he *believes* the scents of the garden behind us. He marks the
40  path of the black-and-white cat as she moves among the roses in search of the bits of chicken sandwich I let fall as I walked from the house to our picnic spot. I can show *that* Fido is alert to the kitty, but not *how*, for my picture-making modes of thought too easily supply falsifyingly
45  literal representations of the cat and the garden and their modes of being hidden from or revealed to me.

10. The phrase "other senses are largely ancillary" (lines 4-5) is used by the author to suggest that

(A) only those events experienced directly can be appreciated by the senses
(B) for many human beings the sense of sight is the primary means of knowing about the world
(C) smell is in many respects a more powerful sense than sight
(D) people rely on at least one of their other senses in order to confirm what they see
(E) the perceptual capacity of an animal is a function of its ability to integrate all of its senses

11. The example in the last paragraph suggests that "principles of phenomenology" mentioned in lines 34-35 can best be defined as

(A) memorable things that happen
(B) behaviors caused by certain kinds of perception
(C) ways and means of knowing about something
(D) rules one uses to determine the philosophical truth about a certain thing
(E) effects of a single individual's perception on what others believe

12. The missing phrase in the incomplete sentence "The dog's—well, we don't know, do we?" (lines 36-37) refers to

(A) color blindness
(B) depth perception
(C) perception of the world
(D) concern for our perceptions
(E) motivation for action

**GO ON TO THE NEXT PAGE**

**13.** The author uses the distinction between "*that*" and
"*how*" (line 43) in order to suggest the difference
between

(A) seeing and believing
(B) a cat's way and a dog's way of perceiving
(C) verifiable hypotheses and whimsical speculation
(D) awareness of presence and the nature of that
     awareness
(E) false representations and accurate representations

**14.** The example in the last paragraph is used to
illustrate how

(A) a dog's perception differs from a human's
(B) human beings are not psychologically rooted in
     the natural world
(C) people fear nature but animals are part of it
(D) a dog's ways of seeing are superior to a cat's
(E) phenomenology is universal and constant

**GO ON TO THE NEXT PAGE**

**Questions 15-24 are based on the following passage.**

*First published in 1976, this passage discusses W.E.B. Du Bois and Marcus Garvey, two leaders of the Black American community in the 1910's and 1920's.*

The concept of two warring souls within the body of the Black American was as meaningful for Du Bois at the end of his years as editor of *Crisis*, the official journal of
Line the National Association for the Advancement of Colored
5 People (NAACP), as when he had first used the image at the start of the century. The tension between race pride and identification with the nation as a whole was nowhere more dramatic than in the most controversial editorial ever printed in *Crisis*, "Close Ranks," which in July 1918 called
10 on Black Americans to "forget our special grievances and close our ranks" with the White people "fighting for democracy" during the First World War. Bitterly criticized by Black people, Du Bois barely modified his statement when, two months later, he set the priorities for his readers:
15 "first your Country, then your Rights!" Perhaps the editor had written more than he intended in using the word "forget," for *Crisis* before and after the editorial showed no diminution in its criticism of racism. But he distinguished between Allied and German ambitions, and declared that
20 defeat of the former would be disastrous for that "United States of the World" to which he was most loyal.

Du Bois nevertheless saw danger in the negation of race pride, by those who did not recognize their own beauty as Black people, for example. The responsibility of *Crisis* was
25 to arbitrate between those who advocated race pride and those who denied any differences between the races. The focal point of the magazine's efforts in this respect came with the rise of Marcus Garvey, the gifted Jamaican leader whose "back-to-Africa" movement, as it was popularly
30 called, was founded on the premise, according to Du Bois, that "a black skin was in itself a sort of patent to nobility."

Garveyism, which flourished during the height of *Crisis'* influence and success, brought a formidable challenge to Du Bois. Garvey and his Universal Negro Improvement
35 Association (UNIA), with its hostility to the interracial ideal and its scheme to have Black Americans emigrate to Africa, threw *Crisis* and the NAACP on the defensive by invoking the specter of self-doubt as characteristic of its Black members. Du Bois had first met Garvey on a visit
40 to Jamaica in 1915, and *Crisis* announced Garvey's arrival in the United States the following year. Almost totally unknown in his new country, Garvey invited Du Bois to preside over his first public lecture; then in 1920 he asked permission to submit Du Bois's name as a candidate in the
45 election of a "leader" of Black America at an international convention organized by the UNIA. Du Bois politely declined the former; "under no circumstances" would he allow the latter. Du Bois saw with amazement Garvey's success in persuading thousands of Black Americans of
50 the legitimacy of his back-to-Africa movement and in collecting funds for the purchase of ships for his Black Star Line to transport people to Africa.

There were superficial similarities between Garvey's and Du Bois's commitment to race consciousness and
55 economic empowerment; both men saw the world as comprising separate cultures, each reflecting a distinct heritage and demanding freedom of expression. But Garvey's fixed belief in the idea of Black racial purity, his obsession with Africa as the solution to the problems
60 of its scattered peoples, and his refusal to allow any liberal idea to deflect his purpose differed greatly from Du Bois's ideals. Du Bois fantasized about Africa in at least one poem and wrote about the continent elsewhere, but he cultivated a scholar's knowledge of the land. He made the first of sev-
65 eral visits there in 1923 and lived in Africa for the last two years of his life (1961-1963). In a cryptic piece in *Crisis* in 1922, Du Bois was surely referring to Garvey when he ominously predicted the rise of a demagogue who would "come to lead, inflame, lie, and steal" and when he com-
70 mented that such a person would "gather large followings and then burst and disappear."

**15.** The primary purpose of the passage is to

(A) account for the rise of Black nationalism in the United States
(B) explain the charismatic appeal of two Black American leaders
(C) explain why Garvey refused to support Du Bois as a leader of Black America
(D) describe differences between the philosophies of Du Bois and Garvey
(E) describe Du Bois's quarrel and eventual reconciliation with Garvey

**16.** The image of "two warring souls" (line 1) refers to the struggle between

(A) democracy and dictatorship
(B) Du Bois's ideals and practical demands
(C) racial and national allegiances
(D) Du Bois's literary and political ambitions
(E) Allied and German goals

**17.** It can be inferred that Du Bois's July 1918 editorial in *Crisis* was "Bitterly criticized" (line 12) because it seemed to

(A) devalue the specific concerns of Black Americans
(B) advocate military service for Black Americans
(C) support Garvey's back-to-Africa movement
(D) insist on racial rather than national priorities
(E) attack the official stance of the NAACP on race pride

**GO ON TO THE NEXT PAGE** ⇨

18. As indicated in lines 15-21 ("Perhaps . . . loyal"), Du Bois advised Black Americans that

   (A) they would be treated more equally in wartime than in peace
   (B) racial harmony in the United States would improve after the war
   (C) despite German military superiority, the Allies would win the war
   (D) wartime provided economic opportunities for both Black and White Americans
   (E) despite American racism, the effects of an Allied defeat would be even worse

19. That to which Du Bois was "most loyal" (line 21) is best described as

   (A) the UNIA
   (B) the NAACP
   (C) *Crisis*
   (D) global democracy
   (E) a new African nation founded by Black Americans

20. According to Du Bois, "the premise" (line 30) underlying Garvey's movement was that

   (A) racial issues are more significant than economic issues in the United States
   (B) an entire group of people is inherently dignified and worthy
   (C) many Black Americans are descended from African royalty
   (D) education is more important than ethnicity in shaping a person's character
   (E) loyalty to one's country takes precedence over all other matters in times of crisis

21. In line 31, "patent to" most nearly means

   (A) copyright of
   (B) safeguard of
   (C) guarantee of
   (D) hope for
   (E) permission for

22. As described in lines 41-46, Garvey's actions suggest that he initially

   (A) scorned Du Bois's advice
   (B) doubted Du Bois's commitment
   (C) envied Du Bois's fame
   (D) admired Du Bois's writings
   (E) appreciated Du Bois's influence

23. The information in lines 62-66 indicates that Du Bois

   (A) valued Africa, but in a very different way than Garvey did
   (B) lived in Africa, but finally returned to the United States to help Black Americans
   (C) read about Africa, but benefited little from his visits there
   (D) fantasized about escaping overseas from demagogues like Garvey
   (E) supported radical solutions to racial problems in the United States

24. The passage implies that over time the relationship between Garvey and Du Bois changed from

   (A) courteous to antagonistic
   (B) professional to personal
   (C) remote to close
   (D) distrustful to ambivalent
   (E) competitive to cooperative

# STOP

**If you finish before time is called, you may check your work on this section only.**
**Do not turn to any other section in the test.**

**SECTION 3**
Time — 25 minutes
18 Questions

**Turn to Section 3 (page 4) of your answer sheet to answer the questions in this section.**

**Directions:** This section contains two types of questions. You have 25 minutes to complete both types. For questions 1-8, solve each problem and decide which is the best of the choices given. Fill in the corresponding circle on the answer sheet. You may use any available space for scratchwork.

Notes

1. The use of a calculator is permitted.
2. All numbers used are real numbers.
3. Figures that accompany problems in this test are intended to provide information useful in solving the problems. They are drawn as accurately as possible EXCEPT when it is stated in a specific problem that the figure is not drawn to scale. All figures lie in a plane unless otherwise indicated.
4. Unless otherwise specified, the domain of any function $f$ is assumed to be the set of all real numbers $x$ for which $f(x)$ is a real number.

Reference Information

    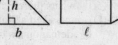    

$A = \pi r^2$
$C = 2\pi r$
$A = \ell w$
$A = \frac{1}{2}bh$
$V = \ell wh$
$V = \pi r^2 h$
$c^2 = a^2 + b^2$
Special Right Triangles

The number of degrees of arc in a circle is 360.
The sum of the measures in degrees of the angles of a triangle is 180.

1. Which of the following numbers is between $\frac{1}{5}$ and $\frac{1}{4}$ ?

(A) 0.14
(B) 0.15
(C) 0.19
(D) 0.21
(E) 0.26

2. The following are coordinates of points in the $xy$-plane. Which of these points is nearest the origin?

(A) $(0, -1)$

(B) $\left(0, \frac{1}{2}\right)$

(C) $\left(\frac{1}{2}, -\frac{1}{2}\right)$

(D) $\left(\frac{1}{2}, \frac{1}{2}\right)$

(E) $(-1, -1)$

**GO ON TO THE NEXT PAGE**

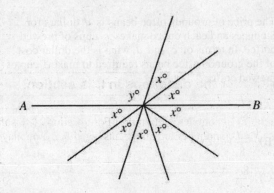

**3.** In the figure above, if $AB$ is a line, what is the value of $y$ ?

(A) 108
(B) 114
(C) 117
(D) 120
(E) 135

**4.** If $6,565 = 65(x + 1)$, then $x =$

(A)    10
(B)    11
(C)    100
(D)    101
(E)    1,001

**5.** If $m^x \cdot m^7 = m^{28}$ and $\left(m^5\right)^y = m^{15}$, what is the value of $x + y$ ?

(A)   7
(B)   12
(C)   14
(D)   24
(E)   31

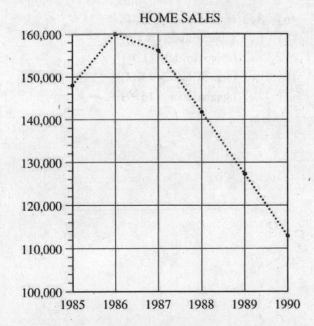

**6.** According to the graph above, which of the following is closest to the decrease per year in the number of homes sold between 1987 and 1990 ?

(A)   7,000
(B)   11,500
(C)   14,000
(D)   17,500
(E)   42,000

**GO ON TO THE NEXT PAGE**

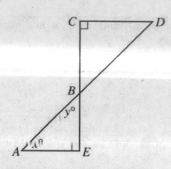

Note: Figure not drawn to scale.

7. In the figure above, $\overline{AE}$ and $\overline{CD}$ are each perpendicular to $\overline{CE}$. If $x = y$, the length of $\overline{AB}$ is 4, and the length of $\overline{BD}$ is 8, what is the length of $\overline{CE}$ ?

(A) $3\sqrt{2}$ (approximately 4.24)
(B) $6\sqrt{2}$ (approximately 8.49)
(C) $8\sqrt{2}$ (approximately 11.31)
(D) $10\sqrt{2}$ (approximately 14.14)
(E) $12\sqrt{2}$ (approximately 16.97)

8. The price of ground coffee beans is $d$ dollars for 8 ounces and each ounce makes $c$ cups of brewed coffee. In terms of $c$ and $d$, what is the dollar cost of the ground coffee beans required to make 1 cup of brewed coffee?

(A) $\dfrac{d}{8c}$

(B) $\dfrac{cd}{0}$

(C) $\dfrac{8c}{d}$

(D) $\dfrac{8d}{c}$

(E) $8cd$

**GO ON TO THE NEXT PAGE**

**Directions:** For Student-Produced Response questions 9-18, use the grids at the bottom of the answer sheet page on which you have answered questions 1-8.

Each of the remaining 10 questions requires you to solve the problem and enter your answer by marking the circles in the special grid, as shown in the examples below. You may use any available space for scratchwork.

Answer: $\frac{7}{12}$

Write answer in boxes.

Grid in result.

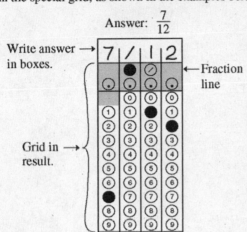

← Fraction line

Answer: 2.5

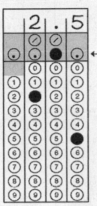

← Decimal point

Answer: 201
Either position is correct.

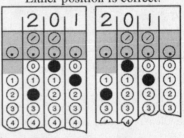

**Note:** You may start your answers in any column, space permitting. Columns not needed should be left blank.

- Mark no more than one circle in any column.

- Because the answer sheet will be machine-scored, **you will receive credit only if the circles are filled in correctly.**

- Although not required, it is suggested that you write your answer in the boxes at the top of the columns to help you fill in the circles accurately.

- Some problems may have more than one correct answer. In such cases, grid only one answer.

- No question has a negative answer.

- **Mixed numbers** such as $3\frac{1}{2}$ must be gridded as 3.5 or 7/2. (If $\boxed{3\,1\,/\,2}$ is gridded, it will be interpreted as $\frac{31}{2}$, not $3\frac{1}{2}$.)

- **Decimal Answers:** If you obtain a decimal answer with more digits than the grid can accommodate, it may be either rounded or truncated, but it must fill the entire grid. For example, if you obtain an answer such as 0.6666..., you should record your result as .666 or .667. **A less accurate value such as .66 or .67 will be scored as incorrect.**

Acceptable ways to grid $\frac{2}{3}$ are:

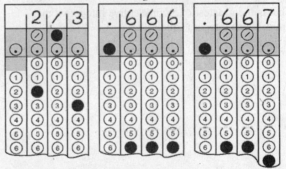

---

9. If $\frac{10}{a} = \frac{b}{12}$, what is the value of $ab$ ?

150, 30, 6, . . .

10. In the sequence above, each term after the 1st term is $\frac{1}{5}$ of the term preceding it. What is the 5th term of this sequence?

**GO ON TO THE NEXT PAGE** →

**11.** Five points, $A$, $B$, $C$, $D$, and $E$, lie on a line, not necessarily in that order. $\overline{AB}$ has a length of 24. Point $C$ is the midpoint of $\overline{AB}$, and point $D$ is the midpoint of $\overline{AC}$. If the distance between $D$ and $E$ is 5, what is one possible distance between $A$ and $E$?

**12.** What is the greatest of 5 consecutive integers if the sum of these integers equals 185 ?

**13.** A salesman's monthly gross pay consists of $1,200 plus 20 percent of the dollar amount of his sales. If his gross pay for one month was $2,500, what was the dollar amount of his sales for that month? (Disregard the $ sign when gridding your answer.)

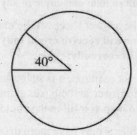

**14.** Naomi makes silver jewelry. For one style of earrings, she cuts wedges from a silver disk, as shown in the figure above. Each wedge makes a 40° angle at the center of the disk. If the weight of each uncut disk is a uniformly distributed 2.5 grams, how many grams does each wedge weigh?

**GO ON TO THE NEXT PAGE**

15. If $x^2 - y^2 = 10$ and $x + y = 5$, what is the value of $x - y$?

17. For all positive integers $j$ and $k$, let $j \boxed{R} k$ be defined as the whole number remainder when $j$ is divided by $k$. If $13 \boxed{R} k = 2$, what is the value of $k$?

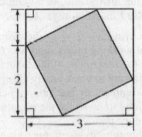

16. In the figure above, what is the area of the shaded square?

18. The average (arithmetic mean) of the test scores of a class of $p$ students is 70, and the average of the test scores of a class of $n$ students is 92. When the scores of both classes are combined, the average score is 86.

What is the value of $\dfrac{p}{n}$?

# STOP

**If you finish before time is called, you may check your work on this section only.**
**Do not turn to any other section in the test.**

## SECTION 4
### Time — 25 minutes
### 35 Questions

**Turn to Section 4 (page 5) of your answer sheet to answer the questions in this section.**

**Directions:** For each question in this section, select the best answer from among the choices given and fill in the corresponding circle on the answer sheet.

The following sentences test correctness and effectiveness of expression. Part of each sentence or the entire sentence is underlined; beneath each sentence are five ways of phrasing the underlined material. Choice A repeats the original phrasing; the other four choices are different. If you think the original phrasing produces a better sentence than any of the alternatives, select choice A; if not, select one of the other choices.

In making your selection, follow the requirements of standard written English; that is, pay attention to grammar, choice of words, sentence construction, and punctuation. Your selection should result in the most effective sentence—clear and precise, without awkwardness or ambiguity.

EXAMPLE:

Laura Ingalls Wilder published her first book <u>and she was sixty-five years old then</u>.

(A) and she was sixty-five years old then
(B) when she was sixty-five
(C) at age sixty-five years old
(D) upon the reaching of sixty-five years
(E) at the time when she was sixty-five

1. The problem of copyright <u>violation, frequently compounded in certain countries because</u> the sale and use of copyrighted materials are not tightly controlled.

(A) violation, frequently compounded in certain countries because
(B) violation, frequently compounded in certain countries and
(C) violation, frequently compounded in certain countries when
(D) violation is frequently compounded in certain countries where
(E) violation is frequently compounded in certain countries so

2. <u>The protesters coming this far, they</u> decided to insist that they meet with the president of the board before leaving the building.

(A) The protesters coming this far, they
(B) They, coming this far, the protesters
(C) Having come this far, the protesters
(D) To come this far, the protesters
(E) The protesters came this far, so that they

3. <u>Our lab instructor gave us the assignment, and we started working busily, and we continued to do so for the remainder of the laboratory period.</u>

(A) Our lab instructor gave us the assignment, and we started working busily, and we continued to do so for the remainder of the laboratory period.
(B) Upon starting to work busily after we were given the assignment by our lab instructor, we continued to do so for the remainder of the laboratory period.
(C) Following our lab instructor's giving us the assignment, we started working busily and continued doing just that for the rest of the laboratory period.
(D) After our lab instructor gave us the assignment, we worked busily for the remainder of the laboratory period.
(E) We worked busily for the remainder of the laboratory period when the assignment had been given to us by our lab instructor.

**GO ON TO THE NEXT PAGE**

Unauthorized copying or reuse of any part of this page is illegal.

**4.** Activist Mumeo Oku campaigned to improve the lot of women in Japan by <u>exposing faulty household products, she successfully demanded that these products be recalled</u>.

(A) exposing faulty household products, she successfully demanded that these products be recalled

(B) exposing faulty household products and successfully demanding their recall

(C) her exposing faulty household products and successful demand of their recall

(D) exposing faulty household products, although successfully demanding that these products be recalled

(E) exposing faulty household products whose recall she was successful in demanding

**5.** In response to the traditional assumption that all readers are basically alike, feminist critics have emphasized <u>that every woman reads from their own unique perspectives</u>.

(A) that every woman reads from their own unique perspectives

(B) that every woman reads from her own unique perspective

(C) that all women reading from a unique perspective of their own

(D) how women reading each have unique perspectives

(E) how the unique perspectives of women are in their readings

**6.** The spirit of the honor code to which each student subscribes <u>requires academic honesty, respectful behavior, and it demands responsibility in action</u>.

(A) requires academic honesty, respectful behavior, and it demands responsibility in action

(B) requires academic honesty, respectful behavior, and responsible action

(C) require academic work that is honest, behavior that is respectful, and action of a responsible nature

(D) requires academic work that is honest, being respectful in behavior, and demands responsible action

(E) require academic honesty, respectful behavior, and the demands of responsible action

**7.** Finding a wide variety of financial services in a small city is usually not as easy as <u>it is</u> in metropolitan areas.

(A) it is

(B) is that

(C) for those

(D) for that

(E) are those

**8.** Television's programming difficulties, <u>already made acute by rising costs, threatens</u> to become even more severe as a result of lobbying by special-interest groups.

(A) already made acute by rising costs, threatens

(B) already made acute by rising costs, threaten

(C) already made acuter by rising costs, threaten

(D) having been made acute by rising costs, threatens

(E) after having been made acute by rising costs, threatens

**9.** Today the primary role of advertising may be to appeal and persuade rather than <u>what it once did, educating and informing</u>.

(A) what it once did, educating and informing

(B) what it once did, which was educating and informing

(C) what it once was, education and information

(D) educating and informing, what it once did

(E) what it once was, to educate and inform

**10.** As an undergraduate at Rutgers University, <u>Paul Robeson developed a serious interest in drama, which eventually led to</u> a distinguished career as an actor during the 1920's and 1930's.

(A) Paul Robeson developed a serious interest in drama, which eventually led to

(B) Paul Robeson's interest in drama developed seriously and eventually led him to

(C) where Paul Robeson developed a serious interest in drama, eventually leading him to

(D) Paul Robeson developed a serious interest in drama, having led him eventually to a

(E) where he developed a serious interest in drama, Paul Robeson, as a result, eventually went on to

**11.** <u>The Roman Empire, often by questionable means, attempted to bring their</u> version of law and order to provinces throughout Europe.

(A) The Roman Empire, often by questionable means, attempted to bring their

(B) The Roman Empire was often questionable in its means in its attempts to bring its

(C) Using means that are often questionable, the Roman Empire, in attempting to bring its

(D) Questionable means were often used by the Roman Empire, in attempting to bring its

(E) Often by questionable means, the Roman Empire attempted to bring its

**GO ON TO THE NEXT PAGE**

The following sentences test your ability to recognize grammar and usage errors. Each sentence contains either a single error or no error at all. No sentence contains more than one error. The error, if there is one, is underlined and lettered. If the sentence contains an error, select the one underlined part that must be changed to make the sentence correct. If the sentence is correct, select choice E. In choosing answers, follow the requirements of standard written English.

EXAMPLE:

The other delegates and him immediately
   A             B       C
accepted the resolution drafted by the
                      D
neutral states. No error
             E

(A) ● (C) (D) (E)

12. Although canoeing through the rapids was exciting,
                A

it was also exhausting, and we were happy for a time
 B

to have the canoe float serene down a smooth stretch
                  C     D

of the river. No error
          E

13. Undoubtedly, more voters in the urban areas

will have voted for Julia Morton if she had taken a
   A          B       C

less conservative stand on zoning codes than she did.
 D

No error
 E

14. Writing about people whose circumstances
    A              B

were deplorable, Dickens used the novel to protest
   C                        D

social conditions in Victorian England. No error
                        E

15. It was fortunate that the doctor, in spite of adverse
     A

medical conditions, was able to examine the patient
             B      C

calm and competently. No error
 D           E

16. In the early days of the steam locomotive,
      A

compassionate engineers would sometimes
     B

have thrown coal overboard in poor neighborhoods.
   C             D
No error
 E

17. According to the store manager, the most important

workers were those which had contributed to the
           A     B

reputation of the store rather than those with the
               C

most impressive sales figures. No error
    D              E

18. The survey showed that most shoppers who drive
       A

prefer the mall more than downtown stores
         B

simply because finding parking is less difficult
   C               D

at the mall. No error
       E

19. For people in many ancient societies, work was
      A

only a means of survival rather than a way
    B         C

to improve your standard of living. No error
  D                  E

**GO ON TO THE NEXT PAGE**

4  4

Unauthorized copying or reuse of any part of this page is illegal.

**20.** The use of irrigation in the once-arid region
A          B

have increased the production of alfalfa and of
C

many other crops as well . No error
D      E

**21.** Unfortunately, the opening of the new library complex,

previously scheduled for next September, would be
A        B            C

delayed for several months because of construction
D

difficulties. No error
E

**22.** Some of the workers who resent the supervisor's
A

authority would probably feel uncomfortable if they
B             C

were to acquire the independence that they demand .
D

No error
E

**23.** Given her strong sense of social justice, Burns
A

vehemently protested over her party's failure
B     C

to support a tax decrease for senior citizens. No error
D                        E

**24.** The friendly competition between my older sister and

I began as soon as we learned that our aunt had
A             B

joked that she might write a will leaving her house
C

to me alone . No error
D      E

**25.** People who wish to be a model should remember that
A

not all modeling is glamorous and that a great deal
B

of it is simply tiring. No error
C    D            E

**26.** Professor Chen repeated her point that the hero, if
A

given the chance to relive the moment, would choose
B           C

to do it . No error
D    E

**27.** The professor's insistence on high standards and

rigorous examinations are not, despite what students
A

think, part of a plan to withhold high grades
B          C

from them . No error
D      E

**28.** Watkins believes that the decline of the essay in the
A           B

United States today is largely due to the decreasing
C

number of inquiring readers . No error
D           E

**29.** Today a medical doctor must often make a choice
A                  B

between engaging in private practice or engaging
C              D

in research. No error
E

**GO ON TO THE NEXT PAGE** ⟶

**Directions:** The following passage is an early draft of an essay. Some parts of the passage need to be rewritten.

Read the passage and select the best answers for the questions that follow. Some questions are about particular sentences or parts of sentences and ask you to improve sentence structure or word choice. Other questions ask you to consider organization and development. In choosing answers, follow the requirements of standard written English.

**Questions 30-35 are based on the following passage.**

This essay was written in response to an assignment to describe an unusual person or an unusual characteristic in a person.

(1) My mother likes to speculate about the infirmities of the great personages of the past. (2) I remember well her analysis of schizophrenia in the Dutch painter, Vincent Van Gogh, and psychological conditions of other famous people. (3) Since I was a young child, I have been fascinated by them. (4) She often engages in these musings during sit-down meals with everyone in the family present to offer contrasting views. (5) Mom's interest in historical aspects of psychology is exciting—more exciting, even, than any of the programs offered by network television. (6) She says that poor programming on the part of the networks is one of the reasons she has felt the need to direct our young minds to other, more engaging avenues. (7) Imagine that her speculation is not only an expression of parental concern for a child's welfare but also an outlet for her creative mind. (8) Mom has this unusual interest, it has made me an authority among my peers. (9) Last week, my American literature teacher launched into a discussion of the writings of Edgar Allan Poe. (10) Before the discussion was over I was asked to give the class a glimpse of the personal life of Poe.

30. In context, what is the best way to deal with sentence 3 ?

(A) Leave it as it is.
(B) Place it after sentence 7.
(C) Insert "On the contrary" at the beginning of the sentence.
(D) Change "them" to "her theories".
(E) Use "and" at the end of sentence 3 to link it with sentence 4.

31. In context, which of the following should be inserted at the beginning of sentence 7 ?

(A) After all,
(B) In fact,
(C) You should
(D) I like to
(E) Then

32. In context, which of the following is the best way to phrase the underlined portion of sentence 8 (reproduced below) ?

*Mom  has this unusual interest, it has made me an authority among my peers.*

(A) (As it is now)
(B) And so it is my mom's unusual interest that has made me such
(C) Because of my mom's unusual interest, I have become
(D) As you can see, having my mom's unusual interest makes me
(E) Naturally, this unusual interest of my mom's should have made me

33. In context, which is the best way to deal with sentence 9 ?

(A) Insert "However," at the beginning of the sentence.
(B) Insert "For example," at the beginning of the sentence.
(C) Insert "her name is Ms. Lumberburd" after "teacher".
(D) Change "into" to "on".
(E) Change "launched" to "launches".

**GO ON TO THE NEXT PAGE**

**34.** Which of the following sentences would be best to add after sentence 10 ?

(A) I confidently related what my mother had taught me about him.

(B) And in fact, you can bet that really made my day.

(C) Indeed, my mother had always encouraged me to do my best on such occasions.

(D) I outlined everything I knew about Poe.

(E) Famous for his tales of terror, Poe has captivated readers for 150 years.

**35.** Where is the most logical place to begin a new paragraph?

(A) After sentence 3
(B) After sentence 5
(C) After sentence 6
(D) After sentence 7
(E) After sentence 10

# STOP

**If you finish before time is called, you may check your work on this section only.**
**Do not turn to any other section in the test.**

## SECTION 5
Time — 25 minutes
24 Questions

**Turn to Section 5 (page 5) of your answer sheet to answer the questions in this section.**

**Directions:** For each question in this section, select the best answer from among the choices given and fill in the corresponding circle on the answer sheet.

Each sentence below has one or two blanks, each blank indicating that something has been omitted. Beneath the sentence are five words or sets of words labeled A through E. Choose the word or set of words that, when inserted in the sentence, <u>best</u> fits the meaning of the sentence as a whole.

**Example:**

Hoping to ------- the dispute, negotiators proposed a compromise that they felt would be ------- to both labor and management.

(A) enforce . . useful
(B) end . . divisive
(C) overcome . . unattractive
(D) extend . . satisfactory
(E) resolve . . acceptable

1. They use language not to explain but to -------; each statement is like a reflection in a warped mirror.

   (A) preserve    (B) distort    (C) enlighten
   (D) negate    (E) destroy

2. Colonial South Carolina was characterized by cultural -------: Europeans, Africans, and Native Americans each absorbed some customs of the other groups.

   (A) tension    (B) conservatism    (C) integrity
   (D) convergence    (E) eradication

3. Anna Freud's impact on psychoanalysis was -------, coming not from one brilliant discovery but from a lifetime of first-rate work.

   (A) tangential    (B) premature    (C) exorbitant
   (D) indiscernible    (E) cumulative

4. Francis learned that by ------- his anger and resentment, and so avoiding -------, he could overcome opponents more successfully than could those who openly defied their adversaries.

   (A) expressing . . hostility
   (B) suppressing . . conflict
   (C) stifling . . temperance
   (D) disguising . . deceit
   (E) rousing . . wrath

5. Sleep actually occurs -------, though one may receive clues signaling its ------- for several minutes before one falls asleep.

   (A) gradually . . abruptness
   (B) erratically . . solace
   (C) temporarily . . length
   (D) inevitably . . approach
   (E) instantaneously . . onset

6. Ellen Swallow Richards, a ------- environmental preservation in the United States, campaigned during the nineteenth century to ------- responsible practices in the discipline that has come to be known as ecology.

   (A) foil for . . expose
   (B) pioneer of . . implement
   (C) resource on . . squelch
   (D) mitigator of . . promote
   (E) critic of . . exploit

7. Laila performed her tasks at the office with -------, completing all her projects in record time.

   (A) alacrity    (B) conformity    (C) deliberation
   (D) recrimination    (E) exasperation

8. Critics say that the autobiographical work *Brothers and Keepers* by John Edgar Wideman is surprising in that it celebrates and yet ------- his own role in the life of his brother.

   (A) censures    (B) exacerbates    (C) explores
   (D) duplicates    (E) delineates

**GO ON TO THE NEXT PAGE** ➔

The passages below are followed by questions based on their content; questions following a pair of related passages may also be based on the relationship between the paired passages. Answer the questions on the basis of what is <u>stated</u> or <u>implied</u> in the passages and in any introductory material that may be provided.

**Questions 9-10 are based on the following passage.**

    During the late nineteenth century in the United States, many people thought it improper for a woman to be a professional artist. Alice Barber Stephens got
*Line*
5  around this prejudice: she succeeded as a book and magazine illustrator by creating art and conducting business with publishers and authors from home. She sold engravings to national magazines and illustrated the books of many novelists, including Louisa May Alcott and Nathaniel Hawthorne. As a young woman,
10  Stephens studied at the Pennsylvania School of the Fine Arts, a member of the first class to admit women. She petitioned for nude drawing classes for women, later instituting such a class at an art school for women. She also founded an organization that fought prejudice
15  against women artists.

**9.** In lines 1-6 ("During . . . home"), the author suggests which of the following?

(A) In late nineteenth-century America, established artists were exclusively male.
(B) It was harder for women artists to work alone than in the studio of an established artist.
(C) It was easier for artists to sell work to magazines than to art dealers.
(D) Stephens found a way to pursue her professional goals and maintain social respectability.
(E) Stephens demonstrated little regard for the opinions of mainstream society.

**10.** Which of the following best characterizes Alice Barber Stephens ?

(A) Materialist and aesthete
(B) Perfectionist and egotist
(C) Pragmatist and activist
(D) Dreamer and revolutionary
(E) Celebrity and philanthropist

**Questions 11-12 are based on the following passage.**

    The first stage of Europe's conquest of northeastern North America was "the traders phase." Casual contacts and exchanges with visiting explorers and fishermen began
*Line*
5  on a basis that was not unfamiliar to the Native Americans. Metal, glass, or cloth items were exchanged for furs in a setting that was unprecedented only in the strangeness of the visitors and their wares. But as casual exchanges became systematic, the Native Americans began altering their subsistence and residential patterns to obtain more
10  furs. As a result, they grew dependent on their European trading partners while frequently entering into competition with one another. In the end, the principles of reciprocity and equality were substantially undermined by the ethics and imperatives of the traders.

**11.** The passage suggests that contact between Native Americans and Europeans ultimately

(A) decreased Native American reliance on the fur trade
(B) distorted relationships among Native Americans
(C) led to Native American economic independence
(D) decimated the population of fur-bearing animals
(E) increased competition among European traders

**12.** Lines 5-7 ("Metal . . . wares") suggest that Native Americans primarily viewed the European traders as

(A) reserved
(B) arrogant
(C) exotic
(D) capricious
(E) grasping

**GO ON TO THE NEXT PAGE**

**Questions 13-24 are based on the following passages.**

*The California museum built by oil billionaire J. Paul Getty (1892-1976) to house his world-class art collection opened in 1974. Passage 1 describes some early reactions to the Getty Museum. Passage 2 is excerpted from Getty's autobiography.*

**Passage 1**

It sits atop a wooded hillside overlooking the Pacific in Malibu, California. Critics have contemptuously compared it to Disneyland. "A plastic paradise in kitsch city," grumped
Line one. "It outstrips any existing monument to expensive,
5 aggressive bad taste, cultural pretension, and self-aggrandizement."

The building that houses the controversial new J. Paul Getty Museum is a re-creation of the Villa dei Papyri in Herculaneum, near Pompeii, which was destroyed by the
10 eruption of Vesuvius in A.D. 79. Visitors and critics alike usually wind up being favorably impressed by the Getty collection, which specializes in classical antiquities. But it is the design of the building rather than the art itself that has ignited the most heated art controversy of the 1970's.

15 Criticism of the museum design is of two types. One school of thought holds that the museum building itself is not sufficiently neutral, that a museum ought not to be, of itself, a work of art, competing with the collection displayed therein. The other school of thought holds that while it is
20 permissible for a museum to be a work of art, the Getty building fails miserably as art because it is neither taste-fully conceived nor accurately reproduced. "It is a faithful replica of nothing that ever existed," wrote architecture critic John Pastier, "re-created by inappropriate technologies
25 and frequently lacking in basic architectural design judg-ment. The details are all based on known Roman examples from various places, but they have been combined and executed in a manner that often negates their nature and purpose or creates an incongruous appearance."

30 Among the specific criticisms offered by Pastier and others dissatisfied with the museum-as-replica is that many interior walls and whole parts of the floor plan of the original villa have been shifted, and an entire wing of the original villa has been omitted. Perhaps the most devas-
35 tating single criticism of the authenticity of the museum design has been that excavation of the original villa site has been so incomplete that there is insufficient knowledge available even to attempt a legitimate re-creation. "No one knows about its precise style and details, how many floors
40 it had, or exactly how tall it was," wrote Pastier. The Getty Museum, he seemed to imply, is merely an exercise in guesswork.

**Passage 2**

Since I personally would be footing the bills for the new museum, the final question was put to me: Expand the
45 existing facilities or construct an entirely new building? I listened to all the pros and cons. "Draw up plans for an entirely new building," I told the trustees. I made one reservation. "I refuse to pay for one of those concrete-bunker-type structures that are the fad among museum
50 architects—nor for some tinted-glass-and-stainless-steel monstrosity." To my delight, the trustees beamed. They, too, wanted the museum building itself to be unique and a work of art.

The flouting of conventional wisdom and refusal to
55 conform carry with them many risks. This is nowhere more true than in the Art World, certain quarters of which tend to be very much doctrinaire and elitist. However, I had calculated the risks—and, I say this with an admitted degree of arrogance, I disregarded them. Thus, I was neither shaken
60 nor surprised when some of the early returns showed that certain critics sniffed at the new museum. The building did not follow the arbitrary criteria for "museum construction." There were those who thought it should have been more conventional—that is, I suppose, that it should have been
65 built to look like some of the museum structures whose architecture can be best described as "Penitentiary Modern." In any event, for the first two months or so, the J. Paul Getty Museum building was called "controversial" in many Art World (or should I say Artsy-Craftsy?) quarters.

70 I have a fortunate capacity to remain unruffled. I also have had more than sufficient experience in many areas of life to know that the shrillest critics are not necessarily the most authoritative (and seldom the most objective). Beyond this, the very shrillness of their cries and howls very quickly
75 exhausts their wind.

13. In line 3, "plastic" most nearly means

   (A) pliable
   (B) artificial
   (C) impermanent
   (D) innovative
   (E) inexpensive

14. The critics mentioned in the first paragraph of Passage 1 most probably consider the comparison of the museum to Disneyland appropriate because they believe that both places

   (A) have aroused controversy in the press
   (B) were built in picturesque areas
   (C) celebrate imagination and innovation
   (D) are garish and inauthentic in design
   (E) were very expensive to maintain

**GO ON TO THE NEXT PAGE**

15. In lines 22-29, Pastier's basic objection to the museum's design is that

(A) its separate parts do not create a coherent whole
(B) it is modeled on a building not worthy of imitation
(C) it does not sufficiently accommodate the needs of modern museum patrons
(D) its architectural style clashes with the styles of the artworks it houses
(E) it is not harmoniously integrated into the landscape that surrounds it

16. Lines 30-42 suggest that the excavation at the site of the Villa dei Papyri had revealed the original structure's

(A) domestic fixtures
(B) architectural embellishments
(C) shell, but not the location of its interior walls
(D) age, but neither its layout nor its purpose
(E) floor plan, but neither its height nor its details

17. Passage 1 indicates that Pastier and like-minded critics have arrived at some of their objections to the Getty Museum by

(A) evaluating the artworks it houses
(B) comparing it to other museums that house antiquities
(C) considering the Roman building on which it is modeled
(D) investigating the sources of Getty's personal fortune
(E) analyzing the character of J. Paul Getty

18. Getty indicates that the trustees "beamed" (line 51) because they were

(A) amused by Getty's cantankerousness
(B) accustomed to Getty's impulsiveness
(C) in accord with Getty's preferences
(D) pleased by Getty's unexpectedly generous donation
(E) impressed with Getty's financial acumen

19. When Getty mentions the "flouting of conventional wisdom" (line 54), he is referring to his opinions about the

(A) design of the museum building
(B) location of the museum
(C) museum's arrangement of displays
(D) financing of the museum
(E) floor plan of the museum building

20. As indicated in Passage 2, Getty considered his choice of museum design an act of

(A) courageous defiance
(B) pointed satire
(C) spiteful mischief
(D) reluctant compromise
(E) justified indignation

21. On the basis of the information in Passage 2, which statement most accurately describes Getty's reaction to the art controversy mentioned in lines 12-14 ?

(A) He tabled plans to expand the museum's facilities.
(B) He felt that his intentions had been misunderstood by critics.
(C) He took the complaints seriously enough to consider redesigning the museum.
(D) He had anticipated the response and decided to ignore it.
(E) He engaged the most vehement of the critics in public debate.

22. Which aspect of the Getty Museum building seems to matter a great deal in Passage 1, but not in Passage 2 ?

(A) Its potential for future expansion
(B) Its convenience for visitors
(C) Its questionable authenticity
(D) Its unusual appearance
(E) Its practicality

**GO ON TO THE NEXT PAGE**

**23.** Which statement best expresses an idea shared by one group of critics in Passage 1 and the trustees in Passage 2?

(A) A museum ought to concentrate on collecting artworks from only one historical period.

(B) Museums can be considered successful only if they attract a large enough segment of the population.

(C) The design of a building in which works of art are shown should resemble the style of those artworks.

(D) It is appropriate for a museum building to be a work of art in its own right.

(E) Museums that collect contemporary art experience fewer difficulties than those that collect classical art.

**24.** The final paragraph of Passage 2 suggests that Getty would predict which of the following about the critics referred to in Passage 1?

(A) Unless they offer more constructive advice, they will lose the chance to contribute.

(B) Unless they start to conform more closely to public opinion, they will lose their audience.

(C) Since they are widely read, they will continue to have an impact on museum attendance.

(D) Since they are taken seriously by the art world, they will continue to influence museum design.

(E) Although they are very loud, their influence will be short-lived.

# STOP

**If you finish before time is called, you may check your work on this section only.**
**Do not turn to any other section in the test.**

**SECTION 7**
Time — 25 minutes
20 Questions

Turn to Section 7 (page 6) of your answer sheet to answer the questions in this section.

**Directions:** For this section, solve each problem and decide which is the best of the choices given. Fill in the corresponding circle on the answer sheet. You may use any available space for scratchwork.

1. In a certain game, points are assigned to every word. Each $q$, $x$, and $z$ in a word is worth 5 points, and all other letters are worth 1 point each. What is the sum of the points assigned to the word "exquisite"?

   (A) 21
   (B) 17
   (C) 16
   (D) 13
   (E) 9

2. If $2x - 10 = 20$, then $x - 5 =$

   (A) 5
   (B) 10
   (C) 15
   (D) 20
   (E) 30

**GO ON TO THE NEXT PAGE** ⇨

3. If $t$ represents an odd integer, which of the following expressions represents an even integer?

(A) $t + 2$
(B) $2t - 1$
(C) $3t - 2$
(D) $3t + 2$
(E) $5t + 1$

SALES OF JEANS IN 2001

Brand $K$ 15%
Brand $J$ 25%
Brand $L$ 15%
Other Brands 20%
Brand $M$ 15%
Brand $N$ 10%

5. The circle graph above represents all the jeans that were sold by a retail store in 2001, according to their brands. If the store sold 900 pairs of jeans other than brands $J$, $K$, $L$, $M$, and $N$, how many pairs of jeans did it sell altogether?

(A) 1,500
(B) 2,250
(C) 3,000
(D) 3,600
(E) 4,500

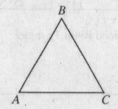
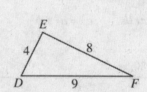

4. For the triangles above, the perimeter of $\triangle ABC$ equals the perimeter of $\triangle DEF$. If $\triangle ABC$ is equilateral, what is the length of $\overline{AB}$?

(A) 4
(B) 5
(C) 7
(D) 9
(E) 15

6. If there is no waste, how many square yards of carpeting is needed to cover a rectangular floor that is 12 feet by 18 feet? (1 yard = 3 feet)

(A) 8
(B) 16
(C) 24
(D) 30
(E) 216

GO ON TO THE NEXT PAGE

**7.** A certain scale only registers weights that are greater than 6 pounds. A person who wanted to know the weights of a puppy, a kitten, and a bunny weighed them in pairs and got the following results.

The kitten and the bunny weighed 7 pounds.
The kitten and the puppy weighed 8 pounds.
The bunny and the puppy weighed 9 pounds.

What is the weight of the puppy?

(A) 2 pounds
(B) 3 pounds
(C) 4 pounds
(D) 5 pounds
(E) 6 pounds

**8.** On a blueprint, $\frac{1}{4}$ inch represents 16 feet. If a driveway is 40 feet long, what is its length, in inches, on the map?

(A) $\frac{3}{8}$

(B) $\frac{5}{8}$

(C) $\frac{3}{4}$

(D) $2\frac{1}{2}$

(E) 10

**9.** In the $xy$-coordinate system, $(p, 0)$ is one of the points of intersection of the graphs of $y = -x^2 + 9$ and $y = x^2 - 9$. If $p$ is positive, what is the value of $p$ ?

(A) 3
(B) 6
(C) 9
(D) 18
(E) 81

**10.** The Smith Metal Company's old machine makes 300 bolts per hour. Its new machine makes 450 bolts per hour. If both machines begin running at the same time, how many <u>minutes</u> will it take the two machines to make a total of 900 bolts?

(A) 36
(B) 72
(C) 120
(D) 144
(E) 180

| $t$ | −1 | 0 | 1 | 2 |
|------|----|---|---|----|
| $g(t)$ | 4 | 2 | 0 | −2 |

**11.** The table above gives values of the linear function $g$ for selected values of $t$. Which of the following defines $g$ ?

(A) $g(t) = \frac{1}{2}t + 1$

(B) $g(t) = -\frac{1}{2}t + 1$

(C) $g(t) = -t + 1$

(D) $g(t) = -t + 2$

(E) $g(t) = -2t + 2$

GO ON TO THE NEXT PAGE

7

7

Unauthorized copying or reuse of
any part of this page is illegal.

**SURVEY RESULTS**

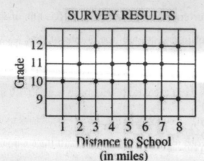

Distance to School
(in miles)

**12.** The results of a survey of 16 students at Thompson High School are given in the grid above. It shows the distance, to the nearest mile, that students at various grade levels travel to school. According to this grid, which of the following is true?

(A) There is only one student who travels 2 miles to school.

(B) Half of the students travel less than 4 miles to school.

(C) More 12th graders than 11th graders travel 6 or more miles to school.

(D) The students who travel less than 3 miles to school are all 12th graders.

(E) Of the students who travel 7 or more miles to school, half are 9th graders.

**13.** How many positive three-digit integers have the hundreds digit equal to 3 and the units digit (ones digit) equal to 4 ?

(A)  10
(B)  19
(C)  20
(D)  190
(E)  200

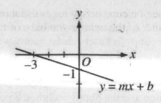

$$y = mx + b$$

**14.** The figure above shows the graph of the line $y = mx + b$, where $m$ and $b$ are constants. Which of the following best represents the graph of the line $y = -3mx + b$ ?

(A)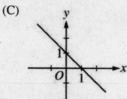

(B)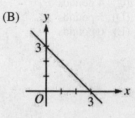

(C)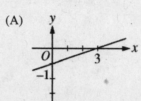

(D)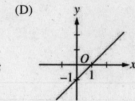

(E)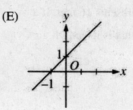

**GO ON TO THE NEXT PAGE**

7 7

Unauthorized copying or reuse of
any part of this page is illegal.

15. If the volume of a cube is 8, what is the shortest distance from the center of the cube to the base of the cube?

    (A)    1
    (B)    2
    (C)    4
    (D)    $\sqrt{2}$
    (E)    $2\sqrt{2}$

16. If $y = \dfrac{5x^3}{z}$, what happens to the value of $y$ when both $x$ and $z$ are doubled?

    (A)  $y$ is not changed.
    (B)  $y$ is halved.
    (C)  $y$ is doubled.
    (D)  $y$ is tripled.
    (E)  $y$ is multiplied by 4.

17. Luke purchased an automobile for $5,000, and the value of the automobile decreases by 20 percent each year. The value, in dollars, of the automobile $n$ years from the date of purchase is given by the function $V$, where $V(n) = 5000\left(\dfrac{4}{5}\right)^n$. How many years from the date of purchase will the value of the automobile be $3,200 ?

    (A)  One
    (B)  Two
    (C)  Three
    (D)  Four
    (E)  Five

**GO ON TO THE NEXT PAGE**

**7**

Unauthorized copying or reuse of
any part of this page is illegal.

**7**

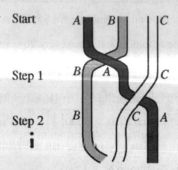

Start

Step 1

Step 2

18. In the figure above, three wires are braided. That
is, by starting in the order *A*, *B*, *C*, the outer left
wire *A* is brought over wire *B* to the middle position,
forming the order shown in step 1, then the outer right
wire *C* is brought to the new middle position shown
in step 2, and so on, alternately bringing each new
left and each new right wire to the middle. At what
numbered step does the braid first repeat the original
order *A*, *B*, *C* ?

(A)  3
(B)  4
(C)  5
(D)  6
(E)  7

19. In a set of eleven different numbers, which of the
following CANNOT affect the value of the median?

(A)  Doubling each number
(B)  Increasing each number by 10
(C)  Increasing the smallest number only
(D)  Decreasing the largest number only
(E)  Increasing the largest number only

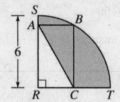

20. In the figure above, arc *SBT* is one quarter of a circle
with center *R* and radius 6. If the length plus the width
of rectangle *ABCR* is 8, then the perimeter of the
shaded region is

(A)   $8 + 3\pi$
(B)  $10 + 3\pi$
(C)  $14 + 3\pi$
(D)   $1 + 6\pi$
(E)  $12 + 6\pi$

# S T O P

**If you finish before time is called, you may check your work on this section only.**
**Do not turn to any other section in the test.**

## SECTION 8
### Time — 20 minutes
### 19 Questions

**Turn to Section 8 (page 7) of your answer sheet to answer the questions in this section.**

**Directions:** For each question in this section, select the best answer from among the choices given and fill in the corresponding circle on the answer sheet.

Each sentence below has one or two blanks, each blank indicating that something has been omitted. Beneath the sentence are five words or sets of words labeled A through E. Choose the word or set of words that, when inserted in the sentence, <u>best</u> fits the meaning of the sentence as a whole.

**Example:**

Hoping to ------- the dispute, negotiators proposed a compromise that they felt would be ------- to both labor and management.

(A) enforce . . useful
(B) end . . divisive
(C) overcome . . unattractive
(D) extend . . satisfactory
(E) resolve . . acceptable

1. Many writers associated with the Harlem Renaissance were not originally from Harlem; drawn by the artistic community it provided, they ------- the place as home.

(A) neglected   (B) adopted   (C) avoided
  (D) criticized   (E) encountered

2. Nicknamed the "contact lens," the device installed on the Hubble telescope successfully ------- its flawed vision, the result of a faulty mirror.

(A) corrected   (B) displayed   (C) generated
  (D) scrutinized   (E) accentuated

3. As an architect who rehabilitates older buildings, Roberta Washington objected to a city policy that resulted in the mass ------- of clearly ------- structures.

(A) demolition . . inconsequential
(B) renovation . . derelict
(C) razing . . salvageable
(D) protection . . venerable
(E) scouring . . grimy

4. The treasurer was intimidated by the ------- demeanor of the auditors who neither spoke nor smiled when they arrived.

(A) amiable   (B) ethical   (C) glacial
  (D) taunting   (E) nondescript

5. Rodolfo Gonzales was once described as ------- in body and mind because of the flexibility and grace apparent in both his boxing and his writing of poetry and plays.

(A) unyielding   (B) tremulous   (C) emphatic
  (D) lithe   (E) fickle

6. On the verge of financial collapse, the museum was granted a -------, receiving a much-needed ------- of cash in the form of a government loan.

(A) reprieve . . infusion
(B) deferment . . inducement
(C) rebate . . advance
(D) hearing . . security
(E) procurement . . account

**GO ON TO THE NEXT PAGE**

The passage below is followed by questions based on its content. Answer the questions on the basis of what is <u>stated</u> or <u>implied</u> in the passage and in any introductory material that may be provided.

**Questions 7-19 are based on the following passage.**

*In this passage from a novel, the narrator has been reading letters of his grandmother, Susan Ward, and is reflecting on the meaning of certain events in her life. In about 1880, Susan Ward was a young woman—a writer and a mother— whose husband Oliver was working as a mining engineer in Leadville, in the West. Here, the narrator imagines Susan Ward as she spends the winter with her family in Milton, New York, before rejoining her husband in the spring.*

From the parental burrow, Leadville seemed so far away it was only half real. Unwrapping her apple-cheeked son after a sleigh ride down the lane, she had difficulty in
Line believing that she had ever lived anywhere but here in Milton.
5      She felt how the placid industry of her days matched the placid industry of all the days that had passed over that farm through six generations. Present and past were less continuous than synonymous. She did not have to come at her grandparents through a time machine. Her own life and that
10 of the grandfather she was writing about showed her similar figures in an identical landscape. At the milldam where she had learned to skate she pulled her little boy on his sled, and they watched a weasel snow-white for winter flirt his black-tipped tail in and out of the mill's timbers. She might
15 have been watching with her grandfather's eyes.
      Watching a wintry sky die out beyond black elms, she could not make her mind restore the sight of the western mountains at sunset from her cabin door, or the cabin itself, or Oliver, or their friends. Who were those glittering people
20 intent on raiding the continent for money or for scientific knowledge? What illusion was it that she bridged between this world and that? She paused sometimes, cleaning the room she had always called Grandma's Room, and thought with astonishment of the memory of Oliver's great revolver
25 lying on the dresser when he, already a thoroughgoing West- erner, had come to the house to court her.
      The town of Milton was dim and gentle, molded by gentle lives, the current of change as slow through it as the seep of water through a bog. More than once she thought how wrong
30 those women in San Francisco had been, convinced that their old homes did not welcome them on their return. Last year when Oliver's professional future was uncertain, she would have agreed. Now, with the future assured in the form of Oliver's appointment as manager of the Adelaide mine in
35 Leadville, the comfortable past asserted itself unchanged. Need for her husband, like worry over him, was tuned low. Absorbed in her child and in the writing of her book, she was sunk in her affection for home. Even the signs of mutability that sometimes jolted her—the whiteness of her mother's
40 hair, the worn patience of her sister's face, the morose silences of her brother-in-law, now so long and black that

the women worried about him in low voices—could not more than briefly interrupt the deep security and peace.
      I wonder if ever again Americans can have that experi-
45 ence of returning to a home place so intimately known, profoundly felt, deeply loved, and absolutely submitted to? It is not quite true that you can't go home again. But it gets less likely. We have had too many divorces, we have consumed too much transportation, we have lived too
50 shallowly in too many places. I doubt that anyone of my son's generation could comprehend the home feelings of someone like Susan Ward. Despite her unwillingness to live separately from her husband, she could probably have stayed on indefinitely in Milton, visited only occasionally
55 by an asteroid husband. Or she would have picked up the old home and remade it in a new place. What she resisted was being a woman with no real home.
      When frontier historians theorize about the uprooted, the lawless, the purseless, and the socially cut-off who emigrated
60 to the West, they are not talking about people like my grand- mother. So much that was cherished and loved, women like her had to give up; and the more they gave it up, the more they carried it helplessly with them. It was a process like ionization: what was subtracted from one pole was added
65 to the other. For that sort of pioneer, the West was not a new country being created, but an old one being repro- duced; in that sense our pioneer women were always more realistic than our pioneer men. The moderns, carrying little baggage of the cultural kind, not even living in traditional
70 air, but breathing into their space helmets a scientific mix- ture of synthetic gases (and polluted at that) are the true pioneers. Their circuitry seems to include no domestic sentiment, they have had their empathy removed, their computers hum no ghostly feedback of Home, Sweet Home.
75 How marvelously free they are! How unutterably deprived!

**7.** In line 1, the phrase "parental burrow" suggests

(A) a lack of luxurious accommodations
(B) an atmosphere of peaceful security
(C) the work required to sustain a home
(D) a lack of interest and stimulation
(E) the loss of privacy

**8.** It can be inferred that Ward "did not have to come at her grandparents through a time machine" (lines 8-9) because

(A) her parents had frequently told her stories of them
(B) she was deeply immersed in the history and liter- ature of the period of their lives
(C) her life in Milton closely resembled theirs
(D) as a writer she could intuitively sense their lives
(E) she possessed written accounts of their lives

**GO ON TO THE NEXT PAGE** ⟶

9. The reference to the grandfather's eyes in line 15 indicates that Ward

   (A) longed to see nature as her ancestors did
   (B) was unable to come to terms with her own life
   (C) felt that her grandfather would approve of her life choices
   (D) was seeing something her grandfather himself might well have seen
   (E) longed to let her grandfather know what she was experiencing

10. The reference to a bog in line 29 serves to convey a sense of the

   (A) natural setting of the town of Milton
   (B) way in which Milton's residents earned their livelihoods
   (C) deliberate pace of life in Milton
   (D) confinement that Ward first felt in Milton
   (E) vague foreboding that permeated Milton

11. Ward came to feel differently from "those women in San Francisco" (line 30) because

   (A) the rigors of life in the West made life in the East seem more pleasant
   (B) the problems in her sister's life made her more content with the situation in her own life
   (C) she had more free time as her son began to grow out of infancy
   (D) her own career as a writer had become more important to her
   (E) she was free to enjoy her surroundings now that she was confident about her husband's professional future

12. The word "sunk" in line 38 conveys the degree to which Ward

   (A) is depressed about being separated from her husband
   (B) is concerned about her son's social development
   (C) feels powerless to help her sister's troubled marriage
   (D) allows herself to be filled with a particular emotion
   (E) lets down her defenses to free her creativity

13. The "feelings" referred to in line 51 might best be defined as

   (A) an unwillingness to travel far
   (B) the importance of property to self-esteem
   (C) the emotional presence of one's ancestors
   (D) deep knowledge and love of a place
   (E) a yearning to recapture childhood

14. The narrator refers to "frontier historians" (line 58) primarily in order to

   (A) add the weight of their authority to his assertion
   (B) show his respect for their research
   (C) suggest that instinct must be supplemented by formal training
   (D) introduce a viewpoint he contradicts
   (E) illustrate the nature of his own education

15. The narrator characterizes the migration by people like his grandmother as chiefly a process of

   (A) recreating a domestic haven
   (B) developing new skills for physical survival
   (C) shedding now-irrelevant concerns over status
   (D) instilling a love of place in the young
   (E) preserving the beauty of unspoiled nature

16. The reference to "little baggage" in lines 68-69 serves to suggest which of the following about the narrator's view of modern people?

   (A) They are not burdened by physical possessions.
   (B) They are not affected by the values of the past.
   (C) They are not interested in artistic tradition.
   (D) They are not bearing their portion of responsibility.
   (E) They are not respectful of the opinions of others.

17. In lines 71-75, the narrator describes members of the modern generation as the "true pioneers" because they

   (A) have worthier motivations for breaking new ground
   (B) build on the achievements of earlier generations
   (C) have superior technology and training
   (D) live in a violent and uncertain world
   (E) regard life as no previous generation has done

**GO ON TO THE NEXT PAGE** ⇨

18. The narrator apparently believes which of the following about the idea of home held by the new pioneers?

(A) They long to achieve their own sense of place.
(B) They scoff at the earlier generation's sense of place.
(C) They are free from hypocritical rhetoric about home.
(D) They are unable to experience the earlier generation's attachment to home.
(E) They are as deeply attuned to home as the earlier generation but in a distinctly different way.

19. What parallel between the narrator and Susan Ward does the passage reveal?

(A) Both openly resent the signs of change around them.
(B) Both have lived in many parts of the country.
(C) Both are writing about the life of a grandparent.
(D) Both feel alienated from their spouses.
(E) Both prefer solitude to company.

# STOP

**If you finish before time is called, you may check your work on this section only.**
**Do not turn to any other section in the test.**

## SECTION 9
Time — 20 minutes
16 Questions

---

**Turn to Section 9 (page 7) of your answer sheet to answer the questions in this section.**

---

**Directions:** For this section, solve each problem and decide which is the best of the choices given. Fill in the corresponding circle on the answer sheet. You may use any available space for scratchwork.

---

Notes

1. The use of a calculator is permitted.

2. All numbers used are real numbers.

3. Figures that accompany problems in this test are intended to provide information useful in solving the problems. They are drawn as accurately as possible EXCEPT when it is stated in a specific problem that the figure is not drawn to scale. All figures lie in a plane unless otherwise indicated.

4. Unless otherwise specified, the domain of any function $f$ is assumed to be the set of all real numbers $x$ for which $f(x)$ is a real number.

---

Reference Information

   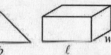  

$A = \pi r^2$
$C = 2\pi r$ $A = \ell w$ $A = \frac{1}{2}bh$ $V = \ell wh$ $V = \pi r^2 h$ $c^2 = a^2 + b^2$ **Special Right Triangles**

The number of degrees of arc in a circle is 360.

The sum of the measures in degrees of the angles of a triangle is 180.

---

**1.** For which of the following values of $m$ will the value of $3m - 1$ be greater than 10 ?

(A) 4
(B) 3
(C) 2
(D) 1
(E) 0

**2.** If $a \times k = a$ for all values of $a$, what is the value of $k$ ?

(A) $-a$
(B) $-1$
(C) $0$
(D) $1$
(E) $a$

---

GO ON TO THE NEXT PAGE ▷

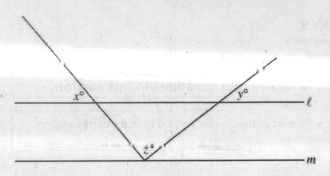

Note: Figure not drawn to scale.

3. In the figure above, $\ell \parallel m$. If $x = 80$ and $y = 70$, what is the value of $z$ ?

(A) 30
(B) 60
(C) 75
(D) 90
(E) 150

4. The scenic route from Mia's home to her office is 5 kilometers longer than the direct route. When she goes by the scenic route and returns by the direct route, the round trip is 35 kilometers. How many kilometers is the direct route?

(A) 5

(B) $12\frac{1}{2}$

(C) 15

(D) 20

(E) $22\frac{1}{2}$

5. A complete cycle of a traffic light takes 80 seconds. During each cycle, the light is green for 40 seconds, amber for 10 seconds, and red for 30 seconds. At a randomly chosen time, what is the probability that the light will not be red?

(A) $\frac{7}{8}$

(B) $\frac{5}{8}$

(C) $\frac{1}{2}$

(D) $\frac{3}{8}$

(E) $\frac{1}{8}$

6. For a certain hot-water heater, the increase in heating expenses is directly proportional to the increase in water-temperature setting. If heating expenses increase by $24 when the water-temperature setting is increased by 20 degrees Fahrenheit, by how much will heating expenses increase when the water-temperature setting is increased by 15 degrees Fahrenheit?

(A) $16
(B) $18
(C) $19
(D) $20
(E) $21

GO ON TO THE NEXT PAGE

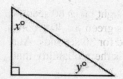 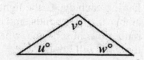

**7.** In the triangles above, what is the average (arithmetic mean) of $u$, $v$, $w$, $x$, and $y$ ?

(A) 21
(B) 45
(C) 50
(D) 52
(E) 54

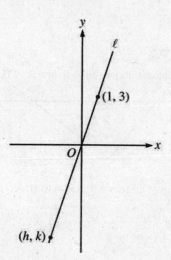

**9.** In the figure above, line $\ell$ passes through the origin. What is the value of $\dfrac{k}{h}$ ?

(A) 3

(B) 2

(C) $\dfrac{3}{2}$

(D) $-\dfrac{3}{2}$

(E) $-3$

**8.** If $x$, $x^2$, and $x^3$ lie on a number line in the order shown above, which of the following could be the value of $x$ ?

(A) $-2$

(B) $-\dfrac{1}{2}$

(C) $\dfrac{3}{4}$

(D) $1$

(E) $\dfrac{3}{2}$

**GO ON TO THE NEXT PAGE**

$$|m - 3| = 5$$
$$|k + 7| = 15$$

10. In the equations above, $m < 0$ and $k < 0$. What is the value of $m - k$ ?

(A) −24
(B) −14
(C) 8
(D) 16
(E) 20

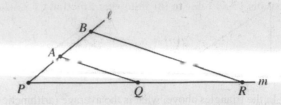

Note: Figure not drawn to scale.

12. In the figure above, points $P$, $A$, and $B$ are equally spaced on line $\ell$ and points $P$, $Q$, and $R$ are equally spaced on line $m$. If $PB = 4$, $PR = 6$, and $AQ = 4$, what is the perimeter of quadrilateral $QABR$ ?

(A) 13
(B) 14
(C) 15
(D) 16
(E) 17

RATINGS OF CAR ENGINE OIL

| Rating | Relative Speed of Flow |
|--------|------------------------|
| 10W | Half as fast as 5W oil |
| 15W | Half as fast as 10W oil |
| 20W | Half as fast as 15W oil |

11. According to the table above, car engine oil with a rating of 5W flows how many times as fast as car engine oil with a rating of 20W?

(A) 2
(B) 4
(C) 8
(D) 16
(E) 32

GO ON TO THE NEXT PAGE

**Questions 13-14 refer to the following functions $g$ and $h$.**

$$g(n) = n^2 + n$$
$$h(n) = n^2 - n$$

**13.** $g(5) - h(4) =$

(A)  0
(B)  8
(C)  10
(D)  18
(E)  32

**14.** Which of the following is equivalent to $h(m+1)$?

(A) $g(m)$
(B) $g(m) + 1$
(C) $g(m) - 1$
(D) $h(m) + 1$
(E) $h(m) - 1$

**15.** A store charges $28 for a certain type of sweater. This price is 40 percent more than the amount it costs the store to buy one of these sweaters. At an end-of-season sale, store employees can purchase any remaining sweaters at 30 percent off the store's cost. How much would it cost an employee to purchase a sweater of this type at this sale?

(A) $8.40
(B) $14.00
(C) $19.60
(D) $20.00
(E) $25.20

**16.** In rectangle $ABCD$, point $E$ is the midpoint of $\overline{BC}$. If the area of quadrilateral $ABED$ is $\dfrac{2}{3}$, what is the area of rectangle $ABCD$?

(A) $\dfrac{1}{2}$

(B) $\dfrac{3}{4}$

(C) $\dfrac{8}{9}$

(D) $1$

(E) $\dfrac{8}{3}$

# STOP

**If you finish before time is called, you may check your work on this section only.
Do not turn to any other section in the test.**

10

Unauthorized copying or reuse of
any part of this page is illegal.

10

## SECTION 10
Time — 10 minutes
14 Questions

**Turn to Section 10 (page 7) of your answer sheet to answer the questions in this section.**

**Directions:** For each question in this section, select the best answer from among the choices given and fill in the corresponding circle on the answer sheet.

The following sentences test correctness and effectiveness of expression. Part of each sentence or the entire sentence is underlined; beneath each sentence are five ways of phrasing the underlined material. Choice A repeats the original phrasing; the other four choices are different. If you think the original phrasing produces a better sentence than any of the alternatives, select choice A; if not, select one of the other choices.

In making your selection, follow the requirements of standard written English; that is, pay attention to grammar, choice of words, sentence construction, and punctuation. Your selection should result in the most effective sentence—clear and precise, without awkwardness or ambiguity.

EXAMPLE:

Laura Ingalls Wilder published her first book and she was sixty-five years old then.

(A) and she was sixty-five years old then
(B) when she was sixty-five
(C) at age sixty-five years old
(D) upon the reaching of sixty-five years
(E) at the time when she was sixty-five

1. At the beginning of George Eliot's novel *Silas Marner*, a linen weaver has been driven by a false charge of theft away from his home and taking refuge in the village of Raveloe.

   (A) taking refuge in the village of Raveloe
   (B) has taken refuge in the village of Raveloe
   (C) the village of Raveloe
   (D) being in the village of Raveloe
   (E) Raveloe, a village that is his refuge

2. Serving as either business tools or recreational devices, computers, they are increasingly popular.

   (A) computers; they are increasingly popular
   (B) their popularity has increased
   (C) they have become more popular
   (D) computers are increasingly popular
   (E) computers, they are popular

3. One often coming upon passages in letters often that are memorable for their thought or their form, or both.

   (A) One often coming upon passages in letters often that are
   (B) One often comes upon passages in letters that are
   (C) One often comes upon a passage in letters that you find
   (D) Often one comes upon a passage in letters; it is
   (E) Often one comes upon a passage in letters in which it is

4. Finding political support, designing a campaign, and, above all, the securing of financial backing are the challenging tasks faced by candidates.

   (A) the securing of financial backing are
   (B) the security of financial backing are
   (C) to secure financial backing is
   (D) securing financial backing is
   (E) securing financial backing are

5. Although only two inches long, the shrew is a mammal and therefore a relative of elephants and giraffes.

   (A) Although only
   (B) Whereas only
   (C) Despite a size
   (D) While its size is
   (E) Since it is

GO ON TO THE NEXT PAGE

**10**

Unauthorized copying or reuse of
any part of this page is illegal.

**10**

6. Many prospective actors in the area auditioned for roles in the movie, and only a few were selected.

(A) Many prospective actors in the area auditioned for roles in the movie, and only a few were selected.
(B) Many prospective actors, having auditioned for roles in the movie, only a few in the area were selected.
(C) Many prospective actors in the area auditioned for roles in the movie, but only a few were selected.
(D) Only a few were selected, many prospective actors in the area having auditioned for roles in the movie.
(E) After many prospective actors in the area auditioned for role in the movie, only a few being selected.

7. The author, taking the reader on a chronological journey through her native land, skillfully combining history and legend with fragments of fiction.

(A) The author, taking the reader on a chronological journey through her native land, skillfully
(B) The reader is taken on a chronological journey through the author's native land by skillfully
(C) The reader is taken on a chronological journey through her native land by the author who is skillfully
(D) The author, who takes the reader on a chronological journey through her native land, skillfully
(E) The author takes the reader on a chronological journey through her native land, skillfully

8. The practice of renaming a street Martin Luther King Boulevard has been adopted through many cities in honoring the civil rights leader.

(A) through many cities in honoring
(B) through many cities to honor
(C) in many cities; it was to honor
(D) by many cities to honor
(E) by many cities in honoring

9. During the 1980's, the income gap between the richest and the poorest Americans widened significantly, while continuing to expand in the 1990's.

(A) significantly, while continuing to expand
(B) significantly, and it continued to expand
(C) significantly with continuing expansion
(D) significantly, it continued expanding
(E) significantly, continuing expanding

10. The Basque language, possibly one of Europe's oldest, whose origins are hotly debated.

(A) The Basque language, possibly one of Europe's oldest, whose origins are hotly debated.
(B) The Basque language, possibly one of Europe's oldest, its origins are hotly debated.
(C) Possibly one of Europe's oldest languages, the origins of Basque are hotly debated.
(D) The origins of the Basque language, possibly one of Europe's oldest, are hotly debated.
(E) Basque is hotly debated as a language whose origins are possibly Europe's oldest.

11. Because the workers approached their jobs with very little interest and almost no energy, their productivity was, not surprisingly, very low.

(A) their productivity was, not surprisingly, very low
(B) this lowered, not surprisingly, their productivity
(C) not to anyone's surprise their productivity was very low
(D) their very low productivity was not to anyone's surprise
(E) their productivity, being very low, was not surprising

12. Many changes occurred while she was president of the college, and they increased its educational quality as well as effectiveness.

(A) college, and they increased its educational quality as well as effectiveness
(B) college, they both increased the educational quality and effectiveness of the college
(C) college, which both increased its educational quality as well as increased its effectiveness
(D) college; these changes increased its educational quality and effectiveness
(E) college; these changes increased both the educational quality and effectiveness of the college

**GO ON TO THE NEXT PAGE**

10  10

Unauthorized copying or reuse of
any part of this page is illegal.

13. <u>Although the global food crisis is most obvious in the tropics, the</u> temperate zones may have a similar problem soon.

(A) Although the global food crisis is most obvious in the tropics, the

(B) The global food crisis being most obvious in the tropics, the

(C) Notwithstanding the fact that the global food crisis is most obvious in the tropics, nevertheless the

(D) Although the global food crisis had been most obvious in the tropics, the

(E) Even if the global food crisis was most obvious in the tropics, nevertheless the

14. High school graduates usually do not end up earning as much income as college graduates <u>do, this being why so many high school students</u> go on to pursue college degrees.

(A) do, this being why so many high school students

(B) do, this is why so many high school students

(C) do; this fact explains why so many high school students

(D) do; this fact explaining the reason for why so many high school students

(E) do, explaining why so many high school students

## STOP

**If you finish before time is called, you may check your work on this section only.
Do not turn to any other section in the test.**

# Correct Answers and Difficulty Levels
## SAT Practice Test #8

## CRITICAL READING

### Section 2
**Multiple-Choice Questions**

| Correct Answer | Difficulty Level | Correct Answer | Difficulty Level |
|---|---|---|---|
| 1 D | E | 13 D | M |
| 2 E | M | 14 A | M |
| 3 C | M | 15 D | M |
| 4 B | H | 16 C | M |
| 5 C | H | 17 A | M |
| 6 D | M | 18 E | M |
| 7 E | M | 19 D | M |
| 8 C | M | 20 B | M |
| 9 D | H | 21 C | M |
| 10 B | M | 22 E | M |
| 11 C | M | 23 A | M |
| 12 C | E | 24 A | M |

Number correct _____

Number incorrect _____

### Section 5
**Multiple-Choice Questions**

| Correct Answer | Difficulty Level | Correct Answer | Difficulty Level |
|---|---|---|---|
| 1 B | M | 13 B | E |
| 2 D | M | 14 D | M |
| 3 E | M | 15 A | M |
| 4 B | M | 16 E | M |
| 5 B | M | 17 C | M |
| 6 B | M | 18 C | M |
| 7 A | M | 19 A | E |
| 8 A | H | 20 A | M |
| 9 D | H | 21 D | M |
| 10 C | H | 22 C | M |
| 11 B | H | 23 D | M |
| 12 C | M | 24 E | M |

Number correct _____

Number incorrect _____

### Section 8
**Multiple-Choice Questions**

| Correct Answer | Difficulty Level | Correct Answer | Difficulty Level |
|---|---|---|---|
| 1 B | E | 11 E | M |
| 2 A | E | 12 E | M |
| 3 C | M | 13 D | M |
| 4 C | H | 14 D | M |
| 5 D | H | 15 D | M |
| 6 A | H | 16 B | M |
| 7 B | M | 17 E | M |
| 8 C | M | 18 D | M |
| 9 D | E | 19 C | H |
| 10 C | M | | |

Number correct _____

Number incorrect _____

## MATHEMATICS

### Section 3

**Multiple-Choice Questions**

| Correct Answer | Difficulty Level |
|---|---|
| 1 D | E |
| 2 B | E |
| 3 A | E |
| 4 C | E |
| 5 D | M |
| 6 C | M |
| 7 B | M |
| 8 A | H |

**Student-Produced Response Questions**

| Correct Answer | Difficulty Level |
|---|---|
| 9 120 | E |
| 10 6/25, .24 | E |
| 11 1,11 | M |
| 12 39 | M |
| 13 6500 | M |
| 14 5/18, .277, .278 | M |
| 15 2 | H |
| 16 5 | M |
| 17 11 | H |
| 18 3/8, .375 | H |

Number correct _____

Number correct (9-18) _____

Number incorrect _____

### Section 7
**Multiple-Choice Questions**

| Correct Answer | Difficulty Level | Correct Answer | Difficulty Level |
|---|---|---|---|
| 1 B | E | 11 E | M |
| 2 B | E | 12 C | M |
| 3 E | E | 13 A | M |
| 4 C | E | 14 D | M |
| 5 E | E | 15 A | M |
| 6 C | E | 16 E | M |
| 7 D | M | 17 B | H |
| 8 B | M | 18 D | M |
| 9 A | M | 19 E | H |
| 10 B | M | 20 B | H |

Number correct _____

Number incorrect _____

### Section 9
**Multiple-Choice Questions**

| Correct Answer | Difficulty Level | Correct Answer | Difficulty Level |
|---|---|---|---|
| 1 A | E | 9 A | M |
| 2 D | E | 10 E | M |
| 3 A | E | 11 C | M |
| 4 C | E | 12 E | M |
| 5 B | E | 13 D | M |
| 6 B | M | 14 A | H |
| 7 E | M | 15 B | H |
| 8 C | M | 16 C | H |

Number correct _____

Number incorrect _____

## WRITING

### Section 1
**Essay**

Essay Score* (0-6) _____

### Section 4
**Multiple-Choice Questions**

| Correct Answer | Difficulty Level | Correct Answer | Difficulty Level |
|---|---|---|---|
| 1 D | E | 19 D | E |
| 2 C | E | 20 C | M |
| 3 D | E | 21 C | M |
| 4 B | E | 22 E | M |
| 5 B | M | 23 C | M |
| 6 B | E | 24 A | M |
| 7 A | E | 25 A | M |
| 8 B | E | 26 D | M |
| 9 E | M | 27 A | M |
| 10 A | M | 28 E | H |
| 11 E | M | 29 D | H |
| 12 C | E | 30 D | E |
| 13 A | E | 31 D | M |
| 14 E | E | 32 C | E |
| 15 D | E | 33 B | E |
| 16 C | E | 34 A | E |
| 17 A | E | 35 D | M |
| 18 B | E | | |

Number correct _____

Number incorrect _____

### Section 10
**Multiple-Choice Questions**

| Correct Answer | Difficulty Level |
|---|---|
| 1 B | E |
| 2 D | E |
| 3 B | E |
| 4 E | E |
| 5 A | E |
| 6 C | E |
| 7 E | M |
| 8 D | M |
| 9 B | E |
| 10 D | M |
| 11 A | M |
| 12 E | H |
| 13 A | M |
| 14 C | H |

Number correct _____

Number incorrect _____

**NOTE:** Difficulty levels are E (easy), M (medium), and H (hard).

\* To score your essay, use the SAT scoring guide in Chapter 9 and the free sample essays available online at www.collegeboard.org/satonlinecourse. On this practice test, your essay score should range from 0 to 6. (Keep in mind that on the actual SAT, your essay will be read by two readers and you will receive a score of 0 to 12 on your score report.)

# The SAT Scoring Process

**Scoring.** The computer compares the circle filled in for each question with the correct response. Each correct answer receives one point; omitted questions do not affect your score. For each wrong answer to a multiple-choice question, one-fourth of a point is subtracted to correct for random guessing. The SAT critical reading section has 67 questions. If, for example, a student has 44 right, 20 wrong, and 3 omitted, the resulting raw score is determined as follows:

$$44 \text{ right} - \frac{20 \text{ wrong}}{4} = 44 - 5 = 39 \text{ raw score points}$$

Obtaining raw scores frequently involves the rounding of fractions to the nearest whole number. For example, a raw score of 39.25 is rounded to 39, the nearest whole number. A raw score of 39.50 is rounded upward to 40. **For the WRITING SECTION**, your essay raw score counts approximately 30% and your multiple-choice raw score counts approximately 70%.

**Converting to reported scaled score.** Raw scores are then placed on the College Board scale of 200 to 800 through a process that adjusts scores to account for minor differences in difficulty among different versions of the test. This process, known as equating, is performed so that a student's reported score is not affected by the version of the test taken or by the abilities of the group with whom the student takes the test. As a result of placing SAT scores on the College Board scale, scores earned by students at different times can be compared. For example, an SAT critical reading score of 400 on a test taken at one administration indicates the same level of developed critical reading ability as a 400 score obtained on a different version of the test taken at another time.

**Note:** Since this test has not been previously administered, score ranges are provided for each possible raw score.

# How to Score Practice Test #8

## SAT Critical Reading Sections 2, 5, and 8

**Step A:** Count the number of correct answers for *Section 2* and record the number in the space provided on the Scoring Worksheet. Then do the same for the incorrect answers. (Do not count omitted answers.)

**Step B:** Count the number of correct answers and the number of incorrect answers for *Section 5* and record the numbers in the spaces provided on the Scoring Worksheet. (Do not count omitted answers.)

**Step C:** Count the number of correct answers and the number of incorrect answers for *Section 8* and record the numbers in the spaces provided on the Scoring Worksheet. (Do not count omitted answers.)

**Step D:** Total the number of correct responses. Total the number of incorrect responses. Enter the resulting figures on the Scoring Worksheet. To determine A, use the formula:

$$\text{Number correct} - \frac{\text{Number incorrect}}{4} = A$$

**Step E:** To obtain B, your Rounded Critical Reading Raw Score, round A to the nearest whole number. (For example, any number from 44.50 to 45.49 rounds to 45.) Enter the resulting figure on the Scoring Worksheet.

**Step F:** To find your Critical Reading Scaled Score Range, look up the Total Rounded Raw Score you obtained in step E in the Critical Reading Conversion Table (Table 1). Enter this range in the box on the Scoring Worksheet.

## SAT Mathematics Sections 3, 7, and 9

**Step A:** Count the number of correct answers and the number of incorrect answers for the multiple-choice questions (*questions 1 through 8*) in *Section 3* and record the numbers in the spaces provided on the Scoring Worksheet. (Do not count omitted answers.)

**Step B:** Count the number of correct answers for the student-produced response questions (*questions 9 through 18*) in *Section 3* and record the number in the space provided on the Scoring Worksheet.

**Step C:** Count the number of correct answers and the number of incorrect answers for *Section 7* and record the number in the space provided on the Scoring Worksheet. (Do not count omitted answers.)

**Step D:** Count the number of correct answers and the number of incorrect answers for *Section 9* and record the numbers in the spaces provided on the Scoring Worksheet. (Do not count omitted answers.)

**Step E:** Total the number of correct responses. Total the number of incorrect responses. Enter the resulting figures on the Scoring Worksheet. To determine A, use the formula:

$$\text{Number correct} - \frac{\text{Number incorrect}}{4} = A$$

**Step F:** To obtain B, your Mathematics Rounded Raw Score, round A to the nearest whole number. (For example, any number from 44.50 to 45.49 rounds to 45.) Enter the resulting figure on the Scoring Worksheet.

**Step G:** To find your Mathematics Scaled Score Range, use the Mathematics Conversion Table (Table 2) to look up the Total Rounded Raw Score you obtained in step F. Enter this range in the box on the Scoring Worksheet.

## SAT Writing Sections 1, 4, and 10

**Step A:** Enter your Essay Score for *Section 1* in the box on the Scoring Worksheet. (On this practice test, your essay score should range from 0 to 6. Keep in mind that on the actual SAT, two readers will read your essay and you will receive a total score of 0 to 12 on your score report.)

**Step B:** Count the number of correct answers and the number of incorrect answers for *Section 4* and record the numbers in the spaces provided on the Scoring Worksheet. (Do not count omitted answers.)

**Step C:** Count the number of correct answers and the number of incorrect answers for *Section 10* and record the numbers in the spaces provided on the Scoring Worksheet. (Do not count omitted answers.)

**Step D:** Total the number of correct responses. Total the number of incorrect responses. Enter the resulting figure on the Scoring Worksheet. To determine A, use the formula:

$$\text{Number correct} - \frac{\text{Number incorrect}}{4} = A$$

**Step E:** To obtain B, your Writing Multiple-Choice (MC) Rounded Raw Score, round A to the nearest whole number. (For example, any number from 44.50 to 45.49 rounds to 45.) Enter the resulting figure on the Scoring Worksheet.

**Step F:** To find your overall Writing Scaled Score Range, use Table 3. Look up the Total MC Rounded Raw Score you obtained in Step E in the left side of Table 3 and the Essay Score entered in Step A across the top of the table. Enter this range in the box on the Scoring Worksheet.

**Step G:** To find your Writing MC Subscore Range, look up the Total MC Rounded Raw Score you obtained in Step E on the Writing Multiple-Choice Conversion Table (Table 4). Enter this range in the box on the Scoring Worksheet.

**Note:** For the **WRITING SECTION**, your Essay Raw Score counts approximately 30% and your Multiple-Choice Raw Score counts approximately 70%.

# SAT Practice Test #8 Scoring Worksheet

## SAT Critical Reading Section

A. Section 2:

_____      _____
no. correct          no. incorrect

+                  +

B. Section 5:

_____      _____
no. correct          no. incorrect

+                  +

C. Section 8:

_____      _____
no. correct          no. incorrect

=                  =

D. Total Unrounded Raw Score

_____ $-$ ( _____ $\div 4$) = _____
no. correct          no. incorrect        A

E. Total Rounded Raw Score
(Rounded to nearest whole number)

_____
B

F. Critical Reading Scaled Score Range
(See Table 1)

$$\boxed{\qquad - \qquad}$$

Critical
Reading Scaled
Score Range

## SAT Mathematics Section

A. Section 3:
Questions 1-8

_____      _____
no. correct          no. incorrect

+

B. Section 3:
Questions 9-18

_____
no. correct

+                  +

C. Section 7:

_____      _____
no. correct          no. incorrect

+                  +

D. Section 9:

_____      _____
no. correct          no. incorrect

$-$                  =

E. Total Unrounded Raw Score

_____ $-$ ( _____ $\div 4$) = _____
no. correct          no. incorrect        A

F. Total Rounded Raw Score
(Rounded to nearest whole number)

_____
B

G. Mathematics Scaled Score Range
(See Table 2)

$$\boxed{\qquad - \qquad}$$

Mathematics
Scaled
Score Range

## SAT Writing Section

**A. Section 1:**

$\boxed{\phantom{XXXXX}}$
Essay Score

**B. Section 4:**

$\underline{\phantom{XXXXXX}}$     $\underline{\phantom{XXXXXX}}$
no. correct        no. incorrect

$+$           $+$

**C. Section 10:**

$\underline{\phantom{XXXXXX}}$     $\underline{\phantom{XXXXXX}}$
no. correct        no. incorrect

$=$          $=$

**D. Total MC Unrounded Raw Score**

$\underline{\phantom{XXXXXX}}$ $-$ ( $\underline{\phantom{XXXXXX}}$ $\div 4$ ) $=$ $\underline{\phantom{XXXXXX}}$
no. correct       no. incorrect       A

**E. Total MC Rounded Raw Score**
   (Rounded to nearest whole number)

$\underline{\phantom{XXXXXX}}$
B

**F. Writing Scaled Score Range**
   (See Table 3)

$\boxed{\phantom{XXX} - \phantom{XXX}}$
Writing Scaled
Score Range

**G. Writing MC Subscore Range**
   (See Table 4)

$\boxed{\phantom{XXX} - \phantom{XXX}}$
Writing MC
Subscore Range

| Table 1. Critical Reading Conversion Table | | | |
|---|---|---|---|
| Raw Score | Scaled Score | Raw Score | Scaled Score |
| 67 | 800 | 30 | 470-530 |
| 66 | 770-800 | 29 | 470-530 |
| 65 | 740-800 | 28 | 460-520 |
| 64 | 720-800 | 27 | 450-510 |
| 63 | 700-800 | 26 | 450-510 |
| 62 | 690-790 | 25 | 440-500 |
| 61 | 670-770 | 24 | 440-500 |
| 60 | 660-760 | 23 | 430-490 |
| 59 | 660-740 | 22 | 420-480 |
| 58 | 650-730 | 21 | 420-480 |
| 57 | 640-720 | 20 | 410-470 |
| 56 | 630-710 | 19 | 400-460 |
| 55 | 630-710 | 18 | 400-460 |
| 54 | 620-700 | 17 | 390-450 |
| 53 | 610-690 | 16 | 380-440 |
| 52 | 600-680 | 15 | 380-440 |
| 51 | 610-670 | 14 | 370-430 |
| 50 | 600-660 | 13 | 360-420 |
| 49 | 590-650 | 12 | 350-410 |
| 48 | 580-640 | 11 | 350-410 |
| 47 | 580-640 | 10 | 340-400 |
| 46 | 570-630 | 9 | 330-390 |
| 45 | 560-620 | 8 | 310-390 |
| 44 | 560-620 | 7 | 300-380 |
| 43 | 550-610 | 6 | 290-370 |
| 42 | 550-610 | 5 | 270-370 |
| 41 | 540-600 | 4 | 260-360 |
| 40 | 530-590 | 3 | 250-350 |
| 39 | 530-590 | 2 | 230-330 |
| 38 | 520-580 | 1 | 220-320 |
| 37 | 510-570 | 0 | 200-290 |
| 36 | 510-570 | -1 | 200-290 |
| 35 | 500-560 | -2 | 200-270 |
| 34 | 500-560 | -3 | 200-250 |
| 33 | 490-550 | -4 | 200-230 |
| 32 | 480-540 | -5 | 200-210 |
| 31 | 480-540 | -6 and below | 200 |

| Table 2. Mathematics Conversion Table | | | |
|---|---|---|---|
| Raw Score | Scaled Score | Raw Score | Scaled Score |
| 54 | 800 | 23 | 460-520 |
| 53 | 750-800 | 22 | 450-510 |
| 52 | 720-800 | 21 | 440-500 |
| 51 | 700-780 | 20 | 430-490 |
| 50 | 690-770 | 19 | 430-490 |
| 49 | 680-740 | 18 | 420-480 |
| 48 | 670-730 | 17 | 410-470 |
| 47 | 660-720 | 16 | 400-460 |
| 46 | 640-700 | 15 | 400-460 |
| 45 | 630-690 | 14 | 390-450 |
| 44 | 620-680 | 13 | 380-440 |
| 43 | 620-680 | 12 | 360-440 |
| 42 | 610-670 | 11 | 350-430 |
| 41 | 600-660 | 10 | 340-420 |
| 40 | 580-660 | 9 | 330-430 |
| 39 | 570-650 | 8 | 320-420 |
| 38 | 560-640 | 7 | 310-410 |
| 37 | 550-630 | 6 | 290-390 |
| 36 | 550-630 | 5 | 280-380 |
| 35 | 540-620 | 4 | 270-370 |
| 34 | 530-610 | 3 | 260-360 |
| 33 | 520-600 | 2 | 240-340 |
| 32 | 520-600 | 1 | 230-330 |
| 31 | 520-580 | 0 | 210-310 |
| 30 | 510-570 | -1 | 200-290 |
| 29 | 500-560 | -2 | 200-270 |
| 28 | 490-550 | -3 | 200-250 |
| 27 | 490-550 | -4 | 200-230 |
| 26 | 480-540 | -5 | 200-210 |
| 25 | 470-530 | -6 and below | 200 |
| 24 | 460-520 | | |

## Table 3. Writing Conversion Table

| MC Raw Score | Essay Score | | | | | | |
|---|---|---|---|---|---|---|---|
| | 0 | 1 | 2 | 3 | 4 | 5 | 6 |
| 49 | 650-690 | 670-720 | 690-740 | 710-770 | 750-800 | 780-800 | 800 |
| 48 | 630-690 | 640-720 | 660-740 | 690-770 | 720-800 | 760-800 | 780-800 |
| 47 | 600-690 | 620-720 | 640-740 | 660-770 | 700-800 | 730-800 | 760-800 |
| 46 | 580-690 | 600-720 | 620-748 | 650-770 | 680-800 | 710-800 | 740-800 |
| 45 | 570-690 | 580-720 | 600-740 | 630-770 | 670-800 | 700-800 | 730-800 |
| 44 | 560-680 | 570-710 | 590-730 | 620-760 | 660-790 | 690-800 | 720-800 |
| 43 | 540-660 | 560-690 | 580-710 | 610-740 | 640-780 | 670-800 | 700-800 |
| 42 | 530-660 | 550-690 | 570-700 | 600-730 | 630-770 | 660-800 | 690-800 |
| 41 | 530-650 | 540-680 | 560-700 | 590-720 | 620-760 | 660-790 | 680-800 |
| 40 | 520-640 | 530-670 | 550-690 | 580-710 | 620-750 | 650-780 | 680-800 |
| 39 | 510-630 | 520-660 | 540-680 | 570-710 | 610-740 | 640-770 | 670-800 |
| 38 | 500-620 | 520-650 | 540-670 | 560-700 | 600-730 | 630-770 | 660-790 |
| 37 | 490-610 | 510-640 | 530-660 | 560-690 | 590-720 | 620-760 | 650-780 |
| 36 | 480-600 | 500-630 | 520-650 | 550-680 | 580-720 | 610-750 | 640-770 |
| 35 | 480-590 | 490-620 | 510-640 | 540-670 | 570-710 | 610-740 | 640-770 |
| 34 | 470-590 | 480-620 | 500-630 | 530-660 | 570-700 | 600-730 | 630-760 |
| 33 | 460-580 | 470-610 | 490-630 | 520-650 | 560-690 | 590-720 | 620-750 |
| 32 | 450-570 | 470-600 | 490-620 | 510-640 | 550-680 | 580-710 | 610-740 |
| 31 | 440-560 | 460-590 | 480-610 | 510-640 | 540-670 | 570-700 | 600-730 |
| 30 | 430-550 | 450-580 | 470-600 | 500-630 | 530-660 | 560-700 | 590-720 |
| 29 | 430-540 | 440-570 | 460-590 | 490-620 | 520-650 | 560-690 | 590-710 |
| 28 | 420-530 | 430-560 | 450-580 | 480-610 | 520-650 | 550-680 | 580-700 |
| 27 | 410-520 | 420-550 | 440-570 | 470-600 | 510-640 | 540-670 | 570-700 |
| 26 | 400-520 | 420-550 | 430-560 | 460-590 | 500-630 | 530-660 | 560-690 |
| 25 | 390-510 | 410-540 | 430-560 | 450-580 | 490-620 | 520-650 | 550-680 |
| 24 | 380-500 | 400-530 | 420-550 | 450-570 | 480-610 | 510-640 | 540-670 |
| 23 | 370-490 | 390-520 | 410-540 | 440-570 | 470-600 | 500-630 | 530-660 |
| 22 | 370-480 | 380-510 | 400-530 | 430-560 | 460-590 | 500-630 | 520-650 |
| 21 | 370-480 | 380-510 | 400-530 | 430-560 | 460-590 | 500-630 | 520-650 |
| 20 | 360-470 | 370-500 | 390-520 | 420-550 | 460-580 | 490-620 | 520-640 |
| 19 | 350-460 | 360-490 | 380-510 | 410-540 | 450-580 | 480-610 | 510-630 |
| 18 | 340-450 | 350-480 | 370-500 | 400-530 | 440-570 | 470-600 | 500-630 |
| 17 | 330-450 | 350-480 | 360-490 | 390-520 | 430-560 | 460-590 | 490-620 |
| 16 | 320-440 | 340-470 | 360-490 | 390-510 | 420-550 | 450-580 | 480-610 |
| 15 | 310-430 | 330-460 | 350-480 | 380-510 | 410-540 | 440-570 | 470-600 |
| 14 | 300-420 | 320-450 | 340-470 | 370-500 | 400-530 | 430-560 | 460-590 |
| 13 | 300-410 | 310-440 | 330-460 | 360-490 | 390-520 | 430-560 | 450-580 |
| 12 | 290-400 | 300-430 | 320-450 | 350-480 | 390-510 | 420-550 | 450-570 |
| 11 | 280-390 | 290-420 | 310-440 | 340-470 | 380-510 | 410-540 | 440-570 |
| 10 | 270-390 | 280-420 | 300-430 | 330-460 | 370-500 | 400-530 | 430-560 |
| 9 | 260-380 | 280-410 | 290-430 | 320-450 | 360-490 | 390-520 | 420-550 |
| 8 | 250-370 | 270-400 | 290-420 | 320-450 | 350-480 | 380-510 | 410-540 |
| 7 | 240-360 | 260-390 | 280-410 | 310-440 | 340-470 | 370-510 | 400-530 |
| 6 | 230-350 | 250-380 | 270-400 | 300-430 | 330-460 | 360-500 | 390-520 |
| 5 | 230-340 | 240-370 | 260-390 | 290-420 | 320-460 | 360-490 | 380-520 |
| 4 | 220-340 | 230-370 | 250-380 | 280-410 | 320-450 | 350-480 | 380-510 |
| 3 | 210-330 | 220-360 | 240-380 | 270-400 | 310-440 | 340-470 | 370-500 |
| 2 | 200-320 | 210-350 | 230-370 | 260-400 | 300-430 | 330-460 | 360-490 |
| 1 | 200-300 | 200-330 | 220-350 | 250-380 | 280-410 | 310-450 | 340-470 |
| 0 | 200-290 | 200-320 | 210-340 | 240-370 | 270-410 | 300-440 | 330-470 |
| -1 | 200-280 | 200-310 | 200-330 | 220-350 | 250-390 | 290-420 | 310-450 |
| -2 | 200-260 | 200-290 | 200-310 | 200-340 | 240-370 | 270-410 | 300-430 |
| -3 | 200-240 | 200-270 | 200-290 | 200-320 | 240-360 | 270-390 | 300-420 |
| -4 | 200-230 | 200-260 | 200-280 | 200-300 | 240-340 | 270-370 | 300-400 |
| -5 | 200 | 200-230 | 200-250 | 200-280 | 240-320 | 270-350 | 300-370 |
| -6 | 200 | 200-220 | 200-240 | 200-270 | 240-310 | 270-340 | 300-370 |
| -7 | 200 | 200-220 | 200-230 | 200-260 | 240-300 | 270-330 | 300-360 |
| -8 | 200 | 200-210 | 200-230 | 200-250 | 240-290 | 270-320 | 300-350 |
| -9 | 200 | 200-210 | 200-230 | 200-250 | 240-290 | 270-320 | 300-350 |
| -10 | 200 | 200-210 | 200-230 | 200-250 | 240-290 | 270-320 | 300-350 |
| -11 | 200 | 200-210 | 200-230 | 200-250 | 240-290 | 270-320 | 300-350 |
| -12 | 200 | 200-210 | 200-230 | 200-250 | 240-290 | 270-320 | 300-350 |

## Table 4. Writing Multiple-Choice Conversion Table

| Raw Score | Scaled Score | Raw Score | Scaled Score |
|---|---|---|---|
| 49 | 78-80 | 21 | 46-56 |
| 48 | 77-80 | 20 | 45-55 |
| 47 | 74-80 | 19 | 44-54 |
| 46 | 72-80 | 18 | 43-53 |
| 45 | 70-80 | 17 | 42-52 |
| 44 | 69-79 | 16 | 41-51 |
| 43 | 67-77 | 15 | 40-50 |
| 42 | 66-76 | 14 | 39-49 |
| 41 | 65-75 | 13 | 38-48 |
| 40 | 64-74 | 12 | 37-47 |
| 39 | 63-73 | 11 | 36-46 |
| 38 | 62-72 | 10 | 35-45 |
| 37 | 61-71 | 9 | 34-44 |
| 36 | 60-70 | 8 | 33-43 |
| 35 | 59-69 | 7 | 32-42 |
| 34 | 58-68 | 6 | 31-41 |
| 33 | 57-67 | 5 | 30-40 |
| 32 | 56-66 | 4 | 29-39 |
| 31 | 55-65 | 3 | 28-38 |
| 30 | 54-64 | 2 | 27-37 |
| 29 | 53-63 | 1 | 25-35 |
| 28 | 52-62 | 0 | 24-34 |
| 27 | 51-61 | -1 | 22-32 |
| 26 | 50-60 | -2 | 20-30 |
| 25 | 49-59 | -3 | 20-28 |
| 24 | 48-58 | -4 | 20-26 |
| 23 | 47-57 | -5 | 20-23 |
| 22 | 46-56 | -6 and below | 20-22 |

# SAT Practice Test #9

 **After this test:**

- Use this book to its full potential! Get exclusive access answer explanations, free practice score reports and free sample student essays to help you score your essay in the Book Owners' Area at www.collegeboard.org/satstudyguide.

- Want more practice? Get 10 more official practice tests, auto essay scoring and lesson plans from the test maker by subscribing to *The Official SAT Online Course*. As a book owner, you're entitled to a $10 discount. Sign up at www.collegeboard.org/satstudyguide.

9

*Note:* Section 7, the variable section, has been omitted from this practice test.

# SAT Reasoning Test — General Directions

## Timing

- You will have 3 hours and 45 minutes to work on this test.
- There are ten separately timed sections:
  - ▶ One 25-minute essay
  - ▶ Six other 25-minute sections
  - ▶ Two 20-minute sections
  - ▶ One 10-minute section
- You may work on only one section at a time.
- The supervisor will tell you when to begin and end each section.
- If you finish a section before time is called, check your work on that section. You may NOT turn to any other section.
- Work as rapidly as you can without losing accuracy. Don't waste time on questions that seem too difficult for you.

## Marking Answers

- Be sure to mark your answer sheet properly.

  COMPLETE MARK ●    EXAMPLES OF INCOMPLETE MARKS ⊘⊗⊖◐ ⊙⊘⊘⊘

- You must use a No. 2 pencil.
- Carefully mark only one answer for each question.
- Make sure you fill the entire circle darkly and completely.
- Do not make any stray marks on your answer sheet.
- If you erase, do so completely. Incomplete erasures may be scored as intended answers.
- Use only the answer spaces that correspond to the question numbers.

## Using Your Test Book

- You may use the test book for scratchwork, but you will not receive credit for anything written there.
- After time has been called, you may not transfer answers to your answer sheet or fill in circles.
- You may not fold or remove pages or portions of a page from this book, or take the book or answer sheet from the testing room.

## Scoring

- For each correct answer, you receive one point.
- For questions you omit, you receive no points.
- For a wrong answer to a multiple-choice question, you lose one-fourth of a point.
  - ▶ If you can eliminate one or more of the answer choices as wrong, you increase your chances of choosing the correct answer and earning one point.
  - ▶ If you can't eliminate any choice, move on. You can return to the question later if there is time.
- For a wrong answer to a student-produced response ("grid-in") math question, you don't lose any points.
- Multiple-choice and student-produced response questions are machine scored.
- The essay is scored on a 1 to 6 scale by two different readers. The total essay score is the sum of the two readers' scores.
- Off-topic essays, blank essays, and essays written in ink will receive a score of zero.

The passages for this test have been adapted from published material. The ideas contained in them do not necessarily represent the opinions of the College Board.

## DO NOT OPEN THIS BOOK UNTIL THE SUPERVISOR TELLS YOU TO DO SO.

**CollegeBoard** SAT

# SAT Reasoning Test™

You must use a No. 2 pencil. Do not use a mechanical pencil. It is very important that you fill in the entire circle darkly and completely. If you change your response, erase as completely as possible. Incomplete marks or erasures may affect your score. It is very important that you follow these instructions when filling out your answer sheet.

---

**1** Your Name:
(Print)

Last                                                First                                                M.I.

I agree to the conditions on the back of the SAT Reasoning Test™ booklet. I also agree to use only a No. 2 pencil to complete my answer sheet.

Signature: _____  Date: ___/___/___

Home Address: _____
(Print)                    Number and Street          City          State     Zip Code

Home Phone: ( )  _____  Center: _____
(Print)                         (Print)           City              State/Country

---

**2** YOUR NAME

Last Name (First 6 Letters) | First Name (First 4 Letters) | Mid. Init.

**3** DATE OF BIRTH

MONTH | DAY | YEAR
Jan Feb Mar Apr May Jun Jul Aug Sep Oct Nov Dec

**5** SEX

○ Female  ○ Male

**6** REGISTRATION NUMBER
(Copy from Admission Ticket.)

○ I turned in my registration form today.

**4** ZIP CODE

**7** SOCIAL SECURITY NUMBER

**Important:** Fill in items 8 and 9 exactly as shown on the back of test book.

**8** FORM CODE
(Copy and grid as on back of test book.)

**9** TEST FORM
(Copy from back of test book.)

**10** TEST BOOK SERIAL NUMBER
(Copy from front of test book.)

**11** TEST CENTER
(Supplied by Test Center Supervisor.)

**FOR OFFICIAL USE ONLY**
0 1 2 3 4 5 6
0 1 2 3 4 5 6
0 1 2 3 4 5 6

00272-36390 • NS75E4600 • Printed in U.S.A.
732652

**PLEASE DO NOT WRITE IN THIS AREA**

**SERIAL #**

9

**Begin your essay on this page. If you need more space, continue on the next page.**

9

SERIAL #

## SECTION 2

| 1 | ⒶⒷⒸⒹⒺ | 11 | ⒶⒷⒸⒹⒺ | 21 | ⒶⒷⒸⒹⒺ | 31 | ⒶⒷⒸⒹⒺ |
| 2 | ⒶⒷⒸⒹⒺ | 12 | ⒶⒷⒸⒹⒺ | 22 | ⒶⒷⒸⒹⒺ | 32 | ⒶⒷⒸⒹⒺ |
| 3 | ⒶⒷⒸⒹⒺ | 13 | ⒶⒷⒸⒹⒺ | 23 | ⒶⒷⒸⒹⒺ | 33 | ⒶⒷⒸⒹⒺ |
| 4 | ⒶⒷⒸⒹⒺ | 14 | ⒶⒷⒸⒹⒺ | 24 | ⒶⒷⒸⒹⒺ | 34 | ⒶⒷⒸⒹⒺ |
| 5 | ⒶⒷⒸⒹⒺ | 15 | ⒶⒷⒸⒹⒺ | 25 | ⒶⒷⒸⒹⒺ | 35 | ⒶⒷⒸⒹⒺ |
| 6 | ⒶⒷⒸⒹⒺ | 16 | ⒶⒷⒸⒹⒺ | 26 | ⒶⒷⒸⒹⒺ | 36 | ⒶⒷⒸⒹⒺ |
| 7 | ⒶⒷⒸⒹⒺ | 17 | ⒶⒷⒸⒹⒺ | 27 | ⒶⒷⒸⒹⒺ | 37 | ⒶⒷⒸⒹⒺ |
| 8 | ⒶⒷⒸⒹⒺ | 18 | ⒶⒷⒸⒹⒺ | 28 | ⒶⒷⒸⒹⒺ | 38 | ⒶⒷⒸⒹⒺ |
| 9 | ⒶⒷⒸⒹⒺ | 19 | ⒶⒷⒸⒹⒺ | 29 | ⒶⒷⒸⒹⒺ | 39 | ⒶⒷⒸⒹⒺ |
| 10 | ⒶⒷⒸⒹⒺ | 20 | ⒶⒷⒸⒹⒺ | 30 | ⒶⒷⒸⒹⒺ | 40 | ⒶⒷⒸⒹⒺ |

## SECTION 3

| 1 | ⒶⒷⒸⒹⒺ | 11 | ⒶⒷⒸⒹⒺ | 21 | ⒶⒷⒸⒹⒺ | 31 | ⒶⒷⒸⒹⒺ |
| 2 | ⒶⒷⒸⒹⒺ | 12 | ⒶⒷⒸⒹⒺ | 22 | ⒶⒷⒸⒹⒺ | 32 | ⒶⒷⒸⒹⒺ |
| 3 | ⒶⒷⒸⒹⒺ | 13 | ⒶⒷⒸⒹⒺ | 23 | ⒶⒷⒸⒹⒺ | 33 | ⒶⒷⒸⒹⒺ |
| 4 | ⒶⒷⒸⒹⒺ | 14 | ⒶⒷⒸⒹⒺ | 24 | ⒶⒷⒸⒹⒺ | 34 | ⒶⒷⒸⒹⒺ |
| 5 | ⒶⒷⒸⒹⒺ | 15 | ⒶⒷⒸⒹⒺ | 25 | ⒶⒷⒸⒹⒺ | 35 | ⒶⒷⒸⒹⒺ |
| 6 | ⒶⒷⒸⒹⒺ | 16 | ⒶⒷⒸⒹⒺ | 26 | ⒶⒷⒸⒹⒺ | 36 | ⒶⒷⒸⒹⒺ |
| 7 | ⒶⒷⒸⒹⒺ | 17 | ⒶⒷⒸⒹⒺ | 27 | ⒶⒷⒸⒹⒺ | 37 | ⒶⒷⒸⒹⒺ |
| 8 | ⒶⒷⒸⒹⒺ | 18 | ⒶⒷⒸⒹⒺ | 28 | ⒶⒷⒸⒹⒺ | 38 | ⒶⒷⒸⒹⒺ |
| 9 | ⒶⒷⒸⒹⒺ | 19 | ⒶⒷⒸⒹⒺ | 29 | ⒶⒷⒸⒹⒺ | 39 | ⒶⒷⒸⒹⒺ |
| 10 | ⒶⒷⒸⒹⒺ | 20 | ⒶⒷⒸⒹⒺ | 30 | ⒶⒷⒸⒹⒺ | 40 | ⒶⒷⒸⒹⒺ |

**CAUTION**  Grid answers in the section below for SECTION 2 or SECTION 3 only if directed to do so in your test book.

## Student-Produced Responses

ONLY ANSWERS THAT ARE GRIDDED WILL BE SCORED. YOU WILL NOT RECEIVE CREDIT FOR ANYTHING WRITTEN IN THE BOXES.

Quality Assurance Mark ●

9, 10, 11, 12, 13

14, 15, 16, 17, 18

9

## SECTION 4

1 Ⓐ Ⓑ Ⓒ Ⓓ Ⓔ   11 Ⓐ Ⓑ Ⓒ Ⓓ Ⓔ   21 Ⓐ Ⓑ Ⓒ Ⓓ Ⓔ   31 Ⓐ Ⓑ Ⓒ Ⓓ Ⓔ
2 Ⓐ Ⓑ Ⓒ Ⓓ Ⓔ   12 Ⓐ Ⓑ Ⓒ Ⓓ Ⓔ   22 Ⓐ Ⓑ Ⓒ Ⓓ Ⓔ   32 Ⓐ Ⓑ Ⓒ Ⓓ Ⓔ
3 Ⓐ Ⓑ Ⓒ Ⓓ Ⓔ   13 Ⓐ Ⓑ Ⓒ Ⓓ Ⓔ   23 Ⓐ Ⓑ Ⓒ Ⓓ Ⓔ   33 Ⓐ Ⓑ Ⓒ Ⓓ Ⓔ
4 Ⓐ Ⓑ Ⓒ Ⓓ Ⓔ   14 Ⓐ Ⓑ Ⓒ Ⓓ Ⓔ   24 Ⓐ Ⓑ Ⓒ Ⓓ Ⓔ   34 Ⓐ Ⓑ Ⓒ Ⓓ Ⓔ
5 Ⓐ Ⓑ Ⓒ Ⓓ Ⓔ   15 Ⓐ Ⓑ Ⓒ Ⓓ Ⓔ   25 Ⓐ Ⓑ Ⓒ Ⓓ Ⓔ   35 Ⓐ Ⓑ Ⓒ Ⓓ Ⓔ
6 Ⓐ Ⓑ Ⓒ Ⓓ Ⓔ   16 Ⓐ Ⓑ Ⓒ Ⓓ Ⓔ   26 Ⓐ Ⓑ Ⓒ Ⓓ Ⓔ   36 Ⓐ Ⓑ Ⓒ Ⓓ Ⓔ
7 Ⓐ Ⓑ Ⓒ Ⓓ Ⓔ   17 Ⓐ Ⓑ Ⓒ Ⓓ Ⓔ   27 Ⓐ Ⓑ Ⓒ Ⓓ Ⓔ   37 Ⓐ Ⓑ Ⓒ Ⓓ Ⓔ
8 Ⓐ Ⓑ Ⓒ Ⓓ Ⓔ   18 Ⓐ Ⓑ Ⓒ Ⓓ Ⓔ   28 Ⓐ Ⓑ Ⓒ Ⓓ Ⓔ   38 Ⓐ Ⓑ Ⓒ Ⓓ Ⓔ
9 Ⓐ Ⓑ Ⓒ Ⓓ Ⓔ   19 Ⓐ Ⓑ Ⓒ Ⓓ Ⓔ   29 Ⓐ Ⓑ Ⓒ Ⓓ Ⓔ   39 Ⓐ Ⓑ Ⓒ Ⓓ Ⓔ
10 Ⓐ Ⓑ Ⓒ Ⓓ Ⓔ   20 Ⓐ Ⓑ Ⓒ Ⓓ Ⓔ   30 Ⓐ Ⓑ Ⓒ Ⓓ Ⓔ   40 Ⓐ Ⓑ Ⓒ Ⓓ Ⓔ

## SECTION 5

1 Ⓐ Ⓑ Ⓒ Ⓓ Ⓔ   11 Ⓐ Ⓑ Ⓒ Ⓓ Ⓔ   21 Ⓐ Ⓑ Ⓒ Ⓓ Ⓔ   31 Ⓐ Ⓑ Ⓒ Ⓓ Ⓔ
2 Ⓐ Ⓑ Ⓒ Ⓓ Ⓔ   12 Ⓐ Ⓑ Ⓒ Ⓓ Ⓔ   22 Ⓐ Ⓑ Ⓒ Ⓓ Ⓔ   32 Ⓐ Ⓑ Ⓒ Ⓓ Ⓔ
3 Ⓐ Ⓑ Ⓒ Ⓓ Ⓔ   13 Ⓐ Ⓑ Ⓒ Ⓓ Ⓔ   23 Ⓐ Ⓑ Ⓒ Ⓓ Ⓔ   33 Ⓐ Ⓑ Ⓒ Ⓓ Ⓔ
4 Ⓐ Ⓑ Ⓒ Ⓓ Ⓔ   14 Ⓐ Ⓑ Ⓒ Ⓓ Ⓔ   24 Ⓐ Ⓑ Ⓒ Ⓓ Ⓔ   34 Ⓐ Ⓑ Ⓒ Ⓓ Ⓔ
5 Ⓐ Ⓑ Ⓒ Ⓓ Ⓔ   15 Ⓐ Ⓑ Ⓒ Ⓓ Ⓔ   25 Ⓐ Ⓑ Ⓒ Ⓓ Ⓔ   35 Ⓐ Ⓑ Ⓒ Ⓓ Ⓔ
6 Ⓐ Ⓑ Ⓒ Ⓓ Ⓔ   16 Ⓐ Ⓑ Ⓒ Ⓓ Ⓔ   26 Ⓐ Ⓑ Ⓒ Ⓓ Ⓔ   36 Ⓐ Ⓑ Ⓒ Ⓓ Ⓔ
7 Ⓐ Ⓑ Ⓒ Ⓓ Ⓔ   17 Ⓐ Ⓑ Ⓒ Ⓓ Ⓔ   27 Ⓐ Ⓑ Ⓒ Ⓓ Ⓔ   37 Ⓐ Ⓑ Ⓒ Ⓓ Ⓔ
8 Ⓐ Ⓑ Ⓒ Ⓓ Ⓔ   18 Ⓐ Ⓑ Ⓒ Ⓓ Ⓔ   28 Ⓐ Ⓑ Ⓒ Ⓓ Ⓔ   38 Ⓐ Ⓑ Ⓒ Ⓓ Ⓔ
9 Ⓐ Ⓑ Ⓒ Ⓓ Ⓔ   19 Ⓐ Ⓑ Ⓒ Ⓓ Ⓔ   29 Ⓐ Ⓑ Ⓒ Ⓓ Ⓔ   39 Ⓐ Ⓑ Ⓒ Ⓓ Ⓔ
10 Ⓐ Ⓑ Ⓒ Ⓓ Ⓔ   20 Ⓐ Ⓑ Ⓒ Ⓓ Ⓔ   30 Ⓐ Ⓑ Ⓒ Ⓓ Ⓔ   40 Ⓐ Ⓑ Ⓒ Ⓓ Ⓔ

**CAUTION** Grid answers in the section below for SECTION 4 or SECTION 5 only if directed to do so in your test book.

## Student-Produced Responses

ONLY ANSWERS THAT ARE GRIDDED WILL BE SCORED. YOU WILL NOT RECEIVE CREDIT FOR ANYTHING WRITTEN IN THE BOXES.

Quality Assurance Mark

9   10   11   12   13

14   15   16   17   18

9

## SECTION 6

1 Ⓐ Ⓑ Ⓒ Ⓓ Ⓔ   11 Ⓐ Ⓑ Ⓒ Ⓓ Ⓔ   21 Ⓐ Ⓑ Ⓒ Ⓓ Ⓔ   31 Ⓐ Ⓑ Ⓒ Ⓓ Ⓔ
2 Ⓐ Ⓑ Ⓒ Ⓓ Ⓔ   12 Ⓐ Ⓑ Ⓒ Ⓓ Ⓔ   22 Ⓐ Ⓑ Ⓒ Ⓓ Ⓔ   32 Ⓐ Ⓑ Ⓒ Ⓓ Ⓔ
3 Ⓐ Ⓑ Ⓒ Ⓓ Ⓔ   13 Ⓐ Ⓑ Ⓒ Ⓓ Ⓔ   23 Ⓐ Ⓑ Ⓒ Ⓓ Ⓔ   33 Ⓐ Ⓑ Ⓒ Ⓓ Ⓔ
4 Ⓐ Ⓑ Ⓒ Ⓓ Ⓔ   14 Ⓐ Ⓑ Ⓒ Ⓓ Ⓔ   24 Ⓐ Ⓑ Ⓒ Ⓓ Ⓔ   34 Ⓐ Ⓑ Ⓒ Ⓓ Ⓔ
5 Ⓐ Ⓑ Ⓒ Ⓓ Ⓔ   15 Ⓐ Ⓑ Ⓒ Ⓓ Ⓔ   25 Ⓐ Ⓑ Ⓒ Ⓓ Ⓔ   35 Ⓐ Ⓑ Ⓒ Ⓓ Ⓔ
6 Ⓐ Ⓑ Ⓒ Ⓓ Ⓔ   16 Ⓐ Ⓑ Ⓒ Ⓓ Ⓔ   26 Ⓐ Ⓑ Ⓒ Ⓓ Ⓔ   36 Ⓐ Ⓑ Ⓒ Ⓓ Ⓔ
7 Ⓐ Ⓑ Ⓒ Ⓓ Ⓕ   17 Ⓐ Ⓑ Ⓒ Ⓓ Ⓔ   27 Ⓐ Ⓑ Ⓒ Ⓓ Ⓔ   37 Ⓐ Ⓑ Ⓒ Ⓓ Ⓔ
8 Ⓐ Ⓑ Ⓒ Ⓓ Ⓔ   18 Ⓐ Ⓑ Ⓒ Ⓓ Ⓔ   28 Ⓐ Ⓑ Ⓒ Ⓓ Ⓔ   38 Ⓐ Ⓑ Ⓒ Ⓓ Ⓔ
9 Ⓐ Ⓑ Ⓒ Ⓓ Ⓔ   19 Ⓐ Ⓑ Ⓒ Ⓓ Ⓔ   29 Ⓐ Ⓑ Ⓒ Ⓓ Ⓔ   39 Ⓐ Ⓑ Ⓒ Ⓓ Ⓔ
10 Ⓐ Ⓑ Ⓒ Ⓓ Ⓔ   20 Ⓐ Ⓑ Ⓒ Ⓓ Ⓔ   30 Ⓐ Ⓑ Ⓒ Ⓓ Ⓔ   40 Ⓐ Ⓑ Ⓒ Ⓓ Ⓔ

## SECTION 7

1 Ⓐ Ⓑ Ⓒ Ⓓ Ⓔ   11 Ⓐ Ⓑ Ⓒ Ⓓ Ⓔ   21 Ⓐ Ⓑ Ⓒ Ⓓ Ⓔ   31 Ⓐ Ⓑ Ⓒ Ⓓ Ⓔ
2 Ⓐ Ⓑ Ⓒ Ⓓ Ⓔ   12 Ⓐ Ⓑ Ⓒ Ⓓ Ⓔ   22 Ⓐ Ⓑ Ⓒ Ⓓ Ⓔ   32 Ⓐ Ⓑ Ⓒ Ⓓ Ⓔ
3 Ⓐ Ⓑ Ⓒ Ⓓ Ⓔ   13 Ⓐ Ⓑ Ⓒ Ⓓ Ⓔ   23 Ⓐ Ⓑ Ⓒ Ⓓ Ⓔ   33 Ⓐ Ⓑ Ⓒ Ⓓ Ⓔ
4 Ⓐ Ⓑ Ⓒ Ⓓ Ⓔ   14 Ⓐ Ⓑ Ⓒ Ⓓ Ⓔ   24 Ⓐ Ⓑ Ⓒ Ⓓ Ⓔ   34 Ⓐ Ⓑ Ⓒ Ⓓ Ⓔ
5 Ⓐ Ⓑ Ⓒ Ⓓ Ⓔ   15 Ⓐ Ⓑ Ⓒ Ⓓ Ⓔ   25 Ⓐ Ⓑ Ⓒ Ⓓ Ⓔ   35 Ⓐ Ⓑ Ⓒ Ⓓ Ⓔ
6 Ⓐ Ⓑ Ⓒ Ⓓ Ⓔ   16 Ⓐ Ⓑ Ⓒ Ⓓ Ⓔ   26 Ⓐ Ⓑ Ⓒ Ⓓ Ⓔ   36 Ⓐ Ⓑ Ⓒ Ⓓ Ⓔ
7 Ⓐ Ⓑ Ⓒ Ⓓ Ⓔ   17 Ⓐ Ⓑ Ⓒ Ⓓ Ⓔ   27 Ⓐ Ⓑ Ⓒ Ⓓ Ⓔ   37 Ⓐ Ⓑ Ⓒ Ⓓ Ⓔ
8 Ⓐ Ⓑ Ⓒ Ⓓ Ⓔ   18 Ⓐ Ⓑ Ⓒ Ⓓ Ⓔ   28 Ⓐ Ⓑ Ⓒ Ⓓ Ⓔ   38 Ⓐ Ⓑ Ⓒ Ⓓ Ⓔ
9 Ⓐ Ⓑ Ⓒ Ⓓ Ⓔ   19 Ⓐ Ⓑ Ⓒ Ⓓ Ⓔ   29 Ⓐ Ⓑ Ⓒ Ⓓ Ⓔ   39 Ⓐ Ⓑ Ⓒ Ⓓ Ⓔ
10 Ⓐ Ⓑ Ⓒ Ⓓ Ⓔ   20 Ⓐ Ⓑ Ⓒ Ⓓ Ⓔ   30 Ⓐ Ⓑ Ⓒ Ⓓ Ⓔ   40 Ⓐ Ⓑ Ⓒ Ⓓ Ⓔ

**CAUTION** Grid answers in the section below for SECTION 6 or SECTION 7 only if directed to do so in your test book.

**Student-Produced Responses** ONLY ANSWERS THAT ARE GRIDDED WILL BE SCORED. YOU WILL NOT RECEIVE CREDIT FOR ANYTHING WRITTEN IN THE BOXES.

Quality Assurance Mark ●

9   10   11   12   13

[Grid-in response fields with digits 0–9]

14   15   16   17   18

[Grid-in response fields with digits 0–9]

**Page 6**

PLEASE DO NOT WRITE IN THIS AREA

SERIAL #

882

**SECTION 8**

| | | | | | | | |
|---|---|---|---|---|---|---|---|
| 1 Ⓐ Ⓑ Ⓒ Ⓓ Ⓔ | 11 Ⓐ Ⓑ Ⓒ Ⓓ Ⓔ | 21 Ⓐ Ⓑ Ⓒ Ⓓ Ⓔ | 31 Ⓐ Ⓑ Ⓒ Ⓓ Ⓔ |
| 2 Ⓐ Ⓑ Ⓒ Ⓓ Ⓔ | 12 Ⓐ Ⓑ Ⓒ Ⓓ Ⓔ | 22 Ⓐ Ⓑ Ⓒ Ⓓ Ⓔ | 32 Ⓐ Ⓑ Ⓒ Ⓓ Ⓔ |
| 3 Ⓐ Ⓑ Ⓒ Ⓓ Ⓔ | 13 Ⓐ Ⓑ Ⓒ Ⓓ Ⓔ | 23 Ⓐ Ⓑ Ⓒ Ⓓ Ⓔ | 33 Ⓐ Ⓑ Ⓒ Ⓓ Ⓔ |
| 4 Ⓐ Ⓑ Ⓒ Ⓓ Ⓔ | 14 Ⓐ Ⓑ Ⓒ Ⓓ Ⓔ | 24 Ⓐ Ⓑ Ⓒ Ⓓ Ⓔ | 34 Ⓐ Ⓑ Ⓒ Ⓓ Ⓔ |
| 5 Ⓐ Ⓑ Ⓒ Ⓓ Ⓔ | 15 Ⓐ Ⓑ Ⓒ Ⓓ Ⓔ | 25 Ⓐ Ⓑ Ⓒ Ⓓ Ⓔ | 35 Ⓐ Ⓑ Ⓒ Ⓓ Ⓔ |
| 6 Ⓐ Ⓑ Ⓒ Ⓓ Ⓔ | 16 Ⓐ Ⓑ Ⓒ Ⓓ Ⓔ | 26 Ⓐ Ⓑ Ⓒ Ⓓ Ⓔ | 36 Ⓐ Ⓑ Ⓒ Ⓓ Ⓔ |
| 7 Ⓐ Ⓑ Ⓒ Ⓓ Ⓔ | 17 Ⓐ Ⓑ Ⓒ Ⓓ Ⓔ | 27 Ⓐ Ⓑ Ⓒ Ⓓ Ⓔ | 37 Ⓐ Ⓑ Ⓒ Ⓓ Ⓔ |
| 8 Ⓐ Ⓑ Ⓒ Ⓓ Ⓔ | 18 Ⓐ Ⓑ Ⓒ Ⓓ Ⓔ | 28 Ⓐ Ⓑ Ⓒ Ⓓ Ⓔ | 38 Ⓐ Ⓑ Ⓒ Ⓓ Ⓔ |
| 9 Ⓐ Ⓑ Ⓒ Ⓓ Ⓔ | 19 Ⓐ Ⓑ Ⓒ Ⓓ Ⓔ | 29 Ⓐ Ⓑ Ⓒ Ⓓ Ⓔ | 39 Ⓐ Ⓑ Ⓒ Ⓓ Ⓔ |
| 10 Ⓐ Ⓑ Ⓒ Ⓓ Ⓔ | 20 Ⓐ Ⓑ Ⓒ Ⓓ Ⓔ | 30 Ⓐ Ⓑ Ⓒ Ⓓ Ⓔ | 40 Ⓐ Ⓑ Ⓒ Ⓓ Ⓔ |

**SECTION 9**

| | | | | | | | |
|---|---|---|---|---|---|---|---|
| 1 Ⓐ Ⓑ Ⓒ Ⓓ Ⓔ | 11 Ⓐ Ⓑ Ⓒ Ⓓ Ⓔ | 21 Ⓐ Ⓑ Ⓒ Ⓓ Ⓔ | 31 Ⓐ Ⓑ Ⓒ Ⓓ Ⓔ |
| 2 Ⓐ Ⓑ Ⓒ Ⓓ Ⓔ | 12 Ⓐ Ⓑ Ⓒ Ⓓ Ⓔ | 22 Ⓐ Ⓑ Ⓒ Ⓓ Ⓔ | 32 Ⓐ Ⓑ Ⓒ Ⓓ Ⓔ |
| 3 Ⓐ Ⓑ Ⓒ Ⓓ Ⓔ | 13 Ⓐ Ⓑ Ⓒ Ⓓ Ⓔ | 23 Ⓐ Ⓑ Ⓒ Ⓓ Ⓔ | 33 Ⓐ Ⓑ Ⓒ Ⓓ Ⓔ |
| 4 Ⓐ Ⓑ Ⓒ Ⓓ Ⓔ | 14 Ⓐ Ⓑ Ⓒ Ⓓ Ⓔ | 24 Ⓐ Ⓑ Ⓒ Ⓓ Ⓔ | 34 Ⓐ Ⓑ Ⓒ Ⓓ Ⓔ |
| 5 Ⓐ Ⓑ Ⓒ Ⓓ Ⓔ | 15 Ⓐ Ⓑ Ⓒ Ⓓ Ⓔ | 25 Ⓐ Ⓑ Ⓒ Ⓓ Ⓔ | 35 Ⓐ Ⓑ Ⓒ Ⓓ Ⓔ |
| 6 Ⓐ Ⓑ Ⓒ Ⓓ Ⓔ | 16 Ⓐ Ⓑ Ⓒ Ⓓ Ⓔ | 26 Ⓐ Ⓑ Ⓒ Ⓓ Ⓔ | 36 Ⓐ Ⓑ Ⓒ Ⓓ Ⓔ |
| 7 Ⓐ Ⓑ Ⓒ Ⓓ Ⓔ | 17 Ⓐ Ⓑ Ⓒ Ⓓ Ⓔ | 27 Ⓐ Ⓑ Ⓒ Ⓓ Ⓔ | 37 Ⓐ Ⓑ Ⓒ Ⓓ Ⓔ |
| 8 Ⓐ Ⓑ Ⓒ Ⓓ Ⓔ | 18 Ⓐ Ⓑ Ⓒ Ⓓ Ⓔ | 28 Ⓐ Ⓑ Ⓒ Ⓓ Ⓔ | 38 Ⓐ Ⓑ Ⓒ Ⓓ Ⓔ |
| 9 Ⓐ Ⓑ Ⓒ Ⓓ Ⓔ | 19 Ⓐ Ⓑ Ⓒ Ⓓ Ⓔ | 29 Ⓐ Ⓑ Ⓒ Ⓓ Ⓔ | 39 Ⓐ Ⓑ Ⓒ Ⓓ Ⓔ |
| 10 Ⓐ Ⓑ Ⓒ Ⓓ Ⓔ | 20 Ⓐ Ⓑ Ⓒ Ⓓ Ⓔ | 30 Ⓐ Ⓑ Ⓒ Ⓓ Ⓔ | 40 Ⓐ Ⓑ Ⓒ Ⓓ Ⓔ |

Quality
●
Assurance
Mark

**SECTION 10**

| | | | | | | | |
|---|---|---|---|---|---|---|---|
| 1 Ⓐ Ⓑ Ⓒ Ⓓ Ⓔ | 11 Ⓐ Ⓑ Ⓒ Ⓓ Ⓔ | 21 Ⓐ Ⓑ Ⓒ Ⓓ Ⓔ | 31 Ⓐ Ⓑ Ⓒ Ⓓ Ⓔ |
| 2 Ⓐ Ⓑ Ⓒ Ⓓ Ⓔ | 12 Ⓐ Ⓑ Ⓒ Ⓓ Ⓔ | 22 Ⓐ Ⓑ Ⓒ Ⓓ Ⓔ | 32 Ⓐ Ⓑ Ⓒ Ⓓ Ⓔ |
| 3 Ⓐ Ⓑ Ⓒ Ⓓ Ⓔ | 13 Ⓐ Ⓑ Ⓒ Ⓓ Ⓔ | 23 Ⓐ Ⓑ Ⓒ Ⓓ Ⓔ | 33 Ⓐ Ⓑ Ⓒ Ⓓ Ⓔ |
| 4 Ⓐ Ⓑ Ⓒ Ⓓ Ⓔ | 14 Ⓐ Ⓑ Ⓒ Ⓓ Ⓔ | 24 Ⓐ Ⓑ Ⓒ Ⓓ Ⓔ | 34 Ⓐ Ⓑ Ⓒ Ⓓ Ⓔ |
| 5 Ⓐ Ⓑ Ⓒ Ⓓ Ⓔ | 15 Ⓐ Ⓑ Ⓒ Ⓓ Ⓔ | 25 Ⓐ Ⓑ Ⓒ Ⓓ Ⓔ | 35 Ⓐ Ⓑ Ⓒ Ⓓ Ⓔ |
| 6 Ⓐ Ⓑ Ⓒ Ⓓ Ⓔ | 16 Ⓐ Ⓑ Ⓒ Ⓓ Ⓔ | 26 Ⓐ Ⓑ Ⓒ Ⓓ Ⓔ | 36 Ⓐ Ⓑ Ⓒ Ⓓ Ⓔ |
| 7 Ⓐ Ⓑ Ⓒ Ⓓ Ⓔ | 17 Ⓐ Ⓑ Ⓒ Ⓓ Ⓔ | 27 Ⓐ Ⓑ Ⓒ Ⓓ Ⓔ | 37 Ⓐ Ⓑ Ⓒ Ⓓ Ⓔ |
| 8 Ⓐ Ⓑ Ⓒ Ⓓ Ⓔ | 18 Ⓐ Ⓑ Ⓒ Ⓓ Ⓔ | 28 Ⓐ Ⓑ Ⓒ Ⓓ Ⓔ | 38 Ⓐ Ⓑ Ⓒ Ⓓ Ⓔ |
| 9 Ⓐ Ⓑ Ⓒ Ⓓ Ⓔ | 19 Ⓐ Ⓑ Ⓒ Ⓓ Ⓔ | 29 Ⓐ Ⓑ Ⓒ Ⓓ Ⓔ | 39 Ⓐ Ⓑ Ⓒ Ⓓ Ⓔ |
| 10 Ⓐ Ⓑ Ⓒ Ⓓ Ⓔ | 20 Ⓐ Ⓑ Ⓒ Ⓓ Ⓔ | 30 Ⓐ Ⓑ Ⓒ Ⓓ Ⓔ | 40 Ⓐ Ⓑ Ⓒ Ⓓ Ⓔ |

9

## CERTIFICATION STATEMENT

Copy the statement below (do not print) and sign your name as you would an official document.

I hereby agree to the conditions set forth online at www.collegeboard.org and/or in the SAT® Registration Booklet and certify that I am the person whose name and address appear on this answer sheet.

_____

_____

_____

_____

By signing below, I agree not to share any specific test questions or essay topics with anyone by any form of communication, including, but not limited to: email, text messages, or use of the Internet.

Signature _____ Date _____

## SPECIAL QUESTIONS

1 Ⓐ Ⓑ Ⓒ Ⓓ Ⓔ Ⓕ Ⓖ Ⓗ Ⓘ Ⓙ
2 Ⓐ Ⓑ Ⓒ Ⓓ Ⓔ Ⓕ Ⓖ Ⓗ Ⓘ Ⓙ
3 Ⓐ Ⓑ Ⓒ Ⓓ Ⓔ Ⓕ Ⓖ Ⓗ Ⓘ Ⓙ
4 Ⓐ Ⓑ Ⓒ Ⓓ Ⓔ Ⓕ Ⓖ Ⓗ Ⓘ Ⓙ
5 Ⓐ Ⓑ Ⓒ Ⓓ Ⓔ Ⓕ Ⓖ Ⓗ Ⓘ Ⓙ
6 Ⓐ Ⓑ Ⓒ Ⓓ Ⓔ Ⓕ Ⓖ Ⓗ Ⓘ Ⓙ
7 Ⓐ Ⓑ Ⓒ Ⓓ Ⓔ Ⓕ Ⓖ Ⓗ Ⓘ Ⓙ
8 Ⓐ Ⓑ Ⓒ Ⓓ Ⓔ Ⓕ Ⓖ Ⓗ Ⓘ Ⓙ

9

PLEASE DO NOT WRITE IN THIS AREA

◉ ○ ○ ○ ○ ○ ○ ○ ○ ○ ○ ○ ○ ○ ○ ○ ○ ○ ○ ○ ○ ○ ○ ○ ○ ○ ○ ○ ○ ○ ○ ○ ○   **SERIAL #**

884

## ESSAY
### Time — 25 minutes

**Turn to page 2 of your answer sheet to write your ESSAY.**

The essay gives you an opportunity to show how effectively you can develop and express ideas. You should, therefore, take care to develop your point of view, present your ideas logically and clearly, and use language precisely.

Your essay must be written on the lines provided on your answer sheet—you will receive no other paper on which to write. You will have enough space if you write on every line, avoid wide margins, and keep your handwriting to a reasonable size. Remember that people who are not familiar with your handwriting will read what you write. Try to write or print so that what you are writing is legible to those readers.

**Important Reminders:**

- **A pencil is required for the essay.** An essay written in ink will receive a score of zero.
- **Do not write your essay in your test book.** You will receive credit only for what you write on your answer sheet.
- **An off-topic essay will receive a score of zero.**
- **If your essay does not reflect your original and individual work, your test scores may be canceled.**

You have twenty-five minutes to write an essay on the topic assigned below.

Think carefully about the issue presented in the following excerpt and the assignment below.

> "Tough challenges reveal our strengths and weaknesses." This statement is certainly true; adversity helps us discover who we are. Hardships can often lead us to examine who we are and to question what is important in life. In fact, people who have experienced seriously adverse events frequently report that they were positively changed by their negative experiences.

**Assignment:** Do you think that ease does not challenge us and that we need adversity to help us discover who we are? Plan and write an essay in which you develop your point of view on this issue. Support your position with reasoning and examples taken from your reading, studies, experience, or observations.

**BEGIN WRITING YOUR ESSAY ON PAGE 2 OF THE ANSWER SHEET.**

**If you finish before time is called, you may check your work on this section only.**
**Do not turn to any other section in the test.**

## SECTION 2
Time — 25 minutes
18 Questions

**Turn to Section 2 (page 4) of your answer sheet to answer the questions in this section.**

**Directions:** This section contains two types of questions. You have 25 minutes to complete both types. For questions 1-8, solve each problem and decide which is the best of the choices given. Fill in the corresponding circle on the answer sheet. You may use any available space for scratchwork.

Set $X = \{30, 31, 32, 33\}$

Set $Y = \{32, 33, 34, 35, 36\}$

**1.** Sets $X$ and $Y$ are shown above. How many numbers in set $X$ are also in set $Y$ ?

(A) Two
(B) Three
(C) Four
(D) Seven
(E) Nine

**2.** If Peg traveled 10 miles in 2 hours and Linda traveled twice as far in half the time, what was Linda's average speed, in miles per hour?

(A) 5
(B) 10
(C) 20
(D) 30
(E) 40

**GO ON TO THE NEXT PAGE**

3. If $x = k(k - 2)$, then $x + 1 =$

   (A) $k^2 - k$
   (B) $k^2 - 3k$
   (C) $k^2 - 2k + 1$
   (D) $k^2 + 2k + 1$
   (E) $k^2 - 1$

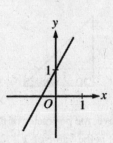

4. The figure above shows the graph of the line $y = ax + b$, where $a$ and $b$ are constants. Which of the following best represents the graph of the line $y = 2ax + b$?

   (A) 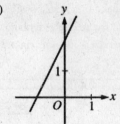     (B)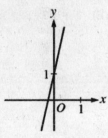

   (C) 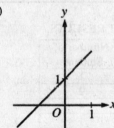     (D)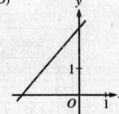

   (E)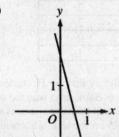

GO ON TO THE NEXT PAGE

5. In the figure above, the perimeter of the triangle is $4 + 2\sqrt{2}$. What is the value of $x$ ?

(A) 2

(B) 4

(C) $\sqrt{2}$

(D) $2\sqrt{2}$

(E) $2 + \sqrt{2}$

7. Ahmad has containers of two different sizes. The total capacity of 16 containers of one size is $x$ gallons, and the total capacity of 8 containers of the other size is also $x$ gallons, and $x > 0$. In terms of $x$, what is the capacity, in gallons, of each of the larger containers?

(A) $4x$

(B) $2x$

(C) $\dfrac{x}{2}$

(D) $\dfrac{x}{8}$

(E) $\dfrac{x}{16}$

**HISTORY TEST RESULTS**

| Score | Number of Students |
|-------|--------------------|
| 100 | 1 |
| 95 | 2 |
| 90 | 4 |
| 85 | 1 |
| 80 | 3 |
| 75 | 2 |
| 70 | 2 |
| 65 | 0 |
| 60 | 1 |

6. The scores on Tuesday's history test for 16 students are shown in the table above. Sam, who was the only student absent on Tuesday, will take the test next week. If Sam receives a score of 95 on the test, what will be the median score for the test?

(A) 90

(B) 87.5

(C) 85

(D) 82.5

(E) 80

8. Rectangle $ABCD$ lies in the $xy$-coordinate plane so that its sides are <u>not</u> parallel to the axes. What is the product of the slopes of all four sides of rectangle $ABCD$ ?

(A) $-2$

(B) $-1$

(C) $0$

(D) $1$

(E) $2$

**GO ON TO THE NEXT PAGE**

**Directions:** For Student-Produced Response questions 9-18, use the grids at the bottom of the answer sheet page on which you have answered questions 1-8.

Each of the remaining 10 questions requires you to solve the problem and enter your answer by marking the circles in the special grid, as shown in the examples below. You may use any available space for scratchwork.

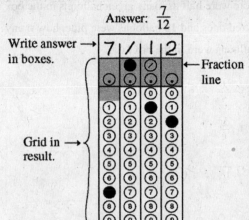

Answer: $\frac{7}{12}$

Write answer → in boxes.

Grid in result.

← Fraction line

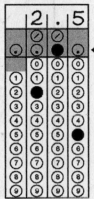

Answer: 2.5

← Decimal point

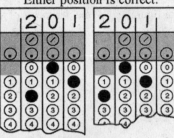

Answer: 201
Either position is correct.

**Note:** You may start your answers in any column, space permitting. Columns not needed should be left blank.

- Mark no more than one circle in any column.

- Because the answer sheet will be machine-scored, **you will receive credit only if the circles are filled in correctly.**

- Although not required, it is suggested that you write your answer in the boxes at the top of the columns to help you fill in the circles accurately.

- Some problems may have more than one correct answer. In such cases, grid only one answer.

- No question has a negative answer.

- **Mixed numbers** such as $3\frac{1}{2}$ must be gridded as

  3.5 or 7/2. (If 3 | 1 | / | 2 is gridded, it will be

  interpreted as $\frac{31}{2}$, not $3\frac{1}{2}$.)

- **Decimal Answers:** If you obtain a decimal answer with more digits than the grid can accommodate, it may be either rounded or truncated, but it must fill the entire grid. For example, if you obtain an answer such as 0.6666..., you should record your result as .666 or .667. **A less accurate value such as .66 or .67 will be scored as incorrect.**

Acceptable ways to grid $\frac{2}{3}$ are:

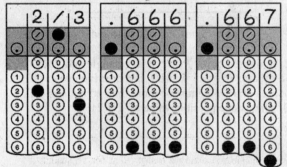

9. An hour-long television program included 20 minutes of commercials. What fraction of the hour-long program was <u>not</u> commercials?

10. If the product of 0.3 and a number is equal to 1, what is the number?

GO ON TO THE NEXT PAGE →

**11.** Let $x \triangle_z^y$ be defined as $x \triangle_z^y = x^y - z^y$ for all positive integers $x$, $y$, and $z$. What is the value of $10 \triangle_5^3$ ?

**12.** In the figure above, $PQST$ is a rectangle and $URST$ is a square. $PU = 5$ and $UT$ is a positive integer. If the area of $PQST$ must be more than 10 but less than 30, what is one possible value of $UT$ ?

```
Q            R    S
┌────────────┬────┐
│            │    │
└────────────┴────┘
P            U    T
```
Note: Figure not drawn to scale.

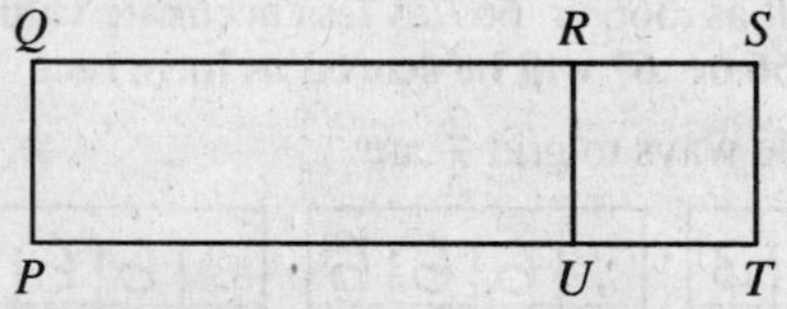

**13.** A company sells boxes of balloons in which the balloons are red, green, or blue. Luann purchased a box of balloons in which $\frac{1}{3}$ of them were red. If there were half as many green balloons in the box as red ones and 18 balloons were blue, how many balloons were in the box?

**14.** The three distinct points $P$, $Q$, and $R$ lie on a line $\ell$; the four distinct points $S$, $T$, $U$, and $V$ lie on a different line that is parallel to line $\ell$. What is the total number of different lines that can be drawn so that each line contains exactly two of the seven points?

**GO ON TO THE NEXT PAGE** ▷

15. If $2^x + 2^x + 2^x + 2^x = 2^7$, what is the value of $x$?

17. Alice and Corinne stand back-to-back. They each take 10 steps in opposite directions away from each other and stop. Alice then turns around, walks toward Corinne, and reaches her in 17 steps. The length of one of Alice's steps is how many times the length of one of Corinne's steps? (All of Alice's steps are the same length and all of Corinne's steps are the same length.)

16. Each of 5 people had a blank card on which they wrote a positive integer. If the average (arithmetic mean) of these integers is 15, what is the greatest possible integer that could be on one of the cards?

18. Let the function $f$ be defined by $f(x) = x^2 + 18$. If $m$ is a positive number such that $f(2m) = 2f(m)$, what is the value of $m$?

# STOP

**If you finish before time is called, you may check your work on this section only.**
**Do not turn to any other section in the test.**

# SECTION 3
## Time — 25 minutes
### 35 Questions

**Turn to Section 3 (page 4) of your answer sheet to answer the questions in this section.**

**Directions:** For each question in this section, select the best answer from among the choices given and fill in the corresponding circle on the answer sheet.

---

The following sentences test correctness and effectiveness of expression. Part of each sentence or the entire sentence is underlined; beneath each sentence are five ways of phrasing the underlined material. Choice A repeats the original phrasing; the other four choices are different. If you think the original phrasing produces a better sentence than any of the alternatives, select choice A; if not, select one of the other choices.

In making your selection, follow the requirements of standard written English; that is, pay attention to grammar, choice of words, sentence construction, and punctuation. Your selection should result in the most effective sentence—clear and precise, without awkwardness or ambiguity.

EXAMPLE:

Laura Ingalls Wilder published her first book <u>and she was sixty-five years old then</u>.

(A) and she was sixty-five years old then
(B) when she was sixty-five
(C) at age sixty-five years old
(D) upon the reaching of sixty-five years
(E) at the time when she was sixty-five

1. While working as a nurse in the streets of Calcutta, <u>that was when Mother Teresa developed a profound love for the poor</u>.

   (A) that was when Mother Teresa developed a profound love for the poor
   (B) Mother Teresa developed a profound love for the poor
   (C) then the development of Mother Teresa's profound love for the poor took place
   (D) Mother Teresa's profound love for the poor developed
   (E) a profound love for the poor developed in Mother Teresa

2. The legislators agreed <u>to return to their districts and they would hold</u> a series of town meetings on the recently passed tax bills.

   (A) to return to their districts and they would hold
   (B) to return to their districts to hold
   (C) to returning to their districts, thereby holding
   (D) with returning to their districts for holding of
   (E) on the return to their districts to the holding

3. Legend has it that medieval Chinese warriors <u>using manned kites to survey enemy troops anticipating</u> modern aerial surveillance.

   (A) using manned kites to survey enemy troops anticipating
   (B) using manned kites to survey enemy troops and anticipate
   (C) using manned kites and surveying enemy troops, they anticipated
   (D) used manned kites to survey enemy troops, a technique anticipating
   (E) used manned kites surveying enemy troops, so anticipating techniques of

4. For months, one of the most popular breakfast foods <u>were selling for so little that people thought something was</u> wrong.

   (A) were selling for so little that people thought something was
   (B) was selling for so little that people thought something were
   (C) were selling for so little; so people thought something has gone
   (D) was selling for so little that people thought something was
   (E) was selling for very little; so people thought of it as

GO ON TO THE NEXT PAGE

5. The programmers always talked of having too much to do, but in truth <u>they had a lesser amount of work to do than</u> their colleagues.

   (A) they had a lesser amount of work to do than
   (B) their work was the least among
   (C) they were having less work to do than
   (D) the amount of work they had to do was the least of
   (E) they had less work to do than

6. Film audiences in the 1950's saw more musicals <u>than</u> the 1960's and 1970's.

   (A) than
   (B) than did
   (C) than the films of
   (D) than with the audiences in
   (E) than did audiences in

7. <u>Unlike American architects who preceded him, Frank Lloyd Wright</u> did not draw on classical or European architecture for inspiration.

   (A) Unlike American architects who preceded him, Frank Lloyd Wright
   (B) Unlike the inspiration of American architects who preceded him, Frank Lloyd Wright
   (C) Frank Lloyd Wright's architecture, unlike American architects who preceded him,
   (D) Different from the American architects who preceded him, Frank Lloyd Wright's designs
   (E) Frank Lloyd Wright's inspirations, different from American architects who preceded him,

8. The revolt against Victorianism was perhaps even more marked in poetry than <u>either fiction or drama</u>.

   (A) either fiction or drama
   (B) either fiction or in drama
   (C) either in fiction or drama
   (D) in either fiction or drama
   (E) in either fiction or in drama

9. <u>Because economic hardship is the real source of many other problems is the reason why</u> the revolutionary government attacked inflation first.

   (A) Because economic hardship is the real source of many other problems is the reason why
   (B) Because economic hardship is the real source of many other problems,
   (C) Economic hardship causes many other problems and is the reason for why
   (D) As a result of economic hardship causing many other problems,
   (E) The fact that economic hardship is the real source of many other problems is why

10. In Germany, foresters discovered that trees killed by acid rain had begun to die four years <u>earlier, even though the trees had shown no signs of disease then</u>.

    (A) earlier, even though the trees had shown no signs of disease then
    (B) earlier, but not showing any signs of disease then
    (C) earlier, no outward signs of disease had been shown then in the trees, however
    (D) earlier without any signs of disease shown then
    (E) earlier, not then having shown any signs of disease, however

11. In the wild, pygmy chimpanzees are found only in an inaccessible region south of the Zaire River, <u>since such is the case, very few are in captivity</u>.

    (A) since such is the case, very few are in captivity
    (B) and very few are in captivity because of that
    (C) no more than a few are in captivity as a result
    (D) the number in captivity is very few for this reason
    (E) and so no more than a few are in captivity

**GO ON TO THE NEXT PAGE** ▷

The following sentences test your ability to recognize grammar and usage errors. Each sentence contains either a single error or no error at all. No sentence contains more than one error. The error, if there is one, is underlined and lettered. If the sentence contains an error, select the one underlined part that must be changed to make the sentence correct. If the sentence is correct, select choice E. In choosing answers, follow the requirements of standard written English.

EXAMPLE:

The other delegates and him immediately
   A            B     C
accepted the resolution drafted by the
                      D
neutral states. No error
          E

(A) ● (C) (D) (E)

12. Although born in the Midwest, Langston Hughes lived

most of his adult life in Harlem, in New York City,

where , like other writers in the 1930's, he had wrote
 A    B                                 C

some of his finest works. No error
         D          E

13. In constant demand as a speaker, Ms. Chernock
            A

has never been more busier than she is now .
   B       C           D
No error
 E

14. During the night, there is usually two German
    A           B

shepherds at the warehouse to guard against robbery
                      C

attempts . No error
  D      E

15. Candy manufacturers applauded the discovery by
                        A

researchers that students which smell chocolate while
                B

studying and again while taking a test are able to
        C              D

recall more material than students not exposed to the

odor of chocolate. No error
           E

16. One can hardly determine which contributes more
   A    B           C       D
to the success of a violinist—innate skill or regular

practice. No error
      E

17. The Red Cross workers had not expected the

refugees from the flooded plain to be as desperate
   A               B

and as undernourished as those whom they had seen
              C             D

earlier in the week. No error
           E

**GO ON TO THE NEXT PAGE**

18. Although naturalists have identified six hundred
    <u>A</u>

    different forms of the corion snail, there <u>is</u> actually
                                              <u>B</u>

    <u>no more than</u> two true species <u>within</u> this genus.
        C                          D

    <u>No error</u>
        E

19. The department of transportation <u>has introduced</u>
                                     A

    pictorial traffic signs because drivers can react to <u>this</u>
                                                         B

    <u>more quickly</u> than <u>to verbal ones</u> . <u>No error</u>
        C              D                      E

20. She claimed that the "representational" actor

    <u>is having to imitate</u> a character's behavior, <u>whereas</u>
              A                                    B

    the "presentational" actor attempts <u>to reveal</u> human
                                         C

    behavior <u>through self-understanding</u> . <u>No error</u>
                         D                      E

21. Many nations, and the United Nations <u>itself</u> ,
                                         A

    <u>has issued</u> stamps <u>that commemorate</u> the fiftieth
        B                   C

    anniversary <u>of the signing of</u> the UN charter.
                        D

    <u>No error</u>
        E

22. The tribal council's program familiarized young people

    <u>with</u> Cherokee history, <u>taught them</u> tribal traditions,
      A                          B

    and <u>they had</u> the <u>opportunity to</u> learn skills used by
           C                D

    ancient artists. <u>No error</u>
                         E

23. Observation of diverse animal species <u>show that</u> the
                                           A

    <u>most successful</u> in the struggle for survival are
        B

    <u>those which</u> are most <u>adaptable to</u> changes in their
        C                      D

    world. <u>No error</u>
               E

24. Far <u>away from</u> having been a diehard conservative,
            A

    <u>Hoover was</u> , some scholars <u>now contend</u> , the leading
        B                            C

    progressive <u>of his day</u> . <u>No error</u>
                    D             E

25. <u>For the past</u> hundred years or more, Yellowstone
        A

    National Park <u>was</u> a kind of sociological laboratory
                  B

    <u>in which</u> North Americans have been exploring
        C

    <u>the meaning of</u> the national-park concept. <u>No error</u>
        D                                          E

**GO ON TO THE NEXT PAGE** ⇒

895

3 3 3 3 3 3

Unauthorized copying or reuse of any part of this page is illegal.

**26.** Alerted by the nervousness and evasiveness of the
       A

witness, the jurors were quick to perceive that his
                                B

statements were inconsistent to those he had made
                    C         D

earlier. No error
         E

**27.** In many respects Anna Karenina and Emma Bovary
       A

are very similar characters, but Bovary has
                            B      C

the most spirit and determination. No error
   D                              E

**28.** Between the sales manager and I existed an easy ,
                              A      B      C

cooperative working relationship; neither of us
                                  D

hesitated to discuss problems. No error
                              E

**29.** As the archbishop of Canterbury, Thomas à Becket
       A

assumed an independence that was intolerable to the
          B                                 C

king, who had long been his friend. No error
           D                       E

**Directions:** The following passage is an early draft of an essay. Some parts of the passage need to be rewritten.

Read the passage and select the best answers for the questions that follow. Some questions are about particular sentences or parts of sentences and ask you to improve sentence structure or word choice. Other questions ask you to consider organization and development. In choosing answers, follow the requirements of standard written English.

**Questions 30-35 are based on the following passage.**

(1) Many people have never heard of Lou Henry Hoover. (2) Of all the wives of United States Presidents since 1900, she is probably the most forgotten. (3) She attended Stanford University, where she met and married another student—a mining engineer named Herbert Hoover—and became one of the first American women to earn a degree in geology. (4) Together they began a life of travel, adventure, and accomplishment.

(5) The Hoovers served on a relief mission in Beijing, China, during the Boxer Uprising of 1900. (6) Lou Hoover held bandages in one hand, a gun in the other. (7) From 1902 to 1916, the Hoovers circled the world five times. (8) In the process Lou Hoover designed for her two young sons a portable crib. (9) It would remain stable during the rocking of a ship. (10) She also learned several languages and published scholarly works on such topics as the gold-mining techniques of the Egyptians.

(11) Lou Hoover being a versatile person, as comfortable in an outdoor camp as she was in a Victorian drawing room. (12) She triumphed over the limits of her position and the times in which she lived. (13) A leader of the Girl Scout movement, she firmly believed that girls should be encouraged to pursue their interests. (14) In 1929 she became the first person to break the racial barrier at the White House. (15) She entertained Jessie DePriest, wife of Oscar DePriest, the African American Congressman from Chicago.

**GO ON TO THE NEXT PAGE**

30. Which is the best version of the underlined portion of sentence 3 (reproduced below) ?

    *She attended Stanford University, where she met and married another student—a mining engineer named Herbert Hoover—and became one of the first American women to earn a degree in geology.*

    (A) (As it is now)
    (B) Attending Stanford University, where she
    (C) At Stanford University, where she
    (D) Having attended Stanford University, she
    (E) She attended Stanford University, she

31. Which of the following is the best version of the underlined portion of sentences 8 and 9 (reproduced below) ?

    *In the process Lou Hoover designed for her two young sons a portable crib. It would remain stable during the rocking of a ship.*

    (A) crib so that it would remain stable
    (B) crib, and it would remain stable
    (C) crib that nevertheless remained stable
    (D) crib that would remain stable
    (E) crib. It was designed to remain stable

32. Which of the following ways to revise the underlined portion of sentence 10 (reproduced below) most effectively links the sentence to the rest of the second paragraph?

    *She also learned several languages and published scholarly works on such topics as the goldmining techniques of the Egyptians.*

    (A) Because as a child she had learned
    (B) Since her time in China she was also learning
    (C) By this time she had also been learning
    (D) And in the midst of all this activity, she learned
    (E) Nevertheless, by now she had also learned

33. In context, which is the best way to deal with sentence 11 ?

    (A) Change "being" to "was".
    (B) Insert "Finally" at the beginning.
    (C) Change "she" to "Lou Hoover".
    (D) Delete "she was".
    (E) Change "was" to "had been".

34. Which of the following is the best version of the underlined portion of sentences 14 and 15 (reproduced below) ?

    *In 1929 she became the first person to break the racial barrier at the White House. She entertained Jessie DePriest, wife of Oscar DePriest, the African American Congressman from Chicago.*

    (A) In 1929 she became the first person to break the racial barrier at the White House, and she entertained
    (B) In addition, in 1929 she became the first person to break the racial barrier at the White House when she entertained
    (C) So in 1929 she becomes the first person to break the racial barrier at the White House by entertaining
    (D) Consequently, the racial barrier at the White House was first broken in 1929 by Hoover's entertaining
    (E) By being the first person to break the racial barrier at the White House in 1929, Hoover entertained

35. Which sentence is best to add after sentence 15 ?

    (A) Lou Henry Hoover was an exceptionally gracious and polished first lady.
    (B) Lou Henry Hoover was an accomplished woman who was truly ahead of her time.
    (C) Lou Henry Hoover's personal papers have only recently been made available to the public.
    (D) Obviously, not a great deal is known about the early life of this extraordinary woman.
    (E) Only historians now know that she was born in Waterloo, Iowa, in 1874.

# STOP

**If you finish before time is called, you may check your work on this section only.**
**Do not turn to any other section in the test.**

4 Unauthorized copying or reuse of any part of this page is illegal. 4

## SECTION 4
### Time — 25 minutes
### 24 Questions

**Turn to Section 4 (page 5) of your answer sheet to answer the questions in this section.**

**Directions:** For each question in this section, select the best answer from among the choices given and fill in the corresponding circle on the answer sheet.

Each sentence below has one or two blanks, each blank indicating that something has been omitted. Beneath the sentence are five words or sets of words labeled A through E. Choose the word or set of words that, when inserted in the sentence, best fits the meaning of the sentence as a whole.

**Example:**

Hoping to ------- the dispute, negotiators proposed a compromise that they felt would be ------- to both labor and management.

(A) enforce . . useful
(B) end . . divisive
(C) overcome . . unattractive
(D) extend . . satisfactory
(E) resolve . . acceptable

1. Initially only the carpeting outside the restroom was ------- by water from the burst pipe; eventually the entire hallway flooded.

(A) diverted    (B) confined    (C) scuttled
(D) cleansed    (E) drenched

2. Communal nests have advantages and disadvantages for animals like voles and mice: they enable the animals to ------- body heat, but leave them more ------- to discovery by predators.

(A) insure . . inclined
(B) maintain . . vulnerable
(C) squander . . liable
(D) stimulate . . resistant
(E) retain . . immune

3. He displayed a nearly pathological -------, insisting on knowing every detail of his friends' lives.

(A) orderliness    (B) credulity    (C) curiosity
(D) shyness    (E) morbidity

4. Despite global efforts to ------- malaria, this mosquito-borne disease continues to -------: the World Health Organization estimates that it still affects up to 500 million people a year.

(A) cure . . flag
(B) foster . . thrive
(C) combat . . abate
(D) scrutinize . . prosper
(E) eradicate . . flourish

5. Although condemned by the review panel, to film critic Pauline Kael the movie seemed entirely ------- and unlikely to offend.

(A) impressionable    (B) innocuous
(C) unsuitable    (D) insensitive
(E) unapproachable

6. The reviewer characterized Madonna Swan-Abdalla's autobiography as a portrait of an ------- person, one who prevailed against great odds.

(A) empathetic    (B) indomitable    (C) expeditious
(D) idiosyncratic    (E) astute

7. Although it stayed in business for several months, the company was actually ------- and met its financial obligations only by engaging in ------- activities.

(A) insolvent . . fraudulent
(B) prudent . . speculative
(C) autonomous . . subordinate
(D) bankrupt . . charitable
(E) stable . . manipulative

8. Mary Shelley's *Frankenstein* centers on a scientist's -------, the overweening pride that makes him believe he can usurp nature.

(A) obstinacy    (B) hubris    (C) impetuosity
(D) valor    (E) callousness

**GO ON TO THE NEXT PAGE**

The passages below are followed by questions based on their content; questions following a pair of related passages may also be based on the relationship between the paired passages. Answer the questions on the basis of what is stated or implied in the passages and in any introductory material that may be provided.

**Questions 9-12 are based on the following passages.**

### Passage 1

American writers Henry Adams (1838-1918) and Samuel Clemens (1835-1910) gradually approached, during their careers, a mood of total despair. Personal
*Line* tragedies have been set forth to explain this development:
5 the deaths of loved ones, the humiliation of family bank-ruptcies. These certainly are contributory causes, but the writings of Adams and Clemens reveal that the despair is in a slow process of incubation from their earliest work, and that it is finally hatched by the growing political
10 discords, moral conflicts, and economic problems of their age. It is not a despair of personal bereavement but of country—and ultimately of humanity—that manifests itself in their works.

### Passage 2

The bankruptcy of Samuel Clemens, the death of his
15 daughter, and the chronic illness of his wife are agonizing as personal history. Our interest, however, is in the works that came out of these disasters. Literary critics are usually unable to say how an author's experience is transformed into art. In Clemens' writings from 1895 onward, how-
20 ever, we can watch while he repeatedly tries and fails to make something of these experiences that were so vitally important to him—and finally we can see him fuse and transform them into a culminating work of art, the book (published posthumously) that we know as
25 *The Mysterious Stranger.*

9. Both authors agree that Clemens

(A) deplored societal and human tendencies
(B) endured painful personal loss
(C) was deeply affected by literary critics
(D) endured hardships much like those of Adams
(E) revealed pessimism in his earliest writings

10. The metaphor in lines 7-11 ("the despair . . . their age") is central to the overall argument of Passage 1 in its suggestion of

(A) literary creativity
(B) gradual development
(C) timeless artistry
(D) reluctant acknowledgement
(E) culminating achievement

11. The author of Passage 2 would most likely view the "contributory causes" mentioned in line 6, Passage 1, as personal experiences that

(A) did not influence Clemens' literary output significantly
(B) affected Clemens early rather than late in his career
(C) were less important than political, moral, and economic factors
(D) were of little interest to literary critics
(E) were eventually molded by Clemens into a meaningful work

12. The author of Passage 1 would most likely regard the "personal history" (line 16, Passage 2) as

(A) essential knowledge for any reader of Clemens' work
(B) more distressing than the personal diffi-culties experienced by Henry Adams
(C) inconsistent with the tone and character of Clemens' literary output
(D) less important than public events as an influence on Clemens' writing
(E) instrumental in making Clemens a unique American writer

**GO ON TO THE NEXT PAGE**

**Questions 13-24 are based on the following passage.**

*This passage is part of an introduction written by a well-known doctor and essayist for his 1996 book about rare neurological disorders.*

I am writing this with my left hand, although I am strongly right-handed. I had surgery to my right shoulder a month ago and am not permitted, not capable of, use of the
Line right arm at this time. I write slowly, awkwardly—but
5 more easily, more naturally, with each passing day. I am adapting, learning, all the while—not merely this left-handed writing, but a dozen other left-handed skills as well. I have also become very adept with my toes, to compensate for having one arm in a sling; I was quite off balance for a
10 few days when the arm was first immobilized, but now I walk differently, I have discovered a new balance. I am developing different patterns, different habits . . . a different identity, one might say, at least in this particular sphere. There must be changes going on with some of the programs
15 and circuits in my brain—altering synaptic weights and connectivities and signals (though our methods of brain imaging are still too crude to show these).

Though some of my adaptations are deliberate, planned, and some are learned through trial and error (in the first
20 week I injured every finger on my left hand), most have occurred by themselves, unconsciously, by reprogram-mings and adaptations of which I know nothing (any more than I know, or can know, how I normally walk). Next month, if all goes well, I can start to readapt again, to regain
25 a full (and "natural") use of the right arm, to reincorporate it back into my body image, myself, to become a dexterous human being once again.

But recovery, in such circumstances, is by no means automatic, a simple process like tissue healing—it will
30 involve a whole nexus of muscular and postural adjustments, a whole sequence of new procedures (and their synthesis), learning, finding, a new path to recovery. My surgeon, an understanding man who has had the same operation himself, said, "There are *general* guidelines, restrictions,
35 recommendations. But all the particulars you will have to find out for yourself." Jay, my physiotherapist, expressed himself similarly: "Adaptation follows a different path in each person. The nervous system creates its own paths. You're the neurologist—you must see this all the time."
40 Nature's imagination, as physicist Freeman Dyson likes to say, is richer than ours, and he speaks, marvellingly, of this richness in the physical and biological worlds, the end-less diversity of physical forms and forms of life. For me, as a physician, nature's richness is to be studied in the
45 phenomena of health and disease, in the endless forms of individual adaptation by which human organisms, people, adapt and reconstruct themselves when faced with the chal-lenges and vicissitudes of life.

Thus while one may be distressed by the trials of devel-
50 opmental disorders or disease, one may sometimes see them as creative too—for if they destroy particular paths, partic-ular ways of doing things, they may force the nervous system into making other paths and ways, force on it an unexpected growth and evolution. This other side of development or
55 disease is something I see, potentially, in almost every patient. That such radical adaptations can occur demands a view of the brain as dynamic and active rather than pro-grammed and static, a supremely efficient adaptive system geared for evolution and change, ceaselessly adapting to the
60 needs of the organism—its need, above all, to construct a coherent self and world, whatever defects or disorders of brain function befall it. That the brain is minutely differen-tiated is clear: there are hundreds of tiny areas crucial for every aspect of perception and behavior (from the percep-
65 tion of color and of motion to, perhaps, the intellectual orientation of the individual). The miracle is how they all cooperate, are integrated together, in the creation of a self.

This sense of the brain's remarkable plasticity, its capac-ity for the most striking adaptations, not the least in the
70 special (and often desperate) circumstances of neural or sen-sory mishap, has come to dominate my own perception of my patients and their lives. So much so, indeed, that I am sometimes moved to wonder whether it may be necessary to redefine the very concepts of "health" and "disease," to
75 see these in terms of the ability of the organism to create a new organization and order, one that fits its special, altered disposition and needs, rather than in the terms of a rigidly defined "norm."

**13.** The passage can primarily be described as

(A) scientific evidence used to refute an established theory
(B) amusing anecdotes countered by a profound insight
(C) skeptical commentary evolving into a detached analysis
(D) a case study followed by a scientific hypothesis
(E) a personal account leading to a general observation

**14.** The author describes himself as "strongly right-handed" (line 2) in order to

(A) convey the ease with which he learned to be ambi-dextrous
(B) contrast his particular abilities and those of other individuals
(C) suggest the difficulties he had to overcome
(D) evoke a sympathetic response from the reader
(E) characterize the sources of his physical strength

**GO ON TO THE NEXT PAGE**

**15.** The author's remark in lines 14-16 ("There must . . . signals") can best be described as

(A) conjecture
(B) irony
(C) inquiry
(D) observation
(E) evidence

**16.** In line 17, "crude" most nearly means

(A) obvious
(B) natural
(C) offensive
(D) undeveloped
(E) vulgar

**17.** The author's parenthetical reference in lines 22-23 serves to

(A) depict his physical capabilities before his accident
(B) highlight the process of learning through experience
(C) explain his continuing inability to perform simple tasks
(D) rationalize the frustration he felt about achieving his goals
(E) illustrate a point about unconscious adaptation

**18.** In lines 34-36 the surgeon advises the author to

(A) become more open-minded about muscular adjustments than he had been
(B) follow a detailed and specific regimen of rehabilitation
(C) find out how others have dealt with the same problem
(D) develop his own procedures for coping
(E) endure patiently until he physically recovers

**19.** The physiotherapist's remarks (lines 36-39) reveal the assumption that

(A) patients have complete control over the progress of their recovery
(B) each neurologist follows a different path to understanding
(C) all neurologists are aware of the nervous system's adaptability
(D) the author is inadequately informed about the intricacies of the muscular system
(E) some neurologists consider both healthy and injured brain processes to be parallel

**20.** In line 42, "richness" most nearly means

(A) biological importance
(B) economic wealth
(C) meaning
(D) variety
(E) resources

**21.** Why does the author mention that he is a physician in lines 43-48 ?

(A) To emphasize his particular point of view
(B) To illustrate the limits of scientific knowledge
(C) To establish that he views brain function strictly from his patients' standpoint
(D) To suggest that his main concern is the surgery he performs on patients
(E) To dispel any doubt about his credentials in the field of neurology

**22.** Lines 49-54 primarily encourage readers to view disease as

(A) a source of psychological harm
(B) an opportunity for productive change
(C) an inevitable fact of human existence
(D) a force that retards evolutionary change
(E) a condition to be dealt with on a spiritual level

**GO ON TO THE NEXT PAGE**

**4**  Unauthorized copying or reuse of any part of this page is illegal. **4**

**23.** It can be inferred from the author's discussion of radical adaptations in lines 56-62 that others may have

(A) believed that adaptations occur only as a response to disease

(B) held that neurological change can occur only as a result of an evolutionary process

(C) viewed the brain as inflexible and unchanging

(D) failed to recognize how minutely differentiated the brain is

(E) recognized that the intellectual orientation of the individual is an organic function

**24.** The main point of the passage is to

(A) explain the most fundamental aspects of brain function

(B) discuss the impact of surgery on the nervous system

(C) invite speculation about how physical rehabilitation complements natural healing

(D) emphasize that current technology to measure brain activity is inadequate

(E) argue that the brain's ability to adapt to changing needs is virtually limitless

# STOP

**If you finish before time is called, you may check your work on this section only.**
**Do not turn to any other section in the test.**

**902**

## SECTION 5
### Time — 25 minutes
### 20 Questions

---

**Turn to Section 5 (page 5) of your answer sheet to answer the questions in this section.**

---

**Directions:** For this section, solve each problem and decide which is the best of the choices given. Fill in the corresponding circle on the answer sheet. You may use any available space for scratchwork.

---

**Notes**

1. The use of a calculator is permitted.

2. All numbers used are real numbers.

3. Figures that accompany problems in this test are intended to provide information useful in solving the problems. They are drawn as accurately as possible EXCEPT when it is stated in a specific problem that the figure is not drawn to scale. All figures lie in a plane unless otherwise indicated.

4. Unless otherwise specified, the domain of any function $f$ is assumed to be the set of all real numbers $x$ for which $f(x)$ is a real number.

**Reference Information**

 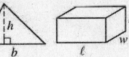   

$A = \pi r^2$
$C = 2\pi r$      $A = \ell w$      $A = \frac{1}{2}bh$      $V = \ell wh$      $V = \pi r^2 h$      $c^2 = a^2 + b^2$      Special Right Triangles

The number of degrees of arc in a circle is 360.
The sum of the measures in degrees of the angles of a triangle is 180.

---

2, 6, 14, 30, . . .

1. In the sequence above, the first term is 2. Each number after the first is obtained by adding 1 to the preceding number and then doubling the result. What is the sixth number in the sequence?

(A) 122
(B) 123
(C) 124
(D) 125
(E) 126

2. If $a(x + y) = 45$ and $ax = 15$, what is the value of $ay$ ?

(A) 3
(B) 5
(C) 15
(D) 25
(E) 30

**GO ON TO THE NEXT PAGE** ⟩

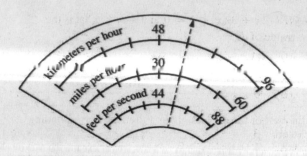

3. On the speedometer above, what is the speed, in miles per hour, indicated by the needle position?

(A) 32.5
(B) 37.5
(C) 40
(D) 55
(E) 60

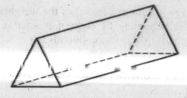

5. The three-dimensional figure represented above consists of rectangular and triangular faces. Each rectangular face has area $r$ and each triangular face has area $t$. What is the total surface area of the figure, in terms of $r$ and $t$?

(A) $2r + t$
(B) $3r + 2t$
(C) $4r + 3t$
(D) $6rt$
(E) $r^3 t^2$

4. How many different positive three-digit integers can be formed if the three digits 4, 5, and 6 must be used in each of the integers?

(A) Three
(B) Four
(C) Six
(D) Eight
(E) Nine

6. If $n$ is a positive integer and $\dfrac{n+1}{2^n} = \dfrac{1}{2}$, then $n =$

(A) 1
(B) 2
(C) 3
(D) 4
(E) 5

GO ON TO THE NEXT PAGE

7. The average (arithmetic mean) of the weights of 14 books is $p$ pounds. In terms of $p$, what is the total weight of the books, in pounds?

(A) $14 + p$

(B) $p - 14$

(C) $\dfrac{p}{14}$

(D) $\dfrac{14}{p}$

(E) $14p$

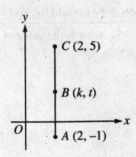

8. Point $B$ is the midpoint of $\overline{AC}$ in the figure above. What is the value of $t$?

(A) 1
(B) 1.5
(C) 2
(D) 2.5
(E) 3

9. If $k(2x + 3)(x - 1) = 0$ and $x > 1$, what is the value of $k$?

(A) $\dfrac{-3}{2}$

(B) 0

(C) $\dfrac{2}{3}$

(D) 1

(E) 2

10. If all men in the Williams family are over six feet tall, which of the following statements must be true?

(A) No man under six feet tall is a member of the Williams family.
(B) All men over six feet tall are members of the Williams family.
(C) All men who are not members of the Williams family are under six feet tall.
(D) Every member of the Williams family over six feet tall is a man.
(E) There is one man in the Williams family under six feet tall.

GO ON TO THE NEXT PAGE

5 ☐ 5 ☐ 5 ☐ 5 ☐ 5

Unauthorized copying or reuse of
any part of this page is illegal.

**11.** What is the radius of a circle that has a circumference of $\pi$ ?

(A) $\dfrac{1}{4}$

(B) $\dfrac{1}{2}$

(C) 1

(D) 2

(E) 4

**12.** If $y$ is directly proportional to $x^2$ and $y = \dfrac{1}{8}$ when $x = \dfrac{1}{2}$, what is the positive value of $x$ when $y = \dfrac{9}{2}$ ?

(A) $\dfrac{3}{4}$

(B) $\dfrac{3}{2}$

(C) $\dfrac{9}{4}$

(D) 3

(E) 9

**13.** If $4x = 6u = 5v = 7w > 0$, which of the following is true?

(A) $x < v < u < w$
(B) $x < u < v < w$
(C) $x < v < w < u$
(D) $w < u < v < x$
(E) $u < v < w < x$

**14.** Let the function $h$ be defined by $h(t) = 2\left(t^3 - 3\right)$. When $h(t) = -60$, what is the value of $2 - 3t$ ?

(A) 35
(B) 11
(C) 7
(D) −7
(E) −11

**GO ON TO THE NEXT PAGE**

**15.** If $x$ is divisible by 3 and $y$ is divisible by 5, which of the following must be divisible by 15 ?

    I. $xy$
   II. $3x + 5y$
  III. $5x + 3y$

  (A) I only
  (B) III only
  (C) I and II only
  (D) I and III only
  (E) I, II, and III

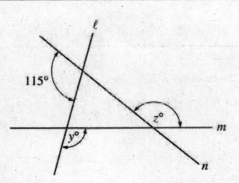

**16.** In the figure above, $y + z =$

  (A) 180
  (B) 195
  (C) 215
  (D) 230
  (E) 245

The sum of three consecutive odd integers is 111.

**17.** If $n$ represents the least of the three integers, which of the following equations represents the statement above?

  (A) $3n = 111$
  (B) $3n + 2 = 111$
  (C) $3n + 4 = 111$
  (D) $3n + 6 = 111$
  (E) $3n + 9 = 111$

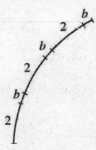

**18.** The figure above shows part of a circle whose circumference is 45. If arcs of length 2 and length $b$ continue to alternate around the entire circle so that there are 18 arcs of each length, what is the <u>degree</u> measure of each of the arcs of length $b$ ?

  (A) 4°
  (B) 6°
  (C) 10°
  (D) 16°
  (E) 20°

**GO ON TO THE NEXT PAGE** ➡

19. The cost of maintenance on an automobile increases each year by 10 percent, and Andrew paid $300 this year for maintenance on his automobile. If the cost $c$ for maintenance on Andrew's automobile $n$ years from now is given by the function $c(n) = 300x^n$, what is the value of $x$?

(A)  0.1
(B)  0.3
(C)  1.1
(D)  1.3
(E)  30

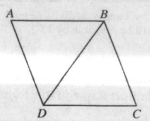

Note:  Figure not drawn to scale.

20. If the five line segments in the figure above are all congruent, what is the ratio of the length of $\overline{AC}$ (not shown) to the length of $\overline{BD}$?

(A)  $\sqrt{2}$ to 1
(B)  $\sqrt{3}$ to 1
(C)  $\sqrt{2}$ to 2
(D)  $\sqrt{3}$ to 2
(E)  $\sqrt{3}$ to $\sqrt{2}$

# STOP
If you finish before time is called, you may check your work on this section only.
Do not turn to any other section in the test.

**SECTION 6**
Time — 25 minutes
24 Questions

**Directions:** For each question in this section, select the best answer from among the choices given and fill in the corresponding circle on the answer sheet.

---

Each sentence below has one or two blanks, each blank indicating that something has been omitted. Beneath the sentence are five words or sets of words labeled A through E. Choose the word or set of words that, when inserted in the sentence, best fits the meaning of the sentence as a whole.

**Example:**

Hoping to ------- the dispute, negotiators proposed a compromise that they felt would be ------- to both labor and management.

(A) enforce . . useful
(B) end . . divisive
(C) overcome . . unattractive
(D) extend . . satisfactory
(E) resolve . . acceptable     Ⓐ Ⓑ Ⓒ Ⓓ ⬤

---

1. May Sarton had a ------- career: it ------- from 1929, when *Poetry* magazine published her early sonnets, to 1994, when her last collection of poems came out.

   (A) limited . . developed
   (B) diverse . . foundered
   (C) variable . . declined
   (D) lengthy . . lasted
   (E) sedate . . soared

2. Recent data recording a bottlenose whale's phenomenal dive of over 4,700 feet ------- earlier ------- that such whales were among the sea's deepest divers.

   (A) refuted . . theories
   (B) challenged . . predictions
   (C) confirmed . . speculations
   (D) validated . . disclaimers
   (E) substantiated . . doubts

3. The residents of the town lived ------- lives; no one indulged in wild or ------- behavior.

   (A) rambunctious . . indecent
   (B) extravagant . . excessive
   (C) secluded . . scrupulous
   (D) circumscribed . . impulsive
   (E) irreverent . . animated

4. The study's warning that monkey populations were declining in Guatemala and Mexico was ------- by new evidence that nearby populations along the Belize River were -------.

   (A) corroborated . . prospering
   (B) confirmed . . extant
   (C) belied . . dwindling
   (D) diminished . . debilitated
   (E) tempered . . thriving

5. The staff complained that management was -------, focusing on short-term profits while disregarding the long-term welfare of the corporation.

   (A) irresolute     (B) officious     (C) rancorous
   (D) punctilious     (E) myopic

GO ON TO THE NEXT PAGE

Each passage below is followed by questions based on its content. Answer the questions on the basis of what is <u>stated</u> or <u>implied</u> in each passage and in any introductory material that may be provided.

**Questions 6-7 are based on the following passage.**

Among the side benefits of the museum's exhibition of early photographs of Egypt is that it can inspire you to read the travel classic *Flaubert in Egypt*. Looking at
*Line*
5  the photographs from the 1850's after reading the book, you should be able to conjure up the French author just outside the picture frame. There is Flaubert in his long white shirt, his shaved head topped by a red tarboosh, settled into the cool shade of an ancient temple, reading poetry, and seeming oh-so-exquisitely bored.

**6.** In context, "conjure up" (line 5) most nearly means

(A) convene
(B) portray
(C) imagine
(D) entreat
(E) recollect

**7.** The characterization of Flaubert in the last sentence chiefly serves to suggest that

(A) Flaubert had an affected manner
(B) Egypt inspired Flaubert to write
(C) Flaubert found the Egyptian climate oppressive
(D) Flaubert was timid about posing for photographs
(E) Egypt's culture was of great interest to Flaubert

**Questions 8-9 are based on the following passage.**

By breaking down the graphic or pictorial vocabulary to a bare minimum, maps achieve a visual minimalism that, physiologically speaking, is easy on the eyes. They turn
*Line*
5  numbers into visual images, create pattern out of measurements, and thus engage the highly evolved human capacity for pattern recognition. Some of the most intense research in the neurosciences today is devoted to elucidating what are described as maps of perception: how perception filters and maps the relentless torrent of information provided by
10  the sense organs, our biotic instruments of measurement. Maps *enable* humans to use inherent biological skills of perception, their "educated" eyes, to separate the message from the static, to see the story line running through random pattern.

**8.** The effect of the "breaking down" (line 1) is to

(A) accentuate selected information
(B) make details small
(C) create momentary confusion
(D) minimize the distinction between words and numbers
(E) eliminate words that would clarify the meaning of images

**9.** In line 8, the phrase "maps of perception" refers to

(A) drawings of the organs of human perception
(B) depictions of how the world actually appears to the human eye
(C) models of the way humans process what they encounter
(D) illustrations of how the human eye functions at the cellular level
(E) representations of a place from one person's perspective

**GO ON TO THE NEXT PAGE** ⟶

**Questions 10-16 are based on the following passage.**

*The passage below was adapted from a 1998 book on the history of Black women in the United States written by two scholars of African American culture.*

We both knew that the story of Black women was a remarkable one. We also knew that a great many people, over the centuries and even over the last few decades,
Line have not wanted it told. Some have dismissed it, saying
5 it wasn't worth telling. Others have actively suppressed it, afraid of what it would reveal. Still others have tried to deny that there was any story particular to Black women. They have insisted that, after you've told the story of African Americans and the story of women, you're finished. Black
10 women are included in those narratives.

But no matter what anyone may say to the contrary, Black women are different. They're different from Black men and they're different from White women. It is true that much of what they have experienced derives from
15 racism and much from sexism. At the same time, however, much of what Black women have experienced and still experience today—bad and good—involves the blending of their separate identities in a way that chemists would call a combination, not just a mixture. Both race and gender
20 are transformed when they are present together, and class is often present as a catalyst.

Unfortunately, both Black men and White feminists have sometimes seen this separate identity as threatening. Many members of both groups want to put their arms
25 metaphorically around the Black woman's shoulder and say, "She's with us." Black women are sought after by Black historians and White feminist historians, by Black political leaders and by White feminist political leaders. But their inclusion is provisionary. They will be valued
30 for their difference so long as they do not mention it too often. It just makes people feel nervous and guilty.

This is a sad situation for everyone, and it is an unnec-essary one. Unity and loyalty do not depend on absolute homogeneity. Maybe it's the American obsession with
35 race that makes it so difficult for us as a nation to get rid of our fear that difference implies, even guarantees, animosity and opposition. But denial of difference is not the road to harmony. It is the road only to a kind of false unity that is so fragile it will splinter at a touch.
40 In a landmark article, "What Has Happened Here," Elsa Barkley Brown compares history to the Louisiana conversational style "gumbo ya ya," in which everyone talks at once and all the stories told interrelate and play off each other. "History," says Barkley Brown, "also is
45 everybody talking at once, multiple rhythms being played simultaneously. The events and people we write about did not occur in isolation but in dialogue with a myriad of other people and events. In fact, at any given moment millions of people are all talking at once." Listening to
50 all those voices at once can be confusing, but silencing

any of them puts in danger the very meaning of the his-torical pursuit. We were sure it was time for the voice of Black women to be heard loud and clear.

10. The purpose of lines 4-10 ("Some . . . narratives") is to

(A) defend diverse perspectives on race and gender
(B) discredit the views of a particular group
(C) introduce a topic of interest to most historians
(D) present a sample of views held by Black women
(E) note the different kinds of resistance to a historical topic

11. The sentence in lines 11-12 ("But . . . different") is best described as

(A) an assertion
(B) an apology
(C) a decision
(D) a concession
(E) a criticism

12. The chemistry metaphor in lines 15-21 ("At . . . catalyst") is used to

(A) characterize the challenges faced by some groups of people
(B) illustrate the connection between scientific and historical studies of race, class and gender
(C) identify the agents for change in a particular social transition
(D) suggest the way certain influences interact to produce a unique perspective
(E) show the similarities between racism and sexism

13. The author suggests that the figurative gesture described in lines 24-26 ("Many . . . us") is one of

(A) misguided affection
(B) calculated self-interest
(C) genuine empathy
(D) uncommon courage
(E) overt arrogance

**GO ON TO THE NEXT PAGE**

**14.** The author suggests that the explanation for the "sad situation" (line 32) is the

(A) resistance that most people exhibit toward political change
(B) fear that most people feel about being held up as role models
(C) differing ways in which men and women behave in positions of power
(D) concern that focusing on differences will lead to disharmony
(E) high value that many people place on nonconformity

**15.** The tone of lines 37-39 ("But . . . touch") is best described as

(A) confiding
(B) defiant
(C) skeptical
(D) resigned
(E) admonishing

**16.** Elsa Barkley Brown's article, described in the last paragraph, emphasizes

(A) multiplicity and inclusion
(B) privacy and mutual respect
(C) self-reliance and individuality
(D) intellectual curiosity
(E) cooperative invention

GO ON TO THE NEXT PAGE →

**Questions 17-24 are based on the following passage.**

*This passage is taken from the beginning of a short story by a nineteenth-century Russian writer.*

In the department of . . . but I had better not mention in what department. There is nothing in the world more readily moved to wrath than a department, a government
Line
office, in fact any sort of official body. And so, to avoid
5 any unpleasantness . . .

In a certain department there was a government clerk, of whom it cannot be said that he was very remarkable; he was short, somewhat pockmarked, with dim, bleary eyes and a small bald patch on the top of his head. As
10 for his grade in the service (for among us the grade is what must be put first), he was what is called a perpetual titular councillor, a class at which, as we all know, various writers who indulge in the habit of attacking those who cannot defend themselves jeer and jibe to
15 their heart's content.

His name was Akaky Akakyevitch. No one has been able to remember when and how long ago he entered the department. However many directors and high officials of all sorts came and went, he was always seen in the
20 same place, at the very same duty, so that they used to declare that he must have been born a perpetual titular councillor in uniform all complete and with a bald patch on his head. The porters, far from getting up from their seats when he came in, took no more notice of him than
25 if a simple fly had flown across the vestibule. His superiors treated him with a sort of domineering chilliness. The head clerk's assistant used to throw papers under his nose without even saying "Copy this" or "Here is an interesting, nice little case," as is usually done in well-behaved offices. And
30 he would take it, gazing only at the papers without looking to see who had put them there and whether he had the right to do so; he would take the papers and at once set to work to copy them. The young clerks made jokes about him to the best of their clerkly wit, and told before his face all
35 sorts of stories of their own invention about him. They would enquire when the wedding was to take place, or would scatter bits of paper on his head, calling them snow. In the midst of all this teasing, Akaky Akakyevitch never answered a word, but behaved as though there were
40 no one there. Only when they jolted his arm and prevented him from going on with his work would he cry out, "Leave me alone! Why do you insult me?" There was something strange in the words and in the voice in which they were uttered, so that one young clerk, new to the office, was
45 cut to the heart, and in those words thought that he heard others: "I am your brother."

It would be hard to find a man who loved his work as did Akaky Akakyevitch. In that copying, he found a varied and agreeable world of his own. If rewards had been given
50 according to the measure of zeal in the service, he might to his amazement have even found himself a civil councillor;

but all he gained in the service, as the wits, his fellow clerks expressed it, was a buckle in his belly button and a pain in his back. It cannot be said, however, that no notice
55 had ever been taken of him. One director, being a good-natured man and anxious to reward him for his long service, sent him something a little more important than his ordinary copying; he was instructed from a finished document to make some sort of report for another office;
60 the work consisted only of altering the headings and in places changing the first person into the third. This cost Akaky Akakyevitch such an effort that it threw him into a regular perspiration: he mopped his brow and said at last, "No, better let me copy something." From that time
65 forth they left him to go on copying forever.

17. The word "unpleasantness" (line 5) most likely refers to

(A) possible consequences resulting from the strong language the author uses when angered
(B) repercussions that might result from identifying Akaky's department
(C) arguments that inevitably occur between different government offices
(D) increased teasing to which Akaky would be subjected by his fellow workers
(E) discomfort that this story might cause for many Russian citizens

18. The reference to how Akaky "must have been born" (line 21) indicates that he

(A) could not escape his basic nature even though he tried to do so continually
(B) would have been viewed differently by others if not for his uniform
(C) could not be imagined any way other than how he appeared at the department each day
(D) had not been working long in the department
(E) was older than he appeared to be

19. The "simple fly" (line 25) is used primarily as an image of something that is

(A) annoying
(B) uncomplicated
(C) fast-moving
(D) easily overlooked
(E) potentially harmful

GO ON TO THE NEXT PAGE

20. The two quotations in lines 28-29 serve as examples of

    (A) typical civilities
    (B) superficial compliments
    (C) unreasonable demands
    (D) unappreciated small talk
    (E) unnecessary explanations

21. In line 35, "invention" most nearly means

    (A) creative experiment
    (B) new device
    (C) fabrication
    (D) discovery
    (E) adeptness

22. The narrator's attitude toward the young clerks in Akaky's office is primarily one of

    (A) disapproval of their cruelty
    (B) annoyance with their disrespect for supervisors
    (C) dissatisfaction with their laziness
    (D) mock sympathy for their lack of challenge
    (E) amusement over their antics

23. The clerk who is "new to the office" (line 44) responds to Akaky's words with

    (A) confusion
    (B) sarcasm
    (C) disbelief
    (D) fear
    (E) compassion

24. It can be inferred from the incident described in lines 55-65 that

    (A) the director was not really trying to reward Akaky for his hard work
    (B) the director understood Akaky better than anyone else in the office did
    (C) Akaky was not really a hard worker
    (D) Akaky wanted a promotion very much
    (E) Akaky feared increased responsibility

# STOP

**If you finish before time is called, you may check your work on this section only.**
**Do not turn to any other section in the test.**

## SECTION 8
**Time — 20 minutes**
**16 Questions**

**Turn to Section 8 (page 7) of your answer sheet to answer the questions in this section.**

**Directions:** For this section, solve each problem and decide which is the best of the choices given. Fill in the corresponding circle on the answer sheet. You may use any available space for scratchwork.

**Notes**

1. The use of a calculator is permitted.
2. All numbers used are real numbers.
3. Figures that accompany problems in this test are intended to provide information useful in solving the problems. They are drawn as accurately as possible EXCEPT when it is stated in a specific problem that the figure is not drawn to scale. All figures lie in a plane unless otherwise indicated.
4. Unless otherwise specified, the domain of any function $f$ is assumed to be the set of all real numbers $x$ for which $f(x)$ is a real number.

**Reference Information**

$A = \pi r^2$
$C = 2\pi r$
$A = \ell w$
$A = \frac{1}{2}bh$
$V = \ell wh$
$V = \pi r^2 h$
$c^2 = a^2 + b^2$
**Special Right Triangles**

The number of degrees of arc in a circle is 360.
The sum of the measures in degrees of the angles of a triangle is 180.

---

**1.** If $6{,}700 = 100(6k + 7)$, then $k =$

(A) $\dfrac{1}{10}$

(B) $1$

(C) $10$

(D) $100$

(E) $1{,}000$

**2.** If 3 more than $n$ is a negative number and if 5 more than $n$ is a positive number, which of the following could be the value of $n$?

(A) $-5$
(B) $-4$
(C) $-3$
(D) $0$
(E) $4$

**GO ON TO THE NEXT PAGE**

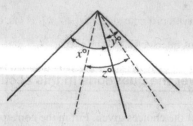

Note: Figure not drawn to scale

3. In the figure above, if $x = 70$ and $y = 40$ and the dotted lines bisect the angles with measures $x°$ and $y°$, what is the value of $z$ ?

(A) 30
(B) 40
(C) 45
(D) 50
(E) 55

4. A piece of fruit is to be chosen at random from a basket of fruit. The probability that the piece of fruit chosen will be an apple is $\frac{2}{5}$. Which of the following could NOT be the number of pieces of fruit in the basket?

(A) 20
(B) 35
(C) 52
(D) 70
(E) 80

5. A square and an equilateral triangle have equal perimeters. If the square has sides of length 3, what is the length of one side of the triangle?

(A) 2
(B) 3
(C) 4
(D) 5
(E) 6

6. If $x = -1$ and $k > 0$, which of the following has the greatest value?

(A) $2kx$
(B) $4kx^2$
(C) $6kx^3$
(D) $8kx^4$
(E) $10kx^5$

GO ON TO THE NEXT PAGE

7. Josephine's daily exercise routine consists of swimming, cycling, and running, in that order. She runs faster than she swims and cycles faster than she runs. If she does not rest between the activities, which of the following could be the graph of the distance she covers during the entire time of her exercise routine?

(A)
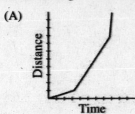

(B)
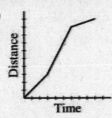

(C)
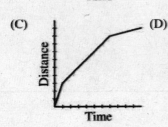

(D)
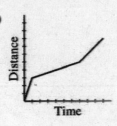

(E)
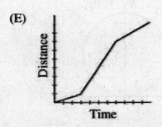

8. In the $xy$-coordinate system, $(\sqrt{6}, k)$ is one of the points of intersection of the graphs $y = x^2 - 7$ and $y = -x^2 + j$, where $j$ is a constant. What is the value of $j$ ?

(A) 5
(B) 4
(C) 3
(D) 2
(E) 1

9. If $|2 - x| < 3$, which of the following is a possible value of $x$ ?

(A) 4
(B) 5
(C) 6
(D) 7
(E) 8

GO ON TO THE NEXT PAGE

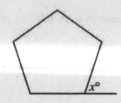

**10.** If all interior angles of the polygon above are congruent, then $x =$

(A) 60
(B) 65
(C) 72
(D) 80
(E) 84

**11.** The length of a drawing of a tool is $\dfrac{3}{8}$ of the length of the actual tool. If the length of the drawing of the tool is 6 inches, what is the length, in inches, of the actual tool?

(A) $2\dfrac{1}{4}$

(B) $8\dfrac{1}{4}$

(C) 16

(D) $18\dfrac{1}{4}$

(E) 22

**12.** If $\dfrac{x+3}{2}$ is an integer, then $x$ must be

(A) a negative integer
(B) a positive integer
(C) a multiple of 3
(D) an even integer
(E) an odd integer

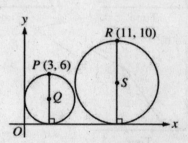

**13.** In the $xy$-plane above, points $Q$ and $S$ are the centers of the circles, which are tangent to the $x$-axis. What is the slope of line $QS$ (not shown)?

(A) $\dfrac{1}{8}$

(B) $\dfrac{1}{4}$

(C) $\dfrac{1}{2}$

(D) $\dfrac{7}{8}$

(E) 1

**GO ON TO THE NEXT PAGE**

**14.** If $n$ and $p$ are integers greater than 1 and if $p$ is a factor of both $n + 3$ and $n + 10$, what is the value of $p$ ?

(A)  3
(B)  7
(C)  10
(D)  13
(E)  30

**16.** If $xy = 7$ and $x - y = 5$, then $x^2 y - xy^2 =$

(A)   2
(B)  12
(C)  24
(D)  35
(E)  70

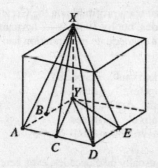

**15.** In the cube shown above, points $B$, $C$, and $E$ are midpoints of three of the edges. Which of the following angles has the least measure?

(A)  $\angle XAY$
(B)  $\angle XBY$
(C)  $\angle XCY$
(D)  $\angle XDY$
(E)  $\angle XEY$

# STOP

**If you finish before time is called, you may check your work on this section only.**
**Do not turn to any other section in the test.**

## SECTION 9
Time — 20 minutes
19 Questions

Turn to Section 9 (page 7) of your answer sheet to answer the questions in this section.

**Directions:** For each question in this section, select the best answer from among the choices given and fill in the corresponding circle on the answer sheet.

Each sentence below has one or two blanks, each blank indicating that something has been omitted. Beneath the sentence are five words or sets of words labeled A through E. Choose the word or set of words that, when inserted in the sentence, best fits the meaning of the sentence as a whole.

**Example:**

Hoping to ------- the dispute, negotiators proposed a compromise that they felt would be ------- to both labor and management.

(A) enforce . . useful
(B) end . . divisive
(C) overcome . . unattractive
(D) extend . . satisfactory
(E) resolve . . acceptable

1. Efforts are finally being made to ------- the traffic congestion that plagues the downtown area.

   (A) engage  (B) alleviate  (C) transport
   (D) regenerate  (E) trivialize

2. Though outwardly -------, the speaker was actually quite disturbed by the tumultuous crowd.

   (A) apprehensive  (B) agitated  (C) furious
   (D) serene  (E) considerate

3. K'ang-hsi, emperor of China from 1661 to 1722, expressed his private thoughts with a ------- rarely found in the usually ------- rulers of great empires.

   (A) peacefulness . . placid
   (B) forthrightness . . reserved
   (C) fairness . . dilatory
   (D) meticulousness . . accessible
   (E) peevishness . . irritable

4. Farming had been profitable on the Great Plains for many decades, but by 1938 ------- agricultural practices and years of inadequate precipitation had ------- the land.

   (A) conscientious . . despoiled
   (B) incompetent . . sustained
   (C) shrewd . . debilitated
   (D) innovative . . fertilized
   (E) imprudent . . denuded

5. Cathedrals usually take decades, even centuries, to complete; thus, no one expected the National Cathedral to be built with -------.

   (A) dispatch  (B) presumption  (C) durability
   (D) deliberation  (E) reverence

6. New York designer Anna Sui creates eclectic clothes that represent an ------- of playful, 1970's funky styles fused with an edgy, urban sensibility.

   (A) induction  (B) amalgam  (C) immersion
   (D) occlusion  (E) estrangement

GO ON TO THE NEXT PAGE

The two passages below are followed by questions based on their content and on the relationship between the two passages. Answer the questions on the basis of what is <u>stated</u> or <u>implied</u> in the passages and in any introductory material that may be provided.

**Questions 7-19 are based on the following passages.**

*The following passages discuss the controversy that surrounded Napster, a service that allowed users to download recordings of music from the Internet at no cost. Both passages were written in 2000 by former songwriters.*

**Passage 1**

In 1950, when I was seventeen, Jerry Lieber and I had our first song recorded. Over the next 50 years, Jerry and I composed many now-familiar songs, like "Hound Dog,"
*Line*
5 "Jailhouse Rock," and "Love Potion No. 9," in many different musical styles, from rhythm and blues to jazz and rock. Our songs were recorded by many great artists, including Ray Charles, Elvis Presley, the Beatles, the Rolling Stones, Peggy Lee, Jimi Hendrix, and the Coasters.

But whatever the style and whoever the artist, there has
10 been one constant: the songs that I have written have been my bread and butter. Writing a song—the music and the lyrics—can take anywhere from ten minutes (as in the case of "Hound Dog") to five years. But no matter how long it takes, it is always a gamble. A songwriter makes
15 nothing until a song is marketed in the form of a recording for sale to the public, and unless that record of the song sells, a songwriter gets nothing for it. Each time a Napster user downloads a copy of a song that I have composed, I am deprived of the royalty that my work should have
20 earned me.

Some say that making music available free of charge on the Web "frees" artists from the control of the recording industry. Many say that since making music is an art, artists like me should do it simply for the love of it. But how free
25 can artists be to do what we love if we must spend most of our days doing something else to make a living? Where would I be today if anyone could have recorded "Hound Dog," and anyone else could have copied that recording, without paying Jerry Lieber and me? I might have occa-
30 sionally written some music for fun, but I would not have had the luxury to compose full time. Who knows what songs I might not have written? I fear for the seventeen-year-old songwriter looking forward to a career in the music business today. Napster and companies like it are
35 threatening not only my retirement, but the future of music itself. In fact, by taking the incentive out of songwriting, Napster may be pushing us closer to a time when there won't be any songs left to swap.

**Passage 2**

In the absence of laws that turn thoughts into things,
40 how will we be assured payment for the work we do with our minds? Must the creatively talented start looking for day jobs?

Nope. Most white-collar jobs already consist of mind work. The vast majority of us live by our wits now,
45 producing "verbs"—that is, ideas—rather than "nouns" like automobiles or toasters. Doctors, architects, executives, consultants, receptionists, and lawyers all manage to survive economically without "owning" their cognition. I take further comfort in the fact that the human species
50 managed to produce pretty decent creative work during the 5,000 years that preceded 1710, when the Statute of Anne, the world's first modern copyright law, passed the British parliament. Sophocles, Dante, da Vinci, Botticelli, Michelangelo, Shakespeare, Newton, Cervantes, Bach—
55 all found reasons to get out of bed in the morning without expecting to own the works they created.

The Grateful Dead, for whom I once wrote songs, learned by accident that if we let fans tape concerts and freely reproduce those tapes—"stealing" our intellectual
60 "property" just like those heinous Napsterians—the tapes would become a marketing virus that would spawn enough Deadheads to fill any stadium in America. Even though Deadheads had free recordings that were often more entertaining than the band's commercial albums, fans still went
65 out and bought records in such quantity that most of them went platinum.

Despite the ubiquity of VCR's, more people go to the movies than ever, and videocassette rentals and sales account for more than half of Hollywood's revenues. The
70 recording industry is unalterably convinced that the easy availability of freely downloadable commercial songs will bring about the apocalypse, and yet since downloadable music began flooding the Net, CD sales have risen by 20 percent. Finally, after giving up copy protection, the
75 software industry expected that widespread piracy would surely occur. And it did. Even so, the software industry is booming. Why? Because the more a program is pirated, the more likely it is to become a standard.

All these examples point to the same conclusion:
80 noncommercial distribution of information increases the sale of commercial information. This is precisely contrary to what happens in a physical economy. When you're selling nouns, there is an undeniable relationship between scarcity and value. But in an economy of verbs, the inverse
85 applies. There is a relationship between familiarity and value. For ideas, fame is fortune. And nothing makes you famous faster than an audience willing to distribute your work for free.

**GO ON TO THE NEXT PAGE**

7. The "great artists" (line 6) in Passage 1 and "The Grateful Dead" (line 57) in Passage 2 both serve to illustrate the two authors'

(A) broad ranges of musical taste
(B) appreciation of musical talent
(C) understanding of songs that appeal to young people
(D) ironic views of what constitutes "quality" in popular music
(E) direct experience with professional songwriting

8. The authors of both passages would most likely agree that

(A) VCR's have increased the public's interest in movies
(B) few people today are able to make a living solely through music
(C) companies such as Napster will ultimately harm the music industry
(D) commercial music sales are necessary to sustain a professional songwriter
(E) artists should free themselves from the demands of the marketplace

9. The "gamble" (line 14) represents a risk that is primarily

(A) financial
(B) artistic
(C) legal
(D) technological
(E) psychological

10. The author of Passage 2 would probably contend that the claim made in lines 17-20 ("Each time . . . me") of Passage 1 is primarily

(A) shortsighted, since downloading free music will ultimately increase an artist's commercial sales
(B) cynical, since most people do believe that artists should be compensated for their efforts
(C) unreasonable, since people cannot be forced to buy music they do not find appealing
(D) discouraging, since downloading drives a wedge between technological innovation and artistic creation
(E) patronizing, because it assumes that people do not understand the function of the Internet

11. The author of Passage 1 presents an argument in lines 24-26 ("But how . . . living?") that can most accurately be called

(A) historical
(B) political
(C) pragmatic
(D) idealistic
(E) facetious

12. Which best summarizes the "fear" (line 32) of the author of Passage 1 ?

(A) Young songwriters will become less devoted to mastering their craft than were songwriters of the past.
(B) Adolescent songwriters will become less popular than they have been in the past.
(C) The increasing demand for music will cause the royalties paid for individual songs to decline.
(D) Young songwriters will no longer be able to earn their living by writing songs.
(E) Technological innovations will one day render music as we now know it obsolete.

13. The primary purpose of Passage 1 is to

(A) challenge a traditional ethical stance
(B) describe a complex technological process
(C) examine an adolescent impulse
(D) urge a radical course of action
(E) argue against a particular practice

14. The quotation marks used in line 22 of Passage 1 and lines 59-60 of Passage 2 both serve to

(A) highlight unique musical theories
(B) acknowledge respected authorities
(C) mock the practices of the music industry
(D) express skepticism about the aptness of particular terms
(E) define unusual phrases for an audience of nonspecialists

15. The use of the phrase "pretty decent" in Passage 2 (line 50) conveys

(A) solemn detachment
(B) cheerful celebration
(C) ironic understatement
(D) lingering doubt
(E) reluctant approval

**GO ON TO THE NEXT PAGE**

**16.** The tone of the author of Passage 2 in lines 59-60 ("stealing . . . Napsterians") is best described as

(A) ebullient
(B) somber
(C) quizzical
(D) irate
(E) satirical

**17.** The attitude of the author of Passage 2 toward the "marketing virus" (line 61) is largely

(A) positive, because it helped make the Grateful Dead more popular
(B) positive, because it made the Grateful Dead's worldview more sophisticated
(C) neutral, because it had little ultimate effect on music critics' views of the Grateful Dead
(D) negative, because it caused the Grateful Dead to focus on monetary gain rather than on artistic integrity
(E) negative, because it created too many fans who could not fully appreciate the Grateful Dead's musical innovations

**18.** The author of Passage 2 discusses VCR's and software in lines 67-77 ("Despite the . . . booming") primarily to

(A) illustrate the vast influence of technology in contemporary life
(B) cite the experiences of other industries to bolster his primary argument about music
(C) offer a personal experience that supports his economic analysis
(D) discourage readers from purchasing CD's and commercial software
(E) show the wide scope of the entertainment industry today

**19.** What might the author of Passage 2 claim would result from the hypothetical situation posed by the author of Passage 1 in lines 26-29 ("Where would . . . me?") ?

(A) Artistic freedom
(B) Musical elitism
(C) Increased renown
(D) Financial injury
(E) Technical knowledge

# STOP

**If you finish before time is called, you may check your work on this section only.**
**Do not turn to any other section in the test.**

**10**  **10**

Unauthorized copying or reuse of
any part of this page is illegal.

# SECTION 10
Time — 10 minutes
14 Questions

Turn to Section 10 (page 7) of your answer sheet to answer the questions in this section.

**Directions:** For each question in this section, select the best answer from among the choices given and fill in the corresponding circle on the answer sheet.

The following sentences test correctness and effectiveness of expression. Part of each sentence or the entire sentence is underlined; beneath each sentence are five ways of phrasing the underlined material. Choice A repeats the original phrasing; the other four choices are different. If you think the original phrasing produces a better sentence than any of the alternatives, select choice A; if not, select one of the other choices.

In making your selection, follow the requirements of standard written English; that is, pay attention to grammar, choice of words, sentence construction, and punctuation. Your selection should result in the most effective sentence—clear and precise, without awkwardness or ambiguity.

EXAMPLE:

Laura Ingalls Wilder published her first book and she was sixty-five years old then.

(A) and she was sixty-five years old then
(B) when she was sixty-five
(C) at age sixty-five years old
(D) upon the reaching of sixty-five years
(E) at the time when she was sixty-five

1. Solar energy, for which there are many potential uses, can be beneficial so that it will produce energy without generating pollution.

(A) beneficial so that it
(B) beneficial because it
(C) beneficial, although it
(D) beneficial in order that it
(E) beneficial because they

2. In her letter, Ms. Kopel stated that she had proof that the treasurer had stolen some of the money.

(A) stated that she had
(B) stated about having
(C) made a statement of having
(D) gave a statement that she had
(E) had a statement there about having

3. As economic conditions improve, the officers of the company maintaining that it will be able to improve sales by increasing exports to other countries.

(A) maintaining that it will be able to improve sales by
(B) maintaining that it, able by improving sales and
(C) maintain that it will improve sales and
(D) maintain that it will be able to improve sales by
(E) maintains that improving sales by

4. For the most part, in the actions of how an animal behaves, instinct is the main determinant.

(A) For the most part, in the actions of how an animal behaves, instinct is the main determinant.
(B) Generally, an animal's behavior and actions are mostly instinctual ones.
(C) An animal's actions, as to behavior, are by and large instinctively determined.
(D) An animal's actions are largely determined by instinct.
(E) Animals mainly have their instinct as a determinant for behavior.

5. Today more and more women are becoming doctors, lawyers, engineers, chemists, or other professions.

(A) or other professions
(B) or they work in other professions
(C) or at work in other professional fields
(D) or professionals in other fields
(E) or in other professional fields

**GO ON TO THE NEXT PAGE**

6. Beginning photographers may choose from among several camera types, there is one which is best for their particular interests.

   (A) there is one which is
   (B) of which there is one
   (C) one of which is
   (D) and one is
   (E) one is

7. In the belief that crossword puzzles stimulated her mind, Dolores will spend hours on them every week.

   (A) Dolores will spend hours on them every week
   (B) Dolores would spend hours on them every week
   (C) hours of every week are spent on them by Dolores
   (D) they occupied hours of every week for Dolores
   (E) every week will find Dolores spending hours on them

8. Enzymes are among the oldest known chemical compounds, as they actually are nonliving protein molecules.

   (A) Enzymes are among the oldest known chemical compounds, as they actually are nonliving protein molecules.
   (B) Among the oldest known chemical compounds, the nonliving protein molecules are actually called enzymes.
   (C) Enzymes, among the oldest known chemical compounds, actually are nonliving protein molecules.
   (D) Enzymes actually are nonliving protein molecules, being among the oldest known chemical compounds.
   (E) Actually, enzymes being nonliving protein molecules, they are among the oldest known chemical compounds.

9. When someone shops by mail or through the Internet, you will be following a tradition begun by the American colonists, who purchased almost everything from Europe.

   (A) you will be following
   (B) it is following
   (C) you will follow
   (D) he or she follows
   (E) it follows

10. Brought to the United States at the age of thirteen to receive a Western education, his first book discusses Lee Yan Phou's childhood in China.

    (A) his first book discusses Lee Yan Phou's childhood in China
    (B) Lee Yan Phou's childhood in China is the subject of his first book
    (C) the subject of his first book is Lee Yan Phou's childhood in China
    (D) Lee Yan Phou discusses his childhood in China in his first book
    (E) Lee Yan Phou, whose childhood was in China, discusses this in his first book

11. Mayor Julia Wilson's daughter told us that she had decided not to run for reelection, even though there is still much to do to improve the downtown district.

    (A) she had decided not to run for reelection
    (B) the decision was that her mother would not run to be reelected
    (C) her mother had decided not to run for reelection
    (D) she decided that she will not run to be reelected
    (E) it was decided about her not running for reelection

12. Although the superintendent has begun to increase the maintenance staff in the schools, she is still being deluged with calls of complaint.

    (A) Although the superintendent has begun to increase the maintenance staff in the schools
    (B) Although beginning to increase, as superintendent, the maintenance staff in the schools
    (C) The superintendent, beginning to increase the maintenance staff in the schools
    (D) The superintendent has begun to increase the maintenance staff in the schools, and
    (E) The superintendent, beginning to increase the maintenance staff in the schools, however

**GO ON TO THE NEXT PAGE** ⟩

**10** 🚫

Unauthorized copying or reuse of
any part of this page is illegal.

🚫 **10**

**13.** When we read, we first form innumerable <u>impressions
and then those impressions are evaluated</u> as we read on.

   (A)  impressions and then those impressions are
           evaluated
   (B)  impressions and then evaluate those impressions
   (C)  impressions, evaluating those impressions then
   (D)  impressions, then we evaluate those impressions
   (E)  impressions, we evaluate those impressions then

**14.** <u>The eerie songs of humpback whales, often lower in
pitch and longer than birds,</u> are intriguing to scientists
partly because whales have no functional vocal cords.

   (A)  The eerie songs of humpback whales, often lower
          in pitch and longer than birds,
   (B)  The eerie songs of humpback whales, which are
          often lower in pitch and last longer than birds,
   (C)  Humpback whales' eerie songs, often pitched
          lower and longer than that of birds,
   (D)  The eerie songs of humpback whales, often lower
          in pitch and lasting longer than those of birds,
   (E)  Often being lower in pitch and lasting longer than
          birds, the eerie songs of humpback whales

# STOP

**If you finish before time is called, you may check your work on this section only.
Do not turn to any other section in the test.**

# Correct Answers and Difficulty Levels
## SAT Practice Test #9

## CRITICAL READING

### Section 4
#### Multiple-Choice Questions

| Correct Answer | Difficulty Level | Correct Answer | Difficulty Level |
|---|---|---|---|
| 1 E | E | 13 B | H |
| 2 B | E | 14 C | E |
| 3 C | E | 15 A | H |
| 4 E | M | 16 D | E |
| 5 B | M | 17 E | M |
| 6 B | M | 18 D | E |
| 7 A | M | 19 C | M |
| 8 B | H | 20 D | M |
| 9 B | H | 21 A | E |
| 10 B | M | 22 B | E |
| 11 E | M | 23 C | M |
| 12 D | H | 24 E | E |

Number correct ____

Number incorrect ____

### Section 6
#### Multiple-Choice Questions

| Correct Answer | Difficulty Level | Correct Answer | Difficulty Level |
|---|---|---|---|
| 1 D | E | 13 B | H |
| 2 C | E | 14 D | M |
| 3 D | H | 15 E | H |
| 4 E | H | 16 A | M |
| 5 E | E | 17 B | M |
| 6 C | E | 18 C | E |
| 7 A | M | 19 D | E |
| 8 A | M | 20 A | M |
| 9 C | M | 21 C | E |
| 10 E | M | 22 A | M |
| 11 A | E | 23 E | M |
| 12 D | M | 24 E | M |

Number correct ____

Number incorrect ____

### Section 9
#### Multiple-Choice Questions

| Correct Answer | Difficulty Level | Correct Answer | Difficulty Level |
|---|---|---|---|
| 1 B | E | 11 C | M |
| 2 D | M | 12 D | D |
| 3 B | M | 13 E | E |
| 4 E | H | 14 D | M |
| 5 A | H | 15 C | M |
| 6 B | H | 16 E | M |
| 7 E | M | 17 A | M |
| 8 D | M | 18 A | M |
| 9 A | E | 19 C | M |
| 10 A | M | | |

Number correct ____

Number incorrect ____

## MATHEMATICS

### Section 2

#### Multiple-Choice Questions

| Correct Answer | Difficulty Level |
|---|---|
| 1 A | E |
| 2 C | E |
| 3 C | E |
| 4 B | M |
| 5 A | M |
| 6 C | M |
| 7 D | H |
| 8 D | H |

#### Student-Produced Response Questions

| Correct Answer | Difficulty Level |
|---|---|
| 9 2/3, .666, .667 | E |
| 10 10/3, 3.33 | M |
| 11 875 | E |
| 12 2, 3 | E |
| 13 36 | M |
| 14 12 | M |
| 15 5 | M |
| 16 71 | M |
| 17 10/7, 1.42, 1.43 | H |
| 18 3 | H |

Number correct ____

Number correct (9-18) ____

Number incorrect ____

### Section 5
#### Multiple-Choice Questions

| Correct Answer | Difficulty Level | Correct Answer | Difficulty Level |
|---|---|---|---|
| 1 E | E | 11 B | M |
| 2 E | E | 12 D | M |
| 3 B | E | 13 D | M |
| 4 C | E | 14 B | M |
| 5 B | E | 15 D | M |
| 6 C | E | 16 E | H |
| 7 E | M | 17 D | M |
| 8 C | M | 18 A | H |
| 9 B | M | 19 C | H |
| 10 A | M | 20 B | H |

Number correct ____

Number incorrect ____

### Section 8
#### Multiple-Choice Questions

| Correct Answer | Difficulty Level | Correct Answer | Difficulty Level |
|---|---|---|---|
| 1 C | E | 9 A | M |
| 2 B | E | 10 C | M |
| 3 E | E | 11 C | M |
| 4 C | E | 12 E | M |
| 5 C | E | 13 B | M |
| 6 D | M | 14 B | H |
| 7 E | M | 15 D | H |
| 8 A | M | 16 D | H |

Number correct ____

Number incorrect ____

## WRITING

### Essay

Essay Score* (0-6) ____

### Section 3
#### Multiple-Choice Questions

| Correct Answer | Difficulty Level | Correct Answer | Difficulty Level |
|---|---|---|---|
| 1 B | E | 19 B | M |
| 2 B | E | 20 A | M |
| 3 D | E | 21 B | M |
| 4 D | E | 22 C | M |
| 5 E | M | 23 A | M |
| 6 E | M | 24 A | M |
| 7 A | M | 25 B | M |
| 8 D | M | 26 C | H |
| 9 B | M | 27 D | M |
| 10 A | M | 28 A | M |
| 11 E | H | 29 E | M |
| 12 C | E | 30 A | M |
| 13 C | E | 31 D | M |
| 14 B | E | 32 D | M |
| 15 B | E | 33 A | M |
| 16 E | E | 34 B | M |
| 17 E | E | 35 B | M |
| 18 B | E | | |

Number correct ____

Number incorrect ____

### Section 10
#### Multiple-Choice Questions

| Correct Answer | Difficulty Level |
|---|---|
| 1 B | E |
| 2 A | E |
| 3 D | E |
| 4 D | M |
| 5 D | M |
| 6 C | M |
| 7 B | M |
| 8 C | M |
| 9 D | M |
| 10 D | M |
| 11 C | M |
| 12 A | M |
| 13 B | M |
| 14 D | H |

Number correct ____

Number incorrect ____

**NOTE:** Difficulty levels are E (easy), M (medium), and H (hard).

* To score your essay, use the SAT scoring guide in Chapter 9 and the free sample essays available online at www.collegeboard.org/satonlinecourse. On this practice test, your essay score should range from 0 to 6. (Keep in mind that on the actual SAT, your essay will be read by two readers and you will receive a score of 0 to 12 on your score report.)

# The SAT Scoring Process

**Scoring.** The computer compares the circle filled in for each question with the correct response. Each correct answer receives one point; omitted questions do not affect your score. For each wrong answer to a multiple-choice question, one-fourth of a point is subtracted to correct for random guessing. The SAT critical reading section has 67 questions. If, for example, a student has 44 right, 20 wrong, and 3 omitted, the resulting raw score is determined as follows:

$$44 \text{ right} - \frac{20 \text{ wrong}}{4} = 44 - 5 = 39 \text{ raw score points}$$

Obtaining raw scores frequently involves the rounding of fractions to the nearest whole number. For example, a raw score of 39.25 is rounded to 39, the nearest whole number. A raw score of 39.50 is rounded upward to 40. **For the WRITING SECTION**, your essay raw score counts approximately 30% and your multiple-choice raw score counts approximately 70%.

**Converting to reported scaled score.** Raw scores are then placed on the College Board scale of 200 to 800 through a process that adjusts scores to account for minor differences in difficulty among different versions of the test. This process, known as equating, is performed so that a student's reported score is not affected by the version of the test taken or by the abilities of the group with whom the student takes the test. As a result of placing SAT scores on the College Board scale, scores earned by students at different times can be compared. For example, an SAT critical reading score of 400 on a test taken at one administration indicates the same level of developed critical reading ability as a 400 score obtained on a different version of the test taken at another time.

**Note:** Since this test has not been previously administered, score ranges are provided for each possible raw score.

# How to Score Practice Test #9

## SAT Critical Reading Sections 4, 6, and 9

**Step A:** Count the number of correct answers for *Section 4* and record the number in the space provided on the Scoring Worksheet. Then do the same for the incorrect answers. (Do not count omitted answers.)

**Step B:** Count the number of correct answers and the number of incorrect answers for *Section 6* and record the numbers in the spaces provided on the Scoring Worksheet. (Do not count omitted answers.)

**Step C:** Count the number of correct answers and the number of incorrect answers for *Section 9* and record the numbers in the spaces provided on the Scoring Worksheet. (Do not count omitted answers.)

**Step D:** Total the number of correct responses. Total the number of incorrect responses. Enter the resulting figures on the Scoring Worksheet. To determine A, use the formula:

$$\text{Number correct} - \frac{\text{Number incorrect}}{4} = A$$

**Step E:** To obtain B, your Rounded Critical Reading Raw Score, round A to the nearest whole number. (For example, any number from 44.50 to 45.49 rounds to 45.) Enter the resulting figure on the Scoring Worksheet.

**Step F:** To find your Critical Reading Scaled Score Range, look up the Total Rounded Raw Score you obtained in step E in the Critical Reading Conversion Table (Table 1). Enter this range in the box on the Scoring Worksheet.

## SAT Mathematics Sections 2, 5, and 8

**Step A:** Count the number of correct answers and the number of incorrect answers for the multiple-choice questions (*questions 1 through 8*) in *Section 2* and record the numbers in the spaces provided on the Scoring Worksheet. (Do not count omitted answers.)

**Step B:** Count the number of correct answers for the student-produced response questions (*questions 9 through 18*) in *Section 2* and record the number in the space provided on the Scoring Worksheet.

**Step C:** Count the number of correct answers and the number of incorrect answers for *Section 5* and record the number in the space provided on the Scoring Worksheet. (Do not count omitted answers.)

**Step D:** Count the number of correct answers and the number of incorrect answers for *Section 8* and record the numbers in the spaces provided on the Scoring Worksheet. (Do not count omitted answers.)

**Step E:** Total the number of correct responses. Total the number of incorrect responses. Enter the resulting figures on the Scoring Worksheet. To determine A, use the formula:

$$\text{Number correct} - \frac{\text{Number incorrect}}{1} = A$$

**Step F:** To obtain B, your Mathematics Rounded Raw Score, round A to the nearest whole number. (For example, any number from 44.50 to 45.49 rounds to 45.) Enter the resulting figure on the Scoring Worksheet.

**Step G:** To find your Mathematics Scaled Score Range, use the Mathematics Conversion Table (Table 2) to look up the Total Rounded Raw Score you obtained in step F. Enter this range in the box on the Scoring Worksheet.

### SAT Writing Sections 1, 3, and 10

**Step A:** Enter your Essay Score for *Section 1* in the box on the Scoring Worksheet. (On this practice test, your essay score should be from 0 to 6. Keep in mind that on the actual SAT, two readers will read your essay and you will receive a total score of 0 to 12 on your score report.)

**Step B:** Count the number of correct answers and the number of incorrect answers for *Section 3* and record the numbers in the spaces provided on the Scoring Worksheet. (Do not count omitted answers.)

**Step C:** Count the number of correct answers and the number of incorrect answers for *Section 10* and record the numbers in the spaces provided on the Scoring Worksheet. (Do not count omitted answers.)

**Step D:** Total the number of correct responses. Total the number of incorrect responses. Enter the resulting figure on the Scoring Worksheet. To determine A, use the formula:

$$\text{Number correct} - \frac{\text{Number incorrect}}{4} = A$$

**Step E:** To obtain B, your Writing Multiple-Choice (MC) Rounded Raw Score, round A to the nearest whole number. (For example, any number from 44.50 to 45.49 rounds to 45.) Enter the resulting figure on the Scoring Worksheet.

**Step F:** To find your overall Writing Scaled Score Range, use Table 3. Look up the Total MC Rounded Raw Score you obtained in Step E in the left side of Table 3 and the Essay Score entered in Step A across the top of the table. Enter this range in the box on the Scoring Worksheet.

**Step G:** To find your Writing MC Subscore Range, look up the Total MC Rounded Raw Score you obtained in Step E on the Writing Multiple-Choice Conversion Table (Table 4). Enter this range in the box on the Scoring Worksheet.

**Note:** For the **WRITING SECTION**, your Essay Raw Score counts approximately 30% and your Multiple-Choice Raw Score counts approximately 70%.

# SAT Practice Test #9 Scoring Worksheet

## SAT Critical Reading Section

A. Section 4:

_____      _____
no. correct         no. incorrect

+                 +

B. Section 6:

_____      _____
no. correct         no. incorrect

+                 +

C. Section 9:

_____      _____
no. correct         no. incorrect

=                 =

D. Total Unrounded Raw Score

_____ $-$ (_____ $\div 4$) = _____
no. correct         no. incorrect       A

E. Total Rounded Raw Score
(Rounded to nearest whole number)

_____
B

F. Critical Reading Scaled Score Range
(See Table 1)

| _ |
|---|

Critical Reading Scaled Score Range

## SAT Mathematics Section

A. Section 2:
Questions 1-8

_____      _____
no. correct         no. incorrect

+

B. Section 2:
Questions 9-18

_____
no. correct

+                 +

C. Section 5:

_____      _____
no. correct         no. incorrect

+                 +

D. Section 8:

_____      _____
no. correct         no. incorrect

=                 =

E. Total Unrounded Raw Score

_____ $-$ (_____ $\div 4$) = _____
no. correct         no. incorrect       A

F. Total Rounded Raw Score
(Rounded to nearest whole number)

_____
B

G. Mathematics Scaled Score Range
(See Table 2)

| _ |
|---|

Mathematics Scaled Score Range

**SAT Writing Section**

A. Section 1:

Essay Score

B. Section 3: _____  _____
   no. correct        no. incorrect

   +                  +

C. Section 10: _____  _____
   no. correct        no. incorrect

   =                  =

D. Total MC Unrounded Raw Score _____ − (_____ ÷ 4) − ___
   no. correct        no. incorrect        A

E. Total MC Rounded Raw Score   ___
   (Rounded to nearest whole number)    B

F. Writing Scaled Score Range
   (See Table 3)

−

Writing Scaled
Score Range

G. Writing MC Subscore Range
   (See Table 4)

−

Writing MC
Subscore Range

| Table 1. Critical Reading Conversion Table | | | |
|---|---|---|---|
| Raw Score | Scaled Score | Raw Score | Scaled Score |
| 67 | 800 | 30 | 470-530 |
| 66 | 770-800 | 29 | 470-530 |
| 65 | 740-800 | 28 | 460-520 |
| 64 | 720-800 | 27 | 450-510 |
| 63 | 700-800 | 26 | 450-510 |
| 62 | 690-790 | 25 | 440-500 |
| 61 | 670-770 | 24 | 440-500 |
| 60 | 660-760 | 23 | 430-490 |
| 59 | 660-740 | 22 | 420-480 |
| 58 | 650-730 | 21 | 420-480 |
| 57 | 640-720 | 20 | 410-470 |
| 56 | 630-710 | 19 | 400-460 |
| 55 | 630-710 | 18 | 400-460 |
| 54 | 620-700 | 17 | 390-450 |
| 53 | 610-690 | 16 | 380-440 |
| 52 | 600-680 | 15 | 380-440 |
| 51 | 610-670 | 14 | 370-430 |
| 50 | 600-660 | 13 | 360-420 |
| 49 | 590-650 | 12 | 350-410 |
| 48 | 580-640 | 11 | 350-410 |
| 47 | 580-640 | 10 | 340-400 |
| 46 | 570-630 | 9 | 330-390 |
| 45 | 560-620 | 8 | 310-390 |
| 44 | 560-620 | 7 | 300-380 |
| 43 | 550-610 | 6 | 290-370 |
| 42 | 550-610 | 5 | 270-370 |
| 41 | 540-600 | 4 | 260-360 |
| 40 | 530-590 | 3 | 250-350 |
| 39 | 530-590 | 2 | 230-330 |
| 38 | 520-580 | 1 | 220-320 |
| 37 | 510-570 | 0 | 200-290 |
| 36 | 510-570 | -1 | 200-290 |
| 35 | 500-560 | -2 | 200-270 |
| 34 | 500-560 | -3 | 200-250 |
| 33 | 490-550 | -4 | 200-230 |
| 32 | 480-540 | -5 | 200-210 |
| 31 | 480-540 | -6 and below | 200 |

| Table 2. Mathematics Conversion Table | | | |
|---|---|---|---|
| Raw Score | Scaled Score | Raw Score | Scaled Score |
| 54 | 800 | 23 | 460-520 |
| 53 | 750-800 | 22 | 450-510 |
| 52 | 720-800 | 21 | 440-500 |
| 51 | 700-780 | 20 | 430-490 |
| 50 | 690-770 | 19 | 430-490 |
| 49 | 680-740 | 18 | 420-480 |
| 48 | 670-730 | 17 | 410-470 |
| 47 | 660-720 | 16 | 400-460 |
| 46 | 640-700 | 15 | 400-460 |
| 45 | 630-690 | 14 | 390-450 |
| 44 | 620-680 | 13 | 380-440 |
| 43 | 620-680 | 12 | 360-440 |
| 42 | 610-670 | 11 | 350-430 |
| 41 | 600-660 | 10 | 340-420 |
| 40 | 580-660 | 9 | 330-430 |
| 39 | 570-650 | 8 | 320-420 |
| 38 | 560-640 | 7 | 310-410 |
| 37 | 550-630 | 6 | 290-390 |
| 36 | 550-630 | 5 | 280-380 |
| 35 | 540-620 | 4 | 270-370 |
| 34 | 530-610 | 3 | 260-360 |
| 33 | 520-600 | 2 | 240-340 |
| 32 | 520-600 | 1 | 230-330 |
| 31 | 520-580 | 0 | 210-310 |
| 30 | 510-570 | -1 | 200-290 |
| 29 | 500-560 | -2 | 200-270 |
| 28 | 490-550 | -3 | 200-250 |
| 27 | 490-550 | -4 | 200-230 |
| 26 | 480-540 | -5 | 200-210 |
| 25 | 470-530 | -6 and below | 200 |
| 24 | 460-520 | | |

## Table 3. Writing Conversion Table

| MC Raw Score | Essay Score | | | | | | |
|---|---|---|---|---|---|---|---|
| | 0 | 1 | 2 | 3 | 4 | 5 | 6 |
| 49 | 650-690 | 670-720 | 690-740 | 710-770 | 750-800 | 780-800 | 800 |
| 48 | 630-690 | 640-720 | 660-740 | 690-770 | 720-800 | 760-800 | 780-800 |
| 47 | 600-690 | 620-720 | 640-740 | 660-770 | 700-800 | 730-800 | 760-800 |
| 46 | 580-690 | 600-720 | 620-740 | 650-770 | 680-800 | 710-800 | 740-800 |
| 45 | 570-690 | 580-720 | 600-740 | 630-770 | 670-800 | 700-800 | 730-800 |
| 44 | 560-680 | 570-710 | 590-730 | 620-760 | 660-790 | 690-800 | 720-800 |
| 43 | 540-660 | 560-690 | 580-710 | 610-740 | 640-780 | 670-800 | 700-800 |
| 42 | 530-660 | 550-690 | 570-700 | 600-730 | 630-770 | 660-800 | 690-800 |
| 41 | 530-650 | 540-680 | 560-700 | 590-720 | 620-760 | 660-790 | 680-800 |
| 40 | 510-640 | 530-670 | 550-690 | 580-710 | 620-750 | 650-780 | 680-800 |
| 39 | 510-630 | 520-660 | 540-680 | 570-710 | 610-740 | 640-770 | 670-800 |
| 38 | 500-620 | 520-650 | 540-670 | 560-700 | 600-730 | 630-770 | 660-790 |
| 37 | 490-610 | 510-640 | 530-660 | 560-690 | 590-720 | 620-760 | 650-780 |
| 36 | 480-600 | 500-630 | 520-650 | 550-680 | 580-720 | 610-750 | 640-770 |
| 35 | 480-590 | 490-620 | 510-640 | 540-670 | 570-710 | 610-740 | 640-770 |
| 34 | 470-590 | 480-620 | 500-630 | 530-660 | 570-700 | 600-730 | 630-760 |
| 33 | 460-580 | 470-610 | 490-630 | 520-650 | 560-690 | 590-720 | 620-750 |
| 32 | 450-570 | 470-600 | 490-620 | 510-640 | 550-680 | 580-710 | 610-740 |
| 31 | 440-560 | 460-590 | 480-610 | 510-640 | 540-670 | 570-700 | 600-730 |
| 30 | 430-550 | 450-580 | 470-600 | 500-630 | 530-660 | 560-700 | 590-720 |
| 29 | 430-540 | 440-570 | 460-590 | 490-620 | 520-650 | 560-690 | 590-710 |
| 28 | 420-530 | 430-560 | 450-580 | 480-610 | 520-650 | 550-680 | 580-700 |
| 27 | 410-520 | 420-550 | 440-570 | 470-600 | 510-640 | 540-670 | 570-700 |
| 26 | 400-520 | 420-550 | 430-560 | 460-590 | 500-630 | 530-660 | 560-690 |
| 25 | 390-510 | 410-540 | 430-560 | 450-580 | 490-620 | 520-650 | 550-680 |
| 24 | 380-500 | 400-530 | 420-550 | 450-570 | 480-610 | 510-640 | 540-670 |
| 23 | 370-490 | 390-520 | 410-540 | 440-570 | 470-600 | 500-630 | 530-660 |
| 22 | 370-480 | 380-510 | 400-530 | 430-560 | 460-590 | 500-630 | 520-650 |
| 21 | 370-480 | 380-510 | 400-530 | 430-560 | 460-590 | 500-630 | 520-650 |
| 20 | 360-470 | 370-500 | 390-520 | 420-550 | 460-580 | 490-620 | 520-640 |
| 19 | 350-460 | 360-490 | 380-510 | 410-540 | 450-580 | 480-610 | 510-630 |
| 18 | 340-450 | 350-480 | 370-500 | 400-530 | 440-570 | 470-600 | 500-630 |
| 17 | 330-450 | 350-480 | 360-490 | 390-520 | 430-560 | 460-590 | 490-620 |
| 16 | 320-440 | 340-470 | 360-490 | 390-510 | 420-550 | 450-580 | 480-610 |
| 15 | 310-430 | 330-460 | 350-480 | 380-510 | 410-540 | 440-570 | 470-600 |
| 14 | 300-420 | 320-450 | 340-470 | 370-500 | 400-530 | 430-560 | 460-590 |
| 13 | 300-410 | 310-440 | 330-460 | 360-490 | 390-520 | 430-560 | 450-580 |
| 12 | 290-400 | 300-430 | 320-450 | 350-480 | 390-510 | 420-550 | 450-570 |
| 11 | 280-390 | 290-420 | 310-440 | 340-470 | 380-510 | 410-540 | 440-570 |
| 10 | 270-390 | 280-420 | 300-430 | 330-460 | 370-500 | 400-530 | 430-560 |
| 9 | 260-380 | 280-410 | 290-430 | 320-450 | 360-490 | 390-520 | 420-550 |
| 8 | 250-370 | 270-400 | 290-420 | 320-450 | 350-480 | 380-510 | 410-540 |
| 7 | 240-360 | 260-390 | 280-410 | 310-440 | 340-470 | 370-510 | 400-530 |
| 6 | 230-350 | 250-380 | 270-400 | 300-430 | 330-460 | 360-500 | 390-520 |
| 5 | 230-340 | 240-370 | 260-390 | 290-420 | 320-460 | 360-490 | 380-520 |
| 4 | 220-340 | 230-370 | 250-380 | 280-410 | 320-450 | 350-480 | 380-510 |
| 3 | 210-330 | 220-360 | 240-380 | 270-400 | 310-440 | 340-470 | 370-500 |
| 2 | 200-320 | 210-350 | 230-370 | 260-400 | 300-430 | 330-460 | 360-490 |
| 1 | 200-300 | 200-330 | 220-350 | 250-380 | 280-410 | 310-450 | 340-470 |
| 0 | 200-290 | 200-320 | 210-340 | 240-370 | 270-410 | 300-440 | 330-470 |
| -1 | 200-280 | 200-310 | 200-330 | 220-350 | 250-390 | 290-420 | 310-450 |
| -2 | 200-260 | 200-290 | 200-310 | 200-340 | 240-370 | 270-410 | 300-430 |
| -3 | 200-240 | 200-270 | 200-290 | 200-320 | 240-360 | 270-390 | 300-420 |
| -4 | 200-230 | 200-260 | 200-280 | 200-300 | 240-340 | 270-370 | 300-400 |
| -5 | 200 | 200-230 | 200-250 | 200-280 | 240-320 | 270-350 | 300-370 |
| -6 | 200 | 200-220 | 200-240 | 200-270 | 240-310 | 270-340 | 300-370 |
| -7 | 200 | 200-220 | 200-230 | 200-260 | 240-300 | 270-330 | 300-360 |
| -8 | 200 | 200-210 | 200-230 | 200-250 | 240-290 | 270-320 | 300-350 |
| -9 | 200 | 200-210 | 200-230 | 200-250 | 240-290 | 270-320 | 300-350 |
| -10 | 200 | 200-210 | 200-230 | 200-250 | 240-290 | 270-320 | 300-350 |
| -11 | 200 | 200-210 | 200-230 | 200-250 | 240-290 | 270-320 | 300-350 |
| -12 | 200 | 200-210 | 200-230 | 200-250 | 240-290 | 270-320 | 300-350 |

## Table 4. Writing Multiple-Choice Conversion Table

| Raw Score | Scaled Score | Raw Score | Scaled Score |
|-----------|--------------|-----------|--------------|
| 49 | 78-80 | 21 | 46-56 |
| 48 | 77-80 | 20 | 45-55 |
| 47 | 74-80 | 19 | 44-54 |
| 46 | 72-80 | 18 | 43-53 |
| 45 | 70-80 | 17 | 42-52 |
| 44 | 69-79 | 16 | 41-51 |
| 43 | 67-77 | 15 | 40-50 |
| 42 | 66-76 | 14 | 39-49 |
| 41 | 65-75 | 13 | 38-48 |
| 40 | 64-74 | 12 | 37-47 |
| 39 | 63-73 | 11 | 36-46 |
| 38 | 62-72 | 10 | 35-45 |
| 37 | 61-71 | 9 | 34-44 |
| 36 | 60-70 | 8 | 33-43 |
| 35 | 59-69 | 7 | 32-42 |
| 34 | 58-68 | 6 | 31-41 |
| 33 | 57-67 | 5 | 30-40 |
| 32 | 56-66 | 4 | 29-39 |
| 31 | 55-65 | 3 | 28-38 |
| 30 | 54-64 | 2 | 27-37 |
| 29 | 53-63 | 1 | 25-35 |
| 28 | 52-62 | 0 | 24-34 |
| 27 | 51-61 | -1 | 22-32 |
| 26 | 50-60 | -2 | 20-30 |
| 25 | 49-59 | -3 | 20-28 |
| 24 | 48-58 | -4 | 20-26 |
| 23 | 47-57 | -5 | 20-23 |
| 22 | 46-56 | -6 and below | 20-22 |

# SAT Practice Test #10

 **After this test:**

- Use this book to its full potential! Get exclusive access answer explanations, free practice score reports and free sample student essays to help you score your essay in the Book Owners' Area at www.collegeboard.org/satstudyguide.

- Want more practice? Get 10 more official practice tests, auto essay scoring and lesson plans from the test maker by subscribing to *The Official SAT Online Course*. As a book owner, you're entitled to a $10 discount. Sign up at www.collegeboard.org/satstudyguide.

10

*Note:* Section 7, the variable section, has been omitted from this practice test.

# SAT Reasoning Test — General Directions

## Timing

- You will have 3 hours and 45 minutes to work on this test.
- There are ten separately timed sections:
  - ▶ One 25-minute essay
  - ▶ Six other 25-minute sections
  - ▶ Two 20-minute sections
  - ▶ One 10-minute section
- You may work on only one section at a time.
- The supervisor will tell you when to begin and end each section.
- If you finish a section before time is called, check your work on that section. You may NOT turn to any other section.
- Work as rapidly as you can without losing accuracy. Don't waste time on questions that seem too difficult for you.

## Marking Answers

- Be sure to mark your answer sheet properly.

COMPLETE MARK ●     EXAMPLES OF INCOMPLETE MARKS

- You must use a No. 2 pencil.
- Carefully mark only one answer for each question.
- Make sure you fill the entire circle darkly and completely.
- Do not make any stray marks on your answer sheet.
- If you erase, do so completely. Incomplete erasures may be scored as intended answers.
- Use only the answer spaces that correspond to the question numbers.

## Using Your Test Book

- You may use the test book for scratchwork, but you will not receive credit for anything written there.
- After time has been called, you may not transfer answers to your answer sheet or fill in circles.
- You may not fold or remove pages or portions of a page from this book, or take the book or answer sheet from the testing room.

## Scoring

- For each correct answer, you receive one point.
- For questions you omit, you receive no points.
- For a wrong answer to a multiple-choice question, you lose one-fourth of a point.
  - ▶ If you can eliminate one or more of the answer choices as wrong, you increase your chances of choosing the correct answer and earning one point.
  - ▶ If you can't eliminate any choice, move on. You can return to the question later if there is time.
- For a wrong answer to a student-produced response ("grid-in") math question, you don't lose any points.
- Multiple-choice and student-produced response questions are machine scored.
- The essay is scored on a 1 to 6 scale by two different readers. The total essay score is the sum of the two readers' scores.
- Off-topic essays, blank essays, and essays written in ink will receive a score of zero.

The passages for this test have been adapted from published material. The ideas contained in them do not necessarily represent the opinions of the College Board.

10

**IMPORTANT:** The codes below are unique to your test book. Copy them on your answer sheet in boxes 8 and 9 and <u>fill in the corresponding circles exactly as shown.</u>

**9  TEST FORM**
(Copy from back of test book.)

**8  FORM CODE**
(Copy and grid as on back of test book.)

## DO NOT OPEN THIS BOOK UNTIL THE SUPERVISOR TELLS YOU TO DO SO.

938

## SAT Reasoning Test™

**1** Your Name:
(Print)

Last                                    First                                    M.I.

I agree to the conditions on the back of the SAT Reasoning Test™ booklet. I also agree to use only a No. 2 pencil to complete my answer sheet.

Signature: _____    Date: __/__/__

Home Address: _____
(Print)                Number and Street              City                    State        Zip Code

Home Phone: ( ) _____    Center: _____
(Print)                                (Print)              City                    State/Country

**2 YOUR NAME**

Last Name (First 6 Letters)    First Name (First 4 Letters)    Mid. Init.

**3 DATE OF BIRTH**

| MONTH | DAY | YEAR |
|---|---|---|
| ○ Jan | | |
| ○ Feb | ⓪⓪ | ⓪ |
| ○ Mar | ①① | ① |
| ○ Apr | ②② | ② |
| ○ May | ③③ | ③ |
| ○ Jun | ④ | ④ |
| ○ Jul | ⑤⑤ | ⑤ |
| ○ Aug | ⑥⑥ | ⑥ |
| ○ Sep | ⑦⑦ | ⑦ |
| ○ Oct | ⑧⑧ | ⑧ |
| ○ Nov | ⑨⑨ | ⑨ |
| ○ Dec | | |

**5 SEX**
○ Female    ○ Male

**6 REGISTRATION NUMBER**
(Copy from Admission Ticket.)

○ I turned in my registration form today.

**Important:** Fill in items 8 and 9 exactly as shown on the back of test book.

**9 TEST FORM**
(Copy from back of test book.)

**8 FORM CODE**
(Copy and grid as on back of test book.)

**10 TEST BOOK SERIAL NUMBER**
(Copy from front of test book.)

**11 TEST CENTER**
(Supplied by Test Center Supervisor.)

**4 ZIP CODE**

**7 SOCIAL SECURITY NUMBER**

**FOR OFFICIAL USE ONLY**
⓪①②③④⑤⑥
⓪①②③④⑤⑥
⓪①②③④⑤⑥

PLEASE DO NOT WRITE IN THIS AREA    ○○○○○○○○○○○○○○○○○○○○○○○○○○○○○○○    **SERIAL #**

10

**SECTION 1**

*IMPORTANT:* **USE A NO. 2 PENCIL. DO NOT WRITE OUTSIDE THE BORDER!**
Words written outside the essay box or written in ink **WILL NOT APPEAR** in the copy sent to be scored, and your score will be affected.

**Begin your essay on this page. If you need more space, continue on the next page.**

Page 3

## SECTION 2

1  Ⓐ Ⓑ Ⓒ Ⓓ Ⓔ     11  Ⓐ Ⓑ Ⓒ Ⓓ Ⓔ     21  Ⓐ Ⓑ Ⓒ Ⓓ Ⓔ     31  Ⓐ Ⓑ Ⓒ Ⓓ Ⓔ
2  Ⓐ Ⓑ Ⓒ Ⓓ Ⓔ     12  Ⓐ Ⓑ Ⓒ Ⓓ Ⓔ     22  Ⓐ Ⓑ Ⓒ Ⓓ Ⓔ     32  Ⓐ Ⓑ Ⓒ Ⓓ Ⓔ
3  Ⓐ Ⓑ Ⓒ Ⓓ Ⓔ     13  Ⓐ Ⓑ Ⓒ Ⓓ Ⓔ     23  Ⓐ Ⓑ Ⓒ Ⓓ Ⓔ     00  Ⓐ Ⓑ Ⓒ Ⓓ Ⓔ
4  Ⓐ Ⓑ Ⓒ Ⓓ Ⓔ     14  Ⓐ Ⓑ Ⓒ Ⓓ Ⓔ     24  Ⓐ Ⓑ Ⓒ Ⓓ Ⓔ     34  Ⓐ Ⓑ Ⓒ Ⓓ Ⓔ
5  Ⓐ Ⓑ Ⓒ Ⓓ Ⓔ     15  Ⓐ Ⓑ Ⓒ Ⓓ Ⓔ     25  Ⓐ Ⓑ Ⓒ Ⓓ Ⓔ     35  Ⓐ Ⓑ Ⓒ Ⓓ Ⓔ
6  Ⓐ Ⓑ Ⓒ Ⓓ Ⓔ     16  Ⓐ Ⓑ Ⓒ Ⓓ Ⓔ     26  Ⓐ Ⓑ Ⓒ Ⓓ Ⓔ     36  Ⓐ Ⓑ Ⓒ Ⓓ Ⓔ
7  Ⓐ Ⓑ Ⓒ Ⓓ Ⓔ     17  Ⓐ Ⓑ Ⓒ Ⓓ Ⓔ     27  Ⓐ Ⓑ Ⓒ Ⓓ Ⓔ     37  Ⓐ Ⓑ Ⓒ Ⓓ Ⓔ
8  Ⓐ Ⓑ Ⓒ Ⓓ Ⓔ     18  Ⓐ Ⓑ Ⓒ Ⓓ Ⓔ     28  Ⓐ Ⓑ Ⓒ Ⓓ Ⓔ     38  Ⓐ Ⓑ Ⓒ Ⓓ Ⓔ
9  Ⓐ Ⓑ Ⓒ Ⓓ Ⓔ     19  Ⓐ Ⓑ Ⓒ Ⓓ Ⓔ     29  Ⓐ Ⓑ Ⓒ Ⓓ Ⓔ     39  Ⓐ Ⓑ Ⓒ Ⓓ Ⓔ
10 Ⓐ Ⓑ Ⓒ Ⓓ Ⓔ     20  Ⓐ Ⓑ Ⓒ Ⓓ Ⓔ     30  Ⓐ Ⓑ Ⓒ Ⓓ Ⓔ     40  Ⓐ Ⓑ Ⓒ Ⓓ Ⓔ

## SECTION 3

1  Ⓐ Ⓑ Ⓒ Ⓓ Ⓔ     11  Ⓐ Ⓑ Ⓒ Ⓓ Ⓔ     21  Ⓐ Ⓑ Ⓒ Ⓓ Ⓔ     31  Ⓐ Ⓑ Ⓒ Ⓓ Ⓔ
2  Ⓐ Ⓑ Ⓒ Ⓓ Ⓔ     12  Ⓐ Ⓑ Ⓒ Ⓓ Ⓔ     22  Ⓐ Ⓑ Ⓒ Ⓓ Ⓔ     32  Ⓐ Ⓑ Ⓒ Ⓓ Ⓔ
3  Ⓐ Ⓑ Ⓒ Ⓓ Ⓔ     13  Ⓐ Ⓑ Ⓒ Ⓓ Ⓔ     23  Ⓐ Ⓑ Ⓒ Ⓓ Ⓔ     33  Ⓐ Ⓑ Ⓒ Ⓓ Ⓔ
4  Ⓐ Ⓑ Ⓒ Ⓓ Ⓔ     14  Ⓐ Ⓑ Ⓒ Ⓓ Ⓔ     24  Ⓐ Ⓑ Ⓒ Ⓓ Ⓔ     34  Ⓐ Ⓑ Ⓒ Ⓓ Ⓔ
5  Ⓐ Ⓑ Ⓒ Ⓓ Ⓔ     15  Ⓐ Ⓑ Ⓒ Ⓓ Ⓔ     25  Ⓐ Ⓑ Ⓒ Ⓓ Ⓔ     35  Ⓐ Ⓑ Ⓒ Ⓓ Ⓔ
6  Ⓐ Ⓑ Ⓒ Ⓓ Ⓔ     16  Ⓐ Ⓑ Ⓒ Ⓓ Ⓔ     26  Ⓐ Ⓑ Ⓒ Ⓓ Ⓔ     36  Ⓐ Ⓑ Ⓒ Ⓓ Ⓔ
7  Ⓐ Ⓑ Ⓒ Ⓓ Ⓔ     17  Ⓐ Ⓑ Ⓒ Ⓓ Ⓔ     27  Ⓐ Ⓑ Ⓒ Ⓓ Ⓔ     37  Ⓐ Ⓑ Ⓒ Ⓓ Ⓔ
8  Ⓐ Ⓑ Ⓒ Ⓓ Ⓔ     18  Ⓐ Ⓑ Ⓒ Ⓓ Ⓔ     28  Ⓐ Ⓑ Ⓒ Ⓓ Ⓔ     38  Ⓐ Ⓑ Ⓒ Ⓓ Ⓔ
9  Ⓐ Ⓑ Ⓒ Ⓓ Ⓔ     19  Ⓐ Ⓑ Ⓒ Ⓓ Ⓔ     29  Ⓐ Ⓑ Ⓒ Ⓓ Ⓔ     39  Ⓐ Ⓑ Ⓒ Ⓓ Ⓔ
10 Ⓐ Ⓑ Ⓒ Ⓓ Ⓔ     20  Ⓐ Ⓑ Ⓒ Ⓓ Ⓔ     30  Ⓐ Ⓑ Ⓒ Ⓓ Ⓔ     40  Ⓐ Ⓑ Ⓒ Ⓓ Ⓔ

**CAUTION**  Grid answers in the section below for SECTION 2 or SECTION 3 only if directed to do so in your test book.

## Student-Produced Responses

ONLY ANSWERS THAT ARE GRIDDED WILL BE SCORED. YOU WILL NOT RECEIVE CREDIT FOR ANYTHING WRITTEN IN THE BOXES.

Quality Assurance Mark

9   10   11   12   13

14   15   16   17   18

Page 4

942

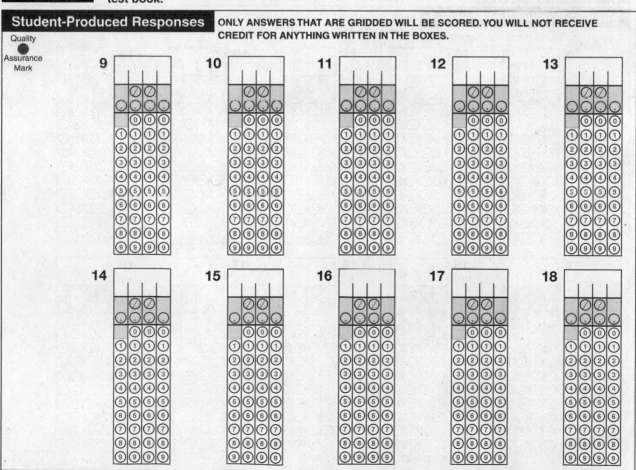

**SECTION 4**

1 Ⓐ Ⓑ Ⓒ Ⓓ Ⓔ     11 Ⓐ Ⓑ Ⓒ Ⓓ Ⓔ     21 Ⓐ Ⓑ Ⓒ Ⓓ Ⓔ     31 Ⓐ Ⓑ Ⓒ Ⓓ Ⓔ
2 Ⓐ Ⓑ Ⓒ Ⓓ Ⓔ     12 Ⓐ Ⓑ Ⓒ Ⓓ Ⓔ     22 Ⓐ Ⓑ Ⓒ Ⓓ Ⓔ     32 Ⓐ Ⓑ Ⓒ Ⓓ Ⓔ
3 Ⓐ Ⓑ Ⓒ Ⓓ Ⓔ     13 Ⓐ Ⓑ Ⓒ Ⓓ Ⓔ     23 Ⓐ Ⓑ Ⓒ Ⓓ Ⓔ     33 Ⓐ Ⓑ Ⓒ Ⓓ Ⓔ
4 Ⓐ Ⓑ Ⓒ Ⓓ Ⓔ     14 Ⓐ Ⓑ Ⓒ Ⓓ Ⓔ     24 Ⓐ Ⓑ Ⓒ Ⓓ Ⓔ     34 Ⓐ Ⓑ Ⓒ Ⓓ Ⓔ
5 Ⓐ Ⓑ Ⓒ Ⓓ Ⓔ     15 Ⓐ Ⓑ Ⓒ Ⓓ Ⓔ     25 Ⓐ Ⓑ Ⓒ Ⓓ Ⓔ     35 Ⓐ Ⓑ Ⓒ Ⓓ Ⓔ
6 Ⓐ Ⓑ Ⓒ Ⓓ Ⓔ     16 Ⓐ Ⓑ Ⓒ Ⓓ Ⓔ     26 Ⓐ Ⓑ Ⓒ Ⓓ Ⓔ     36 Ⓐ Ⓑ Ⓒ Ⓓ Ⓔ
7 Ⓐ Ⓑ Ⓒ Ⓓ Ⓔ     17 Ⓐ Ⓑ Ⓒ Ⓓ Ⓔ     27 Ⓐ Ⓑ Ⓒ Ⓓ Ⓔ     37 Ⓐ Ⓑ Ⓒ Ⓓ Ⓔ
8 Ⓐ Ⓑ Ⓒ Ⓓ Ⓔ     18 Ⓐ Ⓑ Ⓒ Ⓓ Ⓔ     28 Ⓐ Ⓑ Ⓒ Ⓓ Ⓔ     38 Ⓐ Ⓑ Ⓒ Ⓓ Ⓔ
9 Ⓐ Ⓑ Ⓒ Ⓓ Ⓔ     19 Ⓐ Ⓑ Ⓒ Ⓓ Ⓔ     29 Ⓐ Ⓑ Ⓒ Ⓓ Ⓔ     39 Ⓐ Ⓑ Ⓒ Ⓓ Ⓔ
10 Ⓐ Ⓑ Ⓒ Ⓓ Ⓔ    20 Ⓐ Ⓑ Ⓒ Ⓓ Ⓔ     30 Ⓐ Ⓑ Ⓒ Ⓓ Ⓔ     40 Ⓐ Ⓑ Ⓒ Ⓓ Ⓔ

**SECTION 5**

1 Ⓐ Ⓑ Ⓒ Ⓓ Ⓔ     11 Ⓐ Ⓑ Ⓒ Ⓓ Ⓔ     21 Ⓐ Ⓑ Ⓒ Ⓓ Ⓔ     31 Ⓐ Ⓑ Ⓒ Ⓓ Ⓔ
2 Ⓐ Ⓑ Ⓒ Ⓓ Ⓔ     12 Ⓐ Ⓑ Ⓒ Ⓓ Ⓔ     22 Ⓐ Ⓑ Ⓒ Ⓓ Ⓔ     32 Ⓐ Ⓑ Ⓒ Ⓓ Ⓔ
3 Ⓐ Ⓑ Ⓒ Ⓓ Ⓔ     13 Ⓐ Ⓑ Ⓒ Ⓓ Ⓔ     23 Ⓐ Ⓑ Ⓒ Ⓓ Ⓔ     33 Ⓐ Ⓑ Ⓒ Ⓓ Ⓔ
4 Ⓐ Ⓑ Ⓒ Ⓓ Ⓔ     14 Ⓐ Ⓑ Ⓒ Ⓓ Ⓔ     24 Ⓐ Ⓑ Ⓒ Ⓓ Ⓔ     34 Ⓐ Ⓑ Ⓒ Ⓓ Ⓔ
5 Ⓐ Ⓑ Ⓒ Ⓓ Ⓔ     15 Ⓐ Ⓑ Ⓒ Ⓓ Ⓔ     25 Ⓐ Ⓑ Ⓒ Ⓓ Ⓔ     35 Ⓐ Ⓑ Ⓒ Ⓓ Ⓔ
6 Ⓐ Ⓑ Ⓒ Ⓓ Ⓔ     16 Ⓐ Ⓑ Ⓒ Ⓓ Ⓔ     26 Ⓐ Ⓑ Ⓒ Ⓓ Ⓔ     36 Ⓐ Ⓑ Ⓒ Ⓓ Ⓔ
7 Ⓐ Ⓑ Ⓒ Ⓓ Ⓔ     17 Ⓐ Ⓑ Ⓒ Ⓓ Ⓔ     27 Ⓐ Ⓑ Ⓒ Ⓓ Ⓔ     37 Ⓐ Ⓑ Ⓒ Ⓓ Ⓔ
8 Ⓐ Ⓑ Ⓒ Ⓓ Ⓔ     18 Ⓐ Ⓑ Ⓒ Ⓓ Ⓔ     28 Ⓐ Ⓑ Ⓒ Ⓓ Ⓔ     38 Ⓐ Ⓑ Ⓒ Ⓓ Ⓔ
9 Ⓐ Ⓑ Ⓒ Ⓓ Ⓔ     19 Ⓐ Ⓑ Ⓒ Ⓓ Ⓔ     29 Ⓐ Ⓑ Ⓒ Ⓓ Ⓔ     39 Ⓐ Ⓑ Ⓒ Ⓓ Ⓔ
10 Ⓐ Ⓑ Ⓒ Ⓓ Ⓔ    20 Ⓐ Ⓑ Ⓒ Ⓓ Ⓔ     30 Ⓐ Ⓑ Ⓒ Ⓓ Ⓔ     40 Ⓐ Ⓑ Ⓒ Ⓓ Ⓔ

**CAUTION** Grid answers in the section below for SECTION 4 or SECTION 5 only if directed to do so in your test book.

**Student-Produced Responses** ONLY ANSWERS THAT ARE GRIDDED WILL BE SCORED. YOU WILL NOT RECEIVE CREDIT FOR ANYTHING WRITTEN IN THE BOXES.

Quality Assurance Mark

Page 5

943

**SECTION 6**

1 A B C D E　11 A B C D E　21 A B C D E　31 A B C D E
2 A B C D E　12 A B C D E　22 A B C D E　32 A B C D E
3 A B C D E　13 A B C D E　23 A B C D E　33 A B C D E
4 A B C D E　14 A B C D E　24 A B C D E　34 A B C D E
5 A B C D E　15 A B C D E　25 A B C D E　35 A B C D E
6 A B C D E　16 A B C D E　26 A B C D E　36 A B C D E
7 A B C D E　17 A B C D E　27 A B C D E　37 A B C D E
8 A B C D E　18 A B C D E　28 A B C D E　38 A B C D E
9 A B C D E　19 A B C D E　29 A B C D E　39 A B C D E
10 A B C D E　20 A B C D E　30 A B C D E　40 A B C D E

**SECTION 7**

1 A B C D E　11 A B C D E　21 A B C D E　31 A B C D E
2 A B C D E　12 A B C D E　22 A B C D E　32 A B C D E
3 A B C D E　13 A B C D E　23 A B C D E　33 A B C D E
4 A B C D E　14 A B C D E　24 A B C D E　34 A B C D E
5 A B C D E　15 A B C D E　25 A B C D E　35 A B C D E
6 A B C D E　16 A B C D E　26 A B C D E　36 A B C D E
7 A B C D E　17 A B C D E　27 A B C D E　37 A B C D E
8 A B C D E　18 A B C D E　28 A B C D E　38 A B C D E
9 A B C D E　19 A B C D E　29 A B C D E　39 A B C D E
10 A B C D E　20 A B C D E　30 A B C D E　40 A B C D E

**CAUTION** Grid answers in the section below for SECTION 6 or SECTION 7 only if directed to do so in your test book.

**Student-Produced Responses** ONLY ANSWERS THAT ARE GRIDDED WILL BE SCORED. YOU WILL NOT RECEIVE CREDIT FOR ANYTHING WRITTEN IN THE BOXES.

9　10　11　12　13

Quality Assurance Mark

14　15　16　17　18

Page 6

PLEASE DO NOT WRITE IN THIS AREA

**SERIAL #**

COMPLETE MARK ● EXAMPLES OF INCOMPLETE MARKS

You must use a No. 2 pencil and marks must be complete. Do not use a mechanical pencil. It is very important that you fill in the entire circle darkly and completely. If you change your response, erase as completely as possible. Incomplete marks or erasures may affect your score.

SECTION 8

| 1 | A B C D E | 11 | A B C D E | 21 | A B C D E | 31 | A B C D E |
| 2 | A B C D E | 12 | A B C D E | 22 | A B C D E | 32 | A B C D E |
| 3 | A B C D E | 13 | A B C D E | 23 | A B C D E | 33 | A B C D E |
| 4 | A B C D E | 14 | A B C D E | 24 | A B C D E | 34 | A B C D E |
| 5 | A B C D E | 15 | A B C D E | 25 | A B C D E | 35 | A B C D E |
| 6 | A B C D E | 16 | A B C D E | 26 | A B C D E | 36 | A B C D E |
| 7 | A B C D E | 17 | A B C D E | 27 | A B C D E | 37 | A B C D E |
| 8 | A B C D E | 18 | A B C D E | 28 | A B C D E | 38 | A B C D E |
| 9 | A B C D E | 19 | A B C D E | 29 | A B C D E | 39 | A B C D E |
| 10 | A B C D E | 20 | A B C D E | 30 | A B C D E | 40 | A B C D E |

SECTION 9

| 1 | A B C D E | 11 | A B C D E | 21 | A B C D E | 31 | A B C D E |
| 2 | A B C D E | 12 | A B C D E | 22 | A B C D E | 32 | A B C D E |
| 3 | A B C D E | 13 | A B C D E | 23 | A B C D E | 33 | A B C D E |
| 4 | A B C D F | 14 | A B C D E | 24 | A B C D E | 34 | A B C D E |
| 5 | A B C D E | 15 | A B C D E | 25 | A B C D E | 35 | A B C D E |
| 6 | A B C D E | 16 | A B C D E | 26 | A B C D E | 36 | A B C D E |
| 7 | A B C D E | 17 | A B C D E | 27 | A B C D E | 37 | A B C D E |
| 8 | A B C D E | 18 | A B C D E | 28 | A B C D E | 38 | A B C D E |
| 9 | A B C D E | 19 | A B C D E | 29 | A B C D E | 39 | A B C D F |
| 10 | A B C D E | 20 | A B C D E | 30 | A B C D E | 40 | A B C D E |

Quality
● Assurance
Mark

SECTION 10

| 1 | A B C D E | 11 | A B C D E | 21 | A B C D E | 31 | A B C D E |
| 2 | A B C D E | 12 | A B C D E | 22 | A B C D E | 32 | A B C D E |
| 3 | A B C D E | 13 | A B C D E | 23 | A B C D E | 33 | A B C D E |
| 4 | A B C D E | 14 | A B C D E | 24 | A B C D E | 34 | A B C D E |
| 5 | A B C D E | 15 | A B C D E | 25 | A B C D E | 35 | A B C D E |
| 6 | A B C D E | 16 | A B C D F | 26 | A B C D E | 36 | A B C D E |
| 7 | A B C D E | 17 | A B C D E | 27 | A B C D E | 37 | A B C D E |
| 8 | A B C D E | 18 | A D C D E | 28 | A B C D E | 38 | A B C D E |
| 9 | A B C D E | 19 | A B C D E | 29 | A B C D E | 39 | A B C D E |
| 10 | A B C D E | 20 | A B C D E | 30 | A B C D E | 40 | A B C D E |

## CERTIFICATION STATEMENT

Copy the statement below (do not print) and sign your name as you would an official document.

I hereby agree to the conditions set forth online at www.collegeboard.org and/or in the SAT® Registration Booklet and certify that I am the person whose name and address appear on this answer sheet.

_____

_____

_____

_____

By signing below, I agree not to share any specific test questions or essay topics with anyone by any form of communication, including, but not limited to: email, text messages, or use of the Internet.

Signature _____     Date _____

## SPECIAL QUESTIONS

1 Ⓐ Ⓑ Ⓒ Ⓓ Ⓔ Ⓕ Ⓖ Ⓗ Ⓘ Ⓙ
2 Ⓐ Ⓑ Ⓒ Ⓓ Ⓔ Ⓕ Ⓖ Ⓗ Ⓘ Ⓙ
3 Ⓐ Ⓑ Ⓒ Ⓓ Ⓔ Ⓕ Ⓖ Ⓗ Ⓘ Ⓙ
4 Ⓐ Ⓑ Ⓒ Ⓓ Ⓔ Ⓕ Ⓖ Ⓗ Ⓘ Ⓙ
5 Ⓐ Ⓑ Ⓒ Ⓓ Ⓔ Ⓕ Ⓖ Ⓗ Ⓘ Ⓙ
6 Ⓐ Ⓑ Ⓒ Ⓓ Ⓔ Ⓕ Ⓖ Ⓗ Ⓘ Ⓙ
7 Ⓐ Ⓑ Ⓒ Ⓓ Ⓔ Ⓕ Ⓖ Ⓗ Ⓘ Ⓙ
8 Ⓐ Ⓑ Ⓒ Ⓓ Ⓔ Ⓕ Ⓖ Ⓗ Ⓘ Ⓙ

SERIAL #

## ESSAY
### Time — 25 minutes

---

**Turn to page 2 of your answer sheet to write your ESSAY.**

---

The essay gives you an opportunity to show how effectively you can develop and express ideas. You should, therefore, take care to develop your point of view, present your ideas logically and clearly, and use language precisely.

Your essay must be written on the lines provided on your answer sheet—you will receive no other paper on which to write. You will have enough space if you write on every line, avoid wide margins, and keep your handwriting to a reasonable size. Remember that people who are not familiar with your handwriting will read what you write. Try to write or print so that what you are writing is legible to those readers.

**Important Reminders:**

- **A pencil is required for the essay.** An essay written in ink will receive a score of zero.
- **Do not write your essay in your test book.** You will receive credit only for what you write on your answer sheet.
- **An off-topic essay will receive a score of zero.**
- **If your essay does not reflect your original and individual work, your test scores may be canceled.**

You have twenty-five minutes to write an essay on the topic assigned below.

---

Think carefully about the issue presented in the following excerpt and the assignment below.

> Traditionally the term "heroism" has been applied to those who have braved physical danger to defend a cause or to protect others. But one of the most feared dangers people face is that of disapproval by their family, peers, or community. Sometimes acting courageously requires someone to speak out at the risk of such rejection. We should consider those who do so true heroes.

**Assignment:** Should heroes be defined as people who say what they think when we ourselves lack the courage to say it? Plan and write an essay in which you develop your point of view on this issue. Support your position with reasoning and examples taken from your reading, studies, experience, or observations.

---

BEGIN WRITING YOUR ESSAY ON PAGE 2 OF THE ANSWER SHEET.

---

**If you finish before time is called, you may check your work on this section only.
Do not turn to any other section in the test.**

## SECTION 2
### Time — 25 minutes
### 18 Questions

**Turn to Section 2 (page 4) of your answer sheet to answer the questions in this section.**

**Directions:** This section contains two types of questions. You have 25 minutes to complete both types. For questions 1-8, solve each problem and decide which is the best of the choices given. Fill in the corresponding circle on the answer sheet. You may use any available space for scratchwork.

**Notes**

1. The use of a calculator is permitted.
2. All numbers used are real numbers.
3. Figures that accompany problems in this test are intended to provide information useful in solving the problems. They are drawn as accurately as possible EXCEPT when it is stated in a specific problem that the figure is not drawn to scale. All figures lie in a plane unless otherwise indicated.
4. Unless otherwise specified, the domain of any function $f$ is assumed to be the set of all real numbers $x$ for which $f(x)$ is a real number.

**Reference Information**

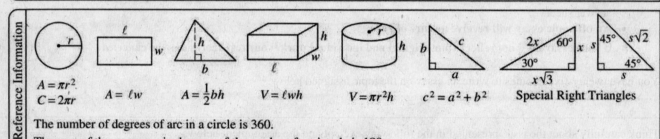

$A = \pi r^2$
$C = 2\pi r$

$A = \ell w$

$A = \frac{1}{2}bh$

$V = \ell wh$

$V = \pi r^2 h$

$c^2 = a^2 + b^2$

Special Right Triangles

The number of degrees of arc in a circle is 360.
The sum of the measures in degrees of the angles of a triangle is 180.

---

**1.** The total cost of 3 equally priced mechanical pencils is $4.50. If the cost per pencil is increased by $0.50, how much will 5 of these pencils cost at the new rate?

(A) $7.50
(B) $8.00
(C) $9.00
(D) $9.50
(E) $10.00

---

| $x$ | 1 | 2 | 3 | 4 |
|-----|---|---|----|----|
| $y$ | 3 | 7 | 11 | 15 |

**2.** The table above represents a relationship between $x$ and $y$. Which of the following linear equations describes the relationship?

(A) $y = x + 1$
(B) $y = x + 4$
(C) $y = 3x$
(D) $y = 4x$
(E) $y = 4x - 1$

---

**GO ON TO THE NEXT PAGE**

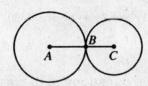

Note: Figure not drawn to scale.

**3.** In the figure above, the two circles are tangent at point $B$ and $AC = 6$. If the circumference of the circle with center $A$ is twice the circumference of the circle with center $C$, what is the length of $\overline{BC}$ ?

(A) 1
(B) 2
(C) 3
(D) 4
(E) 6

**SURVEY RESULTS**

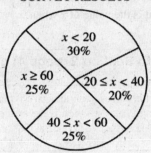

**5.** The chart above shows the results when 1,000 people were asked, "How old are you?" The age they gave is represented by $x$. How many people said that their age was less than 40 ?

(A) 200
(B) 300
(C) 450
(D) 500
(E) 550

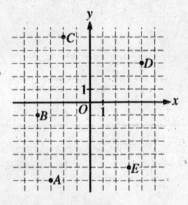

**4.** Which of the lettered points in the figure above has coordinates $(x, y)$ such that $|x| - |y| = 3$ ?

(A) $A$
(B) $B$
(C) $C$
(D) $D$
(E) $E$

**6.** Which of the following could be the remainders when 4 consecutive positive integers are each divided by 3 ?

(A) 1, 2, 3, 1
(B) 1, 2, 3, 4
(C) 0, 1, 2, 3
(D) 0, 1, 2, 0
(E) 0, 2, 3, 0

**GO ON TO THE NEXT PAGE**

**7.** If $y$ is inversely proportional to $x$ and $y = 15$ when $x = 5$, what is the value of $y$ when $x = 25$ ?

(A) $\dfrac{1}{5}$

(B) $\dfrac{1}{3}$

(C) 3

(D) 5

(E) 75

**8.** If $2x + z = 2y$ and $2x + 2y + z = 20$, what is the value of $y$ ?

(A) 5
(B) 8
(C) 10
(D) 15
(E) It cannot be determined from the information given.

GO ON TO THE NEXT PAGE

**Directions:** For Student-Produced Response questions 9-18, use the grids at the bottom of the answer sheet page on which you have answered questions 1-8.

Each of the remaining 10 questions requires you to solve the problem and enter your answer by marking the circles in the special grid, as shown in the examples below. You may use any available space for scratchwork.

Answer: $\frac{7}{12}$      Answer: 2.5      Answer: 201 Either position is correct.

Write answer → in boxes.

← Fraction line

Grid in → result.

← Decimal point

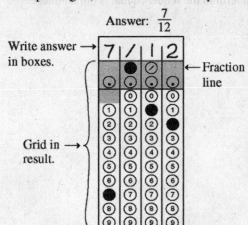

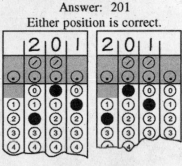

**Note:** You may start your answers in any column, space permitting. Columns not needed should be left blank.

- Mark no more than one circle in any column.

- Because the answer sheet will be machine-scored, **you will receive credit only if the circles are filled in correctly.**

- Although not required, it is suggested that you write your answer in the boxes at the top of the columns to help you fill in the circles accurately.

- Some problems may have more than one correct answer. In such cases, grid only one answer.

- No question has a negative answer.

- **Mixed numbers** such as $3\frac{1}{2}$ must be gridded as 3.5 or 7/2. (If [3|1|/|2] is gridded, it will be interpreted as $\frac{31}{2}$, not $3\frac{1}{2}$.)

- **Decimal Answers:** If you obtain a decimal answer with more digits than the grid can accommodate, it may be either rounded or truncated, but it must fill the entire grid. For example, if you obtain an answer such as 0.6666..., you should record your result as .666 or .667. **A less accurate value such as .66 or .67 will be scored as incorrect.**

Acceptable ways to grid $\frac{2}{3}$ are:

9. If $2(x - 3) = 7$, what is the value of $x$?

10. Point $P$ lies on the line with equation $y - 4 = 3(x - 2)$. If the $x$-coordinate of $P$ is 4, what is the $y$-coordinate of $P$?

**GO ON TO THE NEXT PAGE** →

**11.** Car *A* traveled 60 miles and averaged 20 miles per gallon of gasoline. If car *B* traveled 15 miles for each gallon of gasoline it used, how many miles had car *B* traveled when it had used the same amount of gasoline that car *A* used to travel 60 miles?

**13.** The first term of a sequence is 20 and the second term is 8. The third term and each term thereafter is the average (arithmetic mean) of the two terms immediately preceding it. What is the value of the first term in the sequence that is <u>not</u> an integer?

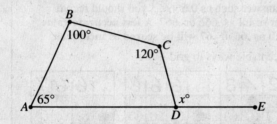

**12.** In the figure above, points *A*, *D*, and *E* lie on the same line. What is the value of *x* ?

**14.** If *x* is $\frac{1}{5}$ of *y*, *y* is $\frac{3}{10}$ of *z*, and $z > 0$, then *x* is what fraction of *z* ?

**GO ON TO THE NEXT PAGE**

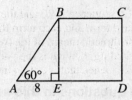

**15.** In the figure above, *EBCD* is a square and *AE* = 8. What is the area of *EBCD* ?

**16.** In a mixture of peanuts and cashews, the ratio by weight of peanuts to cashews is 5 to 2. How many pounds of cashews will there be in 4 pounds of this mixture?

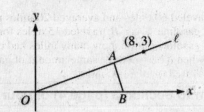

**17.** Line *m* (not shown) passes through *O* and intersects $\overline{AB}$ between *A* and *B*. What is one possible value of the slope of line *m* ?

WESTON HIGH SCHOOL ENROLLMENT

| Year | Number of Students Enrolled |
|------|------------------------------|
| 1992 | *x* |
| 1993 | 1552 |
| 1994 | 1238 |
| 1995 | 1459 |
| 1996 | 1351 |

**18.** The table above shows student enrollment at Weston High School from 1992 through 1996. If the median enrollment for the five years was 1351, and no two years had the same enrollment, what is the greatest possible value for *x* ?

# STOP
**If you finish before time is called, you may check your work on this section only.**
**Do not turn to any other section in the test.**

## SECTION 3
**Time — 25 minutes**
**35 Questions**

---

**Turn to Section 3 (page 4) of your answer sheet to answer the questions in this section.**

---

**Directions:** For each question in this section, select the best answer from among the choices given and fill in the corresponding circle on the answer sheet.

---

The following sentences test correctness and effectiveness of expression. Part of each sentence or the entire sentence is underlined; beneath each sentence are five ways of phrasing the underlined material. Choice A repeats the original phrasing; the other four choices are different. If you think the original phrasing produces a better sentence than any of the alternatives, select choice A; if not, select one of the other choices.

In making your selection, follow the requirements of standard written English; that is, pay attention to grammar, choice of words, sentence construction, and punctuation. Your selection should result in the most effective sentence—clear and precise, without awkwardness or ambiguity.

EXAMPLE:

Laura Ingalls Wilder published her first book <u>and she was sixty-five years old then</u>.

(A) and she was sixty-five years old then
(B) when she was sixty-five
(C) at age sixty-five years old
(D) upon the reaching of sixty-five years
(E) at the time when she was sixty-five

1. Although several groups strongly opposed the new hiring policies of the city council, other groups <u>being enthusiastic in their support of</u> the new rules.

   (A) being enthusiastic in their support of
   (B) were enthusiastic and supportive of
   (C) enthusiastically supported
   (D) enthusiastically supporting
   (E) are enthusiastically supportive of

2. The problem of water <u>pollution, frequently compounded in certain areas because</u> the treatment and release of industrial wastes are not adequately regulated.

   (A) pollution, frequently compounded in certain areas because
   (B) pollution, frequently compounded in certain areas and
   (C) pollution, frequently compounded in certain areas when
   (D) pollution is frequently compounded in certain areas where
   (E) pollution is frequently compounded in certain areas and

3. <u>Having been a victim of malicious rumors,</u> Helen purposely avoided gossips.

   (A) Having been a victim of malicious rumors,
   (B) Her being a victim of malicious rumors,
   (C) Her having been victimized by malicious rumors,
   (D) Because being a victim of malicious rumors,
   (E) Because having been a victim of malicious rumors,

4. In many states, <u>they have laws to allow students to vote wherever</u> they choose, either at their homes or at their college residences.

   (A) they have laws to allow students to vote wherever
   (B) they have laws allowing students to vote where
   (C) their laws allowing students to vote wherever
   (D) the laws allow students to vote wherever
   (E) the laws allow students to vote in the place where

GO ON TO THE NEXT PAGE

5. While driving down the road, the house with the large yard and small pond attracted the family's attention.

(A) the house with the large yard and small pond attracted the family's attention
(B) the house having the large yard and a small pond attracted the attention of the family
(C) the house with the yard and small pond was attractive to the family's attention
(D) the family's attention was attracted by the house with the large yard and small pond
(E) the family was attracted to the house with the large yard and small pond

6. The chestnut, like the oak, is called an immortal tree, the reason is that the trunk and roots remain alive even after the tree has been felled.

(A) tree, the reason is that the trunk and roots remain
(B) tree, which has a trunk and roots that are remaining
(C) tree, the trunk of which and the roots remain
(D) tree because its trunk and roots remain
(E) tree, whose trunk and roots are remaining

7. Both Dr. Henderson and Dr. Ball being widely known for having authored numerous articles in their field.

(A) Both Dr. Henderson and Dr. Ball being widely known for having authored numerous articles in their field.
(B) Both Dr. Henderson and Dr. Ball are widely known for having authored numerous articles in their field.
(C) Widely known for having authored numerous articles in their field being both Dr. Henderson and Dr. Ball.
(D) Having the numerous authored articles in their field widely known are Dr. Henderson and Dr. Ball.
(E) Having authored many widely known articles in their field being Henderson and Ball.

8. Scientists are seeking better ways to predict damage from earthquakes, and they are using supersensitive recorders to study how rock breaks and moves in an earthquake.

(A) Scientists are seeking better ways to predict damage from earthquakes, and they
(B) Scientists who seek better ways to predict damage from earthquakes, they
(C) Scientists seeking better ways to predict damage from earthquakes
(D) Seeking better ways for the prediction of damage from earthquakes, scientists who
(E) Seeking to better predict damage from earthquakes is why scientists

9. Some doctors believe that the types of injuries sustained in contact sports are no different for children than young adults.

(A) are no different for children than young adults
(B) is no different for children than being young adults
(C) are no different for children than for young adults
(D) are no different for children than for those who are young adults
(E) are no different from those for children than young adults

10. The reason for the continued popularity of country-western performers is that it draws on experiences with which almost everyone can identify.

(A) that it draws on
(B) that their music draws on
(C) because the music draws on
(D) because of them drawing from
(E) they will draw from

11. Raised in a large and noisy city, it was only when I went away to college that I realized how delightful life in a small town could be.

(A) it was only when I went away to college that I realized how delightful life in a small town could be
(B) when I went away to college I then realized how delightful life in a small town could be
(C) going away to college made me realize how delightful life in a small town could be
(D) I did not realize how delightful life in a small town could be until I went away to college
(E) delightful life in a small town was unrealized by me until I went away to college

**GO ON TO THE NEXT PAGE**

The following sentences test your ability to recognize grammar and usage errors. Each sentence contains either a single error or no error at all. No sentence contains more than one error. The error, if there is one, is underlined and lettered. If the sentence contains an error, select the one underlined part that must be changed to make the sentence correct. If the sentence is correct, select choice E. In choosing answers, follow the requirements of standard written English.

EXAMPLE:

The other delegates and him immediately
   A                    B        C
accepted the resolution drafted by the
                         D
neutral states. No error
                E

Ⓐ ● Ⓒ Ⓓ Ⓔ

12. At the heart of the program, enthusiastically endorsed
                                 A
by the city's business association, is plans for
                                    B
refurbishing neighborhoods and for making low-
                            C
interest mortgages available to young families.
                        D
No error
E

13. The illustrated books by Dr. Seuss have managed
                                        A
keeping youngsters and adults alike entertained for
  B                           C               D
several decades. No error
                E

14. Introducing new ideas and replacing old ones is
    A                              B       C
always a highly controversial matter, especially when
                                      D
there is already tension between an older and a younger
generation. No error
           E

15. It was fortunate that the inexperienced veterinarian
       A
was able to examine the injured horse calm and with
 B       C                            D
confidence. No error
           E

16. Although the details of the contract has not yet been
                                     A
announced, it is likely that union negotiators accepted
           B
the proposed training program for newly hired
    C                         D
workers. No error
        E

17. Just when those who were watching from the sidelines
             A
feared the worst, the athletes themselves are the
      B                   C         D
most confident. No error
               E

18. Though the statistics on their experiment were
    A                        B              C
neither precise or significant, the biochemists still
                D
published them. No error
               E

GO ON TO THE NEXT PAGE

956

**19.** George Thornton Emmons was one of a handful of
A

ethnographers who committed their life to studying
B          C          D

the Tlingit culture of the Northwest Coast. No error
E

**20.** Before he sprained his back, Morgan spends
A

much of his leisure time engaged in outdoor sports,
B                        C

particularly hiking and canoeing. No error
D                              E

**21.** In a world that the rate of technological and social
A

change accelerates frighteningly, change itself often
B                        C

seems to be the only constant . No error
D              E

**22.** Ms. Tanaka asked Juan and I whether we
A          B

would consider joining our school's quiz bowl
C          D

team. No error
E

**23.** Something of a phenomenon in the entertainment
A                  B

world, political satirists are admired by conservatives
C

and radicals alike . No error
D          E

**24.** In the past, the small nation had been committed to
A

self-managed socialism, a system under which the
B

workers, rather than the state, owns most enterprises.
C              D

No error
E

**25.** Listening at the first song its lead singer ever wrote,
A

the band members did not foresee that this young man
B

would be responsible for bringing them
C

to the attention of the world. No error
D                    E

**26.** The office manager and her coworker, Ms. Andrews,

received equal pay from the company until she
A                              B    C

got a raise for helping to increase productivity.
D

No error
E

**27.** Attaining speeds of up to 60 miles per hour, cheetahs
A          B

are perhaps the fastest of land animals. No error
C          D                    E

**28.** Whether or not they were successful as a candidate ,
A

women such as Geraldine Ferraro and Pat Schroeder

have opened the door to the election of a woman as
B              C      D

President. No error
E

**29.** The often conflicting reports of different polling
A

organizations make it difficult to predict which of the
B

two candidates is more likely to win the election next
C      D

year. No error
E

**GO ON TO THE NEXT PAGE** ⇒

**Directions:** The following passage is an early draft of an essay. Some parts of the passage need to be rewritten.

Read the passage and select the best answers for the questions that follow. Some questions are about particular sentences or parts of sentences and ask you to improve sentence structure or word choice. Other questions ask you to consider organization and development. In choosing answers, follow the requirements of standard written English.

**Questions 30-35 are based on the following passage.**

(1) Elisha Graves Otis did not invent the elevator, even though his name is most closely associated with it. (2) Elevating mechanisms, usually ropes and pulleys, had been used throughout history. (3) Otis is also not credited with developing an elevator large enough and powerful enough to lift heavy loads. (4) They had actually been in use for half of his lifetime. (5) What Otis managed to do in 1854 was to demonstrate an elevator with a built-in safety device. (6) So that the elevator would not plunge to the bottom if the rope used to raise and lower it broke. (7) What was noteworthy about this was that it was then possible for people to use elevators, not just freight.

(8) Prior to this time, hotels and other buildings were a maximum of only four or five stories high. (9) You can imagine why. (10) "Birdcage" elevators were made of open metalwork, just like birdcages. (11) Hotel guests were reluctant to climb many flights of stairs several times daily, rooms on the lower floors were considered premium. (12) In businesses, people as well as desks and other heavy equipment had to be moved up stairs. (13) So when Otis' safe elevator was developed, it meant that buildings could be taller. (14) Before long, hotels and office buildings were nine and ten stories high.

**30.** In context, what is the best way to deal with sentence 4 (reproduced below) ?

*They had actually been in use for half of his lifetime.*

(A) Delete it.
(B) Switch it with sentence 5.
(C) Change "They" to "Such elevators".
(D) Change "his" to "Otis' ".
(E) Insert "supposedly" after "lifetime".

**31.** What is the best way to revise the underlined portion of sentences 5 and 6 (reproduced below) ?

*What Otis managed to do in 1854 was to demonstrate an elevator with a built-in safety <u>device. So that the elevator would not plunge</u> to the bottom if the rope used to raise and lower it broke.*

(A) device, by which the elevator would not plunge
(B) device, and the elevator would not plunge
(C) device because an elevator plunges
(D) device to prevent the elevator from plunging
(E) device, it prevented elevators from plunging

**32.** Which of the following is the best version of sentence 7 (reproduced below) ?

*What was noteworthy about this was that it was then possible for people to use elevators, not just freight.*

(A) (As it is now)
(B) Consequently, it was then possible for elevators to be used for people and freight, and this was noteworthy.
(C) People, not just freight, could use elevators; that this was possible was noteworthy.
(D) This development was noteworthy because elevators could now be used for people as well as for freight.
(E) It is noteworthy that both people and freight can use elevators.

**33.** Which of the following is the best sentence to insert at the beginning of the second paragraph before sentence 8 ?

(A) Freight had always been a major consideration.
(B) Otis' improvement had far-reaching consequences.
(C) So Otis' fame was based entirely in safety.
(D) If Otis had not invented this device, someone else would have.
(E) Elevators can move more than 1,500 feet per minute.

**GO ON TO THE NEXT PAGE** ➡

**34.** Which of the following is the best version of the underlined portion of sentence 11 (reproduced below) ?

*Hotel guests were reluctant to climb many flights of* <u>*stairs several times daily, rooms on the lower floors*</u> *were considered premium.*

(A) (as it is now)
(B) stairs several times daily because rooms on the lower floors
(C) stairs above the rooms on the lower floors several times daily but they
(D) stairs several times daily above the rooms on the lower floors, which
(E) stairs several times daily; as a result, rooms on the lower floors

**35.** Which sentence should be deleted from the essay because it contains unrelated information?

(A) Sentence 1
(B) Sentence 3
(C) Sentence 8
(D) Sentence 10
(E) Sentence 13

# STOP

**If you finish before time is called, you may check your work on this section only.**
**Do not turn to any other section in the test.**

## SECTION 4
Time — 25 minutes
24 Questions

**Turn to Section 4 (page 5) of your answer sheet to answer the questions in this section.**

**Directions:** For each question in this section, select the best answer from among the choices given and fill in the corresponding circle on the answer sheet.

---

Each sentence below has one or two blanks, each blank indicating that something has been omitted. Beneath the sentence are five words or sets of words labeled A through E. Choose the word or set of words that, when inserted in the sentence, best fits the meaning of the sentence as a whole.

**Example:**

Hoping to ------- the dispute, negotiators proposed a compromise that they felt would be ------- to both labor and management.

(A) enforce . . useful
(B) end . . divisive
(C) overcome . . unattractive
(D) extend . . satisfactory
(E) resolve . . acceptable

Ⓐ Ⓑ Ⓒ Ⓓ ●

---

1. Once the principal ------- that the fire alarm had been set off by accident, she apologized to the suspected students and announced that they had been -------.

(A) realized . . exonerated
(B) denied . . reprimanded
(C) perceived . . enlightened
(D) understood . . apprehended
(E) confirmed . . obligated

2. Although the late Supreme Court Justice Thurgood Marshall had ------- that his papers be available only to scholars, the Library of Congress ------- his wishes and exhibited them to the general public.

(A) implied . . publicized
(B) denied . . repealed
(C) stipulated . . disregarded
(D) revealed . . executed
(E) insisted . . honored

3. Royal garments found in the tombs of ancient Egyptians reveal no evidence of having been mended; this discovery suggests that the rulers of Egypt opted for ------- rather than -------.

(A) disposal . . repair
(B) sacrifice . . opulence
(C) wastefulness . . comfort
(D) spirituality . . worldliness
(E) humiliation . . charity

---

4. The author used a rhetorical question as a terminal flourish to ------- the section of text.

(A) disclose (B) rearrange (C) simplify
(D) conclude (E) ascertain

5. "Foamy" viruses cause cells cultured in laboratories to swell but produce no such ------- in cells of living organisms.

(A) compression (B) disintegration
(C) distension (D) deflation
(E) dehydration

6. The two sisters selflessly dedicated their lives to the nursing profession; their ------- made them -------, ones whose ways are worthy of imitation.

(A) aptitude . . eccentrics
(B) morality . . emancipators
(C) erudition . . enigmas
(D) devotion . . egotists
(E) altruism . . exemplars

7. Annoyed by the new employee's excessively ------- manner, the supervisor advised him that such fawning was inappropriate.

(A) obsequious (B) mysterious
(C) lackadaisical (D) argumentative
(E) aggressive

8. Conservationists argue that unconstrained ------- of natural resources, which might deplete them forever, should be replaced with a policy of -------.

(A) dismissal . . preparation
(B) consumption . . dispersion
(C) harvesting . . gathering
(D) exploitation . . husbandry
(E) stockpiling . . extirpation

**GO ON TO THE NEXT PAGE** ➡

960

Each passage below is followed by questions based on its content. Answer the questions on the basis of what is <u>stated</u> or <u>implied</u> in each passage and in any introductory material that may be provided.

**Questions 9-10 are based on the following passage.**

She set out from Poughkeepsie early this morning—
a six-hour ride, but as they headed north, the snowstorm
started, and the traffic slowed to a crawl. She kept checking
*Line* her watch. There was time to spare. Her afternoon class
5 visit was scheduled for four. The presentation itself
wouldn't take place until evening.
    The talk she has prepared is one she will be delivering
countless times this year, the centennial of her mother's
birth. It is academic, and uninspiring, and she knows it.
10 Other scholars can talk about Salomé's poetry and her
pedagogy, but she, Camila, the only daughter, is supposed to shed a different light on the woman.

9. The character's actions in lines 3-4 ("She . . . watch")
   primarily convey her

   (A) fear of traveling in storms
   (B) annoyance at having to make the trip
   (C) concern about arriving on schedule
   (D) eagerness to interact with her colleagues
   (E) excitement about delivering her speech

10. The "light" referred to in line 12 would most likely
    include

   (A) bibliographic information
   (B) direct literary citations
   (C) historical analyses
   (D) personal insights
   (E) scholarly critiques

**Questions 11-12 are based on the following passage.**

Summer 1995. School children collecting frogs
from a pond in Minnesota discover one frog after
another with deformities. The story immediately
*Line* seizes the attention of national media. Is this an
5 isolated occurrence or a widespread trend? What
is causing these deformities?
    Malformations have since been reported in more
than 60 species of amphibians in 46 states. Surprising numbers of deformed amphibians have also been
10 found in Asia, Europe, and Australia. Investigators
have blamed the deformities on amphibians' increased
exposure to ultraviolet radiation, the chemical contamination of water, even a parasite epidemic. Every time
another report appears, the media tout the new position,
15 thus providing a misleading view. Most likely, all of
these factors have been working in tandem.

11. The opening paragraph primarily serves to

   (A) highlight a phenomenon by dramatizing it
   (B) advocate a particular course of action
   (C) illustrate how a story can cause general panic
   (D) compare a local situation to a national one
   (E) demonstrate children's inherent interest in science

12. The author's attitude toward the "media" (line 14)
    might best be described as

   (A) respectful
   (B) indifferent
   (C) ambivalent
   (D) resentful
   (E) critical

**GO ON TO THE NEXT PAGE**

**Questions 13-24 are based on the following passage.**

*This passage is adapted from a 1993 book written by a scientist.*

A physicist, an engineer, and a psychologist are called in as consultants to a dairy farm whose production has been below par. Each is given time to inspect the details of the
*Line* operation before making a report.
5   The first to be called is the engineer, who states: "The size of the stalls for the cattle should be decreased. Efficiency could be improved if the cows were more closely packed, with a net allotment of 275 cubic feet per cow. Also, the diameter of the milking tubes should be increased
10  by 4 percent to allow for a greater average flow rate during the milking periods."
    The next to report is the psychologist, who proposes: "The inside of the barn should be painted green. This is a more mellow color than brown and should help induce
15  greater milk flow. Also, more trees should be planted in the fields to add diversity to the scenery for the cattle during grazing, to reduce boredom."
    Finally, the physicist is called upon. He asks for a blackboard and then draws a circle. He begins: "Assume
20  the cow is a sphere . . ."
    This old joke, if not very funny, does illustrate how, at least metaphorically, physicists picture the world. The set of tools physicists have to describe nature is limited. Most of the modern theories you read about began as simple
25  models by physicists who didn't know how else to start to solve a problem. The class of things that we do know how to solve exactly can be counted on the fingers of one, maybe two, hands. For the most part, physicists follow the same guidelines that have helped keep Hollywood movie
30  producers rich: If it works, exploit it. If it still works, copy it.
    I like the cow joke because it provides an allegory for thinking simply about the world, and it allows me to jump right into an idea that doesn't get written about too much,
35  but that is essential for the everyday workings of science: *Before doing anything else, abstract out all irrelevant details!*
    There are two operative words here: abstract and irrelevant. Getting rid of irrelevant details is the first step in
40  building any model of the world, and we do it subconsciously from the moment we are born. Doing it consciously is another matter. Overcoming the natural desire not to throw out unnecessary information is probably the hardest and most important part of learning physics. This leads us
45  to the second operative word: abstract. Of all the abstract thinking required in physics, probably the most challenging lies in choosing how to approach a problem. The mere description of movement along a straight line—the first major development in modern physics—required enough
50  abstraction that it largely eluded some pretty impressive intellects until Galileo.

Four hundred years ago, Galileo created modern science by describing motion. One of the most obvious traits about the world, which makes a general description of motion
55  apparently impossible, is that everything moves differently. A feather wafts gently down when loosened from a flying bird, but pigeon droppings fall like a rock unerringly on your windshield. Bowling balls rolled haphazardly by a three-year-old serendipitously make their way all the way
60  down the alley, while a lawn mower won't move an inch on its own. Galileo recognized that this most obvious quality of the world is also its most irrelevant, at least as far as understanding motion is concerned. Philosophers before him had argued that a medium—air , water, etc.—is
65  essential to the very existence of motion, but Galileo stated cogently that the essence of motion could be understood only by removing the confusion introduced by the particular circumstances in which moving objects find themselves. "Have you not observed that two bodies which fall in
70  water, one with a speed a hundred times greater as that of the other, will fall in air with speeds so nearly equal that one will not surpass the other by as much as one hundredth part?"
    He claimed, rightly, that if we ignore the effect of the
75  medium, all objects will fall exactly the same way. Moreover, he anticipated the onslaught of criticism from those who were not prepared for his abstraction by defining the very essence of *irrelevant*: "I trust you will not follow the example of many others who divert the discussion from its
80  main intent and fasten upon some statement of mine which lacks a hairbreadth of the truth and, under this hair, hide the fault of another which is as big as a ship's cable."
    This is exactly what he argued that the ancient Greek philosopher Aristotle had done by focusing not on the
85  similarities in the motion of objects but on the differences that are attributable to the effect of a medium. In this sense, a theoretical world in which there was no medium to get in the way was only a "hairbreadth" away from the real one.

13. The engineer, the psychologist, and the physicist respond differently to the situation at the dairy farm because

(A) they have different mathematical training
(B) their specific training causes them to approach problems differently
(C) the psychologist studies the behavior of cows differently than do the engineer and the physicist
(D) the engineer solves the problem, leaving nothing relevant for the psychologist and the physicist to say
(E) only the physicist can successfully eliminate from consideration details irrelevant to the problem

**GO ON TO THE NEXT PAGE**

**14.** A likely consequence of implementing the engineer's proposal (lines 5-11) would be that

(A) large milking tubes would raise the cow's level of discomfort
(B) the dairy farm would be forced to increase in size
(C) the farm's management would emphasize the humane treatment of animals
(D) larger quantities of milk would initially decrease farm profits
(E) the dairy farm would be able to accommodate more cows without additional buildings

**15.** The psychologist's remarks (lines 13-17) are based on the assumption that

(A) any implied psychological similarity between cows and humans is inappropriate
(B) psychology derives insight from current theories of aesthetics
(C) individualized attention to cows will yield measurable increases in milk
(D) contented cows will produce more milk than bored or anxious ones
(E) each cow will respond differently to attempts to increase milk production

**16.** The "old joke" (line 21) primarily plays which role in the passage?

(A) Dramatizing an event
(B) Arguing a point
(C) Introducing a topic
(D) Defining key terms at the outset
(E) Exposing misleading assumptions immediately

**17.** The comparison of physicists to Hollywood producers (lines 28-31) implies that Hollywood producers

(A) do not always know why a film succeeds
(B) do not approach their work with the same dedication as physicists
(C) are more concerned than physicists with solving practical problems
(D) plan their work in a highly systematic fashion
(E) are as conscientious in their own ways as physicists are

**18.** The author suggests that "thinking simply" (line 33) works because

(A) abstract models are more prone to error than are empirical observations
(B) some problems can be solved if details are ignored
(C) scientists should adhere closely to the concerns of the public
(D) empirical facts can never be successfully modeled
(E) events are often self-explanatory

**19.** The statement in lines 39-41 ("Getting . . . born") implies that

(A) a human must have a certain degree of ethical development in order to evaluate details appropriately
(B) learning is delayed when errors are not recognized and eliminated
(C) even human infants seek patterns involving repetition
(D) the basic act of perceiving involves determining which details are important
(E) children must be shown how to construct general models from the abundant data surrounding them

**20.** The author suggests in lines 61-63 ("Galileo . . . concerned") that

(A) Galileo was as much an engineer as a scientist
(B) more careful attention to detail leads to a deeper understanding of science
(C) empirical facts do not always clarify scientific understanding
(D) motion will never be fully understood by non-physicists
(E) the most profound scientific discoveries are sometimes the most obvious

**21.** The "particular circumstances" mentioned in lines 67-68 refer to

(A) the status of science
(B) an object's environment
(C) an individual scientist's predicament
(D) an illogical tradition
(E) a unique problem

**GO ON TO THE NEXT PAGE**

**22.** In line 75, "medium" most nearly means a

(A) mathematical average
(B) middle region
(C) natural habitat
(D) surrounding substance
(E) beneficial environment

**23.** Lines 83-86 reveal which of the following about Galileo?

(A) He respected Aristotle as one of the first philosophers to engage in scientific observation.
(B) He considered Aristotle and others like him mistaken in their approach to motion.
(C) He believed that rival scientists would try to take credit for his discoveries.
(D) He feared that his studies of motion could have religious ramifications.
(E) He conducted significant experiments that served to support his theories.

**24.** The author uses the expression "get in the way" (lines 87-88) to

(A) emphasize the difficulty created by too much information
(B) question the value of elaborate experimental procedures
(C) illustrate a pragmatic approach to a theoretical dilemma
(D) argue that Galileo was many years ahead of his time
(E) suggest the limits of Galileo's physics of motion

# STOP

**If you finish before time is called, you may check your work on this section only.**
**Do not turn to any other section in the test.**

## SECTION 5
### Time — 25 minutes
### 20 Questions

**Turn to Section 5 (page 5) of your answer sheet to answer the questions in this section.**

**Directions:** For this section, solve each problem and decide which is the best of the choices given. Fill in the corresponding circle on the answer sheet. You may use any available space for scratchwork.

Notes

1. The use of a calculator is permitted.
2. All numbers used are real numbers.
3. Figures that accompany problems in this test are intended to provide information useful in solving the problems. They are drawn as accurately as possible EXCEPT when it is stated in a specific problem that the figure is not drawn to scale. All figures lie in a plane unless otherwise indicated.
4. Unless otherwise specified, the domain of any function $f$ is assumed to be the set of all real numbers $x$ for which $f(x)$ is a real number.

Reference Information

    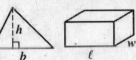    

$A = \pi r^2$
$C = 2\pi r$
$A = \ell w$
$A = \frac{1}{2}bh$
$V = \ell wh$
$V = \pi r^2 h$
$c^2 = a^2 + b^2$
Special Right Triangles

The number of degrees of arc in a circle is 360.
The sum of the measures in degrees of the angles of a triangle is 180.

---

1. If $\dfrac{x}{x-2} = \dfrac{39}{37}$, then $x =$

   (A) 37
   (B) 39
   (C) 41
   (D) 74
   (E) 78

---

### STUDENTS IN AN ADVANCED BIOLOGY CLASS

|        | Juniors | Seniors | Total |
|--------|---------|---------|-------|
| Boys   | $k$     | $n$     | $m$   |
| Girls  | $r$     | $s$     | $t$   |
| Total  | $w$     | $x$     | $z$   |

2. In the table above, each letter represents the number of students in that category. Which of the following must be equal to $z$ ?

   (A) $k + s$
   (B) $m + x$
   (C) $r + s$
   (D) $r + s + t$
   (E) $k + n + r + s$

**GO ON TO THE NEXT PAGE**

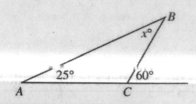

**3.** In $\triangle ABC$ above, what is the value of $x$ ?

(A)  25
(B)  30
(C)  35
(D)  40
(E)  60

**4.** The Martins' refrigerator is broken and it will cost $300 to fix it. A new energy-efficient refrigerator, costing $900, will save the Martins $15 per month on their electric bill. If they buy the new refrigerator, in $x$ months the Martins will have saved an amount equal to the difference between the cost of the new refrigerator and the cost of fixing the old one. What is the value of $x$ ?

(A)  20
(B)  25
(C)  36
(D)  40
(E)  60

**5.** The perimeter of equilateral triangle $ABC$ is 3 times the perimeter of equilateral triangle $DEF$. If the perimeter of $\triangle DEF$ is 10, what is the length of one side of $\triangle ABC$ ?

(A)  $3\frac{1}{3}$

(B)  10

(C)  15

(D)  30

(E)  40

**6.** A machine mints coins at the rate of one coin per second. If it does this for 10 hours each day, approximately how many days will it take the machine to mint 360,000 coins?

(A)       10
(B)      100
(C)    1,000
(D)   10,000
(E)  100,000

**GO ON TO THE NEXT PAGE**

**7.** If the average (arithmetic mean) of $x$ and $3x$ is 12, what is the value of $x$ ?

(A)  2
(B)  4
(C)  6
(D) 12
(E) 24

**8.** At Maple Creek High School, some members of the chess club are on the swim team and no members of the swim team are tenth graders. Which of the following must also be true?

(A)  No members of the chess club are tenth graders.
(B)  Some members of the chess club are tenth graders.
(C)  Some members of the chess club are not tenth graders.
(D)  More tenth graders are on the swim team than are in the chess club.
(E)  More tenth graders are in the chess club than are on the swim team.

**9.** If $3x + n = x + 1$, what is $n$ in terms of $x$ ?

(A)  $4x + 1$
(B)  $2x + 1$
(C)  $2 - x$
(D)  $1 - 2x$
(E)  $1 - 4x$

**10.** If $k$ is a positive integer, let $\boxed{k}$ be defined as the set of all multiples of $k$. All of the numbers in which of the following sets are also in all three of the sets $\boxed{2}$, $\boxed{3}$, and $\boxed{5}$ ?

(A)  $\boxed{5}$
(B)  $\boxed{6}$
(C)  $\boxed{10}$
(D)  $\boxed{21}$
(E)  $\boxed{60}$

**GO ON TO THE NEXT PAGE**

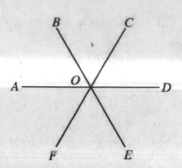

Note: Figure not drawn to scale.

**11.** In the figure above, $\overline{AD}$, $\overline{BE}$, and $\overline{CF}$ intersect at point $O$. If the measure of $\angle AOB$ is 80° and $\overline{CF}$ bisects $\angle BOD$, what is the measure of $\angle EOF$ ?

(A) 40°
(B) 50°
(C) 60°
(D) 70°
(E) 80°

**12.** If $k$ is a positive integer, what is the least value of $k$ for which $\sqrt{\dfrac{5k}{3}}$ is an integer?

(A) 3
(B) 5
(C) 15
(D) 25
(E) 60

**13.** The figures above represent three pieces of cardboard. All angles of the cardboard pieces are right angles, all short sides have length 1, and all long sides have length 2. Which of the following figures could be made from only the three pieces of cardboard without over-lapping or cutting them?

I.

II.

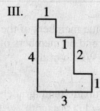

III.

(A) None
(B) I only
(C) II only
(D) III only
(E) I and II

GO ON TO THE NEXT PAGE

**14.** How many integers greater than 20 and less than 30 are each the product of exactly two <u>different</u> numbers, both of which are prime?

(A) Zero
(B) One
(C) Two
(D) Three
(E) Four

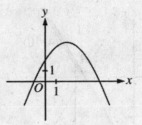

**16.** The figure above shows the graph of a quadratic function $h$ whose maximum value is $h(2)$. If $h(a) = 0$, which of the following could be the value of $a$ ?

(A) −1
(B) 0
(C) 2
(D) 3
(E) 4

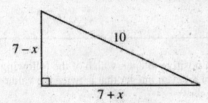

Note: Figure not drawn to scale.

**15.** The figure above is a right triangle. What is the value of $49 + x^2$ ?

(A) 50
(B) 51
(C) 72
(D) 98
(E) 100

**17.** If $k$ and $h$ are constants and $x^2 + kx + 7$ is equivalent to $(x + 1)(x + h)$, what is the value of $k$ ?

(A) 0
(B) 1
(C) 7
(D) 8
(E) It cannot be determined from the information given.

**GO ON TO THE NEXT PAGE** ⇨

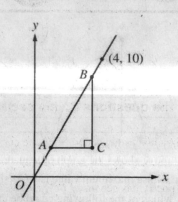

Note: Figure not drawn to scale.

**18.** In the figure above, if the legs of triangle $ABC$ are parallel to the axes, which of the following could be the lengths of the sides of triangle $ABC$ ?

(A) 2, 5, and $\sqrt{29}$

(B) 2, 5, and 7

(C) 3, 3, and $3\sqrt{2}$

(D) 3, 4, and 5

(E) 4, 5, and $\sqrt{41}$

**19.** Let the function $f$ be defined by $f(x) = 2x - 1$.

If $\frac{1}{2} f(\sqrt{t}) = 4$, what is the value of $t$ ?

(A) $\dfrac{3}{\sqrt{2}}$

(B) $\dfrac{7}{2}$

(C) $\dfrac{9}{2}$

(D) $\dfrac{49}{4}$

(E) $\dfrac{81}{4}$

**20.** If $k$ is a positive integer, which of the following must represent an even integer that is twice the value of an odd integer?

(A) $2k$
(B) $2k + 3$
(C) $2k + 4$
(D) $4k + 1$
(E) $4k + 2$

# STOP

**If you finish before time is called, you may check your work on this section only.**
**Do not turn to any other section in the test.**

## SECTION 6
Time — 25 minutes
24 Questions

---

**Turn to Section 6 (page 6) of your answer sheet to answer the questions in this section.**

---

**Directions:** For each question in this section, select the best answer from among the choices given and fill in the corresponding circle on the answer sheet.

---

Each sentence below has one or two blanks, each blank indicating that something has been omitted. Beneath the sentence are five words or sets of words labeled A through E. Choose the word or set of words that, when inserted in the sentence, <u>best</u> fits the meaning of the sentence as a whole.

**Example:**

Hoping to ------- the dispute, negotiators proposed a compromise that they felt would be ------- to both labor and management.

(A) enforce . . useful
(B) end . . divisive
(C) overcome . . unattractive
(D) extend . . satisfactory
(E) resolve . . acceptable

Ⓐ Ⓑ Ⓒ Ⓓ ●

1. Much interpersonal communication is implicit in -------, expressive movements.

   (A) exposés    (B) verbalizations    (C) gestures
      (D) cognitions    (E) intuitions

2. By virtue of her extensive experience and her ------- of practical knowledge, 87-year-old Louisa Vigil was ------- by her family in New Mexico as its chief advice-giver and matriarch.

   (A) store . . condemned
   (B) supply . . dismissed
   (C) wealth . . regarded
   (D) modicum . . abandoned
   (E) deficit . . praised

3. Castillo's poetry has generated only enthusiastic response: praise from the general public and ------- from the major critics.

   (A) condemnation    (B) sarcasm    (C) plaudits
      (D) irony    (E) pathos

4. The twigs of this shrub have a signature ------- whose pungency enables people to ------- the shrub even in winter when its leaves have fallen.

   (A) scent . . cultivate
   (B) flavor . . conceal
   (C) appearance . . recognize
   (D) texture . . locate
   (E) aroma . . identify

5. The announcement that the city would raze the land-mark school building was such a distressing ------- that it provoked an outcry.

   (A) disclosure    (B) evaluation    (C) liberation
      (D) instance    (E) inquiry

---

GO ON TO THE NEXT PAGE ⟩

The passages below are followed by questions based on their content; questions following a pair of related passages may also be based on the relationship between the paired passages. Answer the questions on the basis of what is stated or implied in the passages and in any introductory material that may be provided.

**Questions 6-9 are based on the following passages.**

**Passage 1**

The first three years of life appear to be a crucial starting point—a period particularly sensitive to the protective
mechanisms of parental and family support. For millennia,
Line parents have recognized the newborn's basic need for
5 safety, nourishment, warmth, and nurturing. Now science
has added stunning revelations about human development
from birth to age three, confirming that parents and other
adult caregivers play a critical role in influencing a child's
development. No other period of human life is as suited to
10 learning as are a child's first three years. Babies raised by
caring, attentive adults in safe, predictable environments
are better learners than those raised with less attention
in less secure settings.

**Passage 2**

Much early childhood literature suggests that the first
15 three years of life are the critical years for brain development. Yet new findings in neuroscience suggest that the
brain retains its ability to reorganize itself in response
to experience or injury throughout life: after the loss
of sensory input from an amputated limb, for example,
20 adults are able to learn new motor skills effectively. It
may be useful to question the simplistic view that the
brain becomes unbendable and increasingly difficult
to modify beyond the first few years of life. If so, we
should also be wary of claims that parents have only
25 a single, biologically delimited, once-in-a-lifetime
opportunity to help their children build better brains.

**6.** Which best expresses the relationship between Passage 2 and Passage 1?

(A) Passage 2 urges particular changes as a result of the findings described in Passage 1.

(B) Passage 2 mocks those who support the argument presented in Passage 1.

(C) Passage 2 offers a personal anecdote that casts doubt upon the beliefs espoused in Passage 1.

(D) Passage 2 questions an assumption underlying the ideas expressed in Passage 1.

(E) Passage 2 provides a scientific explanation for the examples cited in Passage 1.

**7.** Both authors would most likely agree with which of the following statements?

(A) The brain becomes increasingly inflexible as a person grows older.

(B) Adults can bounce back from injuries as readily as children can.

(C) Children raised by attentive parents are generally good learners.

(D) It is widely acknowledged that the first three years are important to a child's development.

(E) Most scientists have recently changed their views about human development prior to age three.

**8.** Passage 2 as a whole suggests that its author would most likely react to lines 9-10 in Passage 1 ("No other . . . years") with

(A) indignation
(B) skepticism
(C) humor
(D) ambivalence
(E) approval

**9.** Lines 3-9 of Passage 1 ("For millennia . . . development") draw a parallel between

(A) traditional practices and contemporary critiques
(B) basic human needs and intellectual endeavors
(C) widespread beliefs and scientific findings
(D) parental anxieties and developmental advances
(E) experimental hypotheses and proven theories

**GO ON TO THE NEXT PAGE**

**Questions 10-15 are based on the following passage.**

*The following passage is from a 1988 book on women in the pre-Civil War South. The author discusses Harriet Jacobs and Frederick Douglass, escaped slaves who wrote accounts of their enslavement and escape to freedom.*

In self-consciously writing for a White, northern, middle-class audience, Harriet Jacobs did not differentiate herself from the most celebrated male authors of slave narratives.
Line Frederick Douglass, for example, firmly identified himself
5 with the triumph of manliness and individualism that slavery suppressed. In so doing, he explicitly called upon his northern readers to recognize that the sufferings and inequities to which he had been subjected by the very condition of enslavement directly contravened their deepest
10 principles of individualism. Harriet Jacobs faced a more difficult task. For her, a woman, to claim that enslavement violated the principles of individualism would be to risk having her story dismissed. A few northern White women were beginning to work out the analogy between slavery
15 and the oppression of women, but their view had not won general sympathy. Inequalities between women and men still appeared to many northerners, even those who opposed slavery, as manifestations of natural differences. Northern women who sought improvement in their own condition
20 clung to the discourses of true womanhood and domesticity to make their case. Northern gender conventions differed from southern ones, but they, too, dictated that a woman should address the public modestly and deferentially, if at all. A poignant account of the violation of a woman's virtue
25 stood a much better chance of appealing to northern sensibilities than a pronouncement for woman's individual rights, if only because such an account reaffirmed woman's essentially domestic nature. Perhaps Jacobs would have written differently had she been able to write for an audi-
30 ence of slave women, but few slave women could read, and she could not, in any case, have reached them. Her only hope for a hearing lay in reaching the same people who avidly read Harriet Beecher Stowe.[1] Jacobs left no doubt about her intended readers: "O, you happy free women,
35 contrast *your* New Year's day with that of the poor bond-woman!"

Jacobs shaped her presentation of herself to conform, at least in part, to the expectations of her intended readers. Like Douglass, who invoked the rhetoric of male individ-
40 ualism to encourage identification with his narrative, she had to make her readers take the oppression of slave women personally, to see it as a threat to their own sense of themselves as women. To touch their hearts, she had to address them in their own idiom, tell her story in a way with which
45 they could identify. For her readers to accept her as a woman, she had to present herself as a woman like them. She exposed slavery as a violation of the norms of woman-hood and portrayed slave women as essentially like their northern White sisters in their goals and sensibilities.
50 Slavery, in this portrayal, constituted a crime against woman's essential nature—her yearning for virtue, domesticity, and motherhood. Jacobs followed Douglass in accepting the norms of society as absolutes—the articulations of innate human nature—which were directly
55 contradicted by slavery.

[1] Author of *Uncle Tom's Cabin*, a passionate anti-slavery novel

**10.** The primary purpose of the passage is to

(A) probe the emotional world of a famous author
(B) present a comprehensive history of a particular period
(C) denounce the injustice of slavery
(D) explore the narrative choices of a writer
(E) argue in favor of a particular style of writing

**11.** Frederick Douglass' rhetorical strategy as described in lines 4-10 might best be summarized as

(A) identification with a concept followed by partial rejection
(B) recognition of a group's wrongdoing followed by explicit steps to correct it
(C) elaboration on an unfamiliar argument followed by unusual qualifications
(D) evocation of a revered concept followed by a specific reference to its undermining
(E) analysis of a particular event followed by a subjective plea

**12.** In line 14, "work out" most nearly means

(A) exercise
(B) conciliate
(C) struggle for
(D) formulate
(E) solve

**13.** In the context of lines 18-21 ("Northern women . . . their case"), which of the following might be an argument used by women attempting to improve their condition?

(A) Women are as intelligent and capable as men.
(B) Women who are granted more personal liberties become better mothers.
(C) Allowing women more individual freedom will help them be more productive in society.
(D) Oppressing women is as immoral as owning slaves.
(E) Refusing to allow women certain freedoms violates the principle of self-determination.

**GO ON TO THE NEXT PAGE** →

**14.** The passage suggests that Jacobs' decisions on how best to shape her narrative revealed her willingness to be

(A) pragmatic
(B) disingenuous
(C) scholarly
(D) presumptuous
(E) melodramatic

**15.** The tone of the passage can be described as both

(A) disappointed and critical
(B) analytical and appreciative
(C) regretful and angry
(D) ironic and jocular
(E) hopeful and moralistic

**GO ON TO THE NEXT PAGE** →

**Questions 16-24 are based on the following passage.**

*The following passage is excerpted from a British novel published in the mid-nineteenth century.*

It was interesting to be in the quiet old town once more, and it was not disagreeable to be here and there suddenly recognized and stared after. One or two of the tradespeople
Line even darted out of their shops, and went a little way down
5 the street before me, that they might turn, as if they had forgotten something, and pass me face to face—on which occasions I don't know whether they or I made the worse pretence; they of not doing it, or I of not seeing it. Still, my position was a distinguished one, and I was not at all
10 dissatisfied with it, until Fate threw me in the way of that unlimited miscreant, Trabb's boy.

Casting my eyes along the street at a certain point of my progress, I beheld Trabb's boy approaching, lashing himself with an empty blue bag. Deeming that a serene
15 and unconscious contemplation of him would best beseem me, and would be most likely to quell his evil mind, I advanced with that expression of countenance, and was rather congratulating myself on my success, when suddenly the knees of Trabb's boy smote together,
20 his hair uprose, his cap fell off, he trembled violently in every limb, staggered out into the road, and crying to the populace, "Hold me! I'm so frightened!" feigned to be in a paroxysm of terror and contrition, occasioned by the dignity of my appearance. As I passed him, his
25 teeth loudly chattered in his head, and with every mark of extreme humiliation, he prostrated himself in the dust.

This was a hard thing to bear, but this was nothing. I had not advanced another two hundred yards, when, to my inexpressible terror, amazement, and indignation, I again
30 beheld Trabb's boy approaching. He was coming round a narrow corner. His blue bag was slung over his shoulder, honest industry beamed in his eyes, a determination to proceed to Trabb's with cheerful briskness was indicated in his gait. With a shock he became aware of me, and was
35 severely visited as before; but this time his motion was rotatory, and he staggered round and round me with knees more afflicted, and with uplifted hands as if beseeching my mercy. His sufferings were hailed with the greatest joy by a knot of spectators, and I felt utterly
40 confounded.

I had not got as much further down the street as the post office, when I again beheld Trabb's boy shooting round by a back way. This time, he was entirely changed. He wore the blue bag in the manner of my great-coat,
45 and was strutting along the pavement towards me on the opposite side of the street, attended by a company of delighted young friends to whom he from time to time exclaimed, with a wave of his hand, "Don't know yah!" Words cannot state the amount of aggravation and injury
50 wreaked upon me by Trabb's boy, when, passing abreast of me, he pulled up his shirt collar, twined his side-hair,

stuck an arm akimbo, and smirked extravagantly by, wriggling his elbows and body, and drawling to his attendants, "Don't know yah, don't know yah, 'pon
55 my soul don't know yah!" The disgrace attendant on his immediately afterwards taking to crowing and pursuing me across the bridge with crows, as from an exceedingly dejected fowl who had known me when I was a blacksmith, culminated the disgrace with which I left the town, and
60 was, so to speak, ejected by it into the open country.

**16.** The general organization of the passage is best described by which of the following?

(A) A remembrance of three encounters that lead to ignominious flight
(B) An account of a loosely related series of events
(C) A narration that demonstrates the circular logic behind Trabb's boy's actions
(D) A description of an action from several points of view
(E) A progression from a state of isolation to a state of community and fellowship

**17.** The first paragraph of the passage implies that the narrator felt

(A) apathetic and helpless at being a stranger in town
(B) distanced and smug toward the townspeople
(C) bored and unimportant in a provincial town
(D) confused and disoriented on a busy street
(E) nostalgic and proud on returning to his hometown

**18.** In context, the word "progress" (line 13) implies that the narrator

(A) has noble ideas concerning the future
(B) intends to effect some change in the town
(C) thinks of his stroll as a kind of procession
(D) was not expecting trouble from Trabb's boy
(E) is recollecting a past rise in fortune

**19.** The phrase "that expression of countenance" (line 17) refers to the narrator's

(A) guilty conscience
(B) friendly greeting
(C) feigned indifference
(D) premonition of disaster
(E) recognition of Trabb's boy

**GO ON TO THE NEXT PAGE** ➡

**20.** In context, the word "visited" (line 35) most nearly means

(A) called on
(B) shared an experience with
(C) resided temporarily with
(D) haunted
(E) afflicted

**21.** The sufferings of Trabb's boy "were hailed with the greatest joy" (lines 38-39) because the townspeople

(A) were glad to see a silly boy endure some punishment
(B) were amused by the derision the gestures implied
(C) misunderstood the meaning of the boy's behavior
(D) had always enjoyed the narrator's sense of humor
(E) delighted in the antics between two friends

**22.** The primary motivation behind Trabb's boy's exclamation "Don't know yah" (lines 48 and 54-55) is to

(A) remind the narrator that strangers are not welcome in the town
(B) mock the narrator's demeanor of aloofness
(C) exaggerate the townspeople's desire to deny acquaintance with the narrator
(D) entice the narrator to introduce himself
(E) arouse the sympathy of the townspeople

**23.** The narrator's presentation is most like that of a

(A) novelist commenting on an influential predecessor
(B) mechanic explaining the reason a machine has broken down
(C) social commentator delivering an exhortation
(D) scientist explaining a controversial hypothesis
(E) writer recounting an unpleasant personal experience

**24.** The most pervasive comic strategy of the passage is the

(A) commentary provided by the onlooking townspeople
(B) contrast between the narrator's sense of dignity and the antics of the boy
(C) lack of comprehension shown in retrospect by the narrator
(D) invocation of fate to rationalize human faults
(E) presentation of Trabb's boy as the object of the townspeople's ridicule

# STOP

**If you finish before time is called, you may check your work on this section only.**
**Do not turn to any other section in the test.**

## SECTION 8
### Time — 20 minutes
### 16 Questions

**Turn to Section 8 (page 7) of your answer sheet to answer the questions in this section.**

**Directions:** For this section, solve each problem and decide which is the best of the choices given. Fill in the corresponding circle on the answer sheet. You may use any available space for scratchwork.

**Notes**

1. The use of a calculator is permitted.

2. All numbers used are real numbers.

3. Figures that accompany problems in this test are intended to provide information useful in solving the problems. They are drawn as accurately as possible EXCEPT when it is stated in a specific problem that the figure is not drawn to scale. All figures lie in a plane unless otherwise indicated.

4. Unless otherwise specified, the domain of any function $f$ is assumed to be the set of all real numbers $x$ for which $f(x)$ is a real number.

**Reference Information**

    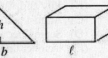    

$A = \pi r^2$
$C = 2\pi r$     $A = \ell w$     $A = \frac{1}{2}bh$     $V = \ell wh$     $V = \pi r^2 h$     $c^2 = a^2 + b^2$     Special Right Triangles

The number of degrees of arc in a circle is 360.
The sum of the measures in degrees of the angles of a triangle is 180.

---

**1.** A restaurant menu lists 8 dinners and 3 desserts. How many different dinner-dessert combinations are possible from this menu?

(A) 24
(B) 12
(C) 11
(D) 8
(E) 3

---

The sum of $3x$ and 5 is equal to the product of $x$ and $\frac{1}{3}$.

**2.** Which of the following equations gives the relationship stated in the problem above?

(A) $3x = \frac{1}{3}x + 5$

(B) $5(3x) = x + \frac{1}{3}$

(C) $3(x + 5) = \frac{1}{3}x$

(D) $3x + 5 = x \div \frac{1}{3}$

(E) $3x + 5 = \frac{1}{3}x$

**GO ON TO THE NEXT PAGE**

977

**3.** A clerk accidentally threw a valuable document into one of 90 trash cans. It is equally likely that the document is in any of these 90 trash cans. If exactly 15 of these 90 trash cans are blue, what is the probability that the document will be in a blue trash can?

(A) $\dfrac{1}{4}$

(B) $\dfrac{1}{5}$

(C) $\dfrac{1}{6}$

(D) $\dfrac{1}{15}$

(E) $\dfrac{1}{90}$

**4.** How many different integer pairs $(x, y)$ satisfy the equation $\dfrac{x}{y} = \dfrac{1}{2}$ ?

(A) One
(B) Two
(C) Three
(D) Four
(E) More than four

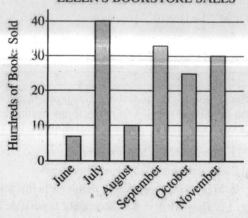

ELLEN'S BOOKSTORE SALES

**5.** According to the graph above, during which of the following two-month periods did Ellen's Bookstore sell the least number of books?

(A) June and July
(B) July and August
(C) August and September
(D) September and October
(E) October and November

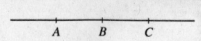

**6.** In the figure above, $AC = 24$ and $AB = BC$. Point $D$ (not shown) is on the line between $A$ and $B$ such that $AD = DB$. What does $DC$ equal?

(A)  6
(B) 12
(C) 16
(D) 18
(E) 20

GO ON TO THE NEXT PAGE

7. If $n$ is a positive integer, then $\left(6 \times 10^{-n}\right) + \left(1 \times 10^{-n}\right)$ must equal

   (A) $\dfrac{7}{10}$

   (B) $\dfrac{7}{10^n}$

   (C) $\dfrac{7}{10^{2n}}$

   (D) $\dfrac{6}{10^n}$

   (E) $\dfrac{6}{10^{2n}}$

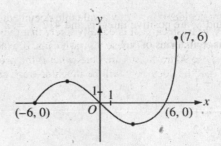

9. Based on the graph of the function $f$ above, what are the values of $x$ for which $f(x)$ is negative?

   (A) $-6 < x < 0$
   (B) $\phantom{-}0 < x < 6$
   (C) $\phantom{-}6 < x < 7$
   (D) $-6 < x < 6$
   (E) $-6 < x < 0$ and $6 < x < 7$

8. How many more degrees of arc are there in $\dfrac{1}{4}$ of a circle than in $\dfrac{1}{5}$ of a circle?

   (A) $\phantom{0}9°$
   (B) $18°$
   (C) $24°$
   (D) $30°$
   (E) $36°$

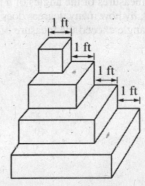

10. The figure above shows the dimensions of a pedestal constructed of 4 layers of marble. Each layer is a rectangular solid that is 1 foot high and has a square base. How many cubic feet of marble make up the pedestal?

    (A) 14
    (B) 16
    (C) 30
    (D) 36
    (E) 80

**GO ON TO THE NEXT PAGE**

11. If $x$ and $y$ are positive integers and $4\left(2^x\right) = 2^y$, what is $x$ in terms of $y$ ?

   (A) $y - 2$
   (B) $y - 1$
   (C) $y$
   (D) $y + 1$
   (E) $y + 2$

12. If the degree measures of the angles of a triangle are in the ratio 2:3:4, by how many degrees does the measure of the largest angle exceed the measure of the smallest angle?

   (A) $20°$
   (B) $30°$
   (C) $40°$
   (D) $50°$
   (E) $60°$

13. The rate for a telephone call between City $A$ and City $B$ is 50 cents for the first minute and 30 cents for each additional minute or portion thereof. Which of the following functions describes the cost, in dollars of a phone call between these two cities that lasts for $n$ minutes, if $n$ is a positive integer?

   (A) $f(n) = 0.80n$
   (B) $f(n) = 0.50 + 0.30n$
   (C) $f(n) = 0.50 + 0.30(n + 1)$
   (D) $f(n) = 0.50 + 0.30(n - 1)$
   (E) $f(n) = 0.50n + 0.30(n - 1)$

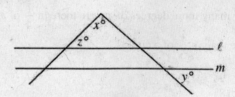

14. In the figure above, if $\ell \parallel m$, what does $z$ equal in terms of $x$ and $y$ ?

   (A) $x + y$
   (B) $x - y$
   (C) $180 - x$
   (D) $180 - x + y$
   (E) $180 - x - y$

**GO ON TO THE NEXT PAGE** ⇨

15. If $\dfrac{n}{n-1} \cdot \dfrac{1}{n} \cdot \dfrac{n}{n+1} = \dfrac{5}{k}$ for positive integers $n$ and $k$, what is the value of $k$?

(A) 1
(B) 5
(C) 24
(D) 25
(E) 26

16. To celebrate a colleague's graduation, the $m$ coworkers in an office agreed to contribute equally to a catered lunch that costs a total of $y$ dollars. If $p$ of the coworkers fail to contribute, which of the following represents the additional amount, in dollars, that each of the remaining coworkers must contribute to pay for the lunch?

(A) $\dfrac{y}{m}$

(B) $\dfrac{y}{m-p}$

(C) $\dfrac{py}{m-p}$

(D) $\dfrac{y(m-p)}{m}$

(E) $\dfrac{py}{m(m-p)}$

# STOP

**If you finish before time is called, you may check your work on this section only.**
**Do not turn to any other section in the test.**

# SECTION 9
**Time — 20 minutes**
**19 Questions**

**Turn to Section 9 (page 7) of your answer sheet to answer the questions in this section.**

**Directions:** For each question in this section, select the best answer from among the choices given and fill in the corresponding circle on the answer sheet.

Each sentence below has one or two blanks, each blank indicating that something has been omitted. Beneath the sentence are five words or sets of words labeled A through E. Choose the word or set of words that, when inserted in the sentence, best fits the meaning of the sentence as a whole.

**Example:**

Hoping to ------- the dispute, negotiators proposed a compromise that they felt would be ------- to both labor and management.

(A) enforce . . useful
(B) end . . divisive
(C) overcome . . unattractive
(D) extend . . satisfactory
(E) resolve . . acceptable

1. Louise Erdrich and Michael Dorris co-wrote *The Crown of Columbus*, a ------- effort successfully mingling their individual styles as writers.

    (A) stratified    (B) fitful    (C) collaborative
        (D) vicarious    (E) corresponding

2. The eager members of the audience found the lecture topic -------, but unfortunately the lecturer's droning voice had a ------- effect.

    (A) interesting . . rousing
    (B) advantageous . . beneficial
    (C) rudimentary . . reassuring
    (D) insipid . . bland
    (E) stimulating . . soporific

3. Displays in the Australian Museum's exhibition on dinosaurs are designed to be touched, offering visitors ------- experience.

    (A) an odoriferous    (B) an archaic    (C) an aural
        (D) a rustic    (E) a tactile

4. The magician's ------- astonished us; her deft performance proved the old saying that the hand is quicker than the eye.

    (A) discernment    (B) tenacity    (C) hilarity
        (D) adroitness    (E) insecurity

5. Although Keller achieved national ------- as a hero, his lamentable ------- in the political arena soon became painfully apparent.

    (A) recognition . . versatility
    (B) ignominy . . inadequacy
    (C) prestige . . finesse
    (D) prominence . . ineptitude
    (E) notoriety . . rectitude

6. The professor argued that every grassroots movement needs -------: without this public declaration of motives, there can be no cohesive organization.

    (A) an invocation    (B) a prospectus
        (C) a manifesto    (D) an arbitration
            (E) a mandate

STOP

If you finish before time is called, you may check your work on this section only. Do not turn to any other section in the test.

GO ON TO THE NEXT PAGE

# 9

   Unauthorized copying or reuse of any part of this page is illegal.

# 9

The two passages below are followed by questions based on their content and on the relationship between the two passages. Answer the questions on the basis of what is <u>stated</u> or <u>implied</u> in the passages and in any introductory material that may be provided.

**Questions 7-19 are based on the following passages.**

*The following passages discuss Colonial Williamsburg, a historically reconstructed village whose residents dress in colonial attire. Visitors to Williamsburg gain a sense of what life may have been like in Virginia's capital in the 1700's. Passage 1 is from a 1960 book by a historian. Passage 2 is from a 1997 book by an architecture critic.*

### Passage 1

Reconstructed with the aid of the money and enthusiasm of John D. Rockefeller, Jr., Colonial Williamsburg is not only a brilliant example of an American style in

*Line*
5 historical monuments; it has become a school for training professionals who will be devotees of popular interpretations of United States history. Meanwhile, academic historians, disturbed by the unorthodoxy and the popular appeal of Williamsburg, have not given it the significance it deserves. Some treat it as simply another example—like

10 William Randolph Hearst's notorious imported castles—of a wealthy man indulging his whim. Some dismiss it as an educational "gadget." Or they treat it condescendingly as a harmless but amusing example of American vulgarity— a kind of patriotic Disneyland. But several visits there have

15 persuaded me that it is significant in ways that its promoters did not advertise.

Williamsburg is a strikingly democratic national monument. It presumes an unspecialized and unaristocratic education. Unless one already knows a great deal, one cannot

20 learn much from visiting the Roman Forum or the Athenian Acropolis. The National Gallery in London seems a jungle of canvas and marble to anyone not already instructed in the different arts and periods represented. These places are planned primarily for the connoisseur or the scholar, not for

25 the citizen.

But because Colonial Williamsburg offers not a segment of the history of a fine art, but a model of an ongoing community, it is intelligible and interesting to nearly everybody. It is a symbol of a culture in which fine arts have become

30 much less important than in other cultures; in which literacy is a higher ideal than literariness. The forbidding ribbon across the antique chair, the "Do Not Touch" sign—these omnipresent features of the European museum have nothing to do with the American restored community. One of the

35 most startling facts to anyone who has toured Europe is that the Williamsburg guides have no set speeches, and are giving visitors their own interpretation of the rigorous course of lectures on colonial life which they are required to attend as part of their training.

40 A Colonial Williamsburg would be impossible in a country that was not wealthy. It is made for a nation of paved roads and family vacations. Williamsburg—like the American spelling bee and educational television shows— symbolizes the American refusal to believe that education

45 need be a chore. Business and pleasure *ought* to be combined. In this sense, Williamsburg is perfectly suited.

### Passage 2

The replacement of reality with selective fantasy is characteristic of that most successful and staggeringly profitable American phenomenon, the reinvention of the

50 environment as themed entertainment. The definition of "place" as a chosen image probably started in a serious way in the late 1920's at Colonial Williamsburg, predating and paving the way for the new world order of Walt Disney Enterprises. Certainly it was in the restoration of Colonial

55 Williamsburg that the studious fudging of facts received its scholarly imprimatur, and that history and place as themed artifact hit the big time. Williamsburg is seen by the connoisseur as a kind of period piece now, its shortsightedness a product of the limitations of the early preservation move-

60 ment. Within those limitations, a careful construct was created: a place where one could learn a little romanticized history, confuse the real and unreal, and have—then and now—a very nice time. Knowledge, techniques, and standards have become increasingly sophisticated since then.

65 But it is the Williamsburg image and example as originally conceived that continue to be universally admired and emulated.

Restoration is a difficult and unclear procedure at best; unreality is built into the process, which requires a highly

70 subjective kind of cosmetic surgery. At Williamsburg, there was instant amputation with the conceit of a "cutoff date" for the restoration—in this case, 1770—an arbitrary determination of when a place should be frozen in time. After the cutoff date had been chosen, the next step was to "restore

75 it back." That means re-creating a place as someone thinks it was—or would like it to have been—at a chosen moment. This usually means moving or destroying a good deal of subsequent architectural history—exactly the stuff of which real history and art are made. In an act of stunning illogic

80 and innocent hubris, a consortium of preservation architects and historical soothsayers plays God.

In the United States, this type of crime against art and history has become an established element of popular culture. It has also given a license to destroy. Approximately

85 730 buildings were removed at Williamsburg; 81 were renovated and 413 were rebuilt on the original sites. Everything later than the chosen time frame had to disappear. So much for reality. And so much for the messy, instructive, invaluable, and irretrievable revelations that are part of the

90 serendipitous record of urban settlements.

**GO ON TO THE NEXT PAGE**

**7.** The authors of both passages would most likely agree that Colonial Williamsburg has

(A) achieved popular acceptance in the United States
(B) served as a prototype for European theme parks
(C) benefited from the input of preservation architects
(D) distorted Americans' sense of a collective past
(E) overcome the limitations of historical reconstruction

**8.** In Passage 1, the Roman Forum, the Athenian Acropolis, and the National Gallery (lines 20-21) are presented as examples of places that

(A) are more interesting to Europeans than to Americans
(B) require expert knowledge to be fully appreciated
(C) educate visitors about different arts and periods
(D) establish aesthetic standards that have been compromised
(E) are interesting to everyone who visits them

**9.** The author of Passage 1 implies that the "ribbon" and the "sign" (lines 31-32) have the effect of

(A) helping people understand the cultural significance of objects that are displayed in museums
(B) preventing damage to antiques that have become both fragile and priceless
(C) restricting architects from re-creating places of historic significance
(D) keeping people away from things that represent a link to their culture and history
(E) conveying the misconception that most people once lived amidst such luxury

**10.** The author of Passage 1 asserts that anyone who has toured Europe would find which of the following most "startling" (line 35) about Colonial Williamsburg?

(A) The participation by tourists in historic reenactments
(B) The obvious wealth of most of the visitors
(C) The freedom accorded to the tour guides
(D) The concept of a make-believe historic village
(E) The expense of training the tourist guides

**11.** The approach to education described in lines 42-45 of Passage 1 ("Williamsburg . . . chore") is most similar to which of the following?

(A) A computer game that teaches geography
(B) A museum that displays historic artifacts
(C) A film that provides comic relief
(D) A textbook that examines controversial issues
(E) A scientific experiment that tests a theory

**12.** In line 55 of Passage 2, the word "studious" serves to emphasize the

(A) hard work that is required to repair historic structures
(B) serious aspects of a place that is designed to provide amusement
(C) ingenuity of those who conceived of Colonial Williamsburg's novel approach
(D) deliberateness with which Colonial Williamsburg was fabricated
(E) academic credentials of the scholars who approve of Colonial Williamsburg

**13.** In line 81, "plays" most nearly means

(A) bets on
(B) competes against
(C) acts as
(D) toys with
(E) takes advantage of

**14.** The author of Passage 2 suggests that "this type of crime" (line 82) is

(A) usual because most people treasure architectural history
(B) alarming because it could threaten the livelihood of artists
(C) exploitive because it takes advantage of the good will of others
(D) negligent because historic landmarks must be regularly maintained
(E) ominous because few people seem to be bothered by it

**15.** The "brilliant example of an American style" (line 3 of Passage 1) would most likely be discredited by the author of Passage 2 on the grounds that

(A) other countries demonstrated a commitment to architectural preservation long before the United States did so
(B) monuments in the United States are striking in appearance but lack true cultural value
(C) nostalgic depictions of history make people yearn for a lifestyle that is no longer possible
(D) attempts to produce a vivid re-creation of the past result in a sanitized version of history
(E) historical restoration is undertaken only when it promises to be profitable

GO ON TO THE NEXT PAGE

**16.** The academic historians whose views are mentioned in lines 12-14 of Passage 1 ("Or . . . Disneyland") would be criticized by the author of Passage 2 because they

(A) overstate the amount of history that people can learn in Williamsburg

(B) assume that themed environments like Williamsburg are commonplace

(C) accept that history needs to be simplified for popular consumption

(D) endorse the creation of replicas over the preservation of original buildings

(E) fail to take seriously the damage done by a cultural trend

**17.** The author of Passage 2 would most likely view the speeches described in lines 34-39 of Passage 1 as evidence of Colonial Williamsburg's

(A) great value for historical preservationists

(B) inability to generate interest in history

(C) excellent reputation among scholars

(D) lack of architectural integrity

(E) tendency to take liberties with historical facts

**18.** Which contrast best describes how the author of each passage views historical reconstructions in the United States?

(A) As escapist in Passage 1; as educational in Passage 2

(B) As lucrative in Passage 1; as unprofitable in Passage 2

(C) As admirable in Passage 1; as lamentable in Passage 2

(D) As stagnant in Passage 1; as dynamic in Passage 2

(E) As diverse in Passage 1; as homogeneous in Passage 2

**19.** The discussion of Colonial Williamsburg in both passages focuses on the challenge of

(A) upgrading the conditions of deteriorating historic buildings

(B) showcasing the diverse architectural styles of a single time period

(C) representing history in an accessible but authentic context

(D) dramatizing the uniqueness of colonial institutions

(E) making historical reconstruction more affordable

# STOP

**If you finish before time is called, you may check your work on this section only.**
**Do not turn to any other section in the test.**

10  10

Unauthorized copying or reuse of
any part of this page is illegal.

## SECTION 10
Time — 10 minutes
14 Questions

**Turn to Section 10 (page 7) of your answer sheet to answer the questions in this section.**

**Directions:** For each question in this section, select the best answer from among the choices given and fill in the corresponding circle on the answer sheet.

The following sentences test correctness and effectiveness of expression. Part of each sentence or the entire sentence is underlined; beneath each sentence are five ways of phrasing the underlined material. Choice A repeats the original phrasing; the other four choices are different. If you think the original phrasing produces a better sentence than any of the alternatives, select choice A; if not, select one of the other choices.

In making your selection, follow the requirements of standard written English; that is, pay attention to grammar, choice of words, sentence construction, and punctuation. Your selection should result in the most effective sentence—clear and precise, without awkwardness or ambiguity.

EXAMPLE:

Laura Ingalls Wilder published her first book and she was sixty-five years old then.

(A)  and she was sixty-five years old then
(B)  when she was sixty-five
(C)  at age sixty-five years old
(D)  upon the reaching of sixty-five years
(E)  at the time when she was sixty-five

1. To fear the act of impeachment and to think of it that it threatens the presidential office is to be misinformed about the Constitution and ignorant of the law.

   (A)  that it threatens the presidential office
   (B)  as a threat to the presidency
   (C)  that a threat exists for the presidency
   (D)  as it were a threat at the presidency
   (E)  as if it were like a threat to the presidency

2. The disposal of nuclear fission's unwanted by-products is one of the thorniest problems in developing nuclear power.

   (A)  The disposal of nuclear fission's unwanted by-products is
   (B)  Unwanted by-products of nuclear fission that need to be disposed of are
   (C)  How nuclear fission's unwanted by-products get to be disposed of is
   (D)  Ridding nuclear fission of unwanted by-products are
   (E)  For nuclear fission to get rid of unwanted by-products is

3. No biographer can attest to absolute accuracy in documenting the activities of his or her subject, this biographer of Cesar Chavez is no exception.

   (A)  subject, this biographer of Cesar Chavez is no exception
   (B)  subject, and this biographer of Cesar Chavez is no exception
   (C)  subject; this biography of Cesar Chavez is no exception
   (D)  subject; such a biography of this one of Cesar Chavez is no exception
   (E)  subject, with this Cesar Chavez biographer being no exception

4. Unlike Charles Lamb, Horace Walpole actually set out to be the historian of his age.

   (A)  Unlike Charles Lamb, Horace Walpole actually set out to be the historian of his age.
   (B)  Unlike Charles Lamb, Horace Walpole was different in that he actually set out to be the historian of his age.
   (C)  Unlike Charles Lamb, Horace Walpole actually set out to be the historian of his age and Lamb did not.
   (D)  Charles Lamb did not, but Horace Walpole's intention was to be the historian of his age.
   (E)  Different from Charles Lamb, for being the historian of his age was the intention of Horace Walpole.

GO ON TO THE NEXT PAGE

**5.** Paradoxically, one way that Shakespeare transcended his era was <u>because of having included it</u> in his plays.

  (A) because of having included it
  (B) when he included it
  (C) through his including of it
  (D) by its inclusion of it
  (E) by including it

**6.** Laughing because they had missed their stop while reading the map, the <u>task for the tourists now was</u> getting off the bus and back to their destination.

  (A) task for the tourists now was
  (B) tourists' task now was
  (C) tourists now facing the task of
  (D) tourists nevertheless now faced the task of
  (E) tourists now faced the task of

**7.** For weeks, one of the company's starring ballerinas <u>were performing so infrequently that dance lovers feared something was</u> wrong.

  (A) were performing so infrequently that dance lovers feared something was
  (B) was performing so infrequently; dance lovers feared something to be
  (C) were performing so infrequently that dance lovers feared something has
  (D) was performing so infrequently that dance lovers feared something was
  (E) was performing very infrequently; so dance lovers fearing something

**8.** When Catherine the Great had a magnificent dinner service of Sèvres porcelain made for her, she was scandalized by its great cost, <u>which became</u> the subject of prolonged controversy.

  (A) which became
  (B) so it was to be
  (C) with a result that it was destined to become
  (D) therefore becoming
  (E) consequently it would become

**9.** <u>Though the damage caused by strip-mining was often irreparable to the natural environment, it</u> was once used to supply half the coal produced annually in the United States.

  (A) Though the damage caused by strip-mining was often irreparable to the natural environment, it
  (B) Though irreparable damage is caused often to the natural environment by strip-mining, it
  (C) Though strip-mining often caused irreparable damage to the natural environment, it
  (D) Despite the fact of often irreparable damage to the natural environment, strip-mining
  (E) In spite of often irreparable damage to the natural environment, strip-mining

**10.** The filibuster on voting-rights legislation went on for three days and <u>nights; senators slept when they could</u> on benches in the hall.

  (A) nights; senators slept when they could
  (B) nights, which meant senators sleeping when possible
  (C) nights; therefore, it meant that senators would sleep when possible
  (D) nights and therefore the senators would be sleeping when able to
  (E) nights; with senators sleeping when they could

**11.** <u>Insofar as so many people were going</u> to the music festival, the highway was jammed with cars.

  (A) Insofar as so many people were going
  (B) With the great many people who are going
  (C) In that there being so many people who went
  (D) Because there was a great many people who went
  (E) Because so many people were going

**12.** The villagers found the visitors <u>equally as fascinating as their customs were</u> mystifying.

  (A) equally as fascinating as their customs were
  (B) equally fascinating and their customs
  (C) as fascinating and their customs
  (D) as fascinating as their customs were
  (E) as fascinating and their customs were

**GO ON TO THE NEXT PAGE** ➡

**13.** Although he played a leading role in planning
spacecraft expeditions, Dr. Carl Sagan refused to
accept praise for the plans he designed nor otherwise
profiting from later advancements in space exploration.

(A) designed nor otherwise profiting
(B) had designed nor otherwise did he profit
(C) has designed nor otherwise to have profited
(D) designed or otherwise profited
(E) had designed or otherwise to profit

**14.** The convenience and widespread availability of
watercolor paint account for its popularity with
amateur artists.

(A) account for its popularity
(B) account for their popularity
(C) accounts for its popularity
(D) is why it is popular
(E) are a reason for its popularity

# S T O P

**If you finish before time is called, you may check your work on this section only.**
**Do not turn to any other section in the test.**

# Correct Answers and Difficulty Levels
## SAT Practice Test #10

## CRITICAL READING

### Section 4
#### Multiple-Choice Questions

| Correct Answer | Difficulty Level | | Correct Answer | Difficulty Level |
|---|---|---|---|---|
| 1 A | E | 13 | B | E |
| 2 C | M | 14 | E | M |
| 3 A | M | 15 | D | E |
| 4 D | M | 16 | C | M |
| 5 C | M | 17 | A | M |
| 6 E | M | 18 | B | M |
| 7 A | H | 19 | D | M |
| 8 D | H | 20 | C | M |
| 9 C | E | 21 | D | M |
| 10 D | M | 22 | D | M |
| 11 A | H | 23 | B | M |
| 12 E | E | 24 | A | M |

Number correct _____

Number incorrect _____

### Section 6
#### Multiple-Choice Questions

| Correct Answer | Difficulty Level | | Correct Answer | Difficulty Level |
|---|---|---|---|---|
| 1 C | E | 13 | D | H |
| 2 C | M | 14 | A | M |
| 3 C | M | 15 | B | M |
| 4 E | M | 16 | A | H |
| 5 A | M | 17 | B | H |
| 6 D | M | 18 | C | E |
| 7 D | E | 19 | C | H |
| 8 B | M | 20 | E | M |
| 9 C | M | 21 | B | M |
| 10 D | M | 22 | B | H |
| 11 D | M | 23 | E | E |
| 12 E | M | 24 | B | M |

Number correct _____

Number incorrect _____

### Section 9
#### Multiple-Choice Questions

| Correct Answer | Difficulty Level | | Correct Answer | Difficulty Level |
|---|---|---|---|---|
| 1 C | E | 11 | A | M |
| 2 E | M | 12 | D | M |
| 3 E | M | 13 | C | E |
| 4 D | M | 14 | E | M |
| 5 D | M | 15 | D | M |
| 6 C | H | 16 | E | H |
| 7 A | M | 17 | E | M |
| 8 B | E | 18 | C | M |
| 9 D | M | 19 | C | M |
| 10 C | M | | | |

Number correct _____

Number incorrect _____

## MATHEMATICS

### Section 2

| Multiple-Choice Questions | | Student-Produced Response Questions | |
|---|---|---|---|
| Correct Answer | Difficulty Level | Correct Answer | Difficulty Level |
| 1 E | E | 9 13/2, 6.5 | E |
| 2 E | E | 10 10 | E |
| 3 B | E | 11 45 | M |
| 4 B | E | 12 105 | M |
| 5 D | M | 13 12.5, 25/2 | M |
| 6 D | M | 14 3/50, .06 | M |
| 7 C | M | 15 192 | M |
| 8 A | H | 16 8/7, 1.14 | H |
| | | 17 0/1<x<3/8, 0<x<.375 | H |
| | | 18 1350 | H |

Number correct _____

Number incorrect _____

Number correct (9-18) _____

### Section 5
#### Multiple-Choice Questions

| Correct Answer | Difficulty Level | | Correct Answer | Difficulty Level |
|---|---|---|---|---|
| 1 B | E | 11 | B | M |
| 2 C | E | 12 | C | M |
| 3 C | E | 13 | C | M |
| 4 D | E | 14 | D | H |
| 5 B | E | 15 | A | M |
| 6 A | M | 16 | A | M |
| 7 C | M | 17 | D | H |
| 8 C | M | 18 | A | H |
| 9 D | M | 19 | E | M |
| 10 E | M | 20 | E | H |

Number correct _____

Number incorrect _____

Number correct (9-18) _____

### Section 8
#### Multiple-Choice Questions

| Correct Answer | Difficulty Level | | Correct Answer | Difficulty Level |
|---|---|---|---|---|
| 1 A | E | 9 | B | M |
| 2 C | E | 10 | C | M |
| 3 C | E | 11 | A | M |
| 4 E | E | 12 | C | M |
| 5 C | E | 13 | D | M |
| 6 D | E | 14 | E | M |
| 7 B | M | 15 | C | H |
| 8 B | M | 16 | E | H |

Number correct _____

Number incorrect _____

## WRITING

### Essay

Essay Score* (0-6) _____

### Section 3
#### Multiple-Choice Questions

| Correct Answer | Difficulty Level | | Correct Answer | Difficulty Level |
|---|---|---|---|---|
| 1 C | E | 19 | C | M |
| 2 D | E | 20 | A | E |
| 3 A | E | 21 | A | M |
| 4 D | E | 22 | A | M |
| 5 E | E | 23 | E | M |
| 6 D | E | 24 | D | M |
| 7 B | E | 25 | A | E |
| 8 C | E | 26 | C | M |
| 9 C | E | 27 | E | H |
| 10 B | E | 28 | A | M |
| 11 D | H | 29 | E | M |
| 12 B | E | 30 | C | M |
| 13 B | E | 31 | D | E |
| 14 E | E | 32 | D | M |
| 15 D | E | 33 | B | M |
| 16 A | E | 34 | E | M |
| 17 D | E | 35 | D | M |
| 18 D | E | | | |

Number correct _____

Number incorrect _____

### Section 10
#### Multiple-Choice Questions

| Correct Answer | Difficulty Level |
|---|---|
| 1 B | E |
| 2 A | E |
| 3 B | E |
| 4 A | E |
| 5 E | E |
| 6 E | M |
| 7 D | E |
| 8 A | E |
| 9 C | E |
| 10 A | E |
| 11 E | M |
| 12 D | M |
| 13 E | M |
| 14 A | H |

Number correct _____

Number incorrect _____

**NOTE:** Difficulty levels are E (easy), M (medium), and H (hard).

\* To score your essay, use the SAT scoring guide in Chapter 9 and the free sample essays available online at www.collegeboard.org/satonlinecourse. On this practice test, your essay score should range from 0 to 6. (Keep in mind that on the actual SAT, your essay will be read by two readers and you will receive a score of 0 to 12 on your score report.)

# The SAT Scoring Process

**Scoring.** The computer compares the circle filled in for each question with the correct response. Each correct answer receives one point; omitted questions do not affect your score. For each wrong answer to a multiple-choice question, one-fourth of a point is subtracted to correct for random guessing. The SAT critical reading section has 67 questions. If, for example, a student has 44 right, 20 wrong, and 3 omitted, the resulting raw score is determined as follows:

$$44 \text{ right} - \frac{20 \text{ wrong}}{4} = 44 - 5 = 39 \text{ raw score points}$$

Obtaining raw scores frequently involves the rounding of fractions to the nearest whole number. For example, a raw score of 39.25 is rounded to 39, the nearest whole number. A raw score of 39.50 is rounded upward to 40. **For the WRITING SECTION**, your essay raw score counts approximately 30% and your multiple-choice raw score counts approximately 70%.

**Converting to reported scaled score.** Raw scores are then placed on the College Board scale of 200 to 800 through a process that adjusts scores to account for minor differences in difficulty among different versions of the test. This process, known as equating, is performed so that a student's reported score is not affected by the version of the test taken or by the abilities of the group with whom the student takes the test. As a result of placing SAT scores on the College Board scale, scores earned by students at different times can be compared. For example, an SAT critical reading score of 400 on a test taken at one administration indicates the same level of developed critical reading ability as a 400 score obtained on a different version of the test taken at another time.

**Note:** Since this test has not been previously administered, score ranges are provided for every possible raw score.

# How to Score Practice Test #10

## SAT Critical Reading Sections 4, 6, and 9

**Step A:** Count the number of correct answers for *Section 4* and record the number in the space provided on the Scoring Worksheet. Then do the same for the incorrect answers. (Do not count omitted answers.)

**Step B:** Count the number of correct answers and the number of incorrect answers for *Section 6* and record the numbers in the spaces provided on the Scoring Worksheet. (Do not count omitted answers.)

**Step C:** Count the number of correct answers and the number of incorrect answers for *Section 9* and record the numbers in the spaces provided on the Scoring Worksheet. (Do not count omitted answers.)

**Step D:** Total the number of correct responses. Total the number of incorrect responses. Enter the resulting figures on the Scoring Worksheet. To determine A, use the formula:

$$\text{Number correct} - \frac{\text{Number incorrect}}{4} = A$$

**Step E:** To obtain B, your Rounded Critical Reading Raw Score, round A to the nearest whole number. (For example, any number from 44.50 to 45.49 rounds to 45.) Enter the resulting figure on the Scoring Worksheet.

**Step F:** To find your Critical Reading Scaled Score Range, look up the Total Rounded Raw Score you obtained in step E in the Critical Reading Conversion Table (Table 1). Enter this range in the box on the Scoring Worksheet.

## SAT Mathematics Sections 2, 5, and 8

**Step A:** Count the number of correct answers and the number of incorrect answers for the multiple-choice questions (*questions 1 through 8*) in *Section 2* and record the numbers in the spaces provided on the Scoring Worksheet. (Do not count omitted answers.)

**Step B:** Count the number of correct answers for the student-produced response questions (*questions 9 through 18*) in *Section 2* and record the number in the space provided on the Scoring Worksheet.

**Step C:** Count the number of correct answers and the number of incorrect answers for *Section 5* and record the number in the space provided on the Scoring Worksheet. (Do not count omitted answers.)

**Step D:** Count the number of correct answers and the number of incorrect answers for *Section 8* and record the numbers in the spaces provided on the Scoring Worksheet. (Do not count omitted answers.)

**Step E:** Total the number of correct responses. Total the number of incorrect responses. Enter the resulting figures on the Scoring Worksheet. To determine A, use the formula:

$$\text{Number correct} - \frac{\text{Number incorrect}}{4} = A$$

**Step F:** To obtain B, your Mathematics Rounded Raw Score, round A to the nearest whole number. (For example, any number from 44.50 to 45.49 rounds to 45.) Enter the resulting figure on the Scoring Worksheet.

**Step G:** To find your Mathematics Scaled Score Range, use the Mathematics Conversion Table (Table 2) to look up the Total Rounded Raw Score you obtained in step F. Enter this range in the box on the Scoring Worksheet.

## SAT Writing Sections 1, 3, and 10

**Step A:** Enter your Essay Score for *Section 1* in the box on the Scoring Worksheet. (On this practice test, your essay score should range from 0 to 6. Keep in mind that on the actual SAT, two readers will read your essay and you will receive a total score of 0 to 12 on your score report.)

**Step B:** Count the number of correct answers and the number of incorrect answers for *Section 3* and record the numbers in the spaces provided on the Scoring Worksheet. (Do not count omitted answers.)

**Step C:** Count the number of correct answers and the number of incorrect answers for *Section 10* and record the numbers in the spaces provided on the Scoring Worksheet. (Do not count omitted answers.)

**Step D:** Total the number of correct responses. Total the number of incorrect responses. Enter the resulting figure on the Scoring Worksheet. To determine A, use the formula:

$$\text{Number correct} - \frac{\text{Number incorrect}}{4} = A$$

**Step E:** To obtain B, your Writing Multiple-Choice (MC) Rounded Raw Score, round A to the nearest whole number. (For example, any number from 44.50 to 45.49 rounds to 45.) Enter the resulting figure on the Scoring Worksheet.

**Step F:** To find your overall Writing Scaled Score Range, use Table 3. Look up the Total MC Rounded Raw Score you obtained in Step E in the left side of Table 3 and the Essay Score entered in Step A across the top of the table. Enter this range in the box on the Scoring Worksheet.

**Step G:** To find your Writing MC Subscore Range, look up the Total MC Rounded Raw Score you obtained in Step E on the Writing Multiple-Choice Conversion Table (Table 4). Enter this range in the box on the Scoring Worksheet.

**Note:** For the **WRITING SECTION**, your Essay Raw Score counts approximately 30% and your Multiple-Choice Raw Score counts approximately 70%.

# SAT Practice Test #10 Scoring Worksheet

**SAT Critical Reading Section**

A. Section 4:

$\underline{\hspace{3cm}}$     $\underline{\hspace{3cm}}$
no. correct     no. incorrect

+       +

B. Section 6:

$\underline{\hspace{3cm}}$     $\underline{\hspace{3cm}}$
no. correct     no. incorrect

+       +

C. Section 9:

$\underline{\hspace{3cm}}$     $\underline{\hspace{3cm}}$
no. correct     no. incorrect

=       =

D. Total Unrounded Raw Score

$\underline{\hspace{3cm}}$ $- ($ $\underline{\hspace{3cm}}$ $\div 4) =$ $\underline{\hspace{3cm}}$
no. correct     no. incorrect     A

E. Total Rounded Raw Score
(Rounded to nearest whole number)

$\underline{\hspace{3cm}}$
B

F. Critical Reading Scaled Score Range
(See Table 1)

$\boxed{\phantom{xx} - \phantom{xx}}$

Critical Reading Scaled Score Range

**SAT Mathematics Section**

A. Section 2:
Questions 1-8

$\underline{\hspace{3cm}}$     $\underline{\hspace{3cm}}$
no. correct     no. incorrect

+

B. Section 2:
Questions 9-18

$\underline{\hspace{3cm}}$
no. correct

+       +

C. Section 5:

$\underline{\hspace{3cm}}$     $\underline{\hspace{3cm}}$
no. correct     no. incorrect

+       +

D. Section 8:

$\underline{\hspace{3cm}}$     $\underline{\hspace{3cm}}$
no. correct     no. incorrect

=       =

E. Total Unrounded Raw Score

$\underline{\hspace{3cm}}$ $- ($ $\underline{\hspace{3cm}}$ $\div 4) =$ $\underline{\hspace{3cm}}$
no. correct     no. incorrect     A

F. Total Rounded Raw Score
(Rounded to nearest whole number)

$\underline{\hspace{3cm}}$
B

G. Mathematics Scaled Score Range
(See Table 2)

$\boxed{\phantom{xx} - \phantom{xx}}$

Mathematics Scaled Score Range

## SAT Writing Section

A. Section 1:

Essay Score

B. Section 3:

_____        _____
no. correct            no. incorrect

+                      +

C. Section 10:

_____        _____
no. correct            no. incorrect

=                      =

D. Total MC Unrounded Raw Score

_____   −   (_____ ÷ 4)   =   _____
no. correct            no. incorrect                    A

E. Total MC Rounded Raw Score
   (Rounded to nearest whole number)

_____
B

F. Writing Scaled Score Range
   (See Table 3)

−

Writing Scaled
Score Range

G. Writing MC Subscore Range
   (See Table 4)

−

Writing MC
Subscore Range

| Table 1. Critical Reading Conversion Table | | | |
|---|---|---|---|
| Raw Score | Scaled Score | Raw Score | Scaled Score |
| 67 | 800 | 30 | 470-530 |
| 66 | 770-800 | 29 | 470-530 |
| 65 | 740-800 | 28 | 460-520 |
| 64 | 720-800 | 27 | 450-510 |
| 63 | 700-800 | 26 | 450-510 |
| 62 | 690-790 | 25 | 440-500 |
| 61 | 670-770 | 24 | 440-500 |
| 60 | 660-760 | 23 | 430-490 |
| 59 | 660-740 | 22 | 420-480 |
| 58 | 650-730 | 21 | 420-480 |
| 57 | 640-720 | 20 | 410-470 |
| 56 | 630-710 | 19 | 400-460 |
| 55 | 630-710 | 18 | 400-460 |
| 54 | 620-700 | 17 | 390-450 |
| 53 | 610-690 | 16 | 380-440 |
| 52 | 600-680 | 15 | 380-440 |
| 51 | 610-670 | 14 | 370-430 |
| 50 | 600-660 | 13 | 360-420 |
| 49 | 590-650 | 12 | 350-410 |
| 48 | 580-640 | 11 | 350-410 |
| 47 | 580-640 | 10 | 340-400 |
| 46 | 570-630 | 9 | 330-390 |
| 45 | 560-620 | 8 | 310-390 |
| 44 | 560-620 | 7 | 300-380 |
| 43 | 550-610 | 6 | 290-370 |
| 42 | 550-610 | 5 | 270-370 |
| 41 | 540-600 | 4 | 260-360 |
| 40 | 530-590 | 3 | 250-350 |
| 39 | 530-590 | 2 | 230-330 |
| 38 | 520-580 | 1 | 220-320 |
| 37 | 510-570 | 0 | 200-290 |
| 36 | 510-570 | -1 | 200-290 |
| 35 | 500-560 | -2 | 200-270 |
| 34 | 500-560 | -3 | 200-250 |
| 33 | 490-550 | -4 | 200-230 |
| 32 | 480-540 | -5 | 200-210 |
| 31 | 480-540 | -6 and below | 200 |

| Table 2. Mathematics Conversion Table | | | |
|---|---|---|---|
| Raw Score | Scaled Score | Raw Score | Scaled Score |
| 54 | 800 | 23 | 460-520 |
| 53 | 750-800 | 22 | 450-510 |
| 52 | 720-800 | 21 | 440-500 |
| 51 | 700-780 | 20 | 430-490 |
| 50 | 690-770 | 19 | 430-490 |
| 49 | 680-740 | 18 | 420-480 |
| 48 | 670-730 | 17 | 410-470 |
| 47 | 660-720 | 16 | 400-460 |
| 46 | 640-700 | 15 | 400-460 |
| 45 | 630-690 | 14 | 390-450 |
| 44 | 620-680 | 13 | 380-440 |
| 43 | 620-680 | 12 | 360-440 |
| 42 | 610-670 | 11 | 350-430 |
| 41 | 600-660 | 10 | 340-420 |
| 40 | 580-660 | 9 | 330-430 |
| 39 | 570-650 | 8 | 320-420 |
| 38 | 560-640 | 7 | 310-410 |
| 37 | 550-630 | 6 | 290-390 |
| 36 | 550-630 | 5 | 280-380 |
| 35 | 540-620 | 4 | 270-370 |
| 34 | 530-610 | 3 | 260-360 |
| 33 | 520-600 | 2 | 240-340 |
| 32 | 520-600 | 1 | 230-330 |
| 31 | 520-580 | 0 | 210-310 |
| 30 | 510-570 | -1 | 200-290 |
| 29 | 500-560 | -2 | 200-270 |
| 28 | 490-550 | -3 | 200-250 |
| 27 | 490-550 | -4 | 200-230 |
| 26 | 480-540 | -5 | 200-210 |
| 25 | 470-530 | -6 and below | 200 |
| 24 | 460-520 | | |

## Table 3. Writing Conversion Table

| MC Raw Score | Essay Score | | | | | | |
|---|---|---|---|---|---|---|---|
| | 0 | 1 | 2 | 3 | 4 | 5 | 6 |
| 49 | 650-690 | 670-720 | 690-740 | 710-770 | 750-800 | 780-800 | 800 |
| 48 | 630-690 | 640-720 | 660-740 | 690-770 | 720-800 | 760-800 | 780-800 |
| 47 | 600-690 | 620-720 | 640-740 | 660-770 | 700-800 | 730-800 | 760-800 |
| 46 | 580-690 | 600-720 | 620-740 | 650-770 | 680-800 | 710-800 | 740-800 |
| 45 | 570-690 | 580-720 | 600-740 | 630-770 | 670-800 | 700-800 | 730-800 |
| 44 | 560-680 | 570-710 | 590-730 | 620-760 | 660-790 | 690-800 | 720-800 |
| 43 | 540-660 | 560-690 | 580-710 | 610-740 | 640-780 | 670-800 | 700-800 |
| 42 | 530-660 | 550-690 | 570-700 | 600-730 | 630-770 | 660-800 | 690-800 |
| 41 | 530-650 | 540-680 | 560-700 | 590-720 | 620-760 | 660-790 | 680-800 |
| 40 | 520-640 | 530-670 | 550-690 | 580-710 | 620-730 | 650-780 | 680-800 |
| 39 | 510-630 | 520-660 | 540-680 | 570-710 | 610-740 | 640-770 | 670-800 |
| 38 | 500-620 | 520-650 | 540-670 | 560-700 | 600-730 | 630-770 | 660-790 |
| 37 | 490-610 | 510-640 | 530-660 | 560-690 | 590-720 | 620-760 | 650-780 |
| 36 | 480-600 | 500-630 | 520-650 | 550-680 | 580-720 | 610-750 | 640-770 |
| 35 | 480-590 | 490-620 | 510-640 | 540-670 | 570-710 | 610-740 | 640-770 |
| 34 | 470-590 | 480-620 | 500-630 | 530-660 | 570-700 | 600-730 | 630-760 |
| 33 | 460-580 | 470-610 | 490-630 | 520-650 | 560-690 | 590-720 | 620-750 |
| 32 | 450-570 | 470-600 | 490-620 | 510-640 | 550-680 | 580-710 | 610-740 |
| 31 | 440-560 | 460-590 | 480-610 | 510-640 | 540-670 | 570-700 | 600-730 |
| 30 | 430-550 | 450-580 | 470-600 | 500-630 | 530-660 | 560-700 | 590-720 |
| 29 | 430-540 | 440-570 | 460-590 | 490-620 | 520-650 | 560-690 | 590-710 |
| 28 | 420-530 | 430-560 | 450-580 | 480-610 | 520-650 | 550-680 | 580-700 |
| 27 | 410-520 | 420-550 | 440-570 | 470-600 | 510-640 | 540-670 | 570-700 |
| 26 | 400-520 | 420-550 | 430-560 | 460-590 | 500-630 | 530-660 | 560-690 |
| 25 | 390-510 | 410-540 | 430-560 | 450-580 | 490-620 | 520-650 | 550-680 |
| 24 | 380-500 | 400-530 | 420-550 | 450-570 | 480-610 | 510-640 | 540-670 |
| 23 | 370-490 | 390-520 | 410-540 | 440-570 | 470-600 | 500-630 | 530-660 |
| 22 | 370-480 | 380-510 | 400-530 | 430-560 | 460-590 | 500-630 | 520-650 |
| 21 | 370-480 | 380-510 | 400-530 | 430-560 | 460-590 | 500-630 | 520-650 |
| 20 | 360-470 | 370-500 | 390-520 | 420-550 | 460-580 | 490-620 | 520-640 |
| 19 | 350-460 | 360-490 | 380-510 | 410-540 | 450-580 | 480-610 | 510-630 |
| 18 | 340-450 | 350-480 | 370-500 | 400-530 | 440-570 | 470-600 | 500-630 |
| 17 | 330-450 | 350-480 | 360-490 | 390-520 | 430-560 | 460-590 | 490-620 |
| 16 | 320-440 | 340-470 | 360-490 | 390-510 | 420-550 | 450-580 | 480-610 |
| 15 | 310-430 | 330-460 | 350-480 | 380-510 | 410-540 | 440-570 | 470-600 |
| 14 | 300-420 | 320-450 | 340-470 | 370-500 | 400-530 | 430-560 | 460-590 |
| 13 | 300-410 | 310-440 | 330-460 | 360-490 | 390-520 | 430-560 | 450-580 |
| 12 | 290-400 | 300-430 | 320-450 | 350-480 | 390-510 | 420-550 | 450-570 |
| 11 | 280-390 | 290-420 | 310-440 | 340-470 | 380-510 | 410-540 | 440-570 |
| 10 | 270-390 | 280-420 | 300-430 | 330-460 | 370-500 | 400-530 | 430-560 |
| 9 | 260-380 | 280-410 | 290-430 | 320-450 | 360-490 | 390-520 | 420-550 |
| 8 | 250-370 | 270-400 | 290-420 | 320-450 | 350-480 | 380-510 | 410-540 |
| 7 | 240-360 | 260-390 | 280-410 | 310-440 | 340-470 | 370-510 | 400-530 |
| 6 | 230-350 | 250-380 | 270-400 | 300-430 | 330-460 | 360-500 | 390-520 |
| 5 | 230-340 | 240-370 | 260-390 | 290-420 | 320-460 | 360-490 | 380-520 |
| 4 | 220-340 | 230-370 | 250-380 | 280-410 | 320-450 | 350-480 | 380-510 |
| 3 | 210-330 | 220-360 | 240-380 | 270-400 | 310-440 | 340-470 | 370-500 |
| 2 | 200-320 | 210-350 | 230-370 | 260-400 | 300-430 | 330-460 | 360-490 |
| 1 | 200-300 | 200-330 | 220-350 | 250-380 | 280-410 | 310-450 | 340-470 |
| 0 | 200-290 | 200-320 | 210-340 | 240-370 | 270-410 | 300-440 | 330-470 |
| -1 | 200-280 | 200-310 | 200-330 | 220-350 | 250-390 | 290-420 | 310-450 |
| -2 | 200-260 | 200-290 | 200-310 | 200-340 | 240-370 | 270-410 | 300-430 |
| -3 | 200-240 | 200-270 | 200-290 | 200-320 | 240-360 | 270-390 | 300-420 |
| -4 | 200-230 | 200-260 | 200-280 | 200-300 | 240-340 | 270-370 | 300-400 |
| -5 | 200 | 200-230 | 200-250 | 200-280 | 240-320 | 270-350 | 300-370 |
| -6 | 200 | 200-220 | 200-240 | 200-270 | 240-310 | 270-340 | 300-370 |
| -7 | 200 | 200-220 | 200-230 | 200-260 | 240-300 | 270-330 | 300-360 |
| -8 | 200 | 200-210 | 200-230 | 200-250 | 240-290 | 270-320 | 300-350 |
| -9 | 200 | 200-210 | 200-230 | 200-250 | 240-290 | 270-320 | 300-350 |
| -10 | 200 | 200-210 | 200-230 | 200-250 | 240-290 | 270-320 | 300-350 |
| -11 | 200 | 200-210 | 200-230 | 200-250 | 240-290 | 270-320 | 300-350 |
| -12 | 200 | 200-210 | 200-230 | 200-250 | 240-290 | 270-320 | 300-350 |

| | Table 4. Writing Multiple-Choice Conversion Table | | |
| --- | --- | --- | --- |
| Raw Score | Scaled Score | Raw Score | Scaled Score |
| 49 | 78-80 | 21 | 46-56 |
| 48 | 77-80 | 20 | 45-55 |
| 47 | 74-80 | 19 | 44-54 |
| 46 | 72-80 | 18 | 43-53 |
| 45 | 70-80 | 17 | 42-52 |
| 44 | 69-79 | 16 | 41-51 |
| 43 | 67-77 | 15 | 40-50 |
| 42 | 66-76 | 14 | 39-49 |
| 41 | 65-75 | 13 | 38-48 |
| 40 | 64-74 | 12 | 37-47 |
| 39 | 63-73 | 11 | 36-46 |
| 38 | 62-72 | 10 | 35-45 |
| 37 | 61-71 | 9 | 34-44 |
| 36 | 60-70 | 8 | 33-43 |
| 35 | 59-69 | 7 | 32-42 |
| 34 | 58-68 | 6 | 31-41 |
| 33 | 57-67 | 5 | 30-40 |
| 32 | 56-66 | 4 | 29-39 |
| 31 | 55-65 | 3 | 28-38 |
| 30 | 54-64 | 2 | 27-37 |
| 29 | 53-63 | 1 | 25-35 |
| 28 | 52-62 | 0 | 24-34 |
| 27 | 51-61 | -1 | 22-32 |
| 26 | 50-60 | -2 | 20-30 |
| 25 | 49-59 | -3 | 20-28 |
| 24 | 48-58 | -4 | 20-26 |
| 23 | 47-57 | -5 | 20-23 |
| 22 | 46-56 | -6 and below | 20-22 |